A Handbook of Foreign Trade: Kelly's Universal Cambist and Commercial Instructor

Volume 1

with Supplements for
1825 and 1835

PATRICK KELLY

THOEMMES PRESS

KYOKUTO SHOTEN LTD

This edition co-published in 1999 by

THOEMMES PRESS
11 Great George Street, Bristol BS1 5RR, United Kingdom

KYOKUTO SHOTEN LTD
12, Kanda-Jimbocho 2-Chome, Chiyoda-Ku, Tokyo, Japan

http://www.thoemmes.com

A HANDBOOK OF FOREIGN TRADE:
KELLY'S UNIVERSAL CAMBIST AND COMMERCIAL INSTRUCTOR
2 volumes : ISBN 1 85506 626 2

1825 supplement reproduced courtesy of Glasgow University Library, Department of Special Collections, Sp Coll g.4.13

PUBLISHER'S NOTE

The publisher has gone to great lengths to ensure the quality of this reprint but points out that some imperfections in the original book may be apparent.
This book is printed on acid-free paper, sewn, and cased in a durable buckram cloth.

- Overstone is an imprint of Thoemmes Press.

A Handbook of Foreign Trade: Kelly's Universal Cambist and Commercial Instructor

OVERSTONE

Printed in England by Pear Tree Imaging Processing, Stevenage

A Handbook of Foreign Trade: Kelly's Universal Cambist and Commercial Instructor

Volume 1

with Supplements for 1825 and 1835

PATRICK KELLY

THOEMMES PRESS

KYOKUTO SHOTEN LTD

This edition co-published in 1999 by

THOEMMES PRESS
11 Great George Street, Bristol BS1 5RR, United Kingdom

KYOKUTO SHOTEN LTD
12, Kanda-Jimbocho 2-Chome, Chiyoda-Ku, Tokyo, Japan

http://www.thoemmes.com

A HANDBOOK OF FOREIGN TRADE:
KELLY'S UNIVERSAL CAMBIST AND COMMERCIAL INSTRUCTOR
2 volumes : ISBN 1 85506 626 2

1825 supplement reproduced courtesy of Glasgow University Library,
Department of Special Collections, Sp Coll g.4.13

PUBLISHER'S NOTE

The publisher has gone to great lengths to ensure the quality of this reprint but points out that some imperfections in the original book may be apparent.
This book is printed on acid-free paper, sewn, and cased in a durable buckram cloth.

- Overstone is an imprint of Thoemmes Press.

THE

UNIVERSAL CAMBIST

AND

Commercial Instructor;

BEING A FULL AND ACCURATE TREATISE ON THE

EXCHANGES, MONIES, WEIGHTS, AND MEASURES,

OF ALL

TRADING NATIONS AND THEIR COLONIES;

WITH

AN ACCOUNT OF THEIR BANKS, PUBLIC FUNDS, AND PAPER CURRENCIES.

BY P. KELLY, LL.D.

MASTER OF THE FINSBURY-SQUARE ACADEMY, LONDON; AUTHOR OF DIFFERENT WORKS ON SCIENTIFIC SUBJECTS; AND MATHEMATICAL EXAMINER TO THE TRINITY HOUSE.

VOL. I.

The Second Edition,

INCLUDING

A REVISION OF FOREIGN WEIGHTS AND MEASURES,

FROM AN ACTUAL COMPARISON OF THEIR STANDARDS,

BY THE ORDER AND AID OF THE BRITISH GOVERNMENT.

LONDON:

PRINTED FOR THE AUTHOR,

AND PUBLISHED BY LACKINGTON AND CO. FINSBURY-SQUARE; LONGMAN AND CO. AND BALDWIN AND CO. PATERNOSTER-ROW; CADELL AND DAVIES, STRAND; R. HUNTER, ST. PAUL'S CHURCH-YARD; AND J. M. RICHARDSON, CORNHILL, OPPOSITE THE ROYAL EXCHANGE.

1821.

TO

THE RIGHT HONOURABLE

THE LORDS OF HIS MAJESTY'S MOST HONOURABLE PRIVY COUNCIL
FOR TRADE AND FOREIGN PLANTATIONS;

THE HONOURABLE

THE DIRECTORS OF THE BANK OF ENGLAND;

AND THE HONOURABLE

THE DIRECTORS OF THE EAST INDIA COMPANY;

THIS SYSTEM OF COMMERCIAL SCIENCE

IS MOST RESPECTFULLY DEDICATED

BY THE AUTHOR,

IN GRATEFUL ACKNOWLEDGMENT OF THE

EARLY ENCOURAGEMENT, IMPORTANT INFORMATION, AND LIBERAL PATRONAGE,

WITH WHICH

THEY HAVE HONOURED AND PROMOTED

THE UNDERTAKING.

PREFACE.

The present Edition of this Work contains the result of an extensive and important operation—that of determining the relative Contents of Foreign Weights and Measures by an actual comparison of their several Standards. This comparison, which has long been considered a *desideratum* in the commercial world, has been effected under the sanction and aid of the British Government; by whose order Foreign Standards, duly verified, have been transmitted to London by the British Consuls abroad, and have been compared with English Standards at His Majesty's Mint.

When this publication was originally undertaken, the Author had three important purposes to accomplish, namely, the *Correction of the Tables of Foreign Coins; of Foreign Exchanges;* and *of Foreign Weights and Measures.* The two former objects were effected in the First Edition; but Weights and Measures could be corrected only by a reference to their Standards which were not then to be obtained in consequence of the war that universally prevailed. When peace, however, was restored, and a New Edition called for, the above Plan of Revision was adopted: but before the particulars are stated, a general view of the Work may be useful.

This Work is divided into Two Volumes. The First is founded on the celebrated publication of *Elert Kruse,* entitled the *Hamburgh Contorist,* which is here modernized and considerably enlarged. It contains a statement of the divisions and proportions of the *Monies, Coins, Weights* and *Measures,* of all Trading Countries, with an account of their *Banks, Public Funds, Paper Currencies, Commercial Allowances,* and various other mercantile regulations.

The SECOND VOLUME is chiefly new both in substance and arrangement. It commences with an Exposition of the Principles and Laws of *Exchange;* after which a regular System is introduced, wherein all the foreign Quotations are explained, and the calculations performed by different methods. *Arbitration of Exchange* is included; and it is presumed, that this ingenious and useful branch of science will be found greatly simplified by illustrations from actual and recent operations. *Arbitration of Bullion and Merchandise* follows, with examples of the use of *Logarithms* and *Fixed Numbers* in abbreviating the calculations of Exchange. This extensive article concludes with Tables of the *Pars of Exchange* and the *Mint Proportions* between Gold and Silver in different countries—documents which were first computed by the Author in 1810, by order of the Bullion Committee of the House of Commons, and which were revised in 1819 for a Committee of the House of Lords.

Tables are next given of the intrinsic value of the Monies of Account of all nations; and these are succeeded by SIR ISAAC NEWTON'S Tables of Assays, which are inserted as an Introduction to the New Tables of Gold and Silver Coins that have been computed expressly for the present Work. When SIR ISAAC NEWTON was Master of the Mint, he caused the principal coins of Europe to be assayed; and his Tables, which were published by order of the Privy Council in 1719, served long as a guide to Bullion Merchants, and as a Standard from which the Par of Exchange was computed: but several of those coins have been since altered, or wholly withdrawn from circulation, and various new ones have been supplied; and even some, that have undergone no change, have been found by modern assays to vary considerably from the original reports.

The *New Tables of Gold and Silver Coins* which follow may be considered as a revision of SIR ISAAC NEWTON'S Tables, and a continuation of his plan. They are computed from Assays made both at London and Paris, which have been, in general, found to verify each other. The London Assays have been made by Robert Bingley, Esq. *F.R.S.*, the King's Assay Master of the Mint; and those at Paris by Pierre Frederic Bonneville, *Essayeur du Commerce*, as published in his elaborate work on the Coins of all Nations. Most of the Foreign Coins, assayed at the London Mint, were supplied for this Work from the Bullion Office, by order of the Bank Directors, and were selected as proper average specimens by John Humble, Esq., the Head of that Office.

An *Explication of Coins* follows, which it is hoped may prove useful to Bullion Merchants, Travellers, and Collectors of Coins in general. Here all the various impressions are explained; and the Legends and other Inscriptions rendered into English, from the Latin, Persian, Arabic, Russian, and other languages. This, it is believed, is the first general Translation of the kind ever published, and has therefore the greater claim to indulgence.

Tables of the Proportion between the Weights and Measures of all Trading Countries are next given, as deduced from the experiments already mentioned. The erroneous state of the old Tables has been always a source of perplexity to merchants, as might indeed be expected from the uncertain manner in which they have been formed. Their origin cannot be traced: it can only be conjectured that they have been gradually collected through a long course of ages from doubtful authorities in different countries; and there is no account that they have ever been corrected or compared on any general or systematic plan. The only attempt of the kind upon record was made by order of the French Government, in 1747, by M. Tillet, at the Paris Mint; but his experiments were confined to a limited number of Money Weights, and there is reason to believe that the standards which he tried were not all duly attested. As to Commercial Weights and Measures, they appear to have been left chiefly to the casual reports of merchants, who could not be supposed always to possess the best means of making accurate experiments.

The great difficulty of effecting a general comparison may account for its omission. It is evident that no individual exertion could accomplish such a task without the aid of a Government possessing very extensive means, and applying them at a moment of universal peace. The present period has proved favourable for the undertaking; and it was reserved for the British Government to avail itself of that peace which its power had established, in thus promoting a plan, which, if duly executed, must be of essential benefit to the commercial world in general. The following account of the origin, progress, and execution of the plan will, it is presumed, shew that it has been undertaken with due deliberation, and conducted with an attention to accuracy commensurate with the importance of the object.

In 1818 the Author of this Work addressed a Letter to the Board of Trade, shewing the erroneous state of the Tables of Foreign Weights and Measures, and submitting a Plan of Correction.* The subject was taken into consideration by the Lords of His Majesty's Privy Council for Coins; and in consequence of their Lordships' recommendation, the following *Circular Dispatch* was issued by *Viscount Castlereagh*, as Principal Secretary of State for Foreign Affairs:—

---

* The plan submitted to the Board of Trade corresponded in substance with the instructions contained in the following Circular; with the addition that the Foreign Weights transmitted by the Consuls should be compared at the London Mint, as an Office of the highest authority for such comparison.

It may be proper further to state, that before this plan was submitted to the Lords of Trade, it was examined and approved by other eminent judges of the subject, particularly by *The Earl of Rosse*, who strongly recommended it to the attention of Government. It was also sanctioned by *The Right Hon. William Wellesley Pole*, Master of the Mint, who, it is well known, zealously promotes all improvements connected with the important establishment over which he presides. Other individuals of high authority on such questions have since recommended and aided the undertaking; among whom should be mentioned *The Earl of Lauderdale.*

It is also important to observe that the East India Company have followed the example of Government in adopting this plan for the comparison of Asiatic Metrology, a Court of Directors having, on the 10th of January, 1821, issued a Circular Letter to the proper authorities throughout India, ordering them to transmit to London verified standards of the weights and measures used in the principal trading places of Asia, as far as their influence may extend. This operation will necessarily be a work of time; and the results must prove a valuable accession to the general stock of commercial knowledge.

COPY OF LORD CASTLEREAGH's CIRCULAR TO THE BRITISH CONSULS ABROAD.

" *Foreign Office, March 10th,* 1818.

" *Sir,*

" *His Majesty's Government being desirous of obtaining every information as to the Standards, in use, for the various weights and measures in Foreign Countries, with a view to ascertain their relative bearings to those in use here, for the benefit of the Commercial Interests of this Country:*

" *I am to desire, that you will use your endeavour to procure, with as little delay as may be, two sets of models, being counterparts in every respect, of the standard pound or mark used at your place of residence for weighing Gold and Silver, and also of other lesser weights used for that purpose.*

" *If, in any place within your Consulate, the standard pound or mark, with its lesser weights, used for weighing Gold or Silver, should differ from those in use at your place of residence, you will procure also two sets of the weights so differing.*

" *You will have the accuracy of all these weights regularly attested by the proper authorities.*

" *You will pack up carefully, and separately, these two sets of weights, complete:— and you will send them to me by separate conveyances, accompanying each set by an explanatory letter, written in duplicate. In that letter you will give a list and description of the weights sent.*

" *You will state the difference and proportion between the pound which is used for weighing Gold and Silver, and that pound used for ordinary articles, which is generally known by the name of the 'commercial pound.'*

" *You will state the contents of the principal measure, used at your place of residence, and at other places within your Consulate, for the measure of Corn, and of the principal measure for Wine, and also of their lesser measures.*

" *You will be so good as to describe the contents of these measures, by stating how many cubic Inches of the place they contain, or how many English Gallons, or how many French Litres.*

" *You will add in your letter such other information as you can collect, or may be in possession of, for throwing light upon the general subject of this instruction.*

"*You will keep an account of the expense to which you may be subjected in the execution of this instruction, and you will send such account, made out in duplicate, in a letter marked 'Separate,' which letter and account may accompany the weights, and the dispatch explanatory of the subject.*

"CASTLEREAGH."

"*To —— His Majesty's Consul at ——.*"

The orders contained in the foregoing *Circular* were executed in due time, in a very correct and satisfactory manner. The packages thus transmitted contained, besides the required Standards, very ample specifications of the divisions and proportions of Weights and Measures, with much new and valuable information on various other commercial subjects. Several of the Consuls likewise sent home Measures of Capacity and of Length from places where their dimensions could not be accurately determined. The dispatches and standards received on this occasion (from upwards of sixty Consuls) were first delivered at the Foreign Office, and thence sent by *Joseph Planta, Esq.*, Under Secretary of State, to the Royal Mint, through the medium of the Board of Trade.

In the beginning of the year 1820 the intended comparisons were carried into effect. These experiments were made by *Robert Bingley, Esq.* who had assayed the Coins, as before stated, and who on every occasion evinced the most zealous attention to scientific accuracy. The apparatus chiefly used for this purpose was the Balance made by *Mr. Bird* in 1758, by order of the House of Commons; and the Standard Weight was the Pound, with its subdivisions, which was adjusted at the same time, and which is commonly called the *Parliamentary Pound.* (See *Introduction,* p. xxiii.)

The Author attended this course of experiments at the Mint; and having registered the results, obtained permission to remove the Standards to his House, with a view of having the comparisons repeated; and, as a further means of verification, to compare the subordinate weights or divisions, the *units* only having been compared at the Mint.

This second course of experiments was made with a fine Balance, recently constructed by *Mr. Troughton* for the London Institution, and with attested standards, both French and English. These comparisons, which were repeated by several competent persons, proved highly satisfactory as corresponding with the Mint experiments. The Measures of Capacity were also carefully ascertained by gauging, and afterwards proved by water measure at Guildhall, by an order from the Lord Mayor, *George Bridges, Esq.*

The results of all the fore-mentioned experiments are inserted in the present Work in their proper places; and in order to render those operations more extensively useful, the contents are computed and expressed in French as well as in English denominations.

The utility of this general comparison will appear manifest, when it is stated that, in almost every article throughout the Work, corrections of Weights or Measures have been found necessary; and considerable errors have been discovered even where least expected, such as in the established proportions between the Weights of England and those of France and Spain. (See *Notes*, Vol. I. pp. 140 and 321; also *Introduction*, p. xxv.)

Besides the revision of Foreign Weights and Measures, the present Edition contains many other corrections and augmentations, rendered necessary by the alterations that have recently taken place in the Monetary Systems, Banking Operations, and Financial Plans, of the different States of Europe.

Much new matter will be likewise found under the extensive articles ***East Indies*** and ***West Indies,*** which has been supplied from official documents, and other authentic communications; and here it may be finally observed that although the most approved written authorities have been consulted on all occasions, yet no articles of importance have been committed to the press, without the inspection and approbation of experienced merchants of the different countries to which those articles respectively relate.

Such is the outline of this publication, and such the peculiar nature of the undertaking, that it could be accomplished only by the co-operation of many men in many countries, and by the sanction and support of a powerful Government.

The Author cannot conclude these remarks without expressing his grateful acknowledgments to the many able and eminent persons who have honoured him with their assistance in the progress of his Work. He would likewise wish to mention their names, and specify their important services, but the list would be inconveniently numerous, and might not be approved by all. He begs only to add, that the valuable time and attention which they so liberally bestowed, and the zeal which they manifested to promote accuracy, besides impressing him with gratitude, constantly stimulated his exertions to render the Work worthy of such distinguished support.—How far his endeavours have been successful, he now with all due deference submits to the decision of the Public.

Finsbury Square,
May 1, 1821.

INTRODUCTION,

CONTAINING AN EXPOSITION OF THE PRINCIPLES OF THE DIFFERENT SUBJECTS COMPRISED IN THIS WORK.

In attempting to explain systematically the theory of *Monies, Coins, Weights,* and *Measures,* the order in which they are generally arranged should be reversed; as it is from Measures that Weights are properly deduced, and Coins are adjusted by Weights; while Imaginary Monies, whether of Account or of Exchange, are valued from their established relation to Coins.

MEASURES.

Measure, in a commercial sense, signifies the dimensions of any thing bought, sold, or estimated.

Measures are of three sorts, namely, Linear, or Long Measure; Square, or Superficial Measure; and Solid, or Cubic Measure.

1. *Linear Measure* is applied to lines; as roads, and distances of all kinds.
2. *Square Measure* is applied to superficies, having both length and breadth; as land, flooring, &c.
3. *Solid Measure* determines the contents of bodies that have length, breadth, and thickness, or depth; as marble, timber, and vessels of all sorts; which last are also called measures of capacity.

Linear Measure is the element of all other measures. *(a)*

Square Measure is determined by multiplying length and breadth together; and Solid Measure, by multiplying length, breadth, and depth together.

(a) The Long Measures of all nations appear from their names to have been taken from some part of the human body, as the Foot, the Fathom, &c.; and the following are the proportions generally observed. The Fathom of a well-proportioned man is reckoned to equal his height or stature; the Girth, or the Pace, $\frac{1}{2}$ of his stature; the Cubit, $\frac{1}{4}$; the Foot, $\frac{1}{6}$; and the Span, $\frac{1}{8}$. The Foot is reckoned equal to 3 times the breadth of the Hand, and 12 times that of the Thumb. Other proportions are occasionally reckoned, as the Nail, the Arm, &c.; and these natural measures are often found convenient where artificial measures are wanted.

WEIGHTS.

Weight may be defined a natural property of matter, proportioned to its bulk and the density of its parts. It is determined by being balanced in a scale against some known or acknowledged weight placed in the opposite scale.

A standard for length being once determined, a standard for weight may be thence deduced: as a vessel of any certain dimensions filled with distilled water, or other homogeneous liquid, will always weigh the same in the same latitude.

The following are the chief properties of weight, as demonstrated by *Sir Isaac Newton:*

1. That the weights of all bodies, at equal distances from the centre of the earth, are directly proportional to the quantity of matter that each contains.

2. On different parts of the earth's surface the weight of the same body is different, increasing from the Equator to the Pole, in proportion to the square of the sine of the latitude.

3. That the weights of the same body, at different distances above the earth, are inversely as the squares of the distances from the centre of the earth.

4. That at different distances within the earth, or below its surface, the weights of the same body are directly as the distances from the earth's centre; so that at half way toward the centre a body would weigh but half as much, and at the very centre it would have no weight at all.

5. That a body immersed in a fluid which is specifically lighter than itself, loses so much of its weight as is equal to the weight of a quantity of the fluid of the same bulk as the body. (b)

(b) From the importance of Weights and Measures as the foundation of law, with respect to property, their adjustments must have been among the first regulations of civil society. *Paucton* observes (in the Introduction to his *Metrologie)* that Standards were generally held sacred by the Ancients, and were therefore deposited in the Sanctuary of the Jews, the Temples of the Heathens, and the Churches of the Primitive Christians. He further states that ancient Standards were generally adjusted by the dimensions of some durable buildings; and thus the base of the largest Pyramid in Egypt was applied, being the 500th part of a degree of the meridian, which had been previously measured for this purpose. He adds, that many of the neighbouring countries of Asia and Europe took their Measures from the Egyptians; and that throughout the Roman Empire uniform Standards were established from the Archetype kept in the Capitol at Rome.

In modern times the general practice has been to commit Standards to the care of the Chief Magistrate of each Government, who sends copies to certain officers of districts, investing them with power to distribute the same and to enforce uniformity.

STANDARDS.

Standards, in a commercial sense, signify any measures or weights of acknowledged authority, by which others are sized or adjusted. They are generally distinguished into *Arbitrary Standards,* and *Invariable Standards from Nature.* The former are those almost universally adopted, and the latter are intended to restore them if lost, or to serve as models for new Systems of Metrology.

From the vague and uncertain origin of Arbitrary Standards, a diversity universally prevails; and this variety has a constant tendency to increase, from the fallibility of workmanship as well as from the decay of all material substances.

With a view to remedy these inconveniences, different methods have been proposed for establishing Standards from some unalterable property in nature; such as the law or force of terrestrial gravitation; the motions of the heavenly bodies; or the measure of some arc or portion of a meridian circle.

Among the various plans tried for this purpose, the two following only have been acted upon with any degree of success, namely—

1. *The length of a pendulum, that vibrates seconds of mean solar time: (c)*
2. *The length of an arc, or portion of the meridian circle.*

If the earth had been a perfect sphere and at rest, these measures would have been the same on all parts of its surface; but its figure is a kind of oblate spheroid, having its equatorial diameter longer than its axis or polar diameter.

From this cause the gravity at the poles is greatest, being nearest to the centre

(c) *Length of the Pendulum vibrating Seconds in different Latitudes.*

Names of Places.	Latitude.	Length of Pendulum.	Names of Observers.
	° ′	*Eng. Inches.*	
Equator	0 0	38,989	Bouguer.
Porto Bello	9 34 N.	38,997	Bouguer.
Jamaica	18 00	39,019	Campbell.
Cape of Good Hope	33 25 S.	39,070	La Caille.
Paris	48 50 N.	39,134	Borda.
Gotha	50 57	39,121	Zach.
London	51 31	39,126	Graham.
London	51 31 8″	39,13929	Kater, 1817.
Petersburg	59 56	39,163	Mallet.
Lapland	66 48	39,172	Academicians.
Lapland	67 04	39,181	Mallet.

of the earth; and it gradually diminishes to the equator. Hence the vibrations of a pendulum are quickest at the poles, and slowest on the equator; and therefore, in order to measure equal portions of time, the pendulum must be gradually lengthened from the equator to the poles. The weight of bodies on the earth is also affected by centrifugal motion, which at the poles is nothing; but it thence increases to the equator, where the force is greatest; and hence the diminution of gravity is proportioned to the distance of bodies from the poles.

From the spheroidical figure of the earth, too, the degrees of the meridian increase from the equator to the poles, in consequence of the increasing curvature of the quadrantal arc.

In order to ascertain the true figure of the earth, and thence to determine an Invariable Standard for Measures, numerous calculations and experiments have been made by the greatest Mathematicians of modern times; and it may be observed that nature seems to oppose great obstacles to the undertaking.

Sir Isaac Newton computed the equatorial diameter to exceed the polar axis in the ratio of 230 to 229, or in other words, that the earth's *ellipticity* was $\frac{1}{230}$; but this calculation, having been made on the supposition that the earth is an entire fluid, is not quite accurate. By actual measurements, the ellipticity has been found to lie between $\frac{1}{291}$ and $\frac{1}{340}$.

The most approved measurements of the Pendulum are contained in the preceding Note (c), and those of the meridian arc in the following Table (d).

(d) Length of a Degree of the Meridian in different Latitudes.

Countries.	Mean Latitude.	Length of Degree.	Measurers.	Dates.
	° ′	*Eng. Miles.*		
Peru	0 0	68,713	Condamine	1744
India	12 32 N.	68,743	Lambton	1803
Cape of Good Hope	33 18 S.	69,076	La Caille	1752
America	39 12 N.	68,895	Mason and Dixon....	1768
Italy	43 00	68,998	Boscovich	1755
France	44 52	68,769	Biot and Arago	1808
France	46 12	69,052	Delambre and Mechain	1793
France	49 22	69,121	Cassini	1740
England..........	51 30	69,146	Mudge	1802
Lapland..........	66 20	69,292	Swanberg	1803

From the foregoing measurement of the meridional arc in France, (Table *d,)* the length of the quadrantal arc was computed; and the ten-millionth part of this Quadrant is the *Metre,* which has been adopted as the standard *unit* for all measures, in the new system in that country.

The standard unit for all weights is the *Gramme,* which is the weight of a cubic vessel of water of the greatest condensation and purity; the side of such cube being the hundredth part of the Metre.

From these two units the other measures and weights are derived by decimal division or multiplication, as explained in this Work under the article *France.*

It should be stated that although the Mathematicians of France chose the meridional arc as the basis of their metrical system, they also recommended the Pendulum as an accurate Standard, and as the most practical means of restoring or repairing the Metre, should it ever be lost, or require correction.

The *Marquis Laplace,* in the *Connoissance des Tems* of 1820, has given the results of *Borda's* experiments on the Pendulum, and of *Mathieu's* investigations of the same, in the following *Formula,* from which the subsequent Table *(e)* is computed:

$$\overset{m}{0}.990787 + \overset{m}{0}.0053982 \text{ Sin}^2 \text{ Lat.}$$

(e) Table, shewing the comparative Weight of Bodies on different parts of the Earth's Surface; with the proportionate Length of the Seconds Pendulum.

	Degrees of Latitude.			Weight of 100lb. in different Latitudes.	Length of the Pendulum.	
					Metres.	English Inches.
	°	′	″			
	0	0	0	100,0000	0,990787	39,0083
	10	0	0	100,0165	0,990950	39,0147
	20	0	0	100,0637	0,991418	39,0331
	30	0	0	100,1362	0,992136	39,0614
	40	0	0	100,2251	0,993017	39,0961
Paris Observatory	48	50	14	100,3088	0,993846	39,1287
	50	0	0	100,3198	0,993955	39,1330
Greenwich Observatory	51	28	40	100,3335	0,994091	39,1383
London, St. Paul's....	51	30	49	100,3338	0,994094	39,1385
	60	0	0	100,4087	0,994836	39,1677
	70	0	0	100,4812	0,995554	39,1960
	80	0	0	100,5284	0,996022	39,2144
	90	0	0	100,5449	0,996185	39,2208

By the foregoing ***Formula*** it appears that the earth's ellipticity is $\frac{1}{311}$, and the increase of weight from the equator to the pole, $\frac{1}{180}$; that is, a body weighing 180lb. at the equator would weigh 181lb. at the pole.

Here it is satisfactory to observe, that the results with respect to the length of the Pendulum, thus finally determined at Paris, perfectly correspond with those ascertained in London, in 1817, by ***Captain Henry Kater, F.R.S.;*** making allowance for the difference of latitudes. These important operations are fully explained in the ***Philosophical Transactions*** of 1818 and 1819.

STANDARDS OF ENGLISH WEIGHTS AND MEASURES.

The original Standards of English Weights and Measures, like those of most other countries, are extremely vague and uncertain. Thus the Standard for Long Measure is said to have been fixed in 1101 by Henry I., who commanded that the ancient ***Ulna*** or Arm, which answers to the modern Yard (the Saxon *Gyrd* or Girth), should be adjusted to the length of his Arm.

The original Standards of Weights, and Measures of Capacity, are equally uncertain. It was enacted in 1266, (3 Edw. 51), "that an English Peny, called a " Sterling, round and without clipping, shall weigh thirty-two wheat corns, from " the midst of the ear; and Twenty Pence to make an Ounce; and Twelve " Ounces, One Pound ;*(f)* and Eight Pound do make One Gallon of wine; and " Eight Gallons of wine do make a London Bushel, which is the eighth part of " a Quarter."

Standards of a more uniform description were established in subsequent reigns: that for long measure, however, has undergone no alteration, except occasional revisions, which time might have rendered necessary; but measures of capacity have been frequently altered. It appears by the above law, that their contents were originally ascertained by weight, which is a practice still used in some countries, and is the most correct method, but not the most convenient.

(f) The ***Pound*** (called by the Romans the ***Pondus*** or Weight, and also the ***Libra*** or Balance), is the most general standard or unit for weights, as the Foot is for measures; and it is to be observed that both have been generally divided into the same number of equal parts, and their divisions were anciently called by the same name, ***Uncia,*** which signifies the twelfth part of a whole. Hence, the *Ounce* and *Inch* have one common derivation, the former being called *Uncia Libræ,* and the latter, *Uncia Pedis.*

As to the original standards of weight, namely, *wheat corns*, it appears that they were, soon after the above period, represented by metallic grains, which are supposed to be the same as the modern Troy Grains. It is however unimportant what their origin might have been, provided that the established standards were kept uniform.

The English standard unit for weight is the Troy Pound; which is one-fourth less than that stated in the foregoing law; the Pennyweight having been reduced to 24 Grains instead of 32. (g)

In 1526 (18 Henry VIII.) the Troy Pound was made the Mint weight, in the room of the Moneyer's Pound or the Pound Tower, which was one-sixteenth less, or 5400 Grains. The weights which were then used for common purposes, were the old Commercial Pound (described Vol. I. page 221); the *Libra Mercatoria* of 15 Ounces; and Avoirdupois Weight. The latter was ordered, by the 24th of Henry VIII. (1532), to be used for meat and other provisions; but this law was repealed in 1541.

In 1588, Queen Elizabeth ordered the Avoirdupois Pound to be placed in the Exchequer as a standard, without any new law on the subject. Her Majesty also directed that a copy of the Troy Pound, belonging to Goldsmiths' Hall, should be deposited at the Exchequer; where it is still used as the legal standard. Copies of this weight were likewise sent to the Mint, and to other Public Offices.

In the year 1758, a select Committee of the House of Commons was appointed to enquire into the state of English Weights and Measures, and to report accordingly. They were assisted in their researches by several eminent Mechanists; among whom may be mentioned *Mr. Bird*, the celebrated Optician, and *Mr. Harris*, the King's Assay Master of the Mint. This Committee, with *Lord Carysfort* at their head, pursued their enquiry with great system and ability, as their Report fully evinces. Their labours, however, were not confined merely to researches and reports: they prepared with great accuracy two standards, namely,

---

(g) There are in most countries two sorts of Pounds, one for the precious metals, and the other for common articles. The former is generally divisible into 12 Ounces, and the latter into 16. The duodecimal scale has the advantage of being divisible by 3 and 6, without remainders; but the binary system, that is, dividing into halves, quarters, eighths, sixteenths, &c. is considered the most simple and convenient, especially in all common operations of domestic trade. It should however be observed that for foreign commerce and scientific calculations, decimal divisions possess superior advantages.

the Yard, and the Pound Troy, which are still carefully preserved, and justly considered of the highest authority.

The Long Measure was adjusted by Mr. Bird from the standards used at the Exchequer, and those belonging to the Royal Society; and the Weight was adjusted by Mr. Harris from the standard Troy Pound kept at the Mint. On this subject a difficulty occurred, as this weight was found to be $1\frac{1}{4}$ Grain heavier than the Exchequer Pound; and in order to know which was correct, the Committee sent to Goldsmiths' Hall for the original Pound, from which both had been copied, but they were informed that no such Standard was known or recollected there. They then resolved to adopt the Mint Standard, as they considered the deficiency of the Exchequer Pound to be the effect of wear. The following are the words of the Report:—

" And considering that the Exchequer weights have been used ever since the " 30th of Queen Elizabeth, 1588 (one hundred and seventy years), to size other " weights by, it is highly probable that the difference may have been occasioned " by the frequent use of the Standard."—(See *Reports from Committees of the House of Commons*, Vol. II. p. 419.)

On the question whether Troy or Avoirdupois Weight should be adopted as the Standard, the former was preferred by the Committee, for the following reasons:

" Because it is the weight best known to our law; that which hath been longest " in use; that by which our coins are measured; that which is best known to the " rest of the world; that to which our learned countrymen have referred, and " compared ancient and modern weights; the weight which hath been subdivided " into the smallest parts. On the other hand, the Avoirdupois Weight is of doubt- " ful authority; and, though unfit to be made a Standard, yet the frequent use of " it renders it necessary to ascertain and declare how many Ounces, Pennyweights, " and Grains, Troy, the Pound Avoirdupois ought to weigh."

The Committee having found the divisions of the Mint Standard inaccurate, caused them to be corrected; and the following is their account of this important operation:

" Your Committee thought it necessary in the first place to obtain, with the " utmost possible exactness, standard weights of the several parts of the Pound " Troy, in order that from thence such other combinations, or proportions of " weight might be formed, as the business or necessities of the subject should "hereafter require. And Mr. Harris was employed to make these several parts, "who accordingly did so, with great skill and attention, by a very curious and "accurate apparatus contrived by Mr. Bird. It was adapted to five different "beams, which ascertained the weights from twelve ounces, or one pound, down "to a grain inclusive; and that with so great exactness as to discern any error in "the pound weight to the 230400th part of the weight, and to the 2000th part "of a single grain.

"By these beams the several parts of the standard Pound were examined and "adjusted by Mr. Harris, in the presence of your Committee, and were found to "be what their denominations import. These several parts were tried in every "progressive combination necessary to discover their proportions to each other; "and appeared so exact, that no greater degree of correctness could, in the nature "of the thing, be expected."

A copy of this standard Pound was delivered to the House of Commons, and another to the King's Assay Master of the Mint, in whose office it is still carefully preserved, with Mr. Bird's weighing apparatus. With this apparatus the late comparisons of Foreign Standards have been made at the Mint, as stated in the foregoing Preface: but it should be observed that certain Standards, which were too heavy for this beam, were weighed by a new Hydrostatic Balance of great accuracy, invented by *John Barton, Esq.* Deputy Comptroller of the Mint.

Before the general comparison was begun, it was deemed proper to compare the Parliamentary Pound with the Exchequer Standard; and for this purpose the latter was taken to the Mint, by an order from the Chancellor of the Exchequer, where it was found to be 1½ Grain lighter than the Parliamentary Pound: and its divisions proved to be still more inaccurate. *(h)*

It should be observed that *Lord Carysfort's* Committee intended to correct this Standard, as appears by their Report; but in 1760, before their plans were completed, Parliament was dissolved—and thus ended their useful labours.

Since that period no alteration has been made in the Standards, though much attention has been paid to the subject, both in and out of Parliament, especially since the adoption of the Metrical System in France.

(h) This comparison between the English standard Weights was made on the 22d of October, 1818, in the presence of the principal Officers of the Mint, and the Chamberlain of the Exchequer; and the results were registered by *James William Morrison, Esq.* Deputy Master of the Mint.

In 1816, in consequence of an Address from the House of Commons to the Prince Regent, His Royal Highness appointed a Commission, to consider the subject of English Weights and Measures; to determine the length of the Pendulum vibrating Seconds in the latitude of London; and to settle the proportion between the Long Measures of England and France.

The Commissioners appointed on this occasion were selected from the Royal Society, and their Reports on the various subjects of enquiry shew them to have been well qualified for the undertaking. The First Report, which was made in June, 1819, contains a comparative view of different systems and standards of Weights and Measures: and appears to be the result of extensive research and mature consideration. No alteration is here proposed to be made in the English Standards of Long Measure or of Weight, those established by the Committee of 1758 having been found quite accurate.

The following opinion of the Commissioners on the Plan which has been often proposed of adopting Foreign Standards, for the purpose of assimilating the systems of different countries, well deserves attention:

"With respect to the actual magnitude of the Standards of Length, it does "not appear to us that there can be any sufficient reason for altering those which "are at present generally employed. There is no practical advantage in having "a quantity commensurable to any original quantity, existing or which may be "imagined to exist, in nature, except as affording some little encouragement to "its common adoption by neighbouring nations. But it is scarcely possible that "the departure from a Standard universally established in a great country, should "not produce much more labour and inconvenience in its internal relations, than "it could ever be expected to save in the operations of foreign commerce and cor-"respondence."

The Second Report contains the final determination of the Commissioners on the Standard of Long Measure, the length of the Pendulum, and of that of the Metre. The following are the concluding words of this decision:

"We prefer the Parliamentary Standard executed by Mr. Bird, in 1760, both "as being laid down in the most accurate manner, and as the best agreeing with "the most extensive comparisons, which have been hitherto executed by various "observers, and circulated throughout Europe; and in particular with the scale "employed by the late *Sir George Shuckburgh*.

"We have therefore now to propose that this Standard be considered as the "foundation of all legal weights and measures; and that it be declared that the "length of the Pendulum vibrating seconds in a vacuum, on the level of the sea, "in London, is 39,1393 Inches, and that of the French Metre, 39,37079 Inches, "the English Standards being employed at 62° of Fahrenheit."

The Third Report of the Royal Commission contains a confirmation of the other two Reports, with respect to Measures of Length: and as to Weights, the Parliamentary Troy Pound of 1758 is recommended to remain unaltered, and the Pound Avoirdupois to continue at 7000 Troy Grains. *(h)*

FRENCH STANDARDS.

The basis of the Metrical System established in France has been already explained in page xix. It remains here to specify the principal Standards, and to shew their proportion to those of England. These are, the ***Metre***, the ***Kilogramme***, and the ***Litre***, which are kept, with other Standards, in the Office of Weights and Measures at Paris.

The length of the Metre, as determined by the Commissioners above-mentioned, may be considered as agreeing with the measurement made by ***Professor Pictet***, in 1802, viz. 39,371 Inches (see Vol. I. p. 134); and the contents of the Litre are of course equally correct. Thus it appears that the ratio between the Measures of England and France has been long accurately determined; but the same cannot be observed of the Weights, as an error of considerable magnitude in their established proportion has been discovered by the late comparisons at the London Mint. The particulars of this extraordinary circumstance are fully explained in a Note, under the article *France*, Vol. I. p. 140: but as certain comparisons and verifications have since taken place on the subject, some further explanation seems necessary.

By that Note it will be seen, that in 1742, the Royal Society of London and the Academy of Sciences at Paris undertook to determine the relative contents of their Weights and Measures, for which purpose they exchanged Standards; and they perfectly agreed in all their experiments, but they had not correct weights to

(h) This important document is dated March the 31st, 1821, and signed by the Commissioners—namely, *Sir George Clerk*, Bart. M. P.; *Davies Gilbert*, Esq. M. P.; *William Hyde Wollaston*, M. D.; *Thomas Young*, M. D.; and *Captain Henry Kater*.

compare, for it has been recently ascertained that the English Pound sent to France, as well as its duplicate kept by the Royal Society, was nearly 4 Grains too light; and this made the French Pound with which it was compared appear 5 English Grains too heavy—an excess which was afterwards transferred by calculation to the Kilogramme, making it about 11 English Grains too much.

That an error of such magnitude should have remained so long undiscovered, seemed incredible: and it was therefore deemed expedient to submit the question to the official authorities of France. For this purpose, an English Troy Pound was verified at the London Mint, by the request of *Thomas Lack, Esq.* Secretary to the Board of Trade; and it was transmitted by *Lord Castlereagh* to Paris to *Count Simeon*, the Minister of the Interior, with the Report of the Mint experiments made on the several Kilogrammes that had been sent to England. By this Report it appeared that their general weight was 15434 Grains each: some were found rather heavier, but none lighter, except the Paris Kilogramme, which weighed only 15433 Grains. Hitherto it had been reckoned at 15444 Grains.

Count Simeon's answer, dated Feb. 28, 1821, contains an official statement of the experiments made on the said English Pound at the Office of Weights and Measures at Paris; and the result perfectly corresponds with that determined at the London Mint respecting the Paris Kilogramme. Thus the Pound was found to weigh 373 Grammes 233 Milligrammes, though hitherto reckoned only at 372,919.

The reason given in this Official Dispatch, why the Kilogrammes from other cities of France were found heavier than the Paris Standard, is as follows:—
" Because they were adjusted according to the laws prescribed for commercial
" weights, that is to say, with *an allowance over*." *(i)*

From this law of sizing weights, it is evident that those used in actual business are something heavier than the original standard; and hence, 15434 Grains may be considered the *Commercial Kilogramme*, and is therefore the Weight adopted in this Work, as that which Merchants universally act upon.

(i) The following are the words of *Count Simeon's* Dispatch: " *Si les résultats obtenus en employant les* " *Kilogrammes que votre gouvernement avait tirés de quelques autres villes de France, ne donnent pas aussi* " *exactement la valeur de ces poids en grains Anglais, ce ne peut être que parcequ' ils étaient ajustés suivant les* " *règles préscrites pour les poids du commerce, c'est à dire avec une tolérance en plus.*"

By " *tolérance en plus*" is to be understood what is commonly called in England *the turn of the scale*, or *the cast of the beam;* and this allowance i the weight of the Kilogramme may be fairly estimated at 1 Grain troy.

COINS.

COINS are pieces of metal, mostly of a round and flat shape, stamped by authority with certain impressions, which are intended to give them a legal and current value, and also to serve as a guarantee for their weight and fineness.

Gold and Silver are the principal metals of which coins are made, being found the fittest for that purpose, both on account of their qualities and their scarcity.

Copper and Billon are likewise used, but always for coins of inferior value.

Gold is the most valuable of all metals, and the most difficult of imitation. It is the least liable to rust or to be altered by fire: it is perfectly malleable, and so ductile, that gold leaf can be reduced to the 300-thousandth part of an inch, and gold gilding to the 10-millionth part.

Silver is next to gold, in value, and in all the above qualities. Silver leaf can be reduced to the 170-thousandth part of an inch: its divisibility is to that of gold as 170 to 300; and the specific gravity of these metals is nearly in the same proportion, being as 105 to 193.

The proportional value of gold and silver is, however, variable; for although they are generally considered as equivalents of other property, and standard measures of value, by which commodities are bought, sold, and estimated, yet, being themselves also saleable articles, they are liable to constant fluctuation in price, as exchanged for each other, as well as with respect to all property. *(k)*

(k) The relative value of gold to silver has varied considerably in different ages, and in different countries at the same period of time. The following may serve as an average statement of those proportions:

	Silver.	Gold.
In Ancient Greece, ... the proportional value was between	15 and	10 to 1.
In Ancient Rome, ... between	12 and	7 to 1.
In England, from the time of the Saxons to the discovery of America, ... between	12 and	10 to 1.
Since that period, the proportion throughout the world has been .... between	17 and	14 to 1.

It should be observed that there have been very great variations from the above average proportions, but not of long continuance. Thus, at some periods of the ancient world, 1 pound of gold was worth nearly 40 of silver; and in England, in the reign of Edward VI., the Mint proportion was as 1 to 5. These extraordinary fluctuations were from political convulsions; but the common cause is the proportional supply from the Mines, which has been computed in modern times at an average of 52lb. of silver for 1lb. of gold. See the Note under the article *Mexico*, Vol. I. p. 254.

For an accurate statement of the relative value of the precious metals, in the principal Mints of the world, see Vol. II. p. 147; and for the periodical variations in the English Mint proportions, see Vol. I. p. xxxi.

Pure gold and silver are invariable in their qualities, from whatever mines they are produced. In their fine state they are considered too flexible to make coins fit for general wear; and hence the practice of mixing with them a certain proportion of harder metal, which is called *Alloy* or *Allay*.

In all regular Governments, there has been a Standard for Coins fixed by law; that is, a certain proportion between the quantity of pure metal and its alloy. Thus, the legal standard for gold in England is $\frac{22}{24}$ or $\frac{11}{12}$; that is, eleven parts of pure metal, and one of alloy. The fineness of gold is generally expressed in Carats; the whole weight being supposed to be divided into 24 equal parts or Carats, 22 of which are of pure metal and 2 of alloy: and hence, English standard gold is said to be 22 Carats fine; and the Carat is divided into 4 parts, called Grains: but these proportions differ in other countries.

The English standard for silver is $\frac{222}{240}$ or $\frac{37}{40}$; that is, 11 oz. 2 dwt. of pure, and 18 dwt. of alloy, making together 1 Pound troy.

The alloy of silver is mostly copper, and that of gold, both silver and copper; but in the computation of coins, the alloy is never reckoned of any value.

Besides this standard fineness of coins, there is also a legal weight fixed according to the Mint Regulations or Rate of Coinage of each country. Thus, in England a Pound troy of standard gold is coined into 44½ guineas, and a Pound of standard silver into 66 shillings; and hence, the Mint price of standard gold is £3 17s. 10½d. per Ounce, and that of standard silver, 66d. per Ounce. Before the year 1816, silver was coined at the rate of 62d. per Ounce; and this is still reckoned the standard price in the valuation of foreign silver coins.

According to the Mint Regulations of most countries, there is an allowance for deviation from the standard weight and fineness of coins, which is called the *Remedy of the Mint*. In some places the Remedy is allowed in the weight, in others in the fineness; but mostly in both weight and fineness. It is considered generally as an allowance for the fallibility of workmanship. In some Mints, however, it is made a source of emolument; and where Governments issue coins at a rate above their intrinsic value, or the market price of the metal, the profit thus made is called *Seignorage*, and charges for Mint expenses are called *Brassage*.

In order further to illustrate the principles and practice of Coinage, and particularly to explain the present state of the English Monetary System, the following historical outline is attempted.

ENGLISH COINS.

The origin of Coins, in almost every country, is involved in great obscurity. In England it has been a question much disputed, and not yet clearly decided, whether the ancient Britons minted any Coins before the arrival of the Romans. It is agreed, however, that the Saxons improved the Roman Coinage, and were authors of the standard of silver, called *Sterling*, *(l)* which has remained since their time unaltered, except some variations, for about ten years, as stated in the following Table, p. xxxi.

The Coinage of William the Conqueror was after the plan established by Charlemagne, in France, in the eighth century, and is supposed to be derived from the Romans, with respect to dividing the Pound into 20 Shillings and the Shilling into 12 Pence. The same proportions are still preserved in the *Lira* of Italy, the *Libra* of Spain, and the *Livre* of France.

The Saxon Pound weight was adopted by King William, and was called the Moneyer's Pound (explained p. xxi.); and from it 20 Shillings were coined, which made 21⅓ to the Pound troy. This number was increased in succeeding reigns until the year 1665 (18th Charles II.), when it was settled at 62 Shillings, at which it continued until the year 1816. It was then altered to 66 Shillings, its present rate.

In the early coinages the Silver Penny or Sterling was minted with a deep cross. When it was broken into two parts, each was called a *Half-penny*, and when into four, each part was called a *Fourth-thing*, or Farthing. Larger silver pieces of Four-pence were also coined, which were called *Greats*, or Groats, and also *Grosses*. There were besides, silver Half-pence and Farthings minted; but no Shillings until the reign of Henry VII. (1504), nor copper coins until the reign of Charles II. (1665).

(l) This is called *Old Sterling*, to distinguish it from *New Sterling*, which is 8 dwt. better. The latter is seldom used, and only in wrought silver.

The name *Sterling* was also given both to the Silver Penny and to the Penny Weight; and it has been since applied to all lawful money of Great Britain. According to *Camden*, *Sterling* is derived from the *Easterlings*, who were expert Refiners from the Eastern parts of Germany, and who first established the standard proportion of silver. The other derivations offered by various authors are numerous, perhaps, beyond the example of any other word; for which, see *Ruding's Annals of the Coinage of Britain*, Vol. I. pp. 21—24.

As to gold coins, the first after the Norman Conquest, according to *Snelling*, was struck by order of Henry III. in the year 1257. It weighed two silver Pence, passed for twenty Pence, and was called the *Gold Pennie*. The same Author observes, " that the King tried this expedient of coining gold through necessity, " and that the City of London made a representation against this measure."

The next gold coinage in England was in the year 1344, when the Florin was struck, which took its name from *Florence*, where it had been first minted in 1252. It was afterwards coined in most countries of Europe. In Germany and Holland it was called the *Gulden*, on account of its having been originally gold. The Florin, however, has been long a silver coin, and also a money of account.

The above Coins are supposed to have been of pure gold; but those minted in the subsequent reigns down to that of Henry VIII. were 23 Carats $3\frac{1}{2}$ Grains fine, with $\frac{1}{2}$ Grain of alloy. This was called the Old Standard to distinguish it from the New or the present Standard, which was first called *Crown Gold*, as being minted into Crown Pieces in 1527.

The principal gold coins of the Old Standard were Nobles of 6s. 8d. each, with halves and quarters: the latter were called *Farthing Nobles*. There were also Marks of 13s. 4d.; Angels of 10 Shillings; and Sovereigns of 20 Shillings each. Sovereigns were first minted by Henry VII. and were frequently altered during the four subsequent reigns; but in the 2d of James I. they were fixed at 22 Carats, at which fineness all gold coins have since been minted. The 20 Shilling Pieces first coined at this rate were called *Unites*, and $33\frac{1}{2}$ Pieces were struck from the lb. Troy; but in the reign of Charles II. (1666) a new coinage of $44\frac{1}{2}$ to the lb. was minted, and these were called *Guineas*, on account of the country from which the gold was originally brought. The Guinea varied in its current price from 20 Shillings up to 30, until the year 1717, when, by the recommendation of Sir Isaac Newton, it was fixed at 21 Shillings, its present rate.

In 1816 a new coinage of 20 Shilling Pieces, called *Sovereigns*, was minted, in due proportion to the Guinea, viz. $46\frac{29}{40}$ Sovereigns to the Pound Troy.

At the same period an extensive Silver coinage took place, at the new rate already stated p. xxix, which affords a *Seignorage*, but its amount must always depend on the market price of the metal.

The following Table may serve to illustrate the foregoing statements.

AN HISTORICAL TABLE OF ENGLISH COINS,

Shewing the Alterations they have undergone from the Reign of WILLIAM *the* CONQUEROR *to that of* GEORGE IV., *with respect both to their Weight and Fineness. Also a Statement of the comparative Value of Gold and Silver, at different periods.*

Date.	Reign.	SILVER. Fineness of Silver Coins.		SILVER. Pound Troy of such Silver coined into			GOLD. Fineness of Gold Coins.		GOLD. Pound Troy of such Gold coined into			Comparative Value of fine Gold and Silver.	
		Oz.	Dwt.	£.	s.	d.	Car.	Gr.	£.	s.	d.	Gold.	Silver.
1066	William I.	11	2	1	1	4	....		....			....	
1280	8 Edward I.	—	—	1	1	4	....		....			....	
1344	18 Edward III.	—	—	1	1	6	23	3½	14	0	10	1	to 12,584
1349	23 ———	—	—	1	3	0	—	—	14	18	8	1	— 11,571
1356	30 ———	—	—	1	6	8	—	—	16	0	0	1	— 11,158
1421	9 Henry V.	—	—	1	12	0	—	—	17	16	0	1	— 10,331
1464	4 Edward IV.	—	—	2	0	0	—	—	22	4	6	1	— 10,331
1465	5 ———	—	—	2	0	0	—	—	24	0	0	1	— 11,158
1470	49 Henry VI.	—	—	2	0	0	—	—	24	0	0	1	— 11,158
1482	22 Edward IV.	—	—	2	0	0	....		24	0	0	1	— 11,158
1509	1 Henry VIII.	—	—	2	0	0	....		24	0	0	1	— 11,158
1527	18 ———	—	—	2	2	8	22	0	24	0	0	1	— 11,268
1543	34 ———	10	0	2	8	0	23	0	28	16	0	1	— 10,434
1545	36 ———	6	0	2	8	0	22	0	30	0	0	1	— 6,818
1546	37 ———	4	0	2	8	0	20	0	30	0	0	1	— 5,000
1547	1 Edward VI.	4	0	2	8	0	20	0	30	0	0	1	— 5,000
1549	3 ———	6	0	3	12	0	22	0	34	0	0	1	— 5,151
1551	5 ———	5	0	3	12	0	23	3½	34	0	0	1	— 11,000
1552	6 ———	11	1	3	0	0	22	0	36	0	0	1	— 11,050
1553	1 Mary	11	0	3	0	0	23	3½	36	0	0	1	— 11,057
1560	2 Elizabeth	11	2	3	0	0	22	0	36	0	0	1	— 11,100
1600	43 ———	—	—	3	2	0	23	3½	36	10	0	1	— 10,904
1604	2 James I.	—	—	3	2	0	22	0	33	10	0	1	— 12,109
1626	2 Charles I.	—	—	3	2	0	—	—	41	0	0	1	— 13,346
1666	18 Charles II.	—	—	3	2	0	—	—	44	10	0	1	— 14,485
1717	3 George I.	—	—	3	2	0	—	—	46	14	6	1	— 15,209
1816	56 George III.	—	—	3	6	0	—	—	46	14	6	1	— 14,287
1821	2 George IV.	—	—	3	6	0	—	—	46	14	6	1	— 14,287

By the above Table it appears that Silver Coins have been diminished in value, during the last 500 years, in the ratio of 99 to 32, and Gold Coins nearly as 3½ to 1. It may be remarked, that within the same period the Silver Coins of France and Spain have been debased in the ratio of about 17 to 1.

Seignorage was charged, but very unequally, until the year 1666, when a law was enacted that any person bringing gold or silver bullion to the Mint, might have it coined free of expense; and this law is still continued with respect to gold, but in 1816 the coinage of silver was wholly undertaken by Government.

Before this change took place, the supply of silver currency was very irregular, and the coins, however correctly minted, soon became greatly deteriorated, insomuch that in the year 1774 they were declared to be no longer a legal tender for more than £25, although they had been previously unlimited in this respect.

The system of both metals being standard measures of value (which they were in virtue of each being a legal tender to any amount), was the source of much disorder; for as their market prices were always subject to variation, one kind of coin had a constant tendency to drive the other out of circulation.

To remedy this great inconvenience, various plans were proposed by different Statesmen. *Sir William Petty* was the first who recommended that "one "metal only should be made the uniform measure of the value of commodities." *Mr. Locke* supported this opinion, and proposed silver. Others recommended gold; and some, both metals, as approved of by *Sir Isaac Newton*.

Such was the diversity of opinion, when, in 1805, a very able Work appeared, which seems to have decided the question. This important publication was *A Treatise on the Coins of the Realm*, by *Charles, Earl of Liverpool*, in which His Lordship maintains, "that coins which are the principal measure of property "should be composed of one metal only; that this metal should be gold (being "that in which the principal payments in England are made); and that the ex-"penses of fabrication should be taken out of the silver and copper coins."

This is in substance the Monetary System established in 1816, at which time the following law was enacted—"That gold coins shall be in future the sole standard "measure of value, and legal tender of payment, without any limitation of amount, "and that silver coins shall be a legal tender for the limited amount of forty shil-"lings only, at any one time." *(m)*

(m) In the history of the English Mint, the Coinage of 1816 will be memorable, not only on account of the important alteration then made in the monetary system, but also for the great accommodation afforded to the public. Thus, after a long period of disorder in the currency, the new silver coins were exchanged for the old on very liberal terms; and, although they amounted to several millions of pounds sterling, the exchange was effected simultaneously throughout the kingdom. The supplies too from the Mint have been since continued, to all parts of the British dominions, with a degree of regularity and dispatch unknown at any former period.

MONIES.

Money is a general term for coin, paper, or any other representative of property that passes current from hand to hand as a circulating medium. (n)

Monies are distinguished into *real* and *imaginary*.

Real monies are coins, bank notes, or any other tokens of credit that have a currency, and are understood to be convertible into property.

Imaginary monies, also called *ideal monies*, are not represented by any coin, but are used in keeping accounts: they are understood to have had their foundation in real coins or in weights, which were the original units adopted as measures of value, and which have been continued under the same denominations, notwithstanding the changes that may have taken place in their intrinsic value.

Although monies of account be not represented by real coins, yet their intrinsic value may be determined by their known relation or proportion to certain coins.

Monies of account may be considered with respect to coins, as weights and measures with respect to goods, or as a mathematical scale with respect to maps, lines, or other geometrical figures. Thus they serve as standards of the value both of merchandize and of the precious metals themselves. It should, however, be remarked, that monies of account, though they are uniform as a scale of divisions and proportions, yet they fluctuate in their intrinsic value with the fluctuation of the coins which they measure or represent.

Monies are further distinguished, in different countries, by particular denominations, as *Cash, Specie, Effective, Currency, Banco, Giro, Moneta di Cambio, Valuta*, &c.; and connected with these are the terms *Agio, Discount, Interest,*

(n) It is worthy of observation, that the progress of metals as representatives of property seems to have kept pace with the increase of wealth and commerce. Thus, iron, brass, and copper, first answered the purposes of money. Silver next succeeded, after which gold was adopted: but the great increase of business in modern times has rendered even the precious metals insufficient as a circulating medium. Paper, therefore, has been substituted in various ways; and it is generally found more convenient and manageable than specie. Where credit cannot be given, the precious metals are necessary; but where well-founded credit exists, paper is greatly preferable: it is exempt from most of the imperfections and disorders of coins, and in many other respects it greatly facilitates the operations of trade and commerce.

Rebate, Exchange, Commission, and *Brokerage,* which may therefore require some explanation.

Cash is a general term for all monies in England, but is a coin in China, Japan, and other countries.

Specie and *Effective* generally mean coin; but in some parts of Germany the word *Specie* is applied to the Rixdollar and its divisions.

Currency generally signifies the common or current money of a place, which in Holland is called *Cassa;* in Venice, *Moneta Piccola;* and in other parts of Italy, *Moneta Lunga:* but in some parts of Germany, and particularly in Augsburg, *Currency* means the money of account, and it has the same meaning in America and the West Indies, where it derives its name from a paper currency, which has been long discontinued.

Banco is the money which is placed in Banks of Deposit, and which is not drawn out, but transferred in the payment of debts and contracts.

Giro, in most parts of Germany, means Money of Exchange, which is called *Moneta di Cambio* in Italy.

The word *Valuta* or *Valeur* is applied on the Continent to the prices or rates at which different kinds of monies are reckoned in commercial transactions.

The difference of one sort of money compared with another is mostly reckoned at so much per cent. When a better sort is given for a worse, the premium or per-centage is called *Agio:* but when the difference or per-centage is considered with regard to the inferior sort of money, it is called *Discount.* Thus formerly, when 100 Florins Banco were given for 104 of Currency, the Agio on Banco was 4 per cent.; but, when the same sum was given for 95 Florins Currency, then Banco was said to be at a discount of 5 per cent.

Discount is likewise a term applied to an allowance of so much per cent. per annum for the payment of money before it becomes due; and this Discount differs from Banco as Agio differs from Interest.

Interest is an allowance of so much per cent. per annum for the use of money, and is therefore an addition to the Principal; but Agio adds nothing to the Capital, being only the actual difference in value between two kinds of money. In the same manner, Discount between various sorts of monies, and Discount for prompt payment, differ. In the former case there is no loss or diminution, but in the latter there is a deduction from the Principal.

There is a third kind of Discount, which is a deduction of so much per cent. from the stipulated price of goods: this is sometimes called REBATE or *Rabbatt*. In many countries there are fixed periods of several months for the payment of certain kinds of goods; and when such contracts are discharged within one month, the Rabbatt is mostly 8 per cent. per annum. This, however, is differently reckoned: in some places 100 is paid for 108, and in others, 92 for 100; the latter is the most general method of deducting all kinds of Discounts. Thus, in England, where the legal interest for money is 5 per cent. per annum, this sum is the Discount taken from a bill of £100 due at twelve months. This is in reality £5 for £95, which is £5 5s. 3d. per cent. per annum.

It should be observed, that the rate of interest in discounting bills on the Continent is not limited by law as in England, but fluctuates according to the plenty or scarcity of money.

Compound Interest is that which arises from any principal and its interest put together, which charge in England is illegal for money lent. It is, however, used in computing annuities, and is also charged on mercantile balances in the ledger when they are not regularly settled, but carried from one year's account to another.

When a sum of money of one kind is given for its amount or equivalent in another sort, the transaction is called an *Exchange*, of which there are two kinds; the one, when the monies are immediately bartered, which is called, in Italy and in many other parts of the Continent, "*Cambio Comune*," or *Common Exchange*, also *Dry Exchange:* but, when a sum of money is paid in one place for a written order for its equivalent in the money of another place, the operation is called "*Cambio Reale*," or *Real Exchange:* and this is what is commonly understood by Foreign Exchange.

Commission is a charge, generally, of so much per *cent.* or per *mille*, made by a Merchant or Factor for any commercial transaction; and *Brokerage* is a similar charge made by a Broker. These charges are either added or subtracted, according to the nature of the transaction. Thus a commission of 1 per cent. on Sales of Goods, or on a Bill of Exchange, will reduce £100 to £99 to the Seller of the Goods, or the Drawer of the Bill: and the like charge on an Invoice, or on a Bill of Exchange, will increase £100 to £101 to the Purchaser of the Goods, or the Remitter of the Bill.

PAPER MONEY, BANKS, AND PAPER CREDIT.

Paper Money or *Paper Currency* consists of promissory notes, bills, or other written obligations or securities, which pass current from hand to hand in payment of debts and contracts, till they are ultimately redeemed by the Issuer.

Paper currency is distinguished into *forced* or *free*, according as it is forced into circulation by authority, or received without any compulsion. Of the former sort are emissions of government paper in some countries; and of the latter, are bank notes and other such issues which are payable to bearer on demand.

Banks are offices for keeping and circulating money: they are generally distinguished into *Banks of Deposit* and *Banks of Circulation.*

Banks of Deposit are so called, because the money lodged in them is not drawn out, but transferred from one person to another: such is the Bank of *Hamburgh.*

Banks of Circulation are such as issue their own notes, and such also as pay the money lodged in them to the order of the owners, as the Bank of England, &c. Such are distinguished into *Public* and *Private Banks,* according as they may have been constituted by public companies and incorporated by law, or established on private credit, without any charter.

Paper Credit is a term which generally comprehends all kinds of paper currency and other written obligations; such as *Bank Notes, Exchequer Navy and Ordnance Bills, Bonds, Promissory Notes, Mortgages, Transfers of Stock, Bills of Exchange, India Bonds,* and in short, all paper securities, both public and private, by which property is transferred from hand to hand, and from nation to nation. Thus, Paper Credit may be considered the instrument by which all the great operations of Trade, Commerce, Banking, Finance, Subsidies, and other Government transactions, are carried on throughout the world.

TABLE OF CONTENTS.

VOLUME I.

ERRATA, VOL. I.

Page.	Line.	
xxi.	2	in the Note, *for* divisible *read* divided.
6	6	*for* 3*s*. 6*d*. *read* 3*s*. 3*d*.
8	6	from the bottom, *for* 5*s*. 10*d*. *read* 5*s*. 6*d*.
11	16	*for* 6 Perches *read* 1 Perch.
18	9	*for* 5238,5 *read* 5234.
18	12	*for* 73,75 *read* 72,77.
25	11	from the bottom, *for* 10 *read* 105.
28	10	*for* the Ecu, the Rixdollar, and the Patagon, *read* the Ecu or Patagon, and the Rixdollar.
35	1	*for* 0,468 *read* 46,8.
35	6	*for* 3189 *read* 3180.
39	6	from the bottom, *for* 4500 *read* 45000.
40	11	*for* 815¼ *read* 814.
47	11	*for* 0,1195 Metres *read* 1,195 Metre.
52	8	*for* Litres *read* Decalitres.
54	10	from the bottom, *for* 4668 *read* 466,8.
55	2	*for* 3669 *read* 3,669.
57	2	*for* 124 *read* 127½.
63	4	*for* Pagoda *read* Mohur; *after which insert*, Pagoda 8*s*. or 16 Schillings.
99	12	*for* Cutcha Seers *read* Pucca Maunds.
120	10	*for* 100 *read* 400.
129	11	from the bottom, *for* $\frac{1}{23}$ *read* $\frac{8}{23}$.
131	2	*for* Bushels *read* Gallons.
137	7	*for* 35,2466 *read* 35,236.
161	3	*for* "the first called Kaysergroschen," &c. to the end of the sentence, *read* "and also into 30 Kaysergroschen of 3 Creutzers, and into 22½ Batzen of 4 Creutzers"
168	3	from the bottom, *for* Sols Banco *read* Shillings Lubs.
208	24	*for* 22,692 *read* 24,041.
208	24	*for* 0,8931 *read* 0,6104.
217	12	*for* ,9125 *read* 9,25.
219	24	*for* Decigrammes *read* Milligrammes.
220	4	*for* Decigrammes *read* Milligrammes.
222	2	*for* 88 *read* 38.
240	30	*for* reduced *read* redeemed.
242	15	*for* 90 *read* 96.
243	2	*for* 65,93 *read* 57,37.
243	3	*for* 249,56 *read* 217,19.
244	9	*for* Litres *read* Decilitres.
255	7	from the bottom, *for* 41,5 *read* 4,15.
255	7	from the bottom, *for* 14,624 *read* 1,4624.
278	6	*for* 149 *read* 151.
278	17	*for* 6,286 *read* 5,564.
278	19	*for* 0,529 *read* 0,657.
280	10	*for* 4,19 *read* 0,419.
280	10	*for* Litres *read* Decilitres.
283	3	*for* 467,711 *read* 233,834.
286	20	*for* 3791 *read* 3797.
336	15	*for* Litres *read* Decilitres.
336	16	*for* Litres *read* Decilitres.
336	18	*for* Litres *read* Decilitres.
342	2	from the bottom, *for* 5494 *read* 5481.
360	5	*for* £5 *read* £5 6*s*. 8*d*. and the divisions of the Doubloon in proportion.
369	2	*for* 28 Shillings *read* 60 Creutzers.
373	last line	*after* Auditor General *insert* at Corfu.

N. B. It is recommended that the above errors be corrected with the pen before the Work is consulted on any question of business.

Explanation of certain Characters used in this Work.

$+$ signifies Addition, as $6 + 2$ denotes that 2 is to be added to 6.
$-$ signifies Subtraction, as $6 - 2$ denotes that 2 is to be subtracted from 6.
$\times$ signifies Multiplication, as 6×2 denotes that 6 is to be multiplied by 2.
$\div$ signifies Division, as $6 \div 2$ denotes that 6 is to be divided by 2 or $\frac{6}{2}$.
$=$ signifies Equality, as $6 + 2 = 8$; $6 - 2 = 4$; $6 \times 2 = 12$: and $6 \div 2 = 3$.
: :: : signifies Proportion, as 2 : 4 :: 6 : 12 denotes that 2 is to 4 as 6 to 12.
The Comma (,) placed before any Figure shews that the Number is a decimal Fraction: thus ,5 denotes $\frac{5}{10}$ or $\frac{1}{2}$; also, 6,25 means $6\frac{25}{100}$ or $6\frac{1}{4}$.

AN ACCOUNT

OF THE

MONIES, COINS, WEIGHTS, MEASURES, BANKS, EXCHANGES,

AND SUNDRY

COMMERCIAL REGULATIONS, OF ALL TRADING COUNTRIES.

ABYSSINIA *(in Africa)*.

THERE are no coins minted in Abyssinia, but those of other countries circulate here, particularly Venetian Sequins, and Imperial or Austrian Dollars. The latter are called *Patakas* or *Patacks*. Spanish Dollars also pass at *Massuah* on the Red Sea, the principal port with which the English have commercial intercourse. Monies and Coins.

Large payments are generally made in Ingots of Gold, which are weighed by the *Wakea* or Abyssinian Ounce; and for small payments Salt Bricks dug out of the mines are adopted, about 80 of which are valued at a Wakea of Gold. Glass Beads also of all colours, perfect and broken, pass for small money, and are called *Borjookes.*

The relative value of monies at Massuah is as follows:

3 Borjookes or Grains make	1 Kibear.	
10 Kibears	....	1 Diwani or Para.
4 Diwanis	....	1 Harf or Dahab.
23 Harfs	....	1 Pataka or Dollar.
$2\frac{1}{4}$ Patakas	....	1 Sequin.

The Pataka is also a money of account, but of fluctuating value. In 1771, according to *Mr. Bruce*, 10 Patakas were worth a Wakea of Gold; but in 1806, according to *Lord Viscount Valentia*, $11\frac{3}{4}$ Patakas were reckoned as the price of the Wakea.

Weights & Measures. The weights are the Derime or Drachm, the Wakea or Ounce, the Mocha, and the Liter, Rottolo or Pound.

10 Drachms make	1	Wakea.
12 Drachms	1	Mocha.
12 Wakeas......	1	Rottolo or Liter.

The Wakea weighs 400 Grains English troy weight, and the Rottolo is therefore 4800 Grains, or 10 Ounces troy, which equal 10 Ounces $15\frac{19}{56}$ Drachms avoirdupois.

The measure for grain is the Ardeb, which, at Gondar, is composed of 10 Madegas, each weighing 12 Ounces Cairo weight, answering to about $\frac{1}{8}$ of an English Bushel. But the Ardeb at Massuah contains 24 Madegas, and is therefore $\frac{1}{3}$ of an English Bushel nearly.

The Cuba, a measure for honey and other articles, contains 62 English cubic Inches, or $2\frac{1}{8}$ English Pints, being very nearly equal to the French *Litre*.

The principal long measure is the Turkish Pic, which is $\frac{3}{4}$ of an English Yard.

AIX LA CHAPELLE (*in Germany*).

Monies of Account. Accounts are kept here in Reichsthalers or Rixdollars current of 54 Marks, each Mark being subdivided into 6 Busches, and each Busche into 4 Hellers.

This Rixdollar is also worth $1\frac{1}{2}$ Gulden or Florin of the Empire, and 6 Schillings or 9 Guldens of Aix la Chapelle.

The Rixdollar Specie, or Effective Rixdollar of the Empire, is worth 72 Marks, and the Schlechthaler 26 Marks.

Coins. The gold coins of the city are Ducats worth $3\frac{1}{3}$ Rixdollars current; and the silver coins, double, single, and half Pieces, called Rathspraesentgers or Presences, of 32, 16, and 8 Marks; also Pieces of 1, 2, and 3 Marks.

The Rixdollar current is equal in value to 303 Dutch Asen, or $224\frac{3}{4}$ English Grains of fine silver; it is therefore worth $31\frac{1}{2}$ pence sterling, and the Rixdollar specie, 3s. 6d. sterling. Other coins, particularly those of France and Prussia, circulate here.

Weights. The weight for merchandise is as follows:

A Shipfund contains 3 Centners, or 300lb. but in the carriage of goods it is reckoned at 318lb. 1lb. = 2 Marks, 16 Ounces, 32 Loths, 128 Quentins, or 512 Pennings. Weights.

30lb. of Aix la Chapelle are nearly equal to 31lb. avoirdupois.

A Malter of Corn contains 6 Fasses; a Fass of Wheat is 4 Kops; a Fass of Oats 6 Kops—a Kop is nearly one-sixth of an English Bushel. Measures.

An Ahm of Wine contains 130 Kannes.

The Ell of Aix la Chapelle measures $26\frac{1}{3}$ English Inches; the Foot $11\frac{5}{12}$ English Inches.

The French decimal system of weights and measures has been introduced here, but not fully established.

Aix la Chapelle exchanges with and gives— Exchanges.

Amsterdam 165 Rixdollars current, more or less, for 100 Rixdollars current.
Antwerp .. 118 Rixdollars specie, more or less, for 100 Rixdrs. of exchange.
Francfort.. 120 Rixdrs. curr. more or less, for 100 Rixdrs. convention curr.
Paris .... 69 Rixdrs. specie, more or less, for 100 Ecus of 60 Sous Tournois.
Vienna.... 120 Rixdrs. current, more or less, for 100 Rixdrs. Vienna curr.

The exchanges of Aix la Chapelle with other places are made chiefly through Amsterdam.

ALEPPO *(in Syria)*,

And its sea port, Alexandretta or Scanderoon, keep accounts in Piastres of 80 Aspers; the Piastre is also divided into 24 Siani. Other coins, however, circulate here at a variable rate, particularly Spanish Dollars, 17 of which should weigh 150 Drams, which makes the Dollar worth 2 Piastres. Monies.

For the coins of Aleppo, see *Constantinople*.

The weights are, the Cantaro of 100 Rottoli, each subdivided into 12 Ounces, or 720 Drams; the great Cantaro of Tripoli, of 175 Rottoli; and the Zurlo, of $27\frac{1}{2}$ Rottoli. This Rottolo, with which most sorts of goods are weighed = 5lb. avoirdupois nearly. Weights.

The Rottolo, with which the silks from Tripoli and other parts of Syria are weighed, is 700 Drams, answering to $4\frac{7}{8}$lb. avoirdupois.

The Rottolo used in weighing the Persian silks is 680 Drams, or $4\frac{3}{4}$lb. avoirdupois nearly.

Weights. The Rottolo of Damascus, with which brass, camphor, benzoin, spikenard, balsam of Mecca, and other drugs, are weighed, contains 600 Drams, or $4\frac{1}{6}$lb. avoirdupois nearly.

Five Rottoli, or 3600 Drams, make what is called a Vesno; and 7 Vesnos make a Cola. A Batman contains 6 Okes, each weighing 400 Drams.

A Metical, with which pearls and ambergris are weighed, is $1\frac{1}{2}$ Dram, or 73 English Grains.

Measures. The long measure, called a Pic, is equal to $26\frac{2}{3}$ English Inches.

Road measure here, and in other parts of the Levant, is estimated by time, that is, the number of hours or days in which a camel, at the ordinary pace, would travel a certain distance.

ALEXANDRIA *(in Egypt)*.

Monies and Coins. Accounts are kept in Piastres current of 40 Medini, each Medino being subdivided into 8 Borbi, or 6 Forli, or 3 Aspers.

A Ducatello is reckoned at 10 Medini; a Griscio or Abuquelp, at 30; and a Zenzerli, at 107 ditto. These are real Egyptian coins.

A Purse is composed of 25000 Medini, or 75000 Aspers.

The Borbi and Forli are copper coins.

The Sequin, called Fundeclee, is worth 146 Medini; that called Zumabob, 120 Medini.

Weights. Goods are sold by the Cantaro, of 100 Rottoli; but the Rottolo is of different sorts. The Rottolo Forforo answers to almost 15 Ounces, or 100 of them to $93\frac{2}{3}$lb. avoirdupois. The Rottolo Zaydino weighs $21\frac{1}{3}$ Ounces, or 100 such = $133\frac{1}{2}$lb. The Rottolo Zauro weighs a little more than 33 Ounces, or 100 = 207lb. The Rottolo Mina weighs $26\frac{2}{3}$ Ounces, or 100 = 167lb. avoirdupois.

A Quintal of coffee from Cairo weighs $103\frac{2}{3}$lb. avoirdupois nearly.

An Oke contains 400 Drams, and the Dram 16 Carats, or 64 Grains; the whole answering to about $42\frac{2}{3}$ Ounces avoirdupois.

Measures. Corn is measured by the Rebebe and the Kisloz; the former $4\frac{1}{2}$ Bushels, the latter $4\frac{7}{8}$ Bushels, English measure.

The Pic or Ell equals 26,8 English Inches.

For further particulars, see *Grand Cairo*.

ALGIERS *(on the Coast of Barbary)*,

Monies and Coins.

Keeps accounts in Saimes or Doubles, of 50 Aspers; also in Patacas Chicas, of 8 Tomins, or 232 Aspers.

A Piastre or Pataca Gourda contains 3 Patacas Chicas; a Tomin, 2 Carubes or 29 Aspers.

A Sultanin passes for $8\frac{1}{2}$ Patacas Chicas, more or less; a Sequin for 10 ditto; a Portuguese Dobraon, or Joanese of 6400 Rees, for 36 ditto.

A Spanish Dollar is worth from $4\frac{3}{4}$ to $4\frac{7}{8}$ Patacas Chicas; hence the said Pataca = $11\frac{1}{2}$d. sterling nearly.

Weights.

The weight called Cantaro is of different sorts. A Cantaro of flax contains 200 Rottoli; of butter, honey, fruit, oil, and soap, 166 Rottoli; of iron, lead, and wool, 150 Rottoli; of almonds, cheese, and cotton, 110 Rottoli; and of copper, brass, wax, and drugs, 100 Rottoli.

The Rottolo contains 16 Ounces; and 100 Rottoli = 119lb. avoirdupois.

Gold, silver, pearls, and diamonds, are weighed with the Metical, which = 73 Grains troy.

Measures.

The measure for corn and dry goods is called Tarrie, and contains something less than $2\frac{1}{4}$ Pecks English measure; 16 Tarries make a Caffise.

The measure for oil, called Metalli, weighs 37lb. 6 oz. avoirdupois.

The measure for cloth, called a Pic, is of two sorts; the Turkish Pic is equal to $24\frac{8}{15}$ English Inches, the Moorish Pic to $18\frac{2}{5}$ English Inches; the former being to the latter as 4 to 3. The Turkish Pic, divided into 8 Robi, is used in measuring cloth; but linen is measured by the Moorish Pic.

ALICANT *(in Spain)*.

Monies and Coins.

Accounts are kept here in Libras of 20 Sueldos; each Sueldo being divided into 12 Dineros.

The Libra, also called the Peso, is worth 10 Reals, and is equal to the Peso de Plata (or of Exchange) of 128 Quartos, which in Spain is reckoned at 272 Maravedis de Plata, or 512 Maravedis de Vellon; hence a Real of Alicant = $27\frac{1}{5}$ Maravedis of Plate, or $51\frac{1}{5}$ Maravedis Vellon.

Monies and Coins.

11 such Reals make a Ducat of Alicant; and $13\frac{4}{5}$ a Ducat of Exchange; or, more exactly, 272 Ducats of Exchange = 375 Libras of 10 Reals.

A Spanish Doubloon passes here for $5\frac{1}{3}$ Libras.

A Peso Duro, or Hard Dollar, equals $13\frac{9}{32}$ Reals, or $26\frac{9}{16}$ Sueldos of Alicant; that is, 32 Dollars are worth 425 Reals; or 42 Libras = 10 Sueldos.

The Libra of Alicant may be valued at 3s. 6d. sterling; and the Real at $4\frac{1}{4}$d. nearly.

Weights.

The Carga of Alicant is $2\frac{1}{2}$ Quintals, or 10 Arrobas or Arroves.

The Quintal is composed of 4 Arrobas, and the Arroba of 24 great Libras, or Pounds of 18 Ounces, or of 36 small Pounds of 12 Ounces each, Castilian weight. The Pound of 18 Ounces is used for weighing wool, fruit, &c.; the Pound of 12 Ounces for spices; but where tolls and other duties are to be paid, the Castilian Pound of 16 Ounces is always used. See *Castile*.

The Ounce is divided into 16 Adarmes, and the Adarme into 36 Grains. $15\frac{1}{2}$ Ounces of the above weight make 16 Ounces of Castilian weight.

The Arroba equals 27lb. 6 oz. avoirdupois.

The King's Weight at the Custom House at Alicant is the Castile Quintal of 4 Arroves; and the Arrove contains 25 Pounds of 16 Ounces each, gold and silver weight.

Corn Measures.

The corn measure is called the Caffise, and contains 12 Barchillas; the Barchilla 8 Medios; and the Medio 2 Quartillos. 1 Caffise equals 7 Winchester Bushels nearly.

Liquid Measure.

Liquors are measured by the Cantaro of 8 Medios; each Medio contains 2 Quartillos. The Cantaro contains $3\frac{1}{19}$ English Wine Gallons.

The Tonelada or Tun, contains 2 Pipes, 80 Arrobas, or 100 Cantaros.

Long Measure.

The measure for cloth is called the Vara, which is subdivided into 4 Palmos; and equals $29\frac{23}{24}$ English Inches. For further particulars, see *Spain*.

ALTONA *(in Danish Holstein)*.

Monies and Coins.

Accounts are kept here in Marks of 16 Shillings Lubs, each subdivided into 12 Pence Lubs, the same as in Hamburgh.

Merchants' books, since the year 1777, must be kept in Marks, Shillings, and Pence Banco; the Specie Thaler, or Rixdollar, being valued at 3 Marks Banco. Monies and Coins.

By a royal edict of 1776, a bank was erected. This bank neither gives nor takes any thing in payment but Fine Silver, or whole and half Danish Specie Rixdollars, each of which must weigh from 537 to 538 Eschen, Cologne weight, or about 445½ English Grains. Bank.

No silver is received or paid under 15 Loths 12 Grains German, or 11 oz. 15 dwts. English.

For every Specie Rixdollar, the person who deposits it, is inscribed for 3 Marks Banco; and for every Mark of Fine Silver, he is inscribed for 27 Marks 12s. Banco.

All bills of exchange, or accounts of any sort, expressed in Altona Banco money, above the value of 100 Marks, cannot be paid any where but at the bank; and in all transactions in current money, the buyer is free to make the payment in Banco, reckoning the Rixdollar Specie at 3 Marks 11s. current, which gives a difference or agio of $22\frac{1}{12}$ per cent.

The bank shuts every year on the 11th of October, and opens again on the 19th; and any bill becoming due during that interval, must be paid before the bank is shut, or be protested.

When the bank directors think proper, they may lend out money on gold, silver, or copper, at 2 per cent. per annum; and then they pay, for gold 15 Carats fine, at least 375 Marks Banco per Mark fine; and for silver from 12 to 15 Loths fine, 27 Marks per Mark fine; for silver from 4 to 12 Loths fine, 26 Marks 12 Shillings per Mark fine; and for a Shipfund, or 280lb. of copper, 120 Marks.

The exchanges, weights, and measures, of Altona, are similar to those of Hamburgh. Exchanges, Weights, &c

AMERICA.

For the Spanish Colonies in South America, see *Mexico;* for those of Portugal, see *Brazil;* and for other places, see *United States, Canada,* and *West Indies.*

AMSTERDAM (*Old System*).*

Monies. Accounts are kept here in Florins or Guilders, also called Gulden. The Florin is divided into 20 Stivers; the Stiver into 16 Pennings, and sometimes into 12 Deniers; it has been also recently divided into Centimes.

Accounts are likewise kept, especially in the business of exchange, in Pounds, Shillings, and Pence Flemish.

The Pound Flemish, or Pondt Vlaams, is divided into 20 Schillings, or Sols de Gros, and the Schilling into 12 Pence, Groots, or Deniers de Gros. 2 Groots = 1 Stiver, 6 Stivers = 1 Schilling Flemish, 40 Groots = 1 Florin, and 6 Florins = 1 Pound Flemish.

The Rixdollar or Daelder, of 50 Stivers or 2½ Guilders, is a money of exchange, and also a coin; and the gold Guilder of 28 Stivers is a money of account, especially in the corn trade.

The monies of Holland were formerly considered under two values, viz. Banco and Currency; but this distinction no longer exists. See *Bank*.

Coins. The gold coins are:

The Ryder, which mostly passes for 14 Florins, or for 29 Francs 40 Centimes, French money, with double and half nearly in proportion. It is worth about £1. 5s. sterling.

The Ducat, which generally passes for 5 Florins 5 Stivers, or 11 Francs ,025 Centimes, with double Ducats in proportion, is worth about 9s. 4d. sterling.

It is to be observed that the gold coins in Holland are subject to variation in their current value, according to the market price of that metal; silver being considered the standard of value. Gold is sold at 355 Florins current per Mark fine, with a fluctuating agio of about 12 per cent. Silver is sold in Florins current per Mark fine, the average price being nearly 26 Florins.

The principal silver coins are:

The Ducatoon or silver Ryder, which passes for 3 Florins 3 Stivers, and is worth 5s. 10d. sterling nearly.

The 3 Florin piece, worth 5s. 6¼d. sterling; and the Florin, worth 1s. 9¾d.

The Florin passes for 2 Francs 10 Centimes French money, with all its multiples and divisions in proportion.

* A now system of monies, weights, and measures, similar to that of France, has been decreed for Holland, Brabant, and Flanders, for which see the article *Netherlands*.

There are, besides the above, the piece of 50 Stivers, and pieces of 30 and 10; the Rixdollar of Zealand of 52 Stivers; the coin of 28 Stivers, the Schilling of 6 Stivers, the Dubbeltje of 2 Stivers, and the Stiver piece. Coins.

The Fineness of Gold is reckoned in Carats and Grains, the weight being divided into 24 Carats, and the Carat into 12 Grains. Fineness of Gold and Silver.

The Fineness of Silver is reckoned in Pennyweights, Deniers, and Grains, the Pennyweight being divided into 12 Deniers, and the Denier into 4 Grains.

Gold and Silver are weighed by the Mark of 8 Ounces; the Ounce is divided into 20 Engels or Esterlins, and the Engel into 32 Az, Azen, or Aas. Thus the Mark contains 5120 Aas, and weighs 246,084 Grammes, or 3798 Grains, English troy weight.* Troy weight

In weighing diamonds or pearls, this Mark is divided into 1200 Carats. Thus 1 Engel = 7½ Carats, which are each subdivided into halves, quarters, eighths, &c. Diamond weight.

Apothecaries' weight is the pound of 12 Ounces or 1½ Mark; but arsenic is weighed by the troy Pound of 16 Ounces, and the Ounce is divided into 8 Drams 24 Scruples, or 480 Grains. Apothecaries' weight.

The Commercial Pound is 40 Aas heavier than the above Pound troy, and therefore weighs 10280 Aas. Hence 256lb. commercial weight = 257lb. Dutch troy. This Pound is divided into 2 Marks, 16 Ounces, 32 Loots, or 128 Drams. Its multiples are 8lb. = 1 Stone, 15lb. = 1 Shipfund, 100lb. = 1 Centner, and 300lb. = 1 Ship-pound. This is commonly called the Amsterdam weight. Commercial weight.

The Commercial Pound weighs 494,09 Grammes, or 7625 English troy Grains. Hence 100lb. of Amsterdam = 108,93lb. avoirdupois.

* Although the Dutch Mark is frequently referred to as a standard of comparison, yet its contents are variously given in works of high authority. It seems therefore proper here to state that the above proportion has been recently determined at the *London Mint* from attested standards transmitted to *Lord Castlereagh* by His Majesty's Consuls, *Mr. Melville* of Amsterdam, and *Mr. Ferrier* of Rotterdam.

It may be added that those standards have been found perfectly to agree with one adjusted at Amsterdam in 1817, for the Author of this work, by *Professor Van Swinden;* and the same proportion is further verified by the publications of this eminent Mathematician and experienced Metrologist.

Corn Measure. The principal measure for corn is the Last, which, though generally uniform in its contents, varies considerably in its divisions.

The Last of Amsterdam is divided into 27 Mudden, 36 Sacks, 108 Schepels, 432 Vierdevats, or 3,456 Coops. The Schepel contains 27,814 Litres, or 6,314 Winchester Gallons; and consequently the Last contains 30,03912 Hectolitres, which equal 85,248 Winchester Bushels.

The Last at Rotterdam is divided into 29 Sacks; at Utrecht into 25; at Flushing into 39; varying in its divisions in above sixty different places in Holland.

Wine Measure. Wine and spirits are generally sold by the Aam, which is divided into 4 Ankers, 8 Steken, 64 Stoops, 128 Mengels, 256 Pints, 1024 Mutsjes.

The Stoop equals 2,425 Litres, or 5,125 Pints English wine measure: hence the Aam contains 41 Gallons English wine measure. There are besides liquid measures of various other denominations, such as the Velt of 3 Stoops, the Oxhoofd of 96, the Legger of 240, and the Vat of 6 Aams or 384 Stoops.

Vessels of several other dimensions for wine, brandy, oil, &c. might be enumerated, which, however, are seldom taken as estimated, but are gauged as occasion may require.

Beer Measure. The Tun of Beer is divided into halves, quarters, and eighths. The eighth part is called the Stekan, and contains 16 Mengels or 32 Pints. The Stekan measures 19,6 Litres or 4,25 Gallons English beer measure: hence the Tun contains 34 Gallons English beer measure, or 41,5 Gallons English wine measure.

Long Measure. There are two kinds of Feet generally used in Holland, viz. the Amsterdam Foot and the Rhineland Foot, which differ in their divisions as well as in their length. The Amsterdam Foot is divided into 11 Inches, and each Inch is divided into quarters and eighths. This Foot equals 0,283133 Metres, or 11,147 English Inches. The Rhineland Foot is divided into 12 Inches, and measures 0,313946 Metres, or 12,36 English Inches.

There are three Ells used in Holland, viz.

The Ell of Amsterdam	= 0,68781 Metres, or	27,0797	English Inches.
Ell of the Hague	= 0,69424	27,333	....
Ell of Brabant	= 0,70066	27,585	....

Road Measure. In Holland, as well as in Flanders and Brabant, itinerary distances are computed by the League, which varies often in the same district.

	English Miles.	Furlongs.	Poles.	
The Dutch League is reckoned 19 to a Degree of the Meridian, and therefore it equals	3	5	4	Road Measure.
The common League of the Netherlands, 22 to a Degree =	3	1	5	
The Flemish League is 20,000 Rhenish Feet = ...	3	7	8	
In the North of Holland, 20 Leagues are reckoned to a Degree = ...	3	3	25	
In Rhineland 1400 Rhenish Perches are a League = ...	3	1	35	

It is also customary throughout the Netherlands to estimate distances by Time, that is, according to the number of hours that carriages, boats, or pedestrians, generally take or require in going a certain distance.

Land is measured in Holland by the Roed, Ruthe, or Perch, which is of various lengths; but the two principal are the Amsterdam Perch of 13 Amsterdam Feet, and the Rhineland Perch of 12 Rhineland Feet; the former being to the latter as 144,91 to 148,32. Land Measure.

600 Square Perches make a Morgen or Acre. Hence the Amsterdam Morgen equals 81,2866 French Ares, or 2 Acres 0 Roods 6 Perches English Statute measure. The Rhineland Morgen contains 85,1579 French Ares or 2 Acres 0 Roods 16 Perches English Statute measure.

In settling the Freight of Ships, certain kinds of goods are paid for by the Last, which is estimated as follows: Ship Lasts.

8 Oxhoofds of Wine.	7 Quartites of Train Oil.
5 Pieces of Brandy.	14 Quartites of Olive Oil.
14 Pieces of Herrings.	20 Chests of Lemons.
12 Casks of Pitch.	4000 lb. of Rice, Iron, or Copper.
13 Casks of Tar.	2000 lb. of Wool, Feathers, or Spices.

Commercial Allowances and other Regulations.

The following Table of the Allowances made at Amsterdam on the Sales and Shipment of Goods, (viz. Draft, Tare, Discount, In-and-Outward Duty, Half-weigh Duty, Brokerage, with further Remarks on sundry Articles,) was printed by authority in 1817, for the information of Merchants who trade from Great Britain and the United States of America to Amsterdam. Allowances, Regulations &c.

☞ *Most of those regulations are of ancient standing, and may therefore be considered as permanently established. The Duties, however, are an exception; but the Table is, notwithstanding, deemed worthy of a place in this work.*

Articles.	*Draft.*	*Tare.*	*Discount.*
Aloe, Cape		14 per ct.	2 per ct. and 1 per ct.
Alum, British	2 per ct.	10 to 11 per ct. or real weight	2 per ct.
Annato	ditto	20 per ct. tare and 4 per ct. for leaves	ditto
Arrack			1 per ct.
Ashes, American Pot and Pearl	ditto	42lb. per barrel	18 months rabat and 1 per ct.
Balsam Capivi		22 per ct.	2 per ct. and 1 per ct.
Barilla	ditto	4 per ct.	2 per ct.
Bark, Jesuit		real weight	2 per ct. and 1 per ct.
Borax		ditto	ditto
Brimstone	ditto	ditto	2 per ct.
Camphire, Cardamoms		ditto	2 per ct. and 1 per ct.
Cassia, Lignea		ditto	ditto
Buds, Fistula, Castorum, China Root		ditto	ditto
Cinnamon	1 p.ct. in chests	13lb. per fardel; real weight of chests	
Coals, Pit			1 per ct.
Cochineal	1½lb. per bale	real weight	4 per ct. add. 1 per ct. deduct
Cocoa		2lb. per bale except Surinam 6 per ct. real weight of casks	2 per ct. and 2 per ct. except Caraccas, Pamaribo and Berbice only 1 per ct.
Coffee, East and West India in general		3 per ct. or 6 per ct. in bales; real weight of casks	2 per ct. 2 per ct. & 1 per ct. for cash
Bourbon		10lb. per original mat	ditto
Java		14 — gunny	1 per ct. for cash
Mocha		24 — bale	1 per ct. and 1 per ct. for ditto
Columba Root		real weight	2 per ct. and 1 per ct.
Copper	1 per ct.		2 per ct.
Copperas	2 per ct.	10 per ct.	ditto
Cotton	ditto	6 per ct. on bales without ropes; 8 per ct. on ditto with ditto	1 per ct.
Elephant Teeth		real weight	2 per ct. and 1 per ct.
Figs, Turkey	1 lb. per mat.	10 per ct.	2 per ct.
Galls, Aleppo		6lb. per bale	2 per ct. and 1 per ct.
Smyrna		20lb. per ditto	
Ginger	4lb. per bale	4 to 8lb. per bale	2 per ct.
Glue, British	2 per ct.	10 per ct. or real weight	ditto
Gum Benzoin, Copal, Stick and Shellack		real weight	2 per ct. and 1 per ct.
Hides, Buenos Ayres	ditto	2lb. per hide	1 per ct.
Jalap, Ipecacuanha		real weight	2 per ct. and 1 per ct.
Indigo		16 to 30lb. per seron, real weight of chests	1 per ct. 2 per ct. and 1 per ct.
Lead	ditto		1 per ct.
Mace	1 per ct.	real weight	
Molasses	2 per ct.	12 to 14 per ct. or real weight	2 per ct.
Nutmegs	1 per ct.	real weight	

Articles.	*Inward Duty.*	*Outward Duty.*	*Half Weigh Duty.*	*Brokerage.*	*Remarks.* SELLS PER
Aloe, Cape	3 per ct. on the value	2 p. ct. on the value	*f.* 1:8 per 1000lb. gr.	1 per ct. on the amount	lb. in *st.*
Alum, British	6 *st.* per 100lb.	6 *st.* per 100lb.	ditto ditto	*f.* 1 per cask	100lb. *s.*
Annato	*f.* 1 per ditto	*f.* 2 per ditto	ditto ditto	ditto	lb. *st.*
Arrack	*f.* 10 per 30 viertels	*f.* 1:10 p. 30 viertels		2 per ct. on the amount	legger *f.*
Ashes, American Pot and Pearl	1 per ct. on the value	1 p. ct. on the value	ditto ditto	12 *st.* per barrel	100lb. *s.*
Balsam Capivi	3 per ct. on ditto	2 per ct. on ditto	ditto ditto	1 per ct. on the amount	lb. *st.*
Barilla	4 *st.* per 100lb.	4 *st.* per 100lb.	ditto ditto	6 *st.* per bale	100lb. *f.*
Bark, Jesuit	3 per ct. on the value	2 p. ct. on the value	ditto ditto	1 per ct. on the amount	lb. *st.*
Borax	*f.* 4 per 100lb.	*f.* 2:10 per 100lb.	*f.* 3:16 ditto	ditto	lb. *st.*
Brimstone	Raw 4 *st.* per ditto Refined *f.* 1:10 p. ditto		*f.* 1:8 ditto	2 *st.* per 100lb.	100lb. *f.*
Camphire Cardamoms	3 per ct. on the value	2 p. ct. on the value	ditto ditto	1 per ct. on the amount	lb. *st.*
Cassia, Lignea	3 *st.* per lb.	2 *st.* per lb.	*f.* 2:17 ditto	ditto	lb. *st.*
Buds Fistula Castorum China Root	3 per ct. on the value	2 p. ct. on the value	ditto ditto	ditto	lb. *st.*
Cinnamon	3 *st.* per lb.	2 *st.* per lb.	*f.* 2:17 ditto	*f.* 3:3 per fardel 1 *st.* per lb. in chests	lb. *st.*
Coals, Pit	free	free		1 per ct. on the amount	hoed *f.*
Cochineal	30 *st.* per 100lb.	30 *st.* per 100lb.	*f.* 28:2 ditto	¼ *st.* per £.	lb. *s.*
Cocoa	*f.* 1 per ditto	*f.* 1 per ditto	*f.* 2:17 ditto	½ p. ct. above 10*st.* p. lb. less 5 *st.* p. 100lb.	lb. *st.*
Coffee, East and West India in general Bourbon Java Mocha	10 *st.* per ditto	free	*f.* 1:8 ditto	½ per ct. on the amount	lb. *st*
Columba Root	3 per ct. on the value	2 p. ct. on the value	ditto ditto	1 per ct. on ditto	lb. *st.*
Copper	4 *st.* per 100lb.	8 *st.* per 100lb.	ditto ditto	½ per ct. on ditto	100lb. *f.*
Copperas	2 *st.* per ditto	2 *st.* per ditto	12 *st.* per cask of about 400lb.	6 *st.* per cask	100lb. *st.*
Cotton	8 *st.* per ditto	15 *st.* per ditto	*f.* 1:8 per 1000lb. gr.	½ per ct. on the amount	lb. *g.*
Elephant Teeth	*f.* 2 per 100lb.	*f.* 1 per 100lb.	ditto ditto	1 per ct. on ditto	lb. *st.*
Figs, Turkey	5 *st.* per ditto	5 *st.* per ditto	ditto ditto	1 *st.* per mat	100lb. *f.*
Galls, Aleppo Smyrna	12 *st.* per ditto	*f.* 1 per ditto	*f.* 2:17 ditto	½ *st.* per £.	100lb. *f.*
Ginger	6 *st.* per ditto	4 *st.* per ditto	*f.* 1:17 ditto	6 *st.* per bale	100lb. *f*
Glue, British	10 *st.* per ditto	5 *st.* per ditto	*f.* 1:8 ditto	2 *st.* per 100lb.	100lb. *f.*
Gum Benzoin Copal Stick and Shellack	3 per ct. on the value	2 p. ct. on the value	ditto ditto	1 per ct. on the amount	lb. *st.*
Hides, Buenos Ayres	1 per ct. on ditto	1 per ct. on ditto	ditto ditto	½ per ct. on ditto	lb. *st.*
Jalap Ipecacuanha	3 per ct. on ditto	2 per ct. on ditto	ditto ditto	1 per ct. on ditto	lb. *st.*
Indigo	20 *st.* per 100lb.	30 *st.* per 100lb.	*f.* 15:15 ditto	½ *st.* per £.	lb. *st.*
Lead	3 *st.* per ditto	free	*f.* 1:8 ditto	1 per ct. on the amount	100lb. *s.*
Mace	3 per ct. on the value	2 p. ct. on the value	*f.* 14:2 ditto	1 *st.* per lb.	lb. *s.*
Molasses	West-India ditto British *f.* 6 per 100lb.	ditto 4 *st.* per 100lb.	*f.* 1:17 ditto	½ per ct. on the amount	lb. *s.*
Nutmegs	3 per ct. on the value	2 p. ct. on the value	*f.* 9:8 ditto	1 *st.* per lb.	lb. *st.*

Articles.	*Draft.*	*Tare.*	*Discount.*
Nux Vomica		8 to 10lb. per bale	2 per ct. and 1 per ct.
Oil Turpentine	2 per ct.	real weight	2 per ct.
Vitriol		ditto	2 per ct. and 2 per ct.
Whale			1 per ct.
Opium		ditto	2 per ct. and 1 per ct.
Orchilla	2 per ct.	10 per ct.	2 per ct.
Pepper		8lb. per bale	2 per ct. for cash
Pimento		6lb. per ditto weighing 100lb. and less, 6 per ct. above 100lb.	2 per ct. and 1 per ct.
Rhubarb		real weight	ditto
Rice, Carolina	2 per ct.	ditto	2 per ct.
Bengal, Brazil	ditto	6lb. per bale	ditto
Rum			1 per ct.
Safflower		4 per ct.	2 per ct. and 2 per ct.
Salt			1 per ct.
Saltpetre		8lb. per single and 12lb. per double bale, or real weight of casks	1 per ct. and 1½ per ct.
Sassafras		real weight	2 per ct. and 2 per ct.
Snake Root, Spermaceti		ditto	2 per ct. and 1 per ct.
Staves			1 per ct. and 1 per ct.
Sugar, West India	2 per ct.	18 to 20 per ct. of casks	2 per ct. except Brazil Muscovade, from which 18 months rabat and 2 per ct. is deducted
East India	ditto	12 per ct. of canisters; 10 per ct. of bales and mats	
Brazil, Havannah	ditto	18 to 20 per ct. of chests	
Refined			only 3 per ct.
Tamarinds		14 per ct.	2 per ct. and 1 per ct.
Tea		20 to 26 per quarter chest	1 per ct.
Tin	ditto		ditto
Tobacco, Varinas		15lb. per canister	2 per ct. and 1 per ct.
Portorico	ditto		2 per ct.
Brazil	ditto	6lb. per roll	ditto
Maryland and Virginia	ditto	weighed without the casks, rafaction, 8 per ct. for stems	1 per ct.
Stems	ditto		ditto
Tortoiseshells		real weight	2 per ct. and 1 per ct.
Turmerick, Java		ditto of casks; 6lb. per bale	2 per ct.
Twist			1 per ct.
Wood, Box, Cedar, Ebony, Pock			2 per ct. and 2 per ct.
Mahogany			1 per ct.
Brazil	ditto		2 per ct.
Fustick, Logwood	ditto	3 per ct. for rot	ditto
Quercitron		real weight	2 per ct. and 2 per ct.

Articles.	Inward Duty.	Outward Duty.	Half Weigh Duty.	Brokerage.	Remarks.
					SELLS PER
Nux Vomica	3 per ct. on the value	2 p. ct. on the value	*f.* 1:8 per 1000lb. gr.	1 per ct. on the amount	lb. *st.*
Oil Turpentine ..	......ditto......	......ditto......	ditto...... ditto ..	... *f.* 1 per cask ...	100lb. *f.*
Vitriol	......ditto......	......ditto......	ditto...... ditto ..	.. 10 *st.* per flask ..	lb. *st.*
Whale	*f.* 3 per quardeel	10 *st.* per quardeel	....	.. 2 *st.* per stekan ..	quardeel *f*
Opium	3 per ct. on the value	2 p. ct. on the value	ditto...... ditto ..	1 per ct. on the amount	lb. *f.*
Orchilla	.. 8 *st.* per 100lb. .	..6 *st.* per 100lb...	ditto...... ditto ..	......ditto......	100lb. *f.*
Pepper	... *f.* 3 per ditto ..	.. *f.* 2 per ditto ..	*f.* 6:3..... ditto ..	... 2 *st.* per bale ...	lb. *g.*
Pimento	3 per ct. on the value	2 p. ct. on the value	*f.* 1:8..... ditto ..	. . 6 *st.* per ditto ..	100lb. *f.*
Rhubarb	......ditto......	......ditto......	ditto...... ditto ..	1 per ct. on the amount	lb. in *st.*
Rice, Carolina....	. $1\frac{1}{2}$ *st.* per 100lb. ..	..4 *st.* per 100lb...	ditto...... ditto ..	.. 10 *st.* per cask }	} 100lb. *s.*
Bengal } Brazil } ..	......ditto......	......ditto......	ditto...... ditto ..	... 6 *st.* per bale . }	} 100lb. *s.*
Rum	*f.* 10 per 30 viertels	*f.* 1:10 p. 30 viertels	....	2 per ct. on the amount	anker *f.*
Safflower........	3 per ct. on the value	3 p. ct. on the value	ditto...... ditto ..	. . *f.* 2 per bale ...	lb. *st.*
Salt	*f.* 12 per hundred	*f.* 3 per hundred	....	*f.* 2:11 per hundred	hund. £.
Saltpetre	.. 10 *st.* per 100lb...	..*f.* 2 per 100lb...	*f.* 3:6..... ditto ..	.... $\frac{1}{2}$ *st.* per £.	100lb. *f.*
Sassafras	3 per ct. on the value	2 p. ct. on the value	*f.* 1:8..... ditto ..	1 per ct. on the amount	100lb. *f.*
Snake Root } Spermaceti }	......ditto......	......ditto......	ditto...... ditto ..	......ditto......	lb. *st.*
Staves	......ditto......	$1\frac{1}{2}$ per ct. on ditto	....	......ditto......	122 ps. *f.*
Sugar, W. India } E. India . } Brazil } Havannah }	.. 6 *st.* per 100lb.	15 *st.* per 100lb. }	} *f.* 2:6..... ditto ..	. $\frac{1}{2}$ per ct. on ditto ..	lb. *g.*
Refined....	..*f.* 10 per ditto ...	.... free .... }	} *f.* 2:6..... ditto ..	. $\frac{1}{2}$ per ct. on ditto ..	lb. *g.*
Tamarinds	3 per ct. on the value	2 p. ct. on the value	*f.* 1:8..... ditto ..	. 1 per ct. on ditto ..	100lb. *f.*
Tea	10 per ct. on ditto	10 *st.* per 100lb.	*f.* 7:10..... ditto ..	......ditto......	lb. *st.*
Tin	. 8 *st.* per 100lb. ..	12 *st.* per ditto	*f.* 3:16..... ditto ..	......ditto......	100lb. *f.*
Tobacco, Varinas	2 p. ct. on the value, *f.* 3:6 excise per canister of about 90lb.	1 p. ct. on the value	*f.* 1:17..... ditto ..	.... $\frac{1}{2}$ *st.* per lb. .... }	} lb. *st.*
Portorico	2 p. ct. on the value, *f* 3:8 excise p. 100lb.	......ditto......	ditto...... ditto ..	... $\frac{1}{4}$ *st.* per ditto .. }	} lb. *st.*
Brazil ..	2 p. ct. on the value, 16 *st.* excise per roll	......ditto......	ditto...... ditto ..	... $\frac{1}{8}$ *st.* per ditto .. }	} lb. *st.*
Maryland and Virginia	2 p. ct. on the value, *f.* 2:10 excise p. cask of about 1000lb.	2 per ct. on ditto	ditto...... ditto ..	... *f.* 1 per cask ... }	} lb. *st.*
Stems. ...	only 2 p. ct. on the val.	......ditto......	ditto...... ditto ..	.. 2 *st.* per 100lb. ..	100lb. *f.*
Tortoiseshells	3 per ct. on ditto	......ditto......	*f.* 1:8..... ditto ..	1 per ct. on the amount	lb. *st.*
Turmerick, Java ..	. *f.* 1 per 100lb. ..	..2 *st.* per 100lb...	ditto...... ditto ..	6 *st.* per 100lb. ..	100lb. *f.*
Twist	1 per ct. on the value	1 p. ct. on the value	....	1 per ct. on the amount	bundle *f.*
Wood, Box } Cedar } Ebony } Pock } ..	2 per ct. on ditto	3 per ct. on ditto	ditto...... ditto ..	......ditto......	100lb. *f.*
Mahogany	......ditto......	......ditto......	....	......ditto......	sq. ft. of 2 inch. thick *st.*
Brazil....	......ditto......	......ditto......	ditto...... ditto ..	... $\frac{1}{2}$ *st.* per £.	100lb. *f.*
Fustick } Logwood }	......ditto......	......ditto......	ditto...... ditto ..	......ditto..... }	} 100lb. *f.*
Quercitron	3 per ct. on ditto	2 per ct. on ditto	ditto...... ditto ..	$\frac{1}{2}$ per ct. on the amt. }	} 100lb. *f.*

Allowances Regulations &c.

"Besides the preceding allowances, there is a small additional charge on the In-and Outward duty, for permits, as also on the half weigh duty for weighing: these expenses, together with those for landing, receiving, and delivering, warehouse rent, cooperage, or similar disbursements, cannot be ascertained, as they depend on the packages the goods are in.

Rabat is reckoned at 8 per cent. per annum, which amounts to $2\frac{1}{7}$ Stivers per Guilder on 18 months.

Rafaction is a deduction from the weight for damage, which is settled by a sworn officer.

Articles of importation are commonly sold here on credit, except Coffee and Pepper, which always sell for ready money.

The customary difference in the weight is, that 112lb. English = 102lb. Dutch; but odd pounds not being counted (except in pepper and some fine goods), and the sworn weighers here, according to the agreement between buyer and seller, weighing the goods with an allowance of 10 to 12lb. per Hogshead, 8lb. per Tierce, 6lb. per Barrel, and 4 to 6lb. per Bale, the loss in the weight may be calculated at about 10 to 11 per cent. on large packages of about 1000lb. and, weighing less, it is proportionably more; so that packages of about 100lb. will lose from 14 to 15 per cent. besides the tare. There are two different modes of selling coffee in Bales, viz. with 3 per cent. tare and about 2lb. per Bale, or with 6 per cent. tare and 4 to 6lb. per Bale allowance; as also Portorico Tobacco, which is sold with 4 to 6lb. allowance on 25 Rolls, or 1lb. is deducted from each Roll: this makes a great difference in the weight, which however is compensated by a higher price.

9 Hoeds of pit coal are about 5 Chaldrons in Newcastle; a Hundred of rock salt is reckoned 26 Tons in Liverpool.

A Legger of arrack of 15 Ankers is about 150 Gallons; an Anker of rum of $5\frac{1}{4}$ Viertels is about 10 Gallons in London.

A Quardel of whale oil of 12 Stekans will render about 61 Gallons."

Explanation of the Marks, &c. in the foregoing Tables.

£. {stands for}	Pound Flemish of 20s. Flemish, is	10s. $10\frac{10}{11}$d. sterl. or	2 Dollars	40 Cents.
s.	Shilling Ditto .. 12 Groats Do.	$6\frac{6}{11}$d. do.		12 "
g.	Groat .... $\frac{1}{2}$ Stiver	$0\frac{6}{11}$d. do.		1 "
f.	Florin or Guilder 20 Stivers	1s. $9\frac{9}{11}$d. do.		40 "
st.	Stiver divided into 16 Parts	$1\frac{1}{11}$d. do.		2 "

The old Bank of Amsterdam was established in 1609, and was long considered the richest in the world. Previous to that period, the monies generally circulating in Holland were of very uncertain and deteriorated value. To remedy this evil, the Bank was established under the guarantee of the city, and it received no coins but according to their intrinsic value. Gold and silver bullion, and other articles of value, were received in the way of pledges; *Recipisses* or receipts, which were transferable, were given for all deposits: as those deposits were seldom drawn out, they accumulated to a considerable amount. Old Bank.

From the high credit of the establishment, Bank money generally bore a premium against currency of about 4 per cent. called the *Agio.*

Such was the flourishing state of this institution until the commencement of the French Revolution, when it rapidly declined; and its deposits are supposed to have been chiefly withdrawn by the proprietors before the invasion of Holland in 1794. Its operations, however, were still continued, but on a very reduced scale, until the year 1814, when they entirely ceased, without any formal declaration of law. A nominal Banco, however, of 2 per cent. Agio was reckoned on settling certain foreign exchanges; but in January, 1820, this practice was ordered to be discontinued.

In 1814 a new Bank was established at Amsterdam, under the name of the *Bank of the Netherlands.* It is not a Bank of deposit, like the old institution, but of circulation, nearly on the plan of the Bank of England. The grant is for 25 years, and no similar institution is to be allowed within that period. New Bank.

The original capital was 5 millions of Florins, divided into shares or *actions* of 1000 Florins each, so that there were in all 5000 shares, and of these the King was always to hold 500. The capital, however, might be doubled whenever the Directors should think proper; and this increase took place in 1819.

This Bank issues notes payable to bearer on demand, discounts bills at 5 per cent. per annum, and lends money at the same rate on pledges. It coins money for the state, and deals in bullion and foreign coins, but in no other kind of property.

The management is under a President, a Secretary, and five Directors, all of whom are paid from the profits of the institution. The qualification of a Director is to hold 10 shares, and every six months he must go out of office, first by lot, and afterwards by seniority of service, but he may be re-elected immediately.

Usances. Usances are in general one month after date, and days of grace, which are nominally six, are seldom taken.

For *Exchanges of Amsterdam,* see Vol. II.

ANCONA *(in Italy).*

Monies of Account. Accounts are kept here in Scudi of 20 Soldi, subdivided into 12 Denari. The Scudo is also divided into 12 Paoli, or 100 Bajocchi ; also into 80 Bolognini, and is worth 4s. 4d. sterling nearly.

For the coins of Ancona see ***Rome.***

Weights. The Roman Pound, which weighs 5238,5 troy Grains, is used here and throughout all the Roman States for gold and silver. The Commercial Pound at Ancona is somewhat lighter than that of Rome. 100lb. of Rome = 102,75lb. of Ancona. Hence 100lb. of Ancona, commercial weight, = 73,75lb. avoirdupois nearly.

Corn Measure. The measures for corn are the Rubbio, the Coppa or Lappe, and the Provenda or Sack.

4 Provende...... = ...1 Coppa.
8 Coppe........ = ...1 Rubbio.

The Rubbio contains 2,861 Hectolitres, which correspond to 7,718 Winchester Bushels.

Wine Measure. The measures for wine are the Soma, Barile, Boccale, and Foglietta.

4 Fogliette...... = ...1 Boccale.
24 Boccali ...... = ...1 Barile.
2 Barili .... = ...1 Soma.

The Soma contains 85,917 Litres, or 22,69 English wine Gallons.

Long Measure. The Ell is called here Braccio, and measures 25,33 English Inches ; hence 27 Braccia of Ancona = 19 English Yards.

Exchanges. Ancona exchanges with and gives (more or less) to—

Amsterdam .... 42 Bajocchi...... for 1 Florin.

Exchanges.

Bologna	1 Scudo	...... for 100	Bolognini.
Florence	118 Scudi	100	Scudi D'oro.
Leghorn	90 Scudi	100	Pezze of 8 Reali.
London	44 Paoli	 1	Pound sterling.
Rome	100 Scudi	100	Scudi Romani.
Venice	91 Scudi	100	Scudi Banco.

The usance for bills drawn from Italy is 15 days, and from France 40 days after date. With respect to other bills, the same usance is adopted as that of the place from whence they are drawn. No days of grace are granted.

ANJENGO, *see East Indies.*

ANTWERP *(Old System).**

Monies of Account.

Accounts are kept here, and in all Brabant and Flanders, in Florins of 20 Stivers; the Stiver being divided into 16 Pennings, but more commonly into 12 Deniers. The Florin has been recently divided into Centimes or Cents, and is then called the New Florin of the Netherlands. Stivers are sometimes called Patars and Sols; Francs and Centimes are also in circulation.

Accounts are likewise kept, especially in exchanges, in Pounds Flemish of 20 Shillings, 120 Stivers, 240 Groots, 1920 Pennings Brabant, or 5760 Miters. The Patacon Rixdollar, or Daalder, is another money of account and of exchange. It is worth $2\frac{2}{5}$ Florins, or 8 Shillings Flemish.

The foregoing monies have two different values, viz. exchange money and current money. The former is also called *Permis,* or *Brabands Wissel,* and the latter *Brabands Current.* 6 Florins of exchange equal 7 Florins current: thus the former money is $16\frac{2}{3}$ per cent. better than the latter.

In all foreign transactions money of exchange is used, but current money in local or domestic trade. The following table shews their values compared with the monies of France and England.

* For the new system of monies, weights, and measures, commenced January 1, 1820, see the article *Netherlands.*

Coins.

GOLD COINS.	Exch. Money.—New Florin of the Netherlds		Current Money of Brabant.			Money of France.		Sterl. Value in Gold.	
	Fl.	Cents.	Fl.	S.	Den.	Fr.	Cents.	S.	D.
Sovereign, with Double and Half in proportion	7	98 525	9	6	3 870	16	90	13	5
Ducat	5	39 595	6	5	10 866	11	42	9	0¾
Double Louis	22	30 200	26	0	4 560	47	20	37	5½
Louis	11	12 738	12	19	7 665	23	55	18	8
Piece of 20 Francs, with Double in proportion	9	45 000	11	0	6 000	20	00	15	10½
SILVER COINS.								Sterl. Value in Silver at 5s. 2d. p. oz.	
Ducatoon, with Double and Half in proportion	2	97 675	3	9	5 440	6	30	5	1
Crown of Brabant, with Halves, &c. in proport[n.]	2	62 710	3	1	3 588	5	56	4	7¾
Crown of France	2	74 050	3	3	11 340	5	80	4	8¼
Half Ditto	1	29 138	1	10	3 825	2	75	2	2¾
Quarter Ditto	0	70 075	0	16	6 450	1	50	1	2½
Escalin of Brabant......	0	28 350	0	6	7 380	0	60	0	5¾
Plaquette, or Half Ditto .	0	14	0	3	3 690	0	30	0	3
Ditto of Liege..........	0	13 230	0	3	11 004	0	28	0	2¾
New Florin of the Netherlands	1	0 000	1	3	4 000	2	11 64	1	8½

Fineness of Gold. The Fineness of Gold is expressed in Carats and Grains; the Mark being 24 Carats, the Carat 12 Grains. The Mark of fine Gold is received at the Mint for 366 Florins 10 Stivers, money of exchange; and the Mark of light Ducats for 358 Florins 10 Stivers, money of exchange.

Fineness of Silver. The Fineness of Silver is expressed in Pennings and Grains; the Mark being 12 Pennings, the Penning 24 Grains. Silver, 10 Pennyweights 9 Grains fine, is received at the Mint for 25 Florins 5 Stivers, the Mark fine; but under that standard, for 24 Florins 19 Stivers, money of exchange.

Troy Weight. The Weight for Gold, Silver, and Coins, is the same as the Dutch Troy Weight, and is divided accordingly; the Mark into 8 Ounces, 160 Engels, or 5120 Azen; and equals 3798 Grains, English Troy Weight.

Of the Commercial Weight, the Shippond is 300lb.; the Centner, 100lb.; the Charge or Load, 400lb.; the Chariot or Cart Load, 165lb.; the Stone, 8lb. The Commercial Pound is divided into 2 Marks, 16 Ounces, and 32 Loots. This weight is about 5 per cent. lighter than Dutch Troy Weight, being 9754 Azen, or 7235,5 English Grains. Hence 100lb. Brabant Weight = 103,35lb. Avoirdupois. The Half Kilogramme equals 1lb. 1,015 oz. Antwerp Commercial Weight. Commercial Weight.

The Corn Measure, called the Viertel, or Raziere, contains 4 Mucken. 37,5 Viertels make 1 Last; and 40 Viertels, 11 English Quarters nearly. Corn is chiefly sold by the Hectolitre, 28,5 of which are computed to equal 10 English Quarters: but the accurate proportion is 28,189 Hectolitres to 80 Bushels Winchester Measure, or 10 Quarters. Corn Measure.

The following are the proportions between the corn measures of different places, as estimated here.

38 Razieres or Viertels of Antwerp =	36	Sacks (1 Last) of Amsterdam;
	30½	Hectolitres of France;
	35¾	Viertels of Malines;
	102	Astlers of Louvain;
	63	Sistres of Brussels;
	29	Common Sacks of Flanders;
	24¾	Great Sacks of Flanders;
	82	Winchester Bushels.

An Aam of wine contains 50 Stoops; and a Boot, 152 Stoops. A Tun of Beer contains 54 Stoops. The Aam is reckoned at 137,4 French Litres, or about 36,5 English Gallons. Some wines are sold by the Velt, which answers to 18,66 Litres, or 5 English Gallons nearly. Wine Measure.

Two different Ells are used at Antwerp; the longest, for silk stuffs, is 0,6939 Metres, or 27,32 English Inches; the shortest, for woollens, is 0,6846 Metres, or 26,966 English Inches. It may be observed, that what is called the Brabant Ell in Hamburgh, is ¾ per 100 less than the Long Ell, or 1 per 100 greater than the Short Ell of the above-mentioned Antwerp Ells. Long Measure.

Antwerp, Brussels, &c. exchange with the following places, and give in money of exchange to— Exchanges.

Exchanges.

Amsterdam	£103 Flemish (more or less)	for	£100 Flemish.
Cologne ...	100 Rixdollars	....	136 Rixdollars specie.
Francfort ..	100 Rixdollars	....	130 Rixdollars current.
Hamburgh	35 Stivers	....	1 Rixdr. of 2 Marks banco.
Lisbon	48d. Flemish	....	1 Crusade of 400 Rees.
London ...	38 Escalins Flemish	....	£1 sterling.
Madrid....	90d. Flemish	....	1 Ducat of 375 Maravedis.
Milan.....	1 Florin	....	56 Soldi Correnti.
Nuremberg	100 Rixdollars	....	127 Rixdollars current.
Paris	100 Francs	....	100 Francs.
Rotterdam	100 Florins of exchange	....	106 Florins current.
Vienna	102 Rixdollars	....	100 Rixdollars specie, or $133\frac{1}{3}$ Rixdollars current.

The Usances, &c. are the same as at *Amsterdam.*

ARRAGON *(a Province of Spain).*

Monies of Account.

Accounts are here kept in Libras Jaquesas of 20 Sueldos, or 320 Dineros de Plata.

The Libra is composed of 10 Reals of Old Plate, or 18 Reals 28 Maravedis Vellon, that is, 640 Maravedis Vellon.

A Sueldo is divided into 8 Quartos, or 16 Dineros; a Dinero, or Ochavo, is worth 2 Maravedis Vellon.

16 Pesos Duros, or Hard Dollars, correspond to 17 Libras Jaquesas; therefore (taking the Dollar at 4s. 4d. sterling) the Libra is worth 4s. 1d. nearly.

Spanish Monies and Coins.

The different Spanish Monies and Coins are valued in Arragon as follows:

The Doubloon de Plata, or Pistole of Exchange, at $3\frac{1}{5}$ Libras, 32 Reals, or 64 Sueldos Arragonese.

The Peso de Plata, or Dollar of Exchange, at 8 Reals, or 16 Sueldos.

The Ducado de Cambio, or Ducat of Exchange, at $11\frac{1}{34}$ Reals.

The Effective Doubloon, of 2 Escudos de Oro, at $42\frac{1}{2}$ Reals.

The Peso Duro, or Hard Dollar, at 21 Sueldos 4 Dineros.

The Peseta, at 4 Sueldos 4 Dineros, or 68 Dineros.

The Real de Plata, at 2 Sueldos 2 Dineros, or 34 Dineros.

Hence, 5 Pistoles of Exchange = 16 Libras Jaquesas.

5 Dollars of Exchange........ = 4 Libras Jaquesas. Spanish Monies and Coins.
68 Ducats of Exchange ...... = 75 ditto.
4 Effective Doubloons........ = 17 ditto.

The Mark, gold and silver weight, contains 8 Ounces, or 32 Quartillos; the Quartillo, 4 Arienses, or 128 Grains. This Grain is $\frac{1}{8}$ heavier than the Castilian Grain; but both Marks are alike, weighing 3550 English Grains. Weights.

The Libra or Pound Pensil, commercial weight, consists of 12 Ounces, and equals 0,3498 Kilogrammes or 5398 Troy Grains. Hence 100lb. of Arragon = 77,1lb. avoirdupois.

The Quintal contains 4 Arrobas or 144lb., and equals 1 cwt. avoirdupois nearly.

The largest measure for corn is called Cahiz, and contains 8 Fanegas, 24 Quartales, 96 Almudas or Celemines, and renders 180,486 Litres or 5,125 Winchester Bushels. Measures.

The Nietro of wine contains 16 Cantaros, and renders 165,8 Litres or 43,8 English Wine Gallons. The Cantaro of brandy = 13,97 Litres or 3,69 English Wine Gallons.

The Vara or Ell = 0,7675 Metres or 30,22 English Inches.*

For Exchanges and other particulars, see *Spain*.

ARABIA, *see Bassora, Betelfagui, and Mocha.*

ARCHANGEL, *see Russia.*

AUGSBURG *(in Germany).*

Accounts are kept in Florins (also called Guilders, Guldens, and Goulds); each Florin being divided into 60 Creutzers, and each Creutzer into 4 Pfenings. Monies of Account.

The Florin is likewise divided into 15 Batzen, or 20 Kaysergroschen.

The Thaler or Rixdollar is $1\frac{1}{2}$ Florin, or 90 Creutzers; it is therefore worth

* These measures of Arragon were ascertained in 1812 by a Commission under *Monsieur Maurin*, and were approved by the Chamber of Commerce at Valencia. They differ in many respects from the measures given by *Marien* and other Spanish authors. The Report of the Commissioners, with other valuable documents on the subject, was transmitted to *Lord Castlereagh* in 1818, by *Mr. Consul Waring*.

Monies of Account.

22,5 Batzen, or 30 Kaysergroschen. These monies are distinguished into *Giro*, *Current*, and *Muntze*.

Giro is the money of exchange, and is 27 per cent. better than Current; thus, 100 Rixdollars Giro are worth 127 Rixdollars Current.

Current money are the convention coins *(see Germany)*, also different other monies, both of gold and silver, the value of which is chiefly regulated by the market price of the precious metals.

Muntze, also called *Wisse Muntzen* or White Money, is composed of inferior coins, against which Current money bears an agio of about 20 per cent.

Coins.

The coins of Augsburg are the following:

Gold.—The Ducat, which is worth 4 Florins 12 Creutzers Current, with a variable agio; and the Gold Guilder which is worth 3 Florins Current.

Silver.—The Reichsthaler Specie of the Constitution, worth 2 Florins 12 Creutzers Current; and the Reichsthaler Specie of the Convention, worth 2 Florins Current.

The Florin of 60 Creutzers, the Half Florin of 30 Creutzers, and pieces of 20, 15, 12, 10, $7\frac{1}{2}$, 5, 4, 3, $2\frac{1}{2}$, 2, and 1 Creutzer, of base silver and copper.

The foreign coins which circulate are generally at a nominal value in Florins Current, which varies according to circumstances.

Value of Monies.

The Rixdollar Giro may be valued at 32,5 Azen or 24,1 English Grains of Fine Gold, and at 463 Azen or 343,4 Grains of Fine Silver; the Rixdollar Current at 25,6 Azen or 19 Grains of Fine Gold, and at 365 Azen or 270,7 Grains of Fine Silver.

100 Rixdollars Hamburgh Banco are worth 114 Rixdollars Augsburg Giro, or $144\frac{3}{4}$ Rixdollars Augsburg Current: hence 100 Marks Hamburgh Banco are worth 57 Florins Augsburg Giro, or $72\frac{2}{5}$ Florins Augsburg Current. Also 1 Florin or 60 Creutzers Augsburg Current = $27\frac{1}{5}$ Shillings Hamburgh Current.

The following valuations may be therefore made, viz.

1 Florin Giro = 2s. 8d. sterling; and 1 Florin Current = 2s. $1\frac{1}{4}$d. Hence £1 sterling = $7\frac{1}{2}$ Florins Giro, or $9\frac{1}{2}$ Florins Current, nearly.

Fineness of Gold and Silver.

The Mark Fine of Gold contains 24 Carats, and the Carat 12 Grains.

The Mark Fine of Silver contains 16 Loths, and the Loth 4 Quintins or 16 Pfenings. Gold and Silver are sold at so many Florins Current per Mark fine.

Gold and Silver are weighed by the Mark of Augsburg, which is composed of 16 Loths, 64 Quintins, or 256 Pfenings; and weighs 236,036 Grammes, or 3643 English Grains. Weights.

The Cologne Mark is likewise used here.

The Centner, commercial weight, contains 100lb. but there are two sorts: the first called the carrier's weight, of which the pound weighs $33\frac{1}{4}$ Loths, and the other the commercial pound, which weighs 32 Loths. The latter weighs 2 Marks and $\frac{5}{8}$ Pfening. Hence 100lb. carrier's weight = $103\frac{29}{32}$lb. commercial weight, or $208\frac{1}{16}$ Marks, gold and silver weight. It also equals 108,28lb. avoirdupois. Thus 24lb. commercial weight equal 25lb. avoirdupois; and 24lb. carrier's weight equal 26lb. avoirdupois nearly.

The corn measure, called a Schaf, contains 8 Metzen, 32 Vierlings, or 128 Maessels. The Schaf equals 4,404 Hectolitres, or $12\frac{1}{2}$ Winchester Bushels. Dry Measure.

The Liquid Measures are as follows: Liquid Measure.

The Fuder contains 8 Jees, 16 Muids, 96 Besons, or 768 Masses. The Mass measures $90\frac{1}{3}$ English cubic Inches; and therefore the Fuder = 11,355 Hectolitres, or 300 English Gallons nearly.

The Ell of Augsburg is of two kinds, the long Ell being 0,6095 Metres, or 24 English Inches, and the short Ell, 0,5923 Metres, or $23\frac{1}{3}$ English Inches: hence, 36 of the long Ells = 24 English Yards, and 54 of the short Ells = 35 English Yards. Long Measure.

The Foot is half the short Ell; and therefore 36 Feet of Augsburg are equal to 35 English Feet nearly.

Augsburg exchanges with, and gives to Exchanges.

Amsterdam	10	Rixdollars giro (more or less) for	100 Rixdollars.
Francfort..	102	Rixdollars current	100 Rixdollars current.
Hamburgh	106	Rixdollars giro	100 Rixdollars banco.
Leipsic ...	99	Rixdollars current	100 Rixdollars current.
London ...	9	Florins 45 Creutzers current....	£1 sterling.
Paris	120	Florins current	100 Ecus of 3 Francs.
Nuremberg	101	Florins current	100 Florins current.
Venice	100	Rixdollars giro	100 Ducats banco.
Vienna....	100	Florins current	106 Florins current.

The Usance is 15 days; half Usance 8 days; double Usance 30 days; $1\frac{1}{2}$ Usance 23 days after sight. Usance.

Days of Grace.

The payment of bills of exchange in Augsburg is generally settled at the *Scontro*, which takes place every Tuesday; and then they are paid on the Wednesday, either in cash, or in *assignations*, or drafts. Thus bills have from 1 to 8 days grace; for such as fall due on the Tuesday must be paid the next day; but such as fall due on the Wednesday are not paid till that day week. Bills, however, drawn *a vista* or at sight, must be paid within 24 hours after being presented; as also any other bills which are not presented until after the Wednesday subsequent to the day on which they become due.

BARBARY STATES, *see Algiers, Tripoli, and Tunis.*

BARCELONA *(in Catalonia, Spain).*

Monies of Account.

Accounts are kept in Libras of 20 Sueldos, 240 Dineros, or 480 Mallas.

The Libra is likewise divided into Reals de Plata Catalan of 3 Sueldos each, and into Reals Ardites of 2 Sueldos each. Hence $6\frac{2}{3}$ of the former, or 10 of the latter, = 1 Libra Catalan.

The different Spanish monies of account here are valued as follows:

The Doubloon de Plata (or of exchange) of 32 Reals de Plata, is valued at 5 Libras 12 Sueldos Catalan.

The Peso de Plata, of 8 Reals de Plata, at 28 Sueldos.

The Ducat of Exchange at 38 Sueldos $7\frac{4}{17}$ Dineros.

The Ducat of 11 Reals Vellon at 20 Sueldos $5\frac{7}{17}$ Dineros.

The Real de Plata at $3\frac{1}{2}$ Sueldos, or 42 Dineros.

Hence 5 Dollars of Exchange make 7 Libras Catalan; 5 Pistoles of Exchange = 28 Libras Catalan; 272 Ducats of Exchange = 525 Libras Catalan.

Coins.

The Spanish Coins are thus valued:

The Effective Doubloon at $7\frac{1}{2}$ Libras Catalan; half, double, and quadruple in proportion.

The Peso Duro, or Hard Dollar, at $37\frac{1}{2}$ Sueldos Catalan; or 8 such Dollars at 15 Libras.

The Peseta Mexicana at 9 Sueldos $4\frac{1}{2}$ Dineros; the Peseta provincial at 7 Sueldos 6 Dineros Catalan.

The Real de Plata provincial at 3 Sueldos 9 Dineros; the Real Vellon at $22\frac{1}{2}$ Dineros.

The Quarto at $5\frac{10}{34}$ Mallas; the Ochavo at $2\frac{22}{34}$ Mallas; the Maravedi de Vellon at $1\frac{11}{34}$ Mallas. *Coins.*

Hence the Libra Catalan is worth 28d. sterling nearly.

The Marc used here for the precious metals is divided into 8 Ounces, 32 Quartos, 192 Arienzos or Adarmes, or 6912 Grains. It is $\frac{1}{6}$ heavier than the Castilian Marc, and therefore equals 272,654 Grammes, or $4141\frac{2}{3}$ troy Grains. *Gold and Silver Weight.*

The Quintal contains 4 Arrobas or 104lb. The Pound is divided into 12 Ounces, 48 Quartos, 192 Arienzos, or 6912 Grains. The Commercial Pound Catalan = 0,40003 Kilogrammes, or 6174 troy Grains. Hence 100lb. Catalan = 88,2 lb. avoirdupois.* *Commercial Weight.*

The Quartera is divided into 12 Cortanes or 48 Picotins, and contains 68,419 Litres, or 1,9416 Winchester Bushels. *Corn Measure.*

The Carga contains 12 Cortanes, 24 Cortarines, or 72 Meitadellas, = 123,756 Litres, or 32,695 English Wine Gallons. The Carga is also divided into 16 Cortanes, or 512 Porrones. The Pipe contains 4 Cargas. *Liquid Measure.*

The Canna contains 8 Palinos or 32 Quartos, and measures 0,535 Metres or 21 English Inches. *Long Measure.*

For exchanges and other particulars, see *Spain*, and *Castile.*

BASIL or BASLE *(in Switzerland).*

Accounts are kept in Livres of 20 Sous, each Sous of 12 Deniers; also in Ecus of 60 Sous, in Rixdollars of 108 Creutzers, and in Florins of 60 Creutzers, the Creutzer being divided into 5 Fenins. *Monies of Account.*

Another mode of keeping accounts was introduced in 1798, into all the Cantons of Switzerland, when they took the name of the Helvetian Republic. This method consists of Franken of 10 Batzen, or 100 Rappen. The following are the proportions of the above monies:—

The Rixdollar or Thaler is worth $1\frac{4}{5}$ Florins, 3 Livres, 27 Good Batzen, 36

* The commercial weight of Catalonia is variously stated by different authors: that here given is deduced from attested standards lately sent to *Lord Castlereagh* by *Mr. Baker,* His Majesty's Vice-Consul at Barcelona; and, from his dispatches, the other proportions in this article have been likewise extracted.

Monies of Account.

Swiss Batzen or Gros, 45 Plapperts or Escalins, 60 Sols, 108 Creutzers, 270 Rappen, 540 Fenins, or 720 Deniers.

The Franken is equivalent to 1½ Franc of the money of France, and also to the Livre of 36 Creutzers. The Rixdollar is therefore worth 4½ Francs, and the Florin 2½ Francs.

There are two sorts of monies here, viz. current money, which is composed of the effective coins of Switzerland; and exchange money, which consists of the coins of foreign countries. Their relative values vary according to circumstances.

Coins.

The coins are, in gold, the Pistole and the Ducat; in silver, the Ecu, the Rixdollar, and the Patagon: for the sterling value of which see the Tables of Coins, Vol. II.

Fineness of Gold and Silver.

The Fineness of Gold is expressed in Carats and Parts, the absolute purity being 24 Carats, and the Carat 32 Parts. The Fineness of Silver is expressed in Deniers and Grains, the absolute fineness being 12 Deniers, and the Denier 24 Grains.

Gold and Silver Weight.

The weight for Gold and Silver is the Cologne Mark of 8 Ounces, 16 Loths, 256 Pfenings, or 4352 German Eschen: and for its proportion to English and French weight see *Cologne.*

Commercial Weight.

The Commercial Weight is the ancient French Poids de Marc, the Pound containing 16 Ounces, 128 Gros, or 9216 Grains. It equals 489,5 Grammes, or 7555 English Grains. Hence 100lb. of Basil = 107,930lb. avoirdupois.

Dry Measure.

The corn measure is the Sack of 8 Muddes or Scheffels, 32 Kupfleins, or 64 Bechers or Goblets. The Sack contains 1,29 Hectolitres, or 3⅔ Winchester Bushels; or, more accurately, 100 Sacks = 45 Quarters 6 Bushels.

Liquid Measure.

The wine measure called the Saum contains 3 Ohms, or 96 Pots, old measure, or 120 Pots new measure. The Ohm is equal to 49,56 Litres, or 13$\frac{1}{11}$ English Gallons.

Cloth Measure.

There are two Ells used here—the long Ell, called Aune, = 1,178 Metres, or 46,38 English Inches; the short Ell, called Brasse, with which ribbons manufactured in Basil are measured, contains 0,544 Metres, or 21,41 English Inches. Cloth Measure.

The Basil Foot is 0,298 Metres, or 11,75 English Inches; 48 Basil Feet are equal to 47 English Feet. A Ruthe, or Perch, is 16 Basil Feet. Long Measure.

A Juchart, or Acre, contains 140 square Ruthes. The Ruthe is divided into 256 square Feet, Basil measure, and equals 245,44 English square Feet. Hence 1 Juchart = 3 Roods 6 Perches, English measure, or 3,1867 Decares of France. Superficial Measure.

Basil exchanges with the following places, and gives in specie, or money of exchange, to Exchanges.

Amsterdam	144	Livres (more or less)	for	100 Florins.
Augsburg	172	Livres		100 Florins current.
Francfort	98$\frac{3}{8}$	Florins		100 Florins.
Geneva	152	Livres		100 Florins.
Genoa	63	Sols		1 Pezza fuori di banco.
Hamburgh	125	Livres		100 Marks banco.
Leghorn	64	Sols		1 Pezza of 8 Reals.
Leipsic	100	Rixdollars		122 Rixdollars current.
London	16	Livres		£1 sterling.
Lyons	99$\frac{1}{2}$	Livres		100 Livres.
Milan	51	Livres		100 Lire correnti.
Nuremberg	100	Rixdollars		122 Rixdollars current.
Paris & Strasburg	99	Livres		100 Livres.
Vienna	130	Livres		100 Guldens.

Bills of exchange on Basil are commonly made payable at a few days sight or date; and no days of grace are allowed.

BASSORA OR BUSSORAH *(near the Persian Gulf)*.

In this city of Arabia, accounts are kept in Mamoodis of 10 Danims, or 100 Floose or Flouches. 100 Mamoodis make 1 Toman, which is valued at 15 Rupees. It must be observed, however, that there are the real and the imaginary Toman and Mamoodi, the latter being only about $\frac{3}{4}$ of the value of the former. Monies of Account.

Coins. Many European as well as Asiatic coins pass here, but their price constantly fluctuates: they are, for instance, much higher during the monsoon than after it, as there is less want of specie when all the foreign ships are gone. The Turkish coins, however, have a fixed value, though merchants, in their dealings with strangers, will generally rate them something above their legal price.

Weights. Gold and silver are weighed by the Cheki of 100 Miscals, or 150 Drams: a Miscal weighs about 72 English Grains. A Miscal of the finest gold is worth about 22½ Mamoodis; gold less fine in proportion. A Cheki of 100 Miscals, or 150 Drams of fine silver, is worth 180 Mamoodis, more or less; hence, the Mamoodi = 3⅕ Grains of fine gold, or 40 Grains of fine silver, or about 5½d. sterling.

The weights for merchandize are the Maund Attary, the Maund Sofy, and the Oka of Bagdat. The Maund Attary contains 25 Vakias Tary (though sometimes reckoned at 24 or 26 Vakias), and weighs 28,5lb. avoirdupois, and the Vakia 19 Ounces avoirdupois. The Rattle is 14½ Vakias Attary.

The Maund Sofy, or Maund Bassorah, contains 24 Vakias Sofy (also called Okas of Bassora), equal to 76 Vakias Tary, or 90lb. 4 oz. avoirdupois.

The Oka of Bagdat is 2½ Vakias Tary, or 47,5 oz. avoirdupois.

In sales of ginger, pepper, and coffee, 26 Vakias are allowed to the Maund; in sales of cardamoms, sugar-candy, and benzoin, 25 Vakias per Maund; and in sales of sugar and metals, 24 Vakias per Maund.

Such are the weights that are made use of by Europeans settled at Bassora: the weights in the bazars, or public markets, are generally different, and vary among themselves. The Vakia Tary (which, according to the above, should be about 115 Miscals) varies from 110 to 118, and the others in proportion: on account of these differences, the buyers give, as much as they can, the preference to the European weights, and most bargains are made accordingly.

Measure. The Guz or Cubit is about 37 English Inches.

BATAVIA, *see East Indies.*

BELGIUM, *see Netherlands.*

BENDER ABASSI, *see Gamron.*

BENGAL, *see East Indies.*

BERGAMO *(in Italy).*

Accounts are kept here in Lire of 20 Soldi or Marchetti, the Soldo being divided into 12 Denari Correnti. Accounts are also kept in Ducats of 24 Grossi, each Grosso being divided into 12 Piccoli or Denari di Ducato. Monies.

A Scudo of Bergamo is worth 7 Lire, or 140 Soldi.

A Ducat current is worth $6\frac{1}{5}$ Lire, or 124 Soldi; and a Ducat banco is worth 9 Lire 4 Soldi.

The Coins of the country will be found under the article *Venice;* but it must be observed that, in Bergamo, they bear an agio of 3 or 4 per cent. above their value in the Moneta Piccola of Venice. Coins.

There are two weights: the Pound *peso sottile,* used in weighing silk, wax, indigo, cochineal, and spices, is divided into 12 Ounces; the Pound *peso grosso,* used in weighing other articles, is divided into 30 of the same Ounces. Weights.

100lb. of the heavy weight = 81,524 Kilogrammes, = 179,84lb. avoirdupois.

100lb. of the light weight = 32,609 .... = 71,93lb. ....

The corn measure, called Soma, is divided into 8 Satari, and contains 1,6419 Hectolitre, or 4,66 Bushels, Winchester measure. Measures.

The Brenta, liquid measure, is divided into 52 Pinte, and contains 71,863 Litres, or 19,25 English Gallons.

The Braccio, or Ell, measures 0,6553 Metres, or 25,8 English Inches.

Bergamo exchanges with, and gives to Exchanges.

Amsterdam	86 Soldi (more or less) for	1 Florin.
Augsburg ...	105 Soldi	1 Florin current.
Genoa	32 Soldi	1 Lira fuori banco.
Hamburgh ..	69 Soldi	1 Mark banco.

Exchanges.

Leghorn	188	Soldi (more or less) for	1 Pezza.
London	45	Lire 16 Soldi	£1 sterling.
Paris & Lyons	120	Soldi	3 Francs.
Milan	210	Soldi	7 Lire correnti.
Naples	165	Soldi	1 Ducato di Regno.
Rome	210	Soldi	1 Scudo Romano.
Venice......	100	Italian Lire..........	105 Italian Lire.
Vienna	104	Soldi	1 Florin current.

Usance. The Usance for foreign bills is here the same as in Venice: for bills drawn from Zurich, however, it is 15 days after acceptance. Bills payable *a vista* or sight, must be paid on being presented: those that are at some days sight, or at usance, must be paid on the very day they become due: 6 days of grace are allowed, in which holidays are not included; and if there is no holiday in the week, Friday is reckoned as such. The holder of the bill must present it for acceptance as soon as he receives it; and if payment be delayed when due, he must have it protested immediately.

BERGEN *(in Norway)*.

Monies. Accounts are kept here in Rixdollars of 6 Marks, the Mark being divided into 16 Skillings Danish. At Christiania, Drontheim, Larwigen, Kopperwyk, and other places in Norway, they reckon in Rixdollars of 4 Orts, each Rixdollar being divided into 24 Skillings Danish.

Coins. The Coins, being those of Denmark, will be found under the Article *Copenhagen.*

Weights. The Shippond is divided into 20 Lisponds, or 320lb. The Centner is 6¼ Lisponds, or 100lb.; the Lispond is 16lb.; the Waag is 3 Bismerponds, or 36lb.

The Pound is divided into 2 Marks, 16 Ounces, 32 Loths, or 128 Quintins. 100lb. in Bergen and all Norway answer to 49,961 Kilogrammes, or 110,23lb. avoirdupois.

Measures. A Last of corn is divided into 12 Tonnes or 144 Krugs. A Last of salt is 18 Tonnes. A Tonne of tar contains 120 Krugs.

The Ell equals 2 Rhineland Feet, and contains 0,62789 Metres, or 24,72 English Inches. Measures.

Masts, and round wood in general, are measured in Palms, three of which are equal to 10$\frac{1}{6}$ Danish Inches, or 10$\frac{1}{2}$ English Inches.

Bergen exchanges with, and gives (more or less) to— Exchanges.

Amsterdam .... 143 Rixdollars Danish current for 100 Rixdollars current.
Copenhagen ...... 100 Rixdollars Danish current for 102 Rixdollars current.
Hamburgh & Lubeck 150 Rixdollars Danish current for 100 Rixdollars current.
London .... 6 Rixdollars current ...... for £1 sterling.

BERLIN *(in Prussia)*.*

Accounts are kept here, and also at Magdeburg, Francfort on the Oder, and throughout the Electorate of Brandenburg, in Thalers or Rixdollars of 24 Good Groschen, each Groschen being divided into 12 Pfenings current. Monies of Account.

But the books of the banks, and the different discounting houses or branch-banks belonging to them, in Berlin, Breslau, and Stettin, must, by an ordinance of the King of Prussia, of 1766, be kept in Pounds or Thalers banco of 24 banco Groschen, subdivided into 12 Pfenings banco. The ordinance likewise extended to merchants' books, which are, however, now kept in currency.

The gold coins are, Ducats, which are either reckoned at 2$\frac{3}{4}$ Rixdollars, and then are about 20 per cent. better than currency, otherwise they pass each for 3 Rixdollars 8 Groschen current, more or less; Double, Single, and Half Fredericks, or Pieces of 10, 5, and 2$\frac{1}{2}$ Rixdollars, which are taken at the bank for 8, 4, and 2 Pounds banco, being thus 25 per cent. worse than banco; but out of the bank the difference is not fixed, nor is it so great. Fredericks bear a premium on currency, which was at first 5 per cent. but it has successively risen to 14 per cent.: thus the single Piece is worth 5 Rixdollars 22 Groschen current. The silver coins are, since the year 1774, Thalers or Rixdollars, halves, thirds, quarters, sixths, and twelfths ditto, or pieces of 24, 12, 8, 6, 4, and 2 Groschen, which form the currency of the country, and are, by the king's edict for the Coins.

* A new system of weights and measures for the Prussian dominions was decreed May 16, 1816, which will be given under the article *Prussia*.

Coins. erection of the bank, 31¼ per cent. worse than banco. There are also base silver pieces of 6, 4, and 3 Pfenings, and copper pieces of 3 and 1 Pfening.

Degrees of Fineness of Gold and Silver. The fineness of gold is valued in Carats and Grains, the Mark being 24 Carats, the Carat 12 Grains; and the Mark of fine gold is worth 192½ Rixdollars, more or less in Fredericks, or 154 Pounds banco. A Mark of light Ducats is worth 188½ Rixdollars, and a Mark of light Louis d'ors and Pistoles, 175 Rixdollars, more or less, in Fredericks.

The Mark of fine silver contains 16 Loths, or 288 Grains, and is worth 14 Rixdollars in Fredericks, or 11⅕ Pounds banco, more or less.

Wrought silver must be 12 Loths fine, and stamped with a sceptre.

Rate of Coinage. From a Cologne Mark of gold, 21¾ Carats fine, 35 Fredericks are to be coined; and from a Cologne Mark of fine silver, 14 Rixdollars of the new currency, in whole pieces, halves, and thirds, are to be coined.

According to the above, the Pound or Rixdollar banco is equivalent to 31,48 German Asen, or 23,35 English Grains of fine gold, and to 456 Asen, or 338,2 Grains of fine silver; the Rixdollars in Fredericks to 25,18 Asen, or 18,66 Grains of fine gold; lastly, the Rixdollar current to 23,8 Asen, or 17,6 Grains of fine gold, and to 347,43 Asen, or 257,68 Grains of fine silver, the proportion of gold to silver being thus as 14$\frac{4}{7}$ to 1.

Value of Monies. Hence it follows that the Rixdollar Prussian current is worth 36d. sterling nearly; the Pound banco, 47¼d. sterling; and the Frederick, 16s. 7d. sterling. Also £1 sterling = 6 Rixdollars 8 Groschen current, or 5 Pounds 2 Groschen banco, or 6 Rixdollars 1 Groschen in Fredericks. *See Table of Coins*, Vol. II.

Gold and Silver Weight. Gold and silver in bars and in coins are weighed by the Mark of 8 Ounces, or 16 Loths. The Loth contains 4 Drams, Quintins, or Gros, 12 Hellers, Pfenings, or Deniers, or 240 Grains. This Mark therefore contains 3840 Prussian Grains, which weigh 233,81 Grammes, or 3608 English Grains.

Commercial Weight. In commercial weight, the Centner or Quintal weighs 5 Stein or Stones, each of 22lb.; the Pound is divided into 2 Marks, 16 Ounces, or 32 Loths; the Loth contains 4 Quintins, 16 Pfenings, or 32 Hellers. The Pound contains 468,53 Grammes, or 7231 English Grains.

A Ship Last contains 12 Ship-funds, each of 20 Lisponds, or 280lb.

Commercial Weight. The Centner of 110lb. of Berlin is equal to 0,468 Kilogrammes, or 113lb. 10 oz. avoirdupois. Hence 100lb. of Berlin = 103,24lb. avoirdupois.

Corn Measure. The measure for corn is called a Wispel. A Last of wheat contains 3 Wispels, a Last of oats 2 Wispels.

The Wispel is divided into 2 Malters, 24 Scheffels, 96 Viertels, or 384 Metzen.

The Scheffel measures 3189 English Inches; it is a common measure all over the country, and weighs, full of rye, about 82lb. of Berlin weight. The Scheffel equals 52,11 Litres, or 1,479 English Bushels.

Liquid Measure. A Fuder of wine is divided into 4 Oxhofts, 6 Ohms, 12 Eimers, 24 Ankers, 768 Masses or Quarts, or 1536 Oessels. An Oxhoft contains 224,696 Litres, or 59,365 English Gallons.

A Gebraude of beer is divided into 9 Kupes, 18 Fasses, 36 Tonnes, 144 Aemgens, 3456 Quarts, or 6912 Oessels. The Gebraude contains 404,23 Litres, or 106,8 English wine Gallons.

Long Measure. The Ell of Berlin measures 0,66681 Metres, or 26,25 English Inches.

The Berlin Foot is divided into 12 Inches, or 96 parts, and measures 0,30972 Metres, or 12,194 English Inches. The Rhineland Foot, used by engineers and land surveyors, is divided into 12 Inches, the Inch being subdivided into 10 Lines, or 100 Points. This Foot measures 0,3139 Metres, or 12,36 English Inches. The Ruthe is 12 Rhineland Feet.

Superficial Measures. A great Hufe, land measure, is divided into 30 great Morgens, or 66⅔ little Morgens or Acres; a Hacken or small Hufe contains 2 great Morgens; a land Hufe is 1 great Morgen.

The great Morgen is composed of 400 square Ruthes or Perches, and the little Morgen of 180. The former contains 56,815 French Ares, or 1 Acre, 1 Rood, 24 Perches, English measure; and therefore the little Morgen contains 25,566 Ares, or 2 Roods 21 Perches English measure.

Exchanges. Besides the places given in Vol. II. page 35, Berlin exchanges with, and gives to—

Constantinople	1	Livre banco (more or less) for	132 Paras.
Copenhagen ..	100	Rixdollars current	123 Rixdollars.
Geneva	100	Rixdollars	76 Ecus current.

Exchanges.

Genoa	1	Livre banco (more or less) for	118¾	Sols.
Lisbon	1	Livre banco	690	Rees.
Milan	1	Livre banco	126	Sols current.
Naples	1	Livre banco	114½	Grani.
Petersburgh	26¼	Good Groschen	1	Rouble.
Rome	1	Livre banco	90	Bajocchi.
Stockholm	1	Livre banco	41	Skillings.
Turin	1	Livre banco	82	Sols.
Venice	1	Livre banco	185	Soldi piccoli.

Usance and Days of Grace.

The usance for bills drawn on Berlin is 14 days after acceptance. Berlin draws on Amsterdam, Breslau, Hamburgh, and Leipsic, at 4 or 5 weeks date, and at sight; on London and Paris at 2 months date.

The days of grace, by the edict of 1751, are three; but if the third day should fall on a Sunday or holiday (or on a Saturday for Jews), the bill must be paid on the preceding day; and should all the three days be holidays, the bill must be paid on the very day on which it is made payable; but a protest for non-payment of such a bill may be delayed without any danger to the holder till the last day of grace.

Banks.

The Banks of Berlin and Breslau were established in 1765. The coins received are Fredericks, 35 of which must weigh a Cologne Mark of gold, 21 Carats 9 Grains fine. Each piece is reckoned at 4 Pounds banco, and the owner is credited for so much in the bank books. Thus banco is 25 per cent. better than Fredericks reckoned at 5 Rixdollars.

All bills of exchange, drafts, &c. on Berlin and Breslau, of 100 Rixdollars and upwards, were formerly expressed in Pounds banco, and paid by inscription at the bank; but, since the year 1787, they have been expressed and paid in Prussian currency.

Since the 1st of January, 1767, bank notes of 10, 20, 50, 500, and 1000 Pounds banco, have been in circulation, with gold and silver coin, though no person is obliged to take them in payment. These notes, though made by the Berlin bank only, are issued by both banks, either in exchange for cash, at the rate of 125 Rixdollars in Fredericks, or 131¼ Rixdollars current in silver, for 100 Pounds banco; or by discounting bills; or on the security of gold and silver bullion, foreign coins, or jewels, that are deposited at the bank. In all the offices for taxes and royal revenues, bank notes are received in payment as cash; and they are also taken as such at the bank from any person who opens an account there. Banks.

At the discounting offices, belonging to the two banks, bills are discounted at ½ per cent. per month; but such bills must have at least 2 months to run, and three persons must be answerable for the payment, the drawer, acceptor, and indorser. The discounting offices or lombards of the banks also advance money for 2 months, at ½ per cent. interest per month, on gold and silver in bars or dust, jewels, and plate, or foreign coins, though never under the value of 400 Pounds banco. Thus they pay for gold in bars, of 21 to 24 Carats fine, 150 Pounds banco per Mark fine; for gold, 16 to 21 Carats fine, 148 Pounds per Mark fine: under that degree of fineness, 140 Pounds per Mark fine. English Guineas, Portugal pieces, and Brabant Souverains, are reckoned at 22 Carats fine; all sorts of gold Ducats, except Turkish and Russian, at 23 Carats 6 Grains; Louis d'ors, at 21 Carats 7 Grains; and Brunswick 5 Rixdollar pieces, at 21 Carats 8 Grains fine.

For silver in bars, of 12 to 16 Loths fine, 9 Pounds 14 Groschen banco per Mark fine are given; for silver, of 6 to 12 Loths fine, 8¾ Pounds banco; under that, 8 Pounds banco per Mark fine. Silver coins are valued as follows, viz. fine pieces of two thirds, at 15 Loths 15 Grains fine; specie Rixdollars, at 14 Loths 2 Grains; common old pieces of two thirds, at 11 Loths 17 Grains; Spanish Dollars and French Ecus, at 14 Loths 9 Grains; and old Louisblancs, at 14 Loths 11 Grains fine.

No loan can be prolonged beyond the settled period of 2 months; and if the pledge is not then redeemed, it must be sold to the best bidder at the borrower's risk. A recepisse is delivered to the borrower, which he must return when he redeems his pledge; and the loan, after deducting the interest, is advanced to him in bank notes.

In December, 1767, notice was given that the bank notes of the royal bank, guaranteed by the edict of 1766, would, from the 1st of January, 1768, he paid off on demand, and that the holders of such notes might at their wish receive the amount of them in specie, without any expence or deduction whatsoever.

These banks, and all the offices belonging to them, shut every year on the last day of May, and re-open on the 14th of June following.

BERMUDA, *see West Indies.*

BERN (*in Switzerland*).

Monies of Account. In this city and canton, accounts are kept in different ways; viz. in Livres, of 20 Sous, the Sou of 12 Deniers; in Livres or Francs, of 10 Batzes, or 40 Creutzers; and in Crowns of 25 Batzes, or 100 Creutzers. In the territory of Argow, accounts are kept in Florins, of 60 Creutzers.

A Rixdollar or Ecu blanc is worth 1⅕ Crown, 2 Florins, 3 Livres, 30 Batzes, 60 Sous, &c.; a Crown, 2½ Livres, 25 Batzes, or 50 Sous; a Florin, 1½ Livre, 15 Batzes, or 30 Sous; a Livre or Franc, 10 Batzes; a Pfund, 7½ Batzes, or 15 Sous; a Batze, 2 Sous, or 4 Creutzers; a Shilling, 1½ Creutzer; a Creutzer, 6 Deniers.

Under the government of the Helvetian Republic, established in 1798, a new mode of keeping accounts was commenced in Francs or Franken of 10 Batzes, each Batze being divided into 10 Rappen; and this mode is still continued, particularly in Government concerns. But these and other new regulations, introduced in all the different cantons, will be explained under the article *Switzerland.*

Coins. The gold coins of the canton of Bern are Double and Single Pistoles, of the same value and fineness as Double and Single Louis of France; and Ducats of 7 Livres 10 Sous, or 75 Batzes.

The silver coins are, Ecus equal to the Ecus of 6 Livres of France; and Patacons of 3 Livres 6 Sous, or 33 Batzes. Also pieces of 10, 5, and 2½ Batzes, or 40, 20, and 10 Creutzers; and baser coins of Single and Half Batzes, and Single and Half Creutzers.

Foreign coins, particularly those of France, circulate here, and vary in their value according to circumstances.

Weights. The Mark used for weighing gold, silver, and other precious articles, is divided into 16 Loths, 64 Quintlins, 256 Pennyweights, or 4608 Grains, and equals 246,877 Grammes, or 3810,3 English Grains. But in expressing the fineness of gold, the Mark is divided into 24 Carats, each of 32 Parts, and of silver into 16 Loths of 18 Grains each.

The Pound, commercial weight, is divided into 16 Ounces, 32 Loths, or 128 Quintlins, and equals 522,330 Grammes, or 8060 English Grains. Hence 100lb. of Bern = 115,14lb. avoirdupois.

Weights. There is, however, a great variety in the weight of the Quintal at the different towns in this canton: thus at Lausanne and Morgis it weighs 97¼lb. Bern weight; at Granson, 96¾lb.; at Nyon 109½lb.; at Iverdun, 103¼lb; at Arau 93½lb; at Thun, 102¼lb. &c.

Dry Measure. The Mutt, the measure for corn and dry goods, is divided into 12 Masses, 48 Immis, 96 Achterlis, or 192 Sechzenerlis; The Mass measures 960 cubic Inches of Bern, answering to 706,33 French cubic Inches, or 857 English cubic Inches. The Mutt = 1,681 Hectolitre, or 4,771 English Bushels.

Liquid Measure. In liquid measures, the Land Fass contains 6 Saums, 24 Brents, or 600 Maases; the common Fass, 4 Saums, 16 Brents, or 400 Maases. A Maas, also called Pinte, is divided into 2 Halves, 4 Quarters, 8 Semi-Quarters or Bechers: this Maas or Measure is a Cylinder, 4 Inches in diameter, and 9 Inches high, and when full of spring water, weighs 51 Ounces 2 Quintlins 2 dwt. Bern weight, or 59 Ounces avoirdupois. The Maas = 1,671 Litre, or 3,532 English Pints.

Long Measure. The Bern Foot is divided into 12 Inches of 12 Lines, subdivided into 10 Seconds, equal to 029,325 Metres, or 11,545 English Inches. But the stone cutter's Foot, which is made use of in the quarries, measures 13 Bernese Inches, or 12½ English Inches nearly.

The Ell of Bern is divided into 2, 4, and 8, or 3 and 6 parts; it is 22 Inches 2 Lines, Bern measure, and = 0,5433 Metres, or 21,4 English Inches. The Clafter or Fathom is 8 Bernese Feet.

Superficial Measure. The Ruthe or Perch contains 10 Feet, which land surveyors divide into 10 Inches. The square Ruthe contains 92¾ English square Feet, and therefore = 8,6 Hectares, or 34 English Perches nearly.

The Juchart or Acre varies in its dimensions; thus the Juchart of Wood is reckoned at 4,500 square Feet of Bern; that of Arable Land, at 40,000; that of Meadow, at 35,000. The Wood Juchart = 38,767 French Ares, or 3 Roods 33 Perches English measure, and the others in proportion.

Exchanges. The exchanges of Bern are regulated by those of Basil or Geneva, according to the proportion between the monies of account of Bern, and those of the above mentioned cities. Most commonly, however, the bills are drawn directly

Exchanges. from thence, instead of being drawn from Bern. There is no established custom respecting usance, nor are there any days of grace allowed.

BETELFAGUI OR BETLEFACKEE *(in Arabia).*

Monies. Accounts are kept here in Piastres of 80 Carats or Cavears, also in Spanish Dollars of 40 Cavears.

Coins. The Coins in which most payments are made are Sequins and Spanish Dollars. The Commassee is a small copper coin, containing a little silver, which is made use of in small payments. A Spanish Dollar is worth from 40 to 80 Commassees. 100 Dollars effective are equal to 121½ Piastres of account; hence the said Piastre may be valued at 3s. 8½d. sterling.

Weights. The Weights are, the Bahar of 40 Farcels, the Farcel or Frazil of 10 Maunds or 20 Rattles. A Farcel weighs 20lb. 6 oz. 4 dr. avoirdupois, or a Bahar, 815¼lb. avoirdupois. 10 Farcels in Betlefackee are equal to 7 Farcels in Mocha.

A Bale of coffee is 14 Farcels, and the allowance for tare, 8 Maunds; 2 Bales are the common burthen of a camel.

A Rattle of coffee contains 14½ Vakias, and a Farcel of ditto, 290 Vakias; of dates, candles, and iron, 16 Vakias are reckoned to a Rattle; of all other sorts of goods, 15 Vakias make a Rattle. The Rattle is used in the *bazar* or market only.

A Tommond of rice contains 40 Kellas, and weighs 168lb. avoirdupois.

Cotton is sold by the Harraff, an imaginary money; 9 Harraffs = 11½ Piastres of account, or 1 Harraff = 1 Piastre 22 Cavears.

Measures. The Gudda, liquid measure, contains about 2 English Gallons; it is divided into 8 Nufieahs, and the Nufieah into 16 Vakias.

A Covid is 18 Inches; a long iron Covid, 27 Inches; a Guz, 25 Inches, English measure.

At Judda, or Jiddah, another sea-port of Arabia on the Red Sea, the Bahar contains 10 Frazils, 100 Maunds, or 500 Rattles, and the Rattle 15 Vakias. The Bahar weighs 222½lb. English troy, or 183lb. avoirdupois, and the Maund, 29 Ounces 4½ Drams avoirdupois; at least such are the regular weights; but as

Measures.

goods are always weighed with the steelyard, after the Turkish manner, and it is said that merchants are not allowed to weigh their goods when bought or sold, even at their own houses.

For further particulars respecting *Arabia*, see *Mocha.*

BILBOA *(in Spain).*

Accounts are kept here in Reals Vellon of 34 Maravedis.

Monies of Account.

An Escudo is worth 10 Reals, or 340 Maravedis Vellon; a Ducado, 11 Reals; a Peso, 8 Reals; a Doubloon, 4 Pesos or 32 Reals.

A Real de Plata is worth 16 Quartos, or 64 Maravedis Vellon; therefore a Peso de Plata is worth 128 Quartos, or 256 Maravedis; and a Doubloon de Plata, 512 Quartos, or 2048 Maravedis Vellon. A Quarto is 4 Maravedis, and an Ochavo, 2 Maravedis Vellon.

For the coins and their value, see *Spain.*

Weights.

There is a great and a lesser weight: the Quintal of the former (with which iron is weighed) is 146lb. of Bilboa, which equal $155\frac{1}{8}$lb. Castilian weight, and answer to 71,458 Kilogrammes, or 157,66lb. avoirdupois; the Quintal of the lesser weight is 100lb. of Bilboa. The Pound weighs 17 Ounces Castilian weight, so that 100lb. of Bilboa = 106,7lb. Castilian, which equal 48,95 Kilogrammes, or 108lb. avoirdupois.

Measures.

Corn is measured by the Fanega, of 12 Celemines. This measure is 6 per cent. larger than the Castilian Fanega; so that 1 Fanega of Bilboa = 60,11 Litres, or 1,706 English Bushel.

The long measures, as well as the measures for wine and other liquids, are the same as the Castilian measures, for which see *Spain.*

Exchanges.

Bilboa exchanges with, and gives (more or less) to

Amsterdam 1 Ducado di Cambio, of 375 Maravedis de Plata, for 97 Grotes Flemish.

London ... 1 Peso de Plata .... 39d. sterling; also

1 Hard Dollar of 20 Reals Vellon.............. 50d. sterling.

Paris ..... 1 Peso de Plata .... 77 Sous in Francs.

BOHEMIA, *see Prague.*

BOLOGNA *(in Italy)*.

Monies of Account. Accounts are kept in Lire of 20 Soldi; each Soldo of 12 Denari.

Also in Scudi of 100 Soldi, Bajocchi, or Bolognini. The Scudo contains 5, Lire, 10 Paoli, 100 Soldi, 500 Quattrini, or 1200 Denari.

These monies have two values; namely, banco, in which the exchanges are reckoned, and Moneta Lunga, or currency: banco is about 2½ per cent. better than currency, but this proportion varies according to circumstances.

The Scudo di Cambio, also called Pezza da Otto Reali, is reckoned at 85 Soldi banco or Bolognini; thus 4 Scudi di Cambio = 17 Lire.

Coins. The coins of Bologna are of the same denomination, weight, and value, as those of Rome. In gold, the Sequin is worth 10 Lire 15 Soldi of Bologna; the Pistole, 15 Lire 15 Soldi. In silver, a Roman or Bologna Scudo is worth 5 Lire; a Testoon, 30 Soldi; a Piastra or Lira, 20 Soldi; a Paolo, 10 Soldi, halves and quarters in proportion. There are also double and single Murajole, of 4 and 2 Soldi; and Bolognini, or single Soldi; likewise copper Soldi, half Soldi, and Quattrini, the 5th part of a Soldo.

Foreign Coins. Foreign coins pass as follows; a Spanish Pistole, for 19 Lire 1 Soldo; a Pistole of Milan for 17 Lire 17 Soldi; of Turin, 25 Lire 16 Soldi; a Florence or Venetian Sequin for 10 Lire 17 Soldi; a Dutch or German Ducat for 10 Lire 13 Soldi; an old French Louis d'or for 22 Lire 19 Soldi 6 Denari; a new one (coined since 1786) for 21 Lire 11 Soldi; a Tuscan Franceschino for 5 Lire; a French Ecu for 5 Lire 6 Soldi; a Savoy Ecu for 6 Lire 8 Soldi; a Spanish Dollar, for 5 Lire; a German Rixdollar for 4 Lire 15 Soldi; a Napoleon, or Louis of 20 Francs, for 18 Lire 5 Soldi; and a Franc for 18 Soldi 3 Quattrini.

Hence the Lira of Bologna may be valued at about 10⅜d. sterling; and the Scudo at 52d. Also the Scudo di Cambio of 4¼ Lire di banco = 49d. sterling.

Weights. The Pound used for gold and silver is divided into 12 Ounces, the Ounce into 8 Ottave, 160 Carats, or 640 Grains.

The same Pound is used for silk and other merchandise; the Ounce is then divided into 16 Ferlini, 160 Carats, or 640 Grains. The Pound of Bologna =

0,361957 Kilogrammes, or 5586 Grains troy; hence 100lb. of Bologna = 79,8lb. avoirdupois. Weights.

The Corba (corn measure) contains 2 Staja, 8 Quartaroli, or 32 Quarticini or Cupi, and must weigh, full of good wheat, 160lb. of Bologna. The Corba holds 73,78 Litres, or 2,094 Winchester Bushels. Measures.

The Corba (wine measure) contains 60 Boccali, or 240 Fogliette; it weighs 200lb. of Bologna, and holds 73,80 Litres, or 19,5 English Gallons.

The Braccio, or Ell, with which woollen cloth is measured, is 0,6350 Metres, or 25 English Inches; the Braccio, with which silk stuffs are measured, is 0,5955 Metres, or 23,4666 English Inches.

The Foot of Bologna, well known all over Italy, is 0,3805 Metres, or 14,99 English Inches; thus, 80 Feet of Bologna = 99 English Feet.

Bologna exchanges with, and gives (more or less) in banco or money of exchange to— Exchanges.

Amsterdam	40 Soldi banco, or Bolognini, for	1 Florin.
Ancona ..	99 ditto	1 Scudo of 10 Paoli.
Augsburg	47 ditto	1 Florin current.
Bolsano..	47 ditto	1 Florin Moneta Lunga.
Florence..	106 Bolognini	1 Ducat of 7 Lire.
France ..	1 Scudo	100 Sous in Francs.
Genoa....	90 Bolognini	6 Lire fuori banco.
Hamburgh	35 ditto	1 Mark banco.
Leghorn..	95 ditto	1 Pezza of 8 Reali.
London ..	46 Paoli	£1 sterling.
Lyons....	54 Bolognini	1 Ecu of 3 Livres.
Milan....	99 ditto	6 Lire correnti.
Naples ..	78 ditto	1 Ducato di Regno.
Novi	85 ditto	1 Scudo d'oro marche.
Rome	99 ditto	1 Scudo Romano.
Sicily....	200 ditto	1 Oncia, of 600 Grains.
Venice ...	97 ditto	1 Ducat current;
Or	1 Scudo di Cambio	116 Soldi banco.
Vienna ...	48 Bolognini	1 Florin current.

Bills of Exchange are paid in banco, except when they are expressly drawn in money fuori banco, or when the acceptor and holder of the bill both agree that Bills how paid.

Bills how paid.

it shall be paid in currency: in the latter case the payment is regulated by the agio on banco.

The Usance on bills drawn on Bologna, from France and the Netherlands, is 2 months after date; from England and the Levant, 3 months after date; from Sicily, 1 month after date; from any part of Italy, bills are usually paid 8 days after acceptance, in which neither the day of acceptance nor the day of payment is included. No other days of grace are allowed. Thus Bills payable after date, or on a determined day, must be paid the first day after their written term.

BOLSANO OR BOTZEN *(in Tyrol)*.

Monies of Account.

Accounts are kept in Florins of 60 Creutzers, or 240 Pfenings. The Rixdollar is worth 1½ Florin, or 90 Creutzers.

There are here three different sorts of money, viz. Moneta del Giro (or money of exchange), Moneta Lunga (or currency), and Mess Valuta (or money of the fair).

Giro money consists of Spanish Pistoles, or the oldest French Louis d'ors (coined before 1726) reckoned at 5 Florins 34 Creutzers Giro, or other gold coins valued in proportion to those Louis. This sort of money is about 30 per cent. better than Moneta Lunga.

Moneta Lunga, or currency, consists of Austrian Rixdollars and their divisions, coined since 1750, reckoned at 2, 1, and ½ Florins. Also pieces of 20, 17, 7, and 3 Creutzers, and several foreign coins of gold and silver. This currency is at par with the Convention coins of the German Empire. *See Germany.*

Mess Valuta signifies the higher value at which the different coins are reckoned in payments made at the Messes, or Fairs; Mess Valuta bears a discount of about 5 per cent. against currency.

The Scudo di Cambio, by which the exchange with Venice is regulated, is reckoned at 90 Creutzers Giro.

Foreign Coins.

As to foreign coins, Dutch Ducats pass for 4 Florins 23 Creutzers; Imperial Ducats for 4 Florins 30 Creutzers; Florence and Venetian Sequins for 4 Florins 26 Creutzers; Max d'ors for 6 Florins 12 Creutzers; old French Louis d'ors for 9 Florins 22 Creutzers; new, for 8 Florins 47 Creutzers; Carolin d'ors for 9 Florins 20 Creutzers; and Souverains for 13 Florins 20 Creutzers; Venetian silver Ducats, for 1 Florin 33 Creutzers; Dutch Albert's Dollars for 2 Florins; Spanish Dollars for 2 Florins 4 Creutzers; Milan Filippi for 2 Florins 12

Creutzers; Milan Scudi for 1 Florin 46 Creutzers; French Ecus for 2 Florins 16 Creutzers; Tuscan Piastres. for 4 Florins 28 Creutzers; Genoa ditto, for 2 Florins 58 Creutzers; all in currency. Foreign Coins.

A Florin, Bolsano currency, is worth 25¼d. sterling, or £1 sterling = 9 Florins 36 Creutzers.

There are two weights used here, the great and the small; by the first iron, and all heavy goods are sold, and by the second spices, and other such wares. The former is to the latter as 100 to 66. Thus the great Quintal answers to 50,060 Kilogrammes, or 110,45lb. avoirdupois; and the Quintal of the lesser weight equals 33,039 Kilogrammes, or 72,89lb. avoirdupois. The Saum is composed of 4 Quintals. Weights.

The measure by which oil is sold is called the Muth, and weighs about 58 Kilogrammes, or 128lb. avoirdupois. Measures.

Long measures are of two sorts; the Ell = 0,79020 Metres, or 31,11 English Inches; the Braccio = 0,54973 Metres, or 21,643 English Inches.

There are four great Fairs held at Bolsano in the year, each of which generally lasts 15 days. Foreign merchants who frequent these fairs, may be admitted to what is called the *matricule* or *contrattation*, which is done by ballot, after the magistrates have made enquiries respecting their persons and the credit of their houses. This gives them different privileges; for instance, their goods on going away from the fair can be carried through the Austrian dominions without impediment; and if there be any failures during the fairs, they are entitled to a dividend of the bankrupts' effects in preference to other persons. Fairs.

Bills payable at such fairs are accepted on the 12th day, and the payments begin on the 13th day, and end two days after the close of the fair. All bills drawn on this place must be payable to one person; all indorsed bills, or bills payable to more persons than one, are forbidden under a fine of 200 Rixdollars.

Bolsano exchanges with, and gives, in Moneta Lunga, to— Exchanges.

Amsterdam	210 Florins (more or less)	for	100 Rixdollars.
Augsburg	100 Florins	....	100 Florins current.
Bergamo..	100 Florins	....	500 Lire piccole.
Bologna ..	1 Florin	....	48 Bolognini.
France ...	63 Rixdollars or 94 Florins	..	100 Ecus of 60 Sous.

Exchanges.

Frankfort	100 Florins (more or less) for ..	100 Florins in Carolins, at 9 Florins 12 Creutzers;
	Or 96 Florins	100 Florins in Carolins, at 9 Florins 42 Creutzers;
	Or 85 Florins	100 Florins in Carolins, at 11 Florins, at the fairs.
Hamburgh	212 Florins	100 Rixdollars banco.
Leghorn ..	100 Florins	54 Pezze of 8 Reali.
Leipsic ..	100 Florins	100 Florins, Leipsic current, at the fairs.
London ..	8 Florins 48 Creutzers	£1 sterling.
Nuremberg	100 Florins	100 Florins current.
Rome	100 Florins	48 Scudi Moneta.
St. Gall ..	98 Florins	100 Florins in Pistoles, at 7½ Florins.
Venice ...	1 Scudo di Cambio	135 Soldi di banco;
	Or 100 Florins Moneta Lunga	500 Lire piccole.
Vienna ...	100 Florins	100 Florins current.

As bills drawn on Bolsano are mostly payable at the fairs, as before mentioned, no regulations have been made with regard to the usance or days of grace.

BOMBAY, *see East Indies.*

BOURDEAUX *(in France).*

Monies. Although the new French system of monies, weights, and measures, is adopted here, yet many of the old customs are partially retained, and therefore some account of them may be useful.

Weights. The old weight of Bourdeaux is the Poids de Marc. Although the Quintal is reckoned at 100lb. it weighs 101lb. Poids de Marc, or 109lb. avoirdupois.*

* Attested standards of these weights have been transmitted to *Lord Castlereagh* by *Mr. Scott,* his Majesty's Consul at *Bourdeaux,* and have been found to weigh about a Grain in the Kilogramme heavier than the Paris weights.

The Boisseau, for corn and other dry commodities, is divided into 16 parts, and contains 76,708 Litres, or 2,177 English Bushels. Measures.

The Tonneau of wine is divided into 4 Barriques, 128 Velts, or 440 Pots. The Barrique contains 229,93 Litres, or 60,748 English Gallons.

Brandy is kept in casks, called Pieces, of 50 Velts, more or less; but it is sold by the Barrique of 32 Velts, or about 60 English Gallons. 5 Velts, proof of Bourdeaux, make 4 Velts proof, by which it is sold in London. At Cognac it is sold by the 27 Velts; and 11 Velts proof of Cognac make 10 Velts proof, by which it is sold in London.

The Foot of Bourdeaux contains 0,35674 Metres, or 14,04 English Inches. The Aune or Ell contains 0,1195 Metres, or 46,93 English Inches. Thus 100 Aunes of Bourdeaux = 130,33 English Yards.

A Journal or Acre of land is divided into 3 Pougnerées, or 216 Escas, and contains 31,924 Decares, or 3 Roods 6 Perches English measure.

Cleft wood is sold by the 124 pieces, deals by the 126, pipe staves by the 1616.

In settling the freight of ships from the port of Bourdeaux, the following quantities are reckoned for a Tonneau or Ton: 4 Barriques of wine, vinegar, honey, and turpentine; 5 Barriques of brandy; 3 Barriques of syrup; 20 Bushels of chesnuts, or 15 Bushels from Perigord; 20 Bushels of corn, beans, linseed, walnuts, &c.; 5 Bales (each of 100lb.) of cork; 5 Bales of skins or feathers (each of 100lb.); 8 Bales of paper; 10 Cubic Feet of marble; 20 Quintals of iron, in bars, or of lead, in pigs; 3 Bales of hemp (each of 200lb.); 20 Quintals, or 150 Rolls of tobacco. Tonnage of Ships.

A Pipe of salt contains 6 Mines, each weighing about 240lb. of Bourdeaux.

The Tare allowed on West India produce is as follows, viz. Tare.

Coffee sold per Pound, real tare.
Martinico Sugar, sold per Hogshead, 2lb. draft, 13 per cent. tare.
St. Domingo Sugar, sold per Hogshead, 2lb. draft, 17 per cent. tare.
Cotton Wool, sold per Quintal, tare 4 per cent. per Bale, 6 per cent. per Bag.
Indigo, sold per Pound, real tare.

There are two great Fairs in Bourdeaux every year; the first begins on the 1st of March, the other on the 15th of October, and each lasts 15 days. Fairs.

For the Exchanges, &c. see *France*.

BRABANT, *see Antwerp.*

BRAZIL *(in South America).*

Monies of Account.

Accounts are kept in Milrees, and Rees; 1000 Rees making a Milree.

For the coins of Brazil, see the article *Rio Janeiro;* also *Portugal.*

Weights & Measures.

The weights and measures of Brazil are nominally those of Portugal, and the weights are in general correctly so, but great variation exists in the measures of capacity. Thus, in the province of Maranham, the Alquiere, the measure for Indian corn, or maize, rice, coffee in husks, salt, and other dry commodities, is computed to contain 2772 English Cubic Inches, which answer to 1¼ Bushel Winchester measure; while in Bahia it is estimated at 1 Bushel only, and in Pernambuco, and Rio Janeiro, it also varies considerably.

Wine and olive oil, imported, pay duty by the Pipe, Hogshead, or Barrel, but there is no fixed standard measure for these liquids. They are retailed by the Frasco, or case bottle, which contains about 4½ Pints, English Wine measure. Cachaça, or Brazil rum, all oils, &c. made in Brazil, are retailed by the standard measure called Quartilho, and its divisions. The Quartilho contains 3 Pints English wine measure. The long measures are the Covado and the Vara, as in Portugal.

For the Exchanges of Brazil, and other particulars, see *Rio Janeiro.*

BREMEN *(in Germany).*

Monies of Account.

Accounts are kept here in Thalers or Rixdollars, of 72 Grotes; the Grote being divided into 5 Swares current.

A Rixdollar is reckoned likewise at 2¼ Bremen Marks, 6 Copsticks, 16 Dutgens, 18 Flinrichs, or 48 Shillings. Rixdollars are generally reckoned at 5 for a Louis d'or.

A Bremen Mark is worth 8 Flinrichs, 32 Grotes, or 160 Swares; a Copstick, 3 Flinrichs, 12 Grotes, or 8 Shillings; a Dutgen, 3 Shillings. Commercial accounts are now kept in banco Marks.

The gold coins are Ducats, which are commonly worth 2¾ Rixdollars current; the silver coins are Specie Rixdollars, reckoned at 1⅓ Rixdollar, or 96 Grotes current; Halves, or Pieces of ⅔ at 48 Grotes; Pieces of ⅓ at 24 Grotes; Copsticks, and Flinrichs; and Pieces of 6, 3, 2, 1, and ½ Grotes; also Swares of copper. Coins.

Bills of exchange are commonly paid in Brunswick Carl d'ors, reckoned at 5 Rixdollars; and good Frederick d'ors, George d'ors, and old Louis d'ors (coined before 1726) pass for the same value; Ducats, at 2¾ Rixdollars, are reckoned about 3 per cent. better; fine Pieces of two-thirds, 12 per cent.; new Pieces, 10 per cent.; old Pieces of 6 Grotes, 6 per cent.; and old French Louisblancs, at 1⅓ Rixdollar, 5 per cent. better than Carl d'ors; but the Convention Coins are exchanged at par, or with a very small agio against Carl d'ors.

The Bremen Rixdollar in gold, is equivalent to 25 German Asen, or 18½ English Grains of fine gold; and the Rixdollar current to 364 Asen, or 270 English Grains of fine silver. Value of Monies.

140 Rixdollars in gold, or 145 Rixdollars current, are equal to 100 Rixdollars Hamburgh banco.

Hence the Bremen Rixdollar current is worth 3s. 2d. sterling; or £1. sterling = 6 Rixdollars 22 Grotes 4 Swares.

Gold and Silver are weighed by the Cologne Mark, and their fineness is valued as in Hamburgh. Weight.

The commercial Pound is divided into 2 Marks, 16 Ounces, 32 Loths, 128 Quentins, or 512 Orts, and contains 498,25 Grammes, or 7690 English Grains. Thus 100lb. of Bremen answer to 49,825 Kilogrammes, or 109,8 avoirdupois.*

Of commercial weight, the Load is 300lb; but waggoners reckon it at 22 Lisponds, or 308lb. The Centner weighs 116lb.; the Shipfund is 2½ Centners, or 290lb.; a Waag of iron is 120lb; a Stone of flax, 20lb; a Stone of wool, or feathers, 10lb; a Lispond, 14lb.

A Tun of butter, great measure, is reckoned at 300lb; and a Tun of ditto, small measure, at 220lb.

* The commercial weight of Bremen is variously stated by different authors. The above proportion has been recently ascertained at the *London Mint,* from an attested standard transmitted to *Lord Castlereagh* by *Francis E. Coleman, Esq.* his Majesty's Vice Consul at Bremen and Oldenburgh.

Dry Measure. A Last of corn is divided into 4 Quarts, 40 Scheffels, 160 Viertels, or 640 Spints. The Last of Bremen answers to 28,43 Hectolitres, or 80,70 Bushels, Winchester measure.

Liquid Measure. The Fuder of wine is divided into 6 Ohms; the Ohm into 20 Viertels, 45 Stubgens, 180 Quarters, or 720 Mingels. The Ohm contains 143,4 Litres, or 37,88 English Gallons.

Brandy is sold by the measure of 30 Viertels, which equals 56¾ English Gallons.

A Tonne of beer contains 48 Stubgens, or 192 Quarters.

A Hogshead of train oil contains 2 Tonnes, 12 Steckans, or 192 Mingels.

Long Measure. The Bremen Foot is divided into 12 Inches, and the Inch into 10 parts. The Foot contains 0,2891 Metres, or 11,38 English Inches. Thus 20 Feet of Bremen are computed to equal 19 English Feet. The Ell is 2 Feet, and contains 22,76 English Inches.

A Clafter is 6 Feet; a Ruthe, 16 Feet.

A Decher is 10 Ells, Pieces, &c.; a Dutzen, 12; a Stiege, 20; a Zimmer, 40; a Schock, 60.

Lastage. In valuing the freight of ships, a Last of salt is reckoned at 4000lb. weight, and a Last of hewn white stone at 5000lb. A Last of herrings or coals is 12 Tonnes.

Exchanges, Usances, &c. For the Exchanges of Bremen, see Vol. II. page 38.

The usance for bills drawn from the other parts of Germany is 14 days sight; from London and Paris, one month after date. The days of grace are 8; but for promissory notes, and bills at short sight, no days of grace are allowed.

BRESLAU *(in Silesia).*

Monies. Accounts are kept in Thalers, or Rixdollars, of 30 silver or Kayser Groschen, each Groschen being divided into 12 Denars or Pfenings current; but accounts in banco money are kept in Pounds of 24 banco Groschen, or 288 Denars banco.

A Rixdollar current is worth 1¼ Silesian Rixdollar, 1½ Gulden or Florin,

24 Good Groschen, 30 Silver Groschen, 45 White Groschen, 90 Creutzers, 120 Groschels, or 360 Denars. Monies.

A specie Rixdollar is worth $1\frac{1}{3}$ Rixdollar current, 2 Florins, 32 Good Groschen, 40 Silver Groschen, 60 White Groschen, or 140 Creutzers.

A Silesian Rixdollar is worth 24 Silver Groschen, 36 White Groschen, or 27 Creutzers.

A Silver Grosche, Kayser Grosche, or Bohemian Grosche, is $1\frac{1}{2}$ White Grosche; a Good Grosche, $1\frac{1}{4}$ Silver Grosche; a White Grosche, 2 Creutzers, 4 Dreyers, or 8 Denars; a Dreyer, 2 Denars or 3 Hellers; a Groschel, 3 Denars.

It is customary to call 60 Silver Groschen a Heavy Schock, and 32 a Heavy Mark, or a Mark of Money; also 32 White Groschen, or $21\frac{1}{3}$ Silver Groschen, a light Mark, or a Mark of Groschen; and 24 White Groschen, or 16 Silver Groschen, a very light Mark.

For an account of the Bank, see *Berlin*.

The coins are Double, Single, and Half Fredericks, and Ducats; Rixdollars current, with halves and thirds; Pieces of 4, 2, and 1 Good Groschen, and 6 Denars; Timpfen, that is, pieces of 6 Silver Groschen, or 18 Polish Groschen; Double and Single Silver Groschen; Double and Single Creutzers; and lastly, Double and Single Grosschel. Coins.

Foreign coins generally pass here as in Berlin. The Imperial or Convention coins bear a premium of from $2\frac{1}{2}$ to 5 per cent. on Prussian currency, except the Pieces of 7 and 17 Creutzers, which are commonly at par with it. Prussian Fredericks, reckoned at 5 Rixdollars, are about 14 per cent. better than Prussian silver. Foreign Coins.

For a valuation of Breslau banco and currency in sterling money, see *Berlin*.

The fineness of gold is expressed in Carats and Grains; the Mark being 24 Carats; the Carat, 12 Grains. The fineness of silver in Loths and Denars; the Mark being 16 Loths; the Loth, 16 Denars. Expression of Fineness.

Gold and silver are weighed by the Mark, which is divided into 8 Ounces, 16 Loths, 64 Quintels, 256 Denars, or 512 Hellers, and contains 204,60 Grammes, or 3158 English Grains. Weights.

The commercial Pound is divided into 16 Ounces, 32 Loths, 128 Quintels, 512 Denars, or 1024 Hellers, and contains 405,27 Grammes, or 6255 English

Weights. Grains. Hence 100lb of Breslau = 89,357lb. avoirdupois; and the Centner of 132lb. = 118lb. avoirdupois.

The Shipfund consists of 3 Centners, 16½ Laeps or Stones, or 396lb.

Measures. The Malter of corn is divided into 12 Scheffels; the Scheffel into 4 Viertels, 16 Metzes, or 64 Maessels. The Scheffel contains 69,89 Litres, or 1,98 Winchester Bushels.

The Eimer of wine is divided into 20 Topfs, 80 Quarts, or 320 Quartiers, and equals 5,5489 Litres, or 14,67 English Gallons.

The Breslau Foot measures 0,2842 Metres, or 11,19 English Inches.

The Silesian Ell contains 0,5759 Metres, or 22,67 English Inches.

A Ruthe is 7½ Silesian Ells, or 14 Feet 2 Inches, English measure.

A Silesian Mile is 1500 Ruthes, and contains 6,476 Kilometres, or 4 English Miles 43 Yards: 17⅕ Silesian Miles are reckoned to make a Degree of the meridian in a mean latitude.

217 Silesian square Ruthes answer nearly to an English Acre.

A Schock of any merchandize contains 4 Mandels, or 60 Pieces. A Zimmer of fox furs is 20 single skins; but of marter furs 20 Pairs. A Bale of woollens contains 12 Tuches or Pieces; and a Saum, 22 Pieces; each Piece of 32 Ells.

Fairs. By a royal edict of 1742, two Fairs are held at Breslau every year; the first beginning on the third Sunday in Lent; the second on the first Monday after Lady-day in September; and each Fair lasts 8 days.

Bills how Paid. Bills of Exchange were formerly paid in Imperial coins, viz. Pieces of 17 and 7 Creutzers, and specie Rixdollars; but, by a royal edict of 1751, they must be all paid in Prussian currency: and if the bill be payable in any other money, the payment must nevertheless be made in the said currency, allowance being made for the agio on the particular money expressed in the bill.

Exchanges. Foreign Exchanges are also settled in Prussian currency; and are similar to those of Berlin.

Usance and Days of Grace. The usance for bills drawn on Breslau is 14 days after acceptance; half usance, 8 days; and the days of grace are three. For bills, however, payable at the fairs, no days of grace are allowed; but such bills must be settled on the last day of payment in those fairs, or else be protested.

Breslau draws on Amsterdam and Hamburgh at sight, or at 4 or 5 weeks date; on Berlin and Konigsberg, at sight, or 8 or 12 days date; on Vienna, Leipsic, and other parts of Germany, at usance of 14 days sight; on Paris and London, at 2 or 3 months after date. Usance Days of Grace.

BRUNSWICK *(in Germany)*,

And also Wolfenbuttle, Hanover, Zell, Luneburgh, and the whole Electorate, and the northern part of Westphalia, keep their accounts in Thalers or Rixdollars, of 36 Marien Groschen, subdivided into 8 Pfenings current. Monies of Account.

The Rixdollar is also reckoned at 1½ Gulden, or Piece of two-thirds; 1⅘ Marien Gulden, 24 Good Groschen, 48 Goesgens, 72 Matthiers, or 288 Pfenings.

A Gulden, Florin, or Piece of two-thirds, is worth 1⅕ Marien Gulden, 16 Good Groschen, 24 Marien Groschen, &c. A Marien Gulden, = 20 Marien Groschen, or 40 Matthiers; a Good Grosche, 3 Matthiers; a Marien Grosche, 2 Matthiers; a Goesgen, 1½ Matthier; a Matthier, 4 Pfenings, or 8 Hellers; a Dreyer, 3 Pfenings, or 6 Hellers.

Thus 2 Rixdollars = 3 Guldens current; 5 Rixdollars = 9 Marien Guldens; 5 current Guldens = 6 Marien Guldens; and 2 Good Groschen = 3 Marien Groschen.

The gold coins are Double, Single, and Half Carl d'ors (coined since 1742), reckoned at 10, 5, and 2½ Rixdollars; and Ducats, at 2¾ Rixdollars. The silver coins are specie and current Rixdollars, at 48 and 36 Marien Groschen; Guldens or Florins, at 24 Marien Groschen; Pieces of ⅓ and ⅙ Rixdollars, at 12 and 6 Marien Groschen; Pieces of 3 and 1½ Marien Groschen, or 2 and 1 Good Groschen; and also of 6 and 4 Pfenings. These silver pieces have been coined since the year 1764 (of the same rate as Convention money), and form the currency of the country. Coins.

There are also the old specie Rixdollars, and fine Pieces of ⅔, ⅓, and ⅙, reckoned at 48, 24, 12, and 6 Marien Groschen, coined after the Leipsic rate of coinage.

It must be observed, however, that Ducats are about 3 per cent. better than currency, so that they pass for 2 Rixdollars 30 Marien Groschen, more or less; and also that the old specie Rixdollars, and fine Pieces of two-thirds, are about

Coins. 12 per cent. better than currency, being worth 54 and 27 Marien Groschen, more or less.

Carl d'ors, old French Louis d'ors, Fredericks, and Spanish Pistoles, are commonly at par with currency.

The Cologne Mark of fine gold is worth 190 Rixdollars, more or less, in Carl d'ors, or currency, and the Cologne Mark of fine silver is worth 13 Rixdollars, more or less, in currency.

Rate of Coinage. Out of a Cologne Mark of gold, $21\frac{3}{4}$ Carats fine, 35 Carl d'ors are coined; and out of a Cologne Mark of fine silver, 13 Rixdollars 12 Marien Groschen are coined.

Thus the Rixdollar in Carl d'ors contains 25,19 Asen, or $18\frac{2}{3}$ English Grains of fine gold; and the Rixdollar silver currency, 364,8 Asen, or $270\frac{1}{2}$ Grains of fine silver; the proportion between gold and silver being as $14\frac{1}{2}\frac{2}{5}$ to 1.

Value of Monies. Hence the Rixdollar, Brunswick currency, is worth 3s. 2d. sterling; or £1 sterling = 6 Rixdollars $11\frac{1}{2}$ Marien Groschen in silver: and the Carl d'or = 16s. $6\frac{1}{4}$d. sterling, in English gold.

Also 100 Rixdollars, Hamburgh banco, are worth 140 Rixdollars, more or less, in Carl d'ors, or $144\frac{3}{4}$ Rixdollars in Brunswick silver currency; and 100 Rixdollars, Hamburgh currency, are worth $117\frac{5}{8}$ Rixdollars, Brunswick currency.

Weight. Gold and silver are weighed by the Cologne Mark, and their fineness is valued as in Hamburgh.

The commercial Pound is divided into 2 Marks, 16 Ounces, 32 Loths, 128 Quentins, 512 Pfenings, or 1024 Hellers, and contains 4668 Grammes, or 7206 English Grains. Hence 100lb. of Brunswick answer to 103lb. avoirdupois; and therefore the Centner of 114lb. of Brunswick = 117lb. 6 oz. avoirdupois. In commercial weight, a Shipfund contains 20 Lisponds, or 280lb.; a Centner, 114lb,; a Lispond is 14lb.; a Stone, 10lb. and sometimes 11lb.

Measures. A Wispel of corn is divided into 4 Scheffels, 40 Himtens, 160 Vierfasses, or 640 Loechers; the Scheffel of oats contains 12 Himtens. The Himten answers to 31,1 Litres, or 0,88 Winchester Bushels, and the Wispel is therefore 4,4 English Quarters.

The Fuder of wine is divided into 4 Oxhofts, 6 Aams, 240 Stubgens, or 1920

Nossels. The Fuder answers to 8807 Litres, or 232,7 English Gallons, and therefore the Stubgen = 3669 Litres, or 0,9695 English Gallons. Measures.

A Fass of beer contains 4 Tonnes; a Tonne, 27 Stubgens.

Hence 100 Stubgens = 96 English Gallons.

The Foot of Brunswick is divided into 12 Inches, and contains 0,2851 Metres, or 11,23 English Inches.

The Ell consists of 2 Shoes or Feet. Hence 8 Ells of Brunswick = 5 English Yards.

A Schock is 3 Steiges, or 60 Ells; a Pack of cloth is 10 Pieces; each Piece 22 Tuches; and the Tuche 22 Ells.

A Last of Herrings is 12 Tonnes, or Barrels; a Last of salt or butter, 18 Tonnes.

Two Fairs are held at Brunswick every year, which last each 10 days; they begin on the Thursdays that fall nearest to Candlemas and St. Laurence's day; that is, to the 2d of February, and 10th of August; but wholesale business begins three days sooner. The acceptance of all bills, payable at those Fairs, must not be delayed beyond the evening of the Friday in the first week of the Fair, but they cannot be protested before that period; and the payment is to be made on the Thursday in the following week. Fairs.

The business of Exchange is chiefly transacted at the Fairs. Brunswick gives (more or less) to Exchanges.

Amsterdam, 141 Rixdollars in Carl d'ors, for 100 Rixdollars.
Hamburgh ..140 .... 100 Rixdollars banco; or
120 .... 100 Rixdollars current.
London ......6 Rixdollars 2 Good Groschen.. £1 sterling.

The Exchanges of Brunswick with other places are like those of Leipsic.

The usance is 14 days after acceptance. Three days are allowed to the holder of a bill to present it for payment; but no days of grace are allowed to the acceptor. Usance and Days of Grace.

BRUSSELS, *see Netherlands*.

CADIZ (*in Spain*).

Monies of Account. Accounts are kept here, and in all Andalusia, in Reals of plate (i. e. old plate,) each Real consisting of 16 Quartos, or 34 Maravedis.

A Peso or Dollar of plate, or of Exchange, is 8 Reals, 128 Quartos, or 272 Maravedis of plate.

A Peso Duro, or hard Dollar, is worth $10\frac{5}{8}$ Reals, 170 Quartos, or $361\frac{1}{4}$ Maravedis of plate.

A Ducado de Plata, or Ducat of plate, is worth 11 Reals; and a Ducado de Cambio, or Ducat of Exchange, 11 Reals 1 Maravedi, or 375 Maravedis; and the latter is commonly divided into 20 Sueldos, or 240 Dineros. The Ducat, by which the freight of ships is sometimes regulated, is reckoned at 12 Reals of plate.

For the coins, and all that relates to gold and silver, see *Spain*.

Weights. The Mark of Castile is the basis of all the weights used here. It is divided into 8 Ounces, 64 Ochavas, 384 Tomines, or 4608 Grains, and contains 230,043 Grammes, or $3550\frac{1}{2}$ English Grains*.

The commercial Pound is composed of 2 Marks, 16 Ounces, or 256 Adarmes, except in weighing fresh meat and fish, for which the Pound of 4 Marks is used.

The Quintal contains 4 Arrobas, or 100lb. and equals 101,43lb. avoirdupois.

Measures. Corn is sold by the Cahiz of 12 Fanegas, each Fanega being divided into 12 Celemines or Almudes, 24 Medios, 48 Quartillos, or 196 Raciones. This is called the standard of Avila; but there is a great diversity of measures throughout the province; 5 Fanegas are computed to equal 1 English Quarter nearly; or, more accurately, 1 Fanega contains 1,599 English Bushel, or 56,346 Litres. A Last of salt contains 4 Cahizes.

The Arroba, when used as a measure for liquids, is divided into 8 Azumbres, or 32 Quartillos, and also into 36 Quartillos; there is the great Arroba and the lesser; 32 of the latter being equal to 25 of the former.

The large Arroba contains 16,07 Litres, or 4,246 English Gallons.

The lesser Arroba contains 12,633 Litres, or 3,337 English Gallons.

* The Mark transmitted from Cadiz by his Majesty's Consul, *R. Matthews, Esq.* has been found, by recent experiments at the *London Mint*, to weigh $3552\frac{1}{2}$ Grains; but as the Castilian Mark is the legal standard for the whole kingdom, its contents, as above, are given under the different heads relating to Spain, with occasional remarks on local variations. *See Note on Castile.*

Measures.

The Botta of wine contains 30 of the greater Arrobas, each weighing 34 Pounds when filled with river water, the whole answering to 124 English Gallons.

The Pipe of oil contains 34 of the lesser Arrobas, each weighing 25 Pounds of oil, or $26\frac{9}{16}$ Castilian Pounds of river water; the whole answering to 864lb. avoirdupois nearly.

Long Measure.

The Vara, or Ell, which is the Castilian measure, is divided into 2 Codos, 4 Palmos, 8 Octavas, or 16 Avas. It is also divided into 3 Feet of Burgos, 36 Inches, or 48 Fingers, and contains 0,8479 Metres, or 33,384 English Inches.

Goods how sold.

Cochineal is sold by the Arroba of 25lb. in Ducats of Plate; tare 22 Ounces per Seron.

Sugar, from the Havannah, by the Arroba in Reals of Plate.

Indigo by the Pound in Reals of Plate, real tare.

Peruvian bark by the Pound in Reals of Plate, real tare.

Cotton wool by the 100lb. in Pesos, or Dollars of Plate.

Copper by the Fanega of 110lb., in Dollars of Plate.

Hides, from South America, by the 35lb. in Reals of Plate.

Brandy by the 30 Arrobas majores in Reals Vellon.

Exchanges, Usance, &c.

For the Exchanges of Cadiz, see Vol. II. page 88.

The usance is, for bills drawn from France, 1 month after date; and 2 months for bills from all the rest of Europe. Six days grace are allowed; on the last day of which bills must be either paid or protested.

For other particulars, see *Spain*, Vol. I.

CAIRO (*in Egypt*).

Monies of Account.

Accounts are kept here in Piastres of 33 Medini, or 80 Aspers. There are, however, other modes of reckoning, and contracts are mostly made in imaginary Pieces of 30, 40, 60, 70, and 73 Medini, and sometimes in Pataccas or Tallari, that is, Imperial Dollars, which formerly passed for 85 Medini, but have been considerably raised. In making bargains, where Pataccas are to be received in payment, it is necessary previously to settle the value of that money.

Contracts are also made in Funducli and Mahbub Sequins. The Funducli

Monies of Account. are reckoned at 146 Medini, and 3 Mahbubs are equal to 4 Pataccas; so that the Mahbub is worth 120 Medini.

Coins. The only coins allowed by the Turkish government to be struck at Cairo are the Mahbub (or Zermahbub) Sequins, and Medini. 40 Medini are valued at $19\frac{1}{4}$d. sterling; so that the Mahbub is worth 4s. $9\frac{3}{4}$d. sterling. Mahbubs, however, of inferior value, are coined by the Beys in Egypt, and generally pass for 110 Medini. Piastres, of inferior value, are likewise coined by the Beys.

The other Turkish coins (all of which are current in Egypt) will be found under the article *Constantinople.*

Weights. The weight called Cantaro, which consists of 100 Rottoli, equals 95lb. avoirdupois, or 43,048 Kilogrammes. The Rottolo is divided into 144 Drams. The Occa is a weight of 400 Drams, and is equal to 2,639lb. avoirdupois, or 1,196 Kilogrammes. 36 Occas = 1 Cantaro.

In Egypt, however, the Cantaro is different for various kinds of goods; and this difference is called the *Tare of Cantaro,* which has no reference to the tare allowed for casks, chests, packages, &c. but is an addition of so much per cent. to the weight, such as 2, 5, 10, 30, 40, &c. per 100 Rottoli.

	Rottoli.		Occas.	Drams.		lb. avoir.
Thus the Cantaro of iron is	$233\frac{1}{3}$	=	84	——	=	$221\frac{2}{3}$
of lead, ...	140		50	160		133
of red lead, ...	130		46	220		$123\frac{1}{2}$
of black lead (barrel included,)	150		54	——		$142\frac{1}{2}$
of gum arabic and balms, ...	133		47	352		$126\frac{1}{3}$
of arsenic and other drugs, ...	125		45	——		$118\frac{3}{4}$
of dye woods, ...	120		43	80		114
of almonds and fruits, ...	115		41	160		$109\frac{1}{4}$
of cloves and nutmegs, salsaparilla, and elephants' teeth,	110		39	240		$104\frac{1}{2}$
of coffee and wire, ...	105		37	320		$99\frac{3}{4}$
of quicksilver, pewter, tin in bars, vermillion, and sugar,	102		36	288		97

Silk is weighed by the Occa or Harsela of 400 Drams; but the silks of Cyprus, Bursa, and Sagoro, are sold by the Occa of 404 Drams.

The principal measure for cloth and silk stuffs in Egypt is the Pic, which contains 26,8 English Inches, or 0,6804 Metres. *Measures.*

The Tares allowed on different articles are as follows: *Tares.*

On red lead, 30 Rottoli per barrel.

On tin in bars, 20 Rottoli per barrel.

On vermillion, 2 Rottoli for paper.

On cloves and nutmegs, the barrel is weighed for tare.

On sugar, for chests or casks, 2 per cent.

On pepper, 19 Rottoli per bag of the larger size; 12 Rottoli per bag of the smaller size.

On cochineal, sold by the Occa, 1 Occa per bag of the larger size; $\frac{3}{4}$ Occa per bag of the smaller size.

CALCUTTA, *see East Indies.*

CANADA *(in North America).*

Accounts are kept in Canada, Halifax, and other provinces of North America belonging to England, in Pounds, Shillings, and Pence currency. This money differs from sterling, being $\frac{1}{10}$ worse, and therefore sterling is $\frac{1}{9}$ better than currency. Thus £100 currency equal £90 sterling, and £100 sterling equal £111$\frac{1}{9}$ currency. *Monies of Account.*

The army pay differs from the above, being $\frac{1}{27}$ higher than sterling. Thus the Dollar of 4s. 6d. is reckoned in all military payments at 4s. 8d.

Accounts are likewise kept in several parts of Canada in Livres, Sous, and Deniers, according to the ancient system of France. This is called old currency.

The proportion between the Shilling and the Livre of these currencies is as 5 to 6; that is, 5 Shillings of the new equal 6 Livres of the old, and their divisions in proportion.

The following table shews the weight and current value of the several gold coins circulating here, and also the current value of the silver coins, according to a law passed by the Provincial Legislature in 1808.

Value of Coins in Canada.

GOLD COINS.	Weight.		Currency.			Old Currency.	
	Dwts.	Grains.	£.	s.	d.	Livres.	Sous.
Doubloon, with half in proportion	17		3	14	6	89	8
Guinea, with its divisions in proportion	5	6	1	3	4	28	
Johanese, with half in proportion	18		4	0	0	96	
Moidore	6	18	1	10		36	
Louis d'or, coined before 1793	5	4	1	2	8	27	4
Pistole, ditto	4	4		18	3	21	18
Eagle, with half in proportion	11	6	2	10		60	
SILVER COINS.							
Crown, English				5	6	6	12
Shilling, Ditto				1	1	1	6
Dollar, Spanish and American				5	0	6	
Pistareen				1	0	1	4
French Crown, coined before 1793				5	6	6	12
French Piece of 4 Livres 10 Sous Tournois				4	2	5	

Any difference of weight in the gold coins is settled by allowing 2¼d. per grain, or 89s. per oz. on English, Portuguese, and American gold; and 2⅕d. per grain, or 87s. 8½d. per oz. on French and Spanish gold, deducting half a grain for each piece when computed by the Ounce.

Weights & Measures.

The weights and measures of France were formerly used here; but in Lower Canada those of England have been legally established in 1808. In the corn trade, however, the French Minot is still retained, 90 of which are estimated at 100 English Bushels, although the true proportion is 90 to 98.

CANARY ISLANDS *(in the Atlantic Ocean).*

Monies of Account.

In these seven islands accounts are kept in Reals Vellon of 8½ Quartos, or 34 Maravedis Vellon. The currency is likewise composed of Quartos, Reales de Plata, and Pesos Corrèntes; the Peso Corrente being divided into 8 Reales de Plata, 10 Reales Correntes, or 128 Quartos. 1 Peso Fuerte, or Hard Dollar, equals 1⅓ Peso Corrente, 10⅔ Reales de Plata, 20 Reals Vellon, 170 Quartos, or 680 Maravedis Vellon.

These monies are imaginary, with the exception of the Hard Dollar and the Quarto, and their sterling value may be computed from the price of the

Dollar. If it be valued at 4s. 4d. the Peso Corrente is worth 39d., and the rest in proportion. Monies of Account.

The Gold coins are the Doubloon or Onza of 16 Hard Dollars, divided into halves, quarters, eighths, and sixteenths. The Silver coins are the Hard Dollar, with the half or Medio Duro, the fourth or Toston, the eighth or half Toston, and the sixteenth or Fisca. Coins.

The Copper coins are the Ochavo of 8 Maravedis, the Quarto of 4, and the Medio Quarto of 2 Maravedis.

The Libra is divided into 16 Ounces, 256 Adarmes, or 6144 Grains. 25lb. = 1 Arroba, 4 Arrobas = 1 Quintal of 100lb. Spanish, which is generally computed at 106lb. avoirdupois; but by a standard weight of 10 Libras, lately sent from Teneriffe to London, the proportion is found to be only 101,48lb. avoirdupois, the said Diez Libras weighing 10lb. 2 oz. 6 Drams avoirdupois, or 4,6 Kilogrammes.* Weights.

Grain of every kind is measured by the Fanega, which is divided into 12 Almudes, or 48 Qnartillos; wheat is sold by struck measurement; but all other sorts of grain, and also salt, by heaped measurement. The Fanega, heaped, is estimated at 2½ Winchester Bushels, and 4½ struck Fanegas answer to 1 English Quarter. Dry Measure.

The Pipe in some of the islands is divided into 12 Barrels, or 480 Quartillos, and is computed to contain from 116 to 124 English Gallons. The Arroba is likewise a measure for liquids, and answers to 4 Gallons 1 Quart English wine measure nearly. Liquid Measure.

The Long Measure is the Castilian Foot, which is divided into 12 Inches, and the Inch into eighths; and equals 11,128 English Inches, or 0,2826 Metres. The Vara is 3 Feet, and the Brasada 2⅙ Varas, or 1,837 Metre = 72,33 English Inches. Long Measure.

Vineyards and corn lands are measured by the Fanegada, which is divided into 12 Almudes or Celemines, and contains 600 square Brasadas. Hence the Fanegada of the Canaries equals half an English Acre, or 2,023 Decares of France.

The Canary Islands give London 90 Reals Vellon for £1 sterling. Exchange.

* This weight, and several other standards belonging to the Canaries, have been transmitted to *Lord Castlereagh* by his Majesty's Consul, *Gilbert Stuart Bruce, Esq.*, from whose dispatches on the occasion the above article is chiefly extracted. It should be noticed, that the Vara sent by him answers to 33,141 English Inches, which is about 7 per cent. less than the Castilian or Burgalese standard, the legal measure for Spain.

CANDIA *(an Island in the Mediterranean).*

Monies. Accounts are here kept in Piastres of 40 Paras.

The coins will be found under the article *Constantinople.*

Weights. The Cantaro contains 100 Rottoli, or 44 Occas, and weighs 116,33lb. avoirdupois, or 52,725 Kilogrammes; the Occa contains 400 Drams; and the Rottolo, 176 Drams.

Measures. The corn Measure is the Carga, which contains 1,523 Hectolitre, or 4,322 English Bushels.

The Mistate of oil at Canea weighs 8½ Occas, which equal 10,198 Kilogrammes, or 22,5lb. avoirdupois, and measures 11,164 Litres, or 2,949 English Gallons. At Retimo, the Mistate weighs 10 Occas.

The Pic or Ell contains 0,6375 Metres, or 25,11 English Inches.

CANTON, *see China.*

CAPE OF GOOD HOPE *(in Africa).*

Monies of Account. There are various modes of keeping accounts in this colony, viz. in Guilders or Florins of 20 Stivers, each Stiver being divided into 16 Pennings; also in Rixdollars, Schillings, and Stivers, the Rixdollar being divided into 8 Schillings, and the Schilling into 6 Stivers. The English mode of keeping accounts is likewise occasionally adopted.

The Rixdollar is a paper currency, which is generally reckoned at 3s. 4d. sterling, but varies in its value according to the plenty or scarcity of cash. Bills on England at 30 days sight are generally considered equal to cash, particularly Government bills.

The English Shilling here passes for 2 Schillings, or 12 Stivers currency, so that the Penny and the Stiver are of one value; and other coins circulate in the same proportion.

The following are the rates at which foreign coins generally pass, both in sterling and currency.

Foreign Coins.

		Sterling.				Schill. Current.
Guinea	=	£1	2	0	=	44
Doubloon	=	4	0	0	=	160
Johannese	=	2	0	0	=	80
Pagoda	=	1	17	6	=	75
Ducat and Sequin	=	0	9	6	=	19
Spanish Dollar	=	0	5	0	=	10
Rupee	=	0	2	6	=	5
PAPER CURRENCY.						
Rixdollar	=	0	3	4	=	8
Dutch Schilling	=	0	0	4½	=	1

The English Weights and Measures are in general use here, except for wines, which are mostly sold by the Leager of 4 Ahms or 388 Cannes, containing 50 English Gallons nearly. Weights & Measures.

CARRARA *(in Italy)*.

Accounts are kept in Lire of 20 Soldi or 240 Denari, Genoa currency. Monies, &c.

The coins, being those of *Genoa*, will be found under that article, as also the weights and measures.

The marble that is found here is measured by the Palmo of 12 Oncie; the Palmo contains 0,2436 Metres, or 9,591 English Inches; and therefore 3¾ Palmi are equal to an English Yard; or 15 Oncie = 1 English Foot. 25 Cubic Palmi of marble make a Carrata, which measures 12¾ English Cubic Feet, or 3,612 French Decisteres, and weighs 1 Ton avoirdupois, or 1 Bar 15,271 Kilogrammes. Solid Measure.

CASSEL *(in Germany)*.

Accounts are kept here in Rixdollars of 32 Albuses, each Albus being divided into 9 Pfenings, or 12 Hellers current. Monies of Account.

This Rixdollar is also reckoned at 1½ Reichsflorin or Florin of the Empire, 24

Monies of Account.

Good Groschen, 36 Marien Groschen, or 90 Creutzers, aud may be valued at 3s. 1¾d. sterling, and the Florin of the Empire at 2s. 1¼d. nearly.

The Specie Rixdollar is worth ⅓ more than the Rixdollar Current.

Coins.

The Gold coins are Double and Single Pistoles, or Pieces of 10 and 5 Rixdollars. The Silver coins are Specie Rixdollars, with Halves and Quarters; Pieces of 6, 4, 3, 2, and 1 Good Groschen, or 8, 5⅓ 4, 2⅔, and 1⅓ Albuses, all coined after the rate of the Convention coins, for which see *Germany*. The copper coins are Pieces of 2 and 1 Albuses, and 4 Hellers or 3 Pfenings.

In 1815, a coinage took place of Gold pieces, called William d'ors, and also of Silver Ecus or Rixdollars, with smaller coins. See *Table of Coins*, Vol. II.

Weights.

The weight for Gold and Silver is the Cologne Mark, which is also sometimes used for common articles. The regular commercial Pound, which is divided into 16 Ounces, or 32 Loths, is nearly 4 per cent. heavier than the Cologne Pound, and weighs 7501 English Grains. Hence 100lb. of Cassel equal 107,14lb. avoirdupois, or 48,56 Kilogrammes. The Centner, or Quintal, is 108lb.

Measures.

The Fuder of Wine is divided into 6 Ohms, 120 Quartlins, or 480 Maass. The Ohm contains 161,52 Litres, or 43,20 English Gallons.

The corn measure, called the Viertel, is divided into 4 Himtens, 16 Metzens, or 64 Maesgens, and contains 1,427 Hectolitre, or 4,05 English Bushels.

The Ell contains 0,5617 Metres, or 22,114 English Inches.

CASTILE *(in Spain)*.

Monies of Account.

Accounts in Madrid, and the whole province of Castile, are kept in Reals Vellon of 34 Maravedis Vellon; but merchants trading with foreign countries mostly keep their accounts in Reals and Maravedis of old Plate (which is always understood by the term Plate, unless new Plate is mentioned), and the royal treasury and its offices keep accounts in Escudos Vellon of 10 Reals, or 340 Maravedis Vellon.

The Real Vellon contains 8½ Quartos, or 17 Ochavos; and the Maravedi, 10 Dineros.

The Real of Plate contains 16 Quartos, 32 Ochavos, 34 Maravedis of Plate, or 64 Maravedis Vellon.

The Escudo Vellon is half a Peso Duro, or Hard Dollar; the Escudo d'oro is half an effective Pistole. Monies of Account.

The Doubloon of Plate (or Pistole of Exchange) is worth 4 Pesos of Plate, or 60 Reals 8 Maravedis Vellon.

The Peso of Plate (or Dollar of Exchange) is worth 8 Reals of Plate, or 15 Reals 2 Maravedis Vellon.

The Ducat of Plate (or Ducat of Exchange) which is divided into 20 Sueldos, or 240 Dineros, is worth 375 Maravedis of Plate, or $705\frac{15}{17}$ Maravedis Vellon.

In the interior trade of the country, the Doubloon is reckoned at 60 Reals; the Peso, at 15 Reals; and the Ducat, at 11 Reals Vellon.

Further particulars respecting the monies of account, and also the coins of the country, will be found under the article *Spain*.

The Mark of Castile, which is the legal weight throughout Spain and its colonies, is divided into 8 Ounces, 64 Ochavas, 128 Adarmes, 384 Tomines, or 4608 Grains, and equals $3550\frac{1}{2}$ English Grains, or 230,043 Grammes.* Weights.

Gold is weighed by the same Mark, but it is divided into 50 Castellanos, 400 Tomines, or 4800 Grains.

For the commercial weight, and the corn, wine, and long measures, &c. of Castile, see *Spain*.

The foreign Exchanges of Madrid may be seen in Vol. II. page 88. Exchanges, &c.

The Exchange of Madrid with Alicant, Barcelona, Cadiz, Carthagena, Seville, Valencia, &c. is about $\frac{1}{2}$ per cent. either above or below par, and at an usance of 8 days after sight; the same takes place with Bilboa, but bills from the latter place are made payable on a specified day.

* Notwithstanding the importance of the Castilian Mark as a standard for weighing a great portion of the precious metals, both in the new and old world, yet its relative contents have not been duly ascertained. According to *Tillet* it answers to 3548 troy Grains, while *Kruse* makes it equal to 3557, and other authors differ between those extremes. See *Nelkenbreker*, p. 509.

By the experiments lately made at the *London Mint* on the Castilian Mark sent from Madrid to *Lord Castlereagh* by the *Hon. John Meade*, His Majesty's Consul General in Spain, it is found to weigh $3550\frac{1}{2}$ Grains, as above, and this result has been verified by the perfect agreement of attested standards received from Barcelona, Carthagena, Corunna, and Malaga. It should however be noticed, that a few weights from other cities of Spain were found heavier, from 1 to 4 Grains; but as they also differed from each other, their variations must be ascribed to inaccurate experiments or the fallibility of workmanship.

Usance. The usance for bills drawn from London, Paris, or Genoa, is 60 days; from Amsterdam, 2 months; and from Rome, 3 months after date.

Days of Grace. Foreign bills, when they are accepted, have 14 days grace allowed, except bills drawn from Rome, which, as well as bills that have not been accepted, must be either paid, or protested, on the very day on which they are made payable.

Bills drawn from Bilboa are allowed 19 days; and from other parts of Spain, 8 days grace.

Bills at sight must be paid on being presented.

For further particulars see *Spain*.

CATALONIA, *see Barcelona.*

CEFALONIA, *see Zante.*

CETTE, *see Montpellier.*

CEYLON, *see East Indies.*

CHINA.

Monies. Accounts are kept here in Tales, Mace, Candarines, and Cash; the Tale being divided into 10 Mace, 100 Candarines, or 1000 Cash.

There is but one kind of money made in China, called *Cash*, which is not coined but cast, and which is only used for small payments: it is composed of 6 parts of copper and 4 parts of lead; it is round, marked on one side, and rather raised at the edges, with a square hole in the middle. These pieces are commonly carried, like beads, on a string or wire. A Tale of fine silver should be worth 1000 Cash; but on account of their convenience for common use, their price is sometimes so much raised that only 750 Cash are given for the Tale.

Foreign coins, however, circulate here, particularly Spanish Dollars; and for small change they are cut into very exact proportions, but afterwards weighed, for which purpose merchants generally carry scales, called Dotchin, made somewhat after the plan of the English steelyards.

The Tale is reckoned at 6s. 8d. sterling in the books of the East India Company; but its value varies, and is generally computed according to the price paid per Ounce for Spanish Dollars in London. The tables given for this proportional value may be calculated in Pence sterling, by the multiplier 1,208. Thus, if the price of the Spanish Dollar be 60d. per Ounce, the value of the Tale will be 60 × 1,208 = 72,48d; if at 66d. the value of the Tale will be 79,728d. and for any other price in the same proportion. Monies.

The fineness of gold and silver is expressed by dividing the weight into 100 parts, called Toques or Touch, similar to the modern practice of France. Thus, if an Ingot be 93 Touch, it is understood to contain 7 parts of alloy, and 93 of pure metal, making in the whole 100. Fineness of Gold and Silver.

The fineness of the precious metals, expressed in these decimal proportions, may be converted into the English mode by the following analogies: Suppose gold is 91,66 Touch, say, as 100 : 91,66 :: 12 : 11 the standard, and *vice versa;* and to convert standard silver into Touch, say, as 240 : 222 :: 100 : 92,5, the Touch of sterling silver. Pure gold or silver without alloy is called by the Chinese, Sycee; and sometimes, when of less purity, the metal is accepted as Sycee.

Silver Ingots are used as money, and weigh from ½ to 100 Tales, their value being determined by their weight. These Ingots are of the best sort of silver, that is, about 94 Touch. Silver Ingots.

Gold is not considered as money, but as merchandise; it is sold in regular Ingots of a determined weight, which the English call *shoes* of gold; the largest of these weigh 10 Tales each, and the gold is reckoned 94 Touch, though it may be only 92 or 93. Gold Ingots.

Gold and Silver are weighed by the Catty of 16 Tales; the Tale is divided into 10 Mace, 100 Candarines, or 1000 Cash. 100 Tales are reckoned to weigh 120 oz. 16 dwt. troy, which make the Tale equal to 579,8 English Grains, or 37,566 Grammes. Weights.

The principal weights for merchandise are the Pecul, the Catty, and the Tale; the Pecul being divided into 100 Catties, or 1600 Tales.

		lb.	oz.	dr.	
1 Tale weighs, avoirdupois		0	1	5,333	= 1⅓oz.
16 Tales	or 1 Catty	1	5	5,333	= 1⅓lb.
100 Catties	or 1 Pecul	133	5	5,333	= 133⅓lb.

Hence the Pecul weighs 60,472 Kilogrammes, or 162lb. 0 oz. 8 dwt. 13 gr. troy.

Weights. The above weights are sometimes otherwise denominated, especially by the natives; thus the Catty is called Gin, the Tale Lyang, the Mace Tchen, the Candarine Fwen, and the Cash Lis.

There are no commercial measures in China, as all dry goods and liquids are sold by weight. In delivering a cargo, English weights are used, and afterwards turned into China Peculs and Catties.

Long Measure. The Long Measure used in China is the Covid or Cobre; it is divided into 10 Punts, and is equal to 0,3713 Metres, or 14,625 English Inches.

The Chinese have four different measures answering to the Foot, viz.

		Metres.		English Inches.
The Foot of the mathematical tribunal	=	0,333	=	13,125
The builders' Foot, called Kongpu	=	0,3228	=	12,7
The tailors' and tradesmen's Foot	=	0,3383	=	13,33
The Foot used by engineers..................	=	0,3211	=	12,65

The Li contains 180 Fathoms, each 10 Feet of the last mentioned length; therefore the Li = 1897½ English Feet; and 192½ Lis measure a mean Degree of the meridian nearly; but European Missionaries in China have divided the Degree into 200 Lis, each Li making 1826 English Feet, which gives the Degree 69,166 English Miles, or 11,131 French Myriametres.

CIVITA VECCHIA, *see Rome.*

CLEVES *(in Germany).*

Monies of Account. In the Duchy of Cleves, in Juliers, and in all the southern parts of Westphalia, accounts are kept in Rixdollars, of 60 Stivers, 480 Pfenings, or 960 Hellers, currency of Cleves.

The Rixdollar current equals 1½ Reichsflorin, 2 Cleves Rixdollars, 3 Cleves Florins, 8 Shillings, 24 Good Groschen, 90 Creutzers, or 120 Fettmangens.

Hence the Reichsflorin, or Florin of the Empire, is two-thirds of the Rixdollar current.

The Cleves Rixdollar is one half of the Rixdollar current; and their respective divisions in proportion.

The Rixdollar current is worth 3s. 1¾d. sterling, and the Florin of the Empire 2s. 1¼d. sterling nearly. Monies of Account.

The Coins will be found under the article *Berlin*.

A Last of corn is divided into 15 Malters, 60 Scheffels, 240 Viertels, or 2880 Kannes. The Malter contains 1,794 Hectolitre, or 5,093 English Bushels. Measures.

The Foot measures 0,2955 Metres, or 11,66 English Inches.

COBLENTZ (*in Germany*).

In this city, and in the whole Electorate of Treves or Triers, accounts are kept in Rixdollars, of 54 Petermangens current. This Rixdollar is worth 1½ Reichsflorin; and the Reichsflorin contains 12 great Petermangens, 36 common ditto, or 60 Creutzers. Monies of Account.

These monies of account are valued either in Convention money, or Müntze, that is, small coins; in the Convention money, the Cologne Mark of fine silver is reckoned at 13⅓ Rixdollars of account, or 20 Florins; in the Müntze, the same Mark is reckoned at 16 Rixdollars of account, or 24 Florins.

The Coins of the Electorate are Rixdollars specie, reckoned at 2 Florins Convention money, or 2⅖ Florins Müntze; Pieces of 20, 10, and 5 Creutzers, or 12, 6, and 3 Petermangens Convention money, or 14⅖, 7½, and 3⅗ Petermangens Müntze. Also baser Pieces of 9 and 12 Petermangens Müntze; the latter are called Copsticks. Coins.

The weights used here are chiefly those of Cologne. Weights & Measures.

The corn measure is the Malter, which contains 4,5305 English Bushels, or 1,5964 Hectolitre.

The Ell of Coblentz and Treves measures 0,558 Metres, or 22 English Inches.

COBURG (*in Germany*).

In Saxe Coburg Saalfeld, and in Anspach, accounts are kept in Florins of the Empire of 60 Creutzers, each Creutzer containing 4 Pfenings. The Thaler of Monies of Account.

Monies of Account. the Empire is worth $1\frac{1}{2}$ Florin of the Empire, $1\frac{1}{5}$ Florin of Franconia, 18 Heavy Batzen, $22\frac{1}{2}$ Light Batzen, 24 Good Groschen, or 90 Creutzers.

The Florin of the Empire is worth 2s. $1\frac{1}{4}$d. sterling, and its divisions in proportion.

Coins. The Gold coins are Ducats, and the Silver coins Crowns of the Convention, with Halves and Quarters; also Pieces of the Convention of 4, 2, and 1 Good Groschen.

Weights. The gold and silver weight is that of Cologne. The commercial Pound contains 0,5098 Kilogrammes, or 7868,9 English Grains. Hence 100lb. of Coburg = 112,4lb. avoirdupois.

Measures. The corn measure is the Simra, which is divided into 4 Quarters or 16 Metzen, and contains 87,727 Litres, or 2,4896 English Bushels.

The Ell contains 0,586 Metres, or 23,07 English Inches.

COLOGNE *(in Germany)*.

Monies of Account. Accounts are kept in Rixdollars specie of 80 Albuses; or Rixdollars current of 78 Albuses; the Albus being divided into 12 Hellers.

The Rixdollar specie is divided into $1\frac{1}{39}$ Florin current, $1\frac{1}{4}$ Rader Florin, $1\frac{1}{2}$ Florin specie (that is, Florin of the Empire, or Piece of two-thirds) 2 Herren Florins, $3\frac{1}{3}$ Cologne Florins, 4 Orts, 8 Shillings, 20 Blafferts, 30 Groschen, 60 Stivers, 80 Cologne Albuses, 90 Creutzers, 100 Light Albuses, 120 Fettmangens, or 960 Hellers.

Value of Monies. The Rixdollar specie = 2s. $7\frac{1}{2}$d. sterling; and the Rixdollar current = 2s. $6\frac{3}{4}$d. sterling. Thus £1 sterling = 7 Rixdollars $49\frac{1}{2}$ Albuses specie, or 7 Rixdollars $63\frac{1}{2}$ Albuses current.

Coins. The Gold coins are Ducats; and the Silver coins effective Specie Rixdollars, Florins, with Halves and Quarters, or Pieces of $\frac{2}{3}$, $\frac{1}{3}$, and $\frac{1}{6}$; Blafferts and Halves, Stivers, Fettmangens, and Albuses.

French coins have a general circulation here, and are reckoned in Exchanges.

Gold and silver are weighed by the Mark of 8 Ounces, 16 Loths, 64 Quintins, 256 Pfenings or Deniers, 4352 Eschen, or 65536 Richtpfenings, and weighs 233,769 Grammes, or 3608 English Grains.* Weights.

The commercial weight is the same as that for gold and silver. Its Pound therefore contains 2 Marks, 16 Ounces, 32 Loths, 128 Quintins, or 512 Pfenings, and equals 467,538 Grammes, or 7216 English Grains. Hence 100lb. of Cologne = 103,086lb. avoirdupois. The Centner is 106lb. Cologne weight.

The Last of corn is divided into 20 Malters, or 480 Fasses, and contains 32,415 Hectolitres, or 91,995 English Bushels. Measures.

The Ohm, wine measure, is divided into 26 Viertels, 104 Maasses, or 416 Pintgers. The Tun is 160 Maasses. The Ohm contains 155,68 Litres, or 41,129 English Gallons.

The Cologne Foot measures 0,275 Metres, or 10,83 English Inches. Hence 100 Feet of Cologne = 90,27 English Feet. The long Ell contains 0,694 Metres, or 27,347 English Inches; the short Ell measures 0,574 Metres, or 22,625 English Inches.

Cologne exchanges with, and gives (more or less) to— Exchanges.

Amsterdam, ...	214 Francs, ...	for 100 Rixdollars.
Augsburg and Nuremberg,	256 Francs, ...	for 100 Rixdollars current.
Brussels and all Brabant,	99 Francs, ...	for 100 Francs.
Francfort and Vienna, ...	215 Francs, ...	for 100 Rixdollars current.
France, ...	99 Francs, ...	for 100 Francs.
Hamburgh, ...	190 Francs, ...	for 100 Rixdollars banco.
London, ...	23 Francs, 80 Cents,	for 1 Pound Sterling.

* THE COLOGNE MARK was, by an edict of the Emperor Charles 5th, in 1524, declared the standard weight for the precious metals throughout Germany, and copies were then deposited in the principal cities of the Empire; but in 1767 they were found by *M. Tillet* (Encyclopédie des Sciences, Supplément, Tome 4.) to have varied in several places from their original uniformity; and even the weight of the archetype kept at Cologne is differently stated by the most accredited authors on the subject, who vary in their reports of its contents from 3606 to 3612 English Grains.

According to the experiments lately made at the *London Mint* on the Cologne Mark transmitted to *Lord Castlereagh* by *Joseph Charles Mellish*, Esq. his Majesty's Consul General at Hamburgh, it was found to weigh 3608 English Grains; which perfectly agrees with the computations of *Kruse.*

It should be observed that the Cologne Mark, which is intended to be the basis of the new Prussian System, is 1 Grain heavier than the Mark used at Hamburgh. Other variations in its weight will be noticed in their proper places.

Usance and Days of Grace. The usance is 14 days sight. Six days grace are allowed, and if the sixth should fall on a Sunday, or holiday, the bill must be either paid or protested on the first day of business following.

CONSTANTINOPLE *(in Turkey)*.

Monies of Account. Accounts are kept in Piastres of 40 Paras, each Para being divided into 3 Aspers. These are real coins, but the Piastre is also an imaginary money, and is sometimes divided into 80, and also into 100 parts, called Aspers or Minas.

The Piastre is mostly called Grouch by the Turks, and Dollar by the English.

A Jux or Juck, is a sum of 100,000 real Aspers; and a Chise or Purse is 500 Piastres.

Gold Coins. The Gold coins of Turkey are the Sequin Funducli, with Halves and Quarters; the Double Sequin, or Yermeebeshlik, the Misseir, and the Rubieh. There are other Sequins besides the above, which bear different names, and their values also vary according to the periods of their coinage.

Silver Coins. The principal Silver coin is the Piastre, which has varied in value from 2s. down to 9d. sterling, its present worth. There are also the Beslik and the piece of 10 Paras, for the value of which, as well as of the gold coins of Turkey, see *Tables of Coins*, Vol. II.

Fineness of Gold and Silver. The fineness of gold is expressed by dividing the weight into 24 Carats, and each Carat into 4 Grains; and the fineness of silver by dividing it into 100 Carats, and each Carat into 4 Grains.

Weights. The Chequee or Pound, with which gold, silver, diamonds, and precious stones are weighed, is divided into 100 Drams; and the Dram into 16 Killos, or 64 Grains. Heavy goods are weighed by the Cantaro or Quintal of 100 Rottoli.

The Cantaro is also divided into 44 Okes, 176 Chequees, or 17600 Drams.

The Kintal of cotton yarn is 45 Okes. Silks from Persia are weighed by the Batman of 6 Okes; and silks from Brussa, by the Taffee of 610 Drams.

The Chequee of opium is 250 Drams, and of goat's wool 800 Drams.

The weight of the Chequee may be reckoned at 4957 English Grains, or 321,173 Grammes; and hence the Oke weighs 2lb. 13 oz. 5 dr. avoirdupois. The Turkish Dram may therefore be taken at 49½ Grains troy; which answer to 64 Turkish Grains.* Weights.

Corn is measured by the Killow, which contains 0,941 of an English Bushel, or 33,148 Litres. 8½ Killows make an English Quarter. The Fortin is composed of 4 Killows. The Killow of rice is reckoned to weigh 10 Okes. Dry Measures.

Oil and other liquids are sold by the Almud or Meter; which renders 1 Gallon 3 Pints, English measure, or 5,227 Litres. The Almud of oil should weigh 8 Okes or 22⅘lb. avoirdupois. Liquid Measures.

The Pic or Pike is of two sorts: the longest, called Halebi or Archim, with which silks and woollens are measured, is 27,9 English Inches, or 0,7083 of a Metre; the other, called Endassè, with which cotton goods and carpets are measured, is 27,06 English Inches, or 0,687 of a Metre: but, in the general course of European trade, the Pike is reckoned at ¾ of an English Yard. Long Measure.

For the exchanges of Constantinople, see Vol. II. page 40. Exchanges.

Bills between Constantinople and the principal trading places of Europe are commonly drawn at 31 days sight; but from one place in Turkey on another, at 11 days sight. Some European merchants pay their bills on the very day on which they become due; and others take as many days grace as are allowed in their own countries respectively. Usance, &c.

Bills are sometimes dated in the Turkish way; for which, see Note, Vol. II. page 210.

* There is much uncertainty in the weights and measures of Turkey; and the standards lately transmitted from that country to London for the present Work, rather increase the perplexity than diminish it. Even duplicates differ from each other, and their subdivisions are likewise out of due proportion.

The Turkish Chequee is stated by *Kruse* as answering to 4923 English Grains; *Tillet* reckons it 4933; *Bonneville*, 4942; and from an average of the late experiments at the *London Mint*, it is 4957, as above.

COPENHAGEN *(in Denmark).*

The Monetary System of Denmark has of late years undergone an entire alteration, and in order to understand the new system, the old should be first explained; it is therefore continued here as it stood in the former edition.

OLD SYSTEM OF MONIES.

OLD SYSTEM. Monies of Account.

Accounts are kept in Rixdollars of 6 Marks, or 96 Skillings.

These Marks and Skillings are of half the value of the same denominations at Hamburgh. Thus 2 Marks Danish are worth 1 Mark Lubs.

This is the general mode of keeping accounts throughout Denmark, except at Elsineur and in the Duchies of Holstein and Sleswig, where the Dollar is divided into 3 Marks and 48 Skillings.

The following are the proportions between the principal monies of Denmark: the Rixdollar equals $1\frac{1}{2}$ Sletdaler, 4 Orts, 6 Marks, 96 Skillings, 192 Fyrkes, 288 Witten, or 1152 Pfenings Danish, and half those denominations in Hamburgh money.

Different Sorts of Money.

The monies are distinguished into five sorts, viz.

1. Specie, in which the bank of Altona keeps its accounts, and in which the effective Rixdollar is reckoned at 6 Marks Danish.

2. Sundish specie, in which the tolls paid to the King of Denmark by all ships passing the Sound are reckoned: this is about $2\frac{5}{8}$ per cent. worse than specie.

3. Crown money, in which the tolls at the Sound are also sometimes reckoned, and which is $15\frac{36}{51}$ per cent. lower than specie.

4. Danish currency, in which the books of merchants and tradesmen are kept: this by the King's edict is $6\frac{1}{4}$ per cent. worse than crown money, that is, $19\frac{17}{32}$ per cent. worse than Sundish specie, and $22\frac{11}{12}$ per cent. worse than specie.

5. Holstein currency, in which accounts are generally kept in the Duchies of Holstein and Sleswig, and which is 25 per cent. below specie.

Coins.

The Gold coins of Denmark are, Ducats specie, which, as well as Dutch Ducats, are worth 14 Marks 12 Skillings Danish currency, more or less; current Ducats, coined since 1757, at 12 Marks Danish currency; Christian d'ors, coined in Holstein since 1775, which are worth about 13 Marks Lubs, or 26 Marks Danish currency.

The Silver coins are, specie Rixdollars, which pass for 7 Marks 6 Skillings

Old System of Coins.

Danish currency, and are commonly reckoned at 6 Marks 12 Skillings crown money, at the toll on the Sound; double, single, and half Crowns, at 8, 4, and 2 Marks crown money, or 8 Marks 8 Skillings, 4 Marks 4 Skillings, and 2 Marks 2 Skillings current; double and single Pieces called Ebrœers or *Justus Judex*, at 28 and 14 Skillings; Ryksorts at 24 Skillings; and Pieces of 15, 10, 8, 4, and 2 Skillings currency.

The Copper coins are, Skillings Danish, Fyrkes or Half Skillings, and Dreylings or Quarter Skillings.

Besides the above, there is the new Holstein currency, coined since the year 1788, consisting of specie Rixdollars, at 48 Shillings specie, or 60 Shillings Holstein currency; and Pieces of 32, 16, 8, 4, and 2 Shillings specie, or 40, 20, 10, 5, and $2\frac{1}{2}$ Shillings Holstein currency. In this money, the Cologne Mark of fine silver is coined into $9\frac{1}{4}$ Rixdollars specie, or $11\frac{9}{16}$ Rixdollars currency.

Rate of Coinage.

The Ducats specie, coined by the King of Denmark as Duke of Holstein, should be of the same weight and fineness as those of the Empire; so that 67 of them are to weigh a Cologne Mark, $23\frac{2}{3}$ Carats fine. $85\frac{3}{8}$ Ducats currency must contain a Cologne Mark of fine gold; and they are little more than 21 Carats fine.

From a Cologne Mark of fine silver, $62\frac{1}{2}$ Marks in Crowns, or 68 Marks in silver currency, should be coined; and, by a Royal Edict of 1776, $9\frac{1}{4}$ Rixdollars specie are to contain a Cologne Mark of fine silver, each piece weighing 537,69 Eschen, Cologne weight, or 447,9 English Grains, and being 14 Lods or $\frac{14}{16}$ fine; so that it contains 390 English Grains of fine silver, and is worth 4s. $6\frac{1}{2}$d. sterling.

NEW SYSTEM OF MONIES.

New System of Monies.

In 1813 a new Monetary System was established, according to which the Cologne Mark of fine silver is coined into $18\frac{1}{2}$ Pieces, called Rigsbank Dollars; so that 2 of these new coins equal 1 of the old Specie Dollars. The new coins are each divided into 8 Marks and 96 Skillings, as the old, but are only half their value.

Thus the new Rigsbank Dollar equals $\frac{5}{8}$ of the old Current Dollar; or 200 Rigsbank equal 125 Current, or 100 Specie Dollars. It contains 195 troy Grains of pure silver, and is therefore worth 2s. $3\frac{1}{4}$d. sterling nearly. See *Bank*, page 79.

Fineness of Gold and Silver.

The fineness of gold is expressed in Carats and Grains; the Mark containing 24 Carats, and the Carat 12 Grains. Danish standard gold is 18 Carats fine; that is, 3 parts of pure gold and 1 part of alloy.

Fineness of Gold and Silver.

The fineness of silver is expressed in Lods and Grains; the Mark being 16 Lods, and the Lod 18 Grains. The Copenhagen standard silver is 13 Lods 6 Grains fine; that is, 5 parts pure and 1 part alloy.

Gold and Silver Weight.

The Pound used for weighing gold and silver is composed of 2 Marks, 32 Lods, 128 Quintins, or 512 Orts; and answers to 7266 English Grains, or 470,778 Grammes. At the Royal Mint alone, the Cologne Pound of 2 Marks is used for the purpose of coining.

Commercial Weight.

The commercial Pound has the same divisions as the gold and silver weight, but is heavier in the proportion of 16 to 17; that is, 16lb. commercial weight equal 17lb. gold and silver weight. Hence the commercial Pound of Denmark equals 7720 English Grains; or 100 such Pounds contain 110,28lb. avoirdupois, or 50,01 Kilogrammes.

The Centner is 100lb.; the Vog or Waag, 36lb.; the Lispond, 16lb.; the Bismerpond, 12lb. The Shippond contains 20 Lisponds or 320lb.

Apothecaries' Weight

Apothecaries' weight is divided as at Hamburgh. Thus, the Pound contains 12 Ounces, 96 Drams, 152 Scruples, or 5760 Grains; and answers to 7452 German Asen, which equal 5527 English Grains, or 358,10 Grammes.

Dry Measures.

The principal measure used throughout Denmark for corn is the Barrel or Toende; which is divided into 8 Skieps or 144 Pots, and also into halves and quarters. The Barrel contains 7776 Danish cubic Inches, or 8488 English cubic Inches; and renders 3,9472 English Bushels, or 1,3908 Hectolitre. Thus the Skiep of corn equals 3,9472 Winchester Gallons, being very nearly half a Bushel.*

---

* These contents of the Toende and Skiep have been verified by experiments of gauging and water measure, on standards transmitted to London in 1820 by *Charles Fenwick, Esq.* His Majesty's Consul General at Elsineur. He transmitted at the same time an account of the cubic Inches of the Holstein Barrel, which answers to that of Copenhagen; with a statement of the contents of 19 different corn measures used in the Duchies of Holstein and Sleswig, which vary from each other between the extremes of 26 and 35 Winchester Gallons.

Several important corrections have been made by means of other standards, transmitted on the same occasion, particularly the Pound for the precious metals; which, by recent experiments at the *London Mint*, weighs 7266 English Grains; whereas *Kruse* reckons it 12 Grains lighter, and *Tillet* 10 Grains heavier.

A Last of corn, French salt, or lime, is 12 Toendes; and therefore contains 47,366 Bushels, or 16,689 Hectolitres. Dry Measures.

A Last of Spanish salt, or of coals, contains 18 Toendes. Norway salt is sold by weight; and the Toende must equal 250lb. Danish, or 275,71lb. avoirdupois.

The Barrel of beer, *Oel Toende*, contains 136 Pots. The Last of oil, butter, herrings, and other fat substances, is composed of 12 Toendes, beer measure, and should weigh 224lb. net.

A Barrel of Norway tar contains 120 Pots; and the Barrel of 32 Stubgens, in Altona and Itzehoa, must be of the same contents.

The measures used for wine and liquors are the following. The Hogshead contains 30 Viertels. The Viertel is divided into 4 Kans, 8 Pots, or 32 Pœgels; and contains 432 Danish cubic Inches, or 471 English cubic Inches. Thus the Viertel answers to 2,041 English Gallons, or 7,7268 Litres. Liquid Measures.

The principal vessels used in the retail trade of wine and spirits are, the Anker of 39 Pots, the half Anker, &c. The Anker contains 2106 Danish cubic Inches; and answers to 9,9513 English Gallons, or 37,666 Litres.

The following liquid measures are also used in some parts of Denmark. The Fuder is divided into 6 Ahms, 24 Ankers, 240 Stubgen, 465 Kannen, 930 Pots, or 3720 Poeles; and contains 237,09 English Gallons, or 897,45 Litres. The Stuckfass is $7\frac{1}{2}$ Ahms, or 30 Ankers; the Fass is 2 Pipes, 4 Oxhofts, 8 Tierces, or 24 Ankers.

The long measure is the Rhineland Foot; which equals 12,356 English Inches, or 0,31382 of a Metre. Long Measure.

The Danish Alen or Ell is composed of 2 Feet, and is divided into 4, 8, and 16 Parts. The Ruthe is 10 Feet.

A Danish Mile measures 2400 Ruthes, or 8244 English Yards: hence 1 Danish Mile = 4,684 English Miles, or 7,5383 Kilometres; and $14\frac{3}{4}$ Danish Miles answer nearly to 1 Degree of the Meridian, in a mean latitude.*

---

* A new standard measure, lately proposed by *Professor Schumacher*, is to be the length of a pendulum vibrating seconds of mean time in latitude 45°, viz. 39,1135 English Inches; the 38th part of which is to be the Danish Inch. This will make the new Foot very nearly equal to the present Rhineland Foot, viz. 12,34 English Inches.

Superficial Measure.

By a Tonne or Toende of hard corn is meant as much land as can be sown with 1 Toende of rye, 1 of barley, or 2 of oats. What is called a Toende of Saatland or arable land contains 560 Danish square Ruthes, or 220 English square Perches, and is one-fourth of the above. Thus the Toende of hard corn is equal to 5½ English Acres, or 22,25 French Ares.

A Danish square Foot contains about 153 English square Inches: thus 16 Danish square Feet = 17 English square Feet nearly.

The fundamental proportion between Danish weights and measures is, that 1 cubic Foot of fresh water is to equal the weight of 62 Pounds, and to contain 32 Pots; whence the Pot equals 54 cubic Inches.

Terms used in reckoning.

A great Thousand contains 10 great Hundreds, 60 Snese, or 1200 Pieces; a great Hundred is 120; a Shock is 60; a Snese or Steige, 20; a Zimmer, 40; a Decher, 10; a Tylt, 12; an Oll or Wall, 80.

Exchanges.

The transactions relating to exchanges are generally made in Danish currency (which includes bank notes); but most of the foreign exchanges are regulated by those of Hamburgh, bills drawn on Copenhagen being sometimes made payable in Hamburgh banco.

The exchanges of Copenhagen have been subject to great variation, in consequence of the depreciation of the paper currency. The metallic par may be computed at about 5⁴⁄₇ Rixdollars for the Pound sterling; but in paper it is more than double that number for the Pound sterling.

The following was the course of exchange on the 15th of February, 1821:

Copenhagen gives to—

Hamburgh ..	264	Rixdollars	for	100	Rixdollars banco.
London	11½	Rixdollars	for	£1	Sterling.
Amsterdam..	244	Rixdollars	for	100	Rixdollars.
France......	40	Skillings	for	1	Franc.
Sweden	60	Skillings	for	1	Rixdollar Swedish.

Usance and Days of Grace.

There is no established usance; but bills are made payable on a certain day. Eight days grace are allowed; and if bills be not paid within that time, they may be protested immediately, and the protest cannot be delayed beyond the tenth day, otherwise the holder of the bill is to bear all risks and expenses. The days of acceptance and protest, as also Sundays and holidays, are included in the ten days; but in Altona, bills may be protested on the eleventh day.

The Bank of Copenhagen has undergone many essential changes since its first establishment; and in order to understand its present state, it may be necessary to take a general view of those alterations. It was originally founded in 1736, as a Bank both of deposit and of circulation. In 1745 it was released from the obligation of discharging its notes in coin; and it continued still to make advances to the State, and to individuals, in paper, by which shares became greatly enhanced in their value. Bank.

This Bank had issued paper to the amount of 11 millions of Rixdollars, when the King returned their deposits to the shareholders, and became himself the sole proprietor. The paper issued was 20 times the amount of the capital, in consequence of which specie disappeared, and notes were issued as low as 1 Rixdollar.

To remedy this inconvenience, in 1791 all further emission of notes was forbidden, and a progressive liquidation of the paper was ordered. A new Bank, called the *Specie Bank*, was created, which was to be independent of the Government. The money deposited might be drawn out at pleasure, or transferred by assignation: and its issue of paper was limited to a certain extent. In 1804 the new notes lost 25 per cent. in exchange with the currency in which they were payable, and the depreciation continued to increase until 1812, when it became excessive.

In 1813 a new Bank was established under the direction of the King, and therefore entitled the *Royal Bank of Denmark.* Its chief object was to reduce the paper then in circulation, which was depreciated to $\frac{1}{6}$ of its nominal value; and in a new issue the Dollar was equivalent to $\frac{5}{8}$ of the old paper Dollar, which reduced the composition to $\frac{5}{48}$. In 1817 this Royal Bank was converted into a National Bank, by making a certain proportion of the property of the kingdom a guarantee for the liquidation of its paper.

For this purpose all property was to pay 6 per cent. to the Bank; and until the capital is paid, the interest charged for each deficiency is $6\frac{1}{2}$ per cent. per annum. Valuation of property in this case is regulated by the public taxes; and all the payments are to be made in silver, or in paper of the full value of silver, according to a certain rate of exchange, which is fixed quarterly; but as this Institution engages to pay off 7 millions of Rigsbank Dollars annually, persons paying in their quota at the Bank are allowed a drawback of $\frac{5}{6}$ of the taxes.

This Bank issues its own notes, which are gradually paid off; and it is intended, when the new paper is entirely reduced, to issue notes payable to bearer on demand. All revenues and great transactions are paid in this paper, according to the rate of exchange. This rate is called Rigsbank Silver value, which may

Bank. be sometimes more and sometimes less than the Rigsbank Dollar. All private contracts and current transactions are understood to be settled in such paper, unless real silver is stipulated for; likewise all payments to public actuaries and to the army; but custom-house duties are settled in real silver.

In January, 1821, the debts of the Bank were computed as follows: 1. Seven millions of Rigsbank Dollars of public stock, which it has undertaken to pay. 2. Seven millions of bonds for the redemption of the former paper money of Holstein, &c. 3. A debt of 7 millions, lately contracted for the diminution of the bank notes in circulation. 4. The bank notes in circulation, which are computed at 22 millions.

The capital is estimated at 33 millions of Rigsbank Dollars; and the Bank is besides computed to possess about 3 millions in silver and in buildings. The surplus of its annual revenue, the principal part of which arises from the interest of its security on real estates, is employed in the reduction of the bank notes in circulation. The contributors of 6 per cent. from estates, as well as voluntary contributors, are share-holders, and are equally entitled to interest, &c.

This Bank advances money on bills of exchange and other paper securities, and on gold and silver bullion.

CORFU, *see Zante.*

CORSICA *(in the Mediterranean).*

The French system of monies, weights, and measures, has been introduced into this Island, but not fully established. The following is that part of the Old System which is still partially retained.

Old Weights & Measures. The old Pound, commercial weight, is divided into 16 Ounces; and 100lb. of this weight are equal to 49,019 Kilogrammes, or 108,137lb. avoirdupois.

The Quintal Metrique of 100 Kilogrammes is equal to 204lb. of Corsica.

The measure for corn, called the Stajo, is divided into 2 Mazzini or 12 Bacini. The Stajo contains 1,5 Hectolitre, or 4,25 English Bushels.

The Barile, wine measure, is divided into 2 Some, 12 Zucche, 108 Pinte or Bocali, or 432 Quarti; and contains 140 Litres, or 36,98 English Gallons.*

* The above statements are chiefly deduced from the despatches and standards recently transmitted to London by *A. P. Palmedo, Esq.* the British Consul at Corsica. They differ essentially from other accounts on the subject; but they are confined to the Commune of Bastia, which, it appears, varies from certain other parts of the Island.

CORUNNA, *see Galicia.*

COURLAND, *see Libau.*

CRACOW, *see Poland.*

CREMONA *(in Italy).*

For the monies of account, coins, &c. see *Milan.* Monies.

The Pound of Cremona weighs 5060 English Grains; thus 100lb. of Cremona = 72,28lb. avoirdupois, or 32,76 Kilogrammes. Weights & Measures.

The Foot measures 0,397 of a Metre, or 15,62 English Inches. The Braccio is 0,6157 of a Metre, or 24,24 English Inches. 6 Feet make 1 Cavezzo.

The Pertica, land measure, contains 24 Tavole, or 96 square Cavezzi; and equals one-fifth of an English Acre, or 8,09 French Ares.

CYPRUS *(an Island in the Levant Sea).*

The monies and coins here are Turkish, for which see *Constantinople.* Monies.

The Occa contains 400 Drams, and weighs 126,79 Grammes, or 1957 English Grains. Weights.

The Rottolo is divided into 12 Ounces, or 750 Drams; and weighs 2,3767 Kilogrammes, or 5,244lb. avoirdupois. The Cantaro contains 100 Rottoli.

The weights at Famagosta are reckoned 4 per cent. heavier than the above.

The corn measure, which is called Medimno, answers to 0,7509 of a Hectolitre, or 2,1312 English Bushels. The measure called Moose weighs 44 Occas, or 123lb. avoirdupois: the Coffino contains half an English Bushel. Measures.

The common measure for wine is the Cass, which contains 4,73 Litres, or 1,25 English Gallon. Oil is sold by a weight of $2\frac{1}{2}$ Occas, or 1000 Drams.

The Pic or Ell measures 0,6715 of a Metre, or 26,45 English Inches.

DAMASCUS *(in Syria).*

Accounts are kept in Piastres of 80 Aspers, as at *Aleppo;* and the coins are the same as at *Constantinople.* Monies and Coins.

Weights & Measures. Silver is sold by the Ounce of 10 Pesi, or $6\frac{2}{3}$ Metecalli, weighing 19 dwt. 4 gr. English troy, or 29,804 Grammes.

The Cantaro weight contains 100 Rottoli; the Rottolo is divided into 600 Pesi, or 400 Metecalli; and weighs 3lb. 15 oz. avoirdupois. Thus the Cantaro equals 178,46 Kilogrammes, or 393,75lb. avoirdupois.

The Pic or Ell measures 0,582 of a Metre, or 22,93 English Inches.

DANTZIC, OR DANTZIG *(in Prussia)*.

Monies of Account. Accounts are kept in Guldens or Florins of 30 Groschen, each Grosche being divided into 3 Schillings, or 18 Pfenings, Dantzic currency.

The Rixdollar is worth 3 Guldens, 90 Groschen, 270 Schillings, or 1620 Pfenings.

Coins. The Gold coins are, Ducats, which are worth 12 Florins, more or less. The Silver coins are, Florins, at 30 Groschen; Tympfen, at 18 Groschen; Sechsers or Shustacks, at 6 Groschen; Dutgens, at 3 Groschen; and pieces of 2 Groschen. The Schilling is a Copper coin.

Prussian currency is $33\frac{1}{3}$ per cent. better than Dantzic currency; that is, 3 Rixdollars Prussian currency are worth 4 Rixdollars Dantzic currency.

Value of Monies. The Rixdollar of 90 Groschen, Dantzic currency, is equal to $260\frac{1}{2}$ German Asen, or 193 English Grains of fine silver; hence a Dantzic Gulden or Florin = 9d. sterling; or £1 sterling = 26 Florins 20 Groschen.

Fineness of Gold and Silver. The Mark of fine gold is divided into 24 Carats, and each Carat into 12 Grains; the Mark of fine silver into 16 Loths, each of 16 Pfenings.

Wrought silver is from 12 Loths 12 Pfenings to 13 Loths fine.

Gold and Silver Weight. The Mark, gold and silver weight, is divided into 8 Ounces, 16 Loths, 24 Schotts or Carats, 64 Quintlins, or 256 Pfenings; and weighs 233,811 Grammes, or 3608 English Grains.

Commercial Weight. The Berlin Pound used here for commercial purposes, is divided into 16 Ounces, 32 Loths, 48 Schotts, 128 Quintlins, or 512 Pfenings; and contains 7231 English Grains. Hence 100lb. of Dantzic = 103,3lb. avoirdupois, or 46,85 Kilogrammes.

The Last of corn is divided into 3¾ Malters, 60 Scheffels, 240 Viertels, or 960 Metzen; and weighs 4860lb. Dantzic weight in rye. The Malter contains 16 Scheffels, 64 Viertels, or 256 Metzen. The Sack Last, which bakers use, is divided into 5 Malters. The Scheffel answers to 0,547 of a Hectolitre, or 1,552 English Bushel. Hence the Last of 60 Scheffels renders 11 Quarters 3 Bushels English. Measures of Capacity.

The Ohm of wine is divided into 2 Eimers, 4 Ankers, or 128 Quarts; and contains 150 Litres, or 39,6 English Gallons. The Hogshead is reckoned at 1½ Ohm, and the Pipe at 2 Ohms.

The Foot of Dantzic is 12 Inches, the Inch being divided into 8 Parts, or 12 Lines. This Foot measures 0,2869 of a Metre, or 11,3 English Inches. Hence 100 Feet of Dantzic = 94,16 English Feet. Long Measures.

The Ell is 2 Feet Dantzic measure. The Arn, with which linens are measured, is half an English Ell; but there is an allowance of 1 per cent. on the number of Arns, or of 2 per cent. on that of English Ells.

The Clafter or Fathom is 6 Feet; the Ruthe or Perch 15 Feet; the Seil is 10 Ruthes, or 150 Feet, Dantzic measure.

A Prussian Mile is 1800 Ruthes, or 27000 Feet Dantzic measure; and equals 7,749 Kilometres, or 4,815 English Miles. 14⅓ Prussian Miles are reckoned to a Degree of the meridian.

The square Ruthe answers to 199½ English square Feet; the Morgen or Acre of land contains 300 square Ruthes, which equal 6650 English square Yards; that is, 1 Acre 1 Rood 20 Perches, English measure, or 55,64 French Ares. The Hube of land is 30 Morgens; and the Polish Hacken, 20 Morgens. Land Measure.

A Last of herrings, Luneburgh salt, honey, pitch, tar, ashes, &c. contains 12 Tonnes or Barrels. Lastage, &c.

A Last of French, Scotch, or Spanish salt, when in a heap all together, contains 18 Tonnes; but when in separate Barrels, only 16.

A Tonne of herrings contains 13 Wahls, each of 80 herrings.

A Last of pipe staves is 4 Schocks, or 240; a Last of timber, 80 cubic Feet. A Load of deck deals is 50 Feet.

The number of loads is found by multiplying the length in Feet by the thickness in Inches, and this by the number of deals; and then dividing the product by 12 and by 50.

Lastage,&c. Of things reckoned by number, a Schock is 60 Pieces; a Zimmer, 40; a Mandel, 15; a Dutze or Dozen, 12; a Decher, 10; a Ring, 4 Schocks; a small Hundred, 2 Schocks, or 120 Pieces; a great Hundred, 12 Rings, or 2880 Pieces.

Goods how Sold. Spices, indigo, saffron, coffee, tobacco, &c. are sold by the Pound.

Sugar, pepper, raisins and figs, oil, lemon-peels, &c. by the Stone of 24lb.

Lead, tin, brimstone, iron ware, logwood, &c. by the Centner of 120lb.

Brandy by the 52 Viertels.

Rapeseed and linseed oil by the Ahm.

Stockfish, potashes, hops, and Swedish iron, by the Shippond.*

Fairs. There are two great fairs at Dantzic, one beginning on the 5th of August, and the other on the 24th of December: the former, which is the most considerable, is called the Fair of St. Dominic, and lasts three weeks; one week of which time is chiefly appropriated to exchange business with foreigners.

For the exchanges of Dantzic, see Vol. II. page 47.

Usance and Days of Grace. The usance is 14 days after acceptance.

The days of grace are 10; and when the tenth day falls on a Sunday or holiday, the bill must be paid on the preceding day. But bills at sight, or such as are presented after the days of grace are elapsed, must be either paid or protested within 24 hours after being presented, which may be done even on a Sunday. Bills at 14 days sight have 3 days grace allowed.

Bills drawn in Dantzic cannot be negotiated there a second time, but must be remitted by the first Holder to the place on which they are drawn.

DEMERARA, *see West Indies.*

DENMARK, *see Copenhagen.*

* The above statements are chiefly deduced from the despatches and standards transmitted to London, in 1818, by *Alexander Gibson, Esq.* the British Consul at Dantzic. He also sent at the same time an account of the new system of weights and measures decreed in 1816 for the Prussian dominions; for which see *Prussia.*

It should be observed that the commercial Pound here, though now that of Berlin, was formerly about 6 per cent. lighter, answering to 6791 English Grains, according to *Kruse, Ricard,* and other authorities. By this computation, 100lb. of Dantzic answer to 97lb. avoirdupois.

DRESDEN, *see Leipsic.*

DUBLIN, *see Ireland.*

DUNKIRK *(in French Flanders).*

Accounts were formerly kept here in three different ways, viz.— Monies and Coins.

1.—In Livres, Sous, and Deniers, as in France.

2.—In Florins, Patards, and Pennings, as at Antwerp ; and

3.—In Pounds, Shillings, and Pence Flemish, in certain exchange computations.

But accounts are now kept chiefly according to the new French system of Francs and Centimes ; and the coins of France are also used here.

The following are the proportions of the old monies of Dunkirk.—

£1 Flemish = 6 Florins = $7\frac{1}{2}$ Livres Tournois = 20 Shillings = 120 Patards = 150 Sous = 240 Pence or Gros = 1800 Deniers = 1920 Pennings.

Although the metrical system of France has been introduced here, with its different modifications, yet certain old weights and measures are retained; and, therefore, some description of them may be useful. Weights & Measures.

The old Pound of Dunkirk is equal to 14 Ounces Poids de Marc ; and hence 100lb. of Dunkirk = 42,8039 Kilogrammes, or 94,44lb. avoirdupois.

The old corn measure is the Raziere, of which there are two sorts ; the sea and the land Raziere ; 8 of the former equal 9 of the latter. The sea Raziere is reckoned at $1\frac{1}{2}$ Hectolitre, or $4\frac{1}{4}$ Winchester Bushels very nearly ; and the land Raziere in proportion.

In the shipment of corn, the Hectolitre is generally used ; 300 of which are reckoned by dealers to render 105 English Quarters, although the correct proportion is nearly $106\frac{1}{2}$.

Wine and brandy are sold in Pots or Lots ; the Lot is divided into 4 Pints, or 16 Potées, and contains 2,302 Litres, or 2,433 English Quarts. Oil is likewise sold by the Pot, each Pot weighing a little more than $4\frac{1}{2}$lb. avoirdupois.

The Dunkirk Ell is 0,6762 of a Metre, or 26,625 English Inches.

The exchanges here are those of Paris, except with Holland and Flanders, where Dunkirk gives 180 Florins, more or less, for 100 Florins Dutch or Flemish money. Exchanges.

EAST INDIES.

General View.

This important article comprehends India on both sides of the Ganges, with the principal Islands in the Indian Ocean.

The monies, weights, and measures of these extensive regions are but partially known, and can only be described, with any degree of accuracy, where Europeans have established settlements, particularly the English, Dutch, Portuguese, French, and Spaniards.

Before these colonies were established, particularly while the Moguls' power prevailed in Hindostan, the monetary system was very simple. There was current throughout those dominions one principal coin of silver, denominated the *Sicca Rupee.* It was of a certain weight called the *Sicca;* which served also as a standard for weighing other articles.

There were, however, gold coins minted, but their price was not fixed, silver being the only standard of value. The principal piece of gold was the *Mohur:* it was of the same weight as the Sicca Rupee, and both are supposed to have been originally coined without any alloy.

These denominations of money are still current in India, but they differ from each other, and all have departed from the original purity. The East India Company, however, have kept as near to it as the necessary firmness of coin seems to require.

The monies of some of the Native Princes are still of a high degree of fineness, but they are subject to frequent alterations; and hence the necessity of *Shroffs,* who are a kind of Money-Brokers and Assayers, appointed to set a value upon the different coins that may require examination.

The principal money of account in India is the *Current Rupee.* It is an imaginary money, to which real coins are generally reduced before they are entered into books of accounts. This reduction is performed by allowing a certain per-centage, called the *Batta,* which varies according to circumstances.

Such is the general system of money in Hindostan, but there are several exceptions; and weights and measures are still more various.*

* The elements of Indian weights and measures bear some analogy to those of Europe. Thus the Barleycorn is the element both of weight and of long measure, as 2 of these grains weigh 1 Soorkh, and 8 of them placed sideways measure an Inch or Finger. In some parts of India, however, certain berries are considered as the elements of weight. See *Dr. Hutton's History of Indian Algebra, in his Tracts on Mathematical and Philosophical Subjects, Vol. II. page* 179.

The element of the measure of time is stated in the same work to be the time in which a word of two letters, as *Ta,* can be uttered 10 times, neither very quickly nor slowly; and this is called the *Pran.*

Its

This extensive article is arranged under two general heads. Arrangement.

The first comprehends the British possessions, commonly called the Three Presidencies, viz. *Bengal*, *Madras*, and *Bombay*.

Under the second general head will be found all the other Trading Places of India, on both sides of the Ganges, which are about 50 in number, arranged in alphabetical order.

BRITISH POSSESSIONS.

The monetary systems of the British possessions in India have undergone various alterations from time to time, as may be seen in the *Table of Coins*, Vol. II.; but the principal object in this place is to shew the Present State of their Monies and Mint Regulations, together with an account of those Weights and Measures that are chiefly used in Commerce.* Monies and Weights.

It should be observed that there are Mints established in each of the Presidencies, where Assay Masters are engaged that have been instructed by the King's Assay Master at the London Mint. These establishments are open to the public as well as to the Company. Thus any person carrying bullion thither may have it coined at a certain per centage, which sometimes varies according to the fineness of the metal. There are likewise subordinate Mints in certain of the provinces, under similar regulations, which will be noticed in their proper places.

CALCUTTA IN BENGAL.

Accounts are commonly kept here in Current Rupees, the Rupee being divided into 16 Annas, and each Anna into 12 Pice. The East India Company, however, keep their accounts in Sicca Rupees, similarly divided, which bear a *batta* of 16 per cent. against Current Rupees; and in their financial statements, Monies of Account.

Its multiples are, 6 Prans make 1 Pul; 60 Puls, 1 Ghurry; and 60 Ghurries, 1 Day. Hence, if the Day be reckoned at 24 Hours mean time, the *Ta* is $\frac{2}{5}$ of a Second; and it is remarkable that this is found to be the best Train of calculation for the beats of a Chronometer; that is, 5 beats in 2 Seconds. This coincidence, it is believed, has never been noticed before.

* The Weights and Measures of India are extremely curious in the minuteness of their subdivisions. Thus the *Ta* in some places is divided into a great number of *Twinklings of an Eye*, and the *Barleycorn* into small Seeds down to an *Atom of the Sunbeam*. For particulars see *Asiatic Researches*, vol. 5, by *H. T. Colebrooke, Esq. F. R. S.* See also the *Algebra of the Hindoos* by the same Author.

Monies of Account.

which are submitted to Parliament, each sum of Sicca Rupees is reduced to Current Rupees, by adding to it this *batta;* and the Current Rupee is then reckoned at 2 Shillings sterling.

Thus a Sicca Rupee of account is worth 2s. $3\frac{7}{8}$d. nearly; but it is commonly reckoned at 2s. 6d.

A Lac of Rupees is 100,000, and a Crore, 100 Lacs or 10 Millions of Rupees.

Accounts are sometimes kept in the inferior departments of business in Cowries, a species of small sea shells, which, as long as they remain unbroken, are used as money in small payments; and 2560 Cowries are generally reckoned for a Current Rupee: but they have intermediate divisions—thus 4 Cowries make 1 Gunda; 20 Gundas 1 Punn; 4 Punns 1 Anna; 4 Annas 1 Cahaun; and 4 Cahauns 1 Current Rupee; but the last proportion is variable.

Coins.

There are under the Presidency of Bengal three Mints, the principal of which is at Calcutta; and the subordinate are, one at Benares, and the other at Furruckabad.

At the Mint of Calcutta there are coined Gold Mohurs, and Silver Sicca Rupees. One of the former is by authority to pass for 16 of the latter.

The fineness of both metals is $\frac{11}{12}$, like English standard gold. The following is a statement of their weight, fineness, and sterling value:*

	Pure Grains.	Alloy Grains.	Gross Wt. Gr.	Sterling Value.
Gold Mohur,	187,651	17,059	204,710	33s. 2,52d.
Sicca Rupee,	175,923	15,993	191,916	2s. 0,56d.

It should be observed that the Sicca Rupee was formerly of the Sicca weight, viz. $179\frac{2}{3}$ English Grains, with $\frac{1}{48}$ part only of alloy, making the pure quantity as above; but in 1819 the alloy was increased to $\frac{1}{12}$, the same as the gold, by which much expense is generally spared in refining.

The charge for coining at the Calcutta Mint is 2 per cent. if the bullion be of the standard fineness; but where it differs, there is a proportional charge made for refining, which varies from $\frac{1}{4}$ to $2\frac{1}{2}$ per cent.

At the subordinate Mints silver only is coined, as follows:

	Pure Grains.	Alloy Grains.	Gross Wt. Gr.	Sterling Value.
Benares Rupee,	168,875	6,125	175	23,58d.
Furruckabad Rupee,	165,220	7,780	173	23,07d.

The charge for coining and refining is the same as for Rupees at Calcutta.

* Sterling value means, throughout this Work, £3 17s. $10\frac{1}{2}$d. per standard Ounce for gold, and 5s. 2d. per standard Ounce for silver.

Gold and silver are weighed by the Dhan or Grain of 4 Punkhos. 25 Grains make 1 Anna; and 32 Grains, 1 Massa. 10 Massa = 1 Sicca weight; which, as before stated, is 179$\frac{2}{3}$ Grains troy, or 6,57066 Drams avoirdupois. *Gold and Silver Weight.*

Thus, 12$\frac{1}{2}$ Massa, or 16 Annas, = 1 Tolah = 224,588 English Grains, or 14,551 French Grammes.

Heavy goods are weighed by the Maund of 40 Seers; and the Seer is divided into 16 Chattacks, or 80 Siccas; also into 4 Pice, or 64 Khanchaas. *Bengal Weights.*

The Maund of the English Factory at Bengal weighs 74lb. 10 oz. 10,666 dr. avoirdupois; the Seer is therefore 1lb. 13 oz. 13,866 dr., and the Chattack, 1 oz. 13,366 dr.

The Bengal Bazar Maund is 10 per cent. heavier than the Factory Maund; it weighs, therefore, 82lb. 2 oz. 2$\frac{2}{15}$ dr. avoirdupois; the Seer is, in this case, 2lb. 0 oz. 13$\frac{2}{3}$ dr., and the Chattack, 2 oz. 0$\frac{5}{6}$ dr.

Grain is sold by the Khahoon of 16 Soallee, or 320 Pallies, which is equal to 40 Maunds. The Pallie is divided into 4 Raiks, 16 Koonkes, or 80 Chattacks; and weighs 9$\frac{1}{12}$lb. avoirdupois. *Measures of Capacity.*

Liquids are sold by the Chattack of 5 Sicca weight: 4 Chattacks make 1 Pouah or Pice; 4 Pouah, 1 Seer; and 40 Seers, 1 Maund.

A Pussaree or Measure is 5 Seers; and 8 Measures equal 1 Maund of the Bazar weight.

3 Jows or Barleycorns lengthwise make 1 Finger; 4 Fingers, 1 Hand; 3 Hands, 1 Span; 2 Spans, 1 Arm or Cubit = 18 English Inches. 4 Cubits = 1 Fathom; and 1000 Fathoms, or 4000 Cubits, make 1 Coss or Bengal Mile, which equals 2000 English Yards, or 1 English Mile 1 Furlong 3 Poles 3$\frac{1}{2}$ Yards. *Long Measure.*

Cloth is measured by the Haut or Cubit, which is divided into 8 Gheria, 24 Angullas, or 72 Joabs; and equals 18 English Inches. The Guz is also used, which equals the English Yard.

Land is measured by the same Haut or Cubit: 5 of those Cubits long and 4 broad make 1 Chattack, which contains, therefore, 45 English square Feet; 16 Chattacks = 1 Cottah; and 20 Cottahs = 1 Biggah = 14400 square Feet. Thus, 30$\frac{1}{4}$ Biggahs = 1 English statute Acre. 40 Biggahs = 1 Madras Cawney. *Square Measure.*

For the exchanges of the Presidencies of India, see Vol. II. p. 103. *Exchanges.*

MADRAS OR FORT ST. GEORGE *(Coromandel Coast)*.

Old System of Monies and Coins.

There are different monetary systems in Madras, which may be distinguished under the heads of the old system and the new.

According to the old system, accounts are kept in Star Pagodas, Fanams, and Cash. 80 Cash = 1 Fanam, and 42 Fanams = 1 Pagoda. The East India Company and other European merchants keep their accounts at 12 Fanams the Rupee, and 42 Fanams or $3\frac{1}{2}$ Rupees the Star Pagoda; but the natives reckon the Rupee at 12 Fanams 60 Cash, and the Star Pagoda at 44 Fanams 50 Cash. The Bazar exchange fluctuates from 35 to 45 Fanams.

The Gold coins are, Star or Current Pagodas; and the Silver coins, Arcot Rupees. Double and Single Fanams, and Copper Pieces of 20 Cash, called Pice, are current here: also, Pieces of 10 and 5 Cash, called Doodee and half Doodee; and single Cash Pieces. These Copper coins are struck in England, and the value is marked upon each.

The Star Pagoda weighs 52,56 English Grains, and the gold is $19\frac{1}{5}$ Carats fine: it contains, therefore, 42,048 Grains of fine gold, and is worth 7s. $5\frac{1}{4}$d. sterling; but it is commonly valued at 8s.

The Arcot Rupee, which is also coined at the Fort St. George Mint, weighs 176,4 Grains, and contains 166,477 Grains of fine silver; its sterling value is, therefore, $23\frac{1}{4}$d. It is divided into 16 Annas or 192 Pice, like the other Rupees.

Many other coins circulate on the Coromandel coast, of which the following are the most generally current:—

The Old Pagoda, with 3 Swamy or Figures, coined at Madras and Negapatam, which is about $20\frac{2}{3}$ Carats fine, and which generally bears a Batta of 10 per cent. against the new coins of the same places.

The New Pagoda of Negapatam and Tutocoryn, which is $18\frac{1}{4}$ Carats fine, and is reckoned about 4 per cent. worse than the Star Pagoda.

The Porto Novo Pagoda, which is $17\frac{3}{4}$ Carats fine, and is about 20 per cent. worse than the Star Pagoda.

The Pondicherry Pagoda, which was originally equal in value to the Star Pagoda, but its standard has been lowered to 17 Carats, and even less. All these different Pagodas are nearly of the same weight.

In 1811 a coinage from Spanish Dollars took place, consisting of Double Rupees, Single Rupees, Halves and Quarters, and Pieces of 1, 2, 3, and 5

Fanams. 1 Rupee weighs 186,70 troy, and contains 166,477 Grains of pure silver, which is the same quantity as is contained in the Arcot Rupee. It is therefore worth 23,247d. sterling. Old System

A silver coinage of Half and Quarter Pagodas, of dollar silver fineness, also took place then. The silver Half Pagoda weighs 326,73 grs. troy, and is equal to $1\frac{3}{4}$ Arcot Rupee.

New System, 1818.

By a proclamation dated January 7th, 1818, the Silver Rupee is in future to constitute the standard coin of this Presidency. The public accounts will in consequence be converted from the Star Pagoda into the Madras Rupee, at the exchange of 350 Rupees for 100 Pagodas; and all engagements of the Government will also be transacted in the same Rupees.

The new coinage of silver will consist of Rupees weighing $7\frac{1}{2}$ dwts. and $\frac{11}{12}$ fine. Thus the Rupee contains 165 Grains of pure silver and 15 Grains of alloy, making together 180 Grains, with half Rupees, quarters, eighths, and sixteenths in proportion. The sixteenth is the Anna; and the eighth, the double Anna.

The new coinage of gold consists of Rupees, halves, and quarters, of the same weight and fineness as the silver Rupee. Thus the former contains 165 Grains of pure gold and 15 Grains of alloy.

The new gold Rupee, valued at the Mint price of gold in England, is worth £1 9s. 2,42d.; and the new silver Rupee, valued at the old Mint price of silver in England, is 1s. 11,04d.; but, as the 15th part of the gold Rupee, it is worth 1s. 11,36d. The coinage of the Pagoda has been discontinued.

The charge for coining at the Madras Mint is 3 per cent. for gold and 4 per cent. for silver, including the charge for refining.

Gold and Silver Weight.

Gold and silver are sometimes weighed by the Star Pagoda weight, which is 52,56 English Grains, as above stated, or 3,405 French Grammes.

Diamond Weight and Valuation.

Diamonds are mostly weighed in India by the Carat, as in England (see *London*, page 220); and rough or unwrought diamonds are generally valued according to the square of their Carat weight, at £2 sterling for each Carat. Thus a rough Diamond weighing 3 Carats is valued at £18; for $3 \times 3 \times 2 = 18$.

Wrought diamonds are supposed to have lost half their original weight, and therefore they are valued according to the square of double their actual

Diamond Weight. weight. Thus a wrought diamond weighing 3 Carats is worth £72; for $6 \times 6 \times 2 = 72$.*

Pearl Weight and Valuation. Pearls are valued by two kinds of weights, real and nominal. By the former they are weighed, and by the latter sold. The real weight used at Madras is the *Mangelin*, which is divided into 16 parts, and is equal to 6 English Grains. The nominal weight is the *Chow*, which is divided into 64 parts; and is deduced from the Mangelin, as follows:—

Rule.—*Square the number of Mangelins, and divide three-fourths of this product by the number of Pearls. The quotient is the number of Chows.*

Thus, to find the number of Chows, and the sterling value of 21 pearls weighing 16 Mangelins, at 12 Pagodas per Chow.—$16 \times 16 \times \frac{3}{4} = 192$, and this divided by $21 = 9$ Chows $9\frac{1}{7}$ Parts, which, at 96s. per Chow, = £43 17s. $8\frac{4}{7}$d.

Commercial Weights. Goods are weighed by the Candy of 20 Maunds; the Maund is divided into 8 Vis, 320 Pollams, or 3200 Pagodas: the Vis is divided into 5 Seers. The Candy of Madras is 500lb. avoirdupois. Hence the Pagoda weighs 2 oz. 3 grs.; and the other weights are in proportion.

These weights have been adopted by the English; but those used in the Jaghire (the territory round Madras belonging to the Company), as also in most other parts of the Coromandel coast, are called the Malabar weights, and are as follows:

The Gursay (called by the English Garce) contains 20 Baruays or Candies; the Baruay, 20 Manungus or Maunds; the Maund, 8 Visay or Vis, 320 Pollams, or 3200 Varahuns. The Varahun weighs $52\frac{3}{4}$ English Grains; therefore, the Visay is 3lb. 3 dr.; the Maund, 24lb. 2 oz.; the Baruay, $482\frac{1}{4}$lb.; and the Gursay, $9645\frac{1}{2}$lb. avoirdupois, or 4 Ton 6 Cwt. nearly.

---

* It may be observed that the diamond Carat, with its divisions, is the only weight that is considered uniform in all countries; there are, however, some small variations. The general estimate is that the diamond Carat weighs $3\frac{1}{5}$ gr. troy; but a nearer proportion seems to be $3\frac{17}{100}$, which has been recently ascertained by comparing a Carat weight, originally adjusted in India, with *De Grave's* standard in London. This verification has been made from weights furnished by *Messrs. J. & G. Sharp*, Diamond Brokers; to whom the Author is indebted for the examples of Chow valuation, both at Madras and Bombay.

The above rule for ascertaining the value of diamonds, though stated in works of authority, is not strictly adhered to, as their quality is too various to admit of uniformity of valuation. Besides, the method of squaring the weight of very large diamonds seems wholly impracticable; as there are some in the possession of certain Sovereigns which must be worth many millions of pounds sterling, if so computed; although they are said to have been purchased for less than the one-fiftieth part of such estimate.

The Garce, corn measure, contains 80 Parahs, or 400 Marcals; and the Marcal, 8 Puddies, or 64 Ollocks. The Marcal should measure 750 cubic Inches, and weigh 27 lb. 2 oz. 2 dr. avoirdupois of fresh spring water; hence, 43 Marcals = 15 English Bushels; and therefore the Garce = $17\frac{1}{2}$ English Quarters nearly. When grain is sold by weight, $9256\frac{1}{2}$lb. are reckoned for 1 Garce, being 18 Candies $12\frac{4}{5}$ Maunds. Measures of Capacity.

The Puddy, by which oil, milk, and some other liquids are sold, is the same as that used for grain: 77 such Puddies = 125 Quarts. The Candy of 20 Maunds = 64 English Gallons; but for wine and spirits, the English measures are used.

A Ground or Mauney, land measure, is 60 English Feet long and 40 broad; and contains, therefore, 2400 square Feet; and 24 Maunies make 1 Cawney or Acre; hence, 121 Cawnies = 160 English Acres; or 1 Cawney = 1 Acre 1 Rood $11\frac{1}{2}$ Poles. Land Measure.

The Covid for cloth is 18 Inches, but the English Yard is generally used.

In the Jaghire, the Ady or Malabar Foot is used, which is 10,46 English Inches; 24 Adies make a Culy; and 100 square Culies, a Canay or Cawney = 4864 English square Yards, or 1 Acre nearly. Such is the legal measure; but in common practice, the Culy is 26 Adies, or $22\frac{2}{3}$ English Feet; so that the customary Cawney contains 5709 English square Yards, or 1 Acre $28\frac{3}{4}$ Perches.

BOMBAY (*Malabar Coast*).

Accounts are kept here in Rupees; each Rupee being divided into 4 Quarters, and each Quarter into 100 Reas. Monies of Account.

The Rupee is also divided into 16 Annas, or 50 Pice. An Urdee is 2 Reas; a Doreea, 6 Reas; a Dooganey or Single Pice, 4 Reas; a Fuddea or Double Pice, 8 Reas. A Paunchea is 5 Rupees; and a Gold Mohur, 15 Rupees. Of these, the Annas and Reas only are imaginary monies.

The coins of Bombay are, the Mohur or Gold Rupee, the Silver Rupee, and their divisions; also the Double and Single Pice, the Urdee, and Doreea, which are Copper coins, with a mixture of tin or lead. Coins.

The old Bombay Rupee was the same as that formerly coined at Surat under the Mogul; it weighed 178,314 English Grains, and contained 1,24 per cent. of alloy. By an agreement of the English government with the Nabob of Surat, the Rupees coined by both were to circulate at an equal value; and they Old System

Coins, Old System.

mutually pledged themselves to keep up the coin to its exact standard of weight and fineness. The Nabob's Rupees, however, were soon after found to contain 10, 12, and even 15 per cent. of alloy: in consequence of which, most of the Bombay Rupees were melted down and re-coined at Surat; the coinage of silver in the Bombay mint was suspended for 20 years, and the Surat Rupees were the only ones seen in circulation. At length, in 1800, the Company ordered the Surat Rupee to be struck at Bombay; and since that period the Rupees of both places have been kept at an equal value, weighing 179 English Grains, and valued at 23d. as below.

In the Company's financial accounts, which are submitted to Parliament, the Bombay Rupee is reckoned at 2s. 3d.; and then it bears a Batta of 16 per cent. against Current Rupees.

In 1774, the Gold Mohur was ordered to be made of the same weight as the Silver Rupee, and to be equal in fineness to a Venetian Sequin: by this, the proportion of gold to silver in the Bombay coins was nearly as 15 to 1. When the Surat Rupees, however, were introduced into circulation, this proportion ceased; and gold, coined according to the regulation of 1774, was exchanged for only 13 times its weight of silver.

In order to remedy this, it was settled in 1800, that the Mohur should be of the same weight and fineness as the Silver Rupee, and that it should pass for 15 such Rupees.

New System.

The following is the New System:

	Pure Grains.	Alloy Gr.	Gross Wt. Gr.	Sterling Value.
Gold Rupee,	164,74	14,26	179	29s. 1,78d.
Silver Rupee,	164,74	14,26	179	1s. 11d.

The charge for coinage in the Bombay Mint is $2\frac{1}{2}$ per cent. for gold, and 3 per cent. for silver, including the charges for refining.

Gold and Silver Weights.

Gold and silver are weighed by the Tola of 40 Valls, 100 Gonze or Bombay Grains, or 600 Chows. 24 Tolas make 1 Seer; and 32 Tolas 13 Valls = 1lb. troy. The Tola is equal in weight to the Silver Rupee.

Pearl Weight and Valuation.

Pearls at Bombay, as at Madras, have a real and nominal weight; see page 92. The real weight is the Tank, which is divided into 24 Ruttee, the Ruttee into 4 Quarters, and the Quarter into 4 Annas; and equals 72 English troy Grains.

The nominal weight is the Chow, which is divided into 4 Quarters, the Quarter into 25 Docra, and the Docra into 16 Buddams. The nominal standard is 1 Tank to 330 Chows. The following is the general rule for reducing the real to the nominal weight:—

Pearl Weight and Valuation.

Rule.—*Multiply the square of the number of Tanks by 330, and divide by the number of Pearls; the quotient is the number of Bombay Chows.*

Suppose it were required to find the number of Chows in 45 pearls, weighing 5 Tanks: then $5 \times 5 \times 330 = 8250$; and this divided by $45 = 183$ Chow, 1 Quarter, 8 Docra, $5\frac{3}{9}$ Buddams.

Again, to find the sterling value of 10 pearls, weighing 1 Tank, 2 Ruttee, 1 Quarter; at 12 Rupees per Chow, the Rupee being valued at 2s.

	CHOW.	QRS.	DOCRA.	BUD.	
	330	0	0	0	Standard of 1 Tank.
	27	2	0	0	Ditto....of 2 Ruttee, $\frac{1}{12}$.
	3	1	18	12	Ditto....of 1 Quarter, $\frac{1}{8}$.
	360	3	18	12	Multiplied again by 1 Tank, 2 Ruttee, 1 Quarter.
Ruttee, $2 = \frac{1}{12}$	30	0	7	13	
Quarter, $1 = \frac{1}{8}$	3	3	0	15	
Pearls 10)	394	3	2	8	
Answer—Chows..	39	1	22	12	at 24s. = £47 7s. $5\frac{1}{2}$d.*

* The foregoing methods of valuing Oriental Pearls are the more fully exemplified, as it does not appear that they have been hitherto explained in any European publication; notwithstanding the curious and complicated nature of those operations.

It may be further useful here to compare the Chows of Bombay with those of Madras; for which purpose, algebraic expressions are adopted as the most convenient.

From the above *Rule* it appears, that if t represents the number of *Tanks*, and n that of *Pearls*, $\frac{330\,t^2}{n}$ = the Bombay Chow. And again, according to the Rule, page 92, if m represents the number of *Mangelins*, and n that of *Pearls*, then $\frac{3\,m^2}{4\,n}$ = the Madras Chow.

Now as 1 Tank equals 12 Mangelins, and as n may, for the sake of illustration, be considered a constant quantity, it will be found, by reducing those expressions to numbers, that 18 Madras Chows weigh 55 Chows of Bombay, a proportion of nearly 3 to 1; but the difference of price is generally about 4 to 1: for, it may be observed, that the Pearls sold at Madras, which are found in the Gulf of Manar, are more highly esteemed in Europe than those from the Persian Gulf, which are sold at Bombay.

Pearls in other countries are sometimes valued, like Diamonds, by the square of their Carat weight; but when several are sold together, they are valued directly as the square of their weight, and inversely as their number. Thus, 10 Pearls of a certain weight and quality, are double the value of 20 of the same weight and quality. To these general rules, however, there are exceptions.

Commercial Weight. The commercial weight is the Candy of 20 Maunds; the Maund is subdivided into 40 Seers; and the Seer into 30 Pice. The Candy is 560lb.; the Maund, 28lb.; and the Seer, $11\frac{1}{5}$ oz. avoirdupois.

Goods are likewise sold by the Surat Maund, and the Pucca or Bengal Maund; so that, in every contract, the particular Maund, or Candy, should be mentioned.

Measures. The Candy, dry measure, contains 8 Parahs; the Parah, 16 Adowlies, 64 Seers, or 128 Tiprees. This serves for wheat, and all grain but rice or batty, which is sold by the batty measure, as follows. The Morah contains 4 Candies, or 25 Parahs; the Parah, 20 Adowlies, 150 Seers, or 300 Tiprees.

A bag of rice weighs 6 Maunds, or 168lb. avoirdupois; and a Candy is equal to 25 Winchester Bushels nearly.

100 Baskets of salt make 1 Anna, or $2\frac{1}{2}$ Tons; and 16 Annas, 1 Rash.

The Haut or Covid, long measure, is 18 English Inches.

Piece goods, and some other articles, are sold by the Corge of 20 pieces.

☞ *In drawing up the foregoing account of the Monies, Weights, and Measures, of the British Possessions in India, much important information has been supplied by official authorities, for which the Writer is greatly indebted to* THOMAS REID, *Esq. F.R.S. Chairman of the East India Company; and it should be particularly acknowledged, that, by his direction, the principal documents relating to the Monetary Systems of the Presidencies have been supplied from the Records of the Company, by* JOSEPH THOMPSON, *Esq. of the East India House.*

SECOND GENERAL HEAD,

Comprehending numerous Trading Places in India, and in the Eastern Ocean, alphabetically arranged.

In preparing the following important article, several publications in different languages have been consulted and compared; among which, particular mention should be made of Mr. BROOKS*'s Work on* "Indian Weights and Measures," *and Mr.* MILBURN*'s* "Oriental Commerce." *Much new and authentic information has been likewise added from official sources, particularly from the Records of the East India Company, from Agency Houses in London, and from Public Offices of Government.*

ACHEEN *(in the Island of Sumatra)*.

Accounts are kept in Tales, Pardows, Mace, Copangs, and Cash. Monies and Coins.

A Tale is 4 Pardows, 16 Mace, or 64 Copangs.

The coins of the country are Mace and Cash. The Mace is a small gold coin weighing 9 Grains, and worth about 14d. sterling. The Cash are small pieces of tin or lead, 2500 of which usually pass for a Mace; but this number often varies.

In the gold dust trade, imaginary coins have been adopted, as Tales of gold, and Mace of gold; and 5 of these are reckoned equal to 4 pieces of the same denomination of the common coin. The gold dust is reckoned 9¼ Touch of Malabar, or 22⅕ Carats fine.

The largest weight is the Bahar of 200 Catties, which equals 423lb. 6 oz. 13 dr. avoirdupois. Weights & Measures.

The Catti is subdivided into 20 Buncalls, 100 Tales, 200 Pagodas, 1600 Mace, or 6400 Copangs; and weighs 30 oz. 17 dwts. 12 gr. troy. Hence the Buncall of 5 Tales, or 80 Mace, weighs 1 oz. 10 dwts. 21 gr. In gold the Buncall is 92 Touch, and is therefore worth £6 0s. 7¾d. sterling.

A Maund of 75lb. of rice contains 21 Bamboos. The Bamboo is 4 Cauls, when it has the king's chop on it; but is commonly reckoned at 5 Cauls.

The principal measure of capacity is the Coyang, which is divided into 10 Gunchas, 100 Nellies, or 800 Bamboos. The Bamboo is divided into 2 Quarters, or 4 Chopas; and weighs 3lb. 10 oz. 10 dr. avoirdupois.

Betel nut is measured by the Parah, swept off with a board, one of which, being counted, serves for a whole cargo.

A Loxa of betel nut is 10,000 nuts, which, when good, should weigh 168lb. avoirdupois.

The Corge of cloth is 20 Pieces.

AMBOYNA *(one of the Molucca Islands)*.

Accounts are kept in Rixdollars; which are divided into 8 Schillings, 12 Dubbeltjees, 48 Stivers, or 192 Doits. The Rixdollar may be valued at 3s. 4d. sterling, and its divisions in proportion. Monies and Coins.

Monies and Coins.

The following are the rates at which different coins pass current:

New Ducatoon, 80 Stivers;	Rixdollar, ... 48 Stivers;
Old Ducatoon, 78 ———	Rupee, ... 30 ———
Spanish Dollar, 64 ———	Star Pagoda, 99 ———
German Crown, 60 ———	Gold Mohur, 480 ———

Weights & Measures.

Gold and silver are weighed by the Catty of 20 Tales; each Tale being subdivided into 16 Mace, or 64 Copangs. This Catty weighs 12288 Dutch Asen, or 18 oz. 19 dwts. 14 gr. English troy weight.

Heavy goods are weighed by Dutch, Chinese, and English weights.

Diamonds are weighed by the Carat of 4 Grains; and 2500 such Carats = 1lb. Dutch troy: hence, 1 Carat = $3\frac{38}{1000}$ English Grains.

The Bahar of cloves, in the Isle of Amboyna, weighs 550lb. Dutch troy, or $596\frac{3}{4}$lb. avoirdupois. A Coyang of rice contains 25 Peculs, 2500 Catties, or 3000lb. Dutch troy = $3255\frac{1}{2}$lb. avoirdupois.

The Kanne, a Dutch liquid measure, of 91 English cubic Inches, or $3\frac{5}{33}$ Pints, and the Covid, a long measure, of $18\frac{2}{15}$ English Inches, are used in all the Molucca Islands.

ANJENGO (*on the Malabar Coast*).

Monies and Coins.

Accounts are kept here in Fanams, Pice, and Budgerooks.

A Fanam is 12 Pice, or 16 Vis; and a Pice, 4 Budgerooks. A silver Rupee is worth 7 old or Travancore Fanams, or 6 new or Gallon Fanams. All these are real coins.

An Anjengo Fanam is reckoned in the Company's accounts to be worth $\frac{4}{5}$ of a Calicut Fanam, or $\frac{1}{5}$ of a Surat Rupee: this gives its intrinsic value about $4\frac{3}{4}$d. sterling.

A full weight Spanish Dollar passes here for 13 Fanams; a Negapatam Pagoda for 20 Fanams; a Madras Pagoda for $19\frac{7}{8}$; a St. Thomas old Pagoda for 17; and a new St. Thomas for $14\frac{1}{2}$ Fanams.

Weights & Measures.

The Maund weight is 28lb. avoirdupois; and the Candy of 20 Maunds, or 560lb. avoirdupois, is 7 Maunds 20 Seers of the Bengal Factory weight.

The Covid is half an English Yard.

AURUNGABUNDAR *(on the hither Peninsula).*

Accounts are kept in Rupees of 50 Carivals, each Carival divided into 12 Pice. Cowries are occasionally circulated at 48 per Pice. The coins of Bombay and various other monies pass here. Monies and Coins.

Gold and silver are weighed by the Tola of 12 Massa; the Massa being divided into 6 Ruttees, and the Ruttee into 24 Moons. The Tola is equal in weight to a silver Rupee, or 179 English Grains nearly. Weights & Measures.

Heavy goods are weighed by the Maund of 40 Pucca Seers. The Seer is divided into 16 Annas, and the Anna into 4 Pice. This Maund weighs 74lb. 5 oz. 7 dr. avoirdupois.

The principal measure for grain is the Carval, which is divided into 60 Cossah, 240 Twiers, or 960 Puttoes. The Carval weighs 24 Cutcha Seers; the Carval of barley 19 Pucca Maunds; the Carval of paddy, 20 Pucca Maunds.

BANDA *(one of the Molucca Islands).*

Accounts are kept in Rixdollars, Schillings, and Stivers; the Rixdollar being divided into 8 Schillings, or 48 Stivers; and the Stiver into 16 Pennings. Spanish Dollars pass current at 100 per 125 Dollars. The Rixdollar may be valued at 3s. 4d. sterling. Monies and Weights.

The Catty weighs $6\frac{1}{10}$lb. avoirdupois; the Bahar is 100 Catties, or 610lb. avoirdupois. A Soekel of nutmeg blossoms is 28 Catties, or $170\frac{4}{5}$lb. avoirdupois. Nutmegs are sold by the Pound Dutch troy, which equals 7596 English troy Grains, or 1lb. 1 oz. $5\frac{3}{4}$ dr. avoirdupois.

BANJAR MASSIN *(in the Island of Borneo).*

Accounts are kept in Rixdollars of 48 Stivers, worth about 3s. 4d. sterling. Spanish Dollars are the chief currency of the Island, and a few Dutch coins from Batavia are used; and also Chinese Cash for small change. The following coins are likewise in circulation: Pillar Dollars, which, if full weight, pass for the same as Spanish Dollars; French Crowns; Ducatoons; and Rupees of various kinds. Monies and Coins.

Weights & Measures.

Gold and silver are weighed by the Tale of 16 Mace, which equals 827$\frac{2}{5}$ Dutch Asen, or 614 English Grains. The Mace is subdivided into 6 Ticas, or 18 Malaborongs.

The weights in common use for gross articles are the Pecul and Catty. The Pecul of pepper is 100 Catties, or 125lb. Dutch troy, which equal 135lb. 10 oz. avoirdupois. The Gantang is 16 Catties.

BANTAM *(in the Island of Java).*

Monies and Coins.

Accounts are kept decimally thus: 10 Peccoes = 1 Laxsan; 10 Laxsans = 1 Catty; 10 Catties = 1 Uta; 10 Utas = 1 Bahar. The Peccoe should contain 1000 Cash, but they are frequently deficient. The price varies from 25 to 35 per Spanish Dollar.

The coins current are Spanish Dollars, Ducatoons, Rupees, Schillings, Dubbeltjees, Doits, and Cash.

Weights & Measures.

The weight for gold, musk, &c. is the Tale, which is 1055 English Grains.

The Bahar of 3 Peculs, or 300 Catties, weighs 396lb. avoirdupois: but the Bahar of pepper is 200 Goelacks, and weighs 375lb. Dutch troy, or 407lb. avoirdupois. A Coyang of rice is 200 Gantams; and the Gantam, 8 Bamboos, or 32 Catties. The Coyang = 8000lb. Dutch troy, or 8681lb. avoirdupois.

The Pecul of 100 Catties at Cheribou weighs 125lb. Dutch troy weight, or 135lb. 10 oz. avoirdupois; and the Tiayang of rice is 2000 Catties, or 2640lb. avoirdupois.

For further particulars, see *Batavia.*

BATAVIA *(in the Island of Java).*

Monies and Coins.

Accounts are kept in Rixdollars, an imaginary money of 48 Stivers, valued at 5s. sterling.

The principal currency is composed of Rupees of 4 Schillings, 12 Dubbeltjees, 15 Cash, 30 Stivers, or 120 Doits.

This Rupee is valued at 3s. 1$\frac{1}{2}$d. sterling; the Cash at 2$\frac{1}{2}$d.; the Stiver at 1$\frac{1}{4}$d.; and the other monies in proportion. There are also Sooka of 2 Satalies, 6 Cash, or 12 Stivers. Certain Chinese denominations are likewise used, especially in the Bazaar. 10 Condorines make 1 Cash; 4 Cash, 1 Mace; and 10 Mace, 1 Tale.

The principal coins of the Island are Patacks and Cash. The Patack is worth 6 Mace, or 24 Cash. Monies and Coins.

There are, besides the above, pieces called Pities, composed of 4 parts of lead and 1 of tin, 50 of which make 1 Stiver.

Foreign coins pass here at a certain number of Stivers each, but these rates are subject to variation; and coins, both of gold and silver, are mostly valued according to their weight and fineness.

Gold and silver are weighed by the Dutch Mark troy; which is divided into 9 Reals, each weighing 422 English Grains. Weights & Measures.

The Dutch troy Pound of 2 Marks is generally used in foreign trade, but the Chinese denominations of weights are mostly adopted in common business. These are the Bahar, Pecul, Catty, and Tale. 16 Tale = 1 Catty; 100 Catties = 1 Pecul: 3 Peculs = 1 small Bahar; and $4\frac{1}{2}$ Peculs = 1 large Bahar. The Pecul weighs 125lb. Dutch troy, which answer to 135lb. 10 oz. English avoirdupois.

Rice and other kinds of grain are sold by the Coyang, which is reckoned at 3300lb. Dutch troy, or 3581lb. avoirdupois. Such are also sold in smaller quantities by the Timbang of 5 Peculs, or 10 Sacks. There is also the Kulack of $7\frac{1}{4}$ Catties, and the Last of 46 Measures.

The most general liquid measure, in all the Dutch settlements, is the Kanne, which is 91 English cubic Inches: thus 33 Kannes = 13 English Gallons.

The Ell is 27 English Inches; and the Foot, 12 Thumbs or Inches, Dutch or Rhineland measure; which equal $12\frac{9}{25}$ English Inches.

For measures of capacity, and other particulars, see *Amsterdam.*

BENCOOLEN *(in the Island of Sumatra).*

Accounts are kept here in Dollars of 4 Soocoos, or 32 Sattalies or Satellers. This Dollar is reckoned at 5s. sterling, and is sometimes called a Rial. Monies, Weights, & Measures.

The Bahar is a weight of 560lb. avoirdupois. The Tale is 26 dwts. 12 gr. troy.

The Coyang measure contains 800 Bamboos, each equal to 1 English wine Gallon. See *Acheen.*

BIRMAN EMPIRE, *see Rangoon.*

BORNEO, *see Banjar Massin.*

BOURBON, ISLE OF, *see Mauritius*.

see Mauritius

CACHAO (*in Tonquin*).

Monies and Coins.

Cash are the only coins here, and are of two sorts, large and small. 600 large, or 1000 small Cash are reckoned at 1 Maradoe. Accounts are kept in Tales, Mace, and Candareens; all of which are regulated by the price of the Maradoes and Copper Cash.

The price of silver coins is variable. All the Mexican and Pillar Dollars imported are run into bar silver; these bars or Ingots should weigh 10 Tales each.

Weights & Measures.

The Tale equals 1 oz. 4 dwts. $14\frac{3}{8}$ gr. English, being about 11 Grains more than the China Tale. The Pecul of 100 Catties = 132lb. avoirdupois.

All goods are weighed by the Chinese Dotchin. For long measure, the Chinese Covid and Punta are in common use.

CALICUT (*Malabar Coast*).

Monies and Coins.

The principal coins in circulation are Tars, Fanams, and Rupees; but accounts are kept in Rupees, Quarters, and Reas, as at Bombay.

16	Tars or Vis	=	1 Fanam.
5	Fanams	=	1 Rupee.
$3\frac{1}{2}$	Rupees..........	=	1 Star Pagoda.
$3\frac{1}{4}$	Rupees..........	=	1 Porto Novo Pagoda.
16	Rupees..........	=	1 Bombay Gold Mohur.

The Fanam is a small gold coin, with a considerable alloy of silver and copper; and the Tar is a small silver coin.

The Calicut Fanams have been found, by assays made at Bombay, to contain $52\frac{1}{2}$ parts of gold, 29 of silver, and $17\frac{1}{2}$ of copper. They are worth 6d. sterling.

Weights & Measures.

The Candy weight contains 20 Maunds; and the Maund, 100 Pools.

The Maund, used here by the English, equals 30lb. avoirdupois, and the Candy 600lb. But the common weights are those of Malabar, the Maund weighing 24lb. 2 oz.; and the Candy, $482\frac{1}{2}$lb. avoirdupois. The Calicut Miscal weighs 2 dwt. 21 gr. troy.

The Covid, long measure, is 18, and the Guz, $28\frac{1}{7}$ English Inches.

CAMBAY (*Malabar Coast*).

Gold Mohurs, Rupees, and Pice are the current coins; the Rupee containing 48 Pice. For small change a species of Almond, called *Baddam*, is used, in the same manner as Cowries at Bengal. These Almonds are imported from Persia, and the general rate is about 60 per Pice. Monies and Weights.

The Maund is 40 Seers, and the Seer 30 Pice. The Maund equals $37\frac{1}{3}$lb. avoirdupois: but in some cases it varies according to particular kinds of goods.

The long measures are the Cubit of 18 English Inches, and the Guz of 28 Inches; or, in the Bazaar, of $28\frac{1}{5}$ Inches.

CAMBODIA (*West of Cochin China*).

The only coin of the country is the Gall, a small piece of silver, with characters on one side only. It is worth about 4d. sterling. Spanish Dollars and China Cash are likewise current. The China Pecul is the common weight in use. Monies and Weights.

CANCAO (*on the East Side of the Gulf of Siam*).

The current coins are the Spanish Dollar and Chinese Cash. All goods are bought and sold by the China Pecul and Catty; and most bargains are made in Spanish Dollars.

CANANOR, *see Tellicherry*.

CARWAR (*Malabar Coast*).

Accounts are kept in Pagodas, Fanams, and Pice. Bargains with the country merchants are made in Fanams of 24 Budgerooks. Monies and Weights.

36 Fanams make a Pagoda, which is also divided into 48 Jettas or Settles; and the Settle is subdivided into 6 Pice, or 36 Budgerooks. A Carwar Pagoda is reckoned equal to $3\frac{3}{5}$ Surat Rupees, or 18 Anjengo Fanams; which gives its value at about 7s. sterling, and the Carwar Fanam = $2\frac{1}{3}$d. sterling.

The Darwar Pagoda, being coined in the province, is most esteemed by the natives, but the Ikeri Pagodas are worth more; they are of the same fineness, but differ in form and weight, $40\frac{1}{2}$ of the latter being equal to $42\frac{1}{2}$ Darwar Pagodas. Spanish Dollars pass current here.

The Seer of 25 Pice equals 8 oz. 19 dwts. troy. 42 Seers make 1 Maund, and 20 Maunds 1 Candy; which makes the Candy about 515lb. avoirdupois, though commonly reckoned at 520lb. The Covid, long measure, is half an English Yard.

CELEBES, *see Macassar*.

CEYLON *(an Island off the Coast of Coromandel)*.

Monies and Weights.

Accounts are kept here in Rixdollars of 48 Stivers Indian. This Rixdollar is an imaginary money, which is used in most of the Dutch settlements, or in such places as have belonged to the Dutch in India: it was formerly valued at 3s. 4d. sterling, but is now worth 1s. 9d. only.

Dutch Ducatoons pass for 80 Stivers; Dutch Shillings for $7\frac{1}{2}$ Stivers; Negapatam Pagodas for 90 Stivers; silver Rupees for 30 Stivers. The Stiver or Cash is a copper coin. All the coins of the Coromandel coast are current in Ceylon.

The weight established by the Dutch is the Bahar or Candy of 480lb. Dutch troy, or $520\frac{4}{5}$lb. avoirdupois.

A Bale of cinnamon is 94lb. Dutch troy, or 102lb. avoirdupois gross; the tare is 14lb. so that the nett weight is 80lb. Dutch troy, or $86\frac{4}{5}$lb. avoirdupois.

An Anna of rice in the husk is 240lb. Dutch troy, or $260\frac{2}{5}$lb. avoirdupois.

The Covid, long measure, is $18\frac{1}{2}$ English Inches.

For further particulars, see *Colombo*.*

CHINA, *see Page* 66.

COCHIN *(Malabar Coast)*.

Monies and Weights.

Accounts are kept here in Rupees of 16 Annas, which are reckoned equal to the Surat Rupees. Accounts are also kept in Fanams, 20 of which equal the Rupee. A Schilling is 4 Fanams.

Venetian Sequins are worth 72 Fanams; Dutch Ducatoons, 50; Spanish Dollars, 40; Dutch Rixdollars, 32; and Negapatam Pagodas, 64 Fanams.

Gold and silver are weighed by the Sicca weight, for which see *Bengal*, p. 88. 31 Fanams equal 1 Sicca; 72 Fanams equal 8 Pagodas, or 1 Dollar weight; and $9\frac{1}{3}$ Fanams equal 1 Sequin weight.

The Maund is here 27lb. $2\frac{4}{5}$ oz. avoirdupois; and the Candy equals 20 Maunds, or 543lb. 8 oz. avoirdupois.

---

* The above is the account of the monies, weights, and measures of Ceylon, as given before the year 1796, when the Island was in the possession of the Dutch. At that period it was captured by the English, and came under the controul of the East India Company; and in 1802 it became entirely a Royal Colony, and has since continued under the direction of the British Government. Hence several alterations have been introduced, which will be found in the article *Colombo*.

COLOMBO *(in the Island of Ceylon).*

Accounts are kept in Rixdollars, Fanams, and Pice; the Rixdollar or Silver Rupee being divided into 12 Fanams, and the Fanam into 4 Pice: the Pice is further divided into 4 English or 3 Dutch Chalies. The Rixdollar is worth 1s. 9d. sterling; and thus £1 = 11 Rixdollars 5$\frac{4}{7}$ Fanams; 1s. = 6 Fanams 3$\frac{4}{7}$ Pice; 1d. = 2$\frac{2}{7}$ Pice; and all other sums in proportion. Monies and Coins.

The Star Pagoda fluctuates from 59 to 61$\frac{1}{2}$ Fanams in bills drawn on Madras. The Sicca Rupee passes for 18 Fanams, either in specie or bills. The Bombay Rupee passes current for 17 Fanams in exchange for bills, and for 18 in the Bazaar. The Spanish Dollar varies from 37 to 39 Fanams, according to the demand. 350 Arcot Rupees equal 400 Ceylon Rupees or Rixdollars, or 100 Star Pagodas.

English weights are in use here. The Candy or Bahar contains 500lb. avoirdupois, or 461lb. Dutch troy weight. 1 complete Bag is 146lb. nett, or 168lb. gross weight. The Garce equals 9256$\frac{1}{2}$lb. or 82 cwt. 2 qrs. 16$\frac{1}{2}$lb. avoirdupois. Weights & Measures.

The dry measure is as follows:—

4 Cut Chundoos = 1 Cut Measure, or Seer; 4$\frac{1}{2}$ Seers = 1 Corney; 2$\frac{2}{3}$ Corneys = 1 Marcal; 2 Marcals = 1 Parrah; 8 Parrahs = 1 Ammonam; 9$\frac{1}{2}$ Ammonams, or 1800 Measures, = 1 Last.

Oil, milk, and ghee, are sold by Chundoos and Measures.

The Parrah measures 16,7 English Inches square, and 5,6 Inches deep; it therefore contains 6$\frac{3}{4}$ English wine Gallons, and its divisions and multiples in proportion. The Parrah is very generally estimated by weight, which varies according to the articles; thus this measure of salt weighs 44lb.; of coffee, pepper, and the like articles, 30lb.

In wine measure, 15 Drams make 1 Quart; 2 Quarts = 1 Canade; 2$\frac{1}{2}$ Canades = 1 Gallon; 5 Canades, or 2 Gallons, = 1 Welt; 75 Welts = 1 Leaguer. Arrack is bought at 80 Welts, and sold at 75 Welts to the Leaguer.

The long and land measures are the same as in England.

FAIFOE *(Coast of Cochin China).*

The only currency of the country is a sort of Cash, made of a white metallic compound called tutenague, 600 of which make a Quan, which is equivalent to Coins.

Coins and Weights. 2 Rupees, or 1 Spanish Dollar: this is divided into 10 Mace of 60 Cash each, the whole strung together, and divided by a knot at each Mace. The King refines and runs all his silver into bars of 10 Tales weight, which are valued at from 16 to 17 Quans each.

The weights are the same as in China, and all goods are weighed with the Dotchin. In the sale of sugars, however, 150 Catties are allowed to the Pecul, instead of 160.

GOA (*Malabar Coast*).

Monies and Coins. Accounts are kept here in Pardos, Tangas, Vintins, and Budgerooks; but there are good and bad Tangas, &c. A Pardo is worth 4 good Tangas, or 5 bad; 16 good Vintins, or 20 bad; 300 good Budgerooks, or 360 bad. The Pardo is also divided into 240 good, or 300 bad Reas.

The coins are—the St. Thomas, a gold piece of nearly the weight of a Ducat, which passes for 11 good Tangas, more or less. The silver coins are the Pardo Xeraphin of 5 good Tangas, and the common Pardo of 4 good Tangas. The copper and tin coins are good and bad Budgerooks.

Venetian Sequins are worth 16 good Tangas; Pagodas, 10 good Tangas; Spanish Dollars, 550 good Budgerooks, all more or less.

A good Tanga is worth about 7½d. sterling; a Pardo, 2s. 6d.; and a Xeraphin, 3s. 1½d. sterling nearly.

Weights & Measures. The Portugal weight is used here; namely, the Quintal of 4 Arrobas, or 128lb. of Lisbon, which equals 129½lb. avoirdupois nearly.

There is also an Indian weight, called the Maund, of 24 Rattles, which equals 24¾lb. avoirdupois; the Candy of 20 Maunds is therefore equal to 495lb. avoirdupois.

Corn and rice are sold by the Candy of 20 Maunds, which renders 14 English Bushels nearly.

The long measures are the Portugal Vara and Covado; the former is 1⅕ English Yard, and the latter, 26⅓ English Inches.

JAVA, *see Bantam and Batavia.*

JUNKCEYLON (*an Island off the Western Coast of Malay*).

Monies and Weights. All kinds of Indian coins pass current here, and likewise Spanish Dollars. There are also certain pieces of tin, called *Poot*, shaped like the under half of a cone, which are used as money, and serve also as weights. Thus 4 Poots make 1 Vis, 10 Vis = 1 Capin, 8 Capins = 1 Bahar, which is equal to 6½ Bengal Factory Maunds, or 485lb. 5 oz. 5⅓ dr. avoirdupois. Monies and Weights.

The China Pecul is also in use here.

MACASSAR *(in the Island of Celebes).*

Accounts are kept in Rixdollars and Stivers. Spanish Dollars are the common coin; but the undermentioned also pass current, at the following rates: Monies, &c.

Ducatoons, ... 13 Schillings,	Bombay Rupees, 5 Schillings,
English Crowns, 10 Ditto,	Madras Rupees, 4 Ditto.

The exchange is 4 Rixdollars for 3 Spanish Dollars. All bargains are made in the former, which is a nominal coin. There is also a kind of Mace, 7 of which go to a Dollar.

Gold and silver are weighed by the Tale of 16 Mace; which equals 827⅗ Dutch Asen, or 614 English Grains. Weights & Measures.

All merchandize is weighed by the Dotchin, and then reduced to other weights. The Pecul is 100 Catties, or 135lb. 10 oz. avoirdupois.

The Gantang among the natives is 7⅔lb. Dutch troy, or 8lb. 5 oz. avoirdupois; but the Gantang used by the Dutch Company is 11½lb. Dutch troy, or 12½lb. avoirdupois.

MAGINDANAO *(one of the Philippine Islands).*

The general currency here, as in Sooloo, is the Chinese Kangan, which is a piece of coarse cloth, thinly woven, 19 inches broad and 6 yards long. A bundle, of 25 pieces, called a Gandang, is valued at 10 Spanish Dollars. There are also used as currency, the Cowsong, a kind of nankeen, dyed black, and the Kompow, a strong white Chinese linen. Monies, Weights, &c.

China Cash are likewise in use; their price varying from 160 to 180 for a Kangan.

The Gantang weighs about 4lb.; 10 Gantangs make a Battell (a cylindrical measure of $13\frac{5}{10}$ Inches high, and the same in diameter); and 3 Battells are commonly sold for a Kangan. In speaking of the value of things here and at Sooloo, it is common to say, such a horse, &c. is worth so many slaves, the usual valuation being 1 slave for 30 Kangans.

MALACCA *(on the Malay Peninsula).*

Monies and Coins.

Accounts are kept in Rixdollars of 8 Schillings, or 48 Stivers; the Stiver is subdivided into 4 Doits.

The Rixdollar is an imaginary money, in which all contracts for goods are made; but the principal current coins are Rupees, Dutch Schillings, Dubbletjies, 2 Stiver Pieces, and Doits.

The Spanish Dollar is from 25 to 40 per cent. better than the Rixdollar of account; hence, at a medium, this Rixdollar is worth 3s. 4d. sterling. A Dutch Ducatoon passes for 13 Schillings; an English Crown for 10 Schillings; a Bombay or Surat Rupee for 5 Schillings; a Madras or Arcot Rupee for 4 Schillings, more or less. A stamped Japan Copang passes for 10 Rixdollars.

Weights & Measures.

Gold is weighed by the Catty of 20 Buncalls, or 320 Miams. The Catty = 29 oz. 17 dwt. 16 gr. English troy.

Heavy goods are weighed by the Pecul of 100 Catties, or 1600 Tales. The Pecul = 135lb. avoirdupois; and 3 Peculs make a Bahar. But, what is called, the China Pecul at Malacca weighs 125lb. avoirdupois.

The Gantang, rice measure, weighs 6lb. Dutch troy, or $6\frac{1}{2}$lb. avoirdupois nearly. The Last of rice contains 50 Maas, or 500 Gantangs, which = 3255lb. avoirdupois; and the Coyang, or 800 Gantangs = 5208lb. avoirdupois. But rice is also sold by the Coyang of 40 Peculs, or 5400lb. avoirdupois.

A Kip of tin contains 15 Bedoors, or 30 Tampangs; it weighs $37\frac{1}{2}$lb. Dutch troy, or 40lb. 11 oz. avoirdupois.

The Covid, long measure, is $18\frac{2}{15}$ English Inches.

MALDIVE ISLANDS *(off Cape Comorin).*

Monies, &c.

The money here, which is called Larin, is of silver wire, and worth about $\frac{1}{4}$ of a Rupee. All other coins pass current by weight. Weights are generally carried for the purpose; and Dollars, Rupees, &c. are frequently cut into pieces, in order to pay for any commodity.

MANGALORE *(Malabar Coast).*

Monies and Weights.

Merchants generally keep their accounts here in Sultanee Pagodas, Rupees, and Annas; the Pagoda being 4 Rupees, and the Rupee, 16 Annas: others divide the Pagoda into 10 Hunas, and the Huna into 16 parts, likewise called Annas. *Monies and Weights.*

The coins current will be found under the article *Seringapatam*.

The Seer or Sida should weigh 24 Bombay Rupees, each of the weight of 178 to 179 English Grains, that is, at a medium, 4284 Grains; but the Seer commonly used in the Bazar has been found by *Dr. Buchanan* to weigh 4297 Grains. The Seer is divided into halves, quarters, eighths, and sixteenths.

The Mana or Maund, by which goods are sold in the market, contains 46 Seers, or 28lb. $3\frac{3}{4}$ oz. avoirdupois: the Maund, by which merchants buy and sell, weighs 16 Rupees more, that is, 28lb. 10 oz. avoirdupois. The Baru or Candy is 20 Maunds.

The measure for corn, salt, pepper, &c. is the Seer, containing $73\frac{633}{1000}$ English cubic Inches. A Mudi or Moray is 38 Seers, or $1\frac{3}{10}$ English Bushel. A Seer of pepper is reckoned to weigh $51\frac{1}{2}$ Bombay Rupees, or 21 oz. avoirdupois.

MANILLA *(in Luconia, one of the Philippine Islands).*

Accounts are kept in Dollars or Pesos of 8 Reals, the Real being divided into 34 Maravedis. The course of exchange between Bengal and Manilla is generally from 38 to 45 Spanish Dollars per 100 current Rupees. *Monies and Coins.*

The small weight is stated by *Mr. Brooks* to be the Mexican Dollar, 16 of which, or 16 Ounces, make 1 Pound, Spanish weight. 8 of these Ounces = 1 Mark of silver; 9 Ounces = 1 Punto of gold or silver thread; 10 Ounces = 1 Tale of gold weight; 11 Ounces = 1 Tale of silk; 22 Ounces = 1 Catty. *Weights & Measures.*

It should be observed that the Spanish Pound weighs $16\frac{1}{4}$ oz. avoirdupois; and that 16 Dollars weigh only $15\frac{1}{4}$ oz. avoirdupois.

According to *Mr. Milburn*, all the Spanish weights are used here, and also the Pecul of China.

MASULIPATAM *(Coromandel Coast).*

Accounts are kept in Pagodas, Rupees, and Annas. The Pagoda is $3\frac{1}{2}$ silver Rupees, and the Rupee 16 Annas. *Monies and Weights.*

The coins are Gold Rupees, which weigh $171\frac{1}{3}$ English Grains; they are about $23\frac{3}{4}$ Carats fine, and are worth £1 10s. sterling; Pagodas, of nearly the value of the Star Pagoda of Madras; and Silver Rupees, $24\frac{1}{4}$ of which weigh a Seer, or

Monies and Weights. 4293 English Grains. The fineness of these Rupees is 11 oz. 12½ dwts. The value, therefore, is 23½d. sterling.

The Candy is 20 Maunds; the Maund, 8 Vis, 40 Seers, 600 Neves, or 900 Dabous. This Maund weighs 24½lb. avoirdupois nearly.

MAURITIUS OR ISLE OF FRANCE *(in the Indian Ocean).*

Monies and Coins. Accounts are kept here in two different ways, namely, in Dollars of 100 Cents, which is the mode generally adopted in public or government accounts; and in Dollars of 10 Livres or 200 Sols, which method is mostly used by merchants. These are called Colonial Livres, 2 of which equal 1 French Franc.

The principal French coin in common currency is the Sol Marqué, which is of copper, and worth 3 Colonial Sols. Hence 66⅔ Marqués equal 1 Dollar.

Thus 2 Sols = 1 Cent; 1 Marqué, 1½ Cent; and 1 Livre, 10 Cents.

Various coins circulate here, particularly those of India, at the following rates of exchange with regard to the Dollar:

2 Sicca Rupees	= 1 Dollar;	10 Ikeri Pagodas	= 17 Dollars;
220 Bombay or 220 Arcot	.. = 100 ——	1 Bombay Gold Mohur	= 7½ ——
		15 Double Fanams ..	= 1 ——
10 Star Pagodas	= 16 ——	4s. 8d. sterling	= 1 ——
10 Porto Novo Pagodas	= 13¼ ——	20 Cash	= 1 Marqué.

Tariff, &c. The following is the Tariff of the current money, and its value in Colonial money, as fixed by Government:

SILVER COINS.

Spanish Dollar .... = 10 Colonial Livres.
Half and Quarter Dollar in proportion.
Sicca Rupee .... = 5 Livres.
Half and Quarter in proportion.
Bombay and Arcot Rupee = 4 Livres 10 Sols.
Half Silver Pagoda .... = 8 Livres.
Quarter in proportion.
Double Fanam .... = 1 Livre 5 Sols.
Fanam .... = 12½ Sols.

The 10 Livre pieces, struck in the Colony under the French Government, the 5 Franc pieces of France, and the German Crown pieces, have the same value in exchange as the Spanish Dollar.

GOLD COINS. Tariff, &c.

Spanish Doubloon	=	160 Livres or 16 Dollars.
Portuguese Half Doubloon	=	80 Livres.
Ikeri Pagoda	=	17 Livres.
Porto Novo Pagoda......	=	13 Livres 5 Sols.
Star Pagoda............	=	16 Livres.
Bombay Gold Mohur....	=	75 Livres.
Bengal Gold Mohur	=	90 Livres.

In computing the sterling value of the above monies, it will be sufficiently correct for ordinary purposes to reckon the Livre at 5½d. sterling, and the Sol at 1 Farthing.

The chief currency of the Isle of France (1820) is Government paper, payable, to bearer on demand, in Spanish Dollars.

The foregoing Tariff is extracted from official documents, and all the coins therein-mentioned are sometimes current; but paper is the principal circulating medium. Even the effective Spanish Dollar (specie Dollar) is generally at an agio, being the most marketable kind of bullion in the East.

The weight used at the Mauritius has been generally the Poids de Marc of France, 100lb. of which are reckoned to equal 108lb. avoirdupois. Weights & Measures.

The measures of capacity are chiefly English; and also those of France according to the ancient system, for which see page 133.

The Isle of Bourbon had the same system of monies, &c. as the Isle of France while in possession of the English before the year 1814; and since that period the French system has been partially established.

MERGUI, *see Rangoon.*

MOLUCCA ISLANDS, *see Amboyna, Banda, Ternate, &c.*

MYSORE COUNTRY.

Accounts are kept in Canteria Pagodas, of 10 Fanams; each Fanam being divided into 16 Cash. Monies and Coins.

The following coins circulate: the Star Pagoda at 45 Fanams, the Bahadre Pagoda at 46 Fanams 29 Cash. The Canteria Pagoda is worth about 6s. 4d. sterling, and the Bahadre Pagoda 8s. 3d. nearly.

Weights & Measures.

The Morah is 40 Pucca Seers; the Batty is 60; and the Garce, 521 Pucca Seers. The Candy equals 560lb. avoirdupois. 9 Trinchinopoly Measures are 50lb.

For a more particular account of the measures, &c. of this extensive country, see *Seringapatam*.

NATAL *(in the Island of Sumatra).*

Monies, Weights, &c.

Rupees and Spanish Dollars are current here, and also single, double, and treble Fanams, coined at Madras. 24 Fanams or Tali are equal to a Spanish Dollar. In this part of the Island, where the traffic in gold is considerable, it is generally employed as currency instead of coin. Small scales are carried by the inhabitants, and purchases of gold are made as low as a Grain of paddy weight.

Various seeds are used as gold weights, particularly the scarlet pea, 24 of which make 1 Mace, and 16 Mace 1 Tale; and the scarlet bean, which is the Candareen of the Chinese, 100 of which make 1 Tale. The Tale differs in the Northern and Southern parts of the Island. At Natal it is 1 oz. 4 dwt. 9 gr. troy; but at Padang and Bencoolen it is 1 oz. 6 dwts. 12 grs. troy.

PALIMBANG *(in the Island of Sumatra).*

Monies and Coins.

Accounts are kept in Rixdollars of 48 Stivers, as in Java: the Spanish Dollar is worth $1\frac{1}{4}$ Rixdollar; and therefore this Rixdollar of account is worth 3s. 6d. sterling.

The currency of the country, and the only money allowed to be received at the King's Treasury, is the Spanish Dollar; but there is also in general circulation a species of small base coin, called Petis, having a square hole in the middle, like the Chinese Cash. They are strung in parcels of 500 each, 16 of which are equivalent to a Spanish Dollar. The exchange between Rixdollars and Spanish Dollars is 5 of the former for 4 of the latter.

Weights & Measures.

Gold and silver are weighed by the Catty of 10 Tales, or $22\frac{1}{2}$ Reals; the Catty weighs 19 oz. 15 dwt. 14 gr. English troy.

The commercial weight is the Baly, which is divided into 10 Gantangs or 60 Catties, and equals 81lb. 6 oz. avoirdupois. The Copang contains 80 Balies.

The Goelack of pepper is $1\frac{1}{4}$ Catty, or 27 Ounces avoirdupois; but the weight used by the Dutch East India Company for pepper is the Pecul, which answers to 133lb. avoirdupois. Weights & Measures.

PEGU *(on the farther Peninsula).*

The trade is here mostly carried on by barter: gold and silver are not coined in the country, but exchanged as merchandize. The Tical, a certain weight of silver, which is sometimes used as a money of account, is divided into 16 Toques or Touch. Monies, Weights, &c.

There is, however, a small coin, called Ganza, which is a mixture of copper, lead, and tin, and worth about $1\frac{1}{4}$d. sterling; but the price varies according to the demand and supply. Gold, silver, pearls, spices, and other valuable articles, are generally paid for in this money.

Gold and silver are weighed by the Tical, and their fineness is expressed by dividing the weight into 16 parts called Touch, answering to 100 Touch in China, or 10 Touch on the Malabar Coast. The Tical weighs $4\frac{1}{2}$ Pagodas, or $237\frac{1}{3}$ English Grains.

The commercial weights are the Vis of 100 Ticals or 1000 Moo, and the Candy of 150 Vis. From the above weight of the Tical, the Candy should weigh $508\frac{1}{2}$lb.: the English, however, reckon it at 6 Maunds 28 Seers of the Bengal Factory, or 500lb. avoirdupois.

Rice is sold by a measure called a Basket, containing 16 Vis, or 54lb. avoirdupois.

PHILIPPINE ISLANDS, *see Magindanao, and Manilla.*

PONDICHERRY *(Coromandel Coast).*

Accounts are kept here in Pagodas of 24 Fanams; and the Fanam is subdivided into 60 Cash. Monies and Coins.

The coins are Gold Pagodas, and Silver Rupees and Fanams, which have been mentioned under the article *Madras*; also Copper Cash, and Dudus, a Copper coin, 20 of which are reckoned to a Fanam.

Gold and silver are weighed by the Seer, Pagoda, Rupee, and Fanam. A Seer weighs $24\frac{3}{8}$ Rupees, $81\frac{1}{4}$ Pagodas, or $731\frac{1}{4}$ Fanams; a Rupee weight equals 30

Weights & Measures. Fanams, or 480 Nellos; a Pagoda weight, 9 Fanams, or 144 Nellos. Thus 3 Rupees are equal in weight to 10 Pagodas. The Seer = 4293 English Grains.

The commercial weight is the Candy of 20 Maunds, or 160 Vis. The Maund equals 25lb. 14 oz. $5\frac{1}{2}$ dr. avoirdupois.

Rice and all other sorts of grain are sold by the Garce of 600 Mercals. 100 Mercals = 18 English Bushels nearly. The Garce therefore equals $13\frac{1}{2}$ English Quarters.

PRINCE OF WALES's ISLAND *(off the Western Coast of Malay).*

Monies and Coins. Accounts are kept in Spanish Dollars, Copangs, and Pice; 10 Pice making 1 Copang, and 10 Copangs 1 Spanish Dollar.

The current Pice are coined in the Island; they are pieces of tin, 16 of which weigh the Catty, or $1\frac{1}{3}$lb. English. On the exchange of Dollars into Pice there is a loss of 2 per cent.; on Dollars without the King's head, 10 per cent.; and from 5 to 10 per cent. on all Dollars defaced.

Weights & Measures. Gold and silver are weighed by the Buncal, which is divided into 16 Miams, and is of the weight of 2 Spanish Dollars nearly, or 1 oz. 9 dwt. $10\frac{7}{12}$ gr. troy. 20 Buncals make 1 Catty, which equals 29 oz. 15 dwt. $11\frac{8}{12}$ gr. troy.

The heavy weights are the Bahar, Coyan, Pecul, Catty, and Tale. There are two Peculs, the large Pecul being 9lb. heavier than the common Pecul. There are also two Catties used in the Bazaar; the Malay Catty weighs 24 Dollars, and the Chinese Catty $22\frac{1}{2}$ Dollars, or $1\frac{1}{3}$lb. avoirdupois. 16 Tales make 1 Catty; 100 Catties, 1 Pecul; 40 Peculs, 1 Coyan. 3 large Peculs make the Bahar, which is equal to 428lb. avoirdupois. Hence the Coyan is 5323lb., and the common Pecul, $133\frac{1}{3}$lb. avoirdupois. A Bag of salt weighs 100lb.; a Bag of rice or dholl, 164lb. The two latter are generally sent from Bengal in Bags of 2 Maunds each; the Maund weighing 82lb. avoirdupois.

The Ganton, by which grain and liquids are sold, equals $1\frac{1}{4}$ English Gallon. 20 Gantons of rice make 1 Bag; 40 Bags or 800 Gantons, 1 Coyan or 5323lb. avoirdupois.

Cloth is sold by the Astah, of 18 English Inches.

Land is measured by the Orlong, which is divided into 20 Jumbas, and equals $1\frac{1}{3}$ English Acre.

RANGOON *(on the farther Peninsula).*

The Birmans, like the Chinese, keep their accounts decimally, and have no coin. Silver bullion, and lead, are the currency of the country. Monies, &c.

The most general piece of silver in circulation is the Tical, which weighs 10 dwt. 10 gr.; and is divided into 4 Maths, 8 Moos, or 16 Tubbees. The Vis is composed of 100 Ticals.

The quantity of alloy in the silver varies in different parts of the Empire. At Rangoon it is adulterated 25 per cent.

The weights are the Moo, Tual, Vis, and Candy; 100 Moos making 1 Tual; 100 Tuals, 1 Vis; and 150 Vis, 1 Candy. The Vis is considered equal to 3lb. 5 oz. 5 dr., and the Candy to 500lb. avoirdupois. Weights & Measures.

Rice is sold by a measure called Basket: the weight of which is 16 Vis.

The measures of length are the Paulgaut, or Inch; 18 of which compose the Taim, or Cubit. The Saundaung, or royal Cubit, is equal to 22 Inches.

The Dha, or Bamboo, consists of 7 royal Cubits; 1000 Dhas make 1 Dain, or Birman League, equal to 2 English Miles 2 Furlongs: the League is also subdivided into tenths.

SALANGORE *(on the West Coast of Malay).*

Imaginary Dollars are the money of account here, which are computed as follows: 8 Tompongs of tin, each of the weight of 8 Catties, make 1 Dollar; 30 Dollars, or 240 Catties, make 1 Bahar, which weighs 324lb. avoirdupois. The Malacca Bahar of 300 Catties, or 405lb. avoirdupois, is also used. Monies, &c.

SCINDY *(Malabar Coast).*

The coins here are Silver Rupees of 16 Annas, or 48 Copper Pice. The shells, called Cowries, are also used for money. 4 Cowries make 1 Dumaree, and 12 Dumarees are commonly worth 1 Copper Pice; but their value is not permanent. Monies and Weights.

Gold and silver are weighed by the Tola of 12 Massa, each Massa being divided into 6 Ruttees; the Tola is equal in weight to a Silver Rupee, or 179 English Grains nearly.

Diamonds and pearls are weighed by the Ruttee of 8 Hublas, and each Hubla = 2 Grains troy weight.

Monies and Weights.

Heavy goods are weighed by the Maund of 40 Seers. There is the Surat or Cutcha Maund, and the Scindy or Pucca Maund; the Cutcha Maund = 37lb. 5 oz. $5\frac{1}{3}$ dr. avoirdupois, and it is divided into 16 Annas, or 32 Pice: the Pucca Maund is double the former, and it is divided into 32 Annas, or 64 Pice.

The Carwall of rice, wheat, and other grain, is 60 Cossah or Copah, 240 Towyah, or 960 Bottwayee; the Bottwayee weighs at Tattah $1\frac{1}{4}$ Cutcha Seer: thus the Carwall is 15 Pucca Maunds; and the Carwall of barley or of paddy, 12 Pucca Maunds.

SERINGAPATAM *(in the Mysore)*.

Monies and Coins.

Accounts are kept here in Canter'raia Pagodas and Palams, called by the English Canteria Pagodas and Fanams. This Pagoda is an imaginary money, and the Fanam, which is a real coin, is the 10th part of the Pagoda, and the Cash the 16th part of the Fanam.

The coins are Gold Mohurs, which pass for 4 Pagodas; Sultany Pagodas, coined by *Tippoo Sultan;* and other Pagodas, coined by *Hyder Ally*, and by the Rajah of Mysore, all passing for 13 Fanams; also Sultany Fanams and Canteria Fanams, two small gold coins of base alloy.

Also Sultany Rupees, and Rajah Rupees, 26 of which pass for 7 Sultany Pagodas: Copper Dudus, called by the English, Dubs; 260 Dudus are the market price for a Sultany Pagoda.

The Shroffs, when they exchange copper for gold or silver, pay at the rate of 234 Dudus for a Pagoda, but when they change gold and silver for copper, they receive 240 Dudus; whilst the price fixed by government is 182 Dudus per Pagoda: the other coins exchange in proportion.

The Mohur weighs 212 English Grains, and is 20 Carats $2\frac{1}{3}$ Grains fine; its intrinsic value is therefore £1 12s. $2\frac{1}{4}$d. sterling; the Half Mohur and the Sultany Pagoda in proportion. The Fanam weighs 6 Grains, and is little more than 14 Carats fine: it is worth $7\frac{1}{2}$d. but passes for something above its intrinsic value. The Sultany Rupee weighs 177 Grains, and is 11 oz. $5\frac{1}{2}$ dwt. fine; it is therefore worth $23\frac{1}{4}$d. sterling nearly.

Weights & Measures.

The following system of weights and measures was adopted by *Tippoo Sultan*, and ordered to be used throughout his dominions.

The Seer is the standard for weights, but there is the Cucha Seer and the Pucca Seer; the former weighs 24 Sultany Rupees, or 4248 English Grains;

the latter, 84 Sultany Rupees, or 14868 English Grains. 5 Cucha Seers make 1 Pansh Seer; 8 Pansh Seers, 1 Maund, or 24lb. 4 oz. $6\frac{1}{4}$ dr. avoirdupois; 20 Maunds, 1 Barua or Candy, or 485lb. 7 oz. $9\frac{1}{2}$ dr. avoirdupois. Weights & Measures.

The Candaca, dry measure, contains 20 Colagas; and the Colaga, 16 Pucca Seers; the Seer measures $74\frac{13}{16}$ English cubic Inches: thus the Candaca = $11\frac{2}{15}$ Winchester Bushels.

The Gujah, long measure, is $38\frac{1}{2}$ Inches. 6000 Gujahs make 1 Hardary or Coss, which equals 3 Miles $5\frac{1}{6}$ Furlongs. 4 Hardaries make 1 Gavada, or Day's Journey; but the Hardary in common use is $\frac{1}{4}$ less: it is therefore equal to 2 Miles $5\frac{19}{24}$ Furlongs.

It should be however observed that the Sultan did not fully succeed in establishing uniformity of weights and measures in his dominions, as a difference still prevails, particularly in corn and land measures, which are said to vary in almost every village.

For a more particular statement of the monies, weights, and measures of this country, the reader is referred to *Dr. Buchanan's Travels through the Mysore*, published in 1807; from which the present article has been chiefly extracted.

SIAM *(on the farther Peninsula).*

Accounts are kept here in Catties, Tales, Ticals or Tuals, Miams, Fouangs, and Cowries, a sort of shell. The Catty is 20 Tales; the Tale, 4 Ticals, 16 Miams, or 32 Fouangs; the Fouang is 800 Cowries. Monies and Coins.

10 Miams are accounted equal to 1 Chinese Tale; so that 5 Tales of Siam = 8 Chinese Tales.

The coins are Gold Ticals, which pass for 10 Silver Ticals: Silver Ticals, Miams, Fouangs, and Sompaies; the latter being the fourth part of a Fouang. The Silver Tical weighs $225\frac{1}{2}$ English Grains, and is from 11 oz. 4 dwt. to 11 oz. 12 dwt. fine; thus it is worth from 29d. to 30d. sterling; but these coins are often adulterated. 2 Ticals pass commonly for 1 Spanish Dollar, and $2\frac{1}{2}$ Ticals for 1 Dutch Ducatoon.

The fineness of gold and silver is expressed, as in China, by dividing the weight into 100 parts, called Toques or Touch.

Gold and silver are weighed by the Tical, which equals 9 dwt. 10 gr. English. Weights & Measures.

The Pecul, the weight for heavy goods, is 50 Catties; the Catty, 20 Tales, or 80 Ticals. The Siam Pecul weighs 129lb. avoirdupois; and the Catty, 41 oz. $4\frac{1}{2}$ dr. avoirdupois.

Weights & Measures. The largest measure for corn is the Cohi, of 40 Sestes; the Seste contains 40 Sats, and weighs 100 Catties, or 258lb. avoirdupois.

Cottons, and other goods of the kind, are commonly sold by the Piece. The long measures are: 2 Soks make 1 Ken; 2 Kens, 1 Vouah; 20 Vouahs, 1 Sen. The Vouah is 1 Inch shorter than the French Toise; it measures, therefore, 6 Feet $3\frac{3}{4}$ Inches, English. 100 Sens, or 2000 Vouahs, make 1 League, called Roeneng, which is 4204 English Yards, or $2\frac{2}{5}$ Miles nearly.

SINKELL *(in the Island of Sumatra).*

Monies, &c. Spanish Dollars are the principal currency here, but accounts are kept in Tales, Soocoos, and Satallies; the Tale being divided into 4 Soocoos, or 16 Satallies. 4 Spanish Dollars are reckoned to the Tale.

Benzoin is sold by the Tompong or Cake, which ought to weigh 20 Catties, each Catty 56 oz. avoirdupois, and for camphire 56 oz. troy weight. The Chinese Pecul is generally used.

SOOLOO *(one of the Sunda Islands).*

Monies. There is no coin at Sooloo; accounts are sometimes reckoned by Spanish money, but commonly by the Sanampoory, Cangan, and Cowsoong. The first is a term only, the second is a coarse Chinese cotton cloth, 6 Fathoms long, which is reckoned equivalent to a Spanish Dollar. The Cowsoong is a piece of nankeen of 4 Fathoms long. Each of these is reckoned at 4 Sanampoories. In small payments, they make use of paddy, that is, rice in the husk.

Weights & Measures. The Sooloo weights are similar to those of China, but differently denominated. The Pecul is divided into 2 Lacksas, 20 Booboots, or 100 Catties. The Catty is divided into 16 Tales, 160 Ammas, and 1600 Choosocks.

The use of paddy as a currency has introduced the custom of measuring instead of weighing grain and some other commodities, as Cowries, &c.

The smallest grain measure is a half cocoa-nut-shell, called a Panching.

8 Panchings............	..make..	1 Gantang.
10 Gantangs		1 Raga.
$2\frac{1}{2}$ Ragas................		1 Pecul.

The Gantang of rice is reckoned to weigh 4 Catties; according to which, $2\frac{1}{2}$ Ragas make 1 China Pecul of $133\frac{1}{3}$lb. avoirdupois.

The measure for cloth is the Fathom, but the Chinese Covid is in common use.

SUCCADANA *(in the Island of Borneo)*.

Spanish Dollars are the only coin in circulation in the trade with Europeans, but accounts among the natives are kept in Tales and Mace. Monies and Weights.

Gold, diamonds, bezoar, and other valuable articles, are weighed by the Tale, which is divided into 4 Pahaws, or 16 Mace; and the Mace into 4 Copangs, or 8 Busucks. Heavy goods are weighed by English weights, and then turned into China Peculs.

SUMATRA, *see Acheen, Bencoolen, Natal, Palimbang, Sinkell, &c.*

SURAT *(Malabar Coast)*.

Accounts are kept in Rupees of 16 Annas, or 64 Pice. Monies and Coins.

The coins are Mohurs or Gold Rupees; and Silver Rupees, with halves and quarters. A Gold Rupee passes for 15 Silver Rupees. There are also Pezas or Pice, of Copper or Lead, 64 of which are reckoned to 1 Silver Rupee.

Padens or Baddams, a sort of bitter almonds from Persia, are also used as money; 60 of which pass for 1 Pice.

The Surat Rupees are now coined at the Bombay mint, and are to be of the same standard as those given under the article *Bombay.*

The weight for gold and silver is the Tola of 32 Valls, or 96 Ruttees. 82½ Valls make 1 Ounce troy; and therefore 31 Tolas = 1lb. troy nearly. Weights & Measures.

Heavy goods are weighed by the Maund, which is 40 Seers; and the Seer, 30 Pice. This Maund is one half of the Bengal Factory Maund; it is therefore equal to 37lb. 5 oz. 5⅓ dr. avoirdupois. There is also the Pucca Maund, which is equal to that of the Bengal Factory. 20 Surat Maunds, or 10 Pucca or Factory Maunds, make 1 Candy, or 746lb. 10 oz. 10 dr. avoirdupois. But these weights are not constant; for, in the sale of many articles, the Maund, instead of 40 Seers, contains from 41 to 46 Seers; neither is the Candy always 20 Maunds. Thus, pepper and sandal-wood are sold by the Bombay Candy of 21 Bombay Maunds, and cotton by the Candy of 21 Surat Maunds.

The long measures are the Guz, of 28⅕ English Inches; the Bazaar Guz, of 28 Inches; the Covid, of 18½ Inches; and the English Yard, with which broad cloth, satin, and velvet, are measured.

The Pherra, corn measure, contains 20 Palies, and weighs about 75lb. avoirdupois.

TAPPANOOLY (*in the Island of Sumatra*).

Monies, &c. Accounts are generally kept in Dollars, of 24 Fanams, or 400 Kepping. Spanish Dollars are the principal coin used in foreign trade; but among the natives, the value of goods is estimated by Tompongs, or cakes, of benzoin; and sometimes by buffaloes, and also by brass wire, beads, and salt. A measure of salt, called a Salup, weighing about 2lb. avoirdupois, is valued at a Fanam, or $2\frac{1}{2}$d. sterling. English weights are used here, and likewise the China Pecul.

TELLICHERRY (*Malabar Coast*).

Monies, Weights, & Measures. Accounts are commonly kept here, as at Bombay, in Rupees, Quarters, and Reas; the Rupee being divided into 100 Reas. The coins are Pagodas, Rupees, Fanams, Pice, and Tars. The Rupee is worth 5 Fanams, 50 Pice, or 100 Tars: hence 4 Reas = 1 Tar; and 80 Reas = 1 Pice. The following is the rate at which gold coins commonly pass.

	Rupees.		Rupees.
Porto Novo Pagoda........	$3\frac{1}{4}$	Venetians	5
Star Pagoda..............	$3\frac{1}{2}$	In paying for goods, 100 Venetians per..........	120
Sultany Pagoda	$4\frac{1}{8}$	Surat Gold Mohurs........	15
In paying for goods, 100 Pagodas per	430	Bombay Ditto	16

The Candy is divided into 20 Maunds, or 400 Pollams, and is generally reckoned at 600lb. avoirdupois; but *Mr. Milburn* states it to be only 570lb.

The long measures are the Covid of 18, and the Guz of $28\frac{2}{5}$ English Inches.

TERNATE (*one of the Molucca Islands*).

Monies and Weights. Accounts are kept in Rixdollars, of 48 Stivers, worth about 3s. 4d. sterling; and in Spanish Dollars. Ducatoons and Crowns also circulate. The rate of exchange is 80 Ducatoons for 100 Spanish Dollars; and 102 Crowns for 100 Spanish Dollars.

Gold and silver are weighed by the Mark, Dutch troy, which is divided into 9 Reals, each Real weighing 422 English Grains.

The Bamboo of rice weighs $1\frac{1}{2}$lb. Dutch troy, or 1lb. 10 oz. avoirdupois: the Pecul and Catty are the same as at Amboyna. The Barotti weighs 11lb. 15 oz.; and the Kaban, $100\frac{1}{3}$lb. avoirdupois.

The Tale of the Isle of Timor weighs $13\frac{1}{4}$ oz. avoirdupois.

TOCOPA *(on the farther Peninsula).*

The only money of this place is tin, which is reckoned by weight, as follows: Monies.

A Capin is 10 Vis, 40 Poots, or 120 Pingas; 8 Capins make 1 Bahar, equal to 6 Maunds 14 Seers 15 Chattacks of the Bengal Factory, or 476lb. avoirdupois.

TONQUIN, *see Cachao.*

TRANGANIA *(on the farther Peninsula).*

The coins here are Mace, a Gold coin, 16 of which are worth 1 Tale in gold dust. The inferior coins are Cossang and Patties; 400 Patties = 1 Cossang; 4 Cossang = 1 Mace; 16 Mace = 1 Tale. Coins, &c.

The common weight is the Pecul, which answers to 140lb. avoirdupois.

TRANQUEBAR *(Coromandel Coast).*

In this Danish settlement, accounts are kept in Rixdollars of 12 Fanams, and also in Rupees of 8 Fanams. The Fanam is divided into 80 Cash. Monies and Weights.

The Rixdollar is an imaginary coin, and is constantly reckoned 18 per cent. below the Danish current Rixdollar; it is therefore worth 37¾d. sterling.

The coins are Silver Rupees, double and single Fanams; and Copper Dudus or Cash.

The coinage of Rupees is here so regulated, that 1302 of them are worth 600 old Spanish Dollars, weighing 43lb. 7 oz. 2 dwt. troy. The value of the Tranquebar Rupee is therefore 24⅝d. sterling.

Star Pagodas are worth 34 Fanams, more or less; and Spanish Dollars, from 19 to 21 Fanams.

The Maund weighs 68lb. Danish, or 74⅘lb. avoirdupois.

TRINCOMALEE, *see Ceylon and Colombo.*

The following Table exhibits, at one view, the proportion between the Weights of the principal trading places in India and those of England and France. A full and accurate Table of the Coins of India will be found in the second volume of this Work, in which their values are given according to assays made at London, Paris, Bombay, &c.; but in the foregoing pages they are computed according to the mint regulations of each place, or legal contents of each coin.

INDIA WEIGHTS COMPARED WITH THOSE OF ENGLAND AND FRANCE.

NOTE.—At Bengal, 16 Chattacks = 1 Seer; 40 Seers = 1 Maund.
At Madras, 40 Pollams = 1 Vis; 8 Vis = 1 Maund.
English avoirdupois, 16 Drams = 1 Ounce; 16 Ounces = 1 Pound.
French weight, 1000 Grammes = 1 Kilogramme.

		Bengal Factory Weight.			Madras Weight.			English Avoirdupois Weight.			French Weight.
		Maunds.	Seers.	Chat.	Maunds.	Vis.	Pollams.	lb.	oz.	dr.	Kilo. Gr.
ACHEEN	Bahar of 200 Catties	5	26	13	16	7	19	423	6	13	192,043
	Guncha of 10 Nellies	2	37	$13\frac{4}{7}$	8	6	16	220	0	0	99,779
ALLAHABAD	Seer of 96 Siccas	0	1	5	0	0	$31\frac{1}{2}$	2	7	$6\frac{3}{4}$	1,117
AMBOYNA	Bahar	7	39	10	23	6	38	596	12	0	270,652
ANJENGO	Candy of 20 Maunds	7	20	0	22	3	8	560	0	0	253,984
AURUNGABUNDAR	Maund of 40 Pucca Seers	0	39	10	2	7	27	74	5	7	33,577
BALLASORE	Maund of 40 Seers	1	0	8	3	0	8	75	10	0	34,299
BANDA	Bahar of 100 Catties	8	6	12	24	3	8	610	0	0	276,661
BANJAR MASSIN	Pecul of 100 Catties	1	32	10	5	3	16	135	10	0	61,511
BANTAM	Bahar of 3 Peculs	5	12	2	15	6	28	396	0	0	179,603
BATAVIA	Pecul of 100 Catties	1	32	10	5	3	16	135	10	0	61,511
BEETLEFACKIE	Bahar of 40 Frazils	10	3	9	32	4	$19\frac{1}{5}$	814	0	0	369,184
BENARES	Seer of 84 Siccas	0	1	$2\frac{1}{2}$	0	0	$27\frac{3}{5}$	2	2	$7\frac{9}{10}$	0,977
BENCOOLEN	Bahar	7	20	0	22	3	8	560	0	0	253,984
BENGAL	Bazaar Maund	1	4	0	3	2	$11\frac{3}{10}$	82	2	$2\frac{2}{15}$	37,250
	Factory Maund	1	0	0	2	7	$35\frac{11}{15}$	74	10	$10\frac{2}{3}$	33,864
BOMBAY	Candy of 20 Maunds	7	20	0	22	3	8	560	0	0	253,984
	Bag of Rice	2	10	0	6	5	$30\frac{2}{5}$	168	0	0	76,195
BUSSORA	Maund Sofy	1	8	$5\frac{4}{7}$	3	4	$35\frac{1}{5}$	90	4	0	40,932
	Maund Attary	0	15	$4\frac{2}{7}$	1	1	$4\frac{4}{5}$	28	8	0	12,926
CALICUT	Maund of 100 Pools	0	16	$1\frac{1}{7}$	1	1	24	30	0	0	13,606
CAMBAY	Maund of 40 Seers	0	20	0	1	3	$37\frac{13}{15}$	37	5	$5\frac{1}{3}$	16,932
CARWAR	Candy of 20 Maunds	6	35	14	20	4	32	515	0	0	233,575
CAZUMBAZAR	Maund of 40 Seers	0	38	6	2	6	39	71	12	0	32,541
CEYLON	Bahar or Candy	6	38	15	20	6	26	520	12	$12\frac{4}{5}$	236,205
CHINA	Pecul of 100 Catties	1	31	6	5	2	26	133	5	$5\frac{1}{3}$	60,472
	Catty of 16 Tales	0	0	$11\frac{17}{40}$	0	0	17	1	5	$5\frac{1}{3}$	0,604
COCHIN	Candy of 20 Maunds	7	11	$2\frac{4}{7}$	21	5	$36\frac{4}{5}$	543	8	0	246,501
COLOMBO	Bahar or Candy	6	28	0	20	0	0	500	0	0	226,772
DACCA	Maund of 40 Seers	1	3	13	3	2	0	81	14	0	37,133
GAMROON	Bazaar Maund	0	4	0	0	2	16	7	8	0	3,401
GOA	Candy of 20 Maunds	6	25	$2\frac{6}{7}$	19	6	16	495	0	0	224,504

Place	Weight	Bengal Factory Weight.			Madras Weight.			English Avoirdupois Weight.			French Weight.
		Maunds.	Seers.	Chat.	Maunds.	Vis.	Pollams.	lb.	oz.	dr.	Kilo. Gr.
HOOGHLEY	Maund of 40 Seers	1	5	0	3	2	$37\frac{1}{2}$	84	2	15	38,182
JUNKCEYLON	Bahar of 8 Capins	6	20	0	19	3	12	485	5	$5\frac{1}{3}$	220,119
LUCKNOW	Seer of 96 Siccas	0	1	5	0	0	$31\frac{1}{2}$	2	7	$6\frac{3}{4}$	1,117
MACASSAR	Pecul of 100 Catties	1	32	10	5	3	16	135	10	0	61,511
MADRAS	Candy of 20 Maunds	6	28	0	20	0	0	500	0	0	226,772
MALACCA	Bahar of 3 Peculs	5	16	15	16	1	24	405	0	0	183,685
MANGALORE	Merchants' Maund	0	15	5	1	1	6	28	10	0	129,826
	Market Maund	0	15	2	1	1	1	28	3	$0\frac{3}{4}$	128,053
MASULIPATAM	Maund of 8 Vis	0	13	0	0	7	33	24	8	0	11,111
MIRZAPORE	Seer of 84 Siccas	0	1	$2\frac{1}{2}$	0	0	$27\frac{3}{5}$	2	2	$7\frac{9}{10}$	0,977
MOCHA	Bahar of 15 Frazils	6	0	1	18	0	0	450	0	0	204,094
MUSCAT	Custom-House Maund	0	4	11	0	2	32	8	12	0	3,968
MYSORE	Candy	7	20	0	22	3	8	560	0	0	253,984
PALIMBANG	Baly of 10 Gantangs	1	3	6	3	1	37	81	6	0	36,754
	Pecul	1	31	4	5	2	22	133	0	0	60,321
PATNA	Maund of 42 Seers	1	3	3	3	1	32	80	10	0	36,566
PEGU	Candy of 150 Vis	6	28	0	20	0	0	500	0	0	226,772
PONDICHERRY	Maund of 160 Vis	0	13	14	0	8	11	25	14	$5\frac{1}{2}$	11,745
PRINCE OF WALES'S ISLAND	Coyan	71	16	6	212	7	14	5323	0	0	2413,204
	Bahar of 3 large Peculs	5	29	4	17	0	38	428	0	0	194,116
	Pecul of 100 Catties	1	31	6	5	2	26	133	5	$5\frac{1}{3}$	60,472
RANGOON	Candy of 150 Vis	6	28	0	20	0	0	500	0	0	226,772
SALANGORE	Bahar of 240 Catties	4	13	9	12	7	27	324	0	0	146,948
SCINDY	Pucca Maund	1	0	0	2	7	$35\frac{1}{15}$	74	10	$10\frac{2}{3}$	33,864
	Cutcha Maund	0	20	0	1	3	$37\frac{13}{15}$	37	5	$5\frac{1}{3}$	16,932
SERAMPORE	Seer of 60 Siccas	0	0	13	0	0	$19\frac{3}{4}$	1	8	$10\frac{1}{4}$	0,698
SERINGAPATAM	Candy	6	20	1	19	3	14	485	7	$9\frac{1}{2}$	220,184
	Maund of 40 Cutcha Seers	0	13	0	0	7	$30\frac{1}{2}$	24	4	$6\frac{1}{4}$	11,009
	Pucca Seer	0	1	2	0	0	27	2	1	$15\frac{3}{4}$	0,963
	Cutcha Seer	0	0	$5\frac{1}{5}$	0	0	$7\frac{67}{80}$	0	9	$11\frac{1}{4}$	0,274
SIAM	Pecul of 50 Catties	1	29	$1\frac{5}{7}$	5	1	$11\frac{1}{5}$	129	0	0	58,507
SURAT	Candy of 20 Maunds	10	0	0	29	6	$37\frac{1}{3}$	746	10	$10\frac{2}{3}$	338,645
	Pucca Maund	1	0	0	2	7	$35\frac{1}{15}$	74	10	$10\frac{2}{3}$	33,864
	Maund of 40 Seers	0	20	0	1	3	$37\frac{13}{15}$	37	5	$5\frac{1}{3}$	16,932
TELLICHERRY	Candy of 20 Maunds	8	0	2	24	0	0	600	0	0	272,126
TERNATE	Kaban	1	13	11	4	0	4	100	5	$5\frac{1}{3}$	45,505
TOCOPA	Bahar of 8 Capins	6	14	15	19	0	12	476	0	0	215,886
TRANGANIA	Pecul	1	35	0	5	4	32	140	0	0	63,496
TRANQUEBAR	Maund	1	0	1	2	7	37	74	12	$12\frac{4}{5}$	33,925

NOTE.—Any of the above weights may be reduced to English troy Grains, by multiplying the number of corresponding Kilogrammes and decimal parts by 15434; which is the number of Grains in each Kilogramme.

BATAVIA, JAVA, &c.*

New Monetary System.

A new system of monies has been recently established here by the King of the Netherlands.

The monetary unit is the new Gulden or Florin of the Netherlands, but instead of decimal divisions it is here divided into 4 Schillings, 12 Dubbels, 24 Dutch Stivers, 30 Indian Stivers, or 120 Doits.

A paper currency has been also established, consisting of Billets of 1000, 600, 300, 100, 50, 25, 10, 5, and 1 Gulden; which are convertible into specie on demand. For this purpose, exchange offices have been established at Batavia, Samarang, and Sourabaya. The two latter places, however, issue no paper of greater value than 100 Guldens.

The following coins are current, and are received in the Government Treasuries at the annexed rates of exchange.

	Doits.		Doits.
Rupee of Java, Surat, & Arcot, at	120	Old Ducatoon	312
Sicca Rupee	126	Milled Ducatoon	320
American Dollar	240	Gold Ducat of the Netherlands	528
Spanish Dollar	264	Gold Rupee	1920

EXCHANGES OF INDIA.

Exchanges of India.

The exchanges between the different trading places of India, as in other countries, are regulated by the intrinsic value of their monies and the proportion that exists between the demand and supply of bills. This kind of business is principally transacted between the three Presidencies, viz. Bengal, Madras, and Bombay; and as there is always the greatest demand for bills on Bengal, being considered the Capital of the English Possessions in India, the course of exchange is mostly in favour of that place.

Calcutta generally exchanges with Madras at 108 Current Rupees for 100 Arcot Rupees; and with Bombay at 110 Current Rupees for 100 Bombay Rupees.

The usual manner in which bills are drawn from those places on London, is stated in Vol. II. page 103; with other particulars respecting Indian exchanges.

* The above account of Batavia, &c. was received after the preceding sheets had been printed, which is the cause of this deviation from alphabetical order. The other accounts, however, of those places are still useful, especially for the weights and measures.

ELSINEUR, OR ELSINORE *(in Denmark).*

Monies and Coins.

Accounts are kept here as in Copenhagen, except that the Rixdollar is divided into 4 Orts instead of 6 Marks: thus 24 Skillings Danish make 1 Ort; and 4 Orts, 1 Rixdollar. The coins are the same as in Copenhagen.

In paying the tolls, however, at the Passage of the Sound, the monies are distinguished into three different values, namely, Specie, Crown, and Current.

Specie-money is that in which the duties of the Sound were fixed in 1701.

Crown-money was the ancient currency of Denmark, in which tolls are sometimes reckoned.

Current-money is the actual currency of the country.

The proportion between these denominations is as follows.

8 Specie Rixdollars are worth 9 Crown Rixdollars. 16 Crown Rixdollars are worth 17 Current Rixdollars: therefore, to reduce Specie-money into Crown-money, add $\frac{1}{8}$; and for the reverse operation, subtract $\frac{1}{9}$.

To reduce Crown-money into Current-money, add $\frac{1}{16}$; and for the reverse operation, subtract $\frac{1}{17}$.

Hence also 128 Specie Rixdollars are worth 144 Crown Rixdollars, or 153 Current Rixdollars; and therefore Specie-money is $12\frac{1}{2}$ per cent. better than Crown-money, and $19\frac{17}{32}$ per cent. better than Current-money.

Weights & Measures.

The weights and measures here are generally the same as those stated under the article *Copenhagen;* but there are certain regulations peculiar to the payment of duties and tolls at the Passage of the Sound, which require explanation.

The Shippond and Russian Berkowitz are reckoned at 300lb.; and the Pood and Stone at 30lb. of Denmark.

The Ship Last used here for the computation of the tolls and duties is that of Amsterdam; which answers to 85,248 English Bushels, or 30,039 Hectolitres, and is called the Sundish Last.

EMBDEN *(in Germany).*

Monies of Account.

In the province of East Friesland, accounts are kept in Rixdollars current of 54 Stivers, the Stiver being 10 Wittens: also in Guldens of 20 Stivers, or 200 Wittens; or in Guldens of 10 Schaafs, each Schaaf containing 20 Wittens.

The Rixdollar current is likewise divided into 3 Marks, 9 Shillings, 18 Flinderkes, 27 Schaafs, 72 Groots, 108 Syferts, 216 Oertgens, or 540 Wittens.

Monies of Account. There are, besides, the Rixdollar specie, which is worth 4 Marks, 12 Shillings, &c., and the base Rixdollar *(Schlecht Thaler)*, which is worth $1\frac{1}{2}$ Gilder, 5 Shillings, &c.

Value of Monies. The Rixdollar, Embden currency, is worth 38 Shillings 10 Pfenings, Hamburgh currency, which is almost 3s. sterling; or, more accurately, £1 sterling = 6 Rixdollars 38 Stivers, or 18 Florins 2 Stivers, Embden currency.

Coins. The Prussian Gold and Silver coins, all of which are current in Embden, have been already described under the article *Berlin*. There are here, besides, Pieces of $\frac{2}{3}$, $\frac{1}{3}$, and $\frac{1}{6}$ Rixdollar, or 36, 18, and 9 Stivers; base Rixdollars, of 30 Stivers; Guldens, with halves and quarters; Pieces of 12, 18, or 36 to a Rixdollar current, that is, of $4\frac{1}{2}$, 3, and $1\frac{1}{2}$ Stivers; Flinderkes, at 3 Stivers; and Malle Flinderkes, at 11 Oertgens; Schaafs, at 2 Stivers, and Malle Schaafs, at 7 Oertgens; Syferts, at 5 Wittens; Krumsterks, at 4 Wittens; Oertgens, and single Wittens of Copper.

The Dutch Florin passes here at 30 Stivers.

Weights & Measures. The Pound, commercial weight, is divided into 32 Loths, and weighs 34 Loths, Cologne weight: hence 100lb. of Embden equal 109,54lb. avoirdupois, or 49,68 Kilogrammes. The Shippond is 300lb. or 3 Centners.

Corn is sold in Tonnes, of 2 Sacks, 4 Verps, 8 Scheffels, or 144 Kruesen. 15 Tonnes, or 60 Verps, make 1 Last, answering to $10\frac{1}{5}$ English Quarters, or 28,686 Hectolitres.

The Foot is 11,66 English Inches, or 0,2961 of a Metre. The Rhineland Foot of 12,356 Inches is also used here. The Ell equals 26,4 English Inches, or 0,6704 of a Metre.

A Diemt or Acre of land, in East Friesland, contains 400 Rhineland square Ruthes: the Ruthe being 12 Rhineland Feet, making 1 Acre 1 Rood 25 Perches English, or 56,74 French Ares.

ERFURT *(in Germany)*.

Monies and Coins. Accounts are kept in Rixdollars of 24 Good Groschen, or 288 Pfenings. The coins are the same as at *Leipsic*, which see.

Weights & Measures. Gold and silver are weighed by the Cologne Mark. The commercial Pound contains 7285 English Grains. Thus 100lb. of Erfurt equal 104lb. avoirdupois, or 47,20 Kilogrammes.

The Malter, corn measure, is divided into 4 Viertels, 12 Scheffels, 48 Metzens, or 192 Masgens. The Scheffel renders 1,70 Winchester Bushel, or 0,6012 of a Hectolitre. Weights & Measures.

The Vat of wine is reckoned at 6 Ohms, or 12 Eimers. The Eimer contains 168 wine, or 144 beer Noszels. The Eimer of wine equals 19,03 English Gallons, or 72,07 Litres; the Eimer of beer equals 19,05 Gallons, or 72,14 Litres.

The Ell is of two sorts, the long Ell being 23,3 English Inches, or 0,594 of a Metre, and the short Ell, 15,9 English Inches, or 0,403 of a Metre.

The Foot is that of Leipsic, which contains 11,11 English Inches, or 0,282 of a Metre. The Ruthe is 14 such feet, and the Morgen, or Acre of land, contains 168 square Ruthes, which equal 2 Roods, 24 Perches English, or 26,223 French Ares.

FERRARA *(in Italy)*.

Accounts are kept in Lire of 20 Soldi, or 240 Denari correnti. Monies and Coins.

The Lira is also divided into 2 Giuli or Paoli; and the Soldo into 6 Quattrini.

The Scudo di Cambio is reckoned at 4 Lire, or 80 Soldi.

The coins will be found under the articles *Bologna* and *Rome*.

The Pound for weighing gold and silver is the same as in all the Roman States, for which see *Rome*. Weights.

The commercial Pound here is 2 per cent. heavier than that of Rome; and therefore contains 5338 English Grains.* Hence 100lb. of Ferrara equal 76,26lb. avoirdupois, or 34,585 Kilogrammes.

The principal corn measure is the Moggio, which is divided into 20 Staja, 80 Quarte, or 160 Quartini. The Moggio contains $2\frac{1}{8}$ Roman Rubbj; and therefore renders 17,757 English Bushels, or 6,257 Hectolitres. Measures.

The principal measure for wine is the Mastello; which is divided into 8 Secchj, or 40 Boccali, and equals $30\frac{3}{4}$ Boccali of Rome. Thus the Mastello answers to 14,63 English Gallons, or 55,378 Litres.

The Foot contains 15,8 English Inches, or 0,4011 of a Metre.

---

* The commercial Pound of Ferrara is stated by *Kruse* to be the same as that of Rome; but *Mr. Parke*, the British Consul for the Roman States, in his despatches on the subject transmitted to *Lord Castlereagh* in 1818, mentions it to be 2 per cent. heavier than the Roman Pound, as above; which agrees with the proportion given by *Ricard*, and other Authors.

Measures. The Braccio for woollens equals 26,3 English Inches, or 0,669 of a Metre: the Braccio for silks is 24,7 English Inches, or 0,628 of a Metre.

Exchanges. The exchanges of Ferrara are for the most part regulated by those of *Rome, Bologna, Venice*, and *Leghorn*, which see.

FEZ, *see Morocco.*

FINLAND, *see Sweden.*

FIUME *(in Istria).*

Monies, &c. The monies and coins here are the same as those of *Trieste*, which see.

Weights. The gold and silver weight used at Fiume is the Marca of Vienna; which is divided into 8 Ounces, and the Ounce into 144 Carats, or 576 Grains. The Marca contains 3684 English Grains, or 238,693 Grammes. Thus the Ounce is $\frac{1}{24}$ part lighter than the English Ounce troy.

The standard commercial Pound is called the Vienna Funti weight. It is divided into 32 Loths, and weighs 8623 English Grains. Hence 100lb. of Fiume answer to 123,18lb. avoirdupois, or 55,87 Kilogrammes.

Measures. The corn measure is the Metzen, divided into halves and quarters. Its dimensions are 3456 cubic Inches of Vienna, or 3813 English cubic Inches. It therefore contains 1,773 English Bushel, or 0,6247 of a Hectolitre.

The principal wine measure is the Orna, or Eimer, which is divided into 32 Buccals, and contains 2949 cubic Inches of Vienna, or 3253 English cubic Inches. Hence the Eimer answers to 14,08 English Gallons, or 53,30 Litres.

The corn Metzen contains $37\frac{1}{2}$ wine Buccals: the proportion, therefore, between the Metzen and the Eimer is as $37\frac{1}{2}$ to 32.

The Venetian weights and measures are occasionally used by the merchants in this district; but the government of Fiume has not any standards of such weights and measures.*

---

* This is a new article, and has been chiefly extracted from the despatches sent to London, in 1818, by *John Leard, Esq.* His Majesty's Consul at Fiume. The weights transmitted on the occasion are generally understood to be the same as those of Vienna. For further particulars on this subject, see the article *Vienna.*

FLORENCE (*in Italy*).

Monies of Account.

There are various modes of keeping accounts in Tuscany. The fundamental money may be considered the ***Lira***, which is divided into 20 Soldi, each of 12 Denari; a similar division is observed in three other monies of account, which are the Scudo, or *Scudo d'oro*, worth 7½ Lire; the Ducato, or *Scudo Corrente*, worth 7 Lire; the ***Pezza da Otto Reali***, also called ***Pezza della Rosa***, or ***Livornina***, worth 5¾ Lire.

Thus the Scudo is divided into 20 Soldi, or 240 Denari di Scudo; the Ducato into 20 Soldi, or 240 Denari di Ducato or Correnti; and the Pezza into 20 Soldi, or 240 Denari di Pezza.

The following monies are likewise used:—the Testone, or Double Lira; the Paolo of $1\frac{1}{2}$ Lira; the Crazia of 20 Denari di Lira; and the Quattrino of 4 Denari di Lira.

From the above statements it appears that 1 Soldo d'oro is worth $1\frac{1}{14}$ Soldo Corrente, $1\frac{7}{23}$ Soldo di Pezza, or $7\frac{1}{2}$ Soldi di Lira.

Hence also 14 Scudi d'oro equal 15 Ducati;
23 ditto .... 30 Pezze da Otto Reali.
23 Ducati .... 28 ditto.
with their respective divisions in the same proportion.

The value of those various monies may be computed from that of the *Lira*, which is worth 84 French Centimes, or $8\frac{1}{8}$d. sterling very nearly.

It should be noticed that the money of Florence is called *moneta buona*, to distinguish it from the *moneta lunga* of Leghorn, being $4\frac{1}{23}$ per cent. better, that is, 23 Lire moneta buona equal 24 Lire moneta lunga. See *Leghorn*.

Gold Coins.

The Gold coins of Tuscany are the ***Ruspone*** or triple Sequin, valued at 40 Lire or 60 Paoli. $32\frac{32}{71}$ Rusponi are minted from 1 Pound of fine gold, and are said to be without alloy or remedy.

The Sequin, also called the Ruspo or Gigliato, is in all respects the third part of the Ruspone.

Silver Coins.

The principal Silver coins are,
The Francescone or Leopoldo of 10 Paoli, or $6\frac{2}{3}$ Lire;
The Piece of 5 Paoli, called Franceschino or Leopoldino;
The Ducatone of 7 Lire;

Silver Coins.

The Tallaro of 6 Lire, with Halves in proportion; the Testone; the Paolo; the Crazia; and Pieces of 20, 10, and 5 Soldi.

The Tallaro is chiefly used in the Levant trade, and is disposed of as merchandize. The Crazia is a coin of the ancient Medicean government, and none have been struck of late years.

Foreign coins, particularly those of France, circulate here at a fluctuating value.

It may be observed that the monetary system of Tuscany underwent some partial change when that Duchy became the Kingdom of Etruria, especially in a coinage of silver in 1803, which however was not extensive. Its particulars will be duly noticed in the *Table of Coins*, Vol. II., where the weight, fineness, and sterling value of all the coins of Tuscany may be found.

Fineness of Gold and Silver.

The fineness of gold is expressed in Carats and Ottavi (eighth parts); the Pound, or other weight of pure gold being reckoned at 24 Carats or 192 Ottavi.

The fineness of silver is expressed in Oncie and Denari; the Pound or other weight of pure silver being reckoned at 12 Oncie, or 288 Denari.

Weights.

The Pound for gold and silver is composed of 12 Ounces, 96 Drams, 288 Denari, or 6912 Grani, and weighs 339,542 Grammes, or 5240 English Grains.* This is likewise the legal weight for all sorts of merchandize. Hence 100lb. of Florence = 74,864lb. avoirdupois. The Quintal is 100lb.

The Cantaro of wool, salt meat and fish, &c. is 160lb.; the Cantaro of other articles is 150lb.

Dry Measure.

The principal measure for corn is the Stajo, which is divided into 2 Mine, 4 Quarti, 32 Mezzette, 64 Quartucci, or 128 Bussoli; and contains 0,2436 Hectolitres, or 0,6913 English Bushels.

---

* The Metrology of Tuscany is variously stated by different authors. Some mention a commercial Pound, 3½ per cent. heavier than that used for the precious metals; even the latter is differently described. *Kruse* makes it 5238 troy Grains, and *Ricard* 5244. Others differ still more widely; but its actual weight, as lately determined at the *London Mint*, is 5240 Grains, as above.

The Libra or Pound, tried on this occasion, was in 1819 verified by the proper authorities in Tuscany, and sent to *Lord Castlereagh* by *John Falconar, Esq.* his Majesty's Consul at Leghorn. He also transmitted attested standards of the Tuscan measures, both of extent and capacity, which have been recently compared by *Mr. Troughton;* and their contents, thus ascertained, are given in the present article.

The Moggio is composed of 24 Staja, and therefore equals 5,847 Hectolitres, or 2 Quarters 4¾ Bushels, English measure. The Sacca contains 3 Staja. **Dry Measure.**

The Barile of wine is divided into 20 Fiaschi, 80 Mezzette, or 160 Quartucci, and contains 45,584 Litres, or 12,042 English Gallons. **Liquid Measure.**

In oil measure the Barile is divided into 16 Fiaschi, 64 Mezzette, or 128 Quartucci, and contains 33,428 Litres, or 8,8313 English Gallons.

The Soma is composed of 2 Barili.

The Long measure is the Braccio, which is divided into 20 Soldi, 60 Quattrini, or 240 Denari, and contains 0,5836 Metres, or 22,98 English Inches. **Long Measure.**

The Tuscan Mile is composed of 566⅗ Canne, each Canna containing 5 Braccia. It therefore equals 1,6536 Kilometre, or 1 Mile 48 Yards English measure.

There is another Braccio used by builders and surveyors, which equals 0,5486 Metres, or 21,6 English Inches, and 5 of these make the Pertica or Perch.

The Saccata of land is composed of 660 square Pertiche, and answers to 4,695 French Decares, or 1 Acre 36 Perches English measure.

Exchanges.

Florence exchanges with, and gives (more or less) to—

Amsterdam, ...	1 Pezza of 5¾ Lire,	for 90 Grotes Flemish.
Augsburgh,......	60 Soldi, ...	for 1 Florin current.
Bologna, ...	1 Ducat of 7 Lire,	for 106 Bolognini.
Cadiz and Madrid,	100 Pezze, ...	for 125 Dollars of exchange.
Genoa, ...	1 Pezza, ...	for 116 Soldi Fuori banco.
Hamburgh, ...	1 Pezza, ...	for 83d. Flemish banco.
Leghorn, ...	100 Ducats of 7 Lire,	for 122 Pezze of 8 Reali.
Lisbon, ...	1 Pezza, ...	for 760 Rees.
London, ...	1 Pezza, ...	for 50d. sterling.
Milan, ...	1 Pezza, ...	for 127 Soldi correnti.
Naples, ...	100 Pezze, ...	for 111 Ducati di Regno.
Palermo & Messina,	1 Pezza, ...	for 11 Tari 10 Grani.
Paris, &c.	1 Pezza, ...	for 98 Sous in Francs.
Rome, ...	100 Francesconi, or 50 Zecchini,	for 103 Scudi Romani;
or	100 Scudi d'oro, ..	for 75 Scudi di Stampa d'oro.
Venice,..........	1 Pezza, ...	for 494 Centimes.
Vienna, ...	60 Soldi, ...	for 1 Florin.

Usances. The following are the usances allowed on Bills of Exchange drawn on Florence and other places in Tuscany, according to the decree of the Grand Duke Ferdinand, dated August 29th, 1814.

Three months after date for bills from America, Denmark, England, Norway, Portugal, Prussia, Russia, Spain, and Sweden.

Two months after date from Bremen, Hamburgh, Holland, Lubec, and the Netherlands.

Fifteen days sight from all other places in Germany, and from Switzerland.

Thirty one days sight from the Barbary States, Egypt, the Levant, and Turkey.

Thirty days sight from the Ionian Islands, Malta, Sardinia, and Sicily.

Eight days sight from Italy, with the exception of Tuscany.

Three days sight for bills drawn from one part of Tuscany on another.

One month after date for France, and all other places not mentioned above.

Bills drawn from Rome, or Venice, on Florence, are accepted on the Saturday, and paid on that day fortnight; but bills from Bologna, which are likewise accepted on Saturday, must be paid on the next Saturday following, or be protested on the same day.

Days of Grace. Florence has no days of grace; but a bill must be paid on the day it becomes due, or it must be protested before the departure of the post for the place where it was drawn.

FRANCE.

General View. In arranging the subjects of this important article, it seems most convenient to depart from the usual plan, by explaining the weights and measures before the monies.

There are three systems of weights and measures to be explained here; namely, the ***Ancient System***, used before the French Revolution; the ***Metrical*** or ***Decimal System***, established in 1795; and the ***Systeme Usuel***, made legal for retail business in the year 1812.

The System of 1795 is the Metrical System, with decimal divisions, and a new vocabulary; and that of 1812 is also the Metrical System, but with binary divisions and the ancient vocabulary, as will be explained in the following pages.

The Decimal System is used in all wholesale and government concerns, and is well calculated to facilitate the operations of commerce; but the Binary System (that is, dividing standards into halves, quarters, eighths, &c.) is found more convenient in the inferior departments of trade, and particularly in retail business. The former system is, both by its divisions and vocabulary, admirably adapted for universal communication among the learned; but it is perhaps too scientific for the common people, to whom the business of weighing and measuring the necessaries of life is chiefly committed in every country. In short, the Decimal and Binary Systems seem to unite advantages, both for foreign and domestic trade, which perhaps no one System could possess. General View.

ANCIENT SYSTEM.*

Weights. The ancient weight of France, called the *Poids de Marc*, was the same for the precious metals as for all merchandize. The Livre or Pound was divided into 2 Marcs, 16 Ounces, 128 Gros, or 9216 Grains. The Ounce was also divided occasionally into 20 Estlins, 40 Mailles, or 80 Felins; and the Gros was sometimes divided into 3 Deniers of 24 Grains each.

Diamonds were weighed by the Ounce of 144 Carats, each Carat being 4 Grains.

Apothecaries' weight was the Poids de Marc of 16 Ounces, 32 Duelles, 128 Siciliques, 192 Sextules, 256 Drachms, 768 Scruples, or 9216 Grains.

The Pound, Poids de Marc, answers to 0,4895 Kilogramme of the new weight, or 7555 English Grains.

Measures of Capacity. The corn measure of Paris was the Muid, which was divided into 12 Setiers, 24 Mines, 48 Minots, or 144 Boisseaux, and the Boisseau into 16 Litrons. The Setier equals 1,56 Hectolitre, or 4,427 English Bushels.

The principal measure for wine was also the Muid, which was divided into 36 Setiers, 144 Quarts, or 288 Pintes. The Muid answered to 2,68 Hectolitres or 70,80 English Gallons.

The Pinte was divided into 2 Chopines, 4 Demi-Setiers, or 8 Boissons; and answered to 0,931 Litres, or 0,2459 English Gallons, being very nearly an English Quart.

* When the weights and measures of a country are altered, a knowledge of the old system, as well as the new, continues long necessary; and in the case of France it is indispensable, as the ancient system is still partially retained, particularly in road measures, and in valuing the work of labourers and mechanics. In land surveying too it is constantly referred to.

Long Measure. The old French Foot (*Pied de Roi*) was divided into 12 Inches, 144 Lines, or 1728 Points; and equalled 0,32484 Metres, or 12,7893 English Inches.

The Aune of Paris was 1,188 Metre, or 46,85 English Inches.

The Toise or Fathom, also called the Toise d'Ordonnance, was 6 Feet Pied de Roi, = 1,949 Metre, or 6,395 English Feet.

The Mile was 1000 Toises, = 1949,036 Metres, or 1 English Mile 1 Furlong 28 Poles. The Lieue or League, legal road measure, is 2000 Toises.

Land Measure. The Arpent or Acre was mostly 100 square Perches, but the Perch varied in different provinces. The following were the principal Land Measures, computed from the length of the Perch:

	Feet.		Ares.	Acre.	R.	P. English.
Arpent d'Ordonnance	22	to the Perch =	51,07.. = ..	1	1	2
Arpent Commun	20	....	42,21	1	0	7
Arpent de Paris	18	....	34,19	0	3	15

The above Acres contain each 100 square Perches, but the *Acre de Normandie* contains 160 Perches of 22 square Feet each, and therefore equals 81,71 *Ares*, or 2 Acres and 2 Perches English.

METRICAL OF DECIMAL SYSTEM.

Metrical Standard. The fundamental standard adopted in France for the metrical system of weights and measures, is a quadrant of the meridian; that is to say, the distance from the equator to the north pole. This quadrant is divided into ten millions of equal parts, and one of these parts or divisions is called the *Metre*, which is adopted as the unit of length, and from which by decimal multiplication and division all other measures are derived. The length of the quadrant has been ascertained by *M. M. Delambre* and *Mechain*, by measuring an arc of the meridian between the parallels of Dunkirk and Barcelona, and has been found to contain 5130740 French Toises. This number, divided by ten millions, gives 36,941328 French Inches, which is the *Metre*, the element of all the other measures, and which is equal to 39,371 English Inches.*

* The above proportion between the measures of France and England was determined by Professor *Pictet*, at the National Institute in 1802, by comparing the Platina Metre with a Brass Yard, made by *Mr. Troughton*. Several comparisons of the Metre and Yard have been since made by other eminent mathematicians, but none differ from the above more than the thousandth part of an Inch.

In order to express the decimal proportions, the following vocabulary of names has been adopted. Vocabulary.

For multipliers, the word *Deca* prefixed means 10 times.
Hecto .... 100 times.
Kilo .... 1000 times.
Myria .... 10,000 times.

On the contrary, for divisors, the word *Deci* expresses the 10th part.
Centi .... 100th part.
Milli .... 1000th part.

It may assist the memory to observe that the terms for multiplying are Greek, and those for dividing, Latin.

Thus *Deca-metre* means 10 Metres.
Deci-metre the 10th part of a Metre.
Hecto-metre 100 Metres.
Centi-metre the 100th part of a Metre, and so on for the rest.

The *Metre* (as before stated) is the element of long measure, and = 39,371 English Inches. Elements Compared.

The *Are*, which is a square *Deca-metre* (or 100 square Metres) is the element of superficial measures. It equals 3,955 English Perches.

The *Stere*, which is a cubic *Metre*, is the element of solid measures, and = 35,317 Cubic Feet English.

The *Litre*, which is the cubic *Deci-metre*, is the element of all liquid measures, and of all other measures of capacity. It equals 0,26419 English Gallons, and Hectolitre = 2,8379 Winchester Bushels.

Lastly the *Gramme*, which is the weight of a cubic *Centi-metre* of distilled water, of the temperature of melting ice, (the greatest condensation) is the element of all weights, and equals 15,434 English Grains troy.*

* The above proportion between the weights of France and England has been recently ascertained at the London Mint, from attested standards sent to *Lord Castlereagh* by *D. R. Morier, Esq.* his Majesty's Consul General at Paris. This proportion has been further verified by the agreement of several attested standards, transmitted by other British Consuls in France, making the Kilogramme equal to 15434 English Grains instead of 15444, which has been hitherto reckoned and acted upon in both countries. For a more particular account of this extraordinary error, see the Note p. 140.

New Weights and Measures of France compared with the old, and also with English Weights and Measures.

LINEAR MEASURE.

Linear Measure.

	French Feet.	English Feet.
Distance from the Equator to the Pole	30784440	32809167
Degree (centesimal)	307844,4	328091,67
Myriametre	30784,44	32809,167
Kilometre	3078,444	3280,9167
Hectometre	307,8444	328,09167
Decametre	30,78444	32,809167
Metre	3,078444	3,2809167
	French Lines.	English Lines.
Decimetre	44,3296	47,2452
Centimetre	4,43296	4,72452
Millimetre	0,443296	,472452

SQUARE OR SUPERFICIAL MEASURE.

Square Measure.

	French Square Feet.	English Square Feet.
Myriare	9476817,46113	10764414,3923
Kilare	947681,746113	1076441,43923
Hectare	94768,1746113	107644,143923
Decare	9476,81746113	10764,4143923
Are	947,681746113	1076,44143923
Deciare	94,7681746114	107,644143923
Centiare (Metre Carré)	9,47681746113	10,7644143923
	F. Square Inches.	E. Square Inches.
Square Decimetre	13,646617	15,500756
	F. Square Lines.	E. Square Lines.
Square Centimetre	19,651134	22,321088
Square Millimetre	0,19651134	0,2232108

MEASURES OF CAPACITY.

Cubic Measure.

	French Cubic Feet.	English Cubic Feet.
Myrialitre	291,738519	353,1714695
Kilolitre (Metre Cube)	29,1738519	35,31714695
Hectolitre	2,91738519	3,5317146945

	Fr. Cubic Inches.	En. Cubic Inches.	
Decalitre	504,124160	610,2802806	Cubic Measure.
Litre (Decimetre Cube)	50,4124160	61,02802806	
Decilitre	5,04124160	6,102802806	
	Cubic Lines.	Cubic Lines.	
Centilitre	871,126926	1054,5643249	

The *Litre*, which is the unit for measures of capacity, = 2,1135 English Pints, wine measure; and therefore 1 Hectolitre equals 26,41906 wine Gallons, or 2,83796 Winchester Bushels. Hence 1 Winchester Bushel = 35,2466 Litres.

SOLID OR CUBIC MEASURE.

	Fr. Cubic Feet.	En. Cubic Feet.
Decastere	291,738519	353,1700
Stere (Metre Cube)	29,1738519	35,3170
Decistere	2,91738519	3,5317

This measure is used for fire-wood, stone, &c. The *Stere* is the same as the Kilolitre in the preceding article.

WEIGHTS. Weights.

	Poids de Marc. livres.	on.	Gros	Grains	Eng. Troy Weight. lb.	oz.	dwt.	grs.
Bar (Cubic Metre of Water)	2042	14	0	14	2679	6	3	8
Myriagramme	20	6	6	63,5	26	9	10	20
Kilogramme	2	0	5	35,15	2	8	3	2
Hectogramme		3	2	10,715		3	4	7,40
Decagramme			2	44,2715			6	10,34
Gramme				18,82715				15,434
Decigramme				1,882715				1,5434
Centigramme				0,1882715				0,15434

The above weights, as before stated, are deduced each from some decimal proportion of the Metre. Thus the Kilogramme corresponds with the contents of a cubic vessel of pure water at the lowest temperature, the side of which cube is the *tenth* part of the Metre (the Decimetre), and the Gramme answers to the contents of a cubic vessel, the side of which is the *hundredth* part of the Metre (the Centimetre); for the contents of all cubic vessels are to each other in a triplicate ratio of their sides (*Euclid*, 33. xi.)

Astronomical Measures.

ASTRONOMICAL MEASURES.

CENTESIMAL DIVISION OF TIME COMPARED WITH SEXAGESIMAL.

Centesimal.		Sexagesimal. H.	M.	S.
	1 second	0	0	0,864
100 seconds	1 minute	0	1	26,4
100 minutes	1 hour	2	24	0
10 hours	1 day	24	0	0

Sexagesimal.		Centesimal. H.	M.	S.
	1 second	0	0	1,1574
60 seconds	1 minute	0	69	54,4
60 minutes	1 hour	1	15	74
24 hours	1 day	10	0	0

CENTESIMAL DIVISION OF THE CIRCLE COMPARED WITH SEXAGESIMAL.

Centesimal.		Sexagesimal. °	′	″
100 seconds	1 minute (of space)	0	0	$32\frac{2}{5}$
100 minutes	1 degree	0	54	0
100 degrees	1 quadrant	90	0	0
400 degrees	1 circle	360	0	0

Sexagesimal.		Centesimal. °	′	″
60 tierces	1 second	0	0	$3\frac{7}{81}$
60 seconds	1 minute of space	0	1	$85\frac{5}{27}$
60 minutes	1 degree	1	11	$11\frac{1}{9}$
90 degrees	1 quadrant	100	0	0
4 quadrants or 360°	1 circle	400	0	0

GEOGRAPHICAL AND ITINERARY MEASURES.

Geographical Measures.

		English Miles.
Quarter of the Terrestrial Meridian	(*10 millions of metres*) =	6213,857
A Degree	(*$\frac{1}{90}$ part*)	69,0429
Marine League	(*$\frac{1}{20}$ of a degree*)	3,4521
Marine Mile	(*minute $\frac{1}{60}$ of a degree*)	1,1507
League of 25 to a Degree		2,7617
A Degree Decimal	(*$\frac{1}{100}$ of the quadrant*)	62,13857
Myriamètre	(*$\frac{1}{10}$ of a degree decimal*)	6,213857
Kilometre	(*minute of a degree decimal*)	0,62138
Mean League	(*$22\frac{1}{2}$ to a degree*)	3,10693
Post League	(*2000 toises*)	2,3000

SYSTÈME USUEL.

The *Système Usuel* has the metrical standards for its basis, but their divisions are binary; and instead of the new nomenclature, the names of the ancient weights and measures are used, annexing the term *Usuel* to each. Thus the Half Kilogramme is called the *Livre Usuelle*, and the Double Metre the *Toise Usuelle*, &c. Système Usuel.

This system was legalized by an Imperial Decree in 1812, for the use of retail traders, and the Decimal System was continued for all other kind of business and measurement; but as the law was left optional it led to many difficulties, insomuch that in 1816 the Système Usuel was enforced by a Royal Decree, in which the use of weights or measures decimally divided is absolutely prohibited in shops or any departments of trade connected with retail business, while the Decimal System is confirmed for all other purposes.

As the Système Usuel has the Metre and Gramme for its basis, any of its divisions may be easily computed from the foregoing tables. The following, however, are the contents of its principal units in English measure:

The *Toise Usuelle* of 2 Metres equals 6 Feet 6¾ Inches English.

The *Pied Usuel* equals $\frac{1}{6}$ of the Toise, and the Inch $\frac{1}{12}$ of the Foot.

The *Aune Usuelle* equals 3 Feet 11¼ Inches English, with all its divisions in proportion.

The long measures are also divided into thirds, sixths, and twelfths, which are easily computed from the foregoing dimension of the Toise and Aune.

The *Boisseau Usuel* is $\frac{1}{8}$ of the Hectolitre, and equals 0,35474 English Bushels, with halves, quarters, &c. in proportion.

The *Litron Usuel* equals 1,074 Paris Pinte, or $2\frac{1}{9}$ English Pints, with halves, quarters, &c. in proportion.

Apothecaries have adopted the Système Usuel in compounding medicines, which weight, in small quantities, scarcely differs from the Poids de Marc.

Diamonds are still weighed by Carats of 4 Grains each, but these Grains differ from the foregoing. Thus 1 Carat equals 3,876 Grains Poids de Marc, or 3,798 Grains Usuels, and also answers to 2,01 Decigrammes, or $3\frac{1}{10}$ English Grains.

The *Livre Usuelle* = 500 Grammes = 9413,575 Grains Poids de Marc, or 7717 English Grains, and all its divisions and multiples in proportion. Hence the Common Pound of France equals 1lb. 1 oz. $10\frac{1}{5}$ Drams avoirdupois; and therefore the *Quintal Metrique* of 100 Kilogrammes answers to 220,486lb.

Système Usuel.

avoirdupois, or 1 cwt. 3 qr. 24½ lb., which is 1000 Grains less than has been hitherto reckoned, on account of the undue proportion allowed to the French weight, as stated in Note, p. 135.*

---

* The error, which has been lately discovered in the established proportion between the weights of England and France, amounts, in money operations, to about £650 per million, or $\frac{1}{15}$ per cent. and it has been acted upon for nearly eighty years.

That an error of such importance should have so long existed seems incredible; and it is the more surprising as having been established by the concurring experiments and calculations of the most scientific men in both countries. The following is an account of its origin.

In 1742 the Royal Society of London and the Royal Academy of Sciences at Paris, prepared each two sets of standards of their respective weights and measures, in order to exchange one set, with a view of determining their relative contents; and it was also agreed that the standards, when thus compared, should be laid up and preserved in the archives of both Societies.

The results of these important comparisons are fully detailed in the Philosophical Transactions of that year (Vol. XLII. p. 185), but for the present purpose it may be sufficient to state that the Societies (who agreed in all their experiments) found the French Pound equal to 7560 English Grains; and this proportion has formed the basis for all subsequent calculations and comparisons between the weights of both countries.

In the late experiments at the London Mint, (March 1820) the French Pound belonging to that institution was found to weigh only 7555 troy Grains. This difference of 5 Grains led to an examination of the standards of 1742, both French and English, which have been carefully preserved by the Royal Society, and their French Pound was ascertained to agree perfectly with that at the Mint; but their troy Pound was found defective, being nearly 4 Grains too light.

As this troy Pound was originally made the standard of comparison, its deficiency gave a proportional preponderance to the French Pound with which it was compared; and this comparative excess was afterwards transferred by calculation to the Kilogramme, making it 10 Grains heavier than it proves to be by actual experiment. For as 9216 : 18827,15 : : 7560 : 15444. (See pp. 133 and 137.)

From the same cause the avoirdupois Pound of the Royal Society was then reckoned at 7004 troy Grains, whereas it is now found to be only 7000, its established weight. This discrepance, however, was noticed in the Phil. Trans. of 1743, p. 541, in reference to the mint weight as the proper criterion; but there the enquiry terminated.

Thus has this extraordinary error been traced to its source: and it is satisfactory to observe that it did not originate in any inaccuracy on the part of the learned Societies, but on that of the Weight-maker, who furnished them with a defective standard.

It may not be improper here to add, that in the former edition of the *Cambist*, Vol. I. page 154, the weight of the Kilogramme was computed (from its arbitrated relation to the standards of other countries) at 15436 English Grains, which is nearly correct; but in Vol. II. page 268, the Author thought it advisable to insert the established weight: for he had not then the means of ascertaining the proportion by the actual comparison of verified standards, such as have been since amply supplied for this work by the British Consuls abroad.

MONETARY SYSTEM.

Accounts are kept here in Francs of 10 Decimes or 100 Centimes. Before the year 1795 they were kept in Livres of 20 Sous or 240 Deniers. The Livre and Franc were formerly of the same value, but the Franc is now $1\frac{1}{4}$ per cent. better; thus 80 Francs equal 81 Livres; and by this proportion the ancient monies have been generally converted into modern. Monies of Account.

But by a decree of 1810 the following proportion has been established:

Pieces of 48 Livres at 47 Fr. 20 C.
of 24...... at 23 .. 55.
of 6...... at 5 .. 80.
of 3...... at 2 .. 75.

Pieces of 30 and 15 Sous pass for 1 Franc 50 Cent. and 75 Cent., but they are not considered a legal standard for more than 5 Francs.

The coins may be considered under two heads; namely, ancient and modern, the ancient Gold coins are Louis of 24 Livres, and Double Louis of different dates, and varying in value as above; and the Silver coins are Ecus of 6 Livres, with halves, quarters, &c. For their intrinsic value see *Tables of Coins*, Vol. II. Coins.

The modern Gold coins are Napoleons of 40 and 20 Francs, and Louis of the same weight, fineness, and current value.

The Silver coins are Pieces of 5 Francs, also of 2, 1, $\frac{3}{4}$, $\frac{1}{2}$, and $\frac{1}{4}$ Francs.

The coins of Billon and Copper are Pieces of 1 and 2 Decimes, and of 1, 2, 3, and 5 Centimes.

In the old system of coinage the absolute fineness of gold was reckoned at 24 Carats, each 32 parts; and of silver at 12 Deniers, each 24 Grains; but in the new system the fineness of both metals is decimally expressed. Fineness of Gold and Silver.

There are three legal degrees of fineness for wrought gold; the first is $\frac{920}{1000}$, or $22\frac{8}{100}$ Carats; the second, $\frac{840}{1000}$, or $20\frac{16}{100}$ Carats; the third, $\frac{750}{1000}$, or 18 Carats. For wrought silver two legal degrees of fineness are allowed; the first is $\frac{950}{1000}$, or $11\frac{2}{5}$ Deniers; the second, $\frac{800}{1000}$, or $9\frac{3}{5}$ Deniers.

According to the law of 1803, $77\frac{1}{2}$ Pieces of 40 Francs, or 150 Pieces of 20 Francs, are to be coined from a Kilogramme of standard gold, of $\frac{9}{10}$ fine. Rate of Coinage.

Rate of Coinage.

The rate for silver coins is, that 200 Francs must be minted from a Kilogramme of standard silver, of $\frac{9}{10}$ fine. Pieces of Billon of 10 Centimes are minted at $\frac{2}{10}$ fine. The fineness of coins is commonly expressed in *Milliemes*.

Remedy of the Mint.

The remedy in the weight and fineness of the coins is as follows:

Pieces of 40 Francs & 20 Francs $\frac{2}{1000}$ in the weight, and the same in the fineness.
Piece of 5 Francs .... $\frac{3}{1000}$ ditto.
Pieces of 2 & 1 Franc .... $\frac{5}{1000}$ ditto.
Pieces of $\frac{3}{4}$ & $\frac{1}{2}$ of a Franc .... $\frac{7}{1000}$ ditto.
Piece of $\frac{1}{4}$ of a Franc .... $\frac{10}{1000}$ ditto.

The remedy is the same, whether the deviation is over or under the standard weight or fineness, being merely considered as an allowance for accidental error.

From the above regulations it appears that Gold Pieces of 898 Millièmes fine, and Silver of 897, are admissible; but it has been found by a trial of the coinages of six successive years, that the average fineness of the Gold coins was 899,740 Millièmes, and that of the Silver coins 899,588, and their weight was found equally correct. (See *Tarbè*, page 372.)

Sterling Value.

The sterling value of these coins may be found by allowing for each Franc, in gold, 9,525d. and in silver, 9,705d. Thus the 40 Franc Piece is worth £1 11s. 8$\frac{3}{4}$d., and the 5 Franc Piece is worth 48$\frac{1}{2}$d. according to the above mint regulations, without however any allowance for remedy.

Proportional Weight & Value of Metals.

In the Monetary System of France, the coins, if accurately minted, may serve also as weights. Thus, 5 Francs in copper, 50 in billon, 200 in standard silver, or 3100 in standard gold, should weigh 1 Kilogramme. Hence the Franc Piece weighs 5 Grammes, and any other Piece in the above proportion.

	Kilogramme.		Kilogrammes.		
Hence also	1	of minted gold is worth	15$\frac{1}{2}$	of silver	or any other weight in the same proportion.
	1	of minted silver is worth	4	of billon	
	1	of minted billon is worth	10	of copper	

Tariff of the Mint.

When gold or silver is carried to the Mint to be coined, or exchanged for new coins, a deduction called *Retenue* is made for expenses, which, according to the *Tariff* of 1803, is as follows:

The price of the Kilogramme of fine gold is fixed at 3434 Francs 44 Cen. $\frac{444}{1000}$, on account of the *Retenue* for Mint expenses; and without the *Retenue* at 3444 Francs 44 Cen. $\frac{444}{1000}$.

Tariff of the Mint.

The price of the Kilogramme of fine silver is fixed at 218 Francs 88 Cen. $\frac{889}{1000}$, on account of the *Retenue*, and at 222 Francs 22 Cen. $\frac{222}{1000}$, without the *Retenue*. Thus the *Retenue* or mint deduction is nearly $\frac{1}{3}$ per cent. on gold, and exactly $1\frac{1}{2}$ per cent. on silver.

Exchange, Usance, &c.

For the Exchanges of France see Vol. II. page 49.

Besides the places stated in that quotation, Paris exchanges with several cities in the Netherlands, Switzerland, and France, in Francs and Centimes, at a variable per centage.

Throughout France the usance of bills is 30 days, not including the date. Bills are drawn at several days' sight, or at a fixed day, at usance, at double usance, and at several usances.

Since the 1st of January, 1808, no days of grace have been allowed in France, and every bill must be paid on the same day that it becomes due. There is, however, in certain cases, a very liberal allowance of time called *Delais*, which, with various other regulations, are explained in the following Laws of Exchange, extracted from the *Code de Commerce*.

Laws of Exchange.

Art. 125. A bill of exchange must be accepted on presentation, or at latest within twenty-four hours after presentation. Non-acceptance is proved by an act called *Protet faute d'acceptation.*

130. A bill of exchange at sight is payable on being presented.

131. The expiration of a bill of exchange at one or more days, at one or more months, at one or more usances, or at sight, is fixed by the date of acceptance, or by that of the protest in default of acceptance.

The months are those fixed by the Gregorian Calendar.

133. A bill of exchange payable at a fair becomes due on the eve of the day fixed for the close of the fair, or on the day of the fair if it lasts only one day.

134. If a bill of exchange falls due on a legal fair day, it is payable on the eve of that day.

160. The holder of a bill of exchange drawn from the continent, or from the islands of Europe, and payable in the European possessions of France, either at sight or at one or more days, months, or usances at sight, must demand payment or acceptance within six months of its date, under penalty of losing all claim on the indorsers, and even on the drawer, if the latter has made provision.

The *delai* is eight months for bills of exchange drawn from the Levant and

Laws of Exchange.

from the northern coasts of Africa, on the European possessions of France; and reciprocally from the continent and the islands of Europe, on the French establishments on the Levant, and on the north coasts of Africa.

The *delai* is one year for bills of exchange drawn from the western coasts of Africa, as far as, and including, the Cape of Good Hope.

One year is also allowed for bills drawn from the continent and islands of the West Indies, on the European possessions of France; and reciprocally from the continent and islands of Europe, on the French possessions or establishments on the western coasts of Africa, and the continent and islands of the West Indies.

The *delai* is two years for bills of exchange drawn from the continent and islands of the East Indies, on the European possessions of France; and reciprocally from the continent and islands of Europe, on the French possessions or establishments on the continent and islands of the East Indies.

The same penalty shall take place against the holder of a bill of exchange at sight, at one or more days, months, or usances at sight, drawn from France, or from the French possessions or establishments, and payable in foreign countries, if he do not demand payment or acceptance within the *delais* above prescribed for each of the respective distances.

The above *delais* of eight months, one year, or two years, are doubled in case of a maritime war.

The above regulations, however, shall not prejudice any contrary stipulations that may intervene between the taker, the drawer, and even the indorsers.

161. The holder of a bill of exchange must demand payment the day that the term expires.

162. Refusal of payment must be proved the morning after the day of expiration, by an act called *Protet faute de paiement*.

If this day fall on a legal fair day, protest is made the following day.

163. The holder is not excused from making protest in case of non-payment, either by the protest in case of non-acceptance, or by the death or failure of the person on whom the bill of exchange is drawn.

In case of the failure of the acceptor before the term of the bill expires, the holder may protest and bring his action.

166. Bills of exchange drawn from France, and payable beyond the continental territory of France in Europe, being protested, the drawers and indorsers residing in France, shall be sued within the following *delais:*

Two months for bills payable in Corsica, the Isle of Elba or Capraia, England, and the States on the confines of France.

Four months for bills payable in other European States. Laws of Exchange.

Six months for bills payable in the ports of the Levant, and the northern coasts of Africa.

One year for bills payable in the western coasts of Africa, extending as far as, and including, the Cape of Good Hope, and also in the West Indies.

Two years for bills payable in the East Indies.

These *delais* shall be observed in the same proportions in proceeding against drawers and indorsers residing in the French possessions not situated in Europe.

The above *delais* of six months, one year, and two years, shall be doubled in times of a maritime war.

BANK OF FRANCE.

In 1716 an Institution was established in Paris, called *The Bank of France*, which in 1718 took the name of the *Royal Bank*. It was planned in some respects like the Bank of Amsterdam, and was intended, among other objects, to pay off certain debts incurred by trading companies, but it did not prove successful. It was afterwards revived under different forms and designations until the year 1803, when it was established on its present footing. Bank of France.

The following is a brief outline of its constitution and operations:

The present Bank of France was established under a grant of 40 years, which will terminate in 1843. Its capital was 70 millions of Francs, divided into 70 thousand shares of 1 thousand Francs each. The shares, which are also called *Actions*, have been lately increased to 90 thousand. The dividends are at 5 per cent. per annum, paid half-yearly. There is also generally a *Reserve* from the bank profits, which is invested in the 5 per cent. consolidated stocks, to be divided among the sharers of bank stock, at the expiration of the grant.

The Bank of France issues its own notes, payable, in specie, to bearer on demand, and no note is circulated for a less sum than 500 Francs (about £20 sterling). It keeps cash for others nearly on the same plan as private bankers; and the accounts thus opened are called *comptes courants*. It discounts bills of exchange and other commercial as well as government paper. The Bank also advances money on pledges of different kinds, such as gold and silver in bars or in coin; also on government or other paper securities, which are convertible into cash at early periods.

The Bank likewise undertakes the care (as deposits in its chest) of different articles of value, such as gold or silver in ingots or in coin, diamonds, foreign

Bank of France. bills, *actions*, *rentes*, title-deeds, and securities of all kinds. The charge for this assurance of safety is the $\frac{1}{8}$ part of 1 per cent. on the value of each deposit, for every period of six months, or under.

No person can open an account at the Bank, either for keeping cash or discounting bills, without a written application to the Governor, accompanied by the recommendation of three merchants known to the Bank.

No bills are discounted that have more than three months to run, and this term is occasionally contracted. All bills thus presented must be guaranteed by three approved signatures; but two are accepted under certain circumstances.

The administration of the affairs of the Bank is vested in a council-general, consisting of 20 members; viz. 17 Regents and 3 Censors, who are nominated by 200 of the principal proprietors. The King appoints the Governor and Deputy-governor: the former must be possessed of 100 Bank shares, and the latter of 50 shares.

The Governor every year makes a Report of the state of the Bank, called the *Compte Rendu*, which contains a full and particular statement of the affairs of the Institution, such as its issues, assets, discounts, loans, *rentes*, *actions*, deposits, &c. From these Reports it appears that the Institution is in a state of very active operation and increasing prosperity.

STOCKS, OR PUBLIC FUNDS.

Stocks, &c. The French Funds, like those of other countries, are certain revenues of the State, set apart for paying the interest of loans raised for the use of Government, on the common principle of the Funding System. The interest or dividends thus paid are called ***Rentes***, and the property, whether in loan or purchase, is so designated. Thus 1000 Francs in the 5 per cents. are called 50 Francs of ***Rente***, a term generally synonymous with income or annuity.

The French Stocks may be considered under three heads, namely, ***Actions***, ***Rentes***, and ***Reconnaissances***.

Actions. The ***Actions*** are Bank shares, as before explained, and they vary in the market price according to the supposed success of the establishment, or the state of public affairs.

Rentes. The ***Rentes*** are generally understood to be the dividends on the national debt, or what is called the 5 per cent. Consolidated Annuities, being the aggregate of various loans, which may be thus briefly noticed:

In 1798, the national debt amounted to 140 millions of Francs Rentes, or 2800 millions principal, at which embarrassed period of public credit the government reduced the payment of those Rentes to one third, about 47 millions. Rentes.

In 1814, the debt was 63 millions; in 1817, 128 millions; and in 1818, on account of subsidies, it was increased to 185 millions; which sum, however, was reduced by means of a Sinking Fund to 173 millions of Rentes, or 3460 millions of Francs capital (about 140 millions of Pounds sterling).

There is another stock, amounting to 15 millions of Rentes, called ***Reconnaissance de Liquidation***, the capital of which (300 millions) is to be paid off by equal instalments in 5 years, beginning in 1821, and the order of payment is to be determined by lot. Reconnaissances.

This stock was created in 1817, to pay certain debts incurred by the Ex-Emperor, and other outstanding arrears.

The acknowledgments or warrants are issued in shares, called *Coupures*, of 10,000, 5000, and 1000 Francs, bearing an interest of 5 per cent. per annum, the same as the other Stock; but its price is always higher on account of the plan of liquidation.

FRANCFORT *on the Maine (in Germany).*

Accounts at Francfort, Darmstadt, Hanau, and Mentz, are kept in Rixdollars of 90 Creutzers, or in Florins of 60 Creutzers, the Creutzer being divided into 4 Pfenings. Monies of Account.

The Rixdollar of account contains $1\frac{1}{2}$ Florin, $4\frac{1}{2}$ Copsticks, $22\frac{1}{2}$ Batzen, 30 Kaysergroschen, 45 Albuses, 90 Creutzers, or 360 Pfenings.

The Rixdollar specie is reckoned at $1\frac{1}{3}$ Rixdollar of account, 2 Florins, 6 Copsticks, 30 Batzen, 40 Kaysergroschen, 60 Albuses, 120 Creutzers, or 480 Pfenings. Thus 3 Rixdollars specie are equal to 4 Rixdollars of account.

Accounts were formerly kept here in Convention money, and in Müntze, the former being to the latter as 6 to 5; but Convention money is now chiefly used in paying taxes. Common accounts are kept in Müntze, and commercial accounts generally in exchange money, which is exclusively used in bill transactions. The proportion is, that 46 Florins exchange money equal 55 Florins Müntze.

There is a fourth way of reckoning, called the 22 Florin rate, in which the

Monies of Account. convention Rixdollar is reckoned at 2 Florins 12 Creutzers. It is only used in paying certain duties or taxes.

Value of Monies. The convention Rixdollar of account = 3s. 2d. sterling; the convention Rixdollar specie = 4s. 2½d. sterling; and £1 sterling = 9 Florins 30 Creutzers convention money, or 11 Florins 24 Creutzers Müntze.

Coins. The Gold coins of the city of Francfort are Ducats; and the Silver coins, convention Rixdollars, with Halves and Quarters; also Copsticks, and Pieces of 1, 5, and 10 Creutzers convention money. The Copper coins are Hellers.

For the weight, fineness, and sterling value of these coins, see *Tables of Coins*, Vol. II.

Fineness of Gold and Silver. The fineness of gold is expressed in Carats, of 12 Grains; the Mark (of 24 Carats) is worth 303 Florins convention money, more or less. The fineness of silver is expressed in Loths of 18 Grains; the Mark (of 16 Loths) is worth about 20 Florins 20 Creutzers, convention money. Wrought silver should be 12 Loths 12⅜ Grains fine.

Weights. The weight for gold and silver is the Cologne Mark, for which see *Cologne*.

The Pound, commercial weight, is divided into 2 Marks, 32 Loths, 128 Quints, 512 Pfenings, or 1024 Hellers. There are two weights, the Centner, and the common weight. 100lb. Centner weight = 108lb. of the common weight. This Centner is equal to 112¼lb. avoirdupois; and 100lb. common weight = 103lb. avoirdupois, or 46,71 Kilogrammes. The Stone is 22lb.

Dry Measure. The corn measure is called Achtel or Malter, and is divided into 4 Simmers, 8 Metzen, 16 Sechters, 64 Gescheides, 256 Makchen, or 1024 Chrotts. The Malter contains 3,064 English Bushels, or 1,0797 Hectolitres.

In Mentz, the Malter contains 4 Simmers, 16 Kimpfes, or 64 Gescheides.

Liquid Measure. The Stück or Piece of wine contains 1¼ Fuder, 7½ Ohms, 150 Viertels, 600 Maas, or 2400 Schopps. The Ohm is equal to 38,96 English Gallons, or 147,45 Litres.

Long Measures. The Foot equals 0,286 Metres, or 11,27 English Inches.

The Ell is 0,539 Metres, or 21,24 English Inches; but French goods are commonly measured by the Paris Ell, and Dutch goods by the Brabant Ell, for which see *France* and *Antwerp*. Long Measures.

The Saum is 22 Pieces, each of 32 Ells.

Two great Fairs are held every year at Francfort, each lasting 3 weeks. The first begins on Easter Tuesday; the second on the nearest Monday to the 8th September. The first week is called the week of acceptance; the second, the week of payment. Fairs.

The time for acceptance begins on the Monday in the first week, and continues till nine in the morning of Tuesday in the second week; if by that time a bill is not accepted, it must be protested, or at least noted; and if an accepted bill is not paid by change time on the Saturday in the week of payment, it must be protested between 2 o'clock and sunset on the same day. Many bills, however, are made payable in the third week, in which the assignations are given; but this circumstance must be expressly mentioned in the bill; otherwise such as are payable at the Fair will be accounted due in the second week.

For the Exchanges of Francfort see Vol. II. page 54.

Bills drawn on Francfort at 1 usance (by which is understood 14 days after acceptance), also bills drawn at 4 days or more after sight, or after date, have 4 days grace allowed, besides Sundays and holidays. But when a bill has no acceptor, or when it is payable by the drawer himself, if not honoured when due, and if the first indorser, or the person to whose order the bill is drawn, refuses to accept it, the bill must be protested on the very day it becomes due. There are no days of grace allowed on bills *a vista* (at sight), or at less than 4 days sight or date. All such bills must be paid within 24 hours of the specified time. Usances, &c.

FRANCFORT *on the Oder, see Berlin.*

GALICIA *(in Spain).*

Accounts are kept in the kingdom of Galicia, the principality of Asturias, and the territory of Santander, in Reals of 34 Maravedis Vellon. Monies of Account.

Monies of Account. The other Spanish monies of account, and the Spanish coins, which are all current here, will be found under the article *Spain;* but though uniform in their monetary system, those places differ much in their weights and measures, except in the weight for the precious metals, which is the Mark of Castile.

Weights of Galicia. The commercial Pound of Galicia contains 20 Ounces Castilian weight, or 8892½ English Grains. Thus 4lb. of Galicia equal 5lb. of Castile, and 100lb. of Galicia equal 127lb. avoirdupois, or 57,60 Kilogrammes.

The Quintal is 4 Arrobas, and the Arroba 25lb.

Measures of Galicia. The Fanega of corn contains 4 Ferrados. The Ferrado is not the same in the different towns of the province; but the Ferrado of Neda (a small hamlet near Ferrol) is best known. This Ferrado is 12 per cent. larger than that of Corunna, and is the third part of a Castilian Fanega. Thus 100 Ferrados of Neda = 33⅓ Castilian Fanegas; 100 Ferrados of Corunna = 29¾ Castilian Fanegas.

The Ferrado of Neda contains 0,1809 Hectolitres, or 0,508 English Bushels.

The Moyo, wine measure, is divided into 4 Canadas, 16 Ollas, 68 Azumbres, or 272 Quartillos, each Quartillo containing 20 Ounces of wine. 17 such Quartillos are equivalent to 20 Quartillos of Castile. Hence the Moyo contains 42,8 English Gallons, or 162 Litres.

The long measures will be found under the article *Spain.*

Weights & Measures of Asturias. The Asturian commercial Pound is composed of 3 Marks, 24 Ounces, 384 Adarmes, or 13824 Grains, Castilian weight. 100 Asturian Pounds make 150 Pounds Castilian, and therefore equal 152,16lb. avoirdupois, or 69,01 Kilogrammes.

The Fanega of Asturias is divided into 12 Celemines or 48 Quartillos, and is ⅓ larger than the Castilian Fanega. It equals 2,055 English Bushels, or 0,7241 Hectolitres.

The Cantara of wine here is divided in the same manner as the Castilian measure, into 8 Azumbres, or 32 Quartillos, but these measures are 16⅔ per cent. greater than those of Castile, bearing the proportion of 6 Asturian to 7 Castilian Quartillos. The Cantara of Asturias therefore equals 4,81 English Gallons, or 18,2 Litres.

100 Varas of Asturias equal 103$\frac{1}{10}$ Castilian. Thus the Vara equals 34,02 English Inches, or 0,863 Metres.

Weights of Santander. The commercial weight varies very much in the territory of Santander; thus the Quintal of 100lb. of bar iron equals 155 Castilian Pounds; that of Newfoundland fish 102; that of cocoa nuts 107.

The dry and liquid measures also vary much; they are regulated or compared by the standards of Avila and Burgos.* See *Spain.*

GALLIPOLI *(in Italy).*

Monies, Coins, &c. The monies, coins, weights, and measures, are the same here as at Naples, with the following exceptions.

Oil Measure. The oil measure, called Salma, is divided into 10 Staja, or 320 Pignatte, and contains 40,948 English Gallons, or 154,99 Litres. The Pipe is $2\frac{4}{5}$ Salme.

The Last for freighting ships is 11 Salme.

Exchanges. Gallipoli exchanges with Naples, at 102 Ducati, more or less, for 100 Ducati di Regno; with other places its exchanges are similar to those of *Naples.*

GAMRON, or GOMROON *(in Persia),*

Monies and Coins. Also called Bender Abassi, near the Persian Gulf; accounts are here kept in Mamoodis current of 20 Gassas; also in Shahees of 10 Coz.

A Toman contains 100 Mamoodis; a new Bassi or Abassee, 2 Mamoodis, or 4 Shatrees or Shahees; a Shahee 10 Cozbaugues or Coz, a small copper coin. For the other coins of the country see *Persia.*

A Mamoodi is to contain $\frac{2}{5}$ silver, and $\frac{3}{5}$ copper; 100 such Mamoodis, coined at Avesa, in Chusistan, weigh $71\frac{3}{4}$ Mussals or Miscals, or 5136 English Grains; hence a Mamoodi contains $20\frac{1}{2}$ Grains of fine silver; and 100 Mamoodis are worth about 24 Shillings, or 1 Mamoodi equals 3d. sterling nearly.

In former times they had better coins here, of the same degree of fineness nearly as the Rupees (that is, 11 oz. 5 dwts.); 8 of these Mamoodis were reckoned for a Spanish Dollar, and 16 for a Venetian Sequin; but they have become very scarce, and are now sold as merchandize, according to their intrinsic value.

---

* The above article is chiefly extracted from the dispatches sent, with the standard weights of Galicia, to *Lord Castlereagh,* by *Richard Allen, Esq.* his Majesty's Consul at Corunna.

Monies and Coins. All bargains are made in Shahees (an imaginary money) worth half a Mamoodi; but the returns for goods are generally made in Abassees or Double Mamoodis.

Weights. Gold and silver are weighed by the Mussal or Miscal, of $71\frac{7}{11}$ English Grains. The larger weights are of different sorts: the Maund Tabree weighs $6\frac{3}{4}$lb. avoirdupois, but in the Bazar, $6\frac{1}{4}$lb.; the Maund Shaw is double the preceding; the Maund Copara, when goods are sold on trust, is $7\frac{3}{4}$lb. but in the Bazar, from $7\frac{1}{4}$ to $7\frac{1}{2}$lb. avoirdupois.

Measure. The long measure is called Guz, 93 of which are computed to equal 100 English Yards.

GENEVA *(in Switzerland)*.

Monies of Account. Accounts are here kept in two different ways; merchants and bankers carry on foreign trade and the business of exchange in Livres of 20 Sols, or 240 Deniers, which is called *current money;* but shopkeepers and other local traders mostly keep their accounts in Florins, each consisting of 12 Sous or Sols, and each Sol of 4 Quarts, or 12 Deniers. These are called Sols and Deniers *of a Florin*, to distinguish them from the current money.

1 Livre equals $3\frac{1}{2}$ Florins; and consequently 1 Florin is worth $\frac{2}{7}$ of a Livre, or $5\frac{5}{7}$ Sous current; also 10 Sous current equal 21 Sous of a Florin.

The Ecu or Patagon, which is sometimes used in accounts, is a real coin worth 3 Livres, or $10\frac{1}{2}$ Florins. The Ecu may be valued at 4s. sterling, and therefore the Livre is worth 1s. 4d. and the Florin $4\frac{1}{2}$d. nearly.

Coins. The Gold coins of Geneva are, the old Pistole of 11 Livres 10 Sols, and the new Pistole, coined since 1752, worth 10 Livres current, or 35 Florins; with double and triple Pistoles in proportion. The Silver coins are the Bajoires of 3 Livres 15 Sols current; Ecus or Patagons, at 3 Livres current; Pieces of 15, 10, and 5 Sous current, or $31\frac{1}{2}$, 21, and $10\frac{1}{2}$ Sous of a Florin. For their intrinsic value, see *Tables of Coins*, Vol. II.

When Geneva was united to France, in 1803, the French system of monies, weights, and measures, was introduced, and is still partially retained.

Fineness of Gold and Silver. The absolute fineness of gold is reckoned at 24 Carats, subdivided into 32 and also into 24 parts. Fine silver is reckoned at 12 Deniers, subdivided into 24 Grains.

The new Pistole contains 79¾ English Grains of fine gold; and the Ecu, 346½ English Grains of fine silver. Hence the Pistole = 14s. 1½d. sterling; the Ecu = 48½d. sterling nearly; and £1 sterling = 14 Livres 17 Sous, or 52 Florins 2 Sous of Geneva. Value of Monies.

The Mark, which is used for weighing the precious metals, is divided into 8 Ounces, 64 Gros, 192 Deniers, or 4608 Grains; and contains 3785 English Grains, or 245,231 Grammes. Gold and Silver Weight.

The commercial weight is of two sorts; the Pound of the greater weight, called *Poids fort*, contains 18 Ounces; and the Pound of the lesser weight, called *Poids foible*, 15 Ounces: the former is to the latter as 5 to 6. The Ounce, in both weights, is divided into 24 Deniers, or 576 Grains. 1lb. of the Poids fort = 1,214lb. avoirdupois, or 550 Grammes; and the Poids foible in proportion. Commercial Weights.

The Coupe, corn measure, weighs in wheat, 110lb.; and in rye, 103lb. Poids fort. The Coupe contains 2,203 English Bushels, or 7,764 Hectolitres. Dry Measure.

The Char, wine measure, is divided into 12 Setiers; the Setier into 24 Quarterons or 48 Pots. The Quarteron holds very little more than two Paris Pintes; and therefore the Setier = 45,22 Litres, or 11,9 English Gallons. Liquid Measure.

Brandy and Italian or Provence oil are sold by the 100lb. with a tare of 14 per cent.

The Foot is 0,4879 Metres, or 19,2 English Inches. Long Measure.

Silk stuffs and linens, sold wholesale, are measured by the Paris Ell; but retail linen drapers measure with the Geneva Ell, which is 45 English Inches, or 1,143 Metre.

The Acre of land at Geneva is 40 French Toises long, and 34 broad; it contains, therefore, 5,163 French Decares, or 1 Acre 1 Rood 4¼ Perches English measure. Superficial Measure.

For the Exchanges of Geneva see Vol. II. page 57. Exchanges.

The usance of bills drawn on this place from Holland, England, and France, is 1 month of 30 days; from Germany and Italy, 15 days sight. In default of Usance and Days of Grace.

Usance and Days of Grace. payment on the maturity of a bill, it must be protested on the 5th day afterwards, exclusive of Sundays.

Geneva draws on Amsterdam, Paris, and London, at 3 months, and sometimes at 2 months date; on Genoa, Leghorn, Milan, and Turin, at 8 days sight; on Lyons at sight and at the payments.

The holder of a protested bill, which had been accepted or indorsed by an inhabitant of Geneva, must prove his debt, and sue for payment, within 8 days, if he (the holder) resides in Geneva; but if in any other part of Switzerland or Savoy, a month is allowed him, and the same if at Lyons; if in any other part of France, or in Italy, Germany, Flanders, or Holland, 2 months: the allowance for a person residing in England, Sweden, or Denmark, is 3 months; and 4 months for a person resident in Spain or Portugal. The same terms are granted when bills drawn from Geneva on the above places have been protested: but if the holder of such bills should neglect to make his demand within the proper time, as above stated, he forfeits all claim on his Genevese debtor.

GENOA *(in Italy)*.

Monies of Account.

Accounts are kept in Lire of 20 Soldi, or 240 Denari di Lira, *fuori banco.* Several other monies are, however, current here; but, in order to describe them, it will be necessary, contrary to the usual plan of this work, first to give some account of the Bank of Genoa, which is the oldest in existence, commonly called the Bank of St. George; and which was formerly remarkable for its wealth and extensive utility, as uniting the advantages both of a bank of deposit and of circulation. It was established in 1345.

Bank.

The government of Genoa having, at different periods, borrowed money from several commercial companies, mortgaged to them the *gabellas* or salt duties, the custom house duties, and the property of the *Porto Franco;* these companies were finally united into one, which was called the *Bank of St. George.*

The constitution of this bank was as follows: it was principally governed by a board of eight persons, called *Protectors*, one half of whom were changed every six months; there were also four inferior boards, each consisting of eight persons. But the more important affairs were decided by a court of proprietors, in which every person, possessed of 10 shares, was entitled to a vote. The government of the republic, having generally a considerable capital in bank stock, was represented in these courts by two senators. Bank.

The stock of the bank was divided into shares, called *Luoghi.* These were transferable by sale, by mortgage, and by will. Every proprietor had an account open at the bank. The books were kept by twelve notaries, whose business it was to register the transfers, and to credit each share-holder for his dividend; also to issue bank notes, or orders on the treasurer, for any sums applied for by those who had money to their credit on the books; such orders signed always by two of the said notaries. In the month of March, every year, the Protectors, after examining and balancing the annual accounts, declared the dividends that were due to each proprietor.

This institution comprehended four banks of deposit, in the books of which the sums lodged in the hands of the treasurer were inscribed; and an account was opened to the credit of each owner of such sums. The person who made the deposit might leave his money in the bank as long as he pleased, or take bank notes for the whole or for part of the amount. These notes were payable to the bearer, and were paid off on demand at the bank; they were therefore current throughout the country. The treasurer was not to receive or pay any other coins than those called *Madonnine,* or such good foreign coins as had their prices stated and fixed in the *Tariffa.*

The *Porto Franco,* including the custom house, is a spacious inclosure, containing above 300 warehouses, and having, besides, other magazines in different parts of the city. Here all sorts of merchandize that come to Genoa, either by sea or land, are to be deposited. Most of these warehouses are let or sold to merchants; some are, however, kept in reserve for the public. The goods are liable to no charge as long as they remain there, but on coming out they pay the custom house duties, if they are intended for Genoa; but if for exportation, they pay a transit duty, which is higher for goods conveyed by land than for those sent by sea. The bank, as before stated, was the owner of the *Porto Franco.*

Bank accounts were kept in three different sorts of money; first, *Banco,* properly so called, which was constantly fixed at 25 per cent. better than *Fuori banco:* the sums inscribed in the bank books, and the notes issued by the bank, were always expressed in this money. Secondly, Moneta di Permesso, sometimes also called Banco, which was 15 per cent. better than *Fuori banco:* the duties paid at the custom house were valued in this money. Thirdly, Numerato or Cartularo, 225 Lire of which money are worth 437 Lire Fuori banco: the

Bank. dividends on the stock of the bank were valued in Cartularo, and they amounted in general to from 42 to 45 Soldi of that money on each share.

Till the year 1746, foreign bills of exchange were paid in banco; but this ceased on the invasion of the Austrians, at which period the bank was in consequence obliged to suspend its payments; and although it afterwards recovered its credit, contracts have been ever since made in *Fuori banco.* In this money all payments are likewise effected, both for bills and merchandize, and the distinction is constantly repeated.

Some time previous to the above period, an alteration was made in the currency by raising the current value of the Crown of 4 Lire to 5, which makes the difference of 25 per cent., but the bank still retained the former currency; hence the origin of the denominations *Banco* and *Fuori banco.*

Such was the state of the Bank of St. George till the year 1800, when the French being besieged in Genoa by the Austrians, the money in the bank was taken out to pay the army, and to answer other calls, in consequence of which, the notes that were then in circulation could not be paid off: the government, therefore, ordered, that the merchants who rented warehouses in the Porto Franco should be compelled to purchase them from the bank, and the purchase money was to be accepted in bank notes. This expedient, however, proved insufficient, as a considerable number of notes were still left in circulation, which came at last to a discount of 50 per cent. When Genoa was annexed to France, it was at first agreed that these notes should be considered as a national debt, and funded as French stock; but this was altered soon after, and the holders were obliged to receive for them Luoghi, or shares of bank stock at the original price.

The Bank of St. George is no longer considered as a place of deposit for money; its only property now consists of the revenues of the Custom-house, from a part of which the dividends are paid: and the Luoghi or shares, which were originally worth upwards of 200 Lire Fuori banco, now sell for 16 or 17 Lire, the annual dividend on each share being fixed at $1\frac{1}{2}$ Lira Fuori banco.

Other Monies of Account. Besides the Lira, Soldo, and Denaro, there are several other monies of account, which it is proper here to explain.

The Scudo d'oro is worth 9 Lire 8 Soldi Permesso, or 10 Lire $16\frac{1}{7}$ Soldi Fuori banco.

The Scudo d'oro marche is nearly 1 per cent. below the value of the Scudo d'oro; or, more correctly, 5814 Scudi d'oro equal 5875 Scudi d'oro marche.

The Scudo d'argento is worth 7 Lire 12 Soldi Permesso, or 8 Lire $14\frac{4}{5}$ Soldi Fuori banco. This Scudo is chiefly used in sales of silver, and it is then valued in two different ways, in *Moneta di Cartularo* and in *Moneta di Paghe.* When silver is sold in bars, its value is expressed in Cartularo; and the Scudo d'argento is reckoned at 4 Lire 10 Soldi di Cartularo. Moneta di Paghe is only used in sales of Spanish Dollars, and the Scudo d'argento is reckoned at 7 Lire 4 Soldi, *Moneta di Paghe.* 72 Lire Moneta di Paghe = 45 Lire di Cartularo, or 76 Lire Permesso. $122\frac{2}{5}$ Scudi d'argento = 100 Scudi d'oro marche. *Other Monies of Account.*

The Scudo di Cambio was formerly reckoned at 4 Lire banco, and afterwards at 4 Lire Permesso, or 4 Lire 12 Soldi Fuori banco.

These Scudi are all imaginary monies; and each of them is divided into 20 Soldi, or 240 Denari, distinguished by the names of Soldi and Denari d'oro, d'oro marche, d'argento, and di Cambio.

The Piastra or Pezza, another imaginary money, is also divided into 20 Soldi, or 240 Denari di Pezza, and is reckoned at 5 Lire Permesso, or 5 Lire 15 Soldi Fuori banco.

The coins of Genoa (valued in money Fuori banco) were as follow, before the year 1790, and as some are still in circulation, it is proper they should be noticed. In Gold, Doppie or Pistoles, at 23 Lire 12 Soldi; halves and quarters, double and quadruple Pistoles, and Pieces of 5 Pistoles in proportion; Genovine d'oro, at 100 Lire, halves, quarters, and eighths in proportion; Sequins, at 13 Lire 10 Soldi. In Silver, Scudi or Genovine, full weight, at 9 Lire 10 Soldi; light Genovine, weighing $32\frac{1}{8}$ Denari, at 9 Lire; Scudi di Giambatista, or Scudi di Cambio (banco value) at 5 Lire, halves and quarters in proportion; Giorgini, at 26 Soldi; double, single, and half Madonnine, at 40, 20, and 10 Soldi. *Coins.*

The above was the legal value of these coins; but they had commonly (except the Madonnine) an abusive value in currency; the Pistole, for instance, passing for 24 Lire 15 Soldi; and so in proportion for the rest.

There were also base silver pieces of 6 Soldi 8 Denari; double and single Parpajole, of 4 and 2 Soldi; and copper Pieces of 8, 4 and 2 Denari.

In 1790, a new coinage took place, consisting of Gold Genovine at 96 Lire; halves, quarters, and eighths; and Silver Scudi at 8 Lire; halves, quarters, and eighths in proportion. *New Coinages.*

In 1797, when Genoa assumed the name of the Ligurian Republic, Gold

New Coinages.

pieces were coined of 4 and 2 Pistoles, or 96 and 48 Lire; and Silver Scudi of 8 Lire, with halves, &c.

Genoa being united to France in 1804, the French coins were introduced there; but the Genoese coins were still allowed to circulate, and the coinage of them is to continue. Even at present (1820), when the country is united to Piedmont, under the government of the King of Sardinia, it still retains the distinct name of the Duchy of Genoa, and continues its coins and nominal currency.

Foreign coins have an extensive circulation here, but are not fixed in their current value.

Sterling Value.

The following is the sterling value, very nearly, of the principal coins here:

The Pistole is worth 16s. 7d. sterling; the Sequin = 9s. 5d.; the old Genovina or Scudo d'Argento = 6s. 7d.; the common Genovina of 9 Lire = 6s. 3d.; the Scudo di Giambatista = 3s. 5d.; the Giorgino = 11d. nearly; the gold Genovina of 96 Lire = 62s. 8d. in gold. The Scudo of 8 Lire = 5s. 4d. in silver; the Lira Fuori banco = 8d.; the Scudo di Cambio of 4 Lire 12 Soldi Fuori banco = 37$\frac{1}{4}$d.; and the Pezza of 5$\frac{3}{4}$ Lire (by which the exchange between Genoa and London is regulated) = 46d.; and £1 sterling = 30 Lire Fuori banco in silver; but in gold, the Pezza is worth 45$\frac{1}{24}$d.; and £1 sterling = 30 Lire 12 Soldi 10 Denari.

For the value of the above coins from assays, see *Table of Coins*, Vol. II.

Fineness of Gold and Silver.

The fineness of gold is expressed in Carats and Ottavi, the weight being divided into 24 Carats, and each Carat into 8 parts or Ottavi. The Pound (of 12 Ounces) of Genoa standard gold is constantly worth 93$\frac{1}{4}$ Scudi d'oro, or 876 Lire 11 Soldi Permesso, with an agio of 9 per cent. more or less; the Pound of fine gold is constantly worth 961 Lire 15 Soldi 4$\frac{5}{6}$ Denari Permesso, with an agio of about 9 per cent.; to each of these valuations must be added a further agio of 15 per cent. in order to express the value in Fuori banco. Hence 72lb. of fine gold = 79lb. of standard gold.

The fineness of silver is expressed in Ounces, each of 24 Denari. The Pound (of 12 Ounces) of fine silver is constantly valued at 38 Lire 3 Soldi 8$\frac{3}{4}$ Denari, with about 10 per cent. agio, in Moneta di Numerato, or at 64 Lire 1 Soldo nearly, in Moneta di Permesso, with the same agio of 10 per cent. more or less.

Weights.

The Pound, gold and silver weight, is divided into 12 Ounces; the Ounce into 24 Denari, or 576 Grani; this Pound weighs 316,963 Grammes, or 4891½ English Grains.*

This weight, called Peso Sottile, is used not only for gold and silver, but for all commodities of small bulk.

Other goods are weighed with the Peso Grosso; the Cantaro of which is divided into 6 Rubbi, 100 Rottoli of 18 Ounces each, or 150lb. of 12 Ounces.

The Cantaro Peso Grosso is 10 per cent. heavier than the Cantaro Peso Sottile. Hence 100lb. Peso Grosso equal 76,875lb. avoirdupois, or 34,86 Kilogrammes; and 100lb. Peso Sottile equal 69,89lb. avoirdupois, or 31,71 Kilogrammes.

Dry Measure.

Corn is measured by the Mina of 8 Quarte, or 96 Gombette. The Mina contains 1,207 Hectolitre, or 3,426 English Bushels. A Mondino of salt contains 8 Mine.

Liquid Measure.

The Mezzarola, wine measure, is divided into 2 Barili 100 Pinte, or 180 Amole, and is reckoned at 18 Rubbi or 450lb. Peso Sottile. The Mezzarola = 148 Litres, or 39,22 English Gallons.

The Barile of oil contains 4 Quarti, or 64 Quarteroni = 7½ Rubbi, or 187½lb. Peso Sottile, rendering 64,647 Litres, or 17,08 English Gallons.

Long Measures.

The Palmo corresponds to 0,24701 Metres, or 9,725 English Inches. The Canna is of three sorts: the Canna Piccola, which tradesmen and manufacturers use, is 9 Palmi, or 87,5 English Inches; the Canna Grossa, which is used by merchants, is 12 Palmi, or 116,7 English Inches; the Canna used at the Custom-house is 10 Palmi, or 97,5 English Inches. The Braccio contains 2⅓ Palmi.

Allowances.

The following are the chief allowances made in the sale of goods in Genoa; viz. alum, copper, hemp, hides, iron, lead, rice, and tin in bars, are sold by the Cantaro of 100 Rottoli or 150lb. Peso Sottile, with real tare only.

Bark, cinnamon, cochineal, cocoa, coffee, cloves, drugs, gums, indigo, liquorice,

* This weight is variously computed by different authors. *Kruse* makes it 4903 English Grains; and *Ricard*, 4898; but the verified standard Pound lately received from *James Sterling, Esq.* his Majesty's Consul at Genoa, has been found at the *London Mint* to weigh only 4891½ English Grains, as above, which corresponds more nearly with *Tillet* and *Bonneville*, who make it equal to 4894 English Grains.

Allowances. nutmegs, tobacco, and tea, are sold by the Pound, with a tret of 6lb. per 106, besides real tare.

Cotton wool, codfish, and stockfish, by the Cantaro Sottile, with 4 per cent. tare.

Raw sugars by the 100lb. with 6 per cent. tret.

Ditto from Lisbon, in chests, with 20 per cent. tare.

Ditto from St. Domingo, in hogsheads, with 13 per cent. tare.

Ditto from Martinico, with 11 per cent. tare.

Ditto Muscovada, with 14 per cent. tare.

Ditto from the Havannah, in boxes, with 14 per cent. tare, besides the tret of 6 in 106.

Loaf sugars have 2 per cent. allowed for paper and string.

Exchanges. For the exchanges of Genoa see Vol. II. page 61.

Usance. The usance for bills drawn on Genoa from Amsterdam, Hamburgh, Spain, and Sicily, is 2 months, and from London and Lisbon, 3 months after date: from Naples, Ancona, and Trieste, 22 days sight; Venice and Rome, 15 days; Augsburg and Vienna, 14 days; Leghorn, Milan, and Turin, 8 days sight; Constantinople and Smyrna, 30 days sight.

Days of Grace. Thirty days are allowed to the holder of a bill to demand payment; but no days of grace are allowed to the acceptor. A bill may be protested on the next day after it becomes due, though it is usual to delay the protest until the first post day for the place from whence the bill came.

GERMANY.

Germany being divided into a number of separate states, the particulars of each will be found in this work, under its proper head. But as there are certain regulations and usages, which are common to most parts of that country, the following general view of them may be useful as well as satisfactory.

Monies of Account. The most common way of keeping accounts is in Rixdollars of 90 Creutzers, or in Guldens or Florins of 60 Creutzers; the Rixdollar of account, or (as it is generally called) Rixdollar *current*, is reckoned at $1\frac{1}{2}$ Florin; and the Rixdollar *specie* or Rixdollar effective, at 2 Florins convention money, or 2 Florins 24 Creutzers Müntze. The Rixdollar current is in some places divided into thirds and fourths, the first called Kaysergroschen of 30 Creutzers, and the second called Batzen of $22\frac{1}{2}$ Creutzers. The above way of keeping accounts prevails in a considerable part of Germany, including Austria and its dependencies, Bohemia, Bavaria, Swabia, and Franconia. In Prussia, Saxony, Hanover, Brunswick, and Luneburg, accounts are kept in Rixdollars of 24 Good Groschen, each Good Grosche being divided into 12 Pfenings; or in Rixdollars of 36 Marien Groschen, each Marien Grosche being divided into 8 Pfenings. Hamburgh, Altona, Lubeck, Holstein, and Mecklenburgh, keep accounts in Marks of 16 Shillings Lubs, each Shilling being divided into 12 Pfenings; and the Rixdollar is reckoned at 3 Marks. The other countries bordering on the Baltic and North Sea, and the countries on the left bank of the Rhine, have various ways of keeping accounts, which are explained each under its proper head. Monies of Account.

Every independent state or city of Germany has its own coins; most of which, however, may be referred to, or compared with the following; namely, in Gold, the Ducat, the Pistole, and the Gold Florin or Gulden; and in Silver, the Rixdollar specie, and its subdivisions. Coins.

The rate of coinage of Ducats is the same all over Germany; 67 Ducats are to weigh a Cologne Mark, and the gold must be $23\frac{2}{3}$ Carats fine; Ducats, however, in most places, are allowed to circulate, provided the deficiency in weight or fineness does not amount, in all, to more than the sixth part of a Carat; and they are then called *Passier Ducats.* Rate of Coinage of Ducats.

Under the name of Pistoles are included the Saxon August d'ors, Prussian Frederick d'ors, Brunswick Carl d'ors, Hanoverian George d'ors, Danish Holstein Christian d'ors, and the Pistoles of Hesse, the Palatinate, Hildesheim, and Mecklenburgh; all reckoned originally at 5 Rixdollars convention money. 35 Pieces of each of these sorts of money are to weigh a Cologne Mark, and the gold to be $21\frac{3}{4}$ Carats fine; so that $38\frac{18}{29}$ Pieces contain a Cologne Mark of fine gold. An allowance is, however, generally made for deficiency in weight and fineness, and they are current in most places, if $35\frac{3}{5}$ Pieces weigh a Cologne Mark of gold, $21\frac{2}{3}$ Carats fine; they are then called *Passier Pistoles;* but the proportional market price of gold to silver having of late years increased, the Pistoles generally yield a premium or agio of from 6 to 10 per cent. Pistoles.

Convention Coins.

The most common standard for Silver coins is the *Convention* or 20 Florin rate of coinage, which, since 1763, has been established throughout the empire, with the exception of Prussia, Hanover, Liege, Swedish Pomerania, Hamburgh, Lubeck, and Holstein. According to this rate, the Cologne Mark of fine silver is valued at 13⅓ Rixdollars of account, or 10 Rixdollars effective, or 20 Florins. The weight and fineness of each Piece is regulated as follows:

8⅓	Specie Rixdollars are to weigh a Cologne Mark,	13 Loths 6 Grains fine.	
16⅔	Florins or Pieces of two-thirds, ...	ditto	ditto.
33⅓	Half Florins, or Pieces of one-third, ...	ditto	ditto.
35	Copfsticks or 20 Creutzers Pieces, ...	ditto 9 Loths 6 Grains fine.	
70	Pieces of 10 Creutzers, ...	ditto 8 Loths fine.	
105	Pieces of 5 Creutzers, ...	ditto 7 Loths fine.	
117$\frac{7}{9}$	Good Groschen, ...	ditto 5 Loths 16 Grains fine.	
137½	Kayser Groschen, ...	ditto 5 Loths 9 Grains fine.	

In small payments, however, the Convention coins are often valued according to the 24 Florin rate, the Cologne Mark of fine silver being then reckoned at 16 Rixdollars of account, or 24 Florins; each of the coins is then rated 20 per cent. higher than its value in Convention money; the specie Rixdollar passes for 2⅖ Florins; the Convention Florin for 1⅕ Gulden; the Copfstuck for 24 Creutzers; and the others in proportion, except the smallest coins, which (being composed of very base metal) do not alter their value. In most parts of the circles of Bavaria, Swabia, Franconia, Upper and Lower Rhine, and Westphalia, current expenses are reckoned according to this rate, and payments are made chiefly in Müntze, that is, small coins. Convention money in those countries is confined to exchanges and wholesale business; but in the Austrian dominions, accounts are, in all cases, kept in Convention money.

Fineness of Gold and Silver.

The fineness of gold is valued (all over Germany) by dividing the Mark fine, or other weight, into 24 Carats, and the Carat into 12 Grains; the fineness of silver, by dividing the Mark fine into 16 Loths, and the Loth into 18 Grains.

Leipsic Rate of Coinage.

The Leipsic rate of coinage had been adopted by an agreement at Leipsic, in 1690, between the Electors of Brandenburg, Saxony, and Brunswick Luneburg; it was established, by an Imperial Decree of 1738, for the common rate of coinage of the empire, and subsisted till the Convention rate was introduced. According to the Leipsic rate, the Cologne Mark of fine silver was valued at 12 Rixdollars of account, 9 effective Rixdollars, or 18 Florins; 8 Specie Rixdollars

Leipsic Rate of Coinage.

were to weigh a Cologne Mark of silver, 14 Loths 4 Grains fine; 13½ Florins or Pieces of ⅔ were to weigh a similar Mark, 12 Loths fine, and the other coins in proportion; except the smallest coins, such as double and single Marien Groschen, in which the Mark of fine silver was coined at the rate of 12⅜ Rixdollars. These coins are also known by the name of *Constitution coins.*

100 Rixdollars, coined after the Leipsic rate, are worth 111⅑ Convention Rixdollars, and such of them as now remain bear an agio accordingly; but they have become very rare.

The rates of coinage established in Prussia, Hamburgh, &c. will be found under each article respectively.

Gold and Silver Weight.

The weight for gold and silver is not the same in all parts of Germany; but the Cologne or Cölnish Mark is every where the standard weight for coins; it is divided into 8 Ounces, 16 Loths, 256 Pfenings, 512 Hellers, 4352 Eschen, or 65536 Richtpfenings. For a more particular account of this weight, see *Cologne, Hamburgh,* and *Prussia.*

Commercial Weight.

The Pfund or Pound of commercial weight is divided into 2 Marks, or 16 Ounces; and the Ounce into 2 Loths, 8 Quentins, 32 Pfenings, or 64 Hellers. Each place has its particular weight. The larger weights are the Shippond, Centner or Quintal, Lispond, and Stein or Stone; but they do not in all places contain the same number of Pounds, as may be seen by a reference to the respective articles.

Apothecaries' Weight

The Pound, apothecaries' weight, contains 12 Ounces; and the Ounce is divided into 8 Drams, 24 Scruples, or 480 Grains. With the exception of Hanover, this weight is the same all over Germany, the Pound being equal to 5527 English Grains, or 358,1 Grammes.

Diamond Weight.

The weight for diamonds, pearls, and precious stones, is the Carat, which is divided into 4 Grains, and also into 64 parts. This Carat weighs 3,171 English Grains, or 2,054 Decigrammes.

Measures.

The measures for corn and liquids are too various to be given under any general head.

The long measures are also very different; but are, in most places, divided in the same manner; namely, the Foot into 12 Inches, and the Inch into 12

Measures. Lines; the Ell most commonly consists of 2 Feet; the Clafter is 6 Feet, and the Ruthe, 12 Feet. The Rhineland Foot, which is used by land surveyors, in most parts of Germany, contains 12,36 English Inches, or 0,3139 Metres.

The German geographical Mile, 15 to a degree, measures 4000 geometrical Paces, and equals 4,60 English Miles, or 7,407 Kilometres.

Of things that are sold by number a gross Thousand is 1200 Pieces; a common Thousand, 1000; a gross Hundred, 120; a common Hundred, 100; a Ring, 240; a Wall, 80; a Webe, 72; a Schock, 60; a Zimmer, 40; a Stiege, 20; a Mandel, 15; a Dozen or Dutzen, 12; a Gross, 12 Dozen or 144; a Decher, 10.

A Bale of paper is 10 Riesses, or 100 Books; each Book containing 24 Sheets of writing paper, or 25 Sheets of printing paper.

A Last of lime, tar, pitch, train oil, butter, &c. is 12 Tonnes or Casks; a Last of herrings is also 12 Tonnes, each Tonne containing about 800; a Roll of stock-fish is 180.

A Pack of cloth is 10 Stuck, or 220 Pieces; a Bale is 12 Pieces; a Stuck or Saum, 22 Pieces; each Piece is 32 Ells; a Fardel is 45 Barchets, each of 22 or 24 Ells.

GHENT, *see Netherlands.*

GIBRALTAR *(in Spain).*

Monies of Account. Accounts are generally kept here in Effective or Hard Dollars, commonly called *Cobs.* The Dollar is divided into 12 Reals, and each Real in 16 Quartos.

Accounts were formerly kept in Current Dollars, which is an imaginary money, valued at two-thirds of the Hard Dollar, and is divided into 8 Reals, each of 16 Quartos, so that the Reals and Quartos of both Dollars are the same.

The estimate par of the Effective Dollar is here 4s. 6d. sterling; and hence the Current Dollar is worth 3s. the Real 4½d. and the Quarto 1⅛ Farthing.

Coins. There are no coins minted here, but those of Spain are used both as money and merchandise, and consist chiefly of Doubloons and Dollars, with their subdivisions; the nominal proportion between them is that 1 Doubloon equals 16 Dollars; but this varies, as Dollars are generally at a premium of from 2 to 5 per cent., and even higher, on account of their convenience for exportation.

Weights & Measures.

The weights and measures both of England and Spain are used here, between which there is the following customary or established proportion.

The Quintal of 100lb. Spanish is reckoned at 101¾lb. avoirdupois. The Arroba, which contains 3⅓ English Gallons, when filled with water, is reckoned to weigh 26lb. avoirdupois.

The principal corn measure is the Fanega, 5 of which are estimated at 8 English Bushels, strake measure; but when heaped, 2 Fanegas are computed at 4⅛ English Bushels.

The wine measures are chiefly those of Cadiz, and the Pipe is estimated at 126 English Gallons.

Exchanges.

Bills from England on Gibraltar are drawn in Current Dollars of 8 Reals; but those from Gibraltar on London have been of late years drawn in Effective Dollars of 12 Reals. Bills on the Treasury of London in time of war are generally at 90 days' sight, and in time of peace at 60 days' sight, which is considered rather shorter than the usual term of mercantile bills on London, which is 90 days' date.

The exchange of Gibraltar on Cadiz, Madrid, and other cities of Spain, is in Hard Dollars, at a per-centage which varies from ⅛ to 8 per cent. mostly in favour of Gibraltar. The governing principle is generally what the Dollar is worth here in sterling, for a bill drawn on London, compared with its sterling value at the place in Spain where it is made payable. Such bills are commonly at 8 days' sight, without days of grace.

All other countries that exchange with Gibraltar pay an uncertain sum of their monies for the Hard Dollar; and in all bill transactions in which Dollars are mentioned, they are understood, whatever may be their current price, to be payable in gold at the rate of 16 to the Doubloon.

The days of grace are three, unless the word *fixed* is inserted, which signifies that the bill must be paid on the day on which the term expires.

Tares or Allowances.

Deductions made from the weight of goods mostly depend on the nature of the packages; and where these cannot be conveniently weighed separately, an allowance is established, which varies in different places. The following are the customary Tares allowed in Gibraltar, and such are generally continued unaltered for the convenience and government of merchants.

Barilla, Alicant, 7lb. per single bag.
12lb. per double bag.

Tares or Allowances. Copperas, Carolina rice, and West India white sugar, in casks, 10 per cent.

Tobacco, in hogsheads, 10 per cent.

Cotton wool, Levant, 5 per cent.

All others in regular packages, 4 per cent.

Indigo, Caraccas, 14lb. per Seroon.

Guyaquil, 18lb. per Seroon.

Steel, Trieste, in boxes, 7 per cent.

Sugar, Havannah, in boxes, as marked, with 4 per cent. thereon; when the mark is erased, 56lb.

Sugar, Brazil, by the tares marked on the chests.

Muscovado, in casks, 12 per cent.

Teas, East India Company's importation, fine, 18lb. per chest; common, 20lb. per chest.

Teas, American importation, Custom-house weights, black mark.

Cinnamon, 7lb. per churla, or 21lb. per double bale.

No tare is allowed on the following goods, when in single or regular bags; viz. cocoa, almond kernels, white beans, East India rice, pepper (American importation,) sumach, Brazil roll tobacco.

Real tares are allowed on the following articles, viz:

Alum, coffee, and cocoa, in casks.

Brimstone, drugs, East India indigo, in boxes.

Butter, lard, soap, in whatever packages.

East India sugars, cochineal, cassia, cloves, nutmegs, Cuba tobacco, wax, English and Dutch cheese, negrohead tobacco.

GOA, *see East Indies.*

GOTHENBURG, *see Sweden.*

GUINEA *(in Africa).*

Shells used for Money. There are no coins minted in this part of Africa; but the inhabitants use for money small shells called by Europeans Cowries, and by Africans Zimbis. 2000 of these shells are called a Macuta. Spanish Dollars, however, and other foreign coins, circulate here.

Gold dust is commonly sold by the Akey, a weight corresponding to $20\frac{1}{32}$ Grains troy. Weights & Measures.

The weight used for merchandize by the Negroes is called Benda, and is divided into 2 Benda-offas, 3 Eggebas, 8 Pisos or Usanos. A Benda = $989\frac{1}{2}$ Grains troy, or 2 oz. $4\frac{5}{16}$drs. avoirdupois.

A Seron is $1\frac{1}{2}$ Piso; and a Piso is subdivided into $1\frac{1}{3}$ Quintos, 2 Agiragues, or 4 Media-tablas.

Linen is sold by the Jacktan of 12 English Feet.

HAMBURGH *(in Germany)*.

Accounts are kept here in Marks, which are divided into 16 Sols or Shillings *Lubs*, and the Shilling into 12 Pfenings. Monies of Account.

Accounts are also kept, particularly in exchanges, in Pounds, Shillings, and Pence *Flemish;* the Pound consisting of 20 Shillings, and the Shilling of 12 Pence or Grotes, Flemish.

The word *Lubs* originally meant money of Lubeck, which is the same as that of Hamburgh, and the term is intended to distinguish this money from the Flemish denominations, and also from the money of Denmark and other neighbouring places.

The Mark Lubs is worth $2\frac{2}{3}$ Shillings Flemish, or 32 Grotes; consequently the Sol Lubs is 2 Grotes Flemish, and the Shilling Flemish 6 Shillings Lubs.

The *Reichsthaler* or Rixdollar specie is 3 Marks, 48 Shillings, or 576 Pfenings.

The Rixdollar of exchange is 2 Marks.

The Pound Flemish is $2\frac{1}{2}$ Rixdollars, $7\frac{1}{2}$ Marks, 20 Shillings Flemish, 120 Shillings Lubs, 240 Grotes Flemish, 720 Dreylings, or 1440 Pfenings.

There are here four different sorts of money, to all of which the above denominations are applied; namely, banco, current money, specie, and light money. Different Sorts of Money.

1. Banco consists of the sums of money deposited by merchants and others in the bank, and inscribed in its books, which sums are not commonly drawn out, but are transferred from one person to another, in payment of a debt or contract.

2. Current money, or Currency, consists of the common coins of the city, in which current expenses are mostly paid.

3. Specie means the old, full weight, *Constitution* Rixdollars, each reckoned at 3 Marks specie; these the bank reckons at 1 per 1000 better than banco, when

Different Sorts of Money.

it receives them, but $1\frac{5}{8}$ per 1000 when it pays them away; and out of the bank, they bear an agio of about $\frac{1}{2}$ per cent. above banco.

4. Light money *(Leichts Geld)* comprehends several foreign coins, to which a nominal value is given; the specie Rixdollars, and also Dutch Alberts Dollars being, for instance, reckoned at 4 Marks light money; old German Florins, and fine Pieces of two-thirds, at 2 Marks; current German Rixdollars, at 3 Marks; Ducats at $8\frac{1}{4}$ Marks; gold Gilders at 6 Marks; Pistoles, Fredericks, Carl d'ors, at 15 Marks, &c. As this is, however, considerably above the value which these coins bear in currency, they are reduced to their real value by deducting a discount, which varies from different causes, such as the agio on the bank, the price of silver, &c.

Banco and Currency being the two principal sorts of money, will be more particularly explained under the head *Bank.*

Coins.

The Gold coins of Hamburgh are Ducats, and Double Ducats, which are coined after the rate of the Empire, of 1559, that is to say, 67 Ducats are minted from a Cologne Mark of gold, of 23 Carats 8 Grains fine, and Double Ducats in proportion. The fineness however in practice is reckoned at $23\frac{1}{2}$, or 47 pure and 1 alloy.

The Silver coins are Rixdollars specie, coined after the rate of the Empire, 8 being minted from a Cologne Mark of silver, of 14 Loths 4 Grains fine, or $\frac{8}{9}$.

The other coins consist of silver currency, which are the coins of the city, minted after the rate fixed by the Convention of Lubeck, viz:

From a Cologne Mark of fine silver are coined

Pieces	of	each Loths fine	or
17 Pieces of	2 Marks, each	12 Loths fine, or	$\frac{3}{4}$.
34	1	12	$\frac{3}{4}$.
68	8 Shillings	10	$\frac{5}{8}$.
136	4	9	$\frac{9}{16}$.
272	2	7	$\frac{7}{16}$.
576	1	6	$\frac{3}{8}$.
1216	6 Pfenings	4	$\frac{1}{4}$.
2432	3	4	$\frac{1}{4}$.

Fineness of Gold, and how sold.

The fineness of gold is expressed in Carats and Grains; the Mark fine, or other weight, being reckoned at 24 Carats, and the Carat at 12 Grains.

Gold is sold by Ducats of $23\frac{1}{2}$ Carats fine, at a variable number of Sols banco per Ducat. The average price for three years, ending in 1819, was $99\frac{3}{4}$ Sols banco per Ducat.

Fineness of Gold.

47 Cologne Marks of Portugal gold, 22 Carats fine, are reckoned at 2948 Ducats; and 43 such Marks of gold, $21\frac{23}{24}$ Carats fine, at 2692 Ducats.

Fineness of Silver, and how sold.

The fineness of silver is expressed in Loths and Grains; the Mark fine being reckoned at 16 Loths, and the Loth at 18 Grains.

The Cologne Mark of fine silver, in bars, is sold in Marks banco per Mark fine. The medium price for three years, ending 1819, was 28 Marks banco. The Mark of fine silver, in Spanish Dollars, valued at $14\frac{2}{3}$ Loths fine, is commonly a few Shillings lower.

Wrought silver in Hamburgh is to be 12 Loths 3 Grains (or 9 oz. $2\frac{1}{2}$ dwts.) fine; and the value of the Loth (or half Ounce) exclusive of the price of labour, is 25 Shillings $10\frac{1}{4}$ Pence Hamburgh currency.

Value of Monies.

The full weight banco specie Rixdollar weighs 2 Loths, or 608 Asen, that is, 451 English Grains, and being 14 Loths 4 Grains fine, (or 10 oz. $13\frac{1}{3}$ dwts.) it contains 540 Asen, or $400\frac{1}{2}$ English Grains of fine silver; the lightest banco Rixdollar weighs 590 Asen, or $437\frac{3}{5}$ English Grains, and the least fine is 14 Loths, (or 10 oz. 10 dwts.) so that the worst banco Rixdollar contains 516 Asen, or $382\frac{3}{4}$ English Grains of fine silver. Therefore, taking a medium between these two valuations, the Hamburgh banco Rixdollar may be considered as containing 528 Asen, or $391\frac{3}{5}$ English Grains of fine silver.

As to currency, the Rixdollar (or more properly the 3 Marks current) in pieces coined since the year 1726, may be valued at 429 Asen, or 318 Grains of fine silver. This would give the proportion of banco to current as 13 to 16, or $23\frac{1}{13}$ for the par of the agio at the bank; this agio, however, fluctuates, according to the variations in the price of silver, and from other causes.

Value in Sterling.

Thus the mean value of the banco Rixdollar is $54\frac{2}{3}$d. sterling; or £1 sterling = 13 Marks $2\frac{5}{7}$ Shillings banco, which would give the par between London and Hamburgh banco at 35s. 1d. Flemish banco nearly for £1 sterling. No permanent par, however, can be fixed between those places, on account of the fluctuation of banco; but from the weight and fineness of the current Marks, it may be computed that £1 sterling = 16 Marks 2 Shillings Hamburgh currency, or that 1 Mark current = $14\frac{4}{5}$d. sterling.

With respect to Hamburgh Ducats, it has been already stated that their value fluctuates, according to the market price of the metal; but as they

Value in Sterling. contain $52\frac{3}{4}$ English Grains of pure gold, they are worth each 9s. 4d. sterling, and the 10 Ducat piece (the Portugaloese), and its divisions, are in proportion.

Specie Rixdollars were first coined at Hamburgh in 1519, and their value was then reckoned at 44 Shillings Lubs; but they rose gradually, during the following century, to 48 Shillings, their present rate; they were, however, in 1620 and 1621, as high as 54s.—but since the year 1622, the Rixdollar, considered either as a real or an imaginary coin, has been reckoned at 48 Shillings; so that a Rixdollar specie, banco, or currency, means 48 Shillings specie, banco, or currency.

Weight for Gold and Silver. Gold, silver, and coins, are weighed by the Cologne weight; the Pound contains 2 Marks, 16 Ounces, or 32 Loths; the Ounce, 2 Loths, 8 Quentins, 32 Pfenings, 544 Eschen, or 8192 Richtpfenings.

The Cologne Mark (as has been stated under the article *Cologne*) weighs 3608 English Grains; so that 480 Ounces, Cologne weight, are equal to 451 Ounces English troy weight.

It is stated by *Kruse*, that in 1742, a standard weight of pure brass was cast at Hamburgh by order of the magistrates, exactly equal to a model which had been brought from Cologne for that purpose; it was stamped with the arms of the bank, where it has been since kept as the standard weight for gold and silver.*

When Ducats are to be weighed in parcels, there are peculiar weights of 1, 2, 4, 8, 16, 32 Ducats, &c. and also of $\frac{1}{2}$, $\frac{1}{4}$, $\frac{1}{8}$, $\frac{1}{16}$, and $\frac{1}{32}$, &c.

For diamond and apothecaries' weight see *Germany*.

Commercial Weight. The commercial Pound is divided into 2 Marks, 16 Ounces, 32 Loths, 128 Quentins, or 512 Pfenings. This Pound answers to 33 Loths, $2\frac{1}{2}$ Pfenings, Cologne weight; that is, $96\frac{1}{2}$lb. Hamburgh weight answer to 100lb. Cologne weight. Thus 100lb. of Hamburgh = 106,81b. avoirdupois, or 48,44 Kilogrammes.

---

* The variations of the Cologne Mark have been already noticed, (page 71,) and a mean of them has been recently taken from the contents of the principal standards of Germany, as determined at the *London Mint* in March 1820. By these experiments and computations it appears that the average weight of the Cologne Mark is about 3609 English Grains, without, however, including the Mark used at Hamburgh, which is one Grain lighter. In making such comparisons, it is indeed difficult to give a preference, although perhaps the greatest reliance may be placed on the Hamburgh standard, from the well known care with which it is preserved; and it may be added, that the copy transmitted for trial to London by the Consul General, was verified for the occasion with particular care by *Richard Parish, Esq.* the President of the Board of Trade of Hamburgh. See *Cologne*.

The Shipfund contains $2\frac{1}{2}$ Centners, 20 Lisponds, or 280lb.; a Stone of flax is 20lb.; of wool or feathers, 10lb; the Lispond is 14lb.; the Centner, 112lb. Hamburgh weight; and the Shipfund = 299lb. avoirdupois, or 135,6 Kilogrammes. Commercial Weight.

The Tonne of butter, small measure, is 224lb; ditto, great measure, 280lb. The Pipe of oil is 820lb.; and the small Tonne of green soap, 60lb.

The Last of wheat or rye is divided into 3 Wispels, 30 Scheffels, 60 Fasses, 120 Himtens, or 480 Spints, and equals 11,20 English Quarters, or 31,585 Hectolitres. Dry Measures.

The standard measure of the Fass is $21\frac{3}{16}$ Inches in diameter, and $10\frac{3}{8}$ Inches deep, Hamburgh measure; its contents are, therefore, 3872 Hamburgh Cubic Inches. Hence 1 Scheffel, or 2 Fasses, = 2,988 Winchester Bushels, or 1,0528 Hectolitres.

The Stock of barley or oats contains 3 Wispels; the Last ditto, 2 Wispels, 20 Scheffels, 60 Fasses, 120 Himtens, or 480 Spints.

The Fass of wheat weighs about 86lb.; of rye, 81lb.; of barley, 68lb.; of malt, 63lb.; of oats, 52lb.; of pease, 100lb.; of beans, 108lb.; Hamburgh commercial weight.

The Fuder is divided into 6 Ahms; the Ahm into 4 Ankers, 5 Eimers, 20 Viertels, 40 Stubgens, 80 Kannen, 160 Quartiers, or 320 Oessels. The Ahm contains 38,25 English Gallons, or 144,7 Litres. Liquid Measures.

The Fass of wine is reckoned at 4 Oxhofts, or 6 Tierces; but the Oxhoft differs according to the kind of liquor; thus for Bourdeaux, or claret wine, it contains from 62 to 64 Stubgen; a Pipe of Spanish wine is from 96 to 100 Stubgen.

The Stuckfass or Piece of brandy is of no determined size, but 30 Viertels are generally reckoned for an Oxhoft, which equals $57\frac{3}{8}$ English Gallons.

A Brew of Hamburgh beer requires 80 Fasses of malt, in 20 sacks, weighing with the sacks 5050lb. and must produce 50 Tonnes or Barrels. A Brew of vinegar requires 74 Fasses, in $18\frac{1}{2}$ sacks. The Tonne of beer contains 48 Stubgen; the small Tonne 32 Stubgen.

The Quarteel of train oil contains 2 Tonnes, or 64 Stubgen, and the Tonne is reckoned at 2 Centners, or 224lb. net weight. The Steekan or Stockan is the sixth part of the Tonne.

The Hamburgh Foot is divided into 12 Inches or 96 Parts, and contains 0,2865 Metres, or 11,289 English Inches. Long Measures.

Long Measures.

The Hamburgh Foot is also divided into 3 Palms, in order to measure the circumference of masts; the Palm is therefore $3\frac{3}{4}$ English Inches nearly.

The Rhineland Foot, which is used by engineers and land surveyors, is divided into 12 Inches, subdivided into 10 Lines, or 100 Parts, and measures $13\frac{1}{7}$ Inches of the Hamburgh measure, or 0,3139 Metres = 12,36 English Inches.

The Hamburgh Ell is 2 Hamburgh Feet, 4 Quarters, or 24 Inches. It is not, however, uniformly 2 Feet, but varies from 3 to 7-tenths of a Line.

The Brabant Ell, with which most kinds of piece goods are measured, contains 0,70066 Metres, or 27,585 English Inches.

A Hamburgh Clafter or Fathom is 3 Ells, or 6 Feet, Hamburgh measure.

A geometrical Pace (of 60000 to a degree) measures about $6\frac{1}{2}$ Feet of Hamburgh, or $6\frac{1}{16}$ English Feet; but an ordinary man's Pace is reckoned at $2\frac{2}{5}$ Feet, Hamburgh measure, or 27 English Inches nearly.

The Ruthe or Perch is of two sorts; one is 7 Ells, or 14 Feet; the other, 8 Ells, or 16 Feet, Hamburgh measure.

The Rhineland Ruthe (12 Rhineland Feet) is $13\frac{1}{7}$ Hamburgh Feet.

A Hamburgh Mile contains 2000 Rhineland Ruthes, or 8244 English Yards, which equal 4,684 English Miles, or 7,538 Kilometres; hence $14\frac{4}{5}$ such Miles answer nearly to a degree of the meridian in the latitude of Hamburgh.

Land Measures.

The Scheffel of corn land is the extent generally sown with a Hamburgh Scheffel of corn. It contains 200 square Ruthes of the longest measure, each 256 Hamburgh square Feet, and equals 1 Acre 6 Perches, English measure, or 4,1984 French Decares.

The Morgen or Acre of land contains 600 square Ruthes, of the shortest measure, each Ruthe 196 Hamburgh square Feet, and equals 2 Acres $6\frac{1}{2}$ Perches, English measure, or 8,2577 French Decares.

Commercial Allowances and other Regulations.

Allowances, Regulations &c.

The following are the customary Allowances on the Sale of Goods at Hamburgh, with the kind of money in which their prices are reckoned. The allowances are Tare and Draft, and the money deductions are Rabat, Discount, and Agio. These important documents have been selected from *Kruse*, *Hedley*, and other good authorities, and have been besides examined and approved by several Hamburgh merchants.

Articles.	*How Sold.*	*Draft.*	*Tare.*
Agaric	per 100lb. in Marks currency	1lb. per cent.	
Almonds	per 100lb. in Marks currency	1lb. per cent.	4lb. per bale.
Aloes	per lb. in Marks currency	½lb. per cent.	4lb. per cent.
Alum	per 100lb. in Marks currency	1lb. per cent.	real tare.
Aniseed	per 100lb. in Marks currency	1lb. per cent.	3 or 4lb. per sack.
Annatto	per lb. in Shillings currency	1lb. per cent.	18 per cent. leaves 2 per cent.
Antimony	per 100lb. in Marks currency	1lb. per cent.	6 per cent.
Arsenic, Yellow / White	per 100lb. in Marks banco	1lb. per cent.	18lb.
Red	per 100lb. in Marks currency	1lb. per cent.	
Bacon	per shipfund of 280lb. in Marks currency.	1lb. per cent.	
Bark	per lb. in Marks or Shillings currency.	½lb. per cent.	real tare.
Bay Berries	per 100lb. in Marks currency	1lb. per cent.	
Bees' Wax	per lb. in Grotes Flemish banco	1lb. per cent.	
Borax	per lb. in Marks currency	1lb. per cent.	
Brandy, French	per 30 viertels in Rixdollars currency	1lb. per cent.	
Brass	per 100lb. in Marks banco	1lb. per cent.	
Brimstone	per 100lb. in Marks currency	1lb. per cent.	10 per cent.
Butter, Danish / Dutch	per 224lb. net in Rixdollars currency	1lb. per cent.	in casks of from 140 to 250lb.—28 to 36lb. 100 to 140lb.—16 to 28lb. 60 to 100lb.— 8 to 16lb.
French / English / Irish	per cask in Rixdollars currency	1lb. per cent.	22 per cent.
Calicos	in sterling, per piece or English yard, also in Shillgs. banco, per Brabant ell	1lb. per cent.	
Camphor	per lb. in Shillings currency	½lb. per cent.	real tare.
Capers	per 100lb. in Marks banco	1lb. per cent.	28 per cent. in casks.
Cardamoms	per lb. in Marks currency	½lb. per cent.	real tare.
Cassia Buds & Cassia Lignea	per lb. in Marks currency	½lb. per cent.	real tare.
Cheese	per shipfund of 280lb. in Marks currency.	1lb. per cent.	
Cinnamon	per lb. in Marks currency	½lb. per cent.	8lb. per single wrapper. 12lb. per double ditto.
Cloves	per lb. in Shillings banco	½lb. per cent.	3lb. per single bag.
Coals	per ton in Marks currency.		
Cochineal	per lb. in Shillings Flemish banco	½lb. per cent.	2lb. per bag.
Cocoa	per lb. in Shillings currency	½lb. per cent.	2lb. per bag. real tare in casks.
Coffee	per lb. in Shillings banco	½lb. per cent.	in bags of 130lb.—2lb. from 131 to 180lb.—3lb. in casks real tare.
Copper	per shipfund in Marks banco	½lb. per cent.	
Corn	per last in Rixdollars currency	1lb. per cent.	
Cotton, Brazil / Georgia	per lb. in Grotes banco	1lb. per cent.	4lb. per cent.
Louisiana / New Orleans / Bourbon	....	1lb. per cent.	6lb. per cent.
Bengal / Surat	....	1lb. per cent.	8lb. per cent.
Cotton Yarn, Levant	per lb. in Shillings Flemish banco	1lb. per cent.	5 per cent. in bales.
Cummin	per 100lb. in Marks currency	1lb. per cent.	3lb. per bag.
Currants	per 100lb. in Marks currency	1lb. per cent.	in barrels......14 per cent. in half ditto....16 per cent. in quarter ditto 18 per cent.

Articles.	*How Sold.*	*Draft.*	*Tare.*
Figs, Smyrna ...... Candia	per 100lb. in Marks currency	1lb. per cent.	10 per cent. in barrels. 2lb. in baskets.
Flax..............	per shipfund of 280lb. in Marks banco.	1lb. per cent.	6 or 7lb. per bag.
Gall Nuts	per 100lb. in Marks banco	1lb. per cent.	6lb. per bag.
Ginger, Jamaica .... Barbadoes..	per lb. in Grotes banco	1lb. per cent.	2lb. per bag weighing from 100 to 120lb.
East India....	....	1lb. per cent.	3lb. per bag of 150lb.
Gum, Arabic ...... Senegal	per 100lb. in Marks currency	1lb. per cent.	10lb. per 300lb.
Hare and Goat Skins .	per 100 pieces in Rixdollars banco....	1lb. per cent.	
Hemp	per shipfund of 280lb. in Marks currency.	1lb. per cent.	
Herrings............	per cask in Rixdollars currency	1lb. per cent.	
Hides, Buenos Ayres .	per lb. in Shillings currency	2lb. per cent.	
Horse........	per 10 pieces in Rixdollars currency.		
Hogs' Bristles	per lb. in Marks currency	1lb. per cent.	
Honey.............	per 336 net in casks in Rixdollars curr.		
Indigo, East India....	per lb. in Shillings Flemish	½lb. per cent.	real tare.
Guatimala .. Caraccas ..	....	½lb. per cent.	24lb. per seron. 20lb. per half ditto.
Ipecacuanha	per lb. in Shillings currency	½lb. per cent.	real tare.
Iron, Russian...... Swedish	per shipfund of 280lb. in Marks currency.	1lb. per cent.	
Iron Wire	in rings of 10lb. in Shillings currency..	1lb. per cent.	
Isinglass	per 100lb. in Marks currency	1lb. per cent.	
Juniper Berries	per 100lb. in Marks currency	1lb. per cent.	2lb.
Laurel Leaves & Berries	per 100lb. in Marks currency	1lb. per cent.	2lb. per bag.
Lead	per shipfund of 280lb. in Marks banco.	1lb. per cent.	12 per cent.
Leather, English .. Hamburgh	per lb. in Shillings currency	1lb. per cent.	4lb. per bale.
Russia	per lb. in Shillings banco	½lb. per cent.	
Lemon & Orange Peels	per 100lb. in Marks currency	1lb. per cent.	8lb. per bale or 6 per cent.
Linen, French........	per stiege of 20 pieces in Marks or Rixdollars banco	1lb. per cent.	
Silesian	per piece in Marks or Rixdollars banco.	1lb. per cent.	
Osnaburg	per 100 double ells in Marks or Rixdollars banco	1lb. per cent.	
Mace	per lb. in Shillings Flemish banco	½lb. per cent.	real tare.
Madder	per 100lb. in Marks currency	1lb. per cent.	
Manna..............	per lb. in Marks currency	1lb. per cent.	
Mats, Russia	per 100 pieces, per shipfund of 280lb. in Marks currency....	1lb. per cent.	
Molasses	per 100lb. in Marks currency	½lb. per cent.	12lb. per cent.
Nankeen............	per piece in Shillings banco	1lb. per cent.	
Nutmegs............	per lb. in Marks banco...............	½lb. per cent.	real tare.
Oak Bark	per 100lb. in Marks currency	1lb. per cent.	
Oil, Greenland .... South Sea	per 6 steekans in Marks currency	1lb. per cent.	
Genoa	per 820lb. in Rixdollars banco	1lb. per cent.	in casks of 1500lb.—14 p. ct. in casks of 900lb.—16 p. ct. in casks of 500lb.—18 p. ct.
Italian	per 820lb. in Rixdollars banco	1lb. per cent.	in casks......14 per cent. half ditto ....16 per cent. quarter ditto..18 per cent.
Malaga	per 820lb. in Rixdollars banco	1lb. per cent.	in casks of 1500lb.—14 p. ct. in pipes of 900lb.—120lb. in pipes of 500lb.— 65lb.
Portugal	per 820lb. in Rixdollars banco	1lb. per cent.	in pipes............125lb.

Articles.	*How Sold.*	*Draft.*	*Tare.*
Oil, Provence........	per 320lb. in Rixdollars banco	1lb. per cent.	in casks of 300lb.—16 per ct.
Seville	per 820lb. in Rixdollars banco	1lb. per cent.	in pipes .... 125lb. half ditto .. 65lb.
Hempseed .... Linseed ...... Rapeseed	per 112lb. in Marks currency	1lb. per cent.	
Pepper	per lb. in Grotes banco..............	½lb. per cent.	6lb. per bag.
Pimento	per lb. in Shillings currency	½lb. per cent.	2lb. per bag of 120lb.
Pitch and Tar........	per last of 12 tonnes in Rixdollars curr.	1lb. per cent.	
Potash...............	per 100lb. in Marks currency	1lb. per cent.	8lb. per cent. in casks.
Prunes, French......	per 100lb. in Marks currency	1lb. per cent.	1½lb. per chest.
Quicksilver	per lb. in Shillings banco	½lb. per cent.	½lb. per cask of 48lb.
Rags	per 105lb. in Marks currency	1lb. per cent.	
Raisins, Malaga	per 100lb. in Marks currency	1lb. per cent.	10lb. per cent.
Smyrna	per 100lb. in Marks currency	1lb. per cent.	12lb. per cent.
Red Lead	per 100lb. in Marks currency	1lb. per cent.	14lb. per barrel.
Rhubarb	per lb. in Marks currency	1lb. per cent.	
Rice, Carolina	per 100lb. in Marks currency	1lb. per cent.	real tare. super tare 4lb. per cask. in barrels super tare 2lb.
East India	....	1lb. per cent.	4lb. per bag.
Rum	per 30 viertels in Rixdollars currency.		
Saffron	per lb. in Marks currency	1lb. per cent.	¼lb. in bags of 25lb.
Sago	per lb. in Marks currency	½lb. per cent.	3lb. per cent.
Sailcloths	per piece in Marks currency	1lb. per cent.	
Sal Ammoniac	per lb. in Marks currency	1lb. per cent.	
Saltpetre	per 112lb. in Rixdollars currency .. .	1lb. per cent.	real tare.
Silk	per lb. in Shillings banco	1lb. per cent.	28 oz. per bale of 60lb.
Soap, Marseilles	per 100lb. in Marks currency	1lb. per cent.	10 per cent. in chests.
Starch	per 100lb. in Marks currency	1lb. per cent.	16lb. per cask.
Staves, Planks, and Timber.......	per gross thousand in Marks banco....	1lb. per cent.	
Steel	in fasses or casks, from 120 to 200lb. in Marks banco	1lb. per cent.	
Sugar, Refined	per lb. in Grotes banco..............	½lb. per cent.	*Double & single loaves.*—Real tare, 1lb. on three loaves for paper and string. *In lumps.*—Real tare and weight of paper and string. *Crushed lumps.*—12 per cent.
Clayed.......	per lb. in Grotes banco.		
Martinico	per lb. in Grotes banco	1lb. per cent.	16lb. per cent.
Havannah	per lb. in Grotes banco	¼lb. per cent.	65lb. per chest, & super tare 5lb. per chest.
Brown ditto ..	per lb. in Grotes banco	¼lb. per cent.	70lb. per chest, & super tare 5lb. per chest.
White Brazil .	per lb. in Grotes banco	¼lb. per cent.	16lb. per cent. & super tare 10lb. per chest.
East India ...	per lb. in Grotes banco..............	1lb. per cent.	single mats 10 per cent. double do. 15 ditto.
Muscovado . Jamaica	per lb. in Grotes banco	1lb. per cent.	18lb. per cent.
Sumach, Portugal	per 100lb. in Marks currency	1lb. per cent.	1 per cent. in bags.
Syrup	per 100lb. in Marks currency	1lb. per cent.	10 per cent. in casks.
Tallow, Muscovy	per shipfund of 280lb. in Marks banco .	1lb. per cent.	10 per cent. in casks.
Tamarinds	per lb. in Marks currency	1lb. per cent.	

Articles.	*How Sold.*	*Draft.*	*Tare.*
Tea, Bohea	per lb. in Shillings currency	½lb. per cent.	in chests of from 100 to 106lb.—28lb. 190 to 200lb.—45lb. 390 to 412lb.—70lb.
Congou	per lb. in Shillings currency	½lb. per cent.	100lb. .... —28lb.
Souchong	per lb. in Shillings currency	½lb. per cent.	80 to 86lb.—24lb. 100 to 110lb.—28lb.
Twankay	per lb. in Shillings currency	½lb. per cent.	96 to 98lb.—28lb.
Hyson	per lb. in Marks currency	½lb. per cent.	80 to 82lb.—24lb.
Gunpowder	per lb. in Marks currency.		
Tin, in Blocks and Bars	per lb. in Shillings currency	½lb. per cent.	
Tobacco, Virginia, Maryland	per lb. in Shillings currency	1lb. per cent.	80lb. per hogshead.
Varinas	per lb in Shillings currency	1lb. per cent.	12lb. per basket.
Turpentine, Venetian	per 100lb. in Marks currency	1lb. per cent.	16lb. per cent.
Twist	per lb. English in Shillings sterling	1lb. per cent.	
Vinegar, Wine	per oxhoft in Rixdollars currency	1lb. per cent.	
Vitriol, White	per 100lb. in Marks banco	1lb. per cent.	55lb. per cask.
Green	per 100lb. in Marks currency	1lb. per cent.	50lb. per cask.
English	per 100lb. in Marks currency	1lb. per cent.	in casks, 10 per cent.
Whalebone	per 100lb. in Rixdollars currency	1lb. per cent.	
Wines	per viertel in Marks currency	1lb. per cent	
Woods, Pernambuco	per 100lb. in Marks banco	1lb. per cent.	
Nicaragua, Logwood, Fustick	per 100lb. in Marks currency	1lb. per cent.	
Wool, Saxony	per lb. in Shillings banco	1lb. per cent.	
Yarn	per bundle in Marks banco	1lb. per cent.	

RABAT, DISCOUNT, AND AGIO.

Rabat, Discount, Agio, &c.

Some sorts of merchandize, when sold in large quantities, have an allowance made of 7, 13, or 16 months Rabat, reckoned at 8 per cent. per annum, which the buyer, when he pays ready money, or pays within 4 weeks of the day of sale, deducts from the nominal price.

English baize, English and Dutch cloth, flannels, kerseymeres, ratteens, serges, shalloons, and refined sugars, are sold with 7 months Rabat, or 4⅔ per cent.; that is, 4⅔ are deducted from 104⅔; or 7 from 157.

Almonds, capers, cinnamon, Silesia cloth, cloves, cochineal, cotton, crape, cummin, currants, gall nuts, ginger, indigo, Russian leather, linen, mace, molasses, nutmegs, rice, Italian silks, Marseilles soap, raw sugars, sumac, Italian tartar, and Turkish yarn, are sold with 13 months Rabat, or 8⅔ per cent. that is, 13 is deducted from 163.

Silks from the Levant, as Ardassete, Barutine, and Cerbaffi, are sold with 16 months Rabat, or 10⅔ per cent.; that is, 8 is deducted from 83.

There is besides a discount generally allowed of 1 per cent.

The Agio on goods sold in currency, and paid for in banco, is *fixed* in certain articles, in others *customary* but subject to variation, and in the rest according to agreement, or to the Agio of the day. Thus alum, gum, logwood, pimento, and rice, have a fixed Agio of 20 per cent. and tobacco, of 25 per cent.

Annatto, bark, cassia, cinnamon, cocoa, molasses, and rum, have a customary Agio of 26 per cent. Hides, Greenland and South Sea oils, and teas, 25 per cent.

FURTHER REGULATIONS AS TO THE SALE AND SHIPMENT OF GOODS.

A Ton in the lading of a ship is generally reckoned at 40 Cubic Feet. Lastage,&c.

The Tonne of Luneburgh salt contains a Shipfund, and measures 7 Himtems of Hamburgh.

The Tonne of lime contains 3 Fasses, or 6 Himtems.

The Tonne of herrings contains about 800 herrings.

The Last of Luneburgh salt, lime, herrings, tar, pitch, train oil, coals, &c. contains 12 Tonnes.

The Tonne of Spanish, Portuguese, and French coarse salt, contains 19 Lisponds, or 266lb. without the wood. The Last ditto, contains 18 Tonnes, or about 4800lb.

A French Hundred of salt is about 11½ Hamburgh Lasts.

Staves are sold in Rings of 4 Schocks and 8 Pieces; 3 Rings of hogshead staves, or 6 Rings of barrel staves, are reckoned equal to 2 Rings of pipe staves.

A Bale of paper contains 10 Reams, or 200 Quires; a Quire of printing paper, 25 Sheets; of writing paper, 24 Sheets.

Oak planks are sold by Schocks of 60 Craveels. The following quantities are reckoned for a Craveel, viz:

24 Feet of plank, 2½ Inches thick.
15 Feet, ...3 Inches thick.
12 Feet, ...3½ Inches thick.
10 Feet, ...4 Inches thick.
9 Feet, ...4½ Inches thick.
8⅓ Feet, ...5 Inches thick.

Of things that are sold by number, a gross Thousand is 1200; a gross Hundred, 120; a Ring, 240; a common or small Thousand, 1000; a small Hundred, 100; a Schock, 60; a Steige, 20; a Webe, 72; a Zimmer, 40; a Dozen, 12; a Decher, 10; a Gross, 12 Dozen. Terms used in Reckoning.

EXCHANGES.

The places with which Hamburgh exchanges, with the denominations of money, and other particulars, are stated in Vol. II. p. 65.

The usance for bills drawn from all parts of Germany is 14 days sight; when bills are drawn at usance, the day of acceptance is reckoned for the first; but Usance.

Usance. when at any other number of days after sight, the day after acceptance is reckoned for the first.

The usance for bills drawn from England, France, and Holland, is 1 month after date; from Spain, Portugal, Trieste, and Italy, 2 months after date.

Days of Grace. Twelve days of grace are allowed for payment or protest: the day on which the bill would become due, if no grace were allowed, is reckoned for the first day; and Sundays and holidays are also included in the 12 days. These regulations, however are more fully explained in the following code; but it may be observed that days of grace are seldom now taken.

EXCHANGE LAWS OF HAMBURGH.

The following laws were first enacted on the 22d of January, 1711, in a convocation of the Senate and Citizens of Hamburgh. They were ordered to be printed for the information of foreign nations, and all proceedings at law have invariably been guided by them up to the present time. Some further elucidation of the 24th and 25th articles was agreed upon the 14th of June, 1798, which will be found at the end.

Brokers to give Notice. *Art.* 1. When a broker negociates a bill of exchange, he shall be bound, at all times and without fail, to give immediate notice in writing thereof to both parties, and put the initials of his name under such notice.

Bills to be drawn in Sets. 2. When a bill of exchange has been negociated, the assignor is bound, generally, to give two, and, in case of need, three or more bills; but, if it be a sole or foreign bill of exchange, the broker shall be obliged, before the final conclusion of such agreement, to inform the taker, or indorsee, thereof; and, if the latter be satisfied with it, the matter shall rest there.

Taker of a Bill to pay the Amount instanter. 3. When a bill of exchange has been negociated, and the taker, or indorsee, does not instantaneously pay the value thereof, Mr. Prætor shall immediately proceed against his person or property, without any judicial decree, and enforce the full and actual payment of the same, by the most effectual execution, without any distinction as to the amount.

Liability of Taker on holding Bills. 4. The taker, or indorsee, may keep the bills he has purchased in his possession and at his disposal, or transmit them to other places, as he thinks proper; yet, in such manner that it be possible to receive the payment thereof in due course of time, on or about the day they fall due, unless the contracting parties should have made a different agreement; that is to say, that the assignor shall immediately transmit the first bill to be accepted; in which case, the broker shall mention it in his notice, and the assignor fulfil the said agreement. Liability of Taker, &c.

5. Whoever accepts a bill of exchange becomes thereby personally bound to pay it, in the same manner as he who may have taken up or received the money. Acceptor bound, &c.

6. If any person takes a bill of exchange into his possession, and promises to pay the same, such person shall thereby be bound and obliged to discharge it, in the same manner as if he had actually accepted it by his signature. Verbal Acceptance binding.

7. If a bill of exchange be handed to any individual, in person, for acceptance, and not returned on the demand of the holder who presented the same, but kept by the former a whole night, he is thereby bound, and the said bill is to be considered as accepted; and, in the same manner, a drawee, who has once accepted a bill of exchange, is no longer at liberty to revoke or cancel his acceptance. Other Modes of Acceptance binding.

8. If a bill be presented to a person for acceptance, such person shall be bound to accept it personally, by subscribing his name and adding the date, if required; but should, if he be absent or in other cases, his clerk, or whom he has empowered for that purpose, make the said acceptance in his name, this shall be done by the name of the master or constituent, as well as the own name of the said clerk or attorney being put to the same, and his power, which is to be a notarial letter of attorney, being actually produced; which being done, the said master or constituent shall be bound, by such acceptance, in the same manner as if it were personally made by him, and obliged to make payment; otherwise, and if the said formality should not be observed at the acceptance, the said bill of exchange should be protested for non-acceptance. Subject continued.

9. If a bill of exchange be remitted from abroad, and addressed to a person for acceptance, and such person refuses to accept it, in this case the holder thereof may immediately cause the said bill to be protested, and return the same, together with the protest; but, should he be willing to wait three days, for the purpose of obliging the drawee, who is to accept the said bill, he may do it without any prejudice or injury to himself; provided that, in the mean time, no regular messenger or mail sets out for the place where the money has been paid. Protests for Non-acceptance.

10. If a bill of exchange be drawn upon the drawer himself, he shall, nevertheless, be bound to accept it. Promissory Note requires Acceptance.

Bills may be accepted for Honour of Drawers or Indorsers

11. If a bill of exchange be presented to a person for acceptance, and such person refuses to accept it, any third person may accept the same, for the honour of the drawer or indorser; who, by virtue of such acceptance, becomes principally bound for the said bill, and, on the other hand, acquires, by the actual payment thereof, the rights of the holder; yet, for the better security of his right, he must previously cause it to be duly protested by the holder, and the protest to be delivered to him, at the time of his accepting the same, on payment of the charges thereof.

Domicilia-tion may be protested.

12. If bills of exchange arrive here, drawn upon foreign drawees, at sight or usance, and payable in this place, and, at the acceptance thereof, it is not specified to whom the holder is to apply here for payment, on the day they fall due, they must, in default of such payment, be duly protested.

Jews not to be molested on their Holidays.

13. If bills of exchange, drawn upon Jews of this place, arrive on a Saturday or other holiday of the Jews, they shall not be molested on such days, yet be bound, if the said bills be drawn at sight, to accept the same, under the date of the day they arrived here.

Regulations as to Indorsements.

14. If a bill of exchange, having no indorsement, be accepted, and the second or third arrives here indorsed, the holder shall present the accepted first bill and indorsed second and third bills to the acceptor, on the day payment becomes due, and then take back his bills; but, at or immediately after the receipt of such payment, every holder shall be bound to deliver the bill or bills of exchange, whether one or more, to the person who made the said payment. If a bill is indorsed, *to order*, these words must not be effaced; but the holder is obliged to indorse the same, either to himself or some other person; and, should he have no folio in the bank-books, he is bound, in this case, to annex a written direction to whom the bill is to be paid.

Subject continued.

15. If the bill with a regular indorsement is thus presented for payment, no other indorsement, made after such presentment, shall be of force, or prejudicial to the acceptor; but, before such presentment, it shall be lawful to negociate a bill, drawn in such a manner as to be payable to order, if it has yet some time to run, to order or to give it in payment.

Days of Grace.

16. And whereas, hitherto, twelve days of grace have been in use, no alteration shall be made in that respect.

17. If a bill is due, the holder is at liberty to protest it within the twelve days of grace, if he thinks proper, or to postpone it until the twelfth day, if it be no Sunday or holiday. Ultimate Date of Protest.

18. If a bill is due, all Sundays and holidays are included in the days of grace of such bill. Holidays.

19. No protest is to be made after sun-set, nor on Sundays or holidays; and, if it be done, such protest shall be considered as null, and as if it had not been made. Protests how made.

20. If bills of exchange, drawn after date or a certain time, do not arrive till after the day of their falling due, they have no more of the days of grace than would be left, according to custom, if they had been here in due time. Days of Grace unalterable.

21. All and every bill of exchange, drawn at months or usance of months, fall due, according to the calendar, the same day and date. Months are Calendar.

22. If a bill of exchange from Germany is drawn at usance, this is understood fourteen days after sight, the day of acceptance making one of such days; but, if it be drawn at sight, the day next ensuing the acceptance is computed as the first. Usances.

23. All bills of exchange, payable at the middle of the month, are considered as falling due on the 15th day of such month, without distinction, whether it has more or less days. Middle of the Month the 15th.

24. Bills of exchange, payable at the bank, which fall due at the end of December or a few days before that time, shall be paid before the bank is shut, without enjoying any farther days of grace; and what is not yet settled, on the first working day after the usual shutting of the bank, at the end of December, shall then be protested. Payment of Bills due before Bank shuts.

25. A bill of exchange, which falls due during the time the bank is shut, has not to enjoy any more days of grace, after the re-opening of the bank, than would be left if the bank had been open, excepting those which fall due the 1st, 2d, or 3d, of January; the payment whereof not being made on the third working day after the opening of the bank, they must then be protested. Bills due whilst Bank shut.

26. If a bill of exchange, at or after sight, should not be accepted immediately on its being presented, but it should be done afterwards, such acceptance is to be considered as made on the first day of presentment. Bills at Sight when due.

Date of Protest when Days of Grace are expired.

27. If a bill of exchange is due, and not protested until after the expiration of the said twelve days, the holder has thereby forfeited his right and claim against the drawer and indorsers, and must resort solely to the acceptor for payment; and, if the twelfth day should happen to be a Sunday or holiday, when it is not lawful to make a protest, it must be done the day before.

Priority of Interference and Protests.

28. If one or more collateral addresses be given in a bill of exchange, the holder must, in default of acceptance or payment, also protest against such addresses, if they refuse acceptance or payment; and the drawer of the bill is bound to pay all such protest-charges, without any objection.

Security on unaccepted Bills.

29. If a person has taken up money, and the bill of exchange given for the same is not accepted, but returned under protest, and the time for payment is elapsed, the drawer is bound to make payment instantaneously, and without delay; in default whereof, he shall be proceeded against with the readiest execution, as above-mentioned, in the third article; but, if the said bill of exchange has yet some time to run, and the drawer is willing to give another order for payment, the holder is bound to accept it, on sufficient security being given him for the amount.

Subject continued.

30. If protests of bills for non-acceptance are received from Spain, Portugal, or other parts, the drawer of such bills is bound, instantaneously and without delay, to give the creditor security for the principal, costs, and damages, by means of sufficient securities, or pledges, until the protest for non-payment, together with the bill of exchange, can arrive by the following mails, on pain of the readiest execution, in case of default, as enacted in the third article.

Bills paid before Expiration unlawful.

31. It shall not be lawful for any person to pay any bill of exchange soever before it is due; for, if it happens that the payee, to whom payment is to be made, at the time the bill falls due, in the mean time becomes a bankrupt, in such case the said payment is for the risk of him who paid the bill before it came due, and he is to bear the loss.

Repayment of protested Bills how regulated.

32. If a bill of exchange, drawn or accepted, is not paid at the precise time it falls due, the holder of such bill is at liberty, after having duly protested the same, to seek his redress against the indorser, of whom he expects to obtain the promptest payment; and, should there be more than one, successively against the others, up to the drawer; but the acceptor remains, nevertheless, bound for the said bill; and it rests entirely with the holder to go against him, in the first instance or afterwards; and the drawer, acceptor, and indorsers, all and every

one of them, remain bound *in solidum*, until full satisfaction shall have been given. Repayment &c.

33. If, on the day a bill of exchange falls due, only a moiety or part thereof be paid, the holder, if he has no express order to the contrary, is obliged to accept the same, but must protest for the remainder, and proceed as before stated, in the thirty-second article. Receipt of partial Payment.

34. In like manner, should the drawer, acceptor, or indorser, either all or one of them, become insolvent, the holder is to resort for payment (the protest being previously duly made) to such of the rest as he thinks proper, and receive, from one or another, as much as he can obtain, until he is completely satisfied for the said bill, together with re-exchange and costs. In Case of general Insolvency, Recovery how had.

35. The party who has paid the sum or moneys mentioned in the bill of exchange, if such bill be not made payable to order, may, as owner of the said bill, as long as the matter remains entire, revoke the charge therein contained, or cause it to be revoked by him, who has written the said bill, prior and before the acceptor has paid the same; save and excepting the case, that the party, who has received the said bill for payment, is not a mere attorney, or agent, of the remitter of such bill, but the said moneys either appertain to him, or he has, with the said bill, got advice and order to receive the sum therein contained for his own benefit and use; or he is able to prove, that he is in advance for the remitter, on account of moneys paid for drafts or similar articles; in which case the above revocation cannot take effect, without the consent and approbation of the holder. Holders of Bills of Exchange in doubtful Cases how to proceed.

36. If a person pays money for a bill of exchange, to another person, for account of a third party, and causes the bill to be made payable to himself or order, such person, in case of a failure, becomes a party to, and bound for, the said bill, by virtue of his indorsement, but not to his constituent, unless he should have obliged himself to guarantee the said bill. Difference of Guarantee to Holders & Constituent.

37. If any person takes up money from another person, to be re-paid at the Francfort, Leipsic, or other, fairs, such person is bound to give the lender a note, under his hand, whereby he acknowledges to have received the money, and promises, in due time, to deliver bills of exchange for the same; in which case, in default of such bills, the above note shall be sufficient to proceed against the maker thereof, according to the laws whereby bills of exchange are governed, and to obtain from Mr. Prætor the most effectual execution. Bills due at Fairs how regulated.

Bills due at Fairs, liable to the Construction of the respective Laws.

38. If bills of exchange, made payable at the fairs of Francfort, Leipsic, Naumburgh, and other fairs and statutes, are negociated here, the holder must, in default of the acceptance or payment thereof, conform himself to the laws whereby matters of exchange are governed in the said places, and cause the protest for non-payment or non-acceptance to be made in due time, and sent thither; but, should he omit doing so in due time, he has forfeited his right of action against the drawer, and is obliged to resort for payment to the acceptor.

Guarantee of Bills protested for Non-acceptance.

39. When a bill of exchange is protested, the drawer thereof is not allowed to accept his own bill, for the honour of such bill, but is obliged, according to the eleventh article, and on pain of the most effectual execution, enacted in the third article, to procure another acceptor, to the satisfaction of the payee, or give sufficient security for the amount.

Limitation of Charges in Acts of Return.

40. When a bill of exchange is returned with protest, no more shall be charged, under the head of re-exchange, than the direct course of exchange back, or a half per cent. per month, according to the option of the holder, together with commission, brokerage, protest-charges, and postage for one letter to, and one from, the place in question, and nothing more, unless it can be proved that more postage has been thereby occasioned.

Irregularity in Indorsements how obviated.

41. When accepted bills of exchange fall due, and there exists an irregularity in the indorsement, the holder thereof must, at the expiration of the days of grace, give sufficient security (if he demands the payment thereof) for procuring, within a certain time, a regular indorsement; which being done, the acceptor shall be bound to pay the same.

Lost Bills to be paid under Guarantee.

42. If an accepted bill of exchange be lost, and the acceptor thereof either acknowledges the debt, or the same is proved against him, the claim founded on the said bill of exchange remains in full force, and he is bound to pay the amount of such bill, on sufficient security being given that the payee, within a certain time, will procure an effectual and legal release from the drawer and indorsers, and deliver it to the acceptor, and fully indemnify the same for all costs and damages, on account of such lost bill of exchange.

Delays in demanding Payment at the Charge of the Holder.

43. If a payee does not demand the amount of a bill of exchange the day it falls due, and, in the mean time, an alteration takes place with regard to the current money, the holder is obliged to accept payment in such value of the money as was current the day on which the bill became due.

44. If bills of exchange are made payable in current money, and no alteration takes place with regard to such currency, they shall be paid in the present current and lawful money, yet without any shillings or smaller coin; and a receipt shall be put on the bill of exchange, stating that the payment thereof has been made. **Payment of Current Money how made.**

45. If the acceptor of a bill of exchange becomes insolvent, the holder thereof is bound to protest, although the said bill be not yet due, as soon as the said failure comes to his knowledge, and to send back the said protest, or give notice thereof to the indorser, according to the disposition of the thirty-second article, in order to seek his redress at the time it falls due; and the drawer and indorser shall be obliged, pursuant to the disposition of the thirty-second article, if the holder of the bill desires it, immediately either to pay the said bill, in ready money, with the discount of half per cent. interest per month, or to give sufficient security that the bill shall be punctually paid, when due. **Protests for better Security.**

46. If bills of exchange are drawn upon a person who has in his possession goods or other effects belonging to the drawer, such drawee must, in case of the bankruptcy of the drawer, and when a commission of bankruptcy is awarded and posted up, give notice to the court of the said goods and effects; yet he retains a right of preference before all other creditors to obtain payment out of the same, as he would do out of things specially mortgaged to him, and he must then deliver the remainder to the other creditors. **Liability of Consigned Goods to pay Drafts drawn against them.**

47. If a person shall have dealt in false bills of exchange, or made a fraudulent bankruptcy, and, with the money thus fraudulently obtained, shall establish himself in other places, he shall be proceeded against, pursuant to the dispositions of the new statute relative to bankrupts. **Fraudulent Bankruptcy**

48. To the foregoing regulations and statutes, respecting matters of exchange, not only all merchants and traders shall be bound to conform, but also other persons, of any country, rank, or condition whatsoever, concerned in bills of exchange drawn, accepted, or indorsed, in this place, either as debtors or creditors; nor shall any evasion or pretence screen them from the same, save and excepting infants and minors, or persons yet serving as apprentices: all bills drawn, accepted, or indorsed, by such persons, shall be considered as not obligatory or binding. And, in particular, in order to check the alarming progress of gambling, all bills of exchange, drawn for money lost or gained by gaming, shall not be admitted by the courts of justice in this city, **Foregoing Laws imperative on all Persons, with the Exceptions specified.**

Laws Imperative. but, on the contrary, cancelled, and, in every respect proceeded against, with regard to the same, pursuant to the tenor of the third and fourth paragraph of the edict against gambling, published the 3d of September, 1709.

Published, the 2d of March, 1711.

Variation in the 24th and 25th Articles of the foregoing Exchange Laws, agreed upon in 1798.

Variation in Art. 24. 24. Bills of exchange, payable in *banco*, which fall due on the last day of December, or which, falling due, have, by virtue of the ordinary days of grace, some time yet to run, shall, nevertheless, be paid before the shutting of the bank, without enjoying any more days of grace; and whatsoever, on the first working day after the last day of December, is not settled, must then be protested.

Variation in Art. 25. 25. Any bills of exchange, falling due during the shutting of the bank, have, on its re-opening, no more days of grace to enjoy than they would have had, had the bank continued open, except those which become due on the 1st, 2d, 3d, 4th, or 5th, of January. If, on the third working day after the re-opening of the bank, they are not found written off, they must then be protested.

BANK.

Bank. The Bank of Hamburgh was established in 1619, on the credit and under the guarantee of the city, as a bank of deposit. Before that period much inconvenience was experienced from the unequal and uncertain value of the currency, which consisted of various coins of the neighbouring states, as well as those of the city; and as foreign bills were paid in such, the exchange was generally unfavourable. In order to remedy this, the bank was established on the plan of receiving only the full standard coins of the state, and paying the same (except a small deduction) when called upon; but such deposits were seldom drawn out, as bills of exchange and other commercial contracts were generally paid in *assignations* on the bank, transferable from one person to another on the common principle of banks of deposit.

At first the bank received only Constitution or Specie Rixdollars, which were written in, or inscribed at 3 Marks banco each, with the *small* Agio of 1 per 1000; but when they were drawn out they were reckoned at the *great* Agio of $1\frac{5}{8}$ per 1000.

In 1770, it was arranged that the bank should receive bullion as well as coin; and since that period it has received silver in bars, and foreign coins as bullion only, of a certain fineness. This renders its money or paper the least variable standard of any in Europe. The silver thus deposited must be 15 Loths 12 Grains, or $\frac{47}{48}$ fine, and then the Cologne Mark of fine silver is inscribed at 27 Marks 10 Shillings banco; but if drawn out, 27 Marks 12 Shillings are reckoned for each Mark fine. A small charge too is occasionally made for refining. Bank.

The following regulations respecting the constitution and operations of the bank are selected and abridged from the *Hamburgh Contorist.* Bank Regulations

1. The bank is under the management of 5 directors, 2 counsellors, 2 treasurers, and 2 of the chief magistrates of the city, and one of each description goes out annually. Thus every director remains in office for five years, and is also president for one year.

2. Every chest or treasury department of the bank has five different locks, and each of the directors is to keep one of the keys, so that no treasury can be opened unless all the five directors are present.

3. No account can be opened at the bank for a less sum than 100 Marks, nor can any transfer be made until the money has been inscribed at least one night in the bank books.

4. All assignations or transfers of banco must be delivered in writing to one of the clerks, and the person by whom the transfer is made must either appear himself, or have a power of attorney duly executed, which however does not hold good beyond the year in which it is made.

5. He that wishes to draw money out of the bank, must procure a printed schedule, fill it up himself, sign it, and present it to the book-keeper, from whom he obtains an immediate order; but should he delay to draw it out, he incurs a fine of $\frac{1}{2}$ per cent. for the first day, 1 per cent. for the second, and so on, the fine being doubled for every successive day of delay.

6. No servant or clerk of the bank can open an account there, or have any dealings with it; and the same law applies to brokers, as they are not allowed at Hamburgh to act as merchants.

7. The money which a person has at the bank cannot be seized, on any account except on his becoming a bankrupt, in which case his banco must be delivered to his creditors.

8. The officers of the bank have the management of the mint and the coins; also the regulation of the public granaries; but all are under well digested statutes.

Bank Regulations

9. No person can open an account with the bank but a native or subject of Hamburgh, or a merchant settled in the city; nor can any citizen, so qualified, open an account in his name for a stranger or any other unqualified person, under very severe penalties.

10. The bank shuts for about 14 days on the 31st of December every year; and when it re-opens, all its creditors or their proper representatives must attend, to settle or agree with the directors what the balance of each account is, before it can be finally carried to their credit.

11. The bank lends money upon pledges of gold and silver, in bars or in coins, also on jewels, &c. to the amount of $\frac{3}{4}$ of their value. The nominal interest is 1 Pfening per month per Mark; but this is variable, being sometimes as low as 2 per cent. per annum.

No sum under 10 Marks is advanced, nor for a shorter term than six months. This branch of the institution is called the *Loan Bank.*

12. The city is answerable for all pledges thus deposited; and such are liable to be sold by auction if they remain a year and six weeks without any interest being paid. If the value be not claimed within three years it is forfeited to the poor. Various other monies, arising from fines, collections, &c. are likewise applied to charitable uses.

General Remarks.

There are, besides the above, numerous regulations stated by *Kruse*, chiefly relating to the duties of clerks and other officers of the establishment, with a list of penalties for irregularity, neglect, or improper disclosures.

All these rules tend to show what has been often observed, that no institution of the kind in any country is better managed than the Bank of Hamburgh. Its business and accounts are always open to proper enquiries, and its Governors are all responsible.

Under this system of laws has the Bank of Hamburgh maintained the highest credit for upwards of 200 years, with the exception of two temporary interruptions; one in 1669, when it was shut for a short time, but re-opened in 1670 under improved regulations. The other was in 1813, when, on the approach of the French forces, most of the deposits were drawn out by the proprietors, and the remainder, amounting to about $7\frac{1}{2}$ millions of Marks banco, was seized upon for the support of the invading army. The bank however soon after resumed its operations with its usual credit, and a restitution has been since made by the French government.

HANOVER *(in Germany.)*

Monies of Account. Accounts are kept in Thalers or Rixdollars of 36 Mariengroschen, each Mariengrosche being divided into 8 Pfenings, as in Brunswick. The Rixdollar also contains $1\frac{1}{2}$ Rixflorin, $1\frac{4}{5}$ Marienflorin, 24 Good Groschen, 36 Mariengroschen, 48 Gosgen, 72 Mathiers, 96 Dreyers, 288 Pfenings, or 576 Hellers.

Coins. The Gold coins of Hanover are the George d'or, of $4\frac{2}{3}$ Rixdollars; the Ducat of $2\frac{2}{3}$ Rixdollars; and the Gulden or Gilder of 2 Rixdollars, with their divisions. Silver coins are the specie Rixdollar of 48 Mariengroschen, with its subdivisions in proportion: also base silver pieces of 3, 2, and 1 Mariengroschen.

Different Sorts of Money. All the foregoing valuations are in the money called Cash, which is the established coin of the state, and that in which the revenues are paid; but there is another kind of money, called Gold value, which is used in certain transactions of trade, and where it is expressly stipulated for.

Cash money reckons the George d'or at $4\frac{2}{3}$ Rixdollars, which in Gold money is reckoned at 5, so that the proportion between them is as 14 to 15. Thus the former is $7\frac{1}{7}$ per cent. better than the latter.

There is a third circulating medium in Hanover, which is Convention money; $13\frac{1}{3}$ Rixdollars of this coin, or 12 of Cash, are coined from the Cologne Mark, and therefore Cash money is to Convention as 9 to 10; or $11\frac{1}{9}$ per cent. better. Hence the proportion between Gold value and Convention money is as 27 to 28, the former being $3\frac{19}{27}$ per cent. better than the latter.

Fineness of Gold and Silver. The absolute fineness of gold is expressed by 24 Carats, the Carat being divided into 12 Grains. That of silver by 16 Loths, each Loth being divided into 18 Grains.

Rate of Coinage. The coins are chiefly minted according to the rate of the Empire; that is—

67 Ducats weigh a Cologne Mark, 23 Carats 8 Grains fine.
35 George d'ors 21 8
72 Gold Guldens 18 10

Double, Quadruple, and Half in proportion.

8 Specie Rixdollars............ 14 Loths. 8 Grains fine.

Also Florins of 24 Mariengroschen, with halves and quarters coined of fine silver, and the Zweydrittel or Piece of two-thirds, which is established at the Leipsic rate.

Sterling Value. The following may be taken as the sterling value nearly of the principal coins: the Ducat, 9s. 4d; the George d'or, 16s. 4½d; the Gold Gulden, 7s; the specie Rixdollar, 4s. 8d; the Rixdollar 3s. 6d; the Piece of two-thirds, 2s. 4d. &c. For a more accurate valuation see *Table of Coins*, Vol. II.

Weights. Gold and silver, as also silk and camel's hair, are weighed with the Cologne Mark. See *Cologne*.

The commercial Pound is divided into 2 Marks, 16 Ounces, 32 Loths, 128 Quentins, or 512 Ortgen. This Pound weighs 7511 English Grains: hence 100lb. of Hanover equal 107,3lb. avoirdupois, or 48,66 Kilogrammes.

The Lispond is 14lb.; the Centner 112lb.; the Shipfund 280lb.; 12 Shipfunds are reckoned for 1 Last; the Stone of flax is 20lb; of wool 10lb.

The apothecaries' weight is ¾ of the commercial weight; the Pound is divided into 12 Ounces, and the Ounce into 8 Drams, 60 Scruples, or 480 Grains. It therefore answers to 5633 English Grains, or 365 French Grammes.

Corn Measure. All kinds of corn in Hanover are to be measured, according to a regulation of 1757, with the Brunswick measure, called Himten; the Last being reckoned at 2 Wispels, 16 Malters, or 96 Himtens. The Himten is, in most places, divided into 3, but in some places into 4 Metzen.

The cylindrical measure which is to serve as a standard for the Brunswick Himten, one of which is kept in each of the cities of Hanover, weighs, full of the best rye, 48lb. of Hanover, and measures 0,8825 Winchester Bushels, or 0,3109 Hectolitres.

Liquid Measures. The Fuder of wine is divided into 4 Oxhofts, 6 Ahms, or 15 Eimers; the Ahm contains 4 Ankers, 40 Stubgens, 80 Kannen, 160 Quartiers, or 320 Nössels; the Quartier must, according to a regulation of 1713, hold 2lb. of spring water. The Ahm contains 41,095 English Gallons, or 155,54 French Litres.

The Tonne or Barrel of honey contains 25½ Stubgens, and weighs 300lb.

A Brew of beer contains 43 Fasses, and the Fass 104 Stubgens, or 208 Kannen.

Long Measures. The Hanoverian Foot is divided into 12 Inches; the Inch into 8 Parts, and sometimes into 12 Lines; the Foot measures 11,454 English Inches, or 0,2908 Metres. A Clafter is 3 Ells, and an Ell 2 Feet, Hanoverian measure.

These measures are to be the same throughout the electoral dominions. A standard Ell is kept in each of the principal cities, by which all the other measures are to be regulated; and, when they have been examined and found to agree with the standard, they are stamped with a lion, and with the arms of the city to which they belong. Long Measures.

The old Calemberg Foot, which was formerly used in Hanover, measures 11,533 English Inches, or 0,2926 Metres.

The Hanoverian, or Zellish Ruthe, is 16 Hanoverian Feet, or 15 Feet 3 Inches English measure.

A legal Mile of the electorate contains 2274 such Ruthes, and equals 6,567 English Miles, or 10,57 Kilometres.

The Morgen, or Acre of land, is 60 Ruthes long and 2 broad; it contains, therefore, 120 square Ruthes, and equals 2 Roods $22\frac{1}{2}$ Perches English measure, or 26,014 French Ares. Superficial Measures.

The exchanges of Hanover are chiefly effected at the Fairs, and are similar to those of *Brunwick*, which see.

HOLLAND, *see Amsterdam.*

HOLSTEIN *(a Duchy belonging to Denmark).*

Accounts are kept here in Rixdollars of 48 Shillings, or Marks of 16 Shillings, as in *Hamburgh*. The coins will be found under the article *Copenhagen*. Monies and Coins.

Gold and silver are weighed by the Cologne Mark; and drugs are retailed by the German apothecaries' weight, but when sold wholesale the Lubeck weight is used. Weights & Measures.

The Lubeck weight, which is $\frac{1}{4}$ per cent. lighter than Hamburgh weight, is established throughout Holstein. The Shipfund is divided into 20 Lisponds, or 280lb.; the Centner into 112lb.; the Pound into 16 Ounces, 32 Loths, 128 Quentins, or 512 Ortgens; 100lb. of this weight = $106\frac{1}{2}$lb. avoirdupois, or 48,30 Kilogrammes.

The Ell is the same as at Hamburgh; the measure for corn is the same as that of Copenhagen; namely, the Tonne of 8 Scheffels, or 32 Viertels, 100 of which Tonnes yield about 49 English Quarters. Flour and hops are sold by weight.

For wine and brandy, the Hamburgh measures are used here.

A Tonne of beer contains 128 Quartiers, or 25 English beer Gallons.

Weights & Measures. All persons must be provided with weights and measures, duly stamped; and any article, bought and sold by other weights or measures, must be confiscated: besides which a fine of 50 Rixdollars is imposed on each person so offending against the law.

HUNGARY.

Monies of Account. Accounts are kept here in Imperial Florins *(Reichsguldens)* each Florin being divided into 20 Groschen, or 60 Creutzers.

The Specie Rixdollar is reckoned at 2 Imperial Florins, $2\frac{2}{7}$ Hungarian Florins, 20 Shostacks, 40 Imperial Groschen, 80 Polturats, 120 Creutzers, 200 Hungarian Groschen, or 400 Reichpfenings.

The Rixdollar current is three fourths of the Rixdollar specie; the Imperial Florin is one half of the Rixdollar specie. 7 Imperial Florins = 8 Hungarian Florins.

A Hungarian Grosche is worth 2 Creutzers in Upper Hungary, but $2\frac{2}{5}$ Creutzers in Lower Hungary: thus 5 Groschen in Upper Hungary, or 6 Groschen in Lower Hungary, = 1 Imperial or Kayser Grosche.

Coins. The gold coins of Hungary are the Kremnitz Ducat, marked K. B. coined from the gold of the mines of Kremnitz; 67 such Ducats weigh a Cologne Mark, and the gold is $23\frac{3}{4}$ Carats fine; they pass for $4\frac{1}{2}$ Imperial Florins, and are worth 9s. 5d. sterling nearly. The silver coins are Convention Rixdollars (called in the Hungarian language *Egistaler);* Imperial Florins *(Zlaty;)* half Florins *(Pul-Zlaty);* Copsticks, of 20 Creutzers; Pieces of 17, 10, 7, 5, and 3 Creutzers: in all these the Cologne Mark is coined at the rate of 20 Florins. The Convention Rixdollar is worth 4s. 2d. sterling. The baser coins are Hungarian Groschen, Creutzers, Polturats, Groschels of 3 Pfenings, and Pfenings; the three last coins sometimes contain a little silver, and sometimes consist entirely of copper.

Weights & Measures. The weights and long measures will be found under the article *Vienna.*

An old Hungarian weight, called Occa, is still used in some places; it answers to $2\frac{1}{4}$lb. of Vienna, 2lb. $6\frac{1}{4}$ oz. avoirdupois, or 1,0842 Kilogramme.

In Upper Hungary the Eimer of wine equals 19,36 English Gallons, or 73,316 Litres. In Lower Hungary it contains 15,03 English Gallons, or 56,891 Litres. Tokay is sold in Casks, called Anthals, which contain each 13,35 English Gallons, or 50,543 Litres.

IONIAN ISLANDS *(in the Mediterranean)*.

Monies and Coins.

Accounts are kept in these Islands in Turkish Piastres of 40 Paras each.

The coins in circulation are principally Venetian Sequins and Ducats, in Gold; and in Silver, Venetian, Spanish, and Imperial Dollars, all of which pass for a variable number of Piastres.

The weights and measures in use are chiefly those of Venice, *which see*.

For further particulars see *Zante*.

IRELAND.

Monies and Coins.

Accounts are kept here in Pounds, Shillings, and Pence, as in England, but Irish currency differs from English in the proportion of 12 to 13. Thus 1s. English is 1s. 1d. Irish; and £1 English, £1 1s. 8d. Irish.

The Gold and Silver coins of Ireland are those of England, but they pass here for $\frac{1}{12}$ more than their British value. Thus the Guinea is worth £1 2s. 9d. Irish, the Crown 5s. 5d. and the smaller coins in proportion. Hence English money is turned to Irish by adding $\frac{1}{12}$, and Irish to English by subtracting $\frac{1}{13}$.

The Copper coins of Ireland are inferior to those of England in the same proportion, 26 Irish Halfpence being equal to 24 English Halfpence, which make the British Shilling.

Bank Tokens.

In 1804, the Bank of Ireland bought in a large quantity of depreciated silver coin; and, as a substitute, issued Spanish Dollars, newly stamped, at 6s. Irish; and also fractions of the Dollar which had been minted for the occasion at the Tower of London, consisting of Five-penny, Ten-penny, and Thirty-penny Pieces Irish, being exactly $\frac{1}{13}$, $\frac{2}{13}$, and $\frac{6}{13}$ of the Dollar. All these coins are called Bank Tokens, the Bank having engaged to receive them again at the issued price; and they have been declared a legal tender in the payment of taxes. Their intrinsic value may be known from that of the Dollar, which is worth 4s. 4d. sterling nearly, though generally reckoned at 4s. 6d.

Weights.

The weights of Ireland are the same as those of England; the measures are also the same, with some exceptions and customary regulations.

Corn, meal, and flour, are sold in Sacks by weight, chiefly by the Stone of 14lb. avoirdupois, and the common appellation of quantity is the *Barrel*, which

Weights. weighs as follows:—20 Stone of wheat, peas, beans, and rye. 16 Stone of barley, bere, and rapeseed. 14 Stone of oats, and in some places 12; and 12 Stone of malt.

By a law of 1734, it was ordered that 41 Stone of wheat and rye, 24 of barley, 22 of oats, or 20 of malt, should be reckoned equivalent to a Quarter, Winchester measure; but these proportions are seldom noticed except in the shipment of corn.

Provisions, for exportation, such as beef and pork, are sold in Tierces, Barrels, and Firkins. The casks are not tared, but the pieces in each must be of the following weight and number.

BEEF——	Navy....304lb.	per Tierce, being	38	Pieces of	8lb. each.
	India....336lb.	.. ditto	42	.. ditto ..	8lb. ditto.
	Mess....304lb.	.. ditto	38	.. ditto ..	8lb. ditto.
	Ditto....200lb.	per Barrel	25	.. ditto ..	8lb. ditto.
	Ditto....100lb.	per Firkin	25	.. ditto ..	4lb. ditto.
PORK——	India....318lb.	per Tierce	53	.. ditto ..	6lb. ditto.
	Navy....320lb.	.. ditto	80	.. ditto ..	4lb. ditto.
	Army ...208lb.	per Barrel	52	.. ditto ..	4lb. ditto.
	Mess....200lb.	.. ditto	50	.. ditto ..	4lb. ditto.
	Ditto....100lb.	per Firkin	25	.. ditto ..	4lb. ditto.

Butter is sold by the Cwt. of 112lb.; tare, the weight of the cask, and tret 1lb. in 28lb. Cheese is also sold by the Cwt.

Dry Measures. Coals and lime are sold by the Bushel, by which also the duty on malt is levied. The coal Bushel is 20 Inches in diameter at the bottom, 21 at the top, and must contain 10 Gallons Winchester measure.

The duties on coals imported are levied by a measure containing a Ton weight.

The lime Bushel was formerly 8 Winchester Gallons; but by a late act, the half Barrel has been adopted, which is to be 21 Inches diameter at the bottom in the clear, 22 at the top, and 12 deep, containing 20 Irish Gallons, or 4352 cubic Inches.

The malt Bushel measures $272\frac{1}{4}$ cubic Inches. It is generally called the Winchester Bushel, though it contains 27,58 cubic Inches more, or about $1\frac{1}{4}$ per cent.

Liquid Measures. The Irish Gallon measures 217,6 cubic Inches; and as that of England is 231 cubic Inches, 100 Gallons of the latter equal $106\frac{1}{6}$ of the former. Dealers generally allow 6 per cent. for the difference.

The Inch, Foot, and Yard, are the same here as in England; but the Irish Perch or Pole is 7 Yards, and that of England only $5\frac{1}{2}$. Hence 11 Irish Miles are equal to 14 English Miles. Long Measures.

The proportion between the land measures of England and Ireland is deduced from the square Perch of each country. Thus $30\frac{1}{4}$ Irish Acres = 49 English Acres. The former is called plantation measure, and the latter statute measure. Land Measures.

1 Irish Acre = 1 Acre 2 Roods $19\frac{21}{121}$ Perches English; and 1 Acre of the latter = 2 Roods $18\frac{38}{49}$ Perches of the former.

The exchanges of Ireland are chiefly with England. The par of exchange is as their monies; that is, £100 English = £108 6s. 8d. Irish; but the course of exchange has been known to vary from 105 to 120 per cent. Exchanges, Usance, &c.

Bills from London on Dublin are mostly drawn at 21 days sight, or, what is considered equivalent, at 31 days date, and such are called *Bills in Course*. If the term be longer, an advance is accordingly made in the price of exchange. Thus bills at 41 days date are charged $\frac{1}{8}$ per cent. more; but, beyond this term, the advance is in a higher proportion, being at the rate of $\frac{1}{2}$ per cent. per month.

Days of grace, and all other usages and laws of exchange, are the same in Ireland as in England, except that when a bill becomes due on Sunday it is not customary here to present it on the preceding Saturday, as in England, but on the Monday following.

BANK OF IRELAND.

In 1784, a National Bank was established in Ireland, nearly after the plan of the Bank of England. The first subscribers advanced a loan to government of £600,000, at 4 per cent. per annum, for which they obtained a charter. Bank of Ireland.

In 1791 they raised a second subscription of £400,000, part of which was applied to the use of the Bank, and the rest given to government in consideration of a renewal of the charter, and of increasing the interest of the first loan $\frac{1}{4}$ per cent.

In 1797 the company advanced another loan to government of £500,000, at an interest of 5 per cent. per annum, with an annuity of £3 12s. 6d. per cent. which was to continue with the charter 19 years. Thus in 1816 the term was to expire, when the corporation might, on receiving a year's notice, be dissolved; but in 1808 the charter was extended 21 years, that is, to 1837, in consideration of a

Bank of Ireland. loan of £1,250,000 advanced to government at 5 per cent. per annum, and also of the Bank having engaged to manage the public debt of Ireland, free of all expense to the state.

The Bank of Ireland is not permitted by its laws to deal in any kind of goods or merchandize; but it can purchase and hold estates, and lend money on mortgages or on pledges. It discounts bills, keeps cash for others, and issues its own notes, after the plan of the Bank of England. No other body corporate or politic, nor any other firm of more than six partners, can transact the same kind of business in Ireland.

The interest charged by the Bank for money advanced is 5 per cent. per annum; though all private banks in Ireland charge 6 per cent. per annum, which is the legal interest of the country.

This Institution is under the management of a Governor, Deputy Governor, and 15 Directors, who are elected annually by the Proprietors. The qualification of a Governor is to be possessed of £4000 bank stock; of a Deputy Governor, £3000; of a Director, £2000; and of Proprietor or Elector, £500; and these sums must have been possessed for three months previous to the election, unless they come by bequest or inheritance.

ISTRIA, *see Fiume and Trieste.*

IVICA, *see Majorca.*

JAPAN.

Monies and Coins. Accounts are here kept in Tales or Tayels, of 10 Mas, or 100 Condorines. The Dutch (the only European nation that trades to Japan) reckon the Tale at 3½ Florins, which is about 6s. 2d. sterling.

The Gold coins of Japan are Itjib or Itchebos, Copangs or Cobans, and Obans; these are flat pieces of gold of an oblong shape, rounded at both ends, bearing various flowers and letters in relief.

The Itchebo is the smallest of these, and its value is about 15 Mas.

The Copang is worth 64 Mas, more or less; the old Copangs weigh 371 Dutch Asen, or 275 English Grains, and the gold is said to be 22 Carats fine;

this would give £2 4s. 7d. sterling for the value of the old Copang; but it must be observed that the Japanese coins are reckoned at Madras only 87 Touch, which is $20\frac{22}{25}$ Carats, and this reduces the value of the old Copang to £2 1s. 10d. sterling. The new Copangs weigh 180 English Grains, and the Gold is about 16 Carats fine, which gives their value 21s. 3d. sterling. Monies and Coins.

The Oban is the largest Gold coin, and is thrice the value of the Copang.

The Schuit is a Silver piece, which weighs 4 Ounces 18 Dwts. 16 Grains, English troy, and is 11 Ounces fine, which gives its value £1 5s. 3d. sterling. The word *Schuit* (a boat) is of Dutch origin, and probably refers to the shape of the piece. Most payments here are made in silver Ingots of different sizes, the values of which are determined by their weight: the largest is about 7 Ounces, and the smallest 84 Grains English troy, and the fineness is $\frac{11}{12}$. There is also a little globular piece of silver, called Kodama, bearing the figure of a Japanese Deity, with several letters. It varies in size and value from 5 to 15 Condorines.

The Sennis or Cashes are small Pieces of iron, copper, or brass, having a square hole in the middle, through which, as in China, they are strung on a wire, or thread, in various numbers, 600 of the smallest sort being reckoned for a Tale.

A Spanish Dollar is valued in payments at from 7 Mas to 74 Condorines, which nearly agrees with the valuation before given of the silver Tale.

The weight called Picul is divided into 100 Catti, the Catti into 16 Tales, and the Tale into 10 Mas, or 100 Condorines. The Picul weighs about 130lb. avoirdupois. The measures for rice are as follow. Weights & Measures.

The Managoga contains 10,000 Ickmagogs; the Ickmagog, 1000 Icgogas; the latter, 100 Gantas, or 300 Cocas.

The long measure called Inc, or Tattamy, is $6\frac{1}{4}$ English Feet nearly, or 1,9 French Metre.

KONIGSBERG *(in Prussia)*,*

And also Memel, on the Baltic, keep accounts in Guldens or Florins, of 30 Groschen, subdivided into 18 Pfenings, Prussian currency. Monies of Account.

---

* A new system of weights and measures was decreed for Konigsberg and all Prussia in May 1816, which will be explained under the article *Prussia*.

Monies of Account. The Gulden is also reckoned at 8 Good Groschen, or 90 Shillings Prussian money.

A Prussian Thaler or Rixdollar is reckoned at 3 Prussian Guldens, 24 Good Groschen, or 90 Prussian Groschen; a Reichsgulden or Piece of two-thirds, at 2 Guldens; a Good Grosche, at $3\frac{3}{4}$ Prussian Groschen; a Prussian Shilling, at 6 Pfenings.

Coins. The only coins peculiar to Konigsberg are Prussian Timpfen of 18 Groschen; Sechsers of 6 Groschen; Dutgens of 3 Groschen; Pieces of 1 Grosche, and of 1 Shilling.

All the Prussian gold and silver coins are current here, for which see *Berlin*.

Gold and Silver Weight. Gold and silver are weighed by the Dantzic Mark: the Konigsberg Mark is, however, something heavier than that of Dantzic, being equal to $3023\frac{1}{2}$ English Grains, or 195,89 French Grammes.

Commercial Weight. The weights and measures of Konigsberg must, according to an edict of 1714, be similar to those of *Berlin*.

The Shipfund, or Shippond, contains 3 Centners, or 330lb. Berlin weight; the Grosse Stone, 33lb.; the Klein Stone, 20lb.; the Lispond, $16\frac{1}{2}$lb. The division of the Pound is into 2 Marks, 16 Ounces, 32 Loths, 128 Quintins, or 512 Dwts. 100lb. of Konigsberg = 103,24lb. avoirdupois, or 46,85 Kilogrammes.

Dry Measures. The Last is divided into 24 Tonnes, $56\frac{1}{2}$ new Scheffels, 60 old ditto, 240 Viertels, or 960 Metzen.

The new Scheffel is divided into 36 Stofs, and contains 3152 English cubic Inches; it must weigh, filled with spring water, 110lb. Berlin weight, and filled with good rye, about 81lb. It answers to 1,465 English Bushel, or 0,5162 Hectolitres.

The Last of Spanish and French salt is reckoned at 18 Tonnes, 60 Quintals, or 6000lb.; the Last of herrings, at 12 Tonnes; of green marbled soap, at 3 Tonnes, or 12 Viertels.

Liquid Measures. The liquid measures are divided as at Dantzic: the Stof, however, is smaller, being $87\frac{1}{2}$ English cubic Inches, and the Quart is $70\frac{1}{5}$ English cubic Inches. Hence 1 Stof = 3 English Pints, or 1,4334 French Litres.

The old Prussian Ell is 22,62 English Inches, or 0,5745 Metres; and the Konigsberg Foot, 12,11 English Inches, or 0,3076 Metres. Hence, 100 such Ells = 63 English Yards nearly, and 108 Feet of Konigsberg = 109 English Feet. The Ell of Berlin, and the Rhineland Foot, are also used here. **Long Measures.**

Konigsberg exchanges with, and gives— **Exchanges, Usances, &c**

Amsterdam, 300 Prussian Groschen, more or less, for £1 Flemish currency.
Berlin, ... 100 Rixdollars Prussian currency, .. for 100 Rixdollars ditto.
Dantzic, .. 100 Prussian Guldens, ... for 124 Polish Guldens.
Hamburgh, 137 Prussian Groschen, ... for 1 Rixdollar banco.
London, .. 19½ Prussian Guldens, ... for £1 sterling.

The usance is 14 days after acceptance, Sundays and holidays included.
There are six days of grace allowed.

LEGHORN *(in Italy.)*

The monies, weights, and measures, of Leghorn have been described generally in the article Florence; but as there are certain regulations peculiar to this place, some additional explanations seem necessary, and such may also tend further to elucidate this complicated system. **Monies of Account.**

The principal money of account, especially among merchants and bankers, is the *Pezza da otto reali*, which is divided into 20 Soldi, or 240 Denari di Pezza.

The *Lira* is another money of account, chiefly used in the inferior departments of business, and in comparing different denominations of money. It is divided into 20 Soldi, or 240 Denari di Lira. 5¾ Lire equal 1 Pezza.

There are two other monies of account here of less frequent use, viz. the *Scudo d'Oro* of 7½ Lire, and the *Scudo Corrente* of 7 Lire, and they are also divided into 20 Soldi and 240 Denari respectively.

Several other denominations circulate in the following proportions to each other. 1 Testone equals 2 Lire, 3 Paoli, 24 Crazie, or 120 Quattrini.

The sterling value of all these monies may be determined by considering the Lira as the fundamental coin, and valuing it at 8⅛d. English silver. This makes the Pezza equal to 46¾d. nearly.

The monies of Leghorn have two values, the one called *moneta buona*, and the other *moneta lunga*. The former is the effective money of the place, as

Monies of Account. already described, and the latter is an imaginary money, adopted probably for simplifying numerical operations. It is formed by reckoning the Pezza of $5\frac{3}{4}$ Lire moneta buona, as 6 Lire moneta lunga; and hence the proportion is as 23 to 24. Thus, moneta buona is converted into moneta lunga by adding $\frac{1}{23}$, and the latter is reduced to the former by subtracting $\frac{1}{24}$. Hence

	Moneta buona.		*Moneta lunga.*
The Pezza =	$5\frac{3}{4}$ Lire	=	6 Lire.
	$8\frac{5}{8}$ Paoli	=	9 Paoli.
	69 Crazie	=	72 Crazie.
	115 Soldi di Lira	=	120 Soldi di Lira.

Coins. The coins here are those of Tuscany, which have been already described under the article *Florence.* The following is their relative value in Leghorn.

		Moneta buona.			*Moneta lunga.*					
		Lire.	Soldi.	Denari.	Lire.	Soldi.	Denari.	Pezze.	Soldi.	Denari.
Gold	Doppia,	23	0	0	24	0	0	4	0	0
	Ruspone,	40	0	0	41	14	9	6	19	$1\frac{1}{2}$
	Sequin,	13	6	8	13	18	3	2	6	$4\frac{1}{2}$
Silver	Francescone,	6	13	4	6	19	2	1	3	$2\frac{1}{2}$
	Half ditto,	3	6	8	3	9	7	0	11	$7\frac{1}{2}$
	Testone,	2	0	0	2	1	9	0	6	$11\frac{1}{2}$
	Paolo,	0	13	4	0	13	11	0	2	4
	Crazia,	0	1	8	0	1	9	0	0	$3\frac{1}{2}$

The sterling value of the above monies may be found from that of the Lira in moneta buona, as before stated. For the intrinsic value of these coins from assays, see *Table of Coins*, Vol. II. and their value in French money may be found by allowing for each Lira 84 Centimes.

The fineness of gold is expressed by dividing the weight into 24 Carati, and the Carato into 8 Ottavi, and that of silver by dividing the weight into 12 Oncie, each of 24 Denari.

Gold in bars is sold per Ounce fine, and silver in bars per Pound fine, and the price of each is regulated in Lire effective.

Spanish Dollars are sold at about $14\frac{1}{2}$ Pezze per Pound weight; and $12\frac{9}{16}$ such Dollars weigh 1lb. or 1000 Dollars equal 79lb. 7 oz. Leghorn weight.

The divisions and accurate contents of the weights and measures of Leghorn are stated under the article *Florence*, and the following are the customary or generally estimated proportions acted upon by merchants. Weights & Measures.

It is computed that 100lb. of Leghorn equal 77lb. avoirdupois, although 75lb. of the latter is the nearest weight (see page 130). In mercantile comparisons, however, there is much uncertainty here, on account of the various deductions made from the weight of goods for Tares and other allowances. Thus it is found that the English Cwt. seldom renders more than 145lb. at Leghorn, though it equals 150lb. The Quintal or Centinajo is 100lb.

The Cantaro is, generally, 150lb.; that of sugar is 151lb.; of oil, 88lb;. of brandy, 120lb.; of stock fish, and some other articles, 160lb. The Rottolo is 3lb.

In weighing gold and silver the beam and scales are used, and also for silk, coral, cochineal, rhubarb, scammony, and spices; all other goods are weighed with the *Stadera* or steelyard.

Diamonds and precious stones are weighed by the Carat of 4 Tuscan Grains, which answer to $3\frac{7}{216}$ English Grains.

The principal measure for corn and salt is the Sacco, 380 of which are estimated at 100 English Quarters. 1 Sack $= 2\frac{1}{16}$ English Bushels.

The Barile of wine is computed at 12 English Gallons; and 9 English Gallons of oil weigh 88lb. of Leghorn, or 66lb. avoirdupois.

In cloth measure 155 Braccia equal 100 English Yards; and hence the Canna of 4 Braccia $=$ 93 English Inches.

Allowances, Tares, and other Regulations in the Sale of Goods.

The following tables contain an account of the kind of money in which goods are generally sold, and the customary tares or deductions made for packages. There are, however, other deductions, which are not comprised in the tables, such as the Tare of *Uso* or Usance, of 2 per cent., which is first taken off, and a final allowance, commonly $\frac{1}{2}$ to 1 per cent., is deducted, called *Courtesy*. Allowances, Tares, &c.

Where customary tare is not established, real tare is understood, for packages, ropes, &c. when there are such, though they are not inserted in the table.

Charges on sales, including commission, are generally from 6 to 8 per cent.; on fish, from 8 to 10. The commission is mostly 2 per cent., and guarantee of debts 2 per cent.

A discount of 3 per cent. is allowed on commodities in general, and of 4 per cent. on all cotton manufactures.

Articles.	*How Sold.*	*Tare.*
Almonds, sweet and bitter	per 100lb. in Lire Moneta lunga.	
Aloes	per 100lb. in Pezze.	
Alum, English, Levant, and Swedish..	per cantaro of 150lb. in Paoli.	
Roman	per cantaro of 150lb. in Moneta buona.	
Anchovies, in casks from 270 to 300lb..	in Pezze.	
Arsenic, yellow and white	per 100lb. in Pezze.	
Assafœtida	per 100lb. in Pezze.	
Bacon	per 100lb. in Lire Moneta buona, no disc^t.	
Barilla, Alicant	per 1000lb. in Pezze.	
Benzoin and Borax	per lb. in Lire Moneta lunga.	
Blue, Prussian	per lb. in Lire Moneta lunga	4 per cent.
Brandy, French or Italian	per barile, in Pezze, no discount.	
Brimstone	per 1000lb. in Lire Moneta lunga.	
Camphor	per lb. in Lire Moneta lunga.	
Cantharides, Cassia, & Cream of Tartar.	per 100lb. in Pezze.	
Cavear, Russian	per 100lb. in Lire Moneta buona	18 per cent.
Cheese, Roman and Parmesan	per 100lb. in Lire Moneta buona.	
Cinnamon	per 100lb. in Ducats	24lb. per bale.
Cloves, Mace, and Nutmegs	per lb. in Lire Moneta lunga.	
Cochineal	per lb. in Lire Moneta lunga	2lb. per bag.
Cocoa	per 100lb. in Pezze.	
Cod Fish	per cantaro of 160lb. in Paoli.	
Coffee, Mocha, per bale	per 100lb. in Pezze	2¼ per cent.
Copal	per 100lb. in Pezze.	
Copper, from Smyrna and Syria	per 100lb. in Pezze.	
per 100 sheaths	per 100lb. in Lire Moneta buona.	
Cotton Wool and Yarn, from the Levant	per 100lb. in Pezze.	
Cumine, Malta	per 100lb. in Lire Moneta lunga.	
Dragon's Blood	per lb. in Lire Moneta lunga.	
Figs and Raisins, Smyrna and Calabria.	per 100lb. in Paoli Moneta lunga.	
Flax, Levant	per 100lb. in Lire Moneta lunga	50lb. per bale.
Muscovy and Riga	per 100lb. in Lire Moneta lunga	4 per cent.
Frankincense	per 100lb. in Pezze	8 per cent.
Galbanum and Galls	per 100lb. in Pezze.	
Gum Ammoniac and Lac	per 100lb. in Pezze.	
Arabic	per 100lb. in Pezze	8 per cent.
Tragacanth	per 100lb. in Pezze.	
Hemp, Bologna	per 100lb. in Lire Moneta lunga	12lb. per bale.
Herrings, Yarmouth red	per cask or barrel, in Pezze.	
Hides, Brazil and Buenos Ayres	per piece, in Pezze.	
Indigo	per lb. in Lire Moneta lunga	40lb. per seron.
Ipecacuanha	per lb. in Lire Moneta lunga.	
Iron, Russian and Swedish	per 100lb. in Lire Moneta buona.	
Juniper Berries, per bale	per 100lb. in Lire Moneta buona, no disc^t.	
Lead, English, in pigs	per 1000lb. in Ducats	1 per cent.
in balls	per 100lb. in Lire Moneta buona.	
Leather, English and Spanish tanned ..	per lb. in Soldi di Lira	1lb. per hide.
Morocco	per lb. in Soldi Moneta buona.	
Russia	per lb. in Soldi di Lira.	
Smyrna raw	per lb. in Soldi di Lira	1lb. per hide.
Lemon Juice	per barile, in Moneta buona, no discount.	
Liquorice	per 100lb. in Pezze	3lb. per Rottolo, marked on the barrel.
Logwood, Brazil	per 1000lb. in Pezze.	
Manna, Sicily	per lb. in Crazie	2½lb. per Rottolo, marked on the box.

Articles.	*How Sold.*	*Tare.*
Oil, Calabria, Genoa, Levant, Tunis, and Tuscany	per barile of 88lb. in Lire Moneta buona.	
Lucca	per jar of 264lb. in Pezze.	
Whale	per 100lb. in Pezze.	
of Vitriol	per lb. in Lire Moneta lunga.	
Opium	per lb. in Lire Moneta lunga.	
Pepper, black, from England	per 100lb. in Ducats	10lb. per bale.
Goa	per 100lb. in Ducats	2lb. per bag.
Holland	per 100lb. in Ducats	18lb. per bale.
Pitch and Rosin	per 100lb. in Paoli.	
Potashes, Sicily	per 1000lb. in Pezze.	
Rhubarb	per lb. in Lire Moneta lunga.	
Rice	per 100lb. in Lire Moneta lunga.	
Rocou, Cayenne	per lb. in Lire Moneta lunga	20 per cent.
Rum	per gallon, in Lire Moneta buona.	
Saffron	per 100lb. in Pezze	6lb. per bale, & 4 per cent.
Sal Ammoniac and Salsaparilla	per 100lb. in Pezze.	
Salmon, pickled	per cask or barrel, in Pezze.	
Salt Fish and Stock Fish	per cantaro of 160lb. in Pezze.	
Saltpetre, Sandrac, and Sponge	per 100lb. in Pezze.	
Scammony	per lb. in Lire Moneta lunga.	
Senna, per bale	per 100lb. in Pezze	10 per cent.
Silk, raw	per lb. in Paoli.	
Organzini	per bale of 320lb. in Pezze.	
Soap, white and marbled	per 100lb. in Lire Moneta buona, no disc[t].	
Steel	per 100lb. in Lire Moneta buona.	
Sugar, West India, in hogsheads	per cantaro of 151lb. in Pezze	12 per cent.
Muscovada, in chests	per cantaro of 151lb. in Pezze	20 per cent.
Ditto from Lisbon	per cantaro of 151lb. in Pezze	18 per cent.
Ditto from Vera Cruz, per bale	per cantaro of 151lb. in Pezze.	
Ditto from Havannah, in chests	per cantaro of 151lb. in Pezze	14 per cent.
Loaf, in Paper	per cantaro of 151lb. in Pezze	4 per cent.
Sumach, Sicilian	per 100lb. in Lire Moneta lunga.	
Tallow	per 100lb. in Lire Moneta buona, no disc[t].	
Tamarinds	per 100lb. in Pezze.	
Tar, Swedish and American, by the cask	per 100lb. in Pezze.	
Tartar	per lb. in Pezze.	
Tea	per lb. in Lire Moneta lunga.	
Tin, English, in casks of 580lb.	per 100lb. in Ducats.	
Tobacco, Brazil	per lb. in Soldi di Lira	20lb. per roll.
Hungary	per 100lb. in Pezze	8lb. per bale.
Salonica	per 100lb. in Pezze	6lb. per bale.
Virginia, in hogsheads	per 100lb. in Pezze	10 per cent.
Tunnies, in casks of about 200lb.	per cask or barrel, in Pezze.	
Turpentine, by the cask of 350lb.	per 100lb. in Pezze.	
Verdigris, French, in bags	per 100lb. in Pezze	2lb. per loaf, and real tare.
Vitriol, English	per 1000lb. in Pezze	10 per cent.
Venetian	per 1000lb. in Pezze	8 per cent.
Wax, yellow, from America, Poland, Salonica, and Smyrna	per 100lb. in Pezze	tare of uso, & 3 per ct. more
Wax, yellow, from Mogadore and Tunis	per 100lb. in Pezze	2¼ per cent.
Wine	per barile of 133¼lb. in Moneta buona, no discount.	
Wool, Barbary and Levant	per cantaro of 160lb. in Pezze.	
Spanish	per 100lb. in Ducats	19 per cent.

Allowances, Tares, &c.

Effective money, in which Tuscan produce is generally sold, implies without discount.

The prices of merchandize are fixed in silver money, with the exception of Italian silks, which are sold in gold money.

Exchanges, &c.

For the exchanges of Leghorn see Vol. II. page 69, and for the usances see *Florence*, Vol. I. page 132.

Foreign bills of exchange on Leghorn are by law payable in gold; and all quotations and calculations of such bills are made in gold money. This is a money of account differing from the silver by a fixed agio of 7 per cent. Thus 100 Pezze gold money are equivalent to 107 Pezze silver money.

Bills how paid.

No days of grace are allowed; but bills are paid three times a week at the *Stanza*, a place where the cashiers meet on Mondays, Wednesdays, and Fridays: thus bills which become due on Tuesdays, Thursdays, or Saturdays, are not payable till the following days of meeting and payment.

When a bill is negotiated in Leghorn on a Monday, the value of it is not paid till the Friday following; and when on the Wednesday or Friday, it is not paid until the following Monday. If, in the interval, the Leghorn merchant, who took the bill, should be declared a bankrupt, and if the bill had been negotiated to answer or effect some commercial transaction ordered from a foreign place, the loss must fall on the merchant at the said foreign place, and not on the merchant of Leghorn, who drew or negotiated the bill.

When the drawer of a bill, accepted in Leghorn, becomes a bankrupt, and the date of his bankruptcy is anterior to that of the acceptance, the acceptance can be declared null and void, and the money may be deposited in the hands of magistrates till the date of the failure has been ascertained.

LEIPSIC *(in Germany)*.

Monies of Account.

Leipsic, Dresden, and all Saxony, keep accounts in Rixdollars of 24 Good Groschen, each Grosche being divided into 12 Pfenings current.

A specie Rixdollar is $1\frac{1}{3}$ Rixdollar current, or 32 Good Groschen.

A Reichsgulden, or Piece of two-thirds, is worth $\frac{2}{3}$ of the Rixdollar current, or 16 Good Groschen; a Meissner Gulden, 21; an old Schock, 20; a new Schock, 60 Good Groschen.

The Gold coins of Saxony are double, single, and half August d'ors, reckoned at 10, 5, and $2\frac{1}{2}$ Rixdollars. Also Ducats worth 2 Rixdollars 20 Groschen. Coins.

The Silver coins are Specie Rixdollars, with halves and quarters; Pieces of 4, 2, and 1 Good Groschen current; and Pieces of 6, 3, and 1 Pfenings, in which the Mark of fine silver is valued at 14 Rixdollars current.

The above coins are minted at the following rate, viz: Rate of Coinage.

35 August d'ors weigh a Cologne Mark of Gold, 21 Carats 8 Grains fine.
$8\frac{1}{3}$ Specie Rixdollars .... of Silver $13\frac{1}{3}$ Loths fine.
$43\frac{1}{3}$ Sechstels or Pieces of 4 Good Groschen .... $8\frac{2}{3}$ Loths fine.
70 Pieces of 2 Groschen .... 7 Loths fine.
$117\frac{1}{7}$ Single Groschen .... 5 Loths 16 Grains fine.
The 6 Pfening Pieces are 5 Loths 2 Grains fine.
The 3 Pfening Pieces .. 3 Loths 4 Grains fine.
The 1 Pfening Piece .. 2 Loths fine.

For the Leipsic rate of coinage see *Germany*, and for the value of the monies see *Tables of Coins*, Vol. II.

The weight for the precious metals is that of *Cologne*, which see. Weights.

The commercial Pound of Leipsic is the standard weight for goods throughout Saxony. It is divided into 2 Marks, 16 Ounces, 32 Loths, 128 Quintlins, 512 Pfenings, or 7680 Grains. This Pound equals 7206 English Grains, and therefore 100lb. of Leipsic = 102,94lb. avoirdupois, or 46,68 Kilogrammes. The Stone is 22lb. the Waag 44lb. and the Centner 110lb.

There is another weight called butchers' or heavy weight, which is about 8 per cent. more than the common weight.

The Wispel, corn measure, is divided into 2 Malters, 24 Scheffels, 96 Viertels, 384 Metzen, or 1536 Masgens. Dry Measure.

In 1719, the Dresden Scheffel was established as the legal measure throughout the country; it is 14 Dresden Inches deep, and a Dresden Ell square; it measures, therefore, 8064 Dresden, or 6456 English cubic Inches, and weighs, full of water, 226lb.; but full of rye, about 166lb. Dresden weight.

The Leipsic Scheffel measures 8481 English cubic Inches, and weighs, full of water, 297lb.; but full of rye, 218lb. Leipsic weight.

Hence the Dresden Wispel, of 24 Scheffels, contains 72 English Bushels, or

Dry Measure. 25,389 Hectolitres; and the Leipsic Wispel, 94,74 English Bushels, or 33,348 Hectolitres.

Liquid Measures. The Fuder of wine contains 12 Eimers; the Fass, 5 Eimers; the Ahm, 2 Eimers; the Oxhoft of French Brandy, 3 Leipsic Eimers, or $3\frac{3}{8}$ Dresden Eimers; the Oxhoft of French wine, $2\frac{2}{3}$ Leipsic Eimers, or 3 of Dresden.

The Leipsic Eimer is divided into 63 Leipsic Kannes, 126 Nössels, or 504 Quartiers; also into 81 Dresden Kannes, or 54 Visier Kannes, and contains 20,10 English Gallons, or 76,09 Litres.

The Dresden Eimer contains 72 Dresden Kannes, 56 Leipsic ditto, or 54 Visier ditto, and answers to 17,87 English Gallons, or 67,63 Litres.

Long Measures. The Leipsic Foot is divided into 12 common Inches, or 10 decimal Inches, and contains 11,11 English Inches, or 0,2822 Metres. The Ell is 2 Feet; the Stab, 4 Feet; the Clafter, 6 Feet.

The Leipsic Builders' Foot equals 11,13 English Inches, or 0,2825 Metres.

The Dresden Foot contains 11,14 English Inches, or 0,2829 Metres.

The Ruthe or Perch is $15\frac{1}{6}$ Feet, Leipsic measure, or $14\frac{1}{8}$ Feet English.

The Saxon Mile is 2000 Ruthes, each of 16 Dresden Feet, or 9905 English Yards; hence 1 Saxon Mile equals 5,628 English Miles, or 9,057 French Kilometres.

Superficial Measures. The Saxon square Ruthe contains $230\frac{1}{36}$ Leipsic Builders' square Feet, or about $197\frac{3}{4}$ English square Feet.

The Saxon Acre of land contains 300 such square Ruthes, or 6590 English square Yards; which equal 1 Acre 1 Rood 18 Perches, English measure, or 5,5075 French Decares.

Fairs. Three great fairs or messes are held at Leipsic every year, viz. at the beginning of the year, at Easter, and at Michaelmas. Each fair lasts 14 days.

New-year's fair begins on the 1st of January; or if this should fall on a Sunday, on the 2d.

Easter or Jubilee fair begins in the afternoon of Jubilee Sunday, that is, the third Sunday after Easter.

Michaelmas fair begins on the afternoon of the first Sunday after the 29th of September.

The opening of each fair is proclaimed on the first day, and on the eighth day the close of the fair is likewise proclaimed. The first week is properly called the fair; during which time all great commercial transactions take place. Fairs.

Bills are presented for acceptance in the four first days of the fair, and the acceptance can be delayed, at new-year's fair, only till the day before the second proclamation; but at the other two fairs, till the Friday in the first week, ten o'clock in the forenoon at the latest; and if the acceptance should not then have taken place, the bills must be protested. Bills payable at the Fairs.

The time of payment of bills of exchange is during the five first days after the close of the fair is proclaimed; so that, at new-year's fair, payment must be made on the 12th of January at latest; and at the other two fairs, on the Thursday in the second week; in default of which, the bills must be then protested before ten o'clock at night, or all recourse is lost against the drawer.

For the exchanges of Leipsic, see *Berlin*, Vol. II. page 35. Exchanges.

The usance in Leipsic is 14 days after acceptance. Usance.

When bills are made payable any number of days after the fair, the time is reckoned from the Monday in the week of payment of the Easter and Michaelmas fair; but at new-year's fair, from the 16th of January.

No days of grace are allowed here; but, on the day a bill becomes due, the holder must demand payment; neither is he permitted, in case of non-payment, to connive at any delay, but must, on the very day, have it protested, with interest, expenses, &c. and return the bill the first opportunity. If he neglects any of these regulations, he loses all claim on the drawer and indorsers.

Bills payable *a vista*, or on demand, may be presented and accepted even on a Sunday or holiday, and must be paid within 24 hours after acceptance.

LEVANT, *see Smyrna, Constantinople, Aleppo.*

LIBAU (*in Russia*).

In this port on the Baltic, and in the whole province of Courland, merchants keep their accounts, as at Riga, in Alberts Dollars of 4 Orts, 80 Ferdings, or 90 Alberts Groschen; but retail traders generally reckon in Guldens of 30 current Groschen. Three Alberts Groschen are worth 4 current Groschen. Monies of Account.

Coins. The coins which chiefly circulate here are Dutch Ducats, and Alberts Dollars; and also Pieces coined in the country of the standard and value of these two coins. The Ferding is an old silver coin, but the Grosche is imaginary.

The Ducat is commonly reckoned at 2 Alberts Dollars, but it bears an agio of about 8 Groschen.

Prussian currency is generally 50 per cent. worse than Alberts Dollars.

The Russian coins are also current here, as at *Riga*.

Weights. The commercial Pound is divided into 32 Loths or Ounces, or 128 Drams, and contains 6449 English Grains. Thus 100lb. of Libau equal 92,13lb. avoirdupois, or 41,78 Kilogrammes. The Shippond contains 20 Lisponds; the Lispond, 20 Pounds.*

Dry Measure. The Lof is the element of dry measures. It contains 4190 English cubic Inches, and answers to 1,948 English Bushel, or 0,686 Hectolitres.

The Last of oats contains 60 Lofs, or 14½ English Quarters; the Last of every other grain is 48 Lofs, or 11,688 English Quarters.

Salt is sold by the Tun, which measures 9648 English cubic Inches, and contains 4,486 English Bushels, or 1,580 Hectolitre. A Tun of linseed is 2 Lofs; a Load of salt 18 Tuns; of lime, herrings, and coals, 12 Tuns.

Liquid Measure. The principal liquid measure is the Stof, which is 80,2 English cubic Inches, and contains 1,388 English Quart, or 1,31 French Litre.

The Oxhoft is divided into 3 Viertels, 6 Ankers, or 180 Stofs, and contains 14436 English cubic Inches, which equal 62½ English Gallons, or 235,8 Litres.

Long Measure. The Foot used here is the Rhenish, which contains 12,36 English Inches, or 0,3139 Metres. The Ell is 22,692 English Inches, or 0,8934 Metres.

A Quart of butter is 80lb. neat, or 100lb. gross.

A Ton of beef is 300lb. gross,—tare from 20 to 25.

A Dekker of skins or hides is 10 Pieces; a Dozen, 12 Pieces; a String, 30 Pieces.

---

* The weight of the Pound of Libau is very differently stated in works of high authority. According to *Kruse*, it answers to 6374 English Grains, while *Marien* makes it nearly 100 Grains heavier, and others vary considerably between those extremes; but by the late experiments at the London Mint, on attested standards, transmitted by *Francis Kienitz, Esq.* the British Consul for Courland, the weight of this Pound is found to be 6449 Grains, as above.

Libau exchanges with and gives— Exchanges.

Amsterdam..100 Alberts Dollars, more or less, for 102 Rixdollars current.
Hamburgh .. 94 Alberts Groschen.......... for 1 Rixdollar banco; or
105 Alberts Dollars............ for 100 Rixdollars banco.
London .... 4 Alberts Dollars 50 Groschen for £1 sterling.

The old style is still used in Libau. See *Russia.*

LIEGE *(in Germany).*

Accounts are kept here, and in most other parts of Westphalia, in Florins current, each Florin being divided into 20 Stivers, and each Stiver into 16 Pfenings. Monies of Account.

Other monies of account are Patacons, Escalins, and Liards, which bear the following proportions to each other:

1 Patacon = 4 Florins, 8 Escalins, 80 Stivers, 320 Liards, or 1280 Pfenings.

The Gold coins are Ducats, minted after the rate of the Empire, which pass for $8\frac{1}{2}$ Current Florins, with double Ducats in proportion. Also the Florin d'or or Gold Gulden, which passes for 5 Current Florins. Coins.

The Silver coins are the Patacon, which passes for $4\frac{1}{8}$ Current Florins; the Escalin, worth half a Florin, or 10 Stivers; and the Blamuse, worth 5 Stivers.

The sterling value of the above monies may be found from the Patacon, which weighs 423 English Grains, and is 10 Oz. 5 Dwts. fine. This gives the value 4s. 3d. sterling. Thus the Florin Current may be computed at $12\frac{1}{4}$d., and the other monies in proportion. Sterling Value.

The Pound used for weighing the precious metals is 3799 English Grains, or 246,028 French Grammes. Weights.

The commercial Pound contains 7330 English Grains; thus 100lb. of Liege equal 104,7lb. avoirdupois, or 47,49 Kilogrammes.

The Last of corn contains 96 Setiers, each Setier being equal to 29,93 Litres, or 0,849 English Bushels = 6,79 Winchester Gallons. Measures.

The Foot is 11,32 English Inches, or 0,2876 Metres. The Ell is 21,71 English Inches, or 0,5515 Metres.

Liege, since its connexion with France, has adopted the French denominations of money in the business of exchanges.

LISBON.

Monies of Account.

Lisbon and all Portugal keep accounts in Rees, Reis, or Reas, 1000 of which make a Milree or Milreis.

In the notation of accounts the Milrees are separated from the Rees by a crossed cipher, called *Cifraon*, and the Milrees from the Millions by a colon; thus Rs. 2:700⊕500 means two thousand seven hundred Milrees and five hundred Rees.

The Crusado of exchange, or old Crusado, is 400 Rees; the new Crusado, 480 Rees; the Testoon, 100 Rees; and the Vinten or Vintem, 20 Rees.

Thus the Milree is worth $2\frac{1}{2}$ old Crusados, $2\frac{1}{12}$ new Crusados, 10 Testoons, or 50 Vintens.

Coins.

The coins of Portugal may be distinguished under two heads; viz. those that were minted before the year 1722, and those that have been coined since that period; the former have been raised 20 per cent. in their nominal value.

	was worth Rees.	is now worth Rees.
The Dobraon which	20000	24000
The Half Dobraon	10000	12000
Lisbonnine	4000	4800
Half Lisbonnine	2000	2400
Milree	1000	1200
Crusado	400	480

The coinage since 1722 is as follows:

		Rees.	Portugal Weight.
Gold.	Dobraon worth	12800	1 Ounce.
	Joanese, or Half Dobraon	6400	$\frac{1}{2}$
	Quarter Dobraon	3200	$\frac{1}{4}$
	Escudo	1600	$\frac{1}{8}$
	Half Escudo	800	$\frac{1}{16}$
	Crusado Velho	400	$\frac{1}{32}$

Silver. . .The new Crusado of 480 Rees, the half, quarter, and eighth, in proportion.

The Piece of 6 Vintems, or 120 Rees.

The Testoon or Toston of 5 Vintems, or 100 Rees.

Pieces of 60 and 50 Rees.

Copper. Pieces of 5, 3, & $1\frac{1}{2}$ Rees.

At Brazil, Silver coins are minted called Patacons, which are there worth 320 Rees, but in Portugal they pass for 240 only, and the half and quarter Patacon in the same proportion. **Coins.**

The Spanish Patacon, or Hard Dollar, is worth in Portugal 810 Rees, more or less.

The fineness of gold is expressed in Quilates or Carats, and Grains; the Mark fine being 24 Carats; the Carat subdivided into 4 Grains, and the Grain into 8 Outavas. **Fineness of Gold and Silver.**

Portuguese gold coins are 22 Carats, wrought gold is $20\frac{1}{2}$ Carats, and gold dust from $21\frac{3}{4}$ to 22 Carats fine.

The fineness of silver is expressed in Dinheiros and Grains; the Mark fine being 12 Dinheiros, and the Dinheiro subdivided into 24 Grains.

Silver coins are 10 Dinheiros 19 Grains fine, and wrought silver $10\frac{1}{4}$ Dinheiros.

From the Mint regulations it appears that 8 Dobraons, 16 Joaneses or Moidores, 32 half Joaneses, 64 Dezeseis Testoons, 128 Oito Testoons, or 256 old Crusados, are to weigh a Portuguese Mark of gold, 22 Carats fine. **Rate of Coinage.**

Hence the Dobraon contains $442\frac{4}{5}$ Grains. These coins, however, are not in general quite 22 Carats fine; but there is a remedy which amounts from $\frac{1}{32}$ to $\frac{3}{32}$ of a Carat, and the new Crusados are found to be only $21\frac{27}{32}$ Carats fine.

The silver coin is 10 Dinheiros 19 Grains fine, as above; and the Mark is coined into $13\frac{1}{3}$ new Crusados; but it appears that this regulation has been of late years departed from, without any known law, while the Crusados of ancient coinage contain $258\frac{1}{3}$ Grains of English standard silver.

The gold Piece of 6400 Rees is worth 35s. 11d. sterling; and the gold Crusado 2s. 3d.; thus the Milree, valued in gold, is worth $67\frac{1}{2}$d. sterling. **Value of Monies.**

The silver Crusado at the foregoing rate is worth about 2s. 9d. sterling; and thus the Milree equals $68\frac{3}{4}$d. sterling; but from the assays made at the London Mint in 1812, on modern Crusados sent for the purpose, the average value of the Milree in silver may be computed at 60d. sterling. See *Table of Coins*, Vol. II.

Gold and silver are weighed by the Marco, which is divided into 8 Onças, 64 Outavas, 192 Escropulos, or 4608 Grãos, and equals $3541\frac{1}{2}$ English Grains, or 229,460 Grammes. See the *Note*, page 212. **Gold and Silver Weight.**

Apothecaries use the same weight, but reckon their Libra at $1\frac{1}{2}$ Mark. Thus their Pound contains 12 Ounces, 96 Eighths, 288 Scruples, or 6912 Grains. **Apothecaries' Weight**

Diamond Weight.

Diamonds, and other precious stones, are weighed by Quilates or Carats, of 4 Grains each, which Grains are heavier than those before stated. Thus 1 Diamond Grain equals 1,033 Grain Peso de Marco; and hence the Diamond Carat equals 4,132 Grains Peso de Marco, which answer to 3,1756 English Grains, or 205,75 Decigrammes. Diamond merchants generally reckon 151 Carats of Portugal to equal 1 Ounce English troy weight. See *London*, page 220.

Commercial Weight.

The commercial weight is the same as that for the precious metals, but with different divisions and multiples. Thus the Arratel, Libra, or Pound, is divided into 2 Marcos, 4 Quartas, 16 Onças, 120 Outavas, or 9216 Grāos. Its multiples are as follow: 32lb. or Arrateis make 1 Arroba; 4 Arrobas, 1 Quintal or 128lb. 13½ Quintals or 54 Arrobas equal 1 Tonelada. The Quintal of the India House is 3½ Arrobas or 112 Arrateis. 100lb. of Portugal equal 101,19lb. avoirdupois, or 45,89 Kilogrammes.*

Dry Measure.

The principal measure for corn, salt, and other dry commodities, is called Moyo, which is divided into 15 Fangas, 60 Alquieres, 240 Quartos, 480 Oitavas, or 1920 Selemines, with halves of several of those measures. The Moyo equals 23,03 English Bushels, or 8,1395 Hectolitres.

Liquid Measure.

The principal liquid measure at Lisbon is the Almude, which is divided into 2 Potes, 12 Canadas, or 48 Quartilhos. 18 Almudes equal 1 Baril; 26 Almudes, 1 Pipe; 52 Almudes, 1 Tonelada. The Almude contains 4,370 English Gallons, or 16,541 Litres.

The standard gauge at the Custom House of London, of a Pipe of Lisbon, is 140 Gallons; and this Pipe is reckoned at 31 Almudes. The standard gauge of a Pipe of Port is 138 Gallons, this Pipe is divided into 21 Almudes of Oporto.

---

* The weights of Portugal have been perhaps more frequently and more accurately compared in foreign mints than those of any other country, and yet authors do not perfectly agree as to their relative contents: according to *M. Tillet*, the Mark of Lisbon answers to 3540 English Grains, while *Kruse* makes it 3542¼, and this latter proportion has been most generally adopted; but by the late experiments at the *London Mint*, on several attested standards transmitted from Portugal and the Brazils, the Mark was found to be 3541½ English Grains, as above. It is worthy of observation, that this result agrees very nearly with the proportion computed by *Sir Isaac Newton* in 1719, namely, that 83lb. English troy weight = 135 Marks of Portugal; which gives the Mark equal to 3541⅓ English Grains.

Long Measures.

The Long Measures of Portugal are divided as follows:

4	Grãos, (of barley placed sideways)	=	1 Dedo, or Finger.
$1\frac{1}{2}$	Dedo	=	1 Pollegada, Thumb, or Inch.
8	Pollegadas	=	1 Palmo, or Span.
$1\frac{1}{2}$	Palmo, or 12 Inches	=	1 Pe, or Foot.
2	Pes, or 3 Palmos	=	1 Covado, or Cubit.
$1\frac{2}{3}$	Covado, 5 Palmos, or 40 Inches ..	=	1 Vara, or Yard.
$1\frac{1}{2}$	Vara, or 60 Inches	=	1 Passo Geometrico.
$1\frac{1}{3}$	Passo, or 80 Inches	=	1 Braça, or Fathom.
$117\frac{1}{3}\frac{1}{0}$	Braças	=	1 Estadio, Stadium, or Furlong.
8	Estadios	=	1 Milha, or Mile.
3	Milhas, or 28168 Palmos	=	1 Legoa, or League.
18	Legoas	=	1 Grau, or Degree of the Meridian.
360	Degrees	=	the Circumference of the Earth.

The Pe or Foot equals 12,944 English Inches, or 0,3285 of a Metre.

The Palmo is, as before stated, 8 Pollegadas which equal 8,64 English Inches; each Pollegada or Inch is divided into 12 Linhas or Lines, and each Linha into 10 Pontos or Points. This is called the *Palmo de Craveira*, or standard Span, being the legal measure of the kingdom; and all other measures derived from it are likewise distinguished by the same term.

The Vara is 5 Palmos de Craveira, or 40 Portuguese Inches, equal to 43,2 English Inches, or 1,096 Metre; but the Covado, which is used for measuring piece goods, is 3 Palmos de Craveira, *avantejados* (or good measure), and is equal to $24\frac{3}{4}$ Inches of Portugal, which equal 26,7 English Inches, or 0,6771 of a Metre.

Each of these measures is likewise divided into 3 Tercas, 4 Quartas, 6 Sexas, and 8 Outavas.

The Mile of Portugal equals $1\frac{1}{4}$ Mile English nearly, or 1,8512 Kilometre.

Land Measure.

Land is surveyed in some parts of Portugal by the Braça, but in most places by the Vara; and the Area is described by the number of these measures in length and breadth. In several places 4840 square Varas, which are equal to 1 Acre 1 Rood $30\frac{2}{5}$ Perches English, or 5,817 French Decares, are reckoned as a Geira or Acre; but arable land in some provinces is estimated by the quantity of seed required in the sowing.

Measures for sundry Articles.

Charcoal is measured by Sacks, which must be 1 Vara 3 Inches in height, and 1 Covado 3 Inches, that is 27 Inches, in circumference.

Pitcoal is sold by the Pipa or Pipe, which is divided in the following manner. 8 Alquieres, heaped up, make a Fanga, and 6 Fangas a Pipe.

Others divide the Pipe of coals into 10 Baldes, and the Balde into 7 Canastras.

The Pipe contains 127 English Bushels, or 3 Chaldrons 19 Bushels, weighing about $4\frac{1}{2}$ Tons Portugal weight.

Lime is sold by the Moyo of 50 Alquieres; and as its bulk is thought to be nearly doubled in burning, limestone is sold by the Moyo of 30 Alquieres.

Salt is sold by the Moyo, containing 60 level Alquieres, which are the same as those used for corn. But old salt weighs more than new; and 2 Moyos of old salt are reckoned to equal 1 Ton of English freight.

Hay and straw are sold by Trusses of 4 Arrobas or 128 Arateis.

Paper is packed in Bales, each of 32 Reams; a Ream is 17 Quires and 3 Sheets; a Quire, 5 Cadernos; and a Caderno, 5 Sheets. A double Ream is 18 Quires and 2 Sheets; the Quire being 4 Cadernos; and the Caderno, 6 Sheets.

Coffee, rice, cocoa, sugar, and almonds, are sold by the Arroba; cotton, indigo, and pepper, by the Pound; oil by the Almude; wine by the Pipe; and corn by the Alquiere.

Lastage.

In reckoning the freight of ships, 4 Chests of Sugar, 4 Pipes of oil, 4000lb. of tobacco, or 3000lb. of sumach, are reckoned for 1 Last.

But when ships sail from one part of Portugal to another, or to the Portuguese colonies, the freight is reckoned by Toneladas of 52 Almudes for liquids, and 54 Arrobas for dry commodities.

Junta Measure for freighting Ships.

Ships are measured by the Ton, being a cylinder 6 Feet high and $3\frac{1}{2}$ Feet in diameter, which gives the contents $57\frac{3}{4}$ cubic Feet nearly. The freight of some ships is regulated by the Palmo da Junta, which was established by royal authority in 1756, to serve as a liquid and dry measure, for regulating the freight of merchandize sent from Portugal to its colonies. This measure was settled by the *Junta da Comercio*, or Board of Trade, whence it derives its name.

The Palmo da Junta is divided into 10 Inches instead of 8, and it is 9 per cent. shorter than the Palmo de Craveira: thus 100 Palmos da Junta = 91 Palmos de Craveira.

This Palmo has been likewise made the standard for liquid measures at

Lisbon. Thus the Pote or half Almude should measure 1000 cubic Inches da Junta, or 1 cubic Palmo da Junta; and hence the Tun of 50 Almudes, which corresponds with the Ton weight or Tonelada of 54 Arrobas, should measure 100 cubic Palmos da Junta, or 100,000 cubic Inches da Junta. Junta Measure.

Although weights and long measures are uniformly established throughout Portugal, great diversity prevails in the measures of capacity; but as their proportions to those of Lisbon are generally known, their relations to the measures of other countries may be thence computed. Their correspondence to English measure is nearly as follows: Measures of Capacity various in Portugal.

		English Gallons.	
Lisbon........	Almude................	$4\frac{37}{100}$	Wine measure.
	Alquiere	$3\frac{7}{100}$	Winchester measure.
Oporto	Almude................	$6\frac{5}{8}$	Wine measure.
	Alquiere	$3\frac{7}{8}$	Winchester measure.
Faro..........	Almude	$4\frac{1}{2}$	Wine measure.
	Alquiere	$3\frac{3}{4}$	Winchester measure.
Figuiera	Almude................	$5\frac{3}{4}$	Wine measure.
	Alquiere	$3\frac{1}{4}$	Winchester measure.
Vianna........	Almude................	$6\frac{1}{2}$	Wine measure.
	Alquiere	$3\frac{7}{8}$	Winchester measure.*

For the exchanges of Lisbon see Vol. II. page 72. Exchanges.

Payments in Portugal have been, of late years, made in what is called legal money, or currency, which consists of one half in effective money or specie, and one half in government paper. The latter is at a discount. Bills how Paid.

The method of converting effective money into currency and into paper, with the reverse operations, is explained and exemplified with the *Exchange Calculations* of *Lisbon*, Vol. II. page 73.

---

* For the above proportions the commercial world is much indebted to the industry and talents of British Consuls in Portugal at different periods, particularly to *John Whitehead, Esq.* formerly Consul at Oporto, who made very extensive and correct comparisons between various measures of capacity, both by gauging and water measure. It should be also added that the despatches lately transmitted to *Lord Castlereagh* (with standards) by *John Jeffery, Esq.*, his Majesty's Consul General at *Lisbon*, contain very full and accurate information on Portuguese Metrology, and from his statements the divisions and proportions in the present article are chiefly deduced.

Usance. The usance for bills drawn from Spain is 15 days sight; from London, 30 days sight; from Germany and Holland, 2 months after date; from France, 60 days after date; from Italy, and from Ireland, 3 months after date.

Days of Grace. Six days grace are allowed on foreign bills, when they have been accepted; but unaccepted bills must be either paid or protested on the day of expiration. Bills drawn from any part of the Portuguese dominions, both in Europe and other parts of the world, are allowed 15 days grace.

LONDON,

Monies of Account. And the whole Island of Great Britain, keep accounts in Pounds, Shillings, Pence, and Farthings, called Sterling or British money, and marked £. *s. d.* and *qrs.*

4 Farthings make 1 Penny; 12 Pence, 1 Shilling; and 20 Shillings, 1 Pound. These are all real coins, as well as monies of account.

Coins. The Gold coins are the Guinea of 21 Shillings; the half Guinea of 10 Shillings and 6 Pence; and the one-third Guinea or 7 Shilling Piece. Also (since 1816), the Sovereign of 20 Shillings, with half and double Sovereigns in proportion.

The Silver coins are the Crown of 5 Shillings; the half Crown of 2 Shillings and 6 Pence; the Shilling of 12 Pence; and the half Shilling or 6 Pence.

The Copper coins are Two-Penny Pieces, Pence, half Pence, and Farthings.

Other coins have been minted here, which are no longer in circulation, though occasionally referred to; namely, the Five-Guinea Piece, the double Guinea, and quarter Guinea; the Mark of 13 Shillings and 4 Pence; the Angel of 10 Shillings; and the Noble of 6 Shillings and 8 Pence; all of Gold. Of Silver, the Groat of 4 Pence; and Three-Penny, Two-Penny, and Penny Pieces.

Certain foreign coins have been current here at different periods, but are now out of circulation, particularly Portugal Gold pieces; viz. the Moidore, which was fixed at 27 Shillings; the Joanese at 36 Shillings; and the smaller coins in proportion. Spanish Dollars, stamped for the occasion, have been of late years circulated by the Bank of England, and received back at the issued prices, which prices varied at different periods.

Fineness of Gold and Silver.

The fineness of gold is expressed in Carats and Grains, the Pound being divided into 24 Carats, and the Carat into 4 Grains, called Carat Grains.

Thus the Carat Pound is the 24th part of the Pound troy, or 10 Pennyweights, and the Carat Grain the 96th part, or 60 Grains troy.

The fineness of silver is expressed in Ounces and Pennyweights, the Pound being divided into 12 Ounces, and the Ounce into 20 Pennyweights.

The standard or legal fineness of gold is 22 Carats; that is, the Pound or other weight should contain 22 parts of pure gold and 2 of alloy. This fineness may be expressed by $\frac{22}{24}$, $\frac{11}{12}$, or ,917.

The standard or legal fineness of silver is 11 oz. 2 dwts. of pure metal, and 18 dwts. of alloy, making together 1 Pound troy, and it may be expressed by $\frac{222}{240} = \frac{37}{40}$, or ,9125.

Rate of Gold Coinage.

From a Pound of standard gold are coined 44½ Guineas, 89 Half Guineas, or 133½ Seven Shilling Pieces. Also 46$\frac{29}{40}$ Sovereigns, with divisions and multiples in proportion. Hence the mint price of gold is £3. 17s. 10½d. per Ounce standard.

Rate of Silver Coinage.

Silver coins may be explained under two heads, viz. the old system and the new. The former, which was used before 1816, was as follows:

From a Pound of standard silver were minted 12$\frac{2}{5}$ Crowns, 24$\frac{4}{5}$ Half Crowns, 62 Shillings, or 124 Sixpences. Thus silver was issued at 5s. 2d. per Ounce, and although the coin has been called in, this is still considered the mint price, in comparing foreign coins; and it agrees very nearly with the average market price at London in ordinary times.

The new coin is minted at 5s. 6d. per Ounce: thus, from a Pound of standard silver 13$\frac{1}{5}$ Crowns, 26$\frac{2}{5}$ Half Crowns, 66 Shillings, or 132 Sixpences, are coined.

From the foregoing regulations it appears that 31 of the old Shillings are equivalent to 33 of the new, which gives a seignorage of 6$\frac{14}{31}$ per cent. on the latter, and therefore all the new silver currency is coined by Government exclusively, while the Mint is open to the public, as heretofore, for the coinage of gold.

It should be stated, that the new silver coin is not a legal tender for any sum above 40 Shillings, and thus gold coin is considered the only standard of value beyond that sum.

Copper money is coined in the proportion of 24 Pence to the Pound avoirdupois. Thus the Penny should weigh 10$\frac{2}{3}$ Drams, or 291$\frac{2}{3}$ troy Grains, and the other pieces in proportion. Copper is not a legal tender for more than 12 Pence.

Weight of Coins.

The following is the full weight of the Gold and Silver Coins:

GOLD COINS.

Old Coinage.	dwts.	grs.	
Guinea	5	9	$\frac{39}{89}$
Half Guinea	2	16	$\frac{64}{89}$
Seven Shilling Piece	1	19	$\frac{13}{89}$
New Coinage.			
Sovereign	5	3	$\frac{171}{623}$
Half Sovereign	2	13	$\frac{397}{623}$
Double Sovereign	10	6	$\frac{342}{623}$
Five Sovereign Piece ..	25	16	$\frac{232}{623}$

SILVER COINS.

Old Coinage.	dwts.	grs.	
Shilling	3	20	$\frac{28}{31}$
Sixpence	1	22	$\frac{14}{31}$
Crown	19	8	$\frac{16}{31}$
Half Crown	9	16	$\frac{8}{31}$
New Coinage.			
Shilling	3	15	$\frac{3}{11}$
Sixpence	1	19	$\frac{7}{11}$
Crown	18	4	$\frac{4}{11}$
Half Crown	9	2	$\frac{2}{11}$

Gold coins are allowed by law to pass under the above full weight. Thus, the Guinea weighing 5 dwts. 8 grs.; the Sovereign, 5 dwts. $2\frac{3}{4}$ grs.; and their divisions in proportion, are a legal tender.

Remedy of the Mint.

The remedy of the Mint, according to the law of 1815, for gold coins is 12 Grains per lb. in the weight, and $\frac{1}{16}$ of a Carat in the fineness; and for silver coins 1 dwt. per lb. in the weight, and the same in the fineness.

The remedy for copper coins is $\frac{1}{40}$ of the weight.

Trial of the Pix.

A small proportion or sample of the coins struck at the Mint is reserved in a box, called the Pix, in order to be assayed and compared with a check piece or standard kept in the Exchequer for the occasion. This operation, which is called the *Trial of the Pix,* is performed with much care and exactness, in the presence of certain members of the Privy Council, the Officers of the Mint, and a Jury of the Goldsmiths' Company: and there is no instance upon record of the coins thus tried having been found under the legal standard.

Wrought Gold and Silver.

Wrought gold has two legal standards; one is 22 Carats, the same as the coin, and the other 18 Carats. The latter commenced in 1798, and is used chiefly in watch cases and rings. Wrought silver has also two legal standards; one is the same as that of the old coin, and the other 8 dwts. better, that is 11 oz. 10 dwts. The latter, which is called New Sterling, is seldom used.

The different standards are thus distinguished: all articles, whether gold or silver, of the money standard, are marked with a Lion; the new gold standard is marked with the number 18; and the new sterling, with the figure of Britannia and a Lion's Head. Wrought Gold and Silver.

Articles of all standards, capable of bearing a stamp, are marked likewise with the initials of the maker's name, the arms or mark of the assay office, and a letter for the date. The letter used by the Goldsmiths' Company shews the date, by beginning the alphabet with 1796, and reckoning on to 20 letters progressively. Thus, 1816 is known by the letter U, and 1820 by D, &c. The mark of the Goldsmiths' office is a Leopard's Head; that of the Assay office of Dublin, a Harp; of Edinburgh, a Thistle; of Newcastle, Three Castles; of Sheffield, a Crown; and of Birmingham, an Anchor.

All articles, except watch cases, are subject to a certain duty, and are marked with the King's Head when the duty is paid.

The cuttings and scrapings of the articles assayed at each office are kept in what is called the *Diet Box*, in order to be melted into a mass and proved, like the Pix, before the proper officers.

WEIGHTS AND MEASURES.

The weight for gold and silver is called troy weight, the Pound of which contains 12 Ounces; the Ounce, 20 Pennyweights; and the Pennyweight, 24 Grains. The Pound is therefore 5760 Grains. Troy Weight.

The Grain troy is composed of 20 Mites, the Mite of 24 Doits, the Doit of 20 Periots, and the Periot of 24 Blanks. These divisions are seldom noticed below Mites, except in calculation; but in weighing, where great nicety is required, decimal divisions are used to the thousandth part of a Grain.

The Pound troy equals 373 Grammes and 202 Decigrammes.*

---

* The above proportion between English and French Weight has been ascertained at the *London Mint* by experiments on several Kilogrammes attested as correct by the proper authorities in France. This has been already noticed, page 135; and here it may be satisfactory to show the authenticity of the British Standard with which those Kilogrammes have been compared.

The troy Pound used on this occasion is the Parliamentary Pound, so called, as having been adjusted by a Committee of the House of Commons in 1758, who caused copies of the same to be distributed. Thus has the uniformity of this weight been very accurately established throughout the British Dominions, and also in the United States of America; as has been recently proved by the general comparisons at the *London Mint*.

Diamond Weight. Diamonds and other precious stones are weighed by Carats, each Carat being divided into halves, quarters, eighths, sixteenths, &c. The Ounce troy weighs 151$\frac{1}{2}$ Diamond Carats; this Carat is therefore 3$\frac{1}{6}$ Grains troy, or 205$\frac{1}{4}$ French Decigrammes.

Pearl Weight. Pearls are weighed by the troy standard; but the Pennyweight is divided into 30 Grains instead of 24, and therefore the Ounce contains 600 pearl Grains. Hence 4 troy Grains equal 5 pearl Grains.

Apothecaries Weight. Apothecaries use the troy Pound, and divide its Ounce into 8 Drams, 24 Scruples, or 480 Grains; but druggists generally use avoirdupois weight.

Avoirdupois Weight. The Pound commercial weight, called avoirdupois, is divided into 16 Ounces, and the Ounce into 16 Drams. It equals 7000 Grains troy, or 453,544 French Grammes.

The Dram or Drachm is sometimes divided into 3 Scruples, and the Scruple into 10 Grains. Thus 1 Grain troy = 1,097 Grain avoirdupois, and 1 Dram avoirdupois equals 27$\frac{11}{32}$ Grains troy. Hence also 144lb. avoirdupois = 175lb. troy, and 192 Ounces avoirdupois = 175 Ounces troy.

The following are the multiples of the Pound avoirdupois: 14lb. = 1 Stone; 8 Stone or 112lb. = 1 Hundredweight; 20 Cwt. = 1 Ton.

Meat, Fish, &c. A Stone of butcher's meat and of fish is 8lb.; a Stone of glass, 5lb; a Seam of glass, 24 Stone or 120lb.

Wool. A Last of wool contains 12 Sacks; a Sack, 2 Weys, 13 Tods, 26 Stone, 52 Cloves, or 364lb; a Pack of wool is 240lb.

Lead. A Fodder of lead in London and Hull is 19$\frac{1}{2}$ Cwt.; at Chester, 20 Cwt.; at Newcastle, 21 Cwt.; at Bawtry, 21$\frac{1}{2}$ Cwt.; at Stockton, 22 Cwt.; at Derby, 22$\frac{1}{2}$ Cwt. The Cwt. of lead at Hull and Chester is 120lb.

Lead ore is, however, sold by a measure called Ore Dish, which is 21,3 Inches long, 6 broad, and 8,4 deep, containing, therefore, about half a Winchester Bushel. 9 Dishes are called a Load, and weigh 3 Cwt. very nearly.

Sundry Articles. A Peck of flour and of salt is 14lb.; a Firkin of butter, 56lb.; and of soap, 64lb.; a Barrel of soap, 256lb.; of candles, 120lb.; of butter, 224lb.; of gunpowder, 100lb.; of anchovies, 30lb.; of raisins, 112lb. A Bushel of rock salt must weigh 65lb.; of crushed rock salt, 56lb.; and of foreign salt, 84lb.

Hay and straw are sold by the Load of 36 Trusses: the Truss of hay is 56lb.; of straw, 36lb. The Truss of new hay is 60lb. until the 1st of September.

The old commercial weight of England, which is still retained in Scotland, and which is said to have been formerly used at Amsterdam, Hamburgh, and Paris, is about $\frac{1}{12}$ heavier than avoirdupois weight, the Pound being 7600 Grains troy, and therefore 35lb. old weight = 38lb. avoirdupois. This has been long the weight in England, by which the assize of bread is fixed by the Magistrates; the Peck Loaf, newly baked, being 16lb. old weight, which answers to 17lb. 6 oz. avoirdupois. The assize in the price however was abolished by an act of 1815, and the rate of the peck loaf left open to the competition of the trade. Old Weight.

The measures for corn and other dry commodities are the following: Dry Measures.

A Last contains 2 Weys, 10 Quarters, 20 Cooms, 40 Strikes, or 80 Bushels, and equals 28,187 Hectolitres.

The Winchester Bushel is 4 Pecks, 8 Gallons, 16 Pottles, 32 Quarts, or 64 Pints, = 35,236 Litres.

The Winchester Bushel, which is the legal measure for corn and seeds, is $18\frac{1}{2}$ Inches in diameter and 8 Inches deep. It therefore measures 2150,42 cubic Inches; and the Winchester Gallon 268,8 cubic Inches.

Corn and seeds are measured in the port of London by striking the Bushel from the brim with a round piece of light wood, about 2 Inches in diameter, and of equal thickness from one end to the other; but it is unlawful to shake the Bushel, so as to increase its virtual capacity.

All other dry goods, sold by measure, are heaped.

There are, besides, two corn Bushels of different shapes, but containing the same quantity; the one, called the Drum Bushel, is generally used for the London Granaries, and is 13 Inches in diameter, and 16,2 Inches in depth; the other, called the Farmers' Bushel, is chiefly used in the country; its diameter is 15,375 and its depth 11,589 Inches. These shapes are chosen for the convenience of working and loading; but the shallow Bushel or standard is adopted to avoid the effects of pressure in filling, which might be increased by the depth of the vessel.

Various corn Bushels are used in different counties and districts of England, notwithstanding the numerous penalties that have been enacted to enforce uniformity. In some places corn is sold by weight, which is considered the fairest mode of dealing, but not the most convenient in practice. Even where measures are used, it is customary to weigh certain quantities or proportions, and to regulate the prices accordingly.

Dry Measures. The average weight of the Bushel of different kinds of grain is reckoned at the London market as follows: wheat, 60lb; rye, 53; barley, 47; oats, 88; peas, 64; beans, 63; clover, 68; canary, 53; and rape, 48lb.

A load of corn for a man is reckoned 5 Bushels, and a cart load 40 Bushels.

Coals. Coals are sold in London by the Chaldron of 4 Vats, 12 Sacks, or 36 Bushels. The coal Bushel is 19½ Inches wide (from the outside), and 8 Inches deep; and contains 8 Winchester Gallons 1 Quart of water, or 2217,6 cubic Inches.

In measuring coals, this Bushel is to be heaped up in the form of a cone, of the height of at least 6 Inches above the brim, the outside of the Bushel being the extremity of the base of such cone. It therefore contains 2814,9 cubic Inches; and 36 of these Bushels (the Chaldron) measure 58,64 cubic Feet.

Sacks for measuring coals must be of certain dimensions, viz. from 50×25 to 52×26 Inches.

All contracts for coals in London above 5 Chaldrons are to be understood as relating to Pool measure, with an ingrain of 1 Chaldron in 20, according to the ancient custom of the port.

The Chaldron of coals at Newcastle is not a measure, but a weight of 53 Cwt. avoirdupois; and this is sometimes found to equal 2 London Chaldrons, but the acknowledged average is, that the Keel, which is 8 Newcastle Chaldrons, equals 15½ London Chaldrons. In such comparisons, however, there can be no precision, as coals not only differ in their specific gravity, but even those of the same quality weigh more, measure for measure, when large, than when broken into smaller parts.

Liquid Measures. A Tun of wine, brandy, or other liquor, contains 2 Pipes, 4 Hogsheads, 3 Puncheons, 6 Tierces, 8 Barrels, 14 Rundlets, or 252 Gallons, = 953,845 French Litres.

The Gallon contains 4 Quarts, 8 Pints, or 32 Gills; and equals 231 English cubic Inches, or 3,785 Litres.

Wine. The following is the standard gauge for foreign wines at the Custom House of London:

	Gallons.		Gallons.
The Pipe of Port	138	The Butt of Mountain........	126
———— Lisbon, Bucella, and Calcavella.	140	Hogshead of Claret	57
		———— Tent	63
———— Madeira	110	The Aum of Hock	36
———— Barcelona & Vidonia	120	———— Teneriffe	120
The Butt of Sherry	120	———— Cape	20

The Gallon used at the Custom House is 7 Inches in diameter, and 6 deep.

The following articles are gauged by wine measure. *Wine Measure.*

The Hogshead of molasses should contain 100 Gallons wine measure.

The Tun of animal oil 252

of vegetable oil 236

The Barrel of herrings 32

of salmon 42

The Gallon of train and seed oil should weigh $7\frac{1}{2}$lb. avoirdupois.

The following are the measures for beer, ale, &c. *Beer Measure.*

The Tun contains 2 Butts, 4 Hogsheads, 6 Barrels, 12 Kilderkins, 24 Firkins, or 216 Gallons, and measures 60912 cubic Inches = 998,092 French Litres.

The beer Gallon measures 282 cubic Inches, and equals 4,6208 French Litres.

Hence 77 beer Gallons, Quarts, or Pints, equal 94 wine Gallons, Quarts, or Pints.

The Firkin of ale, which was formerly 8 Gallons, is, by an act of 1803, made 9 Gallons, the same as the Firkin of beer.

The Foot is divided into 12 Inches, or 36 Barley Corns, and also into tenths. *Long Measures.*

The Inch, in squaring dimensions, is divided into 12 Lines or Parts, each Part into 12 Seconds, and each Second into 12 Thirds. These divisions are called Duodecimals.

The Foot equals ,304799 of the French Metre.

A Palm is 3 Inches, a Hand 4, a Span 9, and a Cubit 18 Inches.

A Yard is 3 Feet, a Pace 5 Feet, a Fathom 6 Feet.

An Ell Flemish is 3 Quarters of a Yard, an Ell English 5 Quarters, an Ell French 6 Quarters. The Quarter is divided into 4 Nails of $2\frac{1}{4}$ Inches each.

A Pole or Perch (also called a Rod, Reed, or Lug) is $5\frac{1}{2}$ Yards, or $16\frac{1}{2}$ Feet, Statute measure; but there are several other Poles, namely:

The Pole, Plantation measure, is 21 Feet; the Woodland Pole, 18 Feet; the Rope, 20 Feet; the Cheshire Pole, 24 Feet; the Sherwood Pole, 25 Feet, &c.

The English Mile is divided into 8 Furlongs, and the Furlong into 40 Poles, Statute measure. The Mile = 1,609,306 French Kilometres.

A Geographical or Sea Mile is $\frac{1}{3}$ of a Sea League, and 20 Sea Leagues make 1 Degree of the Meridian.

A Degree of the Meridian in the Latitude of England, at the medium of 52°,

Long Measures.

was found by Colonel Mudge, in 1800, to equal 69,114 English Miles. A Sea League is therefore 3,4536 English Miles, in the same Latitude.

Land or Superficial Measure.

A square Foot is 144 square Inches; a square Yard, 9 square Feet; and a square Perch, $30\frac{1}{4}$ square Yards. 40 square Perches make 1 Rood, and 4 Roods 1 Acre, Statute measure, which equals 40,466,648 French Ares.

Land is usually measured by a Chain of 4 Poles, 22 Yards, or 792 Inches. It is divided into 100 Links; a Link is therefore $7\frac{92}{100}$ Inches. 10 Chains in length and 1 in breadth make an Acre, or 160 Perches.

30 Acres are called a Yard of land, 100 Acres a Hide of land, and 640 Acres a Mile of land.

Cubic or or Solid Measure.

A cubic Foot is 1728 cubic Inches; a cubic Yard 27 cubic Feet. 42 cubic Feet make 1 Ton of shipping: 40 Feet of rough timber, or 50 Feet of hewn timber, make 1 Load.

The Load, however, of deals and planks is mostly determined by square Feet, which are more or less according to the thickness of the plank.

Thus a Load of 1 Inch plank is 600 square Feet; of 2 Inch plank, 300 square Feet; and of any other thickness in the same proportion.

Deals are mostly sold by the long Hundred; and those from different countries are rated in London according to the following standards:

	Feet long	Inch thick	Inches broad
Russian standard	12	$1\frac{1}{2}$	11
Swedish	14	3	10
Norwegian	12	3	9

Deals from other places are sometimes sold by reducing them to the Russian standard; but oak plank is generally valued by the Load of 50 cubic Feet.

Terms used in Reckoning.

A long Dozen is 13; a long Score, 21; and a long Hundred, 120.

A Roll of parchment is 5 Dozen, or 60 skins.

A Bale of paper is 10 Reams, or 200 Quires, each Quire 24 or 25 Sheets.

A Hundred of salt is 7 Lasts.

A Last of Salt is 18 Barrels; of pot ash, cod fish, herrings, meal, soap, pitch, and tar, 12 Barrels; of flax, or feathers, 17 Hundred weight; a Last of ale or beer, 12 Barrels; and of gunpowder, 24 Barrels.

The following Tables contain the substance of the foregoing statements in a more concise and systematic form.

ENGLISH METROLOGY

COMPARED WITH THAT OF FRANCE.

NOTE.—All numbers on the same line are of equal value.

TROY WEIGHT.

Pound.	Ounces.	Pennyweights.	Grains.	Mites.	Grammes.
1	12	240	5760	115200	= 373,202
	1	20	480	9600	= 31,100
		1	24	480	= 1,555
			1	20	= 0,065
				1	= 0,003

AVOIRDUPOIS WEIGHT.

Ton.	Cwt.	Quarters.	Pounds.	Ounces.	Drams.	Grammes.
1	20	80	2240	35840	573440	= 1015938,836
	1	4	112	1792	28672	= 50796,942
		1	28	448	7168	= 12699,235
			1	16	256	= 453,544
				1	16	= 28,346
					1	= 1,772

LONG MEASURE.

Mile.	Furlongs.	Poles.	Yards.	Feet.	Inches.	Barley Corns.	Metres.
1	8	320	1760	5280	63360	190080	= 1609,3059
	1	40	220	660	7920	23760	= 201,1632
		1	5½	16½	198	594	= 5,0291
			1	3	36	108	= 0,9144
				1	12	36	= 0,3048
					1	3	= 0,0254
						1	= 0,0085

SQUARE OR LAND MEASURE.

Acre.	Roods.	Perches.	Yards.	Feet.	Inches.	Square Metres.
1	4	160	4840	43560	6272640	= 4046,6488
	1	40	1210	10890	1568160	= 1011,6662
		1	30¼	272¼	39204	= 25,2916
			1	9	1296	= 0,8361
				1	144	= 0,0929
					1	= 0,0007

SOLID OR CUBIC MEASURE.

Cubic Yard.	Cubic Feet.	Cubic Inches.	Cubic Metres.
1	27	46656	= 0,7645011
	1	1728	= 0,2831377
		1	= 0,0001638

WINE MEASURE.

Tun.	Pipes.	Puncheons	Hhds.	Tierces.	Gallons.	Quarts.	Pints.		Litres. Decilitres.
1	2	3	4	6	252	1008	2016	=	953,8045
	1	1½	2	3	126	504	1008	=	476,9018
		1	1⅓	2	84	336	672	=	238,4509
			1	1½	63	252	504	=	317,9345
				1	42	168	336	=	158,9673
					1	4	8	=	3,3788
						1	2	=	0,9463
							1	=	0,4731

ALE AND BEER MEASURE.

Butt.	Punc.	Hhds.	Barrels.	Kildks.	Firkins.	Gallons.	Quarts.	Pints.		Litres. Decilitres.
1	1½	2	3	6	12	108	432	864	=	499,0464
	1	1⅓	2	4	8	72	288	576	=	332,6876
		1	1½	3	6	54	216	432	=	249,5232
			1	2	4	36	144	288	=	166,3488
				1	2	18	72	144	=	83,1744
					1	9	36	72	=	41,5872
						1	4	8	=	4,6208
							1	2	=	1,1552
								1	=	0,5776

DRY MEASURE.

Last.	Weys.	Quarters.	Cooms.	Bushels.	Pecks.	Gallons.	Pints.		Litres. Decilitres.
1	2	10	20	80	320	640	5120	=	2818,74432
	1	5	10	40	160	320	2560	=	1409,37216
		1	2	8	32	64	512	=	281,87443
			1	4	16	32	256	=	140,95721
				1	4	8	64	=	35,23830
					1	2	16	=	8,80856
						1	8	=	4,40428
							1	=	0,55053

The contents of the foregoing measures in Cubic Inches are given in the General Tables, Vol. II.; and for the French Metrical System see *France*, Vol. I.

ALLOWANCES, TARES, &c.

Allowances, Tares, &c.

There are certain deductions made from the weight of goods, which are called *Allowances*, and which depend on the nature of the packages, the custom of merchants, and the regulations of public offices. They are mostly distinguished by the terms *Draft, Tare, Trett,* and *Cloff.*

Draft is a deduction from the original or gross weight of goods, and is subtracted before the Tare is taken off.

Tare is an Allowance for the weight of the bag, box, cask, or other package in which goods are weighed.

Real Tare or *Open Tare* is the actual weight of the package.

Customary Tare is an established Allowance for the weight of the package.

Computed Tare is an estimated Allowance agreed upon at the time.

Average Tare is when a few packages only among several are weighed, their mean or average taken, and the rest tared accordingly.

Supertare is an additional Allowance or second Tare, when the commodity, or package, exceeds a certain weight.

When Tare is deducted the remainder is called the *Neat Weight;* but if Trett be allowed it is called the *Suttle Weight.* Allowances, Tares, &c.

Trett is a deduction of 4lb. from every 104lb. of the *Suttle Weight.*

This Allowance, which is said to be for dust or sand, or for the waste or wear of the commodity, was formerly made on most foreign articles sold by the Pound avoirdupois; but it is now nearly discontinued by merchants, or rather allowed in the price. It is wholly abolished at the East India warehouses in London, and neither Trett nor Draft is allowed at the Custom House.

Cloff or *Clough* is another Allowance which is nearly obsolete.—It is stated in books of Arithmetic to be a deduction of 2lb. from every 3 Cwt. of the *Second Suttle* (that is, the remainder after Trett is subtracted); but merchants, at present, know Cloff only as a small deduction, like Draft, from the original weight, and even this only from two or three articles.

As so many Allowances have been abolished, the subject would now become very simple if real Tare could be always ascertained; but as there are several kinds of packages that cannot be conveniently separated from the commodities which they enclose, merchants and public offices have established certain *customary Tares and Allowances,* of which the following pages contain a statement.

The commercial Allowances given in the following tables have been supplied for this work by different mercantile houses of eminence; and as their several statements have been found to agree, it may be concluded that they are correct. Remarks on the following Tables of Allowances.

The Tares, and other Allowances of the Custom House, the East India Warehouses, and the New Docks, may be also relied on, having been supplied by official authorities.

The uncertain and fluctuating state of Allowances heretofore in London may afford a reason why they have never been printed; while, on the other hand, it may be supposed, that their changes and irregularities have arisen from the want of printed regulations. At Amsterdam, Hamburgh, Leghorn, and other commercial cities, Allowances are regularly published, and continue uniform.

It must be highly useful, as well as satisfactory, to every buyer and seller of goods to have the Allowances permanently fixed and publicly known—and therefore those now established in London ought to be adhered to; which may be always done without inconvenience, as any Allowance that should seem inadequate can be corrected, either in the price or in the discount, without altering the established deductions in the weight.

A TABLE OF ALLOWANCES, TARES, &c.

Goods.	*Sold by the*	*Custom-House Allowances.*	*Commercial Allowances.*
Almonds	cwt.	in casks, 14lb. per cwt.; in bags, 4lb. per bag, but mostly real tare; when in shells, two-thirds are allowed for the shells	in serons, 2lb. draft; 12lb. tare per seron, under 3 cwt.; 4lb. draft, and 15lb. tare per seron, above 3 cwt.; in bags or casks, draft as above, and real tare.
Aloes, Socotrina	do.	real tare	in casks under 1 cwt. 1lb. draft; ditto from 1 to 3 cwt. 2lb.; ditto 3 cwt. and upwards, 4lb. real tare.
Epatica	do.	real tare	1lb. draft, 6lb. tare per cwt.
Alum	ton	10 per cent. that is 10 per cwt.	1lb. draft per cwt. and real tare.
Roach	cwt.	real tare	4lb. draft per cask, and 10lb. per cwt. tare.
Annatto	do.	real tare, and 6lb. per cwt. for flags	in casks, 4lb. draft each, and 20lb. per cwt. tare.
Anniseed	do.	real tare	1lb. draft, and real tare.
Argol	do.	10lb. per cwt.	from 2 to 4 cwt. 2lb. draft per cask; 4 cwt. and upwards, 4lb. draft; tare 14lb. per cwt. on Italian argol; on Rhenish, 10lb. per cwt.
Ashes, Pot, American	do.	real tare	2lb. draft per barrel; 14lb. tare per cwt.
Barilla	do.	real tare	4lb. draft per seron; real tare, or 10lb. per cwt. when loose, and 12lb. draft per ton.
Bark, Jesuits	lb.	real tare	2lb. draft per chest; 3lb. per cwt. for dust; and real tare.
Oak	cwt.	real tare	draft 4lb. per cask, and real tare.
Brimstone	ton	in casks, real tare	12lb. draft per ton; or 4lb. per hhd. & real tare
Butter	cwt.	real tare	tare is branded on every cask.
Camphor	lb.	real tare	1lb. draft per cwt. and real tare.
Capers	....	real tare	under 5 cwt. 2lb. draft per cask, and $\frac{2}{3}$ tare; above 5 cwt. 4lb. draft per cask, and $\frac{1}{3}$ tare.
Carraway	cwt.	real tare	1lb. draft, and real tare.
Cassia	do.	real tare	1lb. draft, and real tare.
Castor Oil	gal.	real tare	1lb. draft, and real tare.
Cinnamon	lb.	real tare	tare as per warrants of the East India Company.
Cloverseed	cwt.	real tare	2lb. draft per bag, and 4lb. tare per cwt.
Cloves	lb.	real tare	tare as per warrants.
Cochineal	do.	real tare	real tare.
Cocoa	cwt.	real tare	draft under 1 cwt. 1lb.; from 1 to 3 cwt. 2lb.; from 3 to 5 cwt. 4lb.; 5 cwt. and upwards, 5lb. real tare; and 4lb. per cwt. for garble or dust.
Coffee, West India	do.	real tare	real tare and draft, as for cocoa; otherwise 5lb. draft per cask, 2lb. per barrel or 1lb. per bag.
East India, or Mocha	do.	real tare	tare as per warrants.
Copper, Spanish	do.	none	2lb. draft per cwt.
Turkey	ton	none	2lb. draft per ton.
Copperas, Green	cwt.	real tare	4lb. draft per cask; tare 1 cwt. per cask, or real tare.
White	do.	real tare	
Cotton Wool, W. India & America	lb.	in bags, 4lb. per cent. or 100lb.	1lb. draft, and sometimes 2lb. off per bale; 4lb. per cwt. tare.
Brazil	do.	real tare	ditto.
Smyrna	do.	real tare	1lb. draft per bale, and real tare; if in linen bags, 6lb. tare per cwt.
Spanish	do.	real tare	1lb. draft per bale; 4lb. tare per cwt.
East India	do.	real tare	draft and tare as per warrants.

Goods.	*Sold by the*	*Custom-House Allowances.*	*Commercial Allowances.*
Cotton Yarn	lb.	real tare	1lb. draft per bale; 7lb. tare per cwt.
Currants, Zante	cwt.	16lb. per cwt.	in butts above 17 cwt. draft 2lb. each, and 18lb. tare per cwt.; but if under 17 cwt. 2lb. draft each, and 20lb. tare per cwt.
Leghorn	do.	12lb. per cwt.	
Turkey	do.	real tare	draft 1lb. per case, barrel, or for every 5 drums; and real tare.
Figs	do.	real tare	in chests or casks, 1lb. draft, real tare, and 1lb. above it.
Galls	do.	real tare	1lb. draft per bag; 9lb. tare in hair bags; 6lb. ditto in linen bags; and 2lb. more if roped.
Ginger, Dry	cwt.	real tare	in bags, 1lb. draft each weigh of 2, 3, or 4 bags, and 4lb. per cwt. tare; in casks under 1 cwt. 2lb. draft; if above 1 cwt. 4lb.; real tare.
Green	do.	⅓ for jars	
Glue	do.	real tare	draft, under 3 cwt. 2lb.; above 3 cwt. 4lb.; real tare.
Goats Wool	lb.	real tare	in casks, 4lb. draft, and real tare; in bales, 1lb. draft per bale; and 4lb. tare per cwt. for the shirt.
Gums	cwt.	real tare	in casks, draft 4lb. per cask, and real tare; in chests, draft 2lb. per chest, and real tare; for Turkey and India gums, 1lb. draft per package, and real tare.
Hemp	ton	none	1lb. draft for 5 cwt.
Hides	piece	none	1lb. draft for 10 hides.
Indigo, East India	lb.	real tare	1lb. draft per chest, and real tare.
Spanish	do.	real tare	draft, 1lb.; tare per half seron under 1½ cwt. 17lb.; per seron under 1¼ cwt. 21lb.; above, 25lb.
Ipecacuanha	do.	real tare	1lb. draft per cwt. real tare and trett.
Isinglass	do.	real tare	2lb. draft, and 4 to 5lb. tare per sack, and trett
Jalap	do.	real tare	1lb. draft per cwt. and real tare.
Juniper Berries	cwt.	real tare	1lb. draft per cwt. and real tare.
Liquorice	do.	real tare for the chest and for leaves	2lb. draft per chest, real tare, and 6 per cent. for leaves.
Mace	do.	real tare	draft and tare as per warrants of East India Company.
Madder, Dutch, or Mulls	do.	10lb. per cwt. in fats or casks	4lb. draft per cask; 10lb. tare per cwt.
Turkey Roots	do.	real tare	1lb. draft, and 9lb. tare per bag.
Mohair Yarn	lb.	real tare	1lb. draft per bale; tare 6 to 9lb. each, or 1lb. per 28lb.
Molasses	cwt.	real tare	2lb. draft, and 9lb. cloff per cask.
Nutmegs	lb.	in caroteels the packages are weighed	tare as per warrants; when in shells, ⅓ is allowed for the shells.
Oil, Common	tun	in casks weighing upwards of 3 cwt. tare 18lb. per cwt.; in casks under 3 cwt. 50lb. each	when sold by gauge, no allowance, except for dirt or water; when by weight, 2lb. draft per cask of 9, 10, or 11 cwt.
Train	do.	in barrels, 50lb. each; but in uncertain casks, 18lb. per cwt.	
Opium	lb.	2lb. per cwt. for leaves, & weighed stripped of the outer package	1lb. draft per package, and real tare, after taking away the leaves.
Pepper	do.	real tare	1lb. draft per bag, and real tare; but when sold by the East India Company, tare as per warrants.
Pimento	do.	2 or 3lb. per bag; in casks, real tare	in bags, 1lb. draft per bag, 4lb. tare per cwt. and trett as usual; in casks, 2lb. draft, and 1lb. cloff per cask; real tare and trett.

Goods.	Sold by the	Custom-House Allowances.	Commercial Allowances.
Pitch, American	cwt.	56lb. per barrel	2lb. draft per barrel; tare according to package.
Swedish	do.	36lb. per ditto	
Archangel	do.	93lb. per ditto	
Plumbs, Dry, Portugal	do.	real tare	1lb. draft per chest; average tare, and 1lb. super or above.
Raisins, Denia	do.	real tare	1lb. draft on 5 baskets, 3lb. tare each; in boxes, 1lb. draft on 10 boxes; real tare, and 1lb. above; in jars, 1lb. draft on 5 jars, and tare the same.
Malaga	do.	real tare	
Smyrna Black	do.	real tare	draft, 2lb. per cask; in butts of 12 cwt. and upwards, 16lb. tare per cwt.; in casks under 12 cwt. 18lb. tare per cwt.
Ditto Red	do.	real tare	draft from 1 to 2lb. p. cask; tare 16lb. p. cwt.
Rhubarb	lb.	real tare	India, as per warrants; Russia, 2lb. draft, and real tare.
Rice	cwt.	real tare	draft, 2lb. per barrel, 1lb. per half barrel, and real tare.
Rosin	do.	real tare	in mats or casks, 2lb. draft, and real tare.
Safflower	do.	real tare	draft, 1lb. per bale; tare under 5 cwt. 21lb. above 5 cwt. 36lb. per bale; in scaffers with canes, 1lb. draft each; 10lb. tare per cwt.
Saffron	do.	real tare	draft, 1lb.; real tare.
Sal Ammoniac	do.	real tare	draft, 4lb. per cask, and real tare.
Salsaparilla	lb.	real tare	2lb. draft per bale; real tare and trett.
Saltpetre	cwt.	in bags, 18lb. each; in double bags, 14lb.	tare as per warrants, or 4lb. for single bags; and for double, &c. in proportion.
Scammony	lb.	real tare	1lb. draft, if above 1 cwt.; real tare.
Seeds, Canary	cwt.	30lb. per barrel, or real tare	grain and seeds are generally sold without the package, which, if taken by the buyer, is paid for separately.
Rape	last	real tare } for casks or bags	
Linseed	qr.	real tare } for casks or bags	
Mustard	cwt.	real tare } for casks or bags	
Silks, Bologna	lb.	10 per cent. tare	see pages 233, 234, and 235.
Messina	do.	8 per cent. tare	
Soap	cwt.	real tare	2lb. draft for 3 cwt. and under; above 3 cwt. 4lb.; real tare.
Sugar, Muscovado, from the British West India Isles	do.	in casks of 8 to 12 cwt. 1 cwt.; from 12 to 15 cwt. 1 cwt. 1 qr. 12lb.; from 15 to 17 cwt. $1\frac{1}{2}$ cwt.; 17 cwt. and upwards, $1\frac{3}{4}$ cwt.; under 8 cwt. 14lb. per cwt.	2lb. draft per hogshead; 1lb. ditto per barrel; real tare for home consumption; but for exportation, dock tares are allowed; for which, see page 233.
Martinico	do.	12lb. per cwt.	
Guadaloupe	do.	16lb. per ditto	
St. Domingo	do.	14lb. per ditto	
East India	do.	real tare	tare as per warrants.
Havannah	do.	real tare	draft, 1lb. per chest; real tare.
White Brazil	do.	real tare	draft, 2lb. per chest; 13lb. per cent.
Sugar of Lead	do.	real tare	draft, 4lb. per chest, and real tare.
Sumac	do.	in bags of about $3\frac{1}{4}$ cwt. 4lb.; from 2 to 3 cwt. 3lb.	1lb. draft per bag; 1lb. tare per cwt.
Tallow, Russia	do.	in casks, 12lb. per cwt.	2lb. draft per cask; 12lb. tare per cwt.
Tartar, Cream of	do.	in casks, 11lb. per cwt.	draft, 4lb. per cask, and real tare.
Tobacco, N. America	lb.	transferred to excise	8lb. draft per hogshead from Virginia; 4lb. per ditto from Maryland; shrinkage, 30lb. per hogshead from Virginia; 20lb. ditto from Maryland.
Turmeric	do.	real tare	draft and tare, 4lb. per bag.

Goods.	Sold by the	Custom-House Allowances.	Commercial Allowances.
Turpentine	cwt.	in casks, one fifth part on the gross weight	2s. per cwt. for hard; draft 2lb. and tare 63lb. per cask, if under 2 cwt. 3 qr. 7lb.; but above that weight, draft 3lb. per cask, and tare $\frac{1}{5}$ part.
Valonea	tun	in bulk, no tare; in bags, real tare .	draft, 12lb. per tun; in bulk & in bags, real tare.
Verdigris............	lb.	real tare	1lb. draft per cwt. and 2lb. tare per pod or bag, and trett.
Woad	cwt.	real tare	tare, 1 cwt. per cask.
Woods, in the Log	ton	no tare	draft, 12lb. per ton.
in Casks		real tare	draft, 4lb. per cask, and real tare.
Wool, Spanish	lb.	real tare	2lb. draft per bale; 20lb. tare per bale of 2 cwt.; 22lb. per bale above 2 cwt.
Yellow Berries	do.	real tare	draft, 1lb. per bale; tare, 9lb. per bale, and 2lb. for ropes, if any.

It will be seen by the foregoing Allowances at the Custom House, as compared with those in the former edition of this work, that the practice of ascertaining real tare has greatly increased. It seems now taken on all uncertain packages.

DOCK TARES.

The following are the Tares allowed at the West India and London Docks on Sugars bought for exportation: Dock Tares.

	Cwt.	Cwt.	qr.	lb.	
Under	8	0	0	14	per Cent. or Cwt.
8 Cwt. to	9	1	0	7	on the whole.
9	10	1	0	14	
10	11	1	0	21	
11	12	1	1	0	
12	13	1	1	7	
13	14	1	1	14	
14	15	1	1	21	
15	17	1	2	0	
17 and upwards		1	3	0	

The above Allowances are given on the landing weight.

COMMERCIAL ALLOWANCES ON SILKS.

The following Resolutions were finally agreed upon and signed by the silk merchants of London, on the 11th of June, 1802. Commercial Allowances on Silks.

That all raw silks be sold by the small Pound of 16 Ounces, and that 1lb. Draft per Bale be allowed on all raw silks in general.

That Tares, both on raw and thrown silks, be invariably fixed in the following manner:

ON BALES WEIGHING GROSS,

Commercial Allowances on Silks.

From 100lb.	to 129lb.	4lb.	Tare.		From 210lb.	to 259lb.	8lb.	Tare.
130	149	5	Ditto.		260	309	9	Ditto.
150	179	6	Ditto.		310	339	10	Ditto.
180	209	7	Ditto.		340	369	11	Ditto.

That the Supertares claimed be regulated in the following manner:

That if the Tare of Piedmont Organzine, for which 6lb. is allowed, shall weigh less than 4lb. 8 oz., then no Supertare shall be allowed.

That if the Tare weighs 4lb. 8 oz. or more, and less than 4lb. 12 oz. then to allow ½lb.

That if the Tare weighs 4lb. 12 oz. or more, and less than 5lb. 4 oz. then to allow 1lb.

That if the Tare weighs 5lb. 4 oz. or more, and less than 5lb. 12 oz. then to allow 1½lb. and so on for any greater Supertare.

That if the Tare of any other kind of silk, but Piedmont Organzine, that is to say, of any other kind of thrown silks, and also of raws in general, for which 8lb. is allowed, shall weigh 6lb. 12 oz. then no allowance of Supertares to be made.

That if the Tare weighs more than 6lb. 12 oz. and less than 7lb. then to allow ½lb.

That if the Tare weighs more than 7lb. and less than 7lb. 8 oz. then to allow 1lb.

That if the Tare weighs more than 7lb. 8 oz. and less than 8lb. then to allow 1½lb.

That if the Tare weighs more than 8lb. and less than 8lb. 8 oz. then to allow 2lb. and so on for any greater Supertare.

And that a proportionable Allowance of Supertare, on the above principle, be made, according to the greater or less weight of each Bale.

That on all French raws, in regular packages, not exceeding 179lb. Gross weight, 1lb. for strings (if any) be allowed; and on all above 179lb. Gross weight, 2lb.

That on French raws, coming in irregular packages, such as cases, mats, &c., the Tare and strings be settled at the time of purchase.

That all thrown and raw silks in the Bale be weighed with as many ropes as Pounds Tare allowed, except Bologna, Venetian, Modena, and Rimini thrown silks, which are to be weighed without ropes.

That the usual allowance of 8 Ounces Draft be continued on every Bale or Ballot, when weighed.

That all claims for Supertare, damage, mixture, &c. are to be made by the buyers within one month from the day of delivery; after which time no claims will be allowed. Commercial Allowances on Silks.

That the buyer be requested to weigh the silk on delivery; or in default, the weight per bill of parcels shall be acknowledged right, and no future claim of deficiency shall be allowed.

ALLOWANCES BY THE EAST INDIA COMPANY.

The Allowances made on weighable goods, sold at the Company's warehouses in London, are chiefly Draft and Supertare. Allowances by the East India Company.

The Draft is 1lb. on every package, or quantity of upwards of 28lb.; besides which a two-Ounce weight is placed with the other weights to give the scale a turn in favour of the buyer. If, in weighing, the beam is even, that is, if the scale containing the goods does not preponderate, 1lb. is struck from the weight: this Pound is also allowed by the Customs and Excise; but not the two-Ounce weight, except by the Excise, and that on tea only.

In taring goods, that is, in weighing the packages, the scale in which the weights are placed, is allowed to preponderate.

In making an average Tare, if the mean of the packages tared should prove a fraction, the next whole number above it is taken. Thus, if the average or mean be 28¼lb., the Allowance is 29lb. This is allowed on all goods by the Customs and Excise, as well as by the Company.

On all goods (tea excepted) 1lb. is allowed by the Company, but not by the Customs or Excise, on packages that tare 28lb. or upwards; and if the Tare is taken on an average, and there is a fraction, it is increased to a Pound, as per example, viz.

Actual average Tare	28¾lb.
Fraction wanting	¼
	29
Supertare	1
Tare allowed	30lb.

On Quarter Chests of Tea.—If, on averaging those tared, they turn out even Pounds, no further Allowance is made, unless the Chest weigh gross 84lb. or upwards; in which case, 1lb. for Supertare is allowed on each package; but if there be a fraction, the fraction wanting only is allowed. Thus if the average Tare be 22lb. the Allowance is 23lb.; and it is the same if the average Tare be 22¾lb.

Allowances by the East India Company.

On Half Chests of Tea.—If, on averaging those tared, they turn out even Pounds, 1lb. is allowed for Supertare on each package; and if there be a fraction, it is reckoned a Pound as before. Thus if the average Tare be 36lb. the Allowance is 37lb.; and if 36¼lb. the Allowance is 38lb.

On Whole Chests of Tea.—If, on averaging those tared, they turn out even Pounds, 2lb. are allowed on each package for Supertare; but if there be a fraction, 1lb. only and the fraction wanting are allowed. Thus if the average Tare be 66lb. the Allowance is 68lb.; and it is the same if the average Tare be 66¾lb.

Note. The foregoing Allowances on tea are also made by the Excise; but the Customs allow only the Pound for a fraction, as before stated.

On Silks.—Bengal and China raw silks are weighed in new Hessen Bags, in the following manner:

The large Bengal Bag, containing about 300lb., is tared upon the average at 6lb.; and 2lb. more are allowed for Supertare.

The small Bengal Bag, containing about 150lb., is tared on the average at 3lb., and 1lb. more is allowed for Supertare.

The China Silk Bag, containing about 100lb., is tared on the average at 2lb.; and 1lb. more is allowed for Supertare.

Thus the Allowance on the large Bengal Bag is 8lb.; on the small, 4lb.; and on the China Bag, 3lb.

The two-Ounce weight is invariably put into the scale; and the 1lb. Draft is also allowed; but this Pound Draft not being allowed by the Customs, is charged with duty to the buyers by the Company.

Exchanges.

For the exchanges of London see Vol. II. page 19.

Usances.

The usance for bills drawn from Holland, Germany, and France, is 1 month; from Spain and Portugal, 2 months; and from Italy, 3 months, all after date. The usances with other places will be found under their proper heads respectively.

Days of Grace.

Three days grace are allowed on all bills payable at usance, or after date, or at so many days sight; but if the third day should fall on a Sunday, payment must be made on the preceding Saturday. Bills at sight, or on demand, must be paid on the day they are presented. For the laws and customs relating to bills of exchange, see Vol. II. page 3.

BANK OF ENGLAND.

The Bank of England was established in the year 1694 by a company, who advanced a loan of £1,200,000 to Government, at 8 per cent. per annum, for which they obtained a charter. Various loans have been since advanced by the Company at a lower interest, and sums have been subscribed at different periods for renewals of the charter, amounting (in the year 1820) to £14,686,800. This is called the Permanent Debt, for which various interests are paid by Government, making together 3 per cent. per annum. Bank of England.

The amount of the capital bank stock was increased by a bonus of 25 per cent. in 1816, which makes its present amount £14,553,000, on which dividends are paid of 10 per cent. per annum from the above interest, and the profits of the institution. This capital is transferable like Government stock; and its value fluctuates from political causes, as well as from the supposed success of the Company.

The profits of the bank chiefly arise from discounting bills, keeping cash for others, issuing notes, dealing in bullion, and making temporary advances to the State. It also acts as banker and agent to Government, in whatever relates to the public funds, for which it receives proper remuneration.

The manner of keeping cash at the bank, and the terms for discounting bills, are the same as with a private banker, except that no cash account is begun here with less than £500, nor any discount account opened without the approbation of the Court of Directors. No bill drawn in London of less than £100, or having more than 65 days to run, or 70 days for legal notice, is cashed, but country bills as low as £30 are discounted; each bill, however, must be made payable at a London banking house, and have besides such names on it as are approved by a committee, who allow or reject the bill without assigning any cause; nor is such a refusal to be considered as discreditable to the house or person so refused.

The bank issues no paper without an equivalent, either in cash, bullion, approved bills, or government securities; except for the expenses of the establishment. Its notes are made payable to bearer on demand, and were accordingly paid at sight, until the year 1797, when, on account of the state of public affairs, cash payments were suspended by order of the Privy Council. A resolution was immediately entered into, by the principal merchants and bankers of London, to receive bank notes as cash in all payments. This resolution, together with the favourable report of a committee appointed to inquire into the affairs of the Company, fully upheld the credit of its paper; and the

Bank of England.

restriction from paying in specie, except in certain cases, has been since renewed at different periods by several Acts of Parliament.

In 1819 a law was enacted directing bank notes to be paid, first in Gold Ingots, not weighing less than 60 Ounces each, and at the end of three years in gold coin. The following are the prices of the bullion, and the periods of payment.

From February 1, 1820, to October 1, 1820, at £4. 1s. 0d. per oz. standard,
" October 1, 1820, to May .. 1, 1821, at £3. 19s. 6d. "
" May.... 1, 1821, to May .. 1, 1823, at £3. 17s. 10½d. "

at which time cash payments are to commence. The bank, however, has the option to begin to pay on May 21, 1822; but May 1, 1823, is the definitive period fixed for the resumption of cash payments.

This Corporation is not permitted by its charter to deal in any kind of merchandize, except gold and silver bullion and foreign coins; but it enjoys an exclusive privilege of banking and issuing notes; for no other body politic or corporate, nor any firm of more than six partners, can transact the same kind of business in England.

The business of the bank is divided into two departments; the one under the Chief Cashier, and the other under the General Accountant. The Chief Cashier is the Banker, who transacts all the receipts and payments of money, and issues the bank notes. The General Accountant posts these notes as they are issued, and as they are paid off by the Chief Cashier; and he also keeps the accounts of the Public Funds, and transacts other concerns relating to the National Debt.*

The chief management of the bank is under 24 Directors, with a Governor, and Deputy Governor, who are all annually chosen by the Proprietors. Four general courts are held every year, and others may be convened at the request of nine or more Proprietors. The purpose of these meetings is to make or revise laws, to determine questions relating to the institution, and to elect officers.

The qualification of a Governor is to be possessed of £4000 capital bank stock; of a Deputy Governor, £3000; of a Director, £2000; and of a Proprietor or Elector, £500; and these sums must have been possessed for 6 months previous to the election, unless they come by bequest or inheritance.

---

* A statement of the average amount of Bank of England Notes in circulation for the last 30 years, divided into three equal periods, viz.

	Average Amount.	Lowest Amount.	Highest Amount.
From 1790 to 1800.......	11½ Millions....	8¾ Mil. in 1797	14 Mil. in 1795
—— 1800 — 1810.......	16¾ —— ...	14½ —— 1800	19¾ —— 1809
—— 1810 — 1820.......	25¼ ——	20⅗ —— 1810	31 —— 1817

The above statement is abridged from official documents submitted to Parliament.

There are in London about 70 banking houses; and in the other parts of England nearly 600, which are called Country Banks. The principal business of London bankers is to keep cash for others, but they do not issue their own notes. Their profits arise from laying out part of the money lodged in their hands in good and beneficial securities, such as the Stocks, or other Government paper; but chiefly from discounting bills, by which the most essential support is rendered to trade and commerce. Bankers besides afford great assistance to merchants, in undertaking the management of their bills, and in executing other payments and receipts of money, which they generally perform without any charge, and with the greatest exactness. Private Banks.

Country bankers, like those of London, keep cash for others, and discount bills; but they differ from them in many respects: some pay an interest for money lodged in their hands, on condition of receiving a certain notice before payment is required; and some keep a mutual interest account, and charge commission on their payments.

Many country bankers likewise issue their own notes; that is, in discounting bills, or making advances upon other securities, they give, instead of cash, their own promissory notes, payable to bearer on demand; which notes, having a local currency, so far answer the purposes of coin or any other circulating medium; and when they are brought back for payment, they must be discharged either in cash or Bank of England notes. Most of them are also payable at some London banking house, where the country banker keeps an account, in the same manner as any other customer. Country bank notes must be on stamps, and are not allowed to circulate for more than three years.*

STOCKS OR PUBLIC FUNDS.

Stocks or Public Funds are the loans advanced to Government, for which interest is regularly paid, from revenues set apart for the purpose. This mode of raising supplies by levying taxes for the payment of interest is called the Funding System, and the loans thus raised constitute the National Debt. The debts of Government differ from other contracts in this, that the public creditor can claim only his interest; he may, however, sell his stock—that is, he may transfer his claim, and thus obtain his capital, more or less, according to the price of stock, which fluctuates from a variety of causes. Stocks or Public Funds.

* From the return of stamps, it appears that the average amount of country bank notes in circulation for 10 years, ending in 1819, was about 20 millions; the lowest amount being 15 millions in 1816, and the highest 23 millions nearly in 1814.

Stocks or Public Funds.

The different funds or stocks are variously denominated, according to the terms on which they were established or altered. Thus, some are called the 3 per cents., some the 4 per cents., &c.; and the manner of buying stock is to give a specific sum for a nominal hundred. If, for instance, the price of the 3 per cents. be £60, this sum is paid for £100 stock, which yields a dividend of £3 a year, that is 5 per cent. per annum. When stocks are low, the interest is high, and *vice versâ*. In some funds there is a higher interest than in others, owing chiefly to the preference given to that stock which is the most marketable, or the least likely to be redeemed; for Government has the option to pay off or redeem certain loans, when an advantage may be made by such redemption.

New loans are paid by instalments of 10 or 15 per cent. at stated periods, and they generally comprehend different kinds of stock, which together are called *Omnium*. If these be disposed of separately, before all the instalments are paid, the different articles are called *Scrip*, an abbreviation for *Subscription*.

In raising loans, a *Douceur* is sometimes given by Government of an annuity for a limited time; such are called *Terminable Annuities*, and *Irredeemable;* but the regular stocks on which the common interest is paid, are called *Perpetual Annuities*, and also *Redeemable*.

Loans are called a *Funded Debt*, when taxes are appropriated for paying the interest; but sums raised for which no such provision is yet made, are called the *Unfunded Debt*. Of the latter description are Exchequer, Navy, Victualling, and Ordnance Bills, which are issued by these different offices, and bear an interest until paid off. The interest is from 2d. to 3½d. per day for every £100.

Sinking Fund.

A plan has been adopted for paying off or reducing the National Debt, by means of the Sinking Fund, which is a portion of the revenue set apart for this purpose, and operating on the principle of compound interest. In 1786 it was raised to a million annually, and in 1792 to £1,200,000. A grant was likewise added of 1 per cent. per annum on every new loan that has been since raised. Some impediments, however, have occurred in the progress of the plan, but still it is in useful operation. A sum of nearly 400 Millions has been reduced.

The Sinking Fund is under the management of certain Commissioners, who constantly apply it in buying up or redeeming stock; and the interest accruing on such redeemed stock goes immediately to the increase of the fund, together with all Terminable Annuities as they become extinct.*

* The amount of the National Debt in 1820 was, nominally, about 800 millions; and the interest of the same, including that on the Sinking Fund, was 47 millions nearly.

LUBEC (*in Germany*).

Accounts are kept here in Marks of 16 Schillings Lubs current, each Schilling being divided into 12 Pfenings. Monies of Account.

The Rixdollar is 3 Marks, or 48 Schillings Lubs; and all the other monies of account are the same as in Hamburgh.

The gold coins of Lubec are the Portugalese, and its half, worth 10 and 5 Ducats; the Ducat, worth 7 Marks 6 Schillings, with double, halves, and quarters in proportion. The silver coins are, the specie Rixdollar, at 3 Marks 11 Schillings current, more or less; and the currency of the city, consisting of current Rixdollars at 3 Marks; Pieces of 1 and 2 Marks, of 1, 2, 4, and 8 Schillings; Sechslings and Dreylings, at 6 and 3 Pfenings Lubs. This currency has been coined since 1726; and the current Rixdollar since 1752. The foreign coins that circulate here are very numerous, and vary in their value according to the market prices of the precious metals. Coins.

67 Ducats are to weigh a Cologne Mark of gold, 23 Carats 6 Grains fine; 8 specie Rixdollars are to weigh a Cologne Mark of silver, 14 Loths 4 Grains fine; and the Mark of fine silver is coined into 34 Marks of Lubec currency. Rate of Coinage.

The Rixdollar current may be valued at 429 Asen, or 318 English Grains of fine silver; as to the Rixdollar valued in gold, the price of the Ducat varying with the price of gold, it is sometimes worth more and sometimes less than 29 Asen, or $21\frac{1}{2}$ Grains of fine gold; except, however, when the Danish current Ducat is reckoned at 2 Rixdollars, according to which rate the Rixdollar may be always valued at $28\frac{2}{5}$ Asen, or 21 Grains of fine gold.

The par between Hamburgh and Lubec is $123\frac{1}{13}$ Rixdollars Lubs current for 100 Rixdollars Hamburgh banco, which is commonly reckoned the par between Hamburgh banco and currency; and thus the currencies of both cities are nearly of equal value; this gives 16 Marks 2 Schillings Lubec currency for the value of the Pound sterling; and hence the Lubec Rixdollar current = 3s. 9d. sterling nearly. Value of Monies.

The Lubec Rixdollar specie is worth 3 Marks 12 Schillings 5 Pfenings current, or about 4s. 2d. sterling; and if a Danish current Ducat be reckoned at 6 Marks Lubs, at the same rate a full weight Dutch Ducat is worth 7 Marks 8 Schillings, and a Frederick, 13 Marks 4 Schillings.

Gold and Silver Weight. Gold and silver are weighed by the Cologne Mark, as in Hamburgh.

The Mark of wrought silver must be 12 Loths 3 Grains fine.

The Mark of fine silver is worth 33 Marks current, more or less.

Commercial Weight. The Pound, commercial weight, is divided into 2 Marks, 16 Ounces, 32 Loths, 128 Quentins, or 512 Pfenings, and equals $7479\frac{1}{2}$ English Grains. Hence 100lb. of Lubec = 106,85lb. avoirdupois, or 48,46 Kilogrammes.*

The Centner contains 8 Lisponds, or 112lb.

The Shipfund is $2\frac{1}{2}$ Centners, 20 Lisponds, or 280lb.; but the Shipfund, waggoner's weight, is 20 Lisponds of 16lb., or 320lb.; and sometimes 23 Lisponds of 14lb., or 322lb.

A Shipfund of feathers weighs 20 Lisponds of 16lb. the sacks included.

A Tonne of honey, or of butter, or of Luneburgh salt, great measure, weighs 20 common Lisponds, or 280lb.; a Tonne of butter, small measure, 224lb.

A Stone of flax is 20lb.; a Stone of wool or feathers, 10lb.

Dry Measures. The Last of corn is divided into 8 Dromts, 24 Tonnes or Barrels, 90 Scheffels, or 384 Fasser.

The standard Scheffel, with which wheat and rye are measured, must be $10\frac{7}{12}$ Inches deep, Lubec measure, and $16\frac{19}{24}$ in diameter. Its contents are, therefore, 2343 Lubec cubic Inches, answering to 2041 English cubic Inches. Hence the Scheffel, Lubec measure, is equal to 0,9490 of an English Bushel, or 0,3344 Hectolitres.

The Scheffel for oats is $11\frac{1}{8}$ Inches deep, and $17\frac{3}{4}$ Inches in diameter; it contains therefore 2752 Lubec cubic Inches, answering to 2395 English Inches; thus 20 Scheffels, oat measure, = $23\frac{1}{2}$ Scheffels, wheat measure; and 9 Scheffels, oat measure, = 10 English Bushels nearly.

Liquid Measures. The Fuder contains 6 Ahms, 120 Viertels, 240 Stubgen, 480 Kannes, or 960 Quartiers, and equals 229,5 English Gallons, or 868,2 Litres.

---

* Various statements are given by different authors as to the contents of the commercial Pound of Lubec. *Kruse* makes it answer to 7460 English Grains, and *Nelkenbrecker* gives it 6 Grains less, whereas it appears to be nearly 20 Grains more as above stated. This result has been lately determined at the *London Mint*, from attested standards transmitted to *Lord Castlereagh*, by *William Lewis Behnoke, Esq.*, his Majesty's Consul at Lubec.

Liquid Measures.

Spirits, &c. are likewise sold by the Oxhoft, Ohm, and Anker. The Oxhoft contains $1\frac{1}{2}$ Ohm, 6 Ankers, 30 Viertels, or 240 Quartiers, and answers to 65,93 English Gallons, or 249,56 Litres.

A Pipe of oil is reckoned at 820lb. of Lubec, net weight, which equal 876,17lb. avoirdupois, or 397 Kilogrammes.

Long Measure.

The Ell is generally reckoned at 2 Lubec Feet, or 24 Inches, and contains 22,692 English Inches, or 0,57614 Metres.

Exchanges.

Lubec exchanges with and gives to—

Amsterdam, 117 Rixdollars current, more or less, for 100 Rixdollars.

Hamburgh, 123 Rixdollars current, ... for 100 Rixdollars banco; but Lubec mostly draws on Hamburgh in banco money, at three days date, receiving from $\frac{1}{8}$ to $\frac{1}{4}$ per cent. agio.

With other places Lubec seldom exchanges in a direct way; but bills on foreign countries are drawn in Hamburgh; and bills drawn from foreign countries on Lubec are made payable in Hamburgh banco; and the Lubec merchant is to direct the payment to be made there accordingly.

Usances are the same as at Hamburgh; and 10 days grace are allowed.

LUCCA *(in Italy)*.

Monies of Account.

Accounts are kept in Lire of 20 Soldi or 240 Denari; also in Scudi d'oro, likewise called Scudi di cambio, of 20 Soldi, or 240 Denari di Scudo d'oro. The Scudo d'oro is worth $7\frac{1}{2}$ Lire.

The Lira is also divided into 10 Bajocchi or Bolognini.

The Ducat, Ducatone, or Scudo Corrente, is worth 7 Lire, or 140 Soldi di Lira.

A Ducato della Seta is 7 Lire 18 Soldi 6 Denari.

Coins.

The coins of Lucca are gold Pistoles, of 22 Lire; silver Scudi, of 7 Lire 10 Soldi, halves, thirds, and fifths, in proportion; Lire; Barboni, of 12 Soldi, halves and quarters in proportion; and copper Bolognini, Soldi, and Quattrini.

All the Florentine coins are current here; but they are 10 per cent. higher in value. Thus the Scudo d'oro of Florence is reckoned in Lucca at $8\frac{1}{4}$ Lire; and the Lira of Florence at 22 Soldi.

Coins. Reckoning according to the value of Florentine money, the Scudo d'oro of Lucca is worth 4s. 10¼d. sterling in gold.

Weights. The Pound here is divided into 12 Ounces, and the Ounce into 24 Denari, or 576 Grains. This weight answers to 5213,5 English Grains, or 337,77 Grammes.

There is another weight called Peso grosso, the Pound of which equals 11lb. of Leghorn = 8,234lb. avoirdupois.

Measures. Corn is measured by the Staja, which equals 0,6844 English Bushels, or 0,2411 Hectolitres.

Oil is sold by the Coppo, a measure of 26,37 English Gallons, or 998,13 Litres, reckoned at 24lb. Peso grosso generally, which answers to 197,6lb. avoirdupois.

The Canna, long measure, contains 4 Braccia; the Braccio for woollens is 0,604 Metres, or 23,8 English Inches; and for silk 0,579 Metres, or 22,8 English Inches.

Exchanges. Lucca exchanges with and gives to—

Bologna,	1 Scudo di Cambio, more or less,	for	102 Bolognini.
Bolsano,	53 Bajocchi, ...	for	1 Florin, Moneta lunga.
Florence,	110 Scudi di Cambio, ...	for	100 Scudi d'oro.
Genoa,..	1 Scudo, ...	for	136 Soldi fuori banco.
Leghorn,	6 Lire 6 Soldi,................	for	1 Pezza of 8 Reali.
Lyons,..	52 Scudi, ...	for	100 Ecus of 3 Livres.
Novi, ..	168 ditto,......................	for	100 Scudi d'oro marche.
Rome,..	93 ditto,......................	for	100 Scudi Moneta.
Venice,	86 ditto,......................	for	100 Ducati di banco.

Usance, &c. The usance, and all other regulations respecting bills of exchange, at Lucca, are the same as at Leghorn; and transactions of the kind are most commonly done through that place. Bills of exchange are to be paid in the coins of the city, or in Tuscan coins; and any other kind of money may be refused in payment.

Piombino, Porto-Ferrajo, and Sienna, have the same exchanges as Lucca.

LUNEBURG *(in Germany)*.

Monies of Account.

Accounts are kept in Rixdollars of 24 Good Groschen, each being subdivided into 12 Pfenings.

The Rixdollar is also divided into 36 Mariengroschen, 32 Schwer Schillings, 48 common Schillings, 72 Matthiers, 96 Wittens, 288 Pfenings, or 768 Scherffen.

The coins and money weights here are the same as at *Hanover*, which see.

Weight.

The commercial weight is divided as in Hamburgh, but is something heavier, the Pound weighing 7540 English Grains. Thus 100lb. of Luneburg equal 107,71lb. avoirdupois, or 48,859 Kilogrammes.

Measures.

Corn is measured by the Wispel, containing 20 Scheffels, 40 Himten, or 160 Spints. The Scheffel answers to 1,767 English Bushel, or 0,6226 Hectolitres.

A Tonne or Cask of Luneburg salt weighs a Shipfund, or 280lb., and contains 6 Himtens, or 5⅓ English Bushels. A Cask of honey weighs 300lb., and holds 24½ Stubgens, equal to about 26½ English Gallons.

The Luneburg Foot measures 11,45 English Inches, or 0,2907 Metres; and the Ell is 2 such Feet.

For measures of other descriptions, see *Hanover*.

LYONS *(in France)*.

Monies and Coins.

The coins, and the new weights and measures of this city, will be found under the article *France;* but as several of the old measures are still in use, and are constantly referred to, some account of them is necessary.

Old Weights.

There are three sorts of old weights here, the ***Poids de Marc***, used for weighing precious metals; the ***Poids de Soie***, for weighing silk; and the ***Poids de Ville*** or ***Poids de Table***, for weighing every other kind of goods.

The Pound Poids de Marc, or old French Pound, is 16 Ounces, 15 of which compose the Pound Poids de Soie, and 14 the Pound Poids de Ville. It should be observed, that each of these Pounds is divided into 16 Ounces.

100lb. Poids de Marc = 48,98 Kilogrammes, or 108lb. avoirdupois.
100lb. Poids de Soie = 45,89 Kilogrammes, or 101,25lb. avoirdupois.
100lb. Poids de Ville = 42,85 Kilogrammes, or 94,5lb. avoirdupois.

Old Measures. The corn measure, called *Asnée*, contains 6 Bichets, 24 Coupes, or 96 Picotins; and equals 1,917 Hectolitre, or 5,44 English Bushels.

The wine measure, also called *Asnée*, contains 88 Pots, and equals 82,54 Litres, or 21,8 English wine Gallons.

	Metres.		English Inches.
The Foot of Lyons equals	0,3425	=	13,48.
The Aune	1,174	=	46,2.
The Toise of $7\frac{1}{2}$ Feet....	2,5688	=	101,13.

The Bicherée, in land measure, equals 12,934 Ares, or 3 Acres 31 Perches English; and the Hommé de Vignes is one-third of the Bicherée.

Exchanges, &c. For the exchanges of Lyons see *France*, Vol. II. page 49.

Bills of exchange were formerly settled at the great fairs which were held at Lyons quarterly; but this practice has been discontinued, and bills are now subject to the regulations of the *Code de Commerce*, as in Paris, for which see *France*, page 143.

MADEIRA *(in the Atlantic Ocean)*.

Monies of Account. Accounts are kept here, as in Portugal, in Rees and Milrees, which are imaginary coins. 1000 Rees make a Milree, generally valued at 5s. 6d. sterling.

Coins. The coins current on the island are

Spanish Dollars, which pass for	1000 Rees	=	10 Bits.
Pistareens..................	200	=	2

with halves and quarters in proportion.

The copper coins are Pieces of 20, 10, and 5 Rees.

Weights. The same weights are used for gold and silver, and for all commercial purposes.

The Pound contains $7076\frac{1}{2}$ English Grains.* Thus 100lb. of Madeira equal 101,09lb. avoirdupois, or 45,85 Kilogrammes. The divisions and multiples of the commercial weight are the same as in Portugal.

* The above is the weight of an attested standard of the Madeira Pound, transmitted by *Henry Veitch, Esq.* British Agent and Consul General at *Madeira*, and lately determined at the *London Mint*. It should be observed that this Pound is about 6 English Grains (or nearly 1 per Mille) lighter than the Arratel of Portugal, though they are understood to be equal.

Corn is measured by the Alquiere, $2\frac{1}{2}$ of which are computed to equal the Winchester Bushel. Measures.

The liquid measures are the same as in Portugal. $23\frac{1}{2}$ Almudes are reckoned to equal a Pipe of 110 English Gallons, which makes the Almude of Madeira about $\frac{1}{12}$ more than the Almude of Lisbon.

For the long measures see *Lisbon*.

MADRAS, *see East Indies.*

MADRID, *see Castile and Spain.*

MAJORCA *(in the Mediterranean).*

In this Spanish island, accounts are kept in Pesos of 8 Reales, each Real being divided into 34 Maravedis of Plate. Monies of Account.

Also in Libras of 20 Sueldos, or 240 Dineros.

The Peso and Libra are of the same value, each being worth 128 Quartos, or 512 Maravedis Vellon. Thus 4 Maravedis make 1 Quarto, and 16 Quartos, 1 Real of Plate.

For the other monies of account, and the coins of the Balearic Islands, see *Spain*.

There are two Pounds used here; that for the precious metals is the Castilian Mark, with its divisions. Weights.

The Pound, commercial weight, generally called the Rottolo, is divided into 12 Ounces, and contains 6174 English Grains.* 26lb. make the Arroba, and 4 Arrobas the Quintal or Cantaro, which is equal to 91,73lb. avoirdupois, or 41,6 Kilogrammes. There is also the Cantaro Berberesco of 100 Rottolos. Most

* The weights of the Balearic Islands are variously given by different authors, but all agree in making the commercial Pound of Majorca heavier than that of Minorca, in the proportion of from 4 to 6 per cent. It appears, however, from the dispatches sent to *Lord Castlereagh* in 1818, by *Lewis C. Hargrave, Esq.*, the British Consul for those islands, that the commercial Pound is uniform throughout his Consulate; and he has transmitted an attested standard of the same, which answers to 6174 English Grains, as above. *Marien*, who, as a Spanish author, should be considered a good authority on this subject, makes the Pound of Minorca answer to 6165 English Grains, and that of Majorca to 6483, being a difference of 5 per cent.

Weights. articles are weighed by the latter. The regular Carga of Majorca is 3 Quintals, or 312 Rottolos.

Measures. Corn is sold by the Quartera. The half Quartera, which is the largest measure generally used, is divided into 3 Barcellas, or 18 Almuts, with halves and quarters. The Quartera equals 2 Winchester Bushels nearly, or 0,7047 Hectolitres.

The wine measure is the Quartin, which is divided into 6½ Corters, or 26 Quartas, and equals 7,168 English Gallons, or 27,131 French Litres.

The Quartin of brandy is divided into 4 Quartinillos, or 64 Llivras.

The Quartin or Cortan of oil weighs 9 Rottolos, and 12 Cortans compose an Odor.

The long measure, called Canna, is 1,713 Metre, or 67,5 English Inches.

MALAGA *(in Spain)*.

Monies of Account. Accounts are kept here in Reals of 34 Maravedis Vellon.

The Real Vellon is also divided into 8½ Quartos, 17 Ochavos, 68 Blancas, 136 Cornados, or 340 Dineros.

The Peso or Dollar of Plate, the Doubloon, the Ducat, and other monies of account used here, will be found under the article *Castile*, and the coins under that of *Spain*.

For the weights of Malaga see *Castile* and *Spain*.

Dry Measure. The Fanega is divided into 12 Selemines, 48 Quartillos, or 192 Raciones, and is computed at 1,66 English Bushel, or 0,5637 of a Hectolitre.

Liquid Measure. The Arroba or Cantara is divided into 8 Azumbres, or 32 Quartillos, and contains 4,1875 English wine Gallons, or 15,850 French Litres.*

The regular Pipe of Malaga wine contains 35 Arrobas, but is reckoned at only 34, and is sold by the Arroba. The Bota of wine of Pedro Ximenes contains 53½ Arrobas.

* The contents of the above measures of capacity have been lately determined in London from standards transmitted to the Foreign Office by *W. Laird, Esq.*, his Majesty's Consul at Malaga. The weights which he has sent perfectly agree with those of Castile, and he states them to be uniform throughout Granada, as well as the measures of length and capacity.

The Bota of oil contains 43 Arrobas; and the Pipe about 34 Arrobas, or 860lb. avoirdupois. It is sold either by the Pipe, or by the Arroba. Liquid Measures.

In computing the freight of ships, the following quantities are reckoned for 1 Last, viz. 4 Botas, or 5 regular Pipes of wine or oil; 20 Chests of lemons or oranges; 50 Baskets of raisins; 22 Barrels of almonds or raisins, each of the weight of 8 Arrobas; 32 ditto, of 6 Arrobas; 44 ditto, of 4 Arrobas; 88 ditto, of 2 Arrobas. Lastage.

A Cargo of raisins contains 7 Arrobas; and a Basket half a Cargo.

For the Exchanges of Malaga see *Spain*, Vol. II. page 88. Exchanges.

MALTA *(in the Mediterranean).*

Accounts are kept in this Island in Scudi of 12 Tari, each Taro being divided into 20 Grani. The Taro is likewise divided into 2 Carlini, or 120 Piccioli. Monies of Account.

The Pezza, or Dollar of exchange, contains $2\frac{1}{2}$ Scudi, 30 Tari, 60 Carlini, 600 Grani, or 3600 Piccioli.

The coins in circulation are chiefly Spanish Dollars and Doubloons, and Sicilian Dollars and Ounces. They are valued each at a certain rate, as follows, on which a variable agio is charged. Coins.

The Spanish Dollar	30 Tari 10 Grani.
Spanish Doubloon......	38 Scudi 9 Tari.
Sicilian Dollar	30 Tari.
Sicilian Ounce	6 Scudi 3 Tari.

The coins of the Order of Malta, which are now nearly out of circulation, are the double, single, and half Louis d'or, coined by the Grand Master, worth 20, 10, and 5 Scudi. In silver, the Dollar, and half Dollar, current at 30 and 15 Tari; the Scudo at 12 Tari; and the half Scudo at 6 Tari. The copper coins are pieces of 4, 2, and 1 Tari. These latter coins are greatly over-rated, which formerly led to a distinction between silver and copper money, making the former to the latter as 3 to 2.

The fineness both of gold and silver is expressed in Carats; but the gold is divided into 24 Carats, and the silver into 12. The Carat of each is divided into 32 Grains. Expression of Fineness.

Rate of Coinage. The double Louis d'or is to weigh $\frac{23}{36}$ of an Ounce of Malta, or $260\frac{1}{4}$ English Grains; and the gold, according to the latest regulations, is to be $20\frac{1}{2}$ Carats fine. The Ounce, or Piece of 30 Tari, is to weigh $1\frac{1}{8}$ Ounce of Malta, or $458\frac{1}{4}$ English Grains, and the silver is to be 10 Carats (or $\frac{10}{12}$) fine. The Scudi and inferior silver coins are at most 9 Carats fine.

It does not appear that the forementioned fineness of the Maltese coins was fixed till the year 1782, and therefore a difference is found in the standard of those coined before that period; the old Louis d'ors of the island, in particular, being only from $20\frac{1}{16}$ to $20\frac{3}{8}$ Carats fine.

The single Louis d'or is worth 19s. 8d. sterling; the Piece of 30 Tari, or $2\frac{1}{2}$ Scudi, is worth $53\frac{1}{3}$d. Thus the Scudo, current money, is worth $21\frac{1}{3}$d sterling.

Gold and Silver Weight. Gold and silver are weighed by the Libbra or Pound of 12 Ounces; the Ounce is divided into 16 parts, or into 32 Trapesi; and the Trapeso into 18 Grani. This Pound weighs 4886 English Grains = 316,617 Grammes.

Commercial Weight. The Pound or Rottolo, commercial weight, is divided into 30 Ounces; and equals 12216 English Grains. Hence 100 Rottoli (the Cantar) = 174,5lb. avoirdupois, or 79,14 Kilogrammes. Merchants mostly reckon the Cantar at 175lb. avoirdupois.

Measures. The Salma of corn, stricken measure, is equal to 8,221 English Bushels, or 2,896 Hectolitres. Heaped measure is reckoned 16 per cent. more.

The Caffiso, a measure for oil, contains $5\frac{1}{2}$ English Gallons, or 20,818 Litres. The Barrel is double the Caffiso.

The Foot of Malta is $11\frac{1}{6}$ English Inches, or 0,2836 Metres.

The Canna, long measure, is divided into 8 Palmi, and equals 81,9 English Inches, or 2,079 Metres. Merchants usually convert Malta measure into English, in the proportion of $3\frac{1}{2}$ Palmi to 1 Yard; or $2\frac{2}{7}$ Yards to 1 Canna.

The Sicilian weights and measures are likewise used here, for which see *Sicily*.

Exchanges. Malta exchanges with, and gives to—

Genoa, ...	4 Tari 12 Grani, more or less,	for	1 Lira Fuori Banco.
Leghorn, ..	29 Tari, ...	for	1 Pezza of 8 Reals.
London,....	1 Dollar of Exchange, ...	for	48 Pence sterling.
or as used by Government,	1 Spanish Dollar, ...	for	49 Pence sterling.

Exchanges.

Marseilles, ..	5 Tari 12 Grani, more or less,	for	1 Franc.
Naples, ...	$25\frac{1}{2}$ Tari, ...	for	1 Ducato.
Sicily, ...	$6\frac{1}{4}$ Scudi, ...	for	1 Ounce.
Trieste, ...	$14\frac{1}{2}$ Tari, ...	for	1 Florin.
Turkey, ...	1 Scudo, ...	for	104 Paras.

Usance. Bills on London are usually drawn at 30 and 60 days sight; on Turkey, 31 days sight; on Sicily, 21 days sight; and on all other places at 30 days sight.

MANTUA *(in Italy).*

Monies of Account. Accounts are kept here in Lire of 20 Soldi, the Soldo being divided into 12 Denari. Also in Italian Livres of 100 Centesimi. 20723 Lire Italiane equal 81000 Lire of Mantua, making the latter worth $2\frac{1}{2}$d. sterling very nearly.

A Scudo of account is 6 Lire, or 120 Soldi.

Coins. The coins of Mantua are the Silver Ducatone, of 25 Lire 7 Soldi; the Scudo Bianco, of 19 Lire 7 Soldi; the Tallaro, of 14 Lire 6 Soldi; and pieces of 1, 2, and 3 Lire, and of 5 and 10 Soldi.

The coins of Milan are all current here, but they pass for three times the value in Lire and Soldi of Mantua that they bear in Lire and Soldi of Milan. Austrian, Spanish, French, and Venetian coins pass at a nominal rate, with a fluctuating agio or discount.

Weights & Measures. The weight for gold and silver is the same as at Milan. The commercial Pound contains 4871 English Grains. Thus 100lb. of Mantua equal 69,58lb. avoirdupois, or 31,55 Kilogrammes.

The Stajo of corn weighs 80lb. of Mantua, and contains 0,998 of an English Bushel, or 0,3516 of a Hectolitre.

The Moggio of oil weighs 320lb. of Mantua, and contains 29,45 English Gallons, or 111,48 Litres.

The Braccio is 25 English Inches, or 0,6347 of a French Metre.

MARANHAM, *see Brazil.*

MARBURGH, *see Cassell.*

MARSEILLES *(in France).*

Monies, Weights, &c.

The monies and coins of Marseilles are chiefly those of the rest of France. The decimal system of weights and measures, and also the Système Usuel, are established by law here as at Paris; but in the ordinary transactions of business the ancient system is very generally retained. Thus in mercantile operations of gold and silver, the Poids de Marc is still used; and in weighing common articles the Poids de Table.

The Pound, Poids de Table, is divided into 16 Ounces, 128 Gros, or 9216 Grains, and answers to 6296 English Grains; and hence 100lb. Poids de Table = 89,94lb. avoirdupois, or 40,795 Kilogrammes.

Measures, &c.

The Charge, corn measure, is divided into 8 Panaux, the Panal into 4 Civadiers, and the Civadier into 2 Picotins. The Charge contains 1,6 Hectolitre, or 4½ English Bushels nearly.

Wine is measured by the Millerolle, which is divided into 4 Escandaux, 60 Pots, or 240 Quarts, and equals 64,33 Litres, or 16,99 English Gallons.

The Canne, long measure, is divided into 8 Pans, or 64 Menus, and equals 2,0126 Metres, or 79,238 English Inches.

The Quarterée, land measure, contains 20,509 French Ares, or 2 Roods 1 Perch English.*

For the exchanges of Marseilles see *France*, Vol. I. page 143; also Vol. II. page 49.

MASSUAH, *see Abyssinia.*

MAYENCE, *see Francfort on the Maine.*

MEMEL, *see Konigsberg.*

MESSINA, *see Sicily.*

---

* The foregoing statements are in substance those lately transmitted to *Lord Castlereagh* (with metrical standards), by *A. Turnbull, Esq.*, the British Consul at *Marseilles*, and they have been verified by *M. Ferrier*, the proper official authority of that city.

It is deemed necessary here to mention these particulars, as authors differ very considerably respecting the contents of the *Poids de Table. Nelkenbrecker* makes it about 18¼ per cent. lighter than the *Poids de Marc; Kruse*, 21 per cent.; but according to the proportions given in the above article, it is only 16⅗ per cent. lighter; and this statement is further verified by Tables published in 1803, by *M. Ferogio*, a Member of the Commission of Weights and Measures.

MEXICO *(in North America).*

Accounts are kept here, and in all other parts of Spanish America, in Pesos or Dollars of 8 Reals, the Real being divided into halves and quarters. This Real is occasionally divided into 16 Parts; and also into 34 Maravedis of Mexican Plate. Monies of Account.

The Gold coins are Doubloons of 8 Escudos d'oro, worth 16 Pesos, (with a premium of about 8 per cent.); with halves, quarters, &c. in proportion. The Silver coins are Pesos Mexicanos or Dollars, with halves and quarters. The quarters, in Spain, are called Pecetas Mexicanas. There are also eighths or Reals, which in Spain are valued at $21\frac{1}{4}$ Quartos: also half Reals. Coins.

To express the fineness of gold, the Castellano, or other weight, is divided into 24 Quilates or Carats; the Quilate into 4 Grains; and the Grain into 8 Parts. Fineness of Gold and Silver.

The fineness of silver is expressed in Dineros; the Mark or other weight being divided into 12 Dineros, and each Dinero into 24 Grains.

By the Mint regulations of 1772, the following pieces were to be coined from a Castilian Mark of gold, $21\frac{1}{2}$ Carats fine; viz. $8\frac{1}{2}$ Doubloons of 8 Escudos, 17 Pieces of 4 Escudos, 34 Pistoles, or 68 Escudos. Rate of Coinage.

The following were to be coined from a Mark of silver, $10\frac{3}{4}$ Dineros fine; viz. $8\frac{1}{2}$ Pesos Duros, or 17 Half Dollars; and from a Mark of silver, $9\frac{3}{4}$ Dineros fine, 34 Pecetas, or 68 Reals of Mexican Plate.

The Doubloon, by these regulations, should contain 374 English Grains of pure gold, and be therefore worth £3. 6s. 2d. sterling. The Dollar should contain 374 Grains of pure silver; and its value is therefore 4s. $4\frac{1}{4}$d. sterling nearly. Variations, however, have since been made in a part of this monetary system, which will be explained under the article *Spain.*

Of the silver taken from the new Spanish mines, and brought to the mint at Mexico to be coined, one-fifth formerly belonged to the King of Spain. About 2 Millions of Marks are annually brought to this city, 700,000 of which are struck into Dollars. The owners of such silver pay the expenses of the mint, and also a seignorage to the King of 1 Real per Mark. Though every Spanish subject is at liberty to have his silver coined on those terms, yet merchants are almost the only persons who avail themselves of this privilege. They buy up all Mint.

Mint. the silver they can procure, and deduct from the price 2 Reals per Mark, one for seignorage, and the other for the expenses of the mint.*

Weights, &c. The weights and measures of Mexico are those of *Spain*, which see.

MILAN (*in Italy*).

Monies of Account. Accounts were formerly kept here in Lire of 20 Soldi, or 240 Denari; but by a decree of 1806, they are now kept in Lire Italiane of 100 Centesimi: 20723 Italian Lire equal 27000 Lire Correnti. Thus, reckoning the Italian Livre or French Franc at 9½d. in gold, the Lira of Milan equals 7¼d. sterling nearly.

The Scudo di Cambio or Imperiale is reckoned at 5 Lire 17 Soldi, or 117 Soldi Imperiali; the Scudo Corrente, at 5 Lire 15 Soldi, or 115 Soldi Correnti.

The difference between the value of Imperial and Current money is determined by the Filippo, a coin that is invariably reckoned at 106 Soldi Imperiali, whilst its value in current money has been raised at different periods: in 1755 it was fixed at 7 Lire 10 Soldi, or 150 Soldi Correnti. According to that valuation, 106 Lire Imperiali are equivalent to 150 Lire Correnti, and 1219 Scudi Imperiali to 1725 Scudi Correnti.

Coins. The Gold coins are, Doppie or Pistoles—those coined since 1786 pass for 25 Lire 3 Soldi Correnti; Souverains, at 45 Lire; and Sequins, at 15 Lire 4 Soldi.

---

* The above account of the Mint at Mexico was published in 1781 by *Ricard*, by which it appears that the amount of silver annually coined there at that period was about 6 millions of Dollars; but in 1790 it was 17 millions, according to *Helms;* and, in 1804, above 20 millions, according to *Humboldt*, *Estala*, and other authorities. From statements laid before the Bullion Committee of the House of Commons, in 1810, by *John Allen, Esq.*, it appears that the annual average of both gold and silver, coined in the different mints of Spanish America for some time previously, was nearly as follows:—Mexico, 24 millions of Dollars; Lima, 6 millions; Potosi, 4½ millions; Santa Fé and Santiago, each 1½ million; and Popayan and Guatimala, nearly 1 million; making, in all, about 8 millions sterling.

The proportion of silver to gold coined at all these mints was, on an average of several years, stated to be as 30 to 1; but the proportion of silver to gold produced from all the American mines was estimated as 62 to 1; and from the mines of all countries as 52 to 1.

M. Brongniart computes the value of gold and silver brought annually into circulation from all parts of the world, to be worth nearly 46 millions of Dollars; of which 36 are from Spanish America, 4½ from Portuguese America, and 5½ from the Old World; making the annual increase in all nearly 10 million Pounds sterling. (*Traité Elementaire de Minéralogie, Paris*, 1807.)

The Silver coins are, Ducatoons, valued at 8 Lire 12 Soldi; Filippi, at 7 Lire 10 Soldi; but these are now nearly out of circulation: there is still the Scudo of 6 Lire, with halves, &c. in proportion; also Lire, and halves. Coins.

When the Duchy of Milan took the name of the Cisalpine Republic, it coined money under that title, consisting of silver Scudi, of the same weight and fineness as those above stated. New Coinages.

In 1804, the government of the Italian Republic (afterwards called the Kingdom of Italy) coined gold pieces of the value of 31 Lire, weighing the 125th part of a Pound, and silver coins of the value of 5 and 2 Lire, 1, $\frac{1}{2}$, and $\frac{1}{4}$ Lira; the Lira weighing 4 Denari, or $\frac{1}{6}$ of an Ounce, and the other pieces in proportion.

The coins struck since that period are chiefly silver, according to the regulations of the Paris mint; the *Lira Italiana* (the monetary unit) being equal to the French Franc, with its divisions and multiples in proportion.

Several kinds of foreign coins pass here at rates which are generally printed and circulated. The French gold coins, however, pass as in France. Foreign Coins.

The fineness of gold is expressed by 24 Carats, divided into 24 parts; and the fineness of silver, by 12 Denari, each of 24 Grani. Fineness & Weight of Gold and Silver.

Gold and silver are weighed by the Mark, which is divided into 8 Ounces, 192 Denari, or 4608 Grani, and equals 3627 English Grains, or 235,033 French Grammes.

The commercial Pound, or Libbra, Peso Sottile, is divided into 12 Oncie, 288 Denari, or 6912 Grani, and equals 5044 English Grains. Thus 100lb. of Milan = 72,06lb. avoirdupois, or 32,68 Kilogrammes. Commercial Weights & Measures, Old System

There is another Libbra, of 28 Ounces, called Peso Grosso, 3lb. of which equal 7lb. of the former. Hence 100lb. Peso Grosso equal 168,2lb. avoirdupois, or 76,25 Kilogrammes.

The Moggio is divided into 8 Staja, 32 Quartari, 128 Metà, or 512 Quartini, and contains 41,5 English Bushels, or 14,624 Hectolitres.

The Brenta is divided into 3 Staja, 6 Mine, 12 Quartari, 48 Pinte, or 384 Boccali, and contains 18,86 English Gallons, or 71,38 Litres.

The Rubbio of oil weighs 25lb. of 32 Ounces, Milan weight, or 47$\frac{1}{2}$lb. avoirdupois nearly.

The Braccio is divided into 12 Once, 144 Punti, or 1728 Atomi, and answers to 0,5949 of a French Metre, or 23,42 English Inches.

New System of Weights & Measures. In 1803 a new system of weights and measures was decreed for the kingdom of Italy, and has been partially acted upon. It is founded on the French decimal system, with a vocabulary of Italian names. Thus the Metre is called the *Metro*, and is divided into 10 Palmi, 100 Diti, or 1000 Atomi; the Kilogramme is called the *Libbra nuova Italiana*, and is divided into 10 Oncie, 100 Grossi, 1000 Denari, or 10000 Grani; and the Hectolitre is called the *Soma*, and is divided into 10 Mine, 100 Pinte, or 1000 Coppi.

The proportion of the new weights and measures to the old may be found from the foregoing statements, respecting the French, or may be computed from the following:

The Metro........ = 1 Braccio, 8 Once, 2 Punti;
The Libbra Italiana = 3 Libbre, 17 Denari, 7 Grani;
The Soma........ = 5 Staja, 1 Quartaro, 3½ Metà;
with their decimal divisions and multiples in proportion.

The new system of metrology is used in all public transactions relating to government, but in private business the old system is still continued.

Exchanges. For the Exchanges of *Milan*, see Vol. II. page 76.

Usance. The usance for bills drawn from Genoa, Leghorn, Piedmont, and all Lombardy, is 8 days sight; from Rome, Florence, Augsburg, Vienna, and all Germany, 15 days sight; from Venice, 20 days date; from Naples and Sicily, 20 days sight; from France and Savoy, 1 month after date; from Spain, Holland, and Flanders, 2 months; from London, 3 months after date: the month to be always reckoned at 30 days.

Days of Grace. Bills at sight must be paid on being presented; bills payable at usance, or some days after date or sight, must be paid the day after their written term expires; and if this should fall on a Sunday or holiday, payment is to be made on the next working day. Thus no days of grace can be claimed at Milan; yet the holder of the bill may grant to the person who is to accept it three days: in such a case, however, the bill must be carried to the Notary of the Chamber of Commerce, who writes upon it *seen on such a day;* and when the bill is afterwards accepted, the acceptance is to be dated from the day when it was first presented; but if refused, the protest is to take place on the day marked by the Notary. The same grace may be allowed with regard to payment, when the bill becomes due; but any delay is always at the option of the holder.

MINORCA *(in the Mediterranean).*

Accounts are kept in this Island in Libras of 20 Sueldos, or 240 Denari, as at *Barcelona*. Monies, &c.

For the weights and the dry measures, see *Majorca*.

The liquid measure used here is the Gerra, or Jar, which is divided into 2 Quarters, 4 Half Quarters, &c., and contains 3,187 English Gallons, or 12,063 Litres: 80 Quarters, or 40 Gerras, Mahon wine measure, are computed to equal a Pipe of 126 English Gallons. Liquid Measure.

For further particulars, see *Barcelona* and *Spain*.

MOCHA *(in Arabia).*

Accounts are kept in Piastres of 80 Caveers current. This Piastre is an imaginary coin, but most payments are made in Spanish Dollars, 100 of which pass for $121\frac{1}{2}$ Piastres, which gives the value of the Piastre 3s. $8\frac{1}{2}$d. sterling nearly. Turkish and Italian Sequins, Ducats, &c. are taken in payment according to their weight and fineness. The Venetian Sequin passes commonly for 2 Piastres 25 Caveers. Monies of Account.

Cotton is sold by the Haraff, an imaginary money, valued at 1 Piastre 22 Caveers. Thus 9 Haraffs are equal to $11\frac{1}{2}$ Mocha Piastres of account.

The monies coined in the country are Commassees, which contain but little silver: they are used in small payments, and generally pass at 60 for a Dollar; but their value varies daily, so that sometimes 80, sometimes no more than 40 of them are given for a Dollar. The Carat is a small coin, the seventh part of a Commassee. Coins.

Gold and silver are weighed by the Vakia, of 10 Coffalas, or 160 Carats. 24 Carats make a Miscal, and $1\frac{1}{2}$ Vakia a Beak. 100 Spanish Dollars weigh 87 Vakias; thus the Vakia weighs 1 Ounce English troy weight nearly. Gold and Silver Weight.

The Bahar contains 15 Farzils, or 150 Maunds; the Maund, 40 Vakias. Commercial Weight.

A Rattle is 15 Vakias; but in coffee, $14\frac{1}{2}$ Vakias are reckoned for a Rattle, 2 Rattles for a Maund, and 10 Maunds, or 290 Vakias, for a Farzil. The Rattle is only used in the Bazar.

Commercial Weight. The Bahar of Mocha is stated to be equal to 18 Maunds of Madras, or 450lb. avoirdupois. Others say that it weighs 405lb. French weight, or 437½lb. avoirdupois; but it must be observed that the weights at the Custom-House are generally found to be 2 or 3lb. heavier than the regular weights, and that in the interior divisions of the country the difference is still greater.

Measures. The Teman, dry measure, contains 40 Mecmedas or Kellas, and weighs, in rice, 168lb. avoirdupois.

The Gudda, liquid measure, contains 2 English Gallons nearly; it is divided into 8 Nusfias, and the Nusfia into 16 Vakias.

The long measures are the Guz, of 25 English Inches, and the Cobido, of 19 ditto.

MODENA *(in Italy)*.

Monies of Account. Accounts are kept here in Lire, Soldi, and Denari Correnti; the Lira being divided into 20 Soldi or Bolognini, and the Soldo into 12 Denari: but of late years accounts have been kept in Italian Livres, 20723 of which equal 54000 Lire Correnti. Thus the Lira of Modena is worth 3¾d. sterling.

Coins. The gold coins are, Pistoles of 51 Lire, and Scudini of 9 Lire. The silver coins are, Ducatoons of 17⅔ Lire; Filippi of 15½; Ducats of 8; Scudi of 3¾; new Scudi of 5; Pieces of ½, 1, and 2 Lire; Capelloni of 6 Soldi 8 Denari; Pieces of 5 and 2½ Soldi. For the value of the above coins, see *Tables of Coins*, Vol. II.

The Lira of Reggio is worth two-thirds of the Lira of Modena; so that the above coins are one-third higher when valued in money of Reggio.

Weights. The weights for precious metals are the same as at Milan.

The Quintal weight is reckoned at 100lb. and is 6⅖ per cent. lighter than the same weight in Leghorn: hence 100lb. of Modena are equal to 70,45lb. avoirdupois, or 31,95 Kilogrammes.

Measures. Corn is measured by the Stajo, which equals 2 English Bushels, or 0,704 of a Hectolitre.

The Braccio, long measure, is 2½ Genoese Palmi, and is therefore equal to 24,3 English Inches, or 0,6175 of a Metre.

MOGADORE, *see Morocco*.

MONTE VIDEO, *see Mexico*.

MONTPELLIER *(in France)*.

The monies, coins, weights, and measures of Montpellier, are those of France, which see. The old weights and measures, however, are still partially used, and are as follows:— Monies, &c.

The Quintal (or 100lb. of Montpellier) equals 88lb. avoirdupois, or 39,9 Kilogrammes. Old Weight

The Setier, corn measure, is divided into 2 Emines, or 4 Quarts, and contains $1\frac{1}{2}$ English Bushel, or 0,5285 of a Hectolitre. Old Measures.

The Muid of wine is divided into 18 Setiers, 24 Barrels, or 576 Pots; and contains 161,06 English Gallons, or 609,6 Litres.

Muscat wine is sold by the Muid, and Vin du Rhone by the Barrel; the Cask containing 5 or $5\frac{1}{2}$ Barrels.

Brandy is sold by the weight of 100lb.: $20\frac{1}{2}$lb. of brandy are called a Velte; and a common cask contains about 70 Veltes.

The Charge of Oil is composed of 4 Barrals, 8 Emines, 16 Quartals, or 128 Pots. The Quartal weighs 21lb. of Montpellier, or $18\frac{1}{2}$lb. avoirdupois.

The long measure, called Canne, is divided into 8 Pans, and measures 1,9874 Metre, or 78,24 English Inches.

The Seterée, land measure, is composed of 75 Dextres, and equals 14,175 Ares, or 1 Rood 16 Perches English measure.

In reckoning the freight of ships from the port of Cette, the following quantities are estimated for a Last, viz. 4 Casks of brandy, each containing about 70 Veltes; 8 Hogsheads of Muscat wine, called Frontignac; or 7 Casks of Vin du Rhone, each containing about $5\frac{1}{2}$ Barrals. Lastage.

For the exchanges of Montpellier, see *France*, Vol. II. page 49. Exchanges, &c.

The regulations for the payment or protest of bills, &c. are likewise the same as in other parts of France. See Vol. I. page 143.

MOREA, *see Patras.*

MOROCCO *(in Africa).*

Monies of Account. Accounts are kept here, and in Fez, Mequinez, Sallee, Mogadore, and all the western parts of Barbary, in Mitkuls of 10 Ounces, the Ounce being divided into 4 Blankeels, and the Blankeel into 24 Fluce.

Coins. The principal coins in circulation are Spanish Doubloons and Dollars, with their divisions; also the Madrid, a gold piece worth 10 Dollars, coined at Madrid for the use of the Emperor of Morocco.

The coins of the country are the following:

In gold, the Mitkul (also called Miscal and Ducat), and the Bendiky, or 2 Dollar piece, worth 27 Ounces.

In silver, the Ounce, or Dirhem, $13\frac{1}{2}$ of which make a Dollar;
The 6 Blankeel piece, 9 ditto......ditto;
The Blankeel,...... 54 ditto......ditto.

In copper, pieces of 6 and 4 Fluce.

The above coins are struck in several cities of Barbary, and are not considered as accurately minted.

From their proportion to the Spanish Dollar, the Blankeel may be valued at 1d., the Ounce at 4d., the Ducat at 3s. 4d., and the Bendiky at 9s. sterling.

Weights. The commercial Pound here is generally regulated by the weight of 20 Spanish Dollars, and therefore 100lb. of Barbary, or the Kintal, = 119lb. avoirdupois.

The market Pound for provisions is reckoned 50 per cent. heavier, and therefore equals 30 Dollars, or 1lb. $12\frac{1}{2}$ oz. avoirdupois nearly.

Iron and bees' wax are sold by this weight.

Measures. The corn measures are the Almude and Arroba, commonly called the Mood and Kroba. The Almude of Sallee is reckoned at 40 Selemenes of Castile. The Cahiz, Fanega, and other Spanish measures, are also used, and were probably correct when first introduced; but they are now found too various to be reduced to any certain standard.

The principal long measure at Morocco is the Cubit, or Canna, which answers to 21 English Inches. In other parts of Barbary there is also the Pic, which equals 26 English Inches nearly.

MUNICH *(in Germany)*,

And the whole Electorate of Bavaria, keep accounts in Guldens or Florins, of 60 Creutzers current, the Creutzer being divided into 4 Denari. Monies of Account.

The Florin also contains 15 Batzen, 20 Kaysergroschen, 24 Land Muntze, or 30 Albuses.

A current Rixdollar is worth 1½ Florin; a Batze, 4 Creutzers; a Kaysergrosche, 3; a Land Muntze, 2½; an Albus, 2 Creutzers; and the Creutzer, 4 Pfenings.

Coins.

		FLORINS.	
The gold coins are—	Carolin d'ors, worth	11	halves & quarters in proportion;
	Max d'ors,	7⅓	double and half in proportion;
	Ducats,	5	20 Creutzers;
	Gold Guldens,	3	36 ditto.

The silver coins are—Rixdollars specie, halves, and quarters; Copsticks and halves; all minted after the rate of the Convention coins, but valued 20 per cent. higher in Bavarian money: that is, the Rixdollar passes for 2 Florins 24 Creutzers; the Florin of the Empire for half that sum; and the new Rixdollar for 2 Florins. Thus Bavarian money is to Convention money as 5 to 6.

The value of the current Rixdollar (or Rixdollar of account), as fixed by the latest regulations, answers to 20 German Asen, or 14⅘ English Grains of fine gold, and to 304 Asen, or 225½ Grains of fine silver: the proportion of gold to silver is therefore as 15⅕ to 1. Value of Monies.

Hence the said current Rixdollar is worth 31½d. sterling, and the Florin 21d. sterling; or £1 sterling = 11 Florins 26 Creutzers.

The absolute fineness of gold is 24 Carats, and the Carat is divided into 12 Grains: the absolute fineness of silver is 16 Loths, and the Loth is divided into 18 Grains. Wrought silver is to be 13 Loths fine. Fineness of Gold and Silver.

The weight for the precious metals is considered the Mark of Cologne, but is a shade heavier. It contains 3609,87 English Grains, or 233,891 Grammes. Weights & Measures.

The commercial Pound weighs 8656 English Grains. Thus the Quintal of 100lb. Bavarian weight equals 123,6lb. avoirdupois, or 56 Kilogrammes.

The Scheffel, or Schaff, corn measure, is divided into 6 Metzens, 12 Viertels, or 48 Maessels, and contains 10,29 English Bushels, or 3,626 Hectolitres; the Scheffel of oats is one-seventh larger.

Weights & Measures. The Eimer of wine contains 60 Maass, or 240 Quartels; a Fass of beer contains 25 Eimers, each of 64 Maass. The Maass = 1,30 English Pint, or 0,617 Litres.

The Bavarian Foot measures 11,375 English Inches, or 0,289 Metres; the Ell = 32,9 English Inches, or 0,835 Metres.

MUNSTER *(in Germany)*.

Monies and Coins. Accounts are kept in this part of Westphalia in Rixdollars current of 28 Schillings, the Schilling being divided into 12 Pfenings.

The Rixdollar also contains $1\frac{1}{2}$ Florin, 8 Blamusers, 36 Mariengroschen, 336 Pfenings, or 672 Hellers.

The coins are, Florins and halves, or Pieces of 1 Mark; half Marks of $4\frac{2}{3}$ Schillings, or 6 Mariengroschen; Pieces of 14 and 28 Pfenings.

Weights & Measures. The Cologne weight is used for the precious metals, and the Pound commercial weight = 7353 English Grains. Thus 100lb. of Munster = 105lb. avoirdupois, or 47,64 Kilogrammes.

The Ell measures 31,9 English Inches, or 0,808 of a Metre.

NANTES *(in France)*.

Monies, &c. The monies, weights, and measures here are the same as in the rest of France, with the exception of certain ancient customs, which are still retained, and should therefore be stated.

Old Weights & Measures. The old weight of Nantes is reckoned 1 per cent. heavier than the Poids de Marc. Thus 100lb. of Nantes equal 109lb. avoirdupois, or 49,43 Kilogrammes.

The most general measure for corn is the Setier, which is divided into 16 Boisseaux, and equals 4,063 English Bushels, or 1,431 Hectolitre. The Tonneau is 10 Setiers, and the Muid of salt 4 Quartauts.

The Tonneau of wine is divided into 2 Pipes, 4 Barriques, or 480 Pots. The Barrique contains 63,4 English Gallons, or 240 Litres.

Brandy is sold by the 29 Veltes, in casks of 50 and 60 Veltes. The Velte is divided into 3 Pots, and contains 1,484 English Gallon, or 5,617 Litres.

Train oil is sold by the 30 Veltes.

The Ell measures 55,8 English Inches, or 1,416 French Metre.

Exchanges. For the exchanges of Nantes, see *France*, Vol. I. page 143, and Vol. II. page 49.

NAPLES *(in Italy)*.

Monies of Account.

Accounts are kept here in Ducati di Regno of 100 Grani. The Ducat is divided into 10 Carlini, each of 10 Grani, and, by the public banks, into 5 Tari, of 20 Grani each, making the Ducat always 100 Grani.

There are other monies, both real and imaginary, which bear the following proportions to the Ducat, viz.

The Ducato contains 2 Patacche, 5 Tari, 10 Carlini, 40 Cinquini, 66$\frac{2}{3}$ Pubbliche, 100 Grani, 200 Tornesi, 300 Quartini, 600 Piccioli, or 1200 Cavalli.

Old Coins.

The mint regulations of Naples have undergone several alterations since the year 1750, which are the less necessary to be explained, as a new system of coinage was adopted in 1818, which promises to be permanent.

The old coins still circulate according to their nominal value, or, if much worn, according to weight. Their original value may be known from the *Tables of Coins*, Vol. II.

The gold coins are, Pieces of 2, 4, and 6 Ducati; the Sicilian Onza of 30 Carlini, with double in proportion.

The silver coins are, the Ducato of 10 Carlini, and the half Ducat, or Pataca; the Sicilian Scudo of 12 Carlini, and the half Scudo; Tari of 2 Carlini; Pieces of 12, 13, 24, and 26 Grani; single Carlini, and halves, &c.

Spanish hard Dollars are allowed to pass at the rate of 12 Carlini 4 Grani; and other foreign coins circulate at their intrinsic value, according to a printed ordinance occasionally issued by the Minister of Finance.

New Coins.

The monetary system of 1818 has for its unit the silver Ducat, which weighs 515 Neapolitan Grains (Acini), 354 English Grains, or 22,943 Grammes. It contains 833$\frac{1}{3}$ parts of pure silver, and 166$\frac{2}{3}$ of alloy; that is, five-sixths pure, and one-sixth of alloy, with a remedy of $\frac{3}{1000}$. Its sterling value is therefore 41,2d. There are Pieces of 1, 2, 6, and 12 Carlini in proportion, the Ducat being 10 Carlini.

The gold coins are minted at the fineness of 996 parts of pure in 1000, with a remedy of $\frac{1}{1000}$ in the fineness.

The smallest gold piece is the Oncetta, which weighs 85 Acini, 58,43 English Grains, or 3,786 Grammes. It passes for 3 Ducats, and is worth 10s. 3$\frac{1}{2}$d. sterling, with Pieces of 5 and 10 Oncette in proportion.

New Coins. All coins under the value of the Carlino are represented in copper, of which there are Grani and halves, and Pieces of 2, 3, and 5 Grani. The half Grano, or Torneso, weighs 70 Acini, and the other pieces in proportion.

Fineness of Gold and Silver. By the above mint regulations it will be seen that the fineness of gold and silver is now decimally expressed; but formerly the absolute fineness of gold was expressed by 24 Carats, each Carat being divided into 8 parts, and that of silver by 12 Ounces, the Ounce being divided into 12 Sterlini.

Gold and Silver Wt. Gold and silver are weighed by the Libbra of 12 Ounces, 360 Trapesi, or 7200 Acini; containing 4950 English Grains, or 320,760 French Grammes.

Commercial Weights. The commercial weights are, the Cantaro and Rottolo: the Cantaro Grosso contains 100 Rottoli, each weighing $33\frac{1}{3}$ Ounces of the gold and silver weight, or $31\frac{3}{7}$ Ounces avoirdupois. Hence the Cantaro Grosso = $196\frac{1}{2}$lb. avoirdupois, or 89,1 Kilogrammes.

The Cantaro Piccolo weighs 150lb. of 12 Ounces, and answers to 106lb. avoirdupois, or 48 Kilogrammes.

Dry Measure. The Carro of corn is divided into 36 Tomoli, or 864 Measures: the Tomolo contains 1,451 English Bushel, or 0,5115 of a Hectolitre. A Tomolo of wheat weighs about 45 Rottoli.

Liquid Measure. The Carro of wine or brandy is divided into 2 Botte, 24 Barili, or 1440 Caraffi. The Barile equals 11 English Gallons, or 41,67 Litres. A Pipe of wine contains 14 Barili.

The Salma of oil is composed of 16 Staja, 256 Quarti, 320 Pignate, or 1536 Misurelle: the weight of the Stajo is $10\frac{1}{3}$ Rottoli. Thus the Salma weighs 324,6lb. avoirdupois, or 147,2 Kilogrammes, and measures 42,79 English Gallons, or 162 Litres.

Long Measure. The Canna is divided into 8 Palmi, or 96 Onzie, and equals 6 Feet 11 Inches English. Thus the Palmo is 10,38 English Inches, or 0,264 of a French Metre.

The Moggia, land measure, contains 33,431 French Ares; or 3 Roods 12 Perches English.

In the province of Apulia, 1 Caro = 20 Versure, 120 Catane, 1200 Passi, or 8400 Palmi.

For the exchanges of Naples, see Vol. II. page 80. Exchanges.

The usance for bills drawn from any part of the kingdom of Naples is 15 days after acceptance; and from Sicily, Genoa, Venice, Leghorn, and Rome, 22 days. From Spain, 2 months after date; and from London, 3 months. The acceptance is to take place on the Saturday after the arrival of the post from the place where the bill was drawn. But bills payable at so many days sight or date must be accepted or protested on being presented, without any delay. Usances and Days of Grace.

Three days grace are allowed, except for bills at sight.

NARVA, *see Russia and Pernau.*

NAUMBURG, *see Leipsic.*

NAVARRE (*in Spain*).

Accounts are kept here in various ways, but most commonly in Reals of Old Plate, which, however, are divided into 36 Maravedis instead of 34. See *Spain*. Monies, &c.

Accounts are also kept in Libras of 20 Sueldos, or 240 Dineros.

There are various other monies of account, as Ducados, Tarxas, Gruesos, Ochavos, and Cornados; which render the monetary system of Navarre peculiarly complex. It may, however, be in some measure simplified by considering the Real as the fundamental money, which is worth $4\frac{7}{8}$d. sterling nearly, and valuing all the rest in proportion.

The Real equals $4\frac{1}{2}$ Tarxas, 6 Gruesos, 12 Sueldos, 18 Ochavos, 36 Maravedis, 72 Cornados, or 144 Dineros. 5 Reals = 3 Libras, and therefore

The Libra equals $1\frac{2}{3}$ Real, $7\frac{1}{2}$ Tarxas, 10 Gruesos, 20 Sueldos, 30 Ochavos, 60 Maravedis, 120 Cornados, or 240 Dineros, and is worth $8\frac{1}{3}$d. sterling.

The Ducado equals $6\frac{8}{15}$ Libras, $10\frac{8}{9}$ Reals, and the lesser monies in proportion. It is worth $53\frac{1}{12}$d. nearly.

From the above proportions between the monies of Navarre, their relation to those of Castile may be computed by the Real, which is common to both.

Thus the Doubloon of Exchange of 32 Reals, and the Peso of 8 are known.

Thus also the Ducat of Exchange of 375 Maravedis of Plate is found to be $11\frac{1}{34}$ Reals; for as 34 : 1 :: 375 : $11\frac{1}{34}$.

Also the Ducat Vellon of 374 Maravedis Vellon is found to be $5\frac{27}{32}$ Reals; for as 64 : 1 :: 374 : $5\frac{27}{32}$; always remembering that 34 Maravedis of Plate equal 64 Maravedis Vellon.

Monies, &c. On the same principles the proportions between any of the other monies may be computed. Thus have the following been determined in round numbers:

40 Doubloons of Plate	equal 144	Ducats of Navarre.
49 Pesos of Plate	 36	....
833 Ducats of Exchange	 846	....
5 Doubloons of Plate	 96	Libras of Navarre.
5 Pesos of Plate	 24	....
85 Ducats of Exchange	 564	....

Coins. The coins of Navarre are those of Spain, which see. Their proportion to the monies of account may be computed from the following relations: 1 Hard Dollar equals $6\frac{3}{8}$ Libras, $10\frac{5}{8}$ Reals, $47\frac{13}{16}$ Tarxas, $63\frac{3}{4}$ Gruesos, $127\frac{1}{2}$ Sueldos, $191\frac{1}{4}$ Ochavos, $382\frac{1}{2}$ Maravedis, 765 Cornados, or 1530 Dineros.

784 Hard Dollars equal 765 Ducados of Navarre.

The value of all the divisions and multiples of the Hard Dollar may be of course computed from the same proportion.

Weights & Measures. The Mark of Navarre is divided into 8 Onzas, 32 Quartos, 128 Adarmes, or 4608 Granos. Thus the Mark of Navarre and that of Castile contain the same number of Grains; but the Grain of Navarre is $\frac{1}{16}$ heavier than that of Castile. The Mark of Navarre therefore equals 4896 Castilian Grains, and 16 Marks of Navarre = 17 Marks of Castile. Thus 100lb. of Navarre answer to 107,78lb. avoirdupois, or 48,88 Kilogrammes.

For the measures and other particulars of Navarre, see *Spain*.

NEGROLAND, *see Guinea*.

NETHERLANDS (*Kingdom of the*).

Monies of Account. This New Kingdom, comprehending ***Holland***, ***Brabant***, ***Flanders***, and ***Luxemburgh***, as constituted in 1815, keeps accounts in Florins or Guilders, of 100 Cents. The Guilder is of the same value as that heretofore coined in Holland, being worth 2 Francs $11\frac{64}{100}$ Centimes of France, or $20\frac{1}{8}$d. sterling nearly.

Coins. In 1816 a new system of coinage was decreed, in which the Florin is made the monetary unit, with decimal divisions and multiples. The fineness of the coins is likewise decimally expressed, and no deviation is allowed either in weight or fineness.

Coins.

The Florin must weigh 7 Esterlings, which equal 10,766 Grammes, or 166,17 English Grains, and its fineness is 893 in 1000; with pieces of 3 Florins and of 50 Cents in proportion.

There are also pieces of 25 Cents, weighing 88 As, or 4,25 Grammes, of 569 fine; with pieces of 10 and 5 Cents in proportion.

The new gold coin is called the 10 Florin Piece. It must weigh 140 As, which answer to 6,729 Grammes, or 103,85 English Grains, and its fineness is 900 in 1000: its sterling value is therefore 16s. 6½d. nearly.

The copper coins are Cents of 80 As, or 3,845 Grammes; with half Cents.

Weights & Measures.

In 1816 a new system of weights and measures was decreed for the Kingdom of the Netherlands, to commence in 1820. It is founded on the metrical and decimal system of France, but with an old vocabulary of names. See *Amsterdam*, *Rotterdam*, *Antwerp*, and *France*.

The *Pond* is the unit of weight, and answers to the French *Kilogramme*. Its divisions are the Ons, Lood, Wigtje, and Korrel.

The *Elle*, which is the unit or element of long measure, equals the French *Metre*. Its decimal divisions are the Palm, Duim, and Streep; and its decimal multiples, the Roede and Mijle.

The *Vierkante Elle*, or square Ell, is the unit of superficial measures; and answers to the *Centiare* or *Metre Carré* of France. Its divisions are the Vierkante Palm, Vierkante Duim, and Vierkante Streep; and its multiples, the Vierkante Roede and Vierkante Bunder.

The *Kubicke Elle* is the unit of measures of capacity; and equals the French *Stere*. Its divisions are the Kubicke Palm, Kubicke Duim, and Kubicke Streep.

The term Wisse is given to a Kubicke Elle of fire-wood.

The *Kop* is the unit of measures for dry wares, and is the cube of the Palm; answering to the French *Litre*. Its division is the Maatje, and its multiples the Schepel and Mudde; the latter is also called the *Zak*, and equals the French Hectolitre. 30 Mudde make 1 Last.

The *Kan* is the unit for liquid measure, and is the cube of the Palm; it corresponds to the French *Litre*. Its divisions are the Maatje and Vingerhoed, and 100 Kans make a Vat or Cask, which equals the French Hectolitre.

The Apothecaries' new Pound is divided into 12 Ounces, 96 Drachms, 288 Scruples, or 5760 Grains; and answers to 375 Grammes, or 5787 English Grains.

Table of the Weights and Measures of the Kingdom of the Netherlands, compared with those of France and England.

	NEDERLANDISCH.		FRENCH.		ENGLISH.
Weights.	*Pond*	=	....Kilogramme	=	....15434 Grains.
	Ons	=	....Hectogramme	=	 1543,4
	Lood	=	....Decagramme.........	=	 154,34
	Wigtje	=	....*Gramme*	=	 15,434
	Korrel	=	....Decigramme	=	 1,5434
Long Measure.	Mijle	=	....Kilometre	=	.. 3937,1 Inches.
	Roede	=	....Decametre	=	... 393,71
	Elle	=	....*Metre*	=	 39,371
	Palm	=	....Decimetre	=	 3,9371
	Duim	=	....Centimetre	=	 0,39371
	Streep	=	....Millimetre	=	 0,039371
Square Measure.	Vierkante Bunder	=	....Are	=	...... 3,955 Perches.
	Vierkante Roede .	=	....Deciare	=	 0,3955
	Vierkante Elle..	=	....*Metre Carré*	=	......10,7644 Sq. Feet.
	Vierkante Palm..	=	....Decimetre Carré......	=	......15,500 Sq. Inches.
	Vierkante Duim .	=	....Centimetre Carré.....	=	 1,550
	Vierkante Streep.	=	....Millimetre Carré	=	 0,155
Cubic Measure.	*Kubicke Elle* ...	=	....*Stère, or Mètre Cube*..	=	.....35,3170 Cubic Feet.
	Kubicke Palm ..	=	....Decistere	=	3,5317
	Kubicke Duim ..	=	....Centistere...........	=	0,35317
	Kubicke Streep..	=	....Millistere	=	0,035317
Dry Measure.	Mudde, or Zak ..	=	....Hectolitre	=	......2,8379 Bushels.
	Schepel		.... Decalitre	=	0,28379
	Kop	=	....*Litre*	=	0,028379
	Maatje	=	....Decilitre	=	0,002837
Liquid Measure.	Vat	=	....Hectolitre	=	....26,419 Wine Gallons.
	Kan..........	=	....*Litre*	=	 26419
	Maatje.........	=	....Decilitre	=	 026419
	Vingerhoed	=	....Centilitre	=	 0026419

NEUFCHATEL (*in Switzerland*).

There are different modes of keeping accounts here. The most ancient method is in Livres Foibles, of 12 Gros, or 144 Deniers, which is still partially retained, particularly in rents and inferior departments of business. Monies, Weights, &c.

The second way of keeping accounts, which has been chiefly used by merchants, is in Livres Tournois of Neufchatel, divided into 12 Sous, or 240 Deniers, 1 Livre of which equals 2½ Livres Foibles, and is worth 13½d. sterling nearly.

Another mode was introduced in 1798, which is in Franken of 10 Batzen, or 100 Rappen. This Batze is equal to 1½ French Franc, and is of nearly the same value as the above-mentioned Livre Tournois.

The coins are, silver pieces of 21 and 10½ Batzen; but French monies, as well as those of the surrounding Cantons, circulate here.

Two different weights are used here; namely, the Poids de Marc, or old weight of France, and the Poids de Fer, with which heavy goods are weighed. The Pound of this weight = 17 Ounces French weight, or 8029 English Grains; and therefore 100lb. Poids de Fer = 114,7lb. avoirdupois, or 52,04 Kilogrammes.

The Foot = 0,3000 of a Metre = 11,81 English Inches; the Ell = 1,112 Metre = 43,8 English Inches. For further particulars, see *Switzerland*.

NICE (*in Italy*).

The monies and coins of Nice are the same as those of *Turin*, which see. Monies, Weights, &c.

The weight for gold and silver is the Poids de Marc.

The commercial Pound is composed of 12 Ounces, and is equal to 4809 English Grains. Thus 100lb. of Nice correspond to 68,76lb. avoirdupois, or 31,16 Kilogrammes. 25lb. make the Rubbio, and 6 Rubbi the Quintal.

Corn is measured by the Charge, which is divided into 4 Setiers, 8 Emines, 16 Quartiers, or 64 Motureaux, and equals 1,6 Hectolitre, or 4½ English Bushels.

Wine and oil are sold by the Rubbio, weighing 25lb. of Nice, or 7,79 Kilogrammes; also by the Charge, composed of 12 Rubbi, or 120 Pints. The Rubbio of 10 Pints equals 2,076 English Gallons, or 7,8 Litres.

The element of long measure is the Pan, which equals 0,2615 of a Metre, or 10,29 English Inches. The Trabuc is 12 Pans, and the Canne 8 Pans.

The Ell of Nice equals 1,188 Metre, or 46,77 English Inches.

The square Trabuc equals 0,9885 French Ares, or 3,90 Perches English.*

* The above article is extracted from the dispatches lately sent to *Lord Castlereagh*, with standards, by *P. Lacroix, Esq.* the British Consul at *Nice*.

NORWAY, *see Bergen.*

NOVI, *see Genoa.*

NUREMBERG *(in Germany).*

Monies of Account.

Accounts are kept here in Guldens or Florins of 60 Creutzers.

The Florin also contains 3 Copstucks, 15 Batzen, 20 Kaysergroschen or Schillings, or 240 Pfenings.

The Rixdollar of account is worth 1½ Florin, 4½ Copstucks, 22½ Batzen, 30 Kaysergroschen, 90 Creutzers, or 360 Pfenings. The Rixdollar specie is reckoned at 2 Florins, 30 Batzen, 40 Schillings, or 120 Creutzers.

A Copstuck is 5 Batzen, or 20 Creutzers; a Batze, 4 Creutzers; a Schilling or Kaysergrosche, 3 Creutzers, or 12 Pfenings.

Accounts are kept either in currency, according to the Convention or 20 Florin rate of coinage, in which bills are settled; or in Muntz, according to the 24 Florin rate of coinage, in which goods are paid for.

There was formerly a third sort of money, called Moneta d'oro (or gold money): this money was about 9 per cent. worse than banco, but it is now nearly out of circulation.

Coins.

The gold coins are, Ducats and gold Gilders. The silver coins are, old specie Rixdollars, halves, and quarters; and new specie Rixdollars, Florins, and halves; and Copstucks, coined after the Convention rate, and bearing 20 per cent. agio against Muntz. Also, Pieces of 30, 15, 12, 7½, 6, 5, 4, 3, 2½, 2, and 1 Creutzers, Muntz.

The Ducat is worth 4 Florins 30 Creutzers, in banco or current, or 5 Florins 24 Creutzers, Muntz; the gold Gilder, 3 Florins 12 Creutzers, in banco or current, or 3 Florins 50 Creutzers, in Muntz.

Old full weight specie Rixdollars pass for 2 Florins 40 Creutzers, in small coins; Convention Rixdollars, for 2 Florins current, or 2 Florins 24 Creutzers, in small coins; and the other Convention coins in proportion.

Value of Monies.

The Rixdollar of account, in banco or current, may be valued at about 25⅕ German Asen, or 18⅗ English Grains of fine gold; and at 364 Asen, or 270 Grains of fine silver: the same Rixdollar in small coins may be valued at 21½ Asen, or 16 Grains of fine gold, and at 304 Asen, or 225½ Grains of fine silver.

Hence the Rixdollar, banco or current, is worth 38d. sterling, and the Florin, $25\frac{1}{2}$d. sterling nearly; but in small coins, the Rixdollar is worth only $31\frac{1}{2}$d., and the Florin, 21d. sterling. Value of Monies.

Gold and silver are weighed by the Nuremberg Mark, which is divided into 8 Ounces, 16 Loths, 64 Quintlins, or 256 Pfenings, and equals 3670 English Grains, or 239 French Grammes. Gold and Silver Weight.

The commercial Pound is divided into 2 Marks, 4 Viertungs, 16 Ounces, 32 Loths, 128 Quints, or 512 Pfenings, and answers to 7870 English Grains. Thus 100lb. of Nuremberg equal 112,42lb. avoirdupois, or 50,99 Kilogrammes. Commercial Weight.

The Shipfund contains 3 Centners, or 300lb.

The Malter is divided into 16 Metzen, 32 Diethaufen, or 128 Maass. A Simmer of wheat, rye, and pease, contains 2 Malters; a Simmer of barley or oats, 4 Malters. The Malter answers to 4,74 English Bushels, or 1,671 Hectolitre. Dry Measure.

The Fuder contains 12 Eimers Visiermass, or $12\frac{3}{4}$ Eimers Schenkmass. The Eimer is divided into 32 Viertels, 64 Mass, or 128 Seidels. An Eimer Visiermass contains 17,96 English Gallons, or 67,98 Litres; and an Eimer Schenkmass answers to 16,76 English Gallons, or 63,43 Litres. Liquid Measure.

The Nuremberg Foot of 12 Inches measures 11,96 English Inches, or 0,3036 of a Metre. The Ell is 26 English Inches, or 0,6595 of a Metre. Long Measure.

The long Ruthe, or Perch, is 16 Feet; the short Ruthe, 12 Feet.

The Morgen of land, by which corn land and wood land are measured, contains 200 long square Ruthes, each of 256 square Feet: its contents are therefore equal to 1 Acre 27 Perches, English measure, or 47,295 French Ares. Superficial Measures.

The Morgen, or Acre, by which meadows and pasture land are measured, contains 160 short square Ruthes, each of 144 square Feet: its contents are therefore 2 Roods $4\frac{1}{2}$ Perches, English measure, or 21,372 French Ares.

Nuremberg exchanges with and gives, more or less, to— Exchanges.

Amsterdam, ... 142 Rixdollars banco or current, for 100 Rixdollars.
Augsburg, ... 102 Florins current .... for 100 Florins current.
Breslau, ... 96 Florins current .... for 100 Florins current.

Exchanges.

Francfort, ...	100 Rixdollars current....	for 100 Rixdollars Convention
Hamburgh, ...	148 Rixdollars current....	for 100 Rixdollars banco.
London, ...	9 Florins current	for £1 sterling.
Lyons and Paris,..	101 Francs	for 100 Francs.
Prague and Vienna,	75 Florins current	for 100 Florins current.
Venice, ...	99 Florins current	for 500 Lire Piccole.

Usance.

The common usance for bills of exchange in Nuremberg is 15 days; half usance, 7 days; double usance, 30 days; 1½ usance, 23 days; all reckoning from the day after acceptance. When bills are payable after date, the time is reckoned from the day after that on which the bill was drawn; Sundays and holidays, and vacations of the bank, are included.

When bills are made payable at one or more months after date or sight, they become due on the same day of the month on which they were drawn or accepted.

Days of Grace.

Six days grace are allowed; but if the last of those days should fall on a holiday, payment or protest must take place on the preceding day; or if a bill becomes due when the bank is shut, it must be paid or protested on the day before the shutting of the bank. No days of grace are allowed on bills at sight, or 2, 3, or 4 days sight, or at a shorter date than half usance.

If a bill payable after date should not arrive until after some of the days of grace are elapsed, these days are not to be reckoned from the arrival of the bill, but from the day on which it is made payable; and should all the six days be elapsed, the bill must be paid within 24 hours of its arrival.

ODESSA, *see Russia.*

OLDENBURG *(in Germany).*

Monies of Account.

Accounts are kept in Rixdollars of 72 Grotes, each Grote being divided into 5 Swares.

The Rixdollar is also divided into 48 Schillings, or 54 Stivers; and the Stiver into 4 Ortes: this mode of reckoning is chiefly used in retail trade.

Thus 2 Schillings = 3 Grotes, or 15 Swares; 8 Schillings = 9 Stivers; and 3 Stivers = 4 Grotes.

Coins.

The coins are, silver Pieces of ⅔ and ⅓, or 48 and 24 Grotes, coined at the rate of 12 Rixdollars to the Cologne Mark of fine silver; these bear an agio of

7 to 11 per cent. against the Convention coins, and 25 to 30 per cent. against the smaller coins. Pieces of 6 and 12 Grotes, coined after the rate of the Convention coins, bear an agio of 13 to 16 per cent. against the smaller coins. There are also Pieces of 4, 2, $1\frac{1}{2}$, 1, and $\frac{1}{2}$ Grotes, which are coined at the rate of from $14\frac{1}{2}$ to 15 Rixdollars per Mark of fine silver. Coins.

Wholesale business is transacted in Convention money; and retail business in small coins.

Dutch Ducats pass here at 2 Rixdollars 60 Grotes, Convention money, or 3 Rixdollars 24 Grotes, in small coins, more or less. Pistoles, Fredericks, and other like coins, are reckoned at 5 Rixdollars. French coins are also current here.

The weight for gold and silver is the Cologne Mark. Weights.

The commercial Pound is divided into 32 Loths, and the Loth into 4 Quentins, 16 Pfenings, or 256 Asen. The Pfundschiver is 300lb.; the Shipfund, 290lb.; the Centner, 100lb.

The weight of Oldenburg is equal to that of Hamburgh, of which 100lb. = 106,8lb. avoirdupois, or 48,44 Kilogrammes.

The Last of corn is divided into 12 Molts, 18 Tonnen, or 144 Scheffels; and contains 83,217 English Bushels, or 29,322 Hectolitres. Measures of Capacity.

The Oxhoft of wine is composed of $1\frac{1}{2}$ Ohm, 6 Ankers, 156 Kannes, or 240 Quartiers; and contains 65,93 English Gallons, or 249,56 Litres.

The Foot is divided into 12 Inches, and is equal to 11,65 English Inches, or 0,2959 of a Metre. Long Measures.

The Ell of Oldenburg is equal to that of Bremen, and answers to 22,76 English Inches, or 0,578 of a Metre.

OPORTO, *see Lisbon.*

OSNABURG *(in Germany).*

Accounts are kept here in Rixdollars current of 21 Schillings, each Schilling being divided into 12 Pfenings. Monies of Account.

This Rixdollar is also worth $1\frac{1}{2}$ Florin or Gulden, 36 Mariengroschen, 72 Matthiers, 252 Pfenings, or 504 Hellers.

Monies of Account. The Florin, or Piece of $\frac{2}{3}$, is worth 14 Schillings, or 24 Mariengroschen; a Mariengrosche is 7 Pfenings, or 14 Hellers.

Coins. The coins are, silver specie Rixdollars, with halves and quarters; base silver Pieces, of 6, 4, 3, 2, $1\frac{1}{2}$, and 1 Mariengrosche; of 1 and $1\frac{1}{2}$ Schilling; of 9, 6, 5, 4, and 3 Pfenings; and copper Pieces of 5, 4, 3, $1\frac{1}{2}$, and 1 Pfening. These coins are valued according to the Convention rate of coinage, that is, at the rate of 20 Florins to the Cologne Mark of fine silver. See *Germany*.

Weights. Gold and silver are weighed by the Cologne Mark.

The commercial Pound is divided into 16 Ounces, 32 Loths, 128 Quentins, or 512 Pfenings; and equals 7625 English Grains. Thus 100lb. of Osnaburg answer to 108,9lb. avoirdupois, or 49,4 Kilogrammes.

Measures. The Last of corn contains 100 Scheffels, 400 Viertels, or 1600 Bechers; and the Fuder, 6 Malters, or 72 Scheffels. The Scheffel answers to 0,815 of an English Bushel, or 0,287 of a Hectolitre.

The Fuder of wine contains 6 Ahms, or 168 Viertels; and the Viertel is divided into 4 Kannen, 16 Orts, or 64 Helfgens, and equals 1,29 English Gallon, or 4,88 Litres.

The Foot of Osnaburg equals 11 English Inches, or 0,279 of a Metre.

The Ell is of two sorts; the longer is 23,7 English Inches, or 0,601 of a Metre; the shorter measures 23 English Inches, or 0,583 of a Metre.

Exchanges. The exchanges of this place are chiefly with Amsterdam and Hamburgh: thus Osnaburg gives to—

Amsterdam, 136 Rixdollars, more or less, for 100 Rixdollars.
Hamburgh, 144 Rixdollars, ... for 100 Rixdollars banco.

OSTEND, *see Antwerp.*

OVIEDO, *in Asturias, see Galicia.*

PADUA *(in Italy).*

Monies and Coins. Accounts are kept here in Ducats of 24 Grossi, or 288 Denari; or in Lire of 20 Soldi, or 240 Denari, as at Venice; and the coins are likewise the same.

Accounts are also kept in Italian Livres and Cents.

There are two different weights at Padua as at Venice; and the Peso Grosso is the same in both places; but the Peso Sottile is $12\frac{1}{2}$ per cent. heavier here than the Venetian weight of the same denomination. Hence 100lb. Peso Grosso of Padua = 105,55lb. avoirdupois, or 47,87 Kilogrammes; and 100lb. Peso Sottile = 75lb. avoirdupois, or 34,01 Kilogrammes. Weights.

The Foot of Padua is 13,93 English Inches, or 0,3536 of a Metre. Measures.

The Braccio is of two sorts; one for silk stuffs, which is 25,3 English Inches, or 0,6429 of a Metre; the other for linen and woollens, which is 26,8 English Inches, or 0,6812 of a Metre.

For further particulars, see *Venice*.

PALERMO, *see Sicily.*

PARIS, *see France.*

PARMA *(in Italy).*

Accounts are kept here, and at Placentia and Guastalla, in Lire of 20 Soldi, or 240 Denari; also in Lire Italiane of 100 Centesimi. 757000 Lire of Parma are computed to equal 183481 Francs, or Italian Livres. Thus the Lira of Parma is worth $2\frac{1}{3}$d. sterling nearly. Monies of Account.

6 Lire of Parma = 5 of Placentia; and 24 Lire of Parma = 25 of Guastalla.

The Scudo is reckoned at 7 Lire 6 Soldi.

The Gold coins are, old Doppie, or Pistoles, some reckoned at 72 Lire 12 Soldi, and others at 93 Lire 10 Soldi; but those coined since 1786 pass for 90 Lire; also Sequins at 45 Lire. Coins.

The Silver coins are, Ducatoni, at 21 Lire; Scudi, at 8 Lire 8 Soldi; Testoni, at 6 Lire 6 Soldi; Pieces of 3 Lire; and base Pieces of 20, 10, and 5 Soldi.

French coins also pass here.

The weight for gold and silver is the same as at Milan. Weights.

The commercial Pound of Parma is divided into 12 Ounces, 288 Denari, or 6912 Grani; and weighs 5038 English Grains. Thus 100lb. of Parma equal 71,97lb. avoirdupois, or 32.64 Kilogrammes.

Measures. The Stajo, corn measure, is divided into 16 Quartarole, and contains 1,458 English Bushel, or 0,514 of a Hectolitre.

The Braccio, Silk measure .... = 23,1 English Inches = 0,5865 of a Metre.
Cloth measure ..... = 25,1 .... = 0,6377 ....
Land & Road measure = 21,3 .... = 0,5420 ....

PATRAS *(in the Morea)*.

Monies. Accounts are kept here in Piastres of 80 Aspers.

The Turkish coins are current at Patras, for which see *Constantinople*.

Weights. The Quintal contains 44 Okes, or 132lb.; the Oka is 3lb. 36 Ounces, or 400 Drams. The Pound contains 6168 English Grains. Thus 100lb. of this weight correspond to 88lb. avoirdupois, or 39,95 Kilogrammes.

The Pound, silk weight, is one-fifth heavier, containing 15 Ounces, or 166$\frac{2}{3}$ Drams.

A Sack of currants weighs 140lb. of the common weight, or about 123lb. avoirdupois.

Measures. The corn measure is the Staro, which is composed of 3 Bachels, and equals 2,33 English Bushels, or 0,821 of a Hectolitre.

The Pic, or Ell, is of two sorts; the one being 8 per cent. longer than the other.

The long Pic, used for linens and woollens = 27 English Inches = 0,6855 Metres.
The short Pic, used for silks .... = 25 .... = 0,6347 ......

PERNAU *(in Russia)*.

Monies of Account. Accounts were formerly kept in this part of Livonia in Rixdollars of 64 Wittens, or 80 Copecks, but now in Rubles of 100 Copecks each.

A current Rixdollar is reckoned at 60 Wittens, or 75 Copecks; an Alberts Rixdollar at 80 Wittens, or 100 Copecks.

A Pernau Mark is worth 3 Wittens; a Lettish Mark, 2 Wittens.

Coins. The coins of Russia are current here; and the Russian bank assignations are received at a fluctuating discount, much below their nominal value.

Weights. The commercial Pound is divided into 16 Ounces, 32 Loths, or 128 Quintins; and contains 6430 English Grains. Thus 100lb. of Pernau equal 91,85lb. avoirdupois, or 41,65 Kilogrammes.

The Lispond is 20lb.; the Centner, 120lb.; the Shipfund, 20 Lisponds, or 400lb.

Measures. The Last of corn is divided into 24 Tonnen, 48 Loofs, or 192 Kullmits; and renders 86,25 English Bushels, or 30,39 Hectolitres.

A Last of linseed is reckoned at 12 Tonnen, or 21 Loofs; and a Last of salt at 18 Tonnen, each of 18 Kullmits.

The Ahm of wine is divided into 4 Ankers, 120 Stofs, or 480 Quarters; and equals 40,93 English Gallons, or 154,92 Litres. A Hogshead contains $1\frac{1}{2}$ Ahm; a Fass of beer or brandy, 128 Stofs.

The Pernau Ell answers to 21,6 English Inches, or 0,5486 of a Metre.

PERSIA.

Monies of Account. Accounts are kept in Tomans of 50 Abassis, 100 Mamoodis, 200 Shatrees or Chayés, 1000 Dinars-bisti, 2000 Kasbequis, or 10000 Dinars simple. The Toman and Dinar are imaginary monies.

Coins. Large payments are commonly made in silver; there are, however, some gold coins called Cherassi, which are generally struck for distribution at coronations, and are of different values. Thus the piece of Iman Riza is worth about 4s. 2d. sterling; that of Aboul-Faiz about 12s. 3d.; and that of Kouli Khan £1. 10s. 6d. nearly.

The silver coins of Persia are, Haser Denaries, of 10 Mamoodis; Daezajies, of 5; Larins, of $2\frac{1}{2}$; Albaajers or Abassis, of 2; single Mamoodis; half Mamoodis or Chayés; and copper Kasbequis, of 5 Dinars.

In large payments, the sums are not counted but weighed, mostly in bags of 50 Tomans, or 2500 Abassis; if any of the pieces are thought light, they are weighed in lots of 25 each.

Value of Monies. The weight and fineness of these pieces have been altered in different reigns. *Bonneville* values the present Chayé at 4 Sols 6 Deniers of France, which is about $2\frac{1}{8}$d. sterling; and thus the Toman is worth about 36s. sterling, and the other pieces in proportion.

Weights. Two sorts of weights are used in Persia, the Batman of Cherray, and the Batman of Tauris; the former is exactly double the latter, and their divisions are the same, the Batman containing 6 Rattels, 300 Derhams, or 600 Miscals. The Batman of Cherray weighs 88771 English Grains, or 5751,692 Grammes; and the Batman of Tauris half the above contents, or 6,34lb. avoirdupois.

The Derham, used for weighing gold and silver, equals 149 English Grains, or 9,79 Grammes.

Pearls are weighed by the Abas, which answers to 3,66 diamond Grains English, or 2,25 Troy Grains = ,148 Decigramme.

Long Measures. Of the Guerze, long measure, there are two sorts: the Royal Guerze, also called Monkelser, is 37½ English Inches, or 0,9456 of a Metre. The common Guerze is two-thirds of the Royal.

Another measure is sometimes used, called Arish, which equals 38,27 English Inches, = ,9716 of a Metre.

The Parasang, or Persian League, is the twentieth part of a Degree of the equator; it should therefore equal 3 geographical Miles, or 3 Miles 3 Furlongs 25 Poles English, = 6,286 Kilometres.

Corn Measure. An Artaba of corn contains 25 Capichas, 50 Chenicas, or 200 Sextarios; and equals 1,86 English Bushel, or 0,529 of a Hectolitre.

For further particulars relating to Persia, see *Bassorah* and *Gamron*.

PETERSBURG, *see Russia.*

PIEDMONT, *see Nice and Turin.*

POLAND

Monies of Account. Keeps accounts in Guldens, or Florins of 30 Groschen or Grosz; and each Grosche is divided into 18 Pfenings. Florins are also called *Zloti.*

This Florin contains 2½ Shostacks, 90 Schillings, or 540 Pfenings. The Shostack is worth 12 Groschen, 36 Schillings, or 216 Pfenings.

Little Poland and the kingdom of Prussia also keep their accounts in Guldens and Groschen; but these are double the value of the Polish denominations: thus the Rixdollar, which is reckoned in Great Poland at 6 Florins, or 180 Groschen, is worth only 3 Florins, or 90 Groschen, in Little Poland.

Coins.

The Gold coins in Poland are Ducats, worth 18 Florins Polish.

The Silver coins are specie Rixdollars and halves, at 8 and 4 Florins Polish, or 4 and 2 Florins Prussian; Thalers or Crowns; Pieces of 1, $\frac{1}{2}$, and $\frac{1}{4}$ Florin Polish, or 15, $7\frac{1}{2}$, and $3\frac{3}{4}$ Groschen Prussian.

The Copper coins are Pieces of 3, 1, and $\frac{1}{2}$ Groschen, and 1 Schilling Polish.

All these have been re-coined since 1765; and no other Polish monies have been since current here, except old Casimir Tympfen, at 27 Groschen, and Shostacks, at 10 Groschen Polish.

Rate of Coinage.

In 1765, the coinage was ordered after the rate of the Convention coins of Germany; that is, 67 Ducats were to weigh a Cologne Mark of gold $23\frac{2}{3}$ Carats fine; and 10 Rixdollars, 20 halves, 40 quarters, or 80 Polish Florins, were to contain a Cologne Mark of fine silver.

In 1787, an alteration took place with regard to the silver coins, which were ordered to be minted after the rate of Prussian currency; that is, $10\frac{7}{16}$ Rixdollars, $20\frac{7}{8}$ halves, $41\frac{3}{4}$ quarters, or $83\frac{1}{2}$ Polish Florins were to contain a Cologne Mark of fine silver.

Of the coinages since 1787, $8\frac{1}{2}$ Rixdollars weigh a Cologne Mark, and they are 13 Loths or $\frac{13}{16}$ fine; $25\frac{1}{4}$ double Florins weigh a Cologne Mark, $9\frac{2}{3}$ Loths fine; $44\frac{3}{8}$ single Polish Florins weigh a Cologne Mark, $8\frac{1}{2}$ Loths fine; and 88 Pieces of 10 Polish Groschen weigh a Cologne Mark, $5\frac{2}{3}$ Loths fine.

Value of Monies.

It follows, from the above statements, that the Polish Rixdollar (of 8 Polish Florins) contains $345\frac{3}{5}$ English Grains of fine silver, or $373\frac{3}{5}$ Grains of standard silver; and that it is worth $48\frac{1}{4}$d. sterling, or that £1 sterling = 39 Florins 25 Groschen Polish.

Gold and Silver Weight.

Gold and silver bullion are weighed by the Mark, which is not the same in all parts of Poland: the Warsaw Mark weighs 3113 English Grains, or 201,697 Grammes; the Cracow Mark, 3069 Grains, or 198,846 Grammes; and the Wilna Mark, 3006 Grains, or 194,764 Grammes.

The weight of coins is regulated by the Cologne Mark.

Commercial Weight.

The commercial Pound is divided into 32 Loths, or 48 Skoyciecs: the Pound of Cracow, or common Polish weight, is 8426 Asen, or 6250 English Grains; and the Pound of Warsaw 7863 Asen, or 5832 Grains.

Hence 100lb. of Cracow = 89,3lb. avoirdupois, or 40,49 Kilogrammes.

100lb. of Warsaw = 83,3lb. avoirdupois, or 37,78 Kilogrammes.

Commercial Weight. In 1766, a new weight was established, and ordered to be used throughout Poland; the Pound of which weighs 8408 Asen, or 6236 English Grains. Thus 100lb. of this new weight = 89lb. avoirdupois, or 40,4 Kilogrammes.

The Centner is 5 Stone, and the Stone 32lb.

Dry Measure. The corn measure, called Korzec, contains, at Cracow, 16 Garniecs or Pots; at Sendomir, 24; at Lublin, 28; at Warsaw, 32.

The Last is composed of 60 Korzecs, and answers to 87,04 English Bushels, or 30,67 Hectolitres.

Liquid Measure. The Stangiew is divided into 2 Becska, 72 Garniec, or 288 Quarts. The Garniec contains 4,19 English Gallons, or 15,9 Litres.

The Oxhoft of wine is composed of 60 Garniec, and the Tiercon of 40.

Long Measures. The Cracow Foot measures 14,03 English Inches, or 0,3564 of a Metre.

The Polish Ell, established since 1765, is 24,3 English Inches, or 0,6169 of a Metre.

Exchanges. Warsaw exchanges with, and gives to—

Amsterdam,	1 Ducat, more or less,	for 108	Stivers.
Hamburgh,	1 Ducat............	for 6	Marks banco.
London,....	42 Florins Polish	for £1	sterling.
Paris,......	1 Ducat.............	for 228	Sous.
Vienna, ...	1 Ducat.............	for 4½	Florins Vienna currency.

PORTUGAL, *see Lisbon.*

PRAGUE *(in Germany)*,

Monies of Account. And the whole kingdom of Bohemia, keep accounts in Guldens or Florins of 60 Creutzers, or 240 Pfenings.

This Florin also contains 20 Kaysergroschen or Böhmens, 80 Groschels, or 180 white Pfenings.

A Rixdollar current or of account is worth 1½ Florin, 30 Böhmens, or 90 Creutzers. A specie Convention or effective Rixdollar is worth 1⅓ Rixdollar current, 2 Florins, 40 Böhmens, or 120 Creutzers.

A Schock or Kopy of Bohemian Groschen is 60 Groschen, 3 Florins, or 180 Creutzers; a simple Schock or Kopy is 30 white Groschen, 70 Creutzers, or 210 white Pfenings, also called Bilipeniz; a Bohemian or Kaysergrosche is 3 Creutzers; a white Grosche, $2\frac{1}{3}$ Creutzers, or 7 white Pfenings; a Creutzer, 3 white or 4 common Pfenings. Monies of Account.

The Gold coins which circulate in the country are, Kremnitz Ducats, reckoned since 1786 at 4 Florins 30 Creutzers; Imperial Ducats, at 4 Florins 32 Creutzers; Souverains, at 6 Florins 40 Creutzers, and double in proportion. Coins.

The Silver coins are, Rixdollars of 2 Florins, with halves and quarters; Pieces of 20, 17, 10, and 7 Creutzers; Groschen, and half Groschen.

The Copper coins are, Creutzers, half Creutzers, Groschels, and Pfenings.

For the value of those coins in English money, see *Tables*, Vol. II.

The Prague Mark, used for gold and silver, weighs 165 Engels, Dutch troy weight, or 3916 English Grains = 253,725 Grammes. Weights.

The commercial Pound is divided into 32 Loths, and weighs 10706 Dutch Asen, or 7940 English Grains. Hence 100lb. of Prague answer to 113,4lb. avoirdupois, or 51,44 Kilogrammes.

The Centner contains 6 Stone of 20lb.

Corn is measured by the Strick, which is divided into 4 Viertels, 16 Massels, or 192 Siedels; and contains 3,03 English Bushels, or 1,067 Hectolitre. This measure is something smaller in Prague than in other parts of Bohemia. Dry Measure.

The Fass of wine is composed of 4 Eimers, 128 Pints, or 512 Seidels; and answers to 67,8 English Gallons, or 256,6 Litres. Liquid Measure.

The Foot of Prague measures 11,88 English Inches, or 0,3017 of a Metre. Long Measures.

The Ell is 23,2 English Inches, or 0,5923 of a Metre.

By an Imperial Edict of 1765, the Austrian weights and measures have been introduced throughout the kingdom of Bohemia, for which see *Vienna*.

Prague exchanges with and gives to— Exchanges.

Amsterdam, 144 Rixdollars, more or less, for 100 Rixdollars.

Augsburg, 100 Florins .... for 100 Florins current.

Breslau, ... 95 Rixdollars .... for 100 Rixdollars Prussian current.

Hamburgh, 144 Rixdollars .... for 100 Rixdollars banco.

Exchanges.

Leipsic, ...	101 Rixdollars, more or less,	for 100 Rixdollars current.
Venice, ...	185 Florins	for 100 Ducati di banco.
Vienna, ...	100 Florins	for 100 Florins current.

Usance and Days of Grace.

The usance is called here 14 days after acceptance. Three days grace are allowed, as in all the Austrian dominions. For the other regulations respecting exchanges, see *Vienna*.

PRESBURG, *see Vienna*.

PRUSSIA.

New System of Weights & Measures.

The present article is intended to explain a new and uniform system of weights and measures, decreed in 1816, for all the Prussian dominions.

For an account of the various systems which have been long established in those countries, see ***Aix la Chapelle, Berlin, Breslau, Cologne, Dantzic, Konigsberg, Stettin, &c.***

This new system is founded on standards already used in certain parts of Prussia, and several other places, viz. the Rhineland Foot as the unit for measures, and the Cologne Mark as the unit for weights.

General Regulations

The outline of the plan is as follows.—A new set of standards, both of weights and measures, is to be made, under the direction of scientific and experienced men; these are to be deposited in the office of the Minister of Finance and Commerce at Berlin, and to be henceforth the only authorised standards throughout the Prussian dominions.

From this set three exact copies shall be taken under the same inspectors; one to be deposited in the office of the Commissioners of Public Buildings, a second with the Mathematical Class of the Academy of Sciences, and a third in the Chamber of Justice.

It shall be incumbent on each of these different bodies every ten years, or as often as occasion may require, to examine the standards committed to their care, in order to ascertain their conformity with the originals, and to publish the results of their comparisons.

Under similar regulations, copies are to be duly distributed, and officers appointed for their superintendence.

The following are the principles of this new system.

This Cologne Mark, which has been hitherto used in the Prussian mint, shall be continued for weighing the precious metals. It equals 3609 English Grains, or 467,711 Grammes. (See Note, page 71.) Weights for the Precious Metals.

The fineness of the precious metals is no longer expressed as heretofore in Carats or Loths, but the Mark for this purpose is divided into 288 Grains.

Two Cologne Marks make the new Prussian Pound, which is the 66th part of the weight of a Rhineland cubic Foot of distilled water, the air being of the temperature of 15° of Reaumur. This Pound is divided, for commercial purposes, into 32 Loths, or 128 Quintins. 100lb. of Prussia equal 103,11lb. avoirdupois, or 46,77 Kilogrammes. The Quintal is 110lb., and the Ship Last 4000lb. Commercial Weight.

The apothecaries' Pound is $\frac{3}{4}$ of the commercial Pound, and is divided into 12 Ounces, 96 Drams, 288 Scruples, or 5760 Grains. Thus the apothecaries' Ounce equals 2 Loths; and the Dram, 1 Quintin. Apothecaries Weight.

Jewels are weighed by Carats, which are divided into halves, quarters, eighths, &c.: 100 of such equal 9 Quintins. This Carat therefore weighs 5,075 English troy Grains, or 3,288 French Decigrammes. Diamond Weight.

The principal corn measure is the Scheffel, which is divided into 16 Metzen, or 48 Quarts; and measures 3072 Prussian cubic Inches, or 3353,6 English cubic Inches; and answers to 1,5594 English Bushel, or 0,54943 of a Hectolitre. Dry Measure.

The principal wine measure is the Eimer, which is divided into 2 Ankers, or 60 Quarts; and measures 3840 Prussian cubic Inches, or 4192 English Inches; and contains 18,14 English Gallons, or 68,67 Litres. Thus, from the proportion of Quarts, it appears that 4 Eimers equal 5 Scheffels. Liquid Measure.

2 Eimers make 1 Ohm, and 3 Eimers 1 Oxhoft or Hogshead.

The Tun, beer measure, contains 100 Quarts; and the Tun for salt, lime, coal, and other dry goods, answers to 4 Berlin Scheffels: 9 such Tuns measure 64 Prussian cubic Feet. The liquid Tun is however an exception, and retains its usual contents; which answer to 37$\frac{1}{2}$ Metzen = 129,34 Litres, or 34,17 English Gallons.

The unit for long measure is the Rhineland or Prussian Foot, which is divided into 12 Inches; and answers to 12,356 English Inches, or 0,3138216 of a Metre. Long Measure.

Long Measure. The Prussian Ell contains 25½ Prussian Inches; which equal 26,256 English Inches, or 0,6669 of a Metre.

The Fathom is 6 Prussian Feet; and the Ruthe is 12. These two measures are decimally divided. The Mile is 2000 Ruthes; and it therefore equals 4,68 English Miles, or 7,532 Kilometres.

Land Measure. The Prussian Morgen or Acre contains 180 square Ruthes; and equals 2 Roods 21 Perches English, or 25,526 French Ares.

RAGUSA (*in Dalmatia*).

Monies of Account. Accounts are kept in Ducats of 40 Grossetti, each Grossetto being divided into 6 Soldi.

Formerly the value of the Ducat was fixed, it being a real coin; but of late years it has been merely a money of account, corresponding with the Turkish Piastre: its value has therefore been decreasing, on account of the constant deterioration of the Turkish coins. See *Constantinople*.

Coins. There are no Gold coins struck at Ragusa. The principal Silver coins are, the Tallaro, commonly called Vislino or Ragusina, which is now worth 3s. 1¾d. sterling; the Ducat, of 40 Grossetti, worth 1s. 1¼d. sterling; the Perpero, of 12 Grossetti, worth 4d. nearly; the half Perpero, and the Grossetto in proportion.

Weights. There is no standard peculiar to Ragusa for gold and silver. The weights used are the Venetian Mark, Ounce, and Dram, from which a deduction is made of 7 per cent. Thus 100 Drams Ragusean are equal to 93 Drams Venetian. See *Venice*.

The commercial weight is the Oke of 3½ Pounds, or 42 Ounces; the Ounce being equal to 10 Drams Peso Sottile of Venice. This Oke is 2 Ounces or 20 Drams heavier than that of Turkey, the latter weighing only 400 Venetian Drams. Thus the Oke of Ragusa weighs 2,953lb. avoirdupois, or 1,339 Kilogramme; and the Pound, 13½ oz. avoirdupois nearly.

Measures. Corn is sold by the Stajo, which is divided into 6 Roupells; and renders 4,218 English Bushels, or 1,486 Hectolitre.

Wine and oil are measured by the Barrel of 84 Centlets. The Barrel contains 20,363 English Gallons, or 77,075 Litres.

The Ell is divided into 8 parts; and measures 20,5 English Inches, or 0,5132 of a Metre. Measures.

These are the weights and measures of the ancient government, which are still in use in the circle of Ragusa. At Cattaro, and in all other parts of Dalmatia, the weights and measures correspond with those of Venice.

In Bosnia, Monte Nigro, and other parts of Turkey on the confines of Dalmatia, the weights and measures are regulated by those of Constantinople.*

RATISBON OR REGENSBURG (*in Germany*).

Accounts are kept here, and in the rest of Bavaria, in Florins or Guldens of 60 Creutzers, each Florin being divided into 4 Pfenings. Monies of Account.

The Florin is also divided into 15 Batzen, 20 Kaysergroschen, 24 Landmuntzen, 30 Albuses, 60 Creutzers, 240 Pfenings, or 480 Hellers.

Hence the Rixdollar current, which equals $1\frac{1}{2}$ Florin, contains $22\frac{1}{2}$ Batzen, 30 Kaysergroschen, 36 Landmuntzen, 45 Albuses, 90 Creutzers, 360 Pfenings, or 520 Hellers.

The monies of Ratisbon are distinguished into white money and black money (*Weisse muntze* and *Schwartz muntze*); the former of which is chiefly used in common transactions of business, and the latter in the payment of taxes and other contributions to government.

The divisions of the white money are as above: the black money is divided as follows:

The Pfund is composed of 41 Schillings, 164 Groschen, 492 Ratisboninas, 1230 Pfenings, or 2360 Hellers.

The Pfundfening contains 8 Schillings, 32 Groschen, or 96 Ratisboninas.

The proportion between these monies is as follows:

7 Pfunds, black money, equal 41 Florins, white money.

7 Pfundfenings, black money, equal 8 Florins, white money.

1 Florin, white money, equals 7 Schillings, black money.

A distinction is also made between Convention money and Muntze or small coins; the Cologne Mark of fine silver being reckoned at 20 Florins Convention money, and 24 Florins Muntze.

---

* The above account of the weights and measures of Dalmatia has been chiefly extracted from the dispatches of *Thomas Turner, Esq.* the British Consul at *Ragusa*, as transmitted to *Lord Castlereagh*, in 1818.

Coins.

The coins of the city are, Ducats of 5 Florins 14 Creutzers each; Convention Rixdollars of 2 Florins, Convention money, or 2 Florins 24 Creutzers, in Muntze; Convention Florins of 1 Florin 12 Creutzers, in Muntze; Pieces of 30, 20, and 10 Creutzers, Convention money, or 36, 24, and 12 Creutzers, Muntze.

Foreign coins pass here as in *Munich.*

Value of Monies.

The Rixdollar of account, of 1½ Florin, valued according to the Convention rate of coinage, may be reckoned at 364,8 German Asen, or 270½ English Grains of fine silver; but the same Rixdollar, valued in small coins, answers to 304 Asen, or 225½ Grains of fine silver. Hence the Convention Rixdollar is worth 37½d., and the Rixdollar in small coins, 31½d. sterling.

Weights.

Three different weights are used here for the precious metals:

The first is employed in weighing gold, and is called Crown Weight: it is composed of 128 Crowns, and answers to 6630 English Grains, or 429,592 Grammes.

The second serves to weigh Ducats: it is composed of 11 parts, and corresponds with 64 Ducats; it weighs 3449 English Grains, or 223,507 Grammes.

The third is used for weighing silver: it is the Mark composed of 8 Ounces; the Ounce is divided into halves, quarters, and eighths. The Eighth of the Ounce is called the Drachm, which is divided into halves, quarters, and eighths of a Drachm. This Mark weighs 3791 English Grains, or 246,028 Grammes.

Commercial Weight.

The Pound, commercial weight, is divided into 2 Marks, 16 Ounces, 32 Loths, 128 Quintins, or 512 Pfenings; and answers to 8777 English Grains. Hence 100lb. of Ratisbon equal 125,4lb. avoirdupois, or 56,86 Kilogrammes.

Dry Measure.

The Schaff, corn measure, is divided into 4 Maasses, 16 Vierlings, or 32 Metzen; and renders 29,78 English Bushels, or 10,49 Hectolitres. The Schaff of oats is 28 Vierlings, or 56 Metzen.

Liquid Measure.

The great Eimer of wine is divided into 32 Viertels, 88 Kopfen, or 176 Seidels; and contains 30,01 English Gallons, or 113,6 Litres. The Berg Eimer is 68 Kopfen, or 136 Seidels.

Long Measure.

The Foot of Ratisbon equals 11,42 English Inches, or 0,2899 of a Metre.

The Ell is 31,9 English Inches, or 0,811 of a Metre.

REGGIO, *see Modena.*

REVAL *(in Russia).*

Monies of Account.

Accounts are kept here, as at Petersburg, in Rubles of 10 Grieveners, or 100 Copecks; and sometimes in Rixdollars of 80 Copecks, or 64 Wittens. The Thaler is 52 Wittens, or 65 Copecks. Thus 4 Rubles = 5 Rixdollars, and 4 Wittens = 5 Copecks.

Coins.

The current coins of the country are those of Russia, which see.

There is also the Livonina, coined by order of the Empress Elizabeth in 1757, at 96 Copecks; but raised by the coinage of 1764 to the value of 112 Copecks, with halves and quarters in proportion. There are besides pieces of 4 and 2 Copecks.

Weights.

The Mark, gold weight, is divided into 16 Loths, 64 Quentins, or 256 Oertlins; and contains 3326 English Grains, or 215,498 Grammes.

The Pound, commercial weight, is divided into 32 Loths, and also into halves, quarters, eighths, &c.; and contains 6652 English Grains. Thus 100lb. of Reval answer to 95,03lb. avoirdupois, or 43,1 Kilogrammes. Silver is weighed by this standard.

The Lispond consists of 20lb.; and the Shipfund of 20 Lisponds. The Tonne contains 2 Centners, 12 Lisponds, or 240lb.

Dry Measure.

The Tonne of corn is divided into 3 Lofs, 9 Kulmits, or 108 Stofs. The Last of corn contains 24 Tonnen of 3 Lofs; the Last of salt is 18 Tonnen of 4 Lofs; the Last of herrings 12 Tonnen of 4 Lofs. The Tonne of corn renders 3,356 English Bushels, or 1,182 Hectolitre.

Liquid Measure.

The Stoof is the principal liquid measure, $32\frac{1}{2}$ of which make an Anker; and 4 Ankers, or 130 Stoofs, make a Cask or Ahm. The Stoof contains 1,375 English Quart, or 1,301 Litre; and the Oxhoft is therefore equal to 67,03 English Gallons, or 253,71 Litres.

Long Measures.

The Foot of Reval is divided into 12 Inches; and measures 10,53 English Inches, or 0,2677 of a Metre. The Ell is 2 Feet; the Fathom, 6 Feet.

Weights, &c.

The weights and measures of Reval are used in Hapsal, Baltic Port, Wesenberg, Weissenstein, and all other parts of the government of Esthonia.*

RIGA *(in Russia)*.

Monies of Account.

Accounts are kept here in Rixdollars of 80 Ferdings, or 90 Groschen; and also in Rubles of 100 Copecks, as at Petersburg.

Different Sorts of Money.

The Rixdollar is valued in two different sorts of money; Alberts and Riga currency.

Alberts money consists of Dutch Alberts Dollars, half Dollars and quarters, called Orts. Spanish Dollars were formerly taken for the same value; but those coined since 1772 lose about 6 per cent. against Alberts Dollars. Under this denomination are also included the Saxon, Brandenburg, and Luneburg Pieces of 2 Groschen, and old Swedish 5 Oer Sticks, 16 of which are reckoned for 1 Alberts Dollar, though they commonly bear a discount of about 3 per cent. The Gulden or Florin of 30 Alberts Groschen, is an imaginary money, in which accounts are sometimes kept, as in the oak timber trade.

Riga currency consists of the current coins of the country; and the current Rixdollar is divided into 11¼ Marks of Riga, 30 Marks Ferding, 60 Ferdings, or 90 current Groschen.

Currency is commonly reckoned 33⅓ per cent. worse than Alberts Dollars, the Dollar being valued at 15 Marks of Riga, 40 Marks Ferding, 80 Ferdings, or 120 current Groschen. The agio on Alberts Dollars, however, sometimes rises above 40 per cent., and the Dollar is then worth from 84 to 86 Ferdings.

The current Rixdollar is an imaginary money; the Riga Mark is a very old silver coin, which has long ceased to be current, but of which the name has been preserved as a money of account, particularly in the hempseed trade; the Mark Ferding is another old coin, which is still sometimes to be met with; as is also the Ferding, under which name some old Polish, Prussian, Swedish, and Livonian coins are included.

The Grosche in both sorts of money is imaginary.

* The weights and measures, both of Reval and Riga, as stated in the present edition, are taken from the dispatches and standards transmitted to *Lord Castlereagh* in 1818 by *Sir Daniel Bayley*, His Majesty's Consul General for Russia. They differ in many respects from the statements hitherto published.

139 Rubles are commonly reckoned for 100 Alberts Dollars, or 139 Copecks for 1 Alberts Dollar. Different Sorts of Money.

Coins. The coins chiefly current here are the Russian coins, and the Livonina, which has been mentioned under the article *Reval.* The Livonina, of 112 Copecks, passes for about 70 Ferdings, and the others in proportion.

Dutch Ducats are commonly valued at 2 Alberts Dollars; when they are new and full weight, however, they bear a premium of 3 to 6 Alberts Groschen for each Ducat.

Polish currency passes at the rate of about 180 Polish Groschen for 1 Alberts Dollar.

Value of Monies. The intrinsic value of the Alberts Dollar is 4s. 4½d. sterling; hence £1 sterling = 4 Rixdollars 52 Groschen Alberts; and, taking the difference at 40 per cent. a current Rixdollar of Riga = 37½d. sterling; or £1 sterling = 6 Rixdollars 36 Groschen, Riga currency.

Gold and Silver Weight. Gold and silver are weighed by the Mark. The Mark of fine gold is reckoned at 24 Carats of 12 Grains; and the Mark of fine silver at 16 Loths of 18 Grains, both making in all 288 Grains. Wrought silver must be 13 Loths fine.

This Mark is half a Pound of the Riga commercial weight; and equals 3226 English Grains, or 209,052 Grammes.

The commercial Pound is divided into 2 Marks, or 32 Loths; and also into halves, quarters, &c. It contains 6452 English Grains. Thus 100lb. of Riga answer to 92,17lb. avoirdupois, or 41,80 Kilogrammes.

The Lispound is 20lb.; the Shippound, 20 Lispounds.

Dry Measure. The Loop is the measure for grain, &c.; 48 of which, or 24 Tonnen, make the Last of wheat, barley, and linseed; 45 Loops make the Last of rye; and 60 that of oats. The Loop equals 1,9375 English Bushel, or 0,68269 of a Hectolitre.

Liquid Measure. The Anker consists of 5 Viertels, or 30 Stoofs. The Hogshead is 6 Ankers, 30 Viertels, or 180 Stoofs. The Anker equals 10,33 English Gallons, or 39,1 Litres.

Long Measure. The Foot of Riga contains 12 Inches, and is equal to 10,79 English Inches, or 0,274 of a Metre. The Ell is 2 Feet, and the Clafter 6 Feet.

10 Russian Archeens are equal to 13 Riga Ells.

Long Measure. Masts are measured by Palms of 3 Riga Inches, or 2,7 English Inches.

A Last of French or Portuguese salt, out of the ship, contains 18 Tonnes, each of 18 Lisponds.

A Last of barrelled salt is 16 Tonnes, each of 18 Lisponds.

A Last of fine salt, linseed, potash, herrings, tar, beer, &c. is 12 Tonnes.

A Last of Liverpool white salt is 18 Barrels, and weighs about $2\frac{1}{2}$ Tons avoirdupois.

Exchanges. Riga exchanges with and gives (more or less) to—.

Amsterdam, ...	100 Rixdollars Alberts,	for	103 Rixdollars.
Dantzic, ...	1 Rixdollar Alberts,	for	160 Polish Groschen.
Hamburgh and Lubec,	103 Rixdollars Alberts,	for	100 Rixdollars banco.
Konigsberg, ...	1 Rixdollar Alberts,	for	130 Prussian Groschen.
London, ...	400 Groschen, ...	for	£1 sterling.

For the regulations respecting the payment of bills of exchange, see ***Russia***.

RIO DE JANEIRO (*in Brazil*).

Monies of Account. Accounts are kept here, as in Portugal, in Rees, Reis, or Reas, 1000 making the Milrea: 100,000 being one hundred Milreas; and 1000,000 one thousand Milreas, commonly called a *Conto* of Reis.

Coins. The Gold coins are Pieces of 1,000, 2,000, and 4,000 Rees each; besides the coins of Portugal, for which see ***Lisbon***.

The Silver coins are Pieces of 60, 75, 80, 120, 150, 160, 240, 300, 320, 480, 600, and 640 Rees. The Piece of 320 Reis is called the Pataca, and that of 480 Reis the Cruzado Novo.

The Copper coins are Vintems of 20 Reis, with half and quarter Vintems; and also Two-Vintem Pieces. For the sterling value of these coins see ***Lisbon***.

Foreign Coins. Foreign coins, particularly those of Spain, pass mostly according to their market value; but Spanish Dollars, when re-stamped by the Royal Mint, are issued at 960 Rees, which equal Three Patacas, or a Double Crusado.

Currency in Gold Bars. The metallic circulation of the country is still further increased by the currency of bars or ingots of gold, of various sizes and assays; but each accompanied by its proper certificate of value, which is thus ascertained :—

The gold dust deposited in the beds of the various streams is a common right, but when found is by law bound to be carried to the Royal Smelting Houses *(Cazas de Fundiçao)* established in various districts; where, one-fifth of it being retained *(in natura)* for the Royal *Quinto*, a Bar is made of the remainder, which is weighed, assayed, numbered, stamped, and returned to the owner, accompanied by a certificate, signed by the proper officers, shewing the value of such Bar, calculated at 1,500 Reis per Octave of $\frac{11}{12}$ fine. These Bars serve as a circulating medium, but it is strictly prohibited to export them. They are ultimately carried to the Royal Mint at Rio de Janeiro, where they are received at 1,500 Reis per Octave, and paid for in gold coin valued at 1,600 Reis per Octave; the King retaining a seignorage of $6\frac{2}{3}$ per cent. in addition to the Quinto, or 20 per cent. previously taken on the gold dust. The latter sometimes serves as a circulating medium. Currency in Gold Bars.

The annual produce of gold in Brazil, which is chiefly from the *Minas Geraes*, has been formerly computed at about 300 Arobas (worth about half a million sterling); but it is supposed of late years to have diminished.

This computation has been made from the Quinto paid to the King, which, however, is not considered an accurate criterion of the whole produce.

The weights and measures here are understood to be the same as those of Portugal; but there are exceptions with respect to measures of capacity, especially in other parts of the Brazils, for which see *Brazil.** Weights & Measures.

The exchanges of Rio de Janeiro are similar to those of Portugal, except that no national paper is adopted. Thus London gives to Rio de Janeiro 60d. more or less for the Milrea, reckoned in specie. Exchanges.

ROCHELLE *(in France)*.

Accounts are kept here in Francs and Centimes, as in the rest of France. Monies and Coins.

The coins, and also the weights and measures according to different systems, will be found explained in the article *France.*

* The weights here are very accurately adjusted to those of Portugal, as appears by the different standards lately transmitted to London by *Henry Chamberlain, Esq.* Consul General for Brazil; *Robert Hesketh, Esq.* Consul at Maranham; and *William Pennell, Esq.* Consul at Bahia.

Measures. The ancient measures still in use are the following:

Corn is measured by the Tonneau of 42 Boisseaux. The Boisseau of wheat weighs about 52lb. Poids de Marc; and renders 0,933 of an English Bushel, or 0,3289 of a Hectolitre.

The Hundred of salt contains 28 Muids, each of 24 Boisseaux; it corresponds to $1\frac{3}{4}$ Hondert of Amsterdam, or $12\frac{1}{2}$ Lasts in Hamburgh.

A Muid of coals is 80 Bailles; $11\frac{3}{4}$ Muids = 52 Newcastle Chaldrons.

Brandy from Rochelle, Cognac, Isle de Rhé, and Charente, is in Casks of 3 Barriques, containing in all 75 or 90 Veltes; and is sold by the 27 Veltes. The Velte equals 1,93 English Gallon, or 7,30 Litres.

A Barrique of wine from Rochelle contains 46,04 English Gallons, or 174,27 Litres. The Tonneau is 4 Barriques.

The Aune or Ell measures 46,5 English Inches, or 1,182 Metre.*

ROME *(in Italy)*.

Monies of Account. Accounts are kept here in Crowns or Scudi, called Scudi Romani, and Scudi Moneta; each Scudo is divided into 10 Paoli or Giuli, and each Paolo into 10 Bajocchi.

The Scudo is likewise divided into $3\frac{1}{3}$ Testoni, 500 Quattrini, or 1000 Mezzi Quattrini. Thus 5 Quattrini make 1 Paolo, and 3 Paoli 1 Testone.

The Scudo di Stampa d'Oro, by which many of the foreign exchanges are regulated, is reckoned at 1523 or 1525 Mezzi Quattrini; that is, when a bill is drawn from Rome on a foreign place, the Scudo di Stampa d'Oro is reckoned at 1523 Mezzi Quattrini; but when drawn from another place on Rome, it is reckoned at 1525: this Scudo is divided into 20 Soldi, or 240 Denari.

The Ducato d'Oro di Camera is reckoned at 16 Paoli.

The French monies and weights were introduced here in 1809. The Scudo was reckoned at 5 Francs 35 Cents, answering to 4s. 3d. sterling; and the Franc was therefore valued at 18 Bajocchi 3,45 Quattrini.

Coins. The coins here, even of modern date, are various, as a new coinage is struck by every Pope, and even by the Apostolic Chamber during each Interregnum. The new issues of money, however, in some measure supplant the old, which are

* These proportions are chiefly deduced from the dispatches lately transmitted to London, with standards, by *J. Close, Esq.*, His Majesty's Consul at Charente.

sometimes called in; others are sold by weight; and some kept in the cabinets of the curious as medals. Coins.

The following are the principal Gold coins at present in circulation.

Zecchini or Sequins, at $21\frac{1}{2}$ Paoli, with their doubles and halves in proportion; new Doppie or Pistoles, at $31\frac{1}{2}$ Paoli. The Silver coins are, Scudi Romani, and half ditto; Testoni, at 3 Paoli; Papette, at 2 Paoli; single Paoli; Grossi, and half ditto, at 5 and $2\frac{1}{2}$ Bajocchi. There are, in base silver, double and single Carlini, at 15 and $7\frac{1}{2}$ Bajocchi; double and single Bajocchelli, at 4 and 2 Bajocchi. In Copper, Bajocchi, halves, and Quattrini.

The Sequin is to weigh 2 Denari $21\frac{818}{1000}$ Grains, or $52\frac{9}{10}$ English Grains; and the gold is $23\frac{5}{8}$ Carats fine: thus it contains a little more than 52 Grains of pure gold, and is therefore worth 9s. 3d. sterling. This Sequin being reckoned at $21\frac{1}{2}$ Paoli, the Roman Crown or Scudo is worth about 4s. $3\frac{1}{2}$d. sterling, valued in gold. Value of Coins.

The Scudo weighs 22 Denari $10\frac{73}{100}$ Grains, Roman weight, or $408\frac{15}{100}$ English Grains; and the silver is $10\frac{23}{24}$ Ounces fine in the Pound: it contains, therefore, 403 Grains of English standard silver, and is worth 4s. 4d. sterling. The Scudo di Stampa d'Oro, of 1523 Mezzi Quattrini, is worth 6s. $7\frac{1}{4}$d. sterling; and the Paolo, $5\frac{1}{4}$d. sterling nearly, or £1 sterling = 4 Scudi 62 Bajocchi, valued in silver at 5s. 2d. per oz. standard.

All payments above 5 Scudi are made in Cedole or Schedules, a sort of bank notes, which cannot be refused in payment, and which are constantly at a discount. These Cedole are issued by the two banks, called *Dello Spirito Santo* and *Monte di Pieta*, which never pay but a small proportion of the value in specie (at most 5 per cent.), and give smaller notes for the rest. They are not payable to order, but to bearer, and cannot therefore be indorsed, nor can cash be procured for them without some loss. Bank Notes.

The Roman Pound, or Libra, is divided into 12 Once, 288 Denari, or 6912 Grani; and contains 5234 English Grains, or 339,121 Grammes. Ten Pounds form a weight called the Decina. Gold and Silver Weight.

The medicinal Pound is the same weight as the above, but differently divided. Thus the Ounce is composed of 8 Drams, 24 Scrupoli, or 576 Grani. These Grains correspond to the Grains of the commercial Pound, and are further subdivided into 24 parts. Apothecaries' Weight.

Commercial Weight.

The same Pound weight is used for merchandise as for gold and silver: thus 100 Roman Pounds equal 74,77lb. avoirdupois, or 33,912 Kilogrammes. There are, however, three different Cantaros or Quintals, namely, of 100lb., 160lb., and 250lb., and also the Migliajo of 1000lb.

In all sales of merchandise by the Cantaro, 4lb. per cent. are allowed; 2lb. of which go to the Chamber of Commerce, and 2lb. to the buyer for good weight.

The freight of ships is computed by the weight of the Rubbio of corn, which is 640lb. The Rubbio of salt is 600lb.; the Rubbio of peas, beans, &c. 720lb.; the Peso or Load of quick lime, 400lb.; the Load of hay, 300lb.*

Dry Measure.

The Rubbio contains 4 Quarte, 22 Scorzi, or 88 Quartucci; and is sometimes divided into 12, and also into 16 Stari. The Rubbio answers to 2,9446 Hectolitres, or 8,356 Winchester Bushels.

In measuring salt, the Rubbio is divided into 2 Quarte, 12 Scorzi, or 48 Quartucci. Chalk is sold by the Decina.

Liquid Measure.

The Barile of wine contains 32 Boccali, or 128 Fogliette: it is also divided into halves and quarters. The Barile answers to 58,3416 Litres, or 15,409 English Gallons; consequently the Boccale = 1,926 Quart.

The Botte is composed of 16 Barili.

The Barile of oil is divided into 28 Boccali, 112 Fogliette, or 448 Quartucce; and equals 57,4806 Litres, or 15,18 English Gallons.

The Soma of oil, which is used in wholesale trade, is composed of 80 Boccali; being divided into 2 Pelli or Mastelli, or 20 Cugnatelle, each of 4 Boccali. The Soma corresponds to 164,23 Litres, or 43,38 English Gallons.

---

* The Roman Pound, though very generally known and referred to, is not uniformly described as to its contents. *Ricard* makes it correspond to 5239 English Grains; *Kruse*, to 5236; and *Tillet*, to 5235. Others vary still more; but the standards recently transmitted to London by the British Consuls, *John Parke, Esq.* of Rome, and *Charles Denis, Esq.* of Civita Vecchia, are rather lighter than the above, and nearly agree with its proportion to the Kilogramme, as stated in Tables published by the Commission of Weights and Measures at Rome in 1811. It appears from these documents, that the actual weight of the Roman Pound is 5234 English Grains; which perfectly accords with the computations in *Paucton's Métrologie*, published at Paris in 1780.

It cannot be uninteresting here to take some notice of the ancient Libra of Rome, which perhaps is better ascertained than any other weight of antiquity. According to *Dr. Arbuthnot*, it answered to 5246 English Grains, which, if correct, shews that it has lost about $\frac{1}{4}$ of a Grain per century; and it is worthy of remark that this nearly corresponds with the diminution that has been recently ascertained to have taken place in the English standard Pound used at His Majesty's Exchequer since the year 1588.

The Roman Foot equals 0,297895 of a Metre, or 11,72 English Inches. Long Measure.

The Canna called mercantile = 1,99 Metre, or 78,34 English Inches; and is divided into 8 Palmi, or 24 Parti.

The builders' Canna measures 2,234 Metres, or 87,96 English Inches; and is divided into 10 Palmi, each Palmo into 12 Once, 60 Minuti, or 120 Decimi.

The Roman mile equals 1,4894 Kilometre, or $7\frac{2}{5}$ English Furlongs, or 1628 English Yards. Thus, 40 Roman miles = 37 English miles nearly.

For the exchanges of Rome, see Vol. II. page 86. Exchanges.

Rome draws on most places at usance, which is 3 weeks after acceptance; but bills on Paris are drawn at from 30 to 90 days date, and on London at 3 months. Usance, &c.

Bills drawn on Rome at usance, from any part of the ecclesiastical states, are accepted on the Wednesday or the Saturday: bills from foreign parts are generally accepted on the Saturday in the week in which they are received, except those from the kingdom of Naples, which are accepted on the Friday. Protests for non-acceptance or non-payment are to take place on those days. The usance is properly two weeks after acceptance, and it has been the constant practice of bankers to pay their bills at the expiration of the 14 days; a week of grace, however, is allowed, and merchants and all other traders, except bankers, avail themselves of it. This week is understood in the following manner:—bills accepted on a Friday or Saturday are paid 21 days after acceptance; but the period for bills accepted on a Wednesday is only 18 days. Bills drawn at so many days sight, must be paid on the day their written term expires.

ROSTOCK *(in Germany)*.

Accounts are kept here in Rixdollars of 48 Schillings, or Marks of 16 Schillings current, the Schilling being divided into 12 Pfenings. Monies of Account.

The Rixdollar contains $1\frac{1}{2}$ Reichs Gulden, 2 Mecklenburg Guldens, 3 Marks, 24 Good Groschen, 192 Wittens, or 576 Pfenings.

A Reichs Gulden, or Piece of two-thirds, is worth 2 Marks or 16 Groschen; a Mecklenburg Gulden, $1\frac{1}{2}$ Mark or 12 Groschen; a Grosche, 2 Schillings; a Schilling, 4 Wittens.

The current coins of the Duchy of Mecklenburg are Pieces of 32, 16, 12, 8, 4, 2, and 1 Schillings; and 6 and 3 Pfenings current. Coins.

Coins. The Ducat is here worth 7 Marks 8 Schillings, more or less; the Frederick d'Or, 13 Marks 4 Schillings; and the Piece of two-thirds, coined after the Leipsic rate, 30 Schillings, in the currency of Mecklenburg: or the Ducat is reckoned at $2\frac{3}{4}$ Rixdollars, with about 10 per cent. discount against currency; the Frederick d'Or, at 5 Rixdollars, with about 13 per cent.; and the Piece of two-thirds, at 2 Marks, with about 6 per cent.

Value of Monies. The Cologne Mark of fine silver is coined at the rate of $11\frac{1}{3}$ Rixdollars, or 34 Marks, in Pieces of 2 Schillings to 32 Schillings; thus the Rixdollar contains 429,18 Asen, or $318\frac{1}{3}$ English Grains of fine silver. It is therefore worth 3s. $8\frac{1}{2}$d. sterling, and the Mark about 15d. sterling. Thus the currency of Rostock and Mecklenburg is of the same value as Hamburgh currency.

Weights. Gold and silver are weighed with the Cologne Mark, as at Hamburgh.

The commercial weight is also the same as that of Hamburgh and Lubec.

Besides these weights, ordered by Duke Frederick, in 1757, there is also a public town standard, under the name of the Rostock weight, chiefly used in the trade with Russia, which is 5 per cent. heavier than the above. Thus the Rostock Pound contains 7852 English Grains; and 100lb. of Rostock correspond to 112lb. avoirdupois, or 50,87 Kilogrammes.

The Shippond for merchandise is 20 Lisponds, or 320lb.; the Shippond of lead and iron is 280lb.; the Centner is 8 Lisponds; the Lispond, 20lb.; the Stone of flax, 20lb.; the Stone of wool or feathers, 10lb.

Measures of Capacity. The Scheffel is divided into 4 Fasser, or 16 Spints; and contains 38,89 Litres, or 1,103 English Bushel. The Last is composed of 8 Dromts, or 96 Scheffels.

The Last of oats answers to 41,96 Hectolitres, or 14,91 English Quarters. The Last of other sorts of grain renders 37,334 Hectolitres, or 13,244 English Quarters. The measures for liquids are the same as at Lubec.

Long Measures. The Rostock Foot = 11,38 English Inches = 0,2891 of a Metre. The Mecklenburg Foot = 11,45 English Inches = 0,2909 of a Metre. The Ell is 2 Feet.*

---

* This account of the weights and measures of Mecklenburg is chiefly deduced from documents transmitted in 1818 by *V. S. Brömse, Esq.* His Majesty's Vice Consul at Rostock. It should be observed, that the weight of the commercial Pound, as above given, perfectly agrees with the Tables of *Kruse* and *Nelkenbreker*, but is 35 Grains lighter than the weight stated by *Ricard* and *Dubost*.

ROTTERDAM *(in Holland).*

Accounts were formerly kept here, as at Amsterdam, in Gilders or Florins of 20 Stivers; and the Stiver was divided into 16 Pfenings; but the New Monetary System of the Kingdom of the Netherlands has been lately adopted, for which see *Netherlands*. Monies and Coins.

For the other monies of account, as well as for the real coins of the country, see also *Amsterdam*.

The weight for gold and silver is the Dutch troy, for which see *Amsterdam*, page 9. Weights.

Two different commercial Pounds are used in Rotterdam; one is the Amsterdam weight, 100lb. of which are equal to 108,93lb. avoirdupois, or 49,40 Kilogrammes; the other is 5 per cent. lighter, and is used only by retailers. 100lb. of the latter weight answer to 103,48lb. avoirdupois, or 46,93 Kilogrammes.

The Last of corn contains 29 Sacks, or 87 Agtendeels: a Hoed is $10\frac{2}{3}$ Sacks, or 32 Agtendeels. The Agtendeel is divided into 4 Vierlings or 16 Maats; and equals 0,978 of an English Bushel, or 0,3448 of a Hectolitre. Thus 87 Agtendeels are commonly reckoned for 86 English Bushels. Hence a Last of Rotterdam renders 10,642 English Quarters, or 30 Hectolitres. Dry Measures.

Salt is sold by the Hondert of 404 Maats. The Maat weighs $103\frac{1}{2}$lb. avoirdupois, or 46,94 Kilogrammes.

Coals are sold by the Hoed; and 9 Hoeds answer to 5 Newcastle Chaldrons.

The principal liquid measure is the Stoop, which is divided into 2 Kannes, 4 Pints, or 16 Muschjes; and contains 5,332 English Pints, or 2,523 Litres. The Ahm is 4 Ankers or 60 Stoops; and therefore equals 39,99 English Gallons, or 151,38 Litres. Brandy is sold by the 30 Viertels or Veltes; which equal 59,44 English Gallons, or 225 Litres. Liquid Measures.

Oil of olives and train oil are sold by the Tonne of 340 Stoops. The Stoop weighs 5lb. of Rotterdam, light or retail weight: hence the Tonne weighs about 1763lb. avoirdupois, or 799 Kilogrammes.

Long Measures. The Rhineland Foot is used here, and answers to 12,356 English Inches, or 0,3138 of a Metre. The Ell is 27,2 English Inches, or 0,690 of a Metre.

New Weights & Measures. For the New System of Weights and Measures, see *Netherlands;* and for Exchanges and other particulars, see *Amsterdam*, Vols. I. and II.

Commercial Allowances The commercial allowances established for Holland in 1817, will be found under the article *Amsterdam;* but the following alterations were made in the beginning of the year 1821.

Coffee is to be quoted per half Kilogramme; and the allowances of 2 and 2 per cent. on the money hitherto granted, will be supplied by a simple deduction of 1 per cent. for prompt payment.

Bags and casks are to be weighed in whole Kilogrammes, without taking any account of fractional parts, and without any tacit allowances whatever.

The tare on bags remains at 3 per cent.; and to the real tare of casks, 1 Kilogramme is to be added, and 1 per cent. deducted for overweight.

Cotton will in future be quoted in half Kilogrammes; and the tail allowance of 6lb. per bale will not be deducted.

ROUEN *(in France).*

Monies, &c. For the monies and coins of Rouen, see *France.*

Old Weights. Besides the decimal weights and measures (for which see *France),* the following are used here, namely, the common French Poids de Marc, and a peculiar weight called Poids de Vicomté, 6 per cent. heavier. Thus the Quintal of 100lb. Poids de Vicomté weighs 117,73lb. avoirdupois, or 53,39 Kilogrammes.

Old Measures. The Muid of corn is divided into 12 Setiers, 24 Mines, or 96 Boisseaux; and answers to 60,93 English Bushels, or 21,47 Hectolitres.

Brandy is mostly sold by the Barrique of 120 Pots; which equals 51,688 English Gallons, or 195,64 Litres.

The Aune used for measuring linens is 55 English Inches, or 1,3967 Metre: that used for silks and woollens is 45,8 English Inches, or 1,1639 Metre.

RUSSIA.

Accounts are kept here in Rubles of 100 Copecks. **Monies of Account.**

The Ruble is also divided into 10 Grievens, 33$\frac{1}{3}$ Altins, or 50 Groschen; and the Copeck is divided into 2 Denushkas, or 4 Polushkas.

The Gold coins are, the Imperial, and Half Imperial, of 10 and 5 Rubles, with Ducats double and single; the double Ducat being worth 5 Rubles 60 Copecks, and the single, 2 Rubles 80 Copecks. **Coins.**

The Silver coins are, Rubles of 100 Copecks; Poltins of 50 Copecks; Polpoltins of 25 Copecks; double and single Grieven of 20 and 10 Copecks; also Pieces of 5 Altins or 15 Copecks.

The Copper coins are, Pieces of 10, 5, 2, and 1 Copecks; also Denushkas, or Half Copecks, and Polushkas, or Quarter Copecks.

The fineness both of gold and silver is expressed in Solotnicks; the Pound or other weight being divided into 96 Solotnicks, and the Solotnick subdivided into 96 parts, called Dolis. **Expression of Fineness.**

Several changes have been made here in the rate of coinage: thus, by the *Ukase*, or Edict of 1763, the Imperial was to weigh 3$\frac{3}{44}$ Solotnicks; the Half Imperial, 1$\frac{47}{88}$ Solotnick; and the gold to be 88 Solotnicks, or 22 Carats fine. Also 118 Ducats were to weigh a Russian Pound, 93 Solotnicks, or 23$\frac{1}{4}$ Carats fine. Thus such Imperial, valued in English gold, was worth £1 12s. 9$\frac{1}{2}$d., and the Ducat, 9s. 1d. **Rate of Coinage.**

From the Pound of silver were to be struck 17 Rubles 6$\frac{2}{3}$ Copecks, of the fineness of 72 Solotnicks, or 9 Ounces; making the Ruble worth, in English silver, 3s. 3d. Copper was coined at the rate of 16 Rubles per Pood of 40lb. Russian.

By an Edict of 1801, the Russian Pound of fine silver was coined into 22$\frac{3}{4}$ Rubles of the fineness of 83$\frac{1}{3}$ Solotnicks, or 10 dwt. 8 gr.; which makes the value of the Ruble, in English silver, 3s. 2$\frac{1}{2}$d. The standard of the Imperial and Half Imperial was raised to 94$\frac{1}{2}$ Solotnicks, or 23$\frac{5}{8}$ Carats.

According to the Edict of 1810, the standard fineness of the silver Ruble, and its divisions, denominated Bank Money, was fixed at 83$\frac{1}{3}$ Solotnicks. 100

Rate of Coinage.

Rubles were ordered to be coined out of 5lb. 6 Solotnicks of that standard; each Ruble to contain 4 Solotnicks 21 Dolis of fine silver. Hence from a Pound of Russian standard silver were struck 19 Rubles 75 Copecks nearly; and from a Pound of fine s lver, 22 Rubles $75\frac{1}{2}$ Copecks. Thus the Ruble of 1810 is worth $38\frac{3}{4}$d. sterling very nearly.

The same Edict directed that pieces of 5, 10, and 20 Copecks should be coined, according to the old standard of $\frac{72}{96}$, with smaller pieces in proportion; and that each piece of 20 Copecks should contain $1\frac{12}{96}$ Solotnick of silver, of the standard of $\frac{72}{96}$, or $\frac{81}{96}$ Dolis of fine silver; whence 5 pieces of 20 Copecks or 1 Ruble would contain $4\frac{21}{96}$ Solotnicks of fine silver: but great inconvenience having been experienced from two different standards, the whole of the silver coinage was placed on the same footing of $83\frac{1}{3}$, by the Ukase of August, 1813, and no alteration has since taken place.

The only gold coin at present struck is the Half Imperial, or Five Ruble Piece.

The Ukase of 1817 restores the standard of gold to $\frac{88}{96}$, and directs that each Half Imperial shall contain $1\frac{39}{96}$ Solotnick of pure gold; and that 66 Half Imperials, 2 Rubles, $88\frac{8}{9}$ Copecks, shall be struck out of a Pound of standard gold. Hence the Half Imperial is worth 15s. 8d. sterling nearly, and its gold Ruble the fifth part of that sum.

The copper coinage, as fixed in 1810, consists of pieces of 2 Copecks, 1 Copeck, and half a Copeck. The Pood of 40lb. is coined into 24 Rubles, or 2400 Copecks.

Mint Regulations

It is declared by the Ukase of 1810, that all expenses incident to the coinage of gold and silver, shall be borne by the Crown, except a small deduction for refining, where the fineness of such shall be found to be below the proof of $\frac{64}{96}$, or $\frac{2}{3}$.

Although the regulation of the Mint directs that silver coin shall be delivered for silver received, yet it reserves to itself the option of delivering either gold or silver, when gold is delivered. In those cases where silver is delivered, the regular equivalent for a Solotnick of pure gold is 3 Rubles 55 Copecks of silver coin.

The Mint further reserves to itself the option of delivering for every Pound of gold, of the proof of $\frac{94}{96}$, $117\frac{1}{2}$ Dutch Ducats; and the value of the Ducat is reckoned at 2 Rubles 85 Copecks of silver.

The Russian Pound is the same for gold, silver, and merchandize. It is divided into 32 Loths, or 96 Solotnicks; and answers to 6318,5 English Grains.* Hence 100lb. Russian equal 90,26lb. avoirdupois, or 40,93 Kilogrammes. Weights.

40 Russian Pounds make 1 Pood, and 10 Poods = 1 Berquit or Berkowitz. Thus the Pood weighs 36lb. 1 oz. 11 dr. avoirdupois, or 16,37 Kilogrammes. The ordinary computation among merchants is, that the Pood = 36lb. avoirdupois.

It should be observed that all the Government Hospitals, civil and military, and Apothecaries, make use of the Nuremberg Pound, with its divisions; and for diamonds and other precious stones and pearls, the Dutch Carat is used.

The principal measure for corn is the Chetwert, which is divided into 2 Osmines, 4 Pajacks, 8 Chetwericks, 32 Chetwertkas, or 64 Garnets; and contains 5,952 English Bushels, or 2,0972 Hectolitres. Hence 100 Chetwerts equal 74½ Quarters English. Dry Measure.

The Oxhoft is divided into 6 Ankers, 12 Stekars, 18 Vedros, or 240 Bottles. The Vedro contains 3,246 English Gallons, or 12,289 Litres. Liquid Measure.

The Vedro is divided into 8 Kruskas or Osmins, and the Kruska into 11 Charkeys or Cups; but by an Imperial Ukase it was ordered that the Vedro should be divided into 100 Charkeys, to commence on the 1st January, 1819.

The English Inch is universally adopted throughout the Russian Empire, except in levying the duties on wood destined for exportation, when the Dutch or Rhineland Inch, Foot, and Palm, are ordered to be employed. The Arsheen or cloth measure is divided into 16 parts, called Vershoks; and contains 28 English Inches, or 0,7109 of a French Metre. The Sashine or Fathom is 3 Arsheens, or 7 English Feet. Long Measure.

The Russian Foot is 13,75 English Inches, or 0,3491 of a Metre; and the Moscow Foot, 13,17 English Inches, or 0,3343 of a Metre. The English Foot is very generally used in St. Petersburg, as also the Rhineland Foot.

---

* The Pound of Russia is variously stated by different authors. *Kruse* makes it answer to 6314 English Grains, and *Tillet* to 6324: but the true weight appears to be 6318½, according to experiments lately made at the *London Mint* on standards transmitted by *Sir Daniel Bayley,* the British Consul General at St. Petersburg. He likewise sent home measures of capacity and of length, from which the foregoing results have been deduced; and from his very elaborate despatches, the above account of the monetary system of Russia has been also chiefly extracted.

Long Measure. A Werst or Russian Mile contains 500 Fathoms or 1500 Arsheens, equal to 3500 English Feet. Hence 1 Werst = 5 Furlongs 12 Poles English, or 1,066 French Kilometre; and a Degree of the Meridian is reckoned to be about 104 Wersts.

Superficial Measure. The land measure, called Dessetina, contains 2400 Russian square Fathoms, or 21600 square Arsheens, which equal 13066$\frac{2}{3}$ English square-Yards, or 2 Acres 2 Roods, 32 Perches, answering to 109,26 French Ares.

Goods how sold. Hemp, flax, and tallow, are sold by the Berquet; copper, iron, cordage, horse-hair and tails, linseed and hempseed oil, isinglass, morocco leather, potash, wax, bristles, and tobacco, are sold by the Pood; sail-cloth and mats, by the Piece; diaper and linen, by the 1000 Arsheens.

Banks. During the reign of the Empress Catherine, three different Banks were established at St. Petersburg, namely, the *Loan Bank*, the *Assignation Bank*, and the *Loan Bank for the Nobility and Towns*. During the reign of the Emperor Paul, the *Aid Bank* and the *Discount Office* were formed: and under the Emperor Alexander, a very considerable Institution has been established of such extensive importance as in a great measure to supersede the use of some of the others: it is denominated the *Commercial Bank of Russia.*

The *Loan Bank*, or *Lombard*, lends money on gold, silver, jewels, &c., namely, on gold and silver, three-fourths of the value; on other metals, one-half; and on jewels, a certain proportion, which is fixed according to circumstances. A year's interest is taken in advance, which, agreeably to the legal rate throughout the empire, is 6 per cent. Money may be deposited in this Bank, and drawn out again, on giving two days notice. No interest is paid by the Bank for such money; but if a declaration is made that the money will be left there at least a year, and that three months notice shall be given of the intention to draw it out again, then the legal interest is allowed, and it is paid in the same kind of money in which the deposit was made. The property of this Bank belongs to the Foundling Hospital in St. Petersburg.

The *Loan Bank for the Nobility and Towns*, and the *Aid Bank*, are not establishments of a commercial nature, and their utility is chiefly of a local kind—the bill discount department of the former being now transferred to the *Commercial Bank*, noticed hereafter.

The *Assignation Bank*, which was opened in St. Petersburg and Moscow in 1770, and branches of which have been since extended to all the principal towns in the Russian Empire, issues its notes for 5, 10, 25, 50, and 100 Rubles. This

Bank was converted into an Imperial establishment in 1786, when all the old notes or assignations were called in, and exchanged for new ones; an operation that is now again repeating, in order to substitute a more perfect note. The amount of notes in circulation is not known; but they are become the regular currency of the country; and the European exchanges are quoted in reference to this currency, and to its par in silver, according to the variation of the day. The regulation of paying them off in copper is now discontinued; but the Government is earnestly intent on reducing their amount; and since the year 1817 has contracted loans, partly for the purpose of extinguishing the notes, and partly for that of discharging the floating debt of the State. These loans have been made chiefly against irredeemable rents or annuities. A small part only of the loans are redeemable, and a Sinking Fund is the basis of their liquidation. By means of these loans, a sum of no less than 153,867,010 Rubles had been withdrawn from the paper circulation of Russia, at the end of the year 1820, as officially reported. Banks.

The *Discount Office*, established in 1797, is abolished, and its funds are ordered to be vested in the *Commercial Bank.*

The *Commercial Bank of Russia* was established May 1818, and its provisions are of very extensive utility. It receives deposits in gold or silver, foreign as well as Russian coin, and in bars and ingots. It has a department for transferring the sums deposited in it, on the plan of the Hambro' Bank, from the account of one merchant to that of another, as well in gold and silver as in bank notes at interest. It discounts bills, and lends money on deposits of merchandize, of Russian produce or origin. Its capital consists of 30 Millions of Bank Note Rubles; and it is administered by a Governor and 4 Directors, appointed by Government, and 4 Directors, elected by the Commercial Body of St. Petersburg. The property in the Bank is protected against all taxation, sequestration, or attachment; and it is enacted that subjects of countries with which Russia may be at war, shall be entitled at all times to receive back their deposits, without any reservation. It is also declared, that at no time shall the Bank be called upon for any part of its capital to assist the Government. All deposits must be made for 6 months at least, and be repayable at or before that period, and not be less than 500 Rubles: sums so deposited pay $\frac{1}{4}$ per cent. The deposits, if in bars, ingots, or foreign specie, are estimated in Russian silver coin, and so registered in the attestation; and if not demanded back within 15 days after the expiration of 6 months, or the necessary premium paid for the prolongation, the owner loses the right of claiming his original deposit, and must take its estimated value in Russian silver coin.

Banks. The regulations for deposits at interest are the same as those of the *Loan*, or *Lombard Bank*, and are re-payable on proper notice, which varies from 7 days to 3 months, according to the magnitude of the sum. All bills discounted must be drawn, or accepted, or indorsed, by at least one person of satisfactory credit residing at St. Petersburg. No bills, having less than 8 days, or longer than 6 months to run, are discountable; and the preference is at all times given to bills of the shortest date.

This Bank has branches at *Moscow*, *Archangel*, *Odessa*, *Riga*, &c.

Exchanges. *Petersburg*, *Archangel*, *Moscow*, &c. draw on the following places and give (more or less)

Amsterdam	1 Ruble Bank Notes for	10	Stivers currency, 65 days date.
Hamburg .	1 Ditto..............	9	Shillings banco, ditto.
London ..	1 Ditto.............	10	Pence sterling, 3 months date.
Paris	1 Ditto..............	105½	Cents.

The variable agio of the bank notes, which is now substituted for the silver Ruble, will make these values of exchange fluctuate considerably, as the paper Ruble decreases or improves in value.

The above exchanges are accompanied by the quoted agio of 374 Copecks, or 3 Rubles 74 Copecks paper, per silver Ruble. See Vol. II. page 84.

Days of Grace. Bills drawn in Russia which are payable after date, are allowed 10 days grace, but if payable at sight, three days only: Sundays and holidays are included in both cases. Payment must be demanded in the morning of the day the bill becomes due; and in case of non-payment, the protest should take place at latest on the following day. The 10 days grace are allowed, even though the written term of the bill should be elapsed before it is presented or accepted. But bills payable at so many days after sight are not allowed any days of grace; and if the acceptance be delayed, the term is reckoned from the day on which the bill was presented.

Time how reckoned. Throughout all Russia, the Julian Calendar, or old style, is still retained, which (since the year 1800) is 12 days later than the new style, and in Leap Years 13 days, after the month of February. Thus a Russian bill dated the 1st day of any month, must be reckoned from the 13th day of the same month in England and in every other place where the Gregorian Calendar or new style is used, and the 14th of it be a Leap Year.

ST. GALL *(in Switzerland)*.

Monies of Account.

Accounts are kept in Florins of 60 Creutzers, or 480 Hellers. The Florin is also divided into 10 Schillings or Escalins, or 15 Batzen; a Schilling is worth 6 Creutzers; a Batze, 4 Creutzers.

Accounts are either in specie (that is, money of exchange) or currency; 1190 Florins specie are reckoned for 1383 Florins current; thus the difference is $16\frac{26}{119}$ per cent.

Another method of keeping accounts has been introduced, viz. in Swiss Livres, or Franken of 10 Batzen, or 100 Rappen; for which see *Switzerland*.

Coins.

The coins are, Gold Ducats; Silver Rixdollars, at $2\frac{2}{5}$ Florins; Pieces of 30, 24, 20, 15, 12, 10, and 6 Creutzers; Batzen and half Batzen, at 4 and 2 Creutzers; and single Creutzers.

There are also Silver Pieces of more modern date of 21 and $10\frac{1}{2}$ Batzen; and French coins, as well as those of the other Cantons, circulate here; also Spanish and German coins, which vary in their rates.

Value of Monies.

The Florin, money of exchange, is worth 265 German Asen, or $196\frac{1}{2}$ English Grains of fine silver; and the Florin current, 220 Asen, or 163 English Grains. Hence the Florin specie = $27\frac{1}{2}$d. sterling; and the Florin current, $22\frac{3}{4}$d. sterling; or, more accurately, £1 sterling = 10 Florins 33 Creutzers currency.

The Batze is worth $1\frac{1}{2}$ French Franc, or $14\frac{1}{2}$d. sterling nearly.

Weights & Measures.

Two different weights are used here: 35lb. of the heavier weight = 44lb. of the lighter; and each number answers to 45lb. avoirdupois nearly. Hence 100lb. of the heavier = 128,8lb. avoirdupois, or 58,45 Kilogrammes; and 100lb. of the lighter = 102,5lb. avoirdupois, or 46,49 Kilogrammes.

The Charge, corn measure, renders 2,066 English Bushels, or 0,7279 of a Hectolitre.

The Ell, cloth measure, is 24,2 English Inches, or 0,6158 of a Metre; the Ell, linen measure, is 31,6 English Inches, or 0,8017 of a Metre.

Exchanges.

St. Gall exchanges with and gives (more or less) to—

Amsterdam .... 59 Creutzers current for 1 Florin.
Augsburg & Nuremberg, 119 Florins current .... 100 Florins.

Exchanges.

Bolsano	108 Florins current .... for	100 Florins current.
Francfort	100½ Florins current........	100 Florins in old coins.
Geneva	126 Creutzers current......	1 Ecu of 3 Livres curr.
Genoa	23 Creutzers current......	1 Lira fuori banco.
Hamburgh	157 Creutzers current......	1 Rixdollar banco.
Leghorn	143 Creutzers current......	1 Pezza da 8 Reali.
Leipsic	100½ Florins current........	100 Florins in old coins.
London..............	10 Florins 52 Creutz. curr.	1 Pound sterling.
Lyons and Paris	98 Francs	100 Francs.
Milan	21 Creutzers current......	1 Lira Corrente.
Venice	12 Creutzers current, with 8 per cent. agio	1 Lira Piccola.
Vienna	119 Florins current........	100 Florins current.

Usance and Days of Grace. Usance is 15 days; double usance, 30 days; half usance, 8 days; the day of presentation being reckoned the first. Three days grace are allowed on bills drawn at usance, but two only on bills payable at a longer or shorter term than usance. Sundays and holidays are always included.

ST. HELENA *(an Island in the Southern Atlantic)*.

Monies and Coins. Accounts are kept here in Pounds, Shillings, and Pence sterling; but coins of various denominations pass current, especially those of the East Indies, Spain, and England.

Porto Novo Pagodas pass at 7s. 6d.; Spanish Dollars at 4s. 6d.; but English Guineas and Bank Notes are generally at a premium, especially in exchanging them for East India coins.

English weights and measures are chiefly used here.

ST. MALOES *(in France)*.

Monies, &c. The new system of monies, weights, and measures of France has been established here; but certain old customs are still partially retained, and are as follows.

Old Measures. The old corn measure, called the Tonneau, contains 31¼ Boisseaux; and answers to 39,19 English Bushels, or 13,80 Hectolitres.

Salt is measured by the Jutte, which contains 33 Pots, each Pot being something more than a Paris Pinte. 21 Juttes make a Tonneau, which weighs about 2808lb. avoirdupois, or 1273 Kilogrammes. Old Measures.

The Aune or Ell is 53 English Inches, or 1,347 Metre.

The land measure is the Journal, which contains 20 Sillons, 80 Cordes, or 480 Raies; and equals 48,624 French Ares, or 1 English Acre 32 Perches.

ST. REMO *(in Italy)*.

Accounts are kept here in Lire of 20 Soldi, or 240 Denari, Moneta Corrente. Monies and Coins.

The coins of the country will be found under the article *Genoa*.

The Zecchino of Genoa or Venice is worth 12 Lire 16 Soldi; and 100 Pezze of Leghorn are worth 552 Lire of St. Remo: hence the Lira may be valued at $8\frac{1}{2}$d. sterling in silver. Value of Monies.

The weights and measures are the same here as in Genoa.

St. Remo exchanges with Leghorn, and gives 110 Soldi, more or less, for 1 Pezza da 8 Reali. Bills on other places are negotiated through Genoa. Exchanges.

SALONICA *(Turkey in Europe)*.

Accounts are generally kept in Piastres of 40 Paras, or 120 Aspers. The coins are the same as those described in the article *Constantinople*, but here their intrinsic value is subject to perhaps greater variation. Monies, &c.

The same weight, and the same long measure, are used as in Smyrna; the corn measure, however, differs, the Killow of Salonica corresponding to 3,78 Killows of Smyrna. Thus it renders 5,505 English Bushels, or 1,939 Hectolitre.

SANTANDER *(see Galicia)*.

SARDINIA *(an Island in the Mediterranean)*.

Accounts are kept in Lire of 4 Reali, 20 Soldi, or 240 Denari. A Scudo is worth $2\frac{1}{2}$ Lire, 10 Reali, 50 Soldi, 300 Cagliaresi, or 600 Denari. 5 Lire of Sardinia are equal to 8 Lire of Turin. Monies of Account.

Coins. Before the year 1768, Sardinia had no other coins than those of Piedmont, except Silver Reals and Copper money; but since that period, coins have been struck for this Island at the mint at Turin. These are, in Gold, Carlini of 25 Lire, with halves in proportion; and Doppiette, or Gold Scudi, of 5 Lire. In Silver, Scudi of 2 Lire 10 Soldi, with halves and quarters in proportion. The inferior coins are Reals, Half Reals, and Soldi; and in Copper, Half Soldi, Cagliaresi, and Denari.

Rate of Coinage. The Carlino of 25 Lire is to weigh 12 Denari 12 Grani 20 Granotini, Turin weight, or $247\frac{3}{4}$ English Grains; and the gold is to be 21 Carati 10 Grani, or $21\frac{5}{12}$ Carats fine. The Scudo of $2\frac{1}{2}$ Lire is to weigh 18 Denari 10 Grani of Turin, or 364 English Grains; and the silver to be 10 Denari 18 Grani, or 10 oz. 15 dwts. fine: and the inferior gold and silver coins in proportion. There is no allowance here for remedy. The Carlino is worth 39s. 2d. sterling; the Scudo, $45\frac{1}{4}$d. sterling; and the Lira, 18d. sterling very nearly.

Weights. The weight for gold and silver is the same as in *Turin*, which see.

The commercial Pound is divided into 12 Once, and contains 6125 English Grains. Thus the Cantarello of 100 Libbre equals 87,5lb. avoirdupois, or 39,68 Kilogrammes.

Measures. The Restiere of corn contains 3 Starelli, or 48 Imbuti. The Starello renders 1,389 English Bushel, or 0,4895 of a Hectolitre.

The Raso or Ell equals 21,625 English Inches, or 0,5488 of a Metre; and the Palmo, 9,78 English Inches, or 0,2483 of a Metre.

SAVOY, *see Turin*.

SAYDE, or SIDON *(in Syria)*.

Monies and Weights. Accounts are kept in Piastres, or Medini of 80 Aspers, as at *Aleppo*.

For the different Turkish coins used here, see *Constantinople*.

Silk and cotton yarn are weighed by the Rottolo of 600 Drams; 100 such Rottoli answer to 410,6lb. avoirdupois, or 186,25 Kilogrammes.

Heavy goods are weighed by the Rottolo of Acre, 100 of which equal 482lb. avoirdupois, or 218,60 Kilogrammes.

The Pic, long measure, is 23,8 English Inches, or 0,604 of a Metre.

SCOTLAND.

Accounts are kept in Pounds, Shillings, and Pence sterling, as in England; and since the union in 1707, the same coins are also used as in England. Monies and Coins.

Some computations, however, are still made in Scottish money, which is divided in the same manner as sterling, but is only one-twelfth of its value. Thus a Pound Scottish is equal to 1s. 8d. sterling, a Shilling Scottish to 1d. sterling, and a Penny Scottish to $\frac{1}{12}$ of a Penny sterling. The Penny Scottish is divided into 3 Placks.

At the union, the English weights and measures were introduced into Scotland, and are used chiefly for goods received from England. The old Scottish weights and measures, however, are still retained, of which there is a great variety. Weights & Measures.

The principal standards are distributed among the oldest boroughs, viz. the Elwand or Ell is kept at Edinburgh; the Pound, at Lanark; the Pint, at Stirling; and the Firlot, at Linlithgow: but copies of these are kept in many other towns. The following are their divisions and contents.

Troy or Dutch weight.—16 Drops = 1 Ounce; 16 Ounces = 1 Pound; 16lb. = 1 Stone. Dutch Weight.

This weight is used in many places for iron, hemp, flax, meal, butchers'-meat, unwrought pewter, lead, and most Dutch and Baltic goods. The Pound contains 7600 Grains English Troy weight. Hence 35lb. Dutch weight = 38lb. avoirdupois.

Old or Trone weight is still used for butter, cheese, wool, hay, and some other commodities. The Pound varies in different places, from 20 to 28 Dutch Ounces; it is divided into 16 of its own Ounces, and 16lb. make a Stone. Trone Weight.

Long Measure.—37 Inches = 1 Ell; 6 Ells = 1 Fall; 40 Falls = 1 Furlong; 8 Furlongs = 1 Mile. Long Measure.

The Ell is $37\frac{1}{5}$ English Inches. Hence 30 Scottish Ells = 31 English Yards; and 80 Scottish Miles = 91 English Miles.

Land Measure.—36 square Ells = 1 square Fall; 40 square Falls = 1 Rood; 4 Roods = 1 Acre. The Acre contains 1 Acre 1 Rood $3\frac{1}{3}$ Perches English statute measure. Hence 48 Scottish Acres = equal 61 English Acres. Land Measure.

Dry Measure.

Dry Measure.—4 Lippies = 1 Peck; 4 Pecks = 1 Firlot; 4 Firlots = 1 Boll; 16 Bolls = 1 Chalder.

The Linlithgow Wheat Firlot, which is the standard, contains $21\frac{1}{4}$ Scottish Pints, or $2197\frac{1}{3}$ English cubic Inches. It is used for wheat, rye, pease, beans, salt, and grass seeds. The Barley Firlot, which is used for barley, malt, oats, fruit, and potatoes, contains 31 Scottish Pints, or $3205\frac{1}{2}$ cubic Inches. The former equals $1\frac{1}{48}$, and the latter $1\frac{1}{2}$ Winchester Bushel nearly.

Liquid Measure.

Wine or Liquid Measure.—4 Gills = 1 Mutchkin; 2 Mutchkins = 1 Choppin; 2 Choppins = 1 Pint; 2 Pints = 1 Quart; 4 Quarts = 1 Gallon; 16 Gallons = 1 Hogshead.

The Pint, according to the standard Stirling Jug, is 103,404 English cubic Inches. Hence 105 Scottish Pints = 47 English wine Gallons; and 11 Scottish Pints = 6 English ale Gallons. The Scottish Quart is commonly reckoned about $\frac{1}{10}$ less than the English wine Gallon, and about $\frac{1}{4}$ less than the English ale Gallon.

The foregoing statements are to be considered only as a general outline of the principal weights and measures of Scotland; but to state the various systems that are used in about 30 different counties would greatly exceed the present limits, and vary from the general plan of this work.*

BANKS.

There are in Edinburgh three chartered Banks; namely, *the Bank of Scotland*, *the Royal Bank of Scotland*, and *the British Linen Company*.

Bank of Scotland.

The Bank of Scotland, sometimes denominated the Old Bank, was instituted by Act of Parliament in 1695, and permitted to raise a stock of £1,200,000 Scottish money, or £100,000 sterling. None were allowed to be competent partners or proprietors who did not hold a share equal to £1000 Scottish money; and none could have a larger share than twenty times that sum. The qualification of a Governor was settled at £8000 Scottish money, of a Deputy Governor, £6000, and of a Director, £3000. In the election of officers, £1000 Scottish entitled the proprietor to one vote, £2000 to two votes, and so in proportion

* A full and particular account of the provincial weights and measures of Scotland will be found in a Tract entitled "METROLOGY," published by the Author of the present work in 1816.

up to twenty votes. In 1774 the Bank stock and the qualifications were doubled. Bank of Scotland.

In 1784 the capital was further increased to £3,600,000 Scottish. In 1792 it was doubled, and in 1794 it was augmented to 12 millions Scottish, or 1 million sterling: the qualifications were likewise progressively raised.

In 1804 the capital was again increased to £1,500,000 sterling, and the mode of reckoning by Scottish money abolished.

The qualifications for Governor, Deputy Governor, and Director, are £2000, £1500, and £1000 sterling respectively; and the qualification of a Proprietor is £300 sterling, with liberty, as before, to hold twenty shares and no more.

Royal Bank of Scotland.

The Royal Bank of Scotland was incorporated by Royal Authority in 1727. The original capital was £111,347 19s. 10d. sterling, which was increased in the year 1738 to £150,000.

In 1783 the capital was doubled, and in 1788 it was again doubled, making it £600,000 sterling.

In 1793 it was further increased to £1,000,000 sterling; and the Company were allowed by their charter to augment it to £1,500,000 when they should find occasion.

The qualifications for officers, &c. in the Royal Bank are the same as in the Old Bank, except that here no Proprietor can hold more than four shares.

British Linen Company.

The British Linen Company was incorporated by Royal Authority in 1746, in order to promote the extension of the linen manufactory in Scotland: its capital was at first £100,000 sterling, and by a new charter in 1807 it was increased to £200,000. The qualifications for Governor, Deputy Governor, and Director, are £1000, £500, and £300, respectively. Any partner or proprietor who has a share of £200 is entitled to one vote; if £500, to two votes; and if £1300, he has four votes; but no greater number is allowed.

The Royal Bank has a very considerable establishment or Agency-House at Glasgow. The other two Banks also have Branch Banks in different parts of the country.

Private Banks.

The private Banks in Scotland are numerous, and have been generally conducted with great prudence and safety. They are mostly on a more extensive scale than in England, as the number of partners is not limited; which is sup-

Private Banks. posed to add considerably to their security. They transact business on the same general principle as the English Country Banks, with, however, some exceptions. All these Banks allow 3 per cent. per annum for money lodged with them; and if left in their hands for 6 months, they generally allow 4 per cent.; and some charge a small commission for their banking operations. They charge 5 per cent. per annum for whatever money they advance. These advances are made not only on inland bills of exchange, and bills on London, but also on what is denominated *Cash Accounts*, which are bonds given, with two securities, to a certain amount, on which the customer draws from time to time, never exceeding the sum stipulated. *Cash Accounts* have been found extremely beneficial both to the landed and trading interests of the country.

All Banks in Scotland issue their own notes, payable to bearer on demand. Private bank-notes are generally paid off in public bank-notes; and the latter are ultimately discharged either in cash, Bank-of-England notes, or bills on London; and as each Country Bank has an agent in Edinburgh to pay its notes, such paper has a general currency in all parts of the country.

There are about thirty private Banks, one or two in each principal town, and these have Agency or Branch Banks, amounting to nearly one hundred, in the smaller towns. Each of the latter is confined to the circulation of the notes issued by its principal.

According to a statement submitted to Parliament in 1819, the whole number of Banks in Scotland was 128, and the number of partners 1478; and these computations may be taken as the average for the preceding seven years.

Exchanges. Scotland draws on London at a small exchange or premium, which is always in favour of London. This is allowed in the term of the bill, and 40 days after date are generally reckoned the *par date*. The exchange, however, varies from 40 to 60 days; and small bills are mostly drawn at a longer term than large ones.

Days of Grace. The days of grace and other customs and laws relating to bills of exchange, are the same in Scotland as in England; for which, see the article *London*, page 236.

SEVILLE, *see Cadiz, Castile, Spain, &c.*

SICILY *(an Island in the Mediterranean).*

Accounts are kept in Onzie, of 30 Tari, each Taro being subdivided into 20 Grani. The Taro contains 2 Carlini, 20 Grani, 15 Ponti, or 120 Piccioli. Monies of Account.

The Scudo or Sicilian Dollar is reckoned at 12 Tari; the Fiorino at 6 Tari, or 12 Carlini; and the Ducat at 10 Tari.

The Gold coins are, six Ducat pieces, or double Onzie; and three Ducat pieces, or single Onzie. The Silver coins are, Onzie, of the same value as the above; Sicilian Scudi, of 12 Sicilian Tari; and Pieces of 6, 4, 3, 2, and 1 Sicilian Tari; Carlini, and halves, at 10 and 5 Grani; besides the coins of Naples, which are current here. Coins.

It must be observed, however, that the Sicilian Tari, Carlini, &c. have but half the value of the same denominations in Naples, for the Sicilian Onza passes there for only 15 Tari, the Sicilian Scudo for 6 Tari, &c.

The gold 3 Ducat piece weighs 5 Trapesi, Neapolitan weight; its fineness has varied from $20\frac{1}{2}$ to $21\frac{1}{2}$ Carats: the silver Scudo, or 12 Tari piece, weighs 30 Trapesi $12\frac{3}{4}$ Acini, and is 10 Ounces fine: hence the Sicilian Ounce contains $877\frac{3}{5}$ English Grains of fine silver: it is therefore worth about 10s. $3\frac{1}{2}$d. sterling; the Scudo 4s.; and the Taro about 4d.; or, more accurately, £1 sterling = 1 Onza 28 Tari 15 Grani. Value of Monies.

Three different weights are used here, namely, the Rottolo grosso of 33 Ounces, the Rottolo sottile of 30 Ounces, and the Libra or lb. of 12 Ounces. Weights.

100lb. of Sicily = 70lb. avoirdupois, or 31,74 Kilogrammes.

The Cantaro grosso contains 100 Rottoli grossi, answering to 192,5lb. avoirdupois, or 87,30 Kilogrammes. The Cantaro sottile is 100 Rottoli sottili, and equals 175lb. avoirdupois, or 79,37 Kilogrammes.

The Salma of corn is divided into 4 Bisaccie, 16 Tomoli, or 64 Mondelli: there is, however, the Salma grossa, which is equal to 14 Staja, Leghorn measure; and the Salma generale, equal to $11\frac{1}{4}$ such Staja. Hence the Salma grossa = 9,77 English Bushels, or 3,44 Hectolitres; and the Salma generale = 7,85 English Bushels, or 2,76 Hectolitres. Dry Measure.

Liquid Measures. Wine is measured by the Salma, 4 of which make 1 Botte, and 3 Botti = 1 Tonna. The Salma of Messina is divided into 8 Barili, 16 Quartari, or 320 Quartucci, each weighing 22 or 24 Ounces; and contains 23,06 English Gallons, or 87,36 Litres. The Salma of Syracuse is $\frac{1}{8}$ less than the above. Oil, in Messina and the neighbouring places, is sold by the Caffiso, which weighs 12½ Rottoli, or about 24lb. avoirdupois. 5½ Caffisi are reckoned to equal a Millerolle of Marseilles, or 17 English wine Gallons. Thus the Caffiso answers to 3,09 Gallons, or 11,69 Litres. In Palermo, oil is sold by the Cantaro grosso.

Long Measures. The Canna, long measure, is divided into 8 Palmi: the Palmo measures 9,5 English Inches; and the Canna, therefore, equals 76¼ English Inches, or 1,936 Metre.

Exchanges. For the exchanges of Sicily, see *Palermo*, Vol. II. p. 82.

Usance, &c. Bills are drawn on Leghorn and Genoa at usance of 1 month after acceptance, or at 2 months date, or at a few days sight; on Rome, Venice, and Naples, at 8 or 15 days sight; on London, at 3 months date.

The usance for bills drawn from Naples, Ancona, Rome, and Venice, is 21 days after sight; and from the rest of Italy, 15 days after sight. From France, 30 days after date; from Amsterdam, Antwerp, Hamburgh, Portugal, and Spain, 2 months, and from England, 3 months after date. No days of grace are allowed here in any case.

SMYRNA (*Turkey in Asia*).

Monies and Coins. Accounts are kept in Piastres or Gooroosh, also called Dollars. The Piastre is divided sometimes into 12 Temins, and also into 40 Paras or Medini; but the general division is into Aspers, the number of which varies.

Thus the English and Swedes divide the Piastre into 80 Aspers; the Dutch, French, and Venetians, into 100 Aspers; and the Turks, Greeks, Persians, and Armenians, into 120 Aspers.

The Turkish coins are those chiefly used here, for which see *Constantinople*. Other coins, however, circulate, particularly Spanish and Imperial Dollars; Hungarian and Dutch Ducats; and Venetian Sequins. They are each rated at a certain number of Piastres, which, however, varies according to the fluctuating value of the Piastre. In 1810 it was worth 1 Shilling, and in 1820 about 9d. sterling. Monies and Coins.

The Oke or Oka is used in weighing gold and silver, and in most commercial transactions. It is divided into 4 Chequees; each Chequee is divided into 100 Drams, and each Dram into 64 Grains. Weights.

The Oke weighs 19830 English Grains, or 2lb. 13 oz. 5 dr. avoirdupois, which answer to 1,284 Kilogramme. Thus the Kintal of 45 Okes, or 100 Rottolos, equals 127,48lb. avoirdupois. It is generally reckoned by merchants at about 125lb. The Oke used for retailing commodities is $1\frac{1}{2}$ Dram heavier than the above, that is, about 63 English Grains. According to the above weight of the Oke, 4 Turkish Grains equal 3 English Grains nearly.

The Cantaro or Kintal is the largest commercial weight. It is divided into $7\frac{1}{2}$ Batmans, or 45 Okes; also into 100 Rottoli or Lodra, which is an imaginary weight of 180 Drams, and is chiefly known in the use of the steelyards, by which heavy goods are weighed; but gold, silver, and other precious articles, are weighed by the beam and scales.

It should be observed, that although the Kintal of Smyrna is composed of 45 Okes, or 18000 Drams, that of the surrounding country and of Constantinople is only 44 Okes or 17600 Drams. Several kinds of goods, however, are sold at Smyrna by the Kintal of 44 Okes, as well as by that of 45; others by the Rottolo, the Chequee, and the Oke; and some by the Miscal of $1\frac{1}{2}$ Dram. Various other customs prevail with respect to the purchase and sale of goods, which are subject to variation; and information on these subjects for the time being is generally stated in the Prices Current which are circulated among merchants.

Corn is measured by the circular Killow, which renders 1,456 English Bushel, or $13\frac{1}{2}$ wine Gallons nearly, answering to 51,3 Litres. Measures.

The long measure is the Pic, which equals 27 English Inches, or 0,6855 of a Metre.*

---

* The above account of the weights and measures of Smyrna is chiefly taken from the despatches and standards transmitted to *Lord Castlereagh*, in 1818, by *Mr. Werry*, the British Consul in that city. His statements, which seem very clear and correct, vary in many respects from the accounts hitherto published; but as authors on the subject differ very much among themselves, it may be concluded that Turkish Metrology is not well understood or established.

For an account of these various statements, see the Note on *Constantinople*.

Exchanges. Smyrna exchanges with and gives to—

Amsterdam,	104 Paras, more or less,	for 1	Florin.
France	1 Piastre	for $16\frac{1}{2}$	Sols.
Genoa	44 Paras	for 1	Lira fuori banco.
Leghorn ...	260 Paras	for 1	Piece of 8 Reals.
London ...	28 Piastres of 40 Paras	for £1	sterling.
Vienna	120 Paras	for 1	Florin current.

The exchange of Smyrna with Constantinople is generally done at a variable agio in favour of Constantinople.

SPAIN.

Monies and Coins. Several provinces and colonies of this kingdom have peculiar modes of keeping accounts, which are explained in the present work under the heads *Alicant, Arragon, Barcelona, Bilboa, Canaries, Cadiz, Castile, Galicia, Gibraltar, Malaga, Mexico, Navarre*, and *Valencia:* but as the monies of Spain are more various and complex than perhaps those of any other country, a recapitulation of them is here given, with a comparative view of their divisions, proportions, and sterling value.

The most general mode of keeping accounts in Spain is in *Reals* of 34 Maravedis; but there are nine different Reals, four of which are of general application, and five of local use.

The *Libra* is another money of account, of which there are four varieties. It is always divided into 20 Sueldos or 240 Dineros.

The four principal monies of Spain are *Vellon, New Plate, Old Plate*, and *Mexican Plate;* and in order to obtain a distinct view of them, it may be proper to make the Real Vellon the basis of all the rest. It is the twentieth part of the Hard Dollar (Peso Duro), universally known by the name of the Spanish Dollar. The Real Vellon is also the twentieth part of the gold Dollar (Coronilla), and its value in this metal is $2\frac{1}{2}$d. sterling; but in British silver, at 5s. 2d. per oz. standard, it is worth 2,59d.

The Real *Vellon* or Billon is divided into $8\frac{1}{2}$ Quartos, 17 Ochavos, or 34 Maravedis Vellon.

The Real of *New Plate* is double the Real Vellon, and is divided into 34 Maravedis of New Plate, or 68 of Vellon, with Quartos and Ochavos in proportion. It is a coin but not a money of account in any general way.

Monies and Coins.

The Real of ***Old Plate*** is better than the Real Vellon, in the proportion of 32 to 17. Thus 17 Maravedis of Old Plate equal 32 of Vellon. This Real is also divided into 16 Quartos or 32 Ochavos.

The Real of Old Plate is not a coin; it is a money of account in particular provinces, and is the most general money of exchange. 8 of these Reals make the Peso de Plata, or Piastre, which is also called the Dollar of exchange; and when Plate only is mentioned, Old Plate is understood.

The Real of ***Mexican Plate*** is divided into Halves and Quarters, called Medio and Quartillo. It is the eighth part of the Hard Dollar, and is therefore worth $2\frac{1}{2}$ Reals Vellon, $1\frac{1}{2}$ Real of New Plate, or $1\frac{21}{64}$ Real of Old Plate.

The Real of Mexican Plate is the chief money of account in Spanish America, where it is divided into 16 parts; and in Spain it is sometimes divided into 21 parts.

It may be noticed that Vellon is the root of several other monies employed in domestic and inland trade. Thus 60 Reals Vellon equal the Doubloon de Plata Sencillo; 15 = the Peso Sencillo; and 11 = the Ducado de Vellon.

Besides the above, there are five Reals, which are only of local use. They are not coins but monies of account, and sometimes monies of exchange. Thus—

The Real of Alicant	$13\frac{9}{32}$	of which equal the Hard Dollar.
Real of Catalonia	$12\frac{19}{48}$	" "
Real Ardite of Catalonia	$18\frac{19}{32}$	" "
Real current of Gibraltar	12	" "
Real of Valencia	$17\frac{17}{24}$	" "

Monies of Exchange.

The following are the principal monies of exchange:—

The Peso de Plata or Piastre, before explained, contains 8 Reals or 272 Maravedis of Plate, or 15 Reals 2 Maravedis Vellon.

The Doubloon de Plata or Pistole of exchange is four times the value of the above Piastre.

The Ducado de Plata or Ducat of exchange is worth 11 Reals 1 Maravedi of Plate, or 20 Reals $25\frac{15}{17}$ Maravedis Vellon.

The following Table is a new arrangement of the monies of Spain shewing, at one view, their relations to each other, and their sterling value in silver, that is, at 5s. 2d. per Ounce standard.

A COMPARATIVE VIEW OF SPANISH MONIES,

SHEWING

THEIR PROPORTIONS TO EACH OTHER, AND THEIR STERLING VALUE.

	Hard Dollar.	Dollar of Exchange.	Reals of New Plate	Reals of Old Plate.	Reals Vellon.	Quartos.	Maravedis Old Plate.	Maravedis Vellon.	Sterl. Value d. dec.
Hard Dollar	1	$1\frac{21}{64}$	10	$10\frac{5}{8}$	20	170	$361\frac{1}{4}$	680	51,79
Dollar of Exchange, or of Old Plate	$\frac{64}{85}$	1	$7\frac{9}{17}$	8	$15\frac{1}{17}$	128	272	512	39,00
Real of New Plate	$\frac{1}{10}$	$\frac{17}{128}$	1	$1\frac{1}{16}$	2	17	$36\frac{1}{8}$	68	5,18
Real of Old Plate, or of Exchange	$\frac{8}{85}$	$\frac{1}{8}$	$\frac{16}{17}$	1	$1\frac{15}{17}$	16	34	64	4,87
Real of Vellon	$\frac{1}{20}$	$\frac{17}{256}$	$\frac{1}{2}$	$\frac{17}{32}$	1	$8\frac{1}{2}$	$18\frac{1}{16}$	34	2,59
Quarto	$\frac{1}{170}$	$\frac{1}{128}$	$\frac{1}{17}$	$\frac{1}{16}$	$\frac{2}{17}$	1	$2\frac{1}{8}$	4	0,305
Maravedi of Old Plate	$\frac{4}{1445}$	$\frac{1}{272}$	$\frac{8}{289}$	$\frac{1}{34}$	$\frac{16}{289}$	$\frac{8}{17}$	1	$1\frac{15}{17}$	0,143
Maravedi of Vellon	$\frac{1}{680}$	$\frac{1}{512}$	$\frac{1}{68}$	$\frac{1}{64}$	$\frac{1}{34}$	$\frac{1}{4}$	$\frac{17}{32}$	1	0,076
* Libra of Catalonia	$\frac{8}{15}$	$\frac{85}{48}$	$5\frac{1}{3}$	$5\frac{5}{6}$	$10\frac{2}{3}$	$90\frac{2}{3}$	$198\frac{1}{3}$	$362\frac{2}{3}$	27,62
Libra of Arragon	$\frac{16}{17}$	$1\frac{1}{4}$	$9\frac{7}{17}$	10	$18\frac{14}{17}$	160	340	640	48,75
Libra of Alicant and Valencia	$\frac{64}{85}$	1	$7\frac{9}{17}$	8	$15\frac{1}{17}$	128	272	512	39,00
Libra of Navarre	$\frac{8}{51}$	$\frac{5}{24}$	$1\frac{29}{51}$	$1\frac{2}{3}$	$3\frac{7}{51}$	$26\frac{2}{3}$	$56\frac{2}{3}$	$106\frac{2}{3}$	8,125
Real of Catalonia	$\frac{48}{595}$	$\frac{3}{28}$	$\frac{96}{119}$	$\frac{102}{119}$	$1\frac{73}{119}$	$13\frac{5}{7}$	$29\frac{1}{7}$	$54\frac{6}{7}$	4,18
Real of Valencia	$\frac{24}{425}$	$\frac{51}{680}$	$\frac{48}{85}$	$\frac{3}{5}$	$1\frac{11}{85}$	$9\frac{3}{5}$	$20\frac{2}{5}$	$38\frac{2}{5}$	2,92
Real of Alicant	$\frac{32}{425}$	$\frac{1}{10}$	$\frac{64}{85}$	$\frac{68}{85}$	$1\frac{43}{85}$	$12\frac{4}{5}$	$27\frac{1}{5}$	$51\frac{1}{5}$	3,90
Real Ardite of Catalonia	$\frac{32}{595}$	$\frac{1}{14}$	$\frac{64}{119}$	$\frac{68}{119}$	$1\frac{9}{119}$	$9\frac{1}{7}$	$19\frac{3}{7}$	$36\frac{4}{7}$	2,78
Real of Gibraltar	$\frac{1}{12}$	$\frac{85}{768}$	$\frac{5}{6}$	$\frac{85}{96}$	$1\frac{2}{3}$	$14\frac{1}{6}$	$30\frac{5}{48}$	$56\frac{2}{3}$	4,31

By the inspection of the above Table, the relative values of the different monies may be readily seen, by observing that all the numbers on the same horizontal line are of one value, with reference to the titles at the head of the Table. Thus 1 Hard Dollar, on the first line, equals 20 Reals Vellon, or 51,79 Pence.

It will be also seen, on the last line, that the Real of Gibraltar equals $\frac{1}{12}$ of the Hard Dollar, $\frac{5}{6}$ of a Real of New Plate, $56\frac{2}{3}$ Maravedis Vellon, or 4,31d. sterling; and so of any other numbers.

Note.—The monies above the star are those most generally in use throughout Spain.

The following are the principal coins current in Spain: Coins.

		Vellon Reals.	Maravedis.
In Gold	The Dobloon of 8 Escudos, or Quadruple Pistole, which passes for	320	0
	The Dobloon of 4 Escudos, or double Pistole	160	0
	The Dobloon de Oro, or Pistole..........	80	0
	The Escudo	40	0
	The Coronilla or Veinten de Oro	20	0
In Silver......	The Dollar or Peso Duro................	20	0
	The Half Dollar or Escudo Vellon........	10	0
	The Peseta Mexicana	5	0
	The Real of Mexican Plate..............	2	17
In base Silver..	The Peseta Provincial..................	4	0
	The Real of Provincial Plate	2	0
	The Real Vellon	1	0
In Copper	The Piece of 2 Quartos	0	8
	The Quarto	0	4
	The Ochavo	0	2

The fineness of gold is expressed in Quilates or Carats, and Grains; the Mark or other weight being divided into 24 Carats, the Carat into 4 Grains, and the Grain into 8 parts. Fineness of Gold and Silver.

The fineness of silver is expressed in Dineros and Grains; the Mark or other weight being divided into 12 Dineros, and the Dinero into 24 Grains.

By the royal edict of 1730, $8\frac{1}{2}$ Quadruples or Dobloons of 8 Escudos; 17 Dobloons of 4 Escudos; 34 common Dobloons or Pistoles, or 68 Escudos, were to weigh a Castilian Mark of gold 22 Quilates fine: and $8\frac{1}{2}$ Pesos Duros or Dollars, 17 Half Dollars, 34 Pesetas, or 68 Reals of Mexican Plate, were to weigh a Castilian Mark of silver 11 Dineros fine. Rate of Coinage.

Thus, from 1730 till 1772, the gold was 22 Carats, and the silver 11 Dineros fine; but in 1772, the gold was reduced to $21\frac{1}{2}$ Carats, and the silver to $10\frac{3}{4}$ Dineros fine, except the Pesetas and Reals, which were reduced to $9\frac{3}{4}$ Dineros fine. No alteration has since taken place in the silver coins; but in 1786 the standard of the gold was again reduced to 21 Carats for the different Dobloons and their divisions, and to $20\frac{3}{8}$ Carats for the Coronilla or Veinten de Oro.

The remedy in the weight is 24 Grains per Mark, both for the gold and the silver coins. The remedy in the alloy is $\frac{1}{16}$ of a Carat for the gold coins; 1 Grain,

Rate of Coinage.

or $\frac{1}{24}$ of a Dinero, for the Dollar and its divisions; and 2, or at most 3 Grains for the inferior silver coins.

Value of Monies.

The Quadruple Pistole, or Dobloon of 8 Escudos (coined since 1786), contains $366\frac{1}{6}$ troy Grains of fine gold, and is therefore worth £3 4s. $9\frac{1}{2}$d. valued in English gold coin; and the subdivisions of the quadruple are in proportion.

The Dollar (coined since 1772) should contain $374\frac{7}{8}$ troy Grains of fine silver; and its value, therefore, in English silver coin is 4s. $4\frac{1}{2}$d., and the Half Dollar in proportion.

The value of the Peso of Plate, or Dollar of Exchange, in English silver coin, is $39\frac{1}{2}$d.; of the Dobloon of Plate, or Pistole of Exchange, 13s. 2d.; and of the Ducat of Plate, 4s. $6\frac{1}{2}$d.

The Real of Old Plate is worth about 5d.; and the Real Vellon, $2\frac{3}{5}$d. nearly; or, more accurately, £1 sterling equals 48 Reals $20\frac{2}{3}$ Maravedis of Old Plate, or 91 Reals 17 Maravedis Vellon.

It should be observed, that the above calculations of the value of coins are made according to the mint regulations, without any allowance for remedy; which allowance may be valued at 6d. in the quadruple, and in the Dollar at $\frac{1}{2}$d. sterling.

For the value of those coins according to assays, see *Tables of Coins*, Vol. II.

Weights & Measures.

The original standards of Spanish weights and measures are preserved in the following cities, viz. the standard of long measure, at Burgos; that of dry measure, at Avila; that of liquid measure, at Toledo; and that of weight, in the Archives of the Supreme Senate at Madrid: copies, however, are distributed throughout the kingdom.

There are, however, several kinds of provincial weights and measures, which are described in this work under the heads of the places where such are used; but the following are the legal standards.

Gold and Silver Weight.

Gold is weighed by the Castilian Mark of 50 Castellanos, 400 Tomines, or 4800 Grains. Silver is weighed by the same Mark, but is divided into 8 Ounces, 64 Ochavos, 128 Adarmes, 384 Tomines, or 4608 Grains.

The Castilian Mark, also called the Mark of Colonia and Burgos, contains $3550\frac{1}{2}$ English Grains, or 230,043 Grammes.

1000 Dollars should weigh, according to the Mint regulations, 117 Marks, 5 Ounces, Castilian weight, or 870 oz. English troy weight; but the average weight of this number of Dollars at the Bank of England is found to be 866 Ounces troy, and large quantities are computed accordingly. Gold and Silver Weight.

Diamonds are weighed by the Ounce of 140 Carats or 560 Castilian Grains, which equal 431,48 English Grains. Hence this Carat weighs $3\frac{1}{12}$ English troy Grains, which is nearly $\frac{1}{12}$ of a Grain less than the English Diamond Carat. Diamond Weight.

The Apothecaries' weight is the Castilian; but the Ounce is divided into 8 Drachmas, 24 Escrupulos, 48 Obolos, 144 Caracteres, or 576 Grains.* Apothecaries' Weight

---

* The contradictory accounts hitherto given of the weight of the Mark of Castile, have been already noticed in page 65; but the importance of the correction now offered, seems to demand a further explanation.

In the former edition of the CAMBIST, this weight was stated at 3557 English Grains; and that erroneous statement was made on the authority of *Kruse*, *Nelkenbreker*, and *Gerhart*, who agree in making this Mark 4796 Dutch Aas, which answer to 3557,6 English Grains. *Kruse* further observes that this result had been determined by different experiments made by *Jacob L'Amiral*, the Inspector General of Weights and Measures at Amsterdam.

The following are the results of the late experiments made at the *London Mint* on the Spanish Marks transmitted by different British Consuls to *Lord Castlereagh* in 1818:

Sent from	by	weighing	
Madrid	*Consul Gen. Meade*,	3550	English Grains.
Barcelona	*Mr. Consul Baker*,	3550,75	....
Carthagena	*Amalther*,	3550,5	....
Malaga	*Laird*,	3551	....

The above four weights having been found the most accurately divided, have been chosen to give an average of the Castilian Mark, which is $3550\frac{1}{2}$ English Grains: and this nearly agrees with the determination of *Marien*, a Spanish author of the first authority, who states the English Troy Pound at 7475 Castilian Grains. Hence as 7475 : 5760 : : 4608 : $3550\frac{3}{4}$.

He further states the Spanish Mark to be 10 Castilian Grains heavier than the Mark of Lisbon, which also corresponds very nearly with the present determination.

The following are the results of the other Marks received at the same time from Spain, viz.

Sent from	by	weighing	
Cadiz	*Mr. Consul Matthew*,	3552,3	English Grains.
Alicant	*Athy*,	3537	....
Corunna	*Allen*,	3552	....
Valencia	*Waring*,	3557,6	....

The above weight of the Mark of Valencia agrees exactly with the result given by *Kruse*, &c.; and it is therefore probable that *Jacob L'Amiral's* experiments were made on this Mark. It seems the only way of accounting for so extraordinary an error.

The correction of this error makes a difference of nearly one-fifth per cent. in favour of England.

Commercial Weight.

The commercial Pound is composed of 2 Castilian Marks or 16 Ounces. The Ounce is divided into 8 Drachmas, 16 Adarmes, or 576 Grains. The Quintal of 4 Arrobas or 100lb. answers to 101,44lb. avoirdupois, or 46 Kilogrammes.

Dry Measure.

The Cahiz, a measure for corn, salt, and other dry goods, contains 12 Fanegas; the Fanega, 12 Celemines. The Celemine has many subdivisions, as $\frac{1}{2}$, $\frac{1}{4}$, $\frac{1}{8}$, &c.

The Fanega measures 4322$\frac{3}{4}$ Spanish, or 3439 English cubic Inches; it therefore equals 1,599 English Bushel, or 0,563 of a Hectolitre: hence 5 Fanegas are nearly equal to 8 English Bushels, or 1 Quarter.

Liquid Measure.

The Moyo of wine contains 16 Arrobas or Cantaras; an Arroba, 8 Azumbras, or 32 Quartillos.

The Arroba of wine, or great Arroba, is to be the same all over Spain, being regulated by the standard measure of Toledo, which contains 34lb. of river water (Castilian weight), and measures 1237$\frac{1}{3}$ Spanish, or 981 English cubic Inches; hence 1 Arroba equals 4,245 English wine Gallons, or 16,073 Litres.

The Arroba of oil, or lesser Arroba, should likewise be the same all over the kingdom; and the standard measure of Toledo weighs 25lb. of oil, or 26lb. 9oz. of river water (Castilian weight), and measures 966$\frac{2}{3}$ Spanish, or 771 English cubic Inches. This Arroba is divided into 4 Quartillos, or 100 Quarterones or Panillas, and answers to 3,33 English Gallons, or 12,63 Litres.

A Spanish Botta contains 30 Arrobas of wine, or 38$\frac{1}{2}$ of oil; a Pipe is 27 Arrobas of wine, or 34$\frac{1}{2}$ of oil; thus the Botta equals 127$\frac{1}{2}$ English Gallons, and the Pipe 114$\frac{3}{4}$.

Long Measures.

The Spanish standard Foot (called the Burgalese Foot) is divided into 12 Pulgadas, or 144 Lines; and equals 11,128 English Inches, or 0,2826 of a Metre.

The Palmo measures 9 Pulgadas, or 12 Dedos, which equal 8$\frac{1}{3}$ English Inches: the Palmo de Ribeira, with which masts, &c. are measured, is only 3 Inches.

The Vara, a measure for cloth, linen, and silk, is 3 Feet, or 4 Palmos; and is, therefore, 33,384 English Inches, or 0,847 of a Metre.

The Braza or Toesa is 2 Varas, or 6 Feet; the Passo, 5 Feet; the Estadal, 12 Feet, or 4 Varas; the Cuerda, 8$\frac{1}{4}$ Varas.

The Legua or League is divided into 3 Miles, the Mile into 8 Estadios, and the Estadio into 125 Paces, each of 5 Feet. The League is of very different lengths in the different parts of Spain. On roads made since 1766, the distances are laid down at the rate of 8000 Varas to the League, that is, 7416 English Yards; thus 1 League equals 4,291 English Miles, or 6,78 Kilometres.

The Judicial League is 5000 Varas, or 4635 English Yards; and therefore equals 2,682 English Miles, or 4,238 Kilometres. Long Measures.

The Fanegada, or Acre of corn land, is various in different parts of Spain, and even in different parts of Castile; it is, however, generally understood to be 400 square Estadals, or 6000 square Varas; which equal 1 English Acre 21 Perches, or 45,97 French Ares. Superficial Measures.

The Arranzada (the Acre for vineyards) is the same all over the country; it contains 48400 Spanish square Feet, which equal 3 Roods 33 Perches English, or 38,69 French Ares.

For the exchanges of Spain, see Vol. II. page 88. Exchanges, Usances, and Days of Grace.

The usances and days of grace vary in different parts of the kingdom: thus—

At Madrid and Seville, the usance for bills drawn from England, France, Genoa, and Leghorn, is 60 days after date; from Amsterdam, Hamburgh, and other places in the north of Europe, 2 calendar months.

At Cadiz and Bilboa, the usance from France is 1 month after date; and from the other parts of Europe, 2 months after date.

At Barcelona, the usance for all foreign bills is 60 days after date.

In all parts of Spain, the usance for bills drawn from Rome is 90 days after date, without any days of grace.

The days of grace for all other bills drawn on Madrid, Seville, Bilboa, and Barcelona, are 14 days, provided the bills be accepted before they become due, otherwise no days of grace are allowed: such bills must be protested immediately.

At Cadiz, 6 days' grace are allowed in all cases.

In drawing bills of exchange on Spain it is customary to write "PAYABLE IN EFFECTIVE," in order to distinguish cash from *Vales Reales*, which are of inferior value.

VALES REALES (or Royal Bonds) are a kind of paper currency, which was first issued by the Spanish Government in 1800, in bonds of a certain number of Pesos, transferable by indorsement, and bearing an interest of 4 per cent. per annum. They are still in circulation, at a depreciated and fluctuating value. Vales Reales.

Vales Reales are generally quoted at so many per cent. *loss;* thus they are quoted at 80 per cent. when their real value is 20 per cent. At Cadiz, however, they are valued in Hard Dollars: thus a *Vale* of a certain number of Pesos, is quoted at a variable number of Hard Dollars.

STETTIN *(in Prussian Pomerania).*

Monies and Coins.

Accounts are kept in Rixdollars of 24 Good Groschen, each Grosche being subdivided into 12 Pfenings.

The Rixdollar was also formerly divided into 36 Shillings current, 72 Shillings Sundish, or 144 Wittens; but these monies of account are now nearly discontinued. A Gulden or Florin is worth 16 good Groschen.

The coins being Prussian, will be found under the article *Berlin.*

Weights.

The Centner of the old weight of Stettin consisted of 8 Lisponds, or 112lb.; the Lispond is 14lb.; the Stone, 10lb.; and the Stone of wool, 21lb.

The Pound is divided into 32 Loths, and weighs 7219 English Grains: thus 100lb. of Stettin answer to 103,13lb. avoirdupois, or 46,77 Kilogrammes.*

A Burden of steel is 3 Centners. A Tonne of soap is 4 Viertels, weighing 280lb.

Measures of Capacity.

Corn is measured by the Scheffel of Berlin; a Last is 72 such Scheffels, and the Wispel is 24; but when sold in the market, it is from 26 to 28 Scheffels. A Tonne is 2½ Scheffels. The Scheffel, Berlin measure, equals 1,479 English Bushel, or 0,521 of a Hectolitre; and thus a Last in Stettin equals 13,31 English Quarters, or 37,51 Hectolitres.

The old measure of Stettin is about 11 per cent. less than the Berlin measure; thus the old Scheffel equals 1,395 English Bushel, or 0,4915 of a Hectolitre; a Dromt is composed of 72 such Scheffels.

The Oxhoft of wine is divided into 1½ Ohm, 3 Eimers, or 6 Ankers; the Anker is 30 Quarts of Berlin, and equals 13,70 English Gallons, or 51,85 Litres.

Long Measures.

The Ell of Berlin, and the Rhineland Foot (which is the standard Foot throughout the Prussian dominions) are generally used in Stettin. There is, however, an old Ell of 25,6 English Inches, or 0,6508 of a Metre; and an old Foot of 11,12 English Inches, or 0,2826 of a Metre.

The Pomeranian Ruthe is 16 Feet of the old measure, or 14⅘ Rhineland Feet, which equal 15⅓ English Feet.

---

* The above is the weight of the Pound transmitted to London in 1818 by *F. W. Lutze, Esq.* the British Consul at Stettin. The Foot sent by him has been found to measure about the 100th part of an Inch more than the Rhineland Foot, being 12,365 English Inches.

Superficial Measure. The Pomeranian Morgen or Acre of land contains 300 Pomeranian square Ruthes, which equal 1 Acre 2 Roods $11\frac{2}{3}$ Perches, English statute measure, answering to 63,64 French Ares.

Lastage. A Last of salt is 18 Tonnes; a Hamburgh Last of salt answers to $14\frac{1}{2}$ Tonnes in Stettin; a Hundred of salt from Amsterdam makes $5\frac{1}{2}$ Lasts; and a Hundred of salt from France, $9\frac{2}{3}$ Lasts in Stettin.

The freight of ships is generally valued by the Dutch Ship Last, 5 of which are equal to 4 Lasts of Stettin. The following quantities are reckoned for a Dutch Last, viz. 4000lb. of iron, and other heavy goods; 2000lb. of lighter goods, such as hemp and flax; $56\frac{1}{2}$ Scheffels of corn; 13 Casks of herrings; 8 Hogsheads of wine; 5 Schocks (each of 60 Pieces) of pipe staves; 7 Schocks of hogshead staves; 9 Schocks of barrel staves; 65 cubic Feet of oak timber; or 70 cubic Feet of fir timber.

20 Schocks of pipe staves; 30 Schocks of hogshead staves; 40 ditto of barrel staves; 60 ditto of long-heading, or 80 of short ditto, are called 1 Mille; half that quantity is a Great Hundred. 450 Feet of timber, Rhineland measure, are reckoned equal to 1 Mille of staves.

Exchanges, Usances, and Days of Grace. The exchanges are nearly the same as in Berlin; see page 35, Vol. II.

The usance for bills drawn from London and France is 1 month; from Amsterdam, 6 weeks; from Hamburgh, 4 weeks, after date. Stettin draws generally on Amsterdam, Copenhagen, and Hamburgh at 6 or 8, or sometimes 3 or 4 weeks date; on England and France, at 2 months date.

The days of grace are three, as in Berlin.

STOCKHOLM, *see Sweden.*

STRALSUND (*in Swedish Pomerania*).

Monies of Account. Accounts are kept in Rixdollars of 48 Schillings, each Schilling being divided into 12 Pfenings. Accounts are also kept in Pomeranian Guldens of 24 Schillings current.

The Rixdollar is also reckoned at 2 Guldens, 6 Marks Sundish, 24 Groschen, 48 Schillings, 96 Sechslings, 192 Wittens, or 576 Pfenings current.

The Rixdollar Specie is worth 2 Reichs Guldens or Florins of the Empire, $2\frac{2}{3}$ Pomeranian Guldens, 8 Marks Sundish, or 32 Groschen. The Grosche is divided into 2 Schillings, 4 Sechslings, 8 Wittens, or 24 Pfenings.

Coins. The coins are Silver pieces of 1, $\frac{1}{2}$, and $\frac{1}{4}$ Reichs Gulden, or 16, 8, and 4 Groschen; base Silver coins of 1 and 2 Groschen, and 1 Schilling; and also Copper Wittens; of these, the Single and Double Groschen and Schillings are most common, and with the old Swedish Runsticks, and 5 Oer Pieces (passing here for 4 and 2 good Groschen), they form almost the whole currency of the place.

Weights. The commercial weight of Stralsund is about a quarter per cent. lighter than Hamburgh weight; thus 100lb. of Stralsund equal 106,57lb. avoirdupois, or 48,33 Kilogrammes.

Retailers, however, when they sell under a Lispond, use the Cologne weight, which is $3\frac{1}{2}$ per cent. lighter than that of Stralsund.

The Shippond is 20 Lisponds; the Centner, 8 Lisponds; the Lispond, 14lb. A Stone of wool is 10lb.

Measures. The Last of corn is divided into 8 Dromts, 32 Tonnes, 96 Scheffels, or 384 Fehrts. The Scheffel contains 1,105 English Bushel, or 0,3896 of a Hectolitre: thus the Last of corn renders 13,26 English Quarters.

Liquids are measured by the Stubgen of 4 Pots. 1 Stubgen equals 1,027 English Gallon, or 3,883 Litres.

The Ell is composed of 2 Feet, and equals 22,6 English Inches, or 0,582 of a Metre. The Laken is 24 Ells.

Exchanges. Stralsund exchanges with and gives to—

Amsterdam....130 Rixdollars current, more or less, for 100 Rixdollars.
Hamburgh ....130 Rixdollars current,............for 100 Rixdollars banco.
Stockholm ....132 Rixdollars current,............for 100 Rixdollars specie.

STRASBURG *(in France)*.

Monies and Coins. The monies and coins of France are used here. Accounts are also occasionally kept in Pfunds or Pounds of 20 Schillings; in Rixdollars of 90 Creutzers; or in Florins of 10 Schillings, or 60 Creutzers.

The Pfund is worth 4 Livres; the Ecu or Rixdollar, 3 Livres; the Florin, 2 Livres; the Livre, 5 Schillings, or $7\frac{1}{2}$ Batzen; the Schilling, 4 Sous, or 6 Creutzers; a Batze, 4 Creutzers; a Creutze, 4 Pfenings, or 8 Deniers.

The metrical system of France is introduced here, but there are certain old weights and measures used. Thus the Strasburg Pound, with which goods are weighed when sold retail, equals 7266 English Grains. Hence 100lb. answer to 103,8lb. avoirdupois, or 47,07 Kilogrammes. Old Weights.

The old measure for corn is the Sester or Setier of 4 Quarts, or 16 Massels. There is, however, the land Sester, and the city Sester; the former Sester measures 953 French or 1154 English cubic Inches; and the latter, 924 French or 1118 English cubic Inches: thus the land Sester = 4,29 Winchester Gallons, or 18,9 Litres; and the city Sester = 4,15 Winchester Gallons, or 18,31 Litres. Old Measures.

Corn is also measured by the Sack or Rezal of 6 Boisseaux, weighing about 176lb. old French weight in wheat; such a Sack contains about 3 English Bushels.

The Ohm, liquid measure, is divided into 24 Pots, 48 Pintes, or 96 Chopines, and contains 12,17 English Gallons, or 46 Litres.

The Strasburg Foot is 11,39 English Inches, or 0,2894 of a Metre; and the land Foot is 11,62 English Inches, or 0,2952 of a Metre. The Ell measures 21,2 English Inches, or 0,5382 of a Metre.

Strasburg exchanges with and gives (more or less) to— Exchanges.

Amsterdam ......184 Ecus of 3 Livres, for 100 Rixdollars.
Basil ....164 .... 100 Rixdollars money of exchange.
Francfort ......130 .... 100 Rixdollars convention current.
Hamburgh ......184 .... 100 Rixdollars banco.
Lyons and Paris..100 .... 100 Ecus at sight or usance.

The usance for bills from Germany is 15 days after sight, and from France 30 days after date. Usances and Days of Grace.

The acceptor of a bill cannot claim any days of grace: but the holder may allow 10 days, after which the bill must be either paid or protested.

SURINAM, *see West Indies.*

SWEDEN.

Accounts are kept here in Riksdaler of 48 Skilling, the Skilling being subdivided into 12 Rundstycken or Ore. Monies of Account.

This is a real Specie Riksdaler (commonly called the Swedish Dollar), coined

Monies of Account.

after the rate established in 1664; and, by a royal edict of 1777, it was made a general money of account.

Before that period, accounts were kept in Dahler of 4 Marck, or 32 Ore, either in silver or copper coins, the former being reckoned three times the value of the same denominations of the latter.

Coins.

By the regulations of 1777, the Specie Riksdaler was to pass for the same value that 6 Silver Dahler or 18 Koppar Dahler formerly did; and there were coined whole Riksdaler, and pieces of $\frac{2}{3}$, $\frac{1}{3}$, $\frac{1}{6}$, $\frac{1}{12}$, and $\frac{1}{24}$ of a Riksdaler.

Silver coins of every other denomination were declared to be out of currency; and all persons possessing such were ordered to bring them to the Mint to be exchanged, according to their weight and fineness, for Specie Riksdaler.

The Gold coins here are Double, Single, and Half Ducats. The Single Ducats are to pass for 1 Riksdaler 46 Skilling specie; or 11 Dahler 24 Ore silver; or 35 Dahler 8 Ore koppar.

The Copper coins are, Single and Double Slants, at 1 and 2 Ore silver, or 3 and 6 Ore koppar; and Rundstycken, of 1 Ore koppar; and also Half Rundstycken.

96 Double Slants, 192 Single Slants, or 576 Rundstycken, are to pass for 1 Specie Riksdaler; but in large payments no person is obliged to take more copper coin than the value of half a Riksdaler.

The large copper pieces of the value of 4, 3, 2, 1, $\frac{3}{4}$, and $\frac{1}{2}$ Silver Dahler, or 12, 9, 6, 3, $2\frac{1}{4}$, and $1\frac{1}{2}$ Koppar Dahler, weighing $7\frac{1}{9}$, $5\frac{1}{3}$, $3\frac{5}{9}$, $2\frac{2}{3}$, $1\frac{7}{9}$, $1\frac{1}{3}$, and $\frac{8}{9}$lb. of the Victualie or common weight, are no longer considered as a legal coin, but as a sort of merchandise, which every one is at liberty to sell or export, after paying the duty on exportation. These, in general, but more particularly the 2 Dahler pieces, are called *Plates*.

Rate of Coinage.

According to the regulations of 1777, the following numbers of coins are to weigh a Mark, viz. $60\frac{1}{2}$ Ducats, at 23 Carats 5 Grains fine; $7\frac{1}{5}$ Riksdaler, $10\frac{4}{5}$ Pieces of $\frac{2}{3}$, or $21\frac{3}{5}$ Pieces of $\frac{1}{3}$, at 14 Lods 1 Grain fine; 34 Pieces of $\frac{1}{6}$, at 11 Lods 1 Grain fine; 50 Pieces of $\frac{1}{12}$, at 8 Lods 2 Grains fine; or 76 Pieces of $\frac{1}{24}$, at 6 Lods 2 Grains fine.

Out of a Skeppund of 320lb. of copper, 540 Koppar Dahlers are coined into Plates, and 900 Dahlers into Slants.

Value of Coins.

As the Swedish Ducat weighs $53\frac{3}{4}$ English Grains, and contains $52\frac{4}{7}$ Grains of fine gold, it is, therefore, worth 9s. $2\frac{1}{2}$d. sterling in English gold coin; but in Sweden this Ducat passes for 94 Skilling, which are worth only 9s. 1d. in English silver coin. Value of Coins.

According to the Mint regulations, the Swedish Specie Riksdaler should weigh 609 Swedish Aas, or $451\frac{2}{3}$ English Grains, and contain 535 Aas, or $396\frac{4}{5}$ Grains of fine silver; it is, therefore, worth 4s. $7\frac{1}{2}$d. sterling, and the Skilling, $1\frac{1}{6}$d. nearly; also, the Silver Dahler = $9\frac{1}{4}$d.; and the Koppar Dahler = about 3d. sterling. Hence £1 sterling = 207 Skillings specie; or 25 Dahler 30 Ore silver; or 77 Dahler 26 Ore koppar.

The fineness of gold is expressed in Carats and Grains; the Marck or other weight being divided into 24 Carats, and the Carat into 12 Grains. Fineness of Gold.

Gold is sold by Ducats; and 23 Carats 5 Grains (that is, $\frac{281}{288}$ of a Swedish Marck) of fine gold are reckoned for $60\frac{1}{2}$ such Ducats.

928 Swedish Ducats of gold are commonly reckoned equal to 923 Ducats of gold in Hamburgh; also 869 Swedish Ducats to 12 Marks troy of fine gold in Amsterdam; and 537 Swedish Ducats to 64 Ounces of English standard gold.

Wrought gold is of three sorts, viz. Ducat gold, 23 Carats 5 Grains fine; Pistolet gold, 20 Carats 4 Grains fine, with an allowance of 2 Grains in the Marck for remedy; and Crown gold, 18 Carats 4 Grains fine, with the same allowance.

The fineness of silver is expressed in Lods and Grains; the Marck or other weight being divided into 16 Lods, and the Lod into 18 Grains. Wrought silver should be $13\frac{1}{4}$ Lods fine: an allowance, however, is made of $\frac{1}{8}$ Lod in the Marck for remedy. Fineness of Silver.

The smallest denomination of weight in Sweden is the As, which is the same as that of Amsterdam. Weights.

The Mark for weighing gold and silver is divided into 16 Lods, or 64 Quentins.

There is a particular weight used for Ducats, the Nest of which answers to 128 of those coins.

The Apothecaries' Pound is divided into 12 Ounces; and the Ounce into 8 Drachms, 24 Scruples, or 240 Grains.

There are six other weights in use for different purposes, viz.—

The Victualie or commercial weight, the Skolpund or Pound of which is divided into 32 Lods or 128 Quentins. 20lb. Victualie weight = 1 Lispund;

Weights. 20 Lispunds = 1 Skeppund; 32lb. = 1 Sten; 120lb. = 1 Centner; 165lb. = 1 Waag. 100lb. Victualie weight = 93,76lb. avoirdupois, or 42,52 Kilogrammes.

The Metal weight, called also the Staple Town and Exportation weight, is $\frac{4}{5}$ of the Victualie weight. The Pound is divided into $\frac{1}{4}$, $\frac{1}{8}$, $\frac{1}{16}$, &c. 20lb. make the Lispund; and 20 Lispunds, the Skeppund.

Uppstads-wigt or Inland Town weight.

Bergs-wigt or Miners' weight.

Raw Iron weight; and

Raw Copper weight.

The following Table shews the proportion which these weights bear to English and French weights.

	Swedish As.	English Grains.	French Grammes.
Mint Mark	4384	3252	210,703
Gold or Ducat weight	$9275\frac{29}{121}$	6880	445,768
Silver weight and Commercial Skolpund, called Victualie weight	8848	6563	425,229
Metal weight Skolpund	$7078\frac{2}{5}$	5250	340,196
Medicinal weight Skolpund	7416	5501	356,420
Raw Iron Skolpund	10168	7542	488,661
Raw Copper Skolpund	7853	5825	377,413
Miners' weight Skolpund	$7821\frac{79}{125}$	5801	375,858
Inland Town weight Skolpund	$7450\frac{2}{125}$	5526	358,040

The above are the contents, in Dutch or Swedish Asen, of the different weights, as established and acted upon in business; and writers upon metrology generally have followed those contents.*

Dry Measures. Corn and other dry commodities are measured by the Tunna.

The Barrel or Tunna is divided into 2 Spann, 8 Fjerdingar, 32 Kappar, 56

* It is to be observed that the Mint and Commercial weights transmitted to London, in 1818, by *George Foy, Esq.* British Consul at Stockholm, do not quite agree with the above; the former being 2 English Grains lighter, and the latter 3 Grains. The standards transmitted on the same occasion from Gothenburg, by *J. R. Wise, Esq.* Consul General, vary still more; the Ducat weight being 6854 English Grains, and the Silver weight $6555\frac{1}{2}$. All the other information on Swedish metrology, contained in both dispatches, perfectly agree, and are inserted in the above article.

Kanns, 112 Stop, 448 Quarter, or 1792 Ort or Junkfra. But to every Tunna of wheat, rye, barley, oats, or pease, 4 Kappar are allowed for good measure, making the Tunna 36 Kappar; to every Tunna of malt, 6 Kappar are allowed; and to every Tunna of salt or lime, 2 Kappar. In the sale of coals and other articles, the over measure is taken by heaping the vessel. Dry Measures.

The common Tunna of 32 Kappar contains 4,157 Bushels, or 1,464 Hectolitre.

The Hogshead (Oxhufvud) contains $1\frac{1}{2}$ Am, 3 Eimer, 6 Ankare, 90 Kannor, 180 Stop, 720 Quarter, or 2880 Jungfrur; and answers to 62,23 English Gallons, or 235,58 Litres. Liquid Measures.

Two Oxhufvud make 1 Pipe, and 2 Pipes, 1 Fuder.

The Tunna of liquids or soft substances, and also of flour, meat, and fish, must contain 48 Kanns. A Tunna of pitch or tar may contain 1 Stop, or half a Kann less.

The Kann and its divisions are common to dry and liquid measures: its contents are $159\frac{2}{3}$ English cubic Inches. Hence 100 Kanns equal 69,09 wine Gallons, or 7,42 Bushels, English measure, answering to 2,615 Hectolitres.

The Swedish Foot is commonly divided into 12 Inches, or 144 Lines; but engineers divide it into 10 Inches, 100 Lines, or 1000 Points. This Foot measures 11,684 English Inches, or 0,2968 of a Metre. Long Measures.

The Ell is 2 Feet; the Fathom is 3 Ells; the Rod, 8 Ells.

The Swedish Mile is 6000 Swedish Fathoms, which equal 11700 English Yards. Hence it equals 6,64 English Miles, or 10,698 Kilometres.

A degree of the meridian was formerly reckoned here at $10\frac{23}{50}$ Swedish Miles, answering to $69\frac{1}{2}$ English Miles, and agreeing with the measurement made by *Maupertuis* in Lapland in the year 1736; but in 1802 a more accurate measurement appears to have been made in the same place (lat. 66° 20′ 10″) by *M. Swanberg*, who has determined the degree to be 57196,159 French Toises, or 69,269 English Miles.

A Swedish square Foot contains $136\frac{3}{5}$ English square Inches; a Swedish square Rod, 27 English square Yards; a Swedish square Mile, 44 English square Miles. Superficial Measures.

A Swedish Tunneland or Acre is 56000 Swedish square Feet, or 5900 English square Yards; that is, 1 Acre and 35 Perches English, or 49,31 French Ares.

Lastage. A Last of pitch, pot-ash, Luneburg salt, or beer, is 12 Tunnor; of tar, or train oil, 13 Tunnor; of Spanish and French salt, 18 Tunnor; of fish, 12 Tunnor, or 12000 herrings; of hemp, flax, cordage, tallow, or hops, 6 Skeppunds, or 120 Lispunds, answering nearly to a Ton avoirdupois.

Terms used in Reckoning. A Wahl is 20 Kasts, or 80 Pieces; a Shok is 60 Pieces; a Tiogue or Styk, 20 Pieces; a Tolft, 12 Pieces; a Kast, 4 Pieces.

A Hand of paper is 24 Sheets; a Ream, 20 Hands; a Ballot, 10 Reams.

FINLAND.

Weights & Measures. The weights and measures of Finland correspond with those of Sweden, with the following exceptions:—

In dry measure, the Tunna is divided into 30 Kapps, or 75 Kanns. By an Imperial Decree of April, 1816, the Tunna for all kinds of grain, corn, and salt, is to contain 63 Kanns; and the Tunna for coals, alabaster, lime, and plaster, 56 Kanns.

In liquid measure, the Tunna is subdivided into 4 Furdingar, each of 12 Kanns; the Furdingar into 2 Ottingars, or 4 Sextingars.

In building and trades, the Foot is divided into 2 Quarters, and the Quarter into 6 Inches; so that the Ell contains 4 Quarters or 24 Inches.

The Last of Sweden or of Finland answers to 18 Skeppunds, metal weight, or to 14 Skeppunds 8 Lisponds, Victualie weight: thus the Last corresponds to 3 Tons avoirdupois nearly, or 3064 Kilogrammes.

The following quantities are reckoned for a Last, viz.

24 Tunna of rye; 27 of barley; 30 of oats; 15 of tar; 18 of pitch; and 17 of salt.*

Exchanges of Sweden. For the foreign exchanges of Sweden, see *Stockholm*, Vol. II. p. 91.

Bills of exchange are seldom drawn from abroad on Sweden, as this country, like Russia, generally settles her commercial debts by drawing and remitting foreign bills.

---

* The above specifications of Finland metrology were included in the Russian dispatches transmitted to *Lord Castlereagh*, in 1818, by *Sir Daniel Bayley,* Consul General at Petersburg.

The usance is reckoned at 1 month after sight. Six days of grace are allowed for the payment of bills (Sundays and holidays included): if the sixth day, however, should fall on a Sunday or holiday, the bill must be paid on the preceding day; but those six days are not understood to be granted, except in cases of necessity; and a person who wishes to preserve his credit must not claim any days of grace, but pay his bills on the day they are made payable. Usance, Days of Grace, &c.

Bills payable on demand, or at 2 or 3 days sight, are not allowed any days of grace; bills payable in the middle of a month become due on the 14th, whatever may be the number of days in that month; and the six days of grace are allowed.

When a bill, payable after date, is not presented till 2 or 3 days after its written term is expired, no more days of grace are allowed than may remain unelapsed at the time of presentation.

The Paper Currency of Sweden, which is very extensive, is of two sorts, namely, *Banco* and *Riksgald*. The former is issued by the National Bank, and the latter by the Riksgild Bank, which is under the direction of Government. Banco is 50 per cent. better than Riksgald; that is, 2 Dollars of the former are worth 3 Dollars of the latter. Paper Currency.

Banco is a legal tender, and has been lately declared, by Royal Authority, the national currency. The king or his ministers, however, have no power or control over the Bank, it being entirely under the direction and management of the four Orders which compose the Diet; namely, the Nobility, the Clergy, the Burgesses, and the Bundè or Independent Farmers. From these Orders, Directors, Auditors, and Inspectors of the Bank are chosen.

Bank Notes are issued in great variety, even as low as $\frac{1}{8}$ of a Dollar. No money whatever can be taken out of the Bank without an equivalent; and it is supposed to contain much treasure, especially in silver.

Riksgald is current in all payments; but as no fresh issues of this paper have been lately made by Government, it is continually decreasing in circulation, while Banco increases. Copper only is paid at the Bank in exchange of Notes, which, in mercantile computations, is about half their nominal value in silver or gold.

SWITZERLAND.

Almost every Swiss Canton has a peculiar mode of keeping accounts; as may be seen under the articles *Basil, Bern, Geneva, Neufchatel, St. Gall,* and *Zurich.* Monies of Account.

Monies of Account.

In 1798, when the whole of Switzerland was united under the name of the Helvetic Republic or Confederacy, a uniform way of keeping accounts was introduced, but not fully established, except in Government concerns. It consisted of Franken or Francs of 10 Batzen, each Batze being divided into 10 Rappen. This Franc, which is commonly called the *Swiss Livre*, is equivalent to $1\frac{1}{2}$ Franc of the money of France, and is therefore worth about $14\frac{1}{2}$d. sterling.

Coins.

The old Swiss coins are given under the above articles respectively; but in order to understand those of modern date, it should be stated that from 1798 to 1803, the whole country was united under one government; and the money coined during that period, bearing the stamp of the ***Helvetic Republic***, consisted of gold pieces of 32 and 16 Francs; silver pieces of 40 and 20 Batzen, or 4 and 2 Francs; and base silver pieces of 10 and 5 Batzen. In 1803 Switzerland again became a federative Republic; each Canton was allowed the right of coinage; but the standard of the pieces was to be uniform, and the coins of each Canton were to be current throughout the whole country. These consist of silver pieces of 1, 2, and 4 Francs; and base silver pieces of 5, 1, and $\frac{1}{2}$ Batzen and 1 Rappen.

Coinage of 1804.

In 1804, a silver coinage for all the Cantons of the Helvetic Confederacy was established, under regulations consisting of 29 articles, of which the following are the substance:

The Franc is to contain $127\frac{19}{80}$ Grains of fine silver; and the price of the Mark of fine silver is to be $36\frac{1}{5}$ Francs. The pieces of 1 Franc are to be at the rate of $32\frac{58}{100}$ to the Mark; with pieces of 2 and 4 Francs in proportion: and the fineness, 10 Deniers $19\frac{1}{5}$ Grains, with an allowance of 1 Grain for remedy in the fineness. The remedy of weight in the Francs is 16 Grains per Mark; in the 2 Franc pieces, 12 Grains; and in the 4 Franc pieces, 8 Grains per Mark. The 5 Batze pieces are to be at the rate of 54 to the Mark, 8 Deniers fine; the remedy, $\frac{1}{5}$ of a piece per Mark, and $1\frac{1}{2}$ Grain in the alloy. 90 Batzen, 120 half Batzen, or 360 Rappen, are to weigh a Mark. The Batzen are to contain 1 part of silver in 6; the half Batzen, 3 parts in 32; and the Rappen, 1 part in 24.

No law was then made for gold coins, except that such of the Cantons as may wish to mint them, must regulate the coinage in such a manner, that the Franc may contain $8\frac{1}{5}$ Swiss Grains of fine gold, by which it is worth $14\frac{27}{100}$d. sterling in gold.

Value of Monies.

The silver Franc, according to the law of 1804, is worth $14\frac{57}{100}$d. sterling; or £1 sterling = 16 Francs 4 Batzen 7 Rappen.

Expression of Fineness.

The fineness of gold is expressed in Carats and parts; the Pound or other quantity being divided into 24 Carats, and the Carat into 32 parts.

The fineness of silver is expressed in Deniers and Grains; the Pound or other quantity being divided into 12 Deniers, and the Denier into 24 Grains.

Gold and Silver Weight.

The weight for gold and silver is the old French *Poids de Marc;* the Mark of which is divided into 8 Ounces, 192 Deniers, or 4608 Grains; and answers to 244,751 Grammes, or $3777\frac{1}{2}$ English Grains.

For other particulars, see the different places above quoted.

TENERIFFE, *see Canary Islands.*

TOULON, *see Marseilles and France.*

TRIESTE *(in Istria, on the Adriatic).*

Monies of Account.

Accounts are kept here in Fiorini or Florins of 60 Creutzers; also in Lire of 20 Soldi. The Creutzer is subdivided into 4 Pfenings, and the Soldo into 12 Denari.

These monies of account are valued in three different ways, namely, in Austrian currency, in Trieste currency, and in Valuta di Piazza. The first is chiefly used in foreign exchanges, the second in wholesale trade, and the third in retail business.

The Florin, Austrian currency, is worth $5\frac{5}{17}$ Lire of Trieste currency, or $5\frac{7}{17}$ Lire di Piazza. Thus 17 Florins = 90 current Lire, or 92 Lire di Piazza.

Coins.

The coins will be found under the article *Vienna.* All the Austrian coins pass here at the rate of 90 Lire, Trieste currency, for 17 Florins, Austrian currency, or 30 Soldi for 17 Creutzers, except the 7 Creutzer pieces, which pass for 12 current Soldi.

The Imperial Ducat and Venetian Sequin are reckoned at $4\frac{1}{4}$ Florins, or $22\frac{1}{2}$ current Lire, or 23 Lire di Piazza: but the Sequin bears an agio of about 4 per cent. above that value, which agio is regulated by the exchange of Vienna on Venice. The Ducat of Trieste is an imaginary coin, reckoned at 6 Lire.

Gold and Silver Weight.

The weights and measures chiefly in use at Trieste are those of Vienna and Venice.

In weighing gold and silver, the Venetian Mark is principally used. It is divided into 8 Ounces, 32 Quarters, 192 Denari, 1152 Carats, or 4608 Grains; and answers to 3681½ English Grains, or 238,531 Grammes.*

The Vienna Mark is divided into 16 Loths, 64 Quents, or 256 Denari; and equals 3684 English Grains, or 238,693 Grammes.

Commercial Pound.

The commercial Pound chiefly in use is that of Vienna; but it does not wholly exclude the Pounds Grosso and Sottile of Venice, which are mostly used for Italian goods. It is divided into 4 Quarters, 16 Ounces, 32 Loths, or 128 Quents; and contains 8639 English Grains. Thus 100lb. at Trieste correspond to 123,6lb. avoirdupois, or 55,96 Kilogrammes.

Dry Measures.

The principal measure for corn is the Stajo, which was computed by the French authorities, during their occupation of this place, to equal 826,109 Litres, which answer to 2,344 English Bushels. The Vienna Metzen, which is in use for the military establishments, contains 607,335 Litres, or 1,723 Bushel. There is another measure, called Polonick, which is more generally adopted by the land owners: this renders 303,676 Litres, or 0,861 of an English Bushel.

Liquid Measures.

The Orna, or Eimer, is composed of 40 Boccali, and contains 56,54 Litres, or 14,94 English Gallons. The Barile = 656,25 Litres, or 173,3 English Gallons.

The Orna of oil is divided into 5½ Caffisi, and weighs about 107lb. of Vienna. It contains 17 English Gallons, or 64,34 Litres.

Long Measure.

The Ell, woollen measure, is 26,6 English Inches, or 0,6758 of a Metre. The Ell for silk is 25,2 English Inches, or 0,6406 of a Metre.

---

* The weight of the Mark of Venice, which is used at Trieste, is variously stated by different authors. *Kruse* makes it 3686 English Grains, and *Tillet* 3682. The latter nearly corresponds with the Mark lately sent to *Viscount Castlereagh* by *Edward Stanley, Esq.* His Majesty's Consul at Trieste; which has been found to weigh 3681½ English Grains. His dispatches transmitted on this occasion contain very full statements of the metrology of Trieste. His account, however, of the contents of the measures of capacity (which are here adopted), differ from those hitherto published; and he states them to be the result of actual measurements made by the French authorities while they occupied the place, and which have been recently verified by his own experiments.

Trieste exchanges with, and gives (more or less) to— Exchanges.

Amsterdam	$49\frac{3}{8}$	Kreutzers	for	1 Current Florin.
Augsburg .	$98\frac{3}{8}$	Florins	for	100 Florins, Augsburg currency.
Genoa	$19\frac{13}{32}$	Kreutzers	for	1 Lira fuori banco.
Hamburgh	$43\frac{3}{8}$	Kreutzers	for	1 Marc banco.
London ..	10	Florins	for	£1 sterling.
Naples ...	97	Kreutzers	for	1 Ducat.
Paris	$23\frac{5}{16}$	Kreutzers	for	1 Franc.

TRIPOLI *(on the Coast of Barbary)*.

Accounts are kept in Piastres of 13 Grimellini or 52 Aspers. The Grimellin is valued at 6 Sous Tournois, which makes the Piastre of Tripoli worth 3s. 3d. sterling. Monies of Account.

The Sultanins coined here are of the finest gold, and $\frac{1}{3}$ heavier than those that are minted in Egypt. Coins.

Of foreign coins, Venetian Sequins and Spanish Dollars are most common; but their value is not fixed.

The weight for gold and silver is called Metical, 50 of which equal a Venetian Mark: hence 1 Metical weighs 73,66 English Grains, or 4,77 Grammes. Weights.

The Cantaro weight contains 100 Rottoli, each of 6 Ounces, or 128 Termini. This Cantaro answers to about 112lb. avoirdupois, or 50,79 Kilogrammes.

The corn measure, called Caffiso, contains 20 Tiberi, and is equal to 1,154 English Bushel, or 0,406 of a Hectolitre. Measures.

The oil measure, called Mattaro, weighs 42 Rottoli, or about 47lb. avoirdupois, and equals 21,31 Kilogrammes.

The Pic, or Ell, is equal to 21,8 English Inches, or 0,5536 of a Metre.

TUNIS *(on the Coast of Barbary)*.

Accounts are kept here in Piastres of 16 Carobas or 52 Aspers. Monies of Account.

The Asper, which is an imaginary money, is divided into 2 Bourbes; and therefore $6\frac{1}{2}$ Bourbes make 1 Caroba.

Coins. The only piece of gold coined here is the Mahbub or Sultanin, valued at $4\frac{1}{2}$ Piastres, with halves and quarters.

The Silver coins are, Piastres, with halves and quarters, and Doublas, valued at 24 Aspers.

Value of Coins. Foreign coins have a very uncertain price here, and depend chiefly on the course of exchange. The Spanish Doubloon is generally from 58 to 60 Piastres; the Dollar at 4; and the Venetian Sequin at $8\frac{1}{2}$. Thus the Piastre may be valued at 13d. sterling.

Weights. Gold, silver, and pearls, are weighed by the Ounce of 8 Meticals. 16 of these Ounces make the Tunis Pound, which is used for all kinds of commodities, and answers to $7773\frac{1}{2}$ English Grains;* and therefore the Ounce equals 485,8 English Grains, or 31,475 Grammes.

The principal commercial weight is the Cantaro; which contains 100 Rotuls or Pounds, and answers to 111,05lb. avoirdupois, or 50,36 Kilogrammes.

Dry Measure. The measure for corn is the Caffice; which is divided into 16 Whibas, and the Whiba into 12 Zahs or Sahas. The Caffice renders 15 English Bushels, or 5,28 Hectolitres.

Liquid Measures. The wine measure is the Millerolle of Marseilles; which contains 16,99 English Gallons, or 64,33 Litres. It is here divided into $6\frac{1}{2}$ Mitres.

The principal measure for oil is the Metal or Mettar; which answers to 5,125 English Gallons, or 19,39 Litres, and weighs 34lb. avoirdupois nearly. This measure, however, varies in several parts of the country.

The Metal of Soussa, a village near Tunis, which produces nearly all the oil

* The relative weight of the Tunis Pound has been in general very erroneously stated. According to *Kruse, Ricard,* and *Nelkenbreker,* it answers to 7661 English Grains; *Bonneville* makes it 7755 such Grains; and in the former edition of the Cambist it was stated, from mercantile authority, at 7770: but by the experiments lately made at the *London Mint,* it weighs $7773\frac{1}{2}$ Grains, as above. The Pound, thus examined, was verified by the proper authority at Tunis, in 1820, and transmitted to the *Earl of Bathurst* by *Richard Oglander, Esq.* the British Consul at that city; from whose dispatches on the occasion, addressed to his Lordship, the other particulars of the weights and measures of Tunis, as above stated, have been extracted.

Liquid Measures.

for exportation, is larger than that of Tunis, the Millerolle containing $2\frac{2}{3}$ Metals; but all foreign calculations are made in the above Metal of Tunis.

Long Measure.

The Pic, long measure, is of three sorts: the Pic, woollen measure, is 26,5 English Inches, or 0,6730 of a Metre; the Pic, silk measure, is $\frac{1}{16}$ shorter, and equals 24,8 English Inches, or 0,6298 of a Metre; and the Pic, linen measure, is $\frac{1}{4}$ shorter than the latter, that is, 18,6 English Inches, or 0,4724 of a Metre.

Exchanges.

Tunis exchanges with, and gives to—

Genoa....	1 Piastre, more or less,	for 37 Soldi.
Leghorn..	300 Piastres, ...	for 100 Pezze da 8 Reali.
Marseilles,	1 Piastre, ...	for 30 Sous in silver.

TURIN *(in Piedmont)*.

Monies of Account.

Accounts are kept here in Lire, Soldi, and Denari, Piedmontese currency. 12 Denari make 1 Soldo, and 20 Soldi 1 Lira. Accounts are also kept in Francs and Centimes, as in France. The Lira may be valued at $11\frac{1}{4}$d. sterling.

The following are other monies of account and of exchange: the Florin of Savoy is reckoned at 12 Soldi of Piedmont; the Scudo at 4 Lire; the Ducatoon at 5; the gold Scudo at $7\frac{1}{2}$; the Pistole at 15; and the Louis d'or at 16 Lire.

Coins.

The Gold coins are, Carlini of 5 Doppie or Pistoles, with halves in proportion; also Doppie, with halves and quarters in proportion. The Carlino passes for 120 Lire, and the Doppia for 24 Lire, Piedmontese currency.

The Silver coins are, Scudi of 6 Lire, with halves, quarters, and eighths in proportion.

There are besides, base silver coins of $7\frac{1}{2}$ and $2\frac{1}{2}$ Soldi, and copper coins of 1 Soldo; also pieces of 3 Denari, which are called Quattrini.

French coins not only pass here, but pieces have been coined of the value of the French Franc, which are called Nuove Lire.

Fineness of Gold and Silver.

The fineness of gold is expressed in Carats and Grains; the Ounce or other weight being divided into 24 Carats, and the Carat into 24 Grains.

The fineness of silver is expressed in Denari and Grains; the Ounce or other weight being divided into 12 Denari, and the Denaro into 24 Grains.

Fineness of Gold and Silver.

But in weighing gold or silver, the Ounce is divided into 24 Denari, and the Denaro into 24 Grani, or 576 Granotini.

Rate of Coinage.

The Gold coins are $21\frac{3}{4}$ Carats fine, and the Silver coins, $10\frac{7}{8}$ Denari fine; and no remedy is allowed either in the weight or fineness.

The Doppia weighs 7 Denari 2 Grani 20 Granotini, with its multiples and divisions in proportion. Thus it contains $172\frac{1}{2}$ troy Grains of fine gold, or $139\frac{1}{5}$ Grains of English standard gold, and is therefore worth £1 2s. $6\frac{3}{4}$d. in English gold coin.

The Scudo weighs 27 Denari 10 Grani 23 Granotini, with its subdivisions in proportion. It therefore contains 492 troy Grains of fine silver, or 532 of English standard, and is worth 5s. $8\frac{3}{4}$d. in sterling silver coin.

French Coins, &c.

Before the year 1793, Piedmont, Nice, and Savoy belonged to the crown of Sardinia, and Turin was the chief seat of government, where coins were minted for all parts of those dominions. But at that period, Nice and Savoy were united to France, and Piedmont in 1797. The new French monetary system was therefore introduced into those departments, although the old coins still continued in circulation. In 1815 these dominions were restored to the King of Sardinia.

Weights.

The Mark, gold and silver weight, is divided into 8 Ounces, 192 Denari, or 4608 Grains; and weighs 3795 English Grains, or 245,935 Grammes. The Grain is sometimes divided into 24 Granotti.

The Rubbo, commercial weight, is 25lb. This Pound or Libra contains $1\frac{1}{2}$ Mark, or 12 Ounces of the gold and silver weight; and answers to 5692 English Grains. Thus 100lb. of Turin equal 81,32lb. avoirdupois, or 36,88 Kilogrammes.

Corn Measure.

The Sacco, corn measure, is divided into 3 Staje, 6 Mine, 12 Quartieri, or 48 Copelli; and renders 3,26 English Bushels, or 1,149 Hectolitre.

Liquid Measure.

The Brenta, wine measure, is divided into 6 Rubbi, 36 Pinte, or 72 Boccali. The Rubbo weighs 25lb. of Turin, and contains 2,48 English Gallons, or 9,39 Litres. Oil is likewise sold by the Rubbo of 25lb. of Turin, or $20\frac{1}{3}$lb. avoirdupois. The Carro contains 10 Brente.

The Foot equals 12,72 English Inches, or 0,323 of a Metre. The Raso or Ell equals 23,3 English Inches, or 0,5915 of a Metre. Long Measure.

For the exchanges of Turin, see Vol. II. page 93. Exchanges.

The usance for bills drawn from London is 3 months after date; from Holland, the Netherlands, Hamburgh, Spain, and Portugal, 2 months; and from France, 1 month. Usances.

The period allowed for the payment of bills drawn from any other country besides the foregoing, begins on the day they are presented for acceptance, and ends on the day when an answer can be had, by the regular post, from the place where the bill was drawn or negotiated. Hence the usance for bills drawn in Geneva, Genoa, and Milan, is commonly reckoned at 8 days after sight; for those drawn in Venice, Florence, Leghorn, or Rome, 10 days sight; in Augsburg, Vienna, and other places in Germany, 15 days sight; and for those drawn in Naples and Sicily, at 21 days sight.

The presentation for acceptance of a bill payable at a determined period cannot be delayed beyond 2 months after the date of the bill: the same regulation is observed with regard to claiming the discharge of a bill payable at sight: if it is not claimed within that period, it is supposed that the necessary steps have not been taken to obtain payment.

The day on which a bill is dated is always reckoned in the term it has to run.

The holder of a bill payable after date, is at liberty either to demand payment when it becomes due, or to wait till the fifth day; and if this should fall on a Sunday or holiday, payment is to take place on the next following day of business; but bills at sight must be paid when presented. Days of Grace.

TURKEY, *see Constantinople, Salonica, and Smyrna.*

TUSCANY, *see Florence and Leghorn.*

VALENCIA *(in Spain).*

Accounts are kept in all the kingdom of Valencia in Libras of 20 Sueldos, each Sueldo of 12 Dineros: or sometimes in Reals of New Plate of 24 Dineros. Monies of Account.

Monies of Account.

The Libra is the same as the Peso de Plata or Dollar of Exchange; and therefore its proportions to other Spanish monies and to sterling may be seen in the Table, page 318; where the value of the Real of New Plate may be also found.

The proportions of the divisions of those monies, however, may require some further explanation.

The Real of New Plate is worth 2 Sueldos, $12\frac{4}{5}$ Quartos, or $51\frac{1}{5}$ Maravedis Vellon.

The Real of Old Plate equals $2\frac{1}{2}$ Sueldos or 30 Dineros.

The Real of Valencian Plate is worth $1\frac{1}{2}$ Sueldo or 18 Dineros; and therefore equals $9\frac{3}{5}$ Quartos or $38\frac{2}{5}$ Maravedis Vellon. Hence $13\frac{2}{3}$ Reals of Valencia equal the Libra, and $17\frac{17}{24}$ such Reals equal the Hard Dollar.

The following are other proportions between Castilian and Valencian monies:

	Libras.		Sueldos.		Dineros.
The Doubloon of Exchange of 32 Reals	= 4	=	80	=	960
The Ducat of Exchange of 375 Maravedis Vellon	= $1\frac{103}{272}$	=	$27\frac{39}{68}$	=	$330\frac{15}{17}$
The Doubloon Effective	= $5\frac{5}{16}$	=	$106\frac{1}{4}$	=	1275
The Hard Dollar	= $1\frac{21}{64}$	=	$26\frac{9}{16}$	=	$318\frac{3}{4}$

For the divisions and multiples of all the above monies in proportion, see *Spain*.

Gold and Silver Weight.

The Mark of Valencia, used for gold and silver, is composed of 8 Ounces, 32 Quartos, 128 Adarmes, or 4608 Grains; and answers to 3557,6 troy Grains, or 230,50 Grammes.

Commercial Weight.

The commercial Pound is composed of various numbers of Ounces, according to the different sorts of merchandize to be weighed. For some articles it is divided into 12 Ounces, for others, into 16, 18, or even 36 Ounces. The Arrove, however, is always of the same weight, as the number of Pounds is either increased or diminished according to the number of Ounces they contain. Thus the Arrove invariably weighs 432, and the Quintal, 1728 Ounces.

The Pounds are chiefly distinguished into the ***Libra Sutile***, or light Pound of 12 Ounces, and the ***Libra Grueso***, or heavy Pound of 18 Ounces.

The light Pound is divided into 12 Ounces, 48 Quartos, 192 Adarmes, or 6912 Grains; and equals 5494 English Grains. Hence 100 light Pounds of Valencia equal 78,49lb. avoirdupois, or 35,59 Kilogrammes, and the other Pounds in proportion. A Carga or Carica weighs 3 Quintals, or 12 Arroves. The Arrove = 28,25lb. avoirdupois, or 12,81 Kilogrammes.* Commercial Weight.

Dry Measure.

Corn is measured by the Cahiz, which is divided into 12 Barchillas, 48 Almudes or Celemines, or 96 Medios; and equals 5,825 Winchester Bushels, or 2,0525 Hectolitres.

Liquid Measure.

The Cantara or Arroba is divided into 4 Quartos, or 8 Medios; and equals 3,112 English wine Gallons, or 11,786 Litres. The Carga of wine consists of 15 Arrobas; the Carga of oil, of 12 Arrobas.

Long Measure.

The Vara or Ell is divided into 4 Palmos, or 16 Quartos; and equals 36,626 English Inches, or 0,9303 of a Metre.

Superficial Measure.

The Braza is 2 Varas, and 200 Square Brazas equal the Fanegada. 6 Fanegadas = 1 Cahizada, and 6 Cahizadas = 1 Yugada. Hence the Cahizada = 1 Acre and 8 Perches English, or 42,49 Ares.

Exchanges.

For the exchanges of Valencia, see *Spain*, Vol. II. page 88.

Days of Grace.

Bills are allowed 6 days grace, after which they must be either paid or protested: Sundays or holidays are not included.

Regulations for Protest, &c.

Protests are made by the Fanti or Clerks of the Commercial College, who enter all the bills they have protested, in a book, to which every merchant has free access. Thus many bills, which would otherwise be returned, are accepted and paid for the honor of the drawer or indorser. This practice is likewise useful in giving early notice of approaching insolvency.

* The contents of the Valencian weights are very differently stated in works of authority; and all differ from the above results, which have been lately determined at the *London Mint* by experiments on standards transmitted in 1818 by *Jasper Waring, Esq.* the British Consul at Valencia. These Mint determinations, however, agree very nearly with those of the French authorities in 1812, as noticed in page 23: and the above statements respecting the Measures of Capacity are deduced from the French experiments made at that time.

VENICE *(in Italy)*.

Monies of Account. Accounts are kept here in different ways, which may be arranged under the heads of the *Old System* and the *New*.

Old System. Formerly there were three kinds of money used here, viz. ***Moneta Piccola***, ***Valuta Corrente***, and ***Banco***; and all are still either in use or referred to.

Moneta Piccola has been the general money since the year 1750; Valuta Corrente was that which preceded it; and Banco was the money in which the Bank of Venice kept its accounts: it was 20 per cent. better than Valuta Corrente, and $54\frac{5}{6}$ better than Moneta Piccola.

Accounts are kept in Lire of 20 Soldi or Marchetti; and each Soldo is divided into 12 Denari, Moneta Piccola.

The Ducato Corrente is divided into 24 Grossi, and each Grosso into 12 Grossetti or Denari di Ducato.

The Ducat Banco is also divided into 24 Grossi, each of 12 Denari; and both Ducats are likewise divided into 124 Soldi or Marchetti.

$6\frac{1}{5}$ Lire Piccole equal the Ducat Corrente, and $9\frac{3}{5}$ Lire the Ducat Banco: hence 31 of the latter equal 48 of the former.

New System. The New method of keeping accounts here is in Lire Italiane, each of which is divided into 100 Centesimi, according to the French system; and this Lira is of the same value as the French Franc. The common estimate of this money is, that 405 Venetian Lire Piccole are worth 207 Italian Livres and 23 Centimes; and therefore 100 of the latter equal $195\frac{2}{5}$ of the former, and 100 Lire Piccole equal $51\frac{1}{6}$ Lire Italiane nearly.

Goods of particular kinds are generally sold in certain monies of the Old System; and in settling for them, their value is reduced into Lire Italiane.

Coins. The Gold coins are, Zecchini or Sequins of 22 Lire, with halves and quarters; Doppie or Pistoles of 38 Lire; and Gold Ducats of 14 Lire.

The Silver coins are, the Scudo Veneto or Della Croce of 12 Lire 8 Soldi, with halves and quarters in proportion; the Ducatone or Giustina of 11 Lire; the Ducato Effettivo of 8 Lire, with halves and quarters; and base silver pieces of 30 Soldi, called Lirazze, and of 20, 15, 10, and 5 Soldi. The Tallaro of 10

Lire is a piece coined for the Levant; and the silver Osella is not properly a coin, but a medal distributed occasionally: these, however, have been circulated at 3 Lire 18 Soldi. There are also pieces of 10 Lire, which were coined in 1796. Coins.

The Copper coins are, Soldi and Half Soldi or Bagattini.

New Austrian Coins. When Venice became subject to Austria in 1797, a base silver money was introduced, called *Moneta Provinciale;* but in 1802 it was declared to be out of currency, and a new coinage took place, consisting of pieces of $1\frac{1}{2}$, 1, and $\frac{1}{2}$ Lira, or (in Austrian money) of 18, 12, and 6 Creutzers, which contained only $\frac{1}{4}$ of fine silver, but they were heavier than the former coinage: this money was called *Moneta di Nuovo Stampo.* The Austrian Government also introduced copper pieces of 6 and 3 Creutzers, or 10 and 5 Soldi, and pieces of 2 and 1 Soldi: these were not coined in Venice, but brought from the hereditary dominions of Austria.

Fineness of Gold and Silver. In assaying gold and silver, the Mark or other weight is divided into 1152 Carati, and each Carat into 4 Grani. Gold and silver in bars are sold by the Ounce fine.

Rate of Coinage. $68\frac{1}{4}$ Zecchini or Sequins are to contain a Venetian Mark of fine gold, and are said not to have any alloy; they are, however, found to contain a small but uncertain quantity.

The Scudo Della Croce weighs $153\frac{1}{2}$ Carati; and the Giustina, or Ducat of Justine, 135 Carati; and both are 1056 Carati fine. The silver Ducat weighs 110 Carati, and is 952 Carati fine: the pieces of 10 Lire are of the same standard as the Ducat, but weigh $\frac{1}{5}$ more.

The pieces of 1 Lira, introduced by the Austrian Government, weigh $38\frac{2}{5}$ Carati, with the inferior coins in proportion; and, as before stated, they contain only $\frac{1}{4}$ part of silver.

No remedy was allowed at the Mint of Venice, either in the weight or in the fineness of those coins.

Value of Monies. According to the above regulation, the Venetian Sequin weighs 54 English Grains nearly; and it is therefore worth 9s. 6d. sterling.

The silver Ducat weighs $351\frac{1}{2}$ English Grains, and is 9 oz. $18\frac{1}{3}$ dwt. fine, which gives its value at $40\frac{1}{2}$d. sterling: hence the Ducat of account of $6\frac{1}{5}$ Lire

Value of Monies. Piccole is worth 31½d. nearly, and the Lira about 5d. sterling; or, more accurately, £1 sterling = 47 Lire 8 Soldi Piccoli.

But if the value of the Lira be taken from the coinage introduced by the Austrian Government, it will be found worth about 4¼d.: and £1 sterling, in this case, = 56 Lire 9½ Soldi Piccoli.

For a further valuation of monies, see *Tables of Coins*, Vol. II.

Weights. There are four sorts of weights used here, viz. the Pound Mark for the precious metals; two different weights for merchandize, called the Peso Grosso and Peso Sottile; and lastly, the French Kilogramme, called the *Libbra Italiana*, with which the custom duties are levied, and the other business of Government generally transacted.

The Pound Mark is divided into 8 Ounces, 32 Quarti, 1152 Carati, or 4608 Grani; and equals 3681½ English Grains, or 238,531 Grammes.

The Libbra, Peso Grosso or large weight, which is double the Pound Mark, is divided into 12 Oncie, 72 Sazi, 2304 Carati, or 9216 Grani.

100lb. Peso Grosso equal 105,18lb. avoirdupois, or 47,70 Kilogrammes; and 12lb. Peso Grosso equal 19lb. Peso Sottile.

The Libbra, Peso Sottile or light weight, is divided into 12 Oncie, 72 Sazi, or 1728 Carati, and equals 4650 English Grains; hence 100lb. Peso Sottile equal 66,4lb. avoirdupois, or 30,12 Kilogrammes.

All kinds of drugs, colours, silk, coffee, tea, sugar, rice, and butter, are sold by the Peso Sottile; and every other article, except the precious metals, by the Peso Grosso.

The *Libbra nuova Italiana* is divided into 10 Oncie, 100 Grossi, 1000 Denari, or 10,000 Grani; and equals 15434 English Grains, or 1 Kilogramme. See *France*.

1 Libbra Italiana equals 25,157 Oncie, Peso Grosso, or 39,823 Oncie, Peso Sottile.

Corn Measure. The Moggio is divided into 4 Staja, 16 Quarte, or 64 Quartaroli. The Stajo equals 2,270 Winchester Bushels, or 0,80 of a Hectolitre.

Liquid Measures. The measure for wine, called Anfora, is divided into 4 Bigonzi, 8 Mastelli, 48 Secchj, 192 Bozze, or 768 Quartuzzi. It answers to 136,95 English Gallons, or 518,4 Litres.

The Botte is composed of 5 Bigonzi.

Liquid Measures.

Oil is sold either by weight or by measure. The Botte contains 2 Migliaja, or 80 Miri of 25 Libbre, Peso Grosso. The Miro equals 4,028 English Gallons, or 15,23 Litres.

Long Measures.

The Braccio for woollens equals 26,61 English Inches, or 0,676 of a Metre.

The Braccio for silks is 24,8 English Inches, or 0,630 of a Metre.

The Venetian Foot equals 13,68 English Inches, or 0,347 of a Metre.*

Exchanges and Usance.

For the exchanges of Venice, see Vol. II. page 95.

The usance for bills on this place, drawn from Hamburgh, Holland, France, and Spain, is 2 months' date ; from Lisbon and London, 3 months' date ; from Ancona and Rome, 10 days after acceptance ; from Bergamo, Mantua, Milan, and Modena, 20 days' date ; from Augsburg, Bolsano, Francfort, Genoa, Naples, Nuremberg, Sicily, St. Gall, and Vienna, 15 days after acceptance ; and from Bologna, Ferrara, Florence, Leghorn, and Lucca, 5 days after acceptance.

Bank.

Bills of exchange, as well as most other large commercial transactions, were formerly paid in transfers on the Bank, and though that establishment is discontinued, yet its money is still referred to ; some account of it, therefore, may be useful.

The Bank of Venice is said to have been established before any other in Europe. In 1171 it began on the foundation of a considerable loan, which was advanced to the State, at an interest of 4 per cent. per annum. It afterwards became a bank of deposit, and in 1587 its capital was above 5 millions of Ducats. In 1750 Banco was at an agio of 29 per cent. against Valuta Corrente, and after that period at an agio of 54⅚ per cent. against Moneta Piccola.

Such was the prosperous state of this institution until the year 1797, when the French took possession of the city, and ceded it to the Austrians : from that period the Bank declined. In 1805 the place was incorporated with the kingdom of Italy, and in 1815 it was again restored to the Austrians. In 1808, however, the Bank was discontinued, but some hopes still exist of its re-establishment.

---

* The above account of Venetian weights and measures has been deduced from specifications and standards transmitted to London in 1818 by *R. B. Hoppner, Esq.* His Majesty's Consul General at Venice. His statements on the occasion correct several errors heretofore published, and are corroborated by other authorities. See note on *Trieste,* page 336.

VERONA *(in Italy)*,

Monies. In the Venetian States, keeps accounts in Lire of 20 Soldi, or 240 Denari, Moneta Piccola; for which see *Venice*.

Weights & Measures. There are here a Peso Grosso and a Peso Sottile; 100lb. of the former correspond to 149½lb. of the latter, and equal 109,6lb. avoirdupois, or 49,73 Kilogrammes.

Corn is measured by Minelli; 100 of which equal 45½ Staja of Venice, 103,3 English Bushels, or 36,39 Hectolitres.

The Brenta, wine measure, contains 16 Basse, and answers to 19 English Gallons, or 72,3 Litres.

Oil is sold by the Migliajo of 40 Miri, which weighs 1738lb. Peso Sottile of Verona, or 1274lb. avoirdupois. The Migliajo contains 129 Basse, and equals 154 English Gallons, or 583,32 Litres.

The Braccio, silk measure, is 25,22 English Inches, or 0,6406 of a Metre. The Braccio, woollen measure, equals 25,57 English Inches, or 0,649 of a Metre.

VIENNA *(in Germany)*.

Monies of Account. Accounts are kept in Guldens or Florins, each of 60 Creutzers, and the Creutzer is divided into 4 Phenings.

The Florin is also divided into 20 Groschen, 80 Groschel, or 480 Hellers.

There are two Rixdollars here, one a real money, and the other imaginary. The former, the Rixdollar specie, is worth 2 Florins; and the latter, the Rixdollar current, is worth 1½ Florin.

Hence 1 Rixdollar specie equals 1⅓ Rixdollar current, 2 Florins or Rixguldens, 16 Schillings, 40 Groschen, 120 Creutzers, 160 Groschel, 480 Phenings, or 960 Hellers.

Coins. The principal Gold coins are double Souverains of 26⅔ Florins, with single and half Souverains in proportion; Imperial Ducats of 4½ Florins, with double and quadruple Ducats in proportion; and Kremnitz or Hungarian Ducats, which pass for 4 Florins 32 Creutzers.

The Silver coins are specie Rixdollars of 2 Florins, with Florins and half Florins; also pieces of 20 Creutzers, called Copstucks, and pieces of 10 and 5 Creutzers.

The Copper coins are Creutzers, half Creutzers, and Groschels, or $\frac{3}{4}$ Creutzers; also Phenings and half Phenings, or Hellers. Coins.

For the sterling value of the above coins, see *Tables*, pages 157 and 162, Vol. II.

In the provinces of Gallicia and Lodomeria, formerly belonging to Poland, but now subject to Austria, the Austrian coins are valued in Polish Florins and Groschen: the Austrian Florin passes for 4 Polish Florins, and the other coins in proportion. See *Poland.*

The fineness of gold is expressed in Carats and Grains; the Mark, or other weight, being divided into 24 Carats, and the Carat into 12 Grains. Fineness of Gold and Silver.

The fineness of silver is expressed in Loths and Grains; the Mark being divided into 16 Loths, and the Loth into 18 Grains.

Wrought silver is 14 Loths or $\frac{7}{8}$ fine.

A Mark of gold, 23 Carats 8 Grains fine, is coined into 80$\frac{2}{5}$ Ducats; and as 5 Marks of Vienna equal 6 of Cologne, 67 Ducats must weigh a Cologne Mark. Rate of Coinage.

The current value of the Souverains has been already stated under the article *Antwerp.*

The rate of coinage of the silver coins in Vienna is as follows:—

From an Austrian Mark of Silver..	13$\frac{1}{3}$ Loths fine..	10 Rixdollars are coined
	13$\frac{1}{3}$ Ditto......	20 Florins
	13$\frac{1}{3}$ Ditto......	40 Half Florins
	9$\frac{1}{3}$ Ditto......	42 Pieces of 20 Creutzers
	8$\frac{2}{5}$ Ditto......	46 Ditto .. 17 Ditto
	8 Ditto......	72 Ditto .. 10 Ditto
	6$\frac{1}{1}\frac{3}{8}$ Ditto......	86$\frac{1}{2}$ Ditto .. 7 Ditto

Thus, the Cologne Mark of silver, 13$\frac{1}{3}$ Loths fine, is coined into 8$\frac{2}{3}$ Rixdollars, 16$\frac{2}{3}$ Florins, or 33$\frac{1}{3}$ Half Florins; the same Mark, 9$\frac{1}{3}$ Loths fine, is coined into 35 Copstucks; and so on for the inferior pieces, the Cologne Mark still keeping the proportion of 5 to 6 with the Vienna Mark.

This rate of coinage was established in Austria, Bavaria, and other places, by a Convention in 1753, and it has since been adopted in a great part of Germany; whence the above pieces are sometimes called *Convention Coins.* See *Germany*, page 162.

In the Austrian Dominions, with the exception of the Italian Territories, where the metrical system is introduced, the weight for gold and silver is the Gold and Silver Weight.

Gold and Silver Weight. Vienna Mark, 5 of which are reckoned to equal 6 Cologne Marks; but this is not quite accurate.

The Vienna Mark is divided into 8 Ounces, 16 Loths, 64 Quintins, 256 Phenings, or 65536 Richtphenings. It weighs 4333 troy Grains, or 280,7 Grammes.

The weight of a Ducat is divided into 60 parts, called Mandel weights; and the Mark contains $80\frac{2}{5}$ Ducat weights, or 4824 Mandel weights.

Diamond Weight. Diamonds and precious stones are weighed by the Carat, which equals $48\frac{1}{8}$ Richtphenings, gold and silver weight, 3,18 English Grains, or 2,06 Decigrammes.

Commercial Weight. The Pfund or Pound, commercial weight, is divided into 4 Quarters, 16 Ounces, 32 Loths, 128 Quintins, or 512 Phenings; and weighs 8645 English Grains: hence 100lb. of Vienna equal 123,5lb. avoirdupois, or 56,01 Kilogrammes.

A Stone is 20lb.; a Centner, 100lb.; a Karch, 400lb.; a Saum, 275lb.; but a Saum of steel, 250lb.

Corn Measure. The Muth of corn contains 30 Metzen. The Metzen is divided into 4 Viertels, or 8 Achtels; and equals 1,745 English Bushel, or 0,6148 of a Hectolitre. The Achtel is also divided into 2 Muhlmassels, 4 Fudermassels, or 16 Bechers.

Wine Measure. A Fuder of wine contains 32 Eimers. The Eimer is divided into 4 Viertels, 40 Maasses, 70 Kopfen, or 168 Seidels. The Eimer equals 14,94 English Gallons, or 56,56 Litres. The Dreyling is 30 Eimers.

Long Measure. The Foot of Vienna is 12,45 English Inches, or 0,3161 of a Metre. A Clafter, or Fathom, is 6 Feet Vienna measure.

The Ell of Vienna is 30,66 English Inches, or 0,779 of a Metre; but the Ell in Upper Austria is 31,5 English Inches, or 0,8 of a Metre.

Superficial Measure. By a Joch, or day's work, is understood as much ground as can be ploughed with one team in a day. It is reckoned at 1600 Vienna square Fathoms, or 6889 English square Yards, answering to 1 Acre 1 Rood $27\frac{3}{4}$ Perches English statute measure, or 57,58 Ares.

For the itinerary measures, and terms used in reckoning, see *Germany*.

For the exchanges of Vienna, see Vol. II. page 97. Exchanges, Usance, Days of Grace, &c.

Usance is 14 days after acceptance; half usance, 7 days; $1\frac{1}{2}$ usance, 21 days; double usance, 28 days, including Sundays and holidays; but the day of acceptance is not included.

Bills payable *medio mense* (in the middle of the month) are reckoned due on the 15th; and are allowed, like other bills, 3 days' grace, if necessary.

When the written term of a bill is expired, 3 days of grace are allowed; and if the bill should not be paid by 5 o'clock on the third day, it must be immediately protested and returned. In these days of grace, Sundays and holidays are included; but if the day of payment should fall on a Sunday or holiday, the bill must be paid on the next following day of business. This allowance of 3 days, however, is only made in order that the holder of a bill, if he should not be able to demand payment sooner, may have the advantage of that delay; but a good payee will not avail himself of the days of grace, in order to delay the payment of a bill beyond the written term.

If a bill which is not duly paid is not protested immediately, as above, the holder has no recourse except against the acceptor.

Bills drawn at sight, or on demand, or at less than 7 days' sight or date, are not allowed any days of grace, but must be paid within 24 hours, unless they fall due on a Sunday or holiday.

The Bank of Vienna was originally established in 1703, for commercial as well as State purposes; but it has been for a long time under the sole management of government. Its bonds or actions were vouchers for money borrowed by the State, similar to Exchequer bills in England. Bank of Vienna.

In 1793 it began to issue its own notes, payable to bearer on demand; but in process of time cash payments were discontinued, which caused a considerable depreciation of this paper currency, and it became the only circulating medium of Austria.

In 1816 a new bank was established, entitled the ***Austrian National Bank.*** Its object was twofold—first, to diminish the paper currency; and secondly, to assist trade by advancing money on various securities. Austrian National Bank.

Its capital was to be 100,000 shares, each to consist of 1000 Florins in paper currency, and 100 Florins in coin. The paper currency thus deposited is to be converted into government bonds, bearing an interest of $2\frac{1}{2}$ per cent. per annum, payable in coin; which bonds are not to be sold by the bank without the permission of government.

Austrian National Bank.

For the redemption of those bonds, the treasury is to pay annually to the bank 500,000 Florins, which will redeem 1,000,000 Florins of those actions. These bonds are not to be cancelled, but deposited, and the interest thereon is still to be paid by government; by which plan it is computed that the whole claim of the bank on government will be redeemed in 36 years.

The bank dividends are to be paid half yearly, at 6 per cent. per annum, in coin; and whatever profits may remain are to be divided, one half to be given to the share-holders, and the other to the establishment.

This bank issues its own notes payable to bearer on demand in silver coin. It keeps cash for others; discounts bills payable at Vienna; advances loans on government securities, on gold and silver bullion, and certain merchandise. The interest charged for those advances is 6 per cent. per annum.

It is also decreed, that when the bank shall have sufficient means, it shall have the power to advance money on mortgages of landed property.

This institution proposes to establish branch banks throughout the Empire.

ULM (*in Germany*).

Monies, &c.

Accounts are kept in this part of Suabia in Guldens or Florins of 60 Creutzers.

The Florin is also reckoned at 15 Batzen, or 20 Groschen. The Rixdollar is worth $1\frac{1}{2}$ Florin, 30 Groschen, or 90 Creutzers. A Batze is 4 Creutzers; a Grosche, 3 Creutzers; a Creutzer, 4 Pfenings, or 8 Hellers.

In the wine trade, however, the Gulden is reckoned at 35 Schillings; the Schilling at 6 Pfenings; the Batze at 14 Pfenings; and the Creutzer at 7 Hellers.

The coins of Ulm will be found under the article *Augsburg*.

Weights & Measures.

The Pound is divided into 2 Marks, 32 Loths, or 128 Quints; and contains 7234 English Grains: thus the Centner of 100lb. answers to 103,3lb. avoirdupois, or 46,87 Kilogrammes.

The corn measure, called Immi, is divided into 4 Mittlens, 24 Metzen, or 96 Viertels; and renders 6,519 English Bushels, or 2,29 Hectolitres.

The Foot is divided into 12 Inches, or 144 Scruples; and measures 11,39 English Inches, or 0,289 of a Metre.

The Ell is 22,3 English Inches, or 0,568 of a Metre.

The Ruthe or Rod is 12 Feet.

UTRECHT, *see Amsterdam and Netherlands*.

UNITED STATES OF AMERICA.

Accounts are kept here in different ways, but chiefly in Dollars, which are divided into 10 Dimes, 100 Cents, or 1000 Mills. This is called Federal Money, to distinguish it from the various currencies which were formerly the monies of the United States, and which are still partially retained in domestic traffic; but in foreign commerce and all Government concerns Federal Money is used, which was established by an Act of Congress in 1789, and in which the Dollar is valued at 4s. 6d. sterling. Monies of Account.

Accounts were originally kept, in all the British Colonies of America, as in England; and British coins circulated, as well as Spanish Dollars; but in consequence of excessive issues of paper, various depreciations took place, which were liquidated at different rates of composition. Hence arose the different currencies, which were established by raising the nominal value of the Pound sterling and of the Spanish Dollar, so as to correspond with the depreciations respectively. The following are the different ratios of sterling to currency, and also the proportional values of the Spanish Dollar:

1. In New Hampshire, Massachusetts, Connecticut, Rhode Island, Virginia, Kentucky, Ohio, Tennessee, Indiana, and Mississipi, the ratio is as 3 to 4. Thus £1 sterling = £1 6s. 8d. currency, and £1 currency = 15s. sterling. Hence also the Dollar is worth 6s. currency. Currencies.

2. In New York and North Carolina, the ratio is as 9 to 16; and hence £1 sterling = £1 15s. $6\frac{2}{3}$d. currency, and £1 currency = 11s. 3d. sterling. The Dollar here is therefore worth 8s. currency.

3. In New Jersey, Pensylvania, Delaware, and Maryland, the ratio of currency to sterling is as 3 to 5. Hence £1 sterling = £1 13s. 4d. currency, and £1 currency = 12s. sterling. The Dollar is therefore worth 7s. 6d. currency.

4. In South Carolina and Georgia, the ratio is as 27 to 28; and hence £1 sterling = £1 0s. $8\frac{8}{9}$d. currency, or £1 currency = 19s. $3\frac{3}{7}$d. sterling. The Dollar is therefore worth 4s. 8d. of this currency.

The above currencies may be reduced into each other by the proportional values of the Dollar. Thus, to reduce the currency of New Hampshire to that of New York, multiply by 8 and divide by 6; or, add $\frac{1}{4}$. Currencies Reduced.

Monies of Account.

The following Table shews, at one view, the Currencies of the United States, with their Sterling and Federal Values:

Sterling Value.			New Hampshire, Massachusetts, Rhode Island, Connecticut, Virginia, &c.			New York, North Carolina.			New Jersey, Pensylvania, Delaware, and Maryland.			South Carolina, Georgia.			Federal Value.				
£.	s.	d.	£.	s.	d.	£.	s.	d.	£.	s.	d.	£.	s.	d.	Eagles.	Dollars.	Dimes.	Cents.	Mills.
0	4	6	0	6	0	0	8	0	0	7	6	0	4	8	0	1	0	0	0
1	0	0	1	6	8	1	15	$6\frac{2}{3}$	1	13	4	1	0	$8\frac{8}{9}$	0	4	4	4	4
100	0	0	133	6	8	177	15	$6\frac{2}{3}$	166	13	4	103	14	$0\frac{8}{9}$	44	4	4	4	4
Ratio of Sterling to Currency			3 to 4			9 to 16			3 to 5			27 to 28			From these proportions the Currencies may be easily reduced one into another, and also into Sterling.				
Sterling Value of £1 Currency			= 0	15	0	= 0	11	3	= 0	12	0	= 0	19	$3\frac{3}{7}$					

Coins.

In 1790, the American Government established a Mint, and ordered money to be coined, in gold, silver, and copper, according to the following denominations and values, viz.

Gold Coins.

Eagles—each to be of the value of 10 Dollars, or Units, and to contain $247\frac{1}{4}$ Grains of pure, or 270 Grains of standard, gold, the standard being 22 Carats, or $\frac{11}{12}$ fine. Its intrinsic value in English gold is, therefore, £2 3s. 8d. nearly. Half Eagles and Quarter Eagles were also ordered to be coined in the same proportion.

Silver Coins.

Dollars, or *Units*—each to be of the value of a Spanish Milled Dollar, and to contain $371\frac{1}{4}$ Grains of pure, or 416 Grains of standard, silver, the standard being $\frac{1485}{1664}$ fine, or 10 Ounces 14 Pennyweights nearly. Its intrinsic value in English silver is, therefore, 4s. $3\frac{3}{4}$d. nearly. Half Dollars, Quarter Dollars, Dimes, or Tenths of Dollars, and Half Dimes, were also ordered to be coined in the same proportion.

Copper Coins.

Cents—each to be of the value of the one hundredth part of a Dollar, and to contain 208 Grains of copper. Half Cents were ordered to be coined in the same proportion.

Remedy of the Mint.

The Remedy of the Mint is 1 part in 144. Thus, from every separate mass of standard gold or silver which is coined, a certain number of pieces are set apart to be duly assayed; and if the pieces so tried shall not be found inferior, in their respective standards, more than 1 part in 144 parts, the coinage is deemed lawful. Remedy of the Mint.

The expenses of the Mint being defrayed by the United States, bullion brought thither is coined gratis, or coin is exchanged for bullion, deducting $\frac{1}{2}$ per cent. of the fine for the time which would be required for coining the same, and the advance so made. Bullion coined gratis.

European Gold coins are a legal tender, according to an Act of Congress passed in 1816. They are classed under three heads, and are valued, in English troy weight, according to their standard fineness, in the following manner: European Coins.

	Dol.	Cents.		Cents.	
1. Gold coins of Great Britain and Portugal,	17	78	per oz. standard, or	89	per dwt.
2. .... France	17	45	....	87	....
3. .... Spanish Dominions	16	80	....	84	....

The above proportions are printed by authority in Tables, with intermediate numbers. Other Tables are also printed, in which the divisions of the Dollar are carried to several places of Decimals instead of Cents; but not essentially different from the above, though more accurate as to the proportions. Thus English gold is valued at 17,777, &c., French at 17,4545, &c., and Spanish at 16,842, &c., with their divisions and multiples in proportion. According to the above rate of English gold, the Dollar is valued at $52\frac{9}{16}$d. sterling.

European Silver coins may pass by agreement, but they are no longer a legal tender in the United States.

The weights and measures of the United States are the same as those of England, except that in the States of Virginia, the Carolinas, and Georgia, sales are commonly made by the Quintal of 100lb.* Weights & Measures.

* Standards of the troy and avoirdupois weights of the United States, verified by the proper authorities, have been lately compared with those of England, at the *London Mint*, and were all found perfectly to agree. The experiments were made on standards transmitted to *Viscount Castlereagh*, in 1818, by His Majesty's Consuls in the principal cities of the United States of America: their despatches likewise contained ample specifications of the measures of capacity, all of which correspond in their dimensions with those of England.

Banks.

In 1790, a public Bank was established at Philadelphia, called the *United States Bank.* It was chartered by Congress for 21 years, and invested with power to appoint Branch Banks in the different States. The capital was fixed at ten millions of Dollars, and divided into 25,000 shares of 400 Dollars each; none of the subscribers were to hold more than 1000 shares; one-fourth of the subscription was to be paid in specie, and three-fourths in public stock. These shares were transferable, and yielded a dividend, payable half yearly, of 7 or 8 per cent. per ann. The constitution and government were in other respects nearly on the plan of the Bank of England.

The Charter of this Bank having expired in 1811, it was not renewed, but preparations were made some time after for establishing one upon an enlarged plan, of which the following is an outline.

In 1816, the present Bank of the United States was incorporated by law, and established with a capital of 35 millions of Dollars, divided into 350,000 shares of 100 Dollars each. Seven millions were subscribed by the United States, and the remaining 28 millions by individuals, companies, or corporations.

This Bank issues its own notes, payable to bearer in specie on demand; and no note for a smaller sum than 5 Dollars is issued. It is obliged to pay all its notes, bills, and other obligations, in gold or silver; and if at any time it should refuse, it is chargeable with the payment of interest, at the rate of 12 per cent. per annum.

This Corporation lends money on bills of exchange, and gold and silver bullion, at 6 per cent. per annum.

The management of the affairs of this Institution is under 25 Directors, 5 of whom, being stock-holders, are annually appointed by the President of the United States; and 7 Directors, including the President, constitute a Board. This Institution has Branch Banks established in different cities of the United States, which are all subject to the above laws and regulations.

Exchanges, Regulations, &c.

For the exchanges of the United States, see Vol. II. page 99.

Foreign bills are generally drawn at a certain number of days after sight, and the rate of exchange is sometimes specified.

Bills payable in the United States are mostly deposited in banks; and when the term of a bill is expired, notice is sent from the bank to the acceptor, who must, in three days (the days of grace), take up his bill, or it will be protested.

When bills of exchange are returned to the United States, and protested for non-payment, there are certain damages and interest charged on the original amount of each, besides notarial expenses; and if the holder declines accepting payment in new bills, he is entitled to an equivalent in currency at the actual rate of exchange on the day of settlement. Bills Returned.

The following are the damages and interest charged, in the different States, on foreign bills of exchange, which are returned and protested for non-payment. Damages, &c. on Returned Bills

	DAMAGES.	INTEREST.	TIME CHARGED.
New England	10 per cent.	6 per cent.	From the date of the protest.
New York	20 per cent.	6 per cent.	From presenting the protest.
New Jersey	20 per cent.	6 per cent.	From ditto.
Pensylvania	20 per cent.	6 per cent.	From ditto.
Delaware..........	20 per cent.	6 per cent.	From ditto.
Maryland	15 per cent.	6 per cent.	From the date of the protest.
Virginia	15 per cent.	6 per cent.	From ditto.
North Carolina	15 per cent.	6 per cent.	From ditto.
South Carolina	15 per cent.	6 per cent.	From ditto.
Georgia	15 per cent.	6 per cent.	From ditto.
Louisiana..........	10 per cent.	6 per cent.	From ditto.

WARSAW, *see Poland.*

WEST INDIES.

Under this article are comprehended all the Islands lying in the Caribbean Sea, between North and South America; and, also, a few of the neighbouring Settlements on the Continent. These places, though liable to frequent political changes, still, for the most part, retain the weights, measures, and denominations of money, of the European nations by which they were originally colonized; and they are accordingly classed in the following Table, without any reference to the country or power to which they may at any time eventually belong. Arrangement.

Arrangement.

THE LARGER ISLANDS, OR GREATER ANTILLES, ARE

Jamaica	*English.*	Porto Rico	*Spanish.*
Cuba	*Spanish.*	St. Domingo,	*French and Spanish.*

THE SMALLER ISLANDS, OR LESSER ANTILLES, also called THE CARIBBEE ISLANDS, are divided into LEEWARD and WINDWARD ISLANDS.

THE LEEWARD ISLANDS ARE

Tortola	*English.*	Guadaloupe	*French.*
The Saints	*English.*	Marigalante	*French.*
Barbuda	*English.*	St. Eustatia	*Dutch.*
Antigua	*English.*	St. Martin	*Dutch.*
St. Kitts	*English.*	St. Thomas	*Danish.*
Nevis	*English.*	Santa Cruz	*Danish.*
Montserrat	*English.*	St. John	*Danish.*
Dominica	*English.*	St. Bartholomew	*Swedish.*

THE WINDWARD ISLANDS ARE

Barbadoes	*English.*	Tobago	*English.*
St. Vincent	*English.*	Martinico	*French.*
Grenada	*English.*	St. Lucia	*French.*

ISLANDS ON THE COAST OF TERRA FIRMA.

Trinidad	*Spanish.*	Curaçao	*Dutch.*
Margarita	*Spanish.*	Bonaire	*Dutch.*

SETTLEMENTS ON THE CONTINENT OF SOUTH AMERICA.

Demerara	*Dutch.*	Essequibo	*Dutch.*
Berbice	*Dutch.*	Surinam	*Dutch.*

The monies, coins, exchanges, weights, and measures of the West Indies are classed under the following heads, viz. *English*, *French*, *Danish*, *Dutch*, *Swedish*, and *Spanish* Islands, as arranged in the foregoing Table; and the article will conclude with an account of the *Bermudas* and *Bahama* Islands.

ENGLISH ISLANDS.

Accounts are kept in all the English Islands in Pounds, Shillings, and Pence currency. The Pound is divided into 20 Shillings, and the Shilling into 12 Pence. Monies of Account.

West India currency is an imaginary money, similar to that already described under the article *United States.* It varies in different Islands from 40 to 100 per cent. Thus, in some colonies £140 currency, and in others, £200 currency, must be reckoned for £100 sterling. West India Currency.

The West India currencies had their origin in various causes; such as, the scarcity of specie, the mutilation of coins, and the depreciation of colonial paper. The monies of account, therefore, and the nominal prices of the current coins, have been raised, so as in some measure to correspond with those various depreciations.—Thus, where the currency was settled at 140, the Spanish Dollar (the principal coin in the West Indies) was ordered to pass for 6s. 8d. currency, and other coins in proportion.

The following are the currencies and corresponding values of the Dollar in the different English Islands :

	Currency.		Sterling.		Currency.	
Jamaica	£140	for	£100	Dollar	6s.	8d.
Barbadoes	135*		100		6	3
Windward Islands (except Barbadoes)	175		100		8	3
Leeward Islands	200		100		9	0

Here it should be observed that the above proportions between currency and sterling are seldom acted upon, except in the valuation of silver coins. Even Dollars are sometimes at a premium; and gold coins pass for about 10 per cent. above currency in some of the Islands, as will be shewn in the following pages. The course of exchange, likewise, is generally much higher than currency.

The following are the current coins, and their nominal values, in the principal English Islands. Coins, &c.

* Doubtful—see the article *Barbadoes*, page 362.

JAMAICA.

As the currency of Jamaica is £140, its proportion to sterling is as 7 to 5. Hence, £1 sterling = 28s. currency; and £1 currency = 14s. $3\frac{3}{7}$d. sterling.

Gold Coins. The following are the Gold coins current here, with their weight and legal value in currency:

		dwt.	gr. troy.	Value in Currency.		
SPANISH	Doubloon	17	8	£5	0	0
	Two Pistole Piece .	8	16	2	10	0
	Pistole	4	8	1	5	0
	Half Pistole	2	4	0	12	6
PORTUGUESE	Johanes (called Joe)	18	12	5	10	0
	Half Joe	9	6	2	15	0
	Quarter Joe	4	15	1	7	6
	Moidore	6	22	2	0	0
	Half Moidore	3	11	1	0	0
ENGLISH	Guinea	5	8	1	12	6
	Half Guinea......	2	16	0	16	3
	Sovereign	5	2	1	12	0

Any of the above Gold coins being found light, must pass according to their actual weight; and the deduction is 3d. currency for every Grain of deficiency. Thus, a Doubloon weighing 17 dwt. 6 gr. is worth only £4 19s. 6d. currency.

Silver Coins. The Silver coins of Jamaica are Dollars, with Halves, Quarters, Eighths, and Sixteenths; passing for 6s. 8d. 3s. 4d. 1s. 8d. 10d. and 5d. currency.

Also, Bits or Bitts, which are Spanish Reals, and which pass for $7\frac{1}{2}$d. currency. Thus, 10 Bits and 5d. currency make 1 Dollar; and 1 Bit is worth $5\frac{5}{14}$d. sterling.

Pistereens, or Two Bit Pieces, which are Spanish Pesetas, pass for 1s. 3d. currency, or $10\frac{5}{7}$d. sterling.

English Shillings and Sixpences occasionally pass here as Pistereens and Bits.

Currency compared. From the foregoing values of the different coins, the following is the intrinsic par of the currency of Jamaica with respect to sterling:

According to the English gold coins, £100 sterling = £154 15 0 currency. Currency compared to Sterling.

Spanish ditto	=	156	13	2
Portuguese ditto	=	155	0	0
Dollar	=	154	11	9

It should be observed, that the above calculation on the Spanish gold is made at £5 per Doubloon; but the current price is £5 6s. 8d., though generally printed in Almanacs, &c. as £5.

According to a law of the Assembly of Jamaica, the exchange with England was formerly fixed at 40 per cent.; but it has varied from this considerably. Bills have been sometimes at a premium of 20 per cent. above the legal exchange, and they are seldom under 10. Dollars occasionally bear a premium of 3 or 4 per cent. Exchange.

BARBADOES.

The currency of Barbadoes has been formerly reckoned at $133\frac{1}{3}$, and sometimes at 140 for £100 sterling; but it never was settled by any legal authority, nor does either of these numbers appear to be correct. When these proportions were reckoned, the Spanish Doubloon was valued at £4 10s. Barbadoes currency; but of late Doubloons have been circulated at £5 currency, or 16 Dollars, with their divisions in proportion: and in consequence of this, a rise has taken place in the market from 135 to 150 currency for £100 sterling, and most of the other coins have left the Colony to purchase Doubloons. Currency.

The Silver coins current in Barbadoes are Dollars, with halves, quarters, eighths, and sixteenths; passing for 6s. 3d., 3s. $1\frac{1}{2}$d., 1s. $6\frac{3}{4}$d., $9\frac{1}{2}$d., and $4\frac{3}{4}$d. currency; also Bits, which are Spanish Reals, and which pass for $7\frac{1}{2}$d. currency. Thus, 10 Bits make 1 Dollar, and 1 Bit is worth $5\frac{1}{5}$d. sterling. Silver Coins.

Pistereens, or Two Bit Pieces, which are Spanish Pesetas, pass for 1s. 3d. currency.

There are also French Bits, called *Crimbal*, or *Isle du Vent* Bits, which pass for $7\frac{1}{2}$d. currency.

In all military payments throughout the West Indies, and in most other transactions with the British Government, the Dollar is reckoned at 4s. 8d. sterling, which is generally called the *Army Par*, to distinguish it from the commercial par, which is reckoned at 4s. 6d. sterling.

ENGLISH LEEWARD ISLANDS.

TORTOLA, THE SAINTS, BARBUDA, ANTIGUA, ST. KITT'S, NEVIS, MONTSERRAT, DOMINICA, &c.

Monies and Coins.

The Dollar here is reckoned at 9s., which rate is most generally called the *Leeward currency*.

A small circular piece is mostly cut out of the centre of the Dollar, which is about $\frac{1}{12}$ of its value; but in order to prevent its exportation, it is allowed to pass for $\frac{1}{8}$, and is then stamped, by authority, with the initials of the Island.

The Dollar thus cut passes for 8s. 3d. currency. It is called the ***Cut Dollar*** to distinguish it from the entire piece, which is sometimes called the ***Round Dollar***.

The piece taken from the Dollar is sometimes called the Bit, and sometimes the ***Moco;*** but the regular Bit is the Spanish Real. In some places the Moco is $\frac{1}{4}$ of the Dollar, and in others $\frac{1}{8}$.

Dollars are occasionally cut into Halves, Quarters, &c., and pass accordingly.

There are here small copper coins, called Stampes, Dogs, and Half Dogs.

The following Table shews the value and proportion of the principal coins circulating in these Islands:

				Leeward Currency.		
2	Half Dogs ...... make	1 Dog	=	£0	0	$1\frac{1}{2}$
$1\frac{1}{2}$	Dog	1 Stampe	=	0	0	$2\frac{1}{4}$
6	Dogs or 4 Stampes	1 Bit	=	0	0	9
$1\frac{1}{2}$	Bit	1 Moco	=	0	1	$1\frac{1}{2}$
11	Bits	1 Cut Dollar ..	=	0	8	3
12	Bits or 8 Mocos	1 Round Dollar	=	0	9	0
5	Round Dollars........	1 Guinea	=	2	5	0
8	Cut Dollars	1 Joe	=	3	6	0
16	Round Dollars........	1 Doubloon ...	=	7	4	0

The divisions of the above gold coins pass in proportion; and for any deficiency of weight, a deduction is made of a Round Dollar per Dwt.; that is, $4\frac{1}{2}$d. currency per English Grain.

The exchange with London is generally about 200 per cent.

ENGLISH WINDWARD ISLANDS.

TOBAGO, ST. VINCENT, GRENADA, &c.

The currencies, monies, coins, and exchanges, of these Colonies are nearly the same as those of the Leeward Islands, as described in the last article. There are, however, certain local regulations and customs which should be stated. Currencies, Monies, &c.

The Dollars in St. Vincent are cut into halves and quarters, and pass accordingly, at the rate of 8s. 3d. per Dollar. Stampes and Dogs are not equally used in all the Islands: the former are chiefly current in Tobago, and the latter in St. Vincent and Grenada.

The Bit, which is cut out of the middle of the Dollar, is reckoned the eleventh part: it is mostly issued by the Government of the Islands, and marked accordingly, viz. St. V. for St. Vincent; T. for Tobago; and G. for Grenada.

Bits cut out of the Dollar and not stamped by Government, are, by an act of the Assembly of Grenada, to be taken at only 6d. currency, while the stamped Bit passes for 9d.

The price of gold here is the same as in the Leeward Islands; that is, 1 Round Dollar per Dwt., or 4½d. currency per English Grain.

FRENCH ISLANDS.

MARTINICO, ST. LUCIA, GUADALOUPE, MARIGALANTE, ST. MARTIN, &c.

Accounts are kept by the French settlers here in Livres, Sols, and Deniers; and by the English (particularly in Exchanges) in Pounds, Shillings, and Pence currency; the Livre and Shilling being of one value. Currency, Monies, and Coins.

This currency is the same as that of the English Leeward and Windward Islands: hence the Dollar passes for 9 Livres or Shillings, and other coins in proportion. The names, however, of the same coins are different: thus, the Dog is called here the *Noir;* the Stampe, the *Tempé;* the Bit, the *Escalin;* and the Dollar, the *Gourde.*

The following Table shews the value of the coins, both in Livres and Leeward currency:

Currency, Monies, and Coins.

	Liv.	Sols.	Deniers.		Leeward Currency.		
The Noir, or Dog	0	2	6		£0	0	1½
The Tempé, or Stampe	0	3	9		0	0	2¼
The Trois Tempés	0	11	3		0	0	6¾
The Escalin, or Bit	0	15	0		0	0	9
The Trois petites Pieces	1	2	6		0	1	1½
The Piece de Trente Sols, or Pistereen	1	10	0		0	1	6
The Moco	2	5	0		0	2	9
The Gourde, or Dollar	9	0	0		0	9	0
The Ecu of 6 Livres	9	17	6		0	9	10½
The Louis d'Or	40	10	0		2	0	6
Guinea	45	0	0		2	5	0
Napoleon of 40 Francs	66	13	4		3	6	8
Doubloon	144	0	0		7	4	0

All the divisions of the above gold coins pass in proportion, if full weight.

Gold is weighed by the Gros, which is ⅛th of the old French Ounce (Poids de Marc). The Gros is divided into 72 French Grains, which equal 59 Grains, English troy.

The Doubloon should weigh 7 Gros 3 Gr. or 17 Dwt. 8 Gr. English troy.

And the Napoleon, or Louis, 3 Gros 26 Gr. or 8 Dwt. 6 Gr. ditto.

The following gold coins are taken by actual weight, viz.

Portugal Pieces, at	22 Livres per Gros.
Counterfeit ditto, coined in America, at	20 ditto per Gros.
French and Spanish Coins, deficient in weight, at	£19 15s. per Gros.

English ditto, at 8 Livres 8 Sols per Dwt., that is, 7 Sols per English Grain.

Weights & Measures.

The weights and long measures (with few exceptions) are those of France according to the Old System, for which see *France*.

The Aune, cloth measure, is 44 French Inches, or 46,9 English Inches.

The Carré, land measure, contains 3 Arpents, 78 Perches, 28 square Feet, Paris measure; which answer to 3 English Acres 31 Perches nearly. The Carré is divided into 10,000 square Paces, each Pace being 3½ French Feet, or 3 Feet 8,4 Inches English.

The English Gallon is a common measure for liquids; and it is divided into 2 Pots, 4 Pintes, 8 Chopines, 16 Roquilles, 32 Muces, or 64 Demimuces.

The New System of French Weights and Measures has been partially introduced in these Islands.

ST. DOMINGO, OR HAYTI.

In the French part of St. Domingo, or Hayti, accounts were formerly kept, as above, in Livres, Sols, and Deniers current, and the Dollar was then reckoned at 8 Livres 5 Sous current; but at present, accounts are mostly kept in Dollars and Cents, as in the United States. Monies, &c.

The monies in circulation are nearly the same as in the Leeward Islands. Dollars are valued at 4s. 6d. sterling, with halves and quarters in proportion. 11 Escalins pass for 1 Dollar, and 1 Escalin is reckoned at 9 Cents.

Doubloons pass for 16 Dollars; Joes for 8 ditto; French Crowns for 1 Dollar 9 Cents, and the Half Crowns in proportion. French pieces of 5 Francs pass for 9 Escalins, or 81 Cents.

DUTCH COLONIES.

ST. EUSTATIA, ST. MARTIN, CURAÇOA.

Accounts are kept in these Islands in Pieces of Eight; that is, Piastres current of 8 Reals or Schillings, each Real being subdivided into 6 Stivers. Monies, &c.

The Piastre Gourde or Spanish Dollar passes for 11 Reals or Bits; and thus the current Piastre is worth 3s. 5d. sterling, reckoning the Dollar at 4s. 8d. sterling.

The Joe passes here for 11 Piastres current; the Spanish single Pistole for $4\frac{1}{2}$ Piastres, more or less; the other Spanish and Portuguese gold coins in proportion.

The weights and measures of St. Eustatia and St. Martin are the same as those of Holland, for which see *Amsterdam;* but at Curaçoa they are different, 93lb. of this Island being equal to 100lb. of Amsterdam: hence, 100lb. of Curaçoa = 117lb. avoirdupois.

At Curaçoa the Spanish Vara is used, which answers to $33\frac{3}{8}$ English Inches; and 81 such Varas are equal to 100 Ells of Amsterdam.

SURINAM, BERBICE, DEMERARA, ESSEQUEBO.

Accounts are kept in these Settlements in Guilders of 20 Stivers; the Stiver being divided by some into 8 Duits, and by others into 12 Pennings. Monies, &c.

All the coins of Holland circulate here, and are mostly reckoned at 20 per cent. above their value in Dutch currency.

Monies, &c. The following is their general rate, as well as that of other monies:

	Guilders.	Stivers.		Guilders.	Stivers.
10 Dubbelties .. =	1	0	Spanish Dollar .. =	3	0
The Bit ...... =	0	5	Ducatoon ...... =	3	3
Sestehalf ...... =	0	$5\frac{1}{2}$	Gold Ducat...... =	6	6
Schilling ...... =	0	6	Guinea .... =	14	10
Guilder .... =	1	4	Ryder .... =	16	16
Dalder .... =	1	10	Joe .... =	22	0
Rixdollar ...... =	3	0	Doubloon ...... =	42 to 44	

The chief circulating medium here is paper, issued by Government.

In 1809 a new silver coinage was minted at the Tower of London for these Colonies, consisting of pieces of 3, 2, 1, $\frac{1}{2}$, and $\frac{1}{4}$ Guilders. The larger piece weighs 15 dwt., and is 1 oz. 6 dwt. worse than English standard: its value, therefore, is 3s. 5d. sterling; or, computing it as the Dollar is mostly rated in the West Indies (i. e. at 4s. 8d.), its value is 3s. $8\frac{1}{4}$d., and the smaller pieces in proportion. They are marked on the reverse, *Colonies of Essequebo and Demerara Token*, and the King's head is on the obverse.

The exchange with London should be about 12 Guilders for £1 sterling; but it varies considerably above this, even to 20 Guilders and upwards.

The weights and measures of Amsterdam are used in all these Settlements.

DANISH ISLANDS.

ST. THOMAS, ST. JOHN, SANTA CRUZ.

Monies, &c Accounts are kept here in Piastres or Rixdollars current (also called Pieces of Eight); each Rixdollar being divided into 8 Schillings or Bits, and each Bit into 6 Stivers.

Accounts are also kept in Dollars of 100 Cents, as in America.

The Rixdollar current is commonly reckoned 20 per cent. worse than Danish currency; but, according to the price of most of the Danish coins in these Islands, the difference is 25 per cent.: thus the Danish current Ducat of 2 Rixdollars Danish currency passes here for $2\frac{1}{2}$ Rixdollars or 20 Bits; and the Danish Bank Notes of 5 Rixdollars pass in the same proportion for $6\frac{1}{4}$ Rixdollars.

The Silver coins struck for the Danish Islands are, quadruple, double, and single Bits, and pieces of 1 and 3 Stivers.

The Spanish Dollar passes here for 12½ Bits, and each Bit for 6¼ Stivers; also for 8¼ Shillings, Tortola currency. Monies, &c

The Leeward currency is used in the Danish Islands in the purchase or negotiation of bills on England, though accounts are not so kept. Gold is valued at 1 Dollar per dwt., or 4⅛d. currency per English Grain.

The exchange between London and these Islands is, £100 sterling for £195 Tortola or Leeward currency: it is sometimes much higher.

The Spanish Dollar is given in exchange for the monies of other places.

The weights and measures are those of Denmark, which will be found under the article *Copenhagen;* but the English long measure is also used here.

SPANISH ISLANDS.

CUBA, PORTO RICO, TRINIDAD, and Part of ST. DOMINGO.

The monies, coins, weights, and measures, of the Spanish Islands are the same as in all Spanish America, which have been described under the article *Mexico.* Monies, &c.

Trinidad, however, having been many years in the possession of the English, has chiefly adopted the denominations of money of the English Islands.

Accounts are therefore kept here in Pounds, Shillings, and Pence, Leeward currency; and also in Dollars and Bits, the Bit being the 9th part of the Dollar.

There are likewise Silver pieces of Half Bits and Quarter Bits.

The Spanish, Portuguese, and English gold coins, pass as follow in Trinidad:

	Dwt.	Gr.	Dollars.	Bits.	Leeward Currency.		
The Doubloon	17	8	15	8	£7	4	0
Half Ditto	8	16	7	8½	3	12	0
Joe	7	12	6	8	3	2	0
Guinea	5	8	4	8	2	4	0

Gold is valued at 8s. 3d. Leeward currency per dwt., or 4⅛d. per Grain.

ST. BARTHOLOMEW, a small Swedish Island, uses the monies and currency of the other Leeward Islands. Sundry Islands.

The BERMUDA ISLANDS use the Jamaica currency; and the Gold coins of England, France, Spain, Portugal, and the United States, whether cut or otherwise, pass by law for 2d. sterling per Grain.

The BAHAMA ISLANDS generally use the New York currency; but they reckon the Dollar here at 4s. 8d. sterling; and thus Bahama currency is reduced to sterling by multiplying by 7 and dividing by 12, and *vice versa.*

WEST INDIA EXCHANGES.

DAMAGES ON RETURNED BILLS.

Exchanges. When bills drawn in the West Indies on London are not duly honoured, they are returned to the drawer, with the following charges:

	Damages.	Interest per Annum.	Time how charged.
Jamaica	8 per cent.	6 per cent.	from date of the bill.
Barbadoes	10 per cent.	6 per cent.	from the time of presentation with protest.
Grenada	10 per cent.	6 per cent.	from the bill falling due.
St. Vincent	10 per cent.	8 per cent.	ditto.
Tobago	10 per cent.	8 per cent.	ditto.
Trinidad	10 per cent.	6 per cent.	from date of the protest.
Dominica	10 per cent.	6 per cent.	ditto.
Nevis	10 per cent.	8 per cent.	ditto.
Montserrat	10 per cent.	8 per cent.	ditto.
Antigua	10 per cent.	8 per cent.	ditto.
St. Kitt's	10 per cent.	8 per cent.	ditto.
Tortola	10 per cent.	8 per cent.	ditto.
Demerara, Essequebo, Berbice, Surinam	25 per cent.	6 per cent.	from date of presentation.
St. Thomas, St. John, Santa Cruz	10 per cent.	10 per cent.	from date of the protest.

There are occasionally other charges besides the above, such as postage, notarial expenses, and difference of exchange.

If a bill drawn in the West Indies on any part of Great Britain be noted for non-acceptance, the holder may oblige the drawer, by legal process, to give security in the Island for the amount, without waiting for the bill being protested for non-payment.

WIRTEMBERG *(in Germany)*.

In Wirtemberg and Stutgard, accounts are kept in Guldens or Florins, of 28 Shillings, or 168 Pfenings current. Monies of Account.

This Gulden is reckoned at 15 Batzen, or 60 Creutzers. A Rixdollar current is worth $1\frac{1}{2}$ Gulden, $2\frac{1}{10}$ Pfunds, $22\frac{1}{2}$ Batzen, 30 Kaysergroschen, 42 Schillings, 90 Creutzers, or 252 Pfenings. 7 Shillings are equal to 15 Creutzers; and 5 Creutzers, to 14 Pfenings.

These monies are valued according to the 24 Florin rate, the Cologne Mark of fine silver being 16 Rixdollars. The Florin is therefore worth 21d. sterling.

The Gold coins are, Ducats of 5 Florins, and Carolins d'or of 11 Florins: the Silver coins are, pieces of 24, 12, and 6 Creutzers. The Creutzer is a copper coin, worth about $\frac{1}{3}$ of a Penny. Coins.

The weight for gold and silver is called the Cologne Mark, though it is something heavier; weighing 3610 English Grains, or 233,904 Grammes. Weights.

The commercial Pound is double the gold and silver weight. Thus 100lb. of Wirtemberg answer to 103,1lb. avoirdupois, or 46,78 Kilogrammes.

The Scheffel, corn measure, is divided into 8 Simris, 32 Vierlings or Unzen, 128 Achtels, or 256 Masslein; and renders 5,063 English Bushels, or 1,783 Hectolitre. Measures of Capacity.

The Fuder of wine contains 6 Ohms, 96 Immis, 960 Maass, or 3840 Schoppen.

The Wirtemberg Foot is 11,26 English Inches, or 0,286 of a Metre. Long Measures.

A short Ruthe is 12, and a long Ruthe, 15 Rhineland Feet: the former therefore measures 12,356 Feet, and the latter, 15 Feet $5\frac{1}{2}$ Inches, English measure.

The Stutgard Ell contains 24,08 English Inches, or 0,611 of a Metre.

A great Morgen, or Acre of land, contains 400 short square Ruthes; and is equal to 1 Acre, 1 Rood, 24 Perches English, or 56,74 French Ares. A little Morgen contains 150 great square Ruthes; and measures 3 Roods 11 Perches nearly, or 33,24 French Ares. $1\frac{1}{2}$ Morgen, of the latter measure, is called a Juchart or day's work. Superficial Measures.

WISMAR *(in Germany)*.

Monies, &c. Accounts are kept here in Rixdollars of 48 Schillings, or in Marks of 16 Schillings; the Schilling being divided into 12 Pfenings current.

The Rixdollar is also reckoned at 2 Mecklenburgh Guldens, 3 Marks, 24 Groschen, or 192 Witten.

The coins of Mecklenburgh have been described under the article *Rostock.*

Weights. The same weights and measures are in use as at Hamburgh. There is also a town weight, used chiefly for weighing Russian and Swedish produce, which is reckoned 2 per cent. heavier than that of Hamburgh. It therefore contains 7625 English Grains; and 100lb. of Wismar = 108,93lb. avoirdupois, or 49,40 Kilogrammes.

The Shippond of groceries weighs 20 Lisponds, or 320lb.; the Shippond of iron or lead is 280lb.; a Stone of flax is 20lb.; a Stone of wool or feathers, 10lb.; a Lispond, 16lb.

Measures. The Last of corn is divided into 8 Dromts, or 96 Scheffels. The Scheffel for wheat, rye, pease, and barley, contains 1,15 English Bushel, or 0,4059 of a Hectolitre. The Scheffel for oats is larger; and renders 1,21 English Bushel, or 0,4285 of a Hectolitre. Thus the Last of wheat, &c. answers to 13,82 and the Last of oats to 14,59 English Quarters.*

The measures for wine are the same as at *Rostock.*

The Ell is 2 Feet, each of 11,45 English Inches, or 0,290 of a Metre.

ZANTE *(an Island in the Ionian Sea)*.

This article includes an account of the monies, weights, and measures of all the Ionian Islands, viz. *Corfu, Paxo, Zante, Cephalonia, Santa Maura, Ithaca,* and *Cerigo.*

Monies of Account. Accounts are kept in the Ionian Islands in Dollars of 100 Cents or Oboli. In Cerigo, however, and other places near the Continent, accounts are also kept

* The above statements are chiefly extracted from the despatches transmitted to London in 1818 by *P. Susseroth, Esq.* His Majesty's Vice Consul at Wismar.

in Turkish Piastres of 40 Paras each; and $6\frac{3}{4}$ Piastres equal the Spanish Dollar. Thus the Piastre may be valued at $7\frac{1}{3}$d. sterling. Monies of Account.

The principal Gold coin in these States is the Spanish Doubloon, with its subdivisions. It passes for 15 Spanish Dollars 20 Cents; and its full weight is $416\frac{1}{2}$ Grains troy, being the same weight as the Dollar. Coins.

The Silver coins are, Spanish Pillar Dollars, valued at 100 Cents, with halves and quarters in proportion; Imperial Dollars, with halves, weighing 431 English Grains, and passing for 98 Cents; Venetian Dollars, weighing 432 English Grains, passing for 96 Cents, with halves and quarters in proportion.

The Copper coins are, Cents or Oboli, with double and half pieces, called Dittoboli and Mioboli. The Cent weighs 146 English Grains. A coinage of Quarter Cents, or 400 per Dollar, is in a state of preparation. The Cent is equal to an English Halfpenny nearly.

The weights are Venetian and Turkish. The Pound, Peso Grosso, of 12 Ounces, is reckoned at 7384 troy Grains, or 478,424 Grammes. Hence $94\frac{4}{5}$lb. = 100lb. avoirdupois. The Peso Sottile, for precious metals and drugs, is one-third lighter, weighing 8 Ounces. Weights.

The Oke is used in the Islands to the Southward. It is computed at 18900 English Grains, or $2\frac{7}{10}$lb. avoirdupois. The Levant Cantar or Quintal contains 44 Okes, and therefore answers to 118,8lb. avoirdupois, or 53,88 Kilogrammes.

MEASURES OF THE IONIAN STATES.

The dry measure is the Moggio, which is divided into 8 Misure, and is reckoned at 5 English Bushels. The Misura of Corfu is, in form, the frustrum of a cone, and its dimensions are as follow: the diameter of the top, 11 Inches; of the base, $14\frac{1}{2}$ Inches; and the depth, 10 Inches. Its contents are therefore 1284,78 cubic Inches, answering to 4,78 Winchester Gallons, or 21 Litres. Corfu and Paxo.

Salt is sold by the Centinajo (100lb.), containing 30 Sacchi, each Sacco 2 Mozzette, and each Mozzetta about 70lb. Peso Grosso.

Lime is sold by the Moggio, which has been progressively reduced first to 1 Venetian cubic Foot, and latterly to about half that quantity.

The wine measure is the Barrel, which is divided into 4 Jars or 128 Quartucci; and contains 18 English Gallons, or 68,13 Litres.

The Barrel of oil is divided into 4 Jars, 96 Miltre, or 384 Quartucci.

Measures of Zante. The corn measure is the Bacile, which should contain 72lb. Peso Grosso of best wheat; and estimating the Winchester Bushel at 60lb. avoirdupois, the Bacile equals $1\frac{1}{4}$ Bushel.

The wine Barrel of 120 Quartucci equals $17\frac{5}{8}$ English Gallons.

In oil measure the Barrel is divided into 9 Lire.

The Migliajo (1000lb.) for currants is 1 per cent. lighter than for other articles.

Cephalonia. The Bacile of best wheat should weigh 80lb. Peso Grosso. Thus the Bacile yields $1\frac{2}{5}$ English Bushel.

Salt is sold by the Bacile of 64lb. Peso Grosso.

The wine Barrel is divided into 6 Secchj, 72 Boccali, or 144 Quartucci; and contains 18 English Gallons.

The oil Barrel is divided into 9 Pagliazze.

Santa Maura. The dry measure is the Cado, 4 of which are equal to 3 Moggi of Corfu; and thus the Cado contains $3\frac{3}{4}$ English Bushels.

Salt is sold by the Cariolla of 99lb. Peso Grosso.

The Barrel contains 18 English Gallons. It is divided for wine into 6 Secchj, and for oil into 21 Succali.

Ithaca. The measure for corn is the Bacile, 5 of which make 1 Moggio: consequently the Bacile equals 1 English Bushel.

The liquid measure is the Barrel; which is divided for wine into 64 Boccali, or 128 Quartucci, and for oil into 6 Secchj. The Barrel contains 18 English Gallons.

Cerigo. The Chilo is equal to 1 English Bushel.

The wine Barrel is divided into 30 Bozie, or 60 Agastere; and contains 18 English Gallons.

The oil Barrel contains $14\frac{2}{5}$ English Gallons; and is divided into 24 Bozie.

Long Measures. The Venetian Foot is used in all the Islands: it equals $13\frac{3}{4}$ English Inches.

The Passo is composed of 5 Venetian Feet.

The Braccio for cloths, &c. equals $27\frac{3}{16}$ English Inches.

The Braccio for silks equals $25\frac{3}{8}$ English Inches.

Land is measured by the Misura or Baccile, which is $\frac{1}{8}$ of a Moggio; 400 square Passi being 1 Misura or Baccile, about $\frac{3}{10}$ of an Acre English. Thus the Moggio = 2 Acres 1 Rood 24 Perches, or 97,12 French Ares. Land Measures.

Vineyards are measured by the Zappada; 3 Zappade (a computed day's work of digging) being 1 Misura.

Firewood is measured by the square Passo, usually, however, only 2 Feet thick; this depending on the quality of the wood. Stone is measured by the Passo Cubo.*

ZELL (*in Germany*).

Accounts are kept here in Rixdollars of 36 Mariengroschen, as in *Hanover*, which see. Monies.

The Pound is divided into 32 Loths, or 128 Quentins; and contains 7511 English Grains. Thus 100lb. of Zell = 107,3lb. avoirdupois, or 48,66 Kilogrammes. Weights.

The Lispond is 14lb.; the Centner, 112lb.; the Shippond, 20 Lisponds, or 280lb.; the Last, 12 Shipponds. A Stone of flax is 20lb.; a Stone of wool, 10lb.

A Last of corn contains $2\frac{1}{2}$ Wispels, 10 Scheffels, 100 Himtens, or 400 Spints; a Wispel is 4 Scheffels or 40 Himtens. The Wispel renders 35,30 English Bushels, or 12,43 Hectolitres. Measures of Capacity.

The Stubgen, liquid measure, is divided into 4 Quartiers, or 16 Nossels; and contains 1,025 English Gallon, or 3,888 Litres. A Fass of beer is 4 Tonnes or 104 Stubgens; a Tonne of honey, $25\frac{1}{2}$ Stubgens.

The Foot is 11,45 English Inches, or 0,290 of a Metre. The Ell measures 2 Feet; the Clafter or Fathom, 6 Feet; and the Ruthe, 8 Feet. Long Measures.

* For the foregoing account of the Monies, Weights, and Measures of the Ionian Islands, the Author is indebted to the *Earl of Lauderdale;* at whose request it was transmitted to London, in March, 1821. The statements were signed by *J. Woodhouse, Esq.* Auditor General.

ZURICH *(in Switzerland)*.

Monies of Account.

Accounts are kept here in Florins of 60 Creutzers, or 480 Hellers; or in Florins of 40 Shillings.

The Florin is also divided into 16 Batzen, or 240 Angsters.

A Rixdollar of account is worth $1\frac{1}{2}$ Florin, 60 Shillings, or 90 Creutzers; a Batze, $3\frac{3}{4}$ Creutzers, 10 Rappen, or 15 Angsters; a Creutzer, 4 Angsters, or 8 Hellers; a Rappe, $1\frac{1}{2}$ Angster, or 3 Hellers.

All public accounts relating to the general concerns of the Diet are kept in Swiss Livres of 10 Batzen. See *Switzerland, &c.*

There were formerly here two sorts of money; currency and money of exchange.

Sales of merchandize and all daily transactions took place in currency, in which money the old French Louis d'or (coined before 1786) was reckoned at 9 Florins 45 Creutzers, but it has been raised to 10 Florins; the French Ecu of 6 Livres was reckoned at 2 Florins $26\frac{1}{4}$ Creutzers, and it has been raised to $2\frac{1}{2}$ Florins.

In money of exchange, the value of the oldest French Louis d'or (coined before 1726) was fixed at 7 Florins; the Ducat was reckoned at 3 Florins 54 Creutzers, and the effective Rixdollar or Ecu, at 108 Creutzers.

273 Florins of exchange were commonly reckoned equal to 310 Florins current; but this proportion was not permanent. At present, however, money of exchange is nearly disused, and foreign exchanges, as well as all other commercial transactions, mostly take place in currency.

Coins.

The coins here are Ducats, which, when they weigh $\frac{1}{2}$ Pistole, are reckoned at 4 Florins 15 Creutzers, or 4 Florins 10 Shillings; but when they are of the common weight, at 4 Florins 18 Creutzers, or 4 Florins 12 Shillings; silver Ecus, at 2 Florins; single, half, and quarter Florins, at 60, 30, and 15 Creutzers; Batzen, at $3\frac{3}{4}$ Creutzers; Shillings, halves, and quarters, at 12, 6, and 3 Hellers; and pieces of 2 Hellers.

French Louis d'ors, as mentioned above, pass for 10 Florins, and French Crowns for $2\frac{1}{2}$ Florins.

The modern coins of France, however, have a more general circulation here.

Rate of Coinage.

68 Ducats are to weigh a Cologne Mark of gold, $23\frac{1}{2}$ Carats fine. The Ecus and half Ecus or Florins are to be $13\frac{1}{3}$ Loths (or $\frac{10}{12}$) fine; and 11 Ecus are to contain a Cologne Mark of fine silver. The half Florins are 12 Loths (or $\frac{9}{12}$) fine; and 44 pieces contain a Cologne Mark of fine silver. 94 pieces of 15 Creutzers weigh a Cologne Mark, 8 Loths (or $\frac{6}{12}$) fine.

Thus the Florin, Zurich currency, contains 164 English Grains of fine silver, or $177\frac{3}{10}$ Grains of standard silver, and it is therefore worth 23d. sterling nearly; or £1 sterling = 10 Florins 26 Creutzers.

Wrought gold is to be $19\frac{1}{2}$ Carats fine; and wrought silver, $13\frac{1}{2}$ Loths (or 10 Ounces $2\frac{1}{2}$ Dwt.) fine.

Gold and Silver Weight.

The Mark, gold and silver weight, is divided into 16 Loths, 64 Quintlins, 256 Pennings, or 4352 Zurich Asen; which are equivalent to 4876 Dutch Asen. Hence the Mark of Zurich contains 3616,9 English Grains, or 234,346 Grammes.

Commercial Weights.

The light Pound of 16 Ounces, with which silk is weighed, contains 2 of the above Marks: it weighs therefore 7233 English Grains; and 100lb. of Zurich silk weight = 103,3lb. avoirdupois, or 46,86 Kilogrammes.

The heavy Pound, with which most other sorts of merchandise are weighed, is 18 Ounces or 36 Loths; and weighs therefore 8138 English Grains. Thus 100lb. of Zurich heavy weight = 116,25lb. avoirdupois, or 52,72 Kilogrammes.

Dry Measures.

The measure for all sorts of corn is the Viertel; which contains 1323 Zurich cubic Inches, or 1262 English cubic Inches. The Mutt of corn is divided into 4 Viertels, 16 Vierlings, or 64 Masslings; and renders 2,34 English Bushels, or 0,827 of a Hectolitre. Dry fruits are measured by the Immi, the 9th part of a Viertel.

Pulse is sold by the Malter of 16 Viertels. This Viertel contains 1338 cubic Inches of Zurich, or $1276\frac{1}{3}$ English cubic Inches; and renders 0,593 of an English Bushel, or 0,2091 of a Hectolitre.

Salt is measured by the Maass of 4 Viertels, each containing 1473 cubic Inches of Zurich, or 1406 English cubic Inches. This Viertel therefore equals 0,653 of an English Bushel, or 0,2303 of a Hectolitre.

Liquid Measures.

Wines and other liquids are measured by the Kopf of 2 Maasses. The land Maass contains $116\frac{3}{4}$ cubic Inches of Zurich, or $111\frac{1}{3}$ English cubic Inches; and equals 0,48 of an English Gallon, or 1,82 Litre. The city Maass is $\frac{1}{10}$ less.

A Saum, gross measure, is $1\frac{1}{2}$ Eimer; and an Eimer contains 4 Viertels, 32

Liquid Measures. Kopfs, 64 Maasses, 128 Quartlins, or 256 Stotzes. This Eimer therefore = 30,83 English Gallons, or 116,67 Litres.

A Saum, thin measure, is likewise 1½ Eimer; and the Eimer contains 4 Viertels, 30 Kopfs, 60 Maasses, 120 Quartlins, or 240 Stotzes. This Eimer is therefore about 29 English Gallons, or 109,36 Litres.

The measure for oil and honey contains 88 cubic Inches of Zurich, or 84 English cubic Inches, nearly 3 English Pints, or 1,37 Litre. Oil is also sold by the Pound weight.

Long Measures. The Foot is divided into 12 Inches, and equals 11,81 English Inches, or 0,30 of a Metre. The Ell is 2 Feet; and therefore 99 Ells = 65 English Yards.

The Ruthe or Rod is 10 Feet, each of which, in land surveying, is divided into 10 Inches.

The Clafter or Fathom (the standard measure of which is the space between the two iron hinges of the gate of the late Convent of Nuns in Zurich) measures 73,35 English Inches, or 1,863 Metre.

Exchanges. Zurich exchanges with and gives (more or less) to—

Amsterdam	53 Creutzers	for 1 Florin.
Augsburg	108 Florins	for 100 Florins current.
Francfort	1 per Cent. loss.	
Geneva	2 per Cent. loss.	
Genoa	21 Creutzers	for 1 Lira fuori banco.
Hamburgh	240 Florins	for 100 Rixdollars banco.
Leghorn........	128 Creutzers	for 1 Pezza of 8 Reals.
Leipsic	107 Florins	for 100 Florins in Louis d'ors.
London	11 Florins	for £1 Sterling.
Lyons and Paris,	½ per Cent. profit.	
Milan..........	107 Florins	for 333½ Lire correnti.
Nuremberg	96 Florins	for 100 Florins in small coins.
Venice	13½ Creutzers	for 1 Lira piccola.

The usance on Holland and Germany is 14 days after sight. No days of grace are allowed in Zurich.

END OF VOL. I.

Printed by J. Whiting, 3, Lombard Street.

ADDENDA.

TURKISH METROLOGY.

After the foregoing articles had been printed, a delay occurred in the publication from an important cause—the arrival of a Set of Standard Weights from Constantinople, which had been long expected for the Work; and as they are found more accurately adjusted in their divisions and proportions than any other weights hitherto received from Turkey, their contents are here inserted as supplementary matter or Addenda.

It should be explained that when it became necessary, in the course of the Work, to print the article *Constantinople*, as no Standards had been then received from that place, those of Smyrna were adopted (for the weights of both cities should be equal). Some inaccuracies, however, in their divisions are alluded to (p. 73); and it is now found that the *Oke* of Smyrna is about 1 Grain in 700 heavier than that of Constantinople.

The following are the contents of the Constantinople Weights, as determined at the London Mint August 24, 1821:

The Oke of 400 Turkish Drams = 19800 English Grains troy = 2lb. 13 oz. 4 drams avoirdupois, or 1 Kilogramme 283 Grammes.

Hence the Chequee of 100 Drams = 4950 Grains or 320,75 Grammes, and all its subdivisions and multiples in proportion.

Thus also the Kintal or Cantaro of 45 Okes or 100 Rotoli = 127lb. avoirdupois, or $57\frac{3}{4}$ Kilogrammes, very nearly.

N. B. It is recommended that the foregoing proportions be substituted in the articles *Constantinople* and *Smyrna*, in both Volumes, instead of the contents of the Oke, Chequee, Kintal, &c. already inserted.

This preference is given to the Standards of Constantinople, as being of superior workmanship and materials; and above all, as their subdivisions have been found adjusted with the greatest accuracy.

The correctness, however, of the Smyrna Standards was attested by the *Cadi* of the city on a sheet of parchment, in Turkish characters, and stamped with the *Crescent*.

The Standards of Constantinople are differently verified, that is, by stamps on the weights themselves. Their adjustment was completed by the official authority under the immediate inspection of *M. Frederic Pisani*, Dragoman to His Excellency *Lord Strangford*, the British Ambassador at that city. His Certificate, which is written in French, states—

" That on the 10th of April, 1821, he conveyed the weights in question from the " Maker's Office to the Department of *Conyoumgi Bachi Suleiman Effendi*, the Officer " who has the only authority to verify the accuracy of weights. This Officer having " carefully weighed and adjusted the Standards submitted to him (11 in number), " caused them to be stamped with the cypher of the Sultan *Mahmoud*, and with the " date 1236 (1821)—the weights thus marked being those only which are authorized by " the Turkish Government." He adds, " that at Constantinople the custom is to mark " the date upon all the weights every year."

Such are the means which have been employed by order of the British Government for obtaining a correct knowledge of the Metrology of Turkey. Similar attempts have been made at different periods by the Government of France, but with less satisfactory results. Thus, according to *M. Bonneville* (" *Traité des Monnaies*," p. 196), the Chequee of Constantinople, transmitted by order of the *Duc de Choiseul* to *M. Tillet*, in 1767, was found about $\frac{1}{5}$ per cent. lighter than that brought to Paris by the Ottoman Legation in 1797. The latter Standard is represented by *Bonneville* as defective in workmanship, but he gives no preference to either weight as to accuracy.

The following are the contents of the Turkish Chequee, reduced to English Grains, as stated by different authorities:

	Eng. Gr. Troy.
By *Paucton* and *Soulet*	4922
Kruse, *Ricard*, *Marien*, *Gerhart*, and *Dubost*	4925
Tillet, (transmitted by order of the *Duc de Choiseul*)	4933
Bonneville, (brought by the *Ottoman Legation*)	4942
Nelkenbrecker, p. 507	4969
Smyrna Chequee, transmitted for this Work in 1818	4957
Constantinople Chequee, transmitted for this Work in 1821	4950

The last result seems entitled to the greatest confidence, for the reasons already mentioned.*

* It should be stated that the Standards received from Constantinople were prepared under the superintendence of *John Cartwright, Esq.* the British Consul General at that city, and transmitted by him to *Lord Viscount Castlereagh* (now *The Marquis of Londonderry*), in obedience to the Circular Order addressed by His Lordship to all British Consuls abroad (see Pref. p. xi.)

TRIPOLI *(in Barbary)*.

The following are the contents of the Weights and Measures of Tripoli, as determined in May, 1822, by a series of experiments made by the different authorities mentioned in the foregoing Preface. These experiments were repeated on two sets of verified standards which had been transmitted to London for this Publication; but as they were not received in time for the insertion of their contents in the body of the Work, the present Supplementary Statement is given.

It should be observed that when the article *Tripoli* (p. 337) came to be printed, the Author having no new matter to introduce, reprinted his former account, as given in the first edition of the *Cambist*. That statement was taken from *Kruse*, *Ricard*, and other high authorities, who, though differing on many other subjects, agree in their account of Tripoli, which now appears to be wholly incorrect.*

The largest weight is the Cantar of 100 Rottol, which answers to 109,71lb. avoirdupois, or 49,76 Kilogrammes. Weights.

The Rottol is divided into 16 Ounces (Okie); the Ounce into 10 Drams; and the Dram into 16 Kharouba.

The Rottol weighs 7680 English Grains, and therefore its Ounce equals 480 Grains, which, it is curious to observe, is the English Ounce troy.

The principal weight for wrought gold is the *Metikel*, $6\frac{2}{3}$ of which make an Ounce. It is divided into 24 Kharouba, and therefore answers to 72 English Grains or 4,665 Grammes. This is called the *Metikel Mumini*, to distinguish it from the lesser Metikel, which is called *Aghis*.

The Aghis is used for weighing gold dust. Its contents are 63 English Grains.

Gold lace and gold thread are sold by the Ounce, and also Silver.

---

* The weights and measures examined and proved on this occasion were adjusted at Tripoli in October, 1820, and their correctness certified by the signatures and seals of *Sadi Hamet*, Prime Minister, and *Hagi Hamet Massen*, Governor of the City.

These adjustments and verifications were effected under the care of *Hanmer Warrington, Esq.* Consul General to his Britannic Majesty at Tripoli, who has since transmitted those Standards, with explanatory papers, to *Earl Bathurst*, as Secretary of State for the Colonial Department. He also sent Specimens of the Coins, which are described in the present Article.

In drawing up this account of African Metrology and the Hegira, the Author has to acknowledge much valuable information received from *The Sharif Hassuna D'Ghies*, late of Tripoli; and also from *Mr. Abraham Salamé*, Oriental Interpreter to the British Government.

Measures. Corn, Wine, and Oil. The principal measure for corn is the *Ueba.* It is divided into 4 Temen (quarters), the Temen into 4 Orbah, and the Orbah into 2 Nufs-Orbah.

The Ueba measures 6551 English cubic Inches, and therefore answers to 3,046 Winchester Bushels, or 1,073 Hectolitre. Hence the Temen contains 6,093 Winchester Gallons, and its divisions in proportion.

At Bengasi, in the Regency of Tripoli, corn is measured by the *Saa,* which is divided into 2 Nusfie, and is reckoned 34 per cent. less than the Ueba. It therefore contains 2 Winchester Bushels nearly.

At Bengasi the Cantar is composed of 50 Oke, and answers to 125 Rottol.

The Ueba should weigh 210 Rottol of wheat, or 150 of barley.

[The corn measures are subject to legal variation in years of scarcity.]

The principal measure for wine and spirits is the *Barile.* It is divided into 24 Bozze, which are the same as those of Venice. The Barile answers to 17$\frac{1}{8}$ English Wine Gallons, or 64,75 Litres.

The common measure for oil is the *Caraffa,* which weighs 3$\frac{1}{8}$ Rottol.

The measure for pomatum is the same as for oil, but the Caraffa weighs 4 Ounces more. The *Harbaia* is a measure of 6 Caraffa.

Cloth, Linen, &c. Cloth, linen, silk, cotton, &c. are measured by the Turkish *Dreah* or *Pik,* which is divided into 3 Palmi, and = 26,42 English Inches, or 0,6808 of a Metre.

Ribands of all kinds, and linens of Alexandria, Egypt, and the Levant, and also linens and cloths of the Regency, are measured with the *Arbi Dreah* or *Lesser Pik,* which equals 19,03 English Inches, or 0,483 of a Metre.

Coins. The monies of Tripoli are subject to great variation in their current value: the silver coins are minted much below their nominal price, so that the seignorage is always considerable. The following are specimens of the present coins, which are supposed divisions of the Spanish Dollar, but it will be seen that they are very inferior both in proportional weight, and in fineness.

The *Ghersch,* which is called the Quarter Dollar, is divided into halves and quarters. It is also called the *Real,* and sometimes the *Piastre.*

Assays. The following Assays were made at the London Mint in May, 1822.

	Assay.		Weight.		Standard Weight.		Sterling Value.	
	oz.	dwt.	dwt.	gr.	dwt.	gr.	s.	d.
Ghersch........W.	6	17	7	20	3	0	0	9$\frac{1}{4}$
Half Ghersch...W.	7	8$\frac{1}{2}$	4	2$\frac{1}{2}$	1	8	0	4$\frac{1}{8}$
Quarter Ghersch W.	7	9	1	23	0	15	0	2

The Inscriptions of those Coins are in Arabic, and may be thus translated: Inscriptions.

ON ONE SIDE:

"King of the Two Lands, & Sovereign of the Two Seas, King, Son of a King."

[The "Two Lands" are supposed to mean the continents on each side of the Mediterranean; and "The Two Seas" the Mediterranean and the Black Sea.]

ON THE OTHER SIDE:

"Sultan Mahmoud, Son of Abed-el-Hameed: may his Glory be eternal. Coined in Tripoli of Barbary in 1223."

[The year 1223 of the Hegira* answers to 1808 of the Christian Era.]

---

* The Hegira or Mahometan Era has already been briefly explained (Vol. II. p. 210); but the abstruse nature of the subject, and its extensive application in Eastern commerce, seem to require further elucidation in a Work on Commercial Science. This the Author now deems the more necessary, as he has just discovered that the Tables published in this country for comparing Mahometan and Christian dates, though carried up from the commencement of the Hegira (July 16, A. D. 622) to the year 2000, are correct only to the close of the last century. The following Table is therefore adapted for the present century and the next. Hegira explained.

The necessity of Tables for these comparisons arises from the unequal length of lunar and solar years, as the Mahometans use the former and the Christians the latter. The lunar year contains $354\frac{11}{30}$ days nearly, and the solar year $365\frac{109}{450}$ days. The difference is $10\frac{197}{225}$, but 11 days are used for short intervals; and as there is no embolism adopted for adjusting this difference, the commencement of each lunar year anticipates the conclusion of the solar by 11 days nearly, and thus retrogrades through all its seasons in about $32\frac{1}{2}$ years; or more accurately 32,5848 solar years = 33,5848 lunar years.

In order that lunar years should be reckoned in an integral number of days, the fraction $\frac{11}{30}$ is disposed of by adopting a Cycle of 30 years, 11 of which are reckoned at 355 days, and the others at 354; the former are called *Abounding Years*, and are mixed with the latter, as hereafter explained.

The year is divided into 12 months of 30 and 29 days alternately, except the last month of each Abounding Year, which is reckoned at 30 days; as exemplified at the end of this Note.

There are two modes of measuring the year; the one by the Cycle above described, which is used for historical and other important purposes, and is therefore called the *Political or Chronological Year*. The other, which is called the *Popular Year*, is used for common observances. Its commencement is estimated from the first appearance of the new moon in the beginning of the first month; and thus the successive 12 months are measured, which, on the whole, cannot essentially differ from the Cycle.

The Solar Year is occasionally used in Agriculture, Astronomy, &c. but always according to the Julian Calendar or Old Style, which is at present 12 days behind the Gregorian or New Style. Thus, the date June 1, O. S. answers to June 13, N. S. The difference during the last century was 11 days. It will remain 12 until Feb. 28, 1900; and then continue 13 for two successive centuries.

This suppression of 3 days in 400 years is intended to correct the excess of the civil year, 365*d.* 6*h.* above the solar year, 365*d.* 5*h.* 48*m.* 48*s.*; which is effected by reckoning three successive centenary years as common ones, and the fourth as a leap year. The omission of this Rule, at the periods 1800 and 1900, in reducing the original Table of the Hegira to the New Style, has been the cause of the inaccuracies above mentioned in the English Tables, which are here carefully corrected.

Hegira explained.

It may be satisfactory to add that the following Table perfectly agrees with that published at Paris in 1783, in the celebrated work entitled *L'Art de vérifier les Dates;* and it also corresponds with the Mahometan Calendar published annually at Berlin, in *Professor Bode's Astronomical Year Book.*

TABLE OF THE HEGIRA,

Shewing the Day of the Christian Calendar on which each Mahometan Year begins, from A. D. 1800 *to* A. D. 2000.

An. Heg.	An. Dom.		An. Heg.	An. Dom.		An. Heg.	An. Dom.		An. Heg.	An. Dom.		An. Heg.	An. Dom.	
1215	1800	May 25	1257	1841	Feb. 23	1299	1881	Nov. 23	1341	1922	Aug 24	1383	1963	May 25
1216	1801	May 14	1258	1842	Feb. 12	1300	1882	Nov. 12	1342	1923	Aug. 14	1384	1964	May 13
1217	1802	May 4	1259	1843	Feb 1	1301	1883	Nov. 2	1343	1924	Aug. 2	1385	1965	May 3
1218	1803	Apr. 23	1260	1844	Jan. 22	1302	1884	Oct. 21	1344	1925	July 22	1386	1956	Apr. 22
1219	1804	Apr. 12	1261	1845	Jan. 10	1303	1885	Oct. 10	1345	1926	July 12	1387	1967	Apr. 12
1220	1805	Apr. 1	1262	1845	Dec. 30	1304	1886	Sep. 30	1346	1927	July 1	1388	1968	Mar. 31
1221	1806	Mar. 21	1263	1846	Dec. 20	1305	1887	Sep. 19	1347	1928	June 20	1389	1969	Mar. 20
1222	1807	Mar. 11	1264	1847	Dec. 9	1306	1888	Sep. 7	1348	1929	June 9	1390	1970	Mar. 10
1223	1808	Feb. 28	1265	1848	Nov. 27	1307	1889	Aug. 28	1349	1930	May 29	1391	1971	Feb. 27
1224	1809	Feb. 16	1266	1849	Nov. 17	1308	1890	Aug. 17	1350	1931	May 19	1392	1972	Feb. 16
1225	1810	Feb. 6	1267	1850	Nov. 6	1309	1891	Aug. 7	1351	1932	May 7	1393	1973	Feb. 5
1226	1811	Jan. 26	1268	1851	Oct. 27	1310	1892	July 26	1352	1933	Apr. 26	1394	1974	Jan. 25
1227	1812	Jan. 16	1269	1852	Oct. 15	1311	1893	July 15	1353	1934	Apr 16	1395	1975	Jan. 14
1228	1813	Jan. 4	1270	1853	Oct. 4	1312	1894	July 5	1354	1935	Apr. 5	1396	1976	Jan. 4
1229	1813	Dec. 24	1271	1854	Sep. 24	1313	1895	June 24	1355	1936	Mar. 24	1397	1976	Dec. 23
1230	1814	Dec 14	1272	1855	Sep. 13	1314	1896	June 12	1356	1937	Mar. 14	1398	1977	Dec. 13
1231	1815	Dec. 3	1273	1856	Sep. 1	1315	1897	June 2	1357	1938	Mar. 3	1399	1978	Dec. 2
1232	1816	Nov. 21	1274	1857	Aug. 22	1316	1898	May 22	1358	1939	Feb 21	1400	1979	Nov 21
1233	1817	Nov 11	1275	1858	Aug. 11	1317	1899	May 12	1359	1940	Feb 10	1401	1980	Nov. 10
1234	1818	Oct. 31	1276	1859	July 31	1318	1900	May 1	1360	1941	Jan. 29	1402	1981	Oct. 30
1235	1819	Oct. 20	1277	1860	July 20	1319	1901	Apr. 20	1361	1942	Jan. 19	1403	1982	Oct. 19
1236	1820	Oct. 9	1278	1861	July 9	1320	1902	Apr. 10	1362	1943	Jan. 8	1404	1983	Oct. 9
1237	1821	Sep. 28	1279	1862	June 29	1321	1903	Mar. 30	1363	1943	Dec. 28	1405	1984	Sep. 27
1238	1822	Sep. 18	1280	1863	June 18	1322	1904	Mar. 18	1364	1944	Dec. 17	1406	1985	Sep. 17
1239	1823	Sep. 7	1281	1864	June 6	1323	1905	Mar. 8	1365	1945	Dec. 6	1407	1986	Sep. 6
1240	1824	Aug. 26	1282	1865	May 27	1324	1906	Feb 25	1366	1946	Nov. 25	1108	1987	Aug. 26
1241	1825	Aug. 16	1283	1866	May 16	1325	1907	Feb. 14	1367	1947	Nov. 15	1409	1988	Aug. 15
1242	1826	Aug. 5	1284	1867	May 5	1326	1908	Feb. 4	1368	1948	Nov. 3	1410	1989	Aug. 4
1243	1827	July 25	1285	1868	Apr. 24	1327	1909	Jan. 23	1369	1949	Oct 24	1411	1990	July 24
1244	1828	July 14	1286	1869	Apr. 13	1328	1910	Jan. 13	1370	1950	Oct. 13	1412	1991	July 14
1245	1829	July 3	1287	1870	Apr. 3	1329	1911	Jan. 2	1371	1951	Oct. 2	1413	1992	July 2
1246	1830	June 22	1288	1871	Mar. 23	1330	1911	Dec. 22	1372	1952	Sep. 21	1414	1993	June 21
1247	1831	June 12	1289	1872	Mar. 11	1331	1912	Dec. 11	1373	1953	Sep. 10	1415	1994	June 11
1248	1832	May 31	1290	1873	Mar. 1	1332	1913	Nov 30	1374	1954	Aug 30	1416	1995	May 31
1249	1833	May 21	1291	1874	Feb. 18	1333	1914	Nov. 19	1375	1955	Aug. 20	1417	1996	May 20
1250	1834	May 10	1292	1875	Feb. 7	1334	1915	Nov. 9	1376	1956	Aug. 8	1418	1997	May 9
1251	1835	Apr. 29	1293	1876	Jan. 28	1335	1916	Oct. 28	1377	1957	July 29	1419	1998	Apr 28
1252	1836	Apr. 18	1294	1877	Jan. 16	1336	1917	Oct 17	1378	1958	July 18	1420	1999	Apr. 18
1253	1837	Apr. 7	1295	1878	Jan. 5	1337	1918	Oct. 7	1379	1959	July 7	1421	2000	Apr. 6
1254	1838	Mar. 27	1296	1878	Dec. 26	1338	1919	Sep. 26	1380	1960	June 26			
1255	1839	Mar. 17	1297	1879	Dec. 15	1339	1920	Sep. 15	1381	1961	June 15			
1256	1840	Mar. 5	1298	1880	Dec. 4	1340	1921	Sep. 4	1382	1962	June 5			

☞ From the above Table the general correspondence of dates may be easily determined. Thus, to find the Mahometan month and day answering to December 25, 1822:—the Table shews that in 1822 the year 1238 of the Hegira begins September 18, which is 98 days before Christmas, or 3 Mahometan months and 9 days; that is, the 9th day of Raby second. The following are the names of the months and their number of days respectively:

	Days		Days		Days		Days		Days		Days
1 Moharam...	30	3 Raby awal ...	30	5 Joumad awal .	30	7 Rajab	30	9 Ramadan..	30	11 Delkeda ...	30
2 Safar	29	4 Raby tany ...	29	6 Joumad tany..	29	8 Shahban..	29	10 Shawal....	29	12 Delhiga....	29

The last month has 30 days in each *Abounding Year*, which is found by dividing the date of the Hegira by 30, and the remainder is the year of the Cycle. If it be 2, 5, 7, 10, 13, 16, 18, 21, 24, 26, or 29, it is an Abounding Year.

NEW CODE OF NAVIGATION LAWS.

The principal law for regulating the commercial intercourse between Great Britain and Foreign States, commonly called the "*Navigation Act*," (12 Car. II.) having been in part repealed, together with upwards of 200 subordinate Statutes relating to Trade and Navigation; a New Code has been substituted, of which the following is an Abstract. [*Commencing June* 24, 1822.]

NEW NAVIGATION ACT (3 Geo. IV. cap. 43),

For regulating the Importation of Goods, so far as relates to the Countries or places from whence, and the ships in which such importation shall be made; but not to affect the importation of goods the produce of British Colonies in America or the West Indies.

From ASIA, AFRICA, AND AMERICA *(in British Ships).*

All goods of the growth, produce, or manufacture, may be imported in a British ship only, from any place—but if imported from Europe, *FOR EXPORTATION SOLELY, with the exception of such as are of the growth, produce, or manufacture of any place within the dominions of the Grand Seignor, also raw silk and mohair yarn, the produce or manufacture of Asia; all bullion, prize goods, diamonds, rubies, pearls, emeralds, jewels, and precious stones, and all goods of the growth, produce, or manufacture of the dominions of the Emperor of Morocco, imported direct into Gibraltar from any part of such dominions not to the southward of the port of Mogadore,* (as to which exceptions see explanations under the head of *Europe).*

UNITED STATES OF AMERICA *(in American Ships).*

All goods the growth, produce, or manufacture, (not being prohibited to be imported from any other Country,) may be imported direct in ships of the built of the Country, or in ships legally condemned as prize; such ships being owned by the subjects of the United States, and navigated by a master and three-fourths at least of the mariners thereof.

PORTUGUESE TRANSMARINE TERRITORIES *(in Portuguese Ships).*

All elephants' teeth and ivory, and all goods of the growth, produce, or manufacture of any of the territories or dominions of the Crown of Portugal, (not being prohibited to be imported from other foreign Countries,) may be imported direct from any such territories or dominions in ships built in any of the said territories or dominions, or in ships legally condemned as prize; such ships being owned by the subjects of the said dominions, and navigated by a master and three-fourths at least of the mariners thereof.

SPANISH AMERICA AND WEST INDIES *(in Spanish or other Foreign Ships).*

All goods of the growth, produce, or manufacture of any Country or place in America or the West Indies, *being or having been* a part of the dominions of the King of Spain, (not being prohibited to be imported in a British ship,) may be imported direct from the place of their growth, produce, or manufacture, or from the ports in such Country or place where the same can only be, or have been usually first shipped for transportation, in ships of the built of such Countries or places, and owned by the people thereof, navigated by a master and three-fourths at least of the mariners of such Countries or places; or if such Countries or places are under the dominion of Spain, or if any doubt shall exist thereon, then in ships or vessels of the built of any Country within the dominions of Spain, owned as aforesaid; all which importations in *foreign ships* are to be confined to such Countries and places as aforesaid, where British ships shall be entitled to privileges equal to those granted to foreign ships as above.

TURKISH DOMINIONS IN ASIA AND AFRICA *(in Turkish Ships).*

All goods of the growth, produce, or manufacture of the dominions of Turkey, in *Asia* or *Africa*, may be imported in a ship the built of any Country within the dominions of the *Grand Seignor*, owned by the people thereof, and navigated by a master and three-fourths at least of the mariners of such Country.

EUROPE *(in any Ships*

Subject to Exceptions as to Modes of Importation).

All goods of the growth, produce, or manufacture of Europe, except such manufactured articles as are specially prohibited, and the following, may be imported in *any ships:—*

European masts, timber, boards, salt, pitch, tar, tallow, rosin, hemp, flax, currants, raisins, figs, prunes, olive oil, corn or grain, potashes, wine, sugar, vinegar, brandy, or tobacco, shall be imported only in British ships, or in ships of the built of and belonging to the Country of which they are the growth, produce, or manufacture, or in ships of the built of and belonging to the Country, port, or place in Europe, into which such goods shall have been brought, or imported, *and landed;* all such foreign ships to be navigated by a master and three-fourths at least of the mariners thereof, upon the forfeiture of the goods and of a sum not exceeding £100 by the master of the ship.

All British built ships which shall have been registered and which shall belong to any person not being a subject of His Majesty, shall be considered a ship of the built of the Country (if in Europe) of which such person shall be a subject.

EXPLANATIONS.

Raw silk and mohair yarn, the growth, produce, or manufacture of any part of Asia, may be imported in a British ship direct from any ports or places in the Streights or the Levant Seas, within the dominions of the Grand Seignor.

All goods the growth, produce, or manufacture of any place in Asia or Africa, within the dominions of the Grand Seignor, may be imported in a TURKISH or a British vessel navigated according to law.

All goods the growth, produce, or manufactnre of any place within the dominions of the Emperor of Morocco, imported direct into Gibraltar from any part of such dominions not to the southward of the port of Mogadore, in a British ship or a vessel belonging to the subjects of the said Emperor, may be imported from Gibraltar in a British ship.

Under the New Law no forfeitures attach to British ships with respect to importation, but to the goods only.

WEST INDIA TRADE.

An Act to regulate the trade between His Majesty's Colonies and possessions in America *and the* West Indies, *and other places in* America *and the* West Indies. (3 Geo. IV. cap. 44.)

This Act permits the direct IMPORTATION of the following goods *(in British and certain Foreign Ships).*

Asses, barley, beans, biscuit, bread, beaver and all sorts of fur, bowsprits, calavances, cattle, cocoa, cochineal, coin and bullion, cotton wool, dye woods, drugs, diamonds, flax, fruit, flour, garden seeds, grain, hay, hemp, heading-boards, horses, hogs, hoops, hides, hardwood or mill timber, Indian corn meal, indigo, live stock, lumber, logwood, mahogany and other wood for cabinet wares, masts, mules, neat cattle, oats, precious stones, peas, potatoes, poultry, pitch, rice, rye, staves, skins, shingles, sheep, tar, tallow, tobacco, turpentine, timber, tortoiseshell, vegetables, wool, wheat, and yards,

From any foreign Country on the continent of America, or from any foreign island in the West Indies, whether such Country or island shall be under the dominion of any foreign European Sovereign, or otherwise, in British ships, or in ships of the built of and owned by the inhabitants of any Country or place belonging to or under the dominions of the Sovereign or state of which the said goods are the growth, produce, or manufacture, or in any British built ship which has become the property of the subjects of any such foreign Sovereign or state, (such foreign vessels being navigated with a master, and three-fourths of the mariners, at least, belonging to such Country or places,) into the following Free Ports in the British West Indies and America—the Privy Council having the power to extend the trade to other ports as aforesaid:

Kingston, Savannah Le Mar, Montego Bay, Santa Lucia, Antonio, Saint Ann, Falmouth, Maria, and Morant Bay	in Jamaica	Port Saint George & Port Hamilton	in Bermuda
Saint George	Grenada	Any port where there is a Custom House	in Bahamas
Roseau	Dominica	Bridge Town	Barbadoes
Saint John's	Antigua	Saint John's, Saint Andrew's	New Brunswick
San Josef	Trinidad	Halifax	Nova Scotia
Scarborough	Tobago	Quebec	Canada
Road Harbor	Tortola	Saint John's	Newfoundland
Nassau	New Providence	George Town	Demerara
Pitt's Town	Crooked Island	New Amsterdam	Berbice
Kingston	Saint Vincent	Castries	Saint Lucia
		Basseterre	Saint Kitt's
		Charles' Town	Nevis
		Plymouth	Montserrat.

EXPORT *(in British and certain Foreign Ships).*

And to export from any of the above ports, in any British ship, or in any foreign vessel as aforesaid, any article of the growth, produce, or manufacture of His Majesty's dominions, or any other article legally imported into the said ports; provided that, if the exportation shall take place by a foreign ship, it shall be made direct to the Country in America, or the West Indies, to which such ship shall belong. The exportation is further allowed by British ships from the like ports, of any of the articles before enumerated, which shall have been legally imported, to any other British island, Colony, or plantation in America, or the West Indies, or to any part of the United Kingdom ; but no arms or naval stores are to be exported from the said ports or places in British America or the West Indies, without a licence of His Majesty's Secretary of State. The privileges of trading, granted under this Bill to foreign ships, extends only to the ships of such foreign countries, in whose ports in America, or the West Indies, British ships shall enjoy *equal privileges*.

An Act to regulate the trade between His Majesty's possessions in America *and the* West Indies, *and* other parts of the world. (3 Geo. IV. cap. 45.)

EXPORTS *(in British Ships).*

This Act permits the exportation in British ships, from any British Colonies or possessions in America or the West Indies, direct to any foreign port in Europe, or in Africa, to Gibraltar, Malta, Guernsey, Jersey, Alderney, and Sark, of all goods of the growth, produce, or manufacture of any such Colony or possession, or any goods which shall have been legally imported into the same.

IMPORTS *(in British Ships).*

And also permits the importation into any of the British Colonies or possessions as aforesaid, in British vessels from any foreign port in Europe or in Africa, or from Gibraltar, Malta, Guernsey, Jersey, Alderney, and Sark, of the following articles upon payment of certain duties:

Anchovies, argol, alabaster, rough and worked, anniseed, amber, almonds, biscuit, brandy, bullion, brimstone, boxwood, beans, botargo, cattle, currants, capers, cantharides, corn, cumminseed, coral, cork, cinnabar, cascasoo, caviar, dates, essence of bergamot, essence of citron, essence of lemon, essence of orange, essence of lavender, essence of roses, essence of rosemary, emery stone, flour, fruit dry and wet, preserved in brandy and sugar, and in jars and bottles, figs, garden seeds, gum arabic, gum mastic, gum myrrh, gum Sicily, gum ammoniac, grain, honey, incense, jalap, juniper berries, lava and Malta stone for buildings, lentils, lumber, manna, mosaicworks, medals, meal, musk, marble rough and worked, mill timber, maccaroni, mules, nuts of all kinds, oil of olives, oil of almonds, opium, orris-root, ostrich feathers, ochres, orange buds and peel, olives, pickles in jars and bottles, paintings and prints, pozzolana, precious stones, pearls, punck, pease, pumice stone, parmasan cheese, quicksilver, raisins, rhubarb, rice, salt, sausages, senna, scammony, sarsaparilla, saffron, safflower, shingles, sheep, sponges, staves, vermillion, vermicelli, whetstones, wine, and wood-hoops.

*** For the foregoing well-digested Abstract of the New Code the Author of these Volumes is indebted to *John Hall, Esq.* of London, His Majesty's Consul General for Hanover; whose experience in Trade and Navigation, and knowledge of Commercial Law give the highest authority to the Article. It is therefore considered a valuable appendage to the present Supplement, as affording correct and ready information on Mercantile Regulations of the greatest importance, and thus serving as a Guide and Expositor to the original Acts.

ADDENDA.

ABSTRACT OF AN ACT OF PARLIAMENT,

PASSED JUNE 17, 1824, INTITULED,

"An Act for ascertaining and establishing Uniformity of Weights and Measures."

This is an Act declaratory of the accuracy and legality of the existing Standards, both of Long Measure and Weight; but it orders the abolition of all Measures of Capacity for Wine, Ale, Corn, Coals, &c. and the establishment of one only in their stead, which is to be called *Imperial Measure.*

The operations of this Act are to commence May 1, 1825.

ART.

I. The Standard Yard is declared to be the distance between the centres of the two points on the gold studs in the straight brass rod, now in the custody of the Clerk of the House of Commons, whereon is engraved "Standard Yard, 1760," the brass being at the temperature of 62° by Fahrenheit's thermometer. It is to be called "the Imperial Standard Yard." (For its divisions and multiples, see *Cambist*, vol. 1, page 223 and 226.) Standard of Long Measure.

II. The dimensions for measuring Land are unaltered: they are the Statute Measure, of which the Acre contains 4840 Square Yards. (For its divisions and multiples, see vol. 1, p. 224 and 226.) Land Measure.

III. The Yard, if lost, defaced, or otherwise injured, may be restored by comparing it with the pendulum vibrating seconds of mean time, in the latitude of London, in a vacuum on the level of the sea, the Yard being in the proportion of 36 inches to 39,1393 of the pendulum. (See vol. 1, p. xxv. Introduction). Measure, if lost, how restored.

IV. The Standard Pound is declared to be the standard brass weight of One Pound Troy weight, made in the year 1758, and now in the custody of the Clerk of the House of Commons, and it is denominated "the Imperial Troy Pound." Its subdivisions and relations to Avoirdupois Weight continue, as explained in vol. 1, p. 219 and 225. Standard of Weight.

Pound, if lost, how restored.

V. If the Imperial Pound be lost, defaced, or otherwise injured, it shall be restored by comparison with a cubic inch of distilled water, weighed in air by brass weights, at the temperature of 62° of Fahrenheit's thermometer, the barometer being at 30 inches. Such cubic inch of water is equal to 252.458 grains, the Standard Troy Pound being 5760 such grains; and the Avoirdupois Pound 7000 such grains Troy. All operations of restoring or correcting Standards, are to be made under the directions of the Lord High Treasurer, or the Commissioners of his Majesty's Treasury, or any three of them for the time being.

Standard Gallon.

VI. The Standard Measure of Capacity, as well for liquids as for dry goods, not measured by heaped measure, shall be the Gallon, containing Ten Pounds Avoirdupois Weight of distilled water, weighed in air at the temperature of 62° of Fahrenheit's thermometer, the barometer being at 30 inches; and such brass measure shall be "the Imperial Standard Gallon," and is declared to be the unit and only Standard Measure of Capacity from which all other Measures of Capacity for all sorts of liquids, as well as for dry goods not measured by heaped measure, shall be derived; and that all Measures shall be taken in parts and multiples, the Quart, Pint, Peck, Bushel, and Quarter continuing in the same proportion as heretofore for dry measure. (See vol. 1, page 221 and 228.)

Standard for heaped Measure.

VII. That the Standard Measure of Capacity for coals, culm, lime, fish, potatoes, or fruit, and all other goods and things commonly sold by heaped measure, shall be the Imperial Bushel, containing 80 lb. Avoirdupois of water as aforesaid; the same being made round, with a plain and even bottom, and being 19½ inches from outside to outside. (See vol. 1, page 222.)

How the Bushel shall be heaped.

VIII. That coals and other goods sold by heaped measure, shall be duly heaped up in the said Bushel in the form of a cone, such cone to be of the height of at least 6 inches; and the outside of the Bushel to be the extremity of the base of such cone; and that three Bushels shall be a Sack, and twelve such Sacks a Chaldron. (See vol. 1, p. 222.)

Articles not heaped how stricken.

IX. That for articles not sold by heaped measure, such as corn, pulse, &c. the same shall be stricken with a round stick or roller, straight, and of the same diameter from end to end. (See vol. 1, page 221.)

X. That this law of Imperial Measure is not to extend to Ireland for any articles hitherto sold by weight. (See vol. 1, p. 194) Ireland.

XI. That copies and models of the Standard of Length, Weight, and Measure aforesaid, are to be made and verified within three months after passing the Act, under the direction of the Lords of the Treasury; and that such copies or models shall be deposited in the office of the Chamberlain of the Exchequer at Westminster; and that copies shall be sent to the Lord Mayor of London, and the Chief Magistrate of Edinburgh and of Dublin, and to such other places or persons as the Lord High Treasurer or Commissioners of the Treasury may from time to time direct. Copies of Standards, when and where deposited.

XII. That his Majesty's justices of the peace, in every county of the British Empire, or every town or place, being a county within itself, shall, within six months after passing the Act, purchase a model of each of the Standards aforesaid, with their parts and multiples; and that such shall be compared and verified with the models deposited at the Exchequer, on payment of the usual fees; and that such verified copies shall be placed for custody and inspection with such persons as the magistrates shall chuse to appoint; and that the same shall be produced by the keepers thereof, upon reasonable notice, the persons requiring such production paying the customary charges for the same. Models to be provided for counties, &c.

XIII. The expenses of procuring models for magistrates, counties, &c. are to be raised by the usual modes of taxation. Expenses how paid.

XIV. That when reference cannot be easily had to verified copies of the Standard Measures of Capacity, it may be lawful for any justice of the peace, or magistrate having jurisdiction, to ascertain the content of a Measure of Capacity, by direct reference to the weight of pure or rain water, which such Measure is capable of containing; 10 lb. Avoirdupois weight of such water, at the temperature of 62° by Fahrenheit's thermometer, being the Standard Gallon ascertained by the Act, the same being in bulk equal to 277.274 cubic inches. Measure of Capacity how verified. Contents of Imperial Gallon.

XV. That all Contracts for Sale, &c. by Weight or Measure, shall be according to the Imperial Standard, when no special agreement shall be made to Contracts to be according to the Imperial Measure, unless the contrary is specified.

the contrary; and in all cases where any special agreement shall be made, with reference to any Weight or Measure established by local custom, the proportion which every such local Weight or Measure shall bear to any of the said Standard Weights and Measures, shall be expressly declared and specified, or otherwise such agreement shall be null and void.

Existing Measures to be marked to shew their proportions.

XVI. That existing Measures may be used, being marked so as to shew the proportions which they have to the Imperial Measures; but that after the 1st of May, 1825, no person shall be permitted to make any Weights or Measures, otherwise than according to the provisions of the new Act.

Rents in grain in England or Ireland;

XVII. That for ascertaining Rents, &c. payable in grain or malt in England or Ireland, the amount is to be ascertained according to the Standard by this Act established, by a jury of 12 substantial freeholders.

In Scotland.

XVIII. That for ascertaining Rents, &c. payable in grain or malt in Scotland, such Rents shall be determined according to the New Standard, by such juries as strike the fiar prices of grain.

Tables of Equalization.

XIX. That Tables of Equalization shall be made and constructed under the Commissioners of the Treasury, shewing the proportions between the Weights and Measures heretofore in use and those now established.

Tables for Customs and Excise;

XX. That Tables shall be also constructed for the collection of the Customs and Excise, under the direction of the said Commissioners of the Treasury.

Enforced in England and Scotland;

XXI. The present Act may be enforced in England and Scotland by all the regulations and penalties contained in the following statutes, except such parts of the said statutes, as may be repealed or altered by this present Act, viz. 29 Geo. II. c. 25; 31 Geo. II. c. 17; 35 Geo. III. c. 102; 55 Geo. III. c. 43.

In Ireland.

XXII. The present Act may be enforced in Ireland by all the regulations and penalties contained in the following statutes, except such parts of the said statutes as are repealed or altered by this Act, viz. 4 Anne (*I.*); 11 Geo. II. (*I.*); 25 Geo. II. (*I.*); 27 Geo. III. (*I.*); 28 Geo. III. (*I.*)

XXIII. The repeal of numerous laws is declared in this article; some of uncertain date before the reign of Edward the Third, and many since that period. These are chiefly statutes which fixed the Weight and Measure of certain kinds of goods, such as wool, cheese, salt, wine, beer, fish, fruit, &c.; and also the denominations which determine their quantity, as the Sack, Wey, Load, Tun, Hogshead, Barrel, &c. For the particulars of these statutes, (which are now repealed either wholly or in part), recourse must be had to the originals, as referred to in the margin of the present Act, and which amount to about 60 statutes. Statutes repealed.

XXIV. That this Act shall not extend to affect or alter the rights of the Dean and High Steward of Westminster, to appoint proper officers to sign and seal all Weights and Measures used in the said city and the liberties thereof. Rights of the Dean, &c. of Westminster.

XXV. That gaugeable liquors brought into the port of the city of London shall be gauged as heretofore by the Lord Mayor or his deputies; but the contents shall be ascertained by the Standard Measure directed by this Act. Gaugeable liquors in London.

XXVI. This Act shall not extend to prohibit or diminish the right of the Lord Mayor and Commonalty of the city of London, concerning the office of Gauger of any gaugeable liquors imported within the city of London, or the liberties thereof. Privileges of the City preserved.

HISTORICAL ILLUSTRATIONS.

In order to form a clear notion of the plans and provisions of the new Act, it will be proper to gain some knowledge of the History of English Weights and Measures, as set forth in the Introduction to this volume, p. xx; where it will be seen that, in the year 1588, Standards were placed in the Exchequer by order of Queen Elizabeth, without any legislative enactment; and that, in the year 1758, a Committee of the House of Commons adjusted copies of the same, and placed them in the custody of the Clerk of the House of Commons, with the intention of having them legalized by an Act of the Legislature. But this was not completed, as Parliament was unexpectedly dissolved, and the revised Standards remained unconfirmed by law until the passing of the present Act of 1824

Notwithstanding this delay, copies of those Standards, both of Weight and Long Measure, were found very accurately distributed in 1820, when the general comparison of Weights and Measures took place for this work. Measures of Capacity, however, appeared to be nearly in the same state of diversity as represented in the Report of the Committee of 1758: and here it may not be unworthy of remark, that a similar variety, especially of Corn Measures, prevails more or less in all countries; although it is seldom made a subject of complaint by the parties whom it concerns. On the contrary, all seem tenacious of their respective customs, and in some degree they diminish the inconvenience by adapting prices to estimated quantities. Diversity of Measures, however, has a constant tendency to increase, and therefore any plan calculated to promote uniformity, or even to counteract that tendency, deserves encouragement.

COMPUTATIONS AND PROPORTIONS.

Annexed to the Report of the Committee of the House of Commons, on Weights and Measures (May 28, 1821), are the following Computations and Proportions, which may help to illustrate the new Act for equalizing Measures.

WEIGHT of a Cubic Inch of distilled water in a vacuum at the temperature 62°, as opposed to weights in a vacuum also, = 252.722 grains.

Consequently, a Cubic Foot = 62.3862 lb. Avoirdupois.

Weight of a Cubic Inch of distilled water in air at 62° of temperature with a mean height of the barometer = 252.456 grains.

Consequently, a Cubic Foot = 62.3206 lb. Avoirdupois.

And an Ounce of water = 1.73298 Cubic Inches.

Cubic Inches in the Imperial Gallon, are 277.276.

Diameter of the Cylinder, containing a Gallon at one Inch high, = 18.78933 Inches.

Specific Gravity of Water at different temperatures, that at 62° being taken as unity.

70°	0.99913	62°	1.	52°	1.00076	44°	1.00107
68	0.99936	58	1.00035	50	1.00087	42	1.00111
66	0.99958	56	1.00050	48	1.00095	40	1.00113
64	0.99980	54	1.00064	46	1.00102	38	1.00113

The difference of temperatures between 62° and 39°, where water attains its greatest density, will vary the bulk of a Gallon of water rather less than the third of a Cubic Inch.

And assuming from the mean of numerous estimates the expansion of brass 0.00001044 for each degree of Fahrenheit's thermometer, the difference of temperatures from 62° to 39° will vary the content of a brass Gallon Measure just one-fifth of a Cubic Inch.

It appears that the specific gravity of clear water from the Thames exceeds that of distilled water at the mean temperature, in the proportion of 1.0006 to 1, making a difference of about one-sixth of a Cubic Inch on a Gallon.

Rain water does not differ from distilled water, so as to require any allowance for common purposes. *

* The above proportions have been computed by the Commissioners of Weights and Measures (see Introduction, p. xxiv), who had previously ascertained the Weight of a Cubic Foot of distilled water, at the temperature of 56½° to be exactly 1000 ounces Avoirdupois; and it is remarkable, that a similar result was reported from experiments made on spring water, at Oxford, in 1685, before it was known that the density of water would increase or diminish, according to the temperature. (See Phil. Trans. No. 169.)

COMPARISONS OF OLD AND NEW MEASURES.

The foregoing calculation of the diameter of a Cylinder, which contains 1 Gallon for every Inch in depth, will be found useful in constructing both Corn and Coal Bushels on the new plan of Imperial Measure.

Thus the Corn Bushel, with the diameter 18.78933, and 8 Inches deep, will answer to 2218.192 Cubic Inches, the Imperial Bushel; being about $\frac{1}{32}$ part more than the Winchester Bushel, which is 2150.42 Cubic Inches.

The new Coal Bushel, with the above diameter and depth, and heaped as directed in Art. VIII, the rim being about $\frac{3}{4}$ of an Inch thick, and the diameter $19\frac{1}{2}$ Inches from outside to outside, will measure 2816.459 Cubic Inches, which is only $1\frac{1}{2}$ Inch more than the present Coal Bushel, viz. 2814.9 Cubic Inches. (See vol. 1, p. 222.)

The proportion between the old and new Wine Measures is very simple and convenient, being nearly as 5 to 6. Thus 5 Imperial Gallons equal 6 Wine Gallons and about $\frac{1}{4500}$ of a Gallon over.

The proportion between the old and new Ale Measures is about as 61 to 60; but the following Table will shew the relative contents more accurately, both in Measure and in Weight, the latter having been computed according to the principles stated in the new Act.

TABLE shewing the Contents of the different Gallons, both in Measure and Weight.

	Cubic Inches.	Avoirdupois Weight.			Troy Weight.			
		lb.	oz.	dr.	lb.	oz.	dwt.	gr.
Imperial Gallon	277.274	10	0	0	12	1	16	16
Corn Gallon	268.8	9	10	$1\frac{1}{4}$	11	9	7	12
Wine Gallon	231	8	5	$6\frac{1}{4}$	10	1	9	22
Ale Gallon	282	10	2	$11\frac{1}{2}$	12	4	6	8

The above Table will be found useful in comparing different vessels where gauging cannot be relied on; and although it is computed according to the conditions of temperature, &c. as stated in Art. VI., yet the proportions will answer with sufficient correctness for all common purposes of business, with any kind of fresh water; but where great accuracy is required, it may be determined at any temperature, by means of the Table in the preceding page. Thus to find the weight of the Wine Gallon at 56° Fahrenheit, multiply its weight at 62°, viz. 8.3311 by 1.0005, and the result will be 8.3352, the required weight.

The reduction of the different Measures may be computed with the greatest facility by the help of *Factors* or Multipliers, as in the following Table.

TABLE OF FACTORS,

For converting Old Measures into New, and the contrary.

	By Decimals.			By Vulgar Fractions.		
	Corn Measure.	Wine Measure.	Ale Measure.	Corn Measure.	Wine Measure.	Ale Measure.
To convert Old Measures to New	.96943	.83311	1.01704	$\frac{31}{32}$	$\frac{5}{6}$	$\frac{60}{59}$
To convert New Measures to Old	1.03153	1.20032	.98324	$\frac{32}{31}$	$\frac{6}{5}$	$\frac{59}{60}$

USE OF THE ABOVE TABLE.

EXAMPLE I. Reduce 63 Gallons Wine Measure to Imperial Measure.

$63 \times .83311 = 52.486$; or $63 \times \frac{5}{6} = 52\frac{1}{2}$ Imperial Gallons nearly.

EXAMPLE II. Reduce 8 Bushels Imperial Measure to Winchester Measure.

$8 \times 1.03153 = 8.25224$; or $8 \times \frac{32}{31} = 8\frac{1}{4}$ Winchester Bushels nearly;

Or, more accurately, 8 of the latter $= 7\frac{3}{4}$ of the former.

It should be observed, that the solutions by vulgar Fractions are not quite so accurate as those by decimal Factors; but they will be found sufficiently correct for all practical purposes.

To reduce Foreign Measures of Capacity to Imperial Gallons, and the contrary.

This operation is performed by finding the proportion of Foreign Measures to English, in the Tables of the second volume of this work, page 229, &c. or under the proper heads of places in the first volume, and then by applying the Factors as in the above examples.

EXAMPLE III. Required the number of Imperial Gallons in the Hectolitre of France.

By the Tables, p. 229, &c. it will be seen that the Hectolitre equals 26,419 English Gallons, or 2,837 Winchester Bushels. Hence,

$26.419 \times .83311$ or by $\frac{5}{6} = 22$. Also, $2.837 \times .96943 = 2.75$ or multiplied by $\frac{31}{32} = 2\frac{3}{4}$ Imperial Bushels, or 22 such Gallons, and about $\frac{1}{60}$ of a Gallon over;

OR,

Any Measures, the contents of which are known in English cubic inches, may be reduced to Imperial Gallons by dividing such contents by 277.274, or multiplying them by .003605.

Whiting, Printer, Lombard Street.

SUPPLEMENT FOR 1825.

CONTINUATION OF IMPERIAL MEASURES.

By a Law, passed March 31st, 1825, the commencement of the foregoing Act was postponed to the 1st of January, 1826. This Law (6 Geo. IV. c. 12) confirms all the provisions of the said Act of 1824 (5 Geo. IV. c. 74), and adds the following clause for fixing the dimensions of the subdivisions of the Bushel for heaped measures, as those of the Bushel only are fixed in the first Act (7 and 8, p. 388). The following is the new clause. Act of Postponement.

II. " *That all such measures shall be made cylindrical, and the diameter of such measures shall be at the least double the depth thereof; and the height of the Cone or Heap shall be equal to three-fourths of the depth of the said measure, the outside of the measure being the extremity or base of such Cone.* New clause, 6 Geo. IV. c. 12.

The above is the last enactment on the subject of Imperial Measures, but another regulation respecting their diameters has been since issued, by authority of the Lords of the Treasury, and published in the London Gazette, October 4th, 1825, of which the following is a Copy.

GARRATT, Mayor.

At an Especial Court of Mayor and Aldermen, holden in the Council-Chamber of the Guildhall of the City of London, on the Feast of St. Michael the Archangel, that is to say, Thursday, the 29th day of September, 1825, and in the sixth year of the reign of George the Fourth, of the United Kingdom of Great Britain and Ireland, King, &c.

THE Right Honourable the Lord Mayor communicated to this Court, that numerous applications having been made to him on the difficulties which had occurred, in consequence of the ineffective directions contained in the Acts of Parliament (5 Geo. IV. ch. 74, and 6 Geo. IV. ch. 12), for regulating weights and measures in respect to heaped measures, the diameter of the heaped bushel measure only being defined in the said Acts, and the diameter of all the smaller measures, *viz.* the half bushel, peck, gallon, half gallon, and quart, being thereby rendered uncertain, his Lordship directed a representation to be made to the Lords Commissioners of His Majesty's Treasury on the subject; whereupon the Lords Commissioners referred the matter for the opinion of the Commissioners of Weights and Measures, and received a report from Dr. Wollaston thereon, that it would be unnecessary to express more than the breadth, from outside to outside of the top, of such respective measures, to be as follows:

Diameters of Measures.

The bushel, nineteen inches and an half.
The half bushel, fifteen inches and an half.
The peck, twelve inches and a quarter.
The gallon, or half peck, nine inches and three quarters.
The half gallon, or quartern, seven inches and three quarters.
The half quartern, six inches and one-eighth.

And thereupon the Lords Commissioners declared, that in the absence of any Legislative provision on the subject, they could only issue directions to all persons who might be employed to prepare measures, under their authority, to conform strictly to the proportions pointed out by Dr. Wollaston; and the Lords Commissioners also submitted the expediency of the same course being adopted in the city of London. Directed by the Lords of the Treasury.

Whereupon it is resolved,

That (in order to protect the public from fraud and imposition) directions be given to the proper officers at the Guildhall, London, not to stamp or mark any new measures intended for ascertaining the quantity of such articles as are sold by heaped measures, unless such measures respectively are made strictly conformable to the said proportions specified in Dr. Wollaston's report. By the Lord Mayor of London.

Ordered,

That these proceedings be forthwith published in the London Gazette, for the information of the officers of the several cities and towns corporate in Great Britain, having or directing the adjustment and marking of weights and measures.

Signed, by order of the Court,

Henry Woodthorpe.

TABLE I.

Shewing the Dimensions and Contents of the Imperial Bushel and its divisions—computed in accordance with the foregoing Legal Enactments and Treasury Regulations.—Viz. Making the Diameter of each Measure at least twice the depth, the height of the Cone exactly three-fourths of the depth, and the exterior diameter as directed in the Gazette:—From which *data* the interior diameters and depths are deduced.

	DIMENSIONS.					CONTENTS.			
	Exterior Diameter.	Interior Diameter.	Depth.	Breadth of the Rim.	Height of the Cone.	Contents of the Cylinder.	Contents of the Cone.	Total Contents of Heaped Measure.	Weight of the Cylinder lb avoirdupois
Bushel	19,5	18,789	8	0,355	6	2218,192	597,297	2815,489	80
Half Bushel..	15,5	14,936	6,331	0,282	4,748	1109,096	298,648	1407,744	40
Peck	12,25	11,803	5,071	0,223	3,803	554,548	149,324	703,872	20
Gallon	9,75	9,395	4	0,177	3	277,274	74,662	351,936	10
Half Gallon..	7,75	7,468	3,165	0,141	2,374	138,637	37,331	175,968	5
Quart........	6,125	5,901	2,535	0,112	1,902	69,318	18,666	87,984	2,5

ACTUAL DIMENSIONS OF THE IMPERIAL STANDARDS.

As one great object of the *Cambist* is to give a correct account of the Weights and Measures of all Countries, and as those of England are of peculiar importance at the present time, the Author has considered it his duty to examine the new Standards lately deposited at the Exchequer and at Guildhall; and having gauged the same by permission of the proper Authorities, he found all perfectly correct in their Cylindrical contents, and therefore legal for Liquid or Strike Measures (according to Article VI. p. 388); but for Heaped Measures the Bushel only is perfectly legal, as the clause of 1825 respecting its divisions has not been acted upon. The inaccuracies, however, arising from this omission are too minute to be perceived in practice, and especially in the operation of heaping any kind of goods, where great uncertainty must always prevail. Even the best constructed Measures of Capacity are, from various causes, exposed to unavoidable error, notwithstanding the manifest improvements that have lately taken place in sizing and verifying the Imperial Standards.*

* It may be useful here to state the Plan for the distribution of British Weights and Measures.—Every Corporation or Public Office, duly authorised to distribute such, must have its Standards proved and stamped at his Majesty's Exchequer at Westminster: those even at Guildhall must be so verified, and then all the Weights and Measures used in the City of London are proved and stamped at that Office exclusively.

TABLE II.

Shewing the Dimensions of the new Standards for Imperial Measure, deposited at His Majesty's Exchequer and at Guildhall, as models from which Copies are to be distributed: and although some differ in their depths and diameters, yet all perfectly agree in their Cylindrical Contents, as proved both by Gauging and Water Measure.

	EXCHEQUER STANDARDS.			GUILDHALL TREASURY ORDER.			GUILDHALL WORKING STANDARDS.		
	Exterior Diameter.	Interior Diameter.	Depth.	Exterior Diameter.	Interior Diameter.	Depth.	Exterior Diameter.	Interior Diameter.	Depth.
Bushel	19,5	18,5	8,25	19,5	18,5	8,25	19,5	18,5	8,5
Half Bushel . .	15,4	14,68	6,55	15,5	14,6	6,6	14,9	14,05	7,1
Peck	12,28	11,65	5,19	12,25	11,6	5,4	11	10,25	6,8
Gallon	7,07	7,06	7,06	9,75	9,2	4,3	8	7,4	6,4
Half Gallon . .	5,61	5,61	5,61	7,75	6,1	3,3	6,1	5,6	5,9
Quart	4,45	4,45	4,45	6,125	5,7	2,2	4,7	4,1	5,0

SUMMARY VIEW OF THE IMPERIAL SYSTEM.

From the foregoing Laws and Regulations it appears that no alteration whatever is made in the established system of Weights and Measures, except in Measures of Capacity, commonly called Liquid and Dry Measures. Thus the three different Gallons heretofore used for Wine, Corn, and Ale, are to be converted into one Gallon, which is to hold 10lb. Weight of Water, as before explained, and its divisions and multiples in proportion, which still retain their old names. It will be also seen (p. 394) that in Wine Measure, five of the New Gallons answer to six of the old; in Corn Measure, thirty-one of the new to thirty-two of the old; and in Ale Measure, sixty of the new to fifty-nine of the old. But although no change is made in the Weights, yet some explanation seems necessary with respect to the Avoirdupois Pound, which has been erroneously stated in some publications to contain a few Grains more than the weight long fixed by Law, viz. 7000 Grains Troy. This mistake appears to have originated in the error published in the Philosophical Transactions, as stated in p. 140 of this Volume: but it is proper to repeat, that, in the late Comparison of Weights and Measures for this Work, the Avoirdupois Pound was found accurately distributed not only throughout the British Dominions, but even in the United States of America. *

* It must be also satisfactory to state, that the Troy Pound was then found very correctly established; that is, according to the Standard adjusted in 1758, called the Parliamentary Pound, which was use in the General Comparison of Foreign Weights in 1820, and from which the New Imperial Pound has been copied, and the Old Standards at the Exchequer corrected. (See Introduction, p. XXIII).

Explication

OF THE

NEW COINAGE OF HIS MAJESTY GEORGE IV.

Struck at the Royal Mint in 1825.

These coins are minted on the same principle as those of his late Majesty, with respect to their weight, fineness, and quantity of pure metal, as stated in this Volume, p. 218, and in Vol. II. p. 157, &c. But they differ in their impressions, which are as follow:—

1st. The Five Pound Gold Piece has for the obverse impression the effigy of his Majesty, with the inscription, "*Georgius IV. Dei Gratia,*" and the date of the year; and for the reverse, the ensigns armorial of the United Kingdom contained in a shield mantled, surmounted by the royal crown, with the inscription "*Britanniarum Rex Fid: Def:*" and upon the rim of the piece the words "*Decus et Tutamen,*" and the year of the reign.

2d. The Double Sovereign has the same impressions as the Five Pound Piece.

3d. The Sovereign has likewise the same impressions, except that on the reverse the shield is plain, surmounted with the royal crown, with the inscription, "*Georgius IV. Dei Gratia,*" and a graining on the rim, instead of the above motto.

4th. The Half Sovereign the same as the Sovereign.

5th. The Crown, or Five Shilling Silver Piece, has for the obverse impression the aforesaid effigy, inscription, and date; and for the reverse the ensigns armorial of the United Kingdom contained in a shield, surmounted by the royal crown and helmet with its mantlings, and the motto, "*Dieu et Mon Droit,*" in a scroll beneath, with the inscription, "*Britanniarum Rex Fid: Def:*" and the words on the rim, "*Decus et Tutamen,*" and the year of the reign.

6th. The Half Crown has the same impressions as the Crown, except the rim, which has a graining instead of the motto.

7th. The Shilling has for the obverse impression the aforesaid effigy, inscription, and date; and for the reverse the emblems of the United Kingdom, namely, the Rose, Thistle, and Shamrock, surmounted by the Royal crest, viz. the *Crown and Lion*, with the inscription, "*Britanniarum Rex Fid: Def:*" and a graining upon the rim.

8th. The Sixpence the same as the Shilling.

⁎ For a translation of the different inscriptions, see *Explication of Coins*, Vol. II. p. 182.

ORDER IN COUNCIL,

For giving Currency to, and fixing the Value of, British Silver and Copper Money throughout the British Colonial Possessions in all Parts of the World.

AT THE COURT, AT CARLTON HOUSE,—23d MARCH, 1825.

PRESENT,

THE KING'S MOST EXCELLENT MAJESTY, IN COUNCIL.

British Silver Money made current in all British Colonies. Also the Spanish Dollar at 4*s*. 4*d*. each.

WHEREAS it has been represented to His Majesty at this Board, by the Lords Commissioners of His Majesty's Treasury, that they have given directions that His Majesty's Troops serving in the several British Colonies and Possessions Abroad should in certain cases be paid in British Silver and Copper Money, and that with a view of securing the Circulation of such Money in those Colonies it would be expedient that an Order in Council should be issued declaring that in all those Colonies where the Spanish Dollar is now either by Law, Fact, or Practice, considered as a legal tender for the discharge of Debts, or where the Duties to the Government are rated or collected, or the Individuals have a right to pay in that description of Coin, that a tender and payment of British Silver Money to the amount of Four Shillings and Four Pence should be considered as equivalent to the tender or payment of One Spanish Dollar, and so in proportion for any greater or less amount of Debt.

Paper Rix Dollars at the Cape of Good Hope and at Ceylon exchanged for Silver Currency at 1*s*. 6*d*. each Rix Dollar.

And whereas it has been further represented by the Lords Commissioners of His Majesty's Treasury, that with respect to the Cape of Good Hope, where there are not any Spanish Dollars in Circulation, but where the Circulation consists entirely of Paper Rix Dollars and its proportions; and with respect to Ceylon, where the Circulation consists of Silver and Paper Rix Dollars as well as a variety of other Coins, which are generally received and paid with relation to their value as compared with Rix Dollars, it would be expedient that a tender and payment of 1*s*. 6*d*. in British Silver Money should be considered as equivalent to a tender and payment of one such Rix Dollar so current at the Cape of Good Hope and Ceylon respectively, and so in proportion for any greater or less Sum, and also that British Copper Money should be made a legal tender in all the British Colonies for its due and proper proportions of British Silver Money as by Law established in Great Britain, but that no person should be compelled to take more than 12*d*. in Copper Money at any one payment; His Majesty, having taken the said representation into consideration, is pleased by and with the advice of his Privy Council, to approve of what is therein proposed, and the Right Honourable the Lords Commissioners of His Majesty's Treasury, and the Right Honourable Earl Bathurst, one of His Majesty's Principal Secretaries of State, are to give the necessary directions herein as to them may respectively appertain.

Copper Money.

(Signed) C. C. GREVILLE.

Substance of the Circular.

The foregoing *Order in Council*, it should be observed, approves and confirms certain regulations agreed upon by the Lords Commissioners of His Majesty's Treasury, and issued by their Lordships in a Circular to the proper Authorities in all British Colonies.

This Circular states that His Majesty's Government have determined to transmit to the several Colonies British Silver and Copper Money, for the pay of all Military Officers and Men, and of all the Civil Servants of Government, with a view that such British Money shall become the circulating medium of the Colonies, under the following regulations.

That all British Money shall pass for its nominal value, as in England; that Silver Money shall be a legal tender to any amount, and Copper Money for sums not exceeding 12 pence at any one payment.

The Circular likewise orders the proper Authorities in each Colony, to receive British Silver Money in exchange for Bills on His Majesty's Treasury in London, on the following terms, *viz*:—

That for £103 Silver Money, a Bill for £100 on the Treasury shall be given, but that the said money shall be the proper and legal weight, making allowance for the fair wear of the Coin. The legal weight being 66 shillings to 1lb. Troy, therefore £103 of such Coin shall weigh 31lb. 2oz. 10dwts 21$\frac{9}{11}$grs. Troy.

The Circular likewise orders, that in the event of there not being sufficient British Silver for circulation, Spanish Dollars may circulate at the rate of 4*s.* 4*d.* sterling each, and that other Foreign Coins of the same metal may likewise be received and paid at the Old Standard Value of British Silver, *viz.* 5*s.* 2*d.* per ounce Troy, of 11oz. 2dwts. fine.

Foreign Coins occasionally made current.

A Table of Foreign Silver Coins that may be issued is annexed to the Circular, shewing, 1. their gross weight—2. their contents in pure Silver—3. their value at 5*s.* 2*d.* per ounce Standard—and 4. the rate at which such Coins are to be issued to the Troops. The following are the Coins and the rate at which they are to be issued—the other particulars of gross weight, purity, &c. are stated in the present work (Vol. II. p. 162, &c.)

	s.	*d.*
FRENCH.		
Piece of 5 Francs	4	0
Do. 2 do.	1	8
Do. 1 do.	0	10
SICILIAN.		
Dollar or Scudo	4	1
Piece of 40 Grains	1	5
Do. 20 do.	0	9

	s.	*d.*
SPANISH.		
Dollar	4	4
UNITED STATES OF AMERICA.		
Dollar	4	4
EAST INDIES.		
Calcutta Rupee	2	1
Bombay or Surat do.	1	11

*** The foregoing regulations have been successfully carried into effect.

THE CURRENCY OF IRELAND

ASSIMILATED TO THAT OF ENGLAND.

Abstract and Exposition of an Act of Parliament for the Assimilation of the Currency and Monies of Account throughout the United Kingdom of Great Britain and Ireland, passed June 27, 1825 (6 Geo. IV. c. 79).

Article I. of this Act contains, after a statement of the present proportion between English and Irish Money, an enactment, ordering, in general terms, that the currency of Ireland shall be the currency of Great Britain, and that all dealings shall be held to be made in such currency, unless the contrary be proved.

II. Enacts that all contracts, debts, &c. in Irish currency, made previous to the commencement of this Act, shall be carried into effect by payment in British currency of 12-13ths of the amount, according to Irish currency.

III. Orders that all Public Accounts of Revenues, Duties, Funds, &c. shall be estimated in British currency, and the Accounts thereof kept accordingly.

IV. Provides that this Act shall not affect the real value in Gold or Silver Coin to be paid or payable in reference to any Public Revenues or Debts, or payable under any authority whatsoever.

V. Provides for the Payment of the Fractions of a Penny, British currency, resulting from the converting of Irish currency into British.

This useful operation may be best illustrated by a regular example, thus—

Suppose it were required to reduce $8\frac{3}{4}d.$ Irish currency into British—say

As 52 *qrs.* : 48 *qrs.* :: 35 *qrs.* : $32\frac{16}{52}$ *qrs.*

Now to estimate the remainder $\frac{16}{52}$, or any other fraction, to the nearest Farthing, the following rule must be observed.

If the remainder be .... 8, 12, or 16, then—$\frac{1}{4}$ is to be allowed.

If the remainder be 20, 24, 28, or 32,——— $\frac{1}{2}$

If the remainder be ....36, 40, or 44,——— $\frac{3}{4}$

If the remainder be 48, one penny is allowed, but if 4, nothing.

Hence 35 *qrs.* Irish=32+1, or 33 *qrs.* British.

It should be observed, that remainders must be each a number divisible by 4.

VI. Enacts that, in paying Interest due on the Stocks or Public Funds in Ireland, when the principal shall be converted into British currency, all Pence and Fractions of a Penny, due upon such Dividends, shall be paid with the Dividend at the Bank of Ireland, provided that such shall not exceed one Shilling on any one payment; and thus the principal sum remaining to each proprietor shall be made to consist of Pounds and Shillings only, of the currency of the United Kingdom.

VII. Orders that such Fractional Parts of Shillings shall be repaid to the Bank by Commissioners for the reduction of the National Debt.

VIII. Enacts that, where Annual Sums charged on the Consolidated Fund in Irish currency are converted into British, the Treasury may add sufficient Sums to prevent Fractions of a Penny.

IX. Provides that Contracts may be made according to the currency of Foreign States.

X. Declares that any gifts, debts, or liabilities arising by implication of law, come within the meaning of this Act.

XI. Enacts that, after a day to be named by Proclamation, British Silver and Gold Coin shall be current in Ireland at the same rate of Pence as in Great Britain, and not as heretofore in Ireland.

XII. Orders that, on a like Proclamation, Irish Copper Coins shall be brought into the Bank of Ireland, and exchanged for British Copper Coins, at the rate of 12 Pence British for 13 Pence Irish; and the Irish Copper Coin shall cease to circulate.

XIII. Provides for the payment of Sums under 12 Pence Irish, in British Currency. Thus $1\frac{1}{2}d.$ Irish and under, shall be paid by a like sum in British Copper Coin.

From $1\frac{1}{2}d.$ to $4\frac{3}{4}d.$ by a sum in British Copper Coin less by one Farthing than the expressed Irish account—

From $4\frac{3}{4}d.$ to $8d.$ less by one Halfpenny.
From $8d.$ to $11\frac{1}{4}d.$ less by three Farthings.
From $11\frac{1}{4}d.$ to $12d.$ less by one Penny.

For example—$3d.$ Irish is to be estimated at $2\frac{3}{4}d.$ British; $6d.$ Irish, at $5\frac{1}{2}d.$ British; $10d.$ Irish, at $9\frac{1}{4}d.$ British; and $11\frac{1}{2}d.$ Irish, at $10\frac{1}{2}d.$ British.

XIV. Provides for the re-issuing of certain Bankers' Notes in Ireland, which shall be made payable in British currency; and no Notes payable in Irish currency shall be re-issued after the commencement of this Act, under the penalty of £50 for every such offence.

XV. Enacts that Bankers may deliver into the Stamp Office any re-issuable Notes, paid after the Commencement of this Act, and receive new stamps, on the following conditions:—

To receive the whole amount of the Stamps on the Notes delivered up, if dated within one year previous; or three-fourths, if within two years; and one half, if within three years.

XVI. Authorises the Commissioners of his Majesty's Treasury to publish this Act throughout Ireland, in any way they may think proper.

XVII. Orders the commencement of the Act to take place on the 5th of January, 1826.*

---

* HISTORICAL ILLUSTRATIONS OF THE ABOVE SUBJECT.

THE History of the Currency of Ireland is involved in great obscurity. It is, however, well known that the Monies of that country have for many ages differed from the Currency of England; and also that the difference has proved a great inconvenience to both countries, without producing any real advantage to either.

The best authorities on this subject are *Camden*, *Ware*, and *Simon*, and they agree that Money was coined in Ireland at a very early period, and that, after the English Government had been established there, Mints were erected and Money coined according to the British Standard. Also, that for nearly two centuries the Currencies of both Countries were generally the same; but that, in the reign of Edward III. an Order was issued, that the Silver *Gross*, or *Groat*, which passed in England for 3d. should pass in Ireland for 4d., and all other Monies in the same proportion.

This Rate of Exchange, as it was called, continued for more than a century, during which time Mints were established in the principal cities of Ireland (eleven in number, according to *Ware*, p. 217); but those establishments became nearly useless in the reign of Henry VIII. and were wholly discontinued in the time of Elizabeth; for at those periods much distress prevailed, and such debasement of the Currency as frequently raised the Exchange more than two to one against Ireland.

In 1635, Charles I. ordered Lord Wentworth to assimilate the Currencies of the two Countries, and the plan was undertaken with great zeal, but failed from political misfortunes, and the Monies of Ireland continued for more than half a century in a very degraded and uncertain state.

In 1698, the present proportion of 12 to 13 was established in Silver, and in 1717 in Gold. It was not, however, until the year 1736 that it was regularly fixed in Copper as since continued. But although the Par of Exchange was thus nominally settled at 8⅓ per Cent.; yet the Course of Exchange was sometimes 10 or 12 per Cent. above Par.

In 1804 the Silver Currency of Ireland became so degraded that it was called in, and Spanish Dollars with their divisions (stamped for the occasion) were issued, and have since continued to circulate at a rate of nearly 20 per Cent. above their intrinsic value.

In 1825 the long desired law was introduced, that of assimilating the Currency of the United Kingdom, according to the above regulations. This important measure was planned and conducted by the *Right Honourable Thomas Wallace*, Master of His Majesty's Mint, and it appears to have given universal satisfaction.

SPANISH AMERICA.

New Republics of Spanish America.

As the Spanish Dominions in America have undergone an entire Revolution, and are now formed into several Independent States, alterations have consequently taken place in their commercial regulations, which may require explanation in the present Supplement, and for this purpose the following Statistical Table is constructed.

REPUBLIC OF	FORMERLY CALLED	Number of Inhabitants	CAPITAL	LATITUDE	LONGITUDE
MEXICO	Kingdom of New Spain	6,868,000	Mexico	19° 25′ N	99° 5′ W
United Provinces of CENTRAL AMERICA	Kingdom of Guatemala	1,485,000	Guatemala	14 28 N	92 40 W
COLUMBIA	K. of New Granada and Captain Generalship of Caraccas ...	3,600,000	Santa Fè de Bogotà	4 6 N	78 30 W
PERU, *Upper & Lower*	Vice-Royalty of Lima	1,900,000	Lima	12 2 S	77 7 W
CHILE	Kingdom of Chile	1,200,000	Santiago de Chile	33 26 S	70 44 W
United Provinces of RIO DE LA PLATA	Vice-Royalty of Buenos Ayres	1,500,000	Buenos Ayres	35 34 S	57 24 W

MONIES, EXCHANGES, COINS, &c.

Monies, Exchanges, &c.

Accounts are kept in all the above States in *Pesos*, or Dollars of eight *Reals*. This Peso is an imaginary money of account; but the Real is a Coin which is divided into Halves and Quarters, called *Medios* and *Quartillos;* and likewise multiplied into Double Reals, called *Pesetas*.

These monies are considered the *currency* of the country, and as they are minted on a standard inferior to the hard Dollar (see p. 319), they are estimated 3 per cent. lower than that Coin in law; but in practice the *Fuerte*, or hard Dollar, is sometimes at a premium of from 5 to 10 per cent. against *corriente*, or Currency.

In contracts, however, Currency is generally understood to be the legal money, unless some other coin is stipulated for; and in Exchanges, when current Dollars are the money, the rate must be mentioned, which varies from 40 to 50 Pence sterling per Peso. But Bills on London are generally drawn in Pounds sterling; and the Term is mostly 60 days sight.

The above Real is commonly valued at 6*d.* sterling, and all other current money in the same proportion. It should, however, be observed, that in some parts of Mexico accounts are still kept in Hard Dollars, divided into 8ths, 16ths, &c.

All the new Coins of the Republics, both Gold and Silver, are understood to be minted as heretofore; and such as have been tried in London prove fully correct in their sterling value, though not perfectly uniform in their Mint proportions, as may be seen by the following Assays.

TABLE I.

Shewing the Weight, Fineness, and Sterling Value of the following Coins, deduced from Assays made for this Work at the London Mint, January 21, 1826. New Dollars.

	ASSAY.	WEIGHT.	STERLING VALUE.
	dwt.	dwt. gr.	d.
Dollar of Mexico........ (1823.)	W. 7½	17 9¾	52 . 13
" Central America (1824.)	W. 5½	17 6½	52 . 21
" Chile .... (1823.)	W. 5	17 2½	51 . 83
" Peru .... (1822.)	W. 6	17 10	52 . 5

The Impressions of the above Coins are chiefly Emblems of Liberty, and their Inscriptions are expressive of Justice, Union, Honour, and other virtues; with the names of the Republics and the dates of coinage, &c.

GOLD AND SILVER WEIGHT.

Although the Weights and Measures of Spanish America have been already explained, under the heads *Spain* and *Mexico*, yet some further illustrations here, under different arrangements, may be useful. The Marc of Castile is the Standard Weight for the precious metals. It answers to 3550½ English Grains, or 230,043 French Grammes; but though it is uniform in its contents, it is differently divided for Gold and Silver. Thus— Gold and Silver Weight.

GOLD WEIGHT.		SILVER WEIGHT.	
12 Grains	= 1 Tomine	12 Grains	= 1 Tomine
8 Tomines	= 1 Castellan	3 Tomines	= 1 Adarme
50 Castellanos	= 1 Marc	2 Adarmes	= 1 Ochava
6¼ Castellanos	= 1 Ounce	8 Ochavas	= 1 Ounce
8 Ounces	= 1 Marc	8 Ounces	= 1 Marc

Thus the Marc is divided into 4800 Grains Gold weight, and 4608 Grains Silver weight, and therefore 24 of the latter equal 25 of the former. It should, however, be observed, that Silver Grains are always understood, unless Gold Grains be expressly mentioned.

Diamonds and Pearls are weighed by the Onza of 140 *Quilates*, or 560 Castilian Grains. Hence the Diamond Onza equals 18 dwts. and the Carat $3\frac{1}{12}$ Grains English Troy weight.

COMMERCIAL WEIGHTS AND MEASURES.

Commercial Weights. The Commercial Pound, or *Libra*, equals 2 Marcs, and answers nearly to 1lb. 0 oz. 4 drams Avoirdupois weight. Hence 100 Libras of Spain equal 101lb. 7 oz. Avoirdupois, or 46 Kilogrammes nearly; and thus 1 cwt. English weight, answers to 110lb. 6½ oz. Spanish.

The Libra is divided and multiplied as follows:—

36 Grains	=	1 Adarme
2 Adarmes	=	1 Drachma
8 Drachmas	=	1 Ounce
16 Ounces	=	1 Pound or Libra
25 Pounds	=	1 Arroba
4 Arrobas	=	1 Quintal

Measures. As the Spanish Foot equals 11$\frac{1}{8}$ English Inches; therefore, 89 English Inches, Feet, or Yards, answer to 96 *Pulgados*, *Pies*, or *Varas* Spanish.

For Land and Road Measures, see *Spain*, p. 322. Measures of Capacity should also be of Spanish dimensions; but they are not found to be uniformly established in all South America.

GOLD AND SILVER MINES.

Mines. The annual produce of the Mines of *America* has been long a subject of anxious enquiry, and has, perhaps, never been accurately determined. The most authentic computations on the subject were published in 1811 by *Baron Humboldt*, in his *Essai Politique sur le Royaume de la Nouvelle Espagne*, in which he gives numerous Tables, deduced from official Documents, that is, from the Duties paid during a long period into the Royal Treasury for the produce of all the Mines of Spanish America: this computation, however, he considers below the real amount, on account of smuggling, which he reckons, upon an average, to be about one-sixth or one-seventh of the whole produce.

His Tables show the annual increase of those Mines from the year 1690 down to 1803, from which it appears, that the augmentation was three-fold in fifty years, and six-fold in one hundred; but that the increase was only in Silver, while Gold rather decreased. The proportional produce of the precious Metals during that time he computes at nearly eighty Marcs weight of Silver to one of Gold, and concludes his elaborate researches with the following Table, which, for the sake of simplicity, is here given in English Money and in round numbers, as the chief use of the statement is to shew the Mines which have been the most productive in the different metals.

TABLE II.

Shewing the Annual Produce of all the Mines in Spanish America that paid Duty to the King in the year 1801, computed by *Baron Humboldt.* Produce of Mines.

CHIEF DIVISIONS.	GOLD, Valued in Pounds Sterling.	SILVER, Valued in Pounds Sterling.	Total Annual Produce.
Vice-Royalty of New Spain . .	0,219,000	4,635,000	4,854,000
Vice-Royalty of Peru	0,106,000	1,610,000	1,716,000
Captain-Generalship of Chile . .	0,314,000	0,061,000	0,375,000
Vice-Royalty of Buenos Ayres	0,069,000	0,852,000	0,921,000
Vice-Royalty of New Granada	0,565,000	not much.	0,565,000
Total	1,273,000	7,168,000	8,431,000

Such was the annual produce of the Mines of Spanish America in the beginning of the nineteenth century; but the late revolution which followed put a stop to all means of computation from official documents. This want, however, has been supplied, as well as circumstances would permit, by Mr. JACOB, and the following are the results of his researches, as published in the Second Edition of *Mr. Tooke's* Work on "*High and Low Prices,*" p. 379.

TABLE III.

Shewing the Average Annual Produce of the principal Mines of Spanish America, both in Gold and Silver, from 1800 to 1821, by *William Jacob*, Esq. F.R.S.

	1800 to 1810. Pounds Sterling.	1810 to 1821. Pounds Sterling.
Mexico	6,818,000	1,820,000
Peru	1,245,000	0,455,000
Buenos Ayres	0,827,000	0,340,000
Chile	0,197,000	0,182,000
New Granada	0,621,000	0,455,000
Total Annual Produce	9,708,000	3,252,000

Thus it appears that, during the late war, the Spanish Mines yielded very little more than one-third of their usual produce. It also appears that the Mines of Mexico were more productive in Silver than all the others; and that New Granada was the richest in Gold.

EMPIRE OF BRAZIL.

This extensive territory, formerly a colony belonging to Portugal, is now an independent Empire; and in alliance and commercial intercourse with Great Britain, similar to the other new States of South America.

This political change in the government of Brazil has made no alteration in the commercial regulations of Monies, Weights, or Measures; and, therefore, they will be found correctly explained in this volume, under the heads *Brazil, Lisbon,* and *Rio de Janeiro.* The following proportions, however, in round numbers, may help the memory:—

9 Feet or Inches of Brazil	=	10 Feet or Inches of England.
26 Leagues of ditto	=	100 English Miles.
7 Geiras (Land Measure)	=	10 English Acres.
85 Arratels (Common Weight)	=	86 lb. Avoirdupois.

The Empire of Brazil is in general very rich in vegetable and mineral productions.

Its Diamonds and other precious stones, which are abundant, have never been accurately estimated, as they exclusively belong to the Crown. Also one-fifth of the Gold; from which proportion its annual produce has been computed at nearly a million of pounds sterling in peaceable times.* See vol. i. p. 253.

---

* REMARKS ON THE PROPORTIONS, &c. OF THE PRECIOUS METALS.

From the foregoing documents it appears, that the annual produce of the Mines of America before the late war, might be estimated at nine millions of pounds sterling. This computation is deduced, as before stated, from the works of Baron Humboldt, who estimates the Mines of Europe, including those of Asiatic Russia, at about one million a year. He considers several of the other Mines, both of Asia and Africa, as rich, particularly in Gold, without, however, computing their value; but he expresses astonishment that the great annual increase of the precious metals for so long a time has not been more perceptible in commercial practice. He estimates the annual remittances from America to Europe at seven or eight millions sterling; one-half of which he supposes to have been absorbed in Oriental commerce, one-eighth in European coins, and the rest in plate, jewellery, and other ornaments.

The proportional weight of the precious metals drawn from the Mines he thus estimates:—

	lb. of Silver.		lb. of Gold.
From the Mines of Spanish America	80	to	1
From ditto, reckoning the Gold of Brazil	46	to	1
From the Mines of Europe	40	to	1
From the Mines of Asia and Africa	30	to	1

It may be observed, that the above proportions of weight differ essentially from the Mint proportions of all countries, which, on an average, may be estimated at 15½lb. of Silver to one of Gold. This difference results from the preference given to Silver for general purposes, which thus raises its comparative value. For accurate calculations of the relative proportions of the precious metals, in the principal Mints of all nations, see vol. ii. p. 147; and for their proportions at different periods of antiquity, see Introduction, p. 27.

It may be also remarked, that the above proportions differ from those quoted from other high authorities, p. 254 of this volume; but Humboldt is the latest writer, and his researches and reports on the subject of the precious metals are considered the most elaborate and correct ever published.

NEW EXCHANGES IN ITALY.

A new System of Exchanges has been recently established in *Venice*, and another in *Milan*, of which the following are the quotations and explanations:—

VENICE.

Exchanges are computed in *Lire d'Austria* of 100 Cents. each Lira being divided into 20 Soldi, and each Soldo into 5 Cents. This Lira may be valued at 8*d.* sterling, more or less. For the late Exchanges of *Venice*, see vol. ii. p. 95.

	Variable.	Fixed.
Amsterdam	97 Groots for	6 Lire d'Austria.
Augsburgh	58 Soldi d'Austria	1 Florin Current.
Genoa	63 Soldi fuori banco	3 Lire d'Austria.
Hamburgh	89 Groots	6 Ditto.
Leghorn	97 Soldi	100 Soldi d'Austria.
Lisbon	53 Soldi d'Austria	1 Crusade of 400 Rees.
London	48 Pence Sterling	6 Lire d'Austria.
Milan	60 Soldi d'Austria	3 Ditto.
Naples	60 Grains	3 Ditto.
Paris	85 Cents.	1 Ditto.
Trieste	60 Kreutzers	3 Ditto.
Vienna	60 Kreutzers	3 Ditto.

MILAN.

Exchanges are computed in *Lire Correnti* of 100 Cents. which may be valued as the Lira d'Austria.—For the late Exchanges of Milan, see vol. ii. p. 76.

	Variable.		Fixed.
Amsterdam	2.49	Lire Correnti and Cents. for	1 Florin Current.
Genoa	0.96	Ditto	1 Lira fuori banco.
Hamburgh	2.14	Ditto	1 Marc banco.
Leghorn	5.95	Ditto	1 Dollar of 8 Reals.
London	29.92	Ditto	1 Pound Sterling.
Naples	4.94	Ditto	1 Ducato del Regno.
Paris	1.18	Ditto	1 Franc.
Venice	1.00	Ditto	1 Lira d'Austria.
Vienna	2.98	Ditto	1 Florin eff. of 20 Krs.

100 Lire d'Austria = 87 *Lire Italiche*, and
145 Lire Correnti = 128 *Lire Antica Moneta*.

INDEX

TO THE SUPPLEMENTARY ARTICLES OF THE CAMBIST.

VOL. I.

VOL. II.

Whiting, Printer, Lombard Street.

SUPPLEMENT

TO THE

UNIVERSAL CAMBIST,

CONTINUED TO 1835;

CONTAINING

AN ABSTRACT OF THE ACT OF PARLIAMENT OF 1834,

RELATING TO THE IMPERIAL SYSTEM OF

BRITISH WEIGHTS AND MEASURES,

INCLUDING

Numerous Illustrations,

WITH STATEMENTS OF

ALTERATIONS OF IMPORTANCE IN THE MONIES OF EXCHANGE AND MINT REGULATIONS OF DIFFERENT COUNTRIES;

ALSO AN ACCOUNT OF THE

MONETARY SYSTEM & METROLOGY OF THE NEW KINGDOM OF GREECE.

BY

P. KELLY, LL.D.

WHITING, BEAUFORT HOUSE, LONDON.

SUPPLEMENT TO 1835,

CONTAINING

INTRODUCTORY REMARKS.

This Supplement has become necessary in consequence of recent alterations of importance in the Monies of Exchange and Mint Regulations of different Countries, which are here fully explained.

The leading object, however, of the present Article, is to illustrate the Imperial System of British Weights and Measures, as amended and enforced by the late Act of Parliament, which removes difficulties and enacts penalties, as may be seen in the subsequent Abstract.

The illustrations of the Imperial System which follow, consist chiefly in the reduction of Foreign Measures of Capacity to the Imperial Standard, which is further elucidated by a Table of Factors or Multipliers, for converting the Metrical System of France and the Imperial System of England into each other reciprocally—Systems of great and increasing importance.*

It may be remarked that the numerous Supplements which have been added to this Edition of the Cambist, and which are stated in the preceding Index (p. 410), were rendered indispensably necessary, by various changes which are detailed in their proper places. These augmentations, however, though they must have greatly added to the value of the Work (which had been already essentially improved by the aid of Government) did not produce corresponding advantages to the Author, who considered himself bound to make the Edition keep pace with the improvements of time—and therefore delivered, gratis, to the previous purchasers, copies of each Supplement.

It is intended to pursue the same plan on the present occasion, and with the same view, of constantly keeping the Edition as it were new, and worthy of the Title of "A correct and comprehensive Treatise on the Exchanges, Coins, Weights, and Measures of all Nations."

* The Metrical System is established throughout France, Belgium, and Holland, and has been partially introduced into other States; while the Imperial System is making certain progress throughout the British Empire and its Colonies, and has been also introduced into the United States of America, in order to agree, as formerly, with the English practice. See p. 355 of this Volume.

ABSTRACT OF AN ACT OF PARLIAMENT,

Entitled, "An Act to amend and render more effectual two Acts of the fifth and sixth years of the Reign of his late Majesty, King George the Fourth, relating to Weights and Measures."

Passed 13th August, 1834, and to commence January 1, 1835.

Preamble recites Acts 5 Geo. IV., c. 74, and 6 Geo. IV., c. 12.

Clause 1. Provisions in recited Acts, as to models and copies of standard weights and measures, repealed.

2. Weights and measures stamped at the Exchequer declared legal, although not similar in shape to those required by recited Acts.

3. Superintending officer of the Exchequer may verify and stamp weights and measures of other form than those prescribed by the Act 5 Geo. IV., c. 74.

*4. Heaped measure abolished after 1st January, 1835, also weights made of Lead or Pewter.

5. Copies of the Imperial standards to be provided by order of magistrates in quarter sessions for counties in England and Wales, and by meetings of justices in Scotland.

6. Copies to be provided by grand juries in Ireland.—7. Or by Judges when necessary.

8. Power of providing additional copies when requisite.

9. Return to be made by clerks of the peace on the 1st of March, 1836.

10. Power to magistrates of towns, &c. to provide copies of the Imperial standards.

11. Weigh-masters in Ireland to be supplied with beams and scales and copies by corporate bodies.

12. The stone-weight of 14 lb., hundred-weight of 112 lb, and ton of 20 cwt. to be used and no other.

13. All articles to be sold by avoirdupois weight, excepting gold, silver, platina, diamonds, or other precious stones, also drugs, when retailed, are to be sold by troy weight.

14. All weights and measures to be stamped by inspectors. Penalty for making or using any others.

15. Regulation as to fiar prices of commodities in Scotland.—16. Inspectors to enter into recognizance.

17. Power to magistrates to inspect weights and measures.

18. Penalty for counterfeiting stamps on weights and measures.

19. Copies of the standard weights and measures, which shall have been worn and mended, to be sent to the Exchequer to be re-verified.—20. Officer to keep a register of copies verified.

21. Application of penalties in England and Wales, and in Ireland.—22. Form of conviction.

23. Appeals to be made at the next general quarter sessions of the peace after conviction.

24. Application of penalties in Scotland.

25. Appeals, in Scotland, to be made to the commissioners of justiciary at the next Circuit-court.

26. Acts of 4 Anne (Ireland) and 5 Geo. IV., c. 110, repealed, except so far as they relate to the appointment, duties, and remuneration of weigh-masters.

27. Powers of ward-inquests, &c. in London and Southwark, not to be interfered with.

28. Rights of the Founders' Company of the city of London reserved.

29. Magistrates may plead the general issue in actions brought against them under this Act.

---

* The above Clause which abolishes heaped measure, must extend to the Coal Trade, wherever the Imperial bushel is still used.

It should, however, be stated, that by an Act passed in 1831, Coals are ordered to be sold and delivered in London and its Environs (to the distance of Twenty-five Miles) by weight, instead of measure as heretofore. The legal weight is the ton of 10 sacks, each sack containing 224lb., and when the chaldron is referred to, it is estimated at 25½ cwt.

For Coal Measures, see pp. 222 and 388 of this volume.

ILLUSTRATIONS AND EXAMPLES OF THE IMPERIAL SYSTEM.

It may be again repeated that the Imperial system makes no change whatever in the old system of British Weights and Long Measures.* Its only alteration is in Measures of Capacity, by converting the old "Corn, Wine, and Beer Measures" into one Measure, which is to be tested by the weight of water it contains, as in the following Table, where other proportions are also stated.

CORN MEASURE ACCORDING TO THE IMPERIAL STANDARD,

From which all other Measures of Capacity may be deduced.

MEASURES.	WEIGHT.		CUBIC INCHES.	FRENCH LITRES.
	lb.	*oz.*		
1 Gill = ...	0	5	8,665	0,142
4 Gills = 1 Pint . . .	1	4	34,659	0,568
2 Pints = 1 Quart . .	2	8	69,318	1,136
2 Quarts = 1 Pottle .	5	0	138,637	2,272
2 Pottles = 1 Gallon .	10	0	277,274	4,544
2 Gallons = 1 Peck . .	20	0	554,548	9,087
4 Pecks = 1 Bushel . .	80	0	2218,192	36,347
8 Bushels = 1 Quarter .	640	0	10 Cubic Feet & 2692 In.	290,776

Also, the Last of Corn contains, 2 Weys, 10 Quarters, 20 Cooms, 40 Strikes, or 80 Bushels, and the weight of Water which each contains may be computed from the above Table, which likewise shows the proportion of each to French Measure.

Thus, the Quarter answers to $2\frac{9}{10}$ Hectolitres }
The Hectolitre . . . . $2\frac{3}{4}$ Bushels } nearly, but for greater accuracy, see p. 420.
The Litre . . . . $1\frac{3}{4}$ Pint }

The Foreign Measures of Capacity in the following Tables, are converted to Imperial Measures from the cubic Inches of each, which were procured and verified for this work by order and aid of Government in 1820; and were then converted to Winchester and French Measures, as in the Second Volume of this Edition, p. 229, &c.

---

* The old Standards of Troy and Avoirdupois Weight, and also the ancient Standard Yard, have been recently examined by proper authorities, and found correct. Verified copies, therefore, of the same continue to be distributed, together with the new measures of capacity, and all under the denomination of "Imperial Weights and Measures."

CORN, OR DRY MEASURES,

OF DIFFERENT PLACES, REDUCED TO IMPERIAL BUSHELS,

Intended to correspond with and complete the Table, Page 229, Vol. II.

PLACES.	MEASURES.	English Cubic Inches.	Contents in Imperial Bushels.	PLACES.	MEASURES.	English Cubic Inches.	Contents in Imperial Bushels.
Aix la Chapelle ...	Fass	1461	0,658	Bruges	Hoed	10164	4,581
				Brunswick..	Himten	1898	0,855
Alexandria	Rebebe	9587	4,322	Cadiz......	Fanega	3439	1,550
Algiers	Tarrie	1219	0,549	Calabria ..	Tomolo	3119	1,405
Alicant....	Cahiz......	15038	6,779	Canada	Minot......	2339	1,054
Amersfoort	Mudde	11457	5,153	Canary Isles	Fanega	3821	1,722
Amsterdam	Mudde	6788	3,060	Candia	Carga	9288	4,189
Ancona	Rubbio	17459	7,870	Cassell	Viertel	8710	3,926
Antwerp ..	Hectolitre ..	6102,8	2,751	Cleves	Malter	10954	4,937
Arnheim ..	Malder	8333	3,756	Coblentz ..	Malter	9742	4,391
Arragon ..	Cahiz......	11021	4,968	Coburg	Simra......	5353	2,413
Augsburg ..	Schaf......	26812	12,087	Cologne ..	Malter	9891	4,459
Azores	Alqueire ..	731	0,329	Constantinople ..	Killow	2023	0,912
Barcelona	Quartera ..	4175	1,882				
Basil	Sack	7870	3,554	Copenhagen	Toende	8488	3,826
Bastia	Stajo	9153	4,126	Corunna ..	Ferrado	1022	0,460
Bayonne ..	Conque	2503	1,128	Cyprus	Medimno ..	4583	2,065
Bergamo ..	Soma	10020	4,517	Dantzic....	Scheffel	3337	1,504
Bergen	Toende	8488	3,826	Deventer ..	Mudde	7049	3,177
Berlin	Scheffel....	3180	1,438	Dieppe	Mine	6243	2,814
Bern	Mutt	10260	4,625	Dordrecht	Great Sack	7638	3,443
Bilboa	Fanega	3668	1,654		Little Sack	5728	2,582
Bologna ..	Corba	4503	2,030	Dresden ..	Scheffel....	6455	2,910
Bolsano....	Scheffel....	6657	3,001	Dunkirk ..	Sea Rasiere	9153	4,126
Boulogne ..	Setier	10535	4,748		Land Rasiere	8136	3,667
Bourdeaux	Boisseau ..	4682	2,110	Elbing	Scheffel....	2965	1,335
Breda ...	Viertel	5236	2,360	Embden	Tonne	11697	5,272
Bremen	Scheffel....	4339	1,955	England ..	Imperial Bushel	2218,192	1,000
Breslau	Scheffel	4266	1,922				
Brest	Tonneau ..	84200	37,930	Erfurt	Scheffel....	3668	1,653

PLACES.	MEASURES.	English Cubic Inches.	Contents in Imperial Bushels.	PLACES.	MEASURES.	English Cubic Inches.	Contents in Imperial Bushels.
FARO	Alqueire ..	982	0,442	MARSEILLES	Charge	9763	4,401
FERRARA ..	Stajo	1909	0,859	MECKLENBURG	Scheffel	2591	1,168
FERROL	Ferrado	1042	0,469	MENTZ	Malter	5558	2,505
FIUME	Metze	3813	1,718	MIDDLEBURG	Sack	4417	1,991
FLORENCE ..	Stajo	1486	0,669	MILAN	Stajo	1115	0,502
FRANCE	Setier	9519,9	4,291	MINORCA ...	Quartera ..	4301	1,938
	Hectolitre ..	6102,8	2,751	MODENA	Stajo	4301	1,938
	Boisseau Usuel	762,7	0,343	MONTPELLIER	Setier	3232	1,457
				MUNICH	Scheffel . ..	22130	9,976
FRANCFORT ..	Malter	6590	2,970	NANCY	Carte	2925	1,318
GENEVA	Coupe	4739	2,135	NANTES	Setier	8739	3,939
GENOA	Mina	7367	3,321	NAPLES	Tomolo	3122	1,407
GOES	Sack	4888	2,203	NEDA	Ferrado	1144	0,518
GRONINGEN	Mudden ..	5554	2,504	NEGROPONT	Killow	1849	0,833
HAARLEM .	Sack	4823	2,174	NETHERLANDS	Mudden	6102,8	2,751
HAGUE	Sack	6546	2,946	NICE	Charge	9763	4,401
HAMBURG ..	Scheffel	6426	2,899	NIMEGUEN ..	Scheffel	2546	1,148
HANAU	Malter	6868	3,096	NUREMBERG	Malter	10200	4,598
HANOVER ..	Himtem	1898	0,855	OLDENBURG	Tonne ...	9946	4,483
HEIDELBERG	Malter	6285	2,833	OSNABURG ..	Scheffel	1753	0,790
HILDESHEIM	Scheffel	3164	1,426	OVIEDO	Fanega	4419	1,992
HOLSTEIN ..	Toende	8488	3,826	PARMA	Stajo	3135	1,413
KONIGSBERG	Scheffel	3152	1,420	PATRAS	Staro	5012	2,259
LEGHORN ..	Sacco	4435	1,999	PERNAU	Tonne	7729	3,484
LEIPSIC	Scheffel	8481	3,822	PERSIA	Artaba	4013	1,809
LEWARDEN .	Loop	5092	2,295	POLAND	Korzec	3120,8	1,407
LEYDEN	Sack	4165	1,877	PRAGUE	Strick	6516	2,937
LIBAU	Lof	4190	1,888	PRUSSIA	Scheffel	3353,6	1,512
LIEGE	Setier	1827	0,823	RAGUSA	Stajo	9072	4,089
LISBON	Alqueire ..	824,8	0,372	RATISBON ..	Maass	16016	7,220
LUBEC	Wheat Scheffel	2041	0,920	REVEL	Tonne	7219	3,254
				RIGA	Loop	4166	1,878
	Oat Scheffel	2395	1,079	ROCHELLE ..	Boisseau ...	2007	0,904
LUCCA	Stajo	1472	0,663	ROME	Rubbio	17970	8,100
LUNEBURG ..	Scheffel	3799	1,713	ROSTOCK	Scheffel	2372	1,069
LYONS	Asnée	11706	5,276	ROTTERDAM	Sack	6320	2,849
MAGDEBURGH	Scheffel	3152	1,420	ROUEN	Setier	10920	4,922
MAJORCA ..	Quartera ..	4301	1,937	RUSSIA	Chetwert ..	12800	5,770
MALAGA	Fanega	3439	1,550	ST. GALL ..	Charge	4443	2,003
MALTA	Salma	17678	7,969	ST. MALOES .	Boisseau ..	2697	1,215
MANHEIM ..	Malter	6285	2,833	ST. VALERY	Setier	9356	4,217
MANTUA	Stajo	2146	0,967	SALONICA ..	Killow	1184	0,533
MARANHAM	Alqueire ..	2772	1,248	SARDINIA ..	Starello	2988	1,346

PLACES.	MEASURES.	English Cubic Inches.	Contents in Imperial Bushels.	PLACES.	MEASURES.	English Cubic Inches.	Contents in Imperial Bushels.
SCOTLAND ..	Wheat Firlot	2197,3	0,991	TUNIS	Caffice	32256	14,541
	Barley Firlot	3205,5	1,444	TURIN	Sacco	7015	3,162
SICILY	Salma Grossa	21014	9,473	VALENCIA ..	Cahiz	12526	5,647
	Salma Generale ..	16886	7,611	VENICE	Stajo	4882	2,200
				VERONA	Minello	2221	1,001
SMYRNA	Killow	3132	1,411	VIANNA	Alqueire ..	1031	0,464
SPAIN	Fanega	3439	1,550	VIENNA	Metzen	3753	1,691
STETTIN	Scheffel	3180	1,434	ULM	Immi	14021	6,320
STRALSUND ..	Scheffel	2378	1,072	UTRECHT ..	Sack	5498	2,478
STRASBURG ..	Land Setier	1154	0,520	WIRTEMBERG	Scheffel	10889	4,909
	City Setier	1118	0,504	WISMAR	Wheat Scheffel	2478	1,117
SWEDEN	Tunna of 32 Kappar	8940	4,030		Oat Scheffel	2616	1,178
	Kann	159,6	0,072	ZANTE	Corfu Misura	1284,78	0,579
TEXEL	Loop	3819	1,722	ZEALAND ..	Sack	4556	2,054
TRIESTE	Stajo	5040,6	2,272	ZELL	Himten	1898	0,855
	Metzen	3706	1,670	ZURICH	Mutt	5048	2,275
	Polonick ..	1853	0,835	ZWOLL	Mudden	6851	3,088

RULES FOR CONVERTING DIFFERENT MEASURES INTO EACH OTHER.

To convert ENGLISH CUBIC INCHES *into* IMPERIAL BUSHELS *(as in the foregoing Table).*

Divide the Inches by 2218,192, or multiply them by ,00045082.
For Gallons (as in the following Table), see p. 392.

To convert WINCHESTER MEASURE *into* IMPERIAL MEASURE, *and the contrary.*

Multiply by the Decimal Factors, p. 394, or multiply and divide by any of the following Ratios.

31 Imperial, equal 32 Winchester.
32 ditto 33 ditto.
95 ditto 98 ditto.

These Ratios may be carried to many higher proportions, and the greater the numbers are the nearer they approach to perfect Ratios, which are, however, unattainable in Integers.

Note.—Any one of the above Ratios is sufficiently correct for practical purposes; but, to help the memory, the second seems preferable, as 32 Imperial Quarts make an Imperial Bushel, which answers exactly to the Winchester Bushel and one Winchester Quart over, viz. 33 Winchester Quarts.

WINE, OR LIQUID MEASURES,

OF DIFFERENT PLACES, REDUCED TO IMPERIAL GALLONS,

Intended to correspond with and complete the Table, Page 234, Vol. II.

PLACES.	MEASURES.	English Cubic Inches.	Contents in Imperial Gallons.	PLACES.	MEASURES.	English Cubic Inches.	Contents in Imperial Gallons.
Abyssinia	Cuba	62	0,223	Cologne	Viertel	365	1,316
Alicant	Cantara	704	2,543	Constantinople	Almud	319	1,151
Amsterdam	Wine Stekan	1184	4,270				
	BrandyStekan	1145	4,129	Copenhagen	Viertel	471,5	1,700
	Beer Stekan	1199	4,324		Anker	2298	8,286
Ancona	Soma	5241	18,901	Corfu	Barile	4158	14,995
Antwerp	Stoop	167	0,648	Cyprus	Cass	288,7	1,041
Arragon	Wine Cantaro	629	2,269	Dantzic	Ohm	9142	32,971
	Brandy Cantaro	852	3,074	Dresden	Eimer	4128	14,887
				Dunkirk	Lot	140	0,505
Augsburg	Mass	90,3	0,326	England	Wine Gallon, Old	231	0,833
Barcelona	Carga	7552	27,236				
Bari	Oil Salma	10100	36,425		Beer Gallon, Old	282	1,017
Basil	Ohm	3053	11,010				
Bastia	Barile	8543	30,807	Erfurt	Wine Eimer	4398	15,862
Bayonne	Velte	451	1,554		Beer Eimer	4402	15,876
Bergamo	Brenta	4441	16,018	Faro	Almude	1131	4,078
Berlin	Anker	2285,5	8,243	Ferrara	Mastello	3379,5	12,188
Berne	Mass	102	0,367	Fiume	Orna	3253	11,732
Bologna	Corba	4503	1,624	Florence	Wine Barile	2781,7	10,032
Bourdeaux	Barrique	14033	51,610		Oil Barile	2040	7,357
	Velte	438	1,579	France	Setier	454	1,637
Bremen	Stubgen	194,5	0,701		Hectolitre	6102,8	22,009
Breslau	Eimer	3389	12,222	Francfo	Viertel	450	1,622
Brunswick	Stubgen	224	0,807	Galicia	Moyo	9886	35,654
Burgundy	Quartaut	6275	22,631	Gallipoli	Oil Salma	9459	34,114
Canary Isles	Arroba	981	3,537	Geneva	Setier	2760	9,954
Candia	Oil Mistate	681	2,456	Genoa	Wine Barile	4530	16,337
Cassell	Quartlin	499	1,799		Oil Barile	3946	14,231
Champagne	Quartaut	5496	19,821	Hamburg	Ahm	8836	31,867
Cognac	Brandy Velte	446	1,608	Hanover	Ahm	9493	34,236

PLACES.	MEASURES.	English Cubic Inches.	Contents in Imperial Gallons.
Heidelberg	Maass	140,4	0,506
Hungary, Upper ..	Eimer......	4474	16,135
Hungary, Lower ..	Eimer......	3472	12,522
	Tokay Anthal	3084	11,122
Ireland	Gallon	217,6	0,785
Konigsberg	Stof	87,5	0,315
Leghorn ..	Wine Barile	2781	10,029
	Oil Barile ..	2040	7,357
Leipsic	Eimer......	4644	16,747
Libau	Oxhoft	14436	52,063
Lindau	Quart......	140	0,504
Lisbon	Almude	1009,5	3.641
Lisle	Lot........	126	0,454
Lubec......	Viertel	441,9	1,594
Lucca	Oil Coppo ..	6093	21,974
Lyons	Asnée	5038	18,169
Majorca ..	Quartin	1655,8	5,971
Malaga	Arroba	967	3,487
Malta	Oil Caffiso..	1270	4,580
Mantua	Oil Moggio	6804	24,535
Marseilles	Millerolle ..	3924,7	14,154
Mentz	Maass	114	0,411
Messina	Wine Salma	5331	19,226
	Oil Caffiso ..	714	2,575
Milan	Brenta	4357,5	15,716
Minorca ..	Gerra......	736	2,654
Montpellier	Wine Barrique ..	1550	5,590
	Oil Barrique	2028	7,314
Munich	Wine Eimer	2252	8,122
Nantes	Wine Barrique ..	14645	52,816
	Brandy Velte	343	1,236
Naples	Wine Barile	2544	9,174
	Oil Salma ..	9884	35,647
Netherlands	Vat........	6102,8	22,009
Nice	Rubbio	479,5	1,729
Nuremberg	Eimer Visiermass	4149	14,963
	Eimer Schenkma	3872	13,964
Oldenburg	Oxhoft	15230	54,926
Oporto	Almude	1555	5,608
Osnaburg ..	Viertel	298	1,074
Oviedo	Cantara	1177	4,244
Pernau	Anker	2364	8,525
Poland	Garniec	97	0,349
Prague	Eimer	3916	14,123
Prussia	Eimer......	4192	15,118
Ragusa	Barrel	4704	16,965
Ratisbon ..	Great Eimer	6934	25,007
	Berg Eimer	5359	19,327
Revol	Anker	2580	9,304
Riga	Anker	2386	8,605
Rio de Janeiro ..	Medida	161,7	0,583
Rochelle ..	Wine Barrique ..	10636	38,359
	Brandy Velte	446	1,608
Rome	Wine Barrile	3560,4	12,840
	Oil Barrile..	3507	12,648
Rostock....	Anker	2209	7,966
Rotterdam	Ahm	9238,4	33,318
Rouen	Barrique ..	11940	43,062
Russia	Vedro	750	2,705
Schaffhausen	Mass	80	0,288
Scotland ..	Pint	103,4	0,372
Spain	Wine Arroba	981	3,538
	Oil Arroba	771	2,780
Stralsund ..	Stubgen....	237	0,855
Strasburg ..	Ohm	2813	10,145
Sweden	Kann	159,6	0,576
Trieste	Wine Orna	3452	12,448
Tunis......	Millerolle ..	3924	14,154
	Oil Mettar..	1183	4,269
Turin......	Rubbio	573	2,066
Valencia ..	Arroba	719	2,593
Venice	Secchio	659	2,376
	Oil Miro ..	930	3,354
Verona	Brenta	4417	15,930
	Oil Bassa ..	276	0,995
Vienna	Eimer......	3452	12,449
Wismar....	Viertel	441,9	1,537
Zante	Barile......	4071	14,682
Zell	Stubgen....	237	0,854
Zurich	Laud Maass	111,3	0,401
	City Maass	106,2	0,361
	Oil Maass ..	84	0.302

TABLE OF FACTORS,

FOR CONVERTING THE METRICAL AND IMPERIAL SYSTEMS INTO EACH OTHER RECIPROCALLY.

FRENCH INTO ENGLISH.	Multiply by	ENGLISH INTO FRENCH.	Multiply by
Metres into Yards	1.09364	Yards into Metres	0.914318
Grammes into Grains Troy	15.434	Grains Troy into Grammes	0.064793
Kilogrammes into Pounds Avoirdupois .	2.20486	Pounds Avoirdupois into Kilogrammes .	0.45354
Kilogrammes into Pounds Troy	2.6795	Pounds Troy into Kilogrammes	0.3732
Litres into English Cubic Inches . . .	61.02802	English Cubic Inches into Litres	0.01639
Litres into Imperial Gallons	0.2201	Imperial Gallons into Litres	4.5434
Hectolitres into Imperial Bushels	2.7513	Imperial Bushels into Hectolitres	0.36347
Hectares into Acres	2.47117	Acres into Hectares	0.40467
Kilometres into Miles	0.62138	Miles into Kilometres	1.6102
Lieues de Poste into Miles	2.4222	Miles into Lieues de Poste	0.4128

Examples.

1. Reduce 4 Hectolitres, 54 Litres, 337 Millitres into Imperial Bushels.

4.54,337 × 2.7513 = 12.5 Imperial Bushels.

2. Reduce 12½ Imperial Bushels into Hectolitres.

12.5 × .36347 = 4.54,337 Hectolitres, &c.

3. Reduce 11 Litres 554 Millitres into Imperial Gallons.

11.554 × .2201 = 2.543 Imperial Gallons, &c.

4. Reduce 2.543 Imperial Gallons into Litres.

2.543 × 4.5434 = 11.554 Litres and Millitres.

REFERENCES.

The Metrical System of France and the Imperial System of England are fully explained in different parts of this Work. Thus in vol. i. p. 134, a Scientific Exposition is given of the Metrical System, with a comparison between it and the old systems of France and England. Also in vol. ii. p. 251, another comparison is given under a more simple arrangement, with a statement of the *Système Usuel*, which is partially used in France for retail business.

The Imperial System of England is regularly explained in this Series of Supplements, pp. 387, 394, 397, 414, &c.

Alterations of Importance in the Monies and Mint Regulations of the following places.

AMSTERDAM.—At Amsterdam, Rotterdam, and other cities of Holland, the ancient Flemish monies are nearly discontinued, and exchanges are quoted in Florins current of 20 Stivers, or more generally of 100 Centimes.

ANTWERP.—At Antwerp and other cities of Belgium, exchanges are quoted in Florins current of 100 Centimes; as thus,

	VARIABLE.			FIXED
London . . .	12,02$\frac{1}{2}$	Florins . . .	for	£ 1 Sterling.
Paris	48$\frac{3}{8}$	ditto . . .	for	100 Francs.
Hamburgh . .	35$\frac{7}{16}$	ditto . . .	for	40 Marcs Banco
Francfort . .	36$\frac{3}{16}$	ditto . . .	for	20 Rix Dollars.

GENOA.—Genoa and other cities of the north-west of Italy, have altered their money of exchange from the Lira fuori banco to the Lira nuova, which is of the same value as the French Franc.

HAMBURGH.—At Hamburgh the ancient Flemish monies have been wholly discontinued, and exchanges are negotiated in Marcs Banco of 16 Schillings Banco. An alteration has also taken place in quoting the price of gold. Thus the present quotation is 433 Marcs Banco, more or less, for one Marc weight of fine gold.

LISBON.—In July, 1834, the Portuguese Government decreed the extinction of paper money, and a pure metallic currency was ordered to be substituted. Foreign monies were also ordered to be received as a legal tender at the rate of 4120 Rees for an English Sovereign, and 870 Rees for a Spanish or Mexican Dollar.

New Mint Regulations of the United States of America.

UNITED STATES.—In July, 1834, an alteration was decreed in the Mint regulations of the United States by lowering the weight of the gold coins. Thus the Eagle, which formerly contained 247$\frac{1}{4}$ grains of pure gold, is now reduced to 232 grains, with its divisions in proportion.

This decree changes the Mint proportion between gold and silver from 15 to 1 as heretofore (see p. 147, vol. ii.), to 16 to 1, the new Mint proportion.

The following New Regulations have been also declared.

The gold Coins of Great Britain, Portugal, and Brazil, of not less than 22 carats fine, shall pass current at the rate of 94$\frac{1}{10}$ cents. per dwt.

And the gold Coins of Spain, Mexico, and Columbia, of the fineness of 20 carats, 3$\frac{7}{16}$ grains, shall pass at the rate of 89$\frac{9}{10}$ cents. per dwt.

The Dollars of Mexico, Peru, Chili, and Central America, of not less weight than 415 grains each, and those re-stamped in Brazil of the like weight, of not less fineness than 10 oz. 15 dwts. shall pass at 100 cents. per dollar.

NEW KINGDOM OF GREECE.

Monies of Account.—This new kingdom (comprehending the Morea and other parts of ancient Greece, with numerous islands in the Archipelago, and Athens the Capital) keeps accounts in Drachmas of 100 Centimes, which are valued at nearly $\frac{11}{12}$ of the French Franc, or $8\frac{3}{4}d.$ sterling.

Coins.—The Coins minted for this kingdom, are gold pieces of 20 and 40 Drachmas, $\frac{9}{10}$ fine; the former weighing 89 Grains Troy, or 5,777 French Grammes, and the latter in proportion.

The silver coins are Drachmas, with halves and quarters; also Five Drachma pieces, all minted at $\frac{9}{10}$ fine. The Drachma weighs 69 Grains Troy, or 4,477 Grammes, and the rest in proportion.

Sterling Value.—The sterling value of the Drachma and Pentadrachma has been recently ascertained for this work at the London Mint, and the following is the result at 5*s.* 2*d.* per ounce, English standard.

	ASSAY.	WEIGHT.	STAN. WEIGHT.	CONTENTS IN PURE SILVER.	STERLING VALUE.
	oz. dwt.	dwt. gr.	dwt. gr.	grs.	*s.* *d.*
Drachma	W. 0 6	2 21	2 19.1	62	0 $8\frac{1}{2}$.6
Pentadrachma . . .	W. 0 5	14 $9\frac{1}{2}$	14 2	312.6	3 $7\frac{1}{2}$.8

The value of the gold pieces at the English mint price of gold, is, the smaller piece 14*s.* $2\frac{1}{2}$*d.*, and the larger in proportion.

The copper coins consist of pieces of 1, 2, 5, and 10 Centimes, or hundredths of a Drachma.

Impressions of the Coins.—The gold and silver coins have on the obverse, the head of the king, with the inscription "Otho, King of Greece," and on the reverse the arms of the kingdom, with the current value of the piece, and the date when it was minted.

The copper coins have on one side the arms of the kingdom, with the inscription "Kingdom of Greece;" and, on the other side, the value of the piece, and the date when it was minted.

Weights and Measures.—The system of Weights and Measures decreed for the new kingdom of Greece is the Metrical System of France.—*See Note, p.* 412.

END OF VOL. I.

Whiting, Beaufort House, London.

A Handbook of Foreign Trade: Kelly's Universal Cambist and Commercial Instructor

OVERSTONE

Printed in England by Pear Tree Imaging Processing, Stevenage

A Handbook of Foreign Trade: Kelly's Universal Cambist and Commercial Instructor

Volume 2

with Supplements for 1824 and 1827

PATRICK KELLY

THOEMMES PRESS

KYOKUTO SHOTEN LTD

This edition co-published in 1999 by

THOEMMES PRESS
11 Great George Street, Bristol BS1 5RR, United Kingdom

KYOKUTO SHOTEN LTD
12, Kanda-Jimbocho 2-Chome, Chiyoda-Ku, Tokyo, Japan

http://www.thoemmes.com

A HANDBOOK OF FOREIGN TRADE:
KELLY'S UNIVERSAL CAMBIST AND COMMERCIAL INSTRUCTOR
2 volumes : ISBN 1 85506 626 2

THE UNIVERSAL CAMBIST AND Commercial Instructor;

BEING A FULL AND ACCURATE TREATISE ON THE

EXCHANGES, MONIES, WEIGHTS, AND MEASURES,

OF ALL

TRADING NATIONS AND THEIR COLONIES;

WITH

AN ACCOUNT OF THEIR BANKS, PUBLIC FUNDS, AND PAPER CURRENCIES.

BY P. KELLY, LL.D.

MASTER OF THE FINSBURY-SQUARE ACADEMY, LONDON; AUTHOR OF DIFFERENT WORKS ON SCIENTIFIC SUBJECTS; AND MATHEMATICAL EXAMINER TO THE TRINITY HOUSE.

VOL. II.

The Second Edition,

INCLUDING

A REVISION OF FOREIGN WEIGHTS AND MEASURES,

FROM AN ACTUAL COMPARISON OF THEIR STANDARDS,

BY THE ORDER AND AID OF THE BRITISH GOVERNMENT.

LONDON:

PRINTED FOR THE AUTHOR,

AND PUBLISHED BY LACKINGTON AND CO. FINSBURY-SQUARE; LONGMAN AND CO. AND BALDWIN AND CO. PATERNOSTER-ROW; CADELL AND DAVIES, STRAND; R. HUNTER, ST. PAUL'S CHURCH-YARD; AND J. M. RICHARDSON, CORNHILL, OPPOSITE THE ROYAL EXCHANGE.

1821.

INTRODUCTION (TO VOL. II.),

CONTAINING EXPLANATIONS OF THE CHAIN RULE, WITH SUNDRY ILLUSTRATIONS RELATING TO EXCHANGE AND BULLION OPERATIONS.

EXCHANGE, which forms the leading subject of this volume, is a science of the first importance both in Commerce and Political Economy. By its direct and common application, foreign debts, loans, and subsidies are paid, and the wealth of nations circulated without the trouble or expense of remitting specie; and, by its more complex operations, (called Arbitrations of Exchange,) great profits are frequently made; and not only private fortunes are thus realized, but even public credit has been sometimes sustained by skilful Cambists and Negotiators.

A science, therefore, so highly interesting to nations, governments, and individuals, ought to be studied by Statesmen and Travellers, as well as by Merchants and all other persons concerned in foreign trade.

The Introduction to the First Volume of this work contains an Exposition of the Theory of Monies, Coins, Weights and Measures; and the Principles and Laws of Exchange are stated in the leading pages of the second volume; but, with a view to render the science still more easy and accessible, the chief methods of calculation are explained and illustrated in the present Introduction.

In order to study Exchanges with advantage, the following Rules should be well understood, namely—The Rule of Three, direct and inverse, single and compound; Fractions, vulgar and decimal; and the Chain Rule. The last mentioned only seems to require elucidation in this place, as all the rest are sufficiently well explained in books of common arithmetic.*

---

* THE CHAIN RULE (also called the *Rule of Exchange, Conjoint Proportion,* and the *Rule of Reduction,)* is indispensably necessary in the higher operations of Exchange, as well as in arbitrations of bullion, specie, and merchandise; and yet it does not appear to have been explained by English Authors with that attention which its great utility merits. Foreign Merchants are generally very expert in their application of this rule to commercial computations: and it is, in a great measure, to this that their acknowledged superiority in the science of Exchange may be attributed.

The CHAIN RULE consists of a series of terms which bear a certain proportion to each other, and which are accordingly arranged in two adjoining columns: the first to the left called *Antecedents*, and the second to the right called *Consequents*.

The Terms are arranged in the way of equations, and connected, as it were, like the links of a chain: and, however numerous they may be, the same result is obtained by one operation as by several statings in the Rule of Three.

This Rule, being chiefly useful in exchanges, is generally explained by examples of foreign monies, weights, or measures, but as such are seldom well understood by learners, they tend rather to obscure than to elucidate the subject. The following common articles are therefore first chosen as better adapted for illustration.

EXAMPLE I.—If 3 lb. of tea be worth 4 lb. of coffee, and 6 lb. of coffee worth 20 lb. of sugar, how many pounds of sugar may be had for 9 lb. of tea?

First, by the Double Rule of Three.

	lb. Tea.		lb. Coffee.		lb. Tea.		lb. Coffee.
As	3	:	4	: :	9	:	12

and

	lb. Coffee.		lb. Sugar.		lb. Coffee.		lb. Sugar.
As	6	:	20	: :	12	:	40

Hence, 9lb. of tea are worth 40lb. of sugar.

SOLUTION BY THE CHAIN RULE.

Distinguish the several Terms into Antecedents and Consequents, in the following manner:—

1. Enter on the right the given sum or Term on which the operation is to be performed, (which in the foregoing question is 9lb. of tea,) and call this the *Term of Demand.*

2 On the left of this term, and a step lower, enter the first Antecedent, which must be of the *same kind or name as the Term of Demand, and of the same value as the annexed Consequent*; thus, (according to the question,) 3lb. of tea = 4lb. of coffee.

3. In the same manner, let the second Antecedent be of the same name as

the second Consequent, and of the same value as the third Consequent; and so on for any given number of Terms: thus, 6 lb. of coffee = 20 lb. of sugar.

4. The Terms being thus arranged, divide the product of the Consequents by the Product of the Antecedents, and the quotient will be the answer in the denomination of the *last Consequent*. Thus

		9 lb. tea.
3 lb. tea	=	4 lb. coffee.
6 lb. coffee	=	20 lb. sugar.

Hence $\dfrac{20 \times 4 \times 9}{6 \times 3} = \dfrac{720}{18} = 40$ lb. of sugar,—the answer.

By the above example it will be seen, that, in the arrangement of Antecedents and Consequents, each article is twice entered, except that sort in which the answer is required, and which is called the ***Odd Term.*** Here sugar is the Odd Term, and the answer must be in this denomination.

It should be also observed that no two entries of one denomination are in the same column; and, as they are placed in the way of equations, it is manifest that the quantities on both sides, which are equal to one another, are cancelled in the operation; and, therefore, the quotient or answer will be evidently in the denomination of the Odd Term, or last Consequent.

Proof of the Chain Rule.

This Rule may be proved by reversing the operation, that is, by what is called the *Doctrine of Contraries*, beginning with the Answer as the Term of Demand, and making the last Consequent correspond with the first Antecedent. Thus—

		40 lb. sugar.
20 lb. sugar		6 lb. coffee.
4 lb. coffee	*	3 lb. tea.

Then $\dfrac{40 \times 6 \times 3}{20 \times 4} = \dfrac{3 \times 3}{1 \times 1} = 9$ lb. of tea.

The operation of reducing a statement in this Rule may be abridged by striking out the same numbers when they occur in both columns, or by re-

* The above zigzag line is introduced to exemplify a method sometimes used for connecting the terms of a statement, and is therefore called the *Chain*. Its utility is obvious.

ducing them to a lower denomination where they admit of a common measure or divisor, as in reducing a vulgar fraction to its lowest terms.*

The Chain Rule exemplified by an Operation in Reduction, and also in the Single Rule of Three.

EXAMPLE II.—Let it be required to reduce £2 into farthings, supposing the pound = 20 shillings, the shilling = 12 pence, and the penny = 4 farthings.

		2 Pounds,—Term of Demand.
1 Pound	=	20 Shillings.
1 Shilling	=	12 Pence.
1 Penny	=	4 Farthings,—Odd Term.

Hence, $\frac{2 \times 20 \times 12 \times 4}{1 \times 1 \times 1} = 1920$ Farthings.

These farthings may be reduced to pounds by reversing the operation as before; that is, by making 1920 the Term of Demand, and £2 the Odd Term.

EXAMPLE III.—Let it be required to find the value of 7 yards of cloth, if 3 yards of the same be worth 45 shillings.

7 Yards,—Term of demand.
3 Yards = 45 Shillings,—Odd term.

Hence, $\frac{45 \times 7}{3} = 105s.$

From the above examples the principle of the Chain Rule is obvious, and it may be further demonstrated by an algebraic equation.

Thus, suppose x = the number of Shillings sought,
then x = the value of 7 Yards.
and 3 Yards = 45 Shillings.
Hence, $3x = 45 \times 7 = 315$

$$x = \frac{315}{3} = 105s.$$

Or thus,

As 3 : 45 :: 7 : x
Hence, $3x = 315$ and $x = 105s.$

* In finding a common measure it may be useful to observe the following properties of numbers:—

A number is divisible by 2, if the last figure be even; it is divisible by 4, if the two last figures be divisible by 4; and it is divisible by 8, if the three last figures be divisible by 8.

A number is divisible by 3, if the sum of the digits be divisible by 3; it is divisible by 6, if the last figure of such sum be even; and it is divisible by 9, if the sum of the digits be divisible by 9.

Every number is divisible by 5, if the last figure be a 5 or a cipher; and all ciphers may be equally suppressed at once from the Antecedents and Consequents.

The following investigation of the Chain Rule may be considered more comprehensive than the foregoing:

Suppose A, B, C, D, &c. to be several sorts of goods; and $m, n, p, q,$ &c. given numbers; and the value of these goods are,

Antecedents.		Consequents.
m A	=	n B
p B	=	q C
r C	=	s D
t D	=	v E

To find what quantity of the last sort is equal to a given quantity of the first; and the reverse.

Let z times the last $= y$ times the first; that is, let $z\text{E} = y\text{A}$.

Multiply all these equations together; the first side by the first, and the second by the second. Then we have $m\text{A} \times p\text{B} \times r\text{C} \times t\text{D} \times z\text{E} = n\text{B} \times q\text{C} \times s\text{D} \times v\text{E} \times y\text{A}$. Whence $mprtz = nqsvy$. Then if the quantity of the last sort be required, $z = \frac{nqsvy}{mprt}$. But if the quantity of the first sort be sought, $y = \frac{mprtz}{nqsv}$.

Whence the following general Rule, which is, in substance, that already given.

General Rule.

Place the Terms in two columns, so that there may not be two of a sort in either column. Divide the product of the numbers in the column which has the Odd Term, and the Term of Demand, by the product of the numbers in the other column. The quotient is the quantity of that sort which stands single.

It should be noticed that in the above demonstration there is no Term of Demand, as in the preceding examples; for here that Term is understood to be unity, and it may be placed over either column, according to the conditions of the question; observing that the product of the Terms of such column must be always the dividend.

It may be also remarked that the Term of Demand is, by some Authors, placed under the Consequents, instead of making it the first link of the chain, as in the present work. In both cases the results are the same; but there is this advantage in placing it above, that it serves as a direction to the first Antecedent, which must be of the same denomination.

By the Chain Rule the Proportions or Ratios between the Weights and Measures of different places may be thus determined:

EXAMPLE IV.—Suppose 10 lb. of London = 11 lb. of Rome, and 26 Marks of Spain = 16 lb. of London, what is the Ratio between the Roman Pound and the Spanish Mark?

		1 lb. Rome.
11 lb. Rome	=	10 lb. London.
16 lb. London	=	26 Marks Spain.

Hence $\frac{1 \times 10 \times 26}{11 \times 16} = \frac{65}{44}$. Therefore 44 lb. of Rome = 65 Marks of Spain.

Or thus, let R = Rome, L = London, and S = Spain; then per question,

$$11\,R = 10\,L, \text{ and } 26\,S = 16\,L.$$

Hence $L = \frac{26\,S}{16}$ and $L = \frac{11\,R}{10} \therefore \frac{11\,R}{10} = \frac{26\,S}{16}$ and $176\,R = 260\,S$, or $44\,R = 65\,S$.

EXAMPLE V.—Required the Proportion between the Metre of France and the Foot of Cremona, supposing that 48 of the latter = 56 English Feet, and that the Metre = 39,371 English Inches?

		1 Foot of Cremona.
48 Feet Cremona	=	56 Feet English.
1 Foot English	=	12 Inches.
39,371 Inches	=	1 Metre.

Result, $\frac{14}{39,371}$. Hence 14 Metres = 39,371 Feet, or 1 Metre = 2,812 Feet.

In determining Ratios of this kind, it is indifferent which of the Numbers to be compared is made the Leading Term; but when a given quantity or sum of money is to be reduced to another, it should be made the first consequent.

EXAMPLE VI.—Required the sterling value of a Kilogramme of Gold, $\frac{9}{10}$ fine, at £4 per Ounce Troy, $\frac{11}{12}$ fine?

		1 Kilogramme.
1 Kilogramme	=	15434 Troy Grains.
480 Grains	=	1 Ounce.
10 Ounces Fr. stand.	=	9 Ounces fine.
11 Ounces fine	=	12 English standard.
1 Ounce Eng. stand.	=	4 Pounds.

Result, £126 : 5 : 6

The Chain Rule exemplified by Foreign Monies.

Suppose £1000 sterling is to be remitted to Cadiz, and the direct Exchange is 40d. sterling per Piastre or Dollar of Exchange, but the Remitter wishes to send it through Holland and France; it is required to know which is the most advantageous, the direct or indirect Remittance; the Quotation of the Course of Exchange being as follows?—

London on Amsterdam, 10 Florins 10 Stivers per Pound sterling.
Amsterdam on Paris, 60 Pence Flemish for the Ecu of 3 Francs.
Paris on Cadiz, 15 Francs for 1 Doubloon of 4 Dollars of Exchange.

STATEMENT.

		£1000 Sterling.
1 Pound Sterling	=	$10\frac{1}{2}$ Florins.
1 Florin	=	40 Pence Flemish.
60 Pence Flemish	=	3 Francs.
15 Francs	=	1 Doubloon.
1 Doubloon	=	4 Dollars.

$$\text{Hence } \frac{1000 \times 10{,}5 \times 40 \times 3 \times 4}{60 \times 15} = \frac{50400}{9} = 5600 \text{ Dollars.}$$

PROOF.

		5600 Dollars.
4 Dollars	=	1 Doubloon.
1 Doubloon	=	15 Francs.
3 Francs	=	60 Pence Flemish.
40 Pence Flemish	=	1 Florin.
$10\frac{1}{2}$ Florins	=	1 Pound Sterling.

$$\text{Hence } \frac{5600 \times 15 \times 60}{4 \times 3 \times 40 \times 10{,}5} = \frac{5040000}{5040} = 1000 \text{ Pounds Sterling.}$$

From this operation it appears that, by the indirect exchange, £1000 sterling will produce 5600 Dollars, which gives the Dollar at $42\frac{6}{7}$d. sterling.

Thus, the direct exchange is more profitable than the indirect to the *Remitter*, because he would obtain 6000 Dollars at 40*d.* each; whereas, by the circular remittance, he could receive only 5600: while, on the contrary, the indirect exchange would be most advantageous to the *Drawer* in the same proportion. But these different interests will be more fully exemplified under the article *Arbitration of Exchange.*

*New Arrangement of the Chain Rule.**

From the foregoing Examples it is obvious that the terms of the Chain Rule may be arranged horizontally, in the way of Fractions, making the Consequents the numerators and the Antecedents their denominators respectively; and the result may then be determined by multiplication; that is, by the common operation of reducing a compound fraction to an equivalent simple one.

Thus, let the Term of Demand be the numerator of the first fraction, observing that its denominator be of the same kind, and equal in value to the second numerator: the denominator of the second, of the same kind as its numerator, and of the same value as the third numerator; and so on until you arrive at the numerator of the kind sought, which is the Odd Term, and which is, of course, without a denominator.

This may be exemplified by the foregoing problem, p. xi.

Thus, let $x =$ the number sought,

$$\text{Then } x = \overset{\text{£ sterl.}}{\frac{1000}{1}} \times \overset{\text{S.Flem.}}{\frac{35}{1}} \times \overset{\text{D.Flem.}}{\frac{12}{60}} \times \overset{\text{Fr.}}{\frac{3}{15}} \times \overset{\text{Doub.}}{\frac{1}{1}} \times \overset{\text{Doll.}}{\frac{4}{\ }} = \overset{\text{Doll.}}{5600}.$$

Reverse operation.

$$x = \overset{\text{Doll.}}{\frac{5600}{4}} \times \overset{\text{Doub.}}{\frac{1}{1}} \times \overset{\text{Fr.}}{\frac{15}{3}} \times \overset{\text{D.Flem.}}{\frac{60}{12}} \times \overset{\text{S.Flem.}}{\frac{1}{35}} \times \overset{\text{£ st.}}{\frac{1}{\ }} = 1000.$$

* This method of arranging the Chain Rule has been recently published at Paris, in *M. Soulet's Exchanges*, edited by *M. Garnier*. The following is his *Formula:*

$$x = \frac{a}{a'} \;/\!/\; \frac{b}{b'} \;/\!/\; \frac{c}{c'} \;/\!/\; \frac{d}{\ } \text{ \&c.}$$

By this Formula it is understood that a is the Term of Demand. Also, that a' is of the same kind as a, and in equation with b; that b' is of the same kind as b, and in equation with c; that c' is of the same kind as c, and in equation with d, and so on.

The signs of equality diagonally placed denote the equality between each denominator and the following numerator. The signs, however, of multiplication in the preceding examples seem to be equally proper.

This new method of arrangement is obviously more concise than the old; but what it gains in brevity it perhaps loses in perspicuity. It may, however, be sometimes used with advantage especially by persons who understand the old method.

Another kind of fractional arrangement is given in *Lacroix's Arithmetic*, where the denominators are removed each one place to the right. The following is his method (adopting *Garnier's* symbols)—

$$x = \frac{a}{\ } \times \frac{b}{a'} \times \frac{c}{b'} \times \frac{d}{c'} \text{ \&c.}$$

THE USE OF LOGARITHMS AND FIXED NUMBERS IN BULLION AND EXCHANGE OPERATIONS.

Although the application of Logarithms and Fixed Numbers in Exchange Calculations is explained in the present volume, p. 129, yet some additional illustrations and examples may be useful in this part of the work.

The use of Logarithms in all sciences is to diminish labour, as they perform by addition and subtraction what is obtained by the multiplication and division of common numbers. Hence, in the reduction of a statement of the Chain Rule, *if the Logarithms of the Consequents be added together, and from this sum the amount of the Logarithms of the Antecedents be subtracted, the difference will be the Logarithm of the answer.*

Or, *the same result may be obtained by adding to the said sum of the Consequents the arithmetical complement of the said sum of the Antecedents*, rejecting *ten* in the Index.

Tables of Logarithms are inserted in some books of exchange adapted to the subject; that is, there are negative Logarithms for fractional quantities, as well as positive for whole and mixed numbers; but all such may be deduced from the common tables, by the rules generally given. Thus, the Logarithm of a vulgar fraction is found by *reducing* it *to a decimal;* or by *subtracting the Logarithm of the Denominator from that of the Numerator.** *(See Dr. Hutton's Mathematical Tables, p.* 132.)

When fractions occur in the Chain Rule, the most convenient method is to convert them into whole numbers, by *multiplying the fractional quantity by the denominator, and also any term in the other column by the same figure.* Thus, an antecedent of $\frac{7}{12}$, and a consequent of 9 may stand 7 and 108, without altering the ratio. Or, 5 and $11\frac{3}{4}$ may be converted to 20 and 47. This method of clearing a statement of fractions greatly simplifies the operation; and when Logarithms are used there is no advantage in bringing terms to low denominations, unless such may be reduced to unity or expunged altogether; as it is as easy to find the Logarithm of a large number as of a small one.

---

* Tables of Logarithms, adapted to Exchanges and other commercial purposes, have been published by *Gerhardt,* of Berlin; *Reishammer* of Paris; and by *Bonhote, Dubost,* and *Preston,* of London.

Fixed Numbers are of great utility in exchanges, whether they are used as Logarithms or not. They are peculiarly convenient in bullion operations where the same kind of questions daily occur, as will be exemplified in the remaining part of this Introduction. But before the following Examples are studied, the Rules of Arbitration (p. 107) should be well understood.

In every long statement by the Chain Rule there are several constant or invariable proportions, as the number of shillings in a Pound, or of Penny-weights in an Ounce; and these may, by the rule of Reduction, be converted into one number only, which is called *Fixed.* Thus, in the foregoing example, p. xi., the figures 12, 3, and 4, are constant, and the Fixed Number thence obtained is 144, which, reduced with the other numbers, will give the solution 16 × 50 × 7 = 5600.

In Example VI. page x. there is but one variable number; viz. £4, the price of an ounce of gold; and if the product of the other consequents be divided by that of the antecedents, the result will be 31,569, which will serve as a Fixed Number for all such questions; and this, multiplied by the price per ounce, will give the answer; thus, 31,569 × £4 = £126.276.

Now if the same Kilogramme had been bought at Paris for 3156 Francs 90 Centimes, the ratio between those two prices would give the *Course of Exchange:* for as 126,276 : 3156,90 : : £1 : 25 Fr. Thus the rate would be 25 Francs for 1 Pound sterling; but it should be observed that although the price of Bullion and the Course of Exchange generally regulate each other, yet extraordinary demands cause variations in their computed proportions, which variations, however, have a general tendency to correct themselves.

In Bullion operations the following proportions will be found useful:

		Eng. Oz. Troy.
60 Marks of Hamburgh or Cologne	=	451
80 Marks of Amsterdam	=	633
61 Oz. Paris, Poids de Marc	=	60
1 Kilogramme	=	32,154
31,1 Grammes	=	1
5 Marks of Spain, or 250 Castellanos	=	37
8 Marks of Portugal	=	59
144 Oz. of Leghorn, or Florence	=	131
100 Oz. of Naples	=	86
11 Oz. of Rome	=	10

		Oz. Eng. Stand. fineness.
1000 Spanish Dollars = 866 oz. Troy	=	835
1000 Doubloons = 868 oz. Troy	=	853
1000 Joanese, or Ports	=	460
55 English ounces French Gold	=	54
37 Ditto French Silver	=	36
19 Marks fine Silver, Amsterdam	=	164
34 Marks of Hamburgh Ducats	=	273
8 Marks fine Silver of Hamburgh	=	65
111 Oz. of Dollars	=	107
48 Oz. of do. = 43 oz. of fine Silver.		

GOLD IN BARS.

To calculate the Course of Exchange from the Price of Bullion, and the contrary. Also to find Fixed Numbers for the Solution of such Questions.

EXAMPLE I.—When Gold is sold at Hamburgh at 104 Sols banco per Ducat of $23\frac{1}{2}$ Carats fine, and at London at 78s. 2d. per standard Ounce, what should be the Course of Exchange, supposing that 67 Ducats make 1 Cologne Mark fine, and that 60 Marks weigh 451 Ounces Troy?

		1 Pound sterling.
1 Pound sterling	=	20 Shillings.
$78\frac{1}{6}$ Shillings sterling	=	1 Ounce standard.
451 Ounces standard	=	60 Marks standard.
47 Marks $\frac{44}{48}$	=	44 Marks $\frac{47}{48}$.
1 Mark	=	67 Ducats.
1 Ducat	=	104 Shillings Lubs Banco.
6 Shillings Lubs B°.	=	1 Shilling Flemish.

As the prices of gold are the only variable numbers in the above statement, the Fixed Number may be thus determined:

$$\frac{20 \times 60 \times 44 \times 67}{451 \times 47} = 27{,}815, \text{ the Fixed Number.}$$

Hence, $27{,}815 \times 104 \div 78\frac{1}{6} = 37$ Shillings, Flemish (the Course of Exchange) for £1 sterling.

By the above Fixed Number, with the course of exchange and the price of bullion in one place, it is plain that its price may be found in the other place.

EXAMPLE II.—When Gold is sold at Amsterdam at an advance of 17 per cent. on the Tarif price of 355 Florins per Mark fine, and in London at 78s. per standard Ounce, what is the Course of Exchange, supposing that 80 Marks of Amsterdam weigh 633 Ounces English Troy?

		1 Pound sterling.
1 Pound sterling	=	20 Shillings.
78 Shillings	=	1 Ounce standard.
12 Ounces stand.	=	11 Ounces fine.
633 Ounces fine	=	80 Marks of Amsterdam.
1 Mark	=	355 Florins.
100 Florins	=	117 with the Premium.

The invariable numbers in the above statement are

$\frac{20 \times 11 \times 80 \times 355}{12 \times 633 \times 100} = 3{,}225$ the Fixed Number, which $\times\ 117 \div 78 = 12$ Fl. $6\frac{3}{4}$ St. or 41s. 1d. Flemish per Pound sterling, the Course of Exchange.

EXAMPLE III.—What is the Course of Exchange between Paris and London resulting from the price of Gold; viz. 8 per Mille premium on the Tarif-price, (see vol. i. p. 142,) and 78s. per Ounce English standard?

			1	Pound sterling.
1	Pound sterling	=	20	Shillings.
78	Shillings	=	1	Ounce standard.
12	Ounces standard	=	11	Ounces fine.
32,154	Ounces fine	=	1	Kilogramme fine.
1	Kilogramme fine	=	3434 f. 44 c.	Tarif price.
100	Francs	=	100,8	with the Premium.

The invariable numbers in the above statement are $\frac{20 \times 11 \times 3434\text{ f. }44}{12 \times 32{,}154 \times 100} = 19{,}5823$, the Fixed Number.

Hence $19{,}582 \times 100{,}8 \div 78 = 25$ fr. 30 c. per Pound Sterling, the Course of Exchange.

EXAMPLE IV.—If the price of Gold at Cadiz be 30 Reals per Castellano of $\frac{22\frac{1}{2}}{24}$ fine; and in London 934½d. per ounce standard, (the Mint price,) what is the Course of Exchange, &c.?

		1	Piastre.
1 Piastre	=	8	Reals.
30 Reals	=	1	Castellano.
44 Castellanos $\frac{45}{48}$	=	45	Castellanos $\frac{44}{48}$.
250 Castellanos	=	37	Ounces Troy.
1 Ounce	=	934½	Pence.

Reduced, gives the Course of Exchange = 37¾d. per Piastre.

The invariable Numbers are $\frac{8 \times 45 \times 37}{44 \times 250} = 14{,}531$, the Fixed Number.

EXAMPLE V.—If Gold be sold at Lisbon for 1700 Rees per Outava of $\frac{22}{24}$ fine, and in London at the Mint price, what is the Course of Exchange?

		1	Milree.
1 Milree	=	1000	Rees.
1700 Rees	=	1	Outava.
64 Outavas	=	1	Mark.
8 Marks	=	59	Ounces Troy.
1 Ounce	=	934½	Pence.

Reduced, gives 63⅓d. per Milree, the Course of Exchange.

The invariable Numbers are $\frac{1000 \times 59}{64 \times 8} = 115{,}234$, the Fixed Number.

EXAMPLE VI.—If the price of Gold at Leghorn be 108 Lire per Ounce fine, and in London the Mint price, what is the Course of Exchange, &c.?

		1	Pezza.
4 × 1 Pezza	=	$5\frac{3}{4}$	Lire × 4 = 23.
108 Lire	=	1	Ounce fine of Leghorn.
144 Oz. of Leghorn	=	131	Ounce of London.
11 Oz. fine	=	12	Ounces standard.
1 Oz. standard	=	$934\frac{1}{2}$	Pence.

Reduced, gives 49,37d. per Pezza, the Course of Exchange.

The invariable Numbers are $\frac{23 \times 131 \times 12}{4 \times 144 \times 11} = 5,706$, the Fixed Numbers.

The foregoing Examples solved by Logarithms.

Hamburgh,	Fixed Number,....	27,815	Log.......	1,44428
	Hamburgh Price,..	104	Log.......	2,01703
	London Price, ...	$78\frac{1}{6}$	Ar. Com.*	8,10798
	Course of Exchange	37,091	Log.......	1,56929
Amsterdam,	Fixed Number,....	8,225	Log.......	0,91514
	Amsterdam Price,..	117	Log.......	2,06819
	London Price, ...	78	Ar. Com.	8,10790
	Course of Exchange,	12,338	Log.......	1,09123
Paris,	Fixed Number,....	19,582	Log.......	9,29186
	Paris Price, ...	100,8	Log.......	3,00346
	London Price, ...	78	Ar. Com.	8,10790
	Course of Exchange,	25,30	Log.......	1,40322
Cadiz,	Fixed Number,....	1,201	Log.......	0,08310
	London Price,......	934,5	Log.......	2,97057
	Cadiz Price, ...	30	Ar. Com.	8,52287
	Course of Exchange,	37,72	Log.......	1,57654

* The Arithmetical Complement is found by subtracting the Logarithm of the given Number from 10, and thus the operation is performed by addition only, and with four rows of figures instead of five. See p. 130.

Lisbon,	Fixed Number, ...	115,23	Log.......	2,06156
	London Price,......	934,5	Log.......	2,97057
	Lisbon Price, ...	1700	Ar. Com.	6,76955
	Course of Exchange,	63,34	Log.......	1,80169
Leghorn,	Fixed Number, ...	5,706	Log.......	0,75633
	London Price,......	934,5	Log.......	2,97057
	Leghorn Price, ...	108	Ar. Com.	7,96657
	Course of Exchange,	49,37	Log.......	1,69347

SILVER IN BARS.

To find the Course of Exchange between London and the foregoing Places, resulting from the following Prices of Silver, viz.

Hamburgh,..........	27 Marks Banco, per Cologne Mark fine.
Amsterdam, ...	26 Florins, per Mark fine.
Paris,..............	3 per Cent. Premium on the Tarif price of 218 Fr. 89 c. per Kilogramme fine.
Cadiz,..............	108 Reals of Plate, per Mark fine.
Lisbon, ...	990 Rees, per Ounce fine.
Leghorn, ...	84 Lire, per Libra of 12 Ounces fine.
London,...........	58 Pence, per Ounce $\frac{37}{40}$ fine.

STATEMENTS AND RESULTS, (see p. xii. and xiv. also p. 19, Vol. II.)

	£ ster.		Pence.		Oz. stan.		Oz. fine.		Mks.		Mks Bo.		S.Flem.	Course of Ex.	Fixed Num.
Hamburgh,..	$\frac{1}{1}$	×	$\frac{240}{58}$	×	$\frac{1}{40}$	×	$\frac{37}{451}$	×	$\frac{60}{1}$	×	$\frac{27}{3}$	×	$\frac{8}{}$	= 36,66	78,758
Amsterdam,.	$\frac{1}{1}$	×	$\frac{240}{58}$	×	$\frac{1}{40}$	×	$\frac{37}{633}$	×	$\frac{80}{1}$	×	$\frac{26}{}$ Flor.			= 12,57	28,057
Paris,.....	$\frac{1}{1}$	×	$\frac{240}{58}$	×	$\frac{1}{40}$	×	$\frac{37}{32,154}$	×	$\frac{218,89}{100}$	×	$\frac{103}{}$			= 26,83	15,113
	Piastre.		Reals.		Mks.		Mks fine.		Oz. st.		Pence.				
Cadiz,.....	$\frac{1}{1}$	×	$\frac{8}{104}$	×	$\frac{1}{5}$	×	$\frac{37}{37}$	×	$\frac{40}{1}$	×	$\frac{58}{}$			= 37,72	64,000
	Milree.		Rees.		Oz.		Oz. fine.		Oz. st.		Pence.				
Lisbon, ...	$\frac{1}{1}$	×	$\frac{1000}{990}$	×	$\frac{1}{64}$	×	$\frac{59}{37}$	×	$\frac{40}{1}$	×	$\frac{58}{}$			= 58,38	996,621
	Pezza.		Lire.		Oz. Leg.		Oz. Tr.		Oz. st.		Pence.				
Leghorn,....	$\frac{1}{1}$	×	$\frac{5\frac{3}{4}}{84}$	×	$\frac{12}{144}$	×	$\frac{131}{37}$	×	$\frac{40}{1}$	×	$\frac{58}{}$			= 46,85	67,860

There are three variable numbers in each of the foregoing statements; viz. the price of Foreign Bullion, the London Price, and the Course of Exchange. Now, it is obvious that if any two of these prices be given, the third may thence be found by the help of the Fixed Number. Suppose, for example, in the last statement respecting Paris, that $F =$ the Fixed Number, $p =$ the Paris price, $l =$ the London price, and $c =$ the Course of Exchange, then c, l, or p, may be found, the rest being known. Thus

$$c = \frac{Fp}{l} = \frac{15{,}113 \times 103}{58} = 26{,}83 \text{ Francs for the £1 sterling.}$$

$$l = \frac{Fp}{c} = \frac{15{,}113 \times 103}{26{,}83} = 58 \text{ Pence per Ounce sterling.}$$

$$p = \frac{c\,l}{F} = \frac{26{,}83 \times 58}{15{,}113} = 103 \text{ Francs per Kilogramme fine.}$$

The above Equations will answer for all other places to which London gives the certain, (see p. 13, vol. ii.) but where it gives the uncertain, as to Cadiz, the following will be the Formulæ, supposing s to represent the Spanish or Cadiz price.

$$c = \frac{Fl}{s} = \frac{64 \times 58}{104} = 37{,}72 \text{ Pence per Piastre.}$$

$$s = \frac{Fl}{c} = \frac{64 \times 58}{37{,}72} = 104 \text{ Reals per Mark.}$$

$$l = \frac{s\,c}{F} = \frac{104 \times 37{,}72}{64} = 58 \text{ Pence per Ounce.}$$

These Formulæ will apply to operations in Gold as well as Silver, always reckoning the prices in the denominations here laid down; and where the calculations are laborious Logarithms may be introduced with advantage, but, in ordinary cases, common numbers seem more convenient and intelligible.

When speculations are made in Coins, the readiest method is to find their pure contents from the Table of Assays in the present Volume, p. 157.

ERRATA.—(Vol. II.)

Page xii. lines 17 and 20, for 35*s*. Flemish, read $10\frac{1}{2}$ Florins, and for 12*d*. Flemish, read 40*d*. Flemish.

47, line 5, for 3 Pfenings, read 18.

49, Francfort Exchange, for 75, &c. read 3 per cent. which is an agio or discount in comparing 23 Florins with 60 Livres.

75, column 1, line 10, after 34, insert × 2,312.

95, line 9, for 30,467, read 20,467.

Page 142, line 25, for 62 Pence, read $934\frac{1}{2}$.

142, line 26, for 40 Ounces standard, read 12; and for 37 Ounces fine Silver, read 11 Ounces fine Gold.

143, line 12, for 73 Centimes, read 75.

222, Florence, for 339,542, read 339,510.

226, Milan, for 594,530, read 59,453; and for 665,874, read 66,587.

232, Salonica Killow, for 1184 Cubic Inches, read 11840.

N.B. It is recommended that the above Errors be corrected with the Pen before the Work is consulted on any Question of Business.

TABLE OF CONTENTS.

VOLUME II.

EXCHANGE.

EXCHANGE is the act of paying or receiving the money of one country for its equivalent in the money of another country, by means of Bills of Exchange. This operation, therefore, comprehends both the reduction of monies and the negotiation of bills; it determines the comparative value of the currencies of all nations; and shows how foreign debts are discharged, loans and subsidies paid, and other remittances made from one country to another, without the risk, trouble, or expense of transporting specie or bullion. Exchange.

The subject is here considered under the four following heads:—

1.—*Bills of Exchange;* with customs, laws, and regulations relating to the same.

2.—*Principles of Exchange;* comprehending the *Par of Exchange*, with various views of the subject; and the *Course of Exchange*, with the common causes of its fluctuation.

3.—*Monies of Exchange;* with the quotations explained, and rules and examples of calculation.

4.—*Arbitration of Exchange;* with rules and examples for negotiating bills to the greatest advantage: also operations in specie, bullion, and merchandize.

I.—BILLS OF EXCHANGE.

A BILL of Exchange is a written order for the payment of a certain sum of money at an appointed time. It is a mercantile contract, in which four persons are mostly concerned, *viz.* Bills of Exchange.

1.—The *Drawer*, who receives the value, and is also called the *Maker* and *Seller* of the Bill.

Bills of Exchange.

2.—His debtor in a distant place, upon whom the Bill is drawn, and who is called the *Drawee.* He also is called the *Acceptor*, when he accepts the Bill, which is an engagement to pay it when due.

3.—The person who gives value for the Bill, who is called the *Buyer*, *Taker*, and *Remitter*.

4.—The person to whom it is ordered to be paid, who is called the *Payee*, and who may, by indorsement, pass it to any other person.

Most mercantile payments are made in Bills of Exchange, which generally pass from hand to hand, until due, like any other circulating medium; and the person who at any time has a Bill in his possession, is called the *Holder*.

When the Holder of a Bill disposes of it, he writes his name on the back, which is called *Indorsing*; and the Payee should be the first Indorser. If the Bill be indorsed in favour of any particular person, it is called a *Special Indorsement*, and the person to whom it is thus made payable is called the *Indorsee*, who must also indorse the Bill if he negotiates it. Any person may indorse a Bill, and every Indorser (as well as the Acceptor or Payee) is a security for the Bill, and may therefore be sued for payment.

The *Term* of a Bill varies, according to the agreement between the parties, or the custom of countries. Some Bills are drawn at sight; others at a certain number of days or months after sight or after date; and some at *Usance*, which is the customary or usual term between different places.

Days of Grace are a certain number of days granted to the Acceptor after the term of a Bill is expired. In the British Dominions, three days are allowed.

In reckoning when a Bill, payable after *date*, becomes due, the day on which it is dated is not included; and if it be a Bill payable after *sight*, the day of presentment is not included. When the term is expressed in months, calendar months are understood; and when a month is longer than the succeeding, it is a rule not to go, in the computation, into a third month. Thus, if a Bill be dated the 28th, 29th, 30th, or 31st of January, and payable one month after date, the term equally expires on the last day of February, to which the days of grace must, of course, be added; and, therefore, the Bill becomes due on the 3d of March.

No Bill of Exchange drawn in Great Britain or Ireland can be negotiated, presented for payment, or in any way admitted as good in these countries, that is not written on a proper stamp; and any person drawing, accepting, or paying such a Bill, is liable to a penalty.

LAWS OF EXCHANGE.

The following Laws have been selected from the first legal authorities, and likewise examined and approved by several experienced Merchants, Bankers, and Notaries; and though these Laws apply chiefly to the British Dominions, yet they do not differ essentially from the regulations of other commercial Countries, with respect to ACCEPTING, INDORSING, PAYING, PROTESTING, *and* RECOVERING BILLS.

ACCEPTING BILLS.

WHEN a Bill is presented for acceptance, it is generally left until the next day; and the common way of accepting is for the Drawee to write his name at the bottom or across the body of the Bill, with the word *accepted.* An acceptance, however, in a slighter way, has been heretofore deemed binding; thus had the Drawee written his name upon any part of the Bill, or the initials of his name, or the day of the month, or merely the word *accepted,* he was considered liable; but by an Act of Parliament passed in 1819, it was declared, "that no person shall be bound or charged as Acceptor of an Inland or Foreign Bill of Exchange, otherwise than by an acceptance of such Bill of Exchange written thereon or on some one part of such Bill, if the same shall consist of more than one part." Accepting Bills.

When two or more persons are in partnership, the acceptance of one binds all the others, if the Bill concerns their joint trade; but if it should be made known to the person who receives the Bill that it concerns the Acceptor only in a distinct interest, he alone, as Acceptor, can be sued.

A clerk, or servant, may accept a Bill for his master, when he has authority for that purpose, or if he usually transacts business of this nature for him; and his acceptance binds the master.

But if the Bill be drawn nominally on the servant, directing him to place it to the account of his master, and if the servant should accept it generally, without specifying that he does it for his master's account, the acceptance binds the servant only, and not his employer.

Accepting Bills.

When a Bill is drawn for the account of a third person, and is accepted as such, and he fails without making provision for its payment, the Acceptor must discharge the Bill, and can have no recourse against the Drawer.

A Bill may be accepted to be paid at a longer period than is mentioned in the Bill, or to pay a part of the sum only: such an acceptance is binding on him who makes it; but the Holder is at liberty to take it as it is offered, or to act as if acceptance had been entirely refused.

The acceptance may direct payment to be made at a place different from that mentioned in the Bill, as at the house of a banker; in which case, if the Holder should neglect to demand payment within a reasonable time, and the banker should afterwards fail, the Holder must sustain the loss.

When a Bill has been once accepted, the acceptance cannot be revoked, though the Drawer should be found to have failed before the date of the acceptance.

INDORSING BILLS.

Indorsing Bills.

Bills payable to bearer are transferred by simple delivery, and without any indorsement; but, in order to transfer a Bill payable to order, the Holder must express his order of paying to another person, which is always done by an indorsement.

An indorsement may be blank or special. A *blank indorsement* consists only of the Indorser's name, and the Bill then becomes transferable by simple delivery; a *special indorsement* orders the money to be paid to some particular person, or to his order: a blank indorsement may always be filled up with any person's name, so as to make it special.

An indorsement may take place at any time after the Bill is issued, even after the day of payment is elapsed.

A person who receives a Bill with a blank indorsement may take it as Indorsee, negotiate it again, or demand payment on his own account, or he may receive the money as agent, or for the account of the Indorser; and the latter, notwithstanding his indorsement, may still appear as Holder in an action against the Drawer or Acceptor.

A special indorsement needs not contain the words, *to order*, and the Bill is negotiable; it may also be restrictive, giving authority to the Indorsee to receive the money for the Indorser, but not transfer the Bill again to another.

An indorsement for part of the money only is not valid, except with regard to him who makes it: the Drawer and Acceptor are not bound by it. Indorsing Bills.

When the Holder of a Bill dies, his Executors may indorse it; but, by so doing, they become answerable to their Indorsee personally, and not as Executors.

PAYING BILLS.

Bills should be presented for payment, as well as for acceptance, during the usual hours of business, which are generally considered to be from nine o'clock in the morning till six in the evening. The common mode of payment among merchants is by a draft on a banker for the exact amount of the Bill, and signed by the Drawee; but any paper whatever may be refused, except Bank of England notes; and the Bank receives no other. Paying Bills.

PROTESTING BILLS.

When acceptance or payment has been refused, the Holder of the Bill should give regular and immediate notice to all the parties, to whom he intends to resort for payment; and if, on account of unnecessary delay, a loss should be incurred by the failure of any of the parties, the Holder must bear the loss. Protesting Bills.

With respect to the manner in which notices of non-acceptance or non-payment are to be given, a difference exists between Inland and Foreign Bills.

For Foreign Bills, a Protest is indispensably necessary: thus a Public Notary is to appear with the Bill, and to demand either acceptance or payment; and on being refused, he is to draw up an instrument, called a Protest, expressing that acceptance or payment has been demanded and refused, and that the Holder of the Bill intends to recover any damages which he may sustain in consequence. This instrument is admitted, in foreign countries, as a legal proof of the fact.

The Protest on a Foreign Bill should be made in time to be sent off on the next post-day to the place where it was drawn or negotiated; and if it be for non-payment, the Bill must be sent with the Protest.

As to Inland Bills, a Protest is not absolutely necessary to entitle the Holder to recover the amount of the Bill from the Drawer or Indorsee: it is sufficient that he give notice, by letter or otherwise, that acceptance or payment has been refused, and that he does not mean to give credit to the Drawee.

Protesting Bills.

According to the practice of the London merchants, a Protest is hardly ever made for non-acceptance of an Inland Bill; it is only noted, and, if not paid when it becomes due, it is then protested for non-payment. Notice, however, must be given of the non-acceptance and noting, otherwise the Holder takes the risk upon himself: and if the Protest for non-payment should be omitted, the Holder cannot recover either damages or interest, but merely the amount of the Bill.

If the person who is to accept has absconded, or cannot be found at the place mentioned in the Bill, Protest is to be made in the same manner as if acceptance had been refused.

When an original Bill is lost, and another cannot be had of the Drawer, a Protest may be made on a copy; but if a Bill left for acceptance be lost, the person with whom it was left must bind himself to payment, or else a Protest may be made out immediately.

It is customary, as a precaution against accident or miscarriage, to draw three copies of a Foreign Bill, and to send them by different posts. They are denominated the *First*, *Second*, and *Third of Exchange;* and when any one of them is paid, the rest become void and of no value.

When the Acceptor of a Bill becomes insolvent, or absconds before the term of payment is expired, the Holder may cause a Notary to demand better security, and, on that being refused, to Protest the Bill for want of it. In such cases, however, the most general practice is to wait the regular time till the Bill becomes due.

The damages incurred by non-acceptance and non-payment, besides interest, consist usually of the exchange, re-exchange, commission, and postage, together with the expenses of protest and interest. The exchange is reckoned according to the course at sight, from the place where the Protest is made to the place where the Bill is to be paid by the Drawer; and if it be not paid there, the re-exchange is then reckoned from the same place to that where the Bill is paid, and also double commission. The interest commences from the day when the demand was made.

After a Bill has been protested, it is sometimes accepted by a third person, to save the reputation of the Drawer, or of an Indorser; such an acceptance is called an acceptance *Supra Protest.* The Acceptor then must appear in person, with witnesses, before a Notary, and declare that he accepts it for the honour of such a person, and subscribe the Bill thus—Accepted, *Supra Protest,* in honour of, &c.

The same may happen when the person on whom a Bill is drawn having doubts about the Drawer, protests it, but afterwards accepts it for the honour of one of the Indorsers; in this case the Protest must be sent to the said Indorser without delay. Protesting Bills.

The person for whose honour a Bill was accepted, must reimburse the Acceptor the amount of the Bill, commission, and other charges, even though the acceptance should have taken place without his knowledge. If such a person approves of the acceptance, the Bill may be paid without any further Protest; but if he should return no answer, or express his disapprobation of the acceptance, the Bill must be formally protested for non-payment against him to whom the Bill was directed; and, on his persisting to refuse payment, the Acceptor may safely pay it for his account, as he can recover the amount.

RECOVERING BILLS.

The Drawer, Acceptor, and every Indorser of a Bill, are equally liable to the payment of it; and though the Holder can have but one satisfaction, yet, until such satisfaction is actually had, he may sue any of them, or all of them, either at the same time or in succession, and obtain judgment against them all, till satisfaction be made. Proceedings cannot be staid in any action, but on payment of the debt and of the costs, not only in that action, but in all the others in which judgment has not been obtained; and though the principal sum should be paid by one of the parties, still costs may be recovered in the several actions against the others. Recovering Bills.

When acceptance is refused, and the Bill is returned by protest, an action may be commenced immediately against the Drawer, though the regular time of payment be not arrived. His debt, in such a case, is considered as contracted the moment the Bill is drawn: thus, if before the Bill is returned, the Drawer should become a bankrupt, the debt was contracted before the commission of bankruptcy took place.

Nothing will discharge an Indorser from his engagement but the absolute payment of the money; not even a judgment recovered against the Drawer or any previous Indorser, or an execution against any of them, unless the money be paid in consequence.

The Holder of a Bill, in order to entitle himself to recover against an Indorser,

Recovering Bills.

needs not show that he has made a previous attempt to recover from the Drawer; and this holds good with regard to Inland as well as Foreign Bills.

If any Bill happens to be lost within the time limited for payment, the Drawer is to give another of the same tenor with the first; the person, however, to whom this new Bill is delivered, must give security to indemnify the Drawer against all persons whatsoever, in case the lost Bill should be found.

When a person has indorsed a Bill, and it is re-indorsed to him, he cannot maintain an action against the person to whom he indorsed it.

He that has accepted and duly paid a Bill, without having in his hands any effects of the Drawer, may recover in an action for money paid and laid out for the use of the Drawer.

In an action against the Acceptor of a Bill, it is a general rule that the Drawer's hand-writing is admitted, because the Acceptor is always supposed to be acquainted with the hand-writing of the person whose Bill he accepts. But if the same Bill has been indorsed, the hand-writing of the Indorser or Indorsers must be proved; in case of a blank indorsement, however, the hand-writing of the first Indorser is sufficient. The same takes place in an action by an Indorser against the Drawer.

Proof of the signature of a servant is sufficient to bind the master, when it is proved that the servant has authority to draw, accept, or indorse Bills in his master's name; and a subsequent assent is considered as evidence of such authority. A general custom of the servant's signature and the payment of the master is likewise a sufficient proof of a general authority; and this will continue to bind the master until his determination to the contrary can be generally known.

PROMISSORY NOTES.

Promissory Notes.

Promissory Notes are, in general, considered in the same light as Inland Bills of Exchange: the resemblance between them is greatest when a Promissory Note is indorsed; for such an indorsement is an order to the maker of the Note to pay the sum mentioned in it to a third person. Thus the first Indorser of the Note corresponds to the Drawer of the Bill, and the Maker to the Acceptor; and in that sense all the laws relating to Bills of Exchange may be applied to Promissory Notes; and they have the same allowance of three days' grace for payment.

When the form of a Bill or Promissory Note is incontestably good, the law is the same for both; yet a Note may be valid in some cases, when a Bill of Exchange is not so: thus a Promissory Note can be made payable out of a particular fund then within the power of the Drawer; neither is it necessary that the time of payment of a Note should be absolutely fixed: thus, Notes have been held to be good which were payable at a certain person's death, or after such a ship should be paid off; in short, at the period of an event physically or morally certain; but should the payment depend on a contingency which may never happen, as if it were payable when such a person should marry, the Note cannot be accounted good. Promissory Notes.

BONDS.

A Bond for money is a higher security than a Bill of Exchange or a Promissory Note, as it binds the giver, his heirs and lands, in the first instance; whereas Bills and Notes attach only on personals; and, in case of death, a Bond, as a specialty under seal, is paid before simple contract debts, which Bills and Notes are considered to be. Bonds.

A Bond may be transferred by a deed of assignment, but not by indorsement, and therefore it is not deemed a negotiable security, like a Bill of Exchange or a Promissory Note. In foreign countries, however, Bills of Exchange only are binding, as before noticed.

BILLS, BONDS, AND NOTES, HOW VOID.

It should be observed that the foregoing laws apply only to debts legally contracted. For no Bill, Note, or Bond, made by a bankrupt, or by an insane person, can be valid; neither by a minor, nor a married woman, except in a few particular cases. Neither is any Bill, Note, or Bond binding when the whole or any part of the consideration shall be for money, or other valuable thing, won by gaming or betting, or lent knowingly for such purposes; or for money lent on usury; that is, at more than the legal interest, which is 5 per cent. per annum. Bills &c. how void.

DRAFTS ON BANKERS.

Drafts on Bankers.

DRAFTS or Checks on Bankers are generally received by merchants as ready cash; and if the party receiving them should not, within a reasonable time, demand payment, he must bear the loss in case the Banker or Drawer should fail in the interim: but what shall be deemed a reasonable time has not been precisely fixed, as it must depend on situation; and, therefore, whenever it becomes a question of law, it is left to the jury, or court, to decide according to the circumstances of the case. The general practice is, to present Checks for payment on the day they are received or dated, and during the hours of banking business, which are from nine o'clock in the morning to five in the afternoon.

If a Check on a Banker be refused payment, he who gave it is bound to make it good; and if it be lost, he must also make it good, on receiving a satisfactory security that the lost Draft will not appear against him.

As a precaution against loss, it is customary to write across a Draft, as soon as received, the Firm of the House into which it is to be paid; by which may be understood that it will not be paid to any other house or person without proper inquiry. This practice is also useful in Clearing.

Clearing.

CLEARING is a method adopted by London Bankers for exchanging Drafts and Bills on each other's houses as they become due and settling the differences. This important operation is performed daily at an office, called the Clearing-House, with great correctness and despatch, and with such method that Bills and Drafts to the amount of £5,000,000 on an average are cancelled at each Clearing, with less than one-twentieth part of that sum in Bank of England Notes.

Clearing, though of modern adoption in England, has been long practised in other countries, particularly in settling Bills of Exchange and other Documents of Credit, at the great Fairs on the Continent. The invention of this method is ascribed to the Florentines, but the practice has been greatly improved by the London Bankers.

II.—PRINCIPLES OF EXCHANGE.

INLAND EXCHANGE.

By Inland Exchange is understood the act of remitting Bills to places in the same country; by which means debts are discharged more conveniently than by cash remittances. Inland Exchange.

Suppose, for example, *A.* of London is creditor to *B.* of Edinburgh £100, and *C.* of London debtor to *D.* of Edinburgh £100, both these debts may be discharged by means of one Bill. Thus *A.* draws for this sum on *B.*, and sells his Bill to *C.*, who remits it to *D.*, and the latter receives the amount when due from *B.*—Here, by a transfer of claims, the London debtor pays the London creditor, and the Edinburgh debtor the Edinburgh creditor, and no money is sent from one place to the other. The same would take place if *D.* of Edinburgh drew on *C.* of London, and sold his Bill to *B.* of Edinburgh, who should send it to *A.* of London; the effect, in either case, being merely a transfer of debtors and creditors.*

By the foregoing example, it appears that reciprocal and equal debts, due between two places, may be discharged without remitting specie; and it may be supposed that such an operation is of equal convenience to all parties concerned: but when the debts are unequal, the advantage must be different, as the obligation of remittance is no longer mutual, because the debtor place must pay its balance either by sending Cash or Bills; and as the latter mode is generally preferred, an increased demand for Bills must be the consequence, which enhances their price, as it would that of any other article of sale or purchase.

This is the plain principle of Exchange, and is constantly exemplified in the premium paid for Inland Bills on London, which is the grand emporium of

* In this operation, *A.* is the *Drawer* and *Seller*, *B.* the *Drawee* and *Acceptor*, *C.* the *Buyer* and *Remitter*, and *D.* the *Payee*, if his name be mentioned in the Bill, and he is the Holder when he receives the Bill from *A.*—When *D.*, or any other Holder, presents the Bill for acceptance or payment, he is called the *Presenter*.

Inland Exchange.

commerce that furnishes most other places in the kingdom with foreign merchandize; and being also the seat of Government, to which the revenue is transmitted, and the residence of numerous landlords, whose rents must be remitted to them from the country, it has generally a large balance of debt in its favour; and as this Balance is usually paid in Bills, a demand for them is created, and therefore a premium is the consequence.

The premium on Inland Bills is mostly commuted for time; that is, for a certain number of days after date or after sight, which varies according to circumstances. Thus, the general term for Bills from Edinburgh on London is 40 days' date, which is valued at about ½ per cent., and is called the ***Par Date.*** A similar premium or date is allowed for Bills on London drawn in all other distant parts of Great Britain; but Bills, at sight, on any of those places, may be generally had in London without any premium. Thus, the Inland Exchange is constantly in favour of the capital; and the date or term varies according to the greater or less demand for Bills.

FOREIGN EXCHANGE.

Foreign Exchange.

THE principle of Foreign Exchange is the same as that of Inland, with respect to settling accounts by a transfer of claims, and also by the premium or price of Bills being regulated by the proportion which exists between the demand and supply; but the manner of paying the premium for Foreign Bills differs, and the operation is more complex, owing to the denominations of money not being the same: for, in this case, the value of Bills is estimated by the comparative rate of monies; and the date is, besides, taken into consideration.

In Foreign Exchange, one place always gives another a fixed sum or piece of money for a variable price; the former is called the *certain price,* and the latter the *uncertain price.* Thus, London is said to give to Paris the *certain* for the *uncertain,* that is, the Pound sterling for a variable number of Francs; and to Spain the *uncertain* for the *certain,* that is a variable number of Pence sterling for the Dollar of Exchange. The uncertain price, as quoted at any time, is called the *Rate, or Course of Exchange.*

When the demand in London for Bills on Paris is great, a smaller number of

Francs is given for the Pound sterling, and the contrary; and when there is a demand for Bills on Spain, a greater number of Pence sterling must be given for the Dollar, and the contrary. Foreign Exchange.

Again, if the Course of Exchange between London and Paris be 24 Francs for the Pound sterling, and if this number of Francs contains the same quantity of pure silver as 20 Shillings sterling, then the Exchange is considered *at par;* but if Paris should give a higher price, the Exchange is said to be against France, and in favour of England. This is the general mode of judging whether the Exchange is favourable or unfavourable, though it is not always that on which Merchants act or speculate. But before any further explanation is given of the *Course of Exchange*, or the causes of its fluctuations, it may be necessary to state more fully what is to be understood by the *Par of Exchange*, a subject on which there has been much difference of opinion.

PAR OF EXCHANGE.

THE Par of Exchange may be considered under two general heads, viz. the *Intrinsic Par* and the *Commercial Par*, each of which admits of subordinate divisions and distinctions. Par of Exchange.

The *Intrinsic Par* is the value of the money of one country compared with that of another, with respect both to weight and fineness.

The *Commercial Par* is the comparative value of the monies of different countries, according to the weight, fineness, and market prices of the metals.

Thus two sums of different countries are *intrinsically* at par, when they *contain* an equal quantity of the same kind of pure metal; and two sums of different countries are *commercially* at par, when they can *purchase* an equal quantity of the same kind of pure metal.

This latter equivalence is variously denominated. It has been called by different authors the *Current*, the *Momentary*, the *Rational*, and the *Eventual Par;* and though each of these terms seems to convey a correct idea of its fluctuating and ephemeral nature, yet the word *Commercial* is here adopted as being equally appropriate, and, perhaps, more generally understood.

Par of Exchange.

There are other Pars occasionally noticed by Merchants, such as the ***Nominal*** or ***Estimate Par***, which, though not accurate, is commonly referred to; the ***Monetary Par***, in which the current value fixed by authority is considered; the ***Proportional Par***, which is the equality of two sums of different countries, compared with the rate of Exchange of a third place, and which is also called the ***Arbitrated Price*** and the ***Political Par***. There is, besides, a ***Medium Par*** sometimes reckoned: that is, a mean taken between the Pars of Gold and Silver Coins.

The intrinsic Par of Exchange is, in effect, the Par of Coins or the Metallic Par; for though the Monies of Exchange are, for the most part, imaginary, their value is ascertained by that of the Coins which they represent, or to which they have a known relation or established proportion.

An approximate or average Par, may, however, be computed from the relative proportions between Gold and Silver, as taken from the Mint regulations of the places in question; and it may be further observed, that the Mint proportions are considered the best constituted when deduced from the market prices of the precious metals, taken from an average of several years.

Here the important question comes to be considered, "Whether the Par of Exchange should be computed from gold or from silver coins?" Messrs. Locke, Harris, and other Authors of the last century, agree, that "the equality of Silver expressed by different denominations of coins should constitute the Par of Exchange between any two countries;" but Lord Liverpool, in his "***Treatise on the Coins of the Realm***," maintains, that the proper measure of value should be of that metal in which the principal payments are made, and, therefore that in some countries the Par should be computed from Gold, and in others from Silver, according to the kind of Money in which Bills of Exchange are paid. In England, however, Gold has been made the standard of value, by a law of 1816, which enacts that no payment in Silver above two pounds is a legal tender.

A difference of opinion has also existed as to the correctness of establishing a Par between Gold Coins and Silver Coins, as these two metals are liable to continual fluctuation in their relative prices. It is, however, obvious, that the intrinsic Par of Exchange can be determined only between places which pay their Bills in the same kind of metal It should be even remarked, that the value of the same metal differs considerably in different countries, which must be always the case between two places, where one possesses mines, and supplies the other with materials of coinage, as between Spain and France, or between Portugal and England. The difference in such cases is estimated, in ordinary times, according to the expenses of transporting the precious metals; and, thus, from the intrinsic Par and the various charges and prices, the commercial equivalence is computed. Par of Exchange.

In determining the Intrinsic Par of Exchange, another question occurs; namely, Whether the computation should be made from *Mint regulations* or from *Assays?* The objection to the first is, that all Mints do not keep strictly to their own laws; and to the second, that there can be no assurance that the Coins to be assayed are proper average specimens. The latter is, perhaps, the least objectionable, and therefore a calculation from accredited Assays is generally preferred. In the present work, the computations are made according to both methods.

COURSE OF EXCHANGE.

THE Course of Exchange is the variable price of the money of one country, which is given for a fixed sum of the money of another country; the latter is called the *certain*, and the former the *uncertain* price, as before stated. Course of Exchange.

When London Merchants want to draw or remit Foreign Bills, they meet upon the Royal Exchange, where this kind of business must be transacted. They are distinguished into two classes, called *Drawers* and *Remitters;* the former are also called *Sellers* of Bills and the latter *Buyers* or *Takers*, and like buyers and sellers of all other articles, their interests are opposite. The market is constantly attended by Exchange-Brokers, who generally bring the parties together and settle the price of Exchange for the day, when they have learnt how the market stands with respect to the wants or offers of Buyers and Sellers. It should be observed that the prices of Bullion and Exchange reciprocally determine or at least influence each other.

When the market price of foreign bills is above par, the Exchange is said to

Course of Exchange.

be favourable to the place that gives the certain for the uncertain, and the contrary; thus, if the par between London and Hamburgh be computed at 35 Shillings Flemish, for 1 Pound Sterling, and the Course of Exchange is at 36 Shillings, the Exchange is said to be in favour of London, and against Hamburgh; and the contrary, of course, takes place if the price be under par.

It should, however, be recollected, that when the Exchange is favourable to a place, it is only so to the Buyers and Remitters of Bills, but it is unfavourable to the Drawers and Sellers.

Thus the interest of the Remitter is identified with that of the place where he purchases the bill, and the interest of the Drawer with that of the place where his funds are established and on which he draws.

It is natural to inquire why such prices are considered favourable or unfavourable, if the Drawers and Remitters, whose interests are opposite, are natives of the same country? The usual answer is, that when the Exchange is against a place, it becomes the interest of Remitters to pay their foreign debts in specie or bullion instead of bills, and the exportation of the precious metals is often considered a national disadvantage.

The fluctuations of Exchange are occasioned by various circumstances, both political and commercial. The principal cause is generally stated to be the Balance of Trade: that is, the difference between the commercial exports and imports of any one country with respect to another. Experience, however, shows that the Exchange may be unfavourable to a country when the Balance of Trade is greatly in its favour; for the demand for Bills must chiefly depend on the Balance of such debts as come into immediate liquidation: that is to say, on the *Balance of Payments.*

Besides, it does not follow that large exports are always successful, or quick in their returns; and even should it be the case, the Balance of Payments may be still unfavourable from political causes: such as foreign Loans, Subsidies, Expeditions, or Colonial Establishments. Rich countries are often liable to have the Exchange turned against them, by the sums which they may have to remit to less opulent states on account of their importations of luxuries.

Course of Exchange.

When any alteration takes place in the Coin or Currency of a Country, the Exchange will of course vary, so as to keep pace or correspond with such alteration. This, however, cannot be considered a change in the price of Bills, but in the Money in which they are bought or sold.

In times of peace, the Course of Exchange seldom remains long unfavourable to any country, at least beyond the expenses that might be incurred by the transportation of the precious metals; for Bullion is considered the universal currency of Merchants, and Exchange gives it circulation, and thus tends to maintain the level of Money throughout the commercial world.

Although an unfavourable Course of Exchange is generally considered a disadvantage to the place where it prevails, yet the opinion is not always well founded, as much depends on the quantity of Bullion or specie which the country may have to spare: and there is another consideration that renders the question sometimes doubtful, which is, that an unfavourable rate of Exchange operates as an encouragement to the exportation of goods, and as a check against the importation; for the exporter can afford to sell the goods cheaper in proportion to the premium which he receives for his bill; while, on the contrary, the discount on bills from abroad operates as a tax or duty on importation. Thus, Exchange has a natural tendency to correct itself, and may be considered, in ordinary times, as vibrating to restore an equilibrium.

An unfavourable Course of Exchange may therefore be corrected either by the exportation of Bullion or the shipment of Goods—and another method sometimes offers by negotiating Bills through several places, but the latter remedy must fail, if the Exchange be universally unfavourable.

From what has been said of the causes, both commercial and political, which produce the fluctuations of Exchange, and which sometimes counteract or balance each other, the following simple conclusion may be drawn:—that Bills rise or fall in their prices like any other saleable articles, according to the proportion that exists between the demand and the supply.

III.—MONIES OF EXCHANGE.

Monies of Exchange.

THE Denominations of Money used in the business of Exchange are for the most part Imaginary Monies of Account, varying in some places from those used in domestic trade, and almost universally differing from the Coins from which they originated; for it may be remarked, that coins, as local or national currencies, are subject to frequent alterations, which are easily effected;—while Monies of Exchange, being more widely established, cannot be altered without great inconvenience to the commercial world, and are therefore mostly continued as originally adopted.

This may be exemplified by the Spanish Piastre or Dollar of Exchange, an Imaginary Money of Account, which was at first a Coin (the ***Peso Duro***) of 8 Reals of Old Plate; but in the course of time it was altered to 10, and afterwards to $10\frac{5}{8}$ of the same Reals, while in Foreign Exchanges it has been continued at the original value; and hence it is, that 8 Hard Dollars are worth $10\frac{5}{8}$ Dollars of Exchange.

Most other imaginary monies may be accounted for or traced in a similar way; and as their proportions to real coins are known, their intrinsic value may be thence accurately determined.

The Quotations of Exchange are the Lists of Prices transmitted from one country to another for the advice and government of merchants. In these Lists the figures of the uncertain monies only are given, without stating their denominations, or the certain monies which they purchase: all these omissions are however here supplied. The Places in the Quotations are arranged alphabetically, and the explanations followed by numerous examples of calculation.*

---

* The Calculations of Exchange are performed either by the RULE OF THREE or by the CHAIN RULE. By the former method the sum given to be reduced must be the Third Term of the statement, and the Money into which it is to be reduced, the Second. The First Term must, therefore, be of the same denomination as the Third. Thus, if it be required to reduce 100 Francs into English Money, at 25 Francs per Pound Sterling, say,

As 25 Fr. : 1 £ Ster. :: 100 Fr. : £4

In solving such questions by the CHAIN RULE, *the Sum to be reduced must be the first consequent, and the money into which it is to be reduced, the last consequent. The antecedent must, of course, be of the same denomination as the first consequent.* Thus, to reduee 100 Francs at the above price.

100 Francs.

25 Fr. = £1

Then $\frac{100 \times 1}{25} = £4$

LONDON.

MONIES OF EXCHANGE.

Exchanges are computed in Pounds, Shillings, and Pence sterling; and Farthings are also sometimes reckoned.

4 Farthings = 1 Penny; 12 Pence = 1 Shilling; 20 Shillings = 1 Pound sterling.

COURSE OF EXCHANGE, arranged from Lloyd's List. *January* 1, 1820.			EXPLANATION.	
AMSTERDAM ..	11 16	.. LONDON	receives 11 Florins 16 Stivers.........	for 1 Pound sterling.
DITTO	38 6	.. ———	receives 38 Shill. 6 Pence Flemish Banco	for 1 Pound sterling.
FRANCE	25 15	.. ———	receives 25 Francs 15 Centimes........	for 1 Pound sterling.
FRANCFORT....	149	.. ———	receives 149 Batzen..................	for 1 Pound sterling.
GENOA........	44	.. ———	gives 44 Pence sterling	for 1 Pezza Fuori Banco.
GIBRALTAR....	30	.. ———	gives 30 Pence sterling	for 1 Current Dollar.
HAMBURGH....	36 2	.. ———	receives 36 Shillings 2 Pence Flemish ..	for 1 Pound sterling.
LEGHORN......	51½	.. ———	gives 51½ Pence sterling..............	for 1 Pezza of 8 Reals.
LISBON	52	.. ———	gives 52 Pence sterling................	for 1 Milree, legal money.
MALTA........	46	.. ———	gives 46 Pence sterling	for 1 Dollar of Exchange.
NAPLES	39	.. ———	gives 39 Pence sterling	for 1 Ducato di Regno.
PALERMO......	116	.. ———	gives 116 Pence sterling..............	for 1 Ounce.
RIO JANEIRO ..	56	.. ———	gives 56 Pence sterling................	for 1 Milree, effective.
SPAIN	35	.. ———	gives 35 Pence sterling	for 1 Dollar of Exchange.
VENICE........	27	.. ———	receives 27 Italian Livres.............	for 1 Pound sterling.
VIENNA&TRIESTE	10 15	.. ———	receives 10 Florins 15 Creutzers........	for 1 Pound sterling.
DUBLIN	10½	.. ———	receives 110½ Pounds Irish............	for 100 Pounds British.

[For the usances, days of grace, &c. see LONDON, vol. i.]

LONDON ON AMSTERDAM.

Reduce 2401 Florins 17 Stivers 8 Pennings into English money; exchange at 12 Florins 4 Stivers per £ sterling.

[16 Pennings = 1 Stiver, and 20 Stivers = 1 Florin.]

```
    Fl.  St.   £        Flor.  Stiv. Pen.     £   s. d.
As  12   4  :  1  : :  2401    17    8   :  196  17  6
    20                   20
   ----                -----
   244                 48037
    16                    16
   ----                -----
   3904          3904)768600(£196 17s. 6d.
                      3904
                      -----
                      37820 &c.
```

AMSTERDAM ON LONDON.

Reduce £196 17s. 6d. sterling into Dutch money; exchange at 12 Florins 4 Stivers current per £ sterling.

```
     £   Flor. Stiv.       £   s. d.      Flor. Stiv. Pen.
As   1 :  12    4   : :   196  17  6  :   2401   17    8
          20               20
          --              ----
         244              3937
                            12
                          -----
                          47250
                            244
                         ------(2,0
                 24,0)1152900,0(4803,7½
                                --------
                          2401 Fl. 17 St. 8 Pen.
```

EXCHANGE IN FLEMISH BANCO.

Although the old Bank of Amsterdam has been discontinued, yet Exchanges are sometimes transacted in Banco. The following examples, therefore, may be still useful.

Reduce 8792 Flor. 13 Stiv. 14½ Penn. into English money; exchange at 34s. 4½d. Flemish Banco per £ sterling.

```
    Flemish.     Sterl.       Flor. Stiv. Penn.    £   s. d.
As  34s. 4½d. :  £1    : :   8792   13   14½  :  852  12  6
     12                        20
    ----                     ------
    412½                     175853
      8                          16
    ----                     ------
    3300            33,00)28136,62½(£852 12s. 6d.
                          264
                          ---
                          173
                          165
                          ---
                           86 &c.
```

By the Chain Rule.

```
                 8792 Flor. 13 Stiv. 14½ Penn.
  1 Florin   =     40 Grotes Flemish.
412½ Grotes  =      1 Pound sterling.
                 Result as above.
```

BANCO REDUCED INTO CURRENCY.

Bank money is reduced into currency by saying as 100 : 100 + the Agio : : Banco to currency. Currency is reduced to Banco by the reverse operation.

When the Exchange is expressed in Flemish Banco the operation is as follows—

Reduce £852 12s. 6d. sterling into Dutch money; exchange at 34s. 4½d. Flemish Banco per £ sterling.

```
    Sterling.  Flemish.       £   s. d.    Flor. Stiv. Penn.
As  £1   :  34s. 4½d. : :  852  12  6  :  8792   13   14½
              12            20
            ----          -----
            412½          17052
              8              12
            ----          ------
            3300          204630
                            3300
                        --------(16
           24,0)67527900,0(2813662½
                48            ----------
                ---      2,0)17585,3 14½
                195          ---------
                192 &c.    8792 Fl. 13 St. 14½ Pen.
```

By the Chain Rule.

```
                   £852   12  6
£1 sterling   =    412½ Grotes Flemish.
40 Grotes     =      1  Florin.
           Result as above.
```

LONDON ON FRANCE.

Reduce 4305 Francs 95 Centimes into sterling; exchange at 24 Francs 25 Centimes per £ sterling.

[100 Centimes = 1 Franc.]

Francs : £ :: Francs : £
As 24,25 : 1 :: 4305,95 : 177,565
20
11,300
12
Ans. £177 11s. 3½d. 3,6

FRANCE ON LONDON.

Reduce £177 11s. 3½d. into Francs and Centimes; exchange at 24 Francs 25 Centimes per £ sterling.

11s. 3½d. =,565

£ : Francs Cent. :: £ : Francs
As 1 : 24 25 :: 177,565 : 4305,95

Ans. 4305 Francs 95 Centimes.

LIVRES REDUCED INTO FRANCS.

Exchanges between France and England were formerly transacted by giving about 30 Pence for 1 Ecu of 3 Livres; and of late, Bills have been sometimes drawn in Livres, Sous, and Deniers; in such case, Livres must be reduced to Francs by multiplying by 80 and dividing by 81.

Reduce 16914 Francs 19 Centimes into English money; exchange at 23 Livres 10 Sous per £ sterling.

As 80 : 81 :: Fr. 16914,19 : Liv 17125,625.

Liv. Sous : £ :: Livres Sous Den. : £ s.
As 23 10 : 1 :: 17125 12 6 : 728 15
20 20
470 342512
12 12
5640 564,0)411015,0(£728 15s. *Ans.*
3948
1621 &c.

By the Chain Rule.

16914 Francs 19 Centimes.
80 Francs = 81 Livres.
23½ Livres = £1 sterling.
Result as above.

FRANCS REDUCED INTO LIVRES.

Reduce £728 15s. into Francs and Centimes; exchange at 23 Livres 10 Sous per £ sterling.

£ : Livres Sous :: £ s. : Livres Sous Den.
As 1 : 23 10 :: 728 15 : 17125 12 6
20 20 20
20 470 14575
470
2,0)685025,0
2,0)342512,5
17125 Livres, 12,5 Sous
12
6,0 Deniers
17125,625 Livres
80
81)1370050,000(16914 Francs 19 Centimes. *Ans.*

By the Chain Rule.

£728 15s.
£1 sterling = 23½ Livres.
81 Livres = 80 Francs.
Result as above.

LONDON ON FRANCFORT.

Reduce 8036 Florins 22 Creutzers, Francfort currency, into sterling; exchange at 142½ Batzen per £ sterling.

[4 Creutzers = 1 Batze, 60 Creutzers or 15 Batzen = 1 Florin.]

```
     Batzen    £     Florins Creutzers    £     s.  d.
As 142½   :  1  : :  8036    22     :  845   18   8
    4                  60
   ---              ------
   570           570)482182(£845 18s. 8d.
                     4560
                     ----
                     2618 &c.
```

By the Chain Rule.

		8036 Florins 22 Creutzers.
1 Florin	=	15 Batzen.
142½ Batzen.	=	£1 sterling.

FRANCFORT ON LONDON.

Reduce £845 18s. 8d. into money of Francfort: exchange at 142½ Batzen per £ sterling.

```
     £    Batzen       £    s.  d.    Florins  Cr.
As 1  :  142½   : :  845   18   8  :  8036    22
           4          20
          ---        -----
          570        16918
                        12
                     ------
                     203024
                        570
                  ---------6,0
         24,0)11572368,0(48218,2
              96          -------
              --          8036 Florins 22 Creut.
              197 &c.
```

LONDON ON GENOA.

Reduce 7346 Lire 11 Soldi 8 Denari into sterling; exchange at 45d. sterling per Pezza of 5¾ Lire fuori Banco.

[To turn Lire into Pezze multiply by 4 and divide by 23.]

```
        Lire   Sol. Den. di Lira.
        7346   11   8
                    4
       --------------  Pez.   Sol. Den. di Pez.
   23)29386    6   8(1277   13    4
      23
      --
      63 &c.
         Pez.   d.       Pezze  Sol. Den.     £   s.  d.
Then as 1  :  45   : :  1277   13    4   :  239  11   3
        20              20
       ---             -----
        20             25553
        12                12
       ---             ------
       240             306640
                           45
                   ---------(12
           24,0)1379880,0(57495
                120         ------
                ---     2,0)479,1 3
                179 &c.   ----------
                          £239 11s. 3d.
```

GENOA ON LONDON.

Reduce £239 11s. 3d. into money of Genoa; exchange at 45d. sterling per Pezza of 5¾ Lire fuori Banco.

```
     d.   Pez.      £   s.  d.    Pezze  Soldi  Den. di Pez.
As 45  :  1   : :  239  11   3  :  1277   13     4
                   20
                   ----
                   4791
                     12
                   ------  Pezze  Sol.  Den.
              45)57495(1277    13    4
```

If Lire are required instead of Pezze, say

```
     d.  Liv.  Sol.       £   s.  d.    Lire   Sol.  Den.
As 45  :  5    15   : :  239  11   3  :  7346   11    8
```

By the Chain Rule.

		£239 11s. 3d.
£1 sterling	=	240 Pence.
45 Pence	=	1 Pezza.
4 Pezze	=	23 Lire.

Result as above.

Genoa exchanges also on London by giving 27 Italian Livres more or less for the £ sterling.

LONDON ON HAMBURGH.

Reduce 1416 Marks 1 Schilling 6 Pfenings Banco into English money; exchange at 35 Shillings 4 Grotes or Pence Flemish Banco per £ sterling.

[12 Pfenings = 1 Shilling, 16 Shillings = 1 Mark.]

```
   Flemish.     £      Marks. Schil. Pfen.   £   s. d.
As 35s. 4d. : 1  : :  1416   1    6  : 106  17  6
   12                   16
   ---                -----
   424                22657
   6                    12
   ----               -----
   2544        2544)271890(£106 17s. 6d.
                    2544 &c.
```

By the Chain Rule.

1416 Mks. 1 Schill. 6 Pfen.
1 Mark = 32 Grotes Flemish.
424 Grotes = £1 sterling.
Result as above.

HAMBURGH ON LONDON.

Reduce £106 17s. 6d. sterling into Hamburgh money; exchange at 35 Shillings 4 Grotes or Pence Flemish Banco per £ sterling.

```
Sterling. Flemish.      £   s. d.   Marks. Schil. Pfen.
As £1 : 35s. 4d. : : 106 17 6 : 1416   1   6
        12           20
        ---          ----
        424          2137
                       12
                     -----
                     25650
                       424
               --------(32                 Mks. Schil. Pfen.
        24,0)1087560,0(45315d. Fl. (1416    1    6
               96
```

By the Chain Rule.

£106 17s. 6d.
£1 sterling = 424 Grotes Flemish.
32 Grotes = 1 Mark.
Result as above.

LONDON ON LEGHORN.

Reduce 1876 Pezze 12 Soldi 5 Denari into English money; exchange at 50¼d. sterling per Pezza of 8 Reals.

[12 Denari = 1 Soldo, 20 Soldi = 1 Pezza.]

```
  Pezza  d.       Pezze  Soldi Den.   £   s.  d.
As 1 : 50¼ : : 1876   12    5  : 392  18  4¼
                 20
               -----
               37532
                  12
               ------
               450389
                  50¼
         ---------(12
240)22632047(94300d. sterl.=£392 18s. 4¼d.
```

By the Chain Rule.

1876 Pez. 12 Sol. 5 Den.
1 Pezza = 50¼ Pence.
240 Pence = £1 sterling.
Result as above.

LEGHORN ON LONDON.

Reduce £392 18s. 4¼d. sterling into money of Leghorn; exchange at 50¼d. sterling per Pezza of 8 Reals.

```
   d.   Pez.      £   s.  d.    Pez.  Sol. Den.
As 50¼ : 1 : :  392  18  4¼ : 1876   12   5
   4             20
   ---          -----
   201          7858
                  12
                -----
                94300
                    4
               -------  Pez.  Sol. Den.
          201)377201(1876   12   5
              201 &c.
```

By the Chain Rule.

£392 18s. 4¼d.
£1 sterling = 240 Pence.
50¼ Pence = 1 Pezza.
Result as above.

LONDON ON LISBON.

Reduce 827 Milrees 160 Rees into English money; exchange at 63⅜d. sterling per Milree.

[1000 Rees = 1 Milree, 400 Rees = 1 Crusado.]

	Mil.		d.		Milrees		£	s.	d.
As	1	:	63⅜	: :	827,160	:	218	8	5¼

63,375

12)52421,265

2,0)436,8 5¼

£218 8s. 5¼d.

But if the sum be given in Crusados they are reduced to Rees by multiplying them by 400, thus:

Reduce 7650 Crusados into sterling; exchange at 61½d. sterling per Milree.

7650 × 400 = 30600, then—

	Milree		d.		Milrees		£	s.	d.
As	1	:	61½	: :	3060	:	784	2	6

LISBON ON LONDON.

Reduce £218 8s. 5¼d. into Portugal money; exchange at 63⅜d. sterling per Milree.

	d.		d.		Milree		£ s. d.		M.	R.
As	63⅜	or	63,375	:	1	: :	218 8 5¼	:	827	160

20

4368

12

M. R.

63,375)52421,250(827,160

But if the answer be required in Crusados, two decimals only should be cut off, and the four first figures should be divided by 4, thus:

4)8271,60 Rees(2067 Crusados 360 Rees.

The exchanges of Rio Janeiro are similar to those of Lisbon; there is however a difference in the value of their monies, as that of Lisbon is half cash and half paper, called legal money, and that of Rio Janeiro is effective.

LONDON ON MALTA.

Reduce £728 13s. 6d. into Tari and Grani of Malta; exchange at 49d. per Dollar of 2½ Scudi, or 30 Tari.

[20 Grani = 1 Tari, and 12 Tari = 1 Scudo.]

	d.		Dol.		£	s.	d.		Sc.	Ta.	Gr.
As	49	:	1	: :	728	13	6	:	8922	6	12

2½   240

2½   174882

2½

Scudi Tari Gr.

49)437205(8922 6 12

392

452

441

Rem. × 12 × 20 &c.

MALTA ON LONDON.

Reduce 8922 Scudi 6 Tari 12 Grani into sterling; exchange at 49d. per Dollar.

	Dollar		d.		Scudi	Tari	Gr.		£	s.	d.
As	1	:	49	: :	8922	6	12	:	728	13	6

30   12

30   107070

20   20

600   2141412

49

6,00)1049291,88

12)174882

2,0)1457,3 6

£728 13s. 6d.

LONDON ON NAPLES.

Reduce 1014 Ducati 16 Grani di Regno into English money; exchange at 37½d. sterling per Ducato. This is best done by decimals: thus,

[100 Grani=1 Ducato di Regno.]

	Duc.		d.		Ducati		£	s.	d.
As	1	:	37½	: :	1014,16	:	158	9	3

37,5

24,0)3803,100(£158,4625
24 20

140 &c. 9,2500
12

3,00

NAPLES ON LONDON.

Reduce £158 9s. 3d. into money of Naples; exchange at 640 Grani per £ sterling.

9s. 3d. = ,4625.

	£		Grani		£	s.	d.		Ducati	Grani
As	1	:	640	: :	158	9	3	:	1014	16

240 20

240 3169
12

38031
640

24,0)2433984,0

1,00)1014,16

By Decimals.

9s. 3d. = ,4625.

	£		Grani		£		Ducati	Grani
As	1	:	640	: :	158,4625	:	1014	16

640

Duc. 1014,16

LONDON ON PALERMO.

Reduce 1377 Oncie 14 Grani into English money; exchange at 127d. sterling per Oncia.

[20 Grani=1 Tari, 30 Tari=1 Oncia.]

	On.		d.		On.	Tari	Grani		£	s.	d.
As	1	:	127	: :	1377	0	14	:	728	13	6

30 30

30 41310
20 20

600 826214
127

6,00)1049291,78

÷ 12 & 20)174882

£728 13 6

PALERMO ON LONDON.

Reduce £728 13s. 6d. into Sicilian money; exchange at 127d. sterling per Oncia.

	d.		On.		£	s.	d.		On.	Tari	Gr.
As	127	:	1	: :	728	13	6	:	1377	0	14

× 20 & 12

127)174882(1377 0 14.
127

Remainder × 30 and 20 ÷ 127 gives the Ans. as above.

LONDON ON SPAIN.

Reduce 2375 Dollars 6 Reals 16 Marav. into English money; exchange at 34d. sterl. per Dollar or Piastre.

[34 Mar. = 1 Real, 8 Reals = 1 Dollar of Ex.]

	Dollar		d.		Dollars	Reals	Mar.		£	s.	d.
As	1	:	34	: :	2375	6	16	:	336	11	5½

8   × 8 × 34
——   = 646220
8   34
34   ————
——   2584880
272   1938660
————(12
272)21971480(80777½
2176 ————
——— 2,0)673,1 5½
2114 ————
1904 £336 11s. 5½d.
——
2108 &c.

SPAIN ON LONDON.

Reduce £336 11s. 5½d. sterling into Spanish money; exchange at 34d. sterling per Dollar of Plate, or Piastre.

	d.		Dol.		£	s.	d.		Dollars	Reals	Mar.
As	34	:	1	: :	336	11	5½	:	2375	6	16

20
——
6731
12
——   Dol. Reals Mar.
34)80777½(2375 6 16
68 &c.

And the Remainder multiplied by 8 and divided by 34 gives the Ans.

If the result be required in *Vellon*, multiply the *Plate* by 32 and divide by 17, and *vice versâ*.

Gibraltar exchanges in current Dollars, and also in Hard Dollars. *See* Spain; *also*, Gibraltar, vol. i.

LONDON ON VENICE.

Reduce 14783 Lire 3 Soldi 9 Denari piccoli into sterling; exchange at 59 Lire piccole per £ sterling.

[12 Denari=1 Soldo, 20 Soldi=1 Lira.]

	Lire		£		Lire	Sol.	Den.		£	s.	d.
As	59	:	1	: :	14783	3	9	:	250	11	3

£ s. d.
59)14783 3 9(250 11 3

The above mode of exchange, as formerly used at Venice, has been of late years discontinued, and French Francs, called *Lire Italiane* or *Italian Livres*, substituted in their place. The proportion is, that $40\frac{5}{10}$ Lire piccole of Venice equal $20\frac{723}{1000}$ Lire Italiane. In business the proportion is mostly taken at 23 Lire 9 Soldi for 12 Italian Livres.—*See the annexed Example.*

VENICE ON LONDON.

Reduce £728 13s. 6d. sterling, into Lire Italiane of Venice; exchange at 24 Lire 80 Centimes per £ sterling.

[Italian Livres and Centimes are reduced to sterling, and the contrary, in the same manner as Francs and Centimes of France, according to the given Course of Exchange.]

	£		Lire	Cen.		£	s.	d.		Lire	Cen.
As	1	:	24	80	: :	728	13	6	:	18071	14

To reduce the above Lire Italiane into Lire piccole, say—

	Lire It.		Lire Sol. (piccoli)			Lire It.	Cen.		Lire piccole
As	12	:	23 9	: :		18071	14	:	35314 0 5
	20		20			× 469 ÷ 240			
	——		——			Result as above.			
	240		469						

LONDON ON VIENNA.

Reduce 6451 Florins 50 Creutzers into English money; exchange at 9 Florins 40 Creutzers per £ sterling.

[4 Pfenings = 1 Creutzer, 60 Creutzers = 1 Florin.]

```
   Fl. Cr.     £         Fl.   Cr.        £  s. d.
As 9  40   :   1  : :  6451   50    :   667  8  7½
     60                   60
   ----                --------       £  s. d.
    580              58,0)38711,0(667  8  7½
                          348
                          ---
                          391
                          348
                          ---
                           431
                           406
                           ---
                            25 × 20 and 12 &c.
```

VIENNA ON LONDON.

Reduce £667 8s. 7½d. into money of Vienna; exchange at 9 Florins 40 Creutzers per £ sterling.

```
   £    Fl. Cr.       £  s. d.       Fl.  Cr.
As 1  :  9  40  : :  667  8  7½  :  6451  50
  240    60           20
  ---   ---          -----
  240   580          13348
                        12
                     ------
                     160183,5
                          580
                     --------(6,0
              24,0)9290640,0(38711,0
                     72 &c.   -------
                               6451 Fl. 50 Cr.
```

The Exchange with TRIESTE is similar to that of Vienna.

LONDON ON DUBLIN.

Reduce £879 6s. 6d. Irish into English money; exchange at 11⅝; that is, £100 British for £111⅝ Irish.

```
   £ Irish.  £ British.    £  s. d. Irish.     £   s. British.
As 111⅝  :  100  : :  879  6  6     :   787  15
     8         8       800
   ----      ---    ------
    893      800    703200
5s. = ¼ ....           200
1s. = ⅕ ....            40
6d. = ½ ....            20
                   -------    £    s.
              893)703460(787   15
                  6251 &c.
```

By Decimals.

```
As 111,625 : 100 : : 879,325 : 787,75
                                   20
                               ------
                                15,00
```

DUBLIN ON LONDON.

Reduce £787 15s. English to Irish money; exchange at 11⅝.

```
   £ British.  £ Irish.        £  s. British.    £  s. d. Irish.
As 100  :  111⅝   : :   787  15     :    879  6  6
```

Or thus, by Practice:—

```
              £787   15
                     11⅝
             -----------
              8665    5             £787  15  0
4/8 = ½ ....   393   17   6           91  11  6
1/8 = ¼ ....    98    9   4½        -----------
             ---------------        £879   6  6
             £91,57  11  10½
                20
             ------
              11,51
                 12
             ------
               6,22
```

By Decimals.

As 100 : 111,625 : : 787,75 : 879,325

AMSTERDAM.

MONIES OF EXCHANGE.

Exchanges are computed in Florins, Stivers, and Pennings; or in Pounds, Shillings, and Pence Flemish.

16 Pennings = 1 Stiver; 20 Stivers = 1 Florin or Guilder. Also 12 Grotes or Pence Flemish, or 6 Stivers = 1 Shilling Flemish; 20 Shillings Flemish, or 6 Florins = 1 Pound Flemish; $2\frac{1}{2}$ Florins, or 50 Stivers = 1 Rixdollar.

COURSE OF EXCHANGE. From the Amsterdam Quotation. *January* 7, 1820.			EXPLANATION.		
ANTWERP $4\frac{1}{2}$	per cent.	AMSTERDAM	receives	$104\frac{1}{2}$ Florins	for 100 Florins of exchange.
BRESLAU 144	....	———	receives	144 Rixdollars currency,	for 100 Rixdollars.
FRANCE . 55	....	———	gives	55 Grotes Flemish	for 3 Francs.
FRANCFORT $35\frac{3}{8}$	....	———	receives	$35\frac{3}{8}$ Stivers	for 1 Rixdollar.
GENOA .. 86	....	———	gives	86 Grotes Flemish	for 1 Pezza of $5\frac{3}{4}$ Lire.
HAMBURGH 34	....	———	gives	34 Stivers............	for 1 Rixdollar of 2 Marks.
LEGHORN. 93	....	———	gives	93 Grotes Flemish	for 1 Pezza of 8 Reals.
LISBON .. $40\frac{1}{2}$	....	———	gives	$40\frac{1}{2}$ Grotes Flemish....	for 1 old Crusado.
LONDON . 38	....	———	gives	38 Shillings	for 1 Pound sterling.
NAPLES.. 74	....	———	gives	74 Grotes............	for 1 Ducato di Regno.
SPAIN.... 95	....	———	gives	95 Grotes Flemish	for 1 Ducat of exchange.
VENICE.. 224	....	———	receives	224 Cent. Lire Italiane,	for 1 Florin.
VIENNA.. 14	....	———	gives	14 Stivers............	for 1 Rixdollar paper.
DITTO .. 34	....	———	gives	34 Stivers............	for 1 Rixdollar current effec.

[For the usances, &c. of bills of exchange, see AMSTERDAM, vol. i.]

AMSTERDAM ON LONDON, see page 20.

AMSTERDAM ON FRANCE.

Reduce 475 Florins 10 Stivers, 12 Pennings into French money; exchange at 54 Grotes Flemish per Ecu of 3 Francs.

	Gr. Flem.		Francs		Florins	Stivers	Pen.		Francs	Cents
As	54	:	3	: :	475	10	12	:	1056	75
	8				20					
	432				9510					
					16					
					152172					
					3					

Fr. Cents.
432)456516(1056 75
432 &c.

By the Chain Rule.

475 Flor. 10 St. 12 Pen.
1 Florin = 40 Grotes Flemish.
54 Grotes = 3 Francs.

Result as above.

LONDON ON AMSTERDAM, see page 20.

FRANCE ON AMSTERDAM.

Reduce 1056 Francs 75 Centimes into Dutch money; exchange at 54 Grotes Flemish per Ecu of 3 Francs.

	Fr.		Gr. Fl.		Fr.		Fl.	St.	Pen.
As	3	:	54	: :	1056,75	:	475	10	12
					54				

3)57064,50
4,0)1902,150
475,5375
20
10,7500
16
12,000

By the Chain Rule.

1056,75 Francs.
3 Francs = 54 Grotes Flemish.
40 Grotes = 1 Florin.

Result as above.

AMSTERDAM ON GENOA.

Reduce 4145 Florins 2 Stivers into money of Genoa; exchange at $84\frac{3}{4}$ Grotes Flemish per Pezza of $5\frac{3}{4}$ Lire.

	Grotes		Pezza		Florins	Stivers		Pezze	Soldi	Den.
As	$84\frac{3}{4}$	:	1	: :	4145	2	:	1956	7	9

To reduce Pezze to Lire.

	Pezze	Soldi	Den. di Lira
	1956	7	9
			23
	4)44996	18	3
Ans.	11249	4	7

By the Chain Rule.

4145 Florins 2 Stivers.
1 Florin = 40 Grotes Flemish.
$84\frac{3}{4}$ Grotes = 1 Pezza.
4 Pezze = 23 Lire.

Reduced gives 11249 L. 4 S. 7 D. as above.

GENOA ON AMSTERDAM.

Reduce 11249 Lire 4 Soldi 7 Denari into Dutch money; exchange at $84\frac{3}{4}$ Grotes Flemish per Pezza of $5\frac{3}{4}$ Lire.

To reduce Lire to Pezze.

11249 4 7
4
Pez. Soldi Den. di Pez.
23)44996 18 4(1956 7 9
23 &c. Then

	Pezza		Grotes		Pezze	Soldi	Den.		Florins	Sti.
As	1	:	$84\frac{3}{4}$	: :	1956	7	9	:	4145	2

By the Chain Rule.

11249 Lire 4 Soldi 7 Den.
23 Lire = 4 Pezze.
1 Pezza = $84\frac{3}{4}$ Grotes Flemish.
40 Grotes = 1 Florin.

Reduced gives 4145 Fl. 2 St. as above.

AMSTERDAM ON HAMBURGH.

Reduce 3309 Marks 12 Schillings into Dutch money; exchange at $32\frac{7}{8}$ Stivers per Rixdollar of 2 Marks Hamburgh banco.

	Marks		Stivers		Marks	Sch.		Florins	Stivers
As	2	:	$32\frac{7}{8}$	: :	3309	12	:	2720	4
	16				16				
	32				52956				
					$32\frac{7}{8}$				

$$32)1740928(5440,4 \text{ St.} = 2720 \text{ Fl. } 4 \text{ St.}$$

(2,0 — 160 &c.

By the Chain Rule.

	3309	Mks. 12 Sch.
2 Marks =	$32\frac{7}{8}$	Stivers.
20 Stivers =	1	Florin.

Result as above.

The exchange of Amsterdam on Hamburgh is sometimes done by giving 120 Marks for so many Florins current, the operation is then as follows:

Reduce 4080 Marks banco into Dutch money; exchange at 106 Florins for 120 Marks Hamburgh.

	Marks		Florins		Marks		Florins
As	120	:	106	: :	4080	:	3604

HAMBURGH ON AMSTERDAM.

Reduce 2720 Florins 4 Stivers into Hamburgh money; exchange at $32\frac{7}{8}$ Stivers per Rixdollar of exchange of 2 Marks banco.

	Stivers		Marks		Florins	Sti.		Marks	Sch.
As	$32\frac{7}{8}$	:	2	: :	2720	4	:	3309	12
	8		8		20				
	263		16		54404				
					16				

$$263)870464(3309 \text{ Marks } 12 \text{ Sch.}$$

789 &c.

By the Chain Rule.

	2720	Florins 4 Stivers.
1 Florin =	20	Stivers.
$32\frac{7}{8}$ Stivers =	2	Marks.

Result as above.

The exchange of Hamburgh on Amsterdam is sometimes done at so many Florins current for 120 Marks banco. The operation is then as follows:

Reduce 3604 Florins current into Hamburgh money; exchange at 106 Florins current for 120 Marks Hamburgh banco.

	Florins		Marks		Florins		Marks
As	106	:	120	: :	3604	:	4080

AMSTERDAM ON LEGHORN.

Reduce 9800 Dutch Florins into money of Leghorn; exchange at $87\frac{1}{2}$ Grotes Flemish per Pezza of 8 Reals.

	Gr.		Pezza		Florins		Pezze
As	$87\frac{1}{2}$	:	1	: :	9800	:	4480
	8				20		
	700				196000		
					16		

$$7,00)31360,00$$

$$4480$$

By the Chain Rule.

	9800	Florins.
1 Florin =	20	Grotes.
$87\frac{1}{2}$ Grotes =	1	Pezza.

Result as above.

LEGHORN ON AMSTERDAM.

Reduce 4480 Pezze of 8 Reals into Dutch money; exchange at $87\frac{1}{2}$ Grotes Flemish per Pezza.

	Pezza		Grotes		Pezze		Florins
As	1	:	$87\frac{1}{2}$	: :	4480	:	9800
					$87\frac{1}{2}$		

$$4,0)39200,0 \text{ Grotes.}$$

9800 Florins.

By the Chain Rule.

	4480	Pezze.
1 Pezza =	$87\frac{1}{2}$	Grotes.
20 Grotes =	1	Florin.

Result as above.

AMSTERDAM ON LISBON.

Reduce 557 Mil. 846 Rees into Dutch money; exchange at 46¼ Grotes Flemish per Crusado of 400 Rees.

```
Rees  Grotes     Milrees         Florins  Stiv.  Pen.
As 400 : 46¼ :: 557,846    :    1612     10     8
                  46¼
         4,00)258003,77
          4,0)6450,0944
                                Fl.      St.    Pen.
             1612,5236 =      1612     10     8
```

By the Chain Rule.

```
                557,846  Milrees.
400 Rees    =   46¼   Grotes Flemish.
 40 Grotes  =    1    Florin.
        Result as above.
```

LISBON ON AMSTERDAM.

Reduce 1612 Florins 10 Stivers 8 Pennings into Portugal money; exchange at 46¼ Grotes Flemish per Crusado of 400 Rees.

```
Grotes    Rees      Florins  Stiv.  Pen.    Milrees  Rees
As 46¼  :  400  ::   1612    10     8   :   557     846
    8              ×20×16×400
   370      37,0)20640320,0(557,846
                 185 &c.
```

By the Chain Rule.

```
                 1612  Florins 10 Stivers 8 Pen.
  1  Florin  =     40  Grotes Flemish.
 46¼ Grotes  =    400  Rees.
         Result as above.
```

AMSTERDAM ON SPAIN.

Reduce 956 Dollars 6 Reals of Plate into Dutch money; exchange at 94¼ Grotes Flemish per Ducat of plate.

```
Mar.        Gr.        Dol.  R.        Fl.   St.
As 375  :  94¼  ::    956   6    :    1635   3
              ×8×34×94¼
                       (4,0
       375)24527243(6540,6 Grotes.
           2250
                  1635,15 Florins.
            2027 &c.   20
                     3,00 Stivers.
```

By the Chain Rule.

```
                  956 Dollars 6 Reals.
  1 Dollar    =   272 Maravedis.
375 Marav.    =   94¼ Grotes.
 40 Grotes    =     1 Florin.
         Result as above.
```

SPAIN ON AMSTERDAM.

Reduce 1635 Florins 3 Stivers into Spanish money; exchange at 94¼ Grotes Flemish per Ducat of 375 Maravedis of plate.

```
Gr.       Mar.       Fl.   St.       Dol.  R.
As 94¼  :  375  ::  1635    3    :    956   6
   8               ×20×16×375
                           34       (8
  754      754)196213000(260236(7654 Reals.
                1508       238
                                    956 D. 6 R.
                4541 &c.  222 &c.
```

By the Chain Rule.

```
                     1635 Florins 3 Stivers.
  1  Florin   =        40 Grotes Flemish.
 94¼ Grotes   =       375 Maravedis.
272  Marav.   =         1 Dollar of Plate.
          Result as above.
```

The Exchanges of ANTWERP are similar to those of Amsterdam, for the Monies of Exchange and Regulations of which, see ANTWERP, vol. i.

AUGSBURG.

MONIES OF EXCHANGE.

Exchanges are computed here in Florins and Creutzers; and also in Rixdollars and Creutzers.

60 Creutzers = 1 Florin or Gulden; 90 Creutzers, or 1½ Florin = 1 Rixdollar of account; 100 Rixdollars Giro, or money of exchange = 127 Rixdollars current, or 190½ Florins current; 2 Florins = 1 Rixdollar specie.

COURSE OF EXCHANGE, From the Augsburg Quotation. *January*, 1820.				EXPLANATION.
AMSTERDAM	110	.. AUGSBURG	gives	110 Rixdollars Giro ..... for 100 Rixdollars.
FRANCE	120	.. ———	gives	120 Florins current ...... for 100 Ecus of 3 Francs.
FRANCFORT	102	.. ———	gives	102 Rixdollars current .. for 100 Rixdollars current.
GENOA	62	.. ———	receives	62 Soldi fuori banco .... for 1 Florin current.
HAMBURGH	118	.. ———	gives	118 Rixdollars Giro...... for 100 Rixdollars banco.
LEGHORN	57	.. ———	receives	57 Soldi moneta buona .. for 1 Florin current.
LEIPSIC	99	.. ———	gives	99 Rixdollars current .. for 100 Rixdollars of exchange.
LONDON	9 45	.. ———	gives	9 Flor. 45 Creutzers cur. for £1 sterling.
MILAN	67	.. ———	receives	67 Soldi current........ for 1 Florin current.
NUREMBERG	101	.. ———	gives	101 Florins current...... for 100 Florins current.
VIENNA	106	.. ———	receives	106 Florins .... for 100 Florins current.

[For usances and other particulars relating to bills of exchange, see AUGSBURG, vol. i.]

AUGSBURG ON AMSTERDAM.

Reduce 1197 Florins 18 Stivers $5\frac{1}{2}$ Pennings into Augsburg currency; exchange at 112 Rixdollars money of exchange per 100 Rixdollars of Amsterdam, each $2\frac{1}{2}$ Florins.

	Rixd.		Rixd. of ex.		Florins	Stivers	Pen.		Florins	Cr.cur.
As	100	:	112	: :	1197	18	$5\frac{1}{2}$	:	1022	21
	$2\frac{1}{2}$				20					
	250				23958					
	× 20 × 16				16					

383323,5
112

8,0000)4293,2232

536,6529 Rixdollars.
3

2)1609,9581

804,9798 Florins of exchange.

805 × 127 ÷ 100 = 1022 Florins 21 Cr. cur.

AMSTERDAM ON AUGSBURG.

Reduce 1022 Florins 21 Creutzers, Augsburg currency, into Dutch money; exchange at 112 Rixdollars money of exchange per 100 Rixdollars of Amsterdam.

[127 R. Cur. = 100 R. of Ex.]

	Rixd. cur.		Rixd. of ex.		Florins	Cr.		Fl. of ex.
As	127	:	100	: :	1022	21	:	805
								2

3)1610

$536\frac{2}{3}$

	Rixd. exch.		Rixd.		Rixd.	Cr.		Florins	St.	P.
And as	112	:	100	: :	536	60	:	1197	18	$5\frac{1}{2}$
	90		$2\frac{1}{2}$		90					
	10080		250		48300					
					250					

1008,0)1207500,0(1197 Florins 18 St. $5\frac{1}{2}$ P.
1008

1995 &c.

Remainder × 20 × 16 &c.

AUGSBURG ON FRANCE.

Reduce 2542 Francs 50 Centimes into money of Augsburg; exchange at 124 Rixdollars currency per 100 Ecus of 3 Francs.

	Francs		Rixdollars		Francs		Florins	Cr.
As	300	:	124	: :	2542,50	:	1576	21
					124			

3,00)3152,7000

1050,90
$1\frac{1}{2}$

1576,35
60

21,00

By the Chain Rule.

		2542 Francs 50 Centimes.
300 Francs	=	124 Rixdollars.
2 Rixdollars	=	3 Florins.

Result as above.

FRANCE ON AUGSBURG.

Reduce 1576 Florins 21 Creutzers, Augsburg currency, into French money; exchange at 124 Rixdollars per 100 Ecus of 3 Francs.

	Rixdollars		Francs		Florins	Creutz.		Francs	Centimes
As	124	:	300	: :	1576	21	:	2542	50
	90				60				
	11160				94581				
					300				

1116,0)2837430,0(2542,50
2232

6054 &c.

By the Chain Rule.

		1576 Florins 21 Creutzers.
3 Florins	=	2 Rixdollars.
124 Rixdollars	=	300 Francs.

Result as above.

AUGSBURG ON GENOA.

Reduce 11616 Lire 19 Soldi 10 Denari fuori banco into money of Augsburg; exchange at 62 Soldi per Florin Augsburg currency.

	Soldi		Florin		Lire	Soldi	Denari		Florins	Cr.
As	62	:	1	: :	11616	19	10	:	3747	25
	12				20					
	744				232339					
					12					

744)2788078)3747 Florins 25 Creutzers
2232
5560 &c.

By the Chain Rule.

		11616 Lire 19 Sol. 10 Den.
1 Lira	=	20 Soldi.
62 Soldi	=	1 Florin.

Result as above.

GENOA ON AUGSBURG.

Reduce 3747 Florins 25 Creutzers, Augsburg currency, into money of Genoa; exchange at 62 Soldi fuori banco per Florin.

	Florin		Soldi		Florins	Creutzers		Lire	Sol.	Den.
As	1	:	62	: :	3747	25	:	11616	19	10
					60					
					224845					
					62					

6,0)1394039,0
2,0)23233,9 10
11616 Lire 19 Soldi 10 Denari.

By the Chain Rule.

		3747 Florins 25 Cr.
1 Florin	=	62 Soldi.
20 Soldi	=	1 Florin.

Result as above.

AUGSBURG ON HAMBURGH.

Reduce 3546 Marks 6 Schillings 4 Pfenings banco into money of Augsburg; exchange at 144 Rixdollars Augsburg currency per 100 Rixdollars Hamburgh banco.

[60 Creutzers = 1 Florin; 90 Creutzers = 1 Rixdollar of account.]

	Rixd. H.		Rixd. A.		Marks	Sch.	Pf.		Fl.	Cr.
As	100	:	144	: :	3546	6	4	:	2553	24
	3				16					
	300				56742					
	16				12					
	4800				680908					
	12				144					
	57600									

57600)98050752(170227 Rixd. A.
57600 $1\frac{1}{2}$
404507&c. 2553,40
60
24,00

HAMBURGH ON AUGSBURG.

Reduce 2553 Florins 24 Creutzers, Augsburg currency, into Hamburg banco; exchange at 144 Rixdollars of Augsburg per 100 Rixdollars Hamburgh banco.

	Rixd. A.		Rixd. H.		Florins	Cr.		Marks	Sch.	Pf.
As	144	:	100	: :	2553	24	:	3546	6	4
	90				60					
	12960				153204					
					100					

1296,0)1532040,0(1182 Rixd. H. 2 $1\frac{1}{3}$
1296 3
2360 &c. 3546 6 4

Remainder × 16 × 12 &c.

N.B. The exchanges of Augsburg with LEGHORN are performed on the same principle as the above with Genoa; and those of LONDON with Augsburg are the same as with Vienna, p. 27.

BERLIN AND BRESLAU.

MONIES OF EXCHANGE.

Exchanges are computed here in Rixdollars, good Groschen, and Pfenings, currency.

12 Pfenings = 1 good Grosche; 24 good Groschen = 1 Rixdollar currency, or Rixdollar of account.

COURSE OF EXCHANGE, from the Berlin Quotation. *January*, 1820.		EXPLANATION.
AMSTERDAM	147½	.. BERLIN gives 147½ Rixdollars current for 250 Florins, or 100 Rixd.
AUGSBURG	102	.. ——— gives 102 ——— ...... for 100 Rixd. convention money.
FRANCE	79	.. ——— gives 79 ——— ...... for 100 Ecus of 3 Francs.
FRANCFORT........	105	.. ——— gives 105 ——— ...... for 100 Rixdollars current.
HAMBURGH, in banco	150	.. ——— gives 150 ——— ...... for 100 Rixdollars banco.
KONIGSBERG	100⅔	.. ——— gives 100⅔ ——— ...... for 100 Rixdollars current.
LEIPSIC	104	.. ——— gives 104 ——— ...... for 100 Rixd. convention money.
LONDON	6 14	.. ——— gives 6 ———14Grosc. for 1 Pound sterling.
VIENNA	41	.. ——— gives 41 ——— current for 100 Rixdollars current.

[For the usances and other particulars relating to Bills of Exchange, see BERLIN and BRESLAU, vol. i.]

F 2

BERLIN ON AMSTERDAM.

Reduce 4656 Florins 5 Stivers into Prussian money; exchange at 146 Rixdollars Prussian currency per 100 Rixdollars of Amsterdam.

```
Rixd. Dutch.  Rixd. Prussian.  Florins Stivers    Rixd. Groschen
As 100    :    146    : :     4656    5    :     2719    6
   2½                           20
  ----                        ------
   250                        93125
    20                          146
  ----                        ------
  5000          5,000)13596,250
                      ---------
                        2719,25
                             24
                        -------
                           6,00
```

By the Chain Rule.

		4656 Florins 5 Stivers.
5 Florins	=	2 Rixdollars.
100 Rixdollars	=	146 Prussian Rixdollars.

Result as above.

AMSTERDAM ON BERLIN.

Reduce 2719 Rixdollars 6 good Groschen Prussian currency into Dutch money; exchange at 146 Rixdollars Prussian per 100 Rixdollars Dutch.

```
Rixd. Prussian. Rixd. Dutch.  Rixd. Groschen   Florins Stivers
As 146    :    100    : :    2719    6    :    4656    5
    24          2½             24
  ----         ----          ------
  3504          250          65262
                               250
                         -------------  Florins  Sti.
                   3504)16315500(4656      5
                        14016
                        -----
                        22995 &c.
```

By the Chain Rule.

		2719 Rixdollars 6 Groschen.
146 Prussian Rxds.	=	100 Rxds. of Amsterdam.
2 Rixdollars	=	5 Florins.

Result as above.

BERLIN ON FRANCE.

Reduce 1943 Francs 75 Centimes into Prussian money; exchange at 76 Rixdollars Prussian currency per 100 Ecus of 3 Francs.

```
Francs     Rixd.      Francs  Cen.       Rixd.  Gr.
As 300  :   76   : :   1943    75    :    492   10
                               76
                       ----------
                3,00)1477,25
                     --------
                     492,41667
                            24
                     ---------
                      10,00008
```

FRANCE ON BERLIN.

Reduce 492 Rixdollars 10 Groschen, Prussian currency, into French money; exchange at 76 Rixdollars per 100 Ecus of 3 Francs.

```
Rixd.     Francs     Rixd. Groschen    Francs  Cen.
As 76  :   300   : :  492    10    :   1943    75
   24                  24
  ----               -----
  1824               11818
                       300
                    -------
           1824)3545400(1943,75
                1824
                ----
                17214 &c.
```

BERLIN ON HAMBURGH.

Reduce 1908 Marks 5 Schillings 4 Pfenings banco into Prussian currency; exchange at $145\frac{1}{2}$ Prussian Rixdollars per 100 Rixdollars Hamburgh banco.

Rixd bco.		Rixd. Pr.		Marks.	Sch.	Pf.		Rixd.	Gr.
As 100	:	$145\frac{1}{2}$	: :	1908	5	4	:	925	13
3				16					
300				30533					
16				12					
4800				366400					
12				$145\frac{1}{2}$					
57600		576,00)533112,00(925,54							
		5184 24							
		1471 &c. 12,96							

HAMBURGH ON BERLIN.

Reduce 925 Rixdollars 13 good Groschen Prussian currency into Hamburgh banco; exchange at $145\frac{1}{2}$ Prussian Rixdollars per 100 Rixdollars Hamburgh banco.

Rixd. Pr.		Rixd. bco.		Rixd.	Gr.		Mks.	Sch.	Pf.
As $145\frac{1}{2}$	:	100	: :	925	13	:	1908	5	4
24		3		24					
3492		300		22213					
				300					

Marks Sch. Pf.
3492)6663900(1908 5 4
3492
31719 &c.

Remainder × 16 × 12 &c.

BERLIN ON LONDON.

Reduce £115 13s. 4d. sterling into Prussian currency; exchange at $6\frac{3}{4}$ Rixdollars per £ sterling.

£		Rixd.		£	s.	d.		Rixd.	Gr.
As 1	:	$6\frac{3}{4}$	: :	115	13	4	:	780	13
		24		20					
		162		2313					
				12					
				27760					
				162					

——— 24 Rds. Gr.
24,0)449712,0(18738 Gr.(780 18
24 168
2097 &c. 193 &c.

LONDON ON BERLIN.

Reduce 780 Rixdollars 18 good Groschen Prussian currency into sterling; exchange at $6\frac{3}{4}$ Rixdollars per £ sterling.

Rixd.		£		Rixd.	Gr.		£	s.	d.
As $6\frac{3}{4}$	:	1	: :	780	18	:	115	13	4
24				24					
162									

£ s. d.
162)18738(115 13 4
162
253 &c.

Remainder × 20 × 12 &c.

N.B. The Exchanges between BERLIN and most other cities in GERMANY are computed by a Percentage, like those with Amsterdam and Hamburgh, and the calculations are, of course, similar. Examples of those cities are therefore deemed unnecessary, as well as between places where there is little or no commercial intercourse.

BOLOGNA, *see Rome.*

BOLOGNA, *see Rome.*

BREMEN.

MONIES OF EXCHANGE.

Exchanges are computed in Rixdollars, Grotes, and Swares.

5 Swares = 1 Grote; 32 Grotes = 1 Bremen Mark; 72 Grotes, or 2¼ Marks = 1 Rixdollar of account.

96 Grotes, or 1⅓ Rixdollar of account = 1 Rixdollar specie.

COURSE OF EXCHANGE, From the Bremen Quotation. *January*, 1820.		EXPLANATION.				
AMSTERDAM	143	BREMEN gives	143	Rixdollars	for	100 Rixdollars.
FRANCE	20	——— gives	20	Grotes	for	1 Franc.
FRANCFORT	110	——— gives	110	Rixdollars	for	100 Rixdollars convention money.
HAMBURGH	142	——— gives	142	———	for	100 Rixdollars banco.
LEIPSIC	104	——— gives	104	———	for	100 Rixdollars currency.
LONDON	605	——— gives	605	———	for	£100 sterling.
NUREMBERG	104	——— gives	104	———	for	100 Rixdollars currency.
VIENNA	90	——— gives	90	———	for	100 Rixdollars currency.

[For the usances and days of grace, see BREMEN, vol. i.]

BREMEN ON HAMBURGH.

Reduce 7817 Marks 11 Schillings 4 Pfenings banco into money of Bremen; exchange at 140 Rixdollars Bremen currency per 100 Rixdollars Hamburgh banco.

	Rixd. Ham.		Rixd. Br.		Marks	Sch.	Pf.		Rixd.	Grotes
As	100	:	140	: :	7817	11	4	:	3648	19

100 × 3 = 300; 300 × 16 = 4800; 4800 × 12 = 57600

7817 × 16 = 125083; × 12 = 1501000; × 140

576,00)2101400,00(3648 Rixd. 19 Gr.
1728

3734 &c.

Remainder × 72 &c.

HAMBURGH ON BREMEN.

Reduce 3648 Rixdollars 19 Grotes, Bremen currency, into money of Hamburgh; exchange at 140 Rixdollars Bremen per 100 Rixdollars Hamburgh banco.

	Rixd. Br.		Rixd. Ham.		Rixd.	Grotes		Marks	Sch.	Pf.
As	140	:	100	: :	3648	19	:	7817	11	4

140 × 72 = 10080

100 × 3 = 300

3648 × 72 = 262675; × 300

1008,0)7880250,0(7817 Mks. 11 Sch. 4 Pf.
7056

8242 &c.

Remainder × 16 × 12 &c.

BREMEN ON LONDON.

Reduce £383 6s. 8d. sterling into money of Bremen; exchange at 604½ Rixdollars per £100 sterling.

	£		Rixdollars		£	s.	d.		Rixd.	Grotes
As	100	:	604½	: :	383	6	8	:	2317	18

383 × 20 = 7666; × 12 = 92000; × 604½

24,000)55614,000(2317 Rixd. 18 Gr.
48

76 &c.

LONDON ON BREMEN.

Reduce 2317 Rixdollars 18 Grotes, Bremen currency, into sterling; exchange at 604½ Rixdollars per £100 sterling.

	Rixdollars		£		Rixd.	Grotes		£	s.	d.
As	604½	:	100	: :	2317	18	:	383	6	8

604½ × 72: 1208, 4228, 36 = 43524

2317 × 72

43524)16684200(383 £ 6 s. 8 d.
130572

362700
348192

145080 &c.

Remainder × 20 &c.

The Exchanges between Bremen and other places are similar to the above, as may be seen by the Quotation.

CONSTANTINOPLE.

MONIES OF EXCHANGE.

Exchanges are computed in Piastres, Paras, and Aspers; or in Piastres and Aspers; sometimes in Piastres and half Paras, or in Piastres and Minas.

3 Aspers = 1 Para; 40 Paras, or 120 Aspers = 1 Piastre, or Turkish Dollar.

80 half Paras, or 100 Minas, also called Aspers = 1 Piastre.

COURSE OF EXCHANGE, From the Constantinople Quotation. *January*, 1820.		EXPLANATION.	
AMSTERDAM .. 115	.. CONSTANTINOPLE	gives 115 Paras	for 1 Florin.
FRANCE 14½	.. ————	receives 14½ Sols	for 1 Piastre.
GENOA 44	.. ————	gives 44 Paras	for 1 Lira fuori banco.
HAMBURGH 20	.. ————	receives 20 Grotes Flemish	for 1 Piastre.
LEGHORN 283	.. ————	gives 283 Paras	for 1 Pezza of 8 Reals.
LONDON 35	.. ————	gives 35 Piastres	for £1 sterling.
MALTA 124	.. ————	gives 124 Paras	for 1 Scudo.
RUSSIA 73	.. ————	receives 73 Copecs	for 1 Piastre.
SMYRNA 100½	.. ————	receives 100½ Piastres....	for 100 Piastres.
TRIESTE 140	.. ————	gives 140 Paras	for 1 Florin current.
VENICE 80	.. ————	receives 80 Centimes	for 1 Piastre.
VIENNA 140	.. ————	gives 140 Paras	for 1 Florin current.

[For usances and other customs relating to Bills of Exchange, see CONSTANTINOPLE, vol. i.]

CONSTANTINOPLE ON AMSTERDAM.

Reduce 2904 Florins 12 Stivers 2 Pennings into Turkish money; exchange at 61 Paras per Florin.

	Florin		Paras		Florins	Stivers	Pen.		Dollars	Paras
As	1	:	61	: :	2904	12	2	:	4429	21

20 | 20
20 | 58092
16 | 16
320 | 929474
61

4,0
320)56697914(17718,1
320 &c.

4429 Dol. 21 Paras.

As the Turkish monies are subject to continual variation, the old prices are retained in these questions, being equally proper to exemplify the operations.

AMSTERDAM ON CONSTANTINOPLE.

Reduce 4429 Turkish Dollars 21 Paras into Dutch money; exchange at 61 Paras per Florin.

	Paras		Florin		Dollars	Paras		Florins	Stivers	Pen.
As	61	:	1	: :	4429	21	:	2904	12	2

40

Fl. Sti. Pen.
61)177181(2904 12 2
122
551
549
281 &c.

Remainder × 20 × 16 &c.

CONSTANTINOPLE ON FRANCE.

Reduce 8903 Francs 7 Centimes of France into Turkish money; exchange at 1 Franc 38 Centimes per Piastre.

	Franc	Cen.		Dollar		Francs	Centimes		Dollars	Paras
As	1	38	:	1	: :	8903	7	:	6451	20

1,38)8903,07(6451 20
828
623 &c.

The most general mode of quoting the exchange is in French Sols for the Piastre. The Sol, in such case, is considered as $\frac{1}{20}$ of the Franc, or 5 Centimes: thus—

Reduce 5385 Francs 84 Centimes into Piastres; exchange at 14½ Sols per Piastre.

	Sols		Piastre		Francs	Cen.		Piastres	Paras
As	14,5	:	1	: :	5385	84	:	7428	30

5 | 1
72,5 | 725)5385,84(7428 30
5075
3108 &c.

FRANCE ON CONSTANTINOPLE.

Reduce 6451 Turkish Dollars 20 Paras into French money; exchange at 1 Franc 38 Centimes per Piastre.

	Dollar		Franc	Cen.		Dollars	Paras		Francs	Centimes
As	1	:	1	38	: :	6451	20	:	8903	7

40 | 40
40 | 258060
1,38
4,0)35612,280
8903,07 Francs.

Reduce 7428 Piastres 30 Paras into French money; exchange at 14½ Sols per Piastre.

	Piastre		Sols		Piastres	Paras		Francs	Cen.
As	1	:	14,5	: :	7428	30	:	5385	84

40 | 5 | 40
40 | 72,5 | 297150
72,5
4,0)2154337,50
5385,84

CONSTANTINOPLE ON LEGHORN.

Reduce 264 Pezze 10 Soldi 8 Denari into Turkish money; exchange at 142½ Paras per Pezza.

```
     Pezza   Paras         Pezze Soldi Den.    Dollars Paras
As     1  :  142½  : :     264   10    8   :   942     16
      20                    20
      —                   ————
      20                  5290
      12                    12
     ———                  ————
     240                 63488
                          142½
                   ——————— 4,0
           24,0)904704,0(3769,6
                72        ————
                ——            942 Dol. 16 Paras.
                184 &c.
```

By the Chain Rule.

```
                  264 Pezze 10 Soldi 8 Den.
 1 Pezza    =     142½ Paras.
40 Paras    =       1 Dollar.
```

Result as above.

LEGHORN ON CONSTANTINOPLE.

Reduce 942 Turkish Dollars 16 Paras into money of Leghorn; exchange at 142½ Paras per Pezza of 8 Reals.

```
    Paras   Pez.     Dollars Paras     Pezze Soldi Den.
As  142½  :  1  : :  942     16    :   264   10    8
      2              40
     ——             ————
    285             37696
                       2
                    ————     Pez.   Sol.  Den.
               285)75392(264     10    8
                   570
                   ———
                   1839
                   1710
                   ————
                    1292 &c.
```

By the Chain Rule.

```
                  942 Dollars 16 Paras.
  1 Dollar    =    40 Paras.
142½ Paras    =     1 Pezza.
```

Result as above.

CONSTANTINOPLE ON LONDON.

Reduce £81 2s. 7d. sterling into Turkish money; exchange at 18 Turkish Dollars per £ sterling.

```
     £     Dollars        £   s.  d.       Dollars  Paras
As   1  :  18    : :     81   2   7    :   1460     13
    20                   20
    —                   ———
    20                 1622
    12                   12
   ———                 ————
   240                19471
                         18
                ——————————— Dollars  Paras
             24,0)35047,8(1460     13
                  24
                  ——
                  110 &c.
```

Remainder × 40 &c.

LONDON ON CONSTANTINOPLE.

Reduce 1460 Turkish Dollars 13 Paras into sterling; exchange at 18 Dollars per £ sterling.

```
    Dollars  £       Dollars Paras       £   s.  d.
As  18    :  1  : :  1460    13     :    81  2   7
    40               40
   ———             ———————  £   s.  d.
   720          720)58413(81   2   7
                    5760
                    ————
                     813
                     720
                     ———
                      93
                      20
                     ———
                720)1860(2
                    1440
                    ————
                     420 &c.
```

CONSTANTINOPLE ON VENICE.

Reduce 10420 Lire 13 Soldi 4 Denari Piccoli into Turkish money; exchange at 354 Paras per Sequin of 22 Lire.

	Lire		Paras		Lire	Sol.	Den.		Dollars	Paras
As	22	:	354	: :	10420	13	4	:	4191	38
	20				20					
	440				208413					
	12				12					
	5280				2500960					
					354					

4,0

5280)885339840(16767,8

5280

4191 Dol. 38 Paras.

35733 &c.

The above mode of exchange is partly discontinued, as Venice gives a variable number of Italian Centimes for the Piastre, making the operation the same as with France.

VENICE ON CONSTANTINOPLE.

Reduce 4191 Turkish Dollars 38 Paras into Venetian money; exchange at 354 Paras per Sequin of 22 Lire Piccole.

	Paras		Lire		Dollars	Paras		Lire	Sol.	Den.
As	354	:	22	: :	4191	38	:	10420	13	4
					40					
					167678					
					22					

Lire Sol. Den.

354)3688916(10420 13 4

354

1489

1416

731 &c.

Remainder × 20 × 12 &c.

CONSTANTINOPLE ON VIENNA.

Reduce 3737 Florins 48 Creutzers into Turkish money; the exchange of Vienna with Constantinople being at 50 Paras per Florin.

	Florin		Paras		Florins	Creutzers		Dollars	Paras
As	1	:	50	: :	3737	48	:	4672	10
	60				60				
	60				224268				
					50				

6,0)1121340,0

4,0)18689,0

4672 10

By the Chain Rule.

3737,8 Florins

1 Florin	=	50 Paras.
40 Paras	=	1 Dollar.

Result as above.

VIENNA ON CONSTANTINOPLE.

Reduce 4672 Turkish Dollars 10 Paras into Austrian money; the exchange of Constantinople with Vienna being at 50 Paras per Florin.

	Paras		Florin		Dollars	Paras		Florins	Cr.
As	50	:	1	: :	4672	10	:	3737	48
					40				

5,0)18689,0

3737,8

60

48,0

By the Chain Rule.

4672,25 Dollars.

1 Dollar	=	40 Paras.
50 Paras	=	1 Florin.

Result as above.

COPENHAGEN.

MONIES OF EXCHANGE.

Exchanges are computed here in Rixdollars, Marks, and Skillings Danish; but sometimes in Rixdollars, Marks, and Schillings Lubs. Pfenings are also occasionally reckoned.

12 Pfenings = 1 Skilling.

16 Skillings = 1 Mark.

6 Marks Danish, or 3 Marks Lubs = 1 Ryksdaler, or Rixdollar.

Thus 2 Pfenings, Skillings, or Marks Danish = 1 Pfening, Schilling, or Mark Lubs.

COURSE OF EXCHANGE, From the Copenhagen Quotation.			EXPLANATION.
AMSTERDAM..	143	.... COPENHAGEN	gives 143 Rixdollars Danish currency.. for 100 Rdrs.
FRANCE	25	.... ———	gives 25 Skillings Danish........... for 1 Franc.
HAMBURGH ..	149¼	.... ———	gives 149¼ Rixdollars do. .... for 100 Rdrs. bco.
LONDON......	6 33....	———	gives 6 Rixdollars 33 Skillings...... for £1 sterling.
STOCKHOLM ..	36	.... ———	receives 36 Skillings .... for 1 Rixdollar.

[For days of grace and other particulars relating to Bills of Exchange, see COPENHAGEN, vol. i.]

COPENHAGEN ON AMSTERDAM.

Reduce 1310 Florins 4 Stivers 13 Pennings into Danish money; exchange at 127 Rixdollars Danish per 100 Rixdollars Dutch current, and the agio of banco on current being $3\frac{3}{4}$ per cent.

	Rixd. cur.		Banco		Flor.	Sti.	Pen. bco.		Flor.	Stiv.	Pen. cur.
As	100	:	$103\frac{3}{4}$	: :	1310	4	13	:	1359	7	8

	Rxds. Dutch.		Rxds. Danish.		Flor.	Sti.	Pen.		Rxds.	Mks.	Sk.
And as	100	:	127	: :	1359	7	8	:	690	3	6

$2\frac{1}{2}$ × 20 × 16

250 435000
20 127

5000 8,0000)5524,5000
16

690,5625
80000 6

3,3750
16

6,0000

By the Chain Rule.

		1310 Flor. 4 St. 13 Pen. bco.
100 Florins bco.	=	$103\frac{3}{4}$ Florins current.
$2\frac{1}{2}$ Florins	=	1 Rixdollar.
100 Rxds. cur.	=	127 Rixdollars Danish.

Result as above.

AMSTERDAM ON COPENHAGEN.

Reduce 690 Rixdollars 3 Marks 6 Skillings Danish into Dutch banco; exchange at 127 Rixdollars Danish per 100 Rixdollars Dutch current, and the agio of banco on current being $3\frac{3}{4}$ per cent.

	Rxds. Danish.		Rixds. cur.		Rxds.	Mks.	Sks.		Florins	Sti.	Pen.
As	127	:	100	: :	690	3	6	:	1359	7	8

6 $2\frac{1}{2}$ 6

762 250 4143
16 16

12192 66294
250

12192)16573500(1359 Fl. 7 Sti. 8 Pen. cur.

					Flor.	Sti.	Pen. cur.		Fl.	St.	Pen. bco.
And as	$103\frac{3}{4}$	:	100	: :	1359	7	8	:	1310	4	13

4 4 400

415 400 415)543750(1310 Fl. 4 Sti. 13 Pen.
415 &c.

By the Chain Rule.

		690 Rxds. 3 Mks. 6 Sks.
127 Rxds. Danish	=	100 Rxds. Dutch current.
$103\frac{3}{4}$ Rxds. current	=	100 Rxds. banco.
1 Rixdollar	=	$2\frac{1}{2}$ Florins.

Result as above.

COPENHAGEN ON FRANCE.

Reduce 6698 Francs 36 Centimes into Danish money; exchange at $72\frac{1}{2}$ Rixdollars per 100 Ecus of 3 Francs.

	Francs		Rixdollars		Francs		Rixdollars	Marks	Skil.
As	300	:	$72\frac{1}{2}$	:	6698,36	:	1618	4	10

72,5

3,00)4856,31100

1618,77033
6

4,62198
16

9,95168

FRANCE ON COPENHAGEN.

Reduce 1618 Rixdollars 4 Marks 10 Skillings Danish into French money; exchange at $72\frac{1}{2}$ Rixdollars per 100 Ecus of 3 Francs.

	Rixd.		Francs		Rixd.	Mks.	Skill.		Francs	Cen.
As	$72\frac{1}{2}$	:	300	: :	1618	4	10	:	6698	36

6 6

435 9712
16 16

6960 155402
300

696,0)4662060,0(6698,36 Francs
4176

4860 &c.

COPENHAGEN ON HAMBURGH.

Reduce 12354 Marks 11 Schillings Hamburgh banco into Danish money; exchange at 142 Rixdollars Danish per 100 Rixdollars banco.

Rixd. bco.		Rixd. Dan.		Mks.	Sch.		Rixd.	Mks.	Sks.
As 100	:	142	: :	12354	11	:	5847	5	5
3				16					
300				197675					
16				142					
4800				48,00)280698,50(5847 5 5 (Rxds. Mks. Sks.)					
				240					
				406 &c.					

By the Chain Rule.

12354 Marks 11 Sch.
3 Marks = 1 Rixdollar.
100 Rixdollars = 142 Rixd. Danish.

Result as above.

HAMBURGH ON COPENHAGEN.

Reduce 5847 Rixdollars 5 Marks 5 Skillings Danish into Hamburgh money; exchange at 142 Rixdollars Danish per 100 Rixdollars Hamburgh banco.

Rxds. Danish.		Rxds. banco		Rxds.	Mks.	Sks.		Marks	Sch.
As 142	:	100	: :	5847	5	5	:	12354	11
6		3		6					
852		300		35087					
16				16					
13632				561397					
				300					
				13632)168419100(12354 11 (Mks. Sch. Lubs)					
				13632					
				32099 &c.					

By the Chain Rule.

5847 Rxds. 5 Mks. 5 Sks.
142 Rxds. Danish = 100 Rxds. Hamburgh bco.
1 Rixdollar = 3 Marks.

Result as above.

COPENHAGEN ON LONDON.

Reduce £621 16s. 3d. sterling into Danish money; exchange at 6 Rixdollars 1 Mark Danish per £ sterling.

£		Rxds.	Mark		£	s.	d.		Rxds.	Mks.	Skil.
As 1	:	6	1	: :	621	16	3	:	3834	3	1
		6			20						
		37			12436						
					12						
					149235						
					37						
					6						
					24,0)552169,5(23007						
					48				3834 Rdrs. 3 Mks. 1Sk.		
					72 &c.						

LONDON ON COPENHAGEN.

Reduce 3834 Rixdollars 3 Marks 1 Skilling Danish into sterling; exchange at 6 Rixdollars 1 Mark per £ sterling.

Rdxs.	Mark		£		Rxds.	Marks	Sk.		£	s.	d.
As 6	1	:	1	: :	3834	3	1	:	621	16	3
6					6						
37					23007						
16					16						
592					592)368113(621 16 3 (£ s. d.)						
					3552						
					1291						
					1184						
					1073 &c.						

Remainder × 20 × 12 &c.

DANTZIC.

MONIES OF EXCHANGE.

Exchanges are computed here in Florins, Groschen, and Pfenings.

3 Pfenings = 1 Groschen.
30 Groschen = 1 Florin or Gulden.
3 Florins = 1 Rixdollar.

COURSE OF EXCHANGE, From the Dantzic Quotation. *January*, 1820.		EXPLANATION.			
AMSTERDAM	314	DANTZIC	gives 314	Groschen	for 1 Pound Flemish.
FRANCE	98	——	gives 98	Rixdollars	for 100 Ecus of 3 Francs.
FRANCFORT	88	——	gives 88	Groschen	for 1 Rixdollar.
HAMBURGH	141	——	gives 141	Groschen	for 1 Rixdollar specie.
LEIPSIC	104	——	gives 104	Rixdollars	for 100 Rixdollars.
LONDON	19⅓	——	gives 19⅓	Florins	for £1 sterling.
STOCKHOLM	9½	——	receives 9½	Skillings	for 1 Florin.

[For the usances and other particulars relating to Bills of Exchange, see DANTZIC, vol. i.]

DANTZIC ON AMSTERDAM.

Reduce 1881 Florins 16 Stivers into Dantzic money; exchange at 415 Dantzic Groschen per £ Flemish.

```
£ Flemish  Groschen     Florins Stivers   Florins Grosch. Pfenings
As 1  :  415  : :  1881  16   :  4338   17   15
   6                 20
   —               -----
   6              37636
  20                415
  ——            ---------
 120      12,0)1561894,0
                ---------
          3,0)13015,7  15
              -------
          4338 Flor. 17 Grosch. 15 Pfen.
```

By the Chain Rule.

		1881 Florins 16 Stivers.
6 Dutch Florins	=	1 Pound Flemish.
1 Pound Flemish	=	415 Groschen.
30 Groschen	=	1 Florin Dantzic.

Result as above.

AMSTERDAM ON DANTZIC.

Reduce 4338 Florins 17 Groschen 15 Pfenings Dantzic currency into Dutch money; exchange at 415 Groschen per £ Flemish.

```
Groschen  £ Flemish  Florins  Gr.  Pf.     Florins  Stivers
As 415  :  1  : :  4338  17  15  :  1881  16
    18                30
   ——              ------
  7470             130157
                       18
                  --------      £    s.  d
       747,0)234284,1(313     12   8 Flemish.
             2241 &c.          6
                           --------
                           1881  12
                                  4 St. for 8d.
                           --------
                     Fl. 1881   16 Stivers.
```

By the Chain Rule.

		4338 Fl. 17 Gr. 15 Pf.
1 Florin Dantzic	=	30 Groschen.
415 Groschen	=	1 Pound Flemish.
1 Pound Flemish	=	6 Dutch Florins.

Result as above.

DANTZIC ON HAMBURGH.

Reduce 837 Marks 4 Schillings banco into Dantzic money; exchange at 168 Groschen per Rixdollar banco.

```
Rixd.   Marks  Groschen      Marks Schil.   Florins Groschen
As 1  or 3  :  168  : :  837   4   :  1562   26
         16              16
         —             -----
         48            13396
                         168
                      --------3,0
                 48)2250528(4688,6
                    192       -------
                    ——     1562 Florins 26 Gr.
```

By the Chain Rule.

		837 Marks 4 Schillings.
3 Marks	=	1 Rixdollar.
1 Rixdollar	=	168 Groschen.
30 Groschen	=	1 Florin.

Result as above.

HAMBURGH ON DANTZIC.

Reduce 1562 Florins 26 Groschen Dantzic currency into Hamburgh banco; exchange at 168 Groschen per Rixdollar banco.

```
Groschen  Rixd.  Marks       Florins Groschen   Mks. Sch.
As 168  :  1  or  3  : :  1562   26    :  837   4
                                 30
                              ------
                              46886
                                  3
                              ------      Mks.  Sch.
                        168)140658(837     4
```

By the Chain Rule.

		1562 Florins 26 Groschen.
1 Florin	=	30 Groschen.
168 Groschen	=	1 Rixd. banco.
1 Rixdollar	=	3 Marks.

Result as above.

N.B. The Exchanges of Dantzic with London and Paris are deemed too simple to require illustration. *See* Quotation.

FRANCE.

MONIES OF EXCHANGE.

Exchanges are computed here in Francs and Centimes; or in Livres, Sous, and Deniers.

10 Centimes = 1 Decime; 10 Decimes, or 100 Centimes = 1 Franc; 12 Deniers = 1 Sou or Sol; 20 Sous = 1 Livre Tournois; 80 Francs = 81 Livres; 3 Livres, or 3 Francs = 1 Ecu of exchange.

COURSE OF EXCHANGE, From the Paris Quotation. *January*, 1820.		EXPLANATION.
AMSTERDAM..	53¾	.. PARIS receives 53¾ Grotes Flemish .... for 1 Ecu of 3 Francs.
AUGSBURG ..	249	.. ——— gives 249 Centimes .... for 1 Florin current.
BASIL	1 perte	.. ——— gives 101 Livres .... for 100 Livres.
BERLIN......	3 80	.. ——— gives 3 Francs 80 Centimes . for 1 Rixdollar.
FRANCFORT ..	75	.. ——— receives 75 Rixdollars current .. for 100 Ecus.
GENEVA	162	.. ——— gives 162 Francs .... for 100 Livres current.
GENOA	465	.. ——— gives 465 Centimes .... for 1 Pezza of 5¾ Lire.
HAMBURGH ..	185	.. ——— gives 185 Francs .... for 100 Marks banco.
LEGHORN	503	.. ——— gives 503 Centimes .... for 1 Pezza of 8 Reals.
LISBON	520	.. ——— receives 520 Rees .... for 1 Ecu of 3 Francs.
LONDON	24	.. ——— gives 24 Francs .... for £1 sterling.
MILAN	8 6	.. ——— receives 8 Lire 6 Soldi .... for 6 Francs.
NAPLES	4 20	.. ——— gives 4 Francs 20 Centimes.. for 1 Ducato di regno.
SPAIN	15 40	.. ——— gives 15 Francs 40 Centimes.. for 1 Doubloon of exchange.
VIENNA	257	.. ——— gives 257 Francs .... for 100 Florins effective.

[For the usances and other particulars relating to Bills of Exchange, see FRANCE, vol. I.]

FRANCE ON LONDON, see page 21.
FRANCE ON AMSTERDAM, see page 29.
FRANCE ON AUGSBURG, see page 33.
FRANCE ON GENEVA, see page 58.

FRANCE ON GENOA.

Reduce 1382 Lire 3 Soldi $1\frac{1}{2}$ Denari into French money; exchange at 4 Francs 80 Centimes per Pezza.

1382 3 $1\frac{1}{2}$
4

Pezze Soldi Den. di Pezza
23)5528 12 6(240 7 6
46

92 &c.

Pezza Francs Pezze Sol. Den. Francs Cents.
Then as 1 : 4,80 : : 240 7 6 : 1153 80
4,80

19200
960
5 Soldi = $\frac{1}{4}$ 120
2 Soldi 6 Den. = $\frac{1}{2}$.. 60

1153,80

LONDON ON FRANCE, see page 21.
AMSTERDAM ON FRANCE, see page 29.
AUGSBURG ON FRANCE, see page 33.
GENEVA ON FRANCE, see page 58.

GENOA ON FRANCE.

Reduce 1153 Francs 80 Centimes into money of Genoa; exchange at 4 Francs 80 Centimes per Pezza of $5\frac{3}{4}$ Lire.

Francs Pezza Francs Pezze Soldi D. di Pez.
As 4,80 : 1 : : 1153,80 : 240 7 6
48,0)11538,0(240 7 6
96 &c.

But if the answer be required in Lire, say,

Pezze Sol. D. di P. Lire Sol. D. di L.
As 4 : 23 : : 240 7 6 : 1382 3 $1\frac{1}{2}$
23

720
480
5 Soldi = $\frac{1}{4}$ 5 15
2 Soldi 6 Den. = $\frac{1}{2}$. 2 17 6

4)5528 12 6

1382 3 $1\frac{1}{2}$

FRANCE ON HAMBURGH.

Reduce 3492 Marks 15 Schillings 6 Pfenings banco into French money; exchange at $25\frac{1}{2}$ Schillings Lubs banco, per Ecu of 3 Francs.

Schillings Francs Marks Sch. Pf. Francs
As $25\frac{1}{2}$: 3 : : 3492 15 6 : 6575
12 16

306 55887
12

670650
3

306)2011950(6575
1836

1759 &c.

HAMBURGH ON FRANCE.

Reduce 6575 Francs into Hamburgh money; exchange at $25\frac{1}{2}$ Schillings Lubs banco, per Ecu of 3 Francs.

Francs Sch. Francs Marks Sch. Pf. bco.
As 3 : $25\frac{1}{2}$: : 6575 : 3492 15 6
$25\frac{1}{2}$

3)$167662\frac{1}{2}$

16)$55887\frac{1}{2}$

3492 Marks $15\frac{1}{2}$ Schillings.

Or thus decimally.

Francs Sch. Francs Marks Sch. Pf.
As 3 : 25,5 : : 6575 : 3492 15 6
25,5

3)167662,5

16)55887,5

3492,96875
× 16 × 12

FRANCE ON LEGHORN.

Reduce 760 Pezze 7 Soldi 6 Denari into French money; exchange at 5 Francs 20 Centimes per Pezza of 8 Reals.

	Pezza		Francs		Pezze	Sol.	Den.		Francs	Cent.
As	1	:	5,20	: :	760	7	6	:	3953	95

```
                          5,20
                         -----
                         15200
                         3800
5 Soldi=1/4. . . . . .     130
2 Soldi 6 Denari=1/2.       65
                       -------
                       3953,95
```

Or thus decimally.

760 Pezze 7 Soldi 6 Denari is $760\frac{3}{8}$=760,375

```
As 1  :  5,20  : :  760,375  :  3953,95
                       5,20
                  -----------
                  3953,95000
```

LEGHORN ON FRANCE.

Reduce 3953 Francs 95 Centimes into money of Leghorn; exchange at 5 Francs 20 Centimes per Pezza of 8 Reals.

	Francs		Pezza		Francs		Pezze	Sol.	Den.
As	5,20	:	1	: :	3953,95	:	760	7	6

```
52,0)39539,5(760  7  6
     364
     ---
      313
      312
      ---
        19 × 20 and 12 &c.
```

Or thus decimally.

```
As 5,20  :  1  : :  3953,95  :  760,375
                                     20
                                 ------
                                  7,500
                                     12
                                 ------
                                  6,000
```

FRANCE ON LISBON.

Reduce 617 Mil. 334 Rees into French money; exchange at 465 Rees per Ecu of 3 Francs.

	Rees		Francs		Milrees		Francs	Cents.
As	465	:	3	: :	617,334	:	3982	80

```
                 3
           --------
465)1852002(3982,80
    1395 &c.
```

But if the sum were given in Crusades, they are reduced to Milrees by multiplying by 4, cutting off the last figure, and to this figure adding the first of the Rees, as in the following example.

Reduce 1543 Crusades 134 Rees into Milrees, &c.

```
      4
  -----
  617,2
    134
  -----
   ,334
```

Ans. 617 Mil. 334 Rees.

LISBON ON FRANCE.

Reduce 3982 Francs 80 Centimes into money of Portugal; exchange at 465 Rees per Ecu of 3 Francs.

	Francs		Rees		Francs	Cents.		Milrees	Rees
As	3	:	465	: :	3982	80	:	617	334

```
         465
  ----------
3)1852002,00
  ----------
     617,334
```

But if the answer were required in Crusades, the last two figures should be cut off, and the others divided by 4: thus,

```
4)6173,34
 --------
1543 Crusades 134 Rees.
```

FRANCE ON MILAN.

Reduce 4536 Lire 17 Soldi 6 Denari into French money; exchange at 7 Lire 10 Soldi per 6 Francs.

	Lire	Soldi		Francs		Lire	Soldi	Den.		Francs	Cen.
As	7	10	:	6	: :	4536	17	6	:	3629	50

```
    20              20
   ----           -------
   150            90737
    12               12
   ----           -------
   1800           1088850
                        6
                 ---------
          18,00)65331,00(3629,50
               54 &c.
```

Exchanges have been recently transacted between Milan and France by giving Italian Livres for Francs, with a Percentage on the latter; as in the annexed example.

MILAN ON FRANCE.

Reduce 3629 Francs 50 Centimes into money of Milan; exchange at 7 Lire 10 Soldi per 6 Francs.

	Francs		Lire	Soldi		Francs		Lire	Sol.	Den.
As	6	:	7	10	: :	3629,50	:	4536	17	6

```
                         7
                     -------
                     2540650
10 Soldi = ½ . . . .  181475
                     -------
                  6)27221,25
                    --------
                    4536,875
                          20
                     -------
                      17,500
                          12
                     -------
                        6,00
```

Reduce 3629 Francs 50 Centimes into Italian Livres; exchange at 99 Francs for 100 Italian Livres.

	Francs		It. Livres		Francs		It. Livres
As	99	:	100	: :	3629,50	:	3666,06

FRANCE ON NAPLES.

Reduce 580 Ducats 56 Grains into French money; exchange at 4 Francs 25 Centimes per Ducato di regno.

	Ducat		Francs	Cen.		Ducats		Francs	Cen.
As	1	:	4	25	: :	580,56	:	2467	38

```
      4,25
   -------
    290280
   116112
  232224
 ---------
 2467,3800
```

NAPLES ON FRANCE.

Reduce 2467 Francs 38 Centimes into money of Naples; exchange at 4 Francs 25 Centimes per Ducato di regno.

	Francs		Ducat		Franes		Ducats	Gr.
As	4,25	.	1	: :	2467,38	:	580	56

```
425)2467,38(580  56
    2125
    ----
     3423
     3400
     ----
      2380 &c.
```

FRANCE ON SPAIN.

Reduce 1777 Dollars 7 Reals 2 Maravedis of plate into French money; exchange at 14 Francs 45 Centimes per Doubloon of Exchange of 4 Dollars of plate.

	Dollars		Francs		Doll.	Reals	Mar.		Francs	Cent.
As	4	:	14,45	: :	1777	7	2	:	6422	60
	× 8 × 34				8					

```
1088              14223
                     34
                 483584
                  14,45
  1088)3987788,80(6422,60
       6528
       4597 &c.
```

By the Chain Rule.

		1777 Doll. 7 Rea. 2 Mar.
4 Dollars	=	1 Doub. of exchange.
1 Doubloon	=	14 Francs 45 Centimes.

Result as above.

SPAIN ON FRANCE.

Reduce 6422 Francs 60 Centimes into Spanish money; exchange at 14 Francs 45 Centimes per Doubloon of exchange of 4 Dollars of Plate.

	Francs		Doll.		Francs		Doll.	Reals	Mar.
As	14,45	:	4	: :	6422,60	:	1777	7	2
					4				

```
                       Dol.  Reals  Mar.
14,45)25690,40(1777     7      2
      1445
      11240 &c.
```

Remainder × 8 × 34 &c.

By the Chain Rule.

		6422 Francs 60 Centimes.
14 Francs 45 Cent.	=	1 Doubl. of exchange.
1 Doubloon	=	4 Dollars of plate.

Result as above.

FRANCE ON VIENNA.

Reduce 6025 Florins 55 Creutzers into French money; exchange at 257 Francs per 100 Florins.

	Florins		Francs		Florins	Cr.		Francs	Cent.
As	100	:	257	: :	6025	55	:	15486	60
	60				60				

```
6000              361555
                     257
      6,000)92919,635
            15486,60
```

By Decimals.

55 Creutzers = $\frac{55}{60}$ = ,916.

	Florins		Francs		Florins		Francs
As	100	:	257	: :	6025,916	:	15486,60
					257		

```
1,00)1548660,412
     15486,60
```

VIENNA ON FRANCE.

Reduce 15486 Francs 60 Centimes into money of Vienna; exchange at 257 Francs per 100 Florins.

	Francs		Florins		Francs		Florins	Cr.
As	257	:	100	: :	15486,60	:	6025	55
					100			

```
257)1548660(6025
    1542
     666
     514
    1520
```

Remainder × 60 &c.

FRANCFORT.

MONIES OF EXCHANGE.

Exchanges are computed in Florins and Creutzers, or in Rixdollars and Creutzers; and also in Florins and Batzen.

4 Pfenings = 1 Creutzer.

4 Creutzers = 1 Batze.

60 Creutzers, or 15 Batzen = 1 Florin.

90 Creutzers, or 1½ Florin = 1 Rixdollar of account.

COURSE OF EXCHANGE, From the Francfort Quotation. *January*, 1820.		EXPLANATION.			
AMSTERDAM..	140¾	.. FRANCFORT gives	140¾	Rixdollars of account	for 100 Rixdollars.
AUGSBURG ..	100¾	.. ——— gives	100¾	Ditto ditto....	for 100 Ditto current.
BASIL	101¼	.. ——— gives	101¼	Ditto	for 100 Ditto in new Ecus.
BREMEN	108½	.. ——— gives	108½	Ditto	for 100 Ditto current.
FRANCE......	79	.. ——— gives	79	Ditto	for 100 Ecus of 3 Livres.
HAMBURGH ..	150	.. ——— gives	150	Ditto of account..	for 100 Rixdollars banco.
LEIPSIC	100½	.. ——— gives	100½	Ditto	for 100 Ditto in Louis d'or.
LONDON......	149	.. ——— gives	149	Batzen............	for £1 sterling.
VIENNA......	40	.. ——— gives	40	Florins............	for 100 Florins current.

[For usances and other particulars relating to Bills of Exchange, see FRANCFORT, vol. i.]

FRANCFORT ON AMSTERDAM.

Reduce 6165 Florins 9 Stivers, 11 Pennings into money of Francfort; exchange at 141 Rixdollars Francfort currency per 100 Rixdollars of Amsterdam.

	Rixd. A.		Rixd. F.		Florins	Stivers	Pen.		Rixd.	Cr.
As	100	:	141	: :	6165	9	11	:	3477	30

```
 2½            20
 ---          ------
 250          123309
  20              16
 ---          -------
 5000         1972955
   16             141
 ----      ----------
 80000  8,0000)27818,6655
             ----------
             3477,3332
                    90
             ---------
               29,9880
```

AMSTERDAM ON FRANCFORT.

Reduce 3477 Rixdollars 30 Creutzers, Francfort currency, into Dutch money; exchange at 141 Rixdollars Francfort per 100 Rixdollars of Amsterdam.

	Rixd. F.		Rixd. A.		Rixd.	Cr.		Fl.	St.	Pen.
As	141	:	100	: :	3477	30	:	6165	9	11

```
   90        2½       90
 -----      ---    -------
 12690      250    312960
                      250
              -----------   Fl.  St. Pen.
        1269,0)7824000,0(6165  9   11
               7614
               ----
               2100 &c.
```

Remainder × 20 × 16 &c.

FRANCFORT ON FRANCE.

Reduce 9137 Francs 45 Centimes into money of Francfort; exchange at 76 Rixdollars per 100 Écus of 3 Livres Tournois.

	Francs		Livres		Francs		Livres
As	80	:	81	: :	9137,45	:	9251,667

```
                              20
                          ------
                          13,340 Sous
                              12
                          ------
                           4,080 Den.
```

	Livres		Rixd.		Livres	Sous	Den.		Florins	Cr.
And as	300	:	76	: :	9251	13	4	:	3515	38

```
   20        1½        20
  ----      ---     ------
  6000      114     185033
    12                  12
  ----              -------
  72000             2220400
                        114
               ------------ Florins  Cr.
      72,000)253125,600(3515    38
         216
```

FRANCE ON FRANCFORT.

Reduce 3515 Florins 38 Creutzers, Francfort currency, into French money; exchange at 76 Rixdollars per 100 Ecus of 3 Livres Tournois.

	Rixd.		Livres		Florins	Creutzers		Livres	Sous	Den.
As	76	:	300	: :	3515	38	:	9251	17	9

```
   90              60
  ----          ------
  6840          210938
                   300
            ----------  Livres  Sous  Den.
      684,0)6328140,0(9251    13    4
            6156
            ----
            1721 &c.
```

	Livres		Francs		Livres	Sous	Den.		Francs	Cen.
And as	81	:	80	: :	9251	13	4	:	9137	45

The exchange between Francfort and Paris is sometimes differently quoted, which simplifies the operation.

FRANCFORT ON HAMBURGH.

Reduce 5929 Marks 9 Schillings 4 Pfenings, Hamburgh banco, into money of Francfort; exchange at 144 Rixdollars Francfort per 100 Rixdollars banco.

```
   Rixd.   Rixd. Fr.        Marks  Sch. Pfen.      Rixd.   Cr.
As 100  :  144  :  :        5929    9    4    :    2846    18
     3                        16
   ---                    ------
   300                     94873
    16                        12
  ----                   -------
  4800                   1138480
    12                       144
 -----              ------------- Rixd.   Cr.
 57600    5760,0)16394112,0(2846   18
               11520
              ------
               48741 &c.

          Remainder × 90 &c.
```

HAMBURGH ON FRANCFORT.

Reduce 2846 Rixdollars 18 Creutzers, Francfort currency, into Hamburgh money; exchange at 144 Rixdollars Francfort per 100 Rixdollars Hamburgh banco.

```
   Rixd. F.   Rixd. bco.      Rixd.   Cr.       Marks  Sch.  Pf.
As 144    :   100    :  :    2846    18    :    5929    9    4
    90          3              90
 -----        ---          ------
 12960        300          256158
                              300
                       ----------  Marks  Sch.  Pf.
             1296,0)7684740,0(5929    9    4
                   6480
                  -----
                  12047 &c.

          Remainder × 16 × 12 &c.
```

FRANCFORT ON LONDON.

Reduce £845 18s. 8d. into money of Francfort; exchange at 142½ Batzen per £ sterling.

```
    £     Batzen         £     s.   d.        Florins   Cr.
As  1  :  142½  :  :    845    18   8    :    8036      22
   20      4             20
   --    ---           ----
   20    570          16918
   12                    12
  ---                ------
  240                203024
                        570
              -----------6,0
         24,0)11572368,0(48218,2
              96         --------
              --      8036 Florins 22 Cr.
              197 &c.
```

LONDON ON FRANCFORT.

Reduce 8036 Florins 22 Creutzers, Francfort currency into sterling; exchange at 142½ Batzen per £ sterling.

```
   Batzen      £        Florins   Cr.          £     s.   d.
As 142½   :    1   :  :   8036     22    :     845   18   8
     4                      60
   ---              ----------  £    s.  d.
   570          57,0)482182(845  18  8
```

By the Chain Rule.

```
                  8036 Florins 22 Creutzers.
       1 Florin =   15 Batzen.
  142½ Batzen =     1 £ sterling.
```

Result as above.

GENEVA.

MONIES OF EXCHANGE.

Exchanges are computed here in Livres, Sous, and Deniers; or in Ecus, Livres, &c.

12 Deniers = 1 Sou or Sol.

20 Sous = 1 Livre current.

3 Livres = 1 Ecu or Patagon.

COURSE OF EXCHANGE, From the Geneva Quotation. *February*, 1820.		EXPLANATION.	
AMSTERDAM .. 92	.. GENEVA	receives 92 Grotes Flemish	for 1 Ecu.
AUGSBURG 128	.. ———	receives 128 Rixdollars current..	for 100 Ecus.
BASLE 162	.. ———	receives 162 Livres Tournois....	for 100 Livres current.
FRANCE 162	.. ———	receives 162 Francs	for 100 Livres current.
GENOA 98	.. ———	gives 98 Ecus	for 100 Pezze of $5\frac{3}{4}$ Lire f.b.
HAMBURGH.... 23	.. ———	gives 23 Sous current.........	for 1 Mark banco.
LEGHORN...... 104	.. ———	gives 104 Ecus	for 100 Pezze of 8 Reals.
LONDON 46	.. ———	receives 46 Pence sterling......	for 1 Ecu of 3 Livres.
MILAN 100	.. ———	gives 100 Ecus	for 640 Lire correnti.
NAPLES ...... $50\frac{3}{4}$	.. ———	gives $50\frac{3}{4}$ Sous	for 1 Ducat.
PALERMO 15 3	.. ———	gives 15 Lire 3 Sous	for 1 Oncia.
SPAIN 44	.. ———	gives 44 Sous current	for 1 Dollar of Plate.
TURIN 84	.. ———	receives 84 Soldi Piemontesi....	for 1 Ecu.
VIENNA 128	.. ———	receives 128 Rixdollars current..	for 100 Ecus.

[For the usances and other particulars relating to Bills of Exchange, see GENEVA, vol. i.]

GENEVA ON AMSTERDAM.

Reduce 2479 Florins 13 Stivers 12 Pennings into money of Geneva; exchange at 92 Grotes Flemish per Ecu of 3 Livres.

	Grotes		Livres		Florins	Stivers	Pen.		Livres	Sous	Den.
As	92	:	3	: :	2479	13	12	:	3234	7	6
	8				20						
	736				49593						
					16						
					793500						
					3						

	Livres	Sous	Den.
736)2380500(	3234	7	6
2208			
1725 &c.			

By the Chain Rule.

		2479 Flor. 13 Stivers 12 Pen.
1 Florin	=	40 Grotes.
92 Grotes	=	3 Livres.

Result as above.

AMSTERDAM ON GENEVA.

Reduce 3234 Livres 7 Sous 6 Deniers Geneva currency into Dutch money; exchange at 92 Grotes Flemish per Ecu of 3 Livres.

	Livres		Grotes		Livres	Sous	Den.		Florins	Sti.	Pen.
As	3	:	92	: :	3234	7	6	:	2479	13	12
	20		8		20						
	60		736		64687						
	12				12						
	720				776250						
					736						

16
72,0)57132000,0(793500
504
673 &c.
2,0)4959,3 12
2479 Fl. 13 Sti. 12 Pen.

By the Chain Rule.

		3234 Livres 7 Sous 6 Den.
3 Livres	=	92 Grotes.
40 Grotes	=	1 Florin.

Result as above.

GENEVA ON FRANCE.

Reduce 1623 Francs 93 Centimes into money of Geneva; exchange at 168 Francs per 100 Livres current.

	Francs		Livres		Francs		Livres	Sous	Den.
As	168	:	100	: :	1623,93	:	966	12	6

168)162393(966 12 6
1512
1119 &c.

Remainder × 20 × 12 &c.

Or thus decimally.

	Francs		Livres		Francs		Livres	Sous	Den.
As	168	:	100	: :	1623,93	:	966	12	6

168)162393,00(966,625
1512
1119 &c.

,625
20
12,500
12
6,0

FRANCE ON GENEVA.

Reduce 966 Livres 12 Sous 6 Deniers Geneva currency into sterling; exchange at 168 Francs per 100 Livres current.

	Livres		Francs		Livres	Sous	Den.		Francs	Cen.
As	100	:	168	: :	966	12	6	:	1623	93
	20				20					
	2000				19332					
	12				12					
	24000				231990					
					168					

24,000)38974,320(1623,93
24
149 &c.

Or thus decimally.

12 Sous 6 Deniers $\frac{150}{240} = \frac{5}{8} =$,625

	Livres		Francs		Livres		Francs	Cen.
As	100	:	168	: :	966,625	:	1623	93

GENEVA ON HAMBURGH.

Reduce 1068 Marks 4 Schillings 2 Pfenings banco into Geneva currency; exchange at 23 Sous current per Mark banco.

```
     Mark   Sous         Marks  Sch. Pf.      Livres  Sous
As    1  :  23  : :      1068   4    2   :    1228    10
     16                    16
     --                 -----
     16                 17092
     12                    12
    ---                ------
    192                205106
                           23
                      -------- 2,0
              192)4717438(2457,0
                  384       ------
                  ---       1228 Livres 10 Sous.
                  877 &c.
```

HAMBURGH ON GENEVA.

Reduce 1228 Livres 10 Sous Geneva currency into Hamburgh money; exchange at 23 Sous current per Mark Hamburgh banco.

```
    Sous   Mark       Livres  Sous       Mks.  Sch.  Pf.
As  23  :   1   : :   1228    10    :    1068   4    2
                        20
                     -------  Marks   Sch.  Pf.
                  23)24570(1068      4     2
                     23
                     ---
                     157
                     138
                     ---
                      190 &c.
```

Remainder × 16 × 12 &c.

GENEVA ON LEGHORN.

Reduce 1480 Pezze 8 Soldi 4 Denari into Geneva currency; exchange at 105 Ecus per 100 Pezze of 8 Reals.

```
   Pezze    Ecus         Pezze  Soldi Den.    Livres  Sous Den.
As 100  :   105   : :    1480   8     4   :   4663    6    3
              3            20
            ---         -----
            315         29608
                           12
                       ------
                       355300
                          315
                  -----------  Livres  Sous Den.
        24,000)111919,500(4663    6    3
                96
                --
                159 &c.
```

By the Chain Rule.

		1480 Pezze 8 Sol. 4 Den.
100 Pezze	=	105 Ecus.
1 Ecu	=	3 Livres.

Result as above.

LEGHORN ON GENEVA.

Reduce 4663 Livres 6 Sous 3 Deniers Geneva currency into money of Leghorn; exchange at 105 Ecus per 100 Pezze of 8 Reals.

```
   Ecus     Pezze       Livres  Sous Den.     Pezze  Soldi Den.
As 105  :   100   : :   4663    6    3   :    1480   8     4
    3                      20
   ---                   -----
   315                   93266
    20                      12
   ----           ------------- Pezze  Sol. Den.
   6300     756,00)1119195,00(1480    8    4
     12            756
   ----            ----
  75600            3631 &c.
```

By the Chain Rule.

		4663 Livres 6 Sous 3 Den.
3 Livres	=	1 Ecu.
105 Ecus	=	100 Pezze of 8 Reals.

Result as above.

GENEVA ON LONDON.

Reduce £458 3s. 11d. sterling into money of Geneva; exchange at 48d. sterling per Ecu of 3 Livres current.

	d.		Livres		£	s.	d.		Livres	Sous	Den.
As	48	:	3	: :	458	3	11	:	6872	18	9

20

9163
12

109967
3

48)329901(6872 Livres 18 Sous 9 Den
288

419 &c.

Remainder × 20 × 12 &c.

By the Chain Rule.

		£458 3s. 11d.
£1 sterling	=	240 Pence.
48 Pence	=	3 Livres.

Result as above.

LONDON ON GENEVA.

Reduce 6872 Livres 18 Sous 9 Deniers Geneva currency into sterling; exchange at 48d. sterling per Ecu of 3 Livres current.

	Livres		d.		Livres	Sous	Den.		£	s.	d.
As	3	:	48	: :	6872	18	9	:	458	3	11

20   20

60   137458
12   12

720   1649505
48

12
72,0)7917624,0(109967
72

2,0)916,3 11
717 &c.

£458 3s. 11d.

By the Chain Rule.

		6872 Livres 18 Sous 9 Den.
3 Livres	=	48 Pence.
240 Pence	=	£1 sterling.

Result as above.

GENEVA ON SPAIN.

Reduce 655 Dollars 7 Reals of plate into Geneva currency; exchange at 44 Sous current per Dollar of plate.

	Dollar		Sous		Dollars	Reals		Livres	Sous	Den.
As	1	:	44	: :	655	7	:	1442	18	6

8   8

8   5247
44

8)230868

2,0)2885,8½

1442 Livres 18 Sous 6 Den.

By the Chain Rule.

		655,875 Dollars.
1 Dollar	=	44 Sous.
20 Sous	=	1 Livre.

Result as above.

SPAIN ON GENEVA.

Reduce 1442 Livres 18 Sous 6 Deniers into Spanish money of plate; exchange at 44 Sous current per Dollar of plate.

	Sous		Dollar		Livres	Sous	Den.		Dollars	Reals
As	44	:	1	: :	1442	18	6	:	655	7

12   20

528   28858
12

528)346302(655 Dollars 7 Reals
3168

2950 &c.

Remainder × 8 &c.

By the Chain Rule.

		1442,925 Livres.
1 Livre	=	20 Sous.
44 Sous	=	1 Dollar.

Result as above.

GENOA.

MONIES OF EXCHANGE.

Exchanges are computed in Lire, Soldi, and Denari di Lira; or in Pezze, Soldi, and Denari di Pezza: all in money fuori banco.

12 Denari = 1 Soldo; 20 Soldi = 1 Lira fuori banco; 5 Lire 15 Soldi fuori banco = 1 Pezza. The Pezza is also divided into 20 Soldi, or 240 Denari di Pezza: thus, 4 Pezze = 23 Lire; 4 Soldi di Pezza = 23 Soldi di Lira; 4 Denari di Pezza = 23 Denari di Lira.

Also, 4 Lire 12 Soldi fuori banco = 1 Scudo di cambio, or Crown of exchange; 10 Lire 16$\frac{1}{3}$ Soldi fuori banco = 1 Scudo d'oro, or gold Crown; 10 Lire 14 Soldi fuori banco = 1 Scudo d'oro marche.

COURSE OF EXCHANGE, from the Genoa Quotation. *March*, 1820.			EXPLANATION.	
AMSTERDAM	89	GENOA	receives 89 Grotes Flemish	for 1 Pezza of 5$\frac{3}{4}$ Lire.
AUGSBURG	61$\frac{1}{2}$	———	gives 61$\frac{1}{2}$ Soldi fuori banco	for 1 Florin current.
CONSTANTINOPLE	16	———	gives 16 Soldi or 80 Centimes	for 1 Piastre.
FRANCE	94$\frac{1}{3}$	———	receives 94$\frac{1}{3}$ Sous in Francs	for 1 Pezza of 5$\frac{3}{4}$ Lire.
HAMBURGH	45$\frac{1}{3}$	———	gives 45$\frac{1}{3}$ Soldi fuori banco	for 1 Mark banco.
LEGHORN	123	———	gives 123 Soldi fuori banco	for 1 Pezza of 8 Reals.
LISBON	868	———	receives 868 Rees	for 1 Pezza of 5$\frac{3}{4}$ Lire.
LONDON	48	———	receives 48 Pence sterling	for Ditto.
DITTO	30	———	gives 30 Lire Italiane	for £1 sterling.
MILAN	87$\frac{1}{4}$	———	receives 87$\frac{1}{4}$ Soldi correnti	for 1 Scudo of 4 Lire fuori banco.
NAPLES	100	———	gives 100 Soldi fuori banco	for 1 Ducato di regno.
PALERMO	36$\frac{1}{2}$	———	receives 36$\frac{1}{2}$ Grani	for 1 Lira fuori banco.
DITTO	15	———	gives 15 Lire fuori banco	for 1 Oncia.
ROME	128	———	gives 128 Soldi fuori banco	for 1 Roman Scudo.
SPAIN	617	———	receives 617 Maravedis of Plate	for 1 Scudo d'oro marche.
TRIESTE	61$\frac{1}{4}$	———	gives 61$\frac{1}{4}$ Soldi fuori banco	for 1 Florin effective.
VENICE	34$\frac{1}{4}$	———	receives 34$\frac{1}{4}$ Soldi piccoli	for 1 Lira fuori banco.
VIENNA	61$\frac{7}{8}$	———	gives 61$\frac{7}{8}$ Soldi fuori banco	for 1 Florin effective.

[For the usances and other particulars relating to Bills of Exchange, see GENOA, vol. i.]

GENOA ON LONDON, see page 22.
GENOA ON AMSTERDAM, see page 29.
GENOA ON FRANCE, see page 50.

GENOA ON HAMBURGH.

Reduce 1789 Marks 10 Schillings 8 Pfenings Hamburgh banco into money of Genoa; exchange at $46\frac{1}{2}$ Soldi di Lira per Mark banco.

	Mark		Soldi		Marks	Sch.	Pf.		Lire	Soldi	Den.
As	1	:	$46\frac{1}{2}$	: :	1789	10	8	:	4160	19	6

```
16        16
——       ————
16       28634
12          12
——       —————
192     343616
           46½
        ———————2,0)
192)15978144(8321,9  6
    1536     ———————
    ————    4160 Lire 19 Sol. 6 Den.
     618 &c.
```

By the Chain Rule.

		1789 Marks 10 Sch. 8 Pf.
1 Mark	=	$46\frac{1}{2}$ Soldi.
20 Soldi	=	1 Lira.

Result as above.

LONDON ON GENOA, see page 22.
AMSTERDAM ON GENOA, see page 29.
FRANCE ON GENOA, see page 50.

HAMBURGH ON GENOA.

Reduce 4160 Lire 19 Soldi 6 Denari into Hamburgh money; exchange at $46\frac{1}{2}$ Soldi di Lira per Mark banco.

	Soldi		Mark		Lire	Soldi	Den.		Marks	Sch.	Pf.
As	$46\frac{1}{2}$	:	1	: :	4160	19	6	:	1789	10	8

```
12        20
——       ————
558      83219
            12
       ————————  Mks.  Sch.  Pf.
  558)998634(1789   10    8
      558
      ———
      4406 &c.

Remainder × 16 × 12 &c.
```

By the Chain Rule.

		4160 Lire 19 Soldi 6 Den.
1 Lira	=	20 Soldi.
$46\frac{1}{2}$ Soldi	=	1 Mark.

Result as above.

GENOA ON LEGHORN.

Reduce 210 Pezze 16 Soldi 8 Denari into money of Genoa; exchange at 124 Soldi fuori banco per Pezza of 8 Reals.

	Pezza		Soldi		Pezze	Sol.	Den.		Lire	Soldi	Den.
As	1	:	124	: :	210	16	8	:	1307	3	4

```
20        20
——       ————
20       4216
12         12
——      —————
240     50600
          124
       ————————2,0)
24,0)627440,0(2614,3
     48      ———————
     ——    1307 Lire 3 Sol. 4 Den.
     147 &c.

Remainder × 12 &c.
```

LEGHORN ON GENOA.

Reduce 1307 Lire 3 Soldi 4 Denari of Genoa into money of Leghorn; exchange at 124 Soldi fuori banco per Pezza of 8 Reals.

	Soldi		Pezza		Lire	Sol.	Den.		Pezze	Sol.	Den.
As	124	:	1	: :	1307	3	4	:	210	16	8

```
12        20
——       ————
1488     26143
            12
       —————————  Pezze  Sol.  Den.
  1488)313720(210    16     8
       2976
       ————
       1612 &c.

Remainder × 20 × 12 &c.
```

GENOA ON LISBON.

Reduce 595 Milrees 184 Rees into money of Genoa; exchange at 736 Rees per Pezza of $5\frac{3}{4}$ Lire fuori banco.

Rees : Lire :: Milrees : Lire Sol. Den.
As 736 : $5\frac{3}{4}$ :: 595,184 : 4649 17 6
$5\frac{3}{4}$

Lire Sol. Den.
736)3422308(4649 17 6
2944

4783 &c.

Remainder × 20 × 12 &c.

LISBON ON GENOA.

Reduce 4649 Lire 17 Soldi 6 Denari fuori banco into money of Portugal; exchange at 736 Rees per Pezza of $5\frac{3}{4}$ Lire fuori banco.

Lire Soldi : Rees :: Lire Sol. Denari : Mil. Rees
As 5 15 : 736 :: 4649 17 6 : 595 184
20 20

115 92997
12 12

1380 1115970
736

Milrees
138,0)82135392,0(595,184
690 &c.

GENOA ON NAPLES.

Reduce 1612 Ducati di regno into money of Genoa; exchange at $104\frac{1}{2}$ Soldi fuori banco per Ducat.

Duc. : Soldi :: Duc. : Lire Sol.
As 1 : $104\frac{1}{2}$ :: 1612 : 8422 14
$104\frac{1}{2}$

2,0)16845,4

8422 Lire 14 Soldi.

NAPLES ON GENOA.

Reduce 8422 Lire 14 Soldi fuori banco into money of Naples; exchange at $104\frac{1}{2}$ Soldi per Ducat.

Soldi : Duc. :: Lire Sol. : Duc.
As $104\frac{1}{2}$: 1 :: 8422 14 : 1612
12 20

1254 168454
12

Ducats
1254)2021448(1612

GENOA ON PALERMO.

Reduce 196 Oncie 24 Tari 2 Grani into money of Genoa; exchange at $34\frac{1}{2}$ Grani per Lira fuori banco.

Grani : Lira :: Oncie Tari Gr : Lire Sol. Den.
As $34\frac{1}{2}$: 1 :: 196 24 2 : 3422 13 4
30

5904
20

Lire Sol. Den.
34,5)118082,0(3422 13 4
1035

1458 &c.

PALERMO ON GENOA.

Reduce 3422 Lire 13 Soldi 4 Denari fuori banco into Sicilian money; exchange at $34\frac{1}{2}$ Grani per Lira fuori banco.

Lira : Gr. :: Lire Sol. Den. : On. Tari Gr.
As 1 : $34\frac{1}{2}$ :: 3422 13 4 : 196 24 2
20

68453
12

821440
$34\frac{1}{2}$

2,0)
24,0)2833968,0(11808,2
240

3,0)590,4
433 &c.

196 On. 24 Tari 2 Gr.

GENOA ON SPAIN.

Reduce 468 Dollars 3 Reals 17 Maravedis of plate into money of Genoa; exchange at 640 Maravedis of plate per Scudo d'oro marche of 10 Lire 14 Soldi fuori banco.

```
    Mar.   Lire  Soldi      Dol. Reals Mar.   Lire   Soldi Den.
As 640  :  10    14   : :  468   3   17  :  2130    4    4
           20               8
          ----
          214             3747
                            34
                          ------
                          127415
                            214
                   -----------20)
           64,0)2726681,0(4260,4  4
                256         -------
                ---        2130 Lire 4 Soldi 4 Den.
                166 &c.
```

By the Chain Rule.

```
                           468 Dol. 3 Reals 17 Mar.
  1 Dollar        =        272 Maravedis.
640 Marav.        =        214 Soldi.
 20 Soldi         =          1 Lira.
```

Result as above.

SPAIN ON GENOA.

Reduce 2130 Lire 4 Soldi 4 Denari fuori banco into Spanish money; exchange at 640 Maravedis of plate per Scudo d'oro marche of 10 Lire 14 Soldi fuori banco.

```
  Lire Soldi    Mar.       Lire  Sol. Den.     Dol.  Reals Mar.
As 10  14   :   640  : :  2130    4    4   :   468    3    17
   20                       20
  ----                    -----
   214                    42604
    12                       12
  ----                    ------
  2568                    511252
                             640
                  -------------34)
            2568)327201280(127415
                 2568         -------
                 ----       8)3747   17
                 7040 &c.     ----
                              468 Dol. 3 R. 17 M.
```

By the Chain Rule.

```
                             2130 Lire 4 Soldi 4 Den.
 10 Lire 14 Soldi     =       640 Maravedis.
272 Maravedis         =         1 Dollar.
```

Result as above.

GENOA ON VENICE.

Reduce 4673 Lire 13 Soldi 8 Denari piccoli into money of Genoa; exchange at 38 Soldi piccoli per Lira fuori banco of Genoa.

```
   Soldi    Lira      Lire  Soldi Den.       Lire   Soldi  Den.
As 38   :   1   : :  4673    13    8   :    2459     16     8
   12                  20
  ----               -----
   456               93473
                        12
                -----------  Lire   Sol.  Den.
           456)1121684(2459    16     8
               912
               ---
               2096 &c.
```

If the Exchanges between Genoa and Venice are transacted in Italian Livres, the operation becomes more simple.

VENICE ON GENOA.

Reduce 2459 Lire 16 Soldi 8 Denari of Genoa into money of Venice; exchange at 38 Soldi piccoli per Lira fuori banco.

```
   Lira    Soldi      Lire  Soldi  Den.      Lire  Soldi  Den.
As 1   :   38   : :  2459   16     8    :   4673   13     8
   20                  20
  ----               -----
   20                49196
   12                   12
  ----               ------
  240                590360
                         38
                   ---------2,0)
           24,0)2243368,0(9347,3  3
                216           ------
                ---        4673 Lire 13 Sol. 8 Den.
                 83 &c.
```

Remainder × 12 &c.

HAMBURGH.

MONIES OF EXCHANGE.

Exchanges are computed in Marks, Schillings, and Pfenings, banco or current; or in Pounds, Shillings, and Pence, Flemish banco.

Banco bears an agio on currency, which is generally from 20 to 25 per cent.

12 Pfenings = 1 Schilling, or Sol Lubs; 16 Schillings Lubs = 1 Mark; 3 Marks = 1 Rixdollar; 6 Pfenings = 1 Grote Flemish; 12 Grotes Flemish, or 6 Schillings Lubs = 1 Shilling Flemish; 20 Shillings Flemish, or 7½ Marks = 1 Pound Flemish.

COURSE OF EXCHANGE, From the Hamburgh Quotation. *January*, 1820.		EXPLANATION.	
AMSTERDAM.. 106	HAMBURGH	receives 106 Rixdollars Dutch currency.	for 100 Rixdollars.
AUGSBURG .. 148½	———	receives 148½ Rixdollars effective	for 100 Rixds. banco.
BASIL 25⅛	———	gives 25⅛ Schillings banco	for 1 Ecu of 3 Francs.
BRESLAU 41	———	receives 41 Rixdollars Prussian currency	for 100 Rixds. banco.
COPENHAGEN. 149	———	receives 149 Rixdollars Danish	for 100 Rixds. banco.
FRANCE...... 25⅞	———	gives 25⅞ Schillings banco	for 1 Ecu of 3 Francs.
FRANCFORT.. 148½	———	receives 148½ Rixdollars effective	for 100 Rixds. banco.
GENOA 80	———	gives 80 Grotes Flemish banco	for 1 Pezza of 5¾ Lire f. b.
LEGHORN 86½	———	gives 86½ Grotes Flemish banco........	for 1 Pezza of 8 Reals.
LISBON 37	———	gives 37 Grotes Flemish banco	for 1 old Crusade.
LONDON 35 9	———	gives 35 Shillings & 9 Pence Flemish bco	for £1 sterling.
PRAGUE 149	———	receives 149 Rixdollars effective	for 100 Rixds. banco.
SPAIN 84¾	———	gives 84¾ Grotes Flemish banco	for 1 Ducat of Plate.
VENICE...... 82	———	receives 82 Soldi Piccoli..............	for 1 Mark banco.
VIENNA...... 149	———	receives 149 Rixdollars effective	for 100 Rixds. banco.

[For the usances, laws, &c. of Bills of Exchange, see HAMBURGH, vol. i.]

HAMBURGH ON LONDON, see page 23.
HAMBURGH ON AMSTERDAM, see page 30.
HAMBURGH ON AUGSBURG, see page 34.
HAMBURGH ON BERLIN, see page 37.
HAMBURGH ON BREMEN, see page 39.
HAMBURGH ON COPENHAGEN, see page 46.
HAMBURGH ON DANTZIC, see page 48.
HAMBURGH ON FRANCE, see page 50.
HAMBURGH ON FRANCFORT, see page 56.
HAMBURGH ON GENEVA, see page 59.
HAMBURGH ON GENOA, see page 62.

LONDON ON HAMBURGH, see page 23.
AMSTERDAM ON HAMBURGH, see page 30.
AUGSBURG ON HAMBURGH, see page 34.
BERLIN ON HAMBURGH, see page 37.
BREMEN ON HAMBURGH, see page 39.
COPENHAGEN ON HAMBURGH, see page 46.
DANTZIC ON HAMBURGH, see page 48.
FRANCE ON HAMBURGH, see page 50.
FRANCFORT ON HAMBURGH, see page 56.
GENEVA ON HAMBURGH, see page 59.
GENOA ON HAMBURGH, see page 62.

HAMBURGH ON LEGHORN.

Reduce 527 Pezze 8 Soldi 8 Denari into Hamburgh money; exchange at 84¾ Grotes Flemish per Pezza of 8 Reals.

```
   Pezza   Grotes       Pezze  Soldi  Den.      Marks  Schillings.
As 1    :  84¾    : :   527    8      8    :    1396   14
   20                   20
   ---                  -----
   20                   10548
   12                      12
   ---                  ------
   240                  126584
                           84¾
                  ----------32)
          24,0)1072799,4(44699,9 Grotes Flemish.
               96         -----
               ---        1396 Mks. 14 Sch.
               112 &c.
```

By the Chain Rule.

```
                527   Pezze 8 Soldi 8 Denari.
 1 Pezza   =    84¾   Grotes Flemish.
32 Grotes  =    1     Mark.
```

Result as above.

LEGHORN ON HAMBURGH.

Reduce 1396 Marks 14 Schillings banco into money of Leghorn; exchange at 84¾ Grotes Flemish banco per Pezza of 8 Reals.

```
   Grotes   Pezza     Marks  Sch.     Pezze  Soldi  Denari.
As 84¾   :  1    : :  1396   14   :   527    8      8
    6                   16
   ----               -----
   508½               22350
     2                   12
   ----               ------
   1017               268200
                           2
                      ------
            1017)536400(527 Pezze 8 Soldi 8 Den.
                 5085
                 ----
                 2790 &c.
```

By the Chain Rule.

```
                 1396  Marks 14 Schillings.
 1  Mark     =   32    Grotes Flemish.
84¾ Grotes   =   1     Pezza.
```

Result as above.

HAMBURGH ON LISBON.

Reduce 234 Mil. 743 Rees into Hamburgh money; exchange at 43¾ Grotes Flemish banco per old Crusado.

```
         Milrees
   4,00)2347,43
        -------
        586,857 Crusados.

Crus.   Grotes      Crus.          Marks Sch. Pf.
As 1  :  43¾   : :  586,857    :   802    5   6
                     43¾
               --------------Marks Sch. Pf.
           32)25674,993(802    5   6
              256
              ---
               74 &c.

    Remainder × 16 × 12 &c.
```

LISBON ON HAMBURGH.

Reduce 802 Marks 5 Schillings 6 Pfenings banco into money of Portugal; exchange at 43¾ Grotes Flemish banco per old Crusado.

```
Grotes   Crus.     Marks Sch. Pf.      Crus.
As 43¾  :  1  : :  802    5   6   :  586,857
    6               16
  ----            -----
  262½            12837
    2                12
  ----            ------
   525            154050
                       2
                  --------Crusados.
             525)308100(586,857
                 2625
                 ----
                 4560 &c.
```

But if the answer be required in Milrees and Rees, the Crusados should be multiplied by 400.

HAMBURGH ON SPAIN.

Reduce 357 Dollars 4 Reals 10 Maravedis of plate into Hamburgh money; exchange at 83¾ Grotes Flemish banco per Ducat of exchange of 375 Maravedis.

```
Mar.    Grotes     Doll. Reals Mar.    Marks Sch. Pf.
As 375 : 83¾   : :  357    4   10  :   678   11   7
                      8
                   ----
                   2860
                     34
                   -----
                   97250
                     83¾
                 -------32)
         375)8144687½(21719⅙
                     --------
                     678 Mks. 23⅙ Grotes.
                               6
                             ---
                          12)139
                             ---
                          11 Sch. 7 Pf.
```

SPAIN ON HAMBURGH.

Reduce 678 Marks 11 Schillings 7 Pfenings banco into Spanish money; exchange at 83¾ Grotes Flemish banco per Ducat of exchange.

```
Grotes    Mar.      Marks Sch. Pfen.    Doll. Reals Mar.
As 83¾  : 375  : :  678    11   7    :  357    4    10
    6                16
  ----             -----
  502½             10859
                      12
                  ------
                  130315
                     375
               ---------34)     8)
     502,5)48868125,0(97250 (2860 Rls. 10 M.
           45225       68    ----
           -----       --    357 Dols. 4 R.
           36431 &c.  292 &c.
```

HAMBURGH ON VENICE.

Reduce 21461 Lire 18 Soldi 7 Denari Piccoli into Hamburgh money; exchange at $78\frac{1}{2}$ Grotes per Ducat banco of 9 Lire 12 Soldi Piccoli.

```
   Duc. Soldi     Grotes        Lire Pic.  Soldi Den.   Marks  Sols
As 1 or 192   :   78½     : :   21461      18   7   :   5484   4
        12                      × 20 × 12
      ----                      ---------
      2304                      5150863
                                   78,5
                           ---------—32)
                 2304)404341945,5(1754956
                                  --------
                                  5484 Marks 4 Sch.
```

If the Venetian sum to be reduced into Hamburgh money be in Lire Italiane, it must be first reduced into Lire Piccole; thus—

```
   Lire It.   Lire Pic.     Lire It.       Lire Pic.  Soldi  Den.
As 240    :   469      : :  10982,65   :   21461      18     7
```

VENICE ON HAMBURGH.

Reduce 5484 Marks 4 Sols Lubs into Venetian money; exchange at $78\frac{1}{2}$ Grotes per Ducat.

```
   Grotes  Ducat           Marks  Sols       Lire   Sol.  Den.
As 78½   :  1       : :    5484   4     :    21461  18    7
    2       9  12            32
  ----    ------           ------
   157      9  12          350992
                              9  12
                           -------
                           3158928
             10 = ½....     175496
              2 = ⅕....      35099  4
                           ----------     Lire   Sol.  Den.
                  157)3369523   4(21461  18    7
```

If the result be required in Lire Italiane, say—

```
   Lire Pic.   Lire It.      Lire   Sol.  Den.    Lire It.  Cent.
As 469     :   240      : :  21461  18    7    :  10982     65
```

HAMBURGH ON VIENNA.

Reduce 2719 Rixdollars 41 Creutzers effective of Vienna into Hamburgh money; exchange at $149\frac{1}{10}$ Rixdollars effective for 100 Rixdollars banco.

```
   Rxds. Eff.   Rxd. Bco.     Rxd. Eff.  Cr.      Marks  Sols Lubs.
As 149,1    :   100       : : 2719       41   :   5471   12
      90          3             90
  -------       ----          ------
  13419,0        300          244751
                                 300
                            ----------  Marks  Sch.
                13419(73425300(5471   12
```

Effective money is reduced to paper money at an agio of so much per cent.

Reduce 2719 Rixdollars 41 Creutzers effective into paper money; agio $66\frac{1}{2}$ per cent.

```
                      Rxd. Eff.  Cr.     Paper Money.
As 33⅓   :  100   : :  2719      41   :   8117,70
```

Paper money is reduced to effective by the reverse analogy: thus—

```
As 100  :  33⅓  : :  8117,70  :  2719  41
```

VIENNA ON HAMBURGH.

Reduce 5471 Marks 12 Sols Lubs into effective money; exchange at $149\frac{1}{10}$ Rixdollars effective for 100 Rixdollars banco.

```
   Rxds. bco.   Rxds. Eff.     Marks          Rxds. Eff.  Cr.
As 100      :   149,1     : :  5471,75     :  2719        41
     3                          149,1
   ----                   ------------
    300             300)815837925(2719,459
                        600              90
                       -----         -------
                        2158 &c.      41,310
```

Effective money is reduced to paper, and the contrary, by the analogies in the annexed examples.

LEGHORN.

MONIES OF EXCHANGE.

Exchanges are computed here in Pezze, Soldi, and Denari di Pezza.

12 Denari di Pezza=1 Soldo di Pezza; 20 Soldi di Pezza=1 Pezza, commonly called Pezza of 8 Reals. 12 Denari di Lira=1 Soldo di Lira; 20 Soldi di Lira=1 Lira. 24 Lire moneta lunga=23 Lire moneta buona. 6 Lire moneta lunga, or 5¾ Lire moneta buona=1 Pezza of 8 Reals.

COURSE OF EXCHANGE, From the Leghorn Quotation. *February*, 1820.		EXPLANATION.	
AMSTERDAM	96	.. LEGHORN receives 96 Grotes Flemish	for 1 Pezza.
ANCONA	129¼	.. ——— receives 129¼ Bajocchi	for 1 Pezza of 8 Reals.
AUGSBURG	201½	.. ——— receives 201½ Florins current....	for 100 Pezze.
BOLOGNA	94	.. ——— receives 94 Bolognini	for 1 Pezza.
CONSTANTINOPLE	296	.. ——— receives 296 Paras	for 100 Pezze.
FLORENCE	123	.. ——— receives 123 Soldi	for 1 Pezza.
FRANCE	102	.. ——— receives 102 Sous in Francs	for 1 Ditto.
GENEVA	109	.. ——— receives 109 Ecus of 3 Livres ..	for 100 Pezze.
GENOA	123	.. ——— receives 123 Soldi fuori banco ..	for 1 Pezza.
HAMBURGH	87¼	.. ——— receives 87¼ Grotes Flemish banco	for 1 Ditto.
LISBON	930	.. ——— receives 930 Rees	for 1 Ditto.
LONDON	48¾	.. ——— receives 48¾ Pence sterling	for 1 Ditto.
MALTA	30½	.. ——— receives 30½ Tari	for 1 Ditto.
MILAN..........	134	.. ——— receives 134 Soldi Correnti	for 1 Ditto.
NAPLES	123¼	.. ——— receives 123¼ Ducati di regno . .	for 100 Pezze of 8 Reals.
NOVI	187	.. ——— gives 187 Pezze	for 1 Scudo d'oro marche.
ODESSA	510	.. ——— receives 510 Rubles	for 100 Pezze.
PALERMO	12 3	.. ——— receives 12 Tari 3 Grani	for 1 Pezza.
PETERSBURGH ..	490	.. ——— receives 490 Rubles	for 100 Pezze.
ROME	128	.. ——— receives 128 Bajocchi	for 1 Pezza.
SMYRNA	296	.. ——— receives 296 Paras	for 1 Ditto.
SPAIN	136	.. ——— receives 136 Pesos of old plate . .	for 100 Pezze.
TRIESTE	200½	.. ——— gives 200½ Soldi moneta buona . .	for 1 Florin current.
TURIN..........	90½	.. ——— receives 90½ Soldi	for 1 Pezza.
VENICE	10½	.. ——— receives 10½ Lire piccoli	for Ditto.
VIENNA	201½	.. ——— gives 201½ Soldi moneta buona . .	for 1 Florin current.

[For the usances and other particulars relating to Bills of Exchange, see LEGHORN, vol. i.]

Leghorn on London, see page 23.
Leghorn on Amsterdam, see page 30.
Leghorn on France, see page 51.
Leghorn on Genoa, see page 62.
Leghorn on Hamburgh, see page 66.

LEGHORN ON LISBON.

Reduce 304 Milrees 205 Rees into money of Leghorn; exchange at 825 Rees per Pezza of 8 Reals.

	Rees		Pezza		Milrees		Pezza	Sol.	Den.
As	825	:	1	: :	304,205	:	368	14	8

825)304,205(368 14 8
2475
———
5670 &c.

Remainder × 20 × 12 &c.

If the sum were given in Crusados, they should be first reduced to Rees by multiplying them by 400: thus, reduce 760 Crusados 205 Rees into money of Leghorn; exchange as above.

760 205
400
———
304000
205
———
304,205 Rees.

London on Leghorn, see page 23.
Amsterdam on Leghorn, see page 30.
France on Leghorn, see page 51.
Genoa on Leghorn, see page 62.
Hamburgh on Leghorn, see page 66.

LISBON ON LEGHORN.

Reduce 368 Pezze 14 Soldi 8 Denari into money of Portugal; exchange at 825 Rees per Pezza of 8 Reals.

	Pezza		Rees		Pezze	Soldi	Den.		Milrees	Rees
As	1	:	825	: :	368	14	8	:	304	205

20 — 20
———
20 — 7374
12 — 12
———
240 — 88496
825
———
Mil.
24,0)7300920,0(304,205
72
———
100 &c.

If the answer were required in Crusados, divide 304,000 by 400 and annex 205 Rees which will give 760 Crusados 205 Rees.

LEGHORN ON NAPLES.

Reduce 425 Ducati 2 Grani di regno into money of Leghorn; exchange at 118½ Ducati di regno per 100 Pezze.

	Ducats		Pezze		Ducats		Pezze	Soldi	Den.
As	118½	:	100	: :	425,02	:	358	13	4

2 — 100
———
237 — 42502
2
———
Pezze Sol. Den.
237)85004(358 13 4
711 &c.

Remainder × 20 × 12 &c.

By Decimals.

	Ducats		Pezze		Ducats		Pezze
As	118,5	:	100	: :	425,02	:	358,667

20
———
13,340 Soldi
12
———
4,08 Den.

NAPLES ON LEGHORN.

Reduce 358 Pezze 13 Soldi 4 Denari into money of Naples; exchange at 118½ Ducati di regno per 100 Pezze of 8 Reals.

	Pezze		Ducats		Pezze	Soldi	Den.		Duc.	Gr.
As	100	:	118½	: :	358	13	4	:	425	2

20 — 20
———
2000 — 7173
12 — 12
———
24000 — 86080
118½
———
24,000)10200,480(425,02

By Decimals.

13 Soldi 4 Den. = ,667

	Pezze		Ducats		Pezze		Ducats
As	100	:	118,5	: :	358,667	:	425,02

118,5
———
1,00)425,02,0395

LEGHORN ON PALERMO.

Reduce 567 Oncie 10 Tari 4 Grani into money of Leghorn; exchange at 12 Tari 10 Grani per Pezza of 8 Reals.

```
   Tari Gr.     Pezza      Oncie Tari Gr.     Pezze  Soldi Den.
As 12  10   :    1   : :    567   10   4  :   1361    12   4
   20                        30
   ---                      -----
   250                      17020
                               20
                           -------- Pezze Soldi Den.
                   25,0)34040,4(1361  12   4
                        25
                        ---
                        90 &c.
```

By the Chain Rule.

```
                        567 Oncie 10 Tari 4 Grani.
 1 Oncia       =         30 Tari.
12½ Tari       =          1 Pezza.
```

Result as above.

PALERMO ON LEGHORN.

Reduce 1361 Pezze 12 Soldi 4 Denari into Sicilian money; exchange at 12 Tari 10 Grani per Pezza of 8 Reals.

```
   Pezza   Tari        Pezze  Soldi Den.     Oncie  Tari  Gr.
As 1   :   12½   : :   1361    12    4   :    567    10    4
                         20
                       -----
                       27232
                          12
                       ------
                       326788
                          12½
                       --------30)
               24,0)408485,0(1702,0
                    24             ------
                    ---       567 On. 10 Tari 4 Gr.
                    168 &c.
```

By the Chain Rule.

```
                     1361 Pez. 12 Sol. 4 Den.
 1 Pezza      =       12½ Tari.
30 Tari       =         1 Oncia.
```

Result as above.

LEGHORN ON SPAIN.

Reduce 1210 Dollars 5 Reals 10 Maravedis of plate into money of Leghorn; exchange at 129½ Dollars of plate per 100 Pezze of 8 Reals.

```
   Doll.     Pezze      Dollars Reals Mar.   Pezze Soldi Den.
As 129½  :   100   : :   1210    5    10  :   934   17    6
     8                      8
   -----                  -----
   1036                    9685
     34                      34
   -----               --------- Pezze  Soldi  Den.
   35224        35224)32930000(934   17     6
                      317016 &c.
```

By Decimals.

5 Reals 10 Marav. $= \frac{180}{272} =$,662.

```
   Dollars      Pezze        Dollars          Pezze
As 129,5   :    100    : :   1210,662    :    934,874
                                                   20
                                              --------
                                               17,480
                                                   12
                                              --------
                                                 5,76
```

SPAIN ON LEGHORN.

Reduce 934 Pezze 17 Soldi 6 Denari into Spanish money; exchange at 129½ Dollars of plate per 100 Pezze of 8 Reals.

```
   Pezze     Dollars        Pezze Sol. Den.     Dollars Reals Mar.
As 100   :   129½     : :   934   17   6    :    1210    5    10
                              20
                            ------
                            18697
                               12
                            ------
                            224370
                             129,5
                         ----------
             24,000)29055,915(1210,663
                    24                8
                    ---          ------
                    50 &c.        5,304
                                     34
                                 ------
                                 10,336
```

LISBON.

MONIES OF EXCHANGE.

Exchanges are computed here in Milrees and Rees ; and also in old Crusados.

1000 Rees = 1 Milree ; 400 Rees = 1 old Crusado, or Crusado of exchange ; 480 Rees = 1 new Crusado.

Three sorts of money are at present used in Portugal; namely,—*Effective Money,* that is, specie; *Paper Money,* which is at a discount; and *Legal Money,* consisting of half specie and half paper. The discount in Feb. 1820, was 22 per cent.

COURSE OF EXCHANGE, From the Lisbon Quotation. *February,* 1820.			EXPLANATION.	
AMSTERDAM..	42	.. LISBON	receives 42 Grotes Flemish ..	for 1 old Crusado.
FRANCE......	540	.. ———	gives 540 Rees	for 3 Francs.
GENOA	746	.. ———	gives 746 Rees	for 1 Pez. of $5\frac{3}{4}$ Lire fuori banco.
HAMBURGH ..	38	.. ———	receives 38 Grotes Flemish bco.	for 1 old Crusado.
LEGHORN	810	.. ———	gives 810 Rees	for 1 Pezza of 8 Reals.
LONDON......	53	.. ———	receives 53 Pence sterling....	for 1 Milree.
SPAIN	2700	.. ———	gives 2700 Rees	for 1 Doubl. of plate or Pistole of ex.
TRIESTE	450	.. ———	gives 450 Rees	for 1 Florin current.
VENICE......	66	.. ———	gives 66 Rees	for 1 Lira Piccola.
VIENNA......	450	.. ———	gives 450 Rees	for 1 Florin current.

[For the usances and other particulars relating to Bills of Exchange, see LISBON, vol. i.]

PAPER MONEY REDUCED TO EFFECTIVE.

Paper money is reduced to effective by saying: as 100 is to 100 less the discount, so is the sum in paper to the sum effective.

Reduce 277 Mil. 240 Rees in paper to effective; the discount being $12\frac{1}{2}$ per cent.

	R. Paper		R. Effective		R. Paper		R. Effective
As	100	:	$87\frac{1}{2}$	: :	277,240	:	242,585

EFFECTIVE MONEY REDUCED TO PAPER.

Effective money is reduced to paper by reversing the foregoing operation: that is, as 100 less the discount is to 100, so is the sum effective to the sum in paper.

Reduce 242 Mil. 585 Rees effective into paper; discount at $12\frac{1}{2}$ per cent.

	R. Effective		R. Paper		R. Effective		R. Paper
As	$87\frac{1}{2}$	:	100	: :	242,585	:	277,240

LEGAL MONEY REDUCED TO EFFECTIVE.

As legal money consists of half paper and half effective, it is reduced to effective by saying: as 100 is to 100 less half the discount, so is the sum in legal money to the sum in effective.

Reduce 28 Mil. 640 Rees legal money to effective; the discount on paper against effective money being 15 per cent.

					R. Legal		R. Effective
As	100	:	$92\frac{1}{2}$	: :	28,640	:	26,492

EFFECTIVE MONEY REDUCED TO LEGAL.

Effective money is reduced to legal by reversing the foregoing operation: that is, as 100 less half the discount is to 100, so is the sum in effective to the sum in legal money.

Reduce 26 Mil. 492 Rees effective to legal money; the discount on paper against effective money being 15 per cent.

					R. Effective		R. Legal
As	$92\frac{1}{2}$	:	100	: :	26,492	:	28,640

PAPER MONEY REDUCED TO LEGAL.

In order to reduce paper money to legal, it should be first reduced to effective, as above. Then, as 100 less half the discount is to 100, so is the sum in effective to the sum in legal money.

Reduce 232 Mil. 650 Rees paper money to legal; discount on paper being 20 per cent.

					Paper		Effective
As	100	:	80	: :	232,650	:	186,120
					Effective		Legal
And as	90	:	100	: :	186,120	:	206,800

Or the above question may be performed by a single statement: thus, as 90 is to 80, so is paper to legal money; that is, as 100 less half the discount is to 100 less the whole discount, so is paper to legal money.

LEGAL MONEY REDUCED TO PAPER.

Legal money is reduced to paper by reversing the foregoing statement: that is, as 100 is to 100 less half the discount, so is the sum in legal money to the sum in effective; and this is reduced to paper as above.

Reduce 206 Mil. 800 Rees legal money to paper: the discount on paper being 20 per cent.

					Legal		Effective
As	100	:	90	: :	206,800	:	186,120
					Effective		Paper
And as	80	:	100	: :	186,120	:	232,650

Or the above question may be performed by a single statement: thus, as 100 less the whole discount is to 100 less half the discount, so is the given sum in legal money to the sum in paper.

LISBON ON LONDON, see page 24.
LISBON ON AMSTERDAM, see page 31.
LISBON ON FRANCE, see page 51.
LISBON ON GENOA, see page 63.
LISBON ON HAMBURGH, see page 67.
LISBON ON LEGHORN, see page 70.

LISBON ON NAPLES.

Reduce 232 Ducats 6 Grains into Portugal money; exchange at 684 Rees per Ducato di regno.

```
     Duc.    Rees       Ducats     Milrees  Rees
As   1   :   684   ::   232,06  :   158     729
                        684
                       ─────────── Mil.   Rees
             1,000)158,729,04(158   729
```

LONDON ON LISBON, see page 24.
AMSTERDAM ON LISBON, see page 31.
FRANCE ON LISBON, see page 51.
GENOA ON LISBON, see page 63.
HAMBURGH ON LISBON, see page 67.
LEGHORN ON LISBON, see page 70.

NAPLES ON LISBON.

Reduce 158 Mil. 729 Rees into money of Naples; exchange at 684 Rees per Ducato di regno.

```
    Rees   Ducat     Rees       Ducats Gr.
As  684  :  1   ::  158,729  :   232   6

               684)158729(232,06
                   1368
                   ────
                    2192 &c.
```

LISBON ON PALERMO.

Reduce 79 Oncie 11 Tari 12½ Grani into Portugal money; exchange at 5 Tari 16 Grani per old Crusado.

```
   Tari Gr.     Rees     On.  Tari  Gr.      Mil.  Rees
As 5    16  :   400  ::  79   11    12½   :  164   250
   20                    30
   ──                   ────
   116                  2381
                          20
                       ──────
                       47632½
                          400
                    ────────── Mil.  Rees
          116)19053000(164   250
```

By the Chain Rule.

```
                      79,3875 Oncie.
  1 Oncia     =       30 Tari.
5,8 Tari      =       400 Rees.
```

Result as above.

PALERMO ON LISBON.

Reduce 164 Mil. 250 Rees into Sicilian money; exchange at 5 Tari 16 Grani per old Crusado.

```
   Rees    Tari Gr.       Rees        On.  Tari  Gr.
As 400  :  5    16  ::  164,250  :   79   11    12½
           20             116
           ──          ─────────
           116    4,00)190530,00
                       ─────────
                    2,0)4763,2½
                       ────────
                    3,0)238,1  12½
                       ─────
                        79 On. 11 Tari 12½ Gr.
```

By the Chain Rule.

```
                   164,250 Milrees.
400 Rees    =        5,8 Tari.
 30 Tari    =          1 Oncia.
```

Result as above.

LISBON ON SPAIN.

Reduce 140 Dollars 3 Reals 18 Maravedis of plate into Portugal money; exchange at 2312 Rees per Doubloon of exchange of 4 Dollars of plate.

```
   Dollars   Rees       Dollars Reals Mar.     Mil.  Rees
As 4    :  2,312  : :   140    3    18    :    81   175
   8                      8
   —                    ———
   32                   1123
   34                     34
  ———                ————————— Mil.  Rees
  1088           1088)88318400(81   175
                      8704
                      ————
                      1278 &c.
```

By the Chain Rule.

		140 Doll. 3 Reals 18 Mar.
4 Dollars	=	1 Doub. of exchange.
1 Doubloon	=	2312 Rees.

Result as above.

SPAIN ON LISBON.

Reduce 81 Mil. 175 Rees into Spanish money; exchange at 2312 Rees per Doubloon of exchange.

```
   Rees     Dollars    Mil. Rees      Doll.  Reals Marav.
As 2,312  :   4   : :  81,175     :   140    3     18
                        4
                    —————————   Doll. Reals Mar.
               2312)324700(140    3     18
                    2312
                    ————
                     9350
                     9248
                     ————
                      1020 &c.

           Remainder × 8 × 34 &c.
```

By the Chain Rule.

		81 Mil. 175 Rees.
2312 Rees	=	1 Doubloon.
1 Doubloon	=	4 Dollars.

Result as above.

LISBON ON VENICE.

Reduce 204 Lire 3 Soldi 7 Denari Piccoli into Portugal money; exchange at 67 Rees per Lira Piccola.

```
   Lira  Rees     Lire  Sol. Den.      Rees
As 1  :  67   ::  204   3    7    :   13,630
   20              20
   —              ———
   20             4083
   12               12
   ——             —————
   240            49003
                     67
              ——————————   Rees
        24,0)328320,1(13,680
              24
              ——
              88 &c.
```

VENICE ON LISBON.

Reduce 13,680 Rees into Venetian money; exchange at 67 Rees per Lira Piccola.

```
   Rees   Lira     Rees       Lire  Sol. Den.
As 67  :   1  : :  13,680  :  204   3    7

              67)13,680(204   3   7
                 134
                 ———
                  280
                  268
                  ———
                   12 &c.

        Remainder × 20 × 12 &c.
```

LEIPSIC.

The monies of exchange and calculations for Leipsic are the same as those for *Berlin*, page 35.

MILAN.

MONIES OF EXCHANGE.

Exchanges are computed here in Lire, Soldi, and Denari correnti or imperiali.

12 Denari = 1 Soldo; 20 Soldi = 1 Lira.
106 Soldi or Lire imperiali = 150 Soldi or Lire correnti.
106 Soldi imperiali, or 150 Soldi correnti = 1 Filippo.
117 Soldi imperiali = 1 Scudo or Crown.

COURSE OF EXCHANGE, From the Milan Quotation. *January*, 1820.			EXPLANATION.	
AMSTERDAM	56	.. MILAN	gives 56 Soldi correnti	for 1 Florin.
AUGSBURG	66	.. ———	gives 66 Ditto	for 1 Florin current.
FRANCE	55	.. ———	gives 55 Soldi imperiali	for 3 Francs.
GENOA	86	.. ———	gives 86 Soldi correnti	for 4 Lire fuori banco.
HAMBURGH	49	.. ———	gives 49 Ditto	for 1 Mark banco.
LEGHORN	132	.. ———	gives 132 Ditto	for 1 Pezza of 8 Reals.
LONDON	32 15	.. ———	gives 32 Lire 15 Soldi correnti	for £1 sterling.
NAPLES	108	.. ———	gives 108 Soldi correnti	for 1 Ducato di regno.
ROME	138	.. ———	gives 138 Ditto	for 1 Scudo Romano.
VENICE	96	.. ———	gives 96 Ditto	for 1 Ducat current.
VIENNA	$67\frac{7}{8}$	.. ———	gives $67\frac{7}{8}$ Ditto	for 1 Florin current.

[For the usances and other particulars relating to Bills of Exchange, see MILAN, vol. i.]

MILAN ON AMSTERDAM.

Reduce 717 Florins 5 Stivers into money of Milan; exchange at 57 Soldi current per Florin.

	Florin		Soldi		Florins	Stivers		Lire	Soldi	Den.
As	1	:	57	: :	717	5	:	2044	3	3
	20				20					
	20				14345					
					57					

2,0)81766,5

2,0)40883,25

2044 Lire 3,25 Soldi
12

3,00

By the Chain Rule.

		717,25 Florins.
1 Florin	=	57 Soldi.
20 Soldi	=	1 Lira.

Result as above.

AMSTERDAM ON MILAN.

Reduce 2044 Lire 3 Soldi 3 Denari current of Milan into Dutch money; exchange at 57 Soldi current per Florin.

	Soldi		Florin		Lire	Soldi	Den.		Florins	Stivers
As	57	:	1	: :	2044	3	3	:	717	5
	12				20					
	684				40883					
					12					

Fl. Sti.
684)490599(717 5
4788

1179 &c.

By the Chain Rule.

		2044,1625 Lire.
1 Lira	=	20 Soldi.
57 Soldi	=	1 Florin.

Result as above.

MILAN ON GENOA.

Reduce 3559 Lire 9 Soldi 4 Denari fuori banco into money of Milan; exchange at 85 Soldi current of Milan for 4 Lire fuori banco of Genoa.

	Lire		Soldi		Lire	Sol.	Den		Lire	Sol.	Den.
As	4	:	85	: :	3559	9	4	:	3781	18	8
	20		12		20						
	80		1020		71189						
	12				12						
	960				854272						
					1020						

—12
96,0)87135744,0(907664
864
2,0)7563,8 8
735 &c.
3781 Lire 18 Sol. 8 Den.

GENOA ON MILAN.

Reduce 3781 Lire 18 Soldi 8 Denari of Milan into money of Genoa; exchange at 85 Soldi current of Milan for 4 Lire fuori banco of Genoa.

	Soldi		Lire		Lire	Soldi	Den.		Lire	Sol.	Den.
As	85	:	4	: :	3781	18	8	:	3559	9	4
	12				20						
	1020				75638						
					12						
					907664						
					4						

Lire Sol. Den.
102,0)363065,6(3559 9 4
306

570 &c.

MILAN ON HAMBURGH.

Reduce 901 Marks 15 Schillings 4 Pfenings banco into money of Milan; exchange at 48 Soldi current per Mark banco.

```
     Mark    Soldi       Marks  Sch. Pfen.        Lire   Soldi
As   1   :   48    ::    901    15   4     :      2164   14
     16                  16
     ——                  ————
     16                  14431
     12                  12
     ——                  ————
     192                 173176
                         48
                  ————————2,0
          192)8312448(43294
              768      ————
              ———      2164 Lire 14 Soldi.
              632 &c.
```

HAMBURGH ON MILAN.

Reduce 2164 Lire 14 Soldi current into money of Hamburgh; exchange at 48 Soldi current per Mark banco.

```
     Soldi   Mark       Lire   Soldi      Mks.  Sch.  Pf.
As   48   :  1    ::    2164   14    :    901   15    4
                        20
                        ————  Mks  Sch.  Pf.
                   48)43294(901    15    4
                      432
                      ———
                        94
                        48
                        ——
                        46
```

Remainder × 16 × 12 &c.

MILAN ON LEGHORN.

Reduce 1233 Pezze 11 Soldi 8 Denari into money of Milan; exchange at 135 Soldi of Milan per Pezza of 8 Reals.

```
     Pezza   Soldi       Pezze  Soldi Den.      Lire   Soldi Den.
As   1   :   135   ::    1233   11    8    :    8326   13    9
             12          20
             ———         ————
             1620        24671
                         12
                         —————
                         296060
                         1620
                  ——————————12
          24,0)47961720,0(1998405
               24          ———————
               ——          2,0)16653,3   9
               239 &c.     ——————————
                           8326 Lire 13 Sol. 9 Den.
```

LEGHORN ON MILAN.

Reduce 8326 Lire 13 Soldi 9 Denari of Milan into money of Leghorn; exchange at 135 Soldi per Pezza of 8 Reals.

```
     Soldi   Pezza      Lire   Soldi Den.     Pezze  Sol. Den.
As   135  :  1    ::    8326   13    9   :    1233   11   8
     12                 20
     ———                ——————
     1620               166533
                        12
                   ————————————  Pezze Sol. Den.
             162,0)199840,5(1233  11   8
                   162
                   ———
                   378 &c.
```

MILAN ON LONDON.

Reduce £143 8s. 2d. sterling into money of Milan; exchange at 31 Lire 10 Soldi current per £ sterling.

	£		Lire	Soldi		£	s.	d.		Lire	Soldi	Den.
As	1	:	31	10	::	143	8	2	:	4517	7	3

20   20
20   2868
12   12
240   34418
31½

240)1084167(4517 Lire 7 Soldi 3 Den.
960
1241 &c.

LONDON ON MILAN.

Reduce 4517 Lire 7 Soldi 3 Denari current of Milan into sterling; exchange at 31 Lire 10 Soldi per £ sterling.

	Lire	Soldi		£		Lire	Soldi	Den.		£	s.	d.
As	31	10	:	1	::	4517	7	3	:	143	8	2

20   20
630   90347
12   12
7560   756,0)108416,7(£143 8s. 2d.
756
3281 &c.

Remainder × 20 × 12 &c.

MILAN ON ROME.

Reduce 2007 Scudi 31¼ Bajocchi into money of Milan; exchange at 136 Soldi of Milan per Scudo.

	Scudo		Soldi		Scudi	Baj.		Lire	Soldi	Den.
As	1	:	136	::	2007	31,25	:	13649	14	6

136
2,0)27299,4,5000
13649 Lire 14,5 Soldi

ROME ON MILAN.

Reduce 13649 Lire 14 Soldi 6 Denari into Roman money; exchange at 136 Soldi of Milan per Roman Scudo or Crown.

	Soldi		Scudo		Lire	Soldi	Den.		Scudi	Baj.
As	136	:	1	::	13649	14	6	:	2007	31¼

12   20
1632   272994
12
1632)3275934(2007 Scudi 31,25 Baj.
3264
11934 &c.

N.B. Milan, like many other parts of Italy, exchanges occasionally in Italian Livres, and the estimated proportion is that 27 Lire of Milan are worth 20,723 French Francs or Lire Italiane.

NAPLES.

MONIES OF EXCHANGE.

Exchanges are computed here in Ducats of 100 Grains.

10 Grani = 1 Carlino; and 10 Carlini = 1 Ducato di regno.

COURSE OF EXCHANGE, From the Naples Quotation. *January*, 1820.				EXPLANATION.	
AMSTERDAM	51	25	NAPLES	gives 51 Grains 25 Centimes	for 1 Florin.
ANCONA	125	50	———	gives 125 Grains 50 Centimes	for 1 Scudo.
AUGSBURG	61	35	———	gives 61 Grains 35 Centimes	for 1 Florin current.
FLORENCE	19	90	———	gives 19 Grains 90 Centimes	for 1 Lira Fiorentine.
FRANCE	24	25	———	gives 24 Grains 25 Centimes	for 1 Franc.
DITTO	433		———	receives 433 Centimes	for 1 Ducat.
GENOA	19	90	———	gives 19 Grains 90 Centimes	for 1 Lira fuori banco.
DITTO	101⅓		———	receives 101⅓ Soldi fuori banco	for 1 Ducat.
HAMBURGH	44	10	———	gives 44 Grains 10 Centimes	for 1 Mark banco.
LEGHORN	122	75	———	gives 122 Grains 75 Centimes	for 1 Pezza of 8 Reals.
LISBON	53	80	———	gives 53 Grains 80 Centimes	for 1 Crusado of 400 Rees.
DITTO	670		———	receives 670 Rees	for 1 Ducat.
LONDON	604		———	gives 604 Grains	for 1 £ sterling.
MILAN	18	30	———	gives 18 Grains 30 Centimes	for 1 Lira corrente.
DITTO	113		———	receives 113 Soldi correnti	for 1 Ducat.
PALERMO	120¾		———	{ gives 120 Grains 75 Centimes	for 1 Scudo of 12 Tari.
				{ or 120¾ Ducats	for 100 Sicilian Scudi.
ROME	127		———	gives 127 Ducats	for 100 Scudi Romani.
SPAIN	121		———	gives 121 Grains	for 1 Dollar of Plate.
TRIESTE	61	25	———	gives 61 Grains 25 Centimes	for 1 Florin of Augsburg.
VENICE	22	90	———	gives 22 Grains 90 Centimes	for 1 Italian Livre.
VIENNA	61	50	———	gives 61 Grains 50 Centimes	for 1 Florin current.

[For the usances and other particulars relating to Bills of Exchange, see NAPLES, vol. i.]

Naples on London, see page 25.
Naples on France, see page 52.
Naples on Genoa, see page 63.
Naples on Leghorn, see page 70.
Naples on Lisbon, see page 75.

NAPLES ON PALERMO.

Reduce 277 Oncie 26 Tari into money of Naples; exchange at 120¾ Ducats per 100 Sicilian Scudi.

	Tari		Ducats		Oncie	Tari		Ducats	Gr.
As	1200	:	120¾	::	277	26	:	838	81

30
————
8336
120¾
————
12,00)10065,72
————
838,81

By the Chain Rule.

		277 Oncie 26 Tari.
1 Oncia	=	30 Tari.
12 Tari	=	1 Scudo.
100 Scudi	=	120¾ Ducats.

Result as above.

London on Naples, see page 25.
France on Naples, see page 52.
Genoa on Naples, see page 63.
Leghorn on Naples, see page 70.
Lisbon on Naples, see page 75.

PALERMO ON NAPLES.

Reduce 838 Ducats 81 Grains into Sicilian money; exchange at 120¾ Ducats per 100 Scudi of 12 Tari.

	Ducats		Tari		Ducats	Gr.		Oncie	Tari
As	120¾	:	1200	::	838	81	:	277	26

100
————
12075

838,81
1200
————3,0)
12075)100657200(833,6
96600
————
40572 &c.
277 On. 26 Tari.

By the Chain Rule.

		838 Ducati 81 Grani.
120¾ Ducati	=	100 Scudi.
1 Scudo	=	12 Tari.
30 Tari	=	1 Oncia.

Result as above.

NAPLES ON SPAIN.

Reduce 3368 Dollars 6 Reals 16 Maravedis of plate into money of Naples; exchange at 312 Maravedis of plate per Ducato di regno.

	Marav.		Ducat		Dollars	Reals	Mar.		Ducats	Grains
As	312	:	1	::	3368	6	16	:	2936	91

8
————
26950
34
———— Ducats
312)916316(2936,91
624
————
2923 &c.

SPAIN ON NAPLES.

Reduce 2936 Ducats 91 Grains into Spanish money; exchange at 312 Maravedis of plate per Ducato di regno.

	Ducat		Mar.		Ducats		Dollars	Reals	Mar.
As	1	:	312	::	2936,91	:	3368	6	16

312
————(8
34)916315,92(26950 16
68
———
236 &c.
3368 Dol. 6 R. 16 M.

PALERMO.

MONIES OF EXCHANGE.

Exchanges are computed here in Oncie, Tari, and Grani; and also in Scudi, Tari, and Grani.

20 Grani or Grains = 1 Tari or Tarin. 30 Tari = 1 Oncia.

12 Tari = 1 Scudo or Sicilian Crown. 5 Scudi = 2 Oncie.

COURSE OF EXCHANGE, From the Palermo Quotation. *January*, 1820.		EXPLANATION.	
AMSTERDAM ..	5½	.. PALERMO gives 5½ Tari	for 1 Florin.
FRANCE	47½	.. ——— gives 47½ Grani	for 1 Franc.
GENOA	39½	.. ——— gives 39½ Grani	for 1 Lira fuori banco.
HAMBURGH......	4 6	.. ——— gives 4 Tari 6 Grani	for 1 Mark banco.
LEGHORN........	12½	.. ——— gives 12½ Tari................	for 1 Pezza.
LISBON..........	6¼	.. ——— gives 6¼ Tari	for 1 old Crusado.
LONDON	60	.. ——— gives 60 Tari	for 1 £ sterling.
NAPLES	121	.. ——— receives 121 Ducati	for 100 Sicilian Crowns.
ROME	12½	.. ——— gives 12½ Tari................	for 1 Roman Scudo.
SPAIN	8¾	.. ——— gives 8¾ Tari	for 1 Peso of Plate.
TRIESTE	5 27	.. ——— gives 5 Tari 27 Grani	for 1 Florin current.

[For the usances and other particulars relating to Bills of Exchange, see SICILY, vol. i.]

PALERMO ON LONDON, see page 25.
PALERMO ON GENOA, see page 63.
PALERMO ON LEGHORN, see page 71.
PALERMO ON LISBON, see page 75.
PALERMO ON NAPLES, see page 81.

PALERMO ON AMSTERDAM.

Reduce 2564 Florins 10 Stivers into Sicilian money; exchange at $5\frac{1}{2}$ Tari per Florin.

	Florin		Tari		Florins	Stivers		Oncie	Tari	Gr.
As	1	:	$5\frac{1}{2}$	: :	2564	10	:	470	4	15

20   20
——   ——
20   51290
$5\frac{1}{2}$
——
2,0)28209,5
——
3,0)1410,4 15
——
470 On. 4 Tari 15 Grani.

LONDON ON PALERMO, see page 25.
GENOA ON PALERMO, see page 63.
LEGHORN ON PALERMO, see page 71.
LISBON ON PALERMO, see page 75.
NAPLES ON PALERMO, see page 81.

AMSTERDAM ON PALERMO.

Reduce 470 Oncie 4 Tari 15 Grani into Dutch money; exchange at $5\frac{1}{2}$ Tari per Florin.

	Tari		Florin		Oncie	Tari	Grani		Florins	Stivers
As	$5\frac{1}{2}$	:	1	: :	470	4	15	:	2564	10

30
——
14104
20
——2,0
5,5)282095(5129,0
——
2564 Florins 10 Stivers.

PALERMO ON SPAIN.

Reduce 4646 Dollars 5 Reals 14 Maravedis of plate into Sicilian money; exchange at $8\frac{1}{2}$ Tari per Dollar of plate.

	Dol.		Tari		Dol.	Reals	Mar.		Oncie	Tari	Gr.
As	1	:	$8\frac{1}{2}$	: :	4646	5	14	:	1316	16	15

8   8
——   ——
8   37173
34   34
——   ——
272   1263896
$8\frac{1}{2}$
——3,0
272)10743116(3949,6 15
816   ——
——   1316 On. 16 Tari 15 Gr.
2583 &c.

SPAIN ON PALERMO.

Reduce 1316 Oncie 16 Tari 15 Grani into Spanish money; exchange at $8\frac{1}{2}$ Tari per Dollar of plate.

	Tari		Dollar		Oncie	Tari	Grani		Dollars	Reals	Mar.
As	$8\frac{1}{2}$	:	1	: :	1316	16	15	:	4646	5	14

20   30
——   ——
170   39496
20
—— Dol. Reals Mar.
17,0)78993,5(4646 5 14
68
——
109 &c.

Remainder × 8 × 34 &c.

PETERSBURG.

MONIES OF EXCHANGE.

Exchanges are computed here in **Rubles** and **Copecks**.

10 Copecks = 1 Grieve or Grievener.

10 Grieves, or 100 Copecks = 1 Ruble.

COURSE OF EXCHANGE, From the Petersburg Quotation. *January*, 1820.		EXPLANATION.	
AMSTERDAM	$9\frac{31}{32}$ ..	PETERSBURG receives $9\frac{31}{32}$ Stivers	for 1 Ruble.
CONSTANTINOPLE..	73 ..	——— gives 73 Copecks	for 1 Piastre.
FRANCE	104 ..	——— receives 104 Centimes	for 1 Ruble.
HAMBURGH	$8\frac{31}{32}$ ..	——— receives $8\frac{31}{32}$ Schillings Lubs banco..	for 1 Ruble.
LEIPSIC	17 ..	——— receives 17 Groschen	for 1 Ruble.
LONDON	$10\frac{1}{32}$ ..	——— receives $10\frac{1}{32}$ Pence sterling	for 1 Ruble.
VIENNA	125 ..	——— receives 125 Creutzers...........	for 1 Ruble.

[For the days of grace and other particulars relating to Bills of Exchange, see RUSSIA, vol. i.]

PETERSBURG ON AMSTERDAM.

Reduce 2655 Florins 13 Stivers $2\frac{1}{2}$ Pennings into Russian money; exchange at $9\frac{5}{8}$ Stivers per Ruble.

	Stivers		Ruble		Florins	Stivers	Pen.		Rubles	Copecks
As	$9\frac{5}{8}$	:	1	: :	2655	13	2,5	:	5518	25

16   20

154   53103

16

154)8498105(5518 Rubles 25 Copecks

770

798 &c.

AMSTERDAM ON PETERSBURG.

Reduce 5518 Rubles 25 Copecks into Dutch money; exchange at $9\frac{5}{8}$ Stivers per Ruble.

	Ruble		Stivers		Rubles	Copecks		Florins	Sti.	Pen.
As	1	:	$9\frac{5}{8}$	: :	5518	25	:	2655	13	$2\frac{1}{2}$

9,625

2,0)5311,315625

2655,6578125

20

13,1562500

16

2,5000000

PETERSBURG ON FRANCE.

Reduce 7077 Francs 67 Centimes into Russian money; exchange at 1 Franc 10 Centimes per Ruble.

	Franc	Cen.		Ruble		Francs	Cen.		Rubles	Cop.
As	1	10	:	1	: :	7077	67	:	6434	25

11,0)70776,7

6434,25

FRANCE ON PETERSBURG.

Reduce 6434 Rubles 25 Copecks into French money; exchange at 1 Franc 10 Centimes per Ruble.

	Ruble		Franc	Cen.		Rubles	Copecks		Francs	Centimes
As	1	:	1	10	: :	6434	25	:	7077	67

1,10

7077,6750

PETERSBURG ON LONDON.

Reduce £131 1s. 1d. sterling into Russian money; exchange at $9\frac{1}{8}$d. per Ruble.

	d.		Ruble		£	s.	d.		Rubles	Copecks
As	$9\frac{1}{8}$	:	1	: :	131	1	1	:	3466	90

20

2621

12

9,125)31453(3446,90 Rubles

LONDON ON PETERSBURG.

Reduce 3446 Rubles 90 Copecks into sterling; exchange at $9\frac{1}{8}$d. per Ruble.

	Ruble		d.		Rubles	Copecks		£	s.	d.
As	1	:	$9\frac{1}{8}$	: :	3446	90	:	131	1	1

3446,90

9,125

240)31452,96250(131,05401

240   20

745 &c.   1,08020

12

0,96240

ROME.

MONIES OF EXCHANGE.

Exchanges are computed in Scudi moneta, and Bajocchi; or in Scudi di stampa, Soldi, and Denari d'oro. Quattrini and Mezzi Quattrini are also sometimes reckoned.

2 Mezzi Quattrini = 1 Quattrino.

5 Quattrini = 1 Bajocco.

10 Bajocchi = 1 Paolo; 10 Paoli, or 100 Bajocchi = 1 Scudo moneta, or Roman Crown.

1523 Mezzi Quattrini, or 152 $\frac{3}{10}$ Bajocchi = 1 Scudo di stampa d'oro, or gold Crown.

12 Denari d'oro = 1 Soldo d'oro; 20 Soldi d'oro = 1 Scudo di stampa d'oro.

COURSE OF EXCHANGE, From the Roman Quotation. *January*, 1820.		EXPLANATION.	
AMSTERDAM	44	.. ROME gives 44 Bajocchi	for 1 Florin.
ANCONA	98	.. ——— gives 98 Scudi Romani	for 100 Scudi of Ancona.
BOLOGNA	102	.. ——— gives 102 Scudi Romani...........	for 100 Scudi of Bologna.
FLORENCE	104¼	.. ——— gives 104¼ Scudi di stampa d'oro	for 100 Scudi d'oro.
FRANCE	105	.. ——— receives 105 Sous in Francs	for 1 Scudo.
GENOA..........	128	.. ——— receives 128 Soldi fuori banco	for 1 Scudo.
LEGHORN	96	.. ——— gives 96 Bajocchi	for 1 Pezza of 8 Reals.
LONDON	47	.. ——— receives 47 Pence sterling..........	for 1 Scudo.
MILAN..........	139¾	.. ——— gives 139¾ Scudi Romani	for 100 Scudi imperiali.
NAPLES	127½	.. ——— receives 127½ Ducati di regno	for 100 Scudi Romani.
VENICE	557	.. ——— receives 557 Centimes.............	for 1 Scudo.

[For the usances and other particulars relating to Bills of Exchange, see ROME, vol. i.]

ROME ON FRANCE.

Reduce 26813 Francs 54 Centimes into Roman money; exchange at 5 Francs 20 Centimes per Scudo moneta.

```
   Francs Cen.   Scudo      Francs  Cen.       Scudi  Baj.
As 5      20   :  1   : :   26813   54     :   5156   45

            52,0(268135,4(5156,45
                 260
                 ---
                  81 &c.
```

FRANCE ON ROME.

Reduce 5156 Scudi 45 Bajocchi into French money; exchange at 5 Francs 20 Centimes per Scudo moneta. The operation is best performed decimally; thus,

```
   Scudo   Francs        Scudi          Francs
As 1   :   5,20    : :   5156,45   :   26813,54
                         5,20
                     ----------
                     26813,5400
```

ROME ON GENOA.

Reduce 4017 Lire 3 Soldi 9 Denari fuori banco into Roman money; exchange at 125 Soldi fuori banco per Scudo moneta.

```
   Soldi   Scudo      Lire  Sol. Den.      Scudi  Baj.
As 125   :  1   : :   4017   3    9    :   642    75
   12                  × 20 × 12
   ----               ----------
   1500       15,00)9641,25
                    ----------
                      642,75
```

GENOA ON ROME.

Reduce 642 Scudi 75 Bajocchi into money of Genoa; exchange at 125 Soldi fuori banco per Scudo moneta.

```
   Scudo  Soldi       Scudi  Baj.       Lire  Sol. Den.
As 1   :  125   : :   642    75    :   4017   3    9

                 642,75
                   125
             ------------
             2,0)8034,375
             ------------
             4017 Lire 3¾ Soldi.
```

ROME ON LONDON.

Reduce £937 11s. 5d. sterling into Roman money; exchange at 52d. sterling per Scudo.

```
   d.    Scudo     £    s.  d.      Scudi  Baj.
As 52  :  1   : :  937  11  5   :   4327   25
                    20
                  -----
                  18751
                     12
                 ------- Scudi Baj.
            52)225017(4327 25
               208
               ---
               170 &c.
```

LONDON ON ROME.

Reduce 4327 Scudi 25 Bajocchi into sterling; exchange at 52d. sterling per Scudo.

```
   Scudo  d.        Scudi Bajoc.      £    s.  d.
As 1   :  52  : :   4327  25     :   937  11  5

              4327,25
                   52
           ----------
         12)225017,00
           ----------
          2,0)1875,1  5
           ----------
           £937 11s. 5d.
```

Rome on Milan, see page 79.

Milan on Rome, see page 79.

SPAIN.

MONIES OF EXCHANGE.

Exchanges are generally computed here in denominations of Plate, which is always understood to be Old Plate, if New Plate be not mentioned.

There are three principal denominations of these imaginary monies in which exchanges are generally transacted; viz. Dollars, Doubloons, and Ducats, and they are divided into Reals and Maravedis of Plate, and sometimes converted into Vellon and other denominations.

The Dollar of Exchange, also called *Peso* or *Piastre de Cambio* or *de Plata,* is divided into 8 Reals of 34 Maravedis of Plate each, and sometimes into 16 Quartos.

The *Doubloon de Plata,* or Pistole of Exchange, is four times the Dollar, and therefore contains 32 Reals or 1088 Maravedis of Plate.

The Ducat of Plate, also called *Ducado de Cambio,* contains 11 Reals 1 Maravedi, or 375 Maravedis of Plate.

At Alicant, Valencia, and Barcelona, exchanges are transacted in Libras of 20 Sueldos, or 240 Dineros.

The Libra of Alicant and Valencia is the Dollar of Plate. This is sometimes divided into 10 Reals of New Plate, which are, of course, equal to 8 Reals of Old Plate.

The Libra of Barcelona, commonly called *Libra Catalan,* is worth $5\frac{5}{7}$ Reals of Plate; hence 7 of those Libras equal 5 Dollars of Plate; and, therefore, 28 Sueldos Catalan equal 1 Dollar.

The Hard Dollar of 20 Reals Vellon is occasionally used in exchanges, and is also divided into 12 Reals, each Real of 16 Quartos. The Current Dollar, which is an imaginary money, valued at two-thirds of the Hard Dollar, is divided into 8 Reals, and the Real into 16 Quartos. The two latter are the principal monies of exchange used at Gibraltar.

COURSE OF EXCHANGE, From the Cadiz Quotation. *February,* 1820.		EXPLANATION.	
AMSTERDAM....	96	.. CADIZ receives 96 Grotes Flemish........	for 1 Ducat of plate.
FRANCE........	14	.. ——— receives 14 Francs................	for 1 Doubloon of plate.
GENOA	125	.. ——— gives 125 Dollars of plate	for 100 Pezze of $5\frac{3}{4}$ Lire.
HAMBURGH	88	.. ——— receives 88 Grotes Flemish banco ..	for 1 Ducat of exchange.
LEGHORN	123	.. ——— gives 123 Dollars of plate	for 100 Pezze of 8 Reals.
LISBON	2700	.. ——— receives 2700 Rees	for 1 Doubloon of plate.
LONDON	$35\frac{3}{8}$	.. ——— receives $35\frac{3}{8}$ Pence sterling........	for 1 Dollar of plate.
NAPLES........	290	.. ——— gives 290 Maravedis of plate	for 1 Ducato di regno.

[For the usances and other particulars relating to Exchange, see SPAIN, also ALICANT, BARCELONA, BILBOA, CADIZ, CASTILLE, and GIBRALTAR, vol. i.]

SPAIN ON AMSTERDAM, see page 31.
SPAIN ON FRANCE, see page 53.
SPAIN ON GENEVA, see page 60.
SPAIN ON GENOA, see page 64.
SPAIN ON HAMBURGH, see page 67.
SPAIN ON LEGHORN, see page 71.
SPAIN ON LISBON, see page 75.
SPAIN ON LONDON, see page 26.
SPAIN ON NAPLES, see page 81.
SPAIN ON PALERMO, see page 83.

AMSTERDAM ON SPAIN, see page 31.
FRANCE ON SPAIN, see page 53.
GENEVA ON SPAIN, see page 60.
GENOA ON SPAIN, see page 64.
HAMBURGH ON SPAIN, see page 67.
LEGHORN ON SPAIN, see page 71.
LISBON ON SPAIN, see page 75.
LONDON ON SPAIN, see page 26.
NAPLES ON SPAIN, see page 81.
PALERMO ON SPAIN, see page 83.

The above are the principal places with which Spain exchanges, and, therefore, any further examples would be unnecessary if Bills were always drawn in Plate, the money in which the Courses of Exchange are quoted. But as they are sometimes drawn in other denominations, such as Reals Vellon, and Libras of Alicant, Valencia, and Barcelona, it remains to show how these several currencies are converted into Plate.

It has been stated, p. 26, that Plate is reduced into Vellon by multiplying by 32 and dividing by 17, and *vice versâ*; but when Bills are drawn in Hard Dollars, Reals, and Maravedis Vellon, which is sometimes done in Bilboa and the adjacent places, the operation becomes more complex, as in the following example.

BILBOA ON LONDON.

Reduce £800 4s. 8d. into Hard Dollars, Reals, and Maravedis; exchange at 52½d. per Hard Dollar.

34 Maravedis = 1 Real, 20 Reals = 1 Hard Dollar.

```
     d.  Hard Dol.         £    s.  d.      Dollars Reals Mar.
As 52½ : 1     :  :      800    4   7¾   :   2754    8    11
    4    8       ×20 × 12 × 4
   ---  --              -------
   210   8              768224
        34                8704
        --          ----------
       272     210)6686621696
        32          ----------
      ----      17)31841055
      8704          --------
                34)1873003
                    -------
               2,0)5508,8   11
                    ------
                  2754 H. Dol. 8 Reals 11 Mar.
```

LONDON ON BILBOA.

Reduce 2754 Hard Dollars 8 Reals 11 Maravedis Vellon into sterling; exchange at 52½d. per Hard Dollar.

```
H. Dol.   d.      H. Dollars Reals Mar.     £    s.  d.
As 1   :  52½  ::   2754     8    11   :  800   4   7¾
   8                  20
   --              -----
   8               55088
  34                  34
  ---            -------
  272            1873003
   32                 17
  ---           --------
 8704           31841051
                     52½
            ------------12
     8704)1671655177½(192055¾
          8704          -------
          -----     2,0)1600,4   7
          80125 &c.     -------
                        £800 4s. 7¾d.
```

EFFECTIVE MONEY REDUCED TO PAPER.

Bills, when they are not made payable in *effective*, are paid in a paper money, called *Vales Reales*, which bears a considerable discount.

Effective money is therefore reduced to paper by saying: as 100 *minus* the discount is to 100, so is the effective sum to the sum in paper.

Reduce 743 Reals 10 Maravedis effective to paper money; discount at 48 per cent.

			Reals	Mar.		Reals	Mar.
As 52	: 100	: :	743	10	:	1429	14
			34				

—34) Reals Mar.

52)2527200(48600(1429 14

208 34

447 &c. 146

PAPER MONEY REDUCED TO EFFECTIVE.

Paper money is reduced to effective by reversing the foregoing operation: that is, as 100 is to 100 less the discount, so is the sum in paper to the effective sum.

Reduce 1429 Reals 14 Maravedis in paper into effective; discount at 48 per cent.

			Reals	Mar.		Reals	Mar.
As 100	: 52	: :	1429	14	:	743	10
			34				

48600

52

Reals Mar.

34)25272,00(743 10

238

147 &c.

LIBRAS OF ALICANT REDUCED TO REALS OF PLATE.

The Libras of Alicant and Valencia being Dollars of plate, are reduced to Reals by multiplying by 8. The Sueldos should be multiplied by 8 and divided by 20, because 20 Sueldos equal 8 Reals.

Reduce 314 Libras 11 Sueldos 3 Dineros of Alicant into Reals of plate.

Libras		Suel.	Din.
314		11	3
8		8	
2512 Reals.		2,0)9,1	
4 Reals 17 Mar.		$4\frac{1}{2}$ Reals.	

Ans. 2516 Reals 17 Mar.

REALS OF PLATE REDUCED TO LIBRAS OF ALICANT.

Reals of plate are reduced to Libras of Alicant and Valencia by dividing them by 8. The remainder, if there is any, should be multiplied by 20, and divided by 8, in order to reduce it to Sueldos.

Reduce 2516 Reals 17 Maravedis into Libras of Alicant.

Reals.

8)$2516\frac{1}{2}$

314 Libras $4\frac{1}{2}$ Reals.

20

Sueld. Din.

8)90(11 3

Ans. 314 Libras 11 Sueldos 3 Dineros.

LIBRAS OF BARCELONA REDUCED TO REALS OF PLATE.

The Libras Catalan are reduced to Reals of plate by saying: as 7 Libras is to 40 Reals, so is the given number of Libras to the number of Reals sought.

Reduce 463 Libras 6 Sueldos 3 Dineros Catalan into Reals of plate.

	Libras		Reals		Libras	Suel.	Din.		Reals	Mar.
As	7	:	40	: :	463	6	3	:	2647	17
					40					

18520

5 Sueldos = $\frac{1}{4}$ 10

1 Sueldo = $\frac{1}{5}$ 2

3 Dineros = $\frac{1}{4}$ ...... $\frac{1}{2}$

7)$18532\frac{1}{2}$

Ans. $2647\frac{1}{2}$ Reals of plate.

REALS OF PLATE REDUCED TO LIBRAS OF BARCELONA.

Reals of plate are reduced to Libras Catalan by reversing the foregoing operation: that is, as 40 Reals is to 7 Libras, so is the given number of Reals to the number of Libras sought.

Reduce 2647 Reals 17 Maravedis of plate to Libras Catalan.

	Reals		Lib.		Reals	Mar.		Libras	Suel.	Din.
As	40	:	7	: :	2647	17	:	463	6	3
					7					

18529

17 Maravedis = $\frac{1}{2}$.. 3,5

4,0)1853,25

Libras Sucl. Din.

463,3125 = 463 6 3

STOCKHOLM.

MONIES OF EXCHANGE.

Exchanges are computed in Rixdollars specie, Skillings, and Fenings.

12 Fenings or Oers = 1 Skilling.

48 Skillings = 1 Rixdollar specie.

COURSE OF EXCHANGE, From the Stockholm Quotation. *January*, 1820.		EXPLANATION.		
AMSTERDAM....	128	STOCKHOLM	gives 128 Skillings..............	for 1 Rixdollar.
COPENHAGEN ..	86	———	gives 86 Skillings	for 1 Rixdollar.
DANTZIC	24	———	gives 24 Skillings	for 1 Florin.
FRANCE	25	———	gives 25 Skillings	for 1 Franc.
HAMBURGH	135	———	gives 135 Skillings..............	for 1 Rixdollar banco.
LEGHORN	114	———	gives 114 Skillings..............	for 1 Pezza.
LISBON	51	———	gives 51 Skillings	for 1 old Crusado.
LONDON	12 10	———	gives 12 Rixdollars 10 Skillings ..	for 1 £ sterling.
PETERSBURG ..	25¼	———	gives 25¼ Skillings..............	for 1 Ruble.
SPAIN	110	———	gives 110 Skillings..............	for 1 Ducat of plate.

[For the usances and other particulars relating to Bills of Exchange, see SWEDEN, vol. i.]

STOCKHOLM ON AMSTERDAM.

Reduce 10845 Florins 12 Stivers 8 Pennings into Swedish money; exchange at 44 Swedish Skillings per Rixdollar of 2½ Florins.

```
   Florins  Skillings      Florins  Stivers Pen.    Rixdollars  Sk.
As 2½    :    44     ::    10845      12     8   :    3976      35
   20                      20
   ---                     ------
   50                      216912
   16                      16
   ---                     ------
   800                     3470600
                           44
                      -----------
              8,00)1527064,00
               ---------- Rixds. Skill.
              48)190883(3976   35
```

AMSTERDAM ON STOCKHOLM.

Reduce 3976 Rixdollars 35 Skillings Swedish into Dutch banco; exchange at 44 Skillings per Rixdollar banco.

```
   Skil.    Rixd.  Fl.       Rxds.   Sk.       Florins  Sti.  Pen.
As 44   :   1 or 2½   ::     3976    35    :   10845    12    8
                             48
                            ------
                            190883
                               2½
                            ------- Florins  Sti.  Pen.
                         44)477207½(10845    12    8
                            44
                            --
                            37 &c.
```

STOCKHOLM ON HAMBURGH.

Reduce 1544 Marks banco into Swedish money; exchange at 46½ Skillings Swedish per Rixdollar banco.

```
   Marks   Skillings     Marks      Rixd.  Skillings
As 3    :    46½     ::   1544   :   498     28
                          46½
                        -------
                        3)71796
                        ------- Rixd.  Skil.
                       48)23932(498    28
                          192
                          ---
                          473 &c.
```

HAMBURGH ON STOCKHOLM.

Reduce 498 Rixdollars 28 Skillings Swedish into Hamburgh money; exchange at 46½ Skillings per Rixdollar of 3 Marks banco.

```
   Skil.    Marks      Rixd.  Skil.      Marks
As 46½   :   3    ::   498    28     :   1544
   2                   48
   --                  -----
   93                  23932
                       3
                       -----
                       71796
                       2
                     ------- Marks.
                  93)143592(1544
                     93 &c.
```

STOCKHOLM ON LONDON.

Reduce £2009 3s. 4d. sterling into Swedish money; exchange at 4 Rixdollars 30 Skillings per £ sterling.

```
   £    Rixds.  Sk.       £     s.  d.      Rixds.  Sk.
As 1  :   4     30   ::  2009   3   4   :   9292    19
          48             20
          ---            -----
          222            40183
                         12
                         ------
                         482200
                         222
               ------------48)
        24,0)10704840,0(446035
             96 &c.     --------
                        9292 Rixd. 19 Sk.
```

LONDON ON STOCKHOLM.

Reduce 9292 Rixdollars 19 Skillings Swedish into sterling; exchange at 4 Rixdollars 30 Skillings per £ sterling.

```
   Rixds. Sk.    £        Rixds.  Sk.       £     s.  d.
As 4      30  :  1   ::   9292    19    :   2009  3   4
   48                     48
   ---                  ------- £     s. d.
   222               222)446035(2009  3  4
                         444
                         ---
                         20 &c.
```

TURIN.

MONIES OF EXCHANGE.

Exchanges are computed here in Lire, Soldi, and Denari.

12 Denari = 1 Soldo.
20 Soldi = 1 Lira.

COURSE OF EXCHANGE, From the Turin Quotation. *January*, 1820.			EXPLANATION.	
AMSTERDAM..	35		.. TURIN gives 35 Soldi	for 1 Florin.
AUGSBURG ..	43¼		.. ——— gives 43¼ Ditto	for 1 Florin current.
FRANCE......	20	1	.. ——— gives 20 Lire 1 Soldo	for 24 Francs.
GENEVA	82		.. ——— gives 82 Soldi	for 3 Livres current.
GENOA	9	10	.. ——— gives 9 Lire 10 Soldi	for 13 Lire 10 Soldi f. b.
HAMBURGH ..	31½		.. ——— gives 31½ Soldi	for 1 Mark banco.
LEGHORN	87½		.. ——— gives 87½ Ditto	for 1 Pezza of 8 Reals.
LONDON......	21	5	.. ——— gives 21 Lire 5 Soldi	for £1 sterling.
MILAN	97½		.. ——— gives 97½ Soldi	for 1 Filippo or 7½ Lire correnti.
NAPLES......	74		.. ——— gives 74 Ditto	for 1 Ducat.
ROME	87		.. ——— gives 87 Ditto	for 1 Scudo Romano.
SPAIN	63		.. ——— gives 63 Ditto	for 1 Dollar of exchange.
VENICE......	94		.. ——— gives 94 Ditto	for 1 Ducat current.
VIENNA	43¼		.. ——— gives 43¼ Ditto	for 1 Florin current.

[For the usances and other particulars relating to Bills of Exchange, see TURIN, vol. i.]

TURIN ON FRANCE.

Reduce 1728 Francs 60 Centimes into money of Turin; exchange at 20 Lire 10 Soldi for 24 Francs.

	Francs		Lire		Francs		Lire	Soldi	Den.
As	24	:	20½	: :	1728,60	:	1476	10	3

20½
———
3457200
864,30
——— Lire Sol. Den.
24)35436,30(1476 10 3
24
——
114 &c.

FRANCE ON TURIN.

Reduce 1476 Lire 10 Soldi 3 Denari of Turin into French money; exchange at 20 Lire 10 Soldi for 24 Francs.

	Lire	Soldi		Francs		Lire	Sol.	Den.		Francs	Cen.
As	20	10	:	24	: :	1476	10	3	:	1728	60

20	20
410	29530
12	12
4920	354363
	24

——— Francs
492,0)850471,2(1728,60
492 &c.

TURIN ON GENOA.

Reduce 14239 Lire 16 Soldi fuori banco into money of Turin; exchange at 9 Lire 5 Soldi of Turin per Sequin of 13½ Lire fuori banco.

	Lire	Soldi		Lire	Soldi		Lire	Soldi		Lire	Sol.
As	13	10	:	9	5	: :	14239	16	:	9756	18

20	20	20
270	185	284796
		185

———2,0
27,0)5268726,0(19513,8
27 ———
—— 9756 Lire 18 Sol.
256 &c.

GENOA ON TURIN.

Reduce 9756 Lire 18 Soldi of Turin into money of Genoa; exchange at 9 Lire 5 Soldi per Sequin of 13½ Lire fuori banco.

	Lire	Soldi		Lire	Soldi		Lire	Soldi		Lire	Sol.
As	9	5	:	13	10	: :	9756	18	:	14239	16

20	20	20
185	270	195138
		270

———2,0
185)52687260(28479,6
370 ———
—— 14239 Lire 16 Sol.
1568 &c.

TURIN ON LONDON.

Reduce £406 16s. 2d. sterling into money of Turin; exchange at 19 Lire 10 Soldi per £ sterling.

	£		Lire	Soldi		£	s.	d.		Lire	Soldi	Den.
As	1	:	19	10	: :	406	16	2	:	7932	15	3

20	20	20
20	390	8136
12		12
240		97634
		390

———2,0)
24,0)3807726,0(15865,5¼
24 ———
—— 7932 Lire 15 Sol. 3 Den.
140 &c.

LONDON ON TURIN.

Reduce 7932 Lire 15 Soldi 3 Denari into sterling; exchange at 19 Lire 10 Soldi per £ sterling.

	Lire	Soldi		£		Lire	Sol.	Den.		£	s.	d.
As	19	10	:	1	: :	7932	15	3	:	406	16	2

20	20
390	158655
12	12

——— £ s. d.
4680 468,0)190386,3(406 16 2
1872
———
3186 &c.

VENICE.

MONIES OF EXCHANGE.

Exchanges have been computed here in Lire, Soldi, and Denari, Moneta piccola, and also in Ducats; but they are now generally computed in Centimes, of Italian Livres, which are similar to those of France.

12 Denari = 1 Soldo. 20 Soldi = 1 Lira. 6 Lire 4 Soldi piccoli = 1 Ducat current, or of account.

8 Lire piccoli = 1 Ducat effective.

100 Centimes = 1 Lira Italiana.

40,000 Lire piccoli = 30,467 Lire Italiane.

COURSE OF EXCHANGE, From the Venetian Quotation. *January*, 1820.		EXPLANATION.	
AMSTERDAM	224	.. VENICE gives 224 Centimes	for 1 Florin.
ANCONA	540	.. ——— gives 540 Centimes	for 1 Scudo.
AUGSBURG	260	.. ——— gives 260 Centimes	for 1 Florin current.
CONSTANTINOPLE	83	.. ——— gives 83 Centimes	for 1 Piastre.
FRANCE	105	.. ——— gives 105 Centimes	for 1 Franc.
GENOA	86	.. ——— gives 86 Centimes	for 1 Lira fuori banco.
HAMBURGH	196	.. ——— gives 196 Centimes	for 1 Mark banco.
LEGHORN	533	.. ——— gives 533 Centimes	for 1 Pezza.
LISBON	66	.. ——— receives 66 Rees	for 1 Lira.
LONDON	26,30	.. ——— gives 26,30 Centimes	for 1 £ sterling.
MILAN	102	.. ——— gives 102 Centimes	for 100 Centimes.
NAPLES	433	.. ——— gives 433 Centimes	for 1 Ducato di regno.
PALERMO	13	.. ——— gives 13 Lire	for 1 Oncia.
ROME	550	.. ——— gives 550 Centimes	for 1 Scudo Romano.
VIENNA	261	.. ——— gives 261 Centimes	for 1 Florin effective.

[For the usances and other particulars relating to Bills of Exchange, see VENICE, vol. i.]

VENICE ON LONDON, see page 26.

VENICE ON CONSTANTINOPLE, see page 43.

VENICE ON GENOA, see page 64.

VENICE ON HAMBURGH, see page 68.

VENICE ON LISBON, see page 75.

VENICE ON FRANCE.

Reduce 3372 Francs 30 Centimes into Venetian money; exchange at 2 Lire 5 Soldi piccoli per Franc.

```
     Franc   Lire Soldi       Francs  Cent.       Lire   Soldi  Den.
As     1   :   2   5    ::    3372    30     :    7587    13     6
              20                      45
              --              -----------
              45         2,0)15175,35,0
                              -----------
                              7587    13    5
                                           12
                                           --
                                          6,0
```

By Practice.

```
                         Francs  Cents.
                          3372    30
                             2 Lire 5 Soldi.
                         --------------
                          6744
5 Soldi       = 1/4  ..    843
20 Centimes   = 1/5  ..      0    9
10 Centimes   = 1/2  ..      0    4    6
                         --------------
                   Ans.   7587   13    6
```

FRANCE ON VENICE.

Reduce 7587 Lire 13 Soldi 6 Denari piccoli into French money; exchange at 2 Lire 5 Soldi piccoli per Franc.

```
     Lire Soldi   Franc        Lire  Soldi  Den.      Francs  Cent.
As    2    5   :    1    ::    7587   13     6    :    3372    30
     20                          20
     --                     --------
     45                      151753
     12                          12
     --                -------------Francs.
    540              54,0)182104,2(3372,30
                          162
                          ---
                          201 &c.
```

By Decimals.

2 Lire 5 Soldi	=	2,25
7587 Lire 13 Soldi 6 Den.	=	7587,675

As 2,25 : 1 :: 7587,675 : 3372,30

LONDON ON VENICE, see page 26.

CONSTANTINOPLE ON VENICE, see page 43.

GENOA ON VENICE, see page 64.

HAMBURGH ON VENICE, see page 68.

LISBON ON VENICE, see page 75.

The above is the mode of exchange formerly used, but as it is in a great measure discontinued, any further examples are deemed unnecessary.

VIENNA.

MONIES OF EXCHANGE.

Exchanges are computed in Florins and Creutzers, or in Rixdollars and Creutzers.

4 Pfenings = 1 Creutzer.

60 Creutzers = 1 Florin or Gulden.

1½ Florin, or 90 Creutzers = 1 Rixdollar of account.

2 Florins, or 120 Creutzers = 1 Rixdollar specie.

COURSE OF EXCHANGE, From the Vienna Quotation. *January*, 1820.		EXPLANATION.		
AMSTERDAM	140	.. VIENNA	gives 140 Rixdollars current	for 100 Rixdollars.
AUGSBURG	100	.. ———	gives 100 Rixdollars current	for 100 Rixds. current.
CONSTANTINOPLE	112	.. ———	gives 112 Florins	for 100 Piastres.
FRANCE	119	.. ———	receives 119 Florins	for 100 Ecus of 3 Francs.
GENOA	30½	.. ———	receives 30½ Soldi fuori banco	for 1 Florin current.
HAMBURGH	148½	.. ———	gives 148½ Rixdollars current	for 100 Rixds. banco.
LEGHORN	57½	.. ———	receives 57½ Soldi moneta buona	for 1 Florin.
LONDON	9 52	.. ———	gives 9 Florins 52 Creutzers	for 1 £ sterling.
MILAN	67¼	.. ———	receives 67¼ Soldi correnti	for 1 Florin current.
PRAGUE	99½	.. ———	gives 99½ Florins	for 100 Florins current.
SMYRNA	112	.. ———	gives 112 Florins	for 100 Piastres.
VENICE	184	.. ———	gives 184 Florins	for 500 Lire piccole.

[For the usances and other particulars relating to Bills of Exchange, see VIENNA, vol. i.]

VIENNA ON CONSTANTINOPLE, see page 43.

VIENNA ON FRANCE, see page 53.

VIENNA ON HAMBURGH, see page 68.

VIENNA ON LONDON, see page 27.

VIENNA ON LEGHORN.

Reduce 2233 Pezze into Austrian money; exchange at 42 Soldi di Lira moneta buona per Austrian Florin.

[$5\frac{3}{4}$ Lire moneta buona = 1 Pezza of 8 Reals.]

```
                   Pezze      Lire   Soldi di Lira
As 4  :  23  : :  2233   :  12839     15
                    23
                  -----
                4)51359
                  -----
                  12839 Lire 15 Soldi.

     Soldi   Florin     Lire   Soldi     Florins  Creutz.
Then, as 42  :  1  : :  12839   15   :   6114     10
                          20
                        ------   Fl.     Cr.
                     42)256795(6114      10
                        252
                        ---
                         47 &c.
```

Remainder × 60 &c.

By the Chain Rule.

		2233 Pezze.
1 Pezza	=	115 Soldi di Lira.
42 Soldi	=	1 Florin.

Result as above.

CONSTANTINOPLE ON VIENNA, see page 43.

FRANCE ON VIENNA, see page 53.

HAMBURGH ON VIENNA, see page 68.

LONDON ON VIENNA, see page 27.

LEGHORN ON VIENNA.

Reduce 6114 Florins 10 Creutzers of Austria into money of Leghorn; exchange at 42 Soldi di Lira moneta buona per Florin.

```
  Florin  Soldi     Florins Creutzers    Lire   Soldi
As 1   :  42   : :  6114    10      :  12839   15
                      60
                    ------
                    366850
                        42
                  ---------
               6,0)1540770,0
                  ---------
                 2,0)25679,5
                   --------
                    12839 Lire 15 Soldi.

                          Lire   Soldi di Lira   Pezze
Then, as 23  :  4  : :   12839      15     :    2233
                            20
                         ------
                         256795
                              4
                         --------20)
                      23)1027180(44660
                         92       -----
                         --        2233
                         107 &c.
```

By the Chain Rule.

		6114 Florins 10 Creutzers.
1 Florin	=	42 Soldi di Lira.
115 Soldi di Lira	=	1 Pezza.

Result as above.

UNITED STATES OF AMERICA.

MONIES OF EXCHANGE.

Exchanges are computed in Dollars, Dimes, and Cents; and in some places in Pounds, Shillings, and Pence currency.

10 Cents = 1 Dime; 10 Dimes, or 100 Cents = 1 Dollar.
The Dollar is also divided into 1000 parts, called Mills.
The par of the Dollar is reckoned at 4s. 6d. sterling.
12 Pence currency = 1 Shilling; 20 Shillings = 1 Pound.

[For the different currencies and values of the Dollar, see UNITED STATES, vol. i. and *Table of Coins*, vol. ii.]

COURSES OF EXCHANGE, FROM DIFFERENT QUOTATIONS.

New York, *January*, 1820.

AMSTERDAM	42 Cents per Florin or Gilder.
BREMEN	78 Cents per Rixdollar.
HAMBURGH	35 Cents per Mark banco.
LONDON, direct	£177½ currency for £100 sterling.
PARIS	5 Francs 40 Centimes per Dollar.

Philadelphia.

AMSTERDAM	40 Cents per Florin or Gilder.
HAMBURGH	35 Cents per Mark banco.
LONDON, 2 per cent. Premium	4s. 6d. sterling per Dollar.

Baltimore.

AMSTERDAM	40 Cents per Florin or Gilder.
HAMBURGH	33⅓ Cents per Mark banco.
LONDON at 60 days sight	101—that is—100 Cents for 4s. 6d. sterling, with 1 per cent. premium.

[For damages on returned bills, and other particulars relating to American Exchanges, see UNITED STATES, vol. i.]

LONDON ON AMERICA.

American money is reduced to sterling *at par* by saying: as 1 Dollar is to 4s. 6d. sterling, so is the given sum to the sum sought.

Reduce 1783 Dollars 80 Cents to sterling, at par.

```
Doll.   s. d.        Doll. Cents        £   s. d.
As 1  : 4 6   : :    1783  80     :    401  7 1
        12             54                 Decimally.
        —             ———                  1783,80
        54           7132                     4,5
                     8915                  ———
80 Cents = 4/5 . .     43                  891900
                     ———                   713520
                  12)96325                 ———
                     ———               2,0)802,7,100
                 2,0)802,7  1                    12
                   ———                     ———
                  £401  7s.  1d.           401,7,1,2
```

If the exchange be not at par, the difference is to be computed before the Dollars are reduced to sterling.

Reduce 4282 Dollars 50 Cents to sterling; exchange at 2 per cent. above par.

				Dollars	Cents		Dollars	Cents
As 100	:	102	: :	4282	50	:	4368	15

Dollar		s.	d.		Dollars	Cents		£	s.	d.
And as 1	:	4	6	: :	4368	15	:	982	16	8

Reduce 3646 Dollars 50 Cents to sterling; exchange at 2 per cent. under par.

				Dollars	Cents		Dollars
As 102	:	100	: :	3646	50	:	3575

Dollar		s.	d.		Dollars		£	s.	d.
And as 1	:	4	6	: :	3575	:	804	7	6

AMERICA ON LONDON.

Sterling is reduced to American money *at par* by reversing the annexed operation: that is, as 4s. 6d. is to 1 Dollar, so is the given sum to the sum sought.

Reduce £401 7s. 1d. sterling to American money, at par.

```
   s.  d.     Dollar        £    s.  d.       Dollars  Cents
As 4   6   :    1    : :   401   7   1    :    1783     80
   12                       20
   —                       ———
   54                      8027
                             12
                           ———
                      54)96325(1783,796
                         54
                         ——
                         423 &c.
```

If the exchange be not at par, the difference is to be computed after the sterling has been reduced to Dollars.

Reduce £982 16s. 8d. to American money; exchange at 2 per cent. above par.

	s.	d.		Dollar		£	s.	d.		Dollars	Cents
As	4	6	:	1	: :	982	16	8	:	4368	15

				Dollars	Cents		Dollars	Cents
And as 102	:	100	: :	4368	15	:	4282	50

Reduce £804 7s. 6d. to American money; exchange at 2 per cent. under par.

	s.	d.		Dollar		£	s.	d.		Dollars
As	4	6	:	1	: :	804	7	6	:	3575

				Dollars		Dollars	Cents
And as 100	:	102	: :	3575	:	3646	50

When the discount or premium is at any of the following rates, the operation may be thus performed.

At 1¼ per cent. discount, *i. e.* under par, multiply the Dollars by 80, and divide by 81.

Rate	Multiply by	Divide by
2	50	51.
2½	40	41.
3¾	80	83.
4	25	26.
5	20	21.
6	50	53.
6¼	16	17.
7½	40	43.
8	25	27.
8¾	80	87.
10	10	11.

If the exchange be at a premium, *i. e.* above par, the rule should be reversed.

The Dollars are afterwards reduced to sterling as above.

AMSTERDAM ON AMERICA.

American money is reduced to Dutch by saying: as the rate of exchange is to 1 Florin, so is the given sum to the sum sought.

[For the Dutch monies of exchange, see page 28.]

Reduce 4964 Dollars 67 Cents to Dutch money; exchange at 36 Cents per Florin.

```
   Cents   Florin    Dollars Cents     Florins Stivers
As 36   :   1   ::   4964    67    :   13790    15

                36)496467(13790   15
                   36
                   ——
                   136 &c.
```

AMERICA ON AMSTERDAM.

Dutch money is reduced to American by reversing the annexed operation: that is, as 1 Florin is to the rate of exchange, so is the given sum to the sum sought.

Reduce 13790 Florins 15 Stivers to American money; exchange at 36 Cents per Florin.

```
   Florin   Cents     Florins Stivers     Dollars Cents
As 1    :   36   ::   13790    15     :   4964    67
   20                    20
   ——                 ——————
   20                 275815
                          36
                     ———————
                 2,0)992934,0
                     ———————
               Ans. 496467 Cents.
```

HAMBURGH ON AMERICA.

American money is reduced to that of Hamburgh by saying: as the rate of exchange is to 1 Mark, so is the given sum to the sum sought.

[For the monies of exchange of Hamburgh, see page 65.]

Reduce 378 Dollars 95 Cents to Hamburgh money; exchange at 33 Cents per Mark banco.

```
    Cents   Mark     Dollars Cents    Marks Schill. Pf.
As  33   :   1   ::   378    95   :   1148    5     4

                   33)37895(1148    5     4
                      33
                      ——
                       48 &c.
```

AMERICA ON HAMBURGH.

Hamburgh money is reduced to American by reversing the annexed operation: that is, as 1 Mark is to the rate of exchange so is the given sum to the sum sought.

Reduce 1148 Marks 5 Schillings 4 Pfenings banco to American money; exchange at 33 Cents per Mark banco.

```
   Mark   Cents     Marks Schill. Pf.     Dollars Cents
As 1   :   33   ::   1148    5     4   :   378     95
   16                  16
   ——                —————
   16                18373
   12                   12
   ——                —————
   192               220480 × 33 ÷ 192 = 378,95
```

FRANCE ON AMERICA.

American money is reduced to French by saying: as 1 Dollar is to the rate of exchange, so is the given sum to the sum sought.

[For the monies of exchange of France, see page 49.]

Reduce 1364 Dollars 60 Cents to French money; exchange at 5 Francs 30 Centimes per Dollar.

```
   Dollar  Francs Cen.     Dollars Cents     Francs Centimes
As 1    :   5     30   ::   1364    60   :   7232    38
```

AMERICA ON FRANCE.

French money is reduced to American by saying: as the rate of exchange is to 1 Dollar, so is the given sum to the sum sought.

Reduce 7232 Francs 38 Centimes to American money; exchange at 5 Francs 30 Centimes per Dollar.

```
   Francs Cen.    Dollar     Francs Centimes     Dollars Cents
As 5      30   :   1    ::   7232    38      :   1364    60
```

WEST INDIES.

MONIES OF EXCHANGE.

12 Pence = 1 Shilling.
20 Shillings = 1 Pound currency.

[For the currencies and monies of the different islands, see the article WEST INDIES, vol. i.]

LONDON ON THE WEST INDIES.

West Indian currency is reduced to sterling by saying: as the rate of exchange is to 100, so is the given sum to the sum sought.

Reduce £778 16s. 4d. currency to sterling; exchange at £166 currency per £100 sterling.

As 166 : 100 :: £778 16s. 4d. (Currency) : £469 3s. 4d. (Sterling)

20
15576
12
12
166)18691600(112600
166
209 &c.
2,0)938,3 4
£469 3s. 4d. sterling.

WEST INDIES ON LONDON.

Sterling is reduced to West Indian currency by reversing the foregoing operation: that is, as 100 is to the rate of exchange, so is the given sum to the sum sought.

Reduce £469 3s. 4d. sterling to West Indian currency; exchange at £166 currency per £100 sterling.

As 100 : 166 :: £469 3s. 4d. (Sterling) : £778 16s. 4d. (Currency)

20
9383
12
112600
166
12)186916,00
2,0)1557,6 4
£778 16s. 4d. currency.

Currency at the following prices may be thus reduced to sterling.

At 50	multiply by 2	& divide by 3	At 75	multiply by 4	& divide by 7
52½	40	61	77½	40	71
55	20	31	80	5	9
57½	40	63	82½	40	73
60	5	8	85	20	37
62½	8	13	87½	8	15
65	20	33	90	10	19
67½	40	67	92½	40	77
70	10	17	95	20	39
72½	40	69	97½	40	79

Sterling at the following prices may be thus reduced to currency.

At 50	multiply by 3	& divide by 2	At 75	multiply by 7	& divide by 4
52½	61	40	77½	71	40
55	31	20	80	9	5
57½	63	40	82½	73	40
60	8	5	85	37	20
62½	13	8	87½	15	8
65	33	20	90	19	10
67½	67	40	92½	77	40
70	17	10	95	39	20
72½	69	40	97½	79	40

[For the damages on returned bills, and other laws and customs relating to Exchanges, see WEST INDIES, vol. i.]

From the first example it will be seen, that it is the interest of the London Buyer or Remitter to pay the highest exchange for a Bill on a place which gives the uncertain price to London; and that the reverse is the interest of the Drawer or Seller. And from the second example it is obvious, that it is the interest of the London Buyer or Remitter to pay the lowest exchange for a Bill on a place to which London gives the uncertain price; and that the reverse is the interest of the Drawer or Seller. Hence the two following rules.

1.—*On a place to which London gives the* CERTAIN PRICE *a Bill should be drawn at the lowest course, and remitted at the highest.*

2.—*On a place to which London gives the* UNCERTAIN PRICE *a Bill should be drawn at the highest course, and remitted at the lowest.*

The above rules apply to any other places as well as London.

REMITTANCES AND RETURNS.

Bills of Exchange are sometimes bought and remitted directly to the place on which they are drawn, with orders to have Bills in return if the prices be favourable: and it should be observed that the reciprocal courses of exchange between two places should always differ, so as to be nearly equal to the interest of money and the expenses of remittance. Thus, the course of London on Dublin should differ about 1 per cent. from that of Dublin on London, in order to afford the Remitter from either place a regular profit on his Remittances and Returns on Bills at 21 days sight, the usual Term.

Suppose, for example, L of London purchases a Bill on Dublin, at 21 days sight, of £112 Irish for £100 English, which he remits to his agent at Dublin, desiring him to make Returns in Bills on London at 21 days sight; and suppose a Bill of £100 English is remitted back, which costs only £111 Irish, there is £1 Irish per cent. gained by the transaction: and the same would take place had the remittance been first made from Dublin on the above terms.

Now, to compute how much the difference here ought to be, the interest of 56 days must be reckoned (the usual time such Bills take in making returns); and this, with brokerage, postage, &c. will amount to 1 per cent. nearly; which is reckoned a *Fair Difference* in the exchange between London and Dublin on Bills of the above date.

It may be observed, however, that the difference is not always equivalent to the interest and expenses, but fluctuates according to circumstances, affording sometimes room for profitable operations.

The following is an example of a Bill sent from London to Hamburgh, to have Returns on London.

£842 12s. 1d. sterling on Hamburgh, at 3 usances, at 31s. 8d. Flemish per £ sterling, ...10,000 Mks. bco.

	Mks. bco.	Sh.		
Commission, ½ per cent.	50	0		
Double brokerage, 2 per mille	20	0		
Postage	3	4		
Discount, 82 days, at 5 per cent.	112	4		
....			185	8
Net proceeds in Marks banco			9814	8

Returns made in 3 Bills, namely:

£	s.	d.		Mks. bco.	Sh.
£500	0	0	sterling, at 3 us. at 30s. 10½d..................	5789	1
200	0	0	at 2 us. at 30s. 11d.	2318	12
146	16	4	at 2 us. at 31s. 0d..................	1706	11
846	16	4	Returns.	9814	8
842	2	1	Remittance.		

£4 14 3 Gain, which is not quite equivalent to the discount and postage of the Returns; but had the course of Hamburgh on London been 30s. 9d. it would have produced the regular profit. Thus, 10d. Flemish per £ sterling may be reckoned a *Fair Difference* between London and Hamburgh at usance.

When the Returns are to be made directly, the remittances are discounted as above; but it may be remarked, that the interest of money on the Continent is not limited as in England, but fluctuates according to the plenty or scarcity of cash or the credit of paper. In exchange operations it is generally reckoned at ½ per cent. per month.

ARBITRATION OF EXCHANGE.

Arbitration of Exchange is a comparison between the courses of exchange of several places, in order to ascertain the most advantageous method of drawing or remitting Bills. It is distinguished into Simple and Compound Arbitration: the former comprehends the exchanges of three places only, and the latter of more than three places.

SIMPLE ARBITRATION

Is a comparison between the exchanges of two places with respect to a third—that is to say, it is a method of finding such a rate of exchange between two places as shall be in proportion to the rates quoted between each of them and a third place. The exchange thus determined is called the *Arbitrated Price.*

If, for example, the course between London and Paris be 24 Francs for £1 sterling, and between Paris and Amsterdam 54d. Flemish for 3 Francs, (that is, 36s. Flemish for 24 Francs,) the arbitrated price between London and Amsterdam through Paris, is evidently 36s. Flemish for £1 sterling; for as 3 Fr. : 54d. Flem. : : 24 Fr. : 36s. Flem.

Now, when the actual or direct price (as seen by a quotation or otherwise advised) is found to differ from the arbitrated price, advantage may be made by drawing or remitting indirectly; that is, by drawing on one place through another, as on Amsterdam through Paris: which may be performed in three different ways.

1.—London may draw on Paris, and order his correspondent there to draw on Amsterdam.

2.—London may draw on Paris, and order his correspondent in Amsterdam to remit the same sum to Paris.

3.—London may order his correspondent at Paris to draw on Amsterdam, and to remit the value to London.

The operation of remitting indirectly, or of remitting to one place through another, as to Amsterdam through Paris, may be likewise performed in three different ways.

P 2

1.—London may remit to Paris, and order his correspondent there to remit the sum to Amsterdam.

2.—London may remit to Paris, and order his correspondent in Amsterdam to draw on Paris.

3.—London may take Bills on Paris, and remit them to Amsterdam, there to be negotiated.

In the foregoing questions, the profit or loss is ascertained on an operation already completed: but in arbitration it is ascertained beforehand, and the different results are compared, in order to determine the most advantageous mode of proceeding.

To exemplify this by familiar illustrations, suppose the arbitrated price between London and Amsterdam to be, as before stated, 36s. Flemish for £1 sterling; and suppose the direct course to be 37s. Flemish; then London, by drawing directly on Amsterdam, must give 37s. Flemish for £1 sterling; whereas, by drawing through Paris he will give only 36s. Flemish for £1 sterling: it is therefore the interest of London to draw indirectly on Amsterdam through Paris.

On the contrary, if London remits directly to Amsterdam he will receive 37s. Flemish for £1 sterling; whereas, by remitting through Paris, he will receive only 36s. Flemish: it is the interest of London, therefore, to remit directly to Amsterdam.

Example 2.—Suppose the exchange of London and Lisbon to be at 68d. per Milree, and that of Lisbon on Madrid 500 Rees per Dollar, the arbitrated price between London and Madrid is 34d. sterling per Dollar; for, as 1000 Rees : 68d. :: 500 Rees : 34d. But if the direct exchange of London on Madrid be 35d. sterling per Dollar, then London, by remitting directly to Madrid, must pay 35d. for every Dollar; whereas, by remitting through Lisbon, he will pay only 34d.: it is, therefore, the interest of London to remit indirectly to Madrid through Lisbon.

On the contrary, if London draws directly on Madrid, he will receive 35d. sterling per Dollar; whereas by drawing indirectly through Lisbon, he will receive only 34d.: it is, therefore, the interest of London to draw directly on Madrid.

From these examples, combined with the principles laid down in page 105, the two following rules are manifest.

RULE 1.—*Where London gives the* CERTAIN PRICE, *draw through that place which produces the lowest arbitrated price, and remit through that which produces the highest.*

RULE 2.—*Where London gives the* UNCERTAIN PRICE, *draw through that place which produces the highest arbitrated price, and remit through that which produces the lowest.*

What is here said of London will equally apply to any other place from whence the operation is made.

In order further to exemplify Simple Arbitration of Exchange, the following places are selected as having the most frequent communication with each other in business of this kind; and London is made the centre of operations.

LONDON AND AMSTERDAM.

PROPORTIONAL EXCHANGE.

LONDON QUOTATION. *(Explained page 19.)*		AMSTERDAM QUOTATION. *(Explained page 28.)*
ON AMSTERDAM . . .	34 7	
GENOA	47	 86
HAMBURGH	34 2	. . . . 33⅛
LEGHORN	51½	. . . . 92¾
LISBON	68	 48
MADRID	42	 96
PARIS	23 8	. . . . 53½

The arbitrated or proportional price of exchange between London and Amsterdam, with respect to any of the above places, is found either by the Rule of Three, or by the Chain Rule, as in the following examples; and from such proportional prices, compared with the direct or actual prices, as stated in the quotations, rules are deduced and examples given, for drawing and remitting to the greatest advantage.

LONDON AND AMSTERDAM THROUGH GENOA.

If the exchange of London on Genoa be 47d. sterling per Pezza of $5\frac{3}{4}$ Lire, and that of Amsterdam on Genoa 86 Grotes Flemish per Pezza, what is the proportional exchange between London and Amsterdam through Genoa? that is, how many Shillings and Grotes Flemish are equal to £1 sterling?

Because 47d. give 1 Pezza, and this Pezza in Amsterdam gives 86 Grotes Flemish, say—

	d.		Grotes		£		Sh.	Gr. Flem.
As	47	:	86	: :	1	:	36	7

86
240
———12)
47)20640(439$\frac{7}{47}$
188 ———
——Ans. 36 Sh. 7 Gr. Flemish
184 &c. for £1 sterling.

By the Chain Rule.

		1 Pound sterling.
1 Pound sterling	=	240 Pence.
47 Pence	=	1 Pezza.
1 Pezza	=	86 Grotes Flemish.
12 Grotes	=	1 Shilling Flemish.

Hence, 1 Pound or 240 Pence multiplied by 86, and divided by 47 and by 12, will give the answer in Shillings Flemish, as above.

Thus, 86
240
————
564)20640(36,7
1692
————
3720
3384
————
336 = 7 Gr. nearly.

LONDON AND AMSTERDAM THROUGH HAMBURGH.

If the exchange of London on Hamburgh be 34 Shillings 2 Grotes Flemish banco per £ sterling, and that of Amsterdam on Hamburgh $33\frac{3}{8}$ Stivers per Rixdollar of 2 Marks, required the proportional exchange between London and Amsterdam through Hamburgh?

Because £1 sterling gives 34 Shillings 2 Grotes Flemish in Hamburgh, and 2 Marks give $33\frac{3}{8}$ Stivers in Amsterdam, say (reducing the Marks and the Stivers into Flemish money)—

	Marks		Stivers		Sh.	Gr. Fl.		Sh.	Gr. Fl.
As	2	:	$33\frac{3}{8}$	: :	34	2	:	35	$7\frac{1}{2}$
	16		2		12				
	32		$66\frac{3}{4}$		410				
	2				$66\frac{3}{4}$				
	64								

———12)
64)27367$\frac{1}{2}$(427$\frac{39}{64}$
256 ———
——Ans. 35 Sh. $7\frac{1}{2}$ Gr. for £1
176 &c. sterling.

By the Chain Rule.

		1 Pound sterling.
1 Pound sterl.	=	34 Shil. 2 Grotes in Hamburgh.
8 Shill. Flem.	=	3 Marks.
2 Marks	=	$33\frac{3}{8}$ Stivers.
6 Stivers	=	1 Shill. Flemish in Amsterdam

Hence, 34 Shillings 2 Grotes Flemish multiplied by 3 and by $33\frac{3}{8}$, and divided by 6, by 2, and by 8; or, (expunging the common divisors,) multiplied by 267, and divided by 256, will give the answer in Shillings Flemish, as above.

LONDON AND AMSTERDAM THROUGH LEGHORN.

If the exchange of London on Leghorn be $51\frac{1}{2}$d. sterling per Pezza, and that of Amsterdam on Genoa $92\frac{3}{4}$ Grotes Flemish per Pezza, what is the proportional exchange between London and Amsterdam through Leghorn?

Because $51\frac{1}{2}$d. in London give 1 Pezza, and this Pezza in Amsterdam gives $92\frac{3}{4}$ Grotes Flemish, say—

	d.		Grotes		d.		Sh.	Grotes
As	$51\frac{1}{2}$	:	$92\frac{3}{4}$	: :	240	:	36	$0\frac{1}{4}$
	2				$92\frac{3}{4}$			
	103				22260			
					2			

$$\begin{array}{l} \underline{\qquad\quad}\text{–}12) \\ 103)44520(432\frac{24}{103} \\ 412\&c. \end{array}$$

Ans. 36 Sh. $0\frac{1}{4}$ Gr. for £1 sterling.

By the Chain Rule.

		£1 sterling.
£1 sterling	=	240 Pence.
$51\frac{1}{2}$ Pence	=	1 Pezza.
1 Pezza	=	$92\frac{3}{4}$ Grotes Flemish.
12 Grotes	=	1 Shilling Flemish.

Result as above.

LONDON AND AMSTERDAM THROUGH LISBON.

If the exchange of London on Lisbon be 68d. sterling per Milree, and that of Amsterdam on Lisbon 48 Grotes Flemish per old Crusado, what is the proportional exchange between London and Amsterdam through Lisbon.

Because 68d. in London give 1 Milree, and 1 old Crusado, or 400 Rees, give 48 Grotes Flemish in Amsterdam, say—

	Rees		Grotes		Rees		Grotes	
As	400	:	48	: :	1000	:	120	
	d.		Grotes		d.		Sh.	Gr. Fl.
And as	68	:	120	: :	240	:	35	$3\frac{1}{2}$
					120			

$$\begin{array}{l} \underline{\qquad\quad}\text{–}12) \\ 68)28800(423\frac{36}{68} \\ 272\&c. \end{array}$$

Ans. 35 Sh. $3\frac{1}{2}$ Gr. for £1 sterling.

By the Chain Rule.

		£1 sterling.
£1 sterling	=	240 Pence.
68 Pence	=	1000 Rees.
400 Rees	=	48 Grotes Flemish.
12 Grotes	=	1 Shilling Flemish.

Result as above.

LONDON AND AMSTERDAM THROUGH MADRID.

If the exchange of London on Madrid be 42d. sterling per Dollar of plate, and that of Amsterdam on Madrid 96 Grotes Flemish per Ducat of plate, what is the proportional exchange between London and Amsterdam through Madrid?

Because 42d. in London give 1 Dollar or 272 Maravedis, and because 1 Ducat or 375 Maravedis give 96 Grotes in Amsterdam, say—

	Maravedis		Grotes		Maravedis		Grotes	
As	375	:	96	: :	272	:	$69\frac{2}{3}$	
	d.		Grotes		d.		Sh.	Gr. Fl.
And as	42	:	$69\frac{2}{3}$	: :	240	:	33	2
					$69\frac{2}{3}$			

$$\begin{array}{l} \underline{\qquad\quad}\text{–}12) \\ 42)16720(398 \\ 126\&c. \end{array}$$

Ans. 33 Sh. 2 Gr. for £1 sterling.

By the Chain Rule.

		£1 sterling.
£1 sterling	=	240 Pence.
42 Pence	=	272 Maravedis.
375 Maravedis	=	96 Grotes Flemish.
12 Grotes	=	1 Shilling Flemish.

Result as above.

LONDON AND AMSTERDAM THROUGH PARIS.

If the exchange of London on Paris be at 23 Livres 8 Sous per £ sterling, and that of Amsterdam on Paris $53\frac{1}{2}$ Grotes Flemish per Ecu of 3 Francs, what is the proportional exchange between London and Amsterdam through Paris?

Because £1 sterling gives 23 Livres 8 Sous in Paris, and because 3 Francs give $53\frac{1}{2}$ Grotes Flemish in Amsterdam, say—

					Livres	Sous		Francs	Cen.
As	81	:	80	: :	23	8	:	23	11
	Francs		Grotes		Francs			Sh.	Gr. Fl.
And as	3	:	$53\frac{1}{2}$	: :	23,11		:	34	$4\frac{1}{8}$
					$53\frac{1}{2}$				

$$\begin{array}{l} \underline{\qquad\qquad}12) \\ 3)1236,38(412,12 \end{array}$$

Ans. 34 Sh. $4\frac{1}{8}$ Gr. for £1 sterling.

By the Chain Rule.

		£1 sterling.
£1 sterling	=	23 Livres 8 Sous.
81 Livres	=	80 Francs.
3 Francs	=	$53\frac{1}{2}$ Grotes.
12 Grotes	=	1 Shilling Flemish.

Result as above.

RECAPITULATION.

LONDON AND AMSTERDAM.

RECAPITULATION of the proportional exchanges, as calculated in the three preceding pages, with rules for drawing and remitting to the greatest advantage.

	Sh.	Grotes	
The arbitrated price through GENOA is	36	7	Flemish—see page 110
through HAMBURGH	35	$7\frac{1}{2}$	110
through LEGHORN	36	$0\frac{1}{2}$	111
through LISBON	35	$3\frac{1}{2}$	111
through MADRID	33	2	111
through PARIS	34	$4\frac{1}{8}$	111
And the direct course of LONDON on AMSTERDAM	34	7	109

As London gives the certain price to Amsterdam, that is, £1 sterling for a variable number of Shillings Flemish, the most advantageous place through which to remit is that which gives the highest price; and, on the contrary, the most advantageous place through which to draw is that which gives the lowest price; according to RULE 1, page 108.

From the above statements, therefore, it appears—1st, that if London has to *remit* to Amsterdam, the indirect courses through Hamburgh, Genoa, Lisbon, and Leghorn, are more advantageous than the direct course, and that Genoa is the most advantageous place through which to remit:—2dly, that if London has to *draw* on Amsterdam, the indirect courses through Madrid and Paris are more advantageous than the direct course, and that Madrid is the most advantageous place through which to draw.

The profit or loss per cent. occasioned by one mode of operation, instead of another, may be known in the following manner.

Thus, in the case of Genoa—As 34 Shill. 7 Grotes : 36 Shill. 7 Grotes :: 100 : $105\frac{65}{83}$, or $105\frac{3}{4}$ nearly.

Hence it appears, that $5\frac{3}{4}$ per cent. will be gained by remitting to Amsterdam through Genoa, instead of remitting directly to Amsterdam; and that the same profit will accrue by drawing directly on Amsterdam, instead of drawing through Genoa; but in computations of this kind allowance should be made for the difference of charges between direct and indirect operations.

The foregoing rules respecting Amsterdam will equally apply to Hamburgh, Paris, or any other place to which London gives the certain; but where London gives the uncertain, the rules must be reversed, as in the following examples of Genoa.

LONDON AND GENOA.

PROPORTIONAL EXCHANGE.

QUOTATION AT LONDON, (*Explained page* 19.)			QUOTATION FROM GENOA, (*Explained page* 61.)
On Genoa	47		
Amsterdam	36	7	85
Hamburgh	34	2	$45\frac{1}{3}$
Leghorn	$51\frac{1}{2}$		$123\frac{3}{4}$
Lisbon	68		718
Madrid	42		617
Paris	23	8	$94\frac{1}{3}$

From the above quotations, it is required to find the proportional exchange between London and Genoa, with respect to each of the other places, and thence to determine through what place it may be most advantageous for London to remit to, or draw on, Genoa, and whether direct or indirect exchange is most favourable.

LONDON AND GENOA THROUGH AMSTERDAM.

If the exchange of London on Amsterdam be 36 Shillings 7 Pence Flemish per £ sterling, and that of Genoa on Amsterdam 85 Grotes Flemish per Pezza of $5\frac{3}{4}$ Lire, what is the proportional exchange between London and Genoa through Amsterdam—that is, how many Pence sterling are equal to 1 Pezza?

Because £1 sterling gives 36 Shillings 7 Grotes Flemish in Amsterdam, and 85 Grotes Flemish in Genoa give 1 Pezza, say—

	Shillings	Grotes		Pence		Grotes		Pence
As	36	7	:	240	: :	85	:	$46\frac{1}{2}$
	12			85				
	439			439)20400($46\frac{206}{439}$				
				1756				
				2840 &c.				

Answer $46\frac{1}{2}$ Pence nearly for 1 Pezza.

By the Chain Rule.

			1 Pezza.
1	Pezza	=	85 Grotes Flemish.
12	Grotes	=	1 Shilling Flemish.
36	Shillings 7 Grotes	=	240 Pence sterling.

Hence, 85 Grotes multiplied by 240, and divided by 12, and by 36 Shillings 7 Grotes—that is, divided by 439, will give the answer in Pence sterling, as above.

LONDON AND GENOA THROUGH LEGHORN.

If the exchange of London on Leghorn be $51\frac{1}{2}$d. sterling per Pezza of 8 Reals, and that of Genoa on Leghorn $123\frac{3}{4}$ Soldi fuori banco per Pezza of 8 Reals, what is the proportional exchange between London and Genoa through Leghorn?

Because $51\frac{1}{2}$d. give 1 Pezza in Leghorn, and this same Pezza in Genoa gives $123\frac{3}{4}$ Soldi, say—

	Soldi		Pence		Pezza of Genoa		Soldi		Pence
As	$123\frac{3}{4}$	:	$51\frac{1}{2}$	: :	1	or	115	:	$47\frac{5}{6}$
	4		4				206		
	495		206		495)23690($47\frac{85}{99}$				
					1980 &c.				

Ans. $47\frac{5}{6}$d. nearly.

By the Chain Rule.

			1 Pezza in Genoa.
1	Pezza in Genoa	=	115 Soldi.
$123\frac{3}{4}$	Soldi	=	1 Pezza in Leghorn.
1	Pezza in Leghorn	=	$51\frac{1}{2}$d. sterling.

Result as above.

LONDON AND GENOA THROUGH HAMBURGH.

If the exchange of London on Hamburgh be 34 Shillings 2 Grotes Flemish per £ sterling, and the exchange of Genoa on Hamburgh $45\frac{1}{3}$ Soldi per Mark banco, what is the proportional exchange between London and Genoa through Hamburgh?

Because £1 sterling gives 34 Shillings 2 Grotes Flemish in Hamburgh, and 1 Mark or 32 Grotes in Genoa give 1 Pezza, say—

	Shillings	Grotes		Pence		Grotes		Pence
As	34	2	:	240	: :	32	:	$18\frac{3}{4}$
	12			32				
	410			41,0)768,0($18\frac{30}{41}$				
				41				
				358 &c.				

	Soldi		Pence		Pezza		Soldi		Pence
And as	$45\frac{1}{3}$	:	$18\frac{3}{4}$	: :	1	or	115	:	$47\frac{1}{2}$ nearly
	3						× $18\frac{3}{4}$ × 3		
	136						136)6468($47\frac{76}{136}$		
							544 &c.		

Ans. $47\frac{1}{2}$ Pence for 1 Pezza.

By the Chain Rule.

			1 Pezza.
1	Pezza	=	115 Soldi.
$45\frac{1}{3}$	Soldi	=	1 Mark.
1	Mark	=	32 Grotes Flemish.
410	Grotes	=	240 Pence sterling.

Result as above.

LONDON AND GENOA THROUGH LISBON.

If the exchange of London on Lisbon be 68d. per Milree, and that of Genoa on Lisbon 718 Rees per Pezza of $5\frac{3}{4}$ Lire, what is the proportional exchange between London and Genoa through Lisbon?

Because 1000 Rees give 68d. in London, and 718 Rees in Genoa give 1 Pezza, say—

	Rees		Pence		Rees		Pence
As	1000	:	68	: :	718	:	$48\frac{5}{6}$
					68		
					1,000)48,824		

Ans. $48\frac{5}{6}$d. nearly.

By the Chain Rule.

			1 Pezza.
1	Pezza	=	718 Rees.
1000	Rees	=	68 Pence.

Result as above.

LONDON AND GENOA THROUGH MADRID.

If the exchange of London on Madrid be 42d. sterling per Dollar of plate, and that of Genoa on Madrid 617 Maravedis of plate per Scudo d'oro, what is the proportional exchange between London and Genoa through Madrid?

Because 42d. sterling give 1 Dollar, or 272 Maravedis of plate, and because 617 Maravedis in Genoa give 1 Scudo d'oro, or 10 Lire 14 Soldi fuori banco, say—

	Maravedis		Pence		Maravedis		Pence
As	272	:	42	: :	617	:	$95\frac{1}{4}$
					42		

272)25914($95\frac{74}{272}$, or $95\frac{1}{4}$ nearly.
2448
1434 &c.

	Lire	Sol.		Pence		Pezza		Lire	Sol		Pence
And as	10	14	:	$95\frac{1}{4}$	: :	1	or	5	15	:	$51\frac{1}{5}$
	20							20			
	214							115			
								$95\frac{1}{4}$			

214)10953 ($51\frac{39}{214}$
1070
253 &c.

Ans. $51\frac{1}{5}$d. sterling for 1 Pezza nearly.

By the Chain Rule.

			1 Pezza.
1	Pezza	=	115 Soldi.
214	Soldi	=	617 Maravedis.
272	Maravedis	=	1 Dollar of plate.
1	Dollar	=	42 Pence.

Result as above.

LONDON AND GENOA THROUGH PARIS.

If the exchange of London on Paris be 23 Livres 8 Sous per £ sterling, and the exchange of Genoa on Paris $94\frac{1}{3}$ Sous in Francs per Pezza of $5\frac{3}{4}$ Lire, what is the proportional exchange between London and Genoa through Paris?

Because £1 sterling gives 23 Livres 8 Sous, and because $94\frac{1}{3}$ Sous in Francs give 1 Pezza in Genoa, say—

					Livres	Sous		Sous in Francs
As	81	:	80	: :	23	8	:	$462\frac{2}{9}$
					20			
					468			
					80			

81)37440($462\frac{2}{9}$
324
504 &c.

	Sous		Pence		Sous		Pence
And as	$462\frac{2}{9}$	:	240	: :	$94\frac{1}{3}$	:	49
	9		$94\frac{1}{3}$				
	4160		22640				
			9				

416,0)20376,0(49
1664
3736

Ans. 49d. sterling for 1 Pezza.

By the Chain Rule.

			1 Pezza.
1	Pezza	=	$94\frac{1}{3}$ Sous in Francs.
80	Sous in Francs	=	81 Sous in Livres.
468	Sous in Livres	=	240 Pence sterling.

Result as above.

RECAPITULATION.

LONDON AND GENOA.

RECAPITULATION of the proportional exchanges, or arbitrated prices, as calculated in the two preceding pages, with rules for drawing and remitting to the greatest advantage.

The arbitrated or indirect price through AMSTERDAM is....	$46\frac{1}{2}$	Pence—see page	114
through HAMBURGH	$47\frac{1}{2}$	....	114
through LEGHORN	$47\frac{5}{6}$	....	114
through LISBON	$48\frac{5}{6}$	....	114
through MADRID	$51\frac{1}{5}$	....	115
through PARIS	49	....	115
And the direct course of LONDON on GENOA is	47	....	113

As London gives the uncertain price to Genoa, that is, a variable number of Pence for 1 Pezza, the most advantageous place through which to remit is that which gives the lowest price; and, on the contrary, the most advantageous place through which to draw is that which gives the highest price; according to RULE 2, page 108.

From the above statements, therefore, it appears—1st, that if London has to *remit* to Genoa, the indirect course through Amsterdam is more advantageous than the direct course:—2dly, that if London has to *draw* on Genoa, the indirect courses through any of the above places, except Amsterdam, are more advantageous than the direct course, and that Madrid is the most advantageous place of all to draw through.

The profit or loss per cent. occasioned by one mode of operation, instead of another, may be thus found, as in the case of Madrid.

$$\text{As } 47 : 51\tfrac{1}{5} :: 100 : 109$$

Hence it appears, that 9 per cent. may be gained by drawing on Genoa through Madrid, instead of drawing directly on Genoa; and that the same profit will be made by remitting directly to Genoa, instead of remitting through Madrid: but in computations of this kind allowance should be made for the difference of charges between direct and indirect operations.

The foregoing rules for negotiating Bills are given after the manner of the most approved writers on Exchange, and though it is presumed they are sufficiently clear as well as correct, yet the following rules and illustrations are added, with a view of reducing the question of Arbitration to a still greater degree of simplicity.

SIMPLE ARBITRATION

Further explained; with new Rules and Illustrations.

SIMPLE ARBITRATION ought to be well understood before any higher Rule is attempted. It is not only the foundation and principle of Compound Arbitration, but is in itself a problem of more real utility and general application, as few speculations in Exchange are extended to more than three places in one operation.

It has been already shewn, that whether the arbitrated price is above or below the advised price, an advantage is equally to be made, and the greater the difference is, the greater will be the profit; but as the Courses of Exchange are liable to continual fluctuation, despatch is necessary in order to secure any favourable prices that may offer; and as an operation between three places can be performed sooner than between any greater number, it is evidently the most safe, as well as the most easy and practicable kind of Arbitration.*

* The following comparison between Simple and Compound Arbitration, made by *M. Corbaux*, in his *Dictionnaire des Arbitrages*, seems here to deserve quotation.

" It is very easy to fancy problems and theories in Compound Arbitration, where great advantages might be " made by numerous combinations of Exchange, but seldom does any opportunity occur in practice of realizing " such speculations. On the contrary, men of experience are satisfied with combining the Exchanges of three " places only (as in Simple Arbitration,) and there are few instances of the kind that will not afford room for a " reasonable profit."

The *Dictionnaire des Arbitrages* may be considered the most elaborate work ever published on this subject. It was printed at Paris in 1802, in two large volumes quarto, and contains, among other useful matter, about 900 pages of tables, which shew the arbitrated price *(pair proportionnel)* between the principal places of exchange in Europe, taken two by two with respect to Paris, this city being made the centre of operation.

Various other tables, both of natural numbers and logarithms, have been published by different persons for the more easy solution of Arbitration, and even triangles have been constructed for this purpose (see *Postlethwayt's Dictionary of Commerce*, vol. 1, page 94); but geometrical diagrams do not seem at all to illustrate the Problem.

A graphic operation, however of a very useful and ingenious description, was published in London a few years ago, in which, scales of the monies of exchange of the principal places in Lloyd's List, are so graduated and arranged, that the arbitrated price between any two of those places with respect to a third, may be immediately found by the application of a right line. The invention is by *William Hyde Wollaston, M.D.—S.* and *F.R.S.*

Another kind of scale, for facilitating operations in Exchange, &c. has been lately invented by *William Blake, Esq. F.R.S.* entitled a Logometric Scale of Exchanges, Bullion, Stocks, Monies, Weights, and Measures. It is constructed on the principle of Gunter's sliding-rule, and is well adapted for the ready solution of many useful problems.

In dwelling so long on the explanations of this problem, numerous repetitions must occur, which are, however, more excusable than omissions. Indeed, in a large work, repetitions are unavoidable where perspicuity is the chief object; and it has been the Author's principal endeavour to render Arbitration of Exchange more easy and accessible than it has been hitherto considered, especially in England, where merchants are said to be inferior to their neighbours on the continent in this branch of commercial science, and perhaps in this alone.

As every branch of science is difficult, in proportion as it is complex, the best mode of simplifying a problem is to divide it, so as to distinguish its component parts, and then to consider each division separately. Now the question before us may be distinguished under the three following heads.

1.—To find the arbitrated price of exchange.
2.—To compare it with the advised price.
3.—To draw and remit according to the comparison.

The arbitrated price would be always obvious without any calculation, if the monies of exchange were of one denomination; for the problem is founded on the FIRST AXIOM OF EUCLID, viz. "*Things that are equal to one and the same thing are equal to one another.*"

Thus, if the exchange of London on Amsterdam be 33 Shillings Flemish, and on Hamburgh 34, these two sums, according to the Axiom, are equal to one another, being both equal to the Pound sterling. Hence the arbitrated price would be 33 Shillings Flemish of Amsterdam for 34 Shillings Flemish of Hamburgh, if those places exchanged with each other in Shillings; but Amsterdam gives Hamburgh an uncertain number of Stivers for the Dollar of Exchange, and therefore the proportion between these different denominations of money must be found by the rule of proportion. Thus, as 33s. of Hamburgh : 34s. of Amsterdam : : 1 Dollar : $31\frac{1}{17}$ Stivers. Hence the arbitrated price is $31\frac{1}{17}$ Stivers of Holland, for 2 Marks of Hamburgh.

The following example contains all the variety that can occur in finding the arbitrated price.

If the exchange of London on Paris be 25, and on Cadiz 40, what is the arbitrated price between Paris and Cadiz—that is, how many Francs should equal the Doubloon of 4 Piastres?

Here the Pound sterling equals 25 Francs, and the same Pound equals 6 Piastres; for, as 40d. : 1 Piastre : : 240d. : 6 Piastres. Hence (per the Axiom,) 6 Piastres = 25 Francs; and therefore 4 Piastres (the Doubloon) = $16\frac{2}{3}$ Francs, the arbitrated price; for, as 6 Piastres : 25 Francs : : 4 Piastres : $16\frac{2}{3}$ Francs.

Or thus, by the Chain Rule.

		1 Doubloon.
1 Doubloon	=	4 Piastres.
1 Piastre	=	40 Pence sterling.
240 Pence	=	25 Francs.

Hence, $\frac{4 \times 40 \times 25}{240} = \frac{50}{3} = 16\frac{2}{3}$ Francs.

The second part of this problem, that of comparing the arbitrated and advised prices, is no more than to observe which price is cheapest or dearest to a place, the same as to an individual.

Thus, suppose the arbitrated price between Paris and Cadiz be, as above, $16\frac{2}{3}$ Francs for the Doubloon, and the advised price 16, the latter is evidently best for Paris, and the former for Cadiz; it being the interest of Paris to buy the Doubloon at the lowest price, and the interest of Cadiz to sell it at the highest price. This being understood, the following is the rule to be observed.

GENERAL RULE.

Draw upon the place where the arbitrated price is better for that place than the advised price; and remit to the place where it is worse.

Thus, in the foregoing comparison, London should draw on Cadiz, where the arbitrated price is better than the advised price; and should remit to Paris, where it is worse.

Suppose London exchanges on Amsterdam at 34 10, and on Hamburgh at 33 5; and suppose the advised course of exchange between Amsterdam and Hamburgh is 32 Stivers for the Dollar; how should London draw and remit, and what profit presents on a bill of £100?

As 33s. 5d. : 34s. 10d. :: 2 Marks : $33\frac{243}{401}$ Stivers, the arbitrated price, which is better for Hamburgh than the advised price; therefore, (according to the above Rule,) draw on Hamburgh, and remit to Amsterdam. Thus, your draft, which sells for £100 at 33 5, will amount to 1253 Marks 2 Sols: this sum, turned into Dutch money at 32 Stivers, will produce 1002 Guilders 10 Stivers; and a bill on Amsterdam for the amount at 34 10 will cost only £95 18s. 8d.

For, as £1 sterling : 33s. 5d. :: £100 : 1253 Marks 2 Sols.

And, as 2 Marks : 32 Stivers :: 1253 Marks 2 Sols : 1002 Guilders 10 Stivers.

Again, as 34s. 10d. : £1 sterling :: 1002 Guilders 10 Stivers : £95 18s. 8d.

Hence, the profit which presents in a draft of £100 sterling is £4 1s. 4d. The money you receive for your draft will pay for your remittance, with the above surplus, and your debit at Hamburgh will be paid by your credit at Amsterdam.

But if, on the contrary, the advised price of exchange had been $34\frac{1}{4}$, this would be better than the arbitrated price for Hamburgh, and therefore you should draw on Amsterdam: thus—£100 at 34 10 = 1045 Guilders, which, at 34¼ Stivers = 1220 Marks 7 S. 6 F.; and this bill at 33 5 will cost only £97 7s. 10d.; the profit, therefore, is £2 12s. 2d. The money you receive for your draft will pay for your remittance, with this surplus, and your debit at Amsterdam will be paid by your credit at Hamburgh.

The following example, which is taken from a real operation, contains as much variety as can occur in Problems of this kind.

In March, 1802, the exchanges were (according to Lloyd's List,) London on Amsterdam 10 16, and on Cadiz 37; and, according to the Quotation of Amsterdam, the exchange of that place on Cadiz was 107.

London purchased bills to the amount of 10,000 Piastres, and remitted them to Cadiz, desiring to have returns in bills on Amsterdam; but when the remittance reached Cadiz, the exchange with Amsterdam had fallen to 104.

London also drew on Amsterdam for the amount, and the operation stood thus—
10,000 Piastres at 37d. = £1541 13s. 4d. which sum, converted to Florins at

		Ducats	Fl. Curr.	Stiv.
10 Florins 16 Stivers per £ sterling	=		16,650	0
10,000 Piastres reduced to Ducats of 375 Maravedis	=	7,253⅓		
Commission, brokerage, and discount	=	217⅓		
		7,036		
7,036 Ducats at 104, drawn for, deducting 3 per cent. discount			17,734	15
Gain			1,084	15

Hence, the profit on this operation was about 7 per cent.; and had the exchange kept up, that is, had the Ducat been negotiated at 107 per Ducat, the gain would have been above 10 per cent.—which shews the necessity of despatch in such speculations.

The reason for thus drawing and remitting is founded on the General Rule, and the arbitrated price is determined in the following manner:

First, find how many Pence sterling the Ducat is worth; thus—

	Maravedis		Pence sterling		Maravedis		Pence sterling.		£		Florins	Stivers		Pence sterling		Pence Flemish.
As	272	:	37	::	375	:	51.—Then,	as	1	:	10	16	::	51	:	91⅘

Or thus, 1 Ducat.

1 Ducat	=	375 Maravedis.
272 Maravedis	=	37 Pence sterling.
240 Pence sterling	=	432 Pence Flemish.

Reduced gives 91⅘d. nearly.

Here the arbitrated price is 91⅘d. Flemish for the Ducat, but the real price is 104. Thus the former is the most favourable for Amsterdam, and therefore, (according to the Rule, page 119,) London should draw on Amsterdam and remit to Cadiz.

COMPOUND ARBITRATION

Is a comparison between the exchanges of more than three places, in order to find how much a remittance passing through them all will amount to in the last place; or to find the arbitrated price between the first place and the last, in order to determine on the most advantageous mode of negotiating bills.

Compound arbitration is therefore a repetition of simple arbitration, and may be solved by a continuation of several statings in the Rule of Proportion, as in the following example:

Suppose the exchange between London and Amsterdam to be 35 Shillings Flemish for £1 sterling; between Amsterdam and Lisbon, 42 Pence Flemish for 1 Old Crusade, and between Lisbon and Paris, 480 Rees for 3 Francs, what is the arbitrated price between London and Paris?

First, As 35s. Flemish : £1 :: 42d. Flemish, or 3½s. Flemish : 2s. sterling = 1 Old Crusade.

Secondly, As 1 Old Crusade, or 400 Rees : 2s. sterling :: 480 Rees : 2s. 4⅘d. sterling = 3 Francs.

Thirdly, As 2s. 4⅘d. sterling : 3 Francs :: £1 sterling : 25 Francs.

Hence the arbitrated price is 25 Francs for £1 sterling.

But all such operations are best performed in the following manner by the Chain Rule:

		1 Pound sterling
1 Pound sterling	=	35 Shillings Flemish
3½ Shillings Flemish	=	1 Old Crusade
1 Old Crusade	=	400 Rees
480 Rees	=	3 Francs

Reduced = 25 Francs as above.

Suppose London has a sum of money to receive in Cadiz, the exchange being at 38d.; but, instead of drawing directly on this place, he draws on Amsterdam, ordering his agent there to draw on Paris; and Paris to draw on Cadiz; the exchange between London and Amsterdam being at 35 Shillings Flemish per Pound sterling; between Amsterdam and Paris 53½ Grotes Flemish per Ecu of 3 Francs; and between Paris and Cadiz, 15 Francs 50 Centimes per Doubloon of Plate; what is the arbitrated price between London and Cadiz?

		1 Dollar of Plate
4 Dollars of Plate	=	1 Doubloon do.
1 Doubloon	=	$15\frac{1}{2}$ Francs
3 Francs	=	$53\frac{1}{2}$ Grotes Flemish
12 Grotes	=	1 Shilling Flemish
35 Shillings Flemish	=	240 Pence sterling

Reduced, gives $39\frac{1}{2}$d. sterling per Dollar of Plate.

The circular operation would, therefore, be most advantageous, as London would get $39\frac{1}{2}$d. instead of 38d. for each Dollar, which he had to receive in Cadiz.

London having a sum to receive in Lisbon, when the exchange is at 64d. sterling per Milree, draws on Lisbon, but remits his bill to Hamburgh to be negotiated; and directs the returns to be made to him in bills on Leghorn—the exchange between Hamburgh and Lisbon being 45 Grotes Flemish per Old Crusade, between Hamburgh and Leghorn 85 Grotes Flemish per Pezza, and between London and Leghorn 52d. sterling per Pezza, what is the arbitrated price between London and Lisbon?

		1000 Rees
400 Rees	=	1 Old Crusade
1 Old Crusade	=	45 Grotes Flemish
85 Grotes	=	1 Pezza
1 Pezza	=	52 Pence sterling

Reduced, gives $68\frac{14}{17}$d. sterling per Milreē.

This circular operation would, therefore, be more advantageous than the direct exchange of London on Lisbon, viz. $68\frac{14}{17}$d., instead of 64d.

London has a sum to pay in Petersburg, and another to receive in Genoa; but there being no regular exchange between these places, London draws on Hamburgh, and remits his bill to Petersburg, directing Hamburgh to draw on Genoa—the exchange between London and Genoa, being $46\frac{1}{2}$d. sterling per Pezza; between Hamburgh and Genoa, 81 Grotes Flemish per Pezza; and between Petersburg and Hamburgh, 23 Schillings Lubs per Ruble; what is the exchange between London and Petersburg resulting from the operation—that is, how many Pence sterling does London pay for the Ruble?

		1 Ruble
1 Ruble	=	23 Schillings Lubs
1 Schilling Lubs	=	2 Grotes Flemish
81 Grotes	=	1 Pezza
1 Pezza	=	$46\frac{1}{2}$ Pence sterling

Reduced, = $26\frac{11}{27}$d. sterling per Ruble.

London has a sum to remit to Paris, the exchange being at 24 Livres 5 Sous per Pound sterling; but instead of taking a bill on Paris, London draws on Hamburgh, and remits his bill to Paris to be negotiated; Hamburgh is directed to draw on Venice, and Venice to draw on London; the exchange between Paris and Hamburgh being 190 Francs per 100 Marks Banco, between Hamburgh and Venice 4 Lire 5 Soldi Piccoli per Mark Banco, and between Venice and London 55 Lire Piccole per Pound sterling; what is the arbitrated price between London and Paris?

		1 Pound Sterling
1 Pound Sterling	=	55 Lire Piccole
$4\frac{1}{4}$ Lire Piccole	=	1 Mark
100 Marks	=	190 Francs
80 Francs	=	81 Livres

Reduced, gives 24 Livres 18 Sous per Pound sterling.

The circular operation is, therefore, more advantageous than the direct exchange, as London pays 24 Livres 18 Sous, with £ 1 sterling, instead of 24 Livres 5 Sous.

Hitherto we have only examined one combination of the exchanges between several places in order to discover one result. In the following example we shall examine different combinations of the same exchanges, to find which is most favourable; and what is here performed with four places only, may be done with any greater number, in the same manner—that is, by trial and comparison.

Suppose the following to be the quotations of exchange:

London on	Amsterdam	35	Shillings Flemish per Pound sterling
	Madrid	38	Pence sterling per Dollar of Plate
	Paris	24	Livres per Pound sterling
Amsterdam on	London	34	Shillings Flemish per Pound sterling
	Paris	53	Grotes per Ecu of 3 Francs
	Madrid	92	Grotes per Ducat of Plate
Paris on	London	$23\frac{1}{2}$	Livres per Pound sterling
	Madrid	16	Francs per Doubloon of Plate
	Amsterdam	54	Grotes Flemish per Ecu of 3 Francs
Madrid on	London	39	Pence sterling per Dollar of Plate
	Amsterdam	94	Grotes per Ducat of Plate
	Paris	$16\frac{1}{2}$	Francs per Doubloon of Plate.

Now if London has a sum to receive in Madrid, what would be the most advantageous mode of operation?

By drawing directly on Madrid as above, London will receive 38d. sterling per Dollar.

First.—Let London draw on Amsterdam, directing Amsterdam to draw on Paris, and Madrid to remit to Paris; then the operation will be as follows:

		1 Dollar of Plate
4 Dollars	=	1 Doubloon of Plate
1 Doubloon	=	$16\frac{1}{2}$ Francs
3 Francs	=	54 Grotes Flemish
12 Grotes	=	1 Shilling Flemish
35 Shillings Flemish	=	240 Pence sterling

Reduced, gives the Dollar equal to $42\frac{3}{7}$d. sterling.

Secondly.—Let London draw on Paris, directing Paris to draw on Amsterdam, and Madrid to remit to Amsterdam; then,

		1 Dollar of Plate
1 Dollar of Plate	=	272 Maravedis
375 Maravedis	=	1 Ducat of Plate
1 Ducat	=	94 Grotes Flemish
53 Grotes	=	3 Francs
80 Francs	=	81 Livres
24 Livres	=	240 Pence sterling

Reduced, gives the Dollar = $39\frac{1}{11}$d.

Thirdly.—Let London draw on Madrid, and remit the bill to Paris to be negotiated, and let the returns be made in a bill on Amsterdam; then

		1 Dollar of Plate.
4 Dollars	=	1 Doubloon of Plate
1 Doubloon	=	16 Francs
3 Francs	=	54 Grotes Flemish
12 Grotes	=	1 Shilling Flemish
35 Shillings Flemish	=	240 Pence sterling.

Reduced, gives $41\frac{1}{7}$d. sterling per Dollar.

Fourthly.—Let London draw on Madrid, and remit to be negotiated in Amsterdam, and order the returns to be made in a bill on Paris; then

		1 Dollar of Plate
1 Dollar	=	272 Maravedis

375 Maravedis	=	1 Ducat of Plate
1 Ducat	=	92 Grotes Flemish
53 Grotes	=	3 Francs
80 Francs	=	81 Livres
24 Livres	=	240 Pence sterling.

Reduced, gives $38\frac{1}{4}$d. sterling per Dollar nearly.

Fifthly.—Let London draw on Amsterdam, Amsterdam on Paris, and Paris on Madrid; then

		1 Dollar of Plate
4 Dollars	=	1 Doubloon of Plate
1 Doubloon	=	16 Francs
3 Francs	=	53 Grotes Flemish
12 Grotes	=	1 Shilling Flemish
35 Shillings Flemish	=	240 Pence sterling.

Reduced, gives $40\frac{8}{21}$d. per Dollar.

Sixthly.—Let Madrid remit to Paris, Paris to Amsterdam, and Amsterdam to London; then

		1 Dollar of Plate
4 Dollars	=	1 Doubloon of Plate
1 Doubloon	=	$16\frac{1}{2}$ Francs
3 Francs	=	54 Grotes Flemish
12 Grotes	=	1 Shilling Flemish
34 Shillings Flemish	=	240 Pence sterling.

Reduced, gives 44d. per Dollar nearly.

Several other combinations might be made; but the foregoing are sufficient for the present illustration.

In recapitulating the different combinations here proposed, we find that

The First	gives	$42\frac{3}{7}$	Pence	sterling	per Dollar of Plate.
The Second	—	$39\frac{1}{11}$	—	—	per Ditto
The Third	—	$41\frac{1}{7}$	—	—	per Ditto
The Fourth	—	$38\frac{1}{4}$	—	—	per Ditto
The Fifth	—	$40\frac{8}{21}$	—	—	per Ditto
The Sixth	—	44	—	—	per Ditto
Whilst the direct course	gives	38	—	—	per Ditto

Hence, it is evident, according to the rule laid down in pages 105 and 108, that the 6th operation would be most advantageous for the London drawer, as he would receive more

Pence for the Dollar than by any other combination; but it must be observed, that in this case, he would have to wait about six months for the remittance from Madrid through Paris and Amsterdam; whereas, by drawing directly on Madrid, he would receive the money immediately—consequently, interest should be deducted from the profit, besides commission, postage, &c. The Profit is, however, so great in this case, as far to exceed the additional expenses; thus—

As 38 : 44 :: 100 : $115\frac{30}{38}$. Profit, $15\frac{5}{6}$ per cent. nearly.

It is also evident, that if London was the debtor, and had to remit to Madrid, the lowest course of exchange, which is here the direct one, should be adopted.

CHARGES ON EXCHANGE OPERATIONS.

In the foregoing examples, no notice is taken of the expenses incident to exchange operations, such as commission, brokerage, interest, &c.; but it is necessary to make allowance for those charges, which is generally done by computing them at so much per cent.; *and then adding the per-centage if the money is to be paid, or subtracting it if to be received.* Suppose the charge to be 1 per cent.; if on a Draft it is 101 for 100, but if on a Remittance, 99 for 100.

Example I.—Suppose a merchant in Liverpool has 10,000 Marks to pay in Hamburgh, for which purpose he orders bills to be bought in London at 34s. 8d. besides which he is charged ½ per cent. for commission and brokerage, how much sterling will he have to pay?

	s.	d. Flem.		£ ster.		Marks.		£	s.	d. ster.
As	34	8	:	1	::	10,000	:	769	4	$7\frac{1}{2}$

			£	s.	d. ster.		£	s.	d. ster.
And as 100	:	$100\frac{1}{2}$ ::	769	4	$7\frac{1}{2}$	:	773	1	$6\frac{1}{2}$

Example II.—A merchant in London negotiates a bill on Leghorn of 6592 Pezze 10 Soldi at $49\frac{1}{2}$d. sterling per Pezza; and pays as usual 1 per 1000 brokerage; how much sterling does he receive?

	Pezza		d. ster.		Pezze	Soldi		£	s.	d. ster.
As	1	:	$49\frac{1}{2}$	::	6592	10	:	1359	14	$0\frac{3}{4}$

				£	s.	d.		£	s.	d.
And as 1000	:	999	::	1359	14	$0\frac{3}{4}$	:	1358	6	$10\frac{1}{2}$

When the operation is performed by the Chain Rule, the charges per cent. must be deducted from 100 the last consequent, if it tends to the diminution of the result, but if to its increase, the same remainder must be an antecedent.

Example III.—London, having a sum to pay in Lisbon, buys bills on Hamburgh at the exchange of 35s. 4d. and remits them to Lisbon, where they are negotiated at 43 Grotes Flemish per Old Crusade. The charges in Lisbon for brokerage, commission, and postage are $\frac{3}{4}$ per cent; what is the arbitrated price between London and Lisbon, resulting from the operation—that is how many Pence sterling should be given for the Milree?

		1000 Rees
400 Rees	=	43 Grotes Flemish
424 Grotes	=	240 Pence sterling
100 Pence	=	100$\frac{3}{4}$ Pence, adding charges.

Answer, 61$\frac{3}{10}$d. sterling per Milree.

In the above question the charges are added to the last consequent as they increase the price of the Milree, which must be the case, the charges being against the Payee.

Example IV.—London takes bills on Madrid at 33$\frac{1}{2}$d. per Dollar of exchange, remits them to Amsterdam with orders to negotiate at 90$\frac{1}{4}$ Grotes Flemish per Ducat of exchange, and to make the returns in bills on Paris at 51$\frac{3}{8}$ Grotes per Ecu of 3 Francs: these bills on Paris are negotiated in London at 25 Livres 18 Sous per Pound sterling; and all the charges (including interest) amount to 1$\frac{1}{8}$ per cent.; how much per cent. is gained or lost by this operation—that is, how much will 100d. sterling produce?

		100 Pence Sterling
33$\frac{1}{2}$ Pence	=	272 Maravedis or 1 Dollar of exchange
1 Ducat of exchange, or 375 Maravedis	=	90$\frac{1}{4}$ Grotes
51$\frac{3}{8}$ Grotes	=	3 Francs
80 Francs	=	81 Livres
1 Livre	=	20 Sous
518 Sous	=	240 Pence
100 Pence	=	98$\frac{7}{8}$ Pence deducting charges.

The result is 105,85d. The profit is, therefore, 5,85 or nearly 5$\frac{7}{8}$ per cent.

In the last example, the interest was to be deducted from the profits, but an example will now be given, in which the interest is to be added, because the drawer gains it; and, in such case, it is to be added to the antecedent instead of being subtracted.

Example V.—London draws bills on Hamburgh at 34 Shillings Flemish per Pound sterling, and orders Hamburgh to draw for his reimbursement on Leghorn, which is done at 86 Grotes Flemish per Pezza; Leghorn draws in the same way on Cadiz at 140 Dollars of

Plate per 100 Pezze; and lastly, Cadiz draws on London at 39 Pence sterling per Dollar; what is the profit or loss on the operation, supposing that the charges in each of the above three foreign places are $\frac{3}{4}$ per cent. (in all $2\frac{1}{4}$ per cent.); but that London, by keeping the money in his hands about 8 months, gains 3 per cent. by the interest?

		100 Pence sterling
240 Pence	=	34 Shillings Flemish
1 Shilling Flemish	=	12 Grotes
86 Grotes	=	1 Pezza
100 Pezze	=	140 Dollars of Plate
1 Dollar of Plate	=	39 Pence
$97\frac{3}{4}$ Pence deducting charges	=	100 Pence
103 Pence with interest	=	100 Pence

The Answer is 107,2d. The loss is, therefore, $7\frac{1}{5}$ per cent. nearly.

As the above example comprehends all the varieties that generally occur in questions of this kind, it is here solved by a series of statings in the Rule of Three, which serves at once to explain the nature of the operation, and to prove the correctness of the Chain Rule. Such illustrations must be highly useful in all problems of arbitration.

London, we will suppose, receives 100 Pence, or any other denomination, by drawing on Hamburgh at 34s. Flemish per Pound sterling.

As 240 d. : 34 s. :: 100 d. : 170 Grotes Flem.

Hamburgh must, therefore, draw on Leghorn for that sum,—thus

As 86 Grotes : 1 Pezza :: 170 Grotes : 1,977 Pezza

Leghorn in the same way reimburses on Cadiz.

As 100 Pezze : 140 Doll. Plate :: 1,977 Pezza : 276,78 Doll. Plate

For which Cadiz thus finally draws on London—

As 1 Doll. : 39 d. :: 276,78 Doll. : 107,94 d. which the drawer must pay.

Then to add the expense to the loss, say

As 97,75 d. : 100 d. :: 107,94 d. : 110,42 d.

And to deduct the interest from the loss, say

As 103 d. : 100 d. :: 110,42 d. : 107,2 d.

If, in the above statement, the drawer or seller had been the buyer or remitter, then the expenses and interest must have been reversed as to their places, both in the Chain Rule and in the Rule of Three.

LOGARITHMS IN EXCHANGE.

Operations in exchange may be sometimes greatly facilitated by the help of Logarithms. Thus, in a statement of arbitration—*if the sum of the Logarithms of the Antecedents, be subtracted from the sum of the Logarithms of the Consequents, the remainder will be the Logarithm of the Answer*.

To apply this rule to Example IV. page 127, let like numbers on both sides be struck out as before; to reduce them to a lower denomination is useless, as the Logarithm of a large number is as easily found as that of a small one: thus—

Antecedents.	Logarithms.	Consequents.	Logarithms.
33,5	1,525045	272	2,434569
125	2,096910	90,25	1,955447
51,375	1,710752	3	0,477121
518	2,714330	81	1,908484
		20	1,301030
	8,047037	98,875	1,995086
		Sum of Log. of Con.	10,071737
		Sum of Log. of Ant.	8,047037
		Answer, 105,85 =	2,024700

The reason of the above operation will be understood by considering that Multiplication and Division of common numbers are performed by Addition and Subtraction of their Logarithms. Laborious calculations, therefore, must be greatly facilitated by the help of Logarithms, and their application in Exchange seems too obvious to require any further illustration.

FIXED NUMBERS IN EXCHANGE.

In every long statement of an exchange operation, there are both fixed numbers and variable numbers: the latter are generally the prices of exchange, and the fluctuating agios, or values of different sorts of money, with the amount of charges, &c.; and the former, that is, the fixed numbers, are the permanent proportions between certain denominations of money, as the number of Pence in a Pound sterling, &c. Now when operations between the same places are to be repeated several times, and at such intervals, as to admit of alterations in the variable numbers, the work may be considerably abridged by reducing all the invariable terms into a fixed number, which may be afterwards used as a constant factor in all such questions.

Thus, in Example III., page 127, among the Antecedents, 400 expressing the number of Rees in an Old Crusade, and 100, which is assumed, in order to find a per centage on the operation, are fixed numbers; and, among the Consequents, 1000, the number of Rees in a Milree, and 240, the number of Pence in a Pound sterling, are likewise fixed numbers. The variable numbers are the exchanges between London and Hamburgh, and between Hamburgh and Lisbon, and the amount of the charges. Then let the fixed numbers be cast up, thus—

400	1000
100	240

By expunging the cyphers, and dividing both sides by 4, the result, or *fixed number*, will be 6 in all questions of the same kind. Then multiply the constant number 6 by the course of exchange of Hamburgh on Lisbon, and by 100 more the charges, and divide by the course of exchange of London on Hamburgh expressed in Grotes Flemish: or, by Logarithms,—to the constant Logarithm of 6, add the Logarithms of the two first-mentioned variable quantities, and subtract the Logarithm of the last: thus—

Logarithm of 6	0,778151
43	1,633468
100,75	2,003245
	4,414864
Logarithm of 424....	2,627366
	1,787498 Log. of 61,3 the arbitrated price, *(found page 127.)*

Now let the exchange of London on Hamburgh be at 34s. 8d. (or 416 Grotes per Pound sterling, and that of Hamburgh on Lisbon at 44 Grotes per Crusade; let also the charges amount to ½ per cent.

Fixed Logarithm	0,778151
Logarithm of 44	1,643453
100,5	2,002166
	4,423770
Logarithm of 416	2,619093
	1,804677 Log. of 63,78, or 63¾ nearly.

In Example IV. page 127, on one side 375 and 80; and on the other side 272, 3,81, 240 are invariable numbers (besides 100 which may be cancelled on both sides), which may be reduced as before to 125......272, 3, 81, 20 give $\frac{1321920}{125}$ = 10575,4 Fixed Number.

The fixed Logarithm is then found as follows:

Logarithm of 272......	2,434569
3......	0,477121
81......	1,908484
20......	1,301030
	6,121204
Logarithm of 125......	2,096910
Fixed Logarithm	4,024294 = 10575,4 Fixed Number.

This may be applied to the questions, page 127, as follows:

Antecedents.	Logarithms.	Consequents.	Logarithms.
33,5	1,525045	90,25	1,955447
51,375	1,710754	98,875	1,995086
518,	2,714330	Fixed Logarithm	4,024294
	5,950127	Sum of Log. of Con.	7,974827
		Sum of Log. of An.	5,950127
		Answer, Log. 105,85	......2,024700 as before.

ARBITRATION OF SPECIE AND BULLION.

THE state of the exchange between two countries is sometimes such, that it is found more advantageous, instead of drawing or remitting bills, to import or export specie or bullion. The profit or loss on operations of this kind may be determined by calculations similar to those used in arbitration of exchange.

s 2

By this rule also the course of exchange is determined from the price of bullion, and *vice versa.*

Example I.—London has a sum to receive in Lisbon, the exchange being at 62; but instead of drawing on Lisbon, he orders a quantity of Johaneses to be bought there, the discount on paper money in Portugal being at the time 12 per cent.; these Johaneses are sold in London at £4 sterling per ounce; the charges, namely, commission, freight, and insurance, amount to 2½ per cent.;—what is the exchange between London and Lisbon resulting from the operation; that is, how many Pence sterling should be given for the Milree, legal money?

		1000 Rees
100 Rees legal money	=	94 Rees effective
6400 Rees effective	=	1 Johanese
1 Johanese	=	220½ Grains
480 Grains in Johanese	=	4 Pounds sterling
1 Pound	=	240 Pence sterling
100 Pence	=	97½ Pence deducting charges.

Reduced, gives 63,15d. per Milree.

The circular operation would therefore be most advantageous to the London Drawer.

Example II.—A quantity of Dollars is imported from Cadiz, for which bills are drawn on London at the exchange of 38¾, and the charges amount to 3 per cent.;—how much per ounce will these Dollars cost in London, supposing 1000 Dollars to weigh 866 Ounces Troy?

		1 Ounce of Dollars
866 Ounces	=	1000 Dollars
1 Dollar	=	10⅝ Reals of Plate
8 Reals of Plate	=	1 Dollar of Exchange
1 Dollar of Exchange	=	38¾ Pence sterling
100 Pence	=	103 Pence with charges.

Reduced, gives 61,21d. or 61¼d. per Ounce nearly.

Example III.—London has a sum to pay in Hamburgh, the exchange being at 34; but instead of remitting bills, he buys a quantity of Spanish Dollars at 60½d. sterling per Ounce, which are sent to Hamburgh, and there sold at 28 Marks Banco per Mark fine; the charges amount to 1½ per cent.;—what is the arbitrated price, or course of exchange, between London and Hamburgh, the Dollars being 10 oz. 15 dwts. fine, and 60 Marks in Hamburgh being equal to 451 Ounces Troy?

Example II.—Suppose the cwt. of coffee in London to cost 65 Shillings on board, and the exchange on Hamburgh to be 34s. 8d.; commission 2 per cent.; and insurance 1 per cent.;—what will the lb. of such coffee come to in Hamburgh Banco, reckoning for freight, brokerage, and other charges $4\frac{1}{2}$ Pfenings Banco per Pound,—112lb. avoirdupois being equal to 105lb. of Hamburgh?

		1 lb. of Hamburgh
105 lb. of Hamburgh	=	1 Hundred Weight Avoirdupois
1 Hundred Weight	=	65 Shillings Sterling
20 Shillings Sterling	=	416 Grotes Flemish Banco
2 Grotes Flemish	=	1 Schilling Lubs
100 Schillings	=	102 Schillings with Commission
100 Schillings	=	101 Schillings with Insurance

Answer, 6 Schillings $7\frac{1}{2}$ Pfenings Banco nearly.
Add. . . . . $4\frac{1}{2}$ Pfenings for Charges in Hamburgh

Ans. 7 Schillings per lb.

Example III.—Irish butter sells at Cork for 50 Shillings Irish per cwt. the exchange of Cork on London is $9\frac{1}{4}$; and that of London on Hamburgh 35;—what price will the cask of 224 lb. come to in Hamburgh currency, reckoning commission and insurance together at $3\frac{1}{2}$ per cent., the charges in Hamburgh at 5 Marks current per cask, and the agio on the Bank 22 per cent?

		224 lb. of Hamburgh
105 lb. of Hamburgh	=	1 Hundred Weight Avoirdupois
1 Hundred Weight	=	50 Shillings Irish
$109\frac{1}{4}$ Shillings Irish	=	100 Shillings Sterling
20 Shillings Sterling	=	35 Shillings Flemish Banco
8 Shillings Flemish	=	3 Marks
100 Marks Banco	=	122 Marks current
100 Marks current	=	$103\frac{1}{2}$ Marks current with Comn. and Inse.

Answer, 80 Marks $14\frac{1}{2}$ Schillings current nearly.
Charges in Hamburgh. . . . 5 Marks

85 Marks $14\frac{1}{2}$ Schillings per Cask.

Example IV.—Pepper is bought in London at $11\frac{1}{2}$d. per lb. net weight, which, with the allowances for draft and tare, comes to $10\frac{3}{4}$d. per lb. gross weight. This pepper is exported to Amsterdam, the exchange being at 36 Shillings Flemish Banco per Pound Sterling; $1\frac{2}{3}$ per cent. is allowed for tare in Amsterdam: freight, insurance, and other charges amount to $6\frac{1}{2}$ per cent. and it is sold there at 28 Grotes Flemish per Pound; but 2 per cent. is allowed for Rabat on the price;—what is the profit or loss on the operation,—56 lb. of Amsterdam being equal to 61 lb. avoirdupois?

		1 lb. Avoirdupois
61 lb. Avoirdupois	=	56 lb. of Amsterdam
$101\frac{2}{3}$lb. Gross Weight	=	100 lb. Net Weight in Amsterdam
1 lb. Net Weight	=	28 Grotes Flemish
102 Grotes	=	100 Grotes, with Rabat
$106\frac{1}{2}$Grotes	=	100 Grotes, with Charges
12 Grotes	=	1 Shilling Flemish
36 Shillings Flemish	=	240 Pence Sterling

	s.	d.	
Reduced, gives....	12	9	sterling per lb.
Prime Cost	11	5	
Profit	1	4	per lb. or $12\frac{4}{23}$ per cent.

Example V.—The Last of wheat at Dantzic costs 620 Florins, and it is computed that it might be sold in London at 90 Shillings per Quarter; Dantzic may draw on Hamburgh for the amount at 166 Groschen per Rixdollar Banco, and the exchange of Hamburgh on London is 34s. 6d.;—what would be the profit or loss on the importation of such wheat, reckoning that the Last of Dantzic equals $10\frac{3}{4}$ English Quarters, that the charges at Dantzic will amount to $12\frac{1}{2}$ per cent., and that the freight, insurance, and all the charges to be paid in London (including commission to the Hamburgh correspondent) will amount to 20 per cent.?

		1 English Quarter
$10\frac{3}{4}$Quarters	=	1 Last in Dantzic
1 Last in Dantzic	=	620 Florins
100 Florins	=	$112\frac{1}{2}$Florins, with charges in Dantzic
1 Florin	=	30 Groschen
166 Groschen	=	1 Rixdollar Hamburgh Banco
1 Rixdollar	=	8 Shillings Flemish
$34\frac{1}{2}$Shillings Flemish	=	1 Pound Sterling
100 Pounds	=	120 Pounds, with Charges
1 Pound	=	20 Shillings

Reduced, gives $65\frac{1}{4}$ Shillings per Quarter.

If therefore the wheat can be sold at 90s. the profit will be $24\frac{3}{4}$s. per Quarter, or about 38 per cent.

The following question will show how to determine between two or more places, in order to find which will give the most advantageous result.

Example VI.—A quantity of Spanish wool has been bought at Bilboa at 325 Reals Vellon per Arroba of 25 lb. with an intention to export it either to London or to Amsterdam; the price of such wool in London is found to be 4 Shillings per lb. allowing 6 months credit; and in Amsterdam 58 Stivers per lb. allowing 21 months rabat, *i. e.* 14 per cent. and 1 per cent. for prompt payment: the exchange of Bilboa on London is 37d. per Dollar, and on Amsterdam 87 Grotes Flemish per Ducat;—which of the two places is the most advantageous to export to?

By a reference to the first volume, it will be found that 100 lb. of Bilboa are equal to 108 lb. avoirdupois, which answer to $99\frac{1}{6}$ lb. of Amsterdam: and that the allowances on Spanish wool in London are 22 lb. per bale of 2 cwt. And suppose the allowances in Amsterdam amount to 20 per cent.

And, to simplify the question, we will suppose the charges to be the same in London as in Amsterdam, so that they need not be taken into account.

Beginning with London, say

1 lb. Avoirdupois.
202 lb. Net Weight = 224 lb. Gross Weight.
108 lb. Avoirdupois = 100 lb. of Bilboa.
25 lb. of Bilboa = 325 Reals Vellon.
32 Reals Vellon = 17 Reals of Plate.
8 Reals of Plate = 1 Dollar of Exchange.
1 Dollar of Exchange = 37 Pence Sterling.

Reduced, gives 2s. $8\frac{3}{4}$d. sterling per lb.

This wool will therefore come to 2s. $8\frac{3}{4}$d. per lb. in London, where it is sold at 4s. per lb. from which, however, six months discount must be deducted; then

As 100 : $97\frac{1}{2}$: : 4s. : 3s. $10\frac{3}{4}$d. the real price.
And as 2s. $8\frac{3}{4}$d. : 3s. $10\frac{3}{4}$d. : : 100 : $142\frac{98}{131}$d.

The profit on the operation to London is therefore $42\frac{98}{131}$d. or nearly $42\frac{2}{3}$ per cent.

Then for Amsterdam, say

1 lb. of Amsterdam.
100 lb. Net Weight = 120 lb. Gross Weight.
$99\frac{1}{6}$ lb. of Amsterdam = 100 lb. of Bilboa.
25 lb. of Bilboa = 325 Reals Vellon.
1 Real = 34 Maravedis.

32 Maravedis Vellon	=	17 Maravedis of Plate.
375 Maravedis of Plate	=	1 Ducat of Exchange.
1 Ducat of Exchange	=	87 Grotes Flemish.
2 Grotes Flemish	=	1 Stiver.

Reduced, gives 32,96 Stivers per lb.

This wool will, therefore, come to 32,96 Stivers per lb. in Amsterdam, where it is sold at 58 Stivers per lb.; but from this 15 per cent. must be deducted for Rabat and prompt payment; then

As 100 : 85 : : 58 Stivers : 49,3 Stivers, the real price.

And as 32,96 : 49,30 : : 100 : $149\frac{237}{412}$.

The profit on the operation to Amsterdam is $49\frac{237}{412}$, which is 7 per cent. more than in London; and, therefore, supposing, as we have done, that the freight, insurance, duty on importation, and other charges would amount to the same sum in both places, Amsterdam must be a more advantageous place to export to than London.

By the foregoing examples may be seen the great advantages which merchants may derive from a knowledge of arbitration, whether of merchandize, bullion, or exchanges; and the following article will likewise show the utility and importance of this science when judiciously applied, on a large scale, to national or political purposes.

EXCHANGE CIRCULATIONS.

Exchange Circulations are a kind of arbitration, in which a merchant negotiates his bills on his correspondent in a foreign place, directing him to draw on a third person for his reimbursement; and further ordering the operation to be continued on the same plan from one place to another, until the last correspondent reimburses himself by drawing on the original negotiator or drawer.

Thus, circular exchange is carried on among several persons on the same principle as drawing and redrawing between two correspondents; that is, when one draws upon the other directing the correspondent to draw on him again for his reimbursement, and each sells his draft for ready money.

Operations in circular exchange afford not only immediate resources, but also considerable profits when judiciously managed. In order, however, to carry on this kind of business with proper effect, it is necessary for the original drawer to establish a proper credit in every place where the bills are to be negotiated; and to be provided likewise with funds to make good, in the end, all his engagements.

Exchange Circulations may be distinguished under two heads :

1st. Operations by which individuals or houses possessed of limited capitals may undertake large negotiations, and thus make their credit supply both immediate funds and future profit.

2dly. Operations to which governments and public establishments have occasional recourse, either to remit subsidies, or to effect a rise or fall in exchanges.

The first kind of circulation has been already explained in compound arbitration; and it is particularly illustrated in Example V. page 127.

The second kind of circulation is carried on precisely on the same principle as the first; but as this is a subject of considerable importance in political economy, as well as commercial speculation, we shall here further illustrate it by a real example.

In 1804 Spain was bound to pay to France a large Subsidy; and, in order to do this, three direct methods presented themselves:—

1. To send Dollars to Paris by land.
2. To remit Bills of Exchange directly to Paris.
3. To authorise Paris to draw directly on Spain.

The first of these methods was tried, but it was found too slow and expensive; and the second and third plans were considered as likely to turn the exchange against Spain. The following method by circular exchange was, therefore, adopted:—

A Merchant, or Banquier, at Paris, was appointed to manage the operation, which he thus conducted: he chose London, Amsterdam, Hamburgh, Cadiz, Madrid, and Paris, as the principal hinges on which the operation was to turn, and he engaged correspondents in each of those cities to support the circulation. Madrid and Cadiz were the places in Spain from whence remittances were to be made, and Dollars were, of course, to be sent where they bore the highest price, for which Bills were to be procured on Paris, or on any other places that might be deemed more advantageous.

The principle having been thus established, it only remained to regulate the extent of the operation so as not to issue too much paper on Spain, and to give the circulation as much support as possible from real business. With this view, London was chosen as a place to which the operation might be chiefly directed, as the price of Dollars was then high in England, a circumstance which rendered the proportional exchange advantageous to Spain. The business was commenced at Paris, where the negotiation of drafts issued on Hamburgh and Amsterdam served to answer the immediate demands of the State; and orders were transmitted to those places to draw for their reimbursements on London, Madrid, or Cadiz, according as the courses of exchange were most favourable. The proceedings were all conducted with judgment and attended with considerable success.

At the commencement of the operation the course of exchange of Cadiz on London was 36d. but by the plan adopted, Spain obtained 39¼d. as may be seen by the following computation:—

The several charges of the consignments of Dollars from Cadiz to London amounted to 11 per cent. and they were sold at 5s. 7d. per oz.—Hence,

		1 Dollar of Exchange.
85 Dollars of Exchange	=	64 Hard Dollars.
1000 Hard Dollars	=	866 Ounces (by common estimate).
1 Ounce	=	67 Pence.
111 Pence	=	100 Pence with charges.

Reduced, gives the exchange 39¼d.

Thus Spain, instead of getting 36d. for the Dollar of Exchange, received 39¼d. and, therefore, gained above 8 per cent. by the remittance of Dollars to London, and considerable advantages were likewise made by the circulation of Bills through the several places on the Continent. Time was also gained for the payment of the subsidy; and the course of Exchange, instead of being turned against Spain, as it must have been by direct remittances, was rather turned in her favour by this circular method of operation.

PAR OF EXCHANGE.

As the Par of Exchange has been already explained under various views, (p. 13,) it remains here to show how the intrinsic Par is computed; which is exemplified between London and the principal trading places of Europe by comparing gold with gold, and silver with silver, which may be done either from the Mint Regulations of each place, or from Assays such as are contained in the Tables of Gold and Silver Coins in this Volume.

In computing the Par of Exchange by the Chain Rule the *certain money* should be the leading term, or first consequent, and the *uncertain money* the term of demand, or last consequent, as in the following examples.

LONDON AND AMSTERDAM.

Required the Par of Exchange between London and Amsterdam resulting from the new 10 Florin Piece, weighing 6,729 Grammes $\frac{9}{10}$ fine, and the British Sovereign, or 20 Shilling Piece? Here the latter is the *certain* and the former the *uncertain* money.

		1 Pound Sterling.
1 Pound Sterling	=	240 Pence.
934½ Pence	=	1 Ounce Standard.
12 Ounces Standard	=	11 Ounces fine Gold.
1 Ounce	=	480 Grains.
15434 Grains	=	1000 Grammes.
6,729 Grammes × $\frac{9}{10}$	=	10 Florins.

Result, 12 Florins 9 Cents. for £1 Sterling, or 40 Shillings 3 Pence Flemish.

The Par of Exchange may be found with less labour than by the above method from Tables of Coins. Thus, in the following Table of Gold Coins it will be seen that the 10 Florin Piece contains 93,46 Grains, and the Sovereign 113 Grains of fine Gold:—then say,

	Gr.		Fl.		Gr.		Fr.	Cent.	
As	93,46	:	1	: :	113	:	12	09	as above.

LONDON AND AMSTERDAM.—Silver.

Required the Par of Exchange between London and Amsterdam, resulting from a comparison of the new Silver Florin and the Pound Sterling?

By a reference to the Table of Coins it will be seen that the Florin contains 148,38 Grains of fine Silver, and the Pound 1718,7 Grains;—hence,

	Gr.		Fl.		Gr.		Fl.
As	148,38	:	1	: :	1718,7	:	11,58

Thus the Par in silver is 11 Florins 58 Cents. for the Pound Sterling, which differs about 4½ per cent. from the gold Par:—they might, however, be made to agree by valuing the English silver at 5s. 3½d. per ounce, instead of 5s. 2d.

LONDON AND HAMBURGH.—Gold.

Required the Par of Exchange resulting from a comparison of the Hamburgh Ducat containing 53 English Grains of pure Gold, and the Sovereign containing 113 Grains, supposing that the Ducat equals 6 Marks Banco, or 16 Shillings Flemish.

	Gr.		Sh.		Gr.		Sh.	d.
As	53	:	16	: :	113	:	34	1,35

Thus the gold Par is 34 Shillings 1,35 Pence Flemish per £1 Sterling; but, from the fluctuating value of the Ducat, the Par cannot be considered permanent: by taking the average price of the Ducat for the last four years, which is 6¼ Marks, the Par would be 35 Shillings 6 Pence Flemish per Pound Sterling.

LONDON AND HAMBURGH.—SILVER.

The Cologne Mark of fine Silver is generally worth 27⅝ Marks Banco, and 60 Marks Cologne weight are equal to 451 ounces Troy;—what is the Par between London and Hamburgh Banco in Silver?

		1	Pound Sterling.
1	Pound Sterling	= 240	Pence.
62	Pence	= 1	Ounce Standard.
40	Ounces Standard	= 37	Ounces fine Silver.
451	Ounces	= 60	Cologne Marks.
1	Cologne Mark fine	= 27⅝	Marks Banco.
3	Marks Banco	= 8	Shillings Flemish Banco.

Reduced, gives 35s. 1d. Flemish Banco, per £ sterling.

But on account of the fluctuations in the prices of the Ducat and of the Mark of fine silver, no permanent Par can be determined between London and Hamburgh.

LONDON AND PARIS.—GOLD.

Required the Par of Exchange between London and Paris, resulting from the Mint Regulations, as stated under the articles France and London, vol. i.

		1	Pound Sterling.
1	Pound Sterling	= 240	Pence.
62	Pence	= 1	Ounce Standard.
40	Ounces Standard	= 37	Ounces fine Silver.
1	Ounce	= 480	Grains.
15434	Grains	= 1	Kilogramme.
1	Kilogramme	= 3444	Francs 44 Cen. 444.

Reduced, gives the Pound Sterling equal to 25 Francs 22 Centimes.

The Par deduced from the Table of Assays is 4 Centimes more than the above:—

	Gr.		Fr.		Gr.		Fr.	Cen.
For as	89,5	:	20	: :	113	:	25	26

See Table of Gold Coins.

LONDON AND PARIS.—Silver.

Required the Par of Exchange between England and France, resulting from the Mint Regulations.

		1 Pound Sterling.
1 Pound Sterling	=	240 Pence.
62 Pence	=	1 Ounce Standard.
40 Ounces Standard	=	37 Ounces fine.
1 Ounce fine	=	480 Grains.
15434 Grains	=	1 Kilogramme.
1 Kilogramme	=	222 Francs 222 Cen. 222.

Reduced, gives the Pound Sterling equal to 24 Francs 73 Centimes.

If English Silver be valued at 63⅛ the Pars of both metals will be alike.

The Par in Silver from the Table of Assays is 24,91.

LONDON AND GENOA.—Gold.

The new gold Genovina contains 357,7 English grains of fine gold, and it passes for 96 Lire fuori Banco ;—what is the Par between London and Genoa in gold ?

		1 Pezza.
1 Pezza	=	5¾ Lire.
96 Lire	=	1 Genovina.
1 Genovina	=	357,7 Grains of fine Gold.
480 Grains	=	1 Ounce.
11 Ounces fine Gold	=	12 Ounces Standard.
1 Ounce Standard	=	934½ Pence Sterling.

Reduced, gives 45½d. Sterling per Pezza.

LONDON AND GENOA.—Silver.

The silver Scudo contains 457½ English grains of fine silver, and it passes for 8 Lire fuori Banco ;—what is the Par between London and Genoa in silver ?

		1 Pezza.
1 Pezza	=	5¾ Lire.
8 Lire	=	457½ Grains of fine Silver.
480 Grains	=	1 Ounce.
37 Ounces fine Silver	=	40 Ounces Standard.
1 Ounce	=	62 Pence Sterling.

Reduced, gives 45,92d. Sterling per Pezza.

LONDON AND LEGHORN.—Gold.

The Sequin contains 53,6 English grains of fine gold, and it passes for $13\frac{1}{3}$ Lire Moneta Buona;—what is the Par between London and Leghorn in gold?

		1 Pezza.
1 Pezza	=	$5\frac{3}{4}$ Lire Moneta Buona.
$13\frac{1}{3}$ Lire Moneta Buona	=	1 Sequin.
1 Sequin	=	53,6 Grains of fine Gold.
480 Grains	=	1 Ounce.
11 Ounces fine Gold	=	12 Ounces Standard.
1 Ounce Standard	=	$934\frac{1}{2}$ Pence Sterling.

Reduced, gives 49,09d. Sterling per Pezza.

LONDON AND LEGHORN.—Silver.

The Silver Scudo, or Leopoldone, contains 384 English grains of fine silver, and it passes for $6\frac{1}{3}$ Lire Moneta Buona;—what is the Par between London and Leghorn in silver?

		1 Pezza.
1 Pezza	=	$5\frac{3}{4}$ Lire Moneta Buona.
$6\frac{1}{3}$ Lire Moneta Buona	=	1 Scudo.
1 Scudo	=	384 Grains of fine Silver.
480 Grains	=	1 Ounce.
37 Ounces fine Silver	=	40 Ounces Standard.
1 Ounce Standard	=	62 Pence Sterling.

Reduced, gives $46\frac{1}{4}$d. Sterling per Pezza.

LONDON AND SPAIN.—Gold.

The Quadruple of 1772 contains 372 English grains of fine gold, and it passes for 320 Reals Vellon;—what is the Par between London and Spain in gold?

		1 Dollar of Plate.
1 Dollar of Plate	=	8 Reals of Plate.
17 Reals of Plate	=	32 Reals Vellon.
320 Reals Vellon	=	1 Quadruple.
1 Quadruple	=	372 Grains of fine Gold.
480 Grains	=	1 Ounce.
11 Ounces fine Gold	=	12 Ounces Standard.
1 Ounce Standard	=	$934\frac{1}{2}$ Pence Sterling.

Reduced, gives 37,16d. sterling per Dollar of Plate.

LONDON AND SPAIN.—Silver.

The Dollar contains 371 English grains of fine silver, and it passes for 20 Reals Vellon; —what is the Par between London and Spain in silver?

		1 Dollar of Plate.
1 Dollar of Plate	=	8 Reals of Plate.
17 Reals of Plate	=	32 Reals Vellon.
20 Reals Vellon	=	1 Hard Dollar.
1 Hard Dollar	=	371 Grains of fine Silver.
480 Grains	=	1 Ounce.
37 Ounces fine Silver	=	40 Ounces Standard.
1 Ounce Standard	=	62 Pence Sterling.

Reduced, gives 39d. Sterling per Dollar of Plate.

LONDON AND LISBON.—Gold.

The piece of 6400 Rees contains 203 English grains of fine gold;—what is the Par between London and Lisbon in gold?

		1000 Rees.
6400 Rees	=	203 Grains of fine Gold.
480 Grains	=	1 Ounce.
11 Ounces fine Gold	=	12 Ounces Standard Gold.
1 Ounce Standard	=	934½ Pence Sterling.

Reduced, gives 67,36d. Sterling per Milree.

According to the above methods, the other Pars, which are contained in the following Table, have been computed; but the statements and operations are left for the exercise of the learner.

It has been already shown (page 141) that when the quantity of pure metal in the monies of exchange is known, the Par is found by division; and it may be also found, by a similar operation, from the Table of Monies of Account, (page 149,) when the monies of exchange are of the same denomination. Thus, to find the Par between France and England, the Franc is worth 9,7 Pence in Silver, and 9,52 Pence in Gold, and therefore, 240 divided by these sums respectively will give the Pars in Gold and Silver as before.

Suppose it were required to find the Par between France and Spain, that is, how many Francs should be given for the Doubloon of Exchange of 4 Piastres? The Sterling value of the Doubloon, according to Table III. is 156 Pence, and this divided by 9,7 (the sterling value of the Franc) will give 16 Francs 19 Centimes, which is the Silver Par between those two countries. By the same method, the Par in Gold will be found to be 15 Francs 60 Centimes.

Thus, the monies of exchange may be found in the foregoing quotations, p. 19 to 103, and their values in the following Tables, by which the Pars may always be determined with sufficient accuracy by a simple operation as above.

TABLE I.

A Table *of the* Par of Exchange *between England and the principal Places in Lloyd's List; computed from the intrinsic Value of their Coins, by comparing Gold with Gold and Silver with Silver, according to their Mint Regulations, and to Assays made at the London and Paris Mints, valuing English Gold at £3 17s. 10½d. per Oz. Standard, and English Silver at 5s. 2d. per Oz. Standard.*

	GOLD.		SILVER.		EXPLANATIONS.
	Mint Regulations.	Assays.	Mint Regulations.	Assays.	
Amsterdam, in Flemish..	40 3	——	38,6	——	Shillings and Pence Flem. per £1 Sterl.
Ditto, in Florins	12 09	——	11,58	——	Florins and Cents. per £1 Sterling.
Hamburgh	34 3,5	34 1,5	35 1	35 1,3	Shillings and Pence Flem. per £1 Sterl.
Paris	25 22	25 26	24 75	24 91	Francs and Centimes per £1 Sterling.
Madrid	37,3	37,2	39,2	39 0	Pence Sterling per Piastre.
Lisbon................	67,4	67,5	——	——	Pence Sterling per Milree.
Leghorn	49,1	49,0	46,46	46,5	Pence Sterling per Pezza.
Genoa	45,5	45,5	45,92	45,92	Pence Sterling per Pezza fuori Banco.
Naples................	41,2	——	41,2	——	Pence Sterling per Ducat.
——otherwise......	582	——	582	——	Grains per £1 Sterling.
Venice................	46,3	46,0	47,5	49,0	Lire Piccole per £1 Sterling.
——otherwise......	23,44	23	24,30	25,07	Italian Livres per £1 Sterling.

These Tables (I. and II.) were originally computed by the author of this work, in 1810, by order of the Bullion-Committee of the House of Commons, and are printed in the Appendix to their Report.

They have been likewise inserted in that of the House of Lords, in 1819, with revisions which became necessary on account of recent alterations in the monies of Holland and Naples.

A further revision is now made in the Par of Exchange between England and France, in consequence of the error lately discovered in their relative weights; as explained vol. i. pp. 135 and 140.

This correction is two Centimes per Pound sterling in favour of England.

TABLE II.

THE RELATIVE VALUE OF GOLD AND SILVER *in the principal Trading Places of the World; computed from the proportional Quantity of pure Metal in their principal Coins, and the legal or current Price of those Coins respectively.*

	By Mint Regulations.	By Assays.	Names of the Coins from which the Proportions are taken.
England, By Old Coinage	15,2096 to 1	Proved correct by the Trials of the Pix.	Per Guinea and Old Shilling.
By New Coinage	14,2878 to 1		Per Sovereign and New Shilling.
Amsterdam........	15,8735 to 1	———	Per 10 Guilder Piece decreed in 1816, and Silver Florin of the same Date.
Hamburgh........	15 to 1 nearly	14,83 to 1	Per Ducato reckoned at 6 Marks Banco and Rixdollar.
Paris	15,5 to 1	15,5 to 1	Per 20 Franc Piece and 5 Franc Piece.
Madrid	16 to 1	15,85 / 16,46 to 1	Per Doubloon and Dollar of different Coinages.
Lisbon............	13,56 to 1	13,33 to 1	Per Joannese and New Silver Crusado.
Leghorn	14,65 to 1	14,32 to 1	Per Ruspono and Francescone.
Genoa............	15,34 to 1	15,35 to 1	Per Genovina and Scudo.
Naples............	15,21 to 1	———	Per Oncetta and Ducato. (Coinage of 1818.)
Venice............	15 to 1 nearly	14,35 to 1	Per Sequin and Ducat.
Petersburgh	15 to 1 nearly	15,25 to 1	Per Ducat and Ruble.
United States......	15 to 1	15,94 to 1	Per Eagle and Dollar.
Bengal............	14,857 to 1	14,827 to 1	Per Gold Mohur and Sicca Rupee.
Madras	13,872 to 1	13,857 to 1	Per Star Pagoda and Current Rupee.
Bombay	15 to 1	15 to 1	Per Gold Rupee and Silver Rupee.
China	14,25 to 1	———	Per Tale of Gold, and the Average Price of Spanish Dollars.

The foregoing Table may be computed by the Chain Rule, in the following manner.

Required the relative proportion between Gold and Silver in the English Coins, according to the Mint Regulations both of the Old and New System?

The question is, to compare the value of any certain quantity, suppose an ounce of pure Gold, with an ounce of pure Silver, at the Mint Price.

Old System.

		1 Ounce pure Gold.
11 Ounces pure	=	12 Ounces Standard.
1 Ounce Standard	=	$934\frac{1}{2}$ Pence.
62 Pence	=	1 Ounce Standard Silver.
40 Ounces Standard	=	37 Ounces Pure.

Reduced, gives $15\frac{2850}{13640}$. Thus Gold, decimally expressed, is to Silver as 15,2096 to 1.

New System.

		1 Ounce Pure Gold.
11 Ounces Pure	=	12 Ounces Standard.
1 Ounce Standard	=	$934\frac{1}{2}$ Pence.
66 Pence	=	1 Ounce Standard Silver.
40 Ounces Standard	=	37 Pure.

Reduced, gives $14\frac{1393}{4840}$. Thus Gold, decimally expressed, is to Silver as 14,2878 to 1.

The operation is more simple when the rate of fineness of both metals is expressed in the same manner. Thus, in the coinage of France, the 20 Franc Piece in Gold weighs 6,4516 Grammes in pure Gold, and 20 Francs in Silver weigh 100 Grammes: hence, the latter divided by the former will give 15,5, as in the Table, p. 147.

When the fineness differs in expression, the comparison may be made from the quantity of pure Gold and of pure Silver in any particular sum, found either by the Mint Regulations or by Assays. Thus, the English Sovereign contains 113 Grains of fine Gold; and 20 Shillings (new coinage) 1614,54 Grains of fine Silver: hence, the latter divided by the former will give the relative value very nearly as above.

MONIES OF ACCOUNT.

In the following Table of Monies of Account it may be observed that some of these monies are real coins, the value of which may be computed from the Mint Regulations or from Assays; but when they are imaginary monies, which is generally the case, their value must be found by their established proportion to real coins.

TABLE OF MONIES OF ACCOUNT.

TABLE III.

Containing the Value of the Monies of Account of different Places, (expressed in Pence Sterling and Decimals of Pence,) according to the Mint Price both of Gold and Silver in England; that is, £3 17s. 10½d. per Oz. Standard for Gold, and 5s. 2d. per Oz. Standard for Silver. (*See* vol. i. p. 217)

		Value in Silver. *d.*		Value in Gold. *d.*
AIX LA CHAPELLE..	Rixdollar current	31, 40	....	31, 43
ALICANT	Libra or Peso	39, 40	....	37, 38
AMSTERDAM	Rixdollar	52, 54	....	variable*
	Florin (Old)	21,	....	ditto
	Florin (New)	20, 72	....	ditto
	Pound Flemish	124, 32	....	ditto
ANTWERP	Pound Flemish (money of exchange)	123, 25	....	123, 87
	Florin (money of exchange)	20, 54	....	20, 64
	Pound Flemish current	105, 65	....	106, 18
	Florin current	17, 60	....	17, 70
ARRAGON..........	Libra Jaquesa	49, 25	....	46, 75
AUGSBURG	Florin Giro, or money of exchange	32,	....	31, 83
	Florin current	25, 20	....	25, 07
BARCELONA	Libra Catalan	28, 14	....	26, 70
BASIL	Rixdollar, or Ecu of exchange	47, 27	....	47,
	Rixdollar current	42, 45	....	42, 20
BERGAMO	Scudo of 7 Lire	35, 67	....	36, 50
BERLIN	Pound Banco	47, 25	....	variable
	Rixdollar current	36,	....	ditto
	Rixdollar in Fredericks	———†	....	39, 68

* In the places marked *variable*, the price of the coins is not fixed; and, therefore, the intrinsic value in gold of the monies of account cannot be ascertained for any length of time.

† Where the columns are marked with a dash, it is to be understood that there is no coin in the metal of that column by which the monies of account can be computed.

		Value in Silver.			Value in Gold.	
		d.			d.	
BERN	Ecu of 3 Livres	42,	64	....	42,	90
	Crown of 25 Batzen	35,	53	....	35,	75
BOLOGNA	Lira corrente	10,	86	....	10,	62
	Lira, money of exchange	11,	12	....	10,	89
BOLSANO	Florin Giro, or money of exchange	33,	26	....	33,	08
	Florin moneta lunga, or currency	25,	20	....	25,	06
BREMEN	Rixdollar current	37,	80	....	variable	
	Rixdollar in Carl d'ors	———		....	39,	68
CANARY ISLANDS	Real current	3,	95	....	3,	66
CASSEL	Rixdollar current	37,	80	....	variable	
COLOGNE	Rixdollar specie of 80 Albuses	31,	38	....	ditto	
	Rixdollar current of 78 Albuses	30,	60	....	ditto	
CONSTANTINOPLE	Piastre, or Dollar, 1819	9,	45	....	uncertain	
DANTZIC	Gulden or Florin	9,		....	9,	
DENMARK	Rixdollar specie	54,	72	....	———	
	Rixdollar Sundish specie	53,	21	....	———	
	Rixdollar Crown money	48,	37	....	———	
	Rixdollar Danish currency	44,	27	....	44,	88
	Rixdollar Holstein currency	43,	78	....	44,	16
ENGLAND	Pound Sterling	240,		....	240,	
FLORENCE	Lira	8,	12	....	8,	53
	Ducat, or Crown current	56,	84	....	59,	71
	Scudo d'oro, or Gold Crown	———		....	63,	97
FRANCE	Livre Tournois	9,	58	....	9,	40
	Franc (new system)	9,	70	....	9,	52
FRANCFORT	Rixdollar, Convention money	37,	80	....	37,	65
	Rixdollar Muntze, or in small coins	31,	50	....	———	
GENEVA	Livre current	16,	13	....	16,	93
	Florin	4,	60	....	4,	84
GENOA	Lira fuori Banco	7,	99	....	7,	83
	Pezza, or Dollar of exchange	45,	92	....	45,	50
	Scudo di cambio, or Crown of exchange	36,	75	....	36,	02
	Scudo d'oro marche	85,	49	....	83,	77

		Value in Silver.			Value in Gold.	
		d.			d.	
GERMANY	Rixdollar current	37,	80	....	variable	
	Rixdollar specie	50,	40	....	ditto	
	Florin of the Empire	25,	20	....	ditto	
	Rixdollar Muntze	31,	50	....	ditto	
	Florin Muntze	21,		....	ditto	
HAMBURGH	Mark Banco (at a medium)	18,	22	....	variable	
	Pound Flemish Banco	136,	65	....	ditto	
	Mark current	14,	82	....	ditto	
	Pound Flemish current	111,	15	....	ditto	
HANOVER	Rixdollar, in cash	42,		....	42,	26
	Rixdollar, gold value	39,		....	39,	24
IRELAND	Pound Irish	221,	54	....	221,	54
KONIGSBERG	Gulden or Florin	12,		....	variable	
LEGHORN	Pezza of 8 Reals	46,	25	....	49,	16
	Lira moneta buona	8,	13	....	8,	55
	Lira moneta lunga	7,	79	....	8,	19
LEIPSIC	Rixdollar Convention money	37,	80	....	variable	
	Rixdollar in Louis d'ors or Fredericks	———		....	39,	68
LUCCA	Lira	7,	40	....	7,	77
	Scudo d'oro	55,	50	....	58,	27
	Scudo corrente	51,	80	....	54,	39
MALTA	Scudo, or Crown	21,	32	....	23,	34
MILAN	Lira Imperiale	10,	41	....	10,	53
	Lira corrente	7,	45	....	7,	30
	Scudo Imperiale	60,	90	....	61,	60
	Scudo corrente	42,	32	....	42,	78
MODENA	Lira	3,	72	....	33,	15
MUNICH	Gulden or Florin	21,		....	21,	28
NANCY	Livre (money of Lorraine)	7,	38	....	7,	26
NAPLES	Ducato di regno	41,	20	....	uncertain	
NAVARRE	Real	4,	90	....	4,	67
	Libra	8,	20	....	7,	79
NEUFCHATEL	Livre Tournois	13,	63	....	13,	40
	Livre foible	5,	45	....	5,	36

		Value in Silver.			Value in Gold.	
		d.			*d.*	
Novi	Scudo d'oro marche	85,	49	....	83,	77
Parma	Lira	2,	35	....	2,	30
Persia	Toman of 100 Mamoodis	287,	60	....	———	
Poland	Gulden or Florin	6,	03	....	6,	27
Portugal	Milree	uncertain		....	67,	34
	Old Crusado	uncertain		....	26,	94
Prague	*(See Vienna.)*					
Riga	Rixdollar Alberts	52,	54	....	variable	
	Rixdollar currency, (agio at 40 per cent.)	37,	53	....	ditto	
Rome	Scudo, or Crown	52,	05	....	51,	63
	Scudo di Stampa d'oro	79,	37	....	78,	73
Russia	Ruble	variable				
St. Gall	Florin, money of exchange	27,	44	....	variable	
	Florin current	22,	76	....	ditto	
St. Remo	Lira	8,	46	....	8,	90
Sardinia	Lira	18,	21	....	18,	82
Sicily	Ounce	123,	54	....	124,	80
	Scudo, or Crown	49,	02	....	49,	92
Spain	Real of old plate	4,	88	....	4,	57
	Real of new plate	5,	18	....	4,	86
	Real of Mexican plate	6,	48	....	6,	07
	Real Vellon	2,	59	....	2,	43
	Dollar of old plate or of exchange	39,		....	37,	30
Stralsund	Rixdollar of account	28,	35	....	variable	
	Pomeranian Gulden	14,	18	....	ditto	
Strasburg	Livre and Franc *(see France.)*					
	Florin	19,	08	....	18,	76
Sweden	Rixdollar	55,	41	....	56,	43
Switzerland	Franc (new system)	22,	14	....	———	
Trieste	Florin, Austrian currency	25,	20	....	25,	05
	Lira, Trieste currency	4,	76	....	4,	73
	Lira di Piazza	4,	65	....	4,	63
Turin	Lira	11,	28	....	11,	23
Valencia	Libra	39,	45	....	36,	59

		Value in Silver.			Value in Gold.
		d.			*d.*
VENICE	Lira piccola (in the old coins)	5,	07	....	variable
	Lira piccola (in the coins introduced by the Austrians)	4,	25	....	ditto
VIENNA	Florin	25,	20	....	25, 05
ZANTE............	Lira	4,	06	....	variable
ZURICH	Florin, money of exchange	25,	85	....	ditto
	Florin current	23,	50	....	ditto

The foregoing Table has been computed from the proportion which the monies of account bear to the coins of each place respectively, valued according to the Mint Regulations, as stated in the first volume of this work. Thus, the intrinsic par of exchange may be calculated both in gold and silver, where the monies of exchange are the same as those of account; but dealers in bills, coin, and bullion generally prefer computations from actual assays, such as are given in the following Tables.

TABLES OF COINS FROM ASSAYS.

The first of the following Tables was computed under the direction of Sir Isaac Newton, in 1717, when he was Master of the Mint, and it served long as a Rule or Standard for Bullion and Exchange Merchants; but, however correct this Table might have originally been, it is no longer to be depended on, as many of the Coins are out of circulation, while others have been considerably altered; and it may be further remarked, that the art of assaying Metals, and even of weighing accurately, has been much improved since the above period.

Although these Assays are now become, in a great measure, obsolete, yet it is thought proper to insert them in this Work by way of introduction to the New Tables which follow, and which may be considered as a revision of Sir Isaac Newton's Tables, and a continuation of his plan.

N.B. In the Assay Column in the following Tables, B. means better, and W. worse than the English Standard. Thus, in the Gold Table, B. 1 2 means 1 Carat 2 Grains better than English standard; that is, 23 Carats 2 Grains fine: and W. 0 1½ means 1½ Grain worse than the English standard, that is, 21 Carats 2½ Grains fine.

Again, in the Silver Table, B. 7 Dwt. means 11 Oz. 9 Dwt. fine, and W. 3 Dwt. is 10 Oz. 19 Dwt. fine. For the English Standards, see vol. i. p. 217.

TABLE IV.

Sir Isaac Newton's Assays, Weights, and Values of most Foreign Silver and Gold Coins, actually made at the London Mint, by Order of the Privy Council, before the Year 1717. *First published in* 1719, *and re-published, by Authority, in* 1740.

FOREIGN SILVER COINS.	Assay. dw.	Weight. dw. gr.	Stand. Weight. dw. gr. mi.	Value. d.
The Piastre of Spain, or Seville Piece of 8 Reals, now reduced to 10..	W. 1	17 12	17 10 2	54
The New Seville Piece of Eight..........................	W. 1½	14	13 21 15	43.11
The Mexico Piece of Eight..............................	W. 1	17 10$\frac{5}{9}$	17 8 14	53.83
The Pillar Piece of Eight..............................	Stand.	17 9	17 9	53.87
The Peru Piece of Eight, coarser but of uncertain allay				
The Old Ecu of France, or Piece of 60 Sols Tournois	W. 1	17 12	17 10 2	54
The New Ecu, or Piece of 5 Livres, or 100 Sols................	W. 1½	19 14½	19 11 12	60.39
The Crusado of Portugal, or Ducat worth 400 Rees, now marked and raised to 480 Rees	W. 2	11 4	11 1 13	34.31
The Patacks, or Patagons of Portugal, worth 500 Rees, now marked and raised to 600				
The Ducatoon of Flanders, or Piece of 60 Sols or Patars	B. 4½	20 22	21 8 2	66.15
The Patagon of Flanders, or Cross Dollar, or Piece of 48 Patars..	W. 12	18 1	17 1 13	52.91
The Ducatoon of Holland, or Piece of 63 Stivers	B. 3	20 21	21 3 15	65.59
The Patagon Legdollar, or Rixdollar of Holland, or Piece of 50 Stivers..	W. 14	18	16 20 17	52.28
The Three Guilder Piece of Holland, or Piece of 60 Stivers......	W. 2	20 8	20 3 12	62.46
The Guilder, Florin, or Piece of 20 Stivers..................	W. 2	6 18½	6 17 1	20.08
The Ten Shilling Piece of Zeland, or Piece of 60 Stivers	W. 2	20 6	20 1 13	62.21
The Lion Dollar of Holland, or ⅔ of the Ducatoon	W. 44	17 14	14 2 7	43.07
The Ducatoon of Cologne.................................	B. 3	20 18	21 — 15	65.02
The Rixdollar, or Patagon of Cologne	W. 13	18	16 22 14	52.53
The Rixdollar, or Patagon of the Bishop of Liege..............	W. 12	17 22½	16 22 5	55.48
The Rixdollar of Mentz	W. 6½	18 8	17 19 18	55.27
The Rixdollar of Francfort................................	W. 9	18 8	17 14 4	54.53
The Rixdollar of the Elector Palatine of the Rhine and Bavaria before 1620..	—	18 5		
The Rixdollar of Nuremberg	W. 6	18 10	17 22 1	55.55
The Old Rixdollar of Lunemburg	W. 10	18 11	17 15 2	54.65
The Old Rixdollar of Hanover	W. 8	18 12	17 20 2	55.03
The Double Gulden of the Elector of Hanover.................	W. 7	18 18	18 3 16	56.29
The Gulden of the Elector of Hanover, or Piece of ⅔	B. 17½	8 10	9 1 18	28.14
The Half Gulden of the Elector of Hanover, or Piece of ⅓	B. 17½	4 5	4 12 19	14.07
The Gulden of the Duke of Zell, or Piece of 16 Gute Groshen ..	W. 43	11 2	8 22 10	27.07
The Gulden of the Bishop of Hildesheim, or Piece of 24 Marien Grosh, now raised to 26..........................	W. 40½	11 22	9 17 17	30.21
The Rixdollar of Magdeburgh..............................	W. 10	18 12	17 16 1	54.27
The Gulden or Guilder of Magdeburgh	W. 44	11 14	9 6	28.67
The Old Rixdollar of the Elector of Brandenburgh.............	W. 9	18 13	17 19 1	55.17
The Old Gulden of Brandenburgh, now raised from 24 to 26 Marien Grosh	W. 43	12 4	9 19 9	30.41
The Gulden of Brandenburgh, or Piece of ⅔..................	W. 43	11 3	8 23 6	27.81
The Half Gulden of Brandenburgh, or Piece of ⅓	W. 43	5 13	4 11 14	13.09
The Gulden of the Elector of Saxony, or Piece of ⅔	W. 41	11 3	9 1 14	28.12

FOREIGN SILVER COINS.	Assay. dw.	Weight. dw.	gr.	Stand. Weight. dw.	gr.	mi.	Value. d.
The Old Bank Dollar of Hamburgh	W. 8	18	9	17	17	4	54.92
The Old Rixdollar of Lubec	W. $8\frac{1}{2}$	18	16	17	22	17	55.54
The Four Mark Piece of Denmark of coarser allay	W. 61	14	8	10	9	10	32.23
The Four Mark Piece of Denmark of finer allay	W. 21	11	$13\frac{1}{2}$	10	11	5	32.45
The Eight Mark Piece of Sweden	Stand.	20		20			62
The Four Mark Piece of Sweden	W. 58	13	12	9	23	7	30.92
The Two Mark Piece of Sweden	W.	6	19				
The Old Dollar of Dantzic	W. $10\frac{1}{2}$	18	9	17	12	4	54.27
The Old Rixdollar of Thorn near Dantzic	W. 12	18	$8\frac{1}{2}$	17	8	15	53.85
The Rixdollar of Sigismund III. and Vladislaus IV. Kings of Poland	W. 10	18	9	17	13	14	54.04
The Rixdollar of the late Emperor Leopold	W. $10\frac{1}{2}$	18	9	17	12	4	54.27
The Rixdollar of his Predecessor Ferdinand III.	W. $10\frac{1}{2}$	18	9	17	12	4	54.27
The Rixdollar of Ferdinand, Archduke of Austria	W. $10\frac{1}{2}$	18	5	17	8	7	53.78
The Rixdollar of Basil	W. $7\frac{1}{2}$	18	$18\frac{1}{2}$	18	3	6	56.24
The Rixdollar of Zune	W. 13	18	1	16	23	13	52.65
The Old Ducat of Venice, with the words *Ducatus Venetus* upon it, a Piece of 6 Old Livres, afterwards raised, I think, to 6 Livres 4 Sols de Piccoli	W. $23\frac{1}{2}$	14	15	13	1	17	40.50
The Half Ducat	W. $23\frac{1}{2}$	7	$7\frac{1}{2}$	6	12	8	20.25
The New Ducat, with the No. 124 upon it, signifying 124 Sols, or 6 Livres 4 Sols de Piccoli	—	18	2				
The Half thereof	—	9	1				
The Crusado, Crosaid, or St. Mark of Venice, with the No. 140 upon it, signifying 140 Sols, or 7 Livres de Piccoli	—	20	6				
The Half Crusado of the same form	—	10	3				
The Quarter Crusado of the same form	—	5	1				
Another Coin of Venice	W. 46	17	10	13	19	8	42.08
The Piece of two Jules	B. 6	3	15	3	17	7	11.05
The Ducat de Banco of Naples, or Piece of 5 Tarins, or 10 Carlins, or 100 Grains	W. 3	14	$0\frac{1}{4}$	13	1		40.43
The Half Ducat	W. 3	7	$0\frac{1}{8}$	6	12	10	20.21
The Tarin, or Fifth Part of the Ducat	W. 3	2	$19\frac{1}{4}$	2	14	12	8.09
The Carlin, or Tenth Part of the Ducat	W. 3	1	$9\frac{1}{2}$	1	7	6	4.04
The Escudi, Ecu, or Crown of Rome, or Piece of 10 Julios, or 100 Bayoches	—	20	$14\frac{1}{2}$				
The Teston of Rome, or Piece of 3 Julios	W. 1	5	$21\frac{1}{2}$	5	20	17	18.32
The Ducat of Florence and Leghorn, or Piece of 7 Lires, or $10\frac{1}{2}$ Julios	B. 8	20	3	20	20	6	64.62
The Julio of Rome		2	5				
The Piastre Ecu, or Crown of Ferdinand II. Duke of Tuscany	W. 1	17	12	17	10	2	54
The Piastre Ecu, or Crown of Cosmus III. present Duke of Tuscany, whose monies are about 4 per cent. lighter than those of his father's; this Piece is $8\frac{1}{2}$ Julios	W. 1	16	18	16	16	4	51.69
The Croisat of Genoa, or Piece of $7\frac{1}{2}$ Lires	B. 7	24	15	25	9	11	78.74
The Ecu d'Argent of Genoa, or Piece of 7 Lires 12 Sols							
The Piastre Ecu, or Crown of Milan	—	17	21				
The Philip of Milan, or Piece of 7 Livres	—	20	20				
The Livre, or 20 Sols Piece of Savoy	—	3	22				
The 10 Sols Piece of Savoy	—	1	23				
A Roupee	B. $16\frac{1}{2}$	7	10	7	23	4	24.07
A Gout Gulden, or Florin d'Or, a Dutch Coin of 28 Stivers	W. 75	12	19	8	11	5	26.26
Another Gout Gulden	W. 48	11	00	8	14	18	26.72
Another	W. 48	12		9	9	15	29.15

GOLD COINS UNWORN.	Assay.			Weight.		Stand. Weight			Value.	
		car.	gr.	dw.	gr.	dw.	gr.	mi.	s.	d.
The Old Louis d'Or	W.	0	$0\frac{1}{2}$	4	8	4	7	8	16	9.3
The Half and Quarter in proportion	W.	0	$0\frac{1}{2}$	2	4	2	3	14	8	5
The New Louis d'Or	W.	0	$1\frac{1}{2}$	5	$5\frac{2}{5}$	5	3	18	20	0.6
The Half and Quarter in proportion	W.	0	$1\frac{1}{2}$	2	$14\frac{7}{10}$	2	13	19	10	0.3
The Old Spanish Double Doubloon	W.	0	$0\frac{1}{2}$	17	8	17	5	·12	67	1.4
The Old Spanish Double Pistole	W.	0	$0\frac{1}{2}$	8	16	8	14	16	33	6.7
The Old Spanish Pistole	W.	0	$0\frac{1}{2}$	4	8	4	7	8	16	9.3
The New Seville Double Pistole	W.	0		8	$16\frac{1}{3}$					
The New Seville Pistole				4	$8\frac{1}{6}$					
The Half and Quarter in proportion.										
The Doppia Moeda, or Double Moeda of Portugal new coined	W.	0	$0\frac{1}{4}$	6	22	6	21	12	26	10.4
The Doppia Moeda as they come into England	W.	0	$0\frac{1}{4}$	6	$21\frac{3}{4}$	6	21	7	26	9.9
The Moeda of Portugal	W.	0	$0\frac{1}{4}$	3	11	3	10	16	13	5.1
The Half Moeda	W.	0	$0\frac{1}{4}$	1	$17\frac{1}{2}$	1	17	8	6	8.5
The Hungary Ducat	B.	1	2	2	$5\frac{2}{3}$	2	9	7	9	3.6
The Ducat of Holland, coined at Legem Imperii	B.	1	2	2	$5\frac{1}{2}$	2	9	3	9	3.2
The Ducat of Campen in Holland	B.	1	2	2	$5\frac{1}{2}$	2	9	3	9	3.2
The Ducat of the Bishop of Bamberg	B.	1	2	2	$5\frac{1}{2}$	2	9	3	9	3.2
The Double Ducat of the Duke of Hanover	B.	1	2	4	$10\frac{1}{2}$	4	17	9	18	4.8
The Ducat of the Duke of Hanover	B.	1	2	2	$5\frac{1}{4}$	2	8	18	9	2.7
The Ducat of Brandenburgh	B.	1	2	2	$5\frac{1}{2}$	2	9	3	9	3.2
The Ducat of Sweden	B.	1	2	2	$5\frac{1}{2}$	2	9	3	9	3.2
The Ducat of Denmark	B.	1	2	2	$5\frac{1}{2}$	2	9	3	9	3.2
The Ducat of Poland	B.	1	2	2	5	2	8	12	9	2.1
The Ducat of Transylvania	B.	1	$1\frac{1}{2}$	2	$4\frac{3}{4}$	2	7	6	8	11.6
The Sequen, Chequin, or Zacheen of Venice	B.	1	$3\frac{1}{2}$	2	$5\frac{3}{4}$	2	10	7	9	5.7
The Old Italian Pistole	W.	0	$0\frac{1}{4}$	4	$6\frac{3}{4}$	4	6	11	16	7.6
The Double Pistole of Pope Urban, 1634	—			8	$14\frac{1}{2}$					
The Half Pistole of Innocent II. 1685	—			2	4					
A Double Pistole of Placentia	—			8	10					
A Double Pistole of Genoa, 1621	—			8	16					
A Double Pistole of Milan	—			8	$13\frac{1}{2}$					
A Single Pistole of Milan	—			4	$6\frac{3}{4}$					
A Pistole of Savoy, 1675	—			4	$8\frac{1}{2}$					
Double Ducats of Castile, Genoa, Portugal, Florence, Hungary, and Venice	B.	1	$2\frac{1}{2}$	4	11	4	18	18	18	7.7
Single Ducats of the same places	B.	1	$2\frac{1}{2}$	2	$5\frac{1}{2}$	2	9	9	9	3.8
Double Ducats of several forms in Germany	B.	1	1	4	11	4	17	1	18	4
Single Ducats of the same places	B.	1	1	2	$5\frac{1}{2}$	2	8	$5\frac{1}{2}$	9	2
Double Ducats of Genoa	B.	1	2	4	11	4	18	6	18	6.5
Single Ducats of Genoa, Besançon, and Zurich	B.	1	2	2	$5\frac{1}{2}$	2	9	3	9	3.2
Pistole of Rome, Milan, Venice, Florence, Savoy, Genoa, Orange, Trevou, Besançon	W.	0	$0\frac{1}{4}$	4	6	4	5	17	16	6.7
A Barbary Ducat, with Arabic letters on both sides in square tablets, without any effigies or escutcheon	W.	2	$1\frac{1}{2}$	2	$16\frac{1}{4}$	2	9	6	9	3.5

NEW TABLE OF GOLD COINS.

TABLE V.

Containing the Assays, Weights, and Values of the principal Gold Coins of all Countries, computed according to the Mint Price of Gold in England, and from Assays made both at London and Paris, which have been found to verify each other.

The London Assays have been made by ROBERT BINGLEY, *Esq. F.R.S. the King's Assay Master of the Mint, and those at Paris by* PIERRE FREDERIC BONNEVILLE, *Essayeur du Commerce, as published in his elaborate Work on the Coins of all Nations.**

		Assay.		Weight.		Stan. Weight			Contents in Pure Gold.	Value in Sterling.	
		car.	gr.	dwt.	gr.	dwt.	gr.	mi	grains.	s.	d.
AMERICA	(*See Portugal, Spain, & United States.*)										
AUGSBURG	Ducat	B. 1	1¾	2	5¼	2	8	8	52, 1	9	2,64
AUSTRIAN DOMINIONS	Souverain	W. 0	0¼	3	14	3	13	15	78, 6	13	10,92
	Double Ducat	B. 1	2¾	4	12	4	20	5	106, 4	18	9,97
	Ducat	B. 1	2¾	2	6	2	10	2	53, 2	9	4,98
	Ducat Kremnitz, or Hungarian	B. 1	3	2	5¾	2	10	3	53, 3	9	5,91
BADEN	Ducat	B. 1	2¾	1	23½	2	3	2	46, 9	8	3,60
BASIL	Ducat	Stand.		2	4½	2	4	10	48, 1	8	6,14
	Pistole	W. 0	2½	4	22	4	18	13	105, 1	18	7,20
BAVARIA	Carolin	W. 3	2	6	5¼	5	5	10	115,	20	4,23
	Max d'or, or Maximilian	W. 3	2¼	4	4	3	14	0	77,	13	7,44
	Ducat	B. 1	2¼	2	5¾	2	19	11	52, 8	9	4,12
	Pistole (*See Manheim*)										
BERN	Ducat (Double, &c. in proportion)	B. 1	1¾	1	23	2	2	1	45, 9	8	1,48
	Pistole	W. 0	1½	4	21	4	19	0	105, 5	18	7,86
BOLOGNA	(*See Rome*)										
BRUNSWICK	Pistole (Double in proportion)	W. 0	1½	4	21¼	4	19	5	105, 7	18	8,48
	Carl d'or, before 1802, (Double in prop.)	W. 0	1½	4	6½	4	4	15	92, 5	16	4,44
	Carl d'or, since 1802, (Double in prop.)	W. 0	2½	4	6½	4	3	11	92,	16	3,38
	Ducat	B. 1	0½	2	5¾	2	8	9	51, 8	9	2
COLOGNE	Ducat	B. 1	2	2	5¾	2	9	8	52, 6	9	3,70
CONSTANTINOPLE	(*See Turkey.*)										
DENMARK	Ducat current	W. 0	3¾	2	0	1	21	19	42, 2	7	5,62
	Ducat specie	B. 1	2	2	5¾	2	9	8	52, 6	9	3,70
	Christian d'or	W. 0	1	4	7	4	5	16	93, 3	16	6,14
EAST INDIES	(*See* p. 161.)										
ENGLAND	Guinea	Stand.		5	9½	5	9	10	118, 7	21	0
	Half Guinea	Stand.		2	16¾	2	16	15	59, 3	10	6
	Seven Shilling Piece	Stand.		1	19	1	19	0	39, 6	7	0

* Specimens of all the foreign coins brought to London for commercial purposes have been supplied for this Work from the Bullion-Office, Bank of England, by order of the *Bank Directors*, and have been selected by *John Humble, Esq.* the chief of that Office, who also examined the Tables in their progress. It may likewise be added, that the Mint Reports of these commercial Coins are chiefly from Average Assays, and that all the computations have been carefully verified by different calculators.

		Assay.	Weight.		Stan. Weight			Contents in Pure Gold.	Value in Sterling.	
		car. gr.	dwt.	gr.	dwt.	gr.	mi.	grains.	s.	d.
ENGLAND	Sovereign	Stand.	5	3¼	5	3	5	113, 1	20	0
FLANDERS	*(See Austrian Dominions.)*									
FLORENCE	*(See Tuscany.)*									
FRANCE	Double Louis (coined before 1786)	W. 0 2	10	11	10	5	6	224, 9	39	9,64
	Louis	W. 0 2	5	5½	5	2	12	112, 4	19	10,71
	Demi Louis	W. 0 2	2	14¾	2	13	6	56, 2	9	11,38
	Double Louis (coined since 1786)	W. 0 1½	9	20	9	15	19	212, 6	37	7,53
	Louis	W. 0 1½	4	22	4	19	19	106, 3	18	9,75
	Double Napoleon, or Piece of 40 Francs	W. 0 1¾	8	7	8	3	0	179,	31	8,36
	Napoleon, or Piece of 20 Francs	W. 0 1¾	4	3½	4	1	10	89, 7	15	10,5
	New Louis (Double, &c.) the same as the Napoleon									
FRANCFORT ON THE MAINE	Ducat	B. 1 2½	2	5¾	2	9	14	52, 9	9	4,34
GENEVA	Pistole, Old	W. 0 2	4	7¼	4	4	18	92, 5	16	4,45
	Pistole, New	W. 0 0½	3	15¾	3	15	4	80,	14	1,9
GENOA	Doppia, or Pistole, (Pieces of 2, 4, &c. in proportion)	W. 0 1½	4	7½	4	5	14	93, 4	16	6,36
	Sequin	B. 1 3½	2	5¾	2	10	6	53, 4	9	5,41
	Genovina of 100 Lire (½ &c. in prop.)	W. 0 1	18	3	17	22	0	394, 2	69	9,20
	New Genovina, of 96 Lire or 4 Pistole Piece of the Ligurian Republic	W. 0 0½	16	4	16	1	15	357, 7	63	3,68
	Ditto of 48 Lire, (Pieces of 24 & 12 in proportion)	W. 0 0½	8	2	8	0	18	178, 9	31	7,95
HAMBURGH	Ducat (Double in proportion)	B. 1 2½	2	5¾	2	9	14	52, 9	9	4,35
HANOVER	George d'or	W. 0 1½	4	6½	4	5	3	92, 6	16	4,66
	Ducat	B. 1 3¼	2	5¾	2	10	3	53, 3	9	5,19
	Gold Florin (Double in proportion)	W. 3 0½	2	2	1	18	6	39,	6	10,83
HESSE CASSEL	Pistole	W. 0 2½	4	7¼	4	4	8	92,	16	3,39
	William d'or of 1815	W. 0 1¾	4	6½	4	4	9	92, 1	16	3,6
HESSE DARMSTADT	Carolin	W. 3 2	3	3	2	15	0	58,	10	3,18
	Ducat	B. 1 3	2	5¾	2	10	0	53, 2	9	4,98
HOLLAND	Double Ryder	Stand.	12	21	12	21	0	283, 2	50	1,46
	Ryder	Stand.	6	9	6	9	0	140, 2	24	9,75
	Half Ryder	Stand.	3	4½	3	4	10	70, 1	12	4,87
	Ducat	B. 1 2¼	2	5¾	2	9	12	52, 8	9	4,13
HUNGARY	*(See Austrian Dominions.)*									
JAPAN	*(See East Indies*, p. 161.)									
LEGHORN	*(See Tuscany.)*									
LEIPSIC	*(See Saxony.)*									
LIEGE	Ducat	B. 1 1½	2	5½	2	8	16	52, 3	9	3,07
LORRAINE	Leopold	W. 0 1	7	5¾	7	3	15	157, 4	27	10,28
	Francis	W. 0 1	4	7¼	4	6	1	93, 6	16	6,78
LUCCA	Pistole	W. 0 0¼	3	13¼	3	13	0	77, 9	13	9,44
MALTA	Double Louis	W. 1 3¼	10	16	9	18	18	215, 3	38	1,25
	Louis	W. 1 3	5	8	4	21	16	108,	19	1,37
	Demi Louis	W. 1 2¼	2	16	2	11	3	54, 5	9	7,75
MANHEIM	Carolin (½ and ¼ in proportion)	W. 3 2	6	4½	5	4	16	114, 4	20	2,96
	Pistole	W. 0 1½	4	6½	4	4	16	92, 3	16	4,02
	Ducat	B. 1 2¼	2	5¾	2	9	10	52, 8	9	4,13
MENTZ	Ducat	B. 1 2½	2	5¾	2	9	12	52, 9	9	4,34
MILAN	Sequin	B. 1 3	2	5¾	2	10	0	53, 2	9	4,98
	Doppia, or Pistole	W. 0 1	4	1½	4	0	8	88, 4	15	7,74

		Assay.		Weight.		Stan. Weight			Contents in Pure Gold.	Value in Sterling.	
		car.	gr.	dwt.	gr.	dwt.	gr.	mi.	grains.	s.	d.
Milan	40 Lire Piece of 1808	W. 0	1¾	8	8	8	4	0	179, 7	31	9,64
Naples	Six Ducat Piece of 1752	W. 1	0¼	5	16	5	9	8	118, 7	21	0,09
	Six Ducat Piece of 1767 and 1772	W. 1	2¾	5	18	5	7	14	116, 8	20	8,06
	Six Ducat Piece of 1783	W. 0	2¼	5	16	5	12	18	121, 9	21	6,89
	Four Ducat Piece, or Pistole, of 1752	W. 1	0¼	3	18¾	3	14	6	79, 2	14	0,20
	Four Ducat Piece of 1767 and 1770	W. 1	2¾	3	18¾	3	11	6	76, 8	13	7,10
	Two Ducat Piece, or Sequin, of 1762	W. 1	2¾	1	20¼	1	16	6	37, 4	6	7,42
	Three Ducat Piece, or Oncetta of 1818	B. 1	3½	2	10¼	2	15	1	58, 1	10	3,40
Netherlands	Souverain *(See Austrian Dominions)*										
	Gold Lion, or 14 Florin Piece	Stand.		5	7¾	5	7	16	117, 1	20	8,69
	Ten Florin Piece (1820)	W. 0	1¾	4	7¾	4	5	15	93, 2	16	5,93
Nuremberg	Ducat (Double, &c. in proportion)	B. 1	2	2	5¾	2	9	8	52, 6	9	3,71
Parma	Quadruple Pistole (Double in prop.)	W. 1	0	18	9	17	12	18	386,	68	3,78
	Pistole or Doppia of 1787	W. 0	3	4	14	4	10	4	97, 4	17	2,85
	Ditto of 1796	W. 1	0¼	4	14	4	8	14	95, 9	16	11,67
	Maria Theresa (1818)	W. 0	1¾	4	3½	4	1	10	89, 7	15	10,5
Persia	*(See East Indies,* p. 161.*)*										
Piedmont	Pistole or Doppia (1741 to 1785)	W. 0	1¼	6	4½	6	2	8	134, 2	23	9,01
	Pistole, coined since 1785 (½ &c. in prop.)	W. 0	1¼	5	20	5	17	0	125, 6	22	2,75
	Sequin (½ in proportion)	B. 1	2½	2	5¾	2	9	12	52, 9	9	4,34
	Carlino, coined before 1785	W. 0	1½	31	0½	30	11	14	670, 8	118	8,64
	Carlino, coined since 1785 (½ &c. in prop.)	W. 0	1¼	29	6	28	20	0	634, 4	112	3,33
	Piece of 20 Francs, called *Marengo*	W. 2	0	4	3¼	3	18	4	82, 7	14	7,63
Poland	Ducat	B. 1	2½	2	5¾	2	9	12	52, 9	9	4,34
Portugal	Dobraon of 24,000 Rees	Stand.		34	12	34	12	0	759,	134	3,96
	Meio Dobraon of 12,000 Rees	Stand.		17	6	17	6	0	379, 5	67	1,98
	Dobra of 12,800 Rees	Stand.		18	6	18	6	0	401, 5	71	0,70
	Joannese of 6400 Rees	W. 0	0¼	9	6½	9	5	16	203, 4	35	11,98
	Half Joannese of 3200 Rees	W. 0	0¼	4	15	4	14	12	101, 5	17	11,56
	Moidore or Lisbonnine (½, &c. in prop.)	Stand.		6	22	6	22	0	152, 2	26	11,24
	Piece of 16 Testoons, or 1600 Rees	W. 0	0⅜	2	6	2	5	14	49, 3	8	8,70
	Piece of 12 Testoons, or 1200 Rees	W. 0	0⅜	1	16¼	1	16	0	36, 7	6	5,94
	Piece of 8 Testoons	W. 0	0⅜	1	4½	1	4	6	26,	4	7,21
	Old Crusado of 400 Rees	W. 0	0½	0	15	0	14	18	13, 6	2	4,88
	New Crusado of 480 Rees	W. 0	0⅝	0	16¼	0	16	2	14, 8	2	7,43
	Milree (coined for the African Colonies, 1755)	Stand.		0	19¾	0	19	15	18, 1	3	2,44
Prussia	Ducat of 1748	B. 1	2½	2	5¾	2	9	14	52, 9	9	4,34
	Ducat of 1787	B. 1	2	2	5¾	2	9	6	52, 6	9	3,71
	Frederick (Double) of 1769	W. 0	1¾	8	14	8	9	18	185,	32	8,90
	Frederick (Single) of 1778	W. 0	1½	4	7	4	5	4	92, 8	16	5,08
	Frederick (Double) of 1800	W. 0	2	8	14	8	9	6	184, 5	32	7,84
	Frederick (Single) of 1800	W. 0	2	4	7	4	4	13	92, 2	16	3,42
Ratisbon	Four Ducat Piece	B. 1	2	8	21	9	11	0	77, 2	36	10,81
Rome	Doppia, or Pistole, of Pius VI.	W. 0	0¾	3	13	3	12	5	77, 2	13	7,59
	Ditto, of Pius VII. 1802 (½ &c. in prop.)	W. 0	1½	3	13	3	11	12	76, 6	13	6,68
	Zecchino, or Sequin, (coined before 1760)	B. 1	2	2	4½	2	8	0	51, 4	9	1,16
	Sequin (coined since 1760)	B. 1	3½	2	4½	2	9	0	52, 2	9	2,86
	Scudo of the Republic	W. 0	1¾	17	0¼	16	16	6	367,	64	11,43
Russia	Ducat of 1751	B. 1	1¼	2	5	2	8	4	51, 5	9	1,37
	Double Ducat of St. Andrew of 1756	B. 1	2½	4	10	4	17	16	104, 4	18	5,72
	Ducat of 1796	B. 1	2½	2	6	2	10	0	53, 2	9	4,98
	Ducat of 1763	B. 1	2	2	5¾	2	9	8	52, 6	9	3,71

		Assay.	Weight.		Stan. Weight.			Contents in Pure Gold.	Value in Sterling.	
		car. gr.	dwt.	gr.	dwt.	gr.	mi.	grains.	s.	d.
RUSSIA	Half Ducat of 1785	W. 0 $0\frac{1}{2}$	1	$14\frac{1}{2}$	1	14	6	35, 1	6	2,54
	Gold Ruble of 1756	Stand.	1	$0\frac{1}{2}$	1	0	10	22, 5	3	11,78
	Ditto of 1799	W. 0 $0\frac{1}{4}$	0	$18\frac{3}{4}$	0	18	14	17, 1	3	0,31
	Gold Póltin of 1777	Stand.		9	0	9	0	8, 2	1	5,41
	Imperial (coined before 1763)	Stand.	10	16	10	16	0	234, 7	41	6,45
	Imperial of 1763	Stand.	8	$9\frac{1}{2}$	8	9	10	184, 7	32	8,06
	Imperial of 1772	W. 0 $0\frac{1}{4}$	8	11	8	10	8	185, 5	32	9,96
	Half Imperial of 1780	W. 0 $0\frac{1}{4}$	4	$2\frac{1}{2}$	4	2	4	90,	15	11,14
	Imperial of 1801	B. 1 $2\frac{1}{4}$	7	$17\frac{1}{4}$	8	6	8	181, 9	32	2,31
	Half Imperial of 1801	B. 1 $2\frac{1}{4}$	3	$20\frac{1}{2}$	4	3	4	90, 9	16	1,05
	Ditto of 1818	B. 0 $0\frac{1}{8}$	4	$3\frac{1}{2}$	4	3	12	91, 3	16	1,98
ST. GALL	Ducat	B. 0 3	21	$20\frac{1}{2}$	22	15	2	497, 9	88	1,44
SALTZBURG	Ducat	B. 1 2	2	$5\frac{3}{4}$	2	9	8	52, 6	9	3,71
SARDINIA	Carlino ($\frac{1}{2}$ in proportion)	W. 0 $2\frac{3}{4}$	10	$7\frac{1}{2}$	9	23	16	219, 8	38	10
	Doppietta	W. 0 $2\frac{3}{4}$	2	$1\frac{1}{4}$	1	23	13	43, 7	7	8,81
SAXONY	Ducat of 1784	B. 1 2	2	$5\frac{3}{4}$	2	9	8	52, 6	9	3,71
	Ducat of 1797	B. 1 $2\frac{1}{2}$	2	$5\frac{3}{4}$	2	9	14	52, 9	9	4,34
	Augustus of 1754	W. 0 $2\frac{5}{8}$	4	$6\frac{1}{2}$	4	3	8	91, 2	16	1,69
	Augustus of 1784	W. 0 $1\frac{3}{4}$	4	$6\frac{1}{2}$	4	4	12	92, 2	16	3,81
SICILY*	Ounce of 1734	W. 0 $2\frac{1}{4}$	2	$20\frac{1}{2}$	2	18	14	61, 2	10	9,97
	Ounce of 1741	W. 0 3	2	$20\frac{1}{2}$	2	18	4	60, 7	10	8,91
	Ounce of 1751	W. 1 $2\frac{1}{2}$	2	$20\frac{1}{2}$	2	15	8	58, 2	10	3,60
	Double Ounce of 1758	W. 1 2	5	17	5	7	14	117,	20	8,48
SPAIN	Quadruple Pistole, or Doubloon, (coined before 1772)	W. 0 $1\frac{1}{2}$	17	$8\frac{1}{2}$	17	1	8	375, 3	66	5,06
	Double Pistole, (before 1772, single and half in proportion)	W. 0 $1\frac{1}{2}$	8	$16\frac{1}{4}$	8	12	14	187, 7	33	2,63
	Quarter Pistole, or Gold Dollar (before 1772)	W. 0 2	1	3	1	2	8	24, 2	4	3,39
	Doubloon of 1772 (Double and Single in proportion)	W. 0 $2\frac{1}{4}$	17	$8\frac{1}{2}$	16	21	16	372,	65	10,05
	Half Pistole of 1772	W. 0 $2\frac{1}{2}$	2	4	2	2	10	46, 3	8	2,33
	Quarter Pistole of 1772	W. 0 3	1	3	1	2	2	23, 9	4	2,75
	Quadruple Pistole of 1801	W. 1 1	17	9	16	9	6	360, 5	63	9,62
	Double Pistole of 1801	W. 1 1	8	$16\frac{1}{2}$	8	4	13	180, 3	31	10,92
	Pistole of 1801	W. 1 1	4	$8\frac{1}{4}$	4	2	6	90, 1	15	11,35
	Coronilla, Gold Doll. or Vintem of 1801	W. 1 $2\frac{1}{2}$	1	3	1	0	18	22, 8	4	0,42
SWEDEN	Ducat	B. 1 2	2	5	2	8	12	51, 9	9	2,22
SWITZERLAND	Ducat of Lucerne	B. 1 2	2	$5\frac{3}{4}$	2	9	8	52, 6	9	3,71
	Double Ducat of Lucerne	W. 1 0	4	$11\frac{1}{2}$	4	6	12	94, 1	16	7,84
	Piece of Five Ducats of Lucerne	W. 0 1	11	3	10	23	18	241, 9	42	9,74
	Ducat of Schwitz	B. 0 2	2	5	2	6	4	49, 7	8	9,55
	Ducat of St. Gall	B. 0 3	2	$5\frac{3}{4}$	2	7	12	51,	9	0,31
	Ducat of Uri	B. 1 1	2	5	2	8	0	51, 4	9	1,16
	Pistole of Lucerne	W. 0 $1\frac{1}{2}$	4	$21\frac{1}{2}$	4	19	9	105, 9	18	8,91
	Pistole of Soleure	W. 0 $1\frac{3}{4}$	4	22	4	19	12	106,	18	9,12
	Pistole of the Helvetic Republic of 1800 *(See also Basil, Bern, Geneva, St. Gall, and Zurich.)*	W. 0 $1\frac{1}{2}$	4	$21\frac{1}{2}$	4	19	9	105, 9	18	8,91
TREVES	Ducat	B. 1 2	2	$5\frac{3}{4}$	2	9	8	52, 6	9	3,71

* Much variation is found in the fineness of the Sicilian gold coins.

		Assay. car.	gr.	Weight. dwt.	gr.	Stan. Weight dwt.	gr.	mt.	Contents in Pure Gold. grains.	Value in Sterling. s.	d.
TURKEY	Sequin Fonducli of Constantinople of 1773	W. 2	2½	2	5¾	1	23	6	43, 3	7	7,94
	Sequin Fonducli of 1789	W. 2	3¼	2	5¾	1	22	16	42, 9	7	7,11
	Double Sequin Mahbub of 1773	B. 1	0	3	4¼	3	7	14	73, 1	12	11,26
	Sequin Mahbub of 1789	W. 2	3	1	12	1	7	10	28, 9	5	1,37
	Sequin of Cairo of 1773	W. 3	0½	1	15¼	1	9	16	31,	5	5,83
	Sequin of Cairo of 1789	W. 5	2½	1	15¼	1	5	6	26, 9	4	9,13
	Half Misseir (1818)	W. 5	3½	0	18¼	0	13	5	12,16	2	1,82
	Sequin Fonducli	W. 2	3	2	5	1	22	7	42, 5	7	6,26
	Rubieh	W. 2	3¼	0	12½	0	10	18	9, 9	1	9
	Yermeebeshlek	B. 0	3½	3	1¾	3	4	13	70, 3	12	5,30
TUSCANY	Ruspone	B. 1	3¾	6	17¼	7	7	8	160, 8	28	5,50
	Zecchino, or Sequin	B. 1	3¾	2	5¾	2	10	14	53, 6	9	5,83
	Ruspone of the Kingdom of Etruria	B. 1	3⅞	6	17¼	7	7	13	161,	28	5,93
UNITED STATES	*Eagle (½ and ¼ in proportion)	W. 0	0½	11	6	11	4	8	246, 1	43	6,66
VENICE	Zecchino, or Sequin, (½ and ¼ in prop.)	B. 1	3¼	2	6	2	10	10	53, 6	9	5,83
	Doppia, or Pistole	W. 0	1	4	8	4	7	0	94, 4	16	8,48
	Scudo d'oro, or Gold Crown	B. 1	3½	26	23	29	6	2	643, 6	113	10,87
	Ducato d'oro, or Gold Ducat	B. 1	3½	1	9½	1	12	6	33, 3	5	10,72
	Osella d'oro	B. 1	3½	8	23½	9	17	18	214, 5	37	11,55
WEST INDIES	(*See* Vol. I.)										
WIRTEMBERG	Carolin	W. 3	2	6	3½	5	4	0	113, 7	20	1,47
	Ducat	B. 1	2	2	5	2	8	12	51, 9	9	2,22
WURTZBURG	Ducat	B. 1	2	2	5¾	2	9	8	52, 6	9	3,71
ZURICH	Ducat (Double and ½ Ducat in prop.)	B. 1	2	2	5¾	2	9	8	52, 6	9	3,71

EAST INDIES.

		Assay. car.	gr.	Weight. dwt.	gr.	Stan. Weight dwt.	gr.	mt.	Contents in Pure Gold. grains.	Value in Sterling. s.	d.
EAST INDIA	Mohur of Shah Allum (1770)	B. 1	2¼	7	22¼	8	11	15	186, 8	33	0,72
	Mohur of the same	B. 1	2¾	7	23	8	13	13	188, 5	33	4,33
	Mohur, Half, (1787) ¼ in proportion	B. 1	2½	3	23½	4	6	10	94,	16	7,64
	Mohur Sicca of Bengal, dated 19th Sun.	B. 1	3⅜	7	23	8	15	0	189, 8	33	7,09
	Mohur of Bombay, old, still in circulation	B. 0	3½	7	10⅓	7	17	8	170,	30	1,04
	Mohur of the Dutch East India Company (1783)	W. 3	3¼	10	2	8	8	0	183, 4	32	5,50
	Mohur of ditto (1797)	W. 4	1	9	20	7	22	8	174, 5	30	10,60
	Mohur, Half ditto (1801)	W. 3	1¼	5	3½	4	18	18	96, 2	17	0,30
	Rupee, Tippoo's	W. 1	2	8	20½	8	6	0	181, 5	32	1,46
	†Rupee, Zodiac	B. 1	3¾	7	0	7	14	16	167, 6	29	7,9
	Rupee, Bombay (1818)	B. 0	0½	7	11	7	11	13	164, 7	29	1,78
	Rupee of Madras (1818)	Stand.		7	12	7	12	0	165,	29	2,42
	Pagoda, Star	W. 3	0	2	4¾	1	21	11	41, 8	7	4,77
	Pagoda, with a crescent and three figures	W. 1	3¼	2	5¼	2	0	18	44, 8	7	11,14
	Pagoda, with a crescent and one figure	W. 2	1¾	2	4	1	22	5	42, 4	7	6,04
	Pagoda, Arcot, old	W. 3	2	2	4½	1	20	4	40, 5	7	2,01
	Pagoda, Arcot, new	W. 7	1	2	4½	1	11	4	32, 4	5	8,59
	Pagoda, Onore	W. 1	3¼	2	4½	2	0	4	44, 2	7	9,87
	Pagoda, Mangalore	W. 1	2½	2	4½	2	0	12	44, 6	7	10,72
	Pagoda, Pondicherry	W. 5	0	2	4½	1	16	6	37, 2	6	7
	Pagoda, Hyderee Hoon	W. 2	1¼	2	4¾	1	23	4	43, 3	7	7,96
	Pagoda, Sultanee Hoon	W. 0	3¼	2	4¾	2	2	16	46, 6	8	2,97
	Saik Sai, a Mahratta coin	W. 1	3¾	6	22½	6	7	16	139, 2	24	7,63
	Tippoo's Faruki	W. 1	2	2	4½	2	0	18	44, 8	7	11,14
	Japan Copang, old	W. 1	2	11	9	10	14	8	233, 2	41	3,27
	Japan Copang, new	W. 6	0	8	9¾	6	2	14	134, 5	23	9,65

* This value of the American Eagle is taken from Average Assays of the Coins of twelve years.
† These Rupees are stamped with the Signs of the Zodiac: they are now very scarce, being only preserved as objects of curiosity.

NEW TABLE OF SILVER COINS.

TABLE VI.

Containing the Assays, Weights, and Values of the principal Silver Coins of all Countries, computed at the rate of 5s. 2d. per Ounce Standard, from Assays made both at the London and Paris Mints, as stated in Page 157.

		Assay.			Weight.		Stan. Weight			Contents in pure Silver.	Value in Sterling.	
			oz.	dwt.	dwt.	gr.	dwt.	gr.	mi.	grains.	s.	d.
AIX LA CHAPELLE	Rathsprœsentger	W.	4	2	4	1½	2	13	9	56, 9	0	7,94
	Double ditto	W.	2	15	6	23¼	5	5	16	116, 3	1	4,24
AMERICA........	*(See Portugal, Spain, & United States.)*											
AUSTRIA	Rixdollar, *Constitution*, before 1753 ..	W.	0	11	18	11½	17	13	10	390,	4	6,45
	Rixdollar, *Convention*, coined since 1753	W.	1	6	18	1	15	22	4	353, 7	4	1,39
	Rixdollar Ditto, of Francis II. 1800 ..	W.	1	5	18	1	16	0	4	355, 5	4	1,64
	Rixdollar of the Kingdom of Hungary..	W.	1	2	18	1	16	6	1	360, 9	4	2,39
	Half Rixdollar, or Florin, *Convention*..	W.	1	3	9	0½	8	2	1	179, 6	2	1,07
	Copfstuck, or 20 Creutzer Piece......	W.	4	3	4	6½	2	16	3	59, 4	0	8,29
	17 Creutzer Piece	W.	4	8	4	0	2	9	18	53, 5	0	7,47
	Halbe Copf, or 10 Creutzer Piece	W.	5	5	2	11	1	7	1	28, 8	0	4,01
BADEN..........	Rixdollar.........................	W.	1	4	18	2	16	3	1	358, 1	4	2
BASIL	Patagon, or Ecu, old	W.	0	14	18	4	17	0	10	377, 9	4	4,76
	Thaler, or Rixdollar, of 1763........	W.	1	2	14	22	13	10	10	298, 4	3	5,66
	Patagon, or Ecu, of 1795, (Double, &c. in proportion .... }	W.	1	0½	16	14	15	1	5	334, 3	3	10,68
	Piece of 10 Batzen	W.	2	2	5	13½	4	12	4	100, 1	1	1,97
BAVARIA........	Rixdollar *Convention* of 1780	W.	1	6	18	1	15	22	4	358, 7	4	1,39
	Rixdollar of 1800, (½ in proportion) ..	W.	1	4½	17	12	15	13	13	345, 6	4	0,25
	Copstuck..........................	W.	4	3	4	6½	2	16	3	59, 4	0	8,29
BERN	Patagon, or Crown, (½ in proportion)..	W.	0	7	18	22	18	7	14	406, 7	4	8,79
	Piece of 10 Batzen	W.	1	2	5	3	4	14	17	102, 5	1	2,31
	Piece of 5 Batzen	W.	2	2	2	15	2	3	2	47, 2	0	6,59
BOLOGNA	*(See Rome)*											
BRANDENBURG ..	*(See Prussia.)*											
BREMEN	Piece of 48 Grotes..................	W.	2	2	11	0	8	22	1	198,	2	3,64
BRUNSWICK	Rixdollar, *Convention*	W.	1	3	18	1	16	4	4	359, 2	4	2,15
	Half Rixdollar	W.	1	3	9	0½	8	2	2	179, 6	2	1,07
	Gulden, or Piece of ⅔, fine, of 1764....	B.	0	16	8	10½	9	1	1	200, 8	2	4,03
	Gulden, common, of 1764	W.	1	2	9	0	8	2	10	180,	2	1,13
	Gulden, ditto, of 1795	W.	2	2	11	1½	8	23	7	199, 1	2	3,80
	Half Gulden, or Piece of ⅓, of 1764..	W.	1	2	4	12	4	1	5	90,	1	0,56
CASSEL..........	*(See Hesse Cassel.)*											
COLOGNE........	Rixdollar, old......................	W.	0	15½	18	1	16	18	15	372, 5	4	4,01
	Rixdollar, *Constitution*.............	W.	0	7	18	19	18	4	14	404,	4	8,41
	Rixdollar, *Convention*	W.	1	6	18	1	15	22	4	353, 7	4	1,39
CONSTANTINOPLE	*(See Turkey.)*											

		Assay.		Weight.		Stan. Weight			Contents in pure Silver.	Value in Sterling.	
		oz.	dwt.	dwt.	gr.	dwt.	gr.	mi.	grains.	s.	d.
DENMARK	Ryksdaler, old, of 6 Marks Danish	W. 1	2	17	$5\frac{1}{4}$	15	12	5	344, 4	4	0,92
	Crone, or old piece of 4 Marks	W. 3	1	14	1	10	4	7	226	2	7,55
	Crone, or Crown, of 1747	W. 1	2	11	$15\frac{1}{2}$	10	10	16	232, 9	2	8,52
	Ryksdaler, specie, of 1798	W. 0	13	18	14	17	11	17	388, 4	4	6,23
	New Piece of 4 Marks	W. 0	12	12	9	11	16	14	259, 8	3	0,27
	Half Ryksdaler	W. 0	13	9	7	8	17	8	194, 2	2	3,11
	Mark, specie, or $\frac{1}{6}$ Ryksdaler	W. 3	1	4	0	2	21	12	64, 4	0	7,59
	Rixdollar, specie of Sleswig and Holstein (pieces of $\frac{2}{3}$ and $\frac{1}{3}$ in prop.)	W. 0	12	18	13	17	12	6	389, 4	4	6,37
	Piece of 24 Skillings	W. 4	7	5	$2\frac{1}{2}$	3	2	10	68, 9	0	9,62
EAST INDIES	(*See* p. 170.)										
ENGLAND	Crown *(old)*	Stand.		19	$8\frac{1}{2}$	19	8	10	429, 7	5	0
	Half-crown	Stand.		9	$16\frac{1}{4}$	9	16	5	214, 8	2	6
	Shilling	Stand.		3	21	3	21	0	85, 9	1	0
	Sixpence	Stand.		1	$22\frac{1}{2}$	1	22	10	42, 9	0	6
	Crown, *(new)*	Stand.		18	$4\frac{1}{4}$	18	4	7	403, 6	4	8,36
	Half-crown	Stand.		9	2	9	2	4	201, 8	2	4,18
	Shilling	Stand.		3	$15\frac{1}{4}$	3	15	6	80, 7	0	11,27
	Sixpence	Stand.		1	$19\frac{3}{4}$	1	19	14	40, 3	0	5,63
FLORENCE	(*See Tuscany.*)										
FRANCE	Ecu of 6 Livres	W. 0	7	18	18	18	7	16	403, 1	4	8,28
	Demi Ecu	W. 0	7	9	9	9	1	18	201, 5	2	4,13
	Piece of 24 Sous (divisions in prop.)	W. 0	7	3	20	3	16	19	83, 4	0	11,64
	Piece of 30 Sous ($\frac{1}{2}$ in proportion)	W. 3	8	6	12	4	12	4	100, 2	1	1,99
	Piece of 5 Francs of the Convention	W. 0	$10\frac{1}{2}$	16	0	15	5	14	338, 3	3	11,24
	Piece of 5 Francs (Napoleon) of 1808	W. 0	7	16	1	15	12	4	344, 9	4	0,16
	Piece of 2 Francs of 1808	W. 0	7	6	11	6	6	2	138, 8	1	7,38
	Franc of 1809	W. 0	7	3	$5\frac{1}{2}$	3	3	1	69, 4	0	9,69
	Demi Franc	W. 0	$8\frac{1}{2}$	1	15	4	13	6	34, 7	0	4,84
	Franc (Louis) of 1818, same as Franc of 1809										
FRANCFORT ON THE MAINE	Rixdollar, Convention of 1772	W. 1	$0\frac{1}{2}$	18	1	16	8	16	363, 5	4	2,75
	Rixdollar, Ditto of 1796	W. 1	2	18	1	16	6	0	360, 8	4	2,38
GENEVA	Patagon	W. 1	0	17	9	15	19	8	351,	4	1,03
	Piece of 21 Sous	W. 2	$3\frac{1}{2}$	3	$1\frac{3}{4}$	2	11	5	54, 8	0	7,65
	Piece of 12 Florins 9 Sous, called Genevoise, or Gros Ecu, (1794)	W. 0	13	19	8	18	4	16	404,	4	8,41
	Ditto of 1796, ($\frac{1}{2}$ in proportion)	W. 0	14	19	15	18	9	6	408, 2	4	9
	Piece of 15 Sous of 1794	W. 2	6	2	$1\frac{1}{4}$	1	15	1	36, 1	0	5,04
GENOA	Scudo della croce	B. 0	7	24	$16\frac{3}{4}$	25	11	8	565, 5	6	6,96
	Scudo di S. Giambatista, of 5 Lire	W. 0	2	13	$8\frac{1}{2}$	13	5	12	293, 8	3	5,02
	Double Madonnina, (single and half in proportion	W. 1	2	5	$19\frac{1}{2}$	5	5	12	116, 2	1	4,22
	Scudo, of 8 Lire, of 1796, ($\frac{1}{2}$, $\frac{1}{4}$, &c. in proportion)	W. 0	8	21	9	20	14	10	457, 4	5	3,87
	Scudo of the Ligurian Republic	W. 0	$9\frac{1}{2}$	21	9	20	11	2	454, 3	5	3,43
HAMBURGH	Rixdollar specie	W. 0	10	18	18	17	21	12	397, 5	4	7,49
	Double Mark, or 32 Schillings Piece, single in proportion)	W. 2	3	11	18	9	11	8	210, 3	2	5,36
	Piece of 8 Schillings	W. 3	12	3	$8\frac{1}{4}$	2	6	4	50, 1	0	6,99
	Piece of 4 Schillings	W. 4	6	2	2	1	6	12	28, 3	0	3,95
HANOVER	Rixdollar, *Constitution*	W. 0	9	18	19	18	0	14	400, 3	4	7,89

		Assay.			Weight.		Stan. Weight			Contents in pure Silver.	Value in Sterling.	
			oz.	dwt.	dwt.	gr.	dwt.	gr.	mi.	grains.	s.	d.
HANOVER	Florin, or Piece of $\frac{2}{3}$, fine	B.	0	16	8	10	9	0	10	200, 3	2	3,96
	Half Florin, or Piece of $\frac{1}{3}$, ditto	B.	0	16	4	4	4	11	4	99, 2	1	1,85
	Quarter, or Piece of 6 good Groschen, do.	B.	0	16	2	1	2	4	10	48, 6	0	6,78
	Florin, or Piece of $\frac{2}{3}$, base	W.	2	1	11	$0\frac{3}{4}$	8	23	15	199, 6	2	3,87
HESSE CASSEL ..	Rixdollar, *Convention*	W.	1	6	18	1	15	22	6	353,	4	1,39
	Florin, or Piece of $\frac{2}{3}$, ($\frac{1}{2}$ in proportion)..	W.	1	6	9	$0\frac{1}{2}$	7	23	3	176, 8	2	0,68
	Thaler, or Rixdollar of account of 1778	W.	2	3	15	$2\frac{1}{2}$	12	4	3	270, 3	3	1,74
	Thaler of 1789	W.	0	$10\frac{1}{2}$	12	$7\frac{1}{4}$	11	17	5	259, 7	3	0,26
	Ecu, *Convention* (1815)............	W.	1	6	17	$23\frac{3}{4}$	15	21	2	349, 3	4	0,77
	Six Bon Gros......................	W.	4	10	8	0	2	23	0	65, 1	0	9,80
	Bon Gros..........................	W.	6	14	1	4	0	11	5	10, 3	0	1,43
HOLLAND	Ducatoon..........................	B.	0	3	20	22	21	4	15	471, 6	5	5,85
	Piece of 3 Florins..................	W.	0	2	20	7	20	2	12	446, 4	5	2,33
	Piece of 3 Florins of Batavia	W.	0	$5\frac{1}{2}$	20	3	19	15	0	435, 7	5	0,84
	Rixdollar (the Assay varies)..........	W.	0	16	18	6	16	20	8	375, 9	4	4,99
	Daalder, or 30 Stiver Piece..........	W.	0	10	10	6	9	18	18	217, 3	2	6,34
	Half Rixdollar	W.	0	16	9	0	8	8	8	185, 4	2	1,89
	Florin, or Guilder, ($\frac{1}{2}$ in proportion) ..	W.	0	$4\frac{1}{2}$	6	18	6	14	14	146, 8	1	8,49
	12 Stiver Piece	W.	0	$16\frac{1}{2}$	4	12	4	3	18	92, 4	1	0,90
	Sesthalf, or $5\frac{1}{2}$ Stiver Piece..........	W.	4	15	3	0	1	17	4	38, 1	0	5,32
	8 Stiver Piece......................	W.	0	17	3	0	2	18	8	61, 5	0	8,58
	Florin of Batavia	W.	0	$5\frac{1}{2}$	6	13	6	9	2	141, 6	1	7,77
	Rixdollar, or 50 Stiver Piece of the Kingdom of Holland	W.	0	$5\frac{1}{2}$	17	0	16	13	18	367, 9	4	3,37
HUNGARY	*(See Austria.)*											
JAPAN	*(See East Indies,* p. 170.)											
LEGHORN........	*(See Tuscany.)*											
LEIPSIC	*(See Saxony.)*											
LIEGE	Ducatoon of 1671	B.	0	2	20	$18\frac{1}{2}$	20	22	18	465, 3	5	4,97
	Patagon, old	W.	0	14	17	$20\frac{3}{4}$	16	17	14	371, 6	4	3,89
	Patagon of 1792....................	W.	0	17	17	15	16	6	11	361, 3	4	2,45
	Escalin of 1771	W.	3	17	3	$3\frac{1}{2}$	2	1	6	45, 6	0	6,36
	Escalin of 1792	W.	4	2	3	1	1	22	0	42, 6	0	5,94
LORRAINE..	Ecu, called Leopold, (1704)..........	W.	0	3	17	11	17	5	6	382, 3	4	5,38
	Ecu (1710)	W.	0	4	19	$14\frac{1}{2}$	19	5	10	426, 9	4	11,61
LUBEC	Rixdollar, specie..................	W.	0	13	18	18	17	15	12	391, 9	4	6,72
	Double Mark	W.	2	3	11	18	9	11	8	210, 3	2	5,36
	Mark	W.	2	3	5	21	4	17	14	105, 1	1	2,67
LUCCA	Scudo	W.	0	3	17	0	16	18	10	372, 3	4	3,98
	Mezzo, or $\frac{1}{2}$ Scudo	W.	0	3	8	3	8	0	7	177, 9	2	0,84
	Terzo, or $\frac{1}{3}$ Scudo................	W.	0	3	5	19	5	17	2	126, 8	1	5,70
	Quinto, or $\frac{1}{5}$ Scudo................	W.	0	3	3	5	3	3	19	70, 3	0	9,81
	Barbone	W.	3	3	1	$20\frac{1}{4}$	1	7	14	29, 3	0	4,09
LUNEBURG	*(See Hanover.)*											
MALTA	Ounce of 30 Tari of Emmanuel Pinto..	W.	2	5	19	$1\frac{1}{2}$	15	4	14	337, 4	3	11,11
	Ounce of Emmanuel de Rohan ($\frac{1}{2}$ in prop.)	W.	1	3	19	$1\frac{1}{2}$	17	2	2	379, 3	4	4,96
	Scudo of the same, (Double in prop.)..	W.	2	5	7	19	6	5	0	137, 9	1	7,25
	Ounce of Ferdinand Hompesch	W.	1	2	19	$1\frac{1}{2}$	17	4	3	381, 3	4	5,24
	2 Tari Piece	W.	2	19	1	2	0	19	2	17, 7	0	2,47
MANHEIM	Rixdollar, fine	B.	0	16	16	16	17	20	6	396, 7	4	7,39
	Florin, or Piece of $\frac{2}{3}$, fine	B.	0	16	8	8	8	22	8	198, 3	2	3,69
	Rixdollar, *Convention*	W.	1	3	18	1	16	4	3	359, 0	4	2,13

		Assay.			Weight.		Stan. Weight.			Contents in pure Silver.	Value in Sterling.	
			oz.	dwt.	dwt.	gr.	dw.	gr.	mi.	grains.	s.	d.
MECKLENBURG ..	Florin, or Piece of $\frac{2}{3}$	W.	2	2	11	$1\frac{1}{2}$	8	23	5	199, 1	2	3,80
MENTZ	Rixdollar	W.	1	2	18	1	16	6	0	360, 8	4	2,38
	Copstuck	W.	4	2	4	$6\frac{1}{2}$	2	16	13	59, 8	0	8,35
MILAN	Scudo of 6 Lire ($\frac{1}{2}$ in proportion)	W.	0	7	14	$20\frac{3}{4}$	14	9	10	319, 6	3	8,62
	Lira, new	W.	4	10	4	0	2	9	0	52, 8	0	7,37
	Lira, old	W.	0	3	2	10	2	9	4	52, 9	0	7,38
	Piece of 30 Soldi, Francis II.	W.	2	18	4	17	3	11	8	77, 2	0	10,78
	Scudo of the Cisalpine Republic	W.	0	7	14	$21\frac{1}{2}$	14	10	4	320, 2	3	8,71
	Piece of 30 Soldi of ditto	W.	2	18	4	17	3	11	8	77, 2	0	10,78
MODENA	Scudo of 15 Lire, 1739 (double, &c. in pro.)	W.	0	14	18	$12\frac{1}{2}$	17	8	9	385, 2	4	5,78
	Scudo of 5 Lire, of 1782	W.	0	3	5	19	5	17	2	126, 8	1	5,70
	Scudo of 1796	W.	3	3	18	$1\frac{3}{4}$	12	22	12	287, 4	3	4,13
NAPLES	Ducat, old ($\frac{1}{2}$ in proportion)	W.	0	4	14	0	13	17	18	305, 2	3	6,61
	Piece of 12 Carlini (before 1784)	W.	0	7	16	7	15	18	12	350, 3	4	0,91
	Ducat, new ($\frac{1}{2}$ in proportion)	W.	1	0	14	15	13	7	8	295, 4	3	5,24
	Piece of 12 Carlini of 1791	W.	1	0	17	15	16	0	18	356,	4	1,71
	Ditto of 1796	W.	1	2	17	$16\frac{3}{4}$	15	22	12	353, 9	4	1,41
	Ditto of the Neapolitan Republic (1799)	W.	1	2	17	$16\frac{3}{4}$	15	22	12	353, 9	4	1,41
	Ditto of 1805 ($\frac{1}{2}$ in proportion)	W.	1	2	17	$18\frac{1}{4}$	15	23	18	355, 2	4	1,60
	Ditto of 10 Carlini (1818)	W.	1	2	14	18	13	7	0	295, 1	3	5,20
NETHERLANDS ..	Ducatoon, old	B.	0	4	21	0	21	9	0	474, 6	5	6,27
	Ducatoon of Maria Theresa	W.	0	14	21	10	20	1	12	445, 5	5	2,20
	Crown ($\frac{1}{2}$, &c. in proportion)	W.	0	14	19	0	17	19	4	395, 2	4	7,18
	Escalin (Double in proportion)	W.	4	4	3	$4\frac{1}{4}$	1	23	8	43, 8	0	6,11
	Plaquette	W.	5	8	1	18	0	21	12	20,	0	2,79
	5 Stiver Piece	W.	6	3	3	4	1	9	18	31, 3	0	4,37
	Silver Lion of 1790	W.	0	13	21	3	19	21	6	441, 5	5	1,65
	Florin of 1790	W.	0	14	5	$23\frac{1}{2}$	5	14	9	124, 3	1	5,35
	Piece of 10 Stivers of 1790	W.	0	16	3	0	2	18	6	61, 8	0	8,62
	Florin of 1816	W.	0	$7\frac{1}{2}$	6	22	6	16	6	148, 4	1	8,72
	Half Florin (with Division in prop.) ..	W.	4	$5\frac{1}{2}$	5	11	3	9	2	75,	0	10,46
NEUFCHATEL	Piece of 21 Batzen	W.	1	11	9	20	8	11	0	187, 8	2	2,22
	Piece of $10\frac{1}{2}$ Batzen	W.	1	11	4	22	4	5	10	93, 9	1	1,11
NUREMBERG	Rixdollar, *Constitution*	W.	0	8	18	19	18	2	15	402, 2	4	8,16
	Rixdollar, *Convention*	W.	1	3	18	1	16	4	2	359, 0	4	2,13
	Copstuck	W.	4	2	4	$6\frac{1}{2}$	2	16	13	59, 8	0	8,35
PARMA	Ducat of 1784	W.	0	9	16	11	15	18	18	350, 6	4	0,95
	Ducat of 1796 ($\frac{1}{2}$ in proportion)	W.	0	$5\frac{1}{2}$	16	$12\frac{3}{4}$	16	2	18	357, 9	4	1,97
	Piece of 3 Lire	W.	1	4	4	14	4	2	2	90, 7	1	0,66
PERSIA	(*See East Indies*, p. 170.)											
PIEDMONT	Scudo (1690)	W.	0	3	17	$9\frac{1}{4}$	17	3	12	380, 7	4	5,16
	Scudo (1733)	W.	0	3	19	3	18	20	16	418, 8	4	10,48
	Scudo (1755,) $\frac{1}{2}$, &c. in proportion	W.	0	$5\frac{1}{2}$	22	14	22	0	10	488, 9	5	8,26
	Scudo, (1770,) $\frac{1}{2}$ and $\frac{1}{4}$ in proportion ..	W.	0	5	22	14	22	1	16	490, 0	5	8,42
	Piece of 2 Lire (1714)	W.	0	$4\frac{1}{2}$	7	$20\frac{1}{2}$	7	16	13	170, 8	1	11,85
	5 Franc Piece (1801)	W.	0	8	16	$1\frac{1}{2}$	15	11	12	343, 7	3	11,99
POLAND	Rixdollar, old	W.	1	2	18	1	16	6	0	360, 8	4	2,38
	Rixdollar, new (1794)	W.	2	17	15	$10\frac{1}{2}$	11	11	6	254, 3	2	11,51
	Florin, or Gulden	W.	4	2	6	0	3	18	16	84,	0	11,72
PORTUGAL	New Crusado (1690)	W.	0	4	11	0	10	19	0	239, 2	2	9,40
	Ditto (1718)	W.	0	$6\frac{1}{2}$	9	8	9	1	0	200, 2	2	3,95
	Ditto (1795)	W.	0	7	9	9	9	1	18	201, 6	2	4,15

		Assay. oz.	Assay. dwt.	Weight. dw.	Weight. gr.	Stan. Weight. dwt.	Stan. Weight. gr.	Stan. Weight. mi.	Contents in pure Silver. grains.	Value in Sterling. s.	Value in Sterling. d.
PORTUGAL	Doze Vintems, or Piece of 240 Rees (1799)	W. 0	7	4	16	4	12	10	100, 4	1	2,01
	Testoon (1799)	W. 0	7	2	0½	1	22	18	43, 4	0	6,06
	New Crusado (1802)................	W. 0	9	9	9	8	23	16	199, 7	2	3,88
	Ditto (1809)................	W. 0	4	9	3	8	23	0	198, 2	2	4,67
	Seis Vintems, or Piece of 120 Rees (1802)	W. 0	9	2	4½	2	2	8	46, 6	0	6,50
	Testoon (1802)	W. 0	9	2	0	1	22	0	42, 5	0	5,93
	Tres Vintems, or Piece of 60 Rees (1802)	W. 0	9	1	2¼	1	1	4	23, 3	0	3,25
	Half Testoon (1802)................	W. 0	9	0	23	0	22	0	20, 4	0	2,84
PORTUGUESE COLONIES....	Pataca of Brazil, old, of 640 Rees....	W. 0	2	12	4¾	12	2	2	268, 3	3	1,46
	Ditto of 600 Rees (1755)............	W. 0	4	11	7½	11	2	12	246, 6	2	10,43
	Ditto of 640 Rees (1768)............	W. 0	4½	11	9¾	11	8	14	252, 3	2	11,23
	Ditto of 640 Rees (1801) ½ and ¼ in prop.	W. 0	7	12	4¾	11	19	10	262, 2	3	0,61
	Piece of 12 Macutas, of Portuguese Africa	W. 0	7	11	7½	10	22	18	243, 2	2	9,96
	Ditto of 8 ditto	W. 0	9	7	12	7	4	14	159, 8	1	10,31
	Ditto of 6 ditto	W. 0	9	5	13	5	7	12	118,	1	4,47
	Ditto of 4 ditto	W. 0	9	3	16	3	12	8	78, 1	0	10,90
PRUSSIA	Florin, old, of the Elector of Brandenburg	W. 2	2	11	9¼	9	5	11	204, 9	2	4,61
	*Rixdollar, Prussian currency (½ in prop.)	W. 2	5	14	6½	11	9	0	252, 6	2	11,27
	Rixdollar, *Convention*	W. 1	3	18	1	16	4	2	359,	4	2,13
	Florin, or Piece of ⅔...............	W. 2	3	11	2	8	22	8	198, 4	2	3,70
	Florin of Silesia....................	W. 2	2	9	11	7	16	0	170, 3	1	11,78
	Drittel, or Piece of 8 good Groschen..	W. 3	3	5	8¾	3	20	4	85, 3	0	11,91
	Piece of 4 Groschen................	W. 5	0	3	9	1	20	10	41, 2	0	5,75
	Piece of 6 Groschen................	W. 2	8	3	14	2	19	6	62, 3	0	8,69
	Rixdollar, old, of Bareuth	W. 2	4	12	13	10	1	6	223, 3	2	7,18
	Piece of ⅔ ditto....................	W. 2	4	7	15¼	6	2	18	135, 9	1	6,97
	Piece of 30 Creutzers ditto	W. 2	2	4	2½	3	7	16	73, 8	0	10,30
	Rixdollar, old, of Anspach..........	W. 2	3	14	0	11	6	18	250, 6	2	10,99
	Piece of ⅔ ditto....................	W. 2	4	8	21	7	2	14	158,	1	10,06
	Rixdollar of Anspach and Bareuth, *Convention*	W. 1	3	18	1	16	4	2	359,	4	2,22
RAGUSA	Tallaro, or Ragusina (1759)..........	W. 4	2	18	7½	11	13	2	256, 4	2	11,80
	Ditto (1774)	W. 4	4	18	8½	11	9	16	253, 3	2	11,37
	Ditto (1794)	W. 3	10	18	17¼	12	1	6	267, 7	3	1,38
	Ducat (1797)	W. 5	11	8	17¾	4	8	16	97,	1	1,54
RATISBON	Rixdollar, specie (½, &c. in prop.)	W. 1	3	18	1	16	4	2	359, 2	4	1,58
ROME	Scudo, or Crown, (before 1753)......	W. 0	4	20	11	20	2	2	446,	5	2,27
	Testone, old	W. 0	4½	5	21	5	18	2	127, 8	1	5,84
	Paolo, old	W. 0	4½	1	22¾	1	21	16	42, 4	0	5,92
	Scudo, or Crown (coined since 1753)..	W. 0	4	17	1	16	17	13	371, 5	4	3,87
	Mezzo Scudo, or Half Crown........	W. 0	4	8	12½	8	8	16	185, 7	2	1,93
	Testone (1770)	W. 0	3½	5	2	5	0	0	111, 1	1	3,51
	Ditto (1785)	W. 0	5	5	2	4	23	4	110, 3	1	3,40
	Paolo (1785)	W. 0	4	1	17	1	16	4	37, 2	0	5,19
	Grosso, or Half Paolo (1785)........	W. 0	5	0	20½	0	20	0	18, 5	0	2,58
	Papetto (1775)	W. 0	4½	3	8¼	3	6	12	72, 7	0	10,15
	Scudo of the Roman Republic (1799)..	W. 0	6	17	1	16	13	18	368, 1	4	3,40
	Scudo of Bologna (Pius VI.)	W. 0	3	17	1	16	19	8	373, 2	4	4,11
	Testone ditto	W. 0	3	5	2	5	0	6	111, 5	1	3,56

* The Prussian Coins having been debased at different periods vary in their reports.

		Assay.		Weight.		Stan. Weight.			Contents in pure Silver	Value in Sterling.	
		oz.	dwt.	dwt.	gr.	dwt.	gr.	mi.	grains.	s.	d.
ROME	Scudo of the City of Bologna	W. 1	0	19	0	17	6	18	383, 9	4	5,60
	Ditto of Pius VII. (1800)	W. 0	1	17	0¼	16	21	4	371, 5	4	3,78
RUSSIA	Ruble of Peter the Great	W. 2	7	18	1	14	1	8	312, 1	3	7,58
	Ditto of Catherine I. (1725)	W. 2	4½	17	11	13	23	0	309, 9	3	7,27
	Ditto of Peter II. (1727)	W. 2	12	18	5¾	13	23	4	310,	3	7,28
	Ditto of Anne (1734)	W. 1	11	16	14½	14	6	16	317, 2	3	8,29
	Ditto of Elizabeth (1750)	W. 1	7	16	12	14	11	16	321, 8	3	8,93
	Ditto of Peter III. (1762)	W. 2	2	15	10	12	12	0	277, 5	3	2,75
	Ditto of Catherine II. (1780)	W. 2	4	15	12	12	10	6	275, 9	3	2,52
	Ditto of Paul (1799)	W. 0	14	13	12	12	15	10	280, 8	3	3,21
	Ditto of Alexander (1802)	W. 0	13	13	1½	17	7	2	273,	3	2,12
	Ditto of ditto (1805)	W. 0	16	13	12	12	12	12	278, 1	3	2,83
	Poltin, or ½ Ruble of Anne	W. 1	10	7	21	6	19	8	151, 2	1	9,11
	Ditto of Elizabeth	W. 1	8	8	2	7	1	10	156, 8	1	9,89
	Ditto of Catherine II.	W. 2	4	7	18	6	5	2	137, 9	1	7,25
	Ditto of Paul	W. 0	15	6	18	6	7	2	139, 7	1	7,50
	Ditto of Alexander (1804)	W. 0	14	6	13½	6	3	10	136, 5	1	7,06
	Polpoltin, or ¼ Ruble, old	W. 2	6	4	1	3	4	18	71, 1	0	9,92
	Ditto of Paul	W. 0	18½	3	7	3	0	8	67,	0	9,35
	Ditto of Alexander (1802)	W. 0	13½	3	9½	3	4	10	70, 8	0	9,88
	20 Copeck Piece (1767)	W. 2	2	3	10¾	2	19	0	62, 6	0	8,74
	Ditto (1784)	W. 2	2	3	3	2	12	18	56, 2	0	7,84
	15 Copeck Piece (1778)	W. 2	2	2	6	1	19	18	40, 5	0	5,65
	10 Copeck Piece	W. 2	6	2	1	1	14	16	35, 9	0	5,11
	Ditto (1798)	W. 0	14½	1	9	1	6	16	28, 5	0	3,97
	Ditto (1802)	W. 0	13	1	8½	1	6	11	28, 3	0	3,95
	5 Copeck Piece (1801)	W. 0	13½	0	16½	0	15	10	15, 3	0	2,13
ST. GALL	Rixdollar (½ in proportion)	W. 1	4	18	1	16	2	4	357, 3	4	1,98
	24 Creutzer Piece	W. 4	2	4	7¼	2	17	2	60, 2	0	8,40
SALTZBURG	Rixdollar, *Convention*	W. 1	2	18	1	16	6	0	360, 8	4	2,38
	24 Creutzer Piece	W. 4	3	4	6½	2	16	4	59, 4	0	8,29
SARDINIA	Scudo, or Crown, (½ and ¼ in prop.)	W. 0	7	15	2½	14	15	0	324, 7	3	9,34
SAXONY	Rixdollar, *Convention* (½ and ¼ in prop.)	W. 1	3	18	0	16	3	4	358, 2	4	2,01
	Old Rixdollar of Dresden	W. 0	9½	18	19	17	23	14	399, 3	4	7,75
	Ditto of Leipsic	W. 2	0	18	19	15	9	16	342,	3	11,75
	Piece of 16 Groschen of Leipsic	W. 2	2	9	9½	7	14	16	169, 1	1	11,61
	Piece of 8 Groschen	W. 2	5	4	20	3	20	8	85, 6	0	11,95
	Rixdollar current of Saxe Gotha	W. 4	4½	18	1	11	4	2	248, 1	2	10,64
	⅙ Thaler of 1804	W. 4	11	3	11	2	0	19	45, 3	0	6,32
	Ditto of 1808	W. 4	11½	3	5½	1	21	8	42, 1	0	5,87
	Ditto of Jerome Buonaparte of 1809	W. 5	4	3	17	1	23	6	43, 7	0	6,10
SICILY	Scudo (½ in proportion)	W. 1	4	17	14	15	16	6	348, 2	4	0,62
	Piece of 40 Grains	W. 1	2	5	21	5	7	2	117, 5	1	4,40
	Ditto of 20 Grains	W. 1	5	3	0	2	15	18	59, 1	0	8,25
SIERRA LEONE COMPANY	Piece of 10 Macutas	W. 1	6	16	21	14	21	12	330, 8	3	10,19
	Ditto of 5 Macutas	W. 1	6	8	13	7	12	18	167, 4	1	11,37
	Ditto of 2 Macutas	W. 1	6	3	7½	2	22	6	65,	0	9,07
	Ditto of 1 Macuta	W. 1	6	1	16	1	11	8	32, 5	0	4,53
SPAIN	Dollar, old Mexican square (1747)	W. 0	4½	17	7	16	22	10	376, 1	4	4,51
	Half ditto	W. 0	4½	8	15½	8	11	5	188,	2	1,25
	Dollar, old, called Sevillan (1731)	W. 0	4½	17	7	16	22	10	376, 1	4	4,51

		Assay.		Weight.		Stan. Weight.			Contents in pure Silver.	Value in Sterling.	
		oz.	dwt.	dwt.	gr.	dwt.	gr.	mi.	grains.	s.	d.
SPAIN	Old Mexican Peceta of two Mexican Reals (1736)	W. 0	4½	4	7¼	4	5	2	93, 6	1	1,07
	Real of Mexican Plate (1746)	W. 0	4½	2	3½	2	2	11	46, 8	0	6,53
	Dollar, Mexican, with globes and pillars, (1765)	W. 0	4½	17	8½	17	0	0	377, 4	4	4,79
	Peceta of two Reals of Plate (1721)	W. 1	7	3	16½	3	5	14	71, 9	0	10,04
	Real of Plate (1721)	W. 1	7	1	20¼	1	14	19	35, 9	0	5,01
	Dollar,* of late coinage	W. 0	8	17	8	16	17	0	370, 9	4	3,79
	Half Dollar, ditto	W. 0	8	8	16	8	8	10	185, 4	2	1,88
	Mexican Peceta (1774)	W. 0	8	4	7½	4	3	16	92, 3	1	0,88
	Real of Mexican Plate (1775)	W. 0	8	2	3¾	2	1	20	46, 1	0	6,43
	Peceta Provincial of 2 Reals of new plate (1775)	W. 1	9½	3	18	3	6	0	72, 2	0	10,08
	Real of new plate (1795)	W. 1	9½	1	21	1	15	0	36, 1	0	5,04
SWEDEN	Rixdollar (1762)	W. 0	12	18	20	17	19	10	395, 5	4	7,22
	Rixdollar of late coinage	W. 0	14⅓	18	17	17	12	0	388, 5	4	6,28
	Double Plott, or Piece of ⅔	W. 0	14⅓	12	12	11	16	12	259, 6	3	0,25
	Single Plott, or Piece of ⅓	W. 0	14⅓	6	6	5	20	6	129, 8	1	6,12
	Piece of 8 Skillings	W. 2	18	3	21½	2	21	2	63, 8	0	8,90
	Ditto of 4 Skillings	W. 5	2	2	15	1	14	0	31, 5	0	4,95
SWITZERLAND	Ecu, or Rixdollar of Lucerne, ½, &c. in proportion (1715)	W. 0	14½	17	8½	16	5	8	360, 1	4	2,28
	Old Gulden, or Florin of Lucerne (1714)	W. 1	19	8	14½	7	2	8	157, 5	1	9,99
	Ecu of 40 Batzen of Lucerne (1796)	W. 0	5	19	0	18	13	14	412, 3	4	9,57
	Half Ditto	W. 1	2	9	20	8	20	12	196, 7	2	3,46
	Florin, or Piece of 40 Schillings of Lucerne (1793)	W. 1	5	4	22	4	8	14	96, 8	1	1,51
	Half Florin of Lucerne	W. 2	2	2	15	2	3	0	47, 3	0	6,60
	Piece of 10 Batzen (1782)	W. 1	12	4	20½	4	3	14	92, 2	1	0,68
	Quarter Rixdollar of Friburg	W. 2	19	6	20¾	5	0	18	111, 9	1	3,62
	Piece of ⅛ Rixdollar of Ditto	W. 3	0	3	7½	2	10	0	53, 6	0	7,48
	Piece of 20 Batzen of Soleure	W. 1	2	9	20	8	20	12	196, 7	2	3,46
	Ditto of 10 Batzen of Ditto	W. 1	2	5	1	4	13	0	101, 5	1	2,17
	Ecu of 40 Batzen of the Helvetic Republic, (1798) ½ in prop.	W. 0	6	18	23	18	10	14	409, 5	4	9,18
	Piece of 10 Batzen	W. 1	4	5	3	4	13	17	100, 5	1	2,03
	Ditto of 5 Batzen	W. 3	2	3	2	2	5	8	49, 3	0	6,88
	Ecu of 4 Franken (1801)	W. 0	7	18	23	18	8	12	407, 6	4	9,18
	(See also Basil, Bern, Geneva, Neufchatel, St. Gall, and Zurich.)										
TREVES	Rixdollar, specie	W. 1	3	18	1	16	4	2	359,	4	2,13
TURKEY	Altmichlic of 60 Paras (1757)	W. 4	2	18	12	11	16	0	259,	3	0,16
	Piastre of Mustapha III. (1757)	W. 4	11	12	7	7	6	0	161,	1	10,48
	Altmichlic of 1773	W. 4	9½	17	5¼	10	6	12	228, 1	2	7,85
	Piastre of Abdul-hamed (1773)	W. 5	2	12	7	6	15	8	147, 5	1	8,59
	Another of the same period	W. 4	9	12	0	7	4	10	159, 6	1	10,28
	Piece of 100 Paras of Selim (1789)	W. 5	9	20	7¾	10	8	4	229, 7	2	8,07
	Double Piastre of Ditto	W. 5	12	16	22¾	8	9	10	186, 4	2	2,03
	Piastre of Selim of 1801	W. 5	6	8	6	4	7	8	95, 7	1	1,36

* This is the coin which is universally circulated under the name of the Spanish Dollar.

		Assay.			Weight.		Stan. Weight.			Contents in pure Silver.	Value in Sterling.	
			oz.	dwt.	dwt.	gr.	dwt.	gr.	mi.	grains.	s.	d.
TURKEY	Half Piastre	W.	6	13	4	1	1	14	16	35, 9	0	5,01
	Piastre of Crim Tartary (1778)	W.	6	13	10	5	4	2	4	90, 9	1	0,69
	Piastre of Tunis (1787).............	W.	6	5½	10	0	4	8	6	96, 5	1	1,47
	Piastre (1818)	W.	5	14	6	6½	3	1	4	67, 7	0	9,45
	Beshlie............................	W.	2	6	15	16½	12	10	8	276,	3	2,54
	Piece of Ten Parahs................	W.	5	14	0	16¾	8	14	0	7, 5	0	1,04
TUSCANY........	Ducatone (1676)....................	B.	0	7	20	2	20	17	4	460,	5	4,23
	Livornina (1723)...................	W.	0	3	17	10¼	17	4	13	381, 7	4	5,30
	Pezza della rosa (1726)............	W.	0	2	16	17¾	16	14	2	368, 2	4	3,41
	Francescone (1738) ½ in proportion ..	W.	0	2	17	13½	17	9	14	386, 4	4	5,95
	Leopoldone (1790)..................	W.	0	4	17	15	17	7	8	384, 3	4	5,66
	Piece of 10 Paoli of the Kingdom of Etruria (1801).............	W.	0	4	17	13½	17	5	18	382, 9	4	5,46
	Scudo Pisa of Ditto (1803)..........	W.	0	2	17	12	17	8	4	385, 0	4	5,76
	Piece of 10 Lire Ditto (1803)........	B.	0	7	25	6½	26	1	12	578, 7	6	8,80
	Ditto of 5 Lire Ditto (1803)..........	B.	0	7	12	15¼	13	0	18	289, 4	3	4,41
	Lira (1803)........................	B.	0	7	2	8	2	9	16	53, 4	0	7,45
UNITED STATES*.	Dollar (1795) ½, &c. in proportion	W.	0	6½	17	8	16	19	16	373, 5	4	4,15
	Dollar (1798)......................	W.	0	7	17	10½	16	21	6	374, 9	4	4,35
	Dollar (1802)......................	W.	0	10½	17	10	16	14	0	368, 3	4	3,42
	Dollar, an average of 8 years	W.	0	8½	17	8	16	16	0	370, 1	4	3,68
	Dime, or $\frac{1}{10}$ Dollar (1796)	W.	0	4	1	19½	1	18	14	39, 5	0	5,71
	Half Dime (1796)...................	W.	0	7	0	21¾	0	21	0	19, 5	0	2,72
VENICE	Scudo della Croce	B.	0	5	20	4½	20	15	8	458, 2	5	3,98
	Giustina, or Ducatone	B.	0	5½	17	12	17	22	8	398, 1	4	6,47
	Ducato†	W.	1	5	14	6	12	15	8	280, 8	3	3,21
	Lirazza, or Piece of 30 Soldi	W.	6	8	4	18¾	2	0	10	44, 9	0	6,26
	Tallaro (½, &c. in proportion).......	W.	1	3	18	10¾	16	12	16	367, 1	4	3,26
	Osella	B.	0	4½	6	6¾	6	9	16	142, 3	1	7,87
	Scudo of 10 Lire (1797)	W.	1	4	18	10¾	16	10	16	365, 2	4	2,99
	Piece of 2 Lire, or 24 Creutzers (1800)	W.	8	4½	5	19½	1	12	2	33, 4	0	4,66
	Ditto of 1 Lira	W.	8	3	2	21	0	18	7	16, 9	0	2,35
	Ditto of 2 Lire, called Moneta provinciale (1808).............	W.	8	3	5	13½	1	11	8	32, 8	0	4,58
	Ditto of 1 Lira	W.	8	5	3	1¾	0	18	8	17, 5	0	2,44
	Ditto of 2 Lire (1802) ½ and ¼ in prop.	W.	8	4	5	6¼	1	8	19	30, 5	0	4,25
WEST INDIES....	(*See* vol. i.)											
WIRTEMBERG ..	Rixdollar, specie	W.	1	3	18	1	16	14	2	359, 1	4	2,14
	Copstuck...........................	W.	4	2	4	6½	2	16	12	59, 8	0	8,35
WURTZBURG	Rixdollar, specie	W.	1	3	18	1¾	16	4	16	359, 7	4	2,22
	Copstuck...........................	W.	4	3	4	6½	2	16	6	59, 3	0	8,28
ZURICH	Rixdollar, or Ecu (1753)............	W.	0	14½	18	1¾	16	21	8	375,	4	4,36
	Half Rixdollar (1753)	W.	0	19½	8	23½	8	4	12	181, 8	2	1,38
	Ecu (1761).........................	W.	1	5	17	23¼	15	22	14	354,	4	1,43
	Half Ecu (1761)	W.	1	5	8	21¼	7	21	4	175,	2	0,43
	Ecu (1773).........................	W.	0	19	17	2	15	14	18	346, 8	4	0,42
	Half Ecu (1773)	W.	0	19	8	13	7	19	9	173, 4	2	0,21
	Ecu (1794).........................	W.	0	19½	16	6¼	14	19	18	329, 3	3	9,98
	Half Ecu (1786)	W.	1	0½	8	4¾	7	10	10	165, 2	1	11,06
	Piece of 20 Schillings (1798)........	W.	3	9½	3	18¾	2	14	6	57, 6	0	8,04

* The American Dollars, and inferior Silver Pieces of late coinage, vary in fineness from W. 4 dwt. to W. 9½ dwt.

† The Venetian Silver Ducats vary in weight from 13 dwt. 18 gr. to 14 dwt. 19 gr. some (of 1763) weighing only 13 dwt. 10 gr. The fineness also varies from W. 1 oz. 6 dwt. to W. 1 oz. 3¾ dwt.

EAST INDIES.	Assay.			Weight.		Stan. Weight			Contents in pure Silver.	Value in Sterling.	
		oz.	dwt.	dwt.	gr.	dwt.	gr.	mi.	grains.	s.	d.
EAST INDIA .... Rupee of Mohammed Shah	B.	0	6½	7	9¼	7	14	9	168, 7	1	11,55
.... of Ahmed Shah	B.	0	12	7	9¼	7	18	16	172, 8	2	0,12
.... of Allum Ghir (1759)	B.	0	13	7	11½	7	22	0	175, 8	2	0,54
.... of Shah Allum (1772)	B.	0	14	7	10	7	21	4	175,	2	0,43
.... of the same (Benares 1774)	B.	0	8	7	6¾	7	13	0	167, 5	1	11,38
.... of the same (1779)	B.	0	14½	7	11½	7	23	8	176, 8	2	0,68
.... Benares (1818)	B.	0	1½	7	7	7	14	5	168, 9	1	11,58
.... , Sicca, coined by the East India Company at Calcutta	B.	0	13	7	11½	7	22	0	175, 8	2	0,54
.... Calcutta (1818)	Stand.			8	0	8	0	0	175, 9	2	0,56
.... Arcot (1759)	B.	0	7	7	9¼	7	14	16	169, 1	1	11,61
.... Ditto (1782)	B.	0	8	7	6	7	12	4	166, 8	1	11,29
.... Ditto (1788)	B.	0	8	7	9¼	7	15	12	169, 8	1	11,71
.... Ditto, of the latest coinages	B.	0	4½	7	8½	7	12	2	166, 5	1	11,25
.... Bombay, old	B.	0	13	7	10⅓	7	21	4	174, 9	2	0,42
.... Bombay, new, or Surat (1818)	W.	0	0¼	7	11	7	10	4	164, 7	1	11,01
.... Lucknow	B.	0	8¾	7	5¼	7	12	2	166, 5	1	11,25
.... Sultanny	B.	0	3½	7	9	7	12	0	166, 3	1	11,22
.... Madepoor, or Nowsee	W.	0	5	7	5¾	7	1	16	157, 1	1	9,93
.... Madras Rajapoor	B.	0	4	7	7	7	10	4	164, 8	1	11,01
.... Jeypoor	B.	0	12	7	7	7	16	8	170, 6	1	11,82
.... Furruckabad (1818)	B.	0	1¼	7	5	7	10	14	165, 3	1	11,07
.... Chanderry	W.	0	0¾	7	5	7	4	8	159, 5	1	10,27
.... Oukery	W.	1	0½	7	7	6	14	0	146, 9	1	8,51
.... Shree Sicca of Poona	W.	0	1½	7	4½	7	3	6	158, 5	1	10,13
.... Halee Sicca	B.	0	12½	7	7¼	7	17	2	171, 2	1	11,90
.... Ougein	B.	0	5	7	6¼	7	10	4	164, 8	1	11,01
.... Maisore, or new Holkar	B.	0	7	7	5	7	10	8	165, 1	1	11,05
.... Indore Holkar	B.	0	4¼	7	5	7	8	6	163, 1	1	10,77
.... Chinsouree	B.	0	2	7	4¾	7	6	6	161, 2	1	10,50
.... Broach, old	W.	0	0½	7	10	7	0	10	164, 3	1	10,94
.... Broach, new	W.	0	10	7	10	7	1	18	157, 2	1	9,95
.... Brodera, old	W.	0	4½	7	10½	7	6	17	161, 8	1	10,59
.... Brodera, new	W.	0	10¼	7	10½	7	2	2	157, 3	1	9,96
.... Ana Sai, coined at Caira	W.	0	10¾	7	8¼	6	23	14	155, 1	1	9,65
.... Ana Sai, coined at Pitlad	W.	0	17½	7	9¼	6	19	4	151,	1	9,08
.... Amedabad Sicca	W.	0	7½	7	10	7	3	18	159, 1	1	10,21
.... Mungull Sai	W.	0	10¼	7	10½	7	2	4	157, 4	1	9,97
.... Mumo Sai	W.	0	8¾	7	9¾	7	2	14	157, 9	1	10,04
.... Seea Sai (coined in Futty Sing's time)	W.	0	9½	7	7¾	7	0	4	155, 6	1	9,72
.... Cambay	W.	0	18½	7	10	6	19	2	150, 9	1	9,07
.... Persian (1745)	B.	0	13	7	9¼	7	19	10	173, 5	2	0,22
.... Ditto (1789)	B.	0	12½	7	10	7	20	0	173, 9	2	0,28
.... Madras (1818)	Gold Stard.			7	12	7	12	0	165,	1	11,04
Fanam, Cananore	W.	0	1¼	1	11¾	1	11	10	32, 9	0	4,5
.... Bombay, old	B.	0	13	1	11¾	1	13	16	35,	0	4,88
.... Pondicherry	B.	0	5½	1	0½	1	1	2	22, 8	0	3,18
.... Ditto, double	W.	0	3	1	13¼	1	18	2	39,	0	5,44
Larin	B.	0	10½	3	2½	3	6	0	72, 1	0	10,06
Bussora Crux	W.	6	0¾	11	16	5	7	14	118, 1	1	4,49
Gulden of the Dutch East India Com. (1820)	W.	0	7½	6	22	6	16	6	148, 4	1	8,72

COMPUTATION OF COINS.

In order to show the principles on which the foregoing Tables are calculated, it may be proper first to explain the manner by which the value of any coin may be determined when its weight and fineness are known. For this purpose, the quantity of standard gold and silver contained in it must be first found; and then its sterling value may be ascertained from the Mint-price of the standard ounce.

GOLD COINS.

What is the sterling value of a French Double Louis d'or, the Report (per table, page 158,) being as follows:—weight 9 dwt. 20 gr. Assay W. $1\frac{1}{2}$ gr. that is, 0 car. $1\frac{1}{2}$ gr. worse than English standard?

car. gr.
From 22 0 the fineness of standard gold,
Subtract 0 $1\frac{1}{2}$

21 $2\frac{1}{2}$

Then, as 22 car. : 21 car. $2\frac{1}{2}$ gr. : : 9 dwt. 20 gr. : 9 dwt. 16 gr. the standard gold contained in the piece.

22	21 $2\frac{1}{2}$	9 20
4	4	24
88	$86\frac{1}{2}$	236
		86,5

(24
88)20414,0(232 grains nearly.
176 216

281 &c. 9 dwt. 16 gr.

Again, as 1 oz. : £3 17s. $10\frac{1}{2}$d. : : 9 dwt. 16 gr. : £1 17s. $7\frac{1}{2}$d. the value of the piece in sterling.

1	3 17 $10\frac{1}{2}$	9 16
20	20	24
20	77	232
24	12	$934\frac{1}{2}$
480	$934\frac{1}{2}$	

(12
48,0)21680,4(451,6
192
2,0)37 $7\frac{1}{2}$
248 &c.
4 £1 17s. $7\frac{1}{2}$d.
&c.

The foregoing calculations may be considerably abridged by using a constant decimal as a multiplier. The following is a general rule for gold coins.

Multiply the carat grains in the fineness by the troy grains in the weight, and again multiply this product by 92182; *cut off nine decimals, which will give the answer in pounds and decimals of a pound sterling.* Thus, in the foregoing question of the Louis d'or,

86,5 × 236 = 20414
92182

1,881803348
20

17,636
12

&c.

Ans. £1 17s. 7½d.

To find the contents of pure gold in the above coin, say,

	car.		car. gr.		dwt. gr.		gr.
As	24	:	21 2½	: :	9 20	:	212,6

Or, the contents in pure gold may be found by multiplying the standard weight by 11, and dividing by 12; and standard gold may be reduced to pure by reversing this operation.

SILVER COINS.

What is the value of a Spanish Dollar, the Report (per table, page 168,) being as follows:—weight, 17 dwt. 8 gr. Assay W. 8 dwt. that is, 0 oz. 8 dwt. worse than English standard?

	oz.	dwt.	
From	11	2	the fineness of standard silver,
Subtract	0	8	
	10	14	

	oz. dwt.		oz. dwt.		dwt. gr.		dwt. gr.	
Then, as	11 2	:	10 14	: :	17 8	:	16 17	the standard silver contained in the Dollar.
	20		20		24			
	222		214		416			
					214			

(24
222)89024(401
888
16 dwt. 17 gr.
224 &c.

	oz. gr.		s. d.		dwt. gr.		s. d.	
Again, as	1 or 480	:	5 2	: :	16 17	:	4 3¾	the value of the Dollar in sterling.
			12		24			
			62		401			
					62			

(12
48,0)2486,2(51,8
2400
4s. 3¾d.
86 &c.

The foregoing operation may be thus abridged.

RULE FOR SILVER COINS.—*Multiply the carat grains in the fineness by the troy grains in the weight, and again multiply this product by* 5818 ; *cut off seven decimals, which will give the answer in pence and decimals of a penny sterling.*

Thus, in the foregoing question of the Spanish Dollar,

$$\begin{array}{r} 214 \times 416 = 89024 \\ 5818 \\ \hline 51{,}7941632 \\ 4 \\ \hline 3{,}1766528 \end{array}$$

Ans. 4s. $3\frac{3}{4}$d.

To find the contents of the Spanish Dollar in pure silver, say—

As 12 oz. : 10 oz. 14 dwt. : : 17 dwt. 8 gr. : 370,9 gr.

Or the contents in pure silver may be found by multiplying the standard weight by 37, and dividing by 40; and, on the contrary, multiplying the contents in pure silver by 40, and dividing by 37, will give the standard weight.

RULES FOR STANDARDING COINS AND BULLION.

THE precious metals in England are mostly bought and sold at so much per ounce standard. It therefore becomes necessary to determine the standard weight ; and this must be calculated from the Assay Master's Report of weight and fineness.

But it may be useful first to explain the characters which are generally used in these Reports.

ASSAYERS' MARKS.

/ *	is	1 Dwt.
ij	..	2 ....
2	..	5 ....
C	..	10 ....
C2	..	15 ....
C2iij	..	18 ....
C/C	..	19 ....
ob (*Obulus*)	..	½ ....

The common method of finding the value of small quantities of gold and silver is by allowing, from the Assay Master's Report, at the rate of 4s. per carat, better or worse, in every ounce weight of gold ; and at the rate of 6d. per ounce, better or worse, in every ounce weight of silver. But when silver is more than 10 dwt. worse, an allowance of 2d. per ounce must be made for refining.

* This mark sometimes stands for 1 ounce as well as 1 pennyweight.

THE FOLLOWING ARE THE SCALES OF ALLOWANCE:

Scale for Gold.	Scale for Silver.
1 car. (4s.	1 oz. (6d.
1 gr. (1s.	15 dwt. (4½d.
½ gr. (6d.	10 dwt. (3d.
¼ gr. (3d.	5 dwt. (1½d.
	2½ dwt. (¾d.

Thus, to find the value of 2 oz. of gold B. 1 car. 1 gr. at £4 per oz.—To £8 (for 2 oz.) add 10s. for better, which gives the value £8 10s.—And to find the value of 12 oz. of silver, W. 10 dwts. at 5s. 6d. per oz. From £3 6s. (for 12 oz.) subtract 3s. for worse, which gives the value £3 3s.

RULES FOR STANDARDING GOLD.

As 22 carats are to the Assay or Report of fineness, so is the gross weight to the quantity that is to be added or subtracted from this gross weight, according as the report is *better* or *worse*. If better, the additional quantity is called (by the trade) *Betterness*, and if worse, the subtractional quantity is called *Worseness*.

Example—How much standard gold is there in an ingot of the following Report, B. 1 car. 3½ grains. Weight, 67 oz. 15 dwt. 8 gr.?

			oz.	dwt.	gr.
As 22	: 1	3½ : :	67	15	8
4	4		20		
88	7		1355		
4	4		24		
352	30		32528		

Or thus, as 22 : 23 3½ :: 67 oz. 15 dwt. 8 gr. : 73 oz. 10 dwt. 20 gr.

32528 × 30 ÷ 352 = 2772 gr. = 5 oz. 15 dwt. 12 gr.

	oz.	dwt.	gr.	
To	67	15	8	Gross Weight.
Add	5	15	12	Betterness.
	73	10	20	Standard.

The following method for standarding gold may be generally used with advantage:—

		oz.	dwt.	gr.	
		67	15	8	Gross Weight B. or W. 1 car. 3½ gr.
2 gr.	= ½	33	17	16	
1	= ½	16	18	20	
½	= ½	8	9	10	
		2)127	1	6	Divided by 22.
		11)63	10	15	
		5	15	12	Betterness or Worseness, as above.

RULES FOR STANDARDING SILVER.

As 11 oz. 2 dwt. to the assay, so is the gross weight to the quantity which is to be added or subtracted, according as the Report is B. or W.

EXAMPLE—In 287 oz. of silver, W. $12\frac{1}{2}$ dwt. how much standard?

```
      oz. dwt.    dwt.        oz.                oz. dwt.                    oz. dwt. gr.
As 11  2   :  12½   : :   287     Or thus, as 11  2 : 10 9½ : : 287  :  270 16 20
   20                      20
   ---                    ----
   222                    2840
                           12½
                          ----
                  222)71750(323 dwt. 4 gr. = 16 oz. 3 dwt. 4 gr.
                          oz. dwt. gr.
                  From   287   0   0 Gross Weight.
                  Subtract 16  3   4 Worseness.
                         ----------
                         270  16  20 Standard.
```

From the last example, the reason of the following rule for standarding silver is obvious.

Multiply half the weight in ounces by the assay in pennyweights, and divide the product by 111, *the quotient will be the betterness or worseness in ounces.*

EXAMPLE—How much standard silver in 160 ounces of B. $18\frac{1}{2}$ dwt.?

```
Half weight 80
            18½
            ---    oz. dwt. gr.                 oz. dwt. gr.
      111)1480(13   6   16              To  160   0   0 Gross.
          111                           Add  13   6  16 Betterness.
          ---                               -----------
          370 &c.                           173   6  16 Standard.
```

It should be observed that there are tables constructed, and sometimes used, for standarding gold and silver, as may be seen in *Postlethwayt's Dictionary of Commerce*, vol. 1, page 388 to 398; but from the simplicity and conciseness of the foregoing examples, it is manifest that such tables cannot much shorten the operation, though they may serve to check or prove the calculation.

RULES FOR CONVERTING THE FOREGOING TABLES OF COINS INTO FRENCH DENOMINATIONS.

To reduce English gold coin into Francs, and the contrary.

RULE—*Multiply the number of Pence by* ,105 : *and, the number of Francs by* 9,525.

EXAMPLE—How many Francs in a Sovereign?

Here 240d. × ,105 = 25 Francs 20 Centimes.

And again, 25 Francs 20 Centimes × 9,525 = 240 Pence.

To reduce English sterling silver into Francs, and the contrary.

RULE—*Multiply the number of Pence by* ,103 : *and, the number of Francs by* 9,709.

EXAMPLE—How many Francs in 240 Pence, silver value?

240 × ,103 = 24 Francs 72 Centimes;

And this number × 9,709 = 240 Pence.

The foregoing results are the Pars, very nearly, in gold and silver value, *see page* 146.

To bring English grains into Grammes, and the contrary.

RULE—*Multiply the number of Grains by* ,064792: *and, the number of Grammes by* 15,434.

EXAMPLE—How many Grammes in a Sovereign, weighing 113,1 English grains of pure gold?

Answer, 7 Grammes 328 Decigrammes, nearly; and this number multiplied by 15,434 equals 113,1 grains.

By the application of the above rules, all the foregoing Tables of Coins may be converted into French Denominations, except the first column, which contains the Assay, and which is thus reduced.

FOR GOLD COINS.

RULE—*Make the Assay Report the numerator, and* 24 *the denominator, and this vulgar fraction reduced to three places of decimals will give the Milliemes, according to the French expression.*

EXAMPLE—To convert English standard gold into Milliemes.

Thus, $\frac{22}{24}$ = 916 Milliemes. If the gold be 1 carat 2 grains worse than standard.

	car.	gr.		
	22	0		
	1	2		
	20	2	24	
	4		4	then $\frac{82}{96}$ = 854 Milliemes.
Carat grains	82		96	

Milliemes are reduced to carats by multiplying by 24 and cutting off three decimals.

FOR SILVER COINS.

To reduce English Assay Reports of silver into French Reports, or Milliemes.

RULE—*Make the number of pennyweights in the Assay Report the numerator, and* 240 *the denominator, and this reduced to a decimal fraction of three places gives the Milliemes.*

EXAMPLE—To reduce English standard silver into Milliemes.

dwt.	gr.
11	2
20	
222	

$\frac{222}{240} = \frac{37}{40}$ = 925 Milliemes.

To reduce Milliemes into English Assay Reports of silver.

RULE—*Multiply by* 240, *and cut off three decimals.* Thus, 891 Milliemes × 240 = 214 = 10 dwt. 14 gr. and this subtracted from 11 dwt. 2 gr. gives 8 dwt. worse than English standard.

EXPLICATION OF MODERN COINS;

*Containing a Description of the Devices and other Impressions of the principal Coins in the foregoing Tables, with Translations of their Inscriptions and Legends.**

AIX LA CHAPELLE.

Silver Coins.

The Rathspræsentger bears on the obverse an eagle within a circle, marked 16 on his breast, (32 on the double piece,) and within another circle the legend

REGVM CVRIA PRINCIPALIS PRIMA,
First and principal court of Kings,

and next the edge,

VRBS AQVENSIS. VRBS REGALIS. REGNI SEDES,
City of Aix; royal city; seat of government.

On the reverse, an altar, with two swords and a crown over it on the double piece, but on the single, a crown and the date within a circle; the legend on each is

LOCVS CORONATIONIS CÆSAREÆ,
The place of Cæsar's coronation:

Cæsar being a general title for the Emperors.

AUGSBURG.

Gold Coin.

The Ducat—Head of the reigning Prince, with name and title: thus,

FRANCISCVS I. D.G. ROM. IMP. S.A.
Francis I. by the grace of God, Emperor of Rome, ever august.

Reverse, arms of the city; legend,

AVGVSTA VINDELICORVM,

(the ancient name of the place and people.)

AUSTRIAN DOMINIONS.

Gold Coins.

The Souverain—Head of the reigning Emperor, with the name and title; thus,

FRANCISC. II. D. G. R. IMP. S. A. GE. HIE. HV. BO. REX.

that is, Franciscus secundus, Dei gratia, Romanus Imperator, semper augustus, Germaniæ, Hierosolymæ, Hungariæ, Bohemiæ, Rex,

Francis II. by the grace of God, Roman Emperor, ever august, King of Germany, Jerusalem, Hungary, and Bohemia.

Reverse, the arms of Austria on a St. Andrew's cross, with the date, and the legend,

ARCH. AVS. DVX BVRG. LOTH. BRAB. COM. FLAN.

that is, Archidux Austriæ, Dux Burgundiæ, Lotharingiæ, Brabantiæ, Comes Flandriæ,

* The words, or initials, on coins are generally thus distinguished. When they occupy the field and are written across the coin, they are called an *Inscription*; but when they run round the margin or on either side of the figure, they are denominated a *Legend*; and they are also thus called when they are upon the *Exergue*, which is the bottom of the piece, commonly separated from the field by a line.

It should be also observed that the side of a coin on which the portrait is delineated, is commonly termed the *Face* or *Obverse*, and the opposite side is called the *Reverse*.

As each description begins with the *Obverse*, the frequent repetition of the word seems unnecessary.

Archduke of Austria, Duke of Burgundy, Lorraine, Brabant, Count of Flanders.

The Double Souverain bears the same impression.

The DUCAT—Head of the reigning Sovereign. Reverse, arms of Austria with the two-headed eagle; the legends are the same as on the Souverain, except that among the titles, Brabant and Flanders are omitted, and the letters D. H. or D. HETR. are inserted; *that is,* Dux Hetruriæ, *Duke of Tuscany.* But the Hungarian Ducats, called *Kremnitz,* bear on the obverse a whole length figure of the Emperor, with the name and titles as above; and on the reverse, the Virgin and Child, with this legend,

S. MARIA MATER DEI PATRONA HVNG.

Holy Mary, mother of God, patroness of Hungary.

SILVER COINS.

The RIXDOLLAR *(Constitution)*—Head of the reigning Emperor, with name and titles; thus,

CAR. VI. D. G. R. I. S. A. G. HI. H. BOH. REX,

that is, Carolus sextus, Dei gratia, Romanus Imperator, &c. as on the Souverain. Reverse, a two-headed eagle crowned, bearing on his breast the arms of Austria, and in his talons a sword and sceptre; legend,

ARCHID. AUST. DUX. BU. M. MOR. COM. TYROL,

Archduke of Austria, Duke of Burgundy, Marquis of Moravia, Count of Tyrol,

with the date; and round the edge of the piece,

CONSTANTER CONTINET ORBEM,

He always guides the globe steadily.

The RIXDOLLAR *(Convention)*—Head of the reigning Sovereign, with name and title; thus,

M. THERESIA, D. GR. IMP. GE. HU. BO. REG.

Maria Theresa, by the grace of God, Empress of Germany, Queen of Hungary and Bohemia.

Reverse, as on the Rixdollar Constitution. The legend round the edge of the piece of Francis I. is,

PRO DEO ET IMPERIO,

For God and the Empire;

Round that of Maria Theresa,

JUSTITIA ET CLEMENTIA,

Justice and Clemency;

And round that of Joseph II.

VIRTUTE ET EXEMPLO,

By virtue and example.

The RIXDOLLAR of Hungary—Head, name, titles, and legend round the edge, as above. Reverse, the Virgin and Child, and the letters K. B.; legend, as on the Hungarian Ducat.

The FLORIN, or Half Rixdollar, bears the same impressions as the Rixdollar; as also, the Half Florin.

The COPSTUCK, or COPSTICK, (the 20 Creutzer piece,) bears the same impressions as the Rixdollar, except that there is no legend round the edge, and it is marked 20 on the reverse; the Half-Copstuck is marked 10.

BADEN.

GOLD COIN.

The DUCAT—A female figure standing by an altar; legend,

OBSEQUIUM JURARE PARATA,

Ready to swear obedience,

and the date. Reverse, the arms of Baden.

SILVER COIN.

The RIXDOLLAR—Head of the reigning Prince, with name and title; thus,

CAROLUS FRID. D. G. MARCHIO BAD. ET. H.

Charles Frederick, by the grace of God, Marquis of Baden, &c.

Reverse, arms of Baden; legend,

AD NORMAM CONVENTIONIS,

According to the rule of the Convention;

and on the exergue, the date, and

X EINE F MARCK,

Ten pieces to a Mark fine.

BASIL.

GOLD COINS.

The DUCAT—A griffin supporting the arms of the Republic; legend,

DOMINE CONSERVA NOS IN PACE,
Lord preserve us in peace.

Reverse,

DUCATUS REIPUBL. BASILEENSIS,
Ducat of the Republic of Basil.

The PISTOLE—Arms of the city; legend,

RESPVBLICA BASILIENSIS.

Reverse, a tripod, with the legend as on the Ducat.

SILVER COINS.

The PATAGON or ECU—A view of the city, over which is the name

BASILEA.

Reverse, a griffin supporting the arms of the city, with legend as on the Ducat. But the Ecus of 1795, &c. bear the arms of the city, and the legend,

RESPVBLICA BASILIENSIS;

and on the reverse, a wreath of oak, surrounding the legend as on the Ducat.

The THALER or RIXDOLLAR—The griffin, arms, and legend, as on the reverse of the Patagon. Reverse, a wreath of laurel, with the legend,

MONETA REIPUB. BASILEENSIS,
Money of the Republic of Basil.

BAVARIA.

GOLD COINS.

The CAROLIN—Head of the reigning Prince; legend,

CA. D. G. V. B. ET P. S. D. C. PR. S. R. I. A. ELL.

That is, Carolus, Dei gratia, utriusque Bavariæ et Palatinatus Dux, Princeps sancti Romani Imperii Archidux et Elector,

Charles, by the grace of God, Duke of both Bavarias and the Palatinate, Prince, Archduke, and Elector of the Holy Roman Empire.

Reverse, the Virgin and Child, supporting the arms of Bavaria; legend,

CLYPEVS OMNIBVS IN TE SPERANTIBVS,
A shield to all who hope in thee,

and the date. The Half and Quarter Carolins bear the same impression.

The MAX D'OR has the same impressions as the Carolin, except that the name is

MAX. JOS.
Maximilian Joseph.

The DUCAT—Head of the reigning Prince, with name and title; thus,

CAR. THEOD. D. G. C. P. R. VTR. BAV. DVX.

Reverse, the arms of Bavaria; legend,

S. R. I. ARCHID. & EL. DVX. I. CL. & M.

These initials mean,

Charles Theodore, by the grace of God, Count Palatine, Duke of both Bavarias, &c.

as on the Carolin; and the letters DVX. I. CL. and M. signify

Duke of Juliers, Cleves, and Munster.

But the Ducats coined since the year 1800, bear, with the head, all the titles as above, and the legend on the reverse is

PRO DEO ET POPULO,
For God and the people.

SILVER COINS.

The RIXDOLLAR—Head of the reigning Prince, with name and titles as on the gold coins. Reverse, arms of Bavaria and the date; and on other pieces, the Virgin and Child, with the legend,

PATRONA BAVARIÆ,
Patroness of Bavaria;

but the new Rixdollar, coined in 1800, bears on the reverse the arms of Bavaria, and the legend,

PRO DEO ET POPULO.

The COPSTUCK bears the same impressions as the Rixdollar.

BERN.

Gold Coins.

The Ducat—Arms of the city; legend,

REIPUBLICA BERNENSIS,
Republic of Bern.

Reverse,

BENEDICTUS SIT JEHOVA DEUS,
Blessed be God Jehovah.

The Pistole—Arms of the Republic; legend,

RESPUBLICA BERNENSIS.

Reverse, a wreath enclosing the words

DEUS PROVIDEBIT,
God will provide.

Other Pistoles have on the reverse a man armed with a battle-axe and resting upon the fasces, with the same legend.

Silver Coins.

The Patagon or Ecu—A man resting on his sword; legend as the Pistole. Reverse, arms of the city; legend,

RESPUBLICA BERNENSIS.

The Piece of 10 Batzen (as well as those of 5 and 2½ Batzen)—Arms of the city, with

RESPUBLICA BERNENSIS.

Reverse, a cross formed by eight B's and four crowns; legend as on the Ecu.

BREMEN.

Silver Coin.

The Piece of ⅔, or of 48 Grotes—A two-headed eagle and a crown, with the name of the reigning Emperor; thus,

FRANCISCUS D. G. ROM. IMP. S. AUG.
Francis, by the grace of God, Emperor of Rome, ever august.

Reverse, arms of the city; with the legend,

MONETA NOVA REIPUBL. BREMENSIS,
New money of the Republic of Bremen.

BRUNSWICK.

Gold Coins.

The Carl d'or—Head of the reigning Prince; legend,

CAROLVS D. G. DVX. BRVNS. ET LVN.
Charles, by the grace of God, Duke of Brunswick and Luneburg.

Reverse, a horse in full speed; legend,

NVNQVAM RETRORSVM,
Never backward, or straight forward.

Such as have been coined since 1796 bear no head, but the arms of Brunswick, with

CAROLVS GVLIELMVS FERDINANDVS;

and on the reverse,

X THALER, or V THALER.

with the date; and the legend as on the Carl d'or.

The Ducat bears the same impressions as the Carl d'or.

Silver Coins.

The Rixdollar (Old)—Head, name, and title of the reigning Prince, as on the gold coins. Reverse, the horse and legend as on the Carl d'or; but on the exergue are the words

X EINE FEINE MARCK CONVEN. M.
Ten pieces to a Mark fine, Convention money.

The Rixdollar of 1795—On the obverse, the words

I SPECIES THALER,

and the date; legend,

X EINE FEINE MARCK, &c.

as above. Reverse, arms of Brunswick, with the name and title of the reigning Prince.

The Piece of ⅔ (fine)—A man holding a tree, with the number 24, and the legend,

NVNQVAM RETRORSVM,

as on the Carl d'or. Reverse, a circle, containing the words

24 MARIENGROSCH. FEIN SILBER,
24 Mariengroschen, fine silver.

Legend, the name and title of the reigning Prince.

The Piece of $\frac{2}{3}$ (base)—Head of the reigning Prince, with name and title. Reverse, the horse and legend as before; and also the words

XX EINE FEINE MARCK, &c.

as on the Rixdollar and Piece of $\frac{2}{3}$ fine. The pieces of 1791 bear no head, but the words

XVI GVTE GROSCH. and XX EINE, &c.

Reverse, arms of Brunswick, with the Prince's name and title. The Pieces of 1795 bear the words

XXIIII MARIENGROSCH.

legend,

NACH DEM LEIPZIGER FVS,
According to the Leipsic rate of coinage.

Reverse, a horse, the Prince's name and title, and the mark $\frac{2}{3}$.

COLOGNE.

Gold Coins.

The Ducat—Head of the reigning Sovereign, with name and title; thus,

CLEM. AUG. ARCHIEP. ET EL. COLON.;

that is, Clemens Augustus Archiepiscopus et Elector Coloniensis,

Clement Augustus, Archbishop and Elector of Cologne.

Reverse, a circle of rays enclosing the legend

NON MIHI SED POPULO,
Not for me but for the people.

The Ducats coined by the City of Cologne bear the head of the reigning Sovereign, with his name and titles; and on the reverse, the arms of the city, with

DUCAT. CIVIT. COLON.
Ducat of the City of Cologne.

Silver Coin.

The Rixdollar—Head of the reigning Sovereign, with his name and titles. Reverse, arms of the city; legend,

MONETA NOVA LIB. ET IMPER. CIVIT. COLON.;

that is, Moneta nova liberæ et imperialis civitatis Coloniensis,

New Coin of the free and imperial City of Cologne,

with the date; and on some Rixdollars,

MON. NOVA LIB. REIPUB. COLONIENSIS,
New coin of the free Republic of Cologne.

DENMARK.

Gold Coins.

The Ducat Current—Head of the reigning King, with name and title, thus:

CHRISTIANVS VII. D. G. REX DAN. NORVEG.
Christian VII. by the grace of God, King of Denmark and Norway.

Reverse, value of the coin, surrounded by a crown; legend,

GLORIA EX AMORE PATRIÆ,
Glory from the love of our country.

The Ducat Specie of 1791—A man resting on a club and bearing a shield; legend,

MONETA AUREA DANICA,
Gold money of Denmark.

Reverse,

1 SPECIES DUCAT. 23½ KARAT. 67 STYKKER. 1 MARK BRUTO,

1 *Ducat specie, 23½ Carats fine, 67 pieces to the Mark gross.*

Ducats of anterior date bear on the obverse the head, name, and title of the reigning King; and on the reverse, the arms of Denmark, and the legend

PRUDENTIA ET CONSTANTIA,
Prudence and Perseverance.

Some bear on the reverse a ship, with the legend

DUCE PRUDENTIA CONSTANTIA COMITE,
Prudence being the guide, and Perseverance the companion.

The CHRISTIAN D'OR—Head, name, and title of the reigning Prince, as above. Reverse, a sun and three crowns, with the legend as on the Ducat Current.

SILVER COINS.

The RYKSDALER (old, coined for Norway,)—Head of the reigning King, with name and title; thus,

FRIDERICVS V. D. G. REX DAN. NOR. V. G. or D. G. DAN. NORV. VAND. GOTH. REX,

Frederick V. by the grace of God, King of Denmark, Norway, the Vandals, and the Goths.

Reverse, a lion and battle-axe, the value of the coin, and the following legend in the Norwegian language, in two concentric circles,

MOD TROSKAB DAPPERHED. OGHVAD DER ÆRE GIVER DEN HEELE VERDENRAND BLANT NORSKE KLIPPER LAERE,

Spirit, loyalty, valour, and whatever is honourable, let the whole world learn among the rocks of Norway.

On the same coin, of a later date, the legend is

TROE LOVE MOD OGHVAD DAN KONGENS GUNST KAND VINDE, MENS NORGE KLIPPE HAR MAND SKAL HOS NORDMAND FINDE;

True lion's heart and whatever can win a Danish Monarch's love, whilst Norway has rocks, shall be found among Norwegians.

The RYKSDALER of 1777—The King's cypher and a crown; legend,

D. G. DAN. NORV. VAND. GOTH. REX,

as before. Reverse, arms of Denmark; legend,

GLORIA EX AMORE PATRIÆ,

Glory from the love of our country,

The RYKSDALER of 1795—Head, name, and titles of the reigning King. Reverse, arms of Denmark, and value of the coin.

The 4 MARK Piece—A man on horseback, with the King's name and title, and value of the coin. Reverse, arms of the King; legend,

DOMINUS MIHI ADJUTOR,

The Lord is my helper,

The CROWN—Head of the reigning King, with name, and

DEI GRATIA.

Reverse, a crown, and the inscription,

PRUDENTIA ET CONSTANTIA,

Prudence and Perseverance;

legend, the King's titles, as above.

The RYKSDALER of Holstein—Head, name, and title, as above. Reverse, arms of Denmark with

60 SCHILLING. SCHLESW. HOLST. COURANT,

60 *Schillings Sleswig and Holstein currency.*

The Piece of 24 SCHILLINGS Danish—The King's cypher, with a crown and the titles, as above. Reverse, arms of Denmark, and over them

24 SKILLING DANSKE.

ENGLAND.

OLD GOLD COINS.

The GUINEA—Head of the Sovereign; legend,

GEORGIUS III. DEI GRATIA,

George III. by the Grace of God.

Reverse, the King's arms; legend,

M. B. F. ET H. REX, F. D. B. ET L. D. S. R. I. AT. ET E.

That is, Magnæ Britanniæ, Franciæ, et Hiberniæ, Rex, Fidei Defensor, Brunswickensis et Luneburgensis Dux, Sancti Romani Imperii Archithesaurarius et Elector,

King of Great Britain, France, and Ireland, Defender of the Faith, Duke of Brunswick and Luneburg, Arch-Treasurer and Elector of the Holy Roman Empire.

But the coins minted since the Union with Ireland (1801) have the legend,

BRITANNIARUM REX, FIDEI DEFENSOR,
King of the British Islands, Defender of the Faith;
and round the shield, the motto of the Garter,

HONI SOIT QUI MAL Y PENSE,
Shame be to him who thinks ill of it.

The HALF GUINEA has the same impressions as the Guinea.

The SEVEN SHILLING PIECE—Head and name of the Sovereign as above. Reverse, a crown with the legend,

MAG. BRI. FR. ET HIB. REX;

and on the pieces coined since the Union with Ireland,

BRITANNIARUM REX FIDEI DEFENSOR.

NEW GOLD COIN.

The SOVEREIGN—Head of the Sovereign, with the legend,

GEORGIUS III. D. G. BRITANNIAR. REX, F. D.

and the date. Reverse, the image of St. George armed, sitting on horseback encountering the dragon with a spear; the said device is placed within the Garter, bearing its motto as above, with a newly-invented graining on the edge of the piece.

OLD SILVER COINS.

The CROWN—Head of the Sovereign, with

GEORGIUS II. DEI GRATIA.

Reverse, four crowned shields, viz. of England, France, Scotland, and Ireland, with a star in the centre; legend,

MAG. BR. FR. ET HIB. REX,

to which (ever since the accession of the House of Hanover) the King's German titles have been added, as on the Guinea. The Crowns of Charles II. have in the angles between the shields, four double linked C's. Those of William and Mary, four interlinked W's and M's. Some of Queen Anne's Crowns have two roses in two of the angles, and the Prince of Wales's plume of feathers in the others. The Crowns of George I. have four sceptres. It may also be observed, that the Crowns of King William have, instead of the stars in the centre, the arms of Nassau; and that round the edge of the pieces coined by King William and Queen Anne, there is the following legend:

DECUS ET TUTAMEN, ANNO REGNI, &c.
Ornament and safety, the year of the King's reign, &c.

The HALF-CROWN bears the same impressions as the Crown.

The SHILLING bears the same impressions as the Crown, but in the Shillings of George II. there are four roses in the angles, on the reverse; and in the Shillings of George III. the four crowns instead of being placed on the shields, are placed in the angles. The SIXPENCE bears the same impressions as the Shilling.

The DOLLAR (issued by the Bank in 1804), bears the King's head, with the legend,

GEORGIUS III. DEI GRATIA REX.

Reverse, an oval, with a crown of towers over it, enclosing a figure of *Britannia*.

NEW SILVER COINS.

The CROWN—Head of the Sovereign, with the legend,

GEORGIUS III. D. G. BRITANNIARUM REX, F. D.

and the date. Reverse, the same as the reverse of the SOVEREIGN. Round the edge of the piece,

DECUS ET TUTAMEN. ANNO REGNI LX.
Ornament and Safety; the 60th year of the King's reign.

The HALF-CROWN—Head of the Sovereign; legend,

GEORGIUS III. DEI GRATIA,

and the date. Reverse, the arms of the United Kingdom contained in a shield surrounded by the Garter, bearing its motto; legend,

BRITANNIARUM REX, FID. DEF.

with a newly-invented graining on the edge.

The SHILLING and SIXPENCE—Head of the Sovereign; legend,

GEOR. III. D. G. BRITT. REX, F. D.

and the date. Reverse, the same as the Half-Crown, except that the legend is omitted.

The NEW HALF-CROWN of GEORGE IV. bears the effigy of his Majesty, with the inscription

GEORGIUS IIII. D. G. BRITANNIAR. REX, F. D.

Reverse, the ensigns armorial of the United Kingdom contained in a shield, surmounted by the royal crown; the rose, thistle, and shamrock being placed round the shield, with the word ANNO and the date of the year. The edge is marked with the the newly-invented graining.

The NEW SHILLING and SIXPENCE of GEORGE IV. bear the same impressions as the new Half-Crown.

FRANCE.

GOLD COINS.

The LOUIS—Head of the reigning King, with his name and title: thus,

LUD. XVI. D. G. FR. ET NAV. REX,

that is, Ludovicus XVI. Dei Gratia, Franciæ et Navarræ Rex,

Louis XVI. by the Grace of God, King of France and Navarre.

Reverse, the arms of France and Navarre, with a crown over them. On the Pieces coined before 1786, there are two dictinct shields; and on those coined since 1786, a double shield; legend,

CHRS. REGN. VINC. IMPER.

that is, Christus regnat, vincit, imperat,

Christ reigns, conquers, governs;

under the arms is a letter, by which the mint where the piece was coined is known. The Double and Half Louis bear the same impressions.

The Pieces struck in the year 1791, have on the obverse the head of the King, with the title,

LOUIS XVI. ROI DES FRANCOIS,

Louis XVI. King of the French;

and on the reverse, the Genius of France writing the Constitution on a tablet resting on a pillar, with a cock on one side, and on the other the fasces and cap of Liberty, with the legend,

REGNE DE LA LOI,

Reign of the law;

and at the bottom,

L' AN 4 DE LA LIBERTE,

The year 4 of liberty.

The Piece of 1793 has, instead of the head, a crown of oak leaves containing the words 24 LIVRES; legend,

REPUBLIQUE FRANÇOISE L'AN II.

French Republic, the year 2.

Reverse, as on the Louis of 1791, except that the date is in figures only.

The Piece of 40 FRANCS, 1802—Head of Bonaparte; legend,

BONAPARTE PREMIER CONSUL,

Bonaparte, first Consul.

Reverse, a wreath of laurel, containing the words 40 FRANCS; legend,

REPUBLIQUE FRANÇOISE AN. XI.

and round the edge of the piece,

DIEU PROTEGE LA FRANCE,

God protect France.

In 1804, on Bonaparte's being declared Emperor, the words round the head were altered to NAPOLEON EMPEREUR. The Piece of 20 Francs bears the same impressions, except the figures that mark its value.

The Piece of 40 FRANCS, 1818—Head of the King, with name and title, thus:

LOUIS XVIII. ROI DE FRANCE.

Reverse, arms of France, and 40 F. within two branches of laurel. Round the edge of the piece,

DOMINE SALVUM FAC REGEM,
O Lord, save the King.

SILVER COINS.

The ECU of 6 LIVRES—Head of the reigning King, with name and title, as on the Louis. Reverse, the arms of France, between two laurel branches; legend,

SIT NOMEN DOMINI BENEDICTUM,
Blessed be the name of the Lord,

and a letter denoting the place where the piece was coined. Round the edge are the words

DOMINE SALVUM FAC REGEM,

as on the 40 Franc Piece. The Ecu of three Livres, the Pieces of 24, 12, and 6 Sous, all bear the same impressions, except that the three last mentioned coins have no motto round the edge.

The ECU of 1791—Head of the King; legend,

LOUIS XVI. ROI DES FRANCOIS.

Reverse, the Genius of France, &c. as on the Louis of the same period. Round the edge,

LA NATION LA LOI ET LE ROI,
The nation, the law, and the King.

The Pieces of 15 and 30 Sols, coined at the same period, bear the same impressions, except that instead of the fasces and cock, their value is marked, and that the motto round the edge is omitted.

The 6 LIVRE Piece of the Republic—The Genius of France, &c. as above. Reverse, a wreath of oak, containing the words SIX LIVRES; legend,

REPUBLIQUE FRANCOISE L'AN II.

and round the edge,

LIBERTE, EGALITE,
Liberty, equality.

The 5 FRANC Piece of the Republic—Three figures, representing Hercules and two young women joining their hands; legend,

UNION ET FORCE,
Union and strength.

Reverse, a wreath of laurel and oak, containing the words 5 FRANCS L'AN 7; legend,

REPUBLIQUE FRANCOISE;

and round the edge,

GARANTIE NATIONALE,
National guarantee.

The 5 FRANC Piece of 1803.—Head of Bonaparte; legend as on the 40 Franc Piece. Reverse, a wreath of laurel, containing the value, 5 FRANCS; legend,

REPUBLIQUE FRANCOISE,

but on pieces coined in 1809,

EMPIRE FRANCOIS.

Round the edge, the words

DIEU PROTEGE LA FRANCE,

as before.

The FRANC of Louis XVIII. bears the same impressions as the 40 Franc Piece of the same period; except the mark of the value.

FRANCFORT ON THE MAINE.

GOLD COINS.

The DUCAT—An eagle, with the legend,

TURRIS FORTISSIMA NOMEN DOMINI,
The name of the Lord is the strongest tower.

Reverse, a cross with ornaments; legend,

DUCATUS REIPUBLICÆ FRANCOFURTENSIS,
Ducat of the Republic of Francfort.

The DUCAT of 1796—View of the city. Reverse, a wreath of laurel surrounding the words

AUS DEN GEFÆSEN DER KIRCHENUND BURGER DER STADT FRANCKFURT,
Out of the Plate of the Churches and of the Citizens.

SILVER COIN.

The RIXDOLLAR—The impressions of these

coins have varied much; most of them bear an eagle; but the reverses and legends are very different in coins of different dates; they may be easily distinguished, by the word

FRANCKFURT or FRANCOFURT,

which is to be found on some part of the Piece, as also the words

AD NORMAM CONVENTIONIS,
According to the rate of Convention money,

and

X E. F. MARK, or X EINE FEINE MARK,
10 *to a Mark of fine silver.*

These last words within a circle or wreath, form the reverse of the more modern pieces, and coins of 1796 bear likewise the German legend,

AUS DEN GEFÆSEN, &c.

as on the Ducat; and on the obverse, an eagle, and the legend,

DER STADT FRANCKFURT,
Of the city of Francfort.

GENEVA.

Gold Coin.

The Pistole—On Pistoles of an ancient date, a two-headed eagle crowned; on those of modern date, a sun with the letters I. H. S. in the centre; legend,

POST TENEBRAS LUX,
After darkness light.

Reverse, the arms of the city, with a sun over them; legend,

RESPUBL. GENEVEN.
Republic of Geneva.

Silver Coins.

The Patagon or Ecu (old) bears the same impression as the Pistole.

The Piece of 21 Sous—The inscription,

POST TENEBRAS LUX.

and under it 21, the whole surrounded with various ornaments, and surmounted by a sun: reverse, as on the Pistole.

The Ecu of 1794—The head of a woman with a mural crown, legend

REPUBLIQUE GENEVOISE,
Republic of Geneva;

and under it,

EGALITE, LIBERTE, INDEPENDANCE,
Equality, liberty, independence.

Reverse, two ears of corn, and the inscription

PRIX DU TRAVAIL, L'AN III. DE L'EGALITE,
The prize of labour, the year 3 of equality;

legend,

APRES LES TENEBRES LA LUMIERE,
After darkness light.

But the Ecus coined since that period, bear on the obverse a sun with the letters I. H. S. in the centre; legend,

POST TENEBRAS LUX,

as above, with

XII FLORINS IX SOLS.

Reverse, the arms of Geneva encircled by a wreath of oak; legend,

GENEVE REPUBLIQUE L'AN V. DE L'EGALITE.

The Half Ecu bears the same impressions, except that it is marked within the sun, VI FLORIN IVS. VId.

The Piece of 15 Sols—A sun, with 15 SOLS in the centre; legend,

EGALITE, LIBERTE, INDEPENDANCE.

Reverse, an eagle within a wreath; legend,

POST TENEBRAS LUX.

The Piece of 6 Sols—A wreath containing the words SIX SOLS; legend,

POST TENEBRAS LUX,

Reverse, as on the new Ecu.

GENOA.

Gold Coins.

The Doppia—The Virgin and Child on a cloud, with a sceptre and a crown of stars; legend,

ET REGE EOS,
And govern them:

with the initials of the Doge's name and the date. Reverse, a cross with 4 stars, or flowers, and the legend,

DVX ET GVB. REIP. GENV.

that is, Dux et Gubernator Reipublicæ Genuensis,

Doge and Governor of the Republic of Genoa.

The Pieces of 2, 4, and 5 Doppie, bear the same impressions.

The Sequin—A figure of St. John the Baptist; legend,

NON SVRREXIT MAJOR,
A greater has not arisen.

Reverse, the arms of Genoa with a crown; legend,

DVX ET GVB. REIP. GENV.

as before.

The Genovina—The Virgin and Child, as on the Doppia, and the same legend. Reverse, arms of Genoa with a crown, and the legend DVX, &c. as above. The old Genovine of 100, 50, and 25 lire, and the new ones of 96, 48, and 24 lire, bear the same impressions.

The Four Pistole Piece of the Ligurian Republic—A woman holding a spear and resting on a shield; legend,

REPUBBLICA LIGURE, ANNO I, L. 96.
Ligurian Republic, year 1, 96 lire.

Reverse, a wreath of laurel, with the fasces and cap of Liberty; legend,

NELL' UNIONE LA FORZA,
Strength in union;

and round the edge of the piece

PESO GRANI 550, BONTA CAR. 22,
Weight 550 grains, fineness 22 carats.

Silver Coins.

The Scudo della Croce—Impressions as on the Doppia.

The Scudo di S. Giambatista (old) of 5 Lire—Figure of St. John the Baptist, with the legend as on the Sequin, and the initials of the Doge's name. Reverse, arms of Genoa; legend, DVX, &c. as on the Doppia.

The Scudo of 8 Lire bears the same impressions as the preceding, except that it is marked L. 8 on the reverse, and its divisions L. 4, L. 2, L. 1.

The Madonnina—A whole length figure of the Virgin; legend,

SVB TVVM PRESIDIVM,
Under thy protection;

with the date; and round the figure,

NE DERELINQ. NOS,
Do not forsake us.

Reverse as on the Scudo di S. Giambatista.

The Scudo of the Ligurian Republic—Two figures, representing a soldier and a woman; legend,

LIBERTA EGUAGLIANZA,
Liberty, equality;

and the date. Reverse, arms of Genoa, encircled by a palm and branch of laurel, and surmounted by the cap of Liberty; legend,

REPUBBLICA LIGURE ANNO I, L. 8.

round the edge,

PESO GRANI 726, BONTA ONCIE 10 16
Weight 726 grains, fineness 10 ounces 16 deniers.

HAMBURGH.

Gold Coins.

The Ducat—The inscription,

MON AVR. HAMBVRGENSIS AD LEGEM IMPERII,
Gold coin of Hamburgh, according to the law of the Empire;

and at the top, a city gate with three towers. Ducats of an old date have the gate in the centre, and round it the legend,

MONETA AVREA HAMBVRGENSIS.

Reverse of both, a two-headed eagle crowned, with the name of the reigning Emperor of Germany, thus:

JOSEPHVS II. D. G. ROM. IMP. SEMP. AVGVST.
Joseph II. by the grace of God, Emperor of Rome, ever august.

SILVER COINS.

The RIXDOLLAR (*Specie, or Banco*)—Arms of Hamburgh; legend,

MONETA NOVA HAMBVRGENSIS,
New coin of Hamburgh;

and at the bottom 48 SCHILL. SPEC. Reverse as on the Ducat.

The Piece of 2 MARKS—The arms of the city; legend,

HAMBURGER CURRENTGELD,
Current money of Hamburgh;

and 32 SCHILL. or the legend is,

32 SCHILLING HAMBURGER COURANT.

Reverse as on the Ducat. The Pieces of 1 Mark and under are marked 16 SCHILLING, 8 SCHILLING, &c.

HANOVER.

GOLD COINS.

The GEORGE D'OR—The King's arms; legend,

GEORG. II. D. G. M. B. F. ET H. REX. F. D.

Reverse,

V THALER,
5 Rixdollars of account;

and the date; legend,

BRUNS. ET LUN. DUX. S. R. I. A. T. H. ET ELECT.

as on the English coins, *which see.*

The DUCAT—The King's arms, with his name and all his titles, as on the Guinea. Reverse, a horse at full speed; and on the exergue,

EX AVRO HERC.
From the gold of the mines of Hartz;

and the date. Ducats of an old date have a horse running over rough ground, and the legend,

NEC ASPERA TERRENT,
Neither do rough places deter him.

Other Ducats bear the head, name, &c. of the reigning King; and on the reverse,

1 DUCAT. N. D. R. FUS,

that is, Nach dem reichs fuss,

According to the rate of the Empire,

and the legend,

BRUNS. ET LUN. DUX. &c.

The GOLD FLORIN, or GOLD GULDEN—The King's arms and title. Reverse, the inscription,

1 GOLD GULDEN 2 THALER,

and the letters N. D. R. FU. as on the Ducat; and the same legends.

SILVER COINS.

The RIXDOLLAR—Arms of the reigning King, with his name and title, as in the English coins. Reverse, a horse running over rough ground; legend,

NEC ASPERA, &c.

as above. Some Rixdollars bear on the reverse, a figure of St. Andrew on the cross; legend, the King's German titles.

The PIECE of $\frac{2}{3}$, (fine)—Some of these bear the head of the reigning King; some, a man holding a tree; others the words

24 MARIEN GROSCH.

Reverse, the King's arms; legend, the King's name and titles, as on the Guinea; and under the arms, $\frac{2}{3}$ in an oval, with,

FEIN SILBER,
Fine silver:

and sometimes also N. D. REICHS F. as on the Ducat. The divisions of this piece are marked $\frac{1}{3}$ and $\frac{1}{6}$, and bear in other respects the same impressions.

The PIECE of $\frac{2}{3}$, (base)—The King's head, name, and title. Reverse, $\frac{2}{3}$ in large figures; legend,

18 STUCK EINE MARK FEIN,
18 *Pieces to a Mark fine.*

HESSE CASSEL.

GOLD COINS.

The PISTOLE—Head of the reigning Prince, with his name and titles, thus:

WILHELMUS IX. D. G. HASS. LANDG. HAN. COM.
William IX. by the grace of God, Landgrave of Hesse, Count of Hanau.

Reverse, a star, and within it the legend,

VIRTVTE ET FIDELITATE,
By courage and fidelity;

in the centre, a lion. Other Pistoles, coined in 1794, &c. bear on the reverse a lion at rest, with standards and military trophies, and over this 5 THALER.

SILVER COINS.

The RIXDOLLAR *(Convention)*—Head of the reigning Prince, with name and title as on the Pistole. Reverse, arms of Hesse Cassel; legend,

X ST. EINE FEINE MARK,
10 *Pieces to a Mark fine;*

and at the bottom, the word

IUSTIRT,
Adjusted, or *verified.*

In Pieces of more modern date, (1796, &c.) this last word is not to be found, but under the above legend, the words

BIBERER SILBER,
Silver of the mine of Biber;

and in some pieces of 1770, the words

EX VISCERIBUS FODINÆ BIEBER,
From the bowels of the mine of Biber.

The Half and Quarter Rixdollars are marked XX ST. &c. and 40 ST. &c. and under the arms $\frac{2}{3}$ or $\frac{1}{3}$.

The THALER, or RIXDOLLAR of account—Head, name, and title, as above. Reverse, a star with a lion in the centre, and the words

VIRTVTE ET FIDELITATE,

as before, or the arms of Hesse; the legend, in both, is

EIN THALER,
1 *Thaler;*

and on the Half piece,

EIN HALBER THALER.

HESSE DARMSTADT.

GOLD COINS.

The CAROLIN—Head of the reigning Prince, with name and titles, thus:

ERNEST LVD. D. G. HASS. LANDG. PR. HERSF.
Ernest Louis, by the grace of God, Landgrave of Hesse, Prince of Hirchsfeld.

Reverse, a cross formed by four crowns, and the letters EL four times repeated; in the centre, an X or V, according as it is a Carolin or a Half Carolin; legend,

OCCULTA PATEBUNT,
Hidden things shall be brought to light.

The DUCAT—Head, name, and titles of the reigning Prince. Reverse, arms of Hesse Darmstadt; legend,

SINCERE ET CONSTANTER,
Sincerely and constantly.

HOLLAND.

GOLD COINS.

The RYDER—An armed horseman above the arms of the province; legend,

MO. AUR. PRO. CONFOED. BELG. ZELAND.

that is, Moneta aureæ provinciæ confœderationis Belgicæ Zelandiæ,

Gold coin of Zealand, a province of the Belgic confederacy.

Reverse, arms of the United Provinces, with

14 GL.

14 *Guilders,* or *Florins ;*

legend,

CONCORDIA RES PARVÆ CRESCUNT,

Small things increase by concord.

The DUCAT—A foot soldier with a drawn sword, and a bundle of arrows ; legend,

CONCOR. RES. PAR. CRES.

as above, and HOL. or ZEL. &c. to distinguish the Province. Reverse, the inscription,

MO. ORD. PROVIN. FŒDER. BELG. AD LEG. IMP.

that is, Moneta ordinarea provinciarum fœderatarum Belgicarum ad legem Imperii,

The common coin of the confederated Belgic Provinces, according to the law of the Empire.

SILVER COINS.

The DUCATOON bears the same impressions as the Ryder, except that the legend instead of MO. AUR. begins with the words

MO. NO. ARG.

Moneta nova argentea,

New silver coin ;

and that the value is omitted.

The FLORIN, or GUILDER—A woman leaning on a book which lies on an altar, and holding in the other hand a lance with the cap of Liberty ; legend,

HANC TVEMVR, HAC NITIMVR,

This we support, on this we depend.

Reverse, arms of the United Provinces, with 1 G. ; legend,

MO. ARG. ORD. FOE. BELG.

that is, Moneta argentea ordinum fœderationis Belgicæ,

The common silver coin of the Belgic confederacy ;

and the name of the particular province, marked thus : HOLL. for Holland ; ZEL. for Zealand ; GEL. & C. Z. for Guelders and the County of Zutphen ; WEST F. for West Friesland ; TRAJ. (Trajectus) for Guilder Utrecht ; TRANSI, for Overyssel ; GRON. for Groningen.

The RIXDOLLAR—A soldier with a drawn sword ; and in his left hand the arms of the Province ; legend,

MO. NO. ARG. &c.

as on the Ducatoon and Ryder. Reverse, arms of the United Provinces, with the date ; legend,

CONCORDIA RES, &c.

as on the Ryder.

The RIXDOLLAR of the KINGDOM of HOLLAND—Head of the reigning King, with name and title, thus :

NAP. LODEW. 1 KON. VAN HOLL.

that is, Napoleon Lodewig, I. Konig van Holland,

Napoleon Louis I. King of Holland.

Reverse, arms of Holland, with 50 Ss. (50 *Stivers ;*) legend,

KONINGRIJK HOLLAND,

Kingdom of Holland.

LIEGE.

GOLD COIN.

The DUCAT—Head of the reigning Bishop, with his name and some of his titles ; and on the reverse, his arms ; legend,

LEOD. EP. PR. FR. RAT.

Leodicensis episcopus princeps,

Prince Bishop of Liege, &c.

Ducats coined during an interregnum bear a mitred head, with the legend,

S. LAMBERTUS PATRO. LEOD.

St. Lambert, Patron of Liege.

Reverse, arms of Liege; legend,

DEC. ET CAPLI. LEOD. SEDE VACANTE,

The Dean and Chapter of Liege, the See being vacant.

SILVER COINS.

The silver coins of Liege bear the same impressions as the gold coins. The legend of the Patagons coined during an interregnum is

MONETA NOVA CAPLI. LEOD. SEDE VACANTE,

as above.

The ESCALIN bears on the reverse a lion supporting a small escutcheon, with the legend,

DEC. ET CAPLI, &c.

LORRAINE.

GOLD COINS.

The LEOPOLD—Head of the reigning Prince, with name and title, thus:

LEOP. I. D. G. D. LOT. BAR. REX. IER.

that is, Leopoldus I. Dei gratia, Dux Lotharingiæ et Barri, Rex Ierosolymæ,

Leopold I. by the grace of God, Duke of Lorraine and Bar, King of Jerusalem.

Reverse, arms of Lorraine; legend,

TE DOMINE SPES MEA,

In Thee, O Lord, is my hope.

SILVER COIN.

The LEOPOLD, or ECU—Bears the same impressions as the Gold Leopold, except the legend on the reverse, which is

IN TE DOMINE SPERAVI,

In Thee, O Lord, have I hoped.

LUBEC.

SILVER COINS.

The RIXDOLLAR or 3 MARK PIECE—A two-headed eagle crowned, with 48 on its breast; legend,

MON. NOVA IMP. CIVITAT. LUBECÆ,

New coin of the imperial city of Lubec.

Reverse, arms of the city; legend,

48 SCHILLING COURANT GELDT ANNO, &c.

48 *Schillings currency, the year, &c.*

The DOUBLE and SINGLE MARK are distinguished by the numbers 32 and 16 on the eagle; and on the reverse, above the arms, there are two palm branches surrounding the words 32 SCHILLING or 16 SCHILLING; legend,

COURANT GELDT.

LUCCA.

GOLD COIN.

The DOPPIA—Head of Jesus crowned; legend,

VULTVS SANCTVS,

Holy countenance.

Reverse, arms of the Republic; legend,

RESPUBLICA LUCENSIS,

Republic of Lucca.

SILVER COINS.

The SCUDO—An armed horseman giving his cloak to a beggar; legend,

SANCTUS MARTINUS,

St. Martin.

Reverse, arms of Lucca; legend,

RESPUBLICA LUCENSIS.

The divisions of the Scudo bear the same impressions; but some pieces, instead of the figure of St. Martin, have a crucifix, with the legend

VULTVS SANCTVS,

as above.

The BARBONE—Head of Jesus crowned; legend,

VULTVS SANCTVS.

Reverse, a cross; legend as on the Scudo.

MALTA.

Gold Coins.

The Louis—Head of the reigning Grand-Master, with his name and title, thus:

EMMANUEL DE ROHAN M. M.

that is, Magister Magnus,

Grand-Master.

Reverse, arms of the order and of the Grand-Master in two separate shields, with a crown over them, and

S. 10,

10 *Scudi,* or *crowns;*

legend,

HOSPITALIS ET S. SEPUL. HIERUSA.

Of the Hospital and Holy Sepulchre of Jerusalem.

Silver Coins.

The Ounce—Head, name, and title of the Grand Master, as on the Louis. Reverse, arms of the order, mostly borne by an eagle, with

T. 30,

30 *Tari;*

legend and date as on the gold coins. The Half Ounce is marked T. XV. But some Ounces of ancient date, bear a figure of St. John the Baptist, with the legend,

NON SVRREXIT MAJOR,

A greater has not arisen;

and T. XXX. at the bottom. Reverse, arms of the order, with the name and title of the Grand Master.

The Scudo bears the same impressions as the Ounce, except that there is no legend on the reverse, but the letters S. I. at the bottom, and a wreath of laurel round the arms.

MANHEIM.

Gold Coins.

The Carolin—Head of the reigning Prince, with the name and title, thus:

CAR. PHILIP D. G. ELEC. PALATINUS,

Charles Philip, by the grace of God, Elector Palatine.

Reverse, arms of the Prince, with four crowns, supported by four C's, interlinked and four P's, the whole forming a cross; legend,

MONETA NOVA AUREA PALATI.

New gold coin of the Palatinate.

The Pistole—Head of the reigning Prince, with name and title, thus:

CAR. THE. C. P. S. R. I. A. T. & EL.

that is, Carolus Theodorus, Comes Palatinus, Sancti Romani Imperii Archi-Thesaurarius et Elector;

Charles Theodore, Count Palatine, Arch-Treasurer and Elector of the Holy Roman Empire.

Reverse, a crown, formed by four crowns and four cyphers of the letters C. T.; legend,

DOMINUS REGIT ME,

God directs me.

The Ducat—The same as the Pistole.

Silver Coins.

The Rixdollar (fine)—Head, name, and title, as on the Pistole. Reverse, arms of the Prince; legend,

EX VISCERIBUS FODINÆ WILDBERG;

From the bowels of the mine of Wildberg,

and

FEIN SILB.

Fine silver.

The Piece of $\frac{2}{3}$ bears the same impressions as the Rixdollar, except that it is marked $\frac{2}{3}$ under the arms. Some pieces of an ancient date, bear no head but $\frac{2}{3}$ in large figures, and under this,

FEIN SILBER;

legend,

DEUS SERVET METALLI FODINAS MONTENSES,

May God preserve the mines of Wildberg;

the names and titles are on the reverse, round the arms.

The Rixdollar (*Convention*)—Head, name,

and titles as on the Pistole. Reverse, arms of the Prince; legend,

AD NORMAM CONVENTIONIS,
According to the rule of the Convention;

or,

10 EINE FEINE MARCK,
10 *to a fine Mark.*

MECKLENBURG.

SILVER COIN.

The PIECE of $\frac{2}{3}$—Arms of the reigning Prince, with name and title, thus:

FRIED. FRAN. ZV. G. G. HERZOG ZV. MECKLENB. SCHWERIN,
Frederic Francis, by the grace of God, Duke of Mecklenburg Schwerin.

Reverse, $\frac{2}{3}$ in large figures; legend,

18 STUCK EINE MARCK FEIN,
18 *pieces to a Mark fine.*

MENTZ.

GOLD COIN.

The DUCAT—Head of the reigning Prince, with name and title, thus:

FRID. CAR. IOS. A. EP. ET EL. MOG. EP. W.

that is, Fredericus Carolus Josephus, Archiepiscopus et Elector Moguntiæ, Episcopus Wormiæ,

Frederic Charles Joseph, Archbishop and Elector of Mentz, Bishop of Worms.

Reverse, arms of the Bishop, with the date; other Ducats bear on the reverse a view of the city of Mentz, with the legend,

AVREA MOGVNTIA,
The golden Mentz.

SILVER COINS.

The RIXDOLLAR—Head of the reigning Prince, with name and titles, thus:

FRID. CAR. IOS. D. G. A. E. MOG. S. R. I. P. G. A. C. ET EL. E. W.

that is, Fredericus Carolus Josephus, Dei gratia, Archiepiscopus Moguntiæ, Sancti Romani Imperii pro Germania Archi Cancellarius et Elector, Episcopus Wormensis;

Frederic Charles Joseph, by the grace of God, Archbishop of Mentz, High Chancellor for Germany and Elector of the Holy Roman Empire, Bishop of Worms.

But the pieces of 1796, &c. have their legend in German, thus:

FRID. CAR. IOS. ERZB. V. KVRF. Z. MAINZ. B. Z. W.

that is, Erzbischoff und Kurfurst zu Mainz, Bischoff zu Worms,

Archbishop and Elector of Mentz, Bishop of Worms.

Reverse, arms of the Bishop; legend,

ZEHEN EINE FEINE MARK,
Ten to a Mark fine.

The COPSTUCK bears the same impressions as the Rixdollar, except that the legend on the reverse is

60 AUF EINE FEINE MARK,

and that it is marked 20 at the bottom.

MILAN.

GOLD COINS.

The SEQUIN—Head of the reigning Emperor of Germany, with name and title, thus:

IOSEP. II. D. G. R. IMP. S. AUG. G. H. ET B. REX. A. A.

Joseph II. by the grace of God, Emperor of Rome, ever august, King of Germany, Hungary, and Bohemia, Archduke of Austria.

Reverse, arms of Milan; legend,

MEDIOLANI ET MANT. DUX,
Duke of Milan and Mantua.

The DOPPIA, or PISTOLE—The same as the Sequin.

The PIECE of 40 LIRE of the new kingdom of Italy—Head of Bonaparte; legend,

NAPOLEON IMPERATORE E RE,
Napoleon Emperor and King.

Reverse, arms of Milan; legend,

REGNO D'ITALIA,
Kingdom of Italy,

and 40 LIRE; round the edge of the piece,

DIO PROTEGGE L'ITALIA,
God protect Italy.

SILVER COINS.

The SCUDO—Impressions the same as the Sequin, except that round the edge of the pieces of Maria Theresa, are the words

JUSTITIA ET CLEMENTIA,
Justice and clemency;

and round those of Joseph II.

VIRTUTE ET EXEMPLO,
By virtue and example.

The LIRA bears the same impressions as the Sequin, except that it is marked UNA LIRA, under the arms: pieces of 30 Soldi of the year 1800 have likewise their values marked.

The SCUDO of the CISALPINE REPUBLIC—An armed woman sitting, and another woman standing before her; legend,

ALLA NAZ. FRAN. LA REP. CISAL. RICONOSCENTE,
To the French Nation, the grateful Cisalpine Republic.

Reverse, a wreath of oak, and within it

SCUDO DI LIRE SEI 27 PRATILE ANNO VIII.
Scudo of 6 Lire, 27th of the month Pratile, year 8;

and round the edge of the piece,

UNIONE E VIRTU,
Union and virtue.

The PIECE of 30 SOLDI of the same Republic—Head of a woman; legend,

REPVBBLICA CISALPINE, SOLDI 30.

Reverse,

PACE CELEBRATA, FORO BONAPARTE FONDATO, ANNO IX,
Peace proclaimed, foundation of Bonaparte's forum.

SILVER COINS.

The SCUDO—Head of the reigning Prince, with name and title, thus:

HERCVLES III. D. G. MVT. REG. MIR. EC. DVX,
Hercules III. by the grace of God, Duke of Modena, Reggio, Mirandola, &c.

Reverse, arms of Modena; legend, in pieces of 1782,

PROXIMA SOLI,
Next to the Sun;

and in those of 1796,

DEXTERA DOMINI EXALTAVIT ME,
The right hand of the Lord hath exalted me.

NAPLES.

GOLD COINS.

The SIX DUCAT PIECE—Head of the reigning King, with name and titles, thus:

FERDINAN. IV. D. G. SICILIAR. ET HIER. REX,
Ferdinand IV. by the grace of God, King of the two Sicilies and of Jerusalem.

Reverse, arms of Naples; legend,

INFANS HISPANIAR.
Infant of Spain.

The FOUR and TWO DUCAT PIECES bear the same impressions.

SILVER COINS.

The PIECE of 12 CARLINI—Impressions the same as the Six Ducat Piece, and the value marked

G. 120,
120 *grains.*

Pieces coined since 1805, have round the head,

FERDINANDVS IV. D. G. REX;

and on the reverse,

VTR. SIC. HIER. HISP. INF.
that is, Utriusque Siciliæ, &c.
Of both Sicilies, &c.

and round the edge,

PROVIDENTIA OPTIMI PRINCIPI,
The precaution of the best Prince.

The piece of 6 Carlini is marked

G. 60,
60 *grains.*

In 1791, two different pieces were coined bearing the profiles of the King and Queen with their names,

FERDINANDVS IV. ET MARIA CAROLINA.

One of these pieces has on the reverse the sun in the zodiac, with the globe of the earth at the bottom, and the legend,

SOLI REDVCI,
To the returning Sun.

The reverse of the other piece represents a man and a woman making a sacrifice on an altar, behind which is a view of Mount Vesuvius; legend,

PRO FAVSTO PP. REDITV,
For the happy return of our Sovereigns.

The DUCAT bears the same impressions as above, except that it is marked on the reverse

DVCATO NAP. GRA. 100;

and round the edge,

PROPUGNACULA FIRMA ADVERSUS FRAUDATORES,
A firm guard against fraudulent persons.

The Half Ducat is marked

ME. D. NAP. G. 50.

The PIECE of 12 CARLINI of the Republic of Naples—A woman with a spear and cap of Liberty in one hand, and supporting the fasces with the other; legend,

REPUBBLICA NAPOLITANA.

Reverse, a wreath containing the value,

CARLINI DODICI,
12 *Carlini;*

legend,

ANNO SETTIMO DELLA LIBERTA,
The seventh year of liberty.

NETHERLANDS.

GOLD COINS.

The SOUVERAIN.—See *Austrian Dominions.*

The GOLD LION of the revolted Netherlands (1790)—A lion supporting a shield, with the word

LIBERTAS;

legend,

DOMINI EST REGNUM,
The kingdom is the Lord's.

Reverse, a sun, with eleven escutcheons round it, and the legend,

ET IPSE DOMINABITUR GENTIUM,
And he himself shall reign over the nations.

The TEN FLORIN PIECE, and its divisions (1818)—Head of the King, with the legend,

WILLEM KONING DER NEDERLANDEN, GROOT HERTOG VAN LUXEMBURG,
William King of the Netherlands, Grand Duke of Luxemburg.

Reverse, the arms of the King between 10 GL.; legend,

MUNT VAN HET KONINGRYK DER NEDERLANDEN,
Coin of the kingdom of the Netherlands,

and the date. Round the edge,

GOD ZY MET ONS,
God be with us,

SILVER COINS.

The DUCATOON bears the same impressions as the Souverain.

The CROWN of Maria Theresa, and its divisions—A cross and four crowns in the angles. Reverse, a two-headed eagle crowned, bearing on its breast the arms of Austria; the legends consist of the

Empress's name and her titles as on the Souverain; and round the edge,

JUSTITIA ET CLEMENTIA,
Justice and clemency.

The CROWN of the Emperors Joseph, Leopold, and Francis II.—Head of the reigning Emperor. Reverse, a cross and three crowns, the golden fleece supplying the place of the fourth; legends as on the Souverain. Round the edge of the pieces of Joseph II. are the words

VIRTUTE ET EXEMPLO,
By virtue and example;

round those of Leopold,

PIETATE ET CONCORDIA,
By piety and concord;

and round those of Francis II.

FIDE ET LEGE,
By faith and the law.

The SILVER LION of the revolted Netherlands (1790) bears the same impressions as the Gold Lion, except that round the edge is the legend,

QUID FORTIUS LEONE,
What is stronger than the lion?

The FLORIN of the revolted Netherlands—Obverse, a lion. Reverse, two joined hands and eleven arrows, with the mark, 1 FLOR.; legends as on the Silver Lion. Some Florins, however, have the legend,

MON. NOV. ARG. PROV. FOED. BELG.
New silver coin of the confederated Belgic Provinces;

and on the reverse,

IN VNIONE SALVS.
Safety in union.

The FLORIN of 1816 bears the same impressions as the 10 Florin Piece.

PIECES of 25, 10, and 5 CENTS, simply bear a W crowned, and on the reverse, the King's arms between 25 CT. 10 CT. &c.

NEUFCHATEL.

SILVER COINS.

The PIECE of 21 BATZEN—A cross with a sun in the centre; legend,

SUUM CUIQUE,
To every one his own.

Reverse, arms of Neufchatel; legend,

F. G. REX BOR. PR. SUP. NOVIC. & VAL.

that is, Fredericus Guglielmus, Rex Borussorum, Princeps Supremus Novicastelli et Valangini,

Frederic William, King of Prussia, Supreme Prince of Neufchatel and Valangin;

and at the bottom, 21 BZ. The Half-Piece is marked 10½ BZ. The Pieces of 1799, bear the head of the reigning King of Prussia, with his name and titles. Reverse, arms of Neufchatel; legend,

SUUM CUIQUE,

and 21 BZ. as before.

NUREMBERG.

GOLD COINS.

The DUCAT of 1700—A lamb standing on the globe, and carrying a standard with the word

PAX,
Peace;

legend,

TEMPORA NOSTRA PATER DONATA PACE CORONA,
Crown our times, O Father! by giving us peace.

Reverse, three escutcheons and a dove at the top; legend,

RESP. NORIMBERGENSIS SECVLVM NOVVM CELEBRAT,
The Republic of Nuremberg celebrates the new century.

The Double and Half Ducat bear the same impressions.

SILVER COINS.

The RIXDOLLAR *(Constitution)*—Head of the reigning Emperor, with name and title, thus:

CAROLVS VI. D. G. ROM. IMP. SEMP. AUG.
Charles VI. by the grace of God, Emperor of Rome, ever august.

Reverse, a view of the city, with an eagle flying over it; legend,

AVGVSTO DOMINO TVTA ET SECVRA PARENTE EST,
It is safe and secure under its august Lord and Father;

and on the exergue,

NORIMBERGA.

The RIXDOLLAR *(Convention)*—The impressions of these coins vary, some bearing the head, name, and title of the reigning Emperor; and others a view of the city, with a sun over it. Reverse, a two-headed eagle crowned, bearing the arms of the city on its breast; or a single-headed eagle with two escutcheons in its talons. The pieces are marked with the letter N, the word NURNBERG, or the legend,

MONETA NOVA REIPVBL. NORIMBERGENSIS,
New coin of the Republic of Nuremberg;

and the words

X EINE FEINE MARCK.
Ten to a Mark fine.

The COPSTUCK—Arms of the city, with 20 on a pedestal: legend,

MONETA NOVA, &c.

as above. Reverse, the two-headed eagle and arms of the city, with the Emperor's name and title.

PARMA.

GOLD COIN.

The DOPPIA—Head of the reigning Prince, with name and title, thus:

FERDINANDVS I. HISPANIAR. INFANS,
Ferdinand I. Infant of Spain,

and a star at the bottom. Reverse, arms of Parma; legend,

D. G. PARMÆ PLAC. ET VASTAL. DUX,
By the grace of God, Duke of Parma, Placentia, and Guastalla.

SILVER COINS.

The DUCAT and HALF DUCAT bear the same impressions as the Doppia. The pieces of 1, 2, and 3 Lire bear on the reverse a wreath containing their value, thus:

LIRE TRE DI PARMA,
Three Lire of Parma.

PIEDMONT.

GOLD COINS.

The DOPPIA, or PISTOLE (coined before 1785)—Head of the reigning Prince, with name and title, thus:

VIC. AM. D. G. REX SAR. CYP. ET IER.

that is, Victor Amadeus, Dei gratia, Rex Sardiniæ, Cypri, et Ierosolimæ,

Victor Amadeus, by the grace of God, King of Sardinia, Cyprus, and Jerusalem.

Reverse, the arms of Piedmont, Sardinia, &c. legend,

DVX SAB. ET MONTISF. PRINC. PED.

that is, Dux Sabandiæ et Montisferrati, Princeps Pedemontanus,

Duke of Savoy and Montferrat, Prince of Piedmont.

The Half Doppia bears the same impressions.

The DOPPIA and HALF DOPPIA (coined since 1785)—Head of the reigning Prince; legend,

VIC. AM. D. G. REX SARDINIÆ.

Reverse, an eagle crowned, with an escutcheon on its breast, and under it a sceptre and staff with the collar of an order; legend,

PRINC. PEDEM. DVX SABAVD.

But those coined since 1797, bear, on the obverse, only the head and the name, thus:

CAROLUS EMMANUEL IV.

and on the reverse

D. G. REX SAR. CYP. ET IER.

with the crowned eagle.

The CARLINO and Half-Carlino bear the same impressions as the Doppia.

The SEQUIN—An eagle as described above; legend,

CAROLVS EMMANUEL D. G. SARDINIÆ REX.

Reverse, the Annunciation of the Blessed Virgin.

The MARENGO, or PIECE OF 20 FRANCS (1801)—Head of a woman with a helmet; legend,

L'ITALIE DELIVREE A MARENGO,
Italy delivered at Marengo.

Reverse, a wreath containing the words

20 FRANCS L'AN 9;

legend,

LIBERTE EGALITE,
Liberty, equality,

and ERIDANIA, the name that was then given to the country.

SILVER COINS.

The SCUDO, and its divisions, bear the same impressions as the Old Doppia. It may be observed, however, that the coins of an ancient date (before 1714) do not contain the title of King of Sardinia, but only those of Duke of Savoy, Prince of Piedmont, and King of Cyprus. On the coins of Charles Emmanuel IV. the only title retained is, King of Sardinia, Cyprus, and Jerusalem.

The MEZZO SCUDO of the Republic of Piedmont—A soldier, with the fasces and cap of Liberty; legend,

LIBERTA, VIRTU, EGUAGLIANZA,
Liberty, virtue, equality.

Reverse,

MEZZO SCUDO,

within a wreath of oak; legend,

ANNO VII. REP. 1 DELLA LIBERTA PIEMONTESE,
The 7th year of the Republic, the 1st of the Liberty of Piedmont.

The FIVE FRANC PIECE (1801)—Two female figures, one of them with a spear and the cap of Liberty; legend,

GAULE SUBALPINE.

Reverse, a wreath, containing the words

5 FRANCS L'AN 9;

legend,

LIBERTE, EGALITE, ERIDANIA,

as on the Marengo.

POLAND.

GOLD COINS.

The DUCAT (1772)—A full length figure of the King, with name and title, thus:

STANISLAUS AUG. D. G. REX POL. M. D. L.;

that is, Stanislaus Augustus, Dei Gratia, Rex Poloniæ, Magnus Dux Lithuaniæ,

Stanislaus Augustus, by the grace of God, King of Poland, Grand Duke of Lithuania.

Reverse,

MONETA AUREA POLONI. AD LEG. IMPER.
Gold coin of Poland, according to the law of the Empire.

The DUCAT (1791)—Head of the King, with name and titles as above. Reverse, a wreath, containing the words,

AUREUS NUMMUS POLONIÆ ANNO, &c.
Gold coin of Poland, in the year, &c.

SILVER COIN.

The RIXDOLLAR—Head of the reigning King, with name and title, as on the Ducat. Reverse, arms of Poland; legend,

X EX MARCA PURA COLONIEN,
Ten from the Mark fine, Cologne weight.

Round the edge,

PIGNUS FIDEI PUBLICÆ,
A pledge of the public faith.

On the Half Rixdollar is

XX EX MARCA, &c.

and on the new Rixdollar

$14\frac{1}{12}$ EX MARCA, &c.

and at the bottom

6 ZL.
6 *Zloti, or Polish Florins.*

PORTUGAL.

GOLD COINS.

The DOBRAON—Arms of Portugal; with 20,000 on one side and five flowers on the other; legend,

JOANNES V. D. G. PORT. ET ALG. REX.
John V. by the grace of God, King of Portugal and Algarve.

Reverse, a cross with four M's in the angles; legend,

IN HOC SIGNO VINCES,
By this sign thou shalt conquer.

The Half-Dobraon bears the same impressions, except that it is marked 10,000.

The MOIDORE—The same as the Dobraon, but is marked 4000, and has four B's in the angles of the cross; but some of an ancient date bear on the reverse a cross, surrounded by four connected semicircles, and a whole circle, with the legend

ET BRASILIÆ DOMINVS ANNO, &c.
and Lord of Brazil, in the year, &c.

The Half and Quarter Moidores are marked 2000 and 1000.

The JOANNESE—Head of the reigning Sovereign, with name and titles, thus:

JOANNES V. D. G. PORT. ET ALG. REX;

or,

MARIA I. D. G. PORT. ET ALG. REGINA.

The pieces coined by the Prince Regent, since 1804, bear his head, with

JOANNES D. G. PORT. ET ALG. P. REGENS.

Reverse, arms of Portugal. The Dobra, or Double Joannese, and its subdivisions all bear the same impressions.

The QUARTINHO—Arms of Portugal, with 1000, and the legend

MARIA, D. G. &c.

Reverse, a cross, with four flowers, and the legend

IN HOC SIGNO VINCES,

as before.

The OLD CRUSADO—Head of the reigning King. Reverse, a crown; legend,

JOAN. V. D. G. P. REX.

as before.

The NEW CRUSADO—Name of the Sovereign, between two palm branches, surmounted by a crown, and beneath it 400. Reverse, the cross and legend as on the Quartinho.

The MILREE, coined for the African colonies,—Arms of Portugal, with 1000 on the side, and the name and title as above. Reverse, a cross, &c. as on the old Moidore; legend,

ET DOMINUS AF. OR. ANNO, &c.

that is, Dominus Africæ Orientalis,
Lord of Eastern Africa.

SILVER COINS.

The NEW CRUSADO (1795)—The arms of Portugal, on one side of which is the date, and on the other 400; legend,

MARIA I. D. G. PORT. ET ALG. REGINA,

as on the Joannese. Reverse, a cross with four flowers in the angles; legend,

IN HOC SIGNO, &c.

as above.

The NEW CRUSADO (1802)—Same impressions as the Crusado of 1795, except the legend on the obverse, which is

JOHANNES D. G. PORT. ALG. P. REGENS,

as on the Joannese.

The divisions of the New Crusado, that is, pieces of 240, 120, and 60 Rees, bear the same impressions, except that the Half Crusado is marked 200.

The TESTOON—A crown, and under it LXXX, with the reigning Sovereign's name and title; the Half Testoon is marked XXXX, and the Vintem XX. Reverse, a plain cross, with four flowers in the angles; legend,

IN HOC SIGNO VINCES,

as before.

SILVER COINS OF THE PORTUGUESE COLONIES.

The PATACA of BRAZIL—Arms of Portugal, with 640 on the side, and the date near the top; legend, the name and title of the reigning Sovereign as above, with the addition of

BRAS D.

Brasiliæ Dominus, *or* Domina,

Lord or Lady of Brazil.

Reverse, an armillary sphere, placed on a cross; legend,

SVBQ. SIGN. NATA STAB.

that is, Subque Signo nata Stabili,

Born under a steady sign.

There is also a Pataca of 600 Rees bearing the letter J. with a Crown over it, 600 on the side, and the date at the bottom. Reverse, an armillary sphere placed on a cross, with an R in the centre; the legend,

SVB. SIGN. &c.

The PIECE of 12 MACUTAS—Arms of Portugal; legend,

MARIA I. D. G. REGINA P. ET D. GUINEÆ,

Mary I. by the grace of God, Queen of Portugal, and Mistress of Guinea.

Reverse, a wreath of oak, and within it, MACUTAS 12; legend,

AFRICA PORTUGUEZA,

Portuguese Africa.

PRUSSIA.

GOLD COINS.

The FREDERICK—Head of the reigning King, with name and title; thus,

FRIDERICVS BORVSSORVM REX,

Frederick, King of Prussia;

but the coins struck since 1795 have the German legend—

FRIED. WILHELM III. KŒNIG VON PREUSSEN,

Frederick-William, King of Prussia.

Reverse, an eagle with a crown and military trophies.

The DUCAT of ancient date has the same impressions as the Frederick; but those coined in 1787 bear the arms of Prussia, with the reigning King's name and title as above. Reverse, 1 DUCAT, surrounded by a wreath and chain, with four crowns in the angles.

SILVER COINS.

The RIXDOLLAR (coined before 1791)—Head of the reigning King, with name and title, as on the Frederick. Reverse, an eagle and military trophies; legend,

EIN REICHS THALER,

1 *Rixdollar.*

The Half Rixdollar bears the same impressions; and its value is marked thus—

2 EINEN R. THALER,

2 *to a Rixdollar.*

The RIXDOLLAR current (coined since 1791)—Head of the reigning King, and the legend in German, as above. Reverse, arms of Prussia, with

EIN THALER ;

but the Rixdollar, Convention money, bears on the reverse the legend—

ZEHN EINE FEINE MARK,
10 *to a Mark fine.*

The FLORIN of SILESIA—Impressions as on the Rixdollar of 1791; but on the reverse it is marked

XXI EINE FEINE MARK.

The PIECE of $\frac{2}{3}$—Arms of Prussia; legend,

FRIED. WILH. KOENIG. V. PR. M. ZU BRAND. D. H. R. R. E. K. U. KURF.

that is, Friederick Wilhelm, Koenig von Preussen Markgraf zu Brandenburg, der Heiligen, Romischen Reichs Erzkammerherr und Kurfust,

Frederick William, King of Prussia, Marquis of Brandenburg, High Chamberlain and Elector of the Holy Roman Empire.

Reverse, $\frac{2}{3}$ in large figures; legend,

18 STUCK EINE MARK FEIN,
18 *Pieces to a Mark fine.*

The Piece of 8 GOOD GROSCHEN—Head, name, and title of the reigning King, as on the Frederick. Reverse, on Pieces of 1756, a military trophy, and above it

8 GUTE GROSCHEN ;

on Pieces of 1773, a wreath containing the words

8 EINEN REICHS THALER ;

on those of 1791, &c. the arms of Prussia; legend,

DREI, *or* 3, EINEN R. THALER.

The Piece of 4 GOOD GROSCHEN—Head, name, and title of the reigning King, as on the Frederick. Reverse, on Pieces of 1766,

6 EINEN REICHS THALER ;

on those of 1791, &c. the arms of Prussia, with

4 GR.

legend,

84 EX MARCA PURA COLON.

84 *Pieces from the Mark fine, Cologne weight.*

The RIXDOLLAR of ANSPACH and BAREUTH—Head of the reigning Prince, with name and title, thus:

ALEXANDER D. G. MARCH. BRAND.
Alexander, by the grace of God, Marquis, or Margrave, of Brandenburg.

Reverse, arms of Anspach, &c. with

ZEHEN EINE FEINE MARK,
10 *to a Mark fine.*

But those of more modern date (1790, &c.) bear the impressions of the Prussian coins, Anspach having been at that period ceded to Prussia.

RAGUSA.

SILVER COINS.

The TALLARO, or RAGUSINA—Head of the chief magistrate called the Rector; legend,

RECTOR REIP. RHAGVSIN,
Reetor of the Republic of Ragusa.

Reverse, arms of the city; legend,

DVCAT. ET SEM. REIP. RAC.

that is, Ducatus et semis Reipublicæ Racusinæ,
Ducat and half of the Republic of Ragusa.

Pieces of 1794 bear the head of a woman, with

RESPVBL. RHACVS.
Republic of Ragusa.

Reverse, a shield with the word

LIBERTAS,

surrounded by two branches, over which is a crown; legend,

DVCE DEO FIDE ET IVST.
Under the guidance of God, Faith, and Justice.

The DUCAT—A whole length figure of a Bishop; legend,

AUSPICIIS TUIS A DEO,

From God, under thy auspices.

Reverse, arms of the city; legend,

DUCAT REIP. RHACUSINE.

RATISBON.

GOLD COIN.

The FOUR DUCAT PIECE—The two-headed eagle crowned; legend,

CAROLVS VI. D. G. ROM. IMP. SEMP. AVG.

Charles VI. by the grace of God, Emperor of Rome, ever august.

Reverse, two keys crossed; legend,

MONETA REIPUBLICÆ RATISBONENSIS,

Coin of the Republic of Ratisbon.

SILVER COIN.

The RIXDOLLAR—Head, name, and title of the reigning Emperor, as on the coins of Hamburgh and Nuremberg. Reverse, a view of the city; legend,

MONETA REIP. RATISBON.

as above; and at the bottom,

X ST. EINE F. C. M.

that is, X Stuck eine feine Collnisch Marck,

10 *Pieces to a Mark fine, Cologne weight.*

The Half and Quarter Rixdollars are marked

XX ST. EINE F. C. M.

and,

XL ST. EINE F. C. M.

ROME.

GOLD COINS.

The SEQUIN—A woman representing the church, with rays of glory round her head, sitting on a rock, and holding two keys in one hand, and a temple in the other; legend,

SVPRA FIRMAM PETRAM,

Upon a firm rock.

On some,

FIAT PAX IN VIRTVTE TVA,

Peace be in thy virtue;

and on others of modern date,

AUXILIVM DE SANCTO,

Help from the sanctuary.

Reverse, arms of the reigning Pope, over which are the cross keys and the tiara. The legend is mostly the name of the reigning Pope, as

PIVS SEXTVS PON. MA.

that is, Pontifex Maximus,

Pius VI. Supreme Pontiff,

with the date of his pontificate. Sequins coined during an interregnum have the words

SEDE VACANTE,

The See being vacant.

Sequins of ancient date (as before 1759) have on the reverse a dove surrounded with rays, and their legends are various: the name of the reigning Pope is on the reverse, round the figure of the church.

The impressions on the Sequins of Bologna vary still more than on those of Rome. Such as have been coined since 1786 bear the arms of the reigning Pope, with the keys, tiara, and name, as above; and on the reverse, a bishop seated on a cloud, supported by two small escutcheons; legend,

S. PETRON. BON. PROT.

St. Petronius, Protector of Bologna.

The Double and Half Sequins bear the same impressions; and the pieces of 10 and 5 Sequins are marked

ZECCH. 10,

and

ZECCH. 5.

The DOPPIA or PISTOLE—St. Peter preaching; legend,

PRINCEPS APOSTOLORUM,

Chief of the Apostles.

Reverse, a lily; legend,

FLORET IN DOMO DOMINI,
It blooms in the house of the Lord;

but the new Pistoles (coined since 1800) bear on the reverse the Pope's arms, with the keys and tiara, and his name and the date of his pontificate.

The Pistoles of Bologna bear two escutcheons, and the legend,

BONONIA DOCET,
Bologna teaches.

Reverse, a lily, with the Pope's name, &c. as above.

The Scudo of the Roman Republic—An eagle, with the legend,

REPUBLICA ROMANA;

on the exergue,

PERUGIA, A. VII.

Reverse, the word Scudo, encircled by a wreath of oak.

Silver Coins.

The impressions and legends of the Silver Coins of Rome are too various to be here described.

They all, however, bear the name of the reigning Pope, and the words

PONT. MAX.

as before; they are mostly distinguished by the cross keys and tiara. The pieces coined during an interregnum have the words

SEDE VACANTE,
The See being vacant;

and commonly a dove, surrounded with rays.

When Rome assumed a republican form of government, in 1798, coins were struck, called Scudi Romani, bearing on the obverse a woman resting on the fasces, and holding in her left hand a lance, with the cap of Liberty; legend,

REPUBLICA ROMANA;

and on the reverse,

SCUDO ROMANO,

encircled by a wreath.

On the restoration of the Papal government, under Pius VII. in 1800, coins were struck, bearing on the obverse the emblem of the church, as on the Sequin; and on the reverse, the arms of the Pope, with his name, title, and the date of his pontificate.

The Silver Coins of Bologna have been subject to the same variations as those of Rome. The word

BONONIA

is to be found on some part of the piece, and sometimes,

BONONIA DOCET.

The pieces coined by the city of Bologna have on the obverse a view of the city, and above it the virgin and child on a cloud; legend,

PRÆSIDIVM ET DECVS,
Protection and Ornament.

Reverse, arms of Bologna; legend,

POPVLVS ET SENATVS BONON.
The People and Senate of Bologna;

and on the exergue

P. 10,
10 *Paoli,*

with the date.

RUSSIA.

Gold Coins.

The Ducat—Head of the reigning Emperor or Empress, with the name and titles in Russian characters, which are thus translated:*

Peter, by the grace of God, Emperor, or *Elizabeth, by the grace of God, Empress, and Sovereign of all the Russias.*

The reverse varies; some Ducats of Peter the Great and Elizabeth bear a figure of St Andrew on the cross, without any legend, or with the words

New Coin, Two Rubles;

* The inscriptions on the Russian Coins are all in the Russian language, and are here given literally in English.

those of the Empress Anne bear an eagle and military trophy; legend,

Glory of the Empire;

but most of the Ducats of Peter and Elizabeth, and also those of Catherine II. have on the reverse a two-headed eagle with an escutcheon on its breast, and the words

Sovereign of all the Russias.

The Gold Ruble, and also the Double and Half Ruble, bear the same impressions as above; but on the reverse the value is written,

New Coin, Two Rubles, or 1 *Ruble;*

and the Half Piece bears on the reverse the cypher of the Empress Elizabeth, with the word

Poltina,

which means Half a Ruble. These coins as well as the Ducats are now nearly out of circulation.

The Imperial—Head of the reigning Sovereign, with name and title as above; reverse, a cross formed by five escutcheons, with the four figures of the year of coinage in the angles; legend,

Imperial Russian Coin, Value Ten Rubles;

and on the Half Imperial,

Value Five Rubles.

But the Half Imperials of Paul I. have on the obverse the inscription,

Not unto us, not unto us, but unto Thy Name.

Reverse, a cross and four crowns, with a capital I in the centre, and the figure 5 in the angles of the cross.

Silver Coins.

The Ruble—Head of the reigning Sovereign, with the name and title as on the gold coins. Reverse, a two-headed eagle crowned, with an escutcheon on its breast; legend,

New Coin, Value 1 *Ruble,*

or simply,

Coin, 1 *Ruble,*

and the date. Some Rubles of Peter I. and Catherine I. bear on the reverse a cross and four crowns, with four I's, or four II's in the angles, and the date within the cross.

The Ruble of Paul I. (1799, &c.) bears the same impressions as the Half Imperial of the same period, except that the legend on the reverse is

Coin, Value 1 *Ruble,*

and that the 5's are omitted in the angles.

The Ruble of Alexander (1802) bears on the obverse the eagle and legend as above; on the reverse,

Coin of the Russian Empire, Ruble,

encircled with a branch of laurel and oak, having a small crown at the top.

The Poltina, or Half Ruble, bears the same impressions as the Ruble, according to the period at which it was coined, except that the inscription contains the word

POLTINA

instead of RUBLE; and the Quarter Ruble is marked

POLUPOLTINICK.

The 20 Copeck Piece—Head, name, and title of the reigning Sovereign, as above. Reverse, a two-headed eagle, with the number 20 on its breast. The 15 Copeck Piece bears the same impressions, but it is marked 15.

The 10 Copeck Piece—The two-headed eagle. Reverse,

10 COPECKS.

The 5 Copeck Piece—A Russian P, with a crown over it, and under which is an I. Reverse,

5 COPECKS,

within two laurel branches.

ST. GALL.

Gold Coin.

The Ducat—Arms of the Abbot, with his name and title, thus:

BEDA D. G. S. R. I. P.

Bede, by the grace of God, Prince of the holy Roman Empire.

Reverse, a bear carrying a short beam, encircled by a palm and laurel branch; legend,

AB. BS. G. E. S. I. A. V. E.

Abbot of St. Gall,

with the initials of particular titles.

Silver Coin.

The Rixdollar bears the same impressions as the Ducat; and also the Half Rixdollar and the Copstuck; but the latter coin is marked 20 on the reverse. Round the edge of the Rixdollar and its divisions, coined since 1780, are the words

FORTITER ET CONSTANTER.

SALTZBURG.

Gold Coin.

The Ducat—Head of the reigning Prince, with name and titles, thus:

HIERONYMVS. D. G. A. & P. S. A. S. L. N. G. PRIM.

that is, Hieronymus, Dei gratia, Archiepiscopus et Princeps Salisburgensis, Germaniæ Primas,

Jerome, by the grace of God, Archbishop and Prince of Saltzburg, Primate of Germany.

Reverse, arms of the Prince. Old Ducats bear on the obverse a full length figure of a bishop, with the legend,

S. RVPERTVS EP. SALISBURG.

St. Rupert, Bishop of Saltzburg.

Reverse, the arms, name, and title, as above.

Silver Coin.

The Rixdollar—The impressions on this coin and its divisions are the same as on the Ducat; and the Copstuck, or 20 Creutzer Piece, differs only in being marked 20 on the reverse.

SARDINIA.

The Coins of Sardinia, both Gold and Silver, bear the same impressions as those of Piedmont: *which see.*

SAXONY.

Gold Coins.

The Ducat—Head of the reigning Prince with name and titles, thus:

FRID. AVGVST. D. G. DVX SAX. ELECTOR,

Frederick Augustus, by the grace of God, Duke and Elector of Saxony.

Reverse, arms of Saxony. In 1808, the title was altered to

FRID. AUGUST. REX. SAXONIÆ,

Frederick Augustus, King of Saxony.

The legend on the obverse of the Ducats of Augustus III. is,

AUGUSTUS III. REX POLONIARUM,

Augustus III. King of Poland;

and on the reverse,

SAC. ROM. IMP. ARCHIM. ET ELECT.

Grand Marshal and Elector of the Holy Roman Empire.

The Augustus bears the same impressions as the Ducat, except that it has on the reverse, under the arms,

5 THALER, or 5 TH.

Silver Coins.

The Rixdollar *(Convention)*—Head, name, and titles of the reigning Prince, as on the Ducat. Reverse, arms of Saxony, with

X EINE FEINE MARCK,

10 to a Mark fine.

The FLORIN, or PIECE OF $\frac{2}{3}$, bears the same impressions as the Rixdollar; but the legend on the reverse is

XX EINE FEINE MARCK, $\frac{2}{3}$;

the Half Florin is marked

XL EINE, $\frac{1}{3}$;

and the Quarter Florin,

LXXX. or ACHZIG EINE, $\frac{1}{6}$.

The RIXDOLLAR of SAXE-GOTHA — Head, name, and title of the reigning Prince, thus:

ERNESTVS D. G. GOTHAN. SAXONVM DVX,

Ernest, by the grace of God, Duke of Saxe-Gotha.

Reverse, arms of Saxe-Gotha, with

X EINE FEINE MARCK,

as above.

SICILY.

GOLD COIN.

The OUNCE—Head of the reigning King, with name and title, thus:

CAROLVS D. G. SIC. ET HIE. REX.

Charles, by the grace of God, King of Sicily and Jerusalem:

some pieces have the addition

HIS. IN.

that is, Hispaniarum Infans,

Infant of Spain;

others the word

VNCIA,

Ounce.

Reverse, a phœnix; legend,

RESVRGIT,

He rises again.

SILVER COINS.

The SCUDO or CROWN—Head of the reigning King, with name and title, as on the Ounce. Reverse, an eagle, bearing an escutcheon on its breast; legend,

HISPANIARUM INFANS,

as before. In pieces of ancient date this last title is omitted, and on the reverse are the titles as above. Pieces of the year 1785 have the legend,

ANNO FAVSTO CORONATIONIS,

In the happy year of the Coronation.

The HALF SCUDO—Head of the reigning King. Reverse, a cross; the legends as on the Scudo.

SIERRA LEONE COMPANY.

SILVER COINS.

The DOLLAR, or PIECE of TEN MACUTAS—On the obverse, two joined hands, with the figures 100 both above and under them; legend,

ONE DOLLAR PIECE.

Reverse, a lion; legend,

SIERRA LEONE COMPANY, AFRICA.

The Half Dollar is marked 50; the $\frac{1}{5}$ Dollar, 20; and the $\frac{1}{10}$ Dollar, 10; with the legends,

HALF DOLLAR PIECE;
TWENTY CENT PIECE;

and

TEN CENT PIECE;

the rest as on the Dollar.

SPAIN.

GOLD COINS.

The DOUBLOON, or PISTOLE—Head of the reigning King, with name and title, thus;

CAROL. III. D. G. HISP. ET IND. REX;

that is, Carolus III. Dei gratia, Hispaniarum et Indiarum Rex,

Charles III. by the grace of God, King of Spain and the Indies.

Reverse, arms of Spain within the collar of the golden fleece; legend, in 1740,

INITIUM SAPIENTIÆ TIMOR DOMINI,

The fear of the Lord is the beginning of wisdom;

in 1762,

NOMINA MAGNA SEQUOR,

I follow great names;

in 1763,

IN UTROQUE FELIX AUSPICE DEO,

Happy in both, under the divine auspices;

there is, also, at the bottom, a letter to mark the place where the piece was coined, thus; M. with a crown over it signifies Madrid, and M. with an O Mexico.

The Double, Quadruple, and Half Pistoles bear the same impressions; but, in modern coins, the Half Pistole is marked

1 S.

1 *Scudo, or gold Crown;*

the single Pistole,

2 S.

and the others in proportion. The pieces coined between 1700 and 1723 bear no head, but have the arms and the King's name, with

DEI GRA.

On the reverse, a cross surrounded with different ornaments; legend,

HISPANIARUM REX.

Those coined before that period are not round, but of an irregular shape, and their impressions are very imperfect; the same may be remarked of the old Dollars coined in America.

The DOUBLOON of 1809, and its divisions—Head of Joseph Bonaparte, with the legend,

JOSEPH NAP. D. GR. HISP. ET IND. R.

Reverse, arms of Spain, with a crown; legend,

IN UTROQUE FELIX DEO AUSPICE,

as before.

The CORONILLA, GOLDEN DOLLAR, or VINTEM, bears the same impressions as the Doubloon, except the legends. Those, however, of an ancient date, have on the obverse the King's head and name, with D. G. and on the reverse, the arms of Spain, with

HISPANIARUM REX;

whilst those coined in 1786, &c. have the head and titles on the same side, and the arms of Spain on the reverse.

SILVER COINS.

The DOLLAR (coined before 1772)—On the obverse the arms of Spain, with the initials of the mint, &c. as on the Doubloon, and, also,

8 R.

8 *Reals;*

legend, the name and title of the reigning King. Reverse, a crown resting on two globes, between two pillars; legend,

VTRAQVE VNVM,

Both one,

and the initials of the mint; on the pillars,

NEC PLVS VLTRA,

Nothing beyond.

The divisions of the Dollar bear the same impressions; but the Half Dollar is marked

4 R.

4 *Reals;*

the Quarter Dollar, or Peceta Mexican,

2 R.

and the Real of Mexican Plate,

1 R.

Dollars and other pieces coined before 1740 bear on the obverse the arms, with the King's name, and D. G. Reverse, a sort of irregular escutcheon, divided into four parts by a cross; legend,

HISPANIARUM REX.

The DOLLAR (coined since 1772)—Head of the reigning King, with his name and DEI GRATIA. Reverse, arms of Spain, which, on pieces coined at Mexico, stand between two pillars, on which are the words,

NEC PLUS ULTRA,

as before; legend round the piece,

HISPAN. ET IND. REX,

with an M. for Mexico;

8 R.

8 *Reals;*

and the initials of the Moneyer's name. These are commonly called Pillar Dollars. Those coined in Europe have no pillars, and the legend is only

HISPANIARUM REX.

SWEDEN.

GOLD COIN.

The DUCAT—Head of the reigning King, with name and title, thus:

GUSTAVUS III. D. G. REX SVECIÆ,
Gustavus III. by the grace of God, King of Sweden;

but on Ducats coined since 1800, the name and titles are in the Swedish language, thus:

GUSTAF IV. ADOLPH. SV. G. OCH W. KONUNG,
Gustavus Adolphus IV. King of Sweden, Gothland, and Westmanland.

Reverse, arms of Sweden; legend, in 1746,

IN DEO SPES MEA,
My hope is in God;

in 1767,

SALUS PUBLICA SALUS MEA,
The public safety is my safety;

in 1774,

FADERNES LANDET,
The land of our fathers;

in 1800,

GUD OCH FOLKET,
God and the people.

SILVER COINS.

The RIXDOLLAR (1752)—Head of the reigning King, with name and title in Latin, as on the old Ducat. Reverse, arms of Sweden; legend,

SALUS PUBLICA SALUS MEA,

as before; and round the edge,

MANIBUS NE LÆDAR AVARIS,
That I may not be hurt by rapacious hands.

The RIXDOLLAR (1779)—Head, name, and title, as before. Reverse, arms of Sweden, with 1 RD. legend,

FADERNES LANDET,

as before. The divisions of the Rixdollar bear the same impressions, but have their value marked. The Rixdollar and other pieces coined since 1795 have the legends on both sides in the Swedish language, as on the new Ducat. Round the edge is

MANIBUS, &c.

as on the old Rixdollar.

SWITZERLAND.

GOLD COINS.

The DUCAT of LUCERNE—Arms of the canton. Reverse,

DUCATUS REIPUBLICÆ LUCERNENSIS,
Ducat of the Republic of Lucerne.

The pieces of 2 and 5 Ducats bear the same impressions.

The DUCAT of SCHWITZ—Arms of the canton, supported by a lion. Reverse,

DUCATUS REIPUBLICÆ SUITENSIS,
Ducat of the Republic of Schwitz.

The DUCAT of URI—A horseman giving his cloak to a beggar; legend,

SANCTVS MARTINVS,
St. Martin.

Reverse, arms of the Canton; legend,

DVCATVS REIPVBLICÆ VRANIÆ,
Ducat of the Republic of Uri.

The PISTOLE of LUCERNE—Arms of the canton, with the legend,

RESPVBLICA LVCERNENSIS.

Reverse, a wreath of laurel, containing

12 MZ. GL.

The PISTOLE of SOLEURE—A warrior bearing a standard; legend,

S. URSUS MARTYR.

Reverse, arms of the city; legend,

RESPUBLICA SOLODORENSIS,
Republic of Soleure.

The Double and Half Pistoles bear the same impressions.

The PISTOLE of the HELVETIC REPUBLIC (1800)—A soldier bearing a standard; legend,

HELVETISCHE REPUBLIK,
Helvetic Republic.

Reverse, a crown of oak, containing

16 FRANKEN.

SILVER COINS.

The ECU of LUCERNE (1715)—A figure of a bishop resting on the arms of the canton; legend,

SANCTVS LEODEGARIVS.

Reverse,

MONETA REIPVB. LVCERNENSIS,
Coin of the Republic of Lucerne;

the whole encircled by a wreath and other ornaments. The Half and Quarter Ecu bear the same impressions, and are marked ½ and ¼ on the obverse.

The ECU of LUCERNE (1796)—The arms of the Canton; legend,

RESPUBLICA LUCERNENSIS,

and

40 BAZ.

Reverse, a cross formed by eight L's, and a small wreath in the centre; legend,

DOMINUS SPES POPULI SUI,
The Lord is the hope of his people.

The Half Ecu is marked

20 BAZ.

The GULDEN, or FLORIN of LUCERNE—Arms of the canton; legend,

MONETA NOVA REIP. LVCERNENSIS.

Reverse,

AVXILIO DEI PROSPERE,
Prosperously by the help of God.

The Florin (1793, &c.) and its divisions bear the arms of the canton, with the legend

MON. NOV. &c.

Reverse as on the new Ecu, except that, in the centre of the cross, the Florin is marked

40,
40 *Schillings;*

the Half and Quarter Florins in proportion.

The RIXDOLLAR of FRIBURG—Arms of the canton; legend,

RESPUBLICA FRIBURGENS.

Reverse, a cross formed by eight F's, and four crowns; legend,

AUXILIUM NOSTR. DEUS,
God is our help.

The Quarter Rixdollar has, on a square in the centre of the cross, the number 36, and the inferior divisions are marked 28, 14, and 7.

The Piece of 20 BATZEN of SOLEURE—A cross with an S over it, and sometimes also a large O; legend,

CUNCTA PER DEUM,
All things through God.

Reverse, arms of the canton; legend,

MONETA REIP. SOLODORENSIS, *or* RESPUBLICA SOLODORENSIS, 20 BAZ.

The ECU of the HELVETIC REPUBLIC (1798)—A soldier bearing a standard; legend,

HELVET. REPUBL. *or* HELVETISCHE REPUBLIK.

Reverse, a wreath of oak, containing the words

40 BATZEN.

But the Ecus of 1799 and 1801 are marked

4 FRANKEN

on the reverse. The pieces of 20, 10, and 5 Batzen have their value expressed on the reverse, and bear in other respects the same impressions as the Ecu.

For the Gold and Silver Coins of BASIL, BERN, GENEVA, NEUFCHATEL, ST. GALL, and ZURICH, *see those articles respectively.*

TREVES.

GOLD COIN.

The DUCAT—Head of the reigning Prince, with name and titles; thus,

CLEM. WENC. D. G. A. EP. TREV. S. R. I. A. C. ET EL.

that is, Clemens Wenceslaus, Dei Gratia, Archi Episcopus Trevirensis, Sancti Romani Imperii Archi Cancellarius et Elector,

Clement Wenceslaus, by the grace of God, Archbishop of Treves, Arch-Chancellor and Elector of the Holy Roman Empire.

Reverse, arms of the Prince; legend, on Ducats of 1773,

EPISC. AUG. APP. COAD. ELEC.
Bishop of Augsburg, &c.

SILVER COIN.

The RIXDOLLAR bears the same impressions and legends as the Ducat, besides which there are, on the reverse, the words,

X EINE MARC F. *or* 10 EINE FEINE MARK,
Ten to a Mark fine.

TURKEY.

GOLD COINS.

As the representation of men and animals is forbidden by the Mahometan law, the Turkish coins have no other impressions than inscriptions stating the names, titles, descent, &c. of the Sultans, with the date of the Hegira, or Mahometan æra.* They are in the Arabic language, and the following translations from the principal coins of Sultan Selim (1789) may serve as a specimen, as there is but little variety in the form or style of these compositions.

The SEQUIN MAHBUB—On the obverse,

Sultan Selim, son of Mustapha Khan, may he be victorious, and his valour be blest, struck at Slambul (Constantinople), in the year 1203;

and on the reverse,

Sultan of the two lands, and Sovereign of the two seas, Sultan by inheritance, son of a Sultan.

The words, *May he be victorious, and his valour be*

* The Hegira began July 16 in the year 622 of the Christian æra; it is reckoned in lunar years, which are nearly 11 days shorter than the solar, making a difference of about one year in 33. The year 1225, therefore, of the Hegira commenced February 5, 1810, of the Christian æra, and on the

27 September	1821 the year	1237 commences
17	1822	1238 . . . . .
6	1823	1239 . . . . .

For a full and accurate calculation of these epochs, with tables, see the article *Hegira* in *Rees's Cyclopædia*.

blest, are occasionally used by the Turks at the end of their prayers. By the *two lands* are meant Europe and Asia, and by the *two seas*, the Black Sea and the Archipelago.

The SEQUIN FONDUCLI—On the obverse,

Sultan Selim, son of Mustapha Khan,

and on the reverse,

Struck at Slambul, in the year 1203.

The impressions on Sequins of different periods mostly answer to either of the foregoing descriptions; but the Sequins coined at Cairo, under Sultan Abdulhamid, in 1773, have their inscriptions as follow:

Sultan Abdulhamid, son of Ahmed Khan, may his valour be blest, struck in Egypt, in the year 1187;

and on the reverse, the titles as on the Sequin Mahbub of the Sultan Selim.

The SEQUINS of the BARBARY STATES are coined in the name of the Grand Seignior, and are distinguished by the words

Struck at Tunis, Tripoli, &c.

They bear on the reverse the titles as on the Sequin Mahbub of Selim.

SILVER COINS.

The PIASTRE and other silver coins bear the same inscriptions as the gold coins, and the same differences exist in them. The inscriptions on the Single, Double, and Half Piastres of Selim of 1789 are similar to those on the Sequin Fonducli of this Prince.

The PIASTRE OF TUNIS bears on the obverse the words

Sultan of the two lands, and Sovereign of the two seas, Sultan Selim Khan, blest with victory;

and on the reverse,

Struck at Tunis, in the year, &c.

TUSCANY.

GOLD COINS.

The RUSPONE—A lily, with the name and title of the reigning Prince, thus:

FERDINANDVS III. D. G. A. A. M. D. ETR.

that is, Dei Gratia, Archidux Austriæ, Magnus Dux Etruriæ,

Ferdinand III. by the grace of God, Archduke of Austria, Grand Duke of Tuscany.

Reverse, a figure of St. John the Baptist; legend,

S. JOANNES BAPTISTA.

Some pieces, coined about the year 1738, bear the head of the reigning Prince; legend,

FRANC. III. D. G. LOTH. BAR. ET M. ETR. D. REX HIER.

Francis III. by the grace of God, Duke of Lorraine and Bar, Grand Duke of Tuscany, King of Jerusalem.

Reverse, arms of the Prince; legend,

IN TE DOMINE SPERAVI,

In thee, O Lord, have I hoped.

The NEW RUSPONE of the Kingdom of Etruria bears the same impressions as above; legend on those coined in 1803,

LUDOVICUS I. D. G. HISP. INF. REX ETRVRIÆ,

Louis I. by the grace of God, Infant of Spain, King of Etruria;

and on those struck in 1804,

CAROLVS I. D. G. REX ET M. ALOYSIA R. RECTRIX,

Charles I. by the grace of God, King of Etruria, and Maria Louisa, Queen Regent.

The SEQUIN of TUSCANY bears the same impressions as the Ruspone.

SILVER COINS.

The DUCATONE—Head of the reigning Prince, with name and title, thus:

COSMOS III. D. G. MA. DVX ETRVRI VI.

Cosmos III. by the grace of God, Grand Duke of Tuscany, the 6th year of his reign.

Reverse, St. John baptizing our Saviour; legend,

FILIVS MEVS DILECTVS,
This is my beloved Son.

The LIVORNINA—Head of the reigning Prince, with name and title, thus:

JOAN. GASTO I. D. G. MAG. DVX ETRVRIÆ VII.
John Gaston, &c.

as above. Reverse, the city gate, over which is a crown, and under it,

FIDES,
Faith;

legend,

ET PATET ET FAVET,
It opens and favours.

In pieces of ancient date there is a view of the port of Leghorn with the same legend.

The PEZZA DELLA ROSA—Arms of Tuscany, with the reigning Prince's name and title, as on the Livornina. Reverse, a rose-tree; legend,

VLTIO QVÆSITA GRATIA OBVIA,
Revenge must be sought after, but forgiveness meets.

On the exergue is

LIEVRNE.

The FRANCESCONE—Impressions as on the Ruspone of 1738, to which, in pieces coined since 1740, are added the initials

R. I. S. A.

that is, Romanus Imperator, semper augustus,
Emperor of Rome, ever august.

Reverse, arms of Tuscany on the breast of a two-headed eagle; legend,

IN TE DOMINE SPERAVI,

as on the Ruspone. Pieces struck at Pisa are marked

PISIS.

The LEOPOLDONE—Head, name, title, &c. as on the Ruspone of 1738, with the addition of the initials

P. R. H. ET B.
Prince Royal of Hungary and Bohemia.

Reverse, arms of Tuscany, with the cross of Malta and order of the golden fleece; legend,

DIRIGE DOMINE GRESSVS MEOS,
O Lord, direct my steps.

The SCUDO of the KINGDOM of ETRURIA (1801)—Head of the reigning King, with name and title, thus:

LVDOVICVS I. D. G. HISP. INF. REX ETRVRIÆ PAR. PLAC. ET. PRIN.
Louis I. by the grace of God, Infant of Spain, King of Etruria, Prince of Parma and Placentia.

Reverse, arms of Tuscany, &c. legend,

VIDEANT PAUPERES ET LŒTENTUR,
Let the poor see and rejoice.

The Scudo of 1803 bears the heads of the Infant King and Queen Mother, with their names and titles, thus:

CAROLVS LVD. D. G. REX ETR. ET M. ALOYSIA R. RECTRIX I. I. H. H.
Charles Louis, by the grace of God, King of Etruria, and Maria Louisa, Queen Regent, Infant of Spain.

Reverse, arms of Tuscany, &c. legend,

DOMINE SPES MEA A JUVENTUTE MEA,
O Lord, my hope from my youth,

with

FLORENTIÆ;

round the edge are the words

DIECI LIRE,
10 *Lire.*

The LIRA of 1803—Arms of Tuscany, &c. legend, the King and Queen's names and titles, as on the Scudo. Reverse,

UNA LIRA,
1 *Lira, or Livre,*

encircled by a wreath.

UNITED STATES OF AMERICA.

Gold Coin.

The Eagle—Head of a woman with the cap of Liberty; legend,

LIBERTY,

with 13 stars. Reverse, an eagle, bearing the arms of the United States on its breast, and a bundle of arrows and an olive-branch in its talons; over its head, are 13 stars and a cloud, and across the neck a scroll, with this legend,

E PLURIBUS UNUM,
One from many;

legend,

UNITED STATES OF AMERICA.

On pieces coined since 1795, the reverse bears an eagle, with a palm-branch in its talons, and a wreath of laurel in its beak.

Silver Coin.

The Dollar and its divisions bear the same impressions as the Eagle, except that the head is without a cap. Round the edge are the words

ONE DOLLAR OR UNIT HUNDRED CENTS;

but the inferior coins have no letters on the edge. On the reverse of pieces of 1795, &c. the Eagle is entirely surrounded with branches of palm and laurel.

VENICE.

Gold Coins.

The Sequin—A man holding a cross and another kneeling before him, with the Doge's name, thus:

LVDO MANIN.

and the letters

S. M. V. M. N. M. T.

one above the other, near the edge of the piece;

that is, Sanctus Marcus Venetus;
St. Mark of Venice;

also, the letters

D. V. X.
Dux,
Duke, or Doge,

placed in the same manner above the kneeling figure. Reverse, a whole length figure of St. Mark, with a book, and surrounded with stars; legend,

SIT T. XPE. DAT. Q. TV. REGIS ISTE DVCA.

This inscription of the Venetian Sequin is the same as that of the Venetian Ducat of 1280, which is thus explained by *Muratori,* in his *Antiquitates Italicæ Medii Ævi,* vol. ii. p. 649.

Sit tibi Christe datum, quod (vel quia) tu regis.
Iste ducatum.

To thee, O Christ, be it (this coin) given, because thou governest (universally). He (St. Mark) governs the Duchy.

This interpretation is doubted even by *Muratori* himself, who supposes that *iste* might have been originally *ipse.* The legend is however curious, as being both an hexameter verse and a monkish rhyme.

The Half and Quarter Sequins bear the same impression, but the legend on the reverse is

EGO SVM LVX MVN.
I am the light of the world.

The Doppia or Pistole—A winged lion, holding a book, with

S. 2;

and the legend,

SANCTVS MARCVS VENETVS,

as on the Sequin. Reverse, a cross, and the Doge's name, thus:

FRANC. CONTARENO DVX VENET,
Francis Contareno, Doge of Venice.

The Scudo d'oro, or Gold Crown bears the same impressions as the Doppia, except that it is marked 140, and the Half Scudo d'oro, 70.

The OSELLA D'ORO—A woman sitting; legend,

PIETAS OPTIMI PRINCIPIS,
The piety of the best Prince,

but the impression varies. Reverse, a wreath, and within it the Doge's name, thus:

PAULI RAINERI PRINC. MUNUS ANNO V.
The gift of Paul Rainier, Prince, the year V. of his government.

The GOLD DUCAT—A man sitting and holding a standard, and another kneeling; legend,

S. M. VEN. LEON. DONAT.
St. Mark of Venice gives a Lion.

Reverse, a winged lion with a book; legend,

DVCATVS REIPUB.
Ducat of the Republic.

SILVER COINS.

The SCUDO DELLA CROCE bears the same impressions as the Scudo d'oro, and the Doppia.

The GIUSTINA—A winged lion, holding a book, and before it a figure with a standard; legend, the name and title of the reigning Doge. Reverse, a woman holding a palm-branch, with a circle over her head, and a sword on her shoulder; background, a view of the sea with ships; legend,

MEMOR ERO TVI JUSTINA VIRG.
I shall remember thee, Virgin Justina,

and

124,
124 *Soldi.*

The DUCAT—A winged lion as before, with a book; legend,

DVCATVS VENETVS,
Venetian Ducat.

Reverse, a figure sitting, and another kneeling and receiving a standard from him; legend,

S. M. V.
St. Mark of Venice,

and the Doge's name, as

PAVL RAINERIVS D.

The Half and Quarter Ducat bear the same impressions; but their legends are

MEDI. DVCAT. VENET.

and

QVAR. DVCAT. VENET.

The LIRAZZA, or Piece of 30 SOLDI—The same as the obverse of the Sequin. Reverse, a woman holding a sword and a pair of scales, with a lion by her side; legend,

JUSTITIAM DILIGITE,
Love justice.

The TALLARO and its divisions—Head of a woman; legend,

RESPUBLICA VENETA,
Republic of Venice.

Reverse, a winged lion and a book; legend, the reigning Doge's name, thus:

PAULO RAINERIO DUCE.

The OSELLA—The impressions on this piece are frequently changed, and are, therefore, too numerous to be here described: the reverse is most commonly the Doge's name, with the date of his government, and also of the Christian era, thus:

LUDOVICI MANIN PRINCIPIS MUNUS. AN. VIII. 1796,

as on the Osella d'oro.

The Piece of 10 LIRE of 1797—A woman, holding in one hand the cap of Liberty on a lance, and the other resting on the fasces; legend,

LIBERTA, EGUALIANZA,
Liberty, equality;

and at the bottom,

Z. V. *or* ZECCA V.

Reverse, the words

LIRE DIECI VENETE.
Ten Lire of Venice.

encircled by a wreath; legend,

ANNO I. DELLA LIBERTA ITALIANA,
The first year of Italian liberty.

The NEW COINS introduced by the Austrians, viz. Pieces of 2 Lire or 24 Creutzers of 1800 have, on the obverse, a two-headed eagle, crowned, bearing on its breast the arms of Austria; legend,

FRANZ. II. ROM. KAI. KON. ZU. HU. U. BO. ERZH ZU OEST,

that is, Franz. II. Römische Kaiser, König zu Hungarn und Böhmen, Erzherzog zu Oesterreich,

Francis II. Emperor of Rome, King of Hungary and Bohemia, Archduke of Austria.

Reverse, above a palm and laurel branch,

24 KREUTZER ERBLAENDISCH,
24 *Creutzers of the Hereditary States.*

The pieces of 1 Lira and ½ Lira, or 12 and 6 Creutzers, bear the same impressions, except that the legend round the eagle is

KAI. KON. ERBLANDISCHE. SCHEID. MUNZ.
Small coins of the Emperor and King's hereditary States,

and that the value is marked on the reverse. The pieces called *Provincial money,* issued in 1801, bear on the obverse the two-headed eagle, with the letters

F. II.
Francis II.

in an oval, on its breast: legend,

MONETA PROVINCIALE IMP. VENETA,
Imperial provincial coin of Venice.

Reverse, the value of the piece, viz.

DUE LIRE VENETE, UNA LIRA VENETA, *or* MEZZA LIRA VENETA,
2, 1, *or ½ Lira of Venice;*

the whole encircled by palm and laurel branches. The coins of 1802 bear, on the obverse, the eagle and arms of Austria, and the name of the Emperor Francis II. and his titles in Latin, as on the Austrian coins, with the addition

D. VENET.
Duke of Venice.

Reverse, the value of the piece.

WIRTEMBURG.

GOLD COINS.

The CAROLIN—Head of the reigning Prince, with name and title, thus:

CAROL. ALEX. D. G. DUX WUR. & T.
Charles Alexander, by the grace of God, Duke of Wirtemburg, &c.

Reverse, arms of Wirtemburg; legend,

CUM DEO ET DIE,
With God and Time;

and in some,

PER ARDUA VIRTUS,
Valour through difficulty.

The DUCAT—Impressions as on the Carolin, except that the legend on the reverse is

PROVIDE ET CONSTANTER,
Providently and constantly.

SILVER COIN.

The RIXDOLLAR—The impressions are the same as on the Ducat; but the reverse bears, besides the legend, the words

10 EINE FEINE MARCK,
Ten to a Mark fine.

The COPSTUCK—Impressions as on the Ducat, except that the head and the arms are each enclosed in a square, and that under the head there is the number 20.

WURTZBURG.

GOLD COIN.

The DUCAT—Head of the reigning Prince, with

name and titles, thus:

FRANC. LUD. D. G. EP. BAM. ET WIR. S. R. I. P. F. O. DUX;

that is, Franciscus Ludovicus, Dei Gratia, Episcopus Bambergii et Wirtsburgii, Sancti Romani Imperii Princeps, Francorum Orientalium Dux,

Francis Louis, by the grace of God, Bishop of Bamberg and Wurtzburg, Prince of the Holy Roman Empire, Duke of East Franconia.

Reverse, arms of the Bishop; legend,

DUCATUS DUCIS FRANCORUM,
Ducat of the Duke of Franconia.

SILVER COINS.

The RIXDOLLAR (coined before 1795) bears the same impressions as the Ducat, except the legend on the reverse,

10 EINE FEINE MARCK,
Ten to a Mark fine;

but the Rixdollar of 1795, &c. bears on the obverse the head of the Bishop, with name and titles as on the Ducat: and on the reverse only the inscription

10 EINE FEINE MARCK,

encircled by 2 branches of laurel, and above it the legend,

PRO PATRIA,
For the country.

The COPSTUCK—The same as the Rixdollar, according to the period at which it was coined, except that the words on the obverse are

LX. EINE FEINE MARCK,

and that it is marked 20.

ZURICH.

GOLD COIN.

The DUCAT—A lion with a sword, supporting the arms of the city; legend,

DUCATUS REIPUBLICÆ TIGURINÆ,
Ducat of the Republic of Zurich.

Reverse,

DOMINE CONSERVA NOS IN PACE,
O Lord, preserve us in peace.

On the Ducat of 1775 the legend on the obverse is

DUCATUS REIPUBLICA TURICENCIS.

Reverse,

JUSTITIA ET CORCORDIA,
Justice and Concord.

On Double Ducats, the arms are supported by two lions, and on some Half Ducats, the words on the reverse are only

ANNO DOMINI.

SILVER COINS.

The ECU or RIXDOLLAR of 1753—A view of the city; legend,

DOMINE CONSERVA NOS IN PACE,

as on the Ducat. Reverse, a lion supporting the arms of the Canton; legend,

MONETA REIPVBLICÆ TIGVRINÆ.

The Half Ecu has no legend over the city, but only the word

TIGURUM.
Zurich;

and it is marked ½ on the reverse.

The ECU of 1761—On the obverse, the legend

DOMINE, &c.

and the date, surrounded by various ornaments. Reverse, a lion, &c. as above.

The ECU of 1773—The inscription

JUSTITIA ET CONCORDIA,

and the date; the whole surrounded by various ornaments. Reverse, as before.

The ECU of 1790—A view of the city, with the legend—

DOMINE, &c.

Reverse, arms of the Canton; legend,

MONETA, &c.

as before.

The ECU of 1794—Arms of the Canton; with the legend—

MONETA, &c.

Reverse, the inscription

XI. AVF. I. FEINE MARK,
11 *to a Mark fine,*

encircled by a wreath. On the Half Ecu, or Florin, the words are

XXII. AVF. I. FEINE MARK;

and on the Half Florin

XX. SCHILLING.

EAST INDIES.

GOLD COINS.

The East India Coins, like those of Turkey, have in general no other impressions than inscriptions, setting forth the names and titles of the Sovereigns, with dates and other particulars, which are all in the Persian language.

The following are translations from the principal Indian coins both of gold and silver.

The MOHUR, or GOLD RUPEE (coined under the reign of the Emperor Shah Allum, which began in 1770) has on one side,

He who is the shadow of God's favour, the protector of the religion of Mahomet, the Emperor Shah Allum, coins money for the seven climates,

with the date of the Hegira. On the other side,

Struck at —— the year —— from the happy accession.

Some Mohurs have only, on one side,

Coin of the Emperor Shah Allum,

with the date of the Hegira; and on the other the year of the reign. The coins struck by the East India Company bear the name of the Mogul Emperor, and those minted of late years (as mentioned in the article *East Indies*, vol. i.) are dated the 19th year of the Emperor's reign, and the number 19 is visible on some part of the piece.

The MOHUR OF TIPPOO—On one side,

The faith of Mahomet, the most excellent in this world, is supported by the splendour of the victories of Hyder. Hyder! exalted in equity; struck at Seringapatam, the year pre-eminent in prosperity;

with the date of the Hegira. On the other side,

He alone is the equitable Sultan; the epoch of the accession was a year of happy omen,

with the date of the reign. Some of Tippoo's coins are dated according to an Indian era which is divided into cycles of 60 years each, of which cycles 81 are supposed to be now elapsed.

The FARUKI, or QUARTER MOHUR of Tippoo has on one side,

Mahomet! He is the only and right Sultan,

with the date; and on the other side,

Faruki, struck at Pattan, (Seringapatam,)

with the date of Tippoo's reign, and a Persian H. the initial of Hyder.

The PAGODA—These Pieces differ in shape from all European coins: they have a convex side, with prominent dots; and a flat side, which generally bears a figure, and in some three figures, of Indian idols.

The Star Pagoda is marked on the convex side with a star; other Pagodas are marked with a crescent, or with an initial letter; the Pagodas of Masulipatam and Pondicherry have nothing on the convex side but the dots. Tippoo's Pagodas have no figures on the flat side, but a legend, which is translated thus:

Mahomet! He is the power of equity.

with the date of the Hegira; on the convex side, the name of the place where it was coined, and generally the initial of Hyder.

The MOHUR of the DUTCH EAST INDIA COMPANY—On one side,

Coin of the Company of Holland;

above which is a cock, and under the legend the date of the Christian era; on the other side, the words,

In the great Island of Java.

The JAPAN COPANG is a flat oblong piece, one side of which is marked with transverse lines, and some characters; on the other side, there is in the centre a small circle in which is a mark of the inspector-general of the mint, and in other parts various marks, made by persons who have assayed the piece.

The ZODIACAL RUPEES are pieces of twelve different impressions, representing the twelve signs of the Zodiac. They were coined between the years 1616 and 1624 of the Christian era, by *Jehangeer*, and have been long out of circulation. They are, however, much sought after, and highly valued as objects of curiosity. Each sign, or figure, is surrounded by rays representing the sun; and on the reverse is the following inscription:

This ornamented Coin in Agra, found its face, (received its impression) *in the year —— from the Sovereign Jehangeer, son of King Akber.*

The Zodiacal Rupees are exceptions to the Mahometan law which forbids the representation or embossment of figures, but it is said that Jehangeer had little respect for his religion; and it is further stated by some writers that his favourite queen *Nour-Mahal* had obtained permission to reign for one day, (others say for one year,) and that she caused these coins to be struck to perpetuate the memory of her short reign. This account, however, cannot be quite correct, as the dates of these Rupees are different.

SILVER COINS.

The SICCA RUPEE—The legends on this coin are nearly the same as on the Mohur, and may be thus translated:—

Struck in the seven climates, (date of the Hegira,) *by the shadow of God's favour, Shah Allum, King, disciple in the faith of Mahomet:*

and on the other side,

Struck at —— in the 19th year of the august and glorious reign of the Emperor, &c.

Some Rupees do not bear the date of the Hegira, but only that of the Emperor's reign; and all the Rupees struck in Bengal of late years, at the Company's mint, have been dated the 19th year of his reign, as above noticed.

The ARCOT RUPEE—On one side,

Blessed coin of the conquering King (the name);

on the other side,

Struck at Arcot in the year —— of the reign,

and the date of the Hegira. But it may be observed that in these and many other Rupees, (except such as are coined by the East India Company,) the legends are often illegible, owing to the edge being clipped or worn, or to the piece having been originally too small to receive the impression.

The RUPEE of the DUTCH EAST INDIA COMPANY—On the obverse,

Coin of the Company of Holland,

and the date of the Christian era. Reverse,

In the great Island of Java.

The GULDEN of the DUTCH EAST INDIA COMPANY—The impressions correspond with those of the Gulden of the Netherlands (of 1818), except that the Piece of Java has the letters

N. O.

next to the Statute on one side; and on the other,

MO. ARG. REG. TOT. BELG. JAV.

that is, Moneta argentea Regni totius Belgicæ Javæ,

Silver Coin of the whole Kingdom of Belgium and Java.

The SULTANEE RUPEE of TIPPOO bears the same impressions and legends nearly as Tippoo's Mohur.

The RUPEE of PERSIA, or Piece of 10 MAMOODIS—The legends on these coins vary. Some bear the Sovereign's name, as

Sultan Shahrokh;

and on the other side,

May God prolong his reign, coined at ——,

the name of the place and date of the Hegira. On other Rupees, the King of Persia styles himself

The servant of the Monarch of the Empire,

that is of the *Iman Riza,* the head of their religion, whom the Persians consider as the real Sovereign of their Empire, and the coins are often struck in the name of the Iman Riza, with this legend,

By the divine decree, the coin of happy omen has been struck in the name of Ally Riza, son of Musa;

and on the other side,

There is no God but God, Mahomet is the Apostle of God, Ally is the favourite of God, struck at ——;

with the date of the Hegira.

The SILVER FANAM of PONDICHERRY bears on one side several fleurs de lys, and an inscription on the other.

The LARIN—This is a Silver wire, about an inch in length, doubled up, and flattened on the inner side to receive the impressions of some characters. It was first made in Arabia; and has become scarce, but is still used as a money of account.

The foregoing translations of the Persian and Indian inscriptions and legends are chiefly taken from M. BONNEVILLE'S Treatise on Coins, who states his authorities to be *Messrs. De Sacy,* and *Langles;* and *Mr. Alexander Hamilton* of Calcutta. The translations from the Turkish Coins have been supplied for this Work by Mr. Duc, formerly Secretary to the Turkish Ambassador in London; and the several translations from the Russian, Norwegian, and Swedish Coins have been likewise supplied by good authorities.

TABLES,

CONTAINING A

COMPARISON OF THE WEIGHTS AND MEASURES

OF ALL TRADING COUNTRIES,

Chiefly from actual Experiments made at the London Mint on Foreign Standards, transmitted to England in 1818 *by the British Consuls abroad, and previously verified by the proper Authorities in each Country.*

THE following Tables are, for the most part, a recapitulation of what has been given in the first Volume of this work; but the places here are more numerous; and these Tables also afford a more convenient and ready reference to any subject for which they may be consulted.

Table I.—Contains the Troy Weight of different nations, that is, the Weight chiefly used for the precious Metals. It shews the Weight of each Mark, &c. in English Troy Grains and in French Grammes; also the proportion which each Mark, &c. bears to 100 lb. English Troy.

Table II.—Contains the Commercial Weights of different countries compared with English Avoirdupois; also the Weight of each foreign Pound, Ounce, &c. in English Troy Grains and in French Grammes.

Table III.—Contains the Corn Measures of different countries. It shews the contents of each measure in English Cubic Inches, in English Bushels, and in French Litres; also the number of measures of each place that correspond to 1 English Quarter.

Table IV.—Contains the Liquid Measures of different nations. It shews the contents of a single measure of each sort in English Cubic Inches, in English Wine Gallons, and in French Litres; also how many Gallons, &c. of each place are equal to 100 English Gallons.

Table V.—Is a comparison of the Cloth Measures of different nations. It shews the length of each measure in English Inches and in French Decimetres ; also the number of Ells, Aunes, &c. of each place that correspond with 100 English Yards.

Table VI.—Contains the Long Measures of different Countries. It shews the length of each measure in English Inches and in French Decimetres ; also the number of Feet, &c. of each place that correspond with 100 English Feet.

Table VII.—Shews the contents of the Square Foot of different countries in English Square Inches and in French Square Decimetres.

Table VIII.—Shews the contents of the Cubic Foot of different countries in English Cubic Inches and in French Decilitres.

Table IX.—Contains the Land Measures of different nations. It gives the area of each measure in English Square Yards and in French Ares ; also the number of Acres, &c. of each place that equal 10 English Acres Statute Measure.

Table X.—Gives the length of the itinerary measures of different countries in English Yards and in French Metres ; also the proportion of the foreign League, &c. to 100 English Miles.

Table XI.—Contains the new Weights and Measures of France, with their proportion to those of England.

Table XII.—Contains an account of Ancient Weights and Measures, with their proportion to the Weights and Measures of England.

Rules and Examples are also given for finding the proportion between the Weights or Measures of any two or more places contained in the Tables.

TROY WEIGHT.

TABLE I.

Containing a Comparison of the Troy, or Gold and Silver Weights of different Countries; and shewing the Weight of a single Pound, Mark, Ounce, &c. in English Troy Grains and in French Grammes; also, the number of Pounds, Marks, Ounces, &c. of each place, that are equal to 100lbs. English Troy.

		Weight of a single lb. Mark, &c.		Number equal to 100 lbs. English Troy.
		Eng. Grains	Fr. Grammes.	
ALEPPO	Metical	73	4,729	7890,410
ALGIERS	Metical	73	4,729	7890,410
AUGSBURG	Mark	3643	236,037	158,111
BASSORA	Miscal	72	4,665	8000,000
BENGAL	Sicca	179,6	11,636	3207,126
BERLIN	Mark	3608	233,769	159,645
BERN	Mark	3810,3	246,877	151,117
BOLOGNA	Libbra	5586	361,957	103,114
BOMBAY	Tola	179	11,597	3217,877
BRESLAU	Mark	3158	204,613	182,393
CAIRO	Rottolo	6654	431,125	86,564
CALICUT	Miscal	69	4,470	8347,826
CHINA	Tale	579,8	37,566	993,446
COLOGNE	Mark	3608	233,769	159,645
CONSTANTINOPLE	Chequee	4957	321,173	116,199
CRACOW	Mark	3069	198,846	187,683
CYPRUS	Occa	1957	126,797	294,327
DAMASCUS	Ounce	460	29,804	1252,173
DENMARK	Mark	3633	235,389	158,546
ENGLAND	Pound	5760	373,202	100,000
FLORENCE	Libbra	5240	339,542	109,923
FRANCE	Poids de Marc	3777,5	244,751	152,481
	Kilogramme	15434	1000,000	37,320
GAMRON	Miscal	71,6	4,639	8044,692
GENEVA	Mark	3785	245,231	152,179
GENOA	Libbra	4891,5	316,963	117,755
GERMANY	Cologne Mark	3608	233,769	159,645
GOTHENBURG	Gold Weight	6854	444,084	84,038
	Silver Weight	6555,5	424,743	87,865
HAMBURG, HANOVER	Cologne Mark	3608	233,769	159,645

		Weight of a single lb. Mark, &c.		Number equal to 100lbs. English Troy.
		Eng. Grains.	Fr. Grammes.	
HOLLAND	Mark, Old Weight	3798	246,080	151,658
	New Pound, Netherlands	15434	1000,000	37,320
KONIGSBERG	Mark	3023,5	195,898	190,507
LEGHORN	Libbra	5240	339,510	109,923
LIEGE	Pound	3797,2	246,028	151,691
MADEIRA	Mark	3538,2	229,250	162,794
MADRAS	Star Pagoda Weight	52,5	3,401	10971,428
MALTA	Libbra	4886,6	316,617	117,873
MILAN	Mark	3627	235,033	158,808
MOCHA	Vakia	478	30,970	1205,020
MUNICH	Mark	3609,8	233,891	159,565
NAPLES	Libbra	4950	320,760	116,363
NUREMBERG	Mark	3670	237,786	156,948
PEGU	Tical	237,3	15,375	2427,307
PERSIA	Derham	151,1	9,790	3812,297
PORTUGAL	Mark	3541,5	229,460	162,642
PRAGUE	Mark	3916	253,725	147,088
PRUSSIA	Mark	3609	233,834	159,600
RATISBON	Crown Weight	6630	429,592	86,877
	Ducat Weight	3449	223,507	167,004
	Silver Weight	3797,2	246,028	151,691
REVAL	Mark	3326	215,498	173,180
RIGA	Mark	3226	209,018	178,548
ROME	Libbra	5234	339,121	110,049
RUSSIA	Pound	6318,5	409,388	91,161
SMYRNA	Chequee	4957,5	321,206	116,187
SPAIN	Mark	3550,5	230,043	162,230
STOCKHOLM	Mark	3250	210,574	177,230
TRIPOLI	Metical	73,6	4,768	7826,086
TUNIS	Metical	60,7	3,932	9489,291
TURIN	Mark	3795,7	245,935	151,750
VALENCIA	Mark	3557,6	230,504	161,906
VENICE	Mark	3681,5	238,531	156,457
VIENNA	Mark	4333	280,743	132,933
WARSAW	Mark	3113	201,697	185,030
WILNA	Mark	3006	194,764	191,616
ZURICH	Mark	3616,9	234,346	159,252

AVOIRDUPOIS WEIGHT.

TABLE II.

Containing a Comparison of the Commercial Weights of different trading Places: the first Column shews the Weight of a single Pound, &c. in English Troy Grains; the second, the Weight in French Grammes; the third, the Number of Pounds, &c. of each Place that are equal to 100 lbs. Avoirdupois; and the fourth, the Number equal to a Hundred Weight.

		Weight of a single lb. Rottolo, &c.		Number equal to 100lb. Avoirdupois.	Number equal to 112lb. Avoirdupois.
		Eng. Grains.	Fr. Grammes.		
ABYSSINIA	Rottolo	4800	311,001	145,833	163,333
AIX LA CHAPELLE	Pound	7234	468,705	96,765	108,377
ALEPPO	Rottolo of 720 Drams	35190	2280,030	19,891	22,277
	Ditto 700	34212	2216,663	20,460	22,915
	Ditto 680	33235	2153,362	21,062	23,589
	Ditto 600	29325	1900,025	23,870	26,734
	Oke 400	19550	1266,683	35,805	40,102
ALEXANDRIA	Rottolo Forfori	6542	423,869	107,000	119,840
	...... Zaydini	9345	605,481	74,906	83,895
	..... Zauri	14485	9385,121	48,325	54,124
	...... Mine	11682	7569,001	59,921	67,111
ALGIERS	Rottolo	8330	539,717	84,033	94,116
ALICANT	Heavy Pound	7983,9	517,292	87,676	98,197
	Light Pound	5322,9	344,881	131,509	147,290
AMSTERDAM	Pound, old Weight	7625	494,090	91,803	102,819
	Pound Flemish	15434	1000,000	45,354	50,796
ANCONA	Libbra	5093,9	330,043	137,419	153,909
ARRAGON	Libra	5398	349,799	129,677	145,238
AUGSBURG	Heavy Pound	7580	491,112	92,348	103,429
	Light Pound	7295	472,657	95,956	107,459
BARCELONA	Libra	6174	400,025	113,378	126,974
BASIL	Livre, Poids de Marc	7555	489,503	92,653	103,771
BASSORA	Vakia Tary	8312,5	538,583	84,210	94,315
BERGAMO	Libbra Peso Grosso	12588,8	8156,535	55,605	62,277
	...... Peso Sottile	5035	326,227	139,026	155,709
BERGEN	Pound	7716	499,935	90,720	101,606
BERLIN	Pound	7231	468,510	96,805	108,421
BERN	Pound	8060	522,223	86,848	97,269
BETELFAGUI	Maund	14273	9247,762	49,043	54,928
BILBOA	Heavy Pound	11037	7151,093	63,423	71,033

		Weight of a single lb. Rottolo, &c.		Number equal to 100lb. Avoirdupois.	Number equal to 112lb. Avoirdupois.
		Eng. Grains.	Fr. Grammes.		
Bilboa	Light Pound	7560	489,827	92,592	103,703
Bologna	Libbra	5586	361,957	125,31	140,347
Bolsano	Heavy Pound	7731,5	500,939	90,538	101,402
	Light Pound	5103	330,633	137,174	153,635
Bremen	Pound	7690	489,250	91,027	101,950
Breslau	Pound	6255	405,273	111,910	125,339
Brunswick	Pound	7206	466,891	97,141	108,798
Cairo	Rottolo	6650	430,866	105,263	117,894
Canary Islands	Libra	7103,6	460,256	98,541	110,366
Candia	Rottolo	8143	527,601	85,963	96,278
Cassel	Pound	7501	486,004	93,320	104,518
China	Catty	9333	604,703	75,002	84,002
Coburg	Pound	7869	509,841	88,956	99,630
Cologne	Pound	7216	467,539	97,006	108,646
Constance	Pound	7285	472,009	96,087	107,617
Constantinople	Oke	19830	1284,825	35,300	39,536
Copenhagen	Pound	7720	500,194	90,673	101,553
Corsica	Pound	7565,6	490,190	92,524	103,626
Cremona	Libbra	5060	327,847	138,339	154,939
Cyprus	Rottolo	36708	2378,384	19,069	21,357
Damascus	Rottolo	27562,5	1785,829	25,396	28,443
Dantzic	Pound	7231	468,510	96,805	108,421
East Indies	*(See Vol. I. p. 122)*				
Elsinore	Pound	7720	500,194	90,673	101,553
Embden	Pound	7668	496,825	91,288	102,242
England	Pound	7000	453,544	100,000	112,000
Erfurt	Pound	7285	472,009	96,087	107,617
Ferrara	Libbra	5338	345,859	131,135	146,871
Fiume	Funti Weight	8623	558,701	81,178	90,919
Florence	Libbra	5240	339,510	133,587	149,609
France	Livre, Poids de Marc	7555	489,503	92,653	103,771
	Kilogramme	15434	1000,000	45,354	50,796
	Livre Usuelle	7717	500,000	90,708	101,593
Francfort	Pound	7210	467,150	97,087	108,737
Galicia	Libra	8892,5	576,122	78,718	88,164
Geneva	Heavy Pound	8498	550,602	82,372	92,256
	Light Pound	7081,6	458,831	98,847	110,709
Genoa	Libbra Peso Grosso	5381	348,645	130,087	145,697
	Libbra, Peso Sottile	4892	316,962	143,090	160,261
Hamburg	Pound	7476	484,384	93,633	104,868
Hanover	Pound	7511	486,652	93,196	104,378
Japan	Catty	9100	589,607	76,923	86,153
Konigsberg	Pound	7231	468,510	96,805	108,421

		Weight of a single lb. Rottolo, &c.		Number equal to 100lb. Avoirdupois.	Number equal to 112lb. Avoirdupois.
		Eng. Grains.	Fr. Grammes.		
LEGHORN	Libbra	5240	339,510	133,587	149,609
LEIPSIC	Pound	7206	466,891	97,141	108,798
LIBAU	Pound	6449	417,843	108,543	121,568
LIEGE	Pound	7330	474,925	95,497	106,956
LUBEC	Pound	7479,5	484,612	93,589	104,819
LUCCA	Libbra, Peso Grosso	5763,8	373,448	121,447	136,020
	Libbra, Peso Sottile	5213	337,770	134,279	150,392
LUNEBURG	Pound	7540	488,531	92,838	103,978
LYONS	Livre, Poids de Soie	7087,5	459,213	98,765	110,617
	Livre, Poids de Table	6615	428,599	105,820	118,518
MADEIRA	Libra	7076,5	458,500	98,919	110,789
MAJORCA	Rottolo	6174	400,026	113,378	126,983
MALTA	Rottolo	12216	791,499	57,302	64,178
MANHEIM	Pound	7638	494,881	91,647	102,644
MANTUA	Libbra	4871	315,602	143,707	160,952
MARSEILLES	Livre, Poids de Table	6296	407,950	111,181	124,523
MECCA	Rottolo	7144	462,874	97,984	109,742
MECKLENBURG	Pound	7458	483,218	93,859	105,122
MILAN	Libbra, Peso Grosso	11774	762,861	594,530	665,874
	Libbra, Peso Sottile	5044	326,811	138,778	155,431
	Libbra Nuova	15434	1000,000	45,354	50,796
MODENA	Libbra	4931,5	319,521	141,944	158,977
MOROCCO	Pound	8330	539,717	84,033	94,117
MUNICH	Pound	8656	560,839	80,868	90,572
MUNSTER	Pound	7353	476,415	95,199	106,623
NAPLES	Cantaro Grosso	13755	891,214	50,890	56,997
	Cantaro Piccolo	7420	480,756	94,339	105,660
NETHERLANDS	New Pound	15434	1000,000	45,354	50,796
NEUFCHATEL	Livre, Poids de Marc	7555	489,503	92,653	103,771
	Livre, Poids de Fer	8029	520,215	87,184	97,646
NICE	Livre	4809	311,584	145,560	163,027
NUREMBERG	Pound	7870	509,913	88,945	99,618
OLDENBURG	Pound	7476	484,384	94,633	104,868
ORAN	Rottolo	7775	503,758	90,032	100,835
ORMUS	Seer	4675	302,902	149,732	167,699
OSNABURG	Pound	7625	494,039	91,803	102,819
OVIEDO	Libra	10651	6990,996	65,721	73,607
PADUA	Libbra, Peso Grosso	7388,5	478,715	94,742	106,111
	Libbra, Peso Sottile	5250	340,158	133,333	149,333
PARMA	Libbra	5038	326,422	138,944	155,617
PATRAS	Pound	6168	399,637	113,488	127,106
PERNAU	Pound	6430	416,612	108,864	121,927
PERSIA	Batman of Cherray	88771	5751,692	78,854	88,316

		Weight of a single lb. Rottolo, &c.		Number equal to 100lb. Avoirdupois.	Number equal to 112lb. Avoirdupois.
		Eng. Grains.	Fr. Grammes.		
PERSIA	Batman of Tauris	44385,5	2875,846	157,709	176,634
POLAND	Cracow Pound	6250	404,950	112,000	125,440
	Warsaw Pound	5832	377,866	120,027	134,430
	New Pound	6236	404,043	112,251	125,721
PORTUGAL	Arratel	7083	458,921	98,828	110,687
PRAGUE	Pound	7940	514,448	88,161	98,740
PRUSSIA	Pound	7218	467,668	96,979	108,617
RAGUSA	Oke	20671	1339,315	33,864	37,927
RATISBON	Pound	8777	568,679	79,753	89,323
RAVENNA	Libbra	4623	299,533	151,417	169,587
REGGIO	Libbra	5092	329,921	137,470	153,966
REVAL	Pound	6652	430,996	105,231	117,858
RIGA	Pound	6452	418,038	108,493	121,512
ROME	Libbra	5234	339,121	133,741	149,790
ROSTOCK	Pound	7852	508,746	89,149	99,846
ROTTERDAM	Pound	7625	494,039	91,803	102,819
	Light Pound	7243	469,288	96,645	108,242
ROUEN	Livre, Poids de Vicomté	8241	533,957	84,941	95,134
RUSSIA	Pound	6318,5	409,388	110,785	124,079
ST. GALL	Heavy Pound	9016	584,164	77,640	86,956
	Light Pound	7175	464,882	97,561	109,268
SALTZBURG	Pound	8642	559,932	80,999	90,718
SARDINIA	Libbra	6125	396,851	114,285	127,999
SAYDE	Rottolo of 600 Drams	28742	1862,251	24,355	272,776
	Rottolo of Acre	33740	2186,082	20,746	23,236
SCOTLAND	Pound, Dutch Weight	7600	492,419	92,105	103,157
SICILY	Rottolo Grosso	13475	8730,720	51,948	58,181
	Rottolo Sottile	12250	7937,020	57,143	64,000
	Libbra	4900	317,481	142,857	159,999
SIENNA	Libbra	6904	447,324	101,390	113,556
SMYRNA	Oke	19830	1284,825	35,300	39,536
SPAIN	Libra	7101	460,088	93,577	110,406
STETTIN	Pound	7219	467,733	96,966	108,602
STRALSUND	Old Livre	7460	483,348	93,833	105,092
STRASBURG	Livre	7266	470,778	96,339	107,899
SWEDEN	Pound, Victualie Weight	6563	425,229	106,658	119,456
	——— Miners' Weight	5801	375,858	120,668	135,148
	——— Uppstads or Inland Town Weight	5526	358,040	126,673	141,874
	——— Metal or Staplestad Weight	5250	340,158	133,333	149,333
TRIESTE	Pound	8639	559,738	81,027	90,750
TRIPOLI, in Syria,	Oke	18691	211,127	37,451	41,945

		Weight of a single lb. Rottolo, &c.		Number equal to 100lb. Avoirdupois.	Number equal to 112lb. Avoirdupois.
		Eng. Grains.	Fr. Grammes.		
TRIPOLI, in Africa,	Rottolo	7840	507,969	89,285	99,999
TUNIS	Rotul	7773,5	503,660	90,049	100,855
TURIN	Libbra	5692	368,796	122,979	137,736
VALENCIA	Heavy Pound	8226	532,978	85,096	95,307
	Light Pound	5484	355,350	127,644	142,961
VENICE	Libbra, Peso Grosso	7363	477,063	95,069	106,772
	Libbra, Peso Sottile	4650	301,282	150,537	168,601
	Libbra, Nuova	15434	1000,000	45,354	50,796
VERONA	Libbra, Peso Grosso	7676	497,343	91,193	102,136
	Libbra, Peso Sottile	5134	332,642	136,345	152,706
VIENNA	Pound	8645	560,126	80,972	90,688
ULM	Pound	7234	468,705	96,765	108,377
WIRTEMBERG	Pound	7220	467,792	96,953	108,586
WISMAR	Pound	7625	494,039	91,803	102,819
WURTZBURG	Pound	7362	476,998	95,083	106,492
ZANTE	(See *Venice*)				
ZELL	Pound	7511	486,652	93,196	104,378
ZURICH	Heavy Pound	8138	527,277	86,016	96,337
	Light Pound	7233	468,640	96,778	108,391

CORN MEASURE.

TABLE III.

Containing a Comparison of the Corn Measures of different Places; namely, the Contents of a single Measure in English Cubic Inches, in Bushels, and in French Litres; also the Number of Measures of each Place, corresponding to Eight Bushels, or One Quarter, Winchester Measure.

Place	Measure	Contents of a single Measure of each sort.			Number of each equal to One English Quarter.
		Cubic Inches.	Bushels.	Fr. Litres.	
Aix la Chapelle	Fass	1461	0,679	23,939	11,782
Alexandria	Rebebe	9587	4,458	157,092	1,794
Algiers	Tarrie	1219	0,567	19,974	14,109
Alicant	Cahiz	15038	6,993	246,412	1,144
Amersfoort	Mudde	11457	5,327	187,744	1,502
Amsterdam	Mudde	6788	3,157	111,256	2,534
Ancona	Rubbio	17459	8,119	286,100	0,985
Antwerp	Hectolitre	6102	2,837	100,000	2,818
Arnheim	Malder	8333	3,875	136,541	2,064
Arragon	Cahiz	11021	5,125	180,486	1,561
Augsburg	Schaf	26812	12,467	439,341	0,641
Azores	Alqueire	731	0,340	11,978	23,530
Barcelona	Quartera	4175	1,941	68,419	4,121
Basil	Sack	7870	3,666	128,957	2,182
Bastia	Stajo	9153	4,256	150,000	1,879
Bayonne	Conque	2503	1,164	41,014	6,872
Bergamo	Soma	10020	4,659	164,187	1,720
Bergen	Toende	8488	3,947	139,084	2,026
Berlin	Scheffel	3180	1,479	52,107	5,409
Bern	Mutt	10260	4,771	168,120	1,676
Bilboa	Fanega	3668	1,706	60,104	4,689
Bologna	Corba	4503	2,094	73,786	3,820
Bolsano	Scheffel	6657	3,095	109,081	2,584
Boulogne	Setier	10535	4,898	172,626	1,633
Bourdeaux	Boisseau	4682	2,177	76,708	3,674
Breda	Viertel	5236	2,435	85,826	3,285
Bremen	Scheffel	4339	2,017	71,098	3,966
Breslau	Scheffel	4266	1,983	69,903	4,034
Brest	Tonneau	84200	39,153	1379,701	0,204
Bruges	Hoed	10164	4,726	166,547	1,692

		Contents of a single Measure of each Sort.			Number of each equal to One English Quarter.
		Cubic Inches.	Bushels.	Fr. Litres.	
BRUNSWICK	Himten	1898	0,882	31,100	9,070
CADIZ	Fanega	3439	1,599	56,351	5,003
CALABRIA	Tomolo	3119	1,450	51,108	5,517
CANADA	Minot	2339	1,088	38,327	7,353
CANARY ISLES	Fanega	3821	1,777	62,611	4,502
CANDIA	Carga	9288	4,322	152,193	1,851
CASSEL	Viertel	8710	4,050	142,722	1,975
CLEVES	Malter	10954	5,093	179,492	1,571
COBLENTZ	Malter	9742	4,530	159,632	1,766
COBURG	Simra	5353	2,489	87,727	3,214
COLOGNE	Malter	9891	4,599	162,073	1,739
CONSTANTINOPLE	Killow	2023	0,941	33,148	8,501
COPENHAGEN	Toende	8488	3,947	139,084	2,026
CORUNNA	Ferrado	1022	0,475	16,746	16,842
CYPRUS	Medimno	4583	2,131	75,097	3,754
DANTZIC	Scheffel	3337	1,552	54,680	5,155
DEVENTER	Mudde	7049	3,278	115,535	2,440
DIEPPE	Mine	6243	2,903	102,297	2,755
DORDRECHT	Great Sack	7638	3,552	125,163	2,252
	Little Sack	5728	2,664	93,872	3,003
DRESDEN	Scheffel	6455	3,002	105,788	2,664
DUNKIRK	Sea Rasiere	9153	4,256	150,000	1,879
	Land Rasiere	8136	3,783	133,316	2,114
ELBING	Scheffel	2965	1,378	48,584	5,805
EMBDEN	Tonne	11697	5,439	191,667	1,470
ENGLAND	Bushel	2150,4	1,000	35,236	8,000
ERFURT	Scheffel	3668	1,706	60,120	4,689
FARO	Alqueire	982	0,456	16,091	17,543
FERRARA	Stajo	1909	0,887	31,281	90,191
FERROL	Ferrado	1042	0,484	17,074	16,529
FIUME	Metze	3813	1,773	62,479	4,512
FLORENCE	Stajo	1486	0,691	24,369	11,577
FRANCE	Setier	9519,9	4,427	156,000	1,807
	Hectolitre	6102	2,837	100,000	2,819
	Boisseau Usuel	762,7	0,354	12,500	22,598
FRANCFORT	Malter	6590	3,064	107,984	2,611
GENEVA	Coupe	4739	2,203	77,653	3,631
GENOA	Mina	7367	3,426	120,716	2,335
GOES	Sack	4888	2,273	80,106	3,519
GRONINGEN	Mudde	5554	2,583	91,028	3,097
HAARLEM	Sack	4823	2,243	79,050	3,566
HAGUE	Sack	6546	3,044	107,282	2,628
HAMBURG	Scheffel	6426	2,988	105,296	2,677

		Contents of a single Measure of each Sort.			Number of each equal to One English Quarter.
		Cubic Inches.	Bushels.	Fr. Litres.	
HANAU	Malter	6868	3,194	112,539	2,501
HANOVER	Himtem	1898	0,882	31,100	9,070
HEIDELBERG	Malter	6285	2,922	102,986	2,737
HILDESHEIM	Scheffel	3164	1,471	51,845	5,438
HOLSTEIN	Toende	8488	3,947	139,084	2,026
KONIGSBERG	Scheffel	3152	1,465	51,648	5,460
LEGHORN	Sacco	4435	2,062	72,672	3,879
LEIPSIC	Scheffel	8481	3,943	138,969	2,029
LEWARDEN	Loop	5092	2,368	83,442	3,378
LEYDEN	Sack	4165	1,937	68,271	4,130
LIBAU	Lof	4190	1,948	68,657	4,106
LIEGE	Setier	1827	0,849	29,937	9,422
LISBON	Alqueire	824,8	0,384	13,515	20,833
LUBEC	Wheat Scheffel	2041	0,949	33,444	8,429
	Oat Scheffel	2395	1,113	39,244	7,187
LUCCA	Stajo	1472	0,684	24,120	11,695
LUNEBURG	Scheffel	3799	1,767	62,250	4,527
LYONS	Asnée	11706	5,443	191,814	1,470
MAGDEBURG	Scheffel	3152	1,465	51,648	5,460
MAJORCA	Quartera	4301	1,999	70,476	4,002
MALAGA	Fanega	3439	1,599	56,351	5,003
MALTA	Salma	17678	8,221	289,672	0,973
MANHEIM	Malter	6285	2,922	102,986	2,737
MANTUA	Stajo	2146	0,998	35,164	8,016
MARANHAM	Alqueire	2772	1,288	45,422	6,211
MARSEILLES	Charge	9763	4,540	160,000	1,762
MECKLENBURG	Scheffel	2591	1,205	42,456	6,639
MENTZ	Malter	5558	2,584	91,073	3,095
MIDDLEBURG	Sack	4417	2,054	72,387	3,895
MILAN	Stajo	1115	0,518	18,270	15,444
MINORCA	Quartera	4301	1,999	70,476	4,002
MODENA	Stajo	4301	1,999	70,476	4,002
MONTPELLIER	Setier	3232	1,503	52,959	5,322
MUNICH	Scheffel	22130	10,290	362,622	0,777
NANCY	Carte	2925	1,360	47,929	5,880
NANTES	Setier	8739	4,063	143,197	1,968
NAPLES	Tomolo	3122	1,451	51,157	5,513
NEDA	Ferrado	1144	0,532	18,745	15,037
NEGROPONT	Killow	1849	0,859	30,297	9,313
NETHERLANDS	Mudde	6102	2,837	100,000	2,819
NICE	Charge	9763	4,540	160,000	1,762
NIMEGUEN	Scheffel	2546	1,184	41,721	6,756
NUREMBERG	Malter	10200	4,744	167,137	1,686

		Contents of a single Measure of each Sort.			Number of each equal to One English Quarter.
		Cubic Inches.	Bushels.	Fr. Litres.	
OLDENBURG	Tonne	9946	4,624	162,975	1,730
OSNABURG	Scheffel	1753	0,815	28,724	9,815
OVIEDO	Fanega	4419	2,055	72,41	3,893
PARMA	Stajo	3135	1,458	51,370	5,487
PATRAS	Staro	5012	2,330	82,126	3,433
PERNAU	Tonne	7729	3,594	126,647	2,225
PERSIA	Artaba	4013	1,866	65,757	4,287
POLAND	Korzec	3120,8	1,451	51,137	5,513
PRAGUE	Strick	6516	3,030	106,771	2,640
PRUSSIA	Scheffel	3353,6	1,559	54,952	5,130
RAGUSA	Stajo	9072	4,218	148,653	1,896
RATISBON	Maass	16016	7,448	262,445	1,074
REVAL	Tonne	7219	3,356	118,290	2,383
RIGA	Loop	4166	1,937	68,269	4,130
ROCHELLE	Boisseau	2007	0,933	32,886	8,574
ROME	Rubbio	17970	8,356	294,465	0,957
ROSTOCK	Scheffel	2372	1,103	38,877	7,253
ROTTERDAM	Sack	6320	2,939	103,583	2,722
ROUEN	Setier	10920	5,077	178,893	1,575
RUSSIA	Chetwert	12800	5,952	209,740	1,344
ST. GALL	Charge	4443	2,066	72,802	3,872
ST. MALOES	Boisseau	2697	1,254	44,193	6,379
ST. VALERY	Setier	9356	4,350	153,307	1,839
SALONICA	Killow	1184	5,505	19,401	1,453
SARDINIA	Starello	2988	1,389	48,961	5,759
SCOTLAND	Wheat Firlot	2197,3	1,022	36,005	7,827
	Barley Firlot	3205,5	1,490	52,525	5,369
SICILY	Salma Grossa	21014	9,771	34,433	0,818
	Salma Generale	16886	7,851	27,669	1,019
SMYRNA	Killow	3132	1,456	51,321	5,494
SPAIN	Fanega	3439	1,599	56,351	5,003
STETTIN	Scheffel	3180	1,479	52,107	5,409
STRALSUND	Scheffel	2378	1,105	38,966	7,239
STRASBURG	Land Setier	1154	0,536	18,909	14,925
	City Setier	1118	0,520	18,319	15,384
SWEDEN	Tunna of 32 Kappar	8940	4,157	146,490	1,924
	Kann	159,6	0,0742	2,615	107,816
TEXEL	Loop	3819	1,776	62,581	4,504
TRIESTE	Stajo	5040,6	2,344	82,611	3,413
	Metzen	3706	1,723	60,733	4,643
	Polonick	1853	0,861	30,367	9,291
TUNIS	Caffice	32256	15,000	528,540	0,533
TURIN	Sacco	7015	3,264	115,000	2,451

		Contents of a single Measure of each Sort.			Number of each equal to One English Quarter.
		Cubic Inches.	Bushels.	Fr. Litres.	
VALENCIA	Cahiz	12526	5,825	205,257	1,373
VENICE	Stajo	4882	2,270	80,000	3,524
VERONA	Minello	2221	1,033	36,393	7,745
VIANNA	Alqueire	1031	0,479	16,894	16,701
VIENNA	Metzen	3753	1,745	61,496	4,584
ULM	Immi	14021	6,519	229,748	1,227
UTRECHT	Sack	5498	2,557	90,116	3,128
WIRTEMBERG	Scheffel	10889	5,064	178,440	1,579
WISMAR	Wheat Scheffel	2478	1,152	40,592	6,944
	Oat Scheffel	2616	1,216	42,852	6,578
ZANTE	Corfu Misura	1284,78	0,597	21,062	13,400
ZEALAND	Sack	4556	2,119	74,660	3,775
ZELL	Himten	1898	0,882	31,099	9,070
ZURICH	Mutt	5048	2,347	82,716	3,408
ZWOLL	Mudde	6851	3,186	112,286	2,511

WINE MEASURE.

TABLE IV.

Containing a Comparison of the Liquid Measures of different Places; viz. 1st, the Contents of a single Measure in English Cubic Inches; 2d, in English Gallons; 3d, in French Litres; and, 4th, the Number of Gallons, &c. of each Place that are equal to 100 English Gallons.

Place	Measure	Contents of a single Measure of each sort.			Number of each equal to 100 English Gallons.
		Cubic Inches.	E. Gallons.	Fr. Litres.	
Abyssinia	Cuba	62	0,268	1,016	373,134
Alicant	Cantara	705	3,052	11,554	32,765
Amsterdam	Wine Stekan	1184	5,126	19,403	19,508
	Brandy Stekan	1145	4,956	18,759	20,177
	Beer Stekan	1199	5,193	19,656	19,256
Ancona	Soma	5241	22,698	85,917	4,405
Antwerp	Stoop	167	0,726	2,748	137,741
Arragon	Wine Cantaro	629	2,724	10,313	36,710
	Brandy Cantaro	852	3,690	13,970	27,100
Augsburg	Mass	90,3	0,391	1,479	255,754
Barcelona	Carga	7552	32,695	123,756	3,058
Bari	Oil Salma	10100	43,718	165,498	2,287
Basil	Ohm	3053	13,215	50,026	7,567
Bastia	Barile	8543	36,986	140,000	2,703
Bayonne	Velte	451	1,952	7,390	51,229
Bergamo	Brenta	4441	19,223	72,761	5,202
Berlin	Anker	2285,5	9,894	37,450	10,107
Berne	Mass	102	0,441	1,671	226,757
Bologna	Corba	4503	19,493	73,782	5,130
Bourdeaux	Barrique	14033	60,748	229,937	1,646
	Velte	438	1,896	7,177	52,742
Bremen	Stubgen	194,5	0,842	3,187	118,764
Breslau	Eimer	3389	14,670	55,532	6,816
Brunswick	Stubgen	224	0,969	3,669	103,199
Burgundy	Quartaut	6275	27,161	102,822	3,685
Canary Isles	Arroba	981	4,245	16,073	23,557
Candia	Oil Mistate	681	2,949	11,164	33,909
Cassel	Quartlin	499	2,160	8,175	46,296
Champagne	Quartaut	5496	23,789	90,057	4,203
Cognac	Brandy Velte	446	1,930	7,308	51,813

		Contents of a single Measure of each Sort.			Number of each equal to 100 English Gallons.
		Cubic Inches.	E. Gallons.	Fr. Litres.	
COLOGNE	Viertel	365	1,580	5,980	63,291
CONSTANTINOPLE	Almud	319	1,381	5,227	72,411
COPENHAGEN	Viertel	471,5	2,041	7,726	48,995
	Anker	2298	9,947	37,655	10,049
CORFU	Barile	4158	18,000	68,133	5,555
CYPRUS	Cass	288,7	1,250	4,731	80,000
DANTZIC	Ohm	9142	39,572	149,756	2,527
DRESDEN	Eimer	4128	17,870	67,639	5,596
DUNKIRK	Lot	140	0,608	2,302	164,473
ENGLAND	Wine Gallon	231	1,000	3,785	100,000
	Beer Gallon	282	1,220	4,621	81,967
ERFURT	Wine Eimer	4398	19,040	72,072	5,252
	Beer Eimer	4402	19,059	72,144	5,249
FARO	Almude	1131	4,896	18,532	20,425
FERRARA	Mastello	3379,5	14,630	55,378	6,835
FIUME	Orna	3253	14,082	53,303	7,101
FLORENCE	Wine Barile	2781,7	12,042	45,584	8,304
	Oil Barile	2040	8,831	33,428	11,323
FRANCE	Setier	454	1,966	7,444	50,864
	Hectolitre	6102,8	26,419	100,000	3,785
FRANCFORT	Viertel	450	1,948	7,373	51,334
GALICIA	Moyo	9886	42,798	161,991	2,336
GALLIPOLI	Oil Salma	9459	40,948	154,992	2,442
GENEVA	Setier	2760	11,948	45,224	8,369
GENOA	Wine Barile	4530	19,610	74,225	5,099
	Oil Barile	3946	17,082	64,657	5,854
HAMBURG	Ahm	8836	38,250	144,786	2,614
HANOVER	Ahm	9493	41,095	155,552	2,433
HEIDELBERG	Maass	140,4	0,607	2,300	164,744
HUNGARY, UPPER	Eimer	4474	19,368	73,316	5,163
HUNGARY, LOWER	Eimer	3472	15,030	56,892	6,653
	Tokay Anthal	3084	13,350	50,534	7,490
IRELAND	Gallon	217,6	0,942	3,565	106,157
KONIGSBERG	Stof	87,5	0,378	1,433	264,550
LEGHORN	Wine Barile	2781	12,042	45,584	8,304
	Oil Barile	2040	8,831	33,428	11,323
LEIPSIC	Eimer	4644	20,102	76,099	4,974
LIBAU	Oxhoft	14436	62,487	236,548	1,600
LINDAU	Quart	140	0,606	2,294	165,016
LISBON	Almude	1009,5	4,370	16,541	22,883
LISLE	Lot	126	0,545	2,064	183,486
LUBEC	Viertel	441,9	1,913	7,241	52,273
LUCCA	Oil Coppo	6093	26,373	99,839	3,791

		Contents of a single Measure of each Sort.			Number of each equal to 100 English Gallons.
		Cubic Inches.	E. Gallons.	Fr. Litres.	
LYONS	Asnée	5038	21,809	82,549	4,585
MAJORCA	Quartin	1655,8	7,168	27,131	13,951
MALAGA	Arroba	967	4,186	15,850	23,889
MALTA	Oil Caffiso	1270	5,497	20,810	18,191
MANTUA	Oil Moggio	6804	29,454	111,489	3,395
MARSEILLES	Millerolle	3924,7	16,990	64,330	5,886
MENTZ	Maass	114	0,493	1,868	202,839
MESSINA	Wine Salma	5331	23,079	87,360	4,333
	Oil Caffiso	714	3,090	11,699	32,362
MILAN	Brenta	4357,5	18,865	71,405	5,301
MINORCA	Gerra	736	3,187	12,063	31,377
MONTPELLIER	Wine Barrique	1550	6,710	25,398	14,903
	Oil Barrique	2028	8,778	33,231	11,392
MUNICH	Wine Eimer	2252	9,750	37,020	10,256
NANTES	Wine Barrique	14645	63,405	240,000	1,577
	Brandy Velte	343	1,484	5,617	67,385
NAPLES	Wine Barile	2544	11,013	41,685	9,080
	Oil Salma	9884	42,783	161,959	2,337
NETHERLANDS	Vat	6102,8	26,419	100,000	3,785
NICE	Rubbio	479,5	2,076	7,857	48,169
NUREMBERG	Eimer Visiermass	4149	17,959	67,984	5,567
	Eimer Schenkmass	3872	16,761	63,439	5,966
OLDENBURG	Oxhoft	15230	65,930	249,558	1,516
OPORTO	Almude	1555	6,731	25,480	14,856
OSNABURG	Viertel	298	1,290	4,883	77,519
OVIEDO	Cantara	1177	5,098	19,286	19,615
PERNAU	Anker	2364	10,233	38,736	9,772
POLAND	Garniec	97	0,419	1,590	238,663
PRAGUE	Eimer	3916	16,950	64,167	5,899
PRUSSIA	Eimer	4192	18,145	68,690	5,511
RAGUSA	Barrel	4704	20,363	77,075	4,911
RATISBON	Great Eimer	6934	30,014	113,620	3,331
	Berg Eimer	5359	23,196	87,812	4,311
REVAL	Anker	2580	11,172	42,276	8,951
RIGA	Anker	2386	10,333	39,097	9,677
RIO DE JANEIRO	Medida	161,7	0,700	2,651	142,857
ROCHELLE	Wine Barrique	10636	46,039	174,279	2,172
	Brandy Velte	446	1,930	7,308	51,813
ROME	Wine Barrile	3560,4	15,413	58,341	6,488
	Oil Barrile	3507	15,185	57,480	6,585
ROSTOCK	Anker	2209	9,562	36,199	10,458
ROTTERDAM	Ahm	9238,4	39,993	151,380	2,500
ROUEN	Barrique	11940	51,688	195,648	1,934

		Contents of a single Measure of each Sort.			Number of each equal to 100 English Gallons.
		Cubic Inches.	E. Gallons.	Fr. Litres.	
RUSSIA	Vedro	750	3,246	12,289	30,807
SCHAFFHAUSEN	Mass	80	0,346	1,311	289,017
SCOTLAND	Pint	103,4	0,447	1,694	223,713
SPAIN	Wine Arroba	981	4,245	16,073	23,557
	Oil Arroba	771	3,337	12,633	29,966
STRALSUND	Stubgen	237	1,027	3,883	97,371
STRASBURG	Ohm	2813	12,176	46,093	8,212
SWEDEN	Kann	159,6	0,691	2,615	144,717
TRIESTE	Wine Orna	3452	14,942	56,564	6,692
TUNIS	Millerolie	3924,7	16,990	64,330	5,886
	Oil Mettar	1183,8	5,125	19,397	19,512
TURIN	Rubbio	573	2,480	9,389	40,322
VALENCIA	Arroba	719	3,112	11,786	32,133
VENICE	Secchio	659	2,853	10,800	35,051
	Oil Miro	930	4,028	15,238	24,826
VERONA	Brenta	4417	19,119	72,377	5,230
	Oil Bassa	276	1,194	4,522	83,752
VIENNA	Eimer	3452	14,942	56,564	6,692
WISMAR	Viertel	441,9	1,913	7,241	52,273
ZANTE	Barile	4071	17,625	66,707	5,673
ZELL	Stubgen	237	1,025	3,883	97,561
ZURICH	Land Maass	111,3	0,481	1,823	207,900
	City Maass	100,2	0,433	1,642	230,946
	Oil Maass	84	0,363	1,376	275,482

CLOTH MEASURE.

TABLE V.

Containing a Comparison of the Cloth Measures of different Countries. It shews the Length of each Measure in English Inches and in French Decimetres; also the Number of Ells, Aunes, &c. of each Place that correspond to 100 *English Yards.*

		Length of a single Measure of each Sort.		Number of each equal to 100 English Yards.
		English Inches.	Fr. Decimetres.	
Abyssinia	Pic	27,00	6,857	133,333
Aix la Chapelle	Ell	26,33	6,687	136,726
Aleppo	Pic	26,66	6,771	135,033
Alexandria	Pic	26,80	6,806	134,328
Algiers, Turkish	Pic	24,53	6,230	146,759
Moorish	Pic	18,40	4,673	195,652
Alicant	Vara	29,95	7,607	120,200
Amsterdam	Ell	27,07	6,878	132,988
Ancona	Braccio	25,33	6,433	142,124
Antwerp	Silk Ell	27,32	6,939	131,771
	Woollen Ell	26,96	6,846	133,531
Arragon	Vara	30,22	7,675	119,126
Augsburg	Long Ell	24,00	6,095	150,000
	Short Ell	23,32	5,923	154,373
Barcelona	Canna	21,06	5,350	170,940
Basil	Aune	46,38	11,780	77,619
	Brasse	21,41	5,438	168,145
Batavia	Ell	27,00	6,857	133,333
Bayonne	Aune	34,80	8,838	103,448
Bengal	Cubit	18,00	4,571	200,000
Bergamo	Braccio	25,80	6,553	139,534
Bergen	Ell	24,71	6,276	145,690
Berlin	Ell	26,25	6,668	137,142
Berne	Ell	21,40	5,433	168,224
Betelfagui	Guz	25,00	6,349	144,000
Bologna	Woollen Braccio	25,00	6,349	144,000
	Silk Braccio	23,46	5,955	153,452
Bolsano	Ell	31,11	7,902	115,718
	Braccio	21,64	5,497	166,358
Bombay	Covid	18,00	4,571	200,000

		Length of a single Measure of each Sort.		Number of each equal to 100 English Yards.
		English Inches.	Fr. Decimetres.	
BOURDEAUX	Aune	46,93	11,959	76,709
BRABANT	Ell	27,58	7,006	130,529
BRAZIL	Vara	43,50	11,048	82,758
BREMEN	Ell	22,76	5,781	158,172
BRESCIA	Ell	18,40	4,673	195,652
BRESLAU	Ell	22,67	5,759	158,800
BRUNSWICK	Ell	22,46	5,704	160,284
CAIRO	Pic	26,80	6,806	134,329
CALEMBERG	Ell	22,90	5,816	157,205
CALICUT	Guz	28,40	7,210	126,760
CANDIA	Pic	25,11	6,377	143,369
CASSEL	Ell	22,11	5,617	162,822
CHINA	Covid	14,62	3,713	246,238
COBLENTZ	Ell	22,00	5,585	163,636
COBURG	Ell	23,07	5,857	156,046
COLOGNE	Long Ell	27,34	6,941	131,675
	Short Ell	22,62	5,745	159,151
CONSTANTINOPLE	Long Pic	27,90	7,083	129,032
	Short Pic	27,06	6,870	133,037
COPENHAGEN	Ell	24,71	6,276	145,690
CREMONA	Braccio	24,24	6,157	148,514
CYPRUS	Pic	26,45	6,715	136,105
DAMASCUS	Pic	22,93	5,822	156,999
DANTZIC	Ell	22,60	5,738	159,292
DRESDEN	Ell	22,28	5,658	161,579
DUNKIRK	Aune	26,62	6,762	135,236
ELBING	Ell	22,30	5,664	161,434
EMBDEN	Ell	26,40	6,704	136,363
ENGLAND	Yard	36,00	9,144	100,000
	Ell	45,00	11,429	80,000
ERFURT	Long Ell	23,38	5,940	153,977
	Short Ell	15,90	4,036	226,415
FERRARA	Woollen Braccio	26,33	6,690	136,726
	Silk Braccio	24,75	6,284	145,454
FLORENCE	Braccio	22,98	5,836	156,657
FRANCE	Aune	46,85	11,886	76,841
	Aune Usuelle	47,24	12,000	76,206
	Metre	39,37	10,000	91,440
FRANCFORT	Ell	21,24	5,392	169,491
GAMRON	Guz	38,70	9,826	93,023
GENEVA	Aune	45,00	11,429	80,000
GENOA	Braccio	22,69	5,764	158,660
	Canna Grossa	116,70	29,630	30,848

		Length of a single Measure of each Sort.		Number of each equal to 100 English Yards.
		English Inches.	Fr. Decimetres.	
GENOA	Canna Piccola	87,52	22,229	41,133
	Custom-House Canna	97,25	24,691	37,018
GUINEA	Jacktan	144,00	36,574	25,000
HAGUE	Ell	27,33	6,942	131,723
HAMBURG	Ell	22,58	5,733	159,433
HANOVER	Ell	22,90	5,816	157,205
HILDESHEIM	Ell	22,10	5,613	162,895
INSPRUCK	Ell	31,00	7,873	116,129
JAPAN	Inc	74,90	19,017	48,064
KIEL	Ell	22,64	5,752	159,010
KONIGSBERG	Ell	22,62	5,745	159,151
LEGHORN	Braccio	23,98	5,836	156,657
LEIPSIC	Ell	22,22	5,644	162,016
LEYDEN	Ell	26,89	6,830	133,878
LIBAU	Ell	24,04	6,104	149,750
LIEGE	Ell	21,71	5,515	165,822
LISBON	Vara	43,20	10,968	83,333
	Covado	26,70	6,781	134,831
	Palmo Avantejado	8,90	2,260	404,494
	Palmo de Craviera	8,64	2,193	416,666
LISLE	Aune	27,70	7,033	129,963
LUBEC	Ell	22,69	5,761	158,660
LUCCA	Woollen Braccio	23,80	6,042	151,260
	Silk Braccio	22,80	5,789	157,894
LUNEBURG	Ell	22,90	5,816	157,205
LYONS	Aune	46,20	11,741	77,922
MADRAS	Covid	18,00	4,571	200,000
MAESTRICHT	Ell	26,91	6,835	133,779
MAJORCA	Canna	67,50	17,138	53,333
MALACCA	Covid	18,13	4,603	198,565
MALTA	Canna	81,90	20,794	43,956
MANHEIM	Ell	21,99	5,558	163,710
MANTUA	Braccio	25,00	6,349	144,000
MARSEILLES	Aune	46,77	11,880	76,972
MEMEL	Ell	22,62	5,745	159,151
MENTZ	Ell	21,60	5,486	166,666
MILAN	Braccio	23,42	5,949	153,714
	Metro	39,37	10,000	91,440
MOCHA	Guz	25,00	6,349	144,000
	Covit	19,00	4,824	189,473
MODENA	Braccio	24,31	6,175	148,087
MONTPELLIER	Canne	78,24	19,874	46,012
MOROCCO	Cubit	21,00	5,332	171,428

		Length of a single Measure of each Sort.		Number of each equal to 100 English Yards.
		English Inches.	Fr. Decimetres.	
Munich	Ell	32,90	8,353	109,422
Munster	Ell	31,84	8,084	113,065
Namur	Ell	26,11	6,632	137,878
Nancy	Aune	25,18	6,397	142,970
Nantes	Aune	55,80	14,166	64,516
Naples	Canna	83,00	21,073	43,373
Narva	Ell	23,55	5,982	152,866
Netherlands	Ell	39,37	10,000	91,440
Neufchatel	Aune	43,80	11,125	82,191
Nice	Ell	46,77	11,875	76,972
Nimeguen	Ell	26,11	6,632	137,878
Nuremberg	Ell	25,96	6,596	138,675
Oldenburg	Ell	22,76	5,781	158,172
Oran	Pic	27,00	6,857	133,333
Osnaburg	Long Ell	23,70	6,017	151,898
	Short Ell	22,95	5,833	156,794
Oudenarde	Ell	26,28	6,677	136,986
Ostend	Ell	27,53	6,993	130,766
Oviedo	Vara	34,02	8,637	105,820
Padua	Woollen Braccio	26,80	6,812	134,328
	Silk Braccio	25,30	6,429	142,292
Parma	Cloth Braccio	25,10	6,377	143,426
	Silk Braccio	23,10	5,865	155,844
	Surveyors' Braccio	21,34	5,420	168,697
Patras	Linen Pic	27,00	6,857	133,333
	Silk Pic	25,00	6,349	144,000
Pernau	Ell	21,60	5,486	166,666
Persia	Royal Guerze	37,21	9,456	96,748
	Arish	38,27	9,716	94,068
Poland	Ell	24,30	6,169	148,148
Prague	Ell	23,32	5,923	154,373
Prince of Wales Island	Astah	18,00	4,571	200,000
Prussia	Ell	26,25	6,669	137,142
Ragusa	Ell	20,20	5,132	178,217
Ratisbon	Ell	31,90	8,110	112,852
Ravenna	Braccio	26,46	6,722	136,054
Reggio	Braccio	20,85	5,295	172,661
Reval	Ell	21,80	5,355	170,616
Rhodes	Pic	29,76	7,559	120,967
Riga	Ell	21,58	5,479	166,821
Rio de Janeiro	Vara	43,50	11,048	82,758
Rochelle	Aune	46,50	11,820	77,419

		Length of a single Measure of each Sort		Number of each equal to 100 English Yards.
		English Inches.	Fr. Decimetres.	
ROME	Canna Mercantile	78,34	19,900	45,953
	Builders' Canna	87,96	22,342	40,927
ROSTOCK	Ell	22,76	5,783	158,172
ROTTERDAM	Ell	27,20	6.902	132,352
ROUEN	Linen Aune	55,00	13,967	65,454
	Silk and Woollen Aune	45,80	11,639	78,602
RUSSIA	Arsheen	28,00	7,109	128,571
SALTZBURG	Linen Ell	39,59	10,056	90,932
	Silk Ell	31,56	8,017	114,068
ST. GALL	Linen Ell	31,56	8,017	114,068
	Cloth Ell	24,20	6,158	148,760
ST. MALOES	Aune	53,00	13,471	67,924
SARDINIA	Ell	21,62	5,488	166,512
SCHAFFHAUSEN	Ell	23,74	6,030	151,642
SCIOS	Long Pic	27,00	6,857	133,333
	Short Pic	25,98	6,600	138,568
SCOTLAND	Ell	37,20	9,445	96,774
SIAM	Voua	75,75	19,239	47,524
SICILY	Canna	76,25	19,360	47,213
SIENNA	Cloth Braccio	14,86	3,776	242,261
	Linen Braccio	23,63	6,002	152,348
SMYRNA	Pic	27,00	6,857	133,333
SPAIN	Vara	33,38	8,475	107,849
STETTIN	Ell	25,62	6,508	140,515
STRALSUND	Ell	22,90	5,820	157,205
STRASBURG	Aune	21,20	5,382	169,811
STUTGARD	Ell	24,08	6,116	149,501
SURAT	Guz	28,20	7,162	127,659
	Covid	18,50	4,698	194,594
SWEDEN	Ell	23,36	5,934	154,109
THORN	Ell	22,42	5,695	160,570
TOULOUSE	Canne	71,67	18,206	50,230
TOURNAY	Ell	24,40	6,195	147,540
TRENT	Cloth Ell	26,64	6,767	135,135
	Silk Ell	24,09	6,119	149,439
TREVES	Ell	21,97	5,581	163,859
TRIESTE	Woollen Ell	26,60	6,758	135,338
	Silk Ell	25,22	6,406	142,743
TRIPOLI, (Barbary)	Pic	21,80	5,536	165,137
TRIPOLI, (Syria)	Pic	26,99	6,857	133,382
TUNIS	Woollen Pic	26,50	6,730	135,849
	Silk Pic	24,83	6,298	144,985
	Linen Pic	18,62	4,727	193,340

		Length of a single Measure of each Sort.		Number of each equal to 100 English Yards.
		English Inches.	Fr. Decimetres.	
TURIN	Raso	23,30	5,915	154,506
VALENCIA	Vara	36,62	9,303	98,307
VALENCIENNES	Aune	25,93	6,587	138,831
VENICE	Woollen Braccio	26,61	6,761	135,287
	Silk Braccio	24,81	6,304	145,102
VERONA	Woollen Braccio	25,57	6,493	140,789
	Silk Braccio	25,22	6,406	142,743
VICENZA	Braccio	26,96	6,848	133,531
VIENNA	Silk Ell	30,66	7,790	117,416
	Ell of Upper Austria	31,50	8,000	114,285
ULM	Ell	22,38	5,682	160,857
WISMAR	Ell	22,90	5,816	157,205
WURTZBURG	Ell	22,80	5,789	157,894
YPRES	Ell	27,53	6,993	130,766
ZANTE	Cloth Braccio	27,18	6,903	132,450
	Silk Braccio	25,37	6,443	141,899
ZELL	Ell	22,90	5,816	157,205
ZITTAU	Ell	22,43	5,698	160,499
ZURICH	Ell	23,62	6,000	152,413

LONG MEASURE.

TABLE VI.

Containing a Comparison of the Foot, and other Measures of Length in different Countries. It shews the Length of a single Measure of each Denomination in English Inches and in French Decimetres; also the Number of Feet, &c. of each Place that correspond to 100 English Feet.

		Length of a single Measure of each Sort.		Number of each equal to 100 English Feet.
		Eng. Inches.	Fr. Decimetres.	
AIX LA CHAPELLE	Foot	11,41	2,896	105,171
AMSTERDAM	Foot	11,14	2,831	107,719
	Rhineland Foot	12,35	3,138	97,166
ANSPACH	Foot	11,72	2,978	102,389
ANTWERP	Foot	11,24	2,855	106,761
AUGSBURG	Foot	11,65	2,959	103,004
BASIL	Foot	11,75	2,983	102,127
BERGAMO	Foot	17,17	4,360	69,889
BERLIN	Foot	12,19	3,097	98,441
BERNE	Foot	11,54	2,932	103,986
BOLOGNA	Foot	14,99	3,805	80,053
BOURDEAUX	Foot	14,04	3,567	85,470
BREMEN	Foot	11,38	2,891	105,448
BRESLAU	Foot	11,19	2,842	107,238
BRUNSWICK	Foot	11,23	2,851	106,856
CAGLIARI	Palmo	7,97	2,025	150,564
CALEMBERG	Foot	11,53	2,926	104,076
CARRARA	Palmo	9,59	2,436	125,130
CHINA	Mathematical Foot	13,12	3,331	91,463
	Builders' Foot	12,71	3,228	94,414
	Tradesmen's Foot	13,33	3,383	90,022
	Land-Surveyors' Foot	12,58	3,196	95,389
CLEVES	Foot	11,63	2,955	103,181
COLOGNE	Foot	10,83	2,750	110,803
COPENHAGEN	Rhineland Foot	12,35	3,138	97,166
CRACOW	Foot	14,03	3,564	85,531
CREMONA	Foot	15,62	3,970	76,824
DANTZIC	Foot	11,30	2,869	106,194
DORDRECHT	Foot	14,17	3,600	84,686
DRESDEN	Foot	11,14	2,831	107,719

		Length of a single Measure of each Sort.		Number of each equal to 100 English Feet.
		Eng. Inches.	Fr. Decimetres.	
EMBDEN	Foot	11,66	2,961	102,915
ENGLAND	Foot	12,00	3,048	100,000
ERFURT	Foot	11,11	2,822	108,010
FERRARA	Foot	15,80	4,011	75,949
FRANCE	Pied de Roi	12,78	3,248	93,896
	Metre	39,37	10,000	30,480
FRANCFORT	Foot	11,28	2,865	106,382
GENEVA	Foot	19,21	4,879	62,467
GENOA	Palmo	9,72	2,470	123,450
GOTTINGEN	Foot	11,45	2,908	104,803
GOTHA	Foot	11,32	2,874	106,007
GRONINGEN	Foot	11,49	2,917	104,438
HAERLEM	Foot	11,25	2,858	106,666
HAMBURG	Foot	11,28	2,865	106,382
HANOVER	Foot	11,45	2,908	104,803
HEIDELBERG	Foot	10,96	2,785	109,489
HILDESHEIM	Foot	11,05	2,806	108,597
INSPRUCK	Foot	12,50	3,176	96,000
KONIGSBERG	Foot	12,11	3,076	99,091
LEIPSIC	Foot	11,11	2,822	108,010
	Builders' Foot	11,13	2,826	107,816
LEYDEN	Foot	12,34	3,135	97,244
LIEGE	Foot	11,32	2,874	106,007
LINDAU	Common Foot	11,40	2,894	105,263
	Long Foot	12,40	3,148	96,774
LISBON	Foot	12,94	3,285	92,735
LORRAINE	Foot	11,30	2,869	106,194
LUBEC	Foot	11,34	2,880	105,820
LUNEBURG	Foot	11,45	2,908	104,803
LYONS	Foot	13,48	3,425	89,020
MAESTRICHT	Foot	11,05	2,806	108,597
MAGDEBURG	Foot	11,16	2,836	107,526
MALTA	Foot	11,16	2,836	107,526
MANHEIM	Foot	11,41	2,896	105,170
MARSEILLES	Canne	79,23	20,126	15,145
MECKLENBURG	Foot	11,45	2,908	104,803
MIDDLEBURG	Foot	11,81	3,000	101,608
MILAN	Builders' Foot	15,62	3,965	76,824
MOSCOW	Foot	13,17	3,343	91,116
MUNICH	Foot	11,37	2,891	105,540
NAPLES	Palmo	10,38	2,637	115,606
NEUFCHATEL	Foot	11,81	3,000	101,608
NICE	Pan	10,29	2,615	116,618

		Length of a single Measure of each Sort.		Number of each equal to 100 English Feet.
		Eng. Inches.	Fr. Decimetres.	
NUREMBERG	Foot	11,96	3,036	100,334
OLDENBURG	Foot	11,65	2,959	103,004
OSNABURG	Foot	11,00	2,792	109,090
PADUA	Foot	13,93	3,536	86,145
PAVIA	Foot	18,30	4,646	65,573
PISA	Palmo	11,74	2,984	102,214
PRAGUE	Foot	11,82	3,002	101,522
PRUSSIA	Rhineland Foot	12,35	3,138	97,166
RATISBON	Foot	11,42	2,899	105,078
REVAL	Foot	10,53	2,677	113,960
RHINELAND	Foot	12,35	3,138	97,166
RIGA	Foot	10,79	2,739	111,214
ROME	Foot	11,72	2,978	102,389
ROSTOCK	Foot	11,38	2,891	105,448
RUSSIA	Foot	13,75	3,491	87,272
SARDINIA	Palmo	9,78	2,483	122,699
SICILY	Palmo	9,53	2,420	125,918
SIENNA	Foot	14,86	3,774	80,753
SPAIN	Foot	11,12	2,826	107,913
STETTIN	Foot	11,12	2,826	107,913
	Rhineland Foot	12,35	3,138	97,166
STRALSUND	Foot	11,45	2,908	104,803
STRASBURG	Foot	11,39	2,894	105,355
	Land Foot	11,62	2,952	103,270
SWEDEN	Foot	11,68	2,968	102,739
TURIN	Foot	12,72	3,230	94,339
VALENCIA	Palmo	9,15	2,325	131,147
VENICE	Foot	13,68	3,473	87,719
VERONA	Foot	13,40	6,403	89,552
VICENZA	Foot	13,63	3,461	88,041
VIENNA	Foot	12,45	3,161	96,385
ULM	Foot	11,39	2,892	105,355
WIRTEMBERG	Foot	11,26	2,860	106,571
WISMAR	Foot	11,45	2,908	104,803
ZANTE	*(See Venice)*			
ZELL	Foot	11,45	2,908	104,803
ZURICH	Foot	11,81	3,000	101,608

SQUARE MEASURE.

TABLE VII.

Shewing the Contents of the Square Foot of different Countries in English Square Inches and in French Square Decimetres.

		Eng. Square Inches.	Fr. Sq. Decimetres.
A Square Foot of Amsterdam contains		124,255	8,0160
Antwerp		126,337	8,1503
Augsburg		135,722	8,7558
Basil		138,062	8,9067
Berlin		148,693	9,5926
Berne		133,287	8,5987
Bologna		224,700	14,4960
Bremen		129,504	8,3546
Breslau		125,216	8,0780
Cologne		117,288	7,5666
Dantzic		127,690	8,2376
Dresden		124,099	8,0059
England		144,000	9,2898
France	Pied de Roi	163,558	10,5516
	Square Metre	1550,075	100,0000
Geneva		369,024	23,8068
Hamburg		127,441	8,2216
Hanover		131,194	8,4637
Konigsberg		146,652	9,4609
Leipsic		123,432	7,9629
Liege		128,142	8,2668
Lisbon		167,547	10,8089
Lubec		128,731	8,3048
Milan		243,984	15,7401
Munich		129,390	8,3473
Nuremberg		143,041	9,2279
Osnaburg		121,000	7,8060
Ratisbon		130,416	8,4135
Reval		110,881	7,1532
Rhineland		152,670	9,8492
Riga		116,424	7,5108
Rome		137,358	8,8614
Spain		123,832	7,9887
Sweden		136,515	8,8069
Turin		161,798	10,4380
Venice		187,142	12,0731
Vienna		155,002	9,9996
Zurich		139,476	8,9980

CUBIC MEASURE.

TABLE VIII.

Shewing the Contents of the Cubic Foot of different Countries in English Cubic Inches and in French Litres, or Cubic Decimetres.

	Eng. Cubic Inches.	Fr. Litres.
A Cubic Foot of AMSTERDAM contains	1385,070	22,695
ANTWERP	1420,027	23,268
AUGSBURG	1581,161	25,908
BASIL	1622,228	26,581
BERLIN	1813,162	29,710
BERNE	1538,798	25,214
BOLOGNA	3368,253	55,191
BREMEN	1473,755	24,141
BRESLAU	1401,167	22,959
COLOGNE	1270,229	20,813
DANTZIC	1442,897	23,643
DRESDEN	1382,463	22,653
ENGLAND	1728,000	28,312
FRANCE	2091,743	34,275
Cubic Decimetre	61,028	1,000
GENEVA	7088,951	116,158
HAMBURG	1438,684	23,574
HANOVER	1502,696	24,623
KONIGSBERG	1775,955	29,100
LEIPSIC	1371,329	22,470
LIEGE	1450,577	23,769
LISBON	2168,728	35,536
LUBEC	1460,582	23,933
MILAN	3811,030	62,447
MUNICH	1471,811	24,117
NUREMBERG	1710,770	28,032
OSNABURG	1331,000	21,809
RATISBON	1489,350	24,404
REVAL	1167,577	19,131
RHINELAND	1886,390	30,911
RIGA	1256,215	20,584
ROME	1609,835	26,378
SPAIN	1378,002	22,579
SWEDEN	1595,041	26,136
TURIN	2058,070	33,723
VENICE	2560,102	41,949
VIENNA	1929,774	31,621
ZURICH	1647,211	26,991

LAND MEASURE.

TABLE IX.

Containing a Comparison of the Land Measures of different Countries; namely, the Area of each Measure in English Square Yards and in French Ares; also the Number of Acres, &c. of each Place that correspond to 10 *English Acres.*

Place	Measure	Contents of a single Measure of each Sort.		Number of each equal to 10 English Acres
		Eng. Sq. Yards.	French Ares.	
AMSTERDAM	Morgen	9722	81,286	4,978
BASIL	Juchart	3816	31,905	12,683
BERLIN	Great Morgen	6786	56,736	7,132
	Little Morgen	3054	25,534	15,848
BERNE	Wood Juchart	4632	38,727	10,449
CANARY ISLES	Fanegada	2422	20,236	19,983
DANTZIC	Morgen	6650	55,642	7,278
ENGLAND	Acre	4840	40,466	10,000
FRANCE	Hectare	11960	100,000	4,046
GENEVA	Arpent	6179	51,661	7,833
HAMBURG	Scheffel of Corn Land	5022	41,984	9,637
	Morgen	11545	96,525	4,192
HANOVER	Morgen	3100	25,918	15,613
IONIAN ISLANDS	Moggio	11616	97,119	4,166
IRELAND	Acre	7840	65,549	6,173
NAPLES	Moggia	3998	33,426	12,106
NETHERLANDS	Vierkantebunder	119,6	1,000	406,722
NUREMBERG	Corn Land Morgen	5654	47,272	8,560
	Meadow Morgen	2544	21,270	19,025
PORTUGAL	Geira	6970	58,275	6,944
PRUSSIA	Morgen	3053	25,526	15,853
RHINELAND	Morgen	10185	85,158	4,752
ROME	Pezza	3158	26,406	15,196
RUSSIA	Dessetina	13066,6	109,248	3,704
SAXONY	Acre	6590	55,098	7,344
SCOTLAND	Acre	6150	51,419	7,869
SPAIN	Fanegada	5500	45,984	8,800
	Arranzada	4623	38,652	10,469
SWEDEN	Tunneland	5900	49,329	8,203
SWITZERLAND	Faux	7855	65,674	6,161
TUSCANY	Quadrato	4074	34,062	11,880
VIENNA	Joch	6889	57,598	7,025
ZURICH	Common Acre	3875,6	32,404	12,488
	Wood Acre	4306	36,004	11,240
	Meadow Acre	3445	28,804	14,049

ROAD MEASURE.

TABLE X.

Being a Comparison of the Miles, Leagues, and other Itinerary Measures of different Countries; namely, the Length of each Mile, &c. in English Yards and in French Kilometres; also, the Number of each answering to 100 English Miles.

Country	Measure	Length of a single Measure of each Sort. English Yards.	Fr. Kilometres.	Number of each equal to 100 English Miles.
ARABIA	Mile	2148	1,964	81,936
BRABANT	League	6076	5,556	28,966
CHINA	Li	632	0,577	278,481
DANTZIC	Mile	8475	7,749	20,767
DENMARK	Mile	8244	7,538	21,348
ENGLAND	Mile	1760	1,609	100,000
	Mile, Geographical	2025	1,851	86,913
FLANDERS	League	6864	6,276	25,641
FRANCE	Kilometre	1093	1,000	161,024
	League of 2000 Toises	4263	3,898	41,285
	League of 25 to the Degree	4860	4,444	36,214
	League, Marine	6076	5,555	28,966
GERMANY	Mile, Geographical	8101	7,407	21,725
	Mile, Long	10126	9,258	17,381
	Mile, Short	6859	6,271	25,659
HAMBURG	Mile	8244	7,538	21,348
HANOVER	Mile	11559	10,569	15,226
HOLLAND	Mile	8101	7,407	21,725
HUNGARY	Mile	9113	8,332	19,313
IRELAND	Mile	2240	2,048	78,571
NETHERLANDS	Mile, Metrical	1093	1,000	161,024
PERSIA	Parasang	6086	5,565	28,918
POLAND	Mile, Long	8101	7,407	21,725
	Mile, Short	6076	5,555	28,966
PORTUGAL	League	6760	6,181	26,035
PRUSSIA	Mile	8237	7,532	21,367
ROME	Mile	1628	1,489	108,108
	Mile, Metrical	1093	1,000	161,024
	Mile, Geographical	2025	1,851	86,913
RUSSIA	Werst	1167	1,066	150,814
SCOTLAND	Mile	1984	1,814	88,709
SPAIN	League, Common	7416	6,781	23,732
	League, Judicial	4635	4,238	37,972
SWEDEN	Mile	11700	10,698	15,042
SWITZERLAND	Mile	9153	8,369	19,228
TUSCANY	Mile	1808	1,653	97,345
TURKEY	Berri	1826	1,669	96,385

COMPARISON OF FRENCH AND ENGLISH METROLOGY.

TABLE XI.

Containing the New Weights and Measures of France, with their Proportion to those of England, both according to the Decimal System, and the Systeme Usuel.

DECIMAL SYSTEM.

LONG MEASURES.

French.	English.
Millimetre	0,03937 Inches.
Centimetre	0,39371 Inches.
Decimetre	3,93710 Inches.
Metre	39,37100 Inches.
Decametre	32,80916 Feet.
Hectometre	328,09167 Feet.
Kilometre	1093,6389 Yards.
Myriametre	10936,38900 Yards, or 6 Miles 1 Furlong 28 Poles.

SUPERFICIAL MEASURES.

French.	English.
Centiare	1,1960 Square Yard
Are (a Square Decametre)	119,6046 Square Yards
Decare	1196,0460 Square Yards
Hectare	11960,4604 Square Yards or 2 Acres, 1 Rood, 35 Perches.

MEASURES OF CAPACITY.

French.	English.
Millitre	0,06103 Cubic Inches.
Centilitre	0,61028 Cubic Inches.
Decilitre	6,10280 Cubic Inches.
Litre (a Cubic Decimetre)	61,02802 Cubic Inches, or 2,1135 Wine Pints.
Decalitre	610,28028 Cubic Inches, or 2,642 Wine Gallons.
Hectolitre	3,5317 Cubic Feet, or 2,838 Winchester Bushels.
Kilolitre	35,3171 Cubic Feet, or 1 Tun & 12 Wine Gal.
Myrialitre	353,17146 Cubic Feet.

SOLID MEASURES.

French.	English.
Decistere	3,5317 Cubic Feet.
Stere (a Cubic Metre)	35,3171 Cubic Feet.
Decastere	353,1714 Cubic Feet.

WEIGHTS.

French.	English.
Milligramme	0,0153 Grains.
Centigramme	0,1543 Grains.
Decigramme	1,5434 Grains.
Gramme	15,4340 Grains.
Decagramme	154,3402 Grains, or 5,64 Drams Avoirdupois.
Hectogramme	3,2154 oz. Troy, or 3,527 oz. Avoirdupois.
Kilogramme	2 lb. 8 oz. 3 dwt. 2 gr. Troy, or 2 lb. 3 oz. 4,428 Drams Avoirdupois.
Myriagramme	26,795 Pounds Troy, or 22,0485 Pounds Avoirdupois.
Quintal	1 cwt. 3 qrs. 25 lb. nearly.
Millier, or Bar	9 tons 16 cwt. 3 qrs. 12 lb.

SYSTEME USUEL.

LONG MEASURES.

Usuel.		Metrical.		English.
Ligne	=	2,31 Millimetres	=	0,091 Inches.
Pouce	=	2,77 Centimetres	=	1,090 Inches.
Pied	=	3,33 Decimetres	=	13,110 Inches.
Aune	=	12 Decimetres	=	3 Feet 11,24 Inches.
Toise	=	2 Metres	=	6 Feet 6,74 Inches.

MEASURE OF CAPACITY.

Boisseau	=	12,5 Litres	=	2,837 Gallons.

WEIGHTS.

Grain	=	5,425 Centigrammes	=	0,837 Grains.
Gros	=	3,906 Grammes	=	60,285 Grains.
Once	=	31,25 Grammes	=	482,312 Grains, or 1 oz. 1,628 Dram Avoirdupois.
Livre	=	500 Grammes	=	1 lb. 4 oz. 1 dwt. 13 gr. Troy, or 1 lb. 1 oz. 10$\frac{1}{5}$ dr. Avoirdupois.

For the Proportions between the subordinate Weights and Measures of England and the Metrology of France, see Vol. i. p. 225.

For the New Astronomical and Geographical Measures of France, see Vol. i. p. 138.

For the Ancient Weights and Measures of France, see Vol. i. p. 133.

EXAMPLES OF THE USE OF THE FOREGOING TABLES.

THE proportion between the Weights and Measures of any two Places in the foregoing Tables may be found by the Rule of Three, or in the following manner by the Chain Rule:

EXAMPLE I.—How many Marks, gold and silver weight of Berlin, are equal to 1120 Marks of Amsterdam or Holland? *See Table I.*

		1120 Marks of Amsterdam.
1 Mark of Amsterdam	=	3798 English Grains.
3608 English Grains	=	1 Mark of Berlin.

Result, 1178,9 Marks of Berlin.

Or, as 3608 : 1 : : 3798 × 1120 : 1178,9

EXAMPLE II.—How many Pounds, commercial weight of Amsterdam, are equal to 276 Pounds of Leghorn? *See Table II.*

		276 Pounds of Leghorn.
1 Pound of Leghorn	=	5240 English Grains.
7625 English Grains	=	1 Pound of Amsterdam.

Result, 189,67 Pounds of Amsterdam.

EXAMPLE III.—How many Spanish Fanegas are equal to 523 Scheffels of Dantzic? *See Table III.*

		523 Scheffels of Dantzic.
1 Scheffel of Dantzic	=	3337 English Cubic Inches.
3439 English Cubic Inches	=	1 Fanega of Spain.

Result, 507,48 Fanegas of Spain.

EXAMPLE IV.—How many Barriques of Bourdeaux are equal to 50 Eimers of Leipsic? *See Table IV.*

		50 Eimers of Leipsic.
1 Eimer of Leipsic	=	4644 English Cubic Inches.
14033 English Cubic Inches	=	1 Barrique of Bourdeaux.

Result, 16,546 Barriques of Bourdeaux.

EXAMPLE V.—How many Varas of Spain are equal to 359½ Ells of Hamburg? *See Table V.*

		359½	Ells of Hamburg.
1 Ell of Hamburg	=	22,58	English Inches.
33,38 English Inches	=	1	Vara of Spain.

Result, 243,18 Varas of Spain.

EXAMPLE VI.—How many Feet of Turin are equal to 160 Rhineland Feet? *See Table VI.*

		160	Rhineland Feet.
1 Rhineland Foot	=	12,35	English Inches.
12,72 English Inches	=	1	Foot of Turin.

Result, 155,34 Feet of Turin.

EXAMPLE VII.—How many Square Feet of Rome are equal to 90 of Lisbon? *See Table VII.*

		90	Square Feet of Lisbon.
1 Square Foot of Lisbon	=	167,547	English Square Inches.
137,358 English Square Inches	=	1	Square Foot of Rome.

Result, 121,97 Square Feet of Rome.

EXAMPLE VIII.—How many Cubic Feet of Cologne are equal to 45 Cubic Feet of Sweden? *See Table VIII.*

		45	Cubic Feet of Sweden.
1 Cubic Foot of Sweden	=	1595,041	English Cubic Inches.
1270,229 English Cubic Inches	=	1	Cubic Foot of Cologne.

Result, 56,507 Cubic Feet of Cologne.

EXAMPLE IX.—How many Geiras of Portugal are equal to 84 Dessetinas of Russia? *See Table IX.*

		84	Dessetinas of Russia.
1 Dessetina of Russia	=	13066,6	English Square Yards.
6970 English Square Yards	=	1	Geira of Portugal.

Result, 157,47 Geiras of Portugal.

EXAMPLE X.—How many Miles of Denmark are equal to 33 Miles of Switzerland? *See Table X.*

		33	Miles of Switzerland.
1 Swiss Mile	=	9153	English Yards.
8244 English Yards	=	1	Danish Mile.

Result, 36,638 Miles of Denmark.

ANCIENT WEIGHTS AND MEASURES.

TABLE XII.

Ancient Weights and Measures explained, and compared with English; from the most approved Authorities.

ANCIENT GREEK LONG MEASURES.

Two sorts of Long Measure were used in Greece; namely, the *Olympic* and the *Pythic*.

The Olympic measure was used in Peloponnesus, Attica, Sicily, and the Greek cities in Italy.

The Pythic measure was used in Thessaly, Illyria, Phocis, and Thrace, and at Marseilles in Gaul.

The divisions were the same in both, and were as follow: 4 Dactyli = 1 Palesta; 4 Palestæ = 1 Foot; 1½ Foot = 1 Cubit.

10 Feet = 1 Decapodon; 600 Feet, or 400 Cubits = 1 Stadium.

The length of the foot is stated as follows:

Olympic foot, properly called Greek, according to	*Hutton*	12,108 English Inches.
	Folkes	12,072
	Cavallo	12,084
Pythic foot, also called natural foot, according to	*Hutton*..........	9,768
	Paucton	9,731

Hence, the Olympic Stadium was 201½ English yards nearly; and the Pythic or Delphic Stadium, 162½ yards nearly, and the other measures in proportion.

The Phyleterian foot is the Pythic cubit or 1½ Pythic foot.

The Macedonian foot was 13,92 English inches; and the Sicilian foot of Archimedes 8,76 English inches.

ANCIENT GREEK SUPERFICIAL MEASURES.

Olympic Land Measure.

36 Olympic square feet = 1 Hexapodon; 64 Hexapoda = 1 Hemihectos; 2 Hemihecti = 1 Hectos or Modius; 6 Modii = 1 Medimnus or Jugerum.

Hence, the Olympic Jugerum is computed to equal 2 Roods 23 Perches, English.

Pythic Land Measure.

$1666\frac{2}{3}$ Square Cubits = 1 Hemihectos ; 2 Hemihecti = 1 Modius ; 6 Modii = 1 Medimnus, or Jugerum. Hence, the Pythic Jugerum = 2 Roods 29 Perches, English.

ANCIENT GREEK LIQUID MEASURES.

$1\frac{1}{2}$ Cyathus = 1 Oxybathon; 6 Cyathi = 1 Cotylus ; 2 Cotyli = 1 Xestes ; 6 Xestes = 1 Chous; 6 Choi = 1 Amphoreus; 2 Amphorei = 1 Keramion or Metretes.

The Keramion is stated by *Paucton* to have been equal to 35 French Pints, which equal $8\frac{2}{3}$ English Gallons; and the inferior measures in proportion.

ANCIENT GREEK CORN MEASURES.

2 Xestes = 1 Chœnix ; 4 Chœnices = 1 Hemihectos; $1\frac{1}{2}$ Hemihectos = 1 Tetarlon ; 2 Hemihecti = 1 Modius ; 6 Modii = 1 Medimnus or Achana.

The Medimnus is stated by *Paucton* to equal $3\frac{1}{2}$ French Boisseaux = $1\frac{1}{4}$ English Bushel, and the inferior measures in proportion.

ANCIENT GREEK WEIGHTS.

6 Chalcoi = 1 Obolus ; 6 Oboli = 1 Drachm ; 2 Drachms = 1 Didrachm.

20 Drachms = 1 Gold Statera, or Aureus; 100 Drachms = 1 Attic Mina.

60 Attic Mine = 1 Attic or Euboic Talent ; 10 Attic Talents = 1 Gold Talent.

There was also a smaller Mina containing 75 Drachms.

Authors vary much in their statements of the Greek weights.

Thus, according to *Arbuthnot*, the Attic Drachm .... = 54,6 English Grains.
the Attic Mina .... = 5464
the Attic Medicinal Mina.. = 6994

According to *Christiani*, the Attic Drachm .... = 51,9
the Attic Mina .... = 5189
the Smaller Attic Mina.... = 3892

According to *Paucton*, the Attic Drachm .... = 69
the Attic Mina .... = 6900

Arbuthnot mentions also a very ancient Greek Drachm, which answered to 146,5 English Grains.

ANCIENT ROMAN LONG MEASURES.

6 Scrupula = 1 Sicilicum; 8 Scrupula = 1 Duellum; $1\frac{1}{2}$ Duellum = 1 Semiuncia.

18 Scrupula = 1 Digitus; $1\frac{1}{3}$ Digitus, or 24 Scrupula = 1 Uncia, or Inch.

3 Unciæ = 1 Palma; 12 Unciæ = 1 Pes, or Foot; $1\frac{1}{2}$ Foot = 1 Cubit.

The fractions of the Foot were denominated as follows:

2 Unciæ = 1 Sextans; 3 Unciæ = 1 Quadrans, or Terruncium; 4 Unciæ = 1 Triens; 5 Unciæ = 1 Quincunx; 6 Unciæ = 1 Sexunx or Semis; 7 Unciæ = 1 Septunx; 8 Unciæ = 1 Bes, or Bessis; 9 Unciæ = 1 Dodrans; 10 Unciæ = 1 Dextans; 11 Unciæ = 1 Deunx.

ANCIENT ROMAN ITINERARY MEASURES.

$2\frac{1}{2}$ Pedes or Feet = 1 Gradus; 2 Gradus = 1 Passus; 2 Passus = 1 Decempeda. 1000 Passus = 1 Mile. The length of the Roman Foot is stated as follows, by different authors.

By *Bernard*........................	11,640	English Inches.
By *Picard* and *Hutton*	11,604	
By *Folkes*..........................	11,592	
By *Raper*, (before Titus)	11,640	
By *Raper*, (after Titus)................	11,580	
By *Shuckburgh*, taken from rules........	11,6064	
By the same, from buildings............	11,6172	
By the same, from a tombstone	11,6352	

Hence, 11,6 English Inches seem to be a medium; and, therefore, the Roman Mile = 1611 English Yards, being 149 Yards less than the English Mile.

ANCIENT ROMAN LAND MEASURES.

100 Square Roman Feet = 1 Scrupulum of land; 4 Scrupula = 1 Sextulus.

$1\frac{1}{5}$ Sextulus = 1 Actus; 6 Sextuli, or 5 Actus = 1 Uncia of land; 6 Unciæ = 1 Square Actus.

2 Square Actus = 1 Jugerum; 2 Jugera = 1 Heredium; 100 Heredia = 1 Centuria.

The Actus was a slip of ground 4 Roman Feet broad and 120 long. The Jugerum was also divided into 12 Unciæ, and its fractions were denominated *Sextans, Quadrans,* &c. as the fractions of the Roman Foot.

Taking the Roman Foot as above, at 11,6 English Inches, the Roman Jugerum was 5980 English Square Yards, or 1 Acre $37\frac{1}{2}$ Perches.

ANCIENT ROMAN CORN MEASURES.

4 Ligulæ = 1 Cyathus ; $1\frac{1}{2}$ Cyathus = 1 Acetabulum ; 4 Acetabula = 1 Hemina, or Trulla.

2 Heminæ = 1 Sextarius ; $1\frac{1}{2}$ Sextarius = 1 Chænix ; 16 Sextarii = 1 Modius.

Paucton states the Sextarius to have been 0,6453 of a French Pint, which is equal to 36,94 English Cubic Inches; hence the Modius was 591 Cubic Inches, or $\frac{8}{29}$ of an English Bushel.

ANCIENT ROMAN LIQUID MEASURES.

In liquid measures, the Sextarius and its divisions were used as above, and the larger measures were as follow:

6 Sextarii = 1 Congius ; 4 Congii = 1 Urna ; 2 Urnæ = 1 Amphora ; 20 Amphoræ = 1 Dolium.

The Sextarius being, as above, 36,94 English Cubic Inches, the Amphora = $7\frac{2}{3}$ English Gallons, and the Dolium = $153\frac{1}{3}$ English Gallons.

ANCIENT ROMAN WEIGHTS.

3 Siliquæ = 1 Simplium ; 6 Siliquæ = 1 Scrupulum ; 3 Scrupula = 1 Denarius of Nero.

$3\frac{3}{7}$ Scrupula = 1 Denarius of Papyrius ; 4 Scrupula = 1 Sextulus ; $1\frac{1}{2}$ Sextulus = 1 Sicilicum.

2 Sextuli = 1 Duellum ; 6 Sextuli, 7 Denarii of Papyrius, or 8 Denarii of Nero = 1 Uncia, or Ounce.

12 Unciæ = 1 Libra or Pound ; 100 Libræ = 1 Centumpondium.

The fractions of the Libra were also distinguished by the names of *Sextans, Quadrans, &c.* as the fractions of the Foot, see p. 257.

The Weight of the Roman Denarius, Ounce, and Pound, are stated as follows, by different authors.

By *Arbuthnot,*	the Denarius, (7th part of the Ounce)........	62,4	English Grains.
	the Ounce	437,2	
	the Pound	5246,4	
By *Christiani,*	the Denarius, (8th part of the Ounce)........	51,9	
	the Ounce	415,1	
	the Pound	4981,2	
By *Paucton,*	the Denarius of Papyrius	61,6	
	the Denarius of Nero	53,9	
	the Ounce	431,2	
	the Pound	5174,4	

ANCIENT JEWISH, OR SCRIPTURE LONG MEASURES.

4 Digits = 1 Palm; 3 Palms = 1 Span; 2 Spans = 1 Cubit; 4 Cubits = 1 Fathom; 2 Fathoms = 1 Arabian Pole; 10 Poles = 1 Shœnus, or measuring line.

The Shœnus = 145 Feet 11 Inches English, and the rest in proportion. Thus the Scripture Cubit was 22 inches nearly.

ANCIENT JEWISH ITINERARY MEASURES.

400 Cubits = 1 Stadium; 5 Stadia = 1 Sabbath-Day's Journey; 10 Stadia = 1 Eastern Mile; 3 Eastern Miles = 1 Parasang; 8 Parasangs = 1 Day's Journey.

1 Day's Journey = $33\frac{1}{6}$ English Miles, and the Sabbath Day's Journey = $\frac{2}{3}$ of an English Mile nearly.

ANCIENT JEWISH DRY MEASURES.

20 Grachal = 1 Cab; $1\frac{4}{5}$ Cab = 1 Gomor; $3\frac{1}{3}$ Gomor = 1 Seah; 3 Seahs = 1 Ephah; 5 Ephahs = 1 Leteeh; 2 Leteeh = 1 Comer.

The Comer = 2 Bushels 1 Pint English, and the subordinate measures in proportion.

ANCIENT JEWISH LIQUID MEASURES.

$1\frac{1}{3}$ Caph = 1 Log; 4 Logs = 1 Cab; 3 Cabs = 1 Hin; 2 Hins = 1 Seah; 3 Seahs = 1 Bath, or Ephah; 10 Ephahs = 1 Chomer, Homer, or Corus.

The Chomer = 75 Gallons 5 Pints English, and the other measures in proportion.

ANCIENT JEWISH WEIGHTS.

60 Shekels = 1 Maneh; 50 Maneh = 1 Talent.

The Talent = 113 lb. 10 oz. 1 dwt. 10 gr. Troy, and the other weights in proportion.

For a more full and particular account of Scripture Weights and Measures, see the *Prologomena to Hewlett's Bible,* from which the above Statement is chiefly extracted.

ANCIENT EGYPTIAN WEIGHTS.

The Talent was the principal weight, as well as money among many of the Eastern nations; but it was not uniform. In Egypt it was divided into 60 Minæ, and each Mina into 100 Drachms, and = 86lb. 8 oz. 16 dwt. English Troy Weight.

The Mina, sometimes called the Pound, was divided into 16 ounces; but there was another pound, called the Litra, or Ratel, which was divided into 12 ounces. This weight was used throughout Arabia and Asia Minor, and answered to 6886 Troy Grains. The ounce was divided into a certain number of Dirhems, each of 12 Carats, and each Carat contained 4 grains. *Bishop Cumberland* deduces the English Avoirdupois Pound from the Mina of Egypt, and the Troy Pound from the Ratel; but authors differ much on this subject.

ANCIENT EGYPTIAN LONG MEASURES.

2 Fingers = 1 Condyle; 2 Condyles = 1 Palm; 4 Palms = 1 Geometrical Foot; 5 Palms = 1 Cubit.

This Cubit was the distance from the elbow to the joint of the wrist, and answered to 13 English Inches nearly. In other countries the cubit was reckoned from the elbow to the end of the middle finger, and was about one-half more than that of Egypt.

The Egyptian cubit was the standard to which many of the ancient nations referred their measures, and, according to *Paucton,* was that mentioned by *Herodotus, Pliny,* and other ancient authors in their scientific computations. He also supposes this to be the cubit mentioned in the Book of Judges, ch. iii. v. 16.

For a more comprehensive and minute account of Ancient Weights and Measures, see *Arbuthnot's Tables; Paucton's Metrologie;* and *Gibbon's Miscellaneous Works.*

A

GENERAL INDEX

AND

COMMERCIAL DICTIONARY,

CONTAINING

General References, and also Definitions of Commercial Terms, including Monies, Coins, Weights, and Measures; which are either explained by immediate definitions, or by references.

N.B. The Roman numerals refer to the volumes; the figures to the pages.

A

AAM, a liquid measure of Amsterdam, Antwerp, &c.; i. 10, 21.

ABANDONMENT, the act of relinquishing or giving up goods to creditors or underwriters, either in lieu of a debt, or to avoid the payment of charges.

ABAS, a Persian weight for pearls; i. 278.

ABASSI, or ABASSEE, a Persian coin; i. 151, 277.

ABATEMENT, a deduction from a debt or contract.

ABUQUELP, the same as *Griscio*, an Egyptian coin; i. 4.

ACCEPTANCE of a BILL; ii. 3.

ACCOMMODATION, a term applied to the acceptance of a bill, when the drawee only lends his name; and the drawer engages to furnish him with the means of payment before the bill becomes due.

ACCOUNT CURRENT, the personal account of a merchant or trader with each of his correspondents or customers, a copy of which account is transmitted to the person whose name it bears, showing how affairs stand between the parties at the current or present time when made out.

ACCOUNT SALES, an account showing the net proceeds of the sale of any cargo or consignment of goods.

ACETABULUM, an ancient Roman corn measure; ii. 258.

ACHANA, an ancient Greek corn measure; ii. 256.

ACHTEL, or ACHTELING, a measure of capacity in Germany; i. 148, 350, 369.

ACHTERLIS, a measure of capacity in Berne; i. 39.

ACINO, a weight for gold and silver in Naples and Sicily; i. 263, 313.

ACQUITTANCE, a discharge, in writing, for a sum of money, acknowledging it to have been paid.

ACRE, a land measure in England, and some parts of the Continent; i. 195, 224, 226, 309; ii. 249.

ACT OF HONOUR, an instrument drawn by a notary when a bill is accepted for the honour of another person; ii. 6.

ACTION, the name for shares in some foreign banks; i. 145.

ACTUS, an ancient Roman land measure; ii. 257.

ADARME, a weight in Spain; i. 6, 56, 266, 321, 342.

ADJUSTMENT, the settling of the averages or losses on policies of insurance; see *Average*.

ADMINISTRATOR, a person who is allowed to administer in the ecclesiastical court, by which he takes charge of the personal effects of one who dies intestate.

ADOWLY, a weight in Bombay; i. 96.

ADVICE, the information given *by letter* of any commercial transaction.

ADULTERATION, the act of debasing by an improper mixture.

ADY, a long measure in the Jaghire territory; i. 93.

AEMGEN, a liquid measure in Prussia; i. 35.

AFFIDAVIT, an oath sworn in writing before some person authorised to receive it.

AFFREIGHTMENT, the act of loading a vessel.

AGASTERA, a liquid measure in some of the Ionian Islands; i. 372.

AGENT, a person duly authorised to act for another.

AGIO; i. Introduction, xxxiv; also, pages 17, 186.

AGIRAGUE, a weight in Guinea; i. 167.

AGTENDEEL, a corn measure in Holland; i. 297.

AHM, a measure for wine in Germany, Holland, &c.; i. 3, 77, 171, 206, 277, 287, 297; ii. 235.

AKEY, an African weight; i. 167.

ALBAAJER, see *Abassi*.

ALBERTS DOLLAR, a Dutch silver coin. It is used also as a money of account at Libau and Riga; i. 207, 288.

ALBERTS GROSCHEN, a money of account in Libau; i. 207.

ALBUS, a small coin and money of account at Cassel, Cologne, and other places in Germany; i. 63, 70, 261, 285.

ALLOTTING of goods, is when several persons buy a cargo or quantity of goods jointly, which they divide into as many parcels or lots as there are buyers, and these lots are afterwards drawn.

ALLOWANCES in sales of goods, in London; i. 228. Amsterdam, 11. Bourdeaux, 47. Cairo, 59. Genoa, 159. Gibraltar, 164. Hamburg, 173. Leghorn, 201. Rotterdam, 298.

ARPENT, a measure for land in the old French system; i. 134; ii. 249.

ARRANZADA, a land measure of Spain; i. 323; ii. 249.

ARRATEL, the Libra or Pound of Portugal; i. 212; ii. 227.

ARROBA, or ARROVE, a weight in Spain and Portugal; i. 6, 23, 212, 322, 342; also a liquid measure in Spain: i. 248, 322, 343; ii. 234, &c.; and a dry measure in Morocco; i. 260.

ARSHEEN, or ARCHIN, a long measure in Russia; i. 301; ii. 242.

ARTABA, a corn measure in Persia; i. 278; ii. 232.

AS, *plur. Asen*, a small Dutch weight, used also at Hamburgh, in Switzerland, and in Sweden; i. 9, 169, 329, 375.

ASNÉE, an old dry and liquid measure at Lyons; i. 246; ii. 231, 236.

ASPER, a small Turkish coin and money of account; i. 3, 4, 5, 57, 72, 276, 307, 314, 337.

ASSAY, a process by which the fineness of bullion or coins is determined, by separating, from any small part of the metal, the alloy from the pure, and ascertaining the proportion; ii. 171.

ASSIGNEE, a person appointed to manage the affairs of a bankrupt.

ASSURANCE, see *Insurance*.

ASTAH, a measure for cloth in the Prince of Wales's Island; ii. 241.

ASTLER, a corn measure in Louvain; i. 21.

ATOMO, a long measure in Italy; i. 256.

ATTACHMENT, the act by which a creditor may claim and seize the goods of his debtor, in whatever hands he finds them.

AVA, a long measure in Cadiz; i. 57.

AVERAGE, a contribution made for losses at sea: it is distinguished into general and particular. *General average* is a proportionable contribution, paid by all the proprietors of a ship and cargo for losses, which are made with a view to safety, such as throwing goods overboard, or cutting away masts to prevent shipwreck. *Particular average* is a contribution for such damages or losses as may happen from the common accidents of the sea; in which case the average must be paid by the proprietors of the article that suffers the damage.

AVERAGE TARE; i. 228.

A VISTA, at sight.

AVOIRDUPOIS, the commercial weight in England; i. Introduction, xxi.; i. 220, 225; ii. 225.

AUGUST, a gold coin of Saxony; i. 161, 205. Assay and value; ii. 160. Impressions; 205.

AUME, see *Aam*, or *Ahm;* also the name for a tierce of wine of 42 gallons.

AUNE, a measure for cloth in France and Switzerland; i. 28, 134, 364; ii. 238, 252.

AUREUS, an ancient Greek weight; ii. 256.

AWARD, the judgment of an arbitrator for terminating a difference.

AZUMBRE, a liquid measure in Spain; i. 56, 150, 248, 322.

B

BACILE, a dry measure, and also a land measure, in the Ionian Islands; i. 372, 373.

BACINE, a dry measure in Corsica; i. 80.

BADDAM, a species of almond, used as money in some parts of India; i. 103, 119.

BACHEL, a corn measure in the Morea; i. 276.

BAG, a measure and weight of various contents.

BAGATTINO, a copper coin of Venice; i. 345.

BAHAR, a weight used in some parts of India and of Arabia; i. 40, 98, 122, 257.

BAILLE, a measure for coals in Rochelle; i. 292.

BAJOCHELLO, a base silver coin at Rome; i. 293.

BAJOCCO, a base coin at Rome, Bologna, &c.; i. 18, 42, 243, 292.

BAJOIRE, a silver coin in Geneva; i. 152.

BALANCE, the difference between the debtor and creditor side of an account.

BALANCE OF TRADE, the difference between the commercial exports and imports of one country, with respect to another.

BALE, a quantity of packed goods.

BALLAST, or KENTILLAGE, any heavy matter placed in the hold of a ship, to make her sink to a proper depth, so that she may carry sufficient sail without the danger of oversetting.

BALLIAGE, a small duty paid to the city of London by aliens and others on the exportation of certain commodities.

BALLOON, 24 Reams of a particular sort of paper manufactured at Marseilles for the Levant.

BALLOT, of Paper, in Sweden, 10 Reams.

BALY, a weight in Sumatra; i. 112, 123.

BAMBOE, a measure for rice in Sumatra, the Molucca Islands, &c.; i. 97, 120.

BANCO, the bank money of Genoa, Hamburg, Venice, &c.; i. Introduction, xxxiv. 155, 167, 344; also the paper currency of Sweden; i. 333.

BAND, a weight used on the Gold Coast for weighing gold dust, and equal to 2 Ounces Troy.

BANKS; i. Introduction, xxxvi.

BANK of Altona; i. 7. Amsterdam, 17. Austria, 351. Berlin and Breslau, 36. Copenhagen, 79. England, 237. France, 145. Genoa, 154. Hamburg, 186. Ireland, 195. Netherlands, 17. Russia, 302. Scotland, 310. Venice, 347. Vienna, 351. United States, 356.

BANK BILL, a note signed by one of the cashiers of the Bank of England, promising to pay a certain sum of money at an appointed time.

BANK NOTE, a promissory note issued by a bank, payable to bearer on demand; i. 237.

BERRI, an itinerary measure in Turkey; ii. 250.

BES, or BESSIS, an ancient Roman long measure; ii. 257.

BESLICK, a small Turkish silver coin; ii. 169.

BESON, a liquid measure at Augsburg; i. 25.

BICE, or BIS, see *Pice*.

BICHERÉE, an old land measure in France; i. 246.

BICHET, an old dry measure at Lyons; i. 246.

BIGGAH, a land measure in the East Indies; i. 89.

BIGONCIA, a liquid measure in Venice; i. 346.

BILL, a term generally applied to a draft, advertisement, or account.

BILL OF ENTRY, a note of the particulars of goods entered at the custom-house.

BILL OF EXCHANGE; ii. 1.

BILLS, EXCHEQUER, securities issued by government, which bear interest until paid off. They are mostly for £100, £500, or £1000 each; some of them bear interest at the rate of 3*d.* others at the rate of 3½*d.* per day for every £100.

BILL OF HEALTH, an account of the health of a crew, given by the captain or master of a vessel.

BILLS, INDIA, bills drawn in India on the East India Company in London, and payable at the India House.

BILLS OF LADING, papers signed by the master of a ship, acknowledging the receipt of certain goods on board his vessel, and promising to deliver them at the intended place. It is customary to make out three bills of lading, one to be left with the shipper, the second to be held by the captain of the ship, and the third to be sent to the person to whom the goods are consigned, by which he can claim them on their arrival.

BILLS, NAVY, bills issued by the navy board in payment of stores for the ships, dock-yards, &c. They are made payable at 90 days, with an interest of 3½*d.* per day on every £100.

BILL OF PARCELS, an account given by the seller to the buyer, containing the particulars of the purchase.

BILL OF SALE, a deed by which a right or interest in certain goods is transferred.

BILL OF STORE, a licence granted at the custom-house to merchants or ship-owners, allowing them to carry, custom free, all provisions and stores for their voyage.

BILL OF SUFFERANCE, a licence granted to a merchant at the custom-house, allowing him to trade from one port to another.

BILLS, VICTUALLING, bills issued by the victualling board, as navy bills are by the navy board.

BILLON, base metal, either of gold or silver, in which copper is predominant.

BISACCIA, a corn measure in Sicily; i. 313.

BISMERPOND, a weight in Norway; i. 32.

BIT, or BITT, a small coin in the West Indies; i. 360, &c.

BLANCA, a money of account in Malaga; i. 248.

BLAFFERT, a small coin at Cologne; i. 70.

C

CAROTEEL, of cloves, from 4 to 5 cwt.; of mace, about 3 cwt.; of nutmegs, from 6 to 7½ cwt.; of currants, from 5 to 9 cwt.

CARRATA, a cubic measure in Carrara; i. 63.

CARRÉ, a land measure in the French West India Islands; i. 364.

CARRO, a dry and liquid measure in Italy; i. 264, 340.

CARTE, a corn measure at Nancy; ii. 231.

CARVAL, or CARWALL, a measure for grain in Aurungabundar, &c.; i. 99, 116.

CARUBE, a money of account in Algiers; i. 5.

CASH, a small coin in China and India; i. 66, 90, 97. Also a general term for real money.

CASH MONEY, the established coin of Hanover; i. 189.

CASHIER, one whose business it is to receive and pay money.

CASK, of sugar, from 8 to 10 cwt.; of almonds, about 3 cwt.; of raisins, about 1 cwt. Also a general name for close wooden vessels.

CASS, a wine measure in Cyprus; i. 81; ii. 235.

CASSA, the name given to current money in Holland; i. Introduction, xxxiv.

CASTELLANO, a weight for gold in Spain; i. 65, 253, 320.

CATANA, a long measure in some parts of Italy; i. 264.

CATTY, a weight at Canton and in India; i. 67, 197; ii. 225. Also a money of account in Java; i. 100.

CAVALLO, a copper coin of Naples; i. 263.

CAVEER, or CABEER, a money of account at Betelfagui and Mocha; i. 40, 257.

CAVEZZO, a long measure in Cremona; i. 81.

CAUL, a measure for rice, &c. in Sumatra; i. 97.

CAWNEY, a land measure at Madras; i. 93.

CEDOLA, a sort of bank note at Rome; i. 293.

CELEMINE, a corn measure in Spain; i. 23, 150, 322, 343.

CENSAL, a broker, so called in the south of France, in Italy, and in the Levant.

CENT, a money of account and copper coin of America; i. 353; in the Ionian Isles; 370; and also in the new monetary system of the Netherlands; ii. 267.

CENTESIMO, a money of account in Italy; i. 251, 254, 344.

CENTIARE, CENTIMETRE, &c. the 100th part of the French are, metre, &c.; i. 135, 136; ii. 251.

CENTIME, a money of account in the new system of France; i. 141.

CENTINAJO, the hundred weight in Italy.

CENTLET, a liquid measure in Ragusa; i. 284.

CENTNER, the hundred weight in Germany, Holland, &c.; i. 9, 21, 25, 34, 84.

CENTUMPONDIUM, an ancient Roman weight; ii. 258.

CENTURIA, an ancient Roman land measure; ii. 257.

CERTIFICATE, a paper certifying any thing. A *Certificate* is granted to a bankrupt, with the consent of his creditors, after he has surrendered and made a full discovery of all his property, according to law. To export goods by *certificate* is when foreign goods which have been imported, are re-exported within the time limited by act of parliament, and a drawback is allowed on them.

CHAIN, for measuring land, generally 4 Poles; i. 224.

CHAIN RULE, explained and exemplified; ii. Introduction, v.

CHALDER, a dry measure in Scotland; i. 310.

CHALDRON, a dry measure in England, particularly for coals; also a weight at Newcastle; i. 222.

CHAMBER OF ASSURANCE, in France, a society of merchants, carrying on the business of insuring.

CHAMBER OF COMMERCE, an assembly of merchants, where the affairs relating to trade are discussed and settled.

CHAR, a wine measure in Geneva; i. 153.

CHARGE, a measure of capacity in France and Switzerland; i. 252, 259, 269, 305; ii. 231. Also a weight at Antwerp; i. 21.

CHARGES, the necessary expenses attending any mercantile transaction.

CHARGES, on exchange operations; ii. 126.

CHARKEY, a Russian liquid measure; i. 301.

CHARTER, a written evidence of some grant or privilege.

CHARTER PARTY, a contract executed between the person who hires a ship, and the owner, setting forth the terms, &c. A ship is said to be chartered, when hired for a voyage.

CHATTACK, a weight and also a land measure in the East Indies; i. 89.

CHATTELS, all kinds of goods and property.

CHAYÉ, a silver coin of Persia; i. 277.

CHECK, an order for money on a banker; ii. 10.

CHENICA, a corn measure in Persia; i. 278.

CHEQUEE, a Turkish weight; i. 30, 72, 315; ii. 222.

CHERASSI, a gold medal stamped in Persia, not properly a coin; i. 277.

CHEST, an uncertain quantity; of isinglass, 3½ cwt.; of cochineal, 1½ cwt.

CHETWERT, CHETWERICK, and CHETWERTKA, three corn measures in Russia; i. 301; ii. 232.

CHEVISANCE, a composition between debtor and creditor.

CHILO, a dry measure in Cerigo; i. 372.

CHISE, see *Purse*.

CHITTACK, see *Chattack*.

CIVADIER, a corn measure at Marseilles; i. 252.

CHŒNIX, an ancient Greek and Roman corn measure; ii. 256, 258.

CHOOSOCK, a weight in the Sunda Isles; i. 118.

CHOPA, a measure of capacity in Sumatra; i. 97.

COMMISSION OF BANKRUPTCY, an order under the great seal, directing five or more commissioners to inquire into the affairs of a bankrupt.

COMPANY, a society or partnership in trade or commerce.

COMPOSITION, part of a debt taken in lieu of the whole.

COMPROMISE, settling a difference by making some concessions on both sides.

CONDORINE, see *Candarine*.

CONDYLE, an ancient Egyptian long measure; ii. 260.

CONGUIS, an ancient Roman liquid measure; ii. 258,

CONQUE, a measure for corn and salt at Bayonne; ii. 229.

CONSIGNEE, the person to whom goods are consigned.

CONSIGNMENT, the sending or delivering over of goods to the care of a factor.

CONSTITUTION COINS, of Germany; i. 163.

CONTINGENT, the proportion that falls to the share of a person in any business or adventure.

CONTO OF REES, one thousand milrees.

CONTRABAND TRADE, that which is prohibited by law.

CONTRACT, a covenant or agreement between two or more persons.

CONTRIBUTION, see *Average*.

CONVENTION COINS, of Germany; i. 162, 189.

CONVOY, ships of war sailing with other ships, in order to protect them.

COOMB, a corn measure in England; i. 221, 228.

COOP, a corn measure in Holland; i. 10.

COPANG, a gold coin in Japan; i. 196. Assay and value; ii. 161. Impressions; 218. Also, a money of account in Sumatra, i. 97.

CO-PARTNERSHIP is when two or more persons unite in trade, and agree to participate in the profits and losses, according to their respective shares in the capital.

COPECK, a money of account and copper coin in Russia; i. 276, 299.

COPELLO, a corn measure in Piedmont; i. 340.

COPPA, a corn measure in Ancona; i. 18.

COPPO, a measure for oil at Lucca; i. 244; ii. 235.

COPSTICK, or COPFSTUCK, a silver coin in many parts of Germany; i. 48, 69, 162, 261, 348. Assay and value; ii. 162, &c. Impressions; 178, &c.

CORBA, a measure of capacity at Bologna and other places in Italy; i. 43; ii. 229, 234, &c.

CORD, a pile of wood, 4 feet long, 4 feet broad, and 8 feet deep.

CORDE, an old French land measure; i. 307.

CORGE, in Bombay, 20 pieces; i. 96.

D

E

F

FRAZIL, a weight in Arabia; i. 40, 257.

FREDERICK, or FREDERICK D'OR, a gold coin in Prussia and Germany; i. 34, 161, 296. Assay and value; ii. 159. Impressions; 200.

FREIGHT, the goods which a ship carries; also the money paid for carrying them.

FUDDEA, a money of account in Bombay; i. 93.

FUDER, a large measure for wine in Germany, Prussia, Denmark, and Sweden; i. 25, 35, 50, 77, 171, 271, 331, 350.

FUDERMASSEL, a corn measure at Vienna; i. 350.

FUND, a stock or capital; that by which any expense is supported.

FUNDS, PUBLIC, or STOCKS; i. 239.

FUNDS, French; i. 146.

FUORI BANCO, out of bank; the current money of Genoa; i. 155.

FURDINGAR, a liquid measure in Finland; i. 332.

FURLONG, a long measure in England; i. 223, 226, 309.

FYRKE, a money of account and copper coin in Denmark; i. 74.

G

GABARAGE, wrappers in which Irish goods are packed up.

GABEL, an old word for a tribute or custom paid to the prince or lord.

GALL, a small piece of silver with characters on one side only, used as coin in Cambodia; i. 103.

GALLEON, a sort of ship, employed by the Spaniards in the West-India trade; and also to bring gold and silver from America to Europe, &c.

GALLON, a measure of capacity in England; i. 194, 221, 222, 227, 228, 310; ii. 235.

GANDANG, 25 pieces of cloth which pass as money in the Philippine Islands; i. 107.

GANTAM, or GANTANG, a measure for rice in some parts of the East Indies; i. 107, 108, 118, 197.

GANZA, a small coin in some parts of India beyond the Ganges; i. 113.

GARBLE, the dust, dross, and refuse of spices and drugs.

GARBLING, picking out the worst of any commodity.

GARCE, a measure for grain, and also a weight at Madras, Pondicherry, and other places in the East Indies; i. 92, 93, 105.

GARI, of Rupees, in the East Indies, about 4000.

GARNET, a corn measure of Russia; i. 301.

GARNIEC, a measure of capacity in Poland; i. 280; ii. 236.

GASSA, a money of account in Persia; i. 151.

GAVADA, a land measure in the Mysore; i. 117.

GAUGER, a person appoint to gauge or ascertain the contents of any excisable commodity.

GE, or JE, a long measure in some parts of the East Indies, equal to about 34½ Dutch ells, or 26 English yards.

GEBRAUDE, a liquid measure at Berlin; i. 35.

GEIRA, a land measure in Portugal; i. 213; ii. 249.

GENEVOISE, a silver coin of Geneva; ii. 163.

GENOVINA, a gold coin of Genoa; i. 157. Assay and value; ii. 158. Impressions; 187.

GEORGE D'OR, a gold coin of Hanover; i. 189. Assay and value; ii. 158. Impressions; 188.

GERRA, or JAR, a liquid measure in Minorca; i. 257; ii. 236.

GESCHEIDE, a corn measure in Franckfort and Mentz; i. 148.

GHERIA, a long measure of Bengal; i. 89.

GHURRY, a division of time in the East Indies; i. 87.

GIGLIATO, the Sequin of Tuscany; i. 129; ii. 161, 211.

GILDER, see *Florin*.

GILL, a liquid measure in Great Britain; i. 222, 310.

GIORGINO, a silver coin of Genoa; i. 157.

GIRO, the name given to the money of exchange at Augsburg, Bolsano, and other places in Germany; i. 24, 44.

GIULIO, a small coin of base silver in Italy; i. 127, 292.

GIUSTINA, a silver coin in Venice; i. 344. Assay and value; ii. 169. Impressions, 214.

GOAD, or GODE, a kind of ell, 27½ inches long, by which Welsh frieze is measured in England.

GOBLET, a dry measure in Basil; i. 28.

GOELACK, a weight in Java; i. 100, 113.

GOESGEN, a money of account at Brunswick and Hanover; i. 53, 189.

GOLD GULDEN, or GOLD GILDER, see *Florin, Gold*.

GOLD MONEY, a money of account at Leghorn; i. 204.

GOLD VALUE, a kind of money used in Hanover; i. 189.

GOLD and SILVER, amount of, brought annually into circulation from all parts of the world; i. note, 254. Relative value of Gold and Silver; i. Introduction, xxvii.; ii. 147. Comparative value of Gold and Silver; i. Introduction, xxxi.

GOMBETTA, a corn measure in Genoa; i. 159.

GOMOR, an ancient Jewish measure of capacity; ii. 259.

GONZE, a small weight for gold and silver at Bombay; i. 94.

GOOD GROSCHE, or GUT GROSCHE, a small coin and money of account in Prussia; and also in Hanover, and other parts of Germany; i. 33, 162, 189.

GOOROOSH, the name given to the Piastre by the Turks.

GOULD, see *Florin*.

H

J

K

KABAN, a weight in the Molucca Isles; i. 120, 123.

KANGAN, a piece of coarse cloth that passes as money in the Philippine and Sunda Isles; i. 107, 118.

KANNA, a dry and liquid measure in Sweden; i. 331; ii. 232, 237.

KANNE, a measure of capacity in Germany; i. 3, 171, 206. Also, a Dutch and Danish liquid measure; i. 77, 98, 297.

KAPP, a corn measure in Sweden; i. 331.

KARCH, in Germany, 400 lb.

KASBEQUIS, a money of account and copper coin in Persia; i. 277.

KAST, in Sweden, 4 pieces; i. 332.

KAYSERGROSCHE, a money of account and base silver coin in Bohemia, and some parts of Germany; i. 23, 50, 161, 261, 281.

KEEL, a coal measure in England; i. 222.

KEG, a vessel for sturgeon, salmon, or other pickled fish, containing 4 or 5 gallons.

KELLA, a dry measure in Arabia; i. 40, 258.

KEN, a long measure at Siam; i. 118.

KENTILLAGE, see *Ballast*.

KEPPING, a money in Sumatra; i. 120.

KERAMION, an ancient Greek liquid measure; ii. 256.

KEY, KAY, or QUAY, a lawful wharf for the landing of goods.

KEYAGE, or WHARFAGE, a toll paid for loading or unloading goods at a key or wharf.

KHAHOON, a measure of capacity in Bengal; i. 89.

KHANCHAA, a weight in the East Indies; i. 89.

KIBEAR, a money of Abyssinia; i. 1.

KILARE, 1000 ares in the new French system; i. 136.

KILDERKIN, half a barrel, a measure for liquids and dry goods; i. 223, 227.

KILLOW, or KISLO, a Turkish corn measure; i. 73, 307, 315; ii. 230.

KILOGRAMME, KILOLITRE, KILOMETRE, 1000 grammes, litres, &c. in the new French system of weights and measures; i. 136, &c. ii. 222, 225, 250, 251.

KIMPFE, a corn measure in Mentz; i. 148.

KINTAL, see *Quintal*.

KIP, a weight at Malacca; i. 108.

KISLOZ, a corn measure of Egypt; i. 4.

L

M

MALTER, a corn measure in various parts of Germany, Prussia, and Switzerland; i. 3, 35, 69, 83, 271, 375; ii. 230.

MAMOODI, or MAMOUDI, a money of account and silver coin of Persia and Arabia; i. 29, 151, 277.

MANA, see *Maund.*

MANDEL, in Germany, 15 pieces, or articles of any goods; i. 52, 164.

MANDELWEIGHT, a weight used for Ducats at Vienna; i. 350.

MANEH, an ancient Jewish weight; ii. 259.

MANGELIN, a weight used in the East Indies for pearls; i. 92.

MANIFEST, a paper containing the particulars of a ship and cargo, which paper must be signed by the master of the vessel, before any goods can be landed.

MANOGOGA, a measure for rice in Japan; i. 197.

MANUFACTURE, a commodity produced by labour or machinery from raw materials.

MARADOE, a coin in Tonquin; i. 102.

MARAVEDI, a Spanish money of account; i. 316.

MARCAL, a corn measure at Madras and Ceylon; i. 93, 105.

MARCHETTO, a copper coin and money of account in some parts of Italy; i. 31.

MARENGO, a gold coin of Piedmont; ii. 159. Impressions; 198.

MARIEN GROSCHE, a small money of account in some parts of Germany; i. 53, 161, 189, 245.

MARIEN GULDEN, a money of account at Brunswick; i. 53.

MARK, MARC, or MARCO, a weight in most parts of the continent, used chiefly for gold and silver; ii. 222. It is likewise an old English weight and gold coin; i. Introduction, xxx.; also page 216.

MARK, a money of account in some parts of Germany, and also in Denmark and Norway; i. 2, 6, 32, 74, 167, 241; ii. 151.

MARK, a silver coin of Hamburg, &c.; i. 168. Assay and value; ii. 163. Impressions; 191. It is likewise a silver coin in Denmark; i. 74. Assay and value; ii. 163.

MARK FERDING, MARK RIGISH, two monies of account at Riga; i. 288.

MARQUÉ, a copper coin in the Mauritius; i. 110.

MART, a great market, fair, or other place of public traffic.

MAS, a money of account in Japan; i. 196.

MASGEN, a corn measure in Germany; i. 127, 205.

MASS, see *Mauss.*

MASSA, a weight in the East Indies; i. 89, 99.

MASSLEIN, a corn measure in Wirtemberg; i. 369.

MASSLING, a corn measure in Switzerland; i. 375.

MASTELLO, a wine measure at Ferrara and Rome; i. 127, 294, 346; ii. 235.

MATH, a money of account at Rangoon; i. 115.

N

O

P

PATACON, Spanish, the same as the Hard Dollar.

PATACON RIXDOLLAR, a money of account and of exchange at Antwerp; i. 19.

PATARD, a copper coin in Flanders; i. 19, 85.

PATTY, a small coin in Tranganìa; i. 121.

PAUNCHEA, a money of account in Bombay; i. 93.

PAYEE, the person to whom a bill is made payable; ii. 2.

PAYEMENTS, or PAYMENTS, certain periods at Lyons and other places on the Continent, at which bills are generally made payable.

PECCO, a money of account in some parts of Java; i. 100.

PECK, a measure for dry commodities in England; i. 220, 221, 227, 310.

PECK LOAF, weight of; i. 221.

PECUL, or PICUL, a weight in China and some parts of the East Indies; i. 67, 93, 122, 197.

PENALTY, a forfeiture or fine for disobedience to certain laws or regulations; a penalty is also occasionally annexed to secure the payment of money, or the performance of any contract.

PENDULUM, SECONDS, length of, in different latitudes; i. Introduction, xvii. xix.

PENNING, a money of account in Holland and the Netherlands; i. 8, 19. Also a small weight in Germany and Switzerland; i. 3, 375.

PENNY, a copper coin in England; i. 216.

PENNY FLEMISH, see *Grote*.

PENNYWEIGHT, a division of the ounce Troy in England and Holland; i. 9, 217.

PERCH, a land measure in England, France, and other countries; i. 11, 195, 223, 226.

PERIOT, a division of the English grain; i. 219.

PERMIS, exchange money in Flanders; i. 19.

PERMIT, a licence or warrant for the passing or selling of goods, which have paid duty or excise.

PERPERO, a silver coin of Ragusa; i. 284.

PERPETUITY, the number of years purchase to be given for an annuity that is to last for ever.

PERTICA, a long measure and land measure in Italy; i. 81, 131.

PES, an ancient Roman long measure; ii. 257.

PESAGE, money paid for weighing goods.

PESETA, a Spanish silver coin; i. 253. Assay and value; ii. 168.

PESETA MEXICAN, a Spanish silver coin, the quarter of the dollar; i. 319. Assay and value; ii. 168. Impressions; 207.

PESETA PROVINCIAL, a base silver coin of Spain; i. 319.

PESO, the Spanish for a dollar. PESO DE PLATA, Dollar of Exchange; PESO DURO, Hard Dollar; i. 318. Assay and value; ii. 168. Impressions; 208.

POLUSHKA, a copper coin of Russia; i. 299.

PONTE, a money of account in Sicily; i. 313.

POOD, a Russian weight; i. 301.

POOL, a weight used on the Malabar coast; i. 102.

POOT, a piece of tin, used as a money and as a weight in Junkceylon; i. 107.

PORRONE, a liquid measure in Barcelona; i. 27.

PORTAGE, money paid for sailors' wages while in port.

PORTERAGE, money paid to porters for their service in landing or shipping goods, &c.

PORT SALE, a sale of goods upon the key. Also a sale to the highest bidder.

PORTUGALESE, a gold coin in Lubec; i. 241.

POSSE, a land measure in Switzerland.

POST ENTRY, an additional entry made by a merchant at the custom-house, when the first entry that he made is found to be too small.

POT, of ale, a liquid measure in England, generally one quart. Also a liquid measure in France, Switzerland, Denmark, &c.; i. 28, 47, 77, 85, 153, 252, 326.

POTE, a liquid measure in Portugal; i. 212.

POTÉE, an old wine measure in France; i. 85.

POTTLE, a measure for corn and other dry commodities in England; i. 221.

POUAH, see *Pice*.

POUCE, a French long measure; ii. 252.

POUGNERÉE, a land measure in some parts of France; i. 47.

POUND, the unit for weights in England, and in most parts of Europe; i. Introduction, xx. 220, 309; ii. 222.

POUND, a money of account in the British islands and colonies, and in North America; i. 59, 216. Also a money of account in Strasburgh, and some parts of Germany; i. 326, 369.

POUND FLEMISH, a money of account in Flanders; and a money of exchange at Amsterdam and Hamburg; i. 8, 19, 167; ii. 28, 65, 149.

POUNDAGE, a duty formerly paid to the king of one shilling in the pound on all goods imported and exported, except such as paid tonnage, and on bullion, diamonds, and a few others.

POWER OF ATTORNEY, see *Letter of Attorney*.

PRAN, a division of time in the East Indies; i. 87.

PRE-EMPTION, a first buying, or buying before others.

PREMIUM, the money paid for insuring ships, goods, houses, &c.

PRICE CURRENT, a list published in commercial places of the current value of commodities.

PRIMAGE, a certain allowance or per centage on freight, paid to the captain and mariners of a ship at their setting out or coming into a port.

PRINCIPAL, the capital sum lent or due.

Q

R

REFACTION, a deduction from the weight for damage; i. 16.

REFUNDING, the paying back of the money received in consideration of a contract that has not been fulfilled.

REGENSBURGER, a money of account of Ratisbon.

REGRATING, buying and selling again in the same market, corn and other provisions.

REICHSFLORIN, or REICHSGULDEN, see *Florin.*

REICHSTHALER, see *Rixdollar.*

RELEASE, the relinquishing of any right of action, which a man has or may claim against another.

REMANCIPATE, to sell or return a commodity to him that first sold it.

REMEDY of the Mint; i. Introduction, xxviii.

REMITTANCE, the act of sending money or bills of exchange to a distant place; ii. 105.

RENTE, in the French funds, a term synonymous with income or annuity; i. 146.

RESCONTRE, or SCONTRO, a manner of settling the payment of bills of exchange in some places on the Continent, as at Augsburg, Bolsano, Novi, &c.; i. 26.

RESPONDENTIA, a bond or contract by which money is borrowed on the security of goods, the same as in bottomry on the security of ships.

RESTIERE, a corn measure of Sardinia; i. 308.

RESTITUTION, is when any money has been paid wrongfully or by mistake, the person so paying has a right to demand it back.

RETAIL, dealing in commodities in small quantities.

RETENUE, a deduction made at the mint of France for coining gold or silver; i. 142.

RETURNS, a term expressing the value, either in goods or in money, returned by the consignee of a cargo or parcel of goods to the consigner. The term is also applied to a return of bills.

RETURNS, in exchange; ii. 105.

REZAL, a measure for corn at Strasburg; i. 327.

RIAL, see *Real.*

RICHTPFENNING, a small division of the Cologne weight; i. 71, 170, 350.

RICKSGOLD, or RICKSGALD, a paper currency in Sweden; i. 333.

RIESSE, a term used in reckoning in Germany; i. 164.

RIGSBANK, of Denmark; i. 79.

RIKSDALER, see *Rixdollar.*

RING, in Germany, signifies 240 pieces; i. 84, 164, 177.

RING, of staves, in Hamburg; i. 177.

RIXDOLLAR, a money of account and silver coin in most countries on the continent; i. 8, 27, 33, 74, 160, 327; ii. 149. Assay and value; ii. 162, &c. Impressions; 178, &c.

RIXFLORIN, see *Florin.*

ROBI, a long measure in Algiers; i. 5.

S

STAND, of pitch, from $2\frac{1}{2}$ cwt. to 3 cwt.

STANDARD, a pattern for weights or measures, that is, a weight or measure of undoubted authority by which others are adjusted.

STANDARD of English coins; i. Introduction, xxviii. also page 217.

STANDARD OF VALUE, money which is a legal tender; i. Introduction, xxxii.

STANDARDS, for English weights and measures; i. Introduction, xvii.; French standards, xxv.

STANDARDING coins and bullion, reducing them to a given standard; ii. 173.

STANDPENNING, see *Ryder*.

STANGIEU, a liquid measure in Poland; i. 280.

STAPLE, a city, town, or place appointed as a public mart or emporium for the sale of goods.

STAPLE GOODS, such as are sold at a staple. The term is also applied to the principal produce of a country, and likewise to goods that are not of a perishable nature, as wool, lead, iron, &c.

STARELLO, a corn measure of Sardinia; i. 308; ii. 232.

STARO, a corn measure in Italy, and in the Morea; i. 276, 294; ii. 232.

STATERA, an ancient Greek measure; ii. 256.

STEIGE, or STIEGE, in Germany, 20 pieces; i. 164.

STEIN, or STEEN, see *Stone*.

STEKAN, a liquid measure in Holland and Germany; i. 10, 50, 171; ii. 234, &c.

STEKAR, a liquid measure in Russia; i. 301.

STELLIONATE, a term applied to tricks in bargaining, and particularly in selling another man's property.

STERE, the unit for solid measures in the new French system; i. 135, 136; ii. 251.

STERLING, English money. The term is supposed to be derived from the *Easterlings;* that is, persons from the eastern parts of Germany who are said to have fixed the English standard of silver in the reign of Richard I. The silver penny was afterwards called a *Sterling;* and the word is now applied to all lawful money of Great Britain.

STERLINO, a weight for silver in Naples; i. 264.

STIVER, a money of account and copper coin in Holland and Germany; i. 8, 19, 68, 209.

STOCK, a fund raised by a commercial company; a principal sum or property employed in trade. Stock in book-keeping, denotes the owner or owners of the books.

STOCK-JOBBER, a person who deals in public funds on his own account.

STOCKS, or public funds; i. 239.

STOF, or STOOF, a measure of capacity in Konigsberg, Libau, Pernau, Reval, and Riga; i. 198, 208, 277, 287, 289; ii. 235.

STONE, a weight in England, Holland, and Germany, varying much; i. 9, 21, 49, 84, 171, 220, 309. The German name is *Stein*.

STOOP, a liquid measure in Holland and Flanders; i. 10, 21, 297; ii. 234, &c.

T

V

U

ULLAGE, what a cask of liquor wants of being quite full.

UMPIRE, a person appointed finally to settle a dispute or difference when the arbitrators cannot agree.

UNCIA, a division both of the weights and of the measures of the ancient Romans; i. Introduction, xx.; ii. 257.

UNDERWRITER, a person who insures ships, cargoes, or other risks, which he performs by writing his name under a policy of insurance.

UNZE, a corn measure in Wirtemberg; i. 369.

URDEE, a base coin and money of account in Bombay; i. 93.

URNA, an ancient Roman liquid measure; ii. 258.

USANO, see *Piso*.

USANCE, the usual term of bills of exchange drawn from one country upon another; ii. 2.

USURY, a charge of interest beyond what is allowed by law.

UTA, a money in some parts of Java; i. 100.

W

WAAG, a weight in Norway, Germany, and Sweden; i. 32, 49, 205, 330.

WAKEA, the Abyssinian ounce; i. 1.

WALL, or WAHL, in Germany and Sweden, 80 pieces; i. 83, 164, 332.

WAREHOUSE GOODS, or bonded goods, are certain articles, which, on being landed, are warehoused upon bond being given by the owner for the payment of duties, &c.

WASTE BOOK, a book containing a regular detail of the transactions of a merchant's or trader's business, set down in the order of time in which they take place.

WEBE, in Germany, 72 pieces.

WEDDRA, see *Vedro*.

WEIGHTS, defined; i. Introduction, xvi. Troy Weight of different countries compared; ii. 222. Avoirdupois Weight; 224. Ancient; 255.

WERSCHOCK, a cloth measure in Russia, see *Vershok*.

WERST, the Russian mile; i. 302; ii. 250.

WEY, or WEIGH, a weight for various articles, and also a measure for corn in England; i. 220, 221, 228.

WHARFAGE, money paid for the use of a wharf.

WHARFINGER, the keeper or owner of a wharf.

WHIBA, a corn measure at Tunis; i. 338.

WILLIAM D'OR, a gold coin of Cassel. Assay and value; ii. 158.

WISPEL, a corn measure in Germany and Prussia; i. 35, 54, 171, 205, 245, 324, 373.

X

Y

Z

THE END.

SUPPLEMENT

TO

THE SECOND EDITION

OF

THE UNIVERSAL CAMBIST;

BEING

An Exposition

OF THE

WEIGHTS, MEASURES, AND MONIES,

OF

THE EAST INDIES,

DEDUCED FROM

A SERIES OF EXPERIMENTS ON ATTESTED STANDARDS,

VERIFIED BY OFFICIAL AUTHORITIES;

INCLUDING

MANY OTHER IMPORTANT DOCUMENTS RELATING TO

Oriental Commerce.

TO

THE HONOURABLE

THE COURT OF DIRECTORS

OF THE

East India Company,

WILLIAM WIGRAM, Esq. M. P. Chairman,

WILLIAM ASTELL, Esq. M. P. Deputy Chairman,

JACOB BOSANQUET, Esq.
Hon. W. FULLARTON ELPHINSTONE,
GEORGE SMITH, Esq. M.P.
EDWARD PARRY, Esq.
SWENY TOONE, Esq.
RICHARD CHICHELEY PLOWDEN, Esq.
JOHN HUDLESTON, Esq.
Sir THOMAS REID, Bart.
JOHN BEBB, Esq.
JAMES PATTISON, Esq.
CAMPBELL MAJORIBANKS, Esq.
Sir G. ABERCROMBIE ROBINSON, Bart.
JAMES DANIELL, Esq.
WILLIAM STANLEY CLARKE, Esq.
JOHN THORNHILL, Esq.
GEORGE RAIKES, Esq.
WILLIAM TAYLOR MONEY, Esq. M.P.
JOHN LOCH, Esq.
CHARLES ELTON PRESCOTT, Esq.
CHARLES MILLS, Jun. Esq.
JOHN BAILLIE, Esq. M.P.
JOHN MASTERMAN, Esq.

A Court

WHOSE ADMINISTRATION HAS BEEN EMINENTLY DISTINGUISHED FOR WISDOM, JUSTICE, AND LIBERALITY;

THIS SUPPLEMENT ON INDIAN METROLOGY

(EXECUTED UNDER THEIR AUSPICES)

IS INSCRIBED,

WITH SENTIMENTS OF THE HIGHEST RESPECT FOR THEIR PRIVATE CHARACTERS,

AND OF ADMIRATION FOR THEIR PUBLIC SERVICES,

BY THEIR VERY FAITHFUL SERVANT,

THE AUTHOR.

Finsbury Square,
February 28, 1824.

SUPPLEMENT.

ON THE WEIGHTS, MEASURES, AND MONIES, OF THE EAST INDIES.

PRELIMINARY DOCUMENTS AND EXPLANATIONS.

THIS extensive Supplement has become necessary in consequence of a general Comparison of the Weights, Measures, and Monies of India having taken place after the Article "*East Indies*" was printed in the first Volume; for although it was drawn up with the greatest care, and with the best information that could be then obtained in London, as stated in page 96, yet it is materially deficient in respect to the number of places, which are more than doubled in this Supplement.

That Article, however, is generally correct as far as it extends, particularly the Account of the Three Presidencies, Bengal, Madras, and Bombay; which Account may therefore be considered a proper Introduction to the whole, and ought to be well understood before any further study of the subject is entered upon.

It should have been premised, that the Circular Order issued by his Majesty's Government in 1818, directing all British Consuls abroad to send home verified standards (see Preface, page x), did not extend to the East Indies, and hence the deficiency above mentioned. With a view, therefore, to remedy this want, and to co-operate with government in completing the general Comparison, the Court of Directors, in 1821, issued the following Order.

Extract of the Public Letter from the Court of Directors to Bengal, dated London, 10th of January, 1821.

"*A commission having been lately issued by the Crown, to consider the subject of Weights and Measures, we are desirous of being enabled to assist the pending enquiry, by the fullest information which can be procured concerning Weights and Measures, in all countries with which England has commercial relations in Asia.*

"*For this purpose we forward a number in the packet, the draft of a Letter of Instructions, which we desire you will issue to commercial residents, collectors of customs, and such other persons under your authority, as may be thought competent to furnish the required information. You will communicate the result to us without delay, forwarding from time to time the information received in pursuance of those instructions, until the enquiry be completed.*"

Draft of Instructions to be issued to Commercial Residents, Collectors of Customs, and other Public Officers, referred to in the foregoing Extract.

You are to procure and forward two sets of models, being accurate counterparts of the standard Weights and Measures in use at your Station, for weighing and measuring goods and merchandize of every description.

In places where different denominations and standards of Weight or Measure are employed for particular articles, distinctly from ordinary commodities, separate counterparts of the various Weights and Measures are to be furnished.

Should Weights or Measures in use at places within your authority vary from those established at your principal station, you will likewise procure distinct sets of Weights or Measures so differing.

It will not be necessary that the sets of models should comprehend subdivisions, nor multiples of the principal Weight or Measure of each series. A model of one in a series will suffice; and a convenient one to be selected for Weights may be that which is nearest to the pound (as the seer and the catty, where maunds and peculs are in use respectively); and in like manner for Measures of length, one that is nearest to the cubit or the ell; and for Measures of capacity, one that is next to the pint or the quart.

To every model should be annexed a specification of the usual subdivisions, or smaller Weights employed as aliquot parts, as well as of the greater Weights used as multiples of that which the model represents. Thus an explanatory note should be annexed to the seer, specifying the number of chattacks contained in it, or other customary divisions; and likewise the number of seers contained in the maund, and of maunds in the candy (where such greater weight also is in use).

Brass, copper, or tutanag are considered to be fit materials of which the models may be made.

The accuracy of the models is to be carefully verified and regularly attested by competent persons.

One set of the models is designed for immediate transmission to England, the other to be retained at the Presidency for subsequent and eventual transmission, as a duplicate in case of miscarriage of the first dispatch. The two sets accordingly are to be assorted and separately packed.

If models of Measures of capacity for meting corn or liquids cannot be provided and forwarded without too great inconvenience, the desired information may be supplied by a careful ascertainment and report of the liquid contents, as corresponding either to a known standard of the like sort, or to cubic inches. Accurate models would however be more satisfactory.

In an explanatory letter accompanying the transmission of the models, you will add such information as you may possess, or can procure, upon the general object of these instructions, with any observations which may occur to you, as throwing light upon the subject. (1821.)

In obedience to the foregoing Circular, numerous packages, containing the required standards, with their specifications, and other explanatory documents, were in due time transmitted to the Court of Directors in London; and, as they arrived, were delivered to the Author of this work for examination and comparison, as intimated by the following letter from the Secretary of the East India Company.

East India House,
2d August, 1822.

Sir,

It having been suggested to the Court of Directors of the East India Company, that several specimens of Weights and Measures, which have been, and are expected to be received from the different Settlements in the East Indies, may be entrusted to you for examination and comparison, I am directed, in accordance with that suggestion, to acquaint you that such of the said specimens as have been received will be delivered to you upon your making application at this house for that purpose, and upon your giving a receipt for the same, specifying that they are the property of the East India Company, and will be returned when required.

A similar communication will be made to you upon the arrival of any further articles of the same description.

I am, Sir,
Your most obedient humble Servant,

To Dr. Kelly.

JOSEPH DART, Sec.

Such were the orders and regulations of the Court of Directors, in pursuance of which all the standards received from India (amounting to more than 300 in number) have been compared with English standards by the Author of this work, or under his immediate superintendence; and afterwards the principal weights were examined, and their contents verified at the Royal Mint, by ***Robert Bingley***, Esq. F. R. S. the King's Assay-Master, whose important assistance throughout the work has so essentially promoted its accuracy. (See Pref. p. xii.)

The results of all these comparisons are comprised in the present Supplement, together with much new and useful information on commercial practice, as communicated in the various dispatches from India, which accompanied the standards.

This Supplement contains the result of another extensive operation, which was also considered a desideratum, namely, a general Assay of the Coins of India. It was executed at the Bombay Mint, in 1821, by *B. Noton*, Esq. Assay-Master to the Company.

This Table of Assays is of peculiar importance to the present undertaking, as it not only shews the Par of Exchange throughout India, but also the weight of each Rupee, which is generally considered an aliquot part of the Seer or other standard of the place to which such Coin belongs. The Report is, therefore, made a leading article here; and with a view to render it still more extensively useful, two columns are added. One is a numerical notation of the Coins, for the convenience of reference; and the other shews their sterling value, according to the Mint price in England, from which their value at any other price may be readily computed. (See Note, p. 332.)

As the Table contains no account of the divisions of the Rupee, this want is supplied in the subsequent pages, by mentioning the Presidency to which each Settlement is subject or subordinate; for it may be inferred, that the Rupee of each place is divided according to the practice of its Presidency.* It will be seen by a reference to the article *East Indies*, vol. 1, that in Bengal the Rupee is divided into 16 Annas, and each Anna into 12 Pice; and that a similar system has been of late adopted at Madras; but at Bombay and most of its subordinates, it is divided into 4 Quarters, and each Quarter into 100 Reas.

---

* This account of the Presidencies to which the Settlements are subordinate (now published for the first time) has been supplied for this work by *William Wright*, Esq. Chief Auditor of Indian Accounts: and here the Author would wish also to acknowledge the able assistance which he has received from many other officers of the Company, but the list of names would be too numerous. He cannot, however, omit to mention one distinguished character, from whose writings and communications he has obtained much important information. This is *General Sir John Malcolm*, G.C.B. K.L.S. whose valuable Work on *Central India* contains a very clear Specification of the Weights, Measures, and Exchanges, of nearly twenty Cities in the newly-acquired Territories of *Malwa* and its surrounding Districts.

The Dispatches from the Civil Officers in India to the Court of Directors, in answer to the Circular of 1821, have furnished matter for more than 100 *new* places for this Supplement, that is to say, places on the Metrology of which nothing had been previously published in the English language. This great accession of commercial knowledge is further augmented and improved by the following Table of Assays.

ASSAY REPORT;

Shewing the Mint Standards of Bombay, Calcutta, Madras, and England; and the Weight, Purity, and intrinsic Value, by Assay, of all the Coins, either current in the Honourable Company's Territories under the Presidency of Bombay, or imported as Bullion.—August 4th, 1821.

	NAMES OF COINS.	ASSAY.			Value of 100 in Bombay Currency.	Sterling Value.	REMARKS.
	GOLD.	Weight.	Touch. *	Pure Metal.			
		Grs. dec.	Per Cent. dec.	Grs. dec.	Rs. dec.	S. dec.	
1	Bombay Mohur	179.—	92.	164.68	1500.—	29.18	New standard, 1 part of gold
2	Calcutta do. } New ..	204.71	91.66	187.65	1709.2233	33.37	being worth 15 of silver.
3	Madras do. } New ..	180.—	91.66	165.—	1502.914	29.10	
4	English Guinea	129.50	91.66	118.70	1081.187	21.00	English stand. See p. 157, vol. ii.
5	Venetian or Seguin ..	53.—	99.25	52.60	479.011	9.31	Full weight, 54 grains.
6	Gubber or Dutch Ducat	53.25	98.25	52.31	476.500	9.26	Do. 53¾ do.
7	Joaneese of Portugal ..	220.75	91.50	201.98	1839.805	35.74	Do. 222½ do.
8	Persian Toman	73.50	97.25	71.47	651.06	12.65	Current in Pers. & Arab. Gulfs.
9	New Ekairee Pagoda	52.85	84.—	44.39	404.390	7.85	Cur. in the Mysore and Carnatic.
10	Old Do. .... do. ..	52.62	84.38	44.40	404.452	7.86	Nearly out of circulation.
11	Bhol Do. .... do. ..	52.69	84.50	44.52	405.50	7.79	Curr. in the S. Mahratta country.
12	Bhoolpuddee do. ..	52.77	85.—	44.85	408.585	7.93	Nearly the same coin as the last.
13	Bahandry .. do. ..	52.72	84.50	44.54	405.768	7.88	Struck by Hyder Ally.
14	Funokee .... do. ..	52.80	84.63	44.68	407.037	7.91	Struck by the Sultan.
15	Guddapuddee do. ..	50.97	76.38	38.93	354.625	6.89	These five coins, as well as the
16	Fudduck ....do. ..	50.77	76.38	38.77	353.234	6.86	six preceding ones, are re-
17	Kudvanajee ..do. ..	50.75	76.38	38.76	353.095	6.86	ceived at the Poona trea-
18	Hallee Sicca ..do. ..	50.90	76.38	38.87	354.139	6.88	sury at a variable rate of ex-
19	Modapuddee ..do. ..	50.55	75.25	38.038	346.500	6.73	change.
20	Rajaram Ekaire do. ..	52.80	84.13	44.42	404.632	7.86	
21	Bhatoree ....do. ..	50.50	75.—	37.87	345.003	6.70	Of limited circulation.
22	Tomancien ..do. ½ ..	26.12	84.63	22.105	201.359	3.91	
23	Bangaloree ..do. ..	52.82	84.25	44.50	405.363	7.87	Struck by Hyder Ally.
24	Mahomed Shaie do. ..	51.50	78.75	40.55	369.431	7.17	
25	Ventrataputkee do. ..	51.50	76.38	39.33	358.313	7.04	Of limited circulation.
26	Herponhilee ..do. ..	50.75	77.50	39.33	358.272	7.61	
27	Pavan Tharokee do. ..	52.89	84.38	44.62	406.496	7.89	
28	Nakar Tharokee do. ..	52.90	85.13	45.03	410.186	7.97	
29	Garava Tharokee do. ..	53.85	85.25	45.18	411.543	7.99	
30	Bhut Padee .. do. ..	52.90	84.75	44.83	408.355	7.93	Current in the Southern Mahratta country.
31	Baha Tapee ..do. ..	54.—	84.75	45.76	416.853	8.09	
32	Joona Elaye ..do. ..	52.50	84.38	44.29	403.500	7.84	
33	Navee Ekee ..do. ..	53.—	84.50	44.78	407.92	7.92	
34	Centeroy Fanams ..	5.82	59.—	3.43	31.278	0.61	
35	Sultana Fanams ..	5.87	58.—	3.40	31.012	0.60	

* The Touch is a decimal notation of the fineness. Thus the Bombay Mohur contains 92 parts of pure gold and 8 of alloy. Hence the Touch, multiplied by the Weight, gives the pure metal. (See p. 67, vol. 1.)

ASSAY REPORT *continued.*

	NAMES OF COINS. SILVER.	ASSAY. Weight. Grs. dec.	Touch. Per Cent dec.	Pure Metal. Grs. dec.	Value of 100 in Bombay Currency.* Rs. dec.	Sterling Value. D. dec.	REMARKS.
36	Bombay Rupee	179.—	92.—	164.68	100.	24.48	Mint Standard.
37	Calcutta do.	191.916	91.66	175.923	106.827	26.15	
38	Madras do.	180.—	91.66	165.—	100.194	24.52	
39	English Crown	436.36	92.5	403.63	245.101	60.00	
40	Spanish Dollar	415.02	89.38	370.95	225.25	55.14	Imported as bullion.
41	German Crown	430.25	83.38	358.74	217.84	53.32	Generally current.
42	Ankosee Rupee	172.50	91.75	158.26	96.105	23.52	Standard coin at Poona, &c. &c.
43	Chandore .. do.	172.25	91.50	157.608	95.705	23.17	Standard coin of Candeish.
44	Thoora .. .. do.	170.—	91.50	155.55	94.425	23.12	Current in Candeish.
45	Jeereeputka .. do.	171.6	91.25	156.58	95.083	23.27	Curr. in the Northern Concan, &c.
46	Belapooree .. do.	171.82	85.—	146.04	88.685	21.71	Curr. at Poona, Ahmednuggur, &c.
47	Batoree .. .. do.	171.3	87.—	149.03	90.495	22.15	Current in the Deccan.
48	Shree Sicca .. do.	172.—	91.50	157.38	95.567	23.40	Coined formerly at Poona.
49	Hallee Sicca .. do.	174.75	96.25	168.19	102.128	24.98	
50	Waubgaum .. do.	172.55	91.50	157.88	95.872	23.46	Coined at Waubgaum.
51	Purkee .. .. do.	178.88	94.25	168.59	102.376	25.06	Current in Candeish.
52	Chambagoondee .. do.	171.—	84.75	144.92	88.—	21.51	Coined as described.
53	Mullarshie do.	172.3	89.—	153.34	93.118	22.79	Do. & curr. in the Dooab & Malwa.
54	Shapooree .. .. do.	174.—	87.—	151.38	91.924	22.50	Coined as described.
55	Kittoor Shapooree do.	174.—	86.25	150.07	91.013	22.30	
56	Ougien, ... do.	173.—	90.25	156.13	94.—	23.20	Do. current throughout Malwa.
57	Indore .. .. do.	174.50	92.50	161.41	98.—	23.99	
58	Govind Buksh .. do.	171.16	78.—	133.50	81.066	19.84	Coined at Aurungabad.
59	Nagpore .. .. do.	166.73	86.5	144.22	87.575	21.43	Coined as described.
60	Broach .. .. do.	177.5	87.62	155.52	94.440	23.12	Current at Broach, Surat, &c.
61	Old Broach .. do.	177.06	94.25	166.88	101.335	24.80	Coined formerly at Broach.
62	Cambay .. .. do.	179.50	81.88	146.97	89.247	21.84	Curr. in Nabob's distr. Kaira, &c.
63	Babasye .. .. do.	177.—	84.88	150.75	91.540	22.40	Coined at Baroda; also current at Kaira.
64	Walkersye .. do.	177.39	87.75	155.65	94.532	24.12	
65	Ashasye .. .. do.	176.50	86.5	152.68	92.705	22.69	
66	Mukunsye .. .. do.	176.62	87.5	154.54	93.842	22.97	
67	Wullubsye .. do.	175.56	85.—	150.07	91.217	22.30	
68	Ahmedabad Sicca do.	179.92	84.—	151.13	91.772	22.46	Coined as described.
69	New do. do. do.	180.75	85.—	153.63	93.292	22.83	Current at Anjar, Cutch, &c.
70	Hallee do. do. do.	174.77	96.25	168.21	102.147	25.00	Coined & only cur. at Ahmedabad.
71	Cutch Kowrie .. do.	72.15	60.75	43.83	26.615	6.51	Coined at Anjar, & cur. in the Cutch
72	Porebunder do. .. do.	74.50	69.75	51.96	31.553	7.72	Coined as described.
73	Persian .. .. do.	159.12	94.50	150.36	91.309	22.35	Imported as bullion, and current in the Persian Gulf.
74	New Persian .. do.	141.3	94.50	133.52	81.083	21.67	

* This column is computed by dividing the number of pure grains in 100 Rupees of any place by the number in one Bombay Rupee. Thus it is found that 100 Rupees of Calcutta are worth 106.827 of Bombay (see No. 37). By a similar operation the Par of Exchange between any other two places in the Table may be determined.

ASSAY REPORT *continued.*

	NAMES OF COINS.	ASSAY.			Value of 100 in Bombay Currency.	Sterling Value. *	REMARKS.
	SILVER CONTINUED.	Weight.	Touch.	Pure Metal.			
		Grs. dec.	per Cent dec.	Grs. dec.	Rs. dec.	D. dec.	
75	Goa Rupee	168.50	86.—	144.91	87.995	21.54	Current in the Persian Gulf, &c.
76	Mysore .. do.	173.56	94.25	163.58	99.390	24.31	Coined formerly at Mysore.
77	Mulkapoor.. .. do.	173.2	71.75	124.27	75.461	18.44	Coined as described.
78	Meritch Hookaree do.	172.6	84.—	144.98	88.039	21.54	Do.
79	Narrainpet .. do.	172.5	80.50	138.86	84.321	20.64	A species of Hydrabad Rupee.
80	Timbourne .. do	171.3	85.50	146.46	88.936	21.77	Coined and circulated as described.
81	Waye Sicca .. do.	171.8	89.50	153.76	92.760	22.85	
82	Jumkundee .. do.	175.—	92.—	161.—	97.765	23.93	
83	Berhanpoore .. do.	178.8	94.75	169.41	102.87	25.19	
84	Phoolsheree .. do.	171.7	91.50	157.10	95.397	23.35	A species of Ankosee Rupee.
85	Pertabghur .. do.	170.40	87.25	148.67	90.278	22.09	
86	Emaumee .. do.	175.—	95.50	167.12	101.484	24.83	Coined as described.
87	Rajah Pondicherry do	176.16	94.75	166.91	101.354	24.81	Formerly struck at the Mysore.
88	Punlee old .. do.	170.60	63.—	107.47	65.264	15.97	Of very little currency.
89	Nepanee Perkanee do.	173.—	75.75	131.—	79.548	19.47	Curr. in district of Padshapoor, &c.
90	Semboo do. do.	172.75	79.75	137.76	83.658	20.47	Curr. in the S. Mahratta country.
91	Moodhole do. do.	173.—	57.50	99.47	60.405	14.78	An old coin of limited circulation.
92	Old Semboo do. do.	174.—	89.75	156.16	94.829	23.2	Do.
93	Toragull Nelkantee do.	170.—	62.—	105.4	64.—	15.66	Do.
94	Tokoshaie .. do.	173.16	94.—	162.77	98.84	24.19	Current in the Ahmednuggur districts.
95	Jyenuggree .. do.	172.68	90.—	155.41	94.37	23.10	
96	Mannashic .. do.	169.50	90.—	152.55	92.634	22.67	
97	Delhi .. .. do.	174.50	97.65	170.57	103.578	25.35	
98	Perkanee Newest do.	177.9	88.75	157.88	95.875	23.46	Coined in the Sawant States.
99	Spanish Indept. Dollar	420.5	89.50	376.34	228.532	55.94	Coined at Chili in 1817.

Bombay Assay Office,
Aug. 4, 1821. (Errors excepted). B. NOTON, ASSAY MASTER.

*** The above Table has been approved and acted upon by Government, and is published with the following additional Signature.

By Order of the Honourable the Governor in Council,

J. FARISH,
SEC. TO GOVERNMENT.

* The sterling value of any Coin is found by multiplying the pure grains, if gold, by 2.1238; and, if silver, by ,14364. The product in either case will be in pence sterling.

EXPOSITION

Of the Weights, Measures, and Monies, of the principal trading Places in India, &c.

Note.—The places already described in this Work are referred to in the Supplement, and are enlarged or corrected where necessary.

*** In the following pages, gr. means Grains Troy, and lb. oz. dr. Pounds, Ounces, and Drams Avoirdupois. Also: throughout the work, 1lb.=7000 gr.; 1 oz.=$437\frac{1}{2}$ gr.; and 1 dr.=$27\frac{11}{32}$ gr. Troy. (See p. 220, vol. 1).

ACHEEN, in Sumatra. See vol. 1, p. 97.

AHMEDABAD,

A City in the province of Gujrat, under the Presidency of Bombay.

For the MONIES of Ahmedabad, see *Assay Report*, No. 68, 69, and 70, p. 330. *

Gold and Silver Weight.

				gr.
		1 Ruttee	=	2.015
3 Ruttees	=	1 Val	=	6.045
32 Vals	=	1 Tola	=	193.440

Commercial Weight.

				lb.	oz.	dr.
		1 Seer	=	1	0	$14\frac{1}{2}$
40 Seers	=	1 Maund	=	42	4	13

The Seer is divided into halves, quarters, eighths, &c.

Long Measure.

	Eng. Inches.
Guz for Cloth	$27\frac{1}{4}$
Ditto for Velvet	$34\frac{1}{4}$
Ditto for Artificers ..	$23\frac{1}{3}$

Grain and liquids in this part of India are sold by weight, and this practice is very general throughout Asia.

AHMEDNUGGUR,

A City in the province of Aurungabad, under the Presidency of Bombay.

For the Monies of Ahmednuggur, see *Assay Report*, No. 94 to 97, p. 333.

Gold and Silver Weight.

				gr.
		1 Gonje	=	1.95
2 Gonjes	=	1 Wall	=	3.9
4 Walls	=	1 Massa	=	15.7
12 Massas	=	1 Tola	=	188.4
24 Tolas	=	1 Seer	=	4521.6

Commercial Weight.

				lb.	oz.	dr.
		1 Chittack	=	0	1	$15\frac{1}{2}$
16 Chittacks	=	1 Seer	=	1	15	8
40 Seers	=	1 Maund	=	78	15	12
3 Maunds	=	1 Pullah	=	236	15	4
20 Maunds	=	1 Candy	=	1577	2	4

Dry Measure.

				lb.	oz.	dr.
18 Tanks	=	1 Pao	=	0	10	13
4 Paos	=	1 Seer	=	2	11	6
2 Seers	=	1 Adholee	=	5	6	12
2 Adholees	=	1 Pylee	=	10	13	8
12 Pylees	=	1 Maund	=	130	2	0
$2\frac{1}{2}$ Maunds	=	1 Pullah	=	325	5	0
8 Pullahs	=	1 Candy	=	2602	8	0

* It should be observed, that in the foregoing Table the Silver Coins are computed at 66d. per oz. the new Mint price in England; whereas, in all other parts of this work, the old price is used, viz. 62d. per oz. (See p. 217, vol. 1). These rates may be converted reciprocally into each other, by the proportion of 31 to 33; and the value of the Indian Coins, at any other price, may be found by the following Rule: *multiply the value in the column by the market price, and divide by the mint price.* Thus, to find the worth of the Bombay Rupee (No. 36) at 60d. per ounce standard, 24,48d.$\times$60$\div$66=$22\frac{1}{4}$d,=the required value.

AHMEDNUGGUR, *continued.*

The Seer of Weight equals 80 Ankosee Rupees, in which there are 73⅓ Tolas, gold weight. (See *Assay Report*, No. 42).

The Seer of Capacity is calculated on the grain called Bajree, of which the Seer weighs 110 Ankosee Rupees.

Oil, sugar, ghee, areca nuts, cocoa nuts, indigo, turmeric, and many other articles, are sold by weight; but there are measures formed for them, which assimilate with the Seer of 80 Rupees.

The Seer of saffron, silk, gold thread, and cochineal, equals 72 Tolas, Goldsmiths' weight = 13550 gr. Troy, or 1 lb. 12 oz. 11 dr. Avoirdupois weight.

Long Measure.

				Eng. Inches.
14 Tussoos	=	1 Hath	=	14
1¾ Hath	=	1 Guz	=	24½

ALLAHABAD, a City in the Province of the same name, under the Presidency of Bengal. See vol. 1, p. 122.

AMBOYNA. See vol. 1, p. 97 and 122.

AMOD, OR AHMOODE,

A Town in the Province of Gujrat, under the Presidency of Bombay.

The Monies of Amod are the same as those of Broach, which see.

Commercial Weights.

				lb.	oz.	dr.
40 Broach Rupees	=	1 Market Seer	=	1	0	3½
40 Seers	=	1 Maund	=	40	8	12
20 Maunds	=	1 Candy	=	810	15	0

For Dry Goods, Kuppas, and Grains.

41 Broach Rps.	=	1 Pergunnah Seer	=	1	0	10
40 Seers	=	1 Maund	=	41	9	5
20 Maunds	=	1 Candy	=	831	10	4

AMOD, *continued.*

Commercial Weights.

For Cotton.

				lb.	oz.	dr.
41 Broach Rupees	=	1 Seer	=	1	0	10
42 Seers	=	1 Maund	=	43	10	10
20 Maunds	=	1 Candy	=	873	4	13

Long Measure or Guz = 27⅛ English Inches.

ANJAR,

A District under the Presidency of Bombay.

For the Monies of this District, see *Assay Report*, No. 69 and 71.

Gold and Silver Weight.

				Gr.
		1 Vall	=	5.6
16 Valls	=	1 Guddiana	=	89.5

Commercial Weight.

				lb.	oz.	dr.
		1 Dokra	=	127.5 gr.		
36 Dokra	=	1 Seer	=	0	10	7¾
10 Seers	=	1 Dus Serrah	=	6	8	14
40 Seers	=	1 Maund	=	27	3	8

Cotton and iron are sold wholesale by the Maund of 48 Seers, which equals 31 lb. 7 oz. 9 dr.

Dry Measure.

				Cubic Inches.
		1 Pallee	=	59.3
8 Pallees	=	1 Mapp	=	474.4
4 Mapps	=	1 Shye	=	1897.6
16 Shyes	=	1 Culsey	=	30361.6 *

Long Measure.

The Guz of 34 Country Inches contains 26.4 English Inches.

* The contents of such Measures of Capacity as are here given in cubic inches, may be determined in gallons, by dividing by 231 for Wine Measure, and 268.8 for Corn Measure. Thus 30361.6 the cubic inches of the Culsey, will be found to equal 131.43 Wine gallons, or 112.9 Corn gallons.

ANJENGO. See vol. 1, p. 98 and 122.

ANKOLA. See *Ahmednuggur*, except for the Seer of Capacity, which is here 4 oz. lighter.

AUMMOODH,

A Pergunnah in the District of Calpee, under the Presidency of Bengal.

		lb.	oz.	dr.
The Seer for cotton	=	1	8	0
The Seer for grain and all other goods		2	0	8

For further particulars, see *Calpee.*

AURUNGABUNDAR. See vol. 1, p. 99 and 122.

AYER BONGHYE, in the Island of Sumatra. See *Natal.*

BAGULKOTA,

A Pettah or small District in the Dooab, under the Presidency of Bombay.

For the Monies of this place, see *Assay Report*, No. 53.

Weights.

The Cutcha Seer is used for groceries, oils, &c. It weighs 20 Madras Rupees, and therefore equals 8 oz. $3\frac{1}{2}$ dr.

Grain is sold by the Pucca Seer, which weighs 133 Madras Rupees, and equals 3 lb. 6 oz. $11\frac{1}{2}$ dr. It measures $116\frac{1}{2}$ Cubic Inches.

Long Measure.

24 Tussoos make 1 Guz. = $32\frac{7}{8}$ English inches.

The Hath, for measuring cloths and turbands, answers to $19\frac{1}{4}$ English Inches.

BAIRSEEAH,

A Town in Central India, under the Presidency of Bengal.

BAIRSEEAH, *continued.*

Weights.

			lb.	oz.	dr.
80 Bhopal Rupees	= 1 Seer	=	1	14	13
5 Seers	= 1 Pusseree	=	9	10	$3\frac{1}{2}$
8 Pusserees	= 1 Maund	=	77	1	12
4 Maunds	= 1 Maunee	=	308	7	0
100 Maunees	= 1 Maniasa	=	30843	12	0

For further particulars, see *Malwa.*

BALLASORE. See vol. 1, p. 122.

BANDA. See vol. 1, p. 99 and 122.

BANJAR MASSIN. See vol. 1, p. 99 and 122.

BANSWARRA. See *Malwa.*

BANTAM. See vol. 1, p. 100, 122, and 124.

BARDOLER,

A District of Surat, under the Presidency of Bombay.

Commercial Weight.

The Maund of Bardoler contains $39\frac{1}{4}$ Seers and 2 Pice of Surat = 37 lb. 4 oz. $4\frac{1}{4}$ dr.

For further particulars, see *Surat*, vol. 1, p. 119 and 123, and also in this Supplement.

BARODA,

A Pergunnah in the District of Broach, under the Presidency of Bombay.

For the Monies, see *Assay Report*, No. 63 to 67.

Commercial Weight.

Pergunnah Seer.

			lb.	oz.	dr.
42 Babashey Rs.	= 1 Pergunnah Seer	=	1	1	2
42 Seers	= 1 Maund	=	44	15	4
20 Maunds	= 1 Candy	=	899	1	0

Town Seer.

			lb.	oz.	dr.
41 Babashey Rupees	= 1 Town Seer	=	1	0	$11\frac{1}{4}$
42 Seers	= 1 Maund	=	43	13	15
20 Maunds	= 1 Candy	=	877	7	0

BARODA, *continued.*

Seer for Sea Samum.

			lb.	oz.	dr.
42 Babashey Rupees	= 1 Seer	=	1	0	15.8
40 Seers	= 1 Maund	=	42	7	10.8
20 Maunds	= 1 Candy	=	849	9	9

The Seer for oil is the Pergunnah weight.

Long Measure.

		Eng. Inches.
24 Tussoos	= 1 Guz.	= $27\frac{1}{8}$

BATAVIA. See vol. 1, p. 100, 122, and 124.

BAULEAH,

Under the Presidency of Bengal.

Commercial Weight.

1 Chittack = $670\frac{3}{4}$ gr. Troy.
16 Chittacks = 1 Seer = 1lb. 8oz. 10dr. Avoir.

Besides the above Seer of 60 Sicca Rupees weight, there is a Seer of 80 Sicca Rupees weight, which equals 2lb. 0 oz. 11 dr.

The Sicca Rupee weight of Bengal is reckoned at $179\frac{2}{3}$ English grains, but it varies two or three grains, more or less. The contents here given are those of the actual weights transmitted.

Measure of Capacity for Liquids.

The Seer of 60 Sicca weight equals 1 lb. 8 oz. 10 dr.

The Cubit is 18 English Inches.

BEEMMAR,

In the District of Calpee, under the Presidency of Bengal.

Weights.

Three different Seers have been received from this place, viz.

		lb.	oz.	dr.
1. Khaus Seer	=	1	7	$2\frac{1}{2}$
2. Omeree Seer	=	1	11	15
3. Channee Seer	=	2	0	10

BEEMMAR, *continued.*

The Long Measure here equals $40\frac{5}{8}$ English Inches.

For further particulars, see *Calpee*.

BELGAM,

A Pettah in the Dooab, under the Presidency of Bombay.

For the Monies of this place, see *Assay Report*, No. 55.

Commercial Weight.

The Cutcha Seer, for weighing oils and groceries, equals $20\frac{1}{4}$ Madras Rupees = 8 oz. 5 dr.

The Pucca Seer for grain, salt, &c. when filled with nine different kinds of grain, equals $106\frac{1}{4}$ Madras Rupees = 2 lb. 11 oz. 8 dr. and measures 93.1 Cubic Inches. See note to *Darwar*.

Long Measure.

	Eng. Inches.
The Guz of 24 Tussoos, for goods not sold by the piece	= $32\frac{7}{8}$
The Hath, for cloths and turbands	= $19\frac{1}{4}$

BENARES,

A City in the Province of Allahabad, under the Presidency of Bengal.

For the Rupee of Benares, see vol. i, p. 88.

Weights.

Three different Seers have been transmitted from this city, viz.

				lb.	oz.	dr.
The Seer of	105	Sicca weight	=	2	10	0
Ditto	103	ditto	=	2	9	2
Ditto	96	ditto	=	2	6	7

The Tola weighs 215 grains.

Long Measure.

		Eng. Inches.
The Tailors' Yard	=	33
The Weavers' ditto	=	$42\frac{1}{2}$
The Cloth Merchants' ditto	=	$37\frac{1}{2}$
The Architects' ditto	=	$25\frac{1}{3}$

BENCOOLEN,

In the Island of Sumatra.

For the mode of keeping Accounts here, and the Commercial Weights, see vol. 1, p. 101.

Gold and Silver Weight.

			oz.	dwt.	gr.
	1 Coondee	=	0	0	1.772
30 Coondees =	1 Keping	=	0	2	5.166
8 Kepings =	1 Ringit	=	0	17	17.333
$1\frac{1}{2}$ Ringit =	1 Tael	=	1	6	14.

Measures of Capacity.

		Cubic Inches.
4 Chupahs =	1 Koolah =	252
800 Koolahs =	1 Coyan =	201600

BENDER ABASSI. See *Gamron*, vol. 1, p. 151.

BENGAL. For the Monies, Weights, and Measures of this Presidency, see the article *Calcutta*, vol. 1, p. 87; and for the Exchanges, see vol. 2, p. 103. See also the *Assay Report* in this Supplement, Nos. 2 and 37.

BETELFAGUI. See vol. 1, p. 40 and 122.

BHEDECK,

A Pergunnah in the District of Calpee, under the Presidency of Bengal.

Weights.

Three Seers have been received from this place, viz.

		lb.	oz.	dr.
The Khaus Seer, for goods in general	=	2	1	15
The Roypore Seer for grain (wholesale)	=	2	8	8
Ditto for grain (retail)	=	2	6	0

The Long Measure = $38\frac{1}{2}$ English Inches.

BHEDH,

A Pergunnah in the District of Calpee, under the Presidency of Bengal.

Weights.

		lb.	oz.	dr.
The Seer (retail)	=	1	14	14
The Seer for grain (wholesale)	=	2	11	3

The Long Measure contains $36\frac{3}{4}$ English Inches.

BHILSA,

A City in Central India, under the Presidency of Bengal.

Coin.

The Bhilsa Rupee is computed here to weigh 167.5 grains. It contains 138.7 grains of pure metal, and is therefore worth about 20d. sterling.

Weights.

			lb.	oz.	dr.
80 Bhilsa Rupees =	1 Seer	=	1	14	10
6 Seers =	1 Pusseree	=	11	7	12
8 Pusserees =	1 Maund	=	91	14	0
30 Pusserees, or $3\frac{3}{4}$ Maunds =	1 Maunee	=	344	8	8
100 Maunees =	1 Maniasa	=	34453	2	0

For dry goods and other articles, the Pusseree consists of 5 Seers only.

For other particulars, see *Malwa*.

BHOOTSUR,

A Pergunnah near Surat, under the Presidency of Bombay.

Weights.

The Maund contains 40 Seers 8 Pice of Surat, and equals 37 lb. 12 oz. Avoirdupois.

Measures.

The only Measure of Capacity is the Pauny Seree of 5 Seers, that is, as much batty or rice in the husk as will, if delivered by weight, amount to

BHOOTSUR, *continued.*

that quantity, and which equals 4 lb. 11 oz. Avoirdupois.

For further particulars, see *Surat,* vol. 1, p. 119 and 123; and also in this Supplement.

BHOPAL,

A City in Malwa, under the Presidency of Bengal.

Coin.

The Rupee weighs 168.75 grains. It contains 150 grains of pure metal, and is worth 21½d. sterling.

Weights.

			lb.	oz.	dr.
80 Bhopal Rupees	= 1 Seer	=	1	14	13¾
6½ Seers	= 1 Pusseree	=	12	8	9
40 Pusserees	= 1 Maunee	=	501	6	8
100 Maunees	= 1 Maniasa	=	50140	10	0

For further information, see *Malwa.*

BIRMAN EMPIRE. See *Rangoon,* vol. 1, p. 115.

BOHARE,

A Pergunnah near Surat, under the Presidency of Bombay.

Weights.

The Maund contains 41½ Seers 4 Pice of Surat, and equals 39 lb. 1 oz. Avoirdupois.

For further particulars, see *Surat.*

BOMBAY.

An Account of the Monies, Weights, and Measures of this Presidency will be found in vol. 1, p. 93 and 122; but as the Dispatches, transmitted with the Standards to the Court of Directors, contain some additional matter, and are in particulars more accurate, their contents are here inserted, with the results of several experiments.

For the Coins of Bombay, &c. see *Assay Report,* p. 331.

Gold and Silver Weight.

			gr.
	1 Wall	=	4.475
40 Walls	= 1 Tola	=	179

Pearl Weight.

			gr.
	1 Tucka	=	0.218
13¾ Tuckas	= 1 Ruttee	=	3
24 Ruttees	= 1 Tank	=	72

For a full account of the Weights and Mode of valuing Pearls, &c. see vol. 1, p. 95.

Commercial Weight.

			lb.	oz.	dr.
	1 Tank	=	0	0	2.488
72 Tanks	= 1 Seer	=	0	11	3.2
40 Seers	= 1 Maund	=	28	0	0

These weights are used for all heavy goods, excepting Salt.

Grain Measure.

			lb.	oz.	dr.
2 Tipprees	= 1 Seer	=	0	11	3.2
4 Seers	= 1 Paily	=	2	12	12.8
7 Pailies	= 1 Parah	=	19	9	9.6
8 Parahs	= 1 Candy	=	156	12	12.8

Batty is reckoned by the Morah of 25 Parahs.

Salt Measure.

			Cubic Inches.
10½ Adowlies	= 1 Parah	=	1607.61
100 Parahs	= 1 Anna	=	160761
16 Annas	= 1 Rash	=	2572176

The Anna weighs 2½ Tons, and the Rash 40 Tons.

BOMBAY, *continued.*

Liquor Measure.

(Spirits and Country Arrack.)

The Seer weighs 60 Bombay Rupees, and equals 1 lb. 8 oz. 8½ dr.; and 50 Seers make the Maund.

Long Measure.

			Eng. Inches.
16 Tussoos	= 1 Hath	=	18
24 Tussoos	= 1 Guz	=	27

All the foregoing Standards are likewise divided into halves, quarters, &c.

The Dispatch, containing the above statements, concludes with the following remark:—

"The preceding Weights and Measures are generally used in Bombay; but it occurs in mercantile transactions, that calculations are made in Pounds, Maunds, and Surat Maunds, which two last weights are sometimes reckoned at 40, 40½, 41, 43¼, and 44 Seers; and sometimes in Surat Candies of 20, 21, and 22 Maunds."

BORNEO. See *Banjar Massin*, vol. 1, p. 99 and 122; and *Succadana*, p. 119.

BOURBON, ISLE OF. See *Mauritius*, vol. 1, p. 110.

BROACH,

A Town and District in the Province of Gujrat, Presidency of Bombay.

For the Monies, &c. see *Assay Report*, p. 330, Nos. 60 and 61.

Commercial Weights.

			lb.	oz.	dr.
40 Broach Rs. Wt.	= 1 Kuppas T. Seer	=	1	0	3½
40 Seers	= 1 Maund	=	40	8	12
20 Maunds	= 1 Candy	=	810	15	0

BROACH, *continued.*

The following Standards are used by Mupparahs, or Grain-Weighers.

			lb.	oz.	dr.
40½ Broach Rupees Wt.	= 1 Seer	=	1	0	5½
40 Seers	= 1 Maund	=	41	1	4
20 Maunds	= 1 Candy	=	821	9	0

Market and Pergunnah Seer for all sorts of Grain, except Sea Samum, which is sold by the Kuppas Town Seer first mentioned.

41 Broach Rupees Wt.	= 1 Seer	=	1	0	10
40 Seers	= 1 Maund	=	41	9	5
20 Maunds	= 1 Candy	=	831	10	14

Market and Pergunnah Seer, used for weighing Cotton only.

41 Broach Rupees Wt.	= 1 Seer	=	1	0	10
42 Seers	= 1 Maund	=	43	10	10
20 Maunds	= 1 Candy	=	873	4	3

Measures of Capacity.

The Seer for Oil and Sea Samum contains 31.87 Cubic Inches, or 0.138 of a Wine Gallon; and is the same as that used at Amod, Dehy, and Jumboosur.

For Castor Oil.

			lb.	oz.	dr.
40 Broach Rupees Wt.	= 1 Seer	=	1	0	3½
42 Seers	= 1 Maund	=	42	9	9½
20 Maunds	= 1 Candy	=	852	0	0

This Seer contains 33.03 Cubic Inches, or 0.143 of a Wine Gallon.

Long Measure.

			Eng. Inches.
24 Tussoos	= 1 Broach Zillah Guz	=	27¼

Another standard of Long Measure has been received from this district, called the Wusa, which contains 89.6 English Inches, and which is very extensively used in India in the measurement of land.

			Eng. Inches.
	1 Wiswusa	=	4.48
20 Wiswusas	= 1 Wusa	=	89.6
20 Square Wusas	= 1 Beega	=	2 Roods 2 Perch.

BUGWARA,

A Pergunnah near Surat, under the Presidency of Bombay.

Weights.

The Maund contains 38¾ Seers 6 Pice of Surat, and equals 36 lb. 8 oz. 5 dr.

The Pauny Seree of 5 Seers weight of batty or rice in the husk, contains 4 lb. 11 oz. Avoirdupois.

For other particulars, see *Surat*.

BULSAR,

A Pergunnah near Surat, under the Presidency of Bombay.

Weights.

The Maund contains 40½ Surat Seers, and equals 37 lb. 15 oz. 8 dr.

The Pauny Seree is the same as that used at Bugwara, which see, as also *Surat*.

BURGONG,

A Pergunnah in the District of Calpee, under the Presidency of Bengal.

Weights.

		lb.	oz.	dr.
The Seer for goods in general	=	2	10	4
The Seer for grain	=	1	12	3

The *Long Measure*, called Guz, contains 42 English Inches.

BUSHIRE, IN PERSIA.

The following Weights and Measures were transmitted to the Court of Directors in 1822, by the Company's Resident at Bushire. The largest weight is the Maund Tabruze, which contains 720 Miscals, and has been found to weigh 53784 Troy Grains, or 7 lb. 10 oz. 15 dr. Avoirdupois. Hence the Miscal answers to 74.7 Troy Grains.

The Miscal (in some places called the Metical) is used in several countries, both in Asia and Africa, and varies from 72 to 75 English Grains. See vol. 2, p. 222.

The Maund Tabruze is divided into halves, quarters, eighths, and sixteenths; but the divisions which have been received do not all answer to their due proportions.

The Long Measures are the Half Guz Shaw, which equals 20 English Inches; and the Half Guz Shaw Bushire, which equals 18.4 English Inches. Thus 23 of the former = 25 of the latter.

BUSSORAH, IN ARABIA,

Has been already described in vol. 1, under the head *Bassora*; but the following information has been recently received from that place by the Court of Directors, and should therefore be given, as containing some additional matter.

Commercial Weight.

		lb.	oz.
1 Vakia	=	4	13⅓
24 Vakias = 1 Bussorah Maund	=	116	0

There is a smaller or *Attary* Maund, for the sale of indigo, spices, &c. which is reckoned at 28 lb. Avoirdupois, and is thus divided:

		lb.	oz.
1 Vakia	=	1	2⅔
24 Vakias = 1 Maund Attary	=	28	0

Long Measures.

Silks and Woollens are measured by the Aleppo Yard, which equals 26½ English Inches.

Cottons and linens are measured by the Hadeed, which contains 34⅕ English Inches.

The Bagdad Yard is also used for both purposes, and measures 31⅝ English Inches.

Articles usually measured by a standard of Capacity are here sold by weight.

CACHAO. See vol. 1, p. 102.

CALCUTTA. For the Monies, Weights, and Measures of this Presidency, see vol. 1, p. 87 and 122; and for the Exchanges, see vol. 2, p. 103. See also *Assay Report* in this Supplement, No. 2 and 37.

CALICUT. See vol. 1, p. 102 and 122.

CALPAR,

A Pergunnah near Surat, under the Presidency of Bombay.

Weights.

The Maund contains 39¼ Seers 2 Pice of Surat, and equals 37 lb. 5 oz. 4 dr.

The other Weights and Measures are the same as those of Surat.

CALPEE,

A Town and District in the Province of Agra, under the Presidency of Bengal.

General Division of Weights.

16 Chittacks = 1 Seer
40 Seers = 1 Maund

	lb.	oz.	dr.
The Seer for sugar, metals, and grain =	2	1	15
for ghee =	2	6	3
for cotton =	2	6	12
for grain wholesale =	2	7	5

Long Measure.

		Eng. Inches.
4 Paueens	= 1 Girrah	= 2½
16 Girrahs	= 1 Guz	= 40

CAMBAY. See vol. 1, p. 103 and 122.

CAMBODIA. See vol. 1, p. 103.

CANANOR. See *Tellicherry*, vol. 1, p. 120.

CANCAO. See vol. 1, p. 103.

CANTON. See *China*, vol. 1, p. 66.

CARWAR. See vol. 1, p. 103 and 122.

CELEBES, ISLE OF. See *Macassar*, vol. 1, p. 107 and 123.

CEYLON, ISLE OF. See vol. 1, p. 104, 105, and 122.

CHANADORE,

A District within the Collectorship of Ahmednuggur, under the Presidency of Bombay.

Commercial Weight.

The Seer weighs 74 Ankosee Rupees and 10 Massas, and equals 1 lb. 13 oz. 8 dr.

Measure of Capacity.

The Seer weighs 95 Ankosee Rupees, and its divisions and multiples are as follow:—

			lb.	oz.	dr.
18 Tanks	= 1 Pao Seer	=	0	9	5½
4 Pao Seers	= 1 Seer	=	2	5	7
2 Seers	= 1 Adholee	=	4	10	14
2 Adholees	= 1 Pylee	=	9	5	13
16 Pylees	= 1 Maund	=	149	13	7
20 Maunds	= 1 Candy	=	2996	12	12

For other particulars, see *Ahmednuggur*.

CHINA. See vol. 1, p. 66 and 122; and also *Fort Marlborough* in this Supplement.

COCHIN. See vol. 1, p. 104 and 122.

COCHIN CHINA. See *Faifoe*, vol. 1, p. 105.

COLOMBO. See vol. 1, p. 105 and 122.

COMMERCOLLY,

In the District of Rajishy, under the Presidency of Bengal.

Weights.

Four different Seers have been transmitted from this Presidency, viz.

			lb.	oz.	dr.
The Seer for brass, copper, &c. of	58 Sicca Weight	=	1	7	9
The Seer of	60 ditto	=	1	8	8
The Seer, Factory Wt.	72 11 An. 7 Pi.	=	1	13	13
The Seer of	78 ditto	=	1	15	12

The above are the actual contents of the Seers received in London, which are lighter than the estimated weight by Rupees. Thus the first is $3\frac{1}{2}$, the second 2, the third $\frac{3}{4}$, and the fourth 3 Drams lighter.

Measures of Capacity.

The Rattan Seer, Dry Measure, and the Bamboo Chungah, Liquid Measure, should each weigh 60 Sicca Weight as above, and contain about $\frac{1}{5}$ of a Wine Gallon.

The *Long Measures* contain, one 24 and another 18 English Inches.

COOLPAHAR,

A Pergunnah in the District of Calpee, under the Presidency of Bengal.

		lb.	oz.	dr.
The Seer equals		3	1	$6\frac{1}{4}$
The Grain Measure weighs 2 Seers 15 Chittacks	=	5	15	$11\frac{1}{2}$

COSSIMBAZAR,

A Town in the Province of Bengal.

The following are the contents of the Weights received from this place:—

COSSIMBAZAR, *continued.*

			lb.	oz.	dr.
The Seer of 76 Sicca Weight		=	1	15	$1\frac{1}{2}$
78	ditto	=	1	15	$14\frac{1}{2}$
80	ditto	=	2	0	12
82 10 An.		=	2	1	14

The actual weight of the several Seers above stated is less than the estimated weight by Rupees. Thus the first three are each $1\frac{1}{2}$ Dram lighter, and the last Seer about $\frac{3}{4}$ of a Dram.

The *Liquid Measure* weighs 1 Seer of 80 Sicca weight, as above.

The *Long Measure*, called the Haut, = $19\frac{1}{8}$ English Inches.

DACCA, a city under the Presidency of Bengal. See vol. 1, p. 122.

DARWAR,

A Pettah in the Dooab, under the Presidency of Bombay.

The New Rupee of the Madras mint (for which see *Assay Report*, No. 38) is taken as the standard.

6 Shabee Pice on an average equal 5 Madras Rupees. Hence the Pice weighs 150 Troy Grains.

Commercial Weight.

The Cutcha Seer for weighing Oil and Spices, equals 20 Madras Rupees = 8 oz. $3\frac{1}{2}$ dr. It is divided into 72 Tanks, each containing 50 Grains Troy.

Grain and Salt Measure.

The Pucka Seer (sometimes called Pao) equals 116 Madras Rupees, when filled with nine kinds of grain mixed together. It weighs 2 lb. 15 oz. $11\frac{1}{2}$ dr.; and measures 101 Cubic Inches.*

4 Pucka Seers = 1 Pylee or Chittee = 11 lb. 14 oz. 14 dr.

* The nine kinds of Grain usually mixed together in this part of India, in order to ascertain the weight of the Seer of Capacity, are Wheat, Toor, Hurburr, Roolthee, Moony, Gored, Joowaree, Paddy, and Mudkee.

DARWAR, *continued.*

Liquid Measure.

4 Dhurra = 1 Mun
20 Muns = 1 Randy.

The Dhurra generally contains 12 Seers, but varies from 10 to 14.

Long Measure.

	Eng. Inches.
The Hath for Turbands and other Cotton Cloths	= 19⅞
The Guz for Broad Cloth, Chintz, &c.	= 32¼

DECKAN POONA,

A City in the Southern Mahratta Country, under the Presidency of Bombay.

For the different Rupees of this place, see *Assay Report*, Nos. 42, 46, 48, and 49.

Goldsmiths' Weight.

			Gr.
2 Whats	= 1 Goonj	=	1.995
2 Goonjees	= 1 Wall	=	3.99
4 Walls	= 1 Massa	=	15.97
12 Massas	= 1 Tolla	=	191.66
24 Tollas	= 1 Seer	=	4600.

Commercial Weight.

The Seer contains 72 Tanks or Tollas, and equals 80 Ankosee Rupees, or 1 lb. 15 oz. 8½ dr.

By this Seer articles of high price, such as silk, saffron, gold-thread, cochineal, spices, &c. are sold.

Ghee, areca-nuts, turmerick, cocoa-nuts, dates, &c. are sold by the Maund of 12½ Seers = 24 lb. 10 oz. 4½ dr.

Copper, brass, tin, pewter, and bell-metal are sold by the Maund of 14 Seers = 27 lb. 9 oz. 9⅔ dr.

Iron, lead, tobacco, salt-petre, brimstone, oil, and some other articles, are sold by the Pullah of 120 Seers = 236 lb. 9 oz. 2 dr.

Vegetables and fruits are sold by the Maund of

DECKAN POONA, *continued.*

40 Seers; and choonam, charcoal, &c. by the Candy of 20 Maunds. The Dhurra is composed of 10 Seers = 19 lb. 11 oz. 6½ dr.

Two other Weights are also used here, viz. the Kucha Punchseery of 2½ Seers, and the Punchseery of 5 Seers.

Dry Measure.

			lb.	oz.	dr.
2 Adpaos or Rolhas	= 1 Pao Seer or Chipta	=	0	7	14
2 Pao Seers	= 1 Adseer or Ashwa	=	0	15	12
2 Adseers	= 1 Seer or Chathwa	=	1	15	8½
2 Seers	= 1 Adholee	=	3	15	1
2 Adholees	= 1 Pylee	=	7	14	2
12 Pylees	= 1 Maund	=	94	9	8
2½ Maunds	= 1 Pullah	=	236	7	12
20 Maunds	= 1 Candy	=	1891	14	0

The Maund is sometimes reckoned at 16 Pylees = 126 lb. 2 oz. Avoirdupois.

There is also another Pullah of 120 Seers = 365 lb. 2 oz. 4 dr.

DEWASS,

A Town in the Province of Malwa, under the Presidency of Bengal.

For the value of the Ougein Rupee, which is current here, see *Assay Report*, No. 56.

Weights.

			lb.	oz.	dr.
80 Ougein Rupees	= 1 Seer	=	1	15	10
4⅛ Seers	= 1 Dhurree	=	8	2	7
16⅔ Seers	= 1 Maund	=	137	8	2
12 Maunds	= 1 Maunee	=	1650	1	8

For further particulars, see *Malwa*.

DINDORE,

A District within the Collectorship of Ahmednuggur, under the Presidency of Bombay.

DINDORE, *continued.*

Weights.

The Seer is divided as at Ahmednuggur, but weighs 76 Ankosee Rupees = 1 lb. 13 oz. 15 dr.

Measures of Capacity.

The Seer of Capacity weighs 100 Ankosee Rupees, and is divided as follows, the Tank being 239½ Grains.

				lb.	oz.	dr.
18 Tanks	=	1 Pao Seer	=	0	9	13⅔
4 Pao Seers	=	1 Seer	=	2	7	6½
2 Seers	=	1 Adholee	=	4	14	13
2 Adholees	=	1 Pylee	=	9	13	10
16 Pylees	=	1 Maund	=	157	10	0
20 Maunds	=	1 Candy	=	3152	8	0

For further particulars, see *Ahmednuggur.*

DOONGURPOOR,

The Capital of a small Principality, in the Province of Gujrat, under the Presidency of Bombay.

The Salim Shye Rupee is computed to weigh 168.75 grains, but accounts differ as to its fineness.

Weights.

				lb.	oz.	dr.
52 Salim Shye Rupees	=	1 Seer	=	1	4	0¾
10 Seers	=	1 Dhurree	=	12	8	7½
40 Seers	=	1 Maund	=	501	2	12
12 Maunds	=	1 Maunee	=	6014	1	0

For further particulars, see *Malwa.*

ESSLAMPORE,

A Pergunnah in the District of Calpee, under the Presidency of Bengal.

Two Seers have been received from this place, which weigh 2 lb. 0 oz. 12 dr. and 2 lb. 3 oz. 15 dr.

ETAWAH, a town in the Province of Agra, under the Presidency of Bengal. See *Calpee.*

FAIFOE. See vol. 1, p. 105.

FORT MARLBOROUGH,

In the Island of Sumatra.

Statements of the Monies, Weights, and Measures, of different parts of Sumatra, are given in vol. 1, with references to each place, p. 119; but the following additional matter, which has been lately transmitted to the Court of Directors, will be also found useful.

Gold and Silver Weight.

				gr.
		1 Coondee	=	1.7722
30 Coondees	=	1 Keping	=	53.166
8 Kepings	=	1 Ringit	=	425.33
1½ Ringit	=	1 Tael	=	638.

The following Weights are used at Moco Moca, and occasionally at Fort Marlborough.

				gr.
		1 Koopang	=	9.967
4 Koopang or Soocoo	=	1 Mas	=	39.875
4 Mas	=	1 Pauh	=	159.5
2⅔ Pauh	=	1 Ringit	=	425.33
1½ Ringit	=	1 Tael	=	638.
16 Taels or 24 Ringits	=	1 Catty	=	10208 =

1 lb. 9 oz. 5 dwt. 8 gr. Troy, or 1 lb. 7 oz. 5 dr. Avoirdupois.

Black pepper is invariably weighed by English standard Weights.

Measures of Capacity.

				Cubic Inches.
		1 Chupah	=	63
4 Chupahs	=	1 Koolah	=	252
800 Koolahs	=	1 Coyan	=	201600

The Koolah for measuring paddy, rice, and peas, is struck; but it is hepead when measuring white pepper, coffee, baked rice, Indian corn, &c.

The Koolah of Malay rice weighs about 7 lb; that of Bengal rice and that of oil, nearly 8 lb. The Koolah of rice is occasionally used as a

FORT MARLBOROUGH, *continued.*

weight; and in this case 17 Koolahs constitute the Pecul of 133⅓ lb. Avoirdupois. The Koolah used in the interior districts is about half the size of that now under consideration.

The Coodee or Corge of tobacco consists of 40 Baskets—of every other article of 20.

Long Measures.

				Eng. Inches.
		1 Tempoh	=	4.5
2 Tempohs	=	1 Jankal	=	9
2 Jankals or Spans	=	1 Esto	=	18
2 Estos or Cubits	=	1 Hailoh	=	36
2 Hailohs	=	1 Depoh	=	72

The Fathom of 6 feet has been established as a Standard of Measure in all places here, under the immediate influence of British authority.

Chinese Weights and Measures used at Fort Marlborough.

Gold Weight.

The Gold Catty is the same as that before referred to, which equals about 1 lb. 7 oz. 5⅓ dr.

Commercial Weight.

The Tael equals 1⅓ oz. Avoirdupois, or 575.625 Grains Troy; and is divided into 10 Chehs, 100 Hoons, 1000 Lees, 10,000 Sees, or 100,000 Hoots.

				lb. Avoirdupois.
16 Taels	=	1 Catty	=	1⅓
100 Catties	=	1 Pecul	=	133⅓

See vol. 1, page 67.

Long Measure.

				Eng. Inches
		1 Hoon	=	0.144
10 Hoons	=	1 Choon	=	1.44
10 Choons	=	1 Cheoh	=	14.4
5 Cheohs	=	1 Gocheoh	=	72
2 Gocheohs or Pointungs	=	1 Tung	=	144

FURRUCKABAD,

A Town and District in the Province of Agra, under the Presidency of Bengal.

The Rupee here weighs 173 Grains, and contains 165.22 Grains of pure metal. It is therefore worth 24½d. sterling, at the new Mint price. See vol. 1, p. 88.

Weights.

			lb.	oz.	dr.
Wholesale Seer of 11	Furrd. Sicca Wt.	=	0	4	5¾
Retail Seer of 14	ditto	=	0	5	8¼
Spice Seer of 82	ditto	=	2	0	7

The Weight of the above Spice Seer has been found 1 Dram heavier than the estimated weight by Rupees.

GAMRON. See vol. 1, p. 122 and 151.

GHOUHOWN,

A Pergunnah in the District of Calpee, under the Presidency of Bengal.

Weights.

		lb.	oz.	dr.
The Seer (wholesale)	=	2	2	0
The Seer (retail)	=	2	4	12¼

GHROWLLE,

A Pergunnah in the District of Calpee, under the Presidency of Bengal.

Weights.

The Seer equals 1 lb. 15 oz. 0¾ dr.

The Grain Measure contains 1 Seer 5 Chittacks = 2 lb. 8 oz. 12 dr.

The Guz measures 39¼ English Inches.

GOA. See vol. 1, p. 106 and 122; and also *Assay Report*, No. 75.

HANSOOT,

A Town in the District of Broach, under the Presidency of Bombay.

For the Monies, see *Assay Report*, Nos. 60 and 61.

Weights.

Market Seer.

		lb.	oz.	dr.
38 Broach Rupees Wt.	=1 Seer =	0	15	7
40 Seers	=1 Maund =	38	9	9
20 Maunds	=1 Candy =	771	15	4

Pergunnah Seer.

		lb.	oz.	dr.
38½ Broach Rupees Wt.	=1 Seer =	0	15	11
40 Seers	=1 Maund =	39	3	10
20 Maunds	=1 Candy =	784	8	8

The Pergunnah Seer, as above stated, is 1 Dram heavier than the estimated weight by Rupees.

Oil Measure.

		lb.	oz.	dr.	
38 Broach Rs. Wt.	=1 Seer =	0	15	7	= 31½ Cubic Inches.
42 Seers	=1 Maund =	40	8	6	
20 Maunds	=1 Candy =	810	7	8	

Sea Samum is weighed by the Market Seer.

Long Measure.

24 Tussoos = 1 Guz = 27⅛ English Inches.

HAVERY,

A Pettah in the Dooab, under the Presidency of Bombay.

Weights.

The Cutcha Seer for weighing ghee, tamarinds, pepper, &c. contains,

		oz.	dr.
In buying, 23¼ Madras Rupees Wt.	=	9	9
In selling, 20⅛ ditto	=	8	4½

The Dhurra for buying is 12⅞ Seers; and for selling, 12 Seers.

HAVERY, *continued.*

The Pucca Seer for grain, salt, &c. contains 82 Cubic Inches; and when filled with nine kinds of grain, mixed together, weighs 94½ Madras Rupees, or 2 lb. 6 oz. 13 dr. *See the note to Darwar.*

The Long Measure is the Guz of 24 Tussoos, which equals 34¾ English Inches.

HOOGHLEY.

See vol. 1, p. 123.

HUMMERPORE,

A Pergunnah in the District of Calpee, under the Presidency of Bengal.

Weights.

The Seer contains 2 lb. 0 oz. 7¾ dr.

The Guz equals 39 English Inches.

HURRUPAUL,

Under the Presidency of Bengal.

The Bazar Seer of 60 Sicca weight has been found to weigh 1 lb. 8 oz. 8¼ dr. which is nearly 2 drams lighter than the estimated weight by Rupees.

The Pao, Dry Measure, contains 31 Sicca weight 14 Annas, and equals 13 oz. nearly.

Liquids are sold by the Seer of 60 Sicca weight, which should equal 1 lb. 8 oz. 10 dr.

HUTARGAM,

A Pergunnah near Surat, under the Presidency of Bombay.

The Maund contains 40 Seers 8 Pice of Surat, and equals 37 lb. 13 oz. 10 dr.

For further particulars, see *Surat*.

INDORE,

A City in the Province of Malwa, under the Presidency of Bengal.

INDORE, *continued.*

For the Monies of Indore, see *Assay Report*, Nos. 56 and 57.

Weights.

			lb.	oz.	dr.
82 Ougien Rups.	= 1 Seer	=	2	0	$6\frac{3}{4}$
5 Seers	= { 1 Pusseree or Dhurree }	=	10	2	$1\frac{1}{4}$
20 Seers	= 1 Maund	=	40	8	6
12 Maunds	= 1 Maunee	=	486	4	8

The above Pusseree is called the Small or Kuranah (Dry Goods) Pusseree, by which every thing is sold in the Bazar; but the Bunniah (Retail Merchant) purchases grain by a larger or Grain Pusseree, which equals 10 lb. 4 oz. 11 dr. The Maund for Grain consists only of 20 Seers; but the Maund for Kuranah, as opium, ghee, spices, oil, and the like, is 40 Seers.

For further information, see *Malwa*.

JAMKHAIR,

A District within the Collectorship of Ahmednuggur, under the Presidency of Bombay.

Commercial Weight.

The Seer weighs 80 Ankosee Rupees, and equals 1 lb. 15 oz. $8\frac{1}{2}$ dr.

Measure of Capacity.

The Seer weighs $93\frac{1}{2}$ Ankosee Rupees and $1\frac{1}{4}$ Massa. Its divisions and multiples are as follow:

			lb.	oz.	dr.
18 Tanks	= 1 Pao Seer	=	0	9	$3\frac{1}{2}$
4 Pao Seers	= 1 Seer	=	2	4	$14\frac{1}{2}$
2 Seers	= 1 Adholee	=	4	9	13
2 Adholees	= 1 Pylee	=	9	3	10
16 Pylees	= 1 Maund	=	147	10	0
20 Maunds	= 1 Candy	=	2952	8	0

For other particulars, see *Ahmednuggur*.

JAPAN. See vol. 1, p. 196.

JAVA. See *Bantam* and *Batavia*, vol. 1, p. 100, 122, and 124.

JUMBOOSUR,

A Town in the Province of Gujrat, and District of Broach, under the Presidency of Bombay.

Commercial Weight.

Market Seer.

			lb.	oz.	dr.
40 Broach Rupees Wt.	= 1 Seer	=	1	0	$2\frac{1}{2}$
40 Seers	= 1 Maund	=	40	6	4
20 Maunds	= 1 Candy	=	807	3	0

The above Seer has been found 1 Dram lighter than the estimated weight by Rupees; and the following Seer has been found $\frac{1}{4}$ of a Dram heavier.

Pergunnah Seer for Dry Goods.

			lb.	oz.	dr.
$40\frac{1}{4}$ Broach Rupees Wt.	= 1 Seer	=	1	0	9
40 Seers	= 1 Maund	=	41	6	8
20 Maunds	= 1 Candy	=	828	2	0

In weighing cotton the Market Seer is used, 42 of which are reckoned to the Maund.

Long Measure.

24 Tussoos = 1 Guz = $27\frac{1}{8}$ English Inches.

For Measures of Capacity, see *Broach*.

JUNGYPORE,

A Town in the Province and under the Presidency of Bengal.

The Seer, which is divided into 16 Chittacks, = 1 lb. 8 oz. $0\frac{1}{2}$ dr.

The Seer, Liquid Measure, contains $50\frac{1}{2}$ Cubit Inches.

The Cubit measures 18 English Inches.

JUNKCEYLON. See vol. 1, p. 106 and 123.

KAIRA,

A District under the Presidency of Bombay.

For the Rupees, see Remarks on *Assay Report*, Nos. 62 to 67.

Two standards only have been received from this place, viz. the Seer and the Guz. The former weighs 1 lb. 0 oz. 15½ dr.; and the latter measures 27¼ English Inches.

KATEE,

A District within the Collectorship of Ahmednuggur, under the Presidency of Bombay.

	lb.	oz.	dr.
The Seer weighs 80 Ankosee Rupees =	1	15	8½
The Seer of Capacity = 95 ditto =	2	5	8

For further particulars, see *Ahmednuggur*.

KOOMBHAREEA,

A Pergunnah near Surat, under the Presidency of Bombay.

The Maund contains 40 Seers 8 Pice of Surat = 37 lb. 13 oz. 10 dr. See *Surat*.

KOTAH,

A City in Malwa, under the Presidency of Bengal.

The Kotah Rupee weighs 174.8 grains, and contains 159.7 grains of pure metal. It is therefore worth 23d. sterling.

Weights.

			lb.	oz.	dr.
30 Kotah Rupees	= 1 Seer	=	0	12	0
5 Seers	= 1 Dhurree	=	3	12	0
40 Seers	= 1 Maund	=	30	0	0
12 Maunds	= 1 Maunee	=	360	0	0

Measures.

48 Pice	= 1 Pye	=	1	14	5½
18 Pye	= 1 Seyn	=	34	2	3
20 Seyn	= 1 Maunee	=	682	11	12

KOTAH, *continued.*

The Kotah Pice, on which this is founded, weighs 18 Massah, or 276.6 Grains.

For other particulars, see *Malwa*.

KOTOOL,

A District within the Collectorship of Ahmednuggur, under the Presidency of Bombay.

The Seer of Capacity weighs 100 Ankosee Rupees = 2 lb. 7 oz. 6½ dr.

The other Weights and Measures are the same as at Ahmednuggur.

KURDAH,

A Town in the Province of Gujrat, under the Presidency of Bombay.

	lb.	oz.	dr.
The Seer weighs 80 Ankosee Rupees =	1	15	8½
The Seer of Capacity 90 ditto =	2	3	7½

For the rest, see *Ahmednuggur*.

KURMULLA,

A District within the Collectorship of Ahmednuggur, under the Presidency of Bombay.

The Seer of Capacity weighs 100 Ankosee Rupees = 2 lb. 7 oz. 6½ dr.

For other particulars, see *Ahmednuggur*.

KUROD,

A Pergunnah near Surat, under the Presidency of Bombay.

The Maund contains 40½ Surat Seers = 37 lb. 15 oz. 8½ dr. See *Surat*.

LUCKIPORE,

A Town in the Province of Bengal.

The following are the actual contents of 4 Seers which have been received from this settlement:—

LUCKIPORE, *continued.*

	An. Pi.		lb.	oz.	dr.
Factory Seer of 72	11 7	Sicca Wt.	=1	14	2½
Seer of 80			=2	1	1
Seer of 82			=2	1	13
Bazar Seer of 82	10		=2	1	14

The last of these Seers agrees very nearly with the estimated weight by Rupees. The first is 4¼ dr. heavier; the second, 3½; and the third, 2¼ dr.

Cloth Measure.

	Eng. Inches.
The Cubit for measuring brown cloth	=19
Ditto washed cloth	=18

LUCKNOW,

A City in the Province of Oude, under the Presidency of Bengal.

Accounts are kept in Rupees. 93 Sicca Rupees, 13 Annas, 6 Pice=100 Lucknose. Thus the Rupee of Lucknow weighs 168.6 grains.

The Seer weighs 2 lb. 7 oz. 6¼ dr.

MACASSAR. See vol. 1, p. 107 and 123.

MADRAS. For the Monies, Weights, and Measures of this Presidency, see vol. 1, p. 90 and 123; for the Exchanges, see vol. 2, p. 103. See also *Assay Report* in this Supplement, Nos. 3 and 38.

MAGINDANAO. See vol. 1, p. 107.

MALACCA. See vol. 1, p. 108 and 123.

MALDA,

A Town in the Province, and under the Presidency of Bengal.

The Standards received from this place are,

			lb.	oz.	dr.
Seer of 100 Sicca Wt.	used at	Malda	=2	9	0
Ditto 96		Mogulbarry	=2	7	5¼
Ditto 82 10 An.		Jellalpore	=2	1	14
Ditto 80		EnglishBazar	=2	0	14¼

MALDA, *continued.*

The three first of the above Seers are each 1 Dram lighter than the estimated weight by Rupees, and the fourth is ½ Dram heavier. Each Seer is divided into 16 for Chittacks, and multiplied by 40 for the Maund.

The Seers of Capacity received, measure,

	Cubic Inches.
Seer of Malda	= 72
Ditto Mogulbarry	= 69.7
Ditto Jellalpore	= 57.7
Ditto English Bazar	= 60

MALDIVE ISLANDS. See vol. 1, p. 108.

MALWA,

An extensive Territory of Central India, under the Presidency of Bengal.

Accounts are kept here in Current Rupees, Annas, and Pice.

In the inferior departments of business each Pice is subdivided into 2 Adillahs, 4 Chedaums, 8 Dumries, 4 Gundas, and 96 Cowries. All these divisions are imaginary Monies, except the Cowries or Shells; for a description of which see the places referred to in the Index, vol. 2, p. 275.

The Silver Rupee varies both in its weight and fineness in the several mints of Malwa; and as the Seer is reckoned to weigh a certain number of the Rupees of the place, the Commercial Weights of Central India are various, as will be stated under different heads in this Supplement.

The only uniform weight in this territory is that for the precious metals, which is reckoned as follows:—

Gold and Silver Weight.

			Gr.
	1 Chawl	=	0.247
8 Chawls	= 1 Ruttee	=	1.979
8 Ruttees	= 1 Massa	=	15.833
12 Massas	= 1 Tolah	=	190.

MALWA, *continued.*

Commercial Weight.

			lb.	oz.	dr.
84 Salim Shye Rupees	=1 Seer	=	2	0	6
5 Seers	=1 Dhurree	=	10	1	14
20 Seers	=1 Maund	=	40	7	8
12 Maunds	=1 Maunee	=	485	10	0

The above is the *Banswarra Weight*, which is extensively known in Malwa; but many other kinds are also used there, as will be shewn in their proper places.

Long Measure.

The *Guz* is the most common measure of length: in some places it equals 28 English Inches, and in others 32 Inches.

The *Wussa* is in general use here, particularly for measuring land; and it answers to 7 Feet 5⅗ Inches, English.

MALWA, *continued.*

Land and Road Measures.

The *Beega*, or Indian Acre, contains 20 Square Wusas, or 60 Square Guz, and therefore varies as follows:—

		A.	R.	P.	
20 Wusas squared	=	0	2	2	English
60 Guz ditto, at 28 Inches	=	0	1	29	
Ditto at 32 ditto	=	0	2	17	

The *Cos*, or Indian Mile, varies here from 1½ to 2 English Miles. *

MANGALORE. See vol. 1, p. 108 and 123.

MANILLA. See vol. 1, p. 109.

MASULIPATAM. See vol. 1, p. 109 and 123.

MAURITIUS. See vol. 1, p. 110.

MERGUI. See *Rangoon*, vol. 1, p. 115.

* As Malwa has but recently become subject to the East India Company, no account of its Metrology has been yet transmitted to the Court of Directors, in answer to their Circular of 1821. This want, however, has been in a great measure supplied by SIR JOHN MALCOLM, in his "*Memoir of Central India,*" published in 1823; and from that important work the different articles in this Supplement, relating to Malwa, have been, by permission, extracted. (See Note, p. 330).

It may be proper here to state, that as that Circular related only to Commercial Weights and Measures, no account has been transmitted respecting the *Road Measures* of India. Much useful information on this subject will, however, be found in the "*Memoir of a Map of Hindostan,*" by MAJOR RENNELL, late Surveyor General of Bengal; and in the "*Asiatic Researches*" (vol. v) by H. T. COLEBROOKE, Esq. late President of the Asiatic Society of Calcutta.

From these authorities, it appears that the *Cos* (also called the *Cros, Crosa*, or *Hardary*) although differing in certain provinces of India, is notwithstanding more uniform than the Mile in several countries of Europe. It is, generally, of two sorts, namely, the *Standard Cos* and the *Common Cos.* The former is deduced from some scientific archetype, such as a degree of the meridian; and the latter from popular computation. Thus the most general standard is 35 Cos to a degree, and some are 37½, 40, and 45. The Common Cos equals, on an average, nearly 2 English Miles; and 6 of these, in a direct and horizontal line, answer to about 7, according to the usual windings of the roads.

It is customary in many parts of India, as in several other countries, to estimate Itinerary Measures by time; that is, by the number of hours required, at an ordinary rate of travelling, to go any given distance. (See vol. 1, p. 11 and 117).

MIRZAPORE. See vol. 1, p. 123.

MOCHA. See vol. 1, p. 257 and 123.

MOCO MOCA. See *Sumatra*.

MOLUCCA ISLANDS. See *Amboyna*, vol. 1, p. 97 and 122; *Banda*, p. 99 and 122; and *Ternate*, p. 120 and 123.

MOTA,

A Pergunnah, near Surat, under the Presidency of Bombay.

The Maund contains 40¾ Seers 2 Pice of Surat =38 lb. 4 oz. 4¾ dr.

For other particulars, see *Surat*.

MOWDHAW,

A Pergunnah in the District of Calpee, under the Presidency of Bengal.

Weights.

		lb.	oz.	dr.
The Seer (wholesale)	=	2	2	15½
Ditto (retail)	=	1	15	1½
The Dry Measure contains				
1 Seer 11 Chittacks	=	3	4	7½

The Cloth Measure = 38¾ English Inches.

MUNDISSOR,

A City in the Province of Malwa, under the Presidency of Bengal.

Weights.

				lb.	oz.	dr.
92 Salim Shye Rupees	=	1 Seer	=	2	3	7¾
4 Seers	=	1 Dhurree	=	8	13	15
15 Seers	=	1 Maund	=	33	4	4¾
12 Maunds	=	1 Maunee	=	399	3	3

For other particulars, see *Malwa*.

MUSCAT. See vol. 1, p. 123.

MYSORE. See vol. 1, p. 111 and 123. See also *Assay Report*, Nos. 9, 76, and 87.

NASSUCK,

A District within the Collectorship of Ahmednuggur, under the Presidency of Bombay.

Weights.

	Ankos.	Rs. Massas.		lb.	oz.	dr.
The Seer weighs	79	4	=	1	15	4½
The Seer of Capacity	99	2	=	2	7	1½

For further particulars, see *Ahmednuggur*.

NATAL,

A Town in the Island of Sumatra.

The Monies of this place have been already described in vol. 1, p. 112, where also a concise view of the Weights will be found; but the following documents are more full and authentic, which have been transmitted with Standards, in obedience to the Circular of 1821.

Gold and Silver Weight.

				Gr.
		1 Rackay	=	1.52
24 Rackays	=	1 Ammas	=	36.5
16 Ammas	=	1 Tael	=	584

Benjamin Weight.

				lb.	oz. Avoir.
		1 Tael	=	0	1⅓
48 Taels	=	1 Catty Ootan	=	4	0
20 Catties Ootan	=	1 Tompong	=	80	0

Camphor Weight.

				lb.	oz. Avoir.
16 Taels	=	1 China Catty	=	1	5⅓
3 China Catties	=	1 Catty Ootan	=	4	0

NATAL, *continued.*

Grain and Liquid Measure.

				Cubic Inches.
		1 Pakha	=	33.575
12 Pakhas	=	1 Sukat	=	402.9
10 Sukats	=	1 Tub	=	4029
80 Tubs	=	1 Coyan	=	322320

NEW HOOBLY,

A Pettah in the Dooab, under the Presidency of Bombay.

Weights.

The Cutcha Seer for weighing oils and groceries equals 20⅝ Madras Rupees = 8 oz. 6 dr.

The Pucka Seer (wholesale) for measuring grain, salt, &c. contains 106½ Madras Rupees = 2 lb. 11 oz. 13 dr.

The Pucka Seer (retail) measures 90 Cubic Inches, and when filled with nine kinds of grain, equals 103¾ Madras Rupees, or 2 lb. 10 oz. 10 dr.

The Dhurra contains 13 Seers. (See Note, p. 341.)

The Guz of 24 Tussoos, for goods not sold by the Piece, measures 31¼ English Inches.

For further particulars, see *Darwar.*

NEYWASSA. See *Ahmednuggur.*

NOLYE,

A Town in the Province of Malwa.

Weights.

					lb.	oz.	dr.
80 Ougein Rupees	=	1 Seer	=		1	15	10
5 Seers	=	1 Dhurree	=		9	14	2
20 Seers	=	1 Maund	=		39	8	8
12 Maunds	=	1 Maunee	=		474	6	0

For further particulars, see *Malwa.*

NOWLGOOND,

A Pettah in the Dooab, under the Presidency of Bombay.

NOWLGOOND, *continued.*

Weights.

The Cutcha Seer for weighing oils and groceries contains 20¾ Madras Rupees = 8 oz. 8½ dr.

The Pucka Seer for measuring grain, salt, &c. measures 96.6 Cubic Inches, and weighs 110¼ Madras Rupees, or 2 lb. 13 oz. 5½ dr.

The Guz of 24 Tussoos = 33 English Inches
The Hath for Cloth = 18¼ ditto.

For further particulars, see *Darwar.*

OCKLESUR,

A Town in the Province of Gujrat, District of Broach, under the Presidency of Bombay.

Weights.

Market Seer.

				lb.	oz.	dr.
38 Broach Rupees Wt.	=	1 Seer	=	0	15	6¾
40 Seers	=	1 Maund	=	38	8	13
20 Maunds	=	1 Candy	=	771	0	4

Pergunnah Seer,

for weighing Kuppas and Grains.

				lb.	oz.	dr.
39¾ Broach Rupees Wt.	=	1 Seer	=	1	0	2¾
40 Seers	=	1 Maund	=	40	6	14
20 Maunds	=	1 Candy	=	808	9	8

The Pergunnah Seer received from this place, as above stated, is 1 Dram heavier than the estimated weight by Rupees.

The Measures for oil and sea samum, and the Long Measure, are the same as at *Hansoot*, which see.

OMUTWARRA,

A District in the Province of Malwa, under the Presidency of Bengal.

OMUTWARRA, *continued.*

Weights.

			lb.	oz.	dr.
81 Salim Shye Rs.	=1 Seer	=	1	15	3¼
3½ Seers	=1 Pusseree	=	6	13	5
2 Pusserees	=1 Dhurree	=	13	10	10
4 Dhurrees	=1 Maund	=	54	10	8
8 Maunds	=1 Maunee	=	437	4	0
100 Maunees	=1 Maniasa	=	43725	0	0

For further particulars, see *Malwa.*

OUGEIN,

A Town in the Province of Malwa, under the Presidency of Bengal.

For the Monies, see *Assay Report,* No. 56.

Weights.

			lb.	oz.	dr.
80 Ougein Rupees	= 1 Seer	=	1	15	10
5¾ Seers	= 1 Dhurree	=	11	5	14
16⅞ Seers	= 1 Maund	=	33	5	13
12 Mannds	= 1 Maunee	=	400	5	12

For further particulars, see *Malwa.*

PAICHAL,

A Pergunnah near Surat, under the Presidency of Bombay.

The Maund contains 48 Seers 8 Pice of Surat =45 lb. 4 oz. Avoirdupois. See *Surat.*

PALIMBANG, a Town in Sumatra. See vol. 1, p. 112 and 123.

PALLODA,

A District within the Collectorship of Ahmednuggur, under the Presidency of Bombay.

The Seer weighs 78 Ankosee Rupees and 10½ Massas=1 lb. 15 oz. 2 dr.

The Seer of Capacity weighs 103½ Ankosee Rupees, and is divided and multiplied as follows, the Tank being equal to 248 Grains.

PALLODA, *continued.*

				lb.	oz.	dr.
18 Tanks	=	1 Pao Seer	=	0	10	3¼
4 Pao Seers	=	1 Seer	=	2	8	13
2 Seers	=	1 Adholee	=	5	1	10
2 Adholees	=	1 Pylee	=	10	3	4
16 Pylees	=	1 Maund	=	163	4	0
20 Maunds	=	1 Candy	=	3265	0	0

For further particulars, see *Ahmednuggur.*

PANDREE,

A Pergunnah in the District of Calpee, under the Presidency of Bengal.

The Seer = 2 lb. 11 oz. 12 dr.

The Long Measure=40¼ English Inches.

PANWARREE,

A Pergunnah in the District of Calpee, under the Presidency of Bengal.

The Seer = 2 lb. 2 oz. 2 dr.

The Measure for Grain contains 2 Seers 13 Chittacks = 6 lb. 0 oz. 2 dr.

The Long Measure = 36⅝ English Inches.

PARNAIR,

A District within the Collectorship of Ahmednuggur, under the Presidency of Bombay.

All the Weights and Measures here are the same as at Ahmednuggur, except the following:

	lb.	oz.	dr.
The Seer weighs 76½ Ankosee Rupees=	1	14	2½
The Seer of Capacity contains 95 Ankosee Rupees and 7 Massas .... =	2	5	2

PARNERE,

A Pergunnah near Surat, under the Presidency of Bombay.

The Weights and Measures of this place agree

PARNERE, *continued.*

with those of Surat, except in the following particular:

The Pauny Seery Measure contains 5 Seers, that is, as much batty or rice in the husk as will, if delivered by weight, amount to that quantity. See Note to *Darwar.*

PATNA,

A City in the Province of Bahar, under the Presidency of Bengal.

100 Patna Rupees = 95 Sicca Rupees 11 Annas.

Goldsmiths' Weight.

		Gr.
The Ruttee	=	$3\frac{1}{20}$
The Massa	=	$18\frac{1}{2}$
The Tolah	=	209

The above Weights, and also the following, have been received without any specification of their divisions or multiples.

			lb.	oz.	dr.
The Seer of	45 Sicca Weight	=	1	2	9
	48 ditto	=	1	3	12
	72 ditto	=	1	13	$10\frac{1}{2}$
	72 11 7	=	1	14	2
	76 ditto	=	1	15	$4\frac{3}{4}$
	80 ditto	=	2	0	$14\frac{1}{2}$
	81 5	=	2	1	$6\frac{3}{4}$

These Seers have been each found to weigh about 1 Dram more than the result, if computed at $179\frac{2}{3}$ Grains to the Sicca Rupee.

Oil and all liquids are sold by the above Seers of 45, 76, and 80 Sicca Weight; and also by Measures, standards of which have been transmitted to London, with the Seers, and have been found respectively to measure $32\frac{1}{2}$, 54.2, and 57.75 Cubic Inches.

Long Measure.

		Eng. Inches.
The Cloth and Carpet Measure	=	33
The Broad Cloth	=	$42\frac{1}{2}$

PATNA, *continued.*

Other Measures have been received of $36\frac{1}{4}$, 40, 41, 42, 47, and 51 Inches; but their purposes are not mentioned.

PEGU. See vol. 1, p. 113 and 123.

PERSIA. See vol. 1, p. 277. See also *Assay Report*, Nos. 8, 73, 74, and 75.

PHILLIPINE ISLANDS. See *Magindanao*, vol. 1, p. 107; and *Manilla*, p. 109.

PERTABGHUR,

A Town in Central India, under the Presidency of Bengal.

For the Rupee see *Assay Report*, No. 85.

Commercial Measures and Weights.

			lb.	oz.	dr.
80 Salim Shye Rupees	= 1 Seer	=	1	14	$13\frac{1}{2}$
5 Seers	= 1 Dhurree	=	9	10	$3\frac{1}{2}$
20 Seers	= 1 Maund	=	38	8	14
12 Maunds	= 1 Maunee	=	462	10	8

For further particulars, see *Malwa.*

PONDICHERRY. See vol. 1, p. 113 and 123.

PRINCE OF WALES' ISLAND.

The mode of keeping accounts here is stated in vol. 1, p. 114; but the description of Weights and Measures in that article is not sufficiently ample, nor is it entirely correct. The following statements are therefore extracted from a very copious Dispatch on the subject, lately transmitted to the Court of Directors with the Standard Weights and Measures.

Goldsmiths' Weight.

			Gr.
12 Sagas	= 1 Mayam	=	52
16 Mayams	= 1 Bongkal, or 2 Span. Dol.	=	832
20 Bongkals	= 1 Catty	=	16640

PRINCE OF WALES' ISLAND, *continued.*

A Catty of gold, it should be observed, is heavier than the common Catty, in the proportion of 105 to 78. At Achet, Siak, Malacca, and places on the east side of the Malay peninsula, the Bongkal and Catty Weights are about 10 per cent. less than the above. There is also a Bongkal *Measure*, which is in frequent use amongst Europeans and Native Traders to the eastward, and which is found to weigh very nearly 2 Dollars, or 832 Troy Grains.

Commercial Weight.

			lb.	oz.	dr.
	1 Tahil	=	(nearly)		23
16 Tahils	=1 Catty	=	1	6	13
100 Catties	=1 Malay Pikul	=	142	10	$10\frac{2}{3}$
3 Pikuls (Mal.)	=1 Bhar	=	428	0	0
40 Pikuls (Chi.)	=1 Koyan	=	5333	0	0

There are two kinds of Catties and Pikuls used in the Bazar—the Malay and the Chinese. The Malay Catty weighs 24 Spanish Dollars; the Chinese, $22\frac{1}{2}$. Hence 15 Catties Malay=16 Chinese. By the Malay or large Pikul of $142\frac{2}{3}$ lb. Avoirdupois, merchants purchase pepper, tin, &c. from the native vessels; but sell by the Chinese, or Bazar Pikul of $133\frac{1}{3}$ lb.

Measures of Capacity.

			Cubic Inches.
4 Chupahs	= 1 Gantang	=	271.65
800 Gantangs	= 1 Koyan	=	217320.

The Chupah is divided into halves and quarters.

There is a Measure used here, as well as in most of the neighbouring countries, termed a Parra, which is nominally a Measure of 10 Gantangs; but sometimes consists of 5, 15, or 20 Gantangs. It is by the Parra, the contents of which being previously settled, that rice, salt, and some other articles, are in general measured; and it is always by a Measure of this description that betel-nut is purchased on the Pedir Coast.

PRINCE OF WALES' ISLAND, *continued.*

Long Measure.

The Hasta or Cubit, which is divided into halves and quarters, equals 18 English Inches; and is used by the Malays and many other natives for measuring cloths. But the Chinese shop-keepers in the Bazar make use of the English Yard.

Land Measure.

			Eng. Yards.
4 Hastas	= 1 Depa	=	2
2 Depas	= 1 Jumba	=	4
20 Jumbas	= 1 Orlong	=	80

Hence the Orlong or 80 Square Yards=1 Acre 1 Rood 12 Perches, English.

RADNAGORE,

Under the Presidency of Bengal.

Weights.

The Seer of 62 Sicca Weight, used in the Bazar =1 lb. 9 oz. $7\frac{1}{4}$ dr.

The Seer of 64 Sicca Weight, used for sugar and jagyry = 1 lb. 10 oz. $3\frac{3}{4}$ dr.

The Seer of 80 Sicca Weight, used for ghee =2 lb. 0 oz. $14\frac{3}{4}$ dr.

The above Seers have been found to differ from their estimated weight in Rupees, as follows:—

The first, $\frac{1}{3}$ Dram heavier; the second, $\frac{3}{4}$ Dram lighter; and the third, $1\frac{1}{4}$ Dram heavier.

Measures of Capacity.

The Baugee, by which paddy is sold, weighs 5 Seers of 62 Sicca Weight, which is, however, subject to variation. The Baugee for rice, weighs 6 Seers of 62 Sicca Weight, which varies according to the season.

			Cubic Inches.
The Seer for oil of 62 Sicca Weight		=	56
Ditto 80 ditto		=	60

The principal Long Measure is the Haut of 18 English Inches.

RAHORY,

A District within the Collectorship of Ahmednuggur, under the Presidency of Bombay.

The Seer of Capacity weighs 115½ Ankosee Rupees=2 lb. 13 oz. 8½ dr.; and that of Weight=77 Ankosee Rupees=1 lb. 14 oz. 5¾ dr.

The other Weights and Measures are the same as at Ahmednuggur.

RAJAO,

A District within the Collectorship of Ahmednuggur, under the Presidency of Bombay.

The Monies, Weights, and Measures here agree with those of Ahmednuggur, except that the Seer of Capacity weighs 100 Ankosee Rupees=2 lb. 7 oz. 6¾ dr.

RANDIER. See *Surat.*

RANEE BEDNORE,

A Pettah in the Dooab, under the Presidency of Bombay.

The Pucka Seer for buying grain, salt, &c. weighs 116½ Madras Rupees=3 lb. Avoirdupois. The Pucka Seer for selling weighs 111½ Madras Rupees. When filled with nine kinds of grain, it equals 2 lb. 13 oz. 13 dr. See Note, p. 341.

The Hath for measuring cloth, turbands, &c. contains 18⅞ English Inches.

For further particulars, see *Darwar*.

RANGOON. See vol. 1, p. 115 and 123.

RAULT,

A Pergunnah in the District of Calpee, under the Presidency of Bengal.

Three Seers have been transmitted from this place, which weigh as follow:

RAULT, *continued.*

		lb.	oz.	dr.
Khaus Seer	=	2	0	14
Avontah Seer, for grain	=	2	8	0
Ditto	=	1	9	14

The Guz contains 37 English Inches.

ROOMBHAREE,

A District within the Collectorship of Ahmednuggur, under the Presidency of Bombay.

The Weights and Measures here are the same as at Ahmednuggur, except the following:

The Seer weighs 74 Ankosee Rupees=1 lb. 13 oz. 2¾ dr.

The Seer of Capacity weighs 102 Ankosee Rupees; and is divided and multiplied as follow:

				lb.	oz.	dr.
18 Tanks	=	1 Pao Seer	=	0	10	0¾
4 Pao Seers	=	1 Seer	=	2	8	3½
2 Seers	=	1 Adholee	=	5	0	6¾
2 Adholees	=	1 Pylee	=	10	0	13½
16 Pylees	=	1 Maund	=	160	13	8
20 Maunds	=	1 Candy	=	3217	9	0

ROONCH,

A Pergunnah in the District of Calpee, under the Presidency of Bengal.

		lb.	oz.	dr.
The Seer for Cotton	=	2	9	10
Grain	=	2	9	6

The Guz measures 38 English Inches.

RUNGYPORE,

A Town in the Province of Bengal.

The Standards received from this factory differ from their estimated Weight in Rupees as follows:—

RUNGYPORE, *continued.*

	Wt. by Rupees. lb. oz. dr.	Real Weight. lb. oz. dr.
Seer of 60 Sicca Wt.	= 1 8 10	1 8 12
65 ditto	= 1 10 11	1 10 10.6
72 11 7	= 1 13 13.8	1 13 10.7
73 ditto	= 1 13 15.6	1 14 1.7
80 ditto	= 2 0 13.6	2 1 1
90 ditto	= 2 4 15.5	2 5 1
160 ditto	= 4 1 11.2	4 2 4

The Guz for measuring Baftae cloths = 63 English Inches.

RUTLAM,

A Town in the Province of Malwa, under the Presidency of Bengal.

Weights.

		lb.	oz.	dr.
84 Salim Shye Rupees	= 1 Seer =	2	0	6
5 Seers	= 1 Dhurree =	10	1	14
20 Seers	= 1 Maund =	40	7	8
12 Maunds	= 1 Maunee =	485	10	0

The above are the weights by which goods are bought, but they are sold by the Seer of 80 Rupees = 1 lb. 14 oz. 13¼ dr.

Spices, betel, &c. are sold by a Seer of 79 Rupees Weight = 1 lb. 14 oz. 7½ dr.

ST. HELENA. See vol. 1, p. 306.

SALANGORE. See vol. 1, p. 115 and 123.

SALLOLPORE,

A Pergunnah in the District of Calpee, under the Presidency of Bengal.

	lb.	oz.	dr.
The Seer, Commercial Weight =	2	4	8
The Seer for Cotton =	2	8	2½

The Long Measures contain 38¾ and 40¾ English Inches.

SANTIPORE,

A Town under the Presidency of Bengal.

The Standards received from this Factory differ from their estimated weight in Rupees as follows:

	Wt. by Rupees. lb. oz. dr.	Real Weight. lb. oz. dr.
Seer of 60 Sicca Wt.	= 1 8 10	1 8 11.8
72 11 7	= 1 13 13.8	1 14 0.8
80 ditto	= 2 0 13.6	2 1 0.4
82 ditto	= 2 1 10.7	2 1 11.4
84 ditto	= 2 2 7.9	2 2 5.4
96 ditto	= 2 7 6.7	2 7 3

Export Warehouse.

	lb.	oz.	dr.
Seer, Factory Weight =	1	13	7.8
Seer, Bazar Weight =	2	0	14.4
Seer of 82 10 =	2	1	15

Import Warehouse.

	lb.	oz.	dr.
Factory Seer =	1	13	13.7
Bazar Seer =	2	0	13.6

Measure of Capacity.

The Seer of 80 Sicca Weight is found to contain 57.75 Cubic Inches.

Long Measure.

Two Measures of Length have been received, the one contains 18, and the other 36 Inches.

SCINDY. See vol. 1, p. 115 and 123.

SEESSOLURH,

A Pergunnah in the District of Calpee, under the Presidency of Bengal.

	lb.	oz.	dr.
The Retail Seer for Grain =	1	15	1
Wholesale =	2	2	9

The Long Measure = 40½ English Inches.

SENNUR,

A District within the Collectorship of Ahmednuggur, under the Presidency of Bombay.

	lb.	oz.	dr.
The Seer weighs 76½ Ankosee Rupees=	1	14	2
The Seer of Capacity weighs 95 Ankosee Rupees and 7 Massas ---- =	2	5	11

For further particulars, see *Ahmednuggur*.

SERAMPORE. See vol. 1, p. 123.

SERINGAPATAM. See vol. 1, p. 116 and 123.

SHEWGAWM,

A District within the Collectorship of Ahmednuggur, under the Presidency of Bombay.

The Weights and Measures here are the same as at Ahmednuggur, except the Seer, which weighs 77 Ankosee Rupees=1 lb. 14 oz. 5¾ dr.; and the Seer of Capacity which weighs 115½ Ankosee Rupees=2 lb. 13 oz. 8½ dr.

SIAM. See vol. 1, p. 117 and 123.

SINKELL. See vol. 1, p. 118.

SOOLOO. See vol. 1, p. 118.

SOOMERPORE,

A Pergunnah in the District of Calpee, under the Presidency of Bengal.

	lb.	oz.	dr.
The Seer (Retail) =	2	0	9¼
(Wholesale) =	2	3	0½

The Cloth Measure = 40⅛ English Inches.

SOONAMOOKY,

A Town under the Presidency of Bengal.

Two Seers have been received from this Factory, viz. one of 58 10 Sicca Weight=1 lb. 8 oz. 0½ dr.; and the other of 60 Sicca Weight=1 lb. 8 oz. 10 dr.

Poorseer Measures.

	lb.	oz.	dr.
Seer of 72 Sicca Weight =	1	13	9½
73 4½ =	1	14	1½
75 =	1	14	12½
82 10 =	2	1	14¾

Long Measures.

	Eng. Inches.
The Corah of the Native Merchants =	52.4
for unbleached Linen =	41.8
for bleached ditto =	41.
The Long Measure used at the Factory =	52.4
for unbleached Linen =	43.4
for bleached ditto =	42.6

SOOPA,

A Pergunnah near Surat, under the Presidency of Bombay.

The Maund contains 40¼ Seers of Surat=38 lb. 3 oz. 4¾ dr.

For other Weights, Measures, &c. see *Surat*.

SOOPAH,

A Pergunnah in the District of Calpee, under the Presidency of Bengal.

	lb.	oz.	dr.
The Seer =	2	0	9½
The Seer of Capacity =	5	1	7¾

The Long Measure=39¾ English Inches.

For further proportions, see *Calpee*.

SUCCADANA. See vol. 1, p. 119.

SUMATRA. See *Acheen*, *Bencoolen*, *Fort Marlborough*, and *Natal*, in this Supplement.—*Palimbang*, vol. 1, p. 112 and 123. *Sinkell*, vol. 1, p. 118. *Tappanooly*, vol. 1, p. 120.

SUNDA ISLES. See *Sooloo*, vol. 1, p. 118.

SUNGANMAIR,

A District within the Collectorship of Ahmednuggur, under the Presidency of Bombay.

The Seer of Capacity weighs 100 Ankosee Rupees = 2 lb. 7 oz. 6½ dr.

The Weights are the same as those of Ahmednuggur.

SURAT,

A City in the Province of Gujrat, under the Presidency of Bombay.

In addition to the account of the Monies, Weights, and Measures of Surat, given in vol. 1, p. 119, the following particulars (which have been recently received by the Court of Directors) are of importance.

Goldsmiths' Weight.

				Gr.
		1 Ruttee	=	1.95
3 Ruttees	=	1 Val	=	5.85
8 Ruttees	=	1 Massa	=	15.6
12 Massas	=	1 Tolla	=	187.5
35 Tollas	=	1 Seer	=	6563 or 15 oz. Avoirdupois.

Weight for Pearls and Precious Stones.

				Gr.
		1 Vassa	=	0.1423
20 Vassas	=	1 Ruttee	=	2.846
3 Ruttees	=	1 Val	=	8.538
8 Vals	=	1 Tank	=	67.3
32 Vals	=	1 Tolla	=	273.216

SURAT, *continued.*

Commercial Weight.

30 Surat Old Pice / 42 Surat New Pice	= 1 Seer
40 Seers	= 1 Maund
7 Maunds	= 1 Small Harra
12 Maunds	= 1 Maunee
20 Maunds	= 1 Candy
21 Maunds	= 1 Large Harra
24 Maunds	= 1 Bhaur

Although the Surat Maund is said to contain only 40 Seers, or about 37½ lb. still it varies from 41 to 46 Seers; nor is the Candy uniformly confined to 20 Maunds.

	lb.	oz.	dr.
Grain of all kinds is sold by the Maund of 40 Seers	=37	8	0
Castor Oil by ditto of 40¼ Seers	=37	11	12¾
Oil, cocoa-nut, ghee, cotton, and spirits by ditto of 42 Seers	=39	6	0¼

Long Measure.

The Cloth Merchants' Guz, as well as that used by Carpenters and Bricklayers, is divided into 24 Tussoos. The former contains 27⅗, the latter 24 English Inches. The Hath or Cubit of 18 Tussoos, or 20.9 English Inches, is used in measuring bamboo mats only. The English Yard is in common use in all sales of European manufactures, and every description of cloth and piece goods.

Indian piece goods and a few other articles, are sold by the Corge of 20 pieces.

Timber Measure.

The Guz contains 20 Vussas or 200 Viswasees, and equals 27⅙ English Inches.

Land Measure.

			Eng. Inches.
4⅕ Tussoos	=	1 Viswasee	= 4.88
20 Viswasees	=	1 Vussa	= 97.6
20 Vussas squared	=	1 Beega	= 2 Roods 17 Perches

SURBHAM,

A Pergunnah near Surat, under the Presidency of Bombay.

The Maund contains 39¼ Seers and 2 Pice of Surat=37 lb. 4 oz. 4¾ dr.

For other particulars, see *Surat*.

TAPPANOOLY. See *Natal*.

TELLICHERRY. See vol. 1, p. 120 and 123.

TERNATE. See vol. 1, p. 120 and 123.

TOCOPA. See vol. 1, p. 121 and 123.

TONQUIN. See *Cachao*, vol. 1, p. 102.

TRANGANIA. See vol. 1, p. 121 and 123.

TRANQUEBAR. See vol. 1, p. 121 and 123.

TRINCOMALEE. See *Ceylon*, vol. 1, p. 104 and 122; and *Columbo*, p. 105 and 122.

TUMBUCK,

A District within the Collectorship of Ahmednuggur, under the Presidency of Bombay.

The Seer weighs 79 Ankosee Rupees and 4 Massas=1 lb. 15 oz. 4½ dr.

TUMBUCK, *continued.*

The Seer of Capacity weighs 99 Ankosee Rupees and 2 Massas=2 lb. 7 oz. 1½ dr.

For further particulars, see *Ahmednuggur*.

TURKESUR,

A Pergunnah near Surat, under the Presidency of Bombay.

The Maund contains 40 Seers 8 Pice of Surat=37 lb. 12 oz. Avoirdupois.

For further particulars, see *Surat*.

UCKLESUR. See *Ocklesur*.

WALOR. See *Turkesur*.

WARUHA,

A Pergunnah near Surat, under the Presidency of Bombay.

The Weights and Measures here are the same as those of Surat, except the Maund, which contains 40½ Seers of Surat=37 lb. 15 oz. 8½ dr.

WUNNU. See *Dindore*.

☞ *As the foregoing Supplement may be considered as a* COMMERCIAL GAZETTEER *for Oriental Settlements, so its Index, which here follows, may serve as a* DICTIONARY *for explaining, by references, the Weights, Measures, and Monies of the East Indies.*

INDEX TO THE SUPPLEMENT.

NOTE.—Such Terms as are contained in the Supplement, but not inserted in this Index, will be found explained in the General Index, p. 261 to 323, of this Volume.

REFERENCES TO THE ADDENDA, Vol. I.

SUPPLEMENT

TO THE

UNIVERSAL CAMBIST

For 1827:

CONTAINING

THE METROLOGY OF SOUTHERN INDIA,

Deduced from Standards lately transmitted by the Government of Madras to the

COURT OF DIRECTORS;

INCLUDING

ILLUSTRATIONS OF INDIAN GEOGRAPHY,

WITH

Maps of the Provinces and Principal Rivers,

AND

CLASSIFICATIONS OF THE STATES AND PRESIDENCIES.

Price 10*s.* 6*d.* to Non-Subscribers; but all Supplementary Matter will be delivered, free of expense, to the previous Purchasers of the *Cambist,* on application to their respective Booksellers. The price of the whole Work, including every Augmentation, remains unaltered, viz. Four Guineas.

Whiting, Printer, Lombard Street.

SUPPLEMENT.

EAST INDIES *(continued)*.

THIS Continuation of Indian Metrology was called for in 1827, in consequence of the recent arrival of a Collection of Standards from the Government of Madras, consisting of attested Models of the principal Weights and Measures of Southern India, with explanatory papers, all of which have been prepared by the proper Authorities, in obedience to the Circular Order issued by the Court of Directors in 1821, as stated in page 325 of this volume.

That extensive Order, it should be explained, was executed in due time throughout the Presidencies of Bengal and Bombay; and in 1824 the results were published in the foregoing part of this Supplement; but in certain provinces, subordinate to Madras, impediments occurred which were not entirely removed until the year 1826, when the Order of the Directors was completed in a very full and satisfactory manner.

As soon as this Collection arrived in London, it was delivered to the Author of the present Work, for the purposes of comparison for which the other Standards had been committed to his care, as stated in Mr. Secretary DART's Letter, page 327; and the following are the results of his experiments, verified by the same Authorities as before, the principal Weights having been proved at the Royal Mint, by the liberal and important labours of Mr. BINGLEY, and the Measures in like manner by Mr. TROUGHTON.—*See Pref.* page xii, &c.

The condition of returning the Standards, mentioned in the Secretary's Letter, has been likewise complied with, and they are accordingly deposited in his Office at the India House, in a commodious Cabinet constructed for the purpose, similar to the Cabinet lately erected at the Royal Mint for preserving the Standard Weights of other Countries, which have been collected and compared for this Work by order of Government.*

* As the East India Company have essentially co-operated with His Majesty's Government in completing the universal comparison of Weights and Measures, so they have adopted the same new plan of laying up their verified Standards for future reference;—a plan which must prove permanently useful to philosophy as well as commerce, by affording the means of correcting Standards that are in wear, and of ascertaining what loss each may sustain in any given portion of time.

For a specimen of the utility of such comparisons, see Note, vol. 1. p. 294, on the diminution of the ancient Roman Pound, as deduced from Dr. Arbuthnot's Computations and the recent experiments at the London Mint.—See also vol. ii. p. 258.

EXPOSITION

*Of the Weights, Measures, and Monies, of Southern India.**

In the following Pages much repetition is avoided, by premising that each place is subordinate to Madras; and that the same Monies circulate throughout the Presidency as those explained in Vol. I. p. 90 and Vol. II. p. 103; and for the Contractions, &c. of the different Weights see ⁂ p. 332.

ARCOT,

A Town and Capital of a District of the same name in the Carnatic.

Commercial Weight.

The Pucka Seer used in weighing common goods, as jaggery, sugar, tamarinds, oil, &c. is divided into halves, quarters, &c. and also into 24 Pollams, and answers to 1 lb. 13 oz. Avoirdupois, and its divisions in proportion. Hence 1 Pollam equals 531 Troy Grains nearly.

Dry Measure.

The measure used for grain of every description is the Puddy, which is divided into halves, quarters, &c. and contains 1⅞ English Quart.

The Puddy of grain streaked weighs 42 Pollams, or 3lb. 2 oz. 12 dr. but when heaped, as is the general practice, it weighs 47 Pollams, or 3 lb. 8 oz. 12 dr.

Long Measure.

The Long Measure is the Cubit, which equals 18 English Inches: The English Yard is also used in selling English Cloths, especially to Europeans.

The same Weights and Measures are in use at Allepay, Arnee, Chittoor, Vellore, and Wallajahbad, in the Carnatic.

BANGALORE,

A Town and Territory in the Eastern Range of the Mysore.

Weights for Jewellery, Gold, and Silver.

The weight of 16 small Grains of Paddy, or 4 Groometries (beans) is reckoned to compose the Gold Canteroy, or Sultany Fanam, which equals 5.87 Grains Troy.

9 Sultany Fanams	= 1 Bahadry or Star Pagoda	= 52.8 Grains Troy.
10 Bahadry Pagodas	= 1 Adpowe or 3 Rupees weight, at 30 Gold Fanams per Rupee	= 528.3 Gr. Troy.
80 Bahadry Pagodas	= 1 Cutcha Seer or 24 Rupees weight	= 4227 Gr. Troy or 9 Oz. 10½ Dr. Avoir.

Weights for Grocery, &c.

3 Rajah Rupees weight	= 1 Polum or Adpowe	= 527 Gr. Troy.		
2 Adpowes	= 1 Powe ..	= 1059 Gr.		
		lb.	oz.	dr.
4 Powes or 24 Rupees	= 1 Cutcha Seer ...	= 0	10	0
5 Seers	= 1 Punj Seer or Vis ..	= 2	8	0

* Southern India comprehends that portion of the Peninsula, which extends from Cape Comorin to the River Kristna. These territories, with a few additional provinces, are under the Presidency of Madras, and those to the North-West of that river are subordinate to Bombay, while the regions to the North-East, which are by far the most extensive, are under Bengal, to which Presidency the other two are, in some degree, subordinate, and all are subject to the Court of Directors in London. But for the Laws and Government of the Presidencies, see *Auber's Analysis of the Constitution of the East India Company*; and for their Geography, see *Hamilton's Indian Gazetteer*, and his *Description of Hindostan*.

BANGALORE, *continued.*

			lb.	oz.	dr.
2 Punj Seers	=1 Duddah	=	12	8	0
4 Duddahs	=1 Maund	=	25	0	0
20 Maunds or 480 Rattles, at 40 Rupees weight each	=1 Candy	=	500	0	0

The Maund of 40 Seers is used in all Revenue transactions and Circar accounts. The Merchants, in their retail dealings, weigh by the Punj Seer or Vis, or at the rate of 42 Seers to the Maund.

Grain Measure.

			Gr.
30 Gold Canteroy or Sultany Fanams weight	=1 Rajah Pondicherry or Arcot Rupee	=	175.4

			lb.	oz.	dr.
5¼ Rupees	=1 Chattack	=	0	2	1½
4 Chattacks	=1 Powe	=	0	8	6½
4 Powes or 3½ Cutcha Seers or 84 Rupees weight of nine sorts of grain	=1 Pucka Seer	=	2	1	10¼
2 Pucka Seers	=1 Kistuaraz Bullah	=	4	3	5½
4 Bullahs	=1 Do. Colagah or Coodom	=	16	13	6¼
20 Colagahs or 160 Pucka Seers	=1 Do. Candagon or Candy	=	336	12	4½
1½ Colagah or 12 Seers	=1 Company's Mercall	=	25	4	2

			cwt.	qr.	lb.
400 Mercalls or 30 Kistuaraz Candies	=1 Garce	=	90	0	23

The Kistuaraz, Colagah, and Candy, have been used in the Circar accounts of the Mysore Territory ever since the capture of Seringapatam. Merchants, however, measure by Mercalls of 9, 10, 12, 16, 64, or 96 Pucka Seers, in wholesale dealings.

Long Measure.

			Inches.
3 Jows or Grains of Rice	=1 Angle	=	$2\frac{11}{90}$

BANGALORE, *continued.*

			Inches.
3 Angles	=1 Gerah	=	$6\frac{11}{30}$
8 Gerahs	=1 Haut or Cubit	=	$19\frac{1}{10}$
2 Hauts	=1 Guz	=	$38\frac{2}{10}$

This Guz is established by the Mysore Government for the measurement of land. See vol. i. p. 89.

BELGAUM,

In the Southern Mahratta Country.

The Weights and Measures principally used at Belgaum and Shapere are the following:—

Weights.

1 Shapere Rupee = 174 Gr.

			lb.	oz.	dr.
24 Rupees weight	=1 Seer	=	0	9	8
11 Seers	=1 Dhuddie	=	6	8	15
4 Dhuddies	=1 Maund	=	26	3	15
20 Maunds	=1 Candy	=	524	14	12

Measures.

			Quarts.
8 Kalary	=1 Paw or Seer	=	$1\frac{5}{16}$
2 Pawaas or quarters	=1 Adholy or half	=	$2\frac{10}{16}$
2 Adholies	=1 Payebee	=	5¼
24 Payebees	=1 Koora	=	31½ Gal.
20 Kooras	=1 Candy	=	630

BELLARY,

A Town and Province in the Ceded Districts.

Gold and Silver Weight.

Gold and Silver are bought and sold by the Mysore Rajah's new, or Company's old or Pondicherry Rupee, weighing 176¼ Grains Troy, and denominated Thollam, the divisions of which are as follow:—

			Gr.
3 Goondoominies (vegetable beads)	=1 Canteroy Fanam	=	5.875
2½ Canteroy Fanams	=1 Mass	=	14.687

BELLARY, *continued.*

		Gr.
9 Cantary Fanams.	=1 Bahadry Pagoda ...	= 52.875
30 Do. do........	=1 Thollam.	= 176.25
24 Thollams or Rupees	=1 Seer	=4230

or 9 Oz. 10 Drams Avoirdupois.

This Table of Weights is applicable to the whole of this range.

Commercial Weights.

Gross goods, such as sugar, tamarinds, meat, oil, ghee, &c. are sold by the undermentioned weights, regulated by the Mysore Rupee.

		lb.	oz.	dr.
	1 Mysore Rupee or Thollam	=0	0	6.445
21 Rupees.....	=1 Seer...	=0	8	7.34
6 Seers	=1 Puncha Seer	=3	2	12
2 Puncha Seers	=1 Dhadium	=6	5	8
4 Dhadiums ..	=1 Maund.	=25	6	0

Thus the Bellary Maund is 6 Oz. more than the Madras Maund, reckoning the Mysore Rupee as above; but reckoning the same Rupee at 176.16 Grains, according to Noton's Table, p. 331 of this volume, the excess of the Bellary Maund would be 5 Oz. only.

Cotton Weight.

Cotton is weighed by the Maund and Miggah; the Dhadium or Quarter Maund being equal to 256 Company's Rupees, new coinage, denominated by the natives Gaaders or Bandy Rupee.

Computing this at 180 Grains, the following is the cotton weight.

		lb.	oz.	dr.
256 Rupees	=1 Dhadium	= 6	9	5
4 Dhadiums ..	=1 Maund	= 26	5	4
12 Maunds ...	=1 Nuggah	=315	15	10

Grain Measure.

The following is the ancient Grain Measure of the country, still used in the districts, and regulated by a Measure called Thealee or Thimmapoo, containing 112 Madras Rupees weight of nine sorts of grain, known by the name of the Nuoadanium measurement.*

		lb.	oz.
112 Rupees.....	=1 Thimmapoo=	2	14
3 Thimmapoos or 4 Giduah	=1 Sollagay =	8	10
4 Sollagays ...	=1 Maanah =	34	8
4 Maanahs....	=1 Pullah =	138	0
4 Pullahs	=1 Collagah =	552	0
5 Collagahs ...	=1 Punchagah=	24c.2q.16lb.	
4 Punchagahs .	=1 Contagah =	98 2 8	

The Giduah is thus equal to the Bellary Pucka Seer of 84 Rupees, which is the measure now generally used for grain of all kinds, and which equals 2 lb. 1 oz. 14 dr.

Chunam is measured by the Mercal, containing 12 Pucka Seers, of 84 Rupees weight, grain measurement, and 5 Mercals make the Parrah.

Long Measure.

Cloths, carpets, &c. are measured as follows:—

12 Inches = 1 Foot
1½ Foot = 1 Cubit
2 Cubits = 1 Yard or Guz =36 Engl. Inches.

CALICUT,

A Town and District on the Malabar Coast.

For the Monies and Money Weights see Vol. I. p. 102.

The Commercial Weight is as follows, and is commonly used in all Malabar.

		lb.	oz.	dr.
10 Surat Rupees	= 1 Pollam =	0	4	1⅓
2 Pollams.....	= 1 Seer . =	0	8	2⅔
2 Seers	= 1 Pound =	1	0	5⅓
34 Pounds.....	= 1 Maund =	34	11	11
20 Maunds.....	= 1 Candy = 6 cwt. 0 qr. 23 lb.			

* These nine sorts of grain are,—Rice, Wheat, Coolty, Pasaloo, Mernoomooloo, Oil Seeds, Bengal Grain, Aunoomooloo, and Nooloo.

CANNANORE,

A Town and District in Malabar.

Commercial Weight.

			lb.	oz.	dr.
10 Surat Rupees	= 1 Pollam..	=	0	4	$1\frac{1}{3}$
2 Pollams.....	= 1 Seer....	=	0	8	$2\frac{2}{3}$
2 Seers......	= 1 Pound ..	=	1	0	$5\frac{1}{2}$
30 Pounds....	= 1 Maund ..	=	30	10	5
20 Maunds ...	= 1 Candy	= 5 cwt. 1 qr. 24 lb.			

CHITTOOR. See *Arcot.*

COCHIN,

A Town and District in Malabar.

Weights.

			lb.	oz.	dr.
$42\frac{1}{2}$ Surat Rupees Weight	=1 Pound..	=	1	1	6
25 Pounds	=1 Maund..	=	27	2	11
20 Maunds or 500 Pounds	=1 Candy..	=	543	6	4

By this weight sugars, spices, and metals are sold; other goods are weighed by the Maund of 30 lb., and the Candy of 600 lb.

Note. The Cochin Standard Pound, recently received from India, weighs 1lb. 2 oz. 2 dr., but the above computation is made from the Surat Rupee, according to the instruction in the accompanying dispatch.

Measures.

The measure of capacity used at Cochin contains $1\frac{1}{4}$ Pint.

The Parrah, used for grain, contains 45 such measures, or 7 Gallons nearly.

The Choadany for oil contains 24 such measures, or $3\frac{3}{4}$ Gallons.

Timber measure is the same as at *Travancore.*

For further particulars, see Vol. 1. p. 104.

COILPATAM. See *Masulipatam.*

COLATCHEY,

A Town in the Province of Travancore.

Weights.

			Gr.		
20 Munjandies	=1 Kullanjee.	=	78		
$13\frac{1}{2}$ Kullanjees	=1 Pollum ..	=	105.3		
			lb.	oz.	dr.
$67\frac{1}{2}$ Kullanjees	=5 Pollums wt.	=	0	12	$0\frac{1}{2}$
100 Pollums .	=1 Toolum ..	=	15	0	11
25 Rautuls or 125 Pollums	=1 Maund...	=	18	12	13
20 Maunds or 500 Rautuls.	=1 Candy ...	=	376	1	2

By the above weight, metals, spices, and sugars, are sold; other goods are weighed by the Maund of 150 Pollums, and the Candy of 600 Rautuls.

DINDIGUL,

A Town and District in the Southern Division.

Weights.

The weight for common articles of provision, and for all kinds of drugs, is $\frac{1}{16}$ of a Toolam, which answers to 1 lb. 3 oz. 8 dr. Avoirdupois; and hence 1.282 Toolam is equal to the Maund of 25 lb. The Toolam is divided into halves, quarters, eighths, and sixteenths. It is also divided into 100 Pullums.

Measures.

The measure for all sorts of grain answers to $1\frac{1}{16}$ English Quart. The Mercal contains 5 Dindigul grain measures, and therefore equals $8\frac{7}{16}$ Quarts.

GANJAM. See *Masulipatam.*

HYDRABAD,

A City in the Nizam's Country.

Grain is sold by the following weights:—The Seer being equal to 13896 Grains Troy.

			lb.	oz.	dr.
5 Hydrabad Rupees ..	=1 Chittack...	=	0	1	$15\frac{3}{4}$
16 Chittacks..	=1 Seer......	=	1	15	12
5 Seers	=1 Punsarry..	=	9	14	12

HYDRABAD, *continued.*

		lb.	oz.	dr.
12 Seers	=1 Small or Cutcha Maund	=23	13	0
40 Ditto	=1 Great or Pucka Maund	=79	6	0
120 Ditto......	=1 Selling Pullah......	=238	2	0
124 Ditto......	=1 Purchasing Pullah......	=246	1	0

The Cloth Measure answers to 35⅓ English Inches.

JAULNAH,

In the Nizam's Country.

Small Bazar *Weights for gold, silver, drugs*, &c.

		Troy Grains.
2 Rice Grains.	=1 Oourd Grain	= .48
2 Oourd Grains	=1 Wheat Grain	= .96
2 Wheat Grains	=1 Ruttee	= 1.92
2 Ruttees	=1 Wall......	= 3.84
4 Walls......	=1 Masha.....	= 15.375
12 Mashas	=1 Tola	= 184.5
4¾ Tolas or 57 Mashas	=1 Chittack...	= 876.7
16 Chittacks ...	=1 Seer ...	= 14027

which is equivalent to the Seer in Pucka Weights, viz. 2 lb. 0 oz. 1 dr.

Bazar *Pucka Weights*, for Grain, &c.

		lb.	oz.	dr.
5¼ Pice...	=1 Chittack	= 0	2	0
16 Chittacks or 80 Rupees	=1 Seer...	= 2	0	1
40 Seers...	=1 Maund	= 80	2	8
3 Maunds.	=1 Pullah.	=240	7	8

Bazar *Cutcha Weights*, for ghee, tobacco, &c.

		lb.	oz.	dr.
16 Chittacks....	=1 Seer	= 2	0	1
12 Seers.......	=1 Maund..	=24	0	12

Liquid Measures.

		lb.	oz.	dr.
16 Chittacks....	=1 Seer.....	= 2	0	1
12 Seers	=1 Maund .	= 24	0	12
10 Maunds.....	=1 Pullah..	=240	7	8

JAULNAH, *continued.*

Cloth Measure.

		English Inches.
3 Unglees	=1 Girrah....	= $2\frac{1}{10}$
8 Girrahs.....	=1 And Guz .	= $16\frac{8}{10}$
2 And Guzes..	=1 Guz	= $33\frac{6}{10}$

KALIAT,

In Malabar.

In this place, and at Kotakul, Quilandy, and Kapaud, the measure used is the Dungaly, which contains 2¼ Quarts English.

KAPAUD. See *Kaliat.*

KOTAKUL. See *Kaliat.*

KOTAR. See *Quilon.*

MADURA,

A City in the Southern Carnatic.

The Weights and Measures here are the same as at Trichinopoly, with the following exceptions:—

The Madura Seer, for weighing gold and silver, contains 80 Madura Pagodas Weight, and answers to 4480.7 Gr. Troy, or 10¼ Oz. Avoirdupois, and 39.244 such Seers are equal to 1 Maund of 25 Pounds. The Seer is divided into 50, 30, 20, &c. parts, down to the 64th part of the Pagoda, which is 56 Gr. nearly.

The Measure used for all sorts of grain, and also for gingely, oil, &c. is equal to $1\frac{7}{64}$ English Quart. Six of these measures make 1 Mercal, or 2⅝ Gallons nearly.

MASULIPATAM,

In the Northern Circars.

The following are the Weights and Measures used at Masulipatam, and other Stations of the Northern Division.

MASULIPATAM, *continued.*

Gold Weight.

					Gr.
$\frac{1}{9}$ of a Madras Pagoda	=1	Chunam	=		5.968
30 Chunams	=1	Tolam	=		179.04
24 Tolams	=1	Seer	=		4296.96

Silver is weighed against Rupees, 24 of which make 1 Seer.

Commercial Weights.

The weight used for iron bars, tin, tobacco, ghee, oil, jaggery, chillies, tamarinds, sugar, &c. from Visagapatam to Ganjam, is the $1\frac{1}{4}$ Cutcha Seer, of 100 Madras Pagodas, containing $12\frac{1}{2}$ Oz. Avoirdupois.

Its multiples and divisions are as follow:

				lb.	oz.
2 Chattaucks	=1	Nowtauk	=	0	$1\frac{1}{4}$
8 Nowtauks	=1	Seer	=	0	10
10 Nowtauks	=	$1\frac{1}{4}$ Seer	=	0	$12\frac{1}{2}$
5 Seers	=1	Viss	=	3	2
40 Seers	=1	Maund	=	25	0
20 Maunds	=1	Candy	=	500	0

There is also a Pucka Seer in use for Moguls Moormen, and generally for persons coming from Calcutta and Hydrabad, viz.

2 Chattaucks	=1	Nowtauk	= $\frac{1}{4}$lb.
8 Nowtauks	=1	Seer	= 2lb.
5 Seers	=1	Viss	= 10lb.
8 Viss	=1	Maund	= 80lb.

The Cutcha Seer of 90 Madras Pagodas, used by Merchants in dealing with each other, is thus divided:

				lb.	oz.
2 Chattaucks	=1	Nowtauk	=	0	$1\frac{3}{32}$
8 Nowtauks	=1	Seer	=	0	$11\frac{1}{4}$
5 Seers	=1	Viss	=	3	$8\frac{1}{4}$
40 Seers	=1	Maund	=	28	2
20 Maunds	=1	Candy	=	562	8

The weight used for brass, copper, and tutenag, is the Seer of 72 Madras Pagodas, which is thus divided:

				lb.	oz.
2 Chattaucks	=1	Nowtauk	=	0	$1\frac{1}{8}$
8 Nowtauks	=1	Seer	=	0	9
40 Seers	=1	Maund	=	22	8
20 Maunds	=1	Candy	=	450	0

The $1\frac{1}{4}$ Seer of 96 Madras Pagodas is used for weighing cotton.

				lb.	oz.
		$1\frac{1}{4}$ Seer	=	0	12
32 $1\frac{1}{4}$ Seers	=1	Maund	=	24	0
20 Maunds	=1	Candy	=	480	0

From Coilpatam to Visagapatam, these weights are in use, under the following denominations and divisions:

				lb.
		1 Yabbolam	=	$0\frac{3}{4}$
2 Yabbolam	=1	Puddalum	=	$1\frac{1}{2}$
16 Puddalum	=1	Maund	=	24
20 Maunds	=1	Candy	=	480

Grain Measure.

				Pints.
2 Giddahs	=1	Arsolah or $\frac{1}{4}$ Seer		$=0\frac{17}{32}$
2 Arsolahs	=1	Solah	$\frac{1}{2}$ do.	$=1\frac{1}{16}$
2 Solahs	=1	Zavah	1 do.	$=2\frac{1}{8}$
2 Zavahs	=1	Mannikah	2 do.	$=4\frac{1}{4}$
6 Mannikahs	=1	Mercal	12 do.	$=3\frac{1}{8}$ gal.
80 Mercals	=1	Candy	960 do.	=250
5 Candys or 400 Mercals	=1	Garce	4800 do.	=1250

The half Mercal of 6 Seers is in general use among the natives.

Cloth Measure.

		1 Palm	= $3\frac{3}{16}$ Inches.
2 Palms	=1	Span	= $6\frac{3}{8}$
3 Spans	=1	Cubit	= $19\frac{1}{8}$
2 Cubits	=1	Yard	= $38\frac{1}{4}$

NEGAPATAM,

In the Southern Carnatic.

Weights.

The weight used for all articles of provision is the Seer, which is equal to $9\frac{3}{8}$ English Ounces;

NEGAPATAM, *continued*.

and therefore 41.558 such Seers are equal to the Maund of 25lb. Avoirdupois: The Seer is divided into 8 Pullums. That received in London weighs 4236 Gr. Troy.

Grain Measure.

The measure used for all kinds of Grain answers to $1\frac{13}{16}$ English Pint, and is divided into halves, quarters, and eighths. The Mercal is equal to 4 Negapatam grain measures, and therefore answers to $7\frac{1}{4}$ Pints.

Oil Measure.

The Oil measure in general use for wholesale and retail, is equal to 1 English Quart, and is divided into halves, quarters, and eighths.

PALAMCOTTAH,

In the Southern Division of the Carnatic.

Gold and Silver Weight.

The Seer used for weighing gold, silver, &c. is 4551 Gr. or $10\frac{3}{4}$ Oz. Avoirdupois; and therefore 38.453 such Seers make the Maund of 25 lb.

There are also weights of 100 Cullengeys, with divisions and subdivisions, down to the 32d part. 56 Cullengeys make the Seer. 1 Cullengey = $81\frac{1}{4}$ Gr. Troy.

Commercial Weights.

The weight used by retail sellers, for drugs and provisions, is the eighth of a Toolam, which equals 1 lb. 9 oz. Avoirdupois; and thus, 2 Toolams make the Maund of 25 lb. 100 Pullums compose the Toolam, which is equal to $12\frac{1}{2}$ lb.

The sixteenth of a Toolam, used for weighing the foregoing articles by wholesale, is equal to 1 lb. 3 oz. and thus, 1.315 Toolam makes the Maund of 25lb.

PALAMCOTTAH, *continued*.

The quarter Puddy, used for weighing brass, copper, pewter, tutenag, &c. equals 1 lb. $3\frac{3}{4}$ oz. and hence 5.63 Puddies make the Maund.

The Puddy therefore contains 4 lb. 15 oz. and is divided into halves, quarters, &c.

The Seer used for weighing tape, rope, &c. answers to 1 lb. 13 oz. and 13.793 such Seers make the Maund of 25 lb.

Grain Measure.

The measure used at the Bazaar and by Merchants, for all kinds of grain, answers to $1\frac{7}{16}$ Quart English, and 6 such measures make 1 Mercal $=1\frac{1}{6}$ Gallon nearly.

The Corn Measure used by the Revenue and by the Farmers, answers to $1\frac{5}{64}$ Quart English, and 8 such measures make the Mercal, or $2\frac{5}{32}$ Gallons.

Both Mercals are divided into halves, quarters, &c.

Long Measures.

The Gajum or Measure used by Cloth Merchants, both here and at Trichinopoly, answers to $36\frac{1}{4}$ English Inches.

The Moora used by Stone-Masons is $29\frac{9}{10}$ such Inches, and that used by Carpenters $32\frac{2}{3}$ Inches.

QUILANDY. See *Kaliat*.

QUILON,

A City in Travancore.

The common weight used here, also at Allepey, Trevandrum, and Kotar, is the Olunda or Dutch Pound, which answers to 7660 English Gr. or 1 lb. 1 oz. 8 dr. Avoirdupois.*

			Eng. Gr.
20	Munjandies	= 1 Kullanjee.	= 77.86
13	Kullanjees	= 1 Pollum ..	= 1012.18

* This Dutch Pound is found to be $1\frac{1}{4}$ Dram heavier than the Commercial Standard of Holland; and here it may be observed, that the Amsterdam Weight has been established, not only in all the Dutch Settlements in the East and West Indies, but anciently in several Countries of Europe, and is still partially retained in Scotland. It is likewise curious to remark that, in England, it was the Commercial Weight before the 15th century, and has been continued down even to the present century in fixing the Assize of Bread.—See vol. i. p. 221. Also pages 9, 309, and 366.

QUILON, *continued.*

		lb.	oz.	dr.
98$\frac{3}{8}$ Kullanjees	=1 Olunda . =	1	1	8 Av.
25 Pounds or Olundas ..	=1 Maund .. =	27	5	8
20 Maunds ..	=1 Candy .. =	546	14	0

The above Maund of 25lb. Dutch is used for metals, spices, and sugars, but for other articles the Maund of 30lb. is employed.

The Kotar of 14lb. is used for weighing articles for the palace at Trevandrum; the Tricoor Toolam of 16lb. and the Toodoovalah Toolam of 18lb. also the Toolam of 20lb. for dammer, wax, and other light goods.

In the District south of Quilon to Tavallay, a Five Pollum weight is used for weighing cotton, thread, tamarinds, jagherry, &c. which weight answers to 5848.3 gr. and is thus divided:—

			lb.	oz.	dr.
20 Munjandees	=1 Kullanjee	=	0	0	2.85
15 Kullanjees.	=1 Pollum .	=	0	2	10.77
75 Kullanjees	=5 Pollums Weight.	=	0	13	5.86
100 Pollums ..	=1 Toolam	=	16	11	5.6

The following are the weights by which spices only are weighed, in which 5 Pollum weight answers to 5457 gr.

			lb.	oz.	dr.
20 Munjandees	=1 Kullanjee.	=	0	0	2.8
14 Kullanjees .	=1 Pollum ...	=	0	2	7.9
70 Kullanjees .	=5 Pollums Wt.	=	0	12	7.5
100 Pollums ...	=1 Toolam ...	=	15	9	7.3

SANKERRYDROOG,

A Town in the Southern Division of the Carnatic.

The Seer for provisions, drugs, &c. weighs 9$\frac{1}{4}$ Oz. Avoirdupois, and 41.256 such Seers = the Maund of 25lb. The Seer contains 8 Pullums, which is divided into halves, quarters, &c.

			English Quarts.
The measure used in the Bazar for grain and oil	=	0	1$\frac{3}{4}$
And that used by Farmers for the same articles	=	0	0$\frac{7}{8}$
4 such measures ... = 1 Vallum. .	=	0	3$\frac{1}{2}$

SEKUNDERABAD,

In the Nizam's Country.

The Seer by which grain, &c. is purchased and retailed in the Cantonment of Sekunderabad, is equal to 14106 English Grains, and is thus divided:—

			lb.	oz.	dr.
5 Company's Rupees ..	= 1 Chattack	=	0	2	0$\frac{1}{16}$
16 Chattacks	= 1 Seer	=	2	0	1
5 Seers	= 1 Punsarrie	=	10	0	4
12 Ditto	= 1 Cutcha Maund ..	=	24	0	10
40 Ditto	=1 Pucka Maund ..	=	80	1	15
120 Ditto	=1 Selling Pullah ..	=	240	6	9
126 Ditto	=1 Purchasing Pullah	=	252	7	14

The Long Measure contains 35$\frac{1}{3}$ English Inches, and is divided into 24 parts; hence, each part equals 1.472 English Inch.

SERINGAPATAM,

A City in the Western Range of the Mysore.

The Monies, Weights, and Measures of Seringapatam, have been generally described, vol. i. p. 116, as deduced from "Dr. Buchanan's Travels through the Mysore;" but the following statements, now received from the Government of Madras, are more regular in their specifications and other particulars.

Weights and Measures.

The Standards established in Mysore by the late Tippoo Sultan are as follow:—

The Cutcha Seer is the basis of the weights, and is equal to 24 Sultany Rupees =4248 Troy Grains, or 9 Oz. 11$\frac{1}{3}$ Dr. Avoirdupois. On this is founded the following set of weights.

			lb.	oz.	dr.
	1 Pollum ..	=	0	1	3$\frac{3}{8}$
8 Pollums ...	=1 Cutcha Seer	=	0	9	11$\frac{1}{3}$
5 Cutcha Seers	=1 Panch Seer	=	3	0	9
8 Panch Seers	=1 Maund ...	=	24	4	8
20 Maunds ...	=1 Candy ...	=	485	10	0

By the above are weighed sugar, jaggery, turmeric, pepper, spices, ghee, oil, &c.

SERINGAPATAM, *continued.*

Note. The foregoing contents of the Cutcha Seer agree with the article before mentioned, vol. i. p. 116, and also with the dispatch recently received; but the model of this Seer, transmitted at the same time, is found lighter by $1\frac{1}{2}$ Dram. It is therefore deemed safer here to adopt the above number of Sultany Rupees as the foundation of the system of weights, than this Standard, especially as agreeing with other high authorities.

The Pucka Seer is formed by mixing equal quantities of nine sorts of grain,* and of this mixture 84 Rupees weight is taken and put into a vessel which will exactly contain it when heaped. This serves as the Standard, from which the following Dry Measure is established.

		lb.	oz.	dr.
16 Chattacks	=1 Sultany Pucka Seer .... =	2	1	$15\frac{3}{4}$
16 Seers ...	=1 Colagah .... =	33	15	12
20 Colagahs.	=1 Candy ..... =	679	11	0

By this Measure grain of all kinds is sold, and also milk.

Cloth and timber are usually measured by the Cubit of 18 English Inches.

SHAPERE. See *Belgaum.*

TAVALLAY. See *Quilon.*

TELLICHERRY,

A Seaport on the Malabar Coast.

		lb.	oz.	dr.
10 Surat Rupees	=1 Pollam... =	0	4	$1\frac{1}{3}$
2 Pollams	=1 Seer .... =	0	8	$2\frac{2}{3}$
2 Seers	=1 Pound... =	1	0	$5\frac{1}{2}$
32 Pounds	=1 Maund... =	32	11	0
20 Maunds	=1 Candy... =	653	12	0

For further particulars, see vol. i. p. 120.

TRAVANCORE,

A Province in the South-West of the Peninsula.

Weights.

The Pootoor, Pound, or Rautul, by which the Circar receives pepper from the inhabitants, contains 6972 Troy Grains, and is thus divided:

		lb.	oz.	dr.
20 Munjandies.	=1 Kullanjee. =	78 Gr.		
$89\frac{1}{4}$ Kullanjees.	=1 Pootoor .. =	0	15	15
20 Pounds	=1 Toolam ... =	19	14	11
20 Toolams ...	=1 Bauram .. =	398	5	12
30 Toolams or 600lb.	=1 Candy .... =	597	8	10

The Rautul or Pound, by which the Circar pepper is sold, equals $7007\frac{1}{2}$ Troy Grains, and is divided as follows:—

		lb.	oz.	dr.
20 Munjandies.	=1 Kullanjee =	78 Gr.		
$89\frac{3}{3}\frac{1}{2}$ Kullanjees.	=1 Rautul or lb. =	1	0	$0\frac{1}{4}$
25 Pounds	=1 Maund .. =	25	0	$6\frac{1}{2}$
20 Maunds ...	=1 Candy .. =	500	8	2

Measures.

The Measure used for grain of every description is the Parah, which is composed of 10 Agarasaulay Dungallys, and contains $1\frac{7}{6}$ Quart.

The Measure for oil, ghee, &c. is as follows:

		Quart.
$11\frac{1}{4}$ Dungallys..	=1 Choradany =	$1\frac{3}{32}$
30 Choradanys.	=1 Candy ... =	$8\frac{1}{6}\frac{3}{4}$ Gall.

The following is the Timber Measure in use both here and at Cochin.

Timber, both round and square, is measured by the Kole of 24 Borrels or Malabar Inches, answering to $29\frac{1}{16}$ English Inches, or more accurately 29.065, and hence 13824 Cubic Borrels make 1 Candy or Cubic Kole, measuring $24553\frac{1}{3}$ Cubic Inches, or 14.209 Cubic Feet English.

The Tooda, by which plank taldoms, &c. are measured, is 576 Borrels square and 2 Borrels

* These nine sorts of Grain are Rice, Wheat, Weodso, Tovary, Hessava, Huruli, Avary, Cavlay, and Eliu.

TRAVANCORE, *continued.*

thick, and therefore contains 1152 Cubic Borrels, answering to 2046 Cubic Inches, or 1.184 Cubic Foot English.

TRIVANDRUM, See *Quilon.*

TRICHINOPOLY,

In the Southern Division of the Carnatic.

Weights.

The weight used for medicine and all Bazar articles of provisions, in retail trade, is the Pucka Seer, which is equal to 13342 English Grains, and is thus divided:

		lb.	oz.	dr.
9 Star Pagodas....	=1 Pullam..	= 0	1	2
27 Pullams	=1 Pucka Seer	= 1	14	8
2 Pucka Seers...	=1 Quarter Toolam ...	= 3	13	0
13.114 Pucka Seers	=1 Maund ..	=25	0	0

The Seer used for weighing the above articles by wholesale, is composed of 27 Pullums of 10 Star Pagodas each, and therefore equals 2lb. 1$\frac{3}{4}$ oz.: hence 11.387 such Seers are equal to 1 Maund of 25lb. The above Seers are divided into halves, quarters, &c.

The Vis is equal to 3lb., and therefore 8$\frac{1}{3}$ of such weights make the Maund.

TRICHINOPOLY, *continued.*

The Seer used for weighing copper, brass, lead, pewter, tin, tutenag, &c. but not iron, whether by wholesale or retail, is equal to 4167.7 Gr. Troy, or 9 oz 8$\frac{1}{2}$ dr., and therefore 41.987 such Seers are equal to 1 Maund.

The Madras weights are used at the Custom House of this station, and also occasionally by Merchants.

Measures.

The Measure used for all kinds of grain is equal to 1$\frac{7}{64}$ Quart, and is subdivided into halves, quarters, and eighths. Four of these Measures make the Mercal, which answers to 1$\frac{1}{8}$ Gallon.

It is to be observed, that grain is never sold by weight at Trichinopoly.

The Measure for oil is equal to $\frac{33}{64}$ of an English Quart, and is divided as above. For wholesale, a brass vessel is used, the contents of which are ascertained by this measure.

The Long Measure is the Moora. That used by Stone-cutters equals 33$\frac{1}{60}$ English Inches, and that employed by Carpenters 34$\frac{1}{15}$ ditto.

The Coloo used by Farmers in measuring land, contains 21$\frac{1}{6}$ English Feet.

VELLORE. See *Arcot.*

VISAGAPATAM. See *Masulipatam.*

WALLAJAHBAD. See *Arcot.*

☞ *In concluding this Second Supplement, it may be satisfactory to sum up the number of articles which both Supplements contain, and which comprehend the Weights, Measures, and Monies, of nearly one hundred and fifty Trading Places, of which nothing authentic had been previously published. This augmentation to Commercial Science will appear the more important, when it is considered that the Metrology of India, antecedently known, was confined to less than one-third of the above number, and very few of these articles were duly authenticated. All, however, have been recently examined, and verified, or corrected, by means of the general comparison of Standards.*

⁂ *The following articles on* INDIAN EXCHANGES *and* GEOGRAPHY *may also prove useful.*

EXCHANGES OF INDIA.

The following Table shews the Course of Exchange between the three Presidencies reciprocally, and between each and London, in the beginning of the year 1827. (*See vol.* 2, *p.* 103.)

	On London, 6 *Months Sight.*	On Bengal, 30 *Days Sight.*	On Madras, 30 *Days Sight.*	On Bombay, 30 *Days Sight.*
CALCUTTA..	1*s.* 10½*d.* *per* Sicca Rupee		92 to 96 Sicca Rupees *per* 100 Madras Rupees	98 Sicca Rupees *per* 100 Bombay Rupees
MADRAS	1*s.* 10*d.* *per* Madras Rupee	107 Madras Rupees *per* 100 Sicca Rupees		100 Madras Rupees *per* 102 Bombay Rupees
BOMBAY	1*s.* 9*d.* *per* Bombay Rupee	105 Bombay Rupees *per* 100 Sicca Rupees	99½ Bombay Rupees *per* 100 Madras Rupees	

INTERNAL EXCHANGES OF MADRAS.

The Rules for computing the above Exchanges of India are deemed too simple to require illustration; but there is an Internal Exchange at Madras, which is of a complex nature, and therefore requires examples of calculation. This is to convert the Old Currency to the New, according to the following divisions and proportions.

Old Currency, { 80 Cash = 1 Fanam; 45 Fanams = 1 Star Pagoda } | New Currency, { 12 Pice = 1 Anna; 16 Annas = 1 Rupee }

The proportion between the Old and New Currency is 3½ Rupees for 1 Pagoda.

From the above data the following new Factors are deduced:—*viz.*

75 Cash, Old Currency, answer to 14 Pice, New Currency.

In comparing these Currencies the given sums must be reduced to the lowest denominations, that is, the Old Currency into Cash, per Table 1; and the New, into Pice, per Table 2.—*Examples:*

Reduce 97 Pagodas, 27 Fanams, 58 Cash (that is, 351418 Cash), Old Currency, into Rupees, Annas, and Pice, New Currency, and the contrary.

	Cash.		Pice.		Cash.		Pice.		Rupees.	Annas.	Pice.	
As	75	:	14	::	361418	:	65598 —	or	341	10	6	New Currency.

Reverse Operation.

	Pice.		Cash.		Pice.		Cash.		Pagodas.	Fanams.	Cash.	
As	14	:	75	::	65598	:	351418 —	or	97	27	58	Old Currency.

Thus also the Old Currency may be converted into Gold Rupees of 15 Silver Rupees each.

INDEX TO THE SECOND SUPPLEMENT.

⁂ *For the other* TERMS *of Indian Metrology see the preceding Index, page* 361, *also that of* 261; *but as the* PLACES *are alphabetically arranged, theg are not inserted in any Index.*

APPENDIX,

CONTAINING

ILLUSTRATIONS OF INDIAN GEOGRAPHY.

The great use of Geographical Illustration has been exemplified in various parts of this Work, particularly in explaining the Metrology of new States and Colonies (see vol. 1, pp. 349, 357, 404, &c.); but in no Article are such elucidations so necessary as in that of the East Indies, where not only the Weights, Measures, and Monies, are new to Europeans in general, but even the Places to which they belong; for the Geography of India is not accurately known, except on the Coasts, and in those Provinces where modern surveys have been made, such as are now in extensive progress.

With a view, therefore, to elucidate and simplify this obscure but important study, Outlines of India are here prepared, on separate plans, together with new Tables so arranged as to afford a clear and comprehensive view of many essential particulars. But, before these Illustrations are given, some general account seems necessary of Situations, Boundaries, and Divisions.

INDIA is comprehended between the 8th and 35th degrees of North Latitude, and the 74th and 94th degrees of East Longitude. It is bounded on the North by the Hemalaya Mountains; on the East, by the Burman Empire and the Bay of Bengal; on the South, by the Indian Ocean; and on the West, by the Arabian Sea and the River Indus.

These Regions were anciently distinguished under two general heads or divisions, namely, South and North India, that is, the Peninsula and the Mainland. They were supposed to be divided by the Nerbudda River, or rather by a Parallel of Latitude coinciding nearly with that River, and continued to the Mouths of the Ganges in the Bay of Bengal. The whole Peninsula was then called *The Deccan* (which means South), and the Northern Division *Hindostan;* but in modern times this latter name has been applied to all India, and the former to the upper part of the Peninsula.

Modern Geographers have likewise distinguished each of these grand Divisions under two heads: thus, that portion of the Peninsula between the Rivers Nerbudda and Kristna is called *The Deccan*, and the remaining Provinces to Cape Comorin, *Southern India*, and sometimes (though incorrectly) *The Peninsula.*

With respect to the Northern Regions, they have been differently divided by high Authorities;* some proposing the line of intersection to be from North to South, and others from West to East. The latter is the division adopted in the following Table (p. 380), as being in accordance with the Southern Divisions, and also as separating the mountainous Districts of the North from the most fertile and improved Provinces of India.

In that Table there are four ranges of Provinces horizontally placed, and three perpendicularly. The first range is called *Northern Hindostan*, and contains six Provinces; the second, *Hindostan Proper*, containing twelve; the third and fourth divisions, namely, *The Deccan*, and *Southern India*, contain nine Provinces each, making in the whole thirty-six.

With respect to the Outlines of the Provinces, although sketched from the best Authorities, they cannot be all considered as strictly accurate; but they are presumed to be sufficiently correct for the purpose of general illustration, for which they are chiefly intended; and the same may be observed of the Rivers, which form so very interesting as well as important a part of Indian Geography.

In the present attempt to promote perspicuity, by *systematic arrangements* and *uncrouded Maps*, many Towns and all Villages are omitted. These, however, are numerously supplied in the large Maps of *Rennell*, *Arrowsmith*, and *Walker*, from which the following Outlines are deduced, and to which they may prove useful as an introduction. Those great Maps may be also elucidated by the aid of a recent Publication, entitled "*An Index to the Maps of India*," which contains the Latitudes and Longitudes of upwards of twelve thousand Places in Hindostan.

* *Major Rennell*, who has thrown the greatest light both on the Geography and History of India, proposes a Meridian Line of Intersection; and that division is followed by *Pennant*, *Pinkerton*, and *Playfair*. But the Line from West to East has been more recently adopted by *Hamilton*, *Myers*, and other Geographers. The first Division seems the most natural, as it assigns to the Ganges and Indus (with their Branches) the Regions which they occupy respectively; but then the Line of Intersection must be imaginary, whereas that of the second plan is real, as it coincides with the Provincial Boundaries.

The Indian States belonging to different Powers may be distinguished under three general heads, viz.

1. INDEPENDENT STATES.
2. STATES UNDER BRITISH PROTECTION.
3. BRITISH POSSESSIONS.

INDEPENDENT STATES.

Lahore, Nepaul, Bootan, Caubul, Sinde, and Scindia's Dominions in Agra and in Malwa; also Pondicherry belonging to the French, Goa to the Portuguese, &c.

STATES UNDER BRITISH PROTECTION.

These Countries (which are also called Tributary States) are chiefly the following:

Sikim, Oude, Cutch, and the Rajpoot States. Also those held by the

Rajah of Bhopal in Malwa.

LIKEWISE

Holcar's Dominions in Malwa. The

Gykwar's Dominions in Gujerat.

Nizam's Dominions in Hyderabad, Beeder, and Aurungabad.

Rajah of Satarah's Dominions in Bejapoor.

Rajah of Berar's Dominions in Berar and Gundwana.

Rajah of Mysore's Dominions in Mysore.

Rajah of Cochin's Dominions in Cochin.

Rajah of Travancore's Dominions in Travancore.

ALSO

Assam, Cachar, Jyntia, and Munnipore, lying between Bengal and the Burmese Frontier.

BRITISH POSSESSIONS.

The Possessions of the East India Company comprehend the whole of Hindostan, except the above Independent and Tributary States. See Outlines, p. 381, &c.

These Possessions are arranged under three Presidencies, which have been established for the general purposes of trade and government. They are

THE PRESIDENCY OF BENGAL.
THE PRESIDENCY OF MADRAS.
THE PRESIDENCY OF BOMBAY.

The *Presidency of Bengal*, or *Fort-William*, superintends all the Territories of Hindostan Proper and Northern Hindostan, except the Independent States beforementioned, and the Provinces hereafter stated as subordinate to Madras and Bombay. It also comprehends the Eastern and Northern Parts of Khandeish, Gundwana, and Orissa.

The Presidency of Madras, or *Fort St. George*, comprehends the whole of Southern India, with those Provinces of the Deccan that are not assigned to Bengal or Bombay. Such are The Northern Circars, and the Dominions of the *Nizam*, and the *Rajah of Berar*.

The Presidency of Bombay comprehends Cutch, Gujerat, and some of the Western Districts of Khandeish, Aurungabad, Bejapoor, and Malwa.

Such are the Outlines of the *three* Presidencies; and a *fourth* has been of late years established for the government of certain Settlements in the Eastern Ocean, namely, Prince of Wales' Island, Singapore, and Malacca; for the constitution of which see *Auber's Analysis*, and for their Metrology see the foregoing Supplement.

The Presidencies are divided into Districts, Stations, Collectorships, Factories, Residences, &c.—names which are sufficiently explanatory of their purposes; but there are other local terms commonly used in India, which seem to require explanation, especially as they are introduced into the present Work, in consequence of having been adopted in the Specifications which accompanied the Indian Weights and Measures to London:—as transmitted in obedience to the Order of the Court of Directors, for which see page 325 of this Volume.*

EXPLANATION OF LOCAL TERMS USED IN INDIA.

Bazar, a daily Market—a Market Place.
Chuckla, a District consisting of several Pergunnahs.
Circar, or *Sirkar*, a State—a Government.
Deh, a Village.
Doab, a Tract of Country lying between two Rivers.
Pergunnah, a small District, containing some Villages.
Pettah, the Suburbs of a fortified Town.
Pollam, a District held by a Polegar or Military Chieftain.
Subah, a Province, comprising several Districts, &c.
Subahdar, a Governor or Viceroy of a Province.
Zemandar, a Landholder under peculiar duties.
Zillah, a District having reference to a Court of Justice.

⁎ For further Explanation of Indian Terms, see *Wilkins' Glossary*, annexed to the fifth Report of the House of Commons on the Affairs of India.

* That important Order has been duly executed throughout the British Possessions in India and other parts of Asia.—Many Standards have been also received in London from several of the Tributary States; and a few only from the Independent Provinces; which will be seen by referring to the various Articles in the preceding Supplement. It may be added, that the relative situations of the above States and Presidencies are to be understood by comparing them with the following Arrangement of the Provinces, and their Outlines respectively, all of which may help to illustrate each other.

	PROVINCES, (Westerly).	Chief Towns.	PROVINCES, (Central).	Chief Towns.	PROVINCES, (Easterly).	Chief Towns.
1. NORTHERN HINDOSTAN.	CASHMERE	Cashmere.	KUMAON, &c.	Almora.	BOOTAN	Tassisudon.
	LAHORE	Lahore.	NEPAUL, &c.	Catmandoo.	ASSAM, &c. ..	Rungpoor.
2. HINDOSTAN PROPER.	MOOLTAN ...	Mooltan and Buhawulpoor.	DELHI	Delhi, Meerut, and Bareilly.	ALLAHABAD ..	Allahabad and Benares.
	AJMEER, &c...	Ajmeer, Odeypoor, & Jeypoor	AGRA	Agra, Bhurtpoor & Furruckabad.	BAHAR	Bahar, Patna, and Dinapoor.
	SINDE & CUTCH	Hyderabad, Tatta, & Bhooj.	OUDE	Oude, Lucknow and Fyzabad.	BENGAL	Calcutta, Dacca, & Moorshedabad
	GUJERAT	Cambay, Surat, & Ahmedabad.	MALWAH ..	Ougein, Bhopal and Indore.	CHITTAGONG..	Chittagong and Ramoo.
3. THE DECCAN.	KHANDEISH ..	Chandore and Boorhanpoor.	GUNDWANA .	Nagpoor and Ruttenpoor.	ORISSA	Balasore and Cuttack.
	AURUNGABAD .	Bombay and Aurungabad.	BERAR......	Ellichpoor and Gawulgurgh.	NTH. CIRCARS	Ganjam and Masulipatam.
	BEJAPOOR	Poonah, Goa, and Bejapoor.	BEEDER	Beeder and Nandeir.	HYDERABAD..	Hyderabad and Golconda.
4. SOUTHERN INDIA.	CANARA	Carwar and Mangalore.	CEDED DISTRICTS	Bellary and Kurnool.	NTH. CARNATIC	Nellore and Ongole.
	MALABAR	Tellicherry & Cannanore.	MYSORE	Seringapatam and Bangalore.	CNL. CARNATIC	Madras, Arcot, & Pondicherry.
	COCHIN and TRAVANCORE	Cochin and Trivandrum.	SALEM and COIMBETOOR	Coimbetoor & Satimungulum.	STH. CARNATIC	Madura, Tanjore, & Trichinopoly.

PRINCIPAL RIVERS OF INDIA.

NORTHERN. SOUTHERN.

Name.	Source.	Course. Eng. Miles.	Falls into.	Name.	Source.	Course. Eng. Miles.	Falls into.
GANGES......	Hemala Mountains	E. S. E. 1500	Bay of Bengal	NERBUDDA. .	Gundwana	W. 750	Gulf of Cambay
BURAMPOOTER	Thibet	E. S. W. 1600	Ganges.	TAPTEE	Beeder...... .	W. S. W. 450	Gulf of Cambay
JUMNA	Hemala Mountains	S. E. 780	Ganges.	MAHANUDDY	Western Ghauts	S. E. S. E. 550	Bay of Bengal.
GOGRA	Kumaon........	S. E. 500	Ganges.	GODAVERY ..	Western Ghauts	E. S. E. 800	Do. lat. 19°
GUNDUCK....	Hemala Mountains	S. E. 500	Ganges.	KRISTNA....	Western Ghauts	E. S. E. 650	Do. lat. 16 15′
GOOMTY	Kumaon........	S. E. 300	Ganges.	PENNAIR....	Mysore	N. S. E. 300	Do. lat. 14 35
HOOGLY	Ganges	S. 150	Bay of Bengal	PALAR......	Mysore	S. E. 220	Do. lat. 12 28
INDUS	Thibet	W. S. 1650	Arabian Sea.	COOLROON ..	Cavery	N. E. 100	Do. lat. 11 27
SUTLEDGE ..	Thibet	W. S. 600	Indus.	CAVERY	Malabar	S. E. S. E. 400	Do. lat. 11 5
HYDASPES ..	Cashmere	W. S. 500	Sutledge.	TOMBUDARA.	Western Ghauts	N. E. 200	Kristna.

WHITING, PRINTER, LOMBARD STREET.

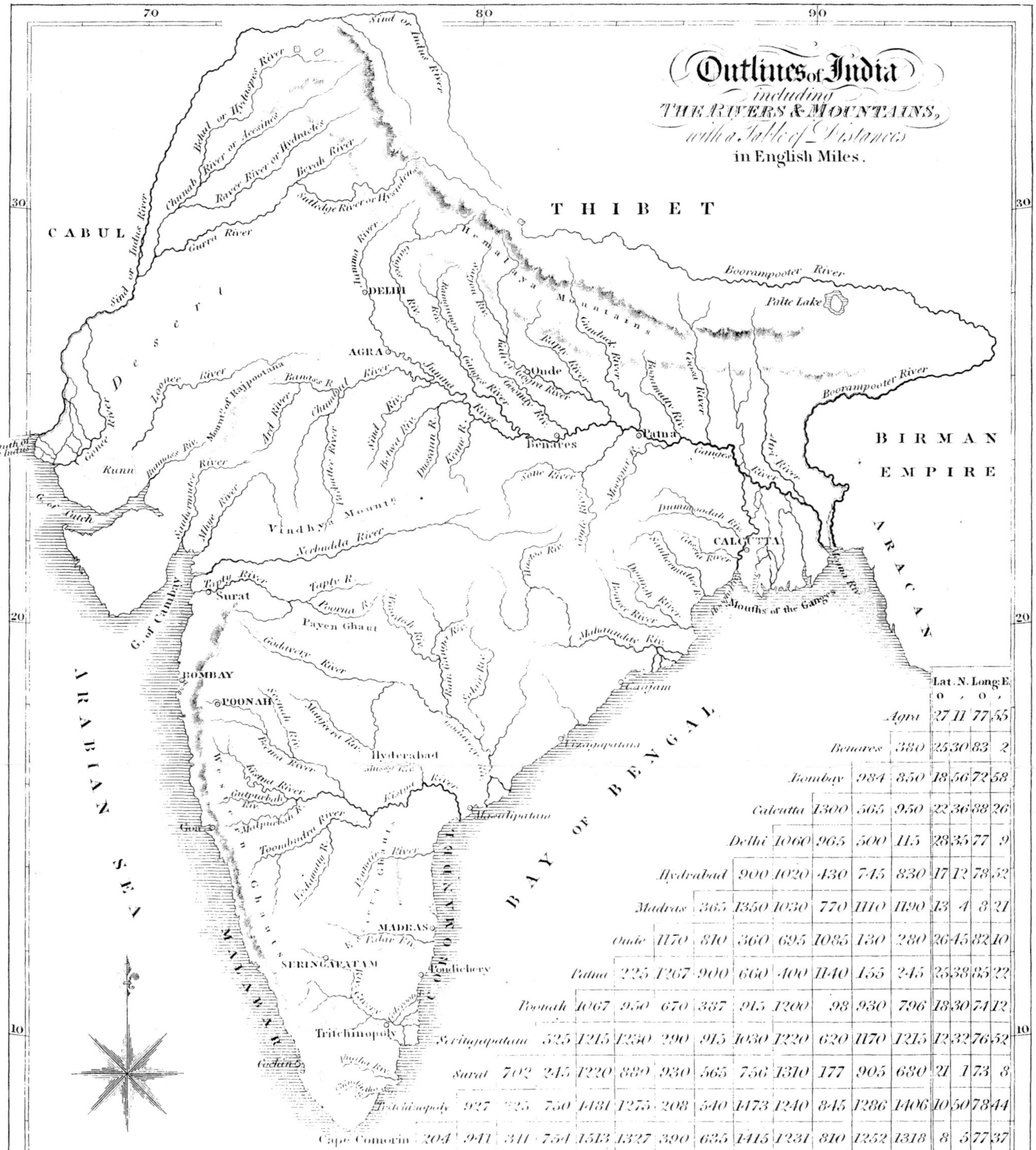

	Tritchinopoly	Surat	Seringapatam	Poonah	Patna	Oude	Madras	Hydrabad	Delhi	Calcutta	Bombay	Benares	Agra	Lat. N. °	Lat. N. ′	Long: E. °	Long: E. ′
Agra														27	11	77	55
Benares													380	25	30	83	2
Bombay												984	850	18	56	72	58
Calcutta											1300	565	950	22	36	88	26
Delhi										1060	965	500	115	28	35	77	9
Hydrabad									900	1020	430	745	830	17	12	78	52
Madras								365	1350	1030	770	1110	1190	13	4	8	21
Oude							1170	810	360	695	1085	130	280	26	45	82	10
Patna						225	1267	900	660	400	1140	155	245	25	38	85	22
Poonah					1067	950	670	387	915	1200	98	930	796	18	30	74	12
Seringapatam				525	1215	1230	290	915	1030	1220	620	1170	1215	12	32	76	52
Surat			702	245	1220	880	930	565	756	1310	177	905	680	21	1	73	8
Tritchinopoly		927	225	750	1481	1275	208	540	1473	1240	845	1286	1406	10	50	78	44
Cape Comorin	204	941	311	754	1513	1327	390	635	1415	1231	810	1252	1318	8	5	77	37

Use of the Table of Distances.

The distance between any two places is contained in the Square where their Columns meet: that is the perpendicular Column of the higher place in the Table, and the horizontal Column of the lower place.

Note. *All the above Distances are taken from the Road Books of India, except the Column belonging to Cape Comorin, which is a new Calculation by Trigonometry and therefore more direct than the others.*

Examples. From Agra to Surat 680 and from Calcutta to Madras 1030.

80 90

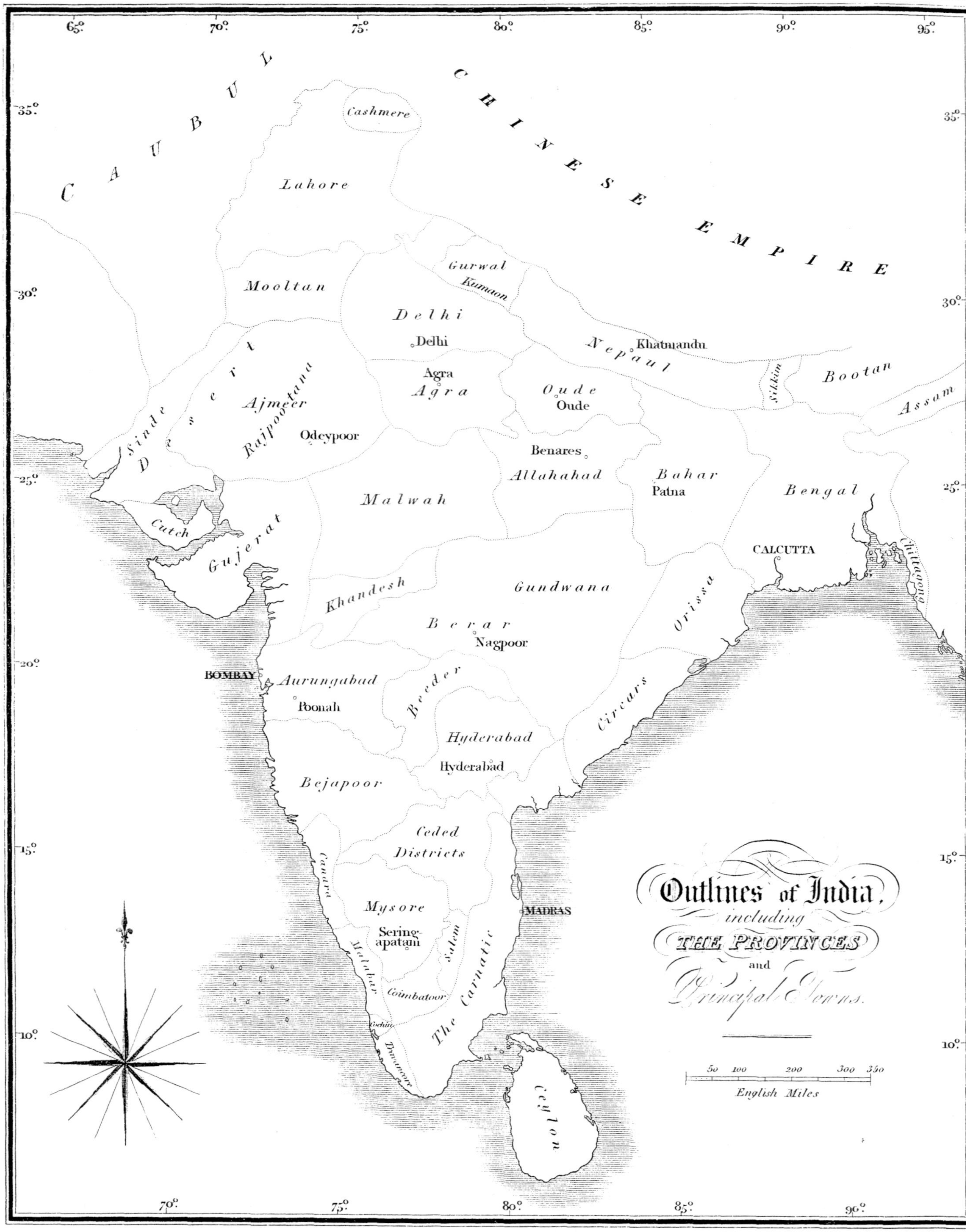

Chas. Walker Sculpt.